Joseph Haydn, Benjamin Vincent

Haydn's Dictionary of Dates

Vol. 3

Joseph Haydn, Benjamin Vincent

Haydn's Dictionary of Dates
Vol. 3

ISBN/EAN: 9783337375225

Printed in Europe, USA, Canada, Australia, Japan

Cover: Foto ©ninafisch / pixelio.de

More available books at **www.hansebooks.com**

R.

RABBITS.

RABBITS, see *New South Wales*, 1887.

RABELAIS CLUB, to promote the study of Rabelais and the illustration of his works; lord Houghton, sir W. Frederick Pollock and his sons, Walter Besant, and others; first meeting, Dec. 1879.

RABIES, see *Hydrophobia*.

RACES, one of the ancient games of Greece; see *Chariots*. Horse-races were known in England in very early times. Fitz-Stephen, in the days of Henry II., mentions the delight taken by the citizens of London in the diversion. In James I.'s reign Croydon in the south, and Garterly in the north, were celebrated courses. Near York there were races, and the prize was a little golden bell, 1607. *Camden.* In the end of Charles I.'s reign, races were performed at Hyde Park. Charles II. patronised them, and instead of bells, gave a silver bowl, or cup, value 100 guineas. William III. added to the plates (as did queen Anne), and founded an academy for riding.

The first racing calendar is said to have been published by John Cheney	1727
Act for suppressing races by ponies and weak horses, 19 Geo. II.	1739
The most eminent races in England are those at Newmarket (*which see*), established by Charles II. 1667; and at Epsom, begun about 1711; by Mr. Parkhurst (annual since 1730, *Allen's Surrey*). [The earl of Derby began the Oaks, 1779; the Derby, 1780 (first won by Diomed)]. See *Derby Day.*	
At Ascot, begun by the duke of Cumberland, uncle to George III.; mentioned	1727
At Doncaster, by col. St. Leger (the *St. Leger* stakes were founded in 1776, and so named in 1777)	1776
At Goodwood, begun by the duke of Richmond, in his park	1802
Lord Stamford, said to have engaged Jemmy Grimshaw, a light-weight jockey, at a salary of 1000*l.* a year. . . . . March,	1865
"Tattersall's," the "high-change of horse-flesh," was established by Richard Tattersall, near Hyde Park Corner (hence termed "the Corner") in 1766, for the sale of horses. The lease of the ground having expired, the new premises at Brompton were erected and opened for business on 10 April,	1865
The *Jockey Club*, which now chiefly regulates races and the betting connected with them, was founded in 1750. Its gradually accumulating rules were modified in 1828 and revised in	1857
Alterations recommended by a committee appointed in April; adopted by the club 16 July following.	1870
Rules revised, Nov. 1876; reforms made	1880
John Scott, a most eminent trainer, died, aged 77, Oct.	1871
Betting. Between 1858 and 1868, 75,000*l.* and 115,000*l.* have been won upon a single race. Betting is now much reprobated; see *Betting.*	
Gate-meetings: Races held in fields by publicans and others; Metropolitan Race-course Act (42 & 43 Vict. c. 18), to check them, passed . 3 July,	1879
Tom Chaloner, celebrated jockey, dies March,	1886
Fred. Archer, very successful jockey, winner of 2,746 races, aged 29, committed suicide with a revolver when in a state of high fever (left by will 70,000*l.*) . . . . 8 Nov.	"
Charles Wood, jockey, v. Cox, for libel in *Licensed Victuallers' Gazette*, charging Wood with pulling the head of Success in two races; nine days' trial in queen's bench division; verdict for	

RADICALS.

plaintiff damages one farthing and no costs allowed . . . . 29 June, 1888
Sir George Chetwynd v. the earl of Durham, see *Trials* . . . . 29 June, 1889

RACE-HORSES

Flying Childers, bred in 1715 by the duke of Devonshire, was allowed by sportsmen to have been the fleetest horse that ever ran at Newmarket, or that was ever bred in the world; he ran four miles in six minutes and forty-eight seconds, or at the rate of 35½ miles an hour, carrying nine stone two pounds. He died in 1741, aged 26 years.

Eclipse was the fleetest horse that ran in England since the time of *Childers*; he was never beaten, and died in February, 1789, aged 25 years. His heart weighed 14 lb., which accounted for his wonderful spirit and courage. *Christie White's Hist. of the Turf.*

On the accession of queen Victoria, the royal stud was sold for 16,476*l.* on . . . . 25 Oct. 1837
The comte de la Grange's stud (in consequence of the war) was sold for 23,730*l. Gladiateur* fetched 5800*l.* 1870
Middle-park stud (property of Mr. Blenkiron, deceased) sold for 102,005 guineas; *Blair Athol*, for 12,000*l.* (to the English Stud Company); 4 days' sale . . . . 26 July, 1872
Lieut. Lubowitz, Hungarian, rode from Vienna to Paris, on his horse Caradoc, in 15 days, winning a wager, arriving . . . . . 9 Nov. 1874
Death of Comte Frédéric Lagrange, eminent French studmaster . . . . . . 22 Nov. 1883
Lord Falmouth's stud sold for 36,420 guineas; (Harvester 8,600 guineas; Busybody 8,800 guineas) 28 April; and for 75,440 guineas . 30 June, 1884

RACK, an engine of torture, for extracting a confession from criminals, mentioned by Demosthenes, *de Coroná*, B.C. 330, and in later times an instrument of the Inquisition. Lord Coke states from tradition that the duke of Exeter, in the reign of Henry VI., erected a rack of torture (thence called the duke of Exeter's daughter, now seen in the Tower, 1447). In the case of Felton, who murdered the duke of Buckingham, the judges of England protested against the proposal of the privy council to put the assassin to the rack, as contrary to the laws, 1628; the use of the rack was abolished 1640. See *Ravaillac* and *Torture.*

RADCLIFFE LIBRARY, OXFORD, founded under the will of Dr. John Radcliffe, an eminent physician. He died 1 Nov. 1714, leaving 40,000*l.* to the university of Oxford for the founding a library, the first stone of which was laid 17 May, 1737, and the edifice was opened 13 April, 1749.—The RADCLIFFE OBSERVATORY, Oxford, founded by the exertions of Dr. Hornsby, Savilian professor of astronomy, about 1771, was completed in 1794. The publication of the observations was commenced in 1842, by Mr. Manuel J. Johnson, the director, appointed in 1839.

RADIATION, see *Heat.*

RADICALS or "RADICAL REFORMERS," persons who professed to aim at procuring a thorough reformation in the government and policy of England, became prominent in 1816, when Hampden clubs were formed, of which sir Francis Burdett, lord Cochrane, major Cartwright, and William Cobbett were prominent members. Samuel Bamford's "Life of a Radical," published in 1842, gives much information; he died 13 April, 1872. Many

radicals were severely punished, 1817-20. Wm. Harris's "History of the Radical Party," published early in 1885.—The "Radicals" in the United States were the party headed by Thaddeus Stevens, bitterly opposed to the policy of president Johnson, as too favourable to the subdued Southern States.

The *Radical Programme*, advocated by the rt. hon. Joseph Chamberlain, widely circulated, first appeared July, 1885, in the *Fortnightly Review;* it included reform of the land laws, free education, increased local government, reform in taxation and finance, improvement of condition of agricultural labourers and of the poor, and religious equality and dis-establishment of national churches. Which tended to disorganise the liberal party.

Mr. C. C. Greville (*Journal*, 25 Aug. 1837) describes "Tory Radicals." Some politicians were so termed in 1885
The National *Radical* Union at its fourth anniversary at Birmingham, Mr. Chamberlain in the chair, changed its name to National *Liberal* Union . . . . 24 April, 1889

RADICLE, see *Compound*.

RADIOMETER, &c. (termed a *light-mill*), a little instrument constructed by Mr. Wm. Crookes, F.R.S., 1873-6. Two little disk arms, mounted on a pivot and placed in an exhausted glass-bulb, revolve when placed in bright light. The motion was attributed to heat-absorption, 1877; see *Light*.

Radiophone. By this apparatus professor Bell, at Philadelphia, showed how a ray of strong light, acting on a selenium cell, conveyed sound 500 feet, Sept. 1884.

RADSTADT, Austria. Here Moreau and the French defeated the Austrians, 5 July, 1796.

RAFFAELLE WARE, see *Pottery*.

RAGGED SCHOOLS, free schools for outcast destitute ragged children, set up in large towns. The instruction is based on the scriptures, and most of the teachers are unpaid. John Pounds, a cobbler, of Portsmouth, who died in 1839, opened a school of this kind; and one was set up by Andrew Walker, in "Devil's Acre," Westminster, in 1839. *Knight*. They did not receive their name till 1844, when the "Ragged school union" was formed, principally by Mr. S. Starey and Mr. Wm. Locke (afterwards hon. secretary). The earl of Shaftesbury was chairman. In 1856 there were 150 Ragged school institutions. Sunday ragged schools reported in London in 1867, 226; in 1878, 177; day schools, in 1867, 204; in 1878, 58; week evening schools, in 1867, 207, in 1878, 147. Ragged school buildings were exempted from rates, 1869. The day schools are being gradually superseded by those established by the London school board; but the sunday and night schools, mother's meetings, &c., are still maintained in very great efficiency (1886). The union has many affiliated institutions (1888). Dr. Guthrie, a founder of ragged schools in Edinburgh, &c., died 24 Feb. 1873. The earl of Shaftesbury presided at the 40th anniversary of the Ragged School Union, 12 May, 1884. See *Shoe-Black*.

RAGMAN ROLL (said to derive its name from Ragimunde, a papal legate in Scotland) contains the records of the homage and fealty to Edward I., sworn to by the nobility and clergy of Scotland at Berwick in 1296. The original was given up to Robert Bruce, king of Scotland, in 1328, when his son David was contracted in marriage to the princess Joanna of England.

RAGUSA, a city on the Adriatic, on the south confines of Dalmatia, was taken by the Venetians, 1171, but became an independent republic, 1358. It suffered much by an earthquake, 1667; was taken by the French in 1806, and given up to Austria in 1814.

RAID OF RUTHVEN, see *Ruthven*.

RAILWAY COMMISSIONERS; see *Railways*, 1873 and 1880.

RAILWAYS. Short roads, in and about Newcastle, laid down by Mr. Beaumont, so early as 1602, are thus mentioned in 1676:—"The manner of the carriage is by laying rails of timber from the colliery to the river, exactly straight and parallel; and bulky carts are made with four rollers fitting those rails, whereby the carriage is so easy that one horse will draw down four or five chaldron of coals, and is an immense benefit to the coal merchants." *Roger North*. They were made of iron at Whitehaven, in 1738. See *Gauges, Tramroads*. For electric railways see *Electricity*.

An iron railway laid down near Sheffield by John Curr (destroyed by the colliers) . . . 1776
The first considerable iron railway was laid down at Colebrook Dale 1786
The first iron railway sanctioned by parliament (except a few undertaken by canal companies as small branches to mines) was the Surrey iron railway (by horses), from the Thames at Wandsworth to Croydon 1801
Trevethick and Vivian obtained a patent for a high pressure *locomotive* engine 1802
William Hedley of Wylam colliery made the first travelling engine (locomotive), or substitute for animal power in a colliery 1813
The first *locomotive* constructed by George Stephenson, travelled at the rate of 6 miles per hour . 1814
The Rocket travelled at the rate of 25 and 35 miles per hour 1829
(It obtained the prize of 500*l*. offered by the directors of the Liverpool and Manchester railway company for the best locomotive, Oct. 1829.)
The Firefly attained a speed of 20 miles per hour . 1834
The North Star moved with a velocity of 37 miles per hour 1839
At the present time locomotives have attained a speed of 70 miles per hour.
Stockton and Darlington railway, constructed by Edw. Pease and George Stephenson, first opened for passengers (see 1875-1881, *below*) . 27 Sept. 1825
The Liverpool and Manchester railway commenced in Oct. 1826, and opened (Wm. Huskisson, M.P., killed) . . . . 15 Sept. 1830
Act for transmission of mails by railways . . 1838
Duty on *Railways*:—½*d*. a mile for 4 passengers (2 & 3 Will. IV. c. 120), 1832; 5 per. cent. on gross receipts (5 & 6 Vict. c. 59) 1842
Railway clearing house established . . . . ,,
The examination of railway schemes, before their introduction into parliament, by the Board of Trade, was ordered 1844
7 & 8 Vict. c. 85, required companies to run *cheap trains* every day, and to permit erection of electric telegraphs, and authorised government, after 1 Jan. 1866, to buy existing railways with the permission of parliament . . . . . ,,
George Hudson, a draper, mayor of York in 1839, by his successful management as chairman of the Leeds and York railway and others, was styled the "railway king" . . . . . . ,,
An act passed 10 Vict. for constituting commissioners of railways, who have since been incorporated with the Board of Trade . . 28 Aug. 1846
The Railway Mania and panic year, when 272 railway acts passed . . . . ,,
Act for compensating families of persons killed by accidents (see *Campbell's Act*) . . . ,,
George Stephenson died . . . 12 Aug. 1848
Act for the better regulation of railways . . 1854
Act to enable railway companies to settle differences with other companies by arbitration . . 1859
Railway Clauses Consolidation act passed . . 1863
Joint committee of both houses of parliament appointed to report on railway schemes . 5 Feb. 1864
Murder of Mr Briggs in a railway carriage (see *Trials* 1864) . . . . . . 9 July, ,,
(See *Atmospheric* and *Street Railways*.)

Period of "contractors' lines" 1859-66
London, Chatham, and Dover company suspend
  payment; directors censured for their policy . 1866
Railway Companies Securities act passed . Aug. ,,
A Welsh railway train (about to start) seized for
  debt . . . . 27 Nov. ,,
250 railway bills passed, 1865; only 98 . . . 1867
Strike of 350 men on London and Brighton line,
  . . . . 25-27 March, ,,
Strike of 500 on North Eastern line, 11 April; overcome by the company . . . . . 25 April, ,,
Railway commission report against the government
  buying the railways, &c. . . . . May, ,,
Railway acts amended by act passed . . 20 Aug. ,,
A climbing locomotive, by means of central rails,
  ascended Mont Cenis in 1865. [The experiments
  were first tried on the High Peak railway, Sept.
  1863 and Feb. 1864.] The railway completed and
  traversed by a locomotive and two carriages, containing Mr. Fell, the inventor of the plan, and
  others; an unexampled journey in regard to steep-
  ness of gradients and the elevation of the summit
  level, 6700 feet, 21 Aug. 1867. After successful
  trials in May, the railway was opened 15 June, 1868
Lord Cairns (on appeal) decides that holders of de-
  bentures are responsible as qualified proprietors,
  . . . . 28 Jan. ,,
Capt. Yolland, government inspector, reports that
  in his opinion electric communication between
  the passengers and the railway servants on trains
  stopping only at long intervals is necessary and
  practicable . . . . March, ,,
Railway Regulation acts passed . . . 1868, 1871
Conference of railway shareholders at Manchester,
  . . . . 14, 15 April, 1868
Southern Railways Amalgamation bill; opposed in
  the lords; withdrawn . . . . . June, ,,
Mont Cenis railway opened for traffic . 15 June, ,,
New act to amend the laws relating to railways,
  30 & 31 Vict. c. 119; (it orders smoking compart-
  ments, and communication between passengers
  and railway servants in certain trains; and prohibits trains for prize-fights, &c.) passed, 31 July, ,,
Midland railway station, St. Pancras (which see),
  opened . . . . 1 Oct. ,,
New route to Liverpool (by a viaduct over the Mersey at Runcorn), opened . . . . 1 April, 1869
Pacific railway: from the Atlantic to the Pacific,
  opened . . . . 12 May, ,,
"Abandonment of Railways act" passed . 11 Aug. ,,
Railway Companies Powers act (1864) and Construction Facilities act (1864) amended by act
  passed . . . . 20 June, 1870
"Railway Association" established: (it consists of
  directors and representatives of shareholders, to
  watch legislation, &c.,) inaugural dinner, 21 July, ,,
Under the London, Dover, and Chatham railway
  act, the arbitrators, the marquis of Salisbury and
  lord Cairns, decide for the amalgamation of the
  general undertaking; extensions for award published . . . . Aug. 1871
Rigi Mountain railway (up to 4000 feet above sea
  level), opened . . . . . . 23 May, ,,
Mansion-house station of the Metropolitan District
  railway inaugurated . . . . . 1 July, ,,
European and North American railway opened at
  Bangor, Maine . . . . . . 18 Oct. ,,
Proposed amalgamation of the Midland and Glasgow and South-Western ,,
Amalgamation of the London and North-Western
  and the Lancashire and Yorkshire railways, voted
  by companies . . . . . . 20 Oct. ,,
Forged telegram announcing proposed amalgamation of the Midland and Manchester, Sheffield,
  and Lincolnshire railways (led to purchase of
  shares, and affected the market), about 23 Nov. ,,
George Hudson, the "railway king," died, 14 Dec. ,,
Strike of porters of London and North-Western
  company; settled . . . . 26, 27 July, 1872
Death of Thos. Brassey, who made 6600 miles of
  railways, which cost 78,000,000l. (able, honest, kind)
Parliamentary committee report in favour of rail-
  way amalgamation, published . . . Aug. ,,
First railway in Japan opened . . . 12 June, ,,
One-rail railway laid down at Paris by M. Larmen-
  jat, reported successful for short distances Aug. ,,
Amalgamations already accomplished: London and

North-Western, 61 branch lines; Great Northern,
  37; Great Eastern, 27; London and Brighton, 22;
  London and South-Western, 22; Midland, 17 . 1872
Railway proposed by M. de Lesseps from Orenburg
  to Peshawur (2500 miles), to connect by means of
  Russian and East Indian railways Calais and
  Calcutta . . . . May, 1873
Bill for amalgamation of London and North-Western
  and Lancashire and Yorkshire companies rejected
  by the commons committee . . . 23 May, ,,
New Regulation of Railways Act passed (commis-
  sioners to be appointed to carry out the Act of
  1854), 21 July; commissioners: sir Frederick
  Peel, Mr. Price, and Mr. Macnamara; met first
  time . . . . 11 Nov. ,,
First railway in Persia begun at Resht . 11 Sept. ,,
Railway accidents investigated by Capt. Tyler; 1871,
  171; in 1872, 246; in the United Kingdom in
  1872, 541 railway servants killed, 499 injured.
Circular from the Board of Trade, by Mr. Chichester
  Fortescue, to the railway companies respecting
  the increase of preventable accidents and un-
  punctuality . . . . 18 Nov. ,,
The justificatory replies of sir Edward Watkin for
  the London and Brighton Co., and of R. Moon
  for the L. and N. W. Co.; from other companies
  . . . . Dec. ,,
Ten railway servants convicted of robbing the luggage, severely sentenced . . . . 19 Nov. ,,
120 persons killed; 48 without their own fault; in
  six months 1873-4
The Board of Trade's reply (by Mr. Malcolm) to
  the railway companies, published about 24 Feb. 1874
The Pullman palace saloon cars (American) introduced on the Midland railway, 21 March; opened
  to the public . . . . 1 June, ,,
Commission to inquire into causes of railway accidents agreed to by government, 27 April; nominated (duke of Buckingham and others) 11 June, ,,
Circular from sir C. Adderley, recommending punctuality and care, to avoid accidents . July, ,,
Railway Travellers' Protection Society organised;
  duke of Manchester, president . . 23 July, ,,
Board of Trade Arbitration Act passed . 30 July, ,,
New standing orders respecting labourers' houses
  removed for making railways, passed 30 July, ,,
Statement of railway servants: that 632 were killed
  in 1872, and 773 killed in 1873; many injured;
  (asserted to be less than the truth) . . Sept. ,,
Midland railway company announces change of
  fares: first-class to 1½d. a mile; second class
  abolished; no return tickets at lower fares;
  began . . . . 1 Jan. 1875
Other companies announce reductions in fares Jan. ,,
Persons employed on railways: England, 228,958;
  Scotland, 31,023; Ireland, 14,554; total, 274,535;
  (L. & N. W. company, about 40,000); announced
  . . . . Jan. ,,
House of lords on appeal decide that railway companies are responsible for negligence in conveying
  persons and goods, although they disclaim it on
  tickets . . . . 1 June, ,,
Great trial of continuous railway brakes on Midland
  railway, near Lowdham; Westinghouse auto-
  matic air pressure break considered the best June ,,
Extension of Metropolitan railway to Great Eastern
  opened, 10 July, ,,
Railway jubilee at Darlington; 50th anniversary of
  opening of the Stockton and Darlington railway;
  statue of Joseph Pease unveiled . . 27 Sept. ,,
Dr. Strousberg, "German railway king," tried for
  fraud, &c., at Moscow 1876
Metropolitan extension to Aldgate opened . 11 Nov. ,,
Elevated street railways erected in New York,
  U.S.A. 1877-8
First railway in China, from Shanghae to Oussoon
  (11 miles), constructed by Europeans; at first
  opposed; trial trip, 16 March; publicly opened,
  30 June, 1876; much opposed; stopped; plant
  taken to Formosa 1877-8
Folkestone and Dover tunnel injured by rains;
  fallings in . . . . . . 12, 15 Jan. 1877
Fusion of South-eastern and London, Chatham, &
  Dover companies, voted by former . . 18 Jan. ,,
Railway accident commission report: recommend
  that the companies' responsibilities be not
  diminished, &c. . . . . Feb. ,,

RAILWAYS. 746 RAILWAYS.

Proposed fusion of the Great Northern and Great Eastern, fails . . . . . June, 1877
Of the Manchester and Sheffield and Lincolnshire with the Great Northern and Midland, falls Nov. ,,
Many embarrassed subsidiary lines purchased by the French government (for about 11,000,000l.) . 1878
Great increase of 3rd-class passengers, receipts, about 7,000,000l. 1869; about 14,000,000l. . . 1879
Sudden strike of goods-guards on Midland railway through alteration of mode of payment, 3 Jan., fails . . . . . . about 20 Jan. ,,
South-Eastern railway company v. Railway Commissioners (who had given orders for enlarging station at Hastings, &c.), Queen's Bench; verdict restricting powers of the commissioners (see above, 1873), two judges against one . . . 13 Jan. 1880
Enlarged dividends on the principal lines for half-year . . . . . 1 Jan. to 30 June, ,,
Expended on railways in the United Kingdom, about 720,000,000l. (since 1829); gross annual receipts about 62,000,000l., net earnings about 30,000,000l. reported . . . . Aug. ,,
Packet of dynamite placed on rails between Bushey and Watford (L. & N. W. Railway), night, 12-13 Sept. ,,
Board of Trade circular respecting precautions against accidents, &c. (accidents of 10, 11 Aug. attributed to neglect) . . . . 20 Sept. ,,
Railway rates select committee meet . 10 March, 1881
Siemens' & Halske's electrical railway at Berlin, 18¼ miles an hour, tried 12 May; opened to the public . . . . 16 May, ,,
Centenary of George Stephenson's birth celebrated at Newcastle, Chesterfield, the Crystal Palace, London, and throughout the counties of Durham and Northumberland . . . . 9 June, ,,
Murder of Mr. Fk. Isaac Gold in a carriage on London and Brighton railway . . 27 June, ,,
[Percy Lefroy alias Mapleton arrested on suspicion, 8 July; committed for trial, 21 July; convicted, 8 Nov.; executed . . . 29 Nov.] ,,
Passenger duty received, 507,076l. for year 1872-3; 736,360l. for year 1875-6; 728,718l. for 1876-7; 741,919l. for 1877-8; 748,506l. for 1880-1; 798,364l. for 1881-2
International congress for the unification of the rolling stock on the railways at Berne opened 16 Oct. 1882
The committee on railway and canal rates for the conveyance of persons, merchandise, &c., defer their report, recommend re-appointment of the committee, and also the establishment of a tribunal to decide questions and enforce decisions; revision of rates, &c., early Aug. 1881; issue report with few recommendations . . 27 July, ,,
A Pullman car burned near Hunslet, Dr. Arthur perishes . . . . 29 Oct. ,,
Caledonian railway strike, traffic partly suspended; Glasgow, &c. . . . . 15, 16, 17 Jan. 1883
A compromise; strike ends . . 21 Jan. ,,
Proposed reduction of duty on third class passengers April, ,,
Metropolitan railway carried 36,753,321 passengers in six months without accident . . . ,,
Association of railway shareholders established; meeting held in London . . . 8 Aug. ,,
Existing: railway and canal, railway companies, railway shareholders, associations . . ,,
Another cheap trains act passed . . 20 Aug. ,,
Northern Pacific railway (2,500 miles) opened 8 Sept. ,,
4,000l. awarded to Rev. Joseph Lloyd Brereton, and 6,500l. to gen. Brereton for injuries caused by derangement of machinery, &c., 28 July, 1882; 25, 26 Feb. 1884
Parks railway bill rejected by committee 20 May, ,,
Railway regulation bill making it a permanent court of record, enlarging powers, &c., read first time, 22 May; dropped . . . 10 July, ,,
M. Lartigue's balance railway, (single rail) reported successful in Normandy . . . June, ,,
Renewed agitation respecting brakes; the board of trade's recommendations neglected . . . ,,
Metropolitan Inner Circle completed; opened 1 Oct. ,,
312,047 railway servants in England . Oct. ,,
Communication of the Canadian Pacific railway (Halifax, Nova Scotia, to Port Moody, British Columbia) 28 May; work completed . 7 Nov. 1885
Death of Dr. R. H. Gilbert, inventor of the ele-

vated rail system used in New York, very poor Aug. 1885
Receipts of twelve leading companies, about 25,084,000l. . . . . . . Jan-June, ,,
Wm. H. Vanderbilt, "Railway King," dies suddenly at New York, aged 64 . . . . 8 Dec. ,,
Lawric v. L. & S. W. Railway; companies may increase their fares on days of extra traffic such as Ascot races . . . . . 11 Dec. ,,
459 railway servants killed in 1886
International railway congress, Brussels, opens 8 Aug. 1885; at Berne, July, 1886; and June, 1887
Mr. Mundella introduces bill for constituting a new court of record for railway affairs with great powers; read first time 11, 12 March; second time 6 May, 1886; introduced (modified) into the lords by lord Stanley . . . . 1 March, ,,
The South-Eastern railway company's present of 1,000l. to the Imperial Institute March; declared to be illegal . . . . . . 6 May, ,,
Midland Railway; strike of 2,713 drivers, firemen, &c.; traffic continued 5 Aug.; strike gradually fails . . . . . . Aug.-Sept. ,,
International railway congress at Rome opens 17 Sept. ,,
Thirty-four principal railway lines of the United Kingdom; net divisible profit for ordinary shareholders first six months, 1886 4,390,517l.; 1887, 5,357,891l. ,,
15th annual congress of Amalgamated society of Railway Servants at Newcastle-on-Tyne; prudent discussion; Midland strike censured 4-7 Oct. ,,
Trumpets employed for signalling near Glasgow, and introduced into the greater lines autumn, ,,
Leinwather, an Austrian, publishes his improvements in portable railways for military purposes Dec. ,,
A railway between Listowel and Ballybunion, county Kerry, on the Lartigue single-rail system opened . . . . . . 27 Feb. 1888
Railway and Canal Traffic Bill passed 14 Aug. ,,
State purchase of the railways negatived by the commons without a division . . 4 May, ,,
L. & N. W. company run trains between London and Edinburgh and Glasgow in 9 hours from 1 June; in eight hours 6 Aug; the Great Northern makes similar reductions June and Aug. ,,
First railway constructed in Persia, from Teheran to Shah-Abdul-Azim, opened . . . 25 June, ,,
Direct railway communication between Constantinople and Vienna completed . . Aug. ,,
Central Asian railway from the Caspian to Samarcand opened . . . . May, ,,
Mr. Justice Wills appointed president of the railway commission . . . . . . Dec. ,,
First regular railway in China, 86 miles, opened Nov. ,,
The new railway and canal commission begins 1 Jan. 1889
Railway up Mount Pilatus, Switzerland, inaugurated . . . . 4 June, ,,

RAILWAYS OF GREAT BRITAIN AND IRELAND.

Year.	Capital paid-up.	Miles opened.	Net Receipts.
1851.	£240,897	6,890	
1854.	286,068,794	8,054	£11,009,519
1860.	348,130,127	10,433	14,579,254
1865.	455,478,143	13,289	18,602,982
1870.	529,908,673	15,537	23,362,618
1875.	630,223,494	16,658	28,016,272
1877.	674,059,048	17,077	29,115,350
1879.	717,003,469	17,696	27,731,430
1880.	728,316,848	17,933	31,890,501
1881.	745,528,162	18,175	32,255,000
1882.	767,899,570	18,457	33,206,683
1883.	784,921,312	18,681	33,693,703
1884.	801,464,367	18,864	33,305,446
1885.	815,858,055	19,163	32,767,817
1886.	828,344,254	19,332	33,073,706
1887.	845,971,654	19,578	33,880,110

Working expenses: 1854, 9,206,205l.; 1861, 13,843,337l.; 1870, 21,715,525l.; 1874, 32,612,722l.; 1877, 33,857,978l.; 1880, 33,601,124l.; 1883, 37,368,562l.; 1887, 37,063,266l.

Number of passengers: 1845, 33,791,253; 1854, 111,206,707; 1860, 163,483,572; 1865, 251,939,862; 1870, 331,701,801; 1874,478,316,761; 1877,549,541,325; 1880, 603,885,025; 1883, 683,718,137; 1887, 733,673,511 (not season-ticket-holders).

RAILWAYS. 747 RAILWAYS.

Miles opened.

	1843.	1361.	1874.	1877.	1879.	1883.	1887.
England & Wales	1775	7820	11,622	12,098	12,547	13,215	13,825
Scotland	225	1626	2,700	2,776	2,864	2,964	3,079
Ireland	31	1423	2,127	2,203	2,285	2,502	2,674

For 1847-9, it was calculated that out of 4,782,188 travellers by railway, one person was killed, from causes beyond his own control; for 1856-9, one in 8,708,411; 1866-8, one in 12,941,170. In 1878, one in 7,503,000. Passengers killed from causes beyond their control: in 1871, 12; 1862-72, 271; 1872, 24; 1876, 811.

United Kingdom.

1874, 1424 killed—211 passengers (not their fault, 86); 788 servants, 425 trespassers; 5041 injured.
1876, 1286 killed—138 (by own fault, 101) passengers; 6112 injured, 1883 passengers.
1877, 1175 killed—126 passengers; 3705 injured, 128 passengers.
1878, 1112 killed; 6507 injured by various causes.
1879, 1032 killed; 160 passengers; 3513 injured, 1307 passengers.
1882, 1,121 killed; 127 passengers; 4,601 injured, 1,739 passengers; 1884, 1135 killed; 4100 injured; 1885, 957 killed, 3,467 injured; 1886, 938 killed, 3,539 injured.
1887, 919 killed, 3,590 injured; 1888, 905 killed, 3,826 injured.

Railway servants killed: annual average (1872-5) 740; 1880, reduced to 483.

Compensation paid for injuries by companies.

	1873.	1883.	1887.
Passengers	£364,509	£247,032	£176,406
Goods	231,707	197,941	169,633

PRINCIPAL RAILWAYS OF THE UNITED KINGDOM.

The railways are generally named after their termini.

Railways.	Date of Opening.
Arbroath and Forfar	3 Jan. 1839
Atmospheric Railway (*which see*)	1840
Bangor and Carnarvon	July, 1852
Belfast and county of Down	April, 1850
Birmingham and Derby	12 Aug. 1839
Birmingham and Gloncester	17 Dec. 1840
Birmingham, Wolverhampton, and Stour Valley,	July, 1852
Brighton and Chichester	8 June, 1846
Brighton and Hastings	27 June, „
Bristol and Exeter	1 May, 1844
Bristol and Gloucester	July, 1845
Caledonian	Feb. 1848
Canterbury and Whitstable	May, 1830
Charing Cross Railway, London, opened	11 Jan. 1864
Cheltenham and Swindon	12 May, 1845
Chester and Birkenhead	22 Sept. 1840
Chester and Crewe	1848
Cockermouth and Workington	28 April, 1847
Colchester and Ipswich	15 June, 1846
Cork and Bandon	8 Dec. 1851
Cornwall	1 May, 1859
Coventry and Leamington	2 Dec. 1844
Croydon and Epsom	17 May, 1847
Devon and Somerset	7 Nov. 1873
Dover and Deal, begun	29 June, 1878
Dublin and Belfast Junction	June, 1852
Dublin and Carlow	10 Aug. 1846
Dublin and Drogheda	26 May, 1844
Dublin and Kingstown	17 Dec. 1834
Dundee and Newtyle	Dec. 1831
Dundee and Perth	22 May, 1847
Durham and Sunderland	28 June, 1839
Eastern Counties	18 June, „
Eastern Union (London and Colchester),	29 March, 1843
East London	10 April, 1876
Edinburgh and Berwick	18 June, 1846
Edinburgh and Glasgow	8 Feb. 1842
Ely and Peterborough	Jan. 1847
Exeter and Plymouth (part)	29 May, 1846
Glasgow and Ayr	19 Sept. 1840
Glasgow and Greenock	24 March, 1841
Glasgow, Garnkirk, and Coatbridge	July, 1845
Gloucester and Chepstow	Sept. 1851
Grand Junction (Birmingham to Newton)	July, 1837
Gravesend and Rochester	10 Feb. 1845
Great Northern	1852
Great Western to Maidenhead, 4 June, 1838; to Bristol	30 June, 1841
Hertford branch of Eastern Counties	31 Oct. 1843
Highland	1865
Inner Circle, London	21 July, 1882-4
Ipswich and Bury St. Edmunds	24 Dec. 1846
Isle of Man	1 July, 1873
Kendal and Windermere	21 April, 1847
Lancaster and Carlisle	16 Dec. 1846
Lancaster and Preston	30 June, 1840
Leeds and Bradford	1 July, 1846
Leeds and Derby	July, 1840
Liverpool and Birmingham	4 July, 1837
Liverpool and Manchester	15 Sept. 1830
Liverpool and Preston	31 Oct. 1838
London and Birmingham	17 Sept. „
London and Blackwall	2 Aug. 1841
London and Brighton	21 Sept. „
London and Bristol	30 June, „
London and Cambridge	30 July, 1845
London, Chatham, and Dover	29 Sept. 1860
London and Colchester	29 March, 1843
London and Croydon	1 June, 1839
London and Dover	7 Feb. 1844
London and Greenwich	26 Dec. 1838
London and Richmond	27 July, 1846
London and Southampton	11 May, 1840
London and Southend	June, 1856
London and Warrington; branch of the Great Northern	Aug. 1850
Lowestoft branch; Norwich and Yarmouth	1847
Lynn and Ely	
Manchester and Birmingham	10 Aug. 1842
Manchester and Leeds	1 March, 1841
Manchester and Sheffield	22 Dec. 1845
Metropolitan, London; act obtained, 1853; construction began, 1860; opened	10 Jan. 1863
Midland Counties	30 June, 1840
Newcastle and Berwick	July, 1847
Newcastle and Carlisle	18 June, 1839
Newcastle and North Shields	18 June, „
Newmarket and Cambridge	Oct. 1851
Northampton and Peterborough	2 June, 1845
North and South-Western Junction	Dec. 1852
North British	1862
North Eastern	July, 1854
Norwich and Yarmouth	1 May, 1844
Nottingham to Grantham	July, 1850
Nottingham and Lincoln	3 Aug. 1846
Nottingham branch; Rugby and Derby	30 May, 1839
Oxford branch of London and Bristol	12 June, 1844
Oxford, Worcester, and Wolverhampton	May, 1852
Penzance to Camborne	Jan. „
Rugby and Derby	July, 1840
Rugby and Leamington	Feb. 1851
St. Andrew's	July, 1852
St. Helen's; first act passed	1830
Salisbury branch of the London and Southampton.	1847
Settle and Carlisle	1 May, 1876
Southampton and Dorchester	1 June, „
South Devon	1850
South Eastern (London and Dover)	7 Feb. 1844
South Eastern; North Kent line	1849
Stockton and Darlington	27 Sept. 1825
Trent Valley	26 June, 1847
Ulster	Aug. 1839
West and East India Docks and Birmingham Junction from the Blackwall railway to Camden Town,	Aug. 1850
Worcester and Droitwich	Jan. 1852
York and Darlington (N. Eastern)	4 Jan. 1841
York and Newcastle	17 June, 1847
York and Normanton	30 June, 1840
York and Scarborough	7 July, 1845
Yarmouth and Norwich	1 May, 1844

Alleged EXTENT OF RAILWAYS (in miles), 1887:—
Austrian dominions, 15,177; Belgium, 2776; Denmark, 1214; France, 20,000; Germany, 25,127; Great Britain and Ireland, 19,578; Greece, 380; Holland, 1,584; India (1888), 14,383; Italy (1888), 7486; Norway, 971; Portugal (1888), 1,192; Prussia (1888), 16,320; Russia (1888), 18,800; Spain, 9,470; Sweden, 4000; Turkey 1261; United States of America, 150,710.

MEMORABLE RAILWAY ACCIDENTS.*

Very many (where only 2 persons killed) are not noted; in nearly all cases a large number were injured.

W. Huskisson, M.P., killed at the opening of the Liverpool and Manchester railway, 15 Sept. 1830
Great Corby (Newcastle and Carlisle); train runs off line; 3 killed . . . . 3 Dec. 1836
Brentwood (Eastern Counties): carriages overturned; 3 killed . . . . 21 Aug. 1840
Cuckfield (London and Brighton): engine runs off line; 4 killed . . . . 2 Oct. 1841
Sonninghill cutting, near Reading: engine forced off line; 8 killed . . . . 24 Dec. ,,
Versailles: carriages take fire, passengers locked in; 52 or 53 lives lost, including admiral D'Urville, 8 May, 1842
Masborough (Midland Counties): collision; Mr. Boteler and others killed, many injured, 20 Oct. 1845
Stratford (Eastern Counties): collision through great carelessness; Mr. Hind killed, many mutilated, 18 July, 1846
Pevensey (Brighton and Hastings): collision; 40 injured . . . . . 24 Aug. ,,
Clifton (Manchester and Bolton): express runs off line; 2 killed, many injured . 15 Dec. ,,
Chester (Chester and Shrewsbury): train runs off bridge; 4 killed; greater number injured, 18 May, 1847
Wolverton (North Western): collision; 7 killed, many injured . . . . 5 June, ,,
Shrivenham (Great Western): collision; 7 killed, many injured . . . . 10 May, 1848
Carlisle (Caledonian): axletree of carriage breaks; 5 killed . . . . 10 Feb. 1849
Frodsham Tunnel (Chester and Warrington Junction): collision; 6 killed . 30 April, 1851
Newmarket Hill (Lewes and Brighton): train runs off line; 4 killed . . . 6 June, ,,
Bicester (Oxfordshire): collision; 6 killed, 6 Sept. ,,
Burnley (Great Northern): collision; 4 killed, 12 July, 1852
Dixonfold (Great Northern): engine wheels broke; 7 killed . . . . 4 March, 1853
Near Straffan (Great Southern and Western, Ireland): collision; 13 killed . 5 Oct. ,,
Near Harting, Norfolk (Eastern Counties): collision; 6 killed . . . . 12 Jan. 1854
Croydon (Brighton and Dover): collision; 3 killed, 24 Aug. ,,
Burlington, between New York and Philadelphia: 21 killed . . . . . 29 Aug. ,,
Reading (Gt. Western): collision; 5 killed, 12 Sept. 1855
Near Paris: collision; 9 killed . . 9 Oct. ,,
Between Thoret and Moret: collision; 16 killed 23 Oct. ,,
Campbell (N. Pennsylvania): collision; above 100 killed . . . . . 17 July, 1856
Dunkett (Waterford and Kilkenny): collision; 7 killed . . . . . 19 Nov. ,,
Kirby (Liverpool and Blackpool): collision; 200 injured; none killed . . 27 June, 1857
Lewisham (North Kent): collision; 11 killed, 28 June, ,,
Between Pyle and Port Talbot: collision; 4 killed 14 Oct. ,,
Attleborough, Warwickshire (North Western): train thrown off the line through a cow crossing the rails; 3 killed . . . 10 May, 1858
Near Mons, Belgium: coke waggon on the rails; 21 killed . . . . . June, ,,
Chilham (South Eastern): either too great speed or broken axletree; 3 killed . 20 June, ,,
Near Round Oak Station (Oxford and Wolverhampton)—excursion train: collision; 14 killed, 23 Aug. ,,
Tottenham (Eastern Counties): engine wheel breaks; 6 killed . . . 20 Feb. 1860
Helmshore (Lancashire and Yorkshire)—excursion train: collision; 11 killed . 4 Sept. ,,
Atherstone (North Western): collision of mail and cattle trains; 11 killed . 16 Nov. ,,
Near Wimbledon; Dr. Daly killed . 28 Jan. 1861
Railway tunnel falls in near Haddon Hall, Derbyshire; 5 men killed . . . 2 July. ,,
Clayton Tunnel (London and Brighton): collision; 23 killed, 176 injured . . 25 Aug. 1861
Kentish Town (Hampstead Junction): 16 killed, 320 injured . . . . 2 Sept. ,,
Market Harborough: collision; 1 killed and 50 injured . . . . . 28 Aug. 1862
Near Winchburgh (Edinburgh and Glasgow): collision; 15 killed, 100 wounded . 13 Oct. ,,
Near Streatham (London and Brighton): explosion of boiler through attempting too great speed; 4 killed; above 30 injured . . 30 May, 1863
Near Lynn (Lynn and Hunstanton): carriages upset through bullock on the line; 5 killed 3 Aug. ,,
Egham (South Western): collision; 5 killed, above 20 injured . . . . 7 June, 1864
Canada: train ran off a bridge at St. Hilaire in crossing; about 83 killed, 200 wounded, 29 June ,,
Blackheath Tunnel: fast train ran into a ballast train; 6 killed . . . . 16 Dec. ,,
Near Rednal (on a branch of Great Western): train ran off insecure rails; 13 killed, about 40 injured, 7 June, 1865
Near Staplehurst (South Eastern): train ran off insecure rails, &c.; 10 killed and about 50 injured, 9 June, ,,
Near Colney Hatch (Gt. Northern): collision with coal trucks; above 50 persons injured. 30 Aug. ,,
Fall of a bridge at Sutton (S. coast line): 6 men killed, 28 April, 1866
Near Caterham junction (London and Brighton): 3 killed, 12 injured . . . 30 April, ,,
In Welwyn Tunnel (Great Northern); a steam tube burst; collision of three goods trains; and a great fire; 2 lives lost . . . 9, 10 June, ,,
Near Royston (Great Northern): train ran off line; 3 lives lost . . . . 2 July, ,,
Brynkir station (Carnarvonshire): points said to have been tampered with; train ran off line; 6 persons killed . . . . 6 Sept. ,,
20 miles from Carlisle (Lancaster and Carlisle): an axle of carriage of goods train broke; collision with another goods train; fire, and explosion of 5 tons of gunpowder; 2 killed . 25 Feb. 1867
Between Bhosawul and Khundwah (Great Indian Peninsular): train precipitated into a chasm made in an embankment by a river torrent; many lives lost . . . . . 26 June, ,,
Walton Junction, Warrington (London and North Western): collision with coal train; error of pointsman; 8 lives lost . . 29 June, ,,
At Brayhead, near Enniscorthy (Dublin, Wicklow, and Wexford): went off the line into a gorge; 2 killed, many injured . . . 9 Aug. ,,
Between New Mills and Peak Forest: 2 collisions; 5 lives lost . . . . . 9 Sept. ,,
French Great Northern, about 14 miles from Paris: several killed, many wounded . . 27 Oct. ,,
Lake Shore railway, New York: embankment fell; 41 persons burnt to death . . 18 Dec. ,,
Carr's Rock, on river Delaware; Erie railway: carriages precipitated down an embankment; 26 persons killed, 52 very seriously injured, 14 April, 1868
Abergele, N. Wales (London and North-Western): collision between Irish mail train and luggage train; barrels of petroleum ignited; 33 persons burnt to death (see *Abergele*) . 20 Aug. ,,
Near Birlingbury station (Rugby and Leamington): carriages went over Draycot embankment; 2 persons killed . . . . 1 Oct. ,,
Near Bull's Pill, S. Wales (Great Western): mail train ran into a cattle train; 1 person and much cattle killed . . . . . 6 Nov. ,,
Near Copenhagen tunnel, Holloway (Great Northern): coal train ran off the line; 2 killed, 18 Jan. 1869
Near Khandalla, Bombay (Great Indian Peninsular): train ran off the line; about 18 killed 26 Jan. ,,
Arch fell in at Bethnal Green (Great Eastern): coal train passing; 5 killed . 25 Feb. ,,
Newcross (London and Brighton): collision; 2 killed, many injured; loss to the company by compensation, about 70,000l. . 23 June, ,,
Near Barnet (Great Northern): collision; 1 man burnt to death . . . . 16 Aug. ,,
Long Eaton Junction (Midland): collision; 7 killed 9 Oct. ,,

* On Dec. 27, 1864, the queen wrote to the directors of the railway companies of London, requesting them "to be as careful of other passengers as of herself."

Near Welwyn (Great Northern): collision; 3 killed . . . . . . 24 Oct. 1869
Eureka, St. Louis, Missouri; collision; 19 killed, 12 May, 1870
Near Newark (Great Northern): collision; a waggon of a goods train, through the breaking of an old axle, went off the rails and met an excursion train; 19 deaths; 1.30 A.M. . 21 June, ,,
Near Carlisle: collision; 5 killed . 10 July, ,,
Tamworth (London and North Western): Irish mail (late), sent into a siding; broke down a buttress and ran into the river Anker (error of a pointsman); 3 deaths . . 4.7 A.M. 14 Sept. ,,
Plessis near Tours: collision; between two trains; several killed . . . . 4 A.M. 20 Sept. ,,
Harrow (London and North-Western): collision with coal waggons; 7 killed . . 26 Nov. ,,
Brockley Whins (North Eastern): collision through mistake of Hedley, a pointsman; 5 killed 6 Dec. ,,
Barnsley (Manchester, Sheffield, and Lincolnshire railway): collision; goods trucks broke loose; 14 killed, many injured . . . 12 Dec. ,,
Bell-bar, near Hatfield (Great Northern): tire of wheel broke; break and carriages overturned; 8 killed . . . . . 26 Dec. ,,
Between Bandol and St. Nizaire: explosion of gun powder in casks; 60 killed . 25 Feb. 1871
Revere (Boston and Portland, U.S.): collision; above 20 killed . . . . 26 Aug. ,,
Near Champigny (Lyons Company): a spring broke; 11 killed . . . 16 Sept. ,,
Ferry-hill (North British): collision; 2 killed, 16 Oct. ,,
Antibes railway between Nice and Cannes: train thrown into the river Brague; 12 said to be killed 24 Jan. 1872
Belleville (Grand Trunk of Canada): engine broke off the line; many burnt, scalded, &c.; about 30 killed . . . . . 22 June, ,,
Connellsville (Baltimore and Pittsburg): collision; many hurt, 3 killed . . . 22 June, ,,
Juvisy (Orleans railway): express ran into luggage train; boiler exploded; 5 burnt to death (including mother of the duchesse of Malakoff) 26 June, ,,
Rose-hill junction (Newcastle and Carlisle): collision; 4 killed . . . . 5 July, ,,
Red-hill junction (Great Western and L. & N. W.), near Hertford; 2 killed . . 29 July, ,,
Clifton Junction (Lancashire and Yorkshire): collision; 4 killed . . . . 3 Aug. ,,
Kirtlebridge, Dumfries (Caledonian): collision; express train late; error of pointsman; 12 killed, 2 Oct. ,,
Kelvedon, near Chelmsford (Great Eastern): locomotive driven off the line by a raised rail; 1 killed, many hurt . . . 17 Oct. ,,
Near Woodhouse junction (Manchester, Sheffield, and Lincolnshire): collision; two killed, 18 Oct. ,,
Corry, Pennsylvania, U.S.: train broke through a bridge; about 20 killed . . 24 Dec. ,,
Near Pesth: train run off line; 21 killed, about 7 May, 1873
Near Shrewsbury (Great Western and London & N. W. Junction): axle of engine broke; carriages driven off the line; 4 killed . 8 May, ,,
Near Higham, Derbyshire (Midland); engine-tire broke; train ran off the line; 2 killed 21 June, ,,
Wigan (London and North Western): carriages thrown off the line; sir John Anson and others (13 persons) killed . . . 23 Aug. ,,
Retford Junction (Great Northern, Manchester, and Sheffield): collision; 3 killed . 23 Aug. ,,
Near Hartlepool (North Eastern): train thrown off the line; 3 killed . . . 2 Sept. ,,
Peamarsh crossing, near Guildford (South Western): collision with a bullock; train thrown off the line; 3 killed . . . . 9 Sept. ,,
Barkston Junction, near Grantham (Great Northern); 2 killed . . . . 10 Jan. 1874
Near Manuel and Bo'ness Junction, between Edinburgh and Glasgow (North British): collision of London express with mineral train; 16 killed 27 Jan. ,,
Euxton Junction, between Preston and Wigan; collision through fog and too great speed; 2 killed 20 Feb. ,,
Merthyr-Tydvil (Great Western): coupling broke,
causing collision; about 40 seriously injured; 1 death . . . . . 18 May, 1874
Bargoed (Rhymney railway): collision; train ran away through brakes not acting; 2 killed; much damage . . . . . 12 Aug. ,,
Thorpe, near Norwich (East Norfolk): collision; two trains met (mistake of Cooper and Robson, telegraph clerks, committed for trial for manslaughter); 26 deaths; about 50 injured; 8.30 p.m. 10 Sept. ,,
[Cost the company above 13,000l., Cooper sentenced to 8 months' imprisonment, 7 April, 1875.]
Shipton, near Oxford (Great Western); tire of carriage-wheel broke; train driven over an embankment; 34 deaths ensued, about 70 injured 24 Dec. ,,
[Verdict of inquiry, accidental deaths; 16 March, 1875.]
Rothbury, near Morpeth (North Eastern): train ran off embankment; 4 killed . 3 July, 1875
Kildwick, near Skipton, Yorkshire (Midland): Scotch express ran into an excursion train; 7 deaths, 11.30 p.m . . . 28 Aug. ,,
Between Mutford and Somerleyton; train ran off the line; 3 killed . . . 1 Jan. 1876
Near Odessa: train ran over embankment; about 68 killed . . . . . 8 Jan. ,,
Abbot's Ripton (Great Northern), near Huntingdon; 2 collisions; first, Scotch express with coal train; and second, with Leeds express from London, whereby 14 deaths; including Mr. Thos. Mure, Scotch advocate, a son of Mr. Noble, the sculptor; a son of Mr. Dion Boucicault, dramatist; brother and 2 nieces of Dr. Burdon Sanderson; during a snow storm . . . 21 Jan. ,,
[Coroner's inquest: verdict, virtually accidental deaths; directors censured for not having a separate line for mineral traffic, 3 Feb. 1876.]
Near Long Ashton (on Great Western), "Flying Dutchman" express: about 57 miles an hour; driver and stoker killed; defective condition of permanent way . . . . 27 July, ,,
Between Radstock and Wellow; about 4 miles from Bath (Somerset and Dorset), single line; collision between excursion trains; 14 killed; about 11 p.m. . . . . . 7 Aug. ,,
[Inquest: verdict, manslaughter against James Sleep, station-master, 12 Sept. 1876.]
Wambrechie, near Lille (French great northern): collision with a conveyance on level crossing, 6 killed . . . . . 5 Nov. ,,
Arlsey siding, near Hitchin (Great Northern): collision of Manchester express with goods train, 5 killed . . . . . 23 Dec. ,,
[Verdict of inquest: neglect of Thos. Pepper, the driver (killed), in not observing the signal, 5 Jan. 1877.]
Near Ashtabula, U.S., Pacific express from New York: a bridge over a creek broke down during a snow storm, above 100 perished by drowning, burning, &c. . . . . 29 Dec. ,,
Near Morpeth (North Eastern): Scotch express went off the line; 5 killed . early 25 March, 1877
Near Billing, Northamptonshire (London and North Western): collision, 2 deaths . 18 Oct. ,,
Buckstone Junction, near Grantham (Gt. Northern): express ran off the rails; 2 killed . 7 Dec. ,,
Holcombe, near Leeds (Midland): collision of trains; 2 killed . . . . . 24 Dec. ,,
Chester: 2 carriages went off rails; 1 death; above 30 hurt . . . . . 8 July, 1878
Newcross: collision between carriages of Brighton and S. Eastern Cos.; several injured, 7.43 p.m. (Bank Holiday) . . . . 5 Aug. ,,
Sittingbourne (London, Chatham, & Dover): cheap fast train, bringing home holyday-makers; run into luggage trucks; mistake of pointsman; midday . . . . . 31 Aug. ,,
[Jacob Moden and Charles Clarke, committed for trial for manslaughter, 3 Sept. 1878.]
Curragheen, near Cork: engine uncoupled; ran off line; 3 killed and many injured . 8 Sept. ,,
Near Pontypridd junction (Rhondda branch of Taff valley line); collision through error of signals; 13 killed; about 40 hurt . . 19 Oct. ,,
Talybont (Brecon and Merthyr); engines uncontrolled; ran down steep descent; 4 killed; great destruction of property . . . 2 Dec. ,,

Bloomfield, near Tipton, Staffordshire (London and North Western); collisions; about 30 severely injured . . . . . . 31 May, 1879
Near Manningtree (Great Eastern); train ran off line; 1 killed; several injured . . 8 Dec. ,,
Tay bridge, Dundee; bridge and train blown into the river; about 74 lives lost . . 28 Dec. ,,
Brickfield siding, Burscough junction (Lancashire and Yorkshire); collision; through error of signalman; 8 deaths . . . 15 Jan. 1880
Argenteuil, near Paris; collision; 7 killed 4 Feb. ,,
Lofthouse, near Wakefield (Great Northern); train runs off line; 2 deaths . . . 20 March, ,,
A bridge fell near Hereford (Midland); 1 death 18 June, ,,
Marshall Meadows, 2 or 3 miles N. of Berwick (North British); "Flying Scotchman" engine ran off the line; carriages precipitated down embankment; guard, driver, and fireman killed much damage to carriages; few passengers; (alleged cause, loose rails), about 11 a.m. 10 Aug. ,,
Near Wennington Junction, 12 miles N. of Lancaster (Midland); train went off the rails; 8 deaths . . . . . . 11 Aug. ,,
Near Manchester (Midland); train went off rails; 17 injured . . . . . . 2 Sept. ,,
Near Nine Elms station, Vauxhall (South Western); collision of train with a left engine; 5 killed; 20 injured . . . . . . 25 Sept. ,,
Kibworth: Leicestershire (Midland); Scotch express; driver by mistake reversed the engine; collision with advancing train; several severely injured . . . . . . 9 Oct. ,,
Leeds (Midland); collision; 2 deaths; many injured . . . . . . 21 Dec. ,,
Dalston Junction (North London); collision; through error in signalling; 2 deaths ensued; about 30 hurt . . . . . 26 Feb. 1881
Mexico; Morelos railway; through fall of bridge near Cuartla; train precipitated into river San Antonio; about 200 lives lost; night of 24 June ,,
Blackburn (Lancashire and Yorkshire); collision; 5 deaths; about 40 injured . . . 8 Aug. ,,
Bow Station (Great Eastern); collision; 2 killed 3 Sept. ,,
Charenton (Lyons Railway); collision; about 20 killed . . . . . . 5 Sept. ,,
Desford, near Leicester (Midland); collision; 5 killed, 22 Oct.; (Butler, pointsman, arrested for manslaughter) . . . . . 6 Nov. ,,
Tayport, Fife (North British); collision with goods train; 4 deaths . . . . 25 Nov. ,,
Highbury Tunnel, near Canonbury (North London); collision of 3 trains; 5 deaths . . 10 Dec. ,,
Slough (Great Western); express runs into a goods train; 12 killed . . . . 24 Dec. ,,
Between Middlesborough and Stockton; explosion of locomotive; 4 deaths . . . 26 Dec. ,,
Hudson river railway, near New York; collision and fire; 8 or 9 killed, including senator Wagner burned to death . . . . 13 Jan. 1882
Hornsey (Great Northern); collision; fog; 2 deaths 25 Jan. ,,
Near Old Ford Station; collision of train with broken up coal trucks; 6 deaths . . . 28 Jan. ,,
Near Cork; collision; about 40 injured . 9 July, ,,
Between Tcherny and Bastigour (Moscow Kursk line); 8 carrriages run off the rails; about 178 killed . . . . . . 13 July, ,,
Streatham Fen (Great Eastern); destruction of the express train, &c., by being thrown off the line 28 July, ,,
Hugstetten, between Freiburg and Colmar, Baden; excursion train ran off the line; about 70 killed . . . . . . 3 Sept. ,,
Crewe (London and North Western); collision; many injured . . . . . 30 Sept. ,,
Bromley (London, Chatham and Dover); fall of a bridge; 7 killed . . . . 24 Nov. ,,
Near Auchterless (Macduff and Turiff section of Great North of Scotland); train wrecked by fall of a bridge; about 5 killed . . 27 Nov. ,,
Vriog, near Barmouth (Cambrian); cliff gave way, part of train falls over; 2 killed . 1 Jan. 1883
Near the Eglinton Street Station, Glasgow; collision; 4 killed . . . . 19 March, ,,
Near Lockerbie (Caledonian); collisions; 8 deaths, 11.30 p.m. . . . . . 14 May, ,,

Watford (London and North Western); express runs into empty carriages; 1 death . . 31 Oct. 1883
Near Toronto, Canada (Grand Trunk); collision; about 31 killed . . . . 2 Jan. 1884
Stepney; collision; about 30 persons injured 22 March, ,,
Between Breamore and Downton (South Western); coupling broke, train falls over embankment; 5 killed and 41 injured . . . 3 June, ,,
Near Sevenoaks Station (South Eastern); collision; of goods trains; 2 killed . . . 7 June, ,,
Bullhouse Bridge, near Penistone (Manchester, Sheffield, and Lincolnshire); express, 55 miles an hour; crank-axle of locomotive engine broke, train wrecked over an embankment; sharp curve; 24 deaths, afternoon . . 16 July, ,,
Near Penistone; coal waggon, by breaking of an axle, thrown into the way of an excursion train; 4 deaths, many injured . . . 1 Jan. 1885
Earl's Court, Kensington (District), collision; one killed . . . . . . 23 Aug. ,,
Whitland and Cardigan Railway, train went off the line through fast driving, 3 lives lost 25 Aug. ,,
Finsbury Park station, collision of Great Northern and North London trains through fog; many injured; 1 death (March) . . 11 Feb. 1886
Roccabrunna, between Monte Carlo and Mentone (Riviera) collision; about 8 killed; many injured 10 March, ,,
Portadown (Great Northern of Ireland), 4 killed 30 June, ,,
Collision near Niagara Falls; 18 killed 14 Sept. ,,
Near Woodstock, Vermont, U.S. (Vermont Central) Boston and Montreal express; carriages fall over a bridge over the White River (frozen) and catch fire; about 45 lives lost . . . 4 Feb. 1887
Near Boston (Boston and Providence) U.S.; train broke through bridge; 32 killed . 14 March, ,,
Ibrox station (Glasgow and Paisley joint line), 4 surfacemen killed by an accident . 22 March, ,,
Collision at St. Thomas's, Ontario; ignition and explosion of petroleum, 14 killed and about 100 injured . . . . . 16 July, ,,
East of Chatsworth, Illinois; excursion to Niagara; train overthrown by a burning bridge; 83 killed and many died afterwards . . 11 Aug. ,,
Hexthorpe, near Doncaster; a Manchester and Sheffield train runs into a Midland excursion train during collection of tickets; 25 deaths 16 Sept; Samuel Taylor (driver) and Robert Davis (fireman) committed for manslaughter 23 Sept.; acquitted; the directors and other officials censured 15 Nov. ,,
Hyde; (Manchester, Sheffield and Lincolnshire); collision with a goods train; 4 women killed, midnight . . . . 14-15 July, 1888
Hampton Wick (London and South Western), collision with a light engine, 4 persons killed near midnight, officers censured for recklessness 6 Aug. ,,
Velars, between Blaisy and Lyons, train went off the rails, 9 persons killed, early . 5 Sept. ,,
Lehigh Valley Railway, collision between excursion trains above Pennhaven; about 61 persons killed 10 Oct.; another collision on the same railway, 14 persons killed . . . . 16 Oct. ,,
Landslip between Salandra and Grassam, Italy; destruction of an excursion train, about 22 persons killed . . . . . . 20 Oct. ,,
Near Borki Station in S. Russia, the engine of the imperial train (with the czar) ran off the line with four carriages (weak rails); 21 persons killed; the czar slightly injured . . 29 Oct. ,,
By the falling in of Abergwynor tunnel of the Rhondda and Swansea Bay railway, 7 persons were killed . . . . 22 Jan. 1889
Near Grönendäl, Brussels; train crushed by collision with a bridge, about 12 lives lost 3 Feb. ,,
Near St. George, Ontario, Canada; by collapse of a bridge, 11 persons killed . . 27 Feb. ,,
Penistone station (Manchester, Sheffield and Lincolnshire), excursion train ran off the line, 1 life lost . . . . . 30 March, ,,
Near Hamilton, Ontario (Grand Trunk), excursion train from Chicago to New York; carriages run off the line and burnt; 17 killed 28 April, ,,
Killooney near Armagh (Gt. Northern of Ireland), collision between Sunday School excursion trains;

about 78 deaths; 400 injured (officials charged with culpable negligence) . . . . . 12 June, 1889

RAINBOW. Its theory was developed by Kepler in 1611, and by René Descartes in 1629; see *Spectrum*.

RAIN-FALL. Mr. G. J. Symons printed a table of rain-fall in Britain for 140 years, 1726-1865, in the Reports of the British Association in 1866; and another table in 1883 for the years 1866—1880. The wettest year was 1852, being 38 per cent. above the average; but 1872 was 58 per cent. He began to publish his "Annual Rainfall in the British Isles" in 1866. In 1867 he published, "*Rain: How, When, Where, Why, it is Measured.*" It contains an attempt at a rainfall table of the world. Rainfall observers in Britain for the tables, 168 in 1860; about 2,000 in 1888. Deficient rainfall in 1887; average yearly fall at Bolton, Lancashire, for 56 years 47·07 in.; in 1887, 27·92 in.

RALEIGH'S CONSPIRACY, termed the *Main Plot* (*which see*).

RAMADAN, the Mahometan month of fasting, in 1889 began 2 May. It is followed by the festival of Bairam (*which see*).

RAMBOUILLET, a royal château, about 25 miles from Paris. Here Francis I. died 31 March, 1547; and here Charles X. abdicated, 2 Aug. 1830. After being owned by the count of Thoulouse and the duc de Penthièvre, it was bought by Louis XVI. 1778.

RAMILLIES (Belgium), the site of a brilliant victory gained by the English under the duke of Marlborough and the allies over the French commanded by the elector of Bavaria and the marshal de Villeroy, on Whitsunday, 23 May (o.s. 12), 1760. The French were soon seized with a panic, and a general rout ensued: about 4000 of the allied army were slain in the engagement. This accelerated the fall of Louvain, Brussels, &c.

RANELAGH (near Chelsea), a public garden for concerts and dancing, occupying the grounds of Ranelagh House (built by Jones, earl of Ranelagh, about 1691), was opened with a breakfast, 5 April, 1742. The music for the orchestra was frequently composed by Dr. Arne. The gardens were closed, and the buildings taken down, in 1804.

RANGOON, maritime capital of the Burmese empire, built by Alompra, 1753, was taken by sir A. Campbell on 11 May, 1824. In Dec. 1826, it was ceded to the Burmese on condition of the payment of a sum of money, the reception of a British resident at Ava, and freedom of commerce. Oppression of the British merchants led to the second Burmese war, 1852. Rangoon was taken by storm by general Godwin, 14 April, and annexed to the British dominions in December. An English bishopric founded, 1877. Destructive fire for two days about 18 April, 1884. Foundation stone of Cathedral laid by lord Dufferin, viceroy, 24 Feb. 1886. See *Burmah*.

RANSOME'S ARTIFICIAL STONE, the invention of Mr. Fred. Ransome, 1848, is made by dissolving common flint (silica) in heated caustic alkali, adding fine sand. The mixture is pressed into moulds and heated to redness.

RANTERS, a sect which arose in 1645, similar to the Seekers, now termed Quakers. The name is now applied to the Primitive Methodists, separated from the main body in 1810; see *Wesleyans*.

RAPE was punished with death by the Jews, Romans, and Goths; by mutilation and loss of eyes in William I.'s reign. This was mitigated by the statute of Westminster 1, 3 Edw. I. 1274. Made felony by stat. Westminster 2, 12 Edw. III.

1338; and without benefit of clergy, 18 Eliz. 1575. Rape made punishable by transportation in 1841; by penal servitude for life, or a less period, 1861.

RAPHIA, a port of Palestine. Here Antiochus III. of Syria was defeated by Ptolemy Philopater king of Egypt, 217 B.C.

RAPHOE, a bishopric in N. Ireland. St. Columb-kille, a man of great virtue and learning, and of royal blood, founded a monastery in this place, and it was afterwards enlarged by other holy men: but it is the received opinion that St. Eunan erected the church into a cathedral, and was the first bishop of the see in the 8th century. Raphoe was united to the bishopric of Derry by act, 3 & 4 Will. IV. 1833; see *Bishops*.

RAPPAHANNOCK, see *Chancellorsville*, and *Trials*, 1865.

RASPBERRY, not named among the fruits early introduced into this country from the continent. The Virginian raspberry (*Rubus occidentalis*) before 1696, and the flowering raspberry (*Rubus odoratus*), about 1700, came from North America.

RASTADT, Baden. Here the preliminaries of a peace were signed, 6 March, 1714, by marshal Villars on the part of the French king, and by prince Eugène on the part of the emperor; the German frontier was restored to the terms of the peace of Ryswick.—The CONGRESS OF RASTADT, to treat of a general peace with the Germanic powers, was commenced 9 Dec. 1797; and negotiations were carried on throughout 1798. The atrocious massacre of the French plenipotentiaries at Rastadt by the Austrian regiment of Szeltzler took place 28 April, 1799.

RATCLIFFE HIGHWAY (now St. George's street), East London. Mr. Marr, a shopkeeper here, with his wife, child, and boy, were brutally murdered in a few minutes, 7 Dec. 1811. In the same neighbourhood, on 11 Dec., Mr. and Mrs. Williamson, their child, and servant, were also murdered. A man, named Williams, arrested on suspicion, committed suicide, 15 Dec.

RATHMINES (near Dublin). Colonel Jones, governor of Dublin castle, made a sally out, routed the marquis of Ormond at Rathmines, killed 4000 men, and took 2517 prisoners, with their cannon, baggage, and ammunition, 2 Aug. 1649.

RATING ACT, 37 & 38 Vict. c. 54, passed 7 Aug. 1874; abolishes exemptions from the poor law act, 43rd of Elizabeth; and provides for the rating of woods, mines, rights of fowling, fishing, &c.

RATIONALISM, the doctrine of those who reject a divine revelation and admit no other means of acquiring knowledge but experience and reason. The leading writers are Reimarus of Hamburg (died 1768), Paulus of Heidelberg, Eichhorn, Reinhard, and Strauss. W. Lecky's "History of Rationalism in Europe" appeared, July, 1865; and Dr. J. Hurst's, April, 1867.

RATISBON (in Bavaria), was made a free imperial city about 1200. Several diets have been held here. A peace was concluded here between France and the emperor of Germany, by which was terminated the war for the Mantuan succession, signed 13 Oct. 1630. In later times, it was at Ratisbon, in a diet held there, that the German princes seceded from the Germanic empire, and placed themselves under the protection of the emperor Napoleon of France, 1 Aug. 1806. Ratisbon was made an archbishopric in 1806; secularised

in 1810; was ceded to Bavaria in 1815; became again an archbishopric in 1817.

RATTENING (from *ratten*, provincial for rat), the removing and hiding workmen's tools as a punishment for nonpayment to trades unions, or opposition to them. Much "rattening" was disclosed at the commission of inquiry at Sheffield in June 1867; and at Manchester Sept. following; see *Sheffield*.

RAUCOUX (Belgium). Here marshal Saxe and the French army totally defeated the allies under prince Charles of Lorraine, 11 Oct. 1746.

RAVAILLAC'S MURDER of Henry IV. of France, 14 May, 1610. The execution of the assassin on 27 May was accompanied by most elaborate tortures.

RAVENNA (on the Adriatic), a city of the Papal states, founded by Greek colonists, fell under the Roman power about 234 B.C. It was favoured and embellished by the emperors, and Honorius made it the capital of the Empire of the West about A.D. 404. In 568 it became the capital of an exarchate. It was subdued by the Lombards in 752, and their king, Astolphus, in 754 surrendered it to Pepin, king of France, who gave it to the pope Stephen, and thus laid the foundation of the temporal power of the holy see. On the 11th of April, 1512, a battle was fought between the French, under Gaston de Foix (duke of Nemours and nephew of Louis XII.), and the Spanish and Papal armies. De Foix perished in the moment of his victory, and his death closed the good fortune of the French in Italy. Ravenna became part of the kingdom of Italy in 1860.

Many of the *Accoltellatori*, a secret society of assassins (said to have been formerly followers of Garibaldi), who long kept the city in terror, arrested, Sept.—Oct.; condemned to life imprisonment . . . . . 12 Dec. 1874

RÉ, ISLE OF (W. coast of France, near Rochelle). Oyster beds planted here in 1862 have flourished. See *Rochelle*.

READERS, a new order of ministrants in the church of England, received the assent of the archbishops and bishops in July, 1866. They were not to be ordained or addressed as reverend.

READING (Berkshire). Here Alfred defeated the Danes, 871. The abbey was founded in 1121 by Henry I. The last abbot was hanged in 1539 for denying the king's supremacy. The palace prison was erected 1850. New town hall, free library, &c. opened 31 May, 1882.

REAL ACTIONS LIMITATION ACT, passed 1874, comes into operation 1 Jan. 1879.

REALISTS, see *Nominalists*.

REAL PRESENCE, see *Transubstantiation*.

REAPING-MACHINES. One was invented in this country early in the present century, but failed from its intricacies. At the meeting of the British Association at Dundee, Sept. 1867, the rev. Patrick Bell stated that he invented a reaping-machine in 1826, which was used in 1827; the principle being that on which the best American machines are now constructed. On 15 Jan. 1868, he was presented with a valuable testimonial, and 1000*l.* in money. McCormick's American machine was invented about 1831, and perfected in 1846; he received a gold medal from the jurors of the Exhibition of 1851; and also at the Royal Agricultural Society's competition at Bristol, 6 Aug. 1878. The sheaves are bound by these reaping machines. About 200 patented; few good. Hussey's machine, also American, exhibited in 1851, was highly commended.

John Ridley, the inventor of the reaping machine largely used in Australia, died 28 Nov. 1887.

REASON was decreed to be worshipped as a goddess by the French republicans, 10 Nov. 1793, and was personified by an actress.—Thomas Paine's "Age of Reason" was published in 1794-5; Immanuel Kant's "Critique of Pure Reason," ("Kritik der reinen Vernunft"), 1781.

REBECCA RIOTS, see *Wales*, 1843, 1878.

REBELLIONS OR INSURRECTIONS IN BRITISH HISTORY. Details of many are given in separate articles. See *Conspiracies*.

Against William the conqueror, in favour of Edgar Atheling, aided by the Scots and Danes, 1069.
By Odo of Bayeux and others, against William II. in favour of his brother Robert, 1088; suppressed, 1090.
In favour of the empress Maude, 1139. Ended, 1153.
The rebellion of prince Richard against his father Henry II. 1189.
Of the Barons, April, 1215. Compromised by the grant of *Magna Charta*, 15 June following.
Of the Barons, 1261-67.
Of the lords spiritual and temporal against Edward II. on account of his favourites, the Gavestons, 1312. Again, on account of the Spencers, 1321.
Of Walter the Tyler, of Deptford, vulgarly called *Wat Tyler*, occasioned by the brutal rudeness of a poll-tax collector to his daughter. He killed the collector in his rage, and raised a party to oppose the tax itself, 1381; see *Tyler*.
In Ireland, when Roger, earl of March, the viceroy and heir presumptive to the crown, was slain, 1398.
Of Henry, duke of Lancaster, who caused Richard II. to be deposed, 1399.
Against king Henry IV. by a number of confederated lords, 1402-3.
Against Henry V. by earl of Cambridge and other lords, 1415.
Of Jack Cade, against Henry VI. 1450; see *Cade's Insurrection*.
In favour of the house of York, 1452, which ended in the imprisonment of Henry VI. and seating Edward IV. of York on the throne, 1461.
Under Warwick and Clarence, 1470, which ended with the expulsion of Edward IV. and the restoration of Henry VI. the same year.
Under Edward IV. 1471, which ended with the death of Henry VI.
Of the earl of Richmond, against Richard III. 1485, which ended with the death of Richard.
Under Lambert Simnel, 1486, who pretended to be Richard III.'s nephew, Edward Plantagenet, earl of Warwick; his army was defeated, leaders slain, and he was discovered to be a baker's son; he was pardoned, and employed by the king as a menial.
Under Perkin Warbeck, 1492; defeated; executed 1499.
Under Thomas Flammock and Michael Joseph, in Cornwall, against taxes levied to pay the Scottish war expenses. They marched towards London, and lord Audley took the command at Wells. They were defeated at Blackheath, 22 June, and the three leaders were executed, 28 June, 1497.
The "Pilgrimage of Grace" against Henry VIII. 1536-7.
Of the English in the West, to restore the ancient liturgy, &c., 1549; suppressed same year.
In Norfolk, headed by Ket, the tanner, but soon suppressed, Aug. 1549.
In favour of lady Jane Grey, against queen Mary. Lady Jane was proclaimed queen of England on the death of Edward VI. 10 July, 1553; but she resigned the crown to Mary a few days afterwards: she was beheaded for high treason, in the Tower, 12 Feb. 1554, aged 17.
Of sir Thomas Wyatt, son of the poet, and others, against queen Mary's marriage with Philip of Spain, &c., fails; he is beheaded 11 April, 1554.
Of the Roman catholic earls of Northumberland and Westmoreland against queen Elizabeth, Nov. and Dec. 1567. The former fled to Scotland, but was given up by the regent Morton and executed.

Of the Irish under the earl of Tyrone, 1599, suppressed in 1601.
Under the earl of Essex, against queen Elizabeth, 1600; it ended in his death, 1601.
Of the Irish under Roger More, sir Phelim O'Neil, &c., against the English in Ireland, 1641-5.
The "Great Rebellion," 1641-60.
Rebellion of the Scots Covenanters, 1666; soon put down.
Under the duke of Monmouth, 1685; executed 15 July.
Of the Scots in favour of the Old Pretender, 1715; quelled in 1716.
Of the Scots under the Young Pretender, 1745; suppressed in 1746; lords Lovat, Balmerino, and Kilmarnock beheaded.
Of the Americans on account of taxation, 1774. This rebellion led to the loss of our chief North American colonies, and the independence of the United States, 1782.
In Ireland, called the *Great Rebellion*, when great numbers took up arms, commenced 24 May, 1798; suppressed next year.
Again in Ireland, under Robert Emmett, a gifted enthusiast, 23 July, 1803, when lord Kilwarden was killed with several others by the insurgents.
Canadian Insurrection (*which see*), Dec. 1837 to Nov. 1838.
Of Chartists at Newport (*which see*), 4 Nov. 1839.
Smith O'Brien's silly Irish rebellion; terminated in the defeat and dispersion of a multitude of his deluded followers by sub-inspector Trant and about sixty police constables, on Boulagh common, Balliugary, co. Tipperary, 29 July, 1848; see *Ireland*.
Sepoy mutiny in India (see *India*), 1857-8.
Of Fenians in Ireland : see *Fenians* and *Ireland*, 1865-7.

RECEIPTS FOR MONEY were first taxed by a stamp duty in 1783. The act was amended in 1784, 1791 *et seq.*, and receipts were taxed by a duty varying according to the amount of the money received, in all transactions. Stamps required on bills of exchange, notes, and receipts in Ireland, by stat. 35 Geo. III. 1795; see *Bills of Exchange*. The uniform stamp of one penny on receipts, for all sums above 2*l.*, was enacted by 16 & 17 Vict. c. 59 (4 Aug. 1853); see *Stamps*. Penny postage-stamps used for receipts after 1 June, 1831.

RECIDIVISTS, the French term for habitual criminals. The proposal of the French government to transmit many of these to New Caledonia, with partial freedom, was opposed in France as dangerous to liberty, and very warmly protested against by our Australian colonies, especially Queensland and New South Wales, fearing their intrusion as dangerous to public security, 1883-4.

French legislation resumed; bill passed 12 May; came into operation . . . . 1 Dec., 1885

RECIPROCITY ASSOCIATION, founded at Manchester Sept. 1869, in consequence of the restrictions on the importation of British manufactures into their territories imposed by foreign governments.

Reciprocity, a form of protection, was advocated by lord Bateman and others in 1878-9. His resolution was negatived by the lords, 29 April, 1879.

RECIPROCITY TREATY between Great Britain and the United States, regulating the relation between the latter and Canada, in regard to trade, fisheries, &c., negotiated by lord Elgin, and ratified 2 Aug. 1854. Its abrogation, proposed by the United States government in 1864, was effected 17 March, 1866. Its renewal was desired in the states in 1867.

RECITATIVE, a species of singing differing but little from ordinary speaking, and used for narratives in operas, is said to have been first employed at Rome by Emilio del Cavaliere, who disputed the claim of Rinuccini to the introduction of the opera, 1600; see *Opera*.

RECORD, Evangelical, or Low Church, weekly newspaper, established 1828.

RECORDER, the principal judicial officer of great corporations. The first recorder of London was Jeffrey de Norton, alderman, 1298; right hon. Russell Gurney, Q.C., recorder, Dec. 1856—Jan. 1878. Sir Thomas Chambers, Feb. 1878. The salary, originally 10*l.* per annum, is now 3000*l.*

RECORDS, PUBLIC, IN ENGLAND, began to be regularly preserved in 1100, by order of Henry I. The repositories which possessed materials the most ancient and interesting to the historian were, the Chapter-house of Westminster Abbey, the Tower of London, the Rolls Chapel, and the Queen's Remembrancer's offices of the exchequer. The early records of Scotland, going from London, were lost by shipwreck in 1298. In Ireland, the council-chamber and most of the records were burned, 1711. Public records Act, 2 Vict. c. 94 (10 Aug. 1838).— A new RECORD OFFICE has been erected on the Rolls estate, between Chancery and Fetter lanes, to which the records have been gradually removed. The Record Commissioners commenced their publications in 1802. Mr. F. Thomas's valuable "Handbooks to the Public Records," was published in 1853; Mr. Ewald's "Our Public Records," in 1873. Acts relating to the Public Records of Ireland, passed 1867 and 1875.

RECREATION, see *Playground*.

The Recreative Evening Schools Association for boys who have left school, founded, under royal patronage, 1886.

RECREATIVE RELIGIONISTS, a name given to an association of gentlemen for diffusing a knowledge of natural religion by the aid of science, formed in Dec. 1866. In Jan. 1867 lectures were given on Sunday evenings at St. Martin's Hall, London, by professor Huxley, Dr. W. B. Carpenter, and others, sacred music being performed at intervals during the evening. This was decided not to be an infraction of the Sunday act, 21 Geo. III. c. 49, in the trial, Baxter *v.* Baxter Langley, 19 Nov. 1868. See *Sunday Lecture Society*.

RECRUITING, see *Army*, 31 Oct. 1866. Recruits: 1878, 28,325; 1879, 25,662; 1880, 25,622; 1881, 26,258; 1882, 23,802; 1883, 33,076 (new regulations); 1884, 35,653; 1885, 39,971; 1886, 39,409; 1887, 31,225; 1888, 25,153.

RECUSANTS, persons who refuse to attend church, 1 Eliz. c. 2. 1559; dissenters relieved from this act, 1689; it was repealed, 1844.

REDAN, a field fortification, consisting of two faces meeting in a salient angle directed towards the enemy; see *Russo-Turkish War*, 1855.

RED CRAG, deposits of fossil remains on the coast of Essex and Suffolk, so designated by Edward Charlesworth about 1835. They are much used in the manure manufacture.

RED CROSS on a white ground, the flag of the Geneva Convention (*which see*). Third international convention at Geneva, 1 Sept. 1884. The Russian Red Cross Society, with others, was very active during the Servian war, July-Aug. 1876. The order of the Royal Red Cross for ladies who have acted as nurses in war, &c., and others, instituted by queen Victoria, 23 April, 1883. The princess of Wales and other ladies nominated, 25 May, 1883.

REDE LECTURE, Cambridge; sir Robert Rede, chief justice of common pleas, in 1524 endowed some lectureships. In 1859 these were replaced by an annual lecture: which has been

given by professors Owen, Phillips, Ansted, Tyndall, and other eminent persons.

REDEMPTORISTS, see *Liguorians.*

REDHILL, see *Reformatory Schools.*

REDISTRIBUTION OF SEATS ACT, see *Reform*, 1885.

REDOWA, a Bohemian dance in 3-4 time, introduced in 1846 or 1847, at Paris, and soon after in London.

RED RIVER SETTLEMENTS, a name given to part of the Hudson bay settlements.

RED SEA. In 1826 Ehrenberg discovered that the colour was due to marine plants, the *Trichodesmium Erythræum;* see *Suez.*

REFERENDUM, the name given to an article in the Swiss constitution of 29 May, 1874, by which certain laws passed by the Cantonal and Federal legislations might be referred to the people at large by *plébiscite.*

REFLECTORS, see *Burning-glass.*

REFORM ASSOCIATION, instituted at Westminster to protect electors, 20 May, 1835.
National Reform Union: at the annual meeting at Manchester it was said to have 411 affiliated societies, 22 May, 1889.

REFORM BANQUETS, see *France,* 1847.

REFORM CLUB, established in 1836, to succeed the Westminster Club, 1834-6. The building in Pall Mall, designed by sir Charles Barry, was completed in 1841.
Jubilee ball; the prince of Wales and son, and above 2,000 persons of all parties present, 15 June, 1887.

REFORM IN PARLIAMENT. Mr. Pitt's motion for a reform in parliament was lost by a majority of 20, 7 May, 1782; of 144, 7 May, 1783; and of 74, 18 April, 1785; see *Radicals.* The measure of reform by earl Grey's administration was proposed in the house of commons by lord John Russell, 1 March, 1831.

BILL OF 1831.
First division; *second* reading: for it, 302; against it, 301; 22 March.
On motion for a committee, general Gascoyne moved an amendment, "that the number of representatives for England and Wales ought not to be diminished." Amendment carried on a division, 299 to 291; 19 April.
The bill abandoned, and parliament dissolved, 23 April.
A new parliament assembled, 14 June. Bill again introduced, 24 June.
Division on *second* reading: for it, 367; against it, 231—majority, 136; 7 July.
Division on *third* reading of the bill: for it, 345; against it, 236—majority, 109; 22 Sept.
In the LORDS:—first division, on *second* reading; lord Wharncliffe moved, "that the bill be read that day six months." For the amendment, 199; against it, 158—majority, FORTY-ONE; 8 Oct. [Parliament prorogued, 20 Oct. 1831.]

ACT OF 1832.*
Read in the COMMONS a *first* time without a division, 12 Dec. 1831. Second reading; division, viz.: for the bill, 324; against it, 162—majority, 162; 17 Dec. 1831. Third reading; division, viz.: for the bill, 355; against it, 239—majority for it, 116; 23 March, 1832.
In the LORDS:—read a *first* time on motion of earl Grey, 27 March. Second reading: for the bill, 184; against it, 175—majority, NINE; 14 April. In the committee lord Lyndhurst moved, "that the question of enfranchisement should precede that of disfranchisement." The division was 151 and 116—majority against ministers, THIRTY-FIVE, 7 May.

* By this "Act to amend the Representation of the People in England and Wales" (2 & 3 Will. IV. c. 45), 56 boroughs in England were disfranchised (schedule A.), 30 were reduced to one member only (B.); 22 new boroughs were created to send two members (C.), and 20 to send one member (D.) and other important changes made.

Resignation of ministers, 9 May; great public excitement ensued, and they were induced to resume office on the king granting them full power to secure majorities by the creation of new peers.
In the LORDS, the bill was carried through the committee, 30 May; read a *third* time: 106 against 22—majority, EIGHTY-FOUR; 4 June. Received the royal assent, 7 June, 1832.
The royal assent given to the Scotch reform bill, 17 July; and to the Irish one, 7 Aug. 1832.

ABORTIVE REFORM BILLS.
Lord John Russell introduced a *new reform bill,* 13 Feb. 1854, which was withdrawn, 11 April, 1854, in consequence of the war with Russia.
On 28 Feb. 1859, Mr. Disraeli brought in a reform bill, which was rejected by the commons on 31 March, by a majority of 39. This led to a dissolution of parliament, and eventually to a change of ministry.
The new government (lords Palmerston and J. Russell) brought forward a new bill, 1 March, 1860; but withdrew it, 11 June. No reform bill was brought forward by the government, 1861-5; see *Commons.*
The discussion respecting parliamentary reform was revived in the autumns of 1864 and 1865.
Mr. Baines' reform bill was rejected by the commons, 8 May, 1865.
Mr. Gladstone introduced a *franchise bill,* 12 March, 1866; after much discussion, it was read a second time, 28 April. A re-distribution of seats bill was introduced, and incorporated with the franchise bill, 7 May; an amendment (on a clause, substituting "rateable" for "clear yearly value") was passed, in opposition to the government, 19 June; which led to the resignation of the government, 26 June; and the withdrawal of the bill (see *Adullam*), 19 July, 1866.
Numerous great reform meetings: London, Hyde-park (riotous), 23, 24 July; Agricultural Hall, 30 July; and Guildhall, 8 Aug.; Manchester, 24 Sept.; Leeds, 8 Oct.; Glasgow, 16 Oct.; Edinburgh, 17 Nov.; Conference at Manchester, 19 Nov. 1866.
Reform demonstration of trades-unions in London; procession of about 25,000; great order observed, 3 Dec., 1866.
Procession of about 18,000 men to Agricultural Hall, Islington: good order kept; 11 Feb. 1867.
Mr. Disraeli announced his plan of proceeding with reform by 13 resolutions, 11 Feb.; these withdrawn, 26 Feb. 1867.
"Ten Minutes' bill" introduced and withdrawn, 25 Feb. 1867.
[It comprised a 6*l.* franchise for boroughs, and 20*l.* for counties. Said by sir John Pakington to have been agreed to in the last ten minutes of a cabinet council.]
New bill (with household suffrage) introduced 18 March; read second time, 27 March, 1867.
The "Ten-room meeting" of liberals (Messrs. Owen Stanley, Dillwyn, Grant Duff, and others), who agree to support the bill in opposition to Mr. Gladstone's resolution, which is withdrawn, and the bill goes into committee, 8 April; Mr. Gladstone's amendment rejected by 22 (for 288, against 310), 12 April, 1867.
Peaceable reform meetings at Birmingham, 22 April; Hyde Park, 6 May; National Reform Union (first meeting), 15 May, 1867.

ACTS OF 1867-8.
The new Reform bill passed by the commons, 15-16 July; by the lords (with amendments, when lord Derby said, that it was "a great experiment," and "a leap in the dark") 6 Aug.; received the royal assent, 15 Aug. 1867.*

* This act is divided into three parts:—
I. FRANCHISES. *Boroughs:* All householders rated for relief of the poor; lodgers, resident for twelve months, and paying 10*l.* a year. *Counties:* Persons of property of the clear annual value of 5*l.*; and occupiers of lands or tenements paying 12*l.* a year. At a contested election for any county or borough represented by three members, no person to vote for more than 2 candidates; in London, to vote for 3 only.
Disfranchised: Totnes; Reigate; Great Yarmouth; Lancaster.
II. DISTRIBUTION OF SEATS: Boroughs with less than 10,000 population, to return one member only (38 in Schedule A.). Manchester, Liverpool, Birmingham, and Leeds, to have 3 members instead of 2.
Chelsea (with Fulham, Hammersmith, and Kensington)

Scotch reform bill introduced by lord advocate, 17 Feb.; passed 13 July, 1868.
Irish bill introduced by the earl of Mayo, 19 March; passed 13 July, 1868.
The Reform league was dissolved 13 March, 1869; revived, Oct. 1876.
Bill for extending household suffrage to counties brought in annually by Mr. G. O. Trevelyan, see *Household Suffrage.*

ACTS OF 1884-5.

New bill for Representation of the People of the United Kingdom extending household and lodger suffrage to counties uniform with boroughs, adding about 2,000,000 voters introduced by Mr. Gladstone, the premier, 28 Feb., read first time 3 March; lord John Manners' amendment, declining to pass the bill without knowledge of re-distribution of seats, 24 March; negatived, (340-210), bill read second time, 7-8 April; third time, 27 June. Lords, first time, 27 June: rejected by earl Cairns's amendment (conservatives led by Marquis of Salisbury), (205-146), 8-9 July; earl of Wemyss's compromise rejected (182-132); earl Cadogan's amendment, (adjournment, instead of prorogation of parliament till the antumn), adopted 17 July. Commons, bill read first time, 24 Oct.; second time, (372-232) 7-8 Nov.; third time, 11 Nov. Lords bill read first time, 14 Nov.; second time, 18 Nov.; (compromise with the government); third time, 5 Dec.; passed 6 Dec. 1884.

Redistribution of Seats Act; commons, read first time, 1 Dec.; second time, 4 Dec. 1884; third time (116-33), 11-12 May, 1885. Lords, read first time, 12 May; second time, 15 May; third time, 12 June; Royal assent, 25 June, 1885.

REDISTRIBUTION OF SEATS ACT.—*Boroughs to cease as such* (having less than 15,000 inhabitants): England, 80; Scotland, 2; Ireland, 22. *To be included in their counties:* Berwick, Lichfield, Carrickfergus, and Drogheda. *Disfranchised for corruption:* Macclesfield, Sandwich. *To lose one member* (having less than 50,000 inhabitants): England, 34, Ireland, 3. *To have additional members* (with more than 50,000 inhabitants): England, 12; Scotland, 3; Ireland, 2. *New boroughs:* England, 43. 160 seats obtained by disfranchisement to be divided among counties and boroughs now underrepresented. Certain boroughs and counties returning more than one member, formed into new subdivisions, returning one member. London only to have two members. Total number of members to be raised from 652 to 670; England to have 6 more, Scotland 12 more.

REFORMATION, THE. Efforts for the reformation of the church may be traced to the reign of Charlemagne, when Paulinus, bishop of Aquileia, employed his voice and pen to accomplish it. The principal reformers were Wickliffe, Huss, Jerome of Prague, Savonarola, Erasmus, Luther, Zuinglius, Tyndal, Calvin, Melanchthon, Cranmer, Latimer, Knox, and Browne. Luther thus characterised himself and his fellow reformers: "Res non Verba—*Luther.*" "Verba non Res—*Erasmus.*" "Res et Verba—*Melanchthon.*" "Nec Verba nec Res—*Carlstadt;*" see *Wickliffites, Protestants, Calvinists, Lutherans, Presbyterianism,* &c. The eras of the reformation are as follows:—

In France (*Albigenses*), said to have been a surviving gnostic sect, not Christian reformers . about 1177
In England (*Wickliffe*) 1360
In Bohemia (*Huss*) 1405
In Italy (*Jerome Savonarola*) 1498
In France (by Farel) . . . . before 1512
In Germany (*Luther*) 1517
In Switzerland (*Zuinglius*) 1519
In Denmark (*Andreas Bodenstein*) . . 1521
In Prussia 1527

made a borough: Merthyr Tydvil, and Salford, to return two members; Tower Hamlets divided into two boroughs—Hackney, and Tower Hamlets. (Other new boroughs in Schedule B.) University of London to return one member.

III. SUPPLEMENTARY PROVISIONS: Registration, &c. Boundary Commissioners (*which see*). Parliament not to be dissolved on any future demise of the crown. Members holding offices of profit from the crown not to vacate their seats on acceptance of another office.

In France (*Calvin*); see *Huguenots* 1529
Protestants first so called . . . . ,,
In Sweden (*Petri*) 1530
In England (*Henry VIII.*) 1534
In Ireland (*Archbishop George Browne*) . . 1535
In England, completed (*Cranmer, Bucer, Fagius,* &c.), 1547; annulled by Mary, 1553; restored by Elizabeth 1558
In Scotland (*Knox*), established 1560
In the Netherlands, established 1562

REFORMATORY SCHOOLS, for juvenile delinquents.* The Reformatory School at Mettray, near Tours in France, was founded in 1839 by M. de Metz, formerly a councillor of Paris, warmly seconded by the vicomte de Courcelles, who gave the estate on which the establishment is placed. The one at Redhill, Surrey, is situated on land purchased in 1849 by the Philanthropic Society, and under the direction of the rev. Sydney Turner. The first stone of the building was laid 30 April, 1849, by the prince consort. The inmates of these establishments are instructed in farm labour, and divided into so-called families. In 1854 the Juvenile Offenders act was passed. In 1851 and 1853 great meetings were held on this subject; and in Aug. 1856, the first grand conference of the National Reformatory Union was held.

North-West London Preventive and Reformatory Institution in the New-road, established: all kinds of trades taught 1852
Reformatory and Refuge Union founded . . 1856
Acts for establishing reformatory schools passed, 1857, 1858, 1866, 1868; amended 1872
Fifty-one reformatory schools in England (and nine in Ireland), 1863; 53 reformatory schools (with 4,674 boys; 1165 girls), 1872; 47 in 1888. In Ireland, 9 in 1887.
An international exhibition of the works of these schools at the Agricultural Hall, Islington, near London, opened by the prince of Wales . . . 1865
Mr. T. Barwick Lloyd Baker, an eminent promoter of the reformatory system, died Dec. 1886.

"REFORMED CHURCH" (Calvinistic), established in Holland and in some parts of Germany. For the Reformed Presbyterian Church in Scotland, see *Cameronians*, note.

REFORMED EPISCOPAL CHURCH, founded in the United States of North America in 1873; in this country a secession from the Free Church of England in 1877.

Dr. Cummins, assistant bishop of Kentucky, after revising the prayer-book, consecrated C. E. Cheney as bishop, 14 Dec. 1873; others since consecrated and churches formed.

REFRACTION, see *Light.*

REFRESHMENT HOUSES for the sale of wine, &c., are licensed in pursuance of an act passed in 1860, amended in 1861: a new act passed in 1864, 1865. See *Licences.*

REFRIGERATORS, see *Provisions.*

REFUGE FOR THE DESTITUTE (criminal young females), Dalston, London, E.; instituted 1805, incorporated 1838.

REFUGEES' BENEVOLENT FUND, instituted in consequence of the Franco-German war, at a great meeting held at the Mansion-house, London, 21 Oct. 1870. It afforded temporary relief to many sufferers.

REFUGES, see *Poor*, 1864. Refuges for Destitute boys and girls, established in Great Queen-street in 1852. See *Chichester.*

* It was calculated (about 1856) that there were in London 30,000, and in England 100,000 youths under 17 leading a vagabond life, and that out of 15,000 of those who were committed for trial nearly half were in custody for the first time.

REGALIA, see *Crown*.

REGATTA. A public boat race, introduced into this country from Venice in 1775; and in that year one took place on the Thames.

REGELATION. See *Ice*.

REGENCY BILLS. One was passed 1751. One was proposed to parliament in consequence of the mental illness of George III., and debated 10 Dec. 1788. It was relinquished on his majesty's recovery, 26 Feb. 1789. The return of the malady led to the prince of Wales (afterwards George IV.) being sworn in before the privy council as regent of the kingdom, 5 Feb. 1811. The Regency Bill providing for the administration of the government, should the crown descend to the princess Victoria while under eighteen years of age, passed 1 Will. IV., 23 Dec. 1830. A Regency Bill appointing prince Albert regent in the event of the demise of the queen, should her next lineal successor be under age; passed 4 Aug. 1840.

REGENTS, see *Protectorates*.

REGENT'S CANAL, begun at Paddington, where it joins a cut to the Grand Junction, passes under Maida-hill, continues its course by the Regent's-park to Islington, where another subterranean excavation, about three-quarters of a mile in length, was formed for its passage. It then proceeds by Hoxton, Hackney, Mile-end, to Limehouse, where it joins the Thames. The whole length of it is nine miles; it comprises twelve locks and thirty-seven bridges. Begun, 1812; opened 1 Aug. 1820. Great explosion of *gunpowder* (*which see*), 2 Oct. 1874. New bridge, near Gloucester gate, Regent's park, opened by the duke of Cambridge, 3 Aug. 1878. Regent's Canal and City Railway Co. act passed, 1882.

REGENT'S PARK, originally part of the grounds belonging to a palace of queen Elizabeth, near to the north end of Tottenham court-road, pulled down in 1791. Since 1600, the property was let to various persons, but the leases having expired it reverted to the crown; and in 1814 great improvements were commenced under the direction of Mr. Nash. The park consists of about 450 acres; within it are the gardens of the Zoological Society and the Royal Botanical Society. During a frost on 15 Jan. 1867, the rotten ice of one of the lakes gave way, and about 200 persons were immersed, of whom above 40 perished. Addition of 20 acres made to the public park, 1883.

Joseph Rumbold was murdered near York Gate, 24 May. Eight youths, George Gallesly, 17, William Elvis, 16, Francis Cole, 18, Peter Lee, 17, William Joseph Graefe, 17, William Henshaw, 16, Charles Henry Govier, 16, and Michael Duling, 15, all described as labourers, were charged with the wilful murder, 1 Aug.; Gallesly was convicted; the rest acquitted of murder, 2 Aug.; they pleaded guilty to minor charges, and were sentenced to various terms of penal servitude, 4 Aug. The evidence disclosed the existence of local bands of young roughs carrying on internecine warfare. Joseph Rumbold was not the intended victim; Gallesly reprieved, Aug. 1888.

REGENT STREET, London, W.; designed and executed by John Nash; authorised by act, 53 George III. 1813. The colonnades of the quadrant were removed in 1848.

REGGIO, see *Rhegium*.

REGICIDES, in English history, are the commissioners appointed to try king Charles I., 150 in number; of whom 70 acted, and 59 signed the death-warrant, Jan. 1649. Of these last, 29 were tried, and 10 executed: Harrison, 13 Oct.; Cook and Peters, 16 Oct.; Scott, Scroop, Clement, and Jones, 17 Oct.; Axtell and Hacker, 19 Oct. 1660. They asserted themselves to be martyrs. Others were imprisoned. See *Assassinations*.

Foreign Regicides.

James I. of Scotland, by nobles		.	20 Feb. 1437
James III.	,,	,,	11 June, 1488
Henry III. of France, by Clement, 1 Aug.;		*d.* 2 Aug.	1589
Henry IV.	,,	by Ravaillac	. 14 May, 1610
Gustavus III. of Sweden, by Ankarström, 16 March;			
			d. 29 March, 1792
Louis XVI.	,,	by convention	. 21 Jan. 1793
Paul of Russia, by nobles		.	24 March, 1801

REGIMENTAL EXCHANGE ACT, passed 28 May, 1875.

REGIMENTS OF INFANTRY were formed in France about 1588; see *Infantry*. The following are the approximate dates of the establishment of several British regiments:—

CAVALRY.

Oxford Blues are erroneously said to have been formed in the reign of Henry VIII.; they derive their name from their colonel, the earl of Oxford, in 1661
Three Indian regiments (19th, 20th, and 21st) added Aug. ,,
The Dragoon Guards, the Royal Irish, and the Scots Greys were formed by James II., about . 1684-6
Several regiments of Light Dragoons were armed with lances and termed *Lancers* . . Sept. 1816

INFANTRY (see *Guards*).

1st Royal or Royal Scots regiment, 1633; the old title resumed . . . . Dec. 1871
Coldstream Guards, established by Monk, in . 1660
3rd Buffs, represent London train bands and have special privileges
2nd Queen's Royal 1661
4th King's Own 1685
5th Northumberland Fusiliers
26th Cameronian 1689
100th Canadian 1858
101st to 109th (Indian) added . . . Aug. 1861
The Highland regiments are the 42nd, 71st, 72nd, 78th, 79th, 92nd, and 93rd. See *Army Organization*.

REGISTERS. The registering of deeds and conveyances disposing of real estates was appointed to be effected in Yorkshire and in Middlesex, 2 Anne, 1703, *et seq.* Greater security was thus given to purchasers and mortgagees; and the value of estates increased in those counties. Wills have been for a series of years kept and registered, in London, at Doctors' Commons; see *Wills*. The registering of shipping in the Thames was commenced, 1786; and throughout England, 1787; and several acts and amendments of acts have since followed for keeping and improving registers. The duties and payments of the Lord Clerk Register of Scotland and his deputy were regulated by 42 & 43 Vict. c. 44 1879

REGISTERS, PAROCHIAL, were established by Cromwell, lord Essex, by which the dates of births, marriages, and burials, became ascertainable, Sept. 1538. This measure was opposed by the people, who feared some new taxation. A stamp-tax was laid on registers in 1784. Laws for their better regulation were enacted in 1813 *et seq.* The great Registration act (introduced by lord John Russell), 6 & 7 Will. IV. c. 86, passed 17 Aug. 1836; see *Bills of Mortality*, &c.

A new registration act for births and deaths, passed 7 Aug. 1874, came into operation . .1 Jan. 1875
Major George Graham, the first registrar-general (1838), was succeeded by sir Brydges Powell Henniker, appointed . . . . . Jan. 1880

REGISTRATION OF VOTERS was enacted by the Reform act, passed 7 June, 1832, and by acts passed in 1868 and 1885; see *Revising Barristers*.
New Parliamentary and Municipal Registration act passed . . . . 22 July, 1878
Births and Deaths Registration act for Ireland passed . . . . 2 Aug. 1880

REGIUM DONUM (Royal gift), an allowance from the sovereign for the maintenance of the Presbyterian ministers in Ireland, commenced by Charles II. in 1672, and revived by William III. in 1690, was commuted by the Irish Presbyterian Church act passed June, 1871. The allowance to certain protestant dissenting ministers in Ireland was given up by them in 1857, in deference to the wishes of English dissenters.

REGULATION OF PUBLIC WORSHIP, see *Public Worship*.

REGULATION OF THE FORCES ACT passed 17 Aug. 1871. See *Army*.

REICHENBACH (Prussia). Here Duroc was killed during the conflicts between the French and the allies, 22 May, 1813; see *Bautzen*. Here was signed a subsidy treaty between Russia, Prussia, and England, whereby the last engaged to provide means for carrying on the war against Napoleon I. on certain conditions, 14, 15 June, 1813. Austria joined the alliance soon after.

REICHSRATH, the representative council of the empire of Austria, reconstituted by decree 5 March; met on 31 May, 1860. In May, 1861, the upper house consisted of 17 spiritual, 55 hereditary, and 39 peers. The lower house consisted of 136 elected deputies. No representatives came from Hungary, Transylvania, Venetia, the Banat, Slavonia, Croatia, and Istria. The Reichsrath was abolished by a rescript, 21 Sept. 1865, with the view of restoring autonomy to Hungary and other provinces. It again met 20 May, 1867. The Reichstag of Germany, the imperial parliament or diet, first met at Berlin, 21 Mar. 1871.

REIGATE (Surrey), sent two members to parliament in the reign of Edward I.; lost one by the Reform Act of 1832, and was wholly disfranchised for corruption by that of 1867.

REIGN OF TERROR. Maximilien Robespierre headed the populace in the Champ de Mars, in Paris, demanding the dethronement of the king, 17 July, 1791. He was triumphant in 1793, and numbers of eminent men and citizens were sacrificed during his sanguinary administration. Billaud Varennes denounced the tyranny of Robespierre in the tribune, 27 July, 1794. The next day he suffered death, with many of his companions; see *France*. This has been termed the *Red* Terror. The reaction after the restoration of the Bourbons, 1815, disgraced by many atrocious acts of wanton cruelty, has been termed the *White* Terror. The Jesuits were then conspicuous in the destruction of their adversaries.

REIGNS OF SOVEREIGNS. The average duration, according to Newton, is 19 years each; according to Hales 22¼ years; that of the sovereigns of England being 23½ years, and that of the popes, 7½ years. Pius IX. was the first pope who reigned above 25 years, 1846-78.

RELICS, the trade in these became general in the 7th century, fragments of bones, &c. being brought from Jerusalem. The sale of relics was prohibited by pope Innocent III. 1198, without effect.

RELIEF CHURCH, a secession from the church of Scotland, founded by Thomas Gillespie, who was deposed from his ministry for opposing the doctrine of passive obedience to the law of the church of Scotland respecting the settlement of ministers, 23 May, 1752. The church was constituted as the "presbytery of relief," 22 Oct. 1761. The Relief and Secession churches were united as the United Presbyterian Church, 13 May, 1847.

RELIEF OF DISTRESS (IRELAND) ACT, 43 & 44 Vict. c. 14, passed 2 Aug. 1880.

RELIGION (from *religo*, I bind again, in the sense of a vow or oath) comprehends a belief in the being and perfections of God, and obedience to his commandments. The Jewish religion is set forth in the Old, and the Christian religion in the New, Testament. Departure from these scriptures has been the origin of all corrupt forms of religion, as foretold in them. Buddhism differs from this. See *Mahometanism*, and other religions and sects under their names. The population of the globe with reference to religious worship, is given by Balbi (who assumed the total population to be 1,050,000,000), and Dieterici (who assumed it to be 1,288,000,000), as follows:

	Balbi (1836)	Dieterici (1859)
Jews	4,500,000	5,000,000
Christians	225,000,000	335,000,000
Roman Catholics	160,000,000	170,000,000
Mahometans	155,000,000	160,000,000
Idolators, &c. not professing the Jewish, Christian, or Mahometan worship	665,500,000	800,000,000

Estimate in 1869: 1,375,000,000.

Roman Catholics	195,460,200
Protestants	100,385,000
Eastern church	81,478,000
Buddhists	360,000,000
Other Asiatic religions	260,000,000
Pagans	200,000,000
Mahometans	165,000,000
Jews	7,000,000

In Europe (estimated) 1869 (*Almanach de Gotha*.)

Roman Catholics	144,000,000
Protestants	68,500,000
Greek Church	68,000,000
Jews	4,400,000
Mahometans	6,642,000

RELIGION OF HUMANITY, see *Positive Philosophy* and *Secularism*.

RELIGIOUS TRACT SOCIETY, founded 1799; receipts (1887), including sales, &c., 203,446*l*.

REMISSION OF PENALTIES ACT, see *Sunday*.

REMONSTRANCE, THE GRAND, drawn up by the house of commons, and presented to king Charles I., 1 Dec. 1641. It consisted of 206 articles, dwelt bitterly on all the king's illegal and oppressive acts, and was printed by order of the house.

REMONSTRANTS, see *Arminians*.

RENAISSANCE, a term applied to the revival of the classic style of art in the 15th and 16th centuries, under the patronage of the Medici and others; see *Painters*, and *Sculptors*.

RENDSBURG (Holstein), was taken by the imperialists in 1627; by the Swedes in 1643; and by the Prussians and confederate troops in 1848. The first diet of Schleswig and Holstein met here 3 April, 1848. It was re-occupied by the Danes in 1852, and taken by the Prussians after a serious conflict, 21 July, 1864.

RENNES (capital of Brittany, N. W. France). Here was established by Henry II., in 1553, the parliament so celebrated for its independence, especially in its struggle with the court, 1788-89. On 20 May, 1788, it declared infamous every one who should take part in the *cour plénière* then proposed, but afterwards suppressed.

RENTS said to have been first made payable in money, instead of in kind, about 1135. Numerous statutes have been enacted in various reigns to define the relations and regulate the dealings between landlord and tenant. 8 & 9 Vict. c. 106 (1845) regulates leases. By the act 8 Anne, 1709, no goods are removable from tenements under an execution until the rent shall have been paid to the landlord by the sheriff, 1709. The rental of England, including land, houses, and mines, was 6,000,000*l.* about the year 1600, and twelve years' purchase the value of land. About 1690, the rental amounted to 14,000,000*l.*, and the land was worth eighteen years' purchase. *Davenant on the Revenues.* The rental of the United Kingdom has been estimated in the present century at 127,000,000*l.*; Great anti-rent agitation in Ireland, 1879, *et seq.*; see *Land and Ireland,* &c.

REPEAL OF THE UNION, IRELAND. An Irish association was formed with this object under the auspices of Mr. O'Connell, in 1829. See *Home Rule and Ireland.*
A proclamation of the lord lieutenant prohibited the meetings of a society "leagued for the purpose of procuring a repeal of the union, under the name of the Irish Society for Legal and Legislative Relief, or the Anti-Union Society" . 18 Oct. 1830
The commons, by a majority of 484, reject Mr. O'Connell's motion for repeal . 27 April, 1834
A new association in 1841, 1842, and 1843 became more violent. Assemblies of the lower classes of the people were held in the last-named year, in various parts of Ireland, some of them amounting to 150,000 persons, and called "monster meetings."
A great meeting at Trim, 16 March ; other meetings were held at Mullingar, Cork, and Longford, on 14, 21, and 28 May, respectively ; at Drogheda, Kilkenny, Mallow, and Dundalk, on 5, 8, 11, and 29 June ; at Donnybrook and Baltinglass, 3 and 20 July ; at Tara, 15 Aug. ; at Loughrea, Clifton, and Lismore, 10, 17, and 24 Sept. ; and at Mullaghmast . . . . . 1 Oct. 1843
A meeting to be held at Clontarf, on 8 Oct. was prevented by government ; and Mr. O'Connell and his chief associates were brought to trial for political conspiracy, 15 Jan. 1844 ; and convicted 12 Feb. ; but the sentence was reversed by the house of lords, 4 Sept. ; see *Trials.*
The association for the repeal of the union continued for some time under the direction of Mr. John O'Connell, but was little regarded.
The total "repeal rent" is said to have amounted to 134,379*l.*
A fruitless attempt was made in Dublin to revive repeal agitation . . . . 4 Dec. 1860

REPLENISHER, see *Electricity (Frictional).*

REPORTING. The publication of the debates in parliament is forbidden as a breach of privilege, but was virtually conceded, after a severe struggle, in 1771.* Reporters' galleries were erected in the houses of parliament after the fire of 1834. To the unfettered liberty of reporting we doubtless owe much of our freedom and good government; see under *Law.* By the verdict for the defendant in the case of Wason *v. The Times* (for libel) reports of parliamentary debates were decided to be privileged, Nov. 1868. For the attempted exclusion of reporters, see *Parliament,* 1875. A commons committee on reporting recommend continuance of Hansard's debates with improvement, May, 1879.
The publication of Hansard's parliamentary debates began 1803 and closed in 1888 ; the publication of the debates was taken up by Messrs. Macrae, Curtice & Co. . . . . . Feb. 1889

REPRESENTATION OF THE PEOPLE ACT FOR ENGLAND, passed 15 Aug. 1867 ; for Ireland and Scotland, 13 July, 1868 ; a new act passed, 6 Dec. 1884. See *Reform.*

"REPTILE BUREAUCRACY," term applied in Germany to certain journalists writing for government pay, 1871, *et seq.*

REPUBLICANS, see *Democrats.* Sir Charles Dilke, M.P. professed himself a republican at public meetings and was much applauded, Nov. 1871 ; but at some places his appearance led to riotous proceedings. His motion for returns respecting the expenditure of the civil list by the queen was negatived in the house of commons (2—276), 19 March, 1872. A national republican conference of delegates was held at Sheffield, 1 Dec. 1872, when a national flag was adopted.

REPUBLICS, see *Athens, Rome, Genoa, Venice, France* (1792, 1848, 1870), and *Spain* (1873).

REQUESTS, COURTS OF; see *Court of Conscience.*

REQUIEM, a solemn mass, sung for the dead, so called from the introit "Requiem Æternam," &c. Palestrina's Requiem was printed at Rome, 1591 ; Vittoria's at Madrid, 1605 ; Mozart's last work was a requiem, 1791.

REREDOS, the screen or decorated portion of the wall behind the altar in a church.
A highly sculptured reredos, designed by sir G. G. Scott, was erected in Exeter cathedral, by subscription 1873
Prebendary Philpotts, the chancellor, and others who objected, brought their objections before the bishop's visitation court, on 7 Jan. ; it was decided that the bishop had jurisdiction in the matter, and he ordered the reredos to be removed, 15 April, 1874. Dean Boyd appealed to the court of arches, and sir R. Phillimore reversed the previous decision . . . . . 6 Aug. 1874
Prebendary Philpotts appealed to the judicial committee of the privy council, who decided that the reredos should remain . . . 24 Feb. 1875
The magnificent reredos set up in St. Paul's Cathedral, London, was protested against as idolatrous by some of the London clergy, April, 1888. An action against the dean having been stopped by the bishop, an action was brought against him in the queen's bench division in Nov. Chief justice Coleridge, justice Manisty, and baron Pollock ordered the bishop to withdraw his veto upon the prosecution . . 1 June, 1889

RESERVE FORCES. In the summer of 1859, acts were passed to provide for the establishment of a military reserve force of men who have been in her majesty's service (not to exceed 20,000), and a volunteer reserve force of seamen not to exceed 30,000. These acts were consolidated and amended in 1867 and 1882. The reserve forces called out by proclamation, on account of possible war with Russia, 2 April, 1878. About 35,000 good soldiers appeared, and were commended. They were disbanded 31

---

* Very inaccurate reports of parliamentary debates were inserted in the *Gentleman's Magazine* and other periodicals in the middle of the last century. Miller, printer of the *London Evening Mail,* was arrested in the city of London, by order of the house of commons, for publishing the debates, but was discharged by the lord mayor, who for doing this was sent to the Tower, where he remained until the end of the session. No opposition was made to the publication of the debates in the next session, 1772.

Aug. 1878. Again called out on account of war in Egypt, 25 July, 1882, and prospect of war with Russia, 27 March, 1885.

RESOLUTE, ship, see *Franklin Search*, 1854.

RESONATOR, a small apparatus, placed in the mouth to strengthen and increase the volume of the voice in singing, invented by signor Alberto Bach, who exhibited its effects at the Royal Academy of Music, 29 June, 1880.

RESPIRATORS, see *Charcoal* and *Fireman*.

RESTITUTION BILL, of Mr. Jesse Collings, proposes the surrender of lands illegally taken from commons, to be given to small cultivators, to become peasant proprietors, Jan. 1885.

RESTORATION, THE, of king Charles II. to the crown of England, after an interregnum of eleven years and four months, between 30 Jan. 1649, when Charles I. was beheaded, and 29 May, 1660, when Charles II. entered London amidst the acclamations of the people. The annual form of prayer, with thanksgiving, then appointed, was ordered to be disused by 22 Vict. c. 2, 25 March, 1849. See *France*, 1814, 1815.

RETREAT OF THE TEN THOUSAND GREEKS, who had joined the army of the younger Cyrus in his revolt against his brother, Artaxerxes Mnemon. The Greeks were victors, but Cyrus was defeated and slain at the battle of Cunaxa, 401 B.C. Artaxerxes having enticed the Greek leaders into his power and killed them, Xenophon was called to the command of his countrymen. Under continual alarms from sudden attacks, he led them across rapid rivers, through vast deserts, over the tops of mountains, till he reached the sea. The Greeks returned home after a march of 1155 parasangs or leagues (3465 miles), which was performed in 215 days, after the absence of fifteen months. This retreat has been immortalised by the account given by its conductor, in his "*Anabasis Cyri*" (Expedition of Cyrus).

REUNION, see *Order*.

REUSS-GREIZ AND **REUSS-SCHLEIZ**, two principalities in central Germany, with a united population of 166,502 in 1885. The reigning family sprang from Ekbert, count of Osterode, in the 10th century. The princely dignity was conferred by the emperor Sigismond in 1426.

1859. Henry XXII., prince of Reuss-Greiz, 8 Nov.; born 28 March, 1846.

REVELATION, see *Apocalypse*.

REVENUE AND EXPENDITURE OF ENGLAND. The revenue collected for the civil list, and for all the other charges of government, as well ordinary as extraordinary, was 1,200,000*l*. per annum, in 1660, the first after the restoration of Charles II. In 1690 it was raised to 6,000,000*l*., every branch of the revenue being anticipated; this was the origin of the funds and the national debt, 2 William and Mary. *Salmon.* The revenue laws were amended in 1861. Previously to 1854 there had been an average *surplus* of 2,500,000*l*. since 1849. In consequence of the Russian war the *deficiency* in 1854 was 3,209,059*l*.; in 1855, 21,141,183*l*.; in 1856, 10,104,412*l*. In 1857 there was a *surplus* of 36,097*l*.; in 1858, of 1,127,657*l*.; in 1859, a *deficiency* of 2,019,584*l*.

PUBLIC REVENUE.

William I. estimated	£400,000
William Rufus	350,000
Henry I.	300,000
Stephen	250,000
Henry II.	200,000
Richard I.	150,000
John	100,000
Henry III.	80,000
Edward I.	150,000
Edward II.	100,000
Edward III.	154,000
Richard II.	130,000
Henry IV.	100,000
Henry V.	76,643
Henry VI.	64,976
Edward IV.	*
Edward V.	100,000
Richard III.	130,000
Henry VII.	400,000
Henry VIII.	800,000
Edward VI.	400,000
Mary	450,000
Elizabeth	500,000
James I.	600,000
Charles I.	895,819
Commonwealth	1,517,247
Charles II.	1,400,000
James II.	2,001,855
William III.	3,895,205
Anne (at the Union)	5,691,803
George I.	6,762,643
George II.	8,522,540
George III., 1788	15,572,971
„ 1800, about	38,000,000
United Kingdom, 1820	65,599,570
George IV., 1825	62,871,300
William IV., 1830	55,431,317
„ 1835	50,494,732
Victoria, 1845, net	53,060,354
„ 1850	52,810,680
„ 1853	54,430,344

	Revenue.	Expenditure.
1855, net	£63,364,605	£65,692,962
1856	68,008,623	88,428,345
1857	66,056,055	75,588,667
1858	61,812,525	68,128,859

	Gross Revenue.	Gross Expenditure, exclusive of Fortifications.
1859, 31 March, gross	£65,477,284	£64,663,883
1860	72,089,669	69,502,289
1863	70,603,561	69,302,008
1864	70,208,964	67,056,286
1865	70,313,437	66,462,207
1866	67,812,292	65,914,357
1867	69,434,568	66,780,396
1868	69,600,219	71,236,242
1869	72,591,991	72,069,961
1870	75,454,252	68,864,752
1871	69,945,220	69,548,539
1872	74,708,314	71,490,020
1873	76,608,770	70,714,448
1874	77,335,057	76,466,510
1875	75,434,252	74,328,040
1876	77,131,693	76,621,773
1877	78,565,036	78,125,227
1878	79,763,298	82,403,495
1879	83,115,972	85,407,789
1880	81,265,055	84,105,754
1881	84,041,288	83,107,924
1882	85,822,282	85,472,556
1883	89,004,456	88,906,278
1884	87,205,184	86,999,564
1885	88,043,660	89,092,883
Vote of Credit, 27 April, 1885		11,000,000
1886	89,581,301	92,223,844
1887	90,772,758	89,996,752
1888	89,802,254	87,423,645
1889	88,473,000	

* Revised in relation to army, navy, and India.

The weekly instead of the quarterly publication of the public revenue and expenditure was begun by Mr. Robert Lowe, the chancellor of the exchequer, 16 Feb. 1870. By an act passed 31 July, 1868, revenue officers are permitted to vote for the election of members of parliament. Above 100 statutes relating to inland revenue fell into disuse 1 Jan. 1871.
The revenue friendly societies, and national debt act, 45 & 46 Vict., c. 72, passed 18 Aug. 1882. New revenue act passed, 1884.

REVEREND, an honorary appellation given to the clergy, since the middle of the 17th century.
In Tamworth parish register the minister is first styled "reverend," in 1657, occasionally afterwards; but regularly so after 1727. It first appears in the registry of All Hallows, Barking . 1732
The prefix on a family tombstone was refused to Mr. Keet, a Wesleyan preacher, by the bishop of Lincoln, but given by the archbishop of Canterbury 1874
On trial, Mr. Walter G. F. Phillimore, the chancellor of Lincoln, decided against Mr. Keet, who gave notice of appeal, 3 June. Sir R. Phillimore gave a similar decision in the court of arches, 31 July, 1875
On appeal to the privy council these decisions were reversed. It was decided that there is no law or usage restricting the epithet to ministers of the Church of England; it is merely laudatory.
21 Jan. 1876

REVIEWS. The *Journal des Scavans*, published on 5 Jan. 1665, by Denis de Salo, under the name of Hédouville, was the parent of critical journals. It was soon imitated throughout Europe, and was itself translated into various languages. It is still published. George III. spoke of this publication to Dr. Johnson, in the private interview with which he was honoured by his majesty, in the library of the queen's house, in Feb. 1767. *Boswell*. The *Bibliothèque Anglaise* came out in 1716-27. For Military REVIEWS, see *Aldershot, Army* and *Volunteers*. For Naval REVIEWS, see *Navy*.

Monthly Review	. 1749	National	. 1855
Critical	. 1756	Saturday	,,
Anti-Jacobin	. 1798	Fortnightly	. 1865
Edinburgh	. 1802	Contemporary	. 1866
Quarterly	. 1809	Academy	. 1869
Eclectic	. 1813	Church Quarterly	. 1875
North American	. 1815	Nineteenth Century	. 1877
Retrospective	. 1820	National Review	. 1883
Westminster	. 1824	Law Quarterly	. 1885
Athenæum	. 1828	English Historical Review	. 1886
Dublin	. 1836		
North British	. 1844	Universal Review	. 1888
British Quarterly	,,	"New Review"	. 1889

REVISERS, see under *Bible*.

REVISING BARRISTERS' COURTS, to examine the lists of voters for members of parliament, were instituted by the Reform Act of 1832.

REVISION, see under *Bible*. Advocates of the revision of the French constitution, chiefly Bonapartists or Jeromists, termed *Revisionists*, Feb. 1884.

REVIVALS on the subject of religion arose in the United States in 1857. In the autumn of 1859, they began in Scotland, the north of Ireland (particularly Belfast), and England. Many meetings were held for prayers and preaching throughout the week, as well as on Sundays. The *"twelve days' mission,"* a series of revival services, took place in many London churches during advent, 1869.

Mr. Moody, preacher, and Mr. Sankey, singer, American Revivalists, visited many towns in the United Kingdom, 1874-5. Their meetings in London began at the Agricultural Hall, 9 March, about 15,000 present; at the Queen's theatre, Haymarket, 12 April-31 May; farewell meeting, 12 July, 1875. Moody and Sankey again in London, 6 Oct. 1881; 3 Nov. 1883-23 June, 1884.

REVOLUTIONARY CALENDAR, see *French Revolution*, and *Calendar*.

REVOLUTIONARY TRIBUNAL, established at Paris, Aug. 1792.
Up to 27 July, 1794, when Robespierre was deposed, it had put to death 2774 persons, including queen Marie Antoinette, the princess Elizabeth, and a large number of nobility and gentry, male and female. The oldest victim was counsellor Dupin, aged 97; the youngest, Charles Dubost, aged 14. From 27 July to 15 Dec. 1794, only Robespierre and his accomplices (about 100) suffered by it.

REVOLUTIONS:—
The Assyrian empire destroyed, and that of the Medes and Persians founded by Cyrus the Great,
B.C.
The Macedonian empire founded on the destruction of the Persian, by the defeat of Darius Codomannus, by Alexander the Great 536
The Roman empire established on the ruins of the republic by Julius Cæsar 331
The empire of the Western Franks begun under Charlemagne 47
	A.D.
In Portugal	800
In England	1640
In Russia	1649 and 1688
In North America	1730 and 1762
In Venice	1775
In Sweden	1797
In Holland, 1795; counter-revolution	1772 and 1809
In Poland	1813
In the Netherlands	1704, 1795, and 1830
In Brunswick	,,
In Brazil	1831
In Hungary	1848
In Rome	1798 and 1848
In France	1789, 1830, 1848, 1851, 1870, and 1871
In Italy	1859 and 1860
In United States	1860-5
In Danubian principalities	1866
In Papal States, suppressed	Oct. 1867
In Spain	Sept. 1868 and Dec. 1874

[See the countries respectively.]
Among the results of the *Revolution* of 1688 in Great Britain, were the toleration act, the establishment of the presbyterian kirk of Scotland, the power of granting supplies limited to the house of commons, the purification of the administration of justice, and unlicensed printing.

REVOLVERS, see *Pistols*.

REVUE DES DEUX MONDES, the French literary and historical periodical published on the 1st and 15th of each month, first appeared in 1831. It includes among its contributors the most eminent writers in France.

REYNARD THE FOX, "REINEKE FUCHS," a satirical epic in low German, in which beasts are actors and speakers, was first printed as Reineke Vos, at Lubeck in 1498, and professes to be written by Hinreck van Alkmer. It has been frequently translated. Goethe's version in High (or literary) German hexameters appeared in 1794. Jacob Grimm has shown that the subject-matter of this "Thier-sage" or "beast-fable" is very ancient, many incidents being found in Pilpay and other oriental writers. The early French had a "Roman de Renart," and "Renart le Nouvel." A poem, entitled "der Reinaert," in Flemish, was known in the 11th century; Caxton's translation in English prose was printed 1481; a poetic English translation of Goethe's version, by T. J. Arnold, appeared in 1855.

REZONVILLE, BATTLE OF, 18 Aug. 1870, see *Metz*.

RHÆTIA (or RÆTIA), an ancient Alpine country, comprising the modern Grisons, Tyrol, and part of Lombardy, inhabited by a wild rapa-

cious people, after a long struggle was conquered by Drusus and Tiberius, B.C. 15.

RHÉ, ISLE OF, see *Ré* and *Rochelle*.

RHEA, see *China Grass*.

RHEGIUM (now Reggio), S. Italy, a Greek colony, flourished in the 5th century, B.C. It was held by the Campanian legion, 281-271, afterwards severely punished for its rebellion. Reggio was taken by Garibaldi, Aug. 1860.

RHEIMS (N. France). The principal church here, built before 406, rebuilt in the 12th century, is now very beautiful. The corpse of St. Remy, the archbishop, is preserved behind the high altar, in a magnificent shrine. The kings of France were crowned at Rheims; probably because Clovis, the founder of the French monarchy, when converted from paganism, was baptized in the cathedral in 496. Several ecclesiastical councils have been held here. The city was taken and retaken several times in the last months of the French war, 1814. University founded by cardinal Lorraine, 1547, suppressed about 1790.

RHEOMETER, see under *Electricity*.

RHETORIC. Rhetorical points and accents were invented by Aristophanes of Byzantium, 200 B.C. Rhetoric was first taught in Latin at Rome by Photius Gallus, about 87 B.C. He taught Cicero, who said "We are first to consider what is to be said; secondly, how; thirdly, in what words; and lastly, how it is to be ornamented." A regius professor of rhetoric was appointed in Edinburgh, 20 April, 1762, when Dr. Blair became first professor.

RHINE (Latin, *Rhenus*; German, *Rhein*; French, *Rhin*), a river, about 760 miles long, rising in Switzerland, receiving the Moselle, Main, Meuse, Neckar, and other rivers, terminating in many arms in Holland, and falling into the German ocean. On its banks are Constance, Basel, Strasbourg, Spires, Mannheim, Cologne, Düsseldorf, Utrecht, and Leyden. The possession of the banks of the Rhine has been the cause of many wars, and it has been crossed by the French above twenty times in a century. In the beginning of the revolutionary war, Custine invaded Germany by crossing it in 1792; and at the close of the war in 1815, France retained the left bank, but lost it at the close of the Franco-Prussian war, 1870-1 (*which see*). A navigation treaty with other powers was signed by France, 17 Oct. 1868. A central committee for the navigation exists, formed by members for Alsace, Lorraine, Baden, Bavaria, Hesse, Holland, and Prussia. Very great damage (about 4,000,000*l*.) and loss of life, caused by the rising of the river through excessive rain, end of November and December, 1882; relieved by government grants.

Becker's German song "They shall not have it, the free German Rhine;" and Alfred de Musset's reply, in French, *Rhin*), "We have had it, your German Rhine," appeared in 1841. Max Schneckenburger, author of "The Watch on the Rhine," died 1851. All were popular during the war, 1870-71.

RHODE ISLAND (N. America), settled by Roger Williams about 1636, was taken in the war of independence by the British, 8 Dec. 1776; but was evacuated by them, 25 Oct. 1779. Population in 1880, 276,531; see *United States*.

RHODES, an island on the coast of Asia Minor, is said to have been peopled from Crete, as early as 916 B.C. The Rhodians were great navigators, and institutors of a maritime code afterwards adopted by the Romans. The city was built about 432 and flourished 300-200 B.C.; see *Colossus*. Rhodes, long an ally of the Romans, was taken by the emperor Vespasian, A.D. 71. It was held by the Knights Hospitallers from 1309 to 1522, when it was conquered by the Turks, who still retain it. The knights retired to Malta (*which see*). Rhodes suffered severely by an earthquake on 22 April, 1863.

RHODIUM, a rare metal, discovered in platinum ore, by Dr. Wollaston in 1804. It has been used for the points of metallic pens.

RHODOPE MOUNTAINS (Turkish, Despoto Dagh), a plateau in Roumelia.

In these about 150,000 Mahometans took refuge during the Russo-Turkish war, on the approach of the Russians in Dec. 1877, and Jan. 1878; and resisted the invaders. The Russians were accused of killing and outraging thousands of men, women, and children. A European commission of inquiry; met 21 July; closed, 26 Aug.; confirmed the statements, but issued no united report; some members seceded 1878
The insurgents asserted that they were not resisting the sultan himself, but maladministration. They are governed by an English chief, col. St. Clair, who receives the taxes, &c., and is styled "commander-in-chief of the national army of the Rhodope" . . . . . . Sept. „
About 40,000 destitute; reported . . 18 Jan. 1879
The insurrection gradually subsided.

RHUBARB. This plant was first cultivated for its stalks to be used as food by Mr. Myall, of Deptford, about 1820, and soon after came into general use.

RHUDDLAN, statute of, see *Wales*, 1283.

RIALTO, BRIDGE OF THE, at Venice (mentioned by Shakspeare in his "*Merchant of Venice*"), built about 1590, consists of a marble arch across the Grand Canal, 90 feet wide and 24 feet high.

RIBBONISM, a term given to the principles of a secret society in Ireland, organised about 1820, to retaliate on landlords any injuries done to their tenants. To the ribbonmen are attributed many of the agrarian murders, 1858-71-79. An act was passed to repress them, 16 June, 1871.

RICE, the *Oryza sativa* of botanists, in the husk termed paddy; largely grown in intertropical regions, occupying the same place as wheat in the warmer parts of Europe. It was conveyed to South Carolina near the end of the 17th century, and its cultivation greatly increased.

The duty on foreign rice, 15s., on colonial rice, 1s. per cwt., was reduced by sir Robert Peel in 1842 to 6s. 3d. and 6½d. respectively. Further reductions were made in 1846, and in 1860 the duty was totally abolished.
Imported into Britain: 1846, 770,604 cwt.; 1856, 3,724,695 cwt.; 1866, 2,309,494 cwt.; 1856, 3,700,124 cwt.; 1866, 2,276,792 cwt.; 1877, 6,617,739 cwt.; 1879, 6,857,330 cwt.; 1881, 8,500,062 cwt.; 1883, 7,747,725 cwt.; 1885, 5,588,650 cwt.; 1887, 5,019,512 cwt.

RICHMOND (Surrey), anciently called Sheen, which in the Saxon tongue signifies *resplendent*. Here stood a palace in which Edward I. and II. resided, and Edward III. died, 1377. Here also died Anne, queen of Richard II., 1394. The palace was repaired by Henry V., who founded three religious houses near it. In 1497 it was destroyed by fire; but Henry VII. rebuilt it, and commanded that the village should be called Richmond, he having borne the title of earl of Richmond (Yorkshire) before he obtained the crown: and here he died in 1509. Queen Elizabeth was a prisoner in this palace for a short time during the reign of her sister. When she became queen it was one of her

favourite places of residence; and here she died 24 March, 1603. It was afterwards the residence of Henry, prince of Wales. The beautiful park and gardens were enclosed by Charles I. The observatory was built by sir W. Chambers in 1769. In Richmond, Thomson "sang the Seasons and their change;" and died 27 Aug. 1748.

The Star and Garter tavern burnt; W. Lever, the manager, perished . . . . 12 Jan. 1870
Mrs. Julia Martha Thomas was murdered at Richmond, her body cut up, put in bags and cast into river Thames, by Katherine Webster, aged 30, about 2 March; John Church, a publican, arrested on suspicion, discharged 17 April; Webster committed for trial, 16 May; convicted, 8 July; confessed; executed at Wandsworth . . 29 July, 1879

RICHMOND (Virginia, U. S.) became the capital of the southern confederate states. The congress adjourned from Montgomery, Alabama, to Richmond, where it met 20 July, 1861. After a siege of 1452 days and many desperate battles, Richmond was evacuated by the confederates, 2 April, 1865; see *United States*. By the fall of the flooring in the state capital building, about 60 persons were killed, 27 April, 1870. A statue of "Stonewall" Jackson (subscribed for by Englishmen), was unveiled here in presence of his wife and child, 26 Oct. 1875. Population 1880, 63,600.

RIDING, see *Races*.

Leon, a Mexican, rode 100 miles, consecutively, in 4 hours 57 minutes, using 6 "Mustang horses," 15 July, 1876; 505 miles in 49 h. 51½ min.
8–10 Feb. 1877

RIFLE CORPS, see *Volunteers*, and *Firearms*. *Rifle Brigade* formed, 1800. International rifle meeting, Washington, began, 26 Sept. 1876. Another at Creedmoor, near New York, began 14 Sept.; the British victors, 1882.

RIGHTS, BILL OF. To the PETITION OF RIGHTS, preferred 17 March, 1627-8, Charles I. answered, "I will that right be done according to the laws and customs of the realm." Both houses addressed the king for a fuller answer to their petition of rights, whereupon he gave them an answer less evasive, "*Soit droit fait comme il est désiré*," 7 June, 1628. The petition thus became a statute 13 Car. I. c. 1. An important declaration was made by the lords and commons of England to the prince and princess of Orange on 13 Feb. 1689, in an act "declaring the rights and liberties of the subject, and settling the succession of the crown." The Bill of Rights, virtually the same as the declaration, was passed by parliament. It totally abolished the dispensing power of the crown, Oct. 1689. See *Claim of Right*.

RIMNIK (near Martinesti, Wallachia). Here the Austrians and Russians under prince Coburg and gen. Suwarrow, gained a great victory over the Turks, 22 Sept. 1789.

RINDERPEST, German for *cattle plague* (*which see*).

RING DES NIBELUNGEN, see *Nibelunge Not*.

RINGS anciently had a seal or signet engraved on them, to seal writings, and they are so used to this day. In Genesis xli. 42, it is said that Pharaoh gave Joseph his ring. Rings are now put upon women's fourth finger at marriage; but the Jews used them at the espousal or contract *before* marriage. Wedding-rings are to be of standard gold by statute, 1855.

RINK (from the Gaelic *rian*, or Saxon *hrine*, a course), a term used in the Scotch game, "curling."
The Belgravia skating rink, London, S.W., was opened to the public . . . . . . 2 Aug. 1875
Others since at Brighton and other places. Skates with rollers (said to have been introduced in a scene of Meyerbeer's "Prophète," at Paris, 16 April, 1849), are used. Mr. Plimpton, an American, patented roller-skates in 1865; his right was affirmed on a trial for infringement. 28 Jan. 1876
See *Glaciarium*.

RIO DE JANEIRO (S. America), discovered by De Sousa, 1 Jan. 1531; see *Brazil*. In 1807 it was made capital of the empire of Brazil.

RIOTS. The riotous assembling of twelve or more persons, and their not dispersing upon proclamation, was first made high treason by a statute enacted 2 & 3 Edw. VI. 1548-9. The present *Riot Act* was passed 1 Geo. I. 1714.

Riots against Jews in London	1189
Some riotous citizens of London demolished the convent belonging to Westminster abbey; the ringleader was hanged, and the rest had their hands and feet cut off, 6 Hen. III.	1221
Goldsmiths' and Tailors' companies fought in the streets of London; several killed; the sheriffs quelled it; and thirteen hanged . . .	1262
A riot at Norwich; the rioters burnt the cathedral and monastery; the king went thither, and saw the ringleaders executed	1271
Riot of Evil May-day (*which see*)	1517
Dr. Lamb killed by the mob . . . . June, 1628
A riot on pretence of pulling down houses of ill-fame; several of the ringleaders hanged . .	1668
Another, at Guildhall, at the election of sheriffs; several considerable persons, who seized the lord mayor, were concerned	1682
At Edinburgh and Dumfries, on account of the Union	1707
In London, on account of Dr. Henry Sacheverel, for preaching two sermons (one 5 Nov. 1709), voted by the house of commons to be scandalous and seditious; several dissenting meeting-houses were broken open and destroyed . . . . Feb.	1710
Riot of the Whig and Tory mobs, called Ormond and Newcastle mobs . . . . . 29 May,	1715
The *Mug-house* riot, in Salisbury-court, between the Whigs and Tories; the riot quelled by the guards; five rioters hanged . . . . . 24 July,	1716
Of the Spitalfields weavers, on account of employing workmen come over from Ireland; quelled by the military, but many lives lost	1736
Porteous riot at Edinburgh (see *Porteous*) 7 Sept.	"
The nailers in Worcestershire march to Birmingham, and make terms with iron merchants there	1737
Of the Spitalfield weavers; the duke of Bedford narrowly escaped death; lives lost . May,	1765
A mob in St. George's-fields, to see Mr. Wilkes in the King's Bench prison; the military aid indiscreetly called for by the justices of the peace, and several innocent persons, particularly young Allen, fired upon, and killed . . . . . 10 May,	1768
Gordon's "No Popery" riots . 10 May, 2-9 June,	1780
At Birmingham, on account of commemorating the French revolution, when several houses were destroyed . . . . 14 July,	1791
In various parts of Scotland, on account of the militia act, when several were killed . Aug.	1797
At Maidstone, at the trial of Arthur O'Connor and others, 22 May, 1798; the earl of Thanet, Mr. Ferguson, and others, were active in endeavouring to rescue O'Connor, for which they were tried and convicted . . . . 25 April,	1799
At Liverpool, occasioned by a quarrel between a party of dragoons and a press-gang . 27 June,	1809
O. P. riot (*which see*) at Covent-garden . Sept.	"
In Piccadilly, in consequence of the house of commons committing sir Francis Burdett to the Tower . . . . 6 April,	1810
Machinery destroyed by rioters at Nottingham from Nov. 1811 to Jan.	1812
In various parts of the north of England, by the Luddites, during . . . . . 1811 and	"

RIOTS.

At Sheffield, during which 800 muskets belonging to the local militia were destroyed . 14 April, 1812
At the Theatre Royal, Dublin, on account of the celebrated *Dog of Montargis*, several nights, Dec. 1814
Alarming riots at Westminster, on account of Corn bill; lasted several days . . . March, 1815
At the depôt at Dartmoor, in quelling which seven American prisoners of war were killed, and thirty-five wounded . . . . . . April, „
Popular meetings at Spa-fields, when the shops of the gunsmiths were attacked for arms. Mr. Platt shot in that of Mr. Beckwith, on Snow-hill (Watson tried for high treason, but acquitted, June, 1817) . . . . . . 2 Dec. 1816
In St. James's park, on the prince-regent going to the house of lords; it was said that an air-gun was fired at him . . . . 28 Jan. 1817
At Manchester, at a popular meeting . 3 March, „
Affray at Manchester, called the " Field of Peterloo" (see *Manchester reform meeting*) . 16 Aug. 1819
At the Theatre Royal, Dublin, of several nights' duration . . . . „
Riot at Paisley and Glasgow; many houses plundered . . . . 16 Sept. „
At Edinburgh, on the acquittal of queen Caroline, 19 Nov. 1820
In London, at the funeral of the queen 14 Aug. 1821
At Knightsbridge, between the military and the populace, on the funeral of Honey and Francis, (killed 14 Aug.) . . . . . 26 Aug. „
At the theatre in Dublin; the riot called the " Bottle conspiracy," against the marquis Wellesley, lord-lieutenant . . . . 14 Dec. 1822
Riot at Ballybay; Lawless arrested . 9 Oct. 1828
Riot at Limerick; the provision-warehouses plundered and mischief done . . 15 June, 1830
Fatal affrays at Castlepollard, 23 May; and Newtownbarry (*which see*) . . . . 18 June, 1831
Alarming riots at Merthyr-Tydvil among the iron-workers; several fired upon by the military, killed and wounded . . . . . 3 June, „
Riot at the Forest of Dean (see *Dean*) . 8 June, „
Nottingham castle burnt by rioters . 10 Oct. „
Reform riots at Bristol (see *Bristol*) . 29 Oct. „
Affray at Castleshock, county Kilkenny, when a number of police, attacked by the populace, were, with their commander, Mr. Gibins, killed, 14 Dec. „
Riot at Boughton, near Canterbury, produced by persons called *Thomites*, headed by a fanatic, Thom, or Courtenay, who, with others, was killed (see *Thomites*) . . . . . 28-31 May, 1838
Great riots throughout the country, occasioned by the chartists; a proclamation . . 12 Dec. „
Riots in Birmingham; much mischief . July, 1839
Chartist riot at Newport (*which see*) . 4 Nov. „
Meditated chartist outbreak at Sheffield, with most destructive objects, providentially discovered, and many persons arrested . . . 11 Jan. 1840
Rebecca riots against turnpikes in Wales . . 1843
Chartist demonstration (see *Chartists*) 10 April, 1848
Fatal affray at Dolly's Brae, near Castlewellan, in Ireland, between the Orangemen and the Roman catholics; several of the latter lost their lives, and some of their houses were ransacked and burnt . . . . 12 July, 1849
Serious riots at Yarmouth, through a dispute between the shipowners and the seamen 23 Feb. 1851
Riots occasioned by a procession of Orangemen at Liverpool, and several lives lost . 14 July, „
Riot at Stockport, Cheshire; two catholic chapels destroyed and houses burnt . . 29 June, 1852
Fierce religious riots at Belfast, in Ireland, occur, 14 July, „
Fatal election riot at Six-mile-bridge, in the county of Clare, in Ireland; five persons shot dead by the military . . . . . . 22 July, „
Riots at Wigan, among the coal-miners, suppressed by the military without loss of life . 28 Oct. 1853
Bread riots at Liverpool . . . 19 Feb. 1855
Riots at Hyde-park, about Sunday bill, July, 1855; about dearness of bread . . . 21, 28 Oct. „
Riots at Belfast through the open-air preaching of the rev. Hugh Hanna . . 6, 13, 20 Sept. 1857
Religious riots at St. George's-in-the-East, London, on Sundays in . . . . Sept. and Nov. 1859
Break-out of the convicts at Chatham, suppressed by the military . . . . . 11 Feb. 1861

Violent riots at Belfast begin, through an Orange demonstration . . . . . 17 Sept. 1862
Fierce rioting (caused by the Irish against the favourers of Garibaldi) at Hyde-park, London, 28 Sept. and 5 Oct.; and at Birkenhead, Cheshire, 8 and 15 Oct. 1862
Rioting at Staleybridge (on account of the mode of relief to the unemployed cotton-workers), principally Irish; put down by the military, 21 March, 1863
Fierce conflicts between Romanists and Protestants at Belfast; 9 persons killed, and about 150 injured 10-27 Aug. 1864
Reform riots in Hyde-park, London; much damage, and many hurt . . . . 23, 24 July, 1866
Anti-popery riots at Birmingham, through the lecturing of Murphy: much damage done to houses, 17, 18 June, 1867
Col. Kelly and Deasy committed for trial as Fenians: rescued from the prisoners' van; Brett, a police sergeant, shot dead . . . . 18 Sept. „
At Wigan; colliers on strike . . end of April, 1868
Fierce riots against a colliery manager at Mold, Flintshire, put down by the military; 4 deaths, 2 June, 1869
Violent rioting at a colliery at Thorncliffe, near Sheffield; quelled by intervention of lord Wharncliffe and others . . . . . 21 Jan. 1870
Rioting at Armathwaite, near Carlisle, between English and Irish navvies . . 15, 16 Oct. „
Violent riots at Belfast . . . 19, 20 Aug. 1872
Riots at Northampton, because Mr. C. Bradlaugh was not elected M. P.; suppressed by military 6 Oct. 1874
At Blackburn, Burnley, Accrington, Preston, and other places, through cotton strike and lock-out; several mills and houses destroyed; riots quelled by the military . . . . 14, 15 May, 1878
At Camborne, Cornwall, against the Irish; a Romanist church destroyed . . 17-18 April, 1882
At Wrexham, of coal miners . . 19 April, „
Westminster rolliery . . . . 19 April, „
In Skye, cottars against rent about 19 April-Sept. „
In Dublin, through resignation of police, suppressed by the military . . . . . 1 Sept. „
At Kidderminster . . . . 4-8 April, 1884
Peaceable mass meeting of the unemployed in Trafalgar-square, joined by the social democrats with red flag led by Hyndman, Burns, and Champion, who, unchecked for about two hours (4 to 6 p.m.), from Pall Mall to Oxford-street and neighbourhood, smash windows, ransack shops, attack and rob private carriages: finally dispersed: police organisation inefficient (except by superintendent Cuthbert); estimated damage 11,000l., 8 Feb.; other meetings; rioting checked 9, 10 Feb.; rioters sentenced to various terms of imprisonment . . . . . March, 1886
Riots at Leicester occasioned by a strike; destruction of factories, &c.; partially checked by the police, 11, 12 Feb.; rioting continued 13-16 Feb. „
Riots Damages Act passed . . . . „
Destructive riot of coal-miners at Plas-Power colliery near Wrexham . . . 30 Sept. „
Violent riots of Lanarkshire miners at Hamilton, Airdrie, &c.; 74 men arrested . 8-10 Feb. 1887
Riot at Lillie Bridge, West Brompton; structures destroyed and burnt by a crowd (about 5,000) disappointed at the non-performance of a race and their money not returned . . 19 Sept. „
Riotous assemblage of the unemployed in Trafalgar-square dispersed 17 Oct.; meeting at Hyde Park dispersed by the police after severe conflict, 18 Oct.; again dispersed 19 Oct.; meeting in Trafalgar-square, about 2,000 went to Westminster Abbey; disorderly, 23 Oct.; quiet meetings 24-27 Oct. and since; arrests for seditious language, &c., 4-8 Nov.; meetings in Trafalgar-square prohibited; 8 and 18 Nov.; processions of disorderly mob dispersed, and meetings in Trafalgar-square prevented by mounted and foot police aided by the 1st life guards; several severe conflicts with men using iron bars and knives; many seriously injured, chiefly police; Mr. Cunninghame Graham, M.P., a magistrate, and Mr. John Burns and many others arrested; moderate conduct of the police; sir C. Warren's arrangements thoroughly successful, Sunday, 13 Nov.; many sentenced to penal servitude . . . . . 14 Nov. „

Funeral procession of Alfred Linnell, a law writer, accidentally killed in a crowd in Northumberland-avenue on Sunday, 20 Nov., from Soho to Bow cemetery: Messrs. Cunninghame Graham, M.P., Wm. Morris the poet, and others present; order was only maintained by a large body of police
18 Dec. 1887
See *Strikes*, 1881; *Ireland*; *Crofters*, 1887-8; and *Belfast*.

RIPON (Yorkshire), an ancient town. About 661 an abbey cell was built here by Eata. Ripon was made a bishopric by archbishop Wilfred, in 690, but did not endure so. It suffered much by the ravages of the Danes, the Normans (1069), and the Scots (1319 and 1323). The present see was erected 5 Oct. 1836, out of the archdeaconry of York in the West Riding. Income 4,200*l*. The cathedral was restored by sir G. G. Scott: the choir was re-opened 27 Jan. 1869. The thousandth anniversary of its incorporation was celebrated 25-27 Aug. 1886.

BISHOPS.
1836. Charles Thos. Longley, trans. to Durham, 1856.
1856. Robert Bickersteth, died 15 April, 1884.
1884. Wm. Boyd Carpenter, May.

RITCHIE'S ACT, see under *Local Government*.

RITUALISTS, a name given in 1866 to a party in the church of England, formerly termed Puseyites, for endeavouring to give a more imposing character to public worship, by the use of coloured vestments, lighted candles, incense, &c., professing to go back to the practices of the church in the time of Edward VI. An exhibition of these things was held during the church congress at York in Oct. 1866, but was not officially connected with it. The practices of the ritualists (said by Mr. Disraeli to be symbolical of doctrines they were bound to renounce), were censured in several episcopal charges in Dec. 1866; in two reports of the ritualistic commission, 19 Aug. 1867, and April, 1868, and by the judicial committee of the privy council on appeal, 23 Dec. 1868. See *Church of England* and *Trials*, 1867-9. At a general convocation of the American episcopal church at Philadelphia, 27, 28 Oct. 1868, after a warm discussion on ritualism, the discussion was adjourned. It was renewed at the convocation 10 Oct. 1874, and the ritualists were decidedly beaten by the evangelical party, a stringent canon on ceremonies being passed 27 Oct. The "Public Worship Regulation Act" was passed 7 Aug. 1874, for the repression of *ritualism* in England. See *Public Worship*.

RIVERS COMMISSIONS, first appointed, 1865, Messrs. R. Rawlinson, J. T. Harrison, and Professor Way; second, 1868; sir Wm. Denison, Mr. J. Chalmers Morton, and Professor Frankland.
Published six blue books 1874
Association for preserving the rivers of Scotland, formed . . . . Jan. 1875
The Pollution of Rivers Act passed . . 15 Aug. 1876

RIVOLI (near Verona, N. Italy). Near here the Austrians defeated the French, 17 Nov. 1796; and were defeated by Bonaparte 14, 15 Jan. 1797. Massena was made duke of Rivoli for his share in the actions.

ROAD CLUB, established in the autumn of 1874 in London, by gentlemen interested in the revival of coaching.

ROAD MURDER. On the night of 29-30 June, 1860, Francis Savile Kent, four years old, was murdered, and his body hid in a garden water-closet at Road. His sister Constance Kent (aged sixteen), and the nurse Elizabeth Gough (the first suspected), were discharged for want of evidence. The coroner was severely blamed for charging the jury improperly, but the court of queen's bench, in Jan. 1861, refused to issue a writ for a new inquiry. Constance Kent, on 25 April, 1865, before sir Thomas Henry at Bow-street, and at her trial at Salisbury, on 21 July following, confessed herself to be guilty of the murder. Her punishment was commuted to penal servitude for life. Let out on ticket-of-leave, 18 July, 1885. Road is near Frome, Somerset.

ROADS, see *Roman Roads*. The first general repair of the highways of this country was directed about 1285. Acts were passed for the purpose in 1524 and 1555, followed by others in Elizabeth's and succeeding reigns. Roads through the Highlands of Scotland were begun by general Wade in 1726. Loudon M°Adam's roads were introduced about 1818. Wooden pavements were tried with partial success in the streets of London: at Whitehall in 1839, and in other streets in 1840; asphalte pavement soon after. An act "for the better management of the highways" was passed in 1862 after much opposition; another, 16 Aug. 1878; also regulated the use of locomotives on roads. Steam road-rollers were tried in 1867; used in London 18 March, 1868: see *Macadamising*, *Tolls*, and *Wooden Pavements*.

ROAD STEAMERS. Mr. R. W. Thomson, of Edinburgh, in 1868, by adding india-rubber to the tires of the wheels of locomotives is considered to have solved the question of steam traction on common roads. Road steamers have been successfully employed in Edinburgh and Leith for drawing heavy waggons up inclined planes, and are adaptable to any draught work. They were tried at Woolwich, 1 Oct. 1870, and reported successful by eminent authorities; and their application to ploughing by lord Dunmore was exhibited 1 Feb. 1871.

ROANOAKE, an island off N. Carolina, U.S., discovered by sir Walter Raleigh, 1584, and settled by him, 1585, without success. Other settlers also failed.

ROASTING ALIVE. An early instance is that of Boechoris, king of Egypt, by order of Sabacon of Ethiopia, 737 B.C. *Lenglet*. Sir John Oldcastle, lord Cobham, was thus put to death in 1418, and Michael Servetus for heresy at Geneva, 27 Oct. 1553; see *Burning Alive*, and *Martyrs*.

ROBBERS were punished with death by Edmund I.'s laws, which directed that the eldest robber should be hanged. Remarkable robbers in England were Robin Hood, 1189 (see *Robin Hood*), and Claud Du Val, "executed at Tyburn," says an historian quaintly, "to the great grief of the women," Jan. 1670. In Ireland, the famous MacCabe was hanged at Naas, 19 Aug. 1691. Galloping Hogan, the rapparee, flourished at this period. Freney, the celebrated highwayman, surrendered himself, 10 May, 1749. The accomplished Barrington was transported, 22 Sept. 1790. See *Trials*.

ROBIN HOOD, captain of a band of robbers, in Sherwood forest, Nottinghamshire; traditionally reported to have been the earl of Huntingdon, disgraced and banished the court by Richard I. at his accession (1189). Robin Hood and Little John and their band are said to have continued their depredations till 1247, when Robin died. *Stow*.

"ROBINSON CRUSOE," by Daniel De Foe; the first part appeared in 1719. See *Juan Fernandez*. Three old ladies, Mary Ann, Jane

Amelia, and Sarah Frances De Foe, lineally descended from De Foe, pensioned by the queen, May, 1877.

ROBURITE, a new German explosive invented by Dr. Carl Roth, reported 1888.

ROCHEFORT (W. France), a seaport on the Charente. The port was made by Louis XIV. in 1666. In Aix-roads or Basque-roads, near Rochefort, capt. lord Cochrane attacked the French fleet and destroyed four ships, 11-12 April, 1809. Near Rochefort, the emperor Napoleon surrendered himself to capt. Maitland of the *Bellerophon*, 15 July, 1815.

ROCHELLE (W. France), a seaport on the Atlantic, belonging to the English for some time, but finally surrendered to the French leader, Du Gueselin, in 1372. As a stronghold of the Calvinist party, it was vainly besieged by the duke of Anjou in 1573; and was taken after a siege of thirteen months by cardinal Richelieu in 1628. The duke of Buckingham was sent with a fleet and army to relieve it; but the citizens declined to admit him. He attacked the isle of Rhé, near Rochelle, and failed, 22 July, 1627. He was repulsed 8 Nov. following. A conspiracy here in 1822 caused loss of life to sergeant Bories and others.

ROCHESTER, in Kent, the Roman *Durobrievæ*. The bishopric, founded by Augustin, 604, is the next in age to Canterbury. The first cathedral was erected by Ethelbert, king of Kent. St. Justus was bishop in 604. Alterations were made in the diocese in 1845. Rochester is valued in the king's books at 358*l*. 3*s*. 2½*d*. per annum. Present income 3,000*l*. The cathedral re-opened after repairs of the choir, 11 June, 1875. The old castle and grounds were purchased for the public by the Corporation, 1883. The "ten churches fund," begun by the bishop, 1884.

RECENT BISHOPS.
1793. Samuel Horseley, trans. to St. Asaph's, 1802.
1802. Thomas Dampier, translated to Ely, 1808.
1809. Walter King, died 22 Feb. 1827.
1827. Hugh Percy, translated to Carlisle, 27 Oct.
1827. George Murray, died 16 Feb. 1860.
1860. Joseph Cotton Wigram, died 6 April, 1867.
1867. Thos. Legh Claughton.
1877. Anthony Wilson Thorold, consecrated, 25 July.

ROCKETS, destructive war implements, were invented by sir William Congreve about 1803. The carcase-rockets were first used at Boulogne, 8 Oct. 1806, when they set the town on fire, their powers being previously demonstrated in the presence of Mr. Pitt and several of the cabinet ministers, 1806. Improved rockets were made by Hales in 1846. Boxer's life-saving rope-carrying rocket, for communicating with stranded vessels, described in 1878.

ROCKINGHAM ADMINISTRATIONS. The first succeeded the administration of Mr. Geo. Grenville; the second succeeded that of lord North.

FIRST ADMINISTRATION, 13 July, 1765 to 30 July, 1766.
Charles, marquis of Rockingham,* *first lord of the treasury*.
William Dowdeswell, *chancellor of the exchequer*.
Earl of Winchilsea and Nottingham, *lord president*.
Duke of Newcastle, *privy seal*.
Earl of Northington, *lord chancellor*.
Duke of Portland, *lord chamberlain*.
Duke of Rutland, *master of the horse*.
Lord Talbot, *lord steward*.

---

* Charles Watson Wentworth, marquis of Rockingham, was born 13 May, 1730; succeeded his father as marquis, 1750. He died without issue, 1 July, 1782; and his estates passed to his nephew, earl Fitzwilliam.

Henry Seymour Conway and the duke of Grafton, *secretaries of state*.
Lord Egmont, *admiralty*.
Marquis of Granby, *ordnance*.
Viscount Barrington, *secretary-at-war*.
Viscount Howe, *treasurer of the navy*.
Charles Townshend, *paymaster of the forces*.
Earl of Dartmouth, *first lord of trade*.
Lords Bessborough and Grantham, lord John Cavendish, Thomas Townshend, &c.
See *Chatham administration*.

SECOND ADMINISTRATION, March to 1 July, 1782, when the marquis died.
Marquis of Rockingham, *first lord of the treasury*.
Lord John Cavendish, *chancellor of the exchequer*.
Lord Camden, *president of the council*.
Duke of Grafton, *privy seal*.
Lord Thurlow, *lord chancellor*.
William, earl of Shelburne and Charles James Fox, *secretaries of state*.
Augustus viscount Keppel, *first lord of the admiralty*
Duke of Richmond, *master-general of the ordnance*.
Thomas Townshend, *secretary-at-war*.
Isaac Barré, Edmund Burke, John Dunning, &c.

ROCROY (N. France). Here, 19 May, 1643, the Spaniards were totally defeated by the French, commanded by the great Condé.

RODNEY'S VICTORIES. Admiral Rodney fought, near Cape St. Vincent, the Spanish admiral, Don Langara, whom he defeated and made prisoner, capturing six of his ships, one of which blew up, 16, 17 Jan. 1780. On 12 April, 1782, he encountered the French fleet in the West Indies, commanded by the count de Grasse, took five ships of the line, and sent the French admiral prisoner to England: Rodney was raised to the peerage, June, 1782.

ROGATION WEEK. Rogation Sunday, the Sunday before Ascension-day, received its title from the Monday, Tuesday, and Wednesday following it, called Rogation days, derived from the Latin *rogare*, to beseech. Extraordinary prayers and supplications for these three days are said to have been appointed in the third century, as a preparation for the devout observance of our Saviour's ascension on the next day succeeding to them, denominated Holy Thursday or Ascension-day. The whole week in which these days happen is styled Rogation week; and in some parts it is still known by the other names of Crop week, Grass week, and Procession week. The perambulations of parishes have usually been made in this week.

ROHAN, an illustrious family, descended from the ancient sovereigns of Brittany. Henri de Rohan, son-in-law of the great Sully, after the death of Henry IV. (14 May, 1610), became head of the Protestant party, and sustained three wars against Louis XIII. He eventually entered the service of the duke of Saxe-Weimar, and died of wounds received in battle in 1638. Of this family was the cardinal de Rohan; see *Diamond Necklace*.

ROHILCUND, a tract of country, N.E. India, was conquered by the Rohillas, an Afghan tribe, who settled here about 1747. After aiding the sovereign of Oude to overcome the Mahrattas, they were treated with much treachery by him, and nearly exterminated. Rohilcund was ceded to the British in 1801. After the great mutiny, Rohilcund was tranquillised in July, 1858.

ROLLER SKATES, see *Rink*.

ROLLING-MILLS, in the metal manufactories, were in use here in the 17th century, and in 1784 Mr. Cort patented his improvements.

ROLLS, see *Master of the Rolls,* and *Records*.

ROLLS' CHAPEL (London), founded by Henry III., about 1233, for receiving Jewish rubbis converted to Christianity. On the banishment of the Jews in 1290 the buildings now called the Rolls, and the chapel, were annexed by patent to the office of the keeper or master of the rolls of chancery, from which circumstance they took their name. A number of public records from the time of Richard III., kept in presses in this chapel, have been removed to the Record Office (*which see*).

ROLT'S ACT, 25 & 26 Vict. c. 42 (1862), relates to the Chancery Court.

ROMAGNA, a province of the papal states, comprised in the legations of Forli and Ravenna. It was conquered by the Lombards; but taken from them by Pepin, and given to the pope, 753. Cæsar Borgia held it as a duchy in 1501, but lost it in 1503. In 1859 the Romagna threw off the temporal authority of the pope, and declared itself subject to the king of Sardinia, who accepted it in March, 1860. It now forms part of the province of Æmilia, in the new kingdom of Italy. See *Rome*.

ROMAINVILLE AND BELLEVILLE, heights near Paris, where Joseph Bonaparte, Mortier, and Marmont were defeated by the allies after a vigorous resistance, 30 March, 1814. The next day Paris capitulated.

ROMAN CATHOLICS, ROMANISTS and **PAPISTS.** Their religion was the established one in Britain till the Reformation. Since then many laws were made against them, which have been repealed; see *Rome, Religion, Leagues, Maynooth*. Among other disabilities, Roman Catholics were excluded from corporate offices, 1667; from parliament, 1691; forbidden to marry protestants, 1708; to possess arms, 1695, &c. The grand church of the Oratory opened at South Kensington, 25 April, 1884.

Roman Catholic Church in England and Wales, 1878; H. E. Manning, archbishop of Westminster, metropolitan, 1865; cardinal, 1875; auxiliary bishop, Wm. Weathers, 1872. 12 bishops (Beverley, Birmingham, Clifton, Hexham, Liverpool, Newport, Northampton, Nottingham, Plymouth, Salford, Shrewsbury, Southwark). *Scotland,* hierarchy revived, 4 March, 1878. *Ireland,* 4 archbishops (metropolitan, Paul Cullen, archbishop of Armagh, 1850; of Dublin, 1852); 24 bishops. England, 17 bishops, 2,380 priests; Scotland, 6 bishops, 341 priests (1888).
Roman Catholics in Great Britain, about 539,500; clergy, 624; churches, 522 in 1840; 1,384,000 persons; 2282 clergy; 1461 churches in 1880.
Bishop Fisher, sir Thomas More, and others, executed for denying the king's supremacy . . 1535
Catholics absolved from their allegiance to the king by Paul III. 1535; by Pius V. 1570
They rebel in . . . . . . 1549 and 1569
The Gunpowder Plot (*which see*) 1605
They suffer by Oates's fictitious popish plot . . 1678
They are excluded from the throne 1689
They suffer by the Gordon riots . . June, 1780
Various disabilities removed in . . 1780 and 1791
Mr. Pitt proposes measures for their relief, which he gives up 1801-4
Roman Catholic Association organised in Ireland, with the object of removing the political and civil disabilities of Roman catholics 1824
Bills in their favour frequently brought in without effect from . . . . . . 1813 to 1828
An act of parliament passed for the suppression of the Catholic Association (it had voted its own dissolution, 12 Feb.) . . . . 5 March, 1829
The duke of Wellington and sir Robert Peel carry the Catholic emancipation bill (10 Geo. IV. c. 7) in the commons, 30 March; in the lords, 10 April; received the royal assent . . . 13 April, ,,

The duke of Norfolk and lords Dormer and Clifford, the first Roman catholic peers, take their seats, 28 April, 1829
The first English R. C. member returned, the earl of Surrey, for Horsham . . . . . 4 May, ,,
Mr. O'Connell elected for Clare, 1828, takes his seat (first Roman catholic M.P. since 1689) . Aug. ,,
Mr. Alexander Raphael, the first Roman catholic sheriff of London . . . . . 28 Sept. 1834
Sir Michael O'Loghlen, the first Roman catholic judge (as Master of the Rolls in Ireland), appointed, 30 Oct. 1836
St. George's cathedral, Southwark, erected by A. W. Pugin; founded 1840
Tablet newspaper established . . . . ,,
Mr. O'Connell elected first Roman catholic lord mayor of Dublin 1841
"Catholic Poor School Committee" established . 1847
The "Papal Aggression" (*which see*); cardinal Nicholas Wiseman appointed archbishop of Westminster . . . . . . 30 Sept. 1850
Roman catholic university, Dublin, originated 5 May, 1851
Univers newspaper established 1860
Agitation in favour of the pope 1860-2
Missionary college founded at Drumcondra, Ireland . . . . . . 20 July, 1862
Roman catholic chaplains permitted for gaols, by Prison Ministers act . . . . July, 1863
Serjeant Wm. Shee made a justice of the Queen's Bench, the first Roman catholic judge since the Reformation [died 19 Feb. 1868] . . 15 Dec. ,,
Death of cardinal Wiseman, aged 63; 7th English cardinal since the Reformation . . 15 Feb. 1865
Henry Manning (formerly an archdeacon in the English church) consecrated archbishop of Westminster . . . . . . 8 June, ,,
Conference of Roman catholic bishops at Dublin; publish resolutions declining state help (in accordance with the papal injunctions, 1801 and 1805), and condemning mixed education and secret societies . . . . . . 17 Oct. 1867
In Great Britain 1639 Roman catholic priests; 1283 chapels and churches; 227 convents for women (principally educational); 21 colleges and large schools . . . . Dec. ,,
A proposal of the Derby government to endow a catholic university for Ireland, Oct. 1867, failed through the catholic bishops claiming the entire practical control . . . . . 31 March, 1868
Mr. Justice Thomas (aft. lord) O'Hagan, appointed lord chancellor of Ireland, is the first Roman catholic who has held that office since the revolution of 1688-9 . . . . . . Dec. ,,
Catholic truth society by Dr. Vaughan, established about ,,
Catholic union of Great Britain, president the duke of Norfolk, constituted 1871
A Roman catholic made M.A. at Oxford, after the abolition of the test . . . . 22 June, ,,
The catholics opposing the dogma of papal infallibility term themselves "old catholics" (*which see*)
The Ecclesiastical Titles act (see *Papal Aggression*) repealed . . . . . . 24 July, ,,
Pastoral issued by the R. C. bishops in Ireland claiming endowment for colleges, &c. under their sole control . . . . Oct. ,,
"Catholic Education Crisis Fund" established . ,,
Two R. C. bishops consecrated at Salford 28 Oct. 1872
"Catholic Union," Dublin, re-organised to obtain education under ecclesiastical control, about 4 Dec. 1873
A catholic union in Dublin formed . . . . ,,
Roman Catholic university senate meet . 21 May, 1874
Archbishop Manning made a cardinal . . 1875
Catholic Congress at Venice met . . 12 June, ,,
The marquis of Ripon becomes a Roman Catholic 7 Sept. ,,
Roman Catholic university college, Kensington; monsignor Capel, principal; opened . 15 Oct. ,,
Several English clergymen secede to Rome . Oct. ,,
New Catholic club opened in London by the duke of Norfolk, lords Denbigh and Petre, and others 27 Nov. ,,
Mr. Gladstone's pamphlet, "The Vatican Decrees," occasions declarations respecting papal infallibility, from abp. Manning, monsig. Capel, the Catholic Union and others for it; from lords Acton, Camoys, and sir George Bowyer, against it, Nov. ,,

R. C. hierarchy re-established in Scotland, by pope Leo XIII . . . . . . 4 March, 1878
For the dissension between Church and State respecting the doctrine of papal infallibility, see *Prussia* and *Germany.*
Church in low state in Germany, 3 dioceses (of 12) occupied: 200 parishes without priests; 1500 priests expelled, reported . . . April, 1879
Lord Petre, a R. C. priest, takes his seat in the house of lords . . . . . . 3 Nov. 1884
Catholic congresses: Madrid, president, archbishop of Saragossa, 25 April *et seq.*; at Vienna, the high clergy and nobility present . . 29 April, 1889

ROMAN LAW, see *Codes;* ROMAN LITERATURE, see *Latin.*

ROMAN ROADS IN ENGLAND. Our historians maintain, but are mistaken, that there were but four of these roads. *Camden.* "The Romans," says Isidore, "made roads almost all over the world, to have their marches in a straight line, and to employ the people;" and criminals were frequently condemned to work at such roads, as we learn from Suetonius, in his life of Caligula. They were commenced and completed at various periods, between the 2nd and 4th centuries, and the Roman soldiery were employed in making them, that inactivity might not give them an opportunity to raise disturbances. *Bede.*

1st, WATLING-STREET, so named from Vitellianus, who is supposed to have directed it, the Britons calling him in their language *Guetalin* (from Kent to Cardigan Bay).
2nd, IKNIELD, or IKENILD-STREET, from its beginning among the *Iceni* (from St. David's to Tynemouth).
3rd, FOSSE, or FOSSE WAY, probably from its having been defended by a fosse on both sides (from Cornwall to Lincoln).
4th, ERMIN-STREET, from *Irmunsul,* a German word, meaning Mercury, whom our German ancestors worshipped under that name (from St. David's to Southampton).

ROMAN WALLS. One was erected by Agricola (79 to 85) to defend Britain from the incursions of the Picts and Scots; the first wall extended from the Tyne to the Solway frith (80 miles); the second from the frith of Forth, near Edinburgh, to the frith of Clyde, near Dumbarton (36 miles). The former was renewed and strengthened by the emperor Adrian (121), and by Septimus Severus (208). It commenced at Bowness, near Carlisle, and ended at Wallsend near Newcastle. It had battlements and towers to contain soldiers. The more northern wall was renewed by Lollius Urbicus, in the reign of Antoninus Pius, about 140. Many remains of these walls still exist, particularly of the southern one; see Bruce's "*Roman Wall,*" published 1853-1868.

ROMANCE, originally a composition in the Romance or Provençal idiom. The term in the middle ages was extended to narrative poetry in general. Heliodorus, a bishop of Tricca, in Thessaly, about 398, was the author of *Æthiopica* (relating to the loves of Theagenes and Charicleia), the first work in this species of writing. The first part of the "Roman de la Rose" was written by Guillaume de Lorres (1226-70); the second, a separate poem, by Jean de Meung (1285-1314), the Decameron of Boccaccio was published, 1358; Don Quixote, by Cervantes, 1605; Gil Blas, by Le Sage, 1715. Dunlop's "History of Fiction," published 1814. See *English Authors;* "*Reynard the Fox.*"

ROME. The foundation of the city, by Romulus, was laid on the 20th April,* according to

* In its original state, Rome was but a small castle on the summit of mount Palatine; and the founder, to give

Varro, in the year 3961 of the Julian period (3251 years after the creation of the world, 753 years before the birth of Christ, 431 years after the Trojan war, and in the fourth year of the sixth Olympiad. Other dates given: Cato, 751; Polybius, 750; Fabius Pictor, 747; Cincius, 728 B.C.) The Romans conquered nearly the whole of the then known world. In the time of Julius Cæsar, the empire was bounded by the Euphrates, Taurus, and Armenia on the east; by Æthiopia on the south; by the Danube on the north; and by the Atlantic on the west. Numerous ecclesiastical councils have been held at Rome, from 197 to 1869-70. Population, 1872, about 240,000; 1877, 250,000; 1881, 300,467. Chiefly through the exertions of Mr. John Henry Parker of Oxford, the Roman exploration fund was established, for the preservation of ancient architectural remains. His "*Archæology of Rome*" (with many photographs) published, 1874-8. The Italian government votes 1200*l.* a year for a similar purpose. The early history of Rome is mythic, and the dates *purely conjectural.*

Foundation of the city by Romulus . . . B.C.	753
The Romans seize on the Sabine women at a public spectacle, and detain them for wives . .	750
The Cæninians defeated, and first triumphal procession	748
Rome taken by the Sabines; the Sabines incorporated with the Romans as one nation .	747
Romulus sole king of the Romans and Sabines .	742
The Circensian games established by him .	732
Romulus murdered by senators . . .	716
Numa Pompilius elected king, 715; institutes the priesthood, the augurs and vestals . .	710
Roman calendar of 10 months reformed and made 12	,,
The Romans and the Albans contesting for superiority, agreed to choose three champions on each part to decide it. The three *Horatii,* Roman knights, overcame the three *Curiatii,* Albans, and united Alba to Rome . . . . about	669
War with the Fidenates; the city of Alba destroyed	665
Ostia, at the mouth of the Tiber, built . .	627
The capital founded	615
The first census of the Roman state taken .	566
Political institutions of Servius Tullius . .	550
The rape of Lucretia by Sextus, son of Tarquin .	510
Royalty abolished: the Patricians establish an aristocratical commonwealth . . .	509
Junius Brutus and Tarquinius Collatinus first consuls; first alliance of the Romans with Carthage	508
The capitol dedicated to *Jupiter Capitolinus* .	507
First dictator Titus Lartius	501
The Latins and the Tarquins declare war against the republic, 501; defeated at lake Regillus 498 or	496
Secession of the Plebeians to the sacred mount; establishment of tribunes of the Plebeians .	494
First agrarian law passed; Spurius Cassius put to death by Patricians	493
C. Martius Coriolanus banished . . .	491
He (with the Volsci) besieges Rome, but withdraws at the suit of his wife and mother . .	488
Contests between the Patricians and Plebeians respecting the agrarian law . . .	486
Quæstors appointed about	484
The Fabii slain (see *Fabii*)	477
Cincinnatus, dictator, defeats the Æqui . .	458
The Secular Games first celebrated . .	456
The Decemviri created	451
Virginius kills his daughter, Virginia, to save her from the decemvir, Appius Claudius; (Appius killed himself in prison; the decemviral government abolished)	449
The Canuleian law passed, permitting marriages between Patricians and Plebeians . . .	445

his followers the appearance of a nation or a barbarian horde, was obliged to erect a standard as a common asylum for criminals, debtors, or murderers, who fled from their native country to avoid the punishment which attended them. From such an assemblage a numerous body was soon collected, and before the death of the founder, the Romans had covered with their habitations the Palatine, Capitoline, Aventine, and Esquiline hills, with Mounts Cœlius and Quirinalis.

ROME.

Event	B.C.
Military tribunes first created	444
Office of censor instituted	443
Rome afflicted with an awful famine, and many persons on account of it drown themselves in the Tiber	440
The Veientes defeated, and their king Tolumnus slain	437
War with the Tuscans	434
A temple is dedicated to Apollo on account of a pestilence	431
Æqui and Volsci defeated by Tubertus, dictator	,,
Two more quæstors appointed	421
Another dreadful famine at Rome	411
Three quæstors are chosen from the Plebeians for the first time	409
Institution of the Lectisternian festival on account of a pestilence	399
Veii taken by Camillus after ten years' siege	396
Banishment of Camillus	391
The Gauls under Brennus, besiege Clusium (see Gauls)	390
They are expelled by Camillus	389
Rome burnt to the ground by the Gauls, who besiege the capitol	387
Rebuilt—Capitoline games instituted	,,
M. Manlius Capitoline thrown from the Tarpeian rock on a charge of aiming at sovereign power	384
The first appointment of curule magistrates	371
Lucius Sextus, the first Plebeian consul	366
Marcus Curtius leaps into the gulf which had opened in the forum	362
The Gauls defeated in Italy	350
Treaty with Carthage to repress Greek piracy	348
War with the Samnites (with breaks) 51 years	343
Latin war	340-338
Embassy to Alexander the Great	324
Defeat at Caudium	321
Priests first elected from the Plebeians	300
Etruscans, Samnites, and others, defeated at Sentinum by Fabius	295
End of the third Samnite war	290
The Gauls invade the Roman territory; siege of Arezzo	284
Etruscans defeated at Vadimonian lake	310 and 283
Pyrrhus of Epirus invades Italy, 281; defeats the Romans at Pandosia, 280; and at Asculum, 279; defeated by them at Benevento	275
All Italy subdued by Rome	266
First Punic war commenced (see *Punic Wars*)	264
First Roman fleet built	260
Attilius Regulus said to be put to a cruel death by the Carthaginians	255
End of first Punic war; Sicily annexed	241
Temple of Janus closed	235
Corsica and Sardinia annexed	231
First Roman embassy to Greece	228
Invasion of the Gauls: beaten by the consuls	225
Second Punic war breaks out	218
The Romans are defeated by Hannibal at Thrasymene, 217; Cannæ 2 Aug.	216
Syracuse taken by Marcellus	212
Marcellus defeated by Hannibal, and slain near Venusia	208
Scipio defeats Hannibal at Zama in Africa	202
The Macedonian wars with Philip begin, 213 and 200; his defeat at Cynoscephalæ	197
Death of Scipio Africanus the elder	185
Third Macedonian war begins 171; Perseus beaten at Pydna; Macedon annexed	168
First public library erected at Rome	167
Philosophers and rhetoricians banished from Rome	161
Third Punic war begins	149
Corinth and Carthage destroyed by the Romans (see *Corinth* and *Carthage*)	146
Celtiberian and Numantine war in Spain	153-133
Attalus III. of Pergamos bequeaths his kingdom and riches to the Romans	133
The Servile war in Sicily	132
Two Plebeian consuls chosen	,,
Agrarian disturbances: Gracchus slain	121
The Jugurthine war	112-106
The Mithridatic war (*which see*)	108-63
The Ambrones defeated by Marius	102
The Social war	90-88
Rome besieged by four armies (viz.: those of Marius, Cinna, Carbo, and Sertorius) and taken	87

Event	B.C.
Sylla defeats Marius; becomes dictator; sanguinary proscriptions, 82; abdicates	79
Bithynia bequeathed to the Romans by king Nicomedes	74
Revolt of Spartacus and the slaves	73-71
Syria conquered by Pompey	65
The Catiline conspiracy suppressed by Cicero	63
The first triumvirate: Cæsar, Pompey, and Crassus	60
Cæsar's campaigns in Gaul, 58; in Britain	55
Crassus killed by the Parthians	53
Gaul conquered and made a province	51
War between Cæsar and Pompey	50
Pompey defeated at Pharsalia (*which see*)	48
Cæsar defeats Pharnaces at Zela; and writes home "Veni, vidi, vici"	,,
Cato kills himself at Utica; Cæsar dictator for ten years	47
Cæsar killed in the senate-house 15 March,	46
Second triumvirate: Octavius, Antony, and Lepidus	44
Cicero killed, proscribed by Antony	43
Battle of Philippi; Brutus and Cassius defeated	,,
Lepidus ejected from the triumvirate, 36; war between Octavius and Antony, 32; Antony defeated totally at Actium 2 Sept.	42

Event	A.D.
Octavius emperor, as *Augustus Cæsar*	31
The empire now at peace with all the world; the temple of Janus shut; JESUS CHRIST born. (See *Jesus*)	27
Varus defeated by Hermann and the Germans 4 April, A.D.	5
Ovid banished to Tomi	9
Death of Ovid and Livy	18
Tiberius retires to Capreæ; tyranny of Sejanus	26
A census being taken by Claudius, the emperor and censor, the inhabitants of Rome are stated to amount to 6,944,000.—[It is now considered that the population of Rome within the walls was under a million.]	
Caractacus brought in chains to Rome	48
St. Paul arrives in bonds at Rome	60
Nero burns Rome to the ground, and charges the crime upon the Christians	64
Seneca, Lucan, &c., put to death	65
Peter and Paul said to be put to death	67
Jerusalem levelled to the ground by Titus 8 Sept.	70
Coliseum founded by Vespasian	75
The Dacian war begins (continues 15 years)	86
Pliny, junior, proconsul in Bithynia, sends Trajan his celebrated account of the Christians	102
Trajan's expedition into the East against the Parthians, &c.; subdues Dacia	106
Trajan's column erected at Rome	114
Adrian resides in Britain, and builds the wall	121
The capitol destroyed by lightning	188
Byzantium taken; its walls razed	196
The Goths are paid tribute	222
[The Goths, Vandals, Alani, Suevi, and other Northern nations attack the empire.]	
Pompey's amphitheatre burnt	248
Invasion of the Goths	250
Pestilence throughout the empire	252
Great victory over the Goths obtained by Claudius II.; 300,000 slain	269
Dacia relinquished to the Goths	270
Palmyra conquered, and Longinus put to death	273
The era of Martyrs, or of Diocletian	284
The Franks settle in Gaul. *Frérot*	287
Constantius dies at York	306
Four emperors reign at one time	308
Constantine the Great, it is said, in consequence of a vision, places the cross on his banners, and begins to favour the Christians	
Constantine defeats Licinius, at Chrysopolis, and reigns alone 18 Sept.	312
He *tolerates* the Christian faith	323
Puts his son Crispus to death	324
Constantine convokes the first general council of Christians at Nice	
The seat of empire removed from Rome to Byzantium, 321; dedicated by Constantine	325
Constantine orders the heathen temples to be destroyed	330
Revolt of 300,000 Sarmatian slaves suppressed	,,
Death of Constantine, soon after being baptized	334
The army under Julian proclaims him emperor	337
Julian, who had been educated for the priesthood, and had frequently officiated, abjures Christianity, and re-opens the heathen temples, becoming the pagan pontiff	360

Julian killed in battle in Persia; Christianity restored by Jovian . . . . . A.D.	363
The empire divided into Eastern and Western by Valentinian and Valens, brothers: the former has the Western portion, or Rome . . .	364
(See *Western and Eastern Empires;* and *Italy.*)	
Rome placed under the exarchate of Ravenna .	404
Taken by Alaric . . . . . 24 Aug.	410
Taken and pillaged by Genseric . . 15 July,	455
Odoacer takes Rome, and becomes king of Italy .	476
Rome recovered for Justinian by Belisarius .	536
Retaken by Totila the Goth, 546; recovered by Belisarius, 547; seized by Totila . . .	549
Recovered by Narses, and annexed to the eastern empire; and the senate abolished . . .	553
Rome at her lowest state . . . . about	600
Rome independent under the popes . . about	728
Pepin of France compels Astolphus, king of the Lombards, to cede Ravenna and other places to the Holy Church	755
Confirmed and added to by Charlemagne .	774
Charlemagne crowned emperor of the West by the pope at Rome . . . . . 25 Dec.	800
Rome taken by Arnulf and the Germans .	896
Otho I. crowned at Rome . . . . 2 Feb.	962
The emperor Henry IV. takes Rome . March,	1084
Arnold of Brescia, endeavouring to reform church and state and to establish a senate, is put to death as a heretic	1155
The pope removes to Avignon	1309
Nicola di Rienzi, tribune of the people, establishes a republic, 20 May; is compelled to abdicate, 15 Dec.	1347
Returns; made senator, 1 Aug.; assassinated, 8 Oct.	1354
Papal court returns to Rome	1377
Rise of the families, Colonna, Orsini, &c. about	,,
Julius II. conquers the Romagna, Bologna, and Perugia	1503-13
The city greatly embellished by pope Leo X.	1513-21
It is captured by the constable de Bourbon, who is slain . . . . . . 6 May,	1527
Ferrara annexed	1597
St. Peter's dedicated . . . . 18 Nov.	1626
Expulsion of the Jesuits . . . 16 Aug.	1773
Harassed by the French, German, and Spanish factions . . from the 16th to the 18th century.	
The French invasion; the Legations incorporated with the Cisalpine republic	1796
The French proclaim the Roman republic, 20 March,	1798
Recovered for the pope by the Neapolitans, Nov.	1799
Retaken by the French, 1800; restored to Pius VII. July,	1801
Annexed by Napoleon to the kingdom of Italy, and declared second city of the empire . May,	1808
Restored to the pope, who returns . 23 Jan.	1814
He re-establishes the Inquisition and the Jesuits, 7 Aug.	,,
The papal government endeavour to annul all innovations, and thus provoke much opposition; the Carbonari increase in numbers . . .	1815-17
Political assassinations in the Romagna . .	1817
The "Young Italy" party established by Joseph Mazzini; temporary insurrections at Bologna suppressed by Austrian aid	1831
Election of Pius IX. . . . . 16 June,	1846
He proclaims an amnesty; and authorises a national guard and municipal institutions . . .	1847
The Romans desire to join the king of Sardinia against the Austrians; the pope hesitates; the Antonelli ministry retires; and the Mamiani ministry is formed	1848
Count Rossi, minister of justice of the pontifical government, assassinated on the staircase of the Chamber of Deputies at Rome . . 15 Nov.	,,
Insurrection at Rome, the populace demand a democratic ministry and the proclamation of Italian nationality the pope (Pius IX.) hesitates, the Romans surround the palace, and a conflict ensues. The pope accepts a popular ministry (Cardinal Palma, the pope's secretary, shot in this conflict) . . . . 16 Nov.	,,
A free constitution published . . 20 Nov.	,,
The pope escapes in disguise from Rome to Gaëta, 24 Nov.	,,
M. de Corcelles leaves Paris for Rome, a French armed expedition to Civita Vecchia having preceded him, to afford protection to the pope, 27 Nov.	,,
Protest of the pope against the acts of the provisional government . . . . 28 Nov.	1848
A constituent assembly meets at Rome . 5 Feb.	1849
The Roman National Assembly divests the pope of all temporal power, and adopts the republican form of government . . . . 8 Feb.	,,
The pope appeals to the Catholic powers, 18 Feb.	,,
Civita Vecchia occupied by the French force under Marshal Oudinot . . . . 26 April,	,,
A French force repulsed with loss . 30 April,	,,
Engagement between the Romans and Neapolitans; the former capture 60 prisoners and 400 muskets, 5 May,	,,
The assembly refuses to receive the French as allies, 19 May,	,,
The French under marshal Oudinot commence an attack on Rome . . . . 3 June,	,,
After a brave resistance, the Romans capitulate to the French army . . . . 30 June,	,,
The Roman assembly dissolved . . 4 July,	,,
An officer from Oudinot's camp arrives at Gaëta, to present the pope with the keys of the two gates of Rome by which the French army had entered the city . . . . . 4 July,	,,
The re-establishment of the pope's authority proclaimed at Rome . . . . 15 July,	,,
Oudinot issues a general order stating that the pope (or his representative) now re-possesses the administration of affairs, but that public security in the pontifical dominions still remains under the special guarantee of the French army, 3 Aug.	,,
The pope arrives at Portici on a visit to the king of Naples . . . . . 4 Sept.	,,
He arrives at Rome; cardinal Antonelli becomes foreign minister . . . . April,	1850
He issues the bull establishing a Roman catholic hierarchy in England (see *Papal Aggression*), 24 Sept.	,,
Important concordat with Austria . 18 Aug.	1855
The pope visits his dominions . . May-Sept.	1857
Insurrection in the Romagna, at Bologna, and Ferrara June,	1859
The pope appeals to Europe for help against Sardinia 12 July,	,,
The Legations form a defensive alliance with Tuscany, Parma, and Modena . 20 Aug.	,,
The queen of Spain engages to send troops to Rome, if the French retire . . 26 Aug.	,,
The assembly at Bologna vote annexation to Piedmont, 7 Sept.; the king engages to support their cause before the great powers, 15 Sept.; the pope annuls the acts of the assembly at Bologna; and announces the punishment due to those who attack the holy see, 26 Sept.; and dismisses the Sardinian chargé d'affaires at Rome . 1 Oct.	,,
The Romagna, Modena, and Parma formed into a province, to be called Æmilia . . 24 Dec.	,,
The Sardinian government annul the Tuscan and Lombard concordats . . 27 Jan., 20 March,	1860
Riots at Rome suppressed by the police with great cruelty . . . . . 19 March,	,,
The pope excommunicates all concerned in the rebellion in his states . . . 26 March,	,,
General Lamoricière takes command of the papal army, March; which is re-organised, and increased by volunteers from Ireland, &c. . May,	,,
Tuscan volunteers enter the papal states and are repulsed . . . . . 19 May,	,,
Irish volunteers are severely treated for insubordination; many dismissed . . . July,	,,
The papal army estimated at 20,000 . . Aug.	,,
Insurrection in the Marches, 8 Sept.; Fossembrone subdued by the papal troops; the people appeal to the Sardinian government, whose troops, under Cialdini and Fanti, enter the Papal States, 11 Sept.	,,
Fanti takes Pesaro, 12 Sept.; and Perugia, including general Schmidt and 1600 prisoners, 14 Sept.	,,
Ancona besieged by sea and land . 17 Sept.	,,
Severe allocution of the pope against France and Sardinia; he appeals to Europe for help, 28 Sept.	,,
Cialdini defeats Lamoricière at Castel-Fidardo, 18 Sept.; and takes Ancona . 29 Sept.	,,
Additional French troops sent to Rome . Oct.	,,
The Marches vote for annexation to Sardinia, Nov.	,,

3 D

Subscriptions raised for the pope in various countries; the formal collection forbidden in France and Belgium; permitted in England . . Nov. 1860
Monastic establishments suppressed in the Legations; the monks pensioned; educational institutions founded . . . . . . Dec. ,,
The French emperor advises the pope to give up his revolted provinces . . . 21 Dec. ,,
Publication of *Rome et les Evêques*, 6 Jan.; and of *La France, Rome et l'Italie*, 15 Feb.; great excitement, and strong advocacy of the pope's temporal government (attacked by prince Napoleon) in the French chambers . . . . March, 1861
Cavour claims Rome as capital of Italy, 27 March, ,,
Petition to the emperor Napoleon to withdraw French troops from Rome . . 10 May, ,,
The emperor of France declines a union with Austria and Spain for the maintenance of the pope's temporal power . . . . June, ,,
Grand ceremony at the canonization of 27 Japanese martyrs (see *Canonization*) . . 8 June, ,,
The pope declares a severe allocution against the Italians . . . . . . 9 June, ,,
Garibaldi calls for volunteers, taking as his watchword, "Rome or death!" . . . 19 July, 1862
Railway between Rome and Naples completed; its opening opposed by the papal government, Nov. ,,
Earl Russell's offer to the pope of a residence at Malta, 25 Oct.; declined . . . 11 Nov. ,,
Antonelli's resignation of his office not accepted, 5 March, 1863
Convention between France and Italy: French troops to quit Rome within two years, 15 Sept. 1864
Encyclical letter of the pope, publishing a "syllabus," censuring 80 errors in religion, philosophy, and politics; (caused much dissatisfaction, and was forbidden to be read in churches in France and other countries) . . . 8 Dec. ,,
Jews persecuted at Rome . . . . Dec. ,,
Fruitless negotiations between the pope and the king of Italy (by Vegezzi); mutual concessions proposed . . . . 21 April to 23 June, 1865
Pope's severe allocution against secret societies (Freemasons, Fenians, &c.) . . 25 Sept. ,,
Merode, the papal minister of war, dismissed, 20 Oct. ,,
A part of the French troops leave the papal dominions Nov. ,,
Rupture with Russia . . . Dec. 1865—Jan. 1866
A Franco-pontifical legion (1200 men) formed at Antibes, arrives; blessed by the pope, 24 Sept. ,,
Pope's severe allocution against Italy and Russia, 29 Oct. ,,
The pope invites all catholic bishops to meet at Rome to celebrate the 18th centenary of the martyrdom of Peter and Paul . . 8 Dec. ,,
The pope's blessing given to French troops, 6 Dec., who all quit Rome . . . . 2-12 Dec. ,,
Rome tranquil . . . . . 13 Dec. ,,
Law prohibiting protestant worship except at embassies in Rome enforced . . 31 Dec. ,,
Negotiation with Italy fruitless; the Italian councillor, Tonello, quits Rome . . . April, 1867
599 bishops and thousands of priests present at the pope's allocution, 26 June; and canonization of 25 martyrs . . . . . 29 June, ,,
The pope receives an album and address from 100 cities of Italy . . . . . 8 July, ,,
Cholera in Rome: death of cardinal Altieri, while assisting the afflicted . . . 11 Aug. ,,
The pope's allocution censures the sacrilegious audacity of the Sub-alpine kingdom, in confiscating ecclesiastical property . . 20 Sept. ,,
Garibaldi arrested at Sinalunga, near the Roman frontier . . . . . 23 Sept. ,,
Irruption of Garibaldians in Viterbo—conflicts with various results; reported appeal of Antonelli for help from the great powers . . . Oct. ,,
Zouave barracks at Rome blown up, many killed, 22 Oct. ,,
Attempt at insurrection in Rome suppressed, 22 Oct.; state of siege proclaimed; Garibaldi within 20 miles of Rome, 24 Oct.; takes Monte Rotondo 26 Oct. ,,
French brigades enter Rome . . . 30 Oct. ,,
Italian troops cross the frontier, 30 Oct.; occupy several posts . . . . . 1 Nov. ,,
Garibaldians defeated by the papal and French troops at Mentana (*which see*) . . 3 Nov. ,,

Italian troops retire from the papal states Nov. 1867
The Roman committee of insurrection issue a narrative, and state that their watchword is "Try again and do better" . . . . Dec. ,,
The papal army increased to about 15,000 . Dec. ,,
The pope's short allocution (thanking and blessing the French government) . . 19 Dec. ,,
Nine cardinals made; Lucien Bonaparte one 13 March, 1868
Sudden death of cardinal Andrea . 15 May, ,,
The pope, in his allocution, censures the Austrian new civil marriage law . . 22 June, ,,
Arrangement respecting the papal debt made with Italy . . . . . . 30 July, ,,
Encyclical letter of the pope, summoning an œcumenical council at Rome on 8 Dec. 1869, and inviting ministers of the Greek and other churches 13 Sept. ,,
The patriarch of the Greek church declined to attend about 3 Oct. ,,
Monti and Tognetti (for complicity in the explosion of the Zouave barracks, 22 Oct. 1867), executed 24 Nov. ,,
The pope celebrates a jubilee . 11 April, 1869
In his allocution he deplores the opposition to the church in Austria and Spain . . 25 June, ,,
He declares, in a letter to archbishop Manning, that no discussions on disputed points can take place at the council . . . . 4 Sept. ,,
The council opened, see *Council XXI.* 8 Dec. ,,
An exhibition of objects of Christian art opened by the pope . . . . . . 7 Feb. 1870
British and American bishops protest against discussing the dogma of papal infallibility in the council, 11 April; the discussion begins 14 May, ,,
Count Arnim, on behalf of the North German confederation, protests against the dogma . May, ,,
Papal infallibility adopted by the council and promulgated (533 for; 2 against; many retire); the council adjourns to 11 Nov. . . 18 July, ,,
Rome completely evacuated by French troops in consequence of the war; 8 mortars and 15,000 shells said to be ceded to the pope, 8 Aug.; the troops sent from Civita Vecchia . 21 Aug. ,,
Conciliatory letter from Victor Emmanuel to the pope 8 Sept. ,,
Agitation in the papal provinces; the Italian troops invited to enter . . about 10 Sept. ,,
The pope refuses terms offered him by the king of Italy (sovereignty of the Leonine city and retention of his income) . . . . 11 Sept. ,,
Skirmish with papal Zouaves; several killed 14 Sept. ,,
The Italians occupy Civita Vecchia without resistance . . . . . about 15 Sept. ,,
Gen. Cadorna crosses the Tiber at Cusale; sends flags of truce to gen. Kanzler, commander of the Zouaves, who refuses to surrender; baron Arnim in vain negotiates between them . 17 Sept. ,,
Letter from the pope to gen. Kanzler directing that a merely formal defence be made at Rome, and that bloodshed be avoided . . 19 Sept. ,,
After a brief resistance from the foreign papal troops, stopped by order of the pope, the Italian troops under Cadorna make a breach and enter Rome amid enthusiastic acclamations of the people . . . . . . 20 Sept. ,,
[Reported Italian loss, about 22 killed, 117 wounded; papal troops, 55 killed and wounded.]
Cardinal Antonelli issues a diplomatic protest against the Italian occupation of Rome 21 Sept. ,,
The papal troops surrender arms; about 8500 foreigners march out with honours of war; they insult the Italians; the native troops retained, 22 Sept. ,,
About 10,000 persons assemble in the Coliseum, choose 44 names for a provisional government (*giunta*) . . . . . 22 Sept. ,,
Protest of the pope . . . . 26 Sept. ,,
Castle of St. Angelo occupied by Italian troops at the pope's request . . . 28 Sept. ,,
Circular letter from the pope to the cardinals complaining of the invasion and of his loss of liberty, and interference with his private post bag 29 Sept. ,,
A giunta of 14 (the duke Gaetani chief) selected from the 44 names chosen; approved by Cadorna 30 Sept. ,,

General Masi in command of Rome and the provinces ; S.P.Q.R. appears on the proclamations 30 Sept. 1870
Plebiscite : out of 167,548 votes, 133,681 for union with the kingdom of Italy ; 1507 against ; the remainder did not vote . . . 2 Oct. ,,
Cardinal Antonelli issues a protest ; published 4 Oct. ,,
The pope said to have accepted 50,000 crowns (his monthly civil list) from the Italian government 4 Oct. ,,
The result of the plébiscite sent to the king, 8 Oct. ; Rome and its provinces incorporated with the kingdom by royal decree . . . 9 Oct. ,,
General La Marmora enters Rome as viceroy ; he proclaims that the pope shall be guaranteed in his sovereign powers as head of the church 11 Oct. ,,
The Roman provinces united into one by decree 19 Oct. ,,
The pope issues an encyclical letter adjourning the meeting of the council . . . 20 Oct. ,,
Antonelli protests against the occupation of the Quirinal by the king . . . 10 Nov. ,,
Bill introduced into the Italian parliament respecting the transfer of the seat of government to Rome in about six months, and the preservation of the spiritual and temporal sovereignty of the pope . . . . . . about 12 Dec. ,,
Inundation of the Tiber; great suffering of the people, 27, 28 Dec. ; the king gives 200,000 lire ; visits Rome suddenly, the city illuminated 4 A.M. 31 Dec. ,,
Law guaranteeing to the pope full personal liberty and honours, a revenue of 3,225,000 livres &c., 13 May ; rejected by the pope in his allocution 15 May, 1871
2624th anniversary of the city kept ; the pope celebrates a jubilee on the 25th anniversary of his election . . . . . 16 June, ,,
The Italian government remove to Rome, 2, 3 July, ,,
Allocation of the pope, appointing some Italian bishops ; still rejecting guarantees . 27 Oct. ,,
Grand reception of the king . 21 Nov. ,,
He opens the parliament, saying, "The work to which we have consecrated our life is completed " 27 Nov. ,,
The pope receives an address from nobles and others 27 Nov. ,,
Commission appointed to dredge the bed of the Tiber to recover antiquities . . Dec. ,,
Easter solemnities not performed by the pope 31 March, 1872
The pope delivers an allocution complaining of persecution of the church in Italy, Germany, and Spain . . . . . . 23 Dec. ,,
American Protestant church dedicated to St. Paul : founded . . . . 25 Jan. 1873
First Anglican church within the walls opened 25 Oct. 1874
Assassination of Raffaele Sonzogno, a republican printer and manager of "Il Capitale," 6 Feb. ; trial of Pio Frezza, the murderer caught in the act with Luciani, Armati, and others, as incitors to the crime ; convicted "with extenuating circumstances ;" penal servitude for life . 13 Nov. 1875
Re-interment on the Janiculum hill of remains of Angelo Brunetti (termed Ciceruacchio) and other unarmed Italian patriots (shot by the Austrians 10 Aug. 1849) . . . . 12 Oct. 1879
International exhibition of fine art, opened 21 Jan. 1883
The German crown prince arrives at Rome, 17 Dec. ; visits the pope . . . . 18 Dec. ,,
2,637th anniversary of the foundation of Rome 21 April, 1884
First Italian "Derby day" . . 24 April, ,,
A sale of part of the Castellani collection, 21 days, about 48,000l. realized . . April, ,,
Dispute ; a cardinal stopped from visiting a cholera hospital without quarantine . . Oct. ,,
Discoveries about the Temple of Vesta in the Forum by Prof. H. Jordan, announced April, 1885
Death of prince Torlonia, a great benefactor, aged 86, 7 Feb. 1886
Statue of Giordano Bruno, philosopher (burnt as a heretic at Venice, 17 Feb. 1600); unveiled, 9 June, 1889
See *Popes*, Pius IX. *et seq*., and *Italy*.

B.C.   KINGS OF ROME.
753. Romulus ; murdered by the senators.
[Tatius, king of the Sabines, had removed to Rome in 747, and ruled jointly with Romulus six years.]
716. [Interregnum.]
715. Numa Pompilius, son-in-law of Tatius the Sabine, elected ; died at the age of 82.
673. Tullus Hostilius ; murdered by his successor, by whom his palace was set on fire ; his family perished in the flames.
640. Ancus Martius, grandson of Numa.
616. Tarquinius Priscus ; son of Demaratus, a Corinthian emigrant, chosen king.
578. Servius Tullius, a manumitted slave : married the king's daughter ; and succeeded by the united suffrages of the army and the people.
534. Tarquinius Superbus, grandson of Tarquinius Priscus : assassinates his father-in-law, and usurps the throne.
510. [The rape of Lucretia, by Sextus, son of Tarquin, and consequent insurrection, leads to the abolition of royalty and the establishment of the consulate.]

REPUBLIC.

510-82. *First period*. From the expulsion of Tarquin to the dictatorship of Sylla.
2-27. *Second period*. From Sylla to Augustus.
48. Caius Julius Cæsar ; perpetual dictator ; assassinated, 15 March, 44 B.C.
31. Octavianus Cæsar.

EMPERORS.

27. AUGUSTUS IMPERATOR, died 19 Aug. A.D. 14.
A.D.
14. Tiberius (Claudius Nero).
37. Caius Caligula : murdered by a tribune.
41. Claudius I. (Tiberius Drusus): poisoned by his wife Agrippina, to make way for
54. Claudius Nero ; deposed ; kills himself, 68.
68. Servius Sulpicius Galba ; slain by the prætorians.
69. M. Salvius Otho ; stabbed himself.
,, Aulus Vitellius ; deposed by Vespasian, and put to death.
,, Titus Flavius Vespasian.
79. Titus (Vespasian), his son.
81. Titus Flavius Domitian, brother of Titus ; last of the *twelve Cæsars* ; assassinated.
96. Cocceius Nerva.
98. Trajan M. Ulpius (Crinitus).
117. Adrian or Hadrian (Publius Ælius).
138. Antoninus Titus, surnamed Pius.
161. Marcus Aurelius (a philosopher) and Lucius Verus, his son-in-law ; the latter died in 169.
180. Commodus (L. Aurelius Antoninus), son of Marcus Aurelius ; poisoned by his favourite mistress, Martia.
193. Publius-Helvius-Pertinax ; put to death by the prætorian band.
[Four emperors now start up : Didianus Julianus, at Rome ; Pescennius Niger, in Syria ; Lucius Septimius Severus, in Pannonia ; and Clodius Albinus, in Britain.]
,, Lucius Septimius Severus ; died at York in Britain, in 211 ; succeeded by his sons,
211. M. Aurelius Caracalla and Septimius Geta. Geta murdered by Caracalla, 212 ; who is slain by his successor
217. M. Opilius Macrinus, prefect of the guards ; beheaded in a mutiny.
218. Heliogabalus (M. Aurelius Antoninus), a youth ; put to death for his enormities.
222. Alexander Severus ; assassinated by some soldiers corrupted by Maximinus.
235. Caius Julius Verus Maximinus ; assassinated in his tent before the walls of Aquileia.
237. M. Antonius Gordianus, and his son ; the latter having been killed in a battle with the partisans of Maximinus, the father strangled himself in a fit of despair, at Carthage, in his 80th year.
238. Balbinus and Pupienus ; put to death.
,, Gordian III., grandson of the elder Gordian, in his 16th year ; assassinated by the guards, at the instigation of his successor.

244. Philip the Arabian ; assassinated by his own soldiers ; his son Philip was murdered at the same time, in his mother's arms.
249. Metius Decius ; he perished with his two sons, and their army, in an engagement with the Goths.
251. Gallus Hostilius, and his son Volusianus ; both slain by the soldiery.
253. Æmilianus ; put to death after a reign of only four months.
 " Valerianus, and his son Gallienus ; the first was taken prisoner by Sapor, king of Persia, and flayed alive.
260. Gallienus reigned alone.
 [About this time thirty pretenders to imperial power arise in different parts of the empire ; of these Cyriades is the first, but he is slain.]
268. Claudius II. (Gallienus having been assassinated by the officers of the guard) succeeds ; dies of the plague.
270. Quintillus, his brother, elected at Rome by the senate and troops ; Aurelian by the army in Illyricum. Quintillus, despairing of success against his rival, who was marching against him, opened his veins and bled himself to death.
 " Aurelianus ; assassinated by his soldiers on his march against Persia, in Jan. 275.
275. [Interregnum of about nine months.]
 " Tacitus, elected 25 Oct. ; died at Tarsus in Cilicia, 13 April, 276.
276. Florianus, his brother ; his title not recognised by the senate.
 " M. Aurelius Probus ; assassinated by his troops at Sirmium.
282. M. Aurelius Carus ; killed at Ctesiphon by lightning ; succeeded by his sons
283. Carinus and Numerianus ; both assassinated, after transient reigns.
284. Diocletian ; who associated as his colleague in the government,
286. Maximianus Hercules ; the two emperors resign in favour of
305. Constantius I. Chlorus and Galerius Maximianus ; the first died at York, in Britain, in 306, and the troops saluted as emperor his son,
306. Constantine, afterwards styled the Great ; whilst at Rome the prætorian band proclaimed
 " Maxentius, son of Maximianus Hercules. Besides these were
 " Maximianus Hercules, who endeavoured to recover his abdicated power.
 " Flavius Valerius Severus, murdered by the last-named pretender ; and
307. Flavius Valerianus Licinius, the brother in-law of Constantine.
 [Of these, Maximianus Hercules was strangled in Gaul, in 310; Galerius Maximianus died wretchedly in 311 ; Maxentius was drowned in the Tiber in 312; and Licinius was put to death by order of Constantine in 324.]
323. Constantine the Great now reigned alone ; died on Whitsunday, 22 May, 337.
337. { Constantine II. / Sons of Constantine ; divided
       Constans. | the empire between them ; the
       Constantius II. | first was slain in 340, and the
                     | second murdered in 350, when
                     | the third became sole emperor.
360. Julian, the Apostate, so called for abjuring Christianity, having been educated for the priesthood ; mortally wounded in a battle with the Persians, 363.
363. Jovian ; reigned eight months ; found dead in his bed, supposed to have died from the fumes of charcoal.
364. Valentinian and Valens.
375. Valens with Gratian and Valentinian II.
379. Theodosius I., &c.
392. Theodosius alone.
395. The Roman empire divided ; see *Eastern Empire*, *Western Empire*, *Popes*, and *Italy*.

ROMILLY'S ACT, SIR SAMUEL, 52 Geo. III. c. 101 (1812) relates to charities.

RONCESVALLES (in the Pyrenees), where, it is said, Charlemagne's paladin, Roland, or Orlando, was surprised, defeated and slain by the Gascons, 778. On 25 July, 1813, marshal Soult was defeated here by the British entering France.

RONDO. A short piece of music having one prominent subject to which returns are made, many composed by Beethoven, Chopin, and others.

ROOF. The largest in the world was said to be that over a riding-school at Moscow, erected in 1791, being 235 feet in span. The roof of the London station of the Midland railway, in Euston-road, London, N.W., is 240 feet wide, 690 feet long, 125 feet high. The extent of ground covered is about 165,000 square feet.

ROPE-MAKING MACHINE. One was patented by Richard March in 1784, and by Edmd. Cartwright, in 1792. Many improvements have been made since.

RORKE'S DRIFT, boundary of British territory of Natal, in South Africa and Zululand. Behind extemporised trenches a handful of British soldiers here successfully resisted a large Zulu army, and probably saved the colony, 22 Jan. 1879. See *Zululand*.

ROSAMOND'S BOWER. Rosamond was daughter of lord Clifford, and mistress of Henry II. about 1154. A conspiracy against her was formed by the queen, prince Henry, and the king's other sons. Henry kept her in a labyrinth at Woodstock, where his queen, Eleanor, it is said, discovered her apartments by the clue of a silk thread, and poisoned her. She was buried at Godstow church, from whence Hugh, bishop of Lincoln, had her ashes removed, 1191.

ROSARY, see *Beads*
In a brief of pope Pius IX., 30 Sept. 1852, it was asserted that 40 repetitions in a rosary of 40 beads of " Sweet Heart of Mary, be my salvation ! " will obtain a large number of days of indulgence for souls in purgatory (23,300 days calculated).

ROSAS (N. E. Spain), BAY OF, where a brilliant naval action was fought by the boats of the *Tigre*, *Cumberland*, *Volontaire*, *Apollo*, *Topaze*, *Philomel*, *Scout*, and *Tuscan*, led by lieut. John Tailour (of the *Tigre*), which ended in the capture or destruction of eleven armed vessels in the bay, 1 Nov. 1809 ; for which purpose lord Collingwood had organised the expedition commanded by capt. Hallowell. Rosas was gallantly defended by lord Cochrane, 27 Nov. ; but surrendered, 4 Dec. 1809.

ROSBACH (Rosebecque), Flanders. Here Charles VI. of France beat the Flemings, who had revolted against their count, 27 Nov. 1382.—At ROSBACH, in Prussia, a great battle was fought between the Prussians, commanded by Frederick the Great, and the combined army of French and Austrians, in which the latter were defeated with severe loss, 5 Nov. 1757.

"ROSCIUS, INFANT," Wm. Henry West Betty, born 13 Sept. 1791. After acting at Belfast, 16 Aug. 1803, and at other places, with much applause, he appeared at Covent-garden, 1 Dec. 1803, as Selim, in " Barbarossa," and is said to have gained in his first season, 17,210*l*.
After several years' retirement, he re-appeared, but soon after left the stage, not being successful. He retired on the fortune he had amassed, and died   Aug. 1874
His portrait may be seen at the Garrick club.

ROSE, see under *Flowers*. The rose, a symbol of silence, gave rise to the phrase *sub rosâ*, " under the rose ; " said, by Italian writers, to have risen

from the circumstance of the pope's presenting consecrated roses, which were placed over the confessionals at Rome, to denote secrecy, 1526. The pope sent a *golden rose* to the queen of Spain, which was given to her with much solemnity, 8 Feb. 1868. A "national rose society" opened its first annual show, St. James's hall, 4 July, 1877.

The *League of the Rose*, under the patronage of the Comtesse de Paris, formed to promote the restoration of the monarchy in France, autumn 1888.

ROSE'S ACT, 33 Geo. III. c. 54 (1793) brought benefit societies under the control of government.

ROSES, WARS OF THE, between the Lancastrians (who chose the red rose as their emblem) and the Yorkists (who chose the white rose), 1455-1485. It is stated that in the Wars of the Roses there perished 12 princes of the blood, 200 nobles, and 100,000 gentry and common people. The union of the roses was effected in the marriage of Henry VII. with the princess Elizabeth, daughter of Edward IV. 1486.

Richard II., who succeeded his grandfather Edward III. in 1377, was deposed and succeeded in 1399 by his cousin Henry IV. (son of John of Gaunt, duke of Lancaster, the fourth son of Edward III.), in prejudice to the right of Roger Mortimer (grandson of Lionel, duke of Clarence, Edward's third son), who was declared presumptive heir to the throne in 1385
Roger's grandson, Richard duke of York, first openly claimed the crown in 1449
Attempts at compromise failed, and the war began in 1455
The Lancastrians were defeated at St. Alban's; the protector Somerset was slain; a truce was made, and Richard was declared successor to Henry VI. 23 May,
The war was renewed, and the Yorkists defeated the Lancastrians at Bloreheath . . 23 Sept. 1459
The Yorkists eventually dispersed, and the duke was attainted.
He defeated his opponents at Northampton, took Henry prisoner, and was declared heir to the crown; but fell into an ambuscade near Wakefield, and was put to death . . . 31 Dec. 1460
His son (Edward) continued the struggle; was installed as king . . . . . 4 March, 1461
Defeated the Lancastrians at Towton . 29 March,
Was deposed by Warwick, who restored Henry VI. Sept. 1470
Edward defeated the Lancastrians at Barnet, 14 April, and finally at Tewkesbury . . 4 May, 1471
The struggle ended with the defeat and death of Richard III. at Bosworth . . . 22 Aug. 1485

ROSETTA (in Egypt), taken by the French in 1798; and by the British and Turks, 19 April, 1801. The Turks repulsed the British here, 22 April, 1807. Near Rosetta was fought the battle of the Nile, 1 Aug. 1798; see *Nile.* Mehemet Ali rendered great service to his country by constructing a canal between Rosetta and Alexandria.

The *Rosetta Stone*, discovered by the French in 1799, was brought from Rosetta in a French vessel, from whence it was taken by Mr. Wm. R. Hamilton, who deposited it in the British Museum. In 1841, Mr. Letronne published the text and a translation of the Greek inscription. It is a piece of black basalt, about 3 feet long and 2½ feet wide, with an inscription in three languages, viz., hieroglyphics, modified hieroglyphics (enchorial), and Greek, setting forth the praises of Ptolemy Epiphanes (about 196 B.C.). It has been studied by Dr. T. Young and Champollion.

ROSICRUCIANS, a sect of mystical philosophers who appeared in Germany in the 14th century. It is asserted that their founder was a noble German monk named Christian Rosencreutz, born 1378, who travelled in Arabia, Egypt, Africa, and Spain; returned to Germany and founded the fraternity of the Rosy Cross, and died aged 102.

The *Fama Fraternitatis* and the *Confessio Rosæ Crucis*, 1615, the latter attributed to Johann Valentin Andreas and others, are important works. They swore fidelity, promised secrecy, and wrote hieroglyphically, and affirmed that the ancient philosophers of Egypt, the Chaldeans, Magi of Persia, and Gymnosophists of the Indies, taught the same doctrine.
Mr. Arthur E. Waite's elaborate work "The Real History of the Rosicrucians" published in 1887.

ROSS, Cork (S. Ireland), a bishopric founded, it is supposed, by St. Fachnan, in the beginning of the 6th century. It was united to Cork in 1340; and Cloyne to both, by the Irish Church Temporalities act (1833); see *Bishops; New Ross.*

ROTA CLUB, a society who met at Miles's Coffee-house in New Palace-yard, Westminster, during the administration of Oliver Cromwell; their plan was that all the great officers of state should be chosen by ballot: and that a certain number of members of parliament should be changed annually by rotation, from whence they took their title. Sir William Petty was one of the members in 1659. *Biog. Brit.*

ROTHESAY CASTLE, see *Wrecks*, 1831.

ROTHSCHILD FAMILY. Meyer Amschel, or Anselm, was born at No. 148, Judengasse (Jew-lane), Frankfort, in 1743. In 1772 he began business as a money-lender and dealer in old coins, in the same house, over which he placed the sign of the red shield (in German, Roth Schild). Having had dealings with the landgrave of Hesse, that prince entrusted him with his treasure (said to have been 250,000*l.*) in 1806, when the French held his country. With this sum as capital, Anselm traded and made a large fortune, and restored the 250,000*l.* to the landgrave in 1815. At his death his sons continued the business as partners. His son, Nathan, begun at Manchester in 1798, removed to London in 1803; and died immensely rich, 28 July, 1836. The baron, James, head of the family, died at Paris, 15 Nov. 1868.
Sir Nathaniel de Rothschild, son of Lionel, created a peer; takes his seat, 9 July, 1885.

ROTTERDAM, the second city in Holland. Its importance dates from the 13th century. The commerce of Antwerp was transferred to it in 1509. In 1572, Rotterdam was taken by the Spaniards by stratagem, and cruelly treated. It suffered much from the French revolutionary wars, and from inundations in 1775 and 1825. Desiderius Erasmus was born here in 1467. The museum and picture-gallery of Rotterdam were destroyed at the fire of the Schieland palace, 16 Feb. 1864.

ROUEN (N. France), an archbishopric, 260, became the capital of Normandy in the 10th century. It was held by the English kings till 1204; and was retaken by Henry V., 19 Jan. 1419. Joan of Arc, the Maid of Orleans, was burnt here, 30 May, 1431. It was taken by Charles VII. of France in 1449; and by the duke of Guise from the Huguenots, Oct. 1562 and 1591. Rouen, after slight conflicts, 4, 5 Dec. 1870, surrendered to general Von Göben, 6 Dec. It was ordered to pay a contribution of 17,000,000 francs.
The theatre, destroyed by fire; many persons injured, and 13 killed . . . . 25 April, 1876

"ROUGH TERROR," a term given in 1874 to the prevalence of brutal assaults on women, children, and unprotected persons among the lower classes, especially in Lancashire and other manufacturing districts, for the repression of which the law appeared to be inadequate.

ROUMANIA, a kingdom, the name assumed by the Danubian principalities (*which see*) on 23 Dec. 1861, when their union was proclaimed at Bucharest and Jassy. Population in 1888, 5,376,000.

M. Catargi, the president of the council of ministers, assassinated as he was leaving the chamber of deputies . . . . 20 June,	1862
The united chambers of the two principalities meet at Bucharest . . . . 5 Feb.	,,
Coup d'état of prince Couza against the aristocrats; a plébiscite for a new constitution, 2 May; which is adopted . . . . 28 May,	1864
Law passed enabling peasants to hold land Aug.	,,
Revolt at Bucharest suppressed, 15 Aug.; amnesty, 11 Sept.,	1865
Revolution at Bucharest; forced abdication of prince Couza; and provisional government established . . . . 22 Feb.,	1866
The offered crown declined by the count of Flanders, Feb.; *prince Charles of Hohenzollern-Sigmaringen* elected hospodar by plébiscite, 20 April; enthusiastically received at Bucharest, 22 May; sworn to observe the constitution 12 July,	,,
Recognised hereditary hospodar by the sultan, and received at Constantinople . . . 24 Oct.	,,
Roumania unsettled; "nationality" projects, Nov.	1867
The legislature proposes to repudiate the just claims of the German shareholders in the Roumanian railways; the prince assents reluctantly; Bismarck appeals to the Porte, which declines to interfere . . . . July-Aug.	1871
Peace between the prince and chambers . Nov.	,,
Austria, Germany, and Russia inform Turkey that they claim the right to conclude separate treaties with Roumania; the sultan objects . . Oct.	1874
Convention with Russia, giving permission to cross Roumania, signed 16 April; Russians enter Moldavia . . . . 24 April,	1877
The Senate vote a declaration of independence and war with Turkey . . . . . . 21 May,	,,
The Roumanians actively engaged before Plevna. See *Russo-Turkish War*, 1877.	
Roumania declared independent by treaties of San Stefano (3 March) and Berlin (losing the part of Bessarabia acquired in 1856, in exchange for the Dobrudscha) . . . . . . 13 July,	1878
Independence recognised by England, France, and Germany . . . . 20 Feb.	1880
The prince and princess crowned king and queen, 23 May,	1881
Temporary rupture with Austria respecting the Danube, about . . . . 1-27 Dec.	,,
Roumanian troops enter Silistria and seize territory, 3 Sept.	1885
Riotous meeting at Bucharest suppressed with loss of life, 25-27 March; M. Bratiano resigns (twelve years minister) . . . about 27 March,	1888
M. Rosetti forms a ministry . . . . 3 April,	,,
Insurrection in the country towns and agricultural districts; increase reported; military called out; Bucharest threatened; revolt said to be encouraged by Russian emissaries 16 April; decrease, 24 April; the elections support the government, Oct.; assembly meets . . 13 Nov.	,,

PRINCES AND KING OF ROUMANIA.

1859. Alexander Couza; abdicated 1866.
1866. Charles I. (of Hohenzollern-Sigmaringen); born 20 April, 1839; elected 20 April, 1866; married Elizabeth, daughter of prince Hermann von Wied, 15 Nov. 1869; nominated KING 26 March, 1881, and crowned with the queen, 23 May, 1881.

Heir, Prince Ferdinand (of Hohenzollern), nephew.

ROUMELIA or **ROMANIA** (Turkey), part of Thrace (*which see*). The Roumelian railway opened 17 June, 1873. Population, 1880, 815,946. By the treaty of Berlin, the province of Eastern Roumelia (termed South Bulgaria in 1886) was constituted, to be partly autonomous, with a Christian governor, nominated by the sultan 13 July, 1878

Sir H. D. Wolff appointed H.M.'s European commissioner for organisation of the province, 10 Aug. ,,

Russian prince Dondoukoff Khorsakoff rules here July-Nov.	1878
Scheme for government of the province approved by the sultan and the allied commissioners Nov.	,,
Russian evacuation begins . . . . 5 May,	1879
Aleko Pasha (prince Alexander Vogorides, a Bulgarian) installed as governor at Philippopolis 30 May,	,,
Much political disorganisation reported . Sept.	,,
Tranquillity restored . . . . Dec.	,,
Great prosperity reported . . . . . Sept.	1883
M. Chrestovitch (Gavril Pasha) appointed governor-general by the Porte, about . . . 10 May,	1884
Bloodless revolution at Philippopolis; reunion with Bulgaria proclaimed 18 Sept.; prince Alexander at Philippopolis; all Bulgaria and Roumelia arming . . . . . Sept.-Oct.	1885
About 75,000 Roumelians armed, . . Nov.	,,
(see *Turkey* and *Bulgaria* for the war.)	
Turkish delegates sent to Philippopolis . 2 Dec.	,,
Prince Alexander appointed governor for five years, (see *Bulgaria*) . . . . . . 5 April,	1886
State of siege at Philippopolis on account of brigandage and Russian agency . . 4 Nov.	,,
Diplomatic rupture with Greece respecting the nationality of a person who died at Bucharest, 13 Nov.	1887
A band of about 150 Montenegrins invading Bourgas repulsed with loss . . . 4 Jan.	1888
Amnesty granted to the insurgent peasantry, 15 Jan.	1889
Impeachment of the Bratiano cabinet voted (141-41), 21 Feb.	,,
M. Catagari forms a ministry . . 10 April,	,,

ROUND. A species of musical canon in regular rhythm. Ancient rounds for six voices were composed in Italy, and introduced into England by the earl of Essex, about 1510. The first printed collection appeared in 1609. Warren's collection published 1763-94. Round, Catch, and Canon club founded in 1843.

ROUND-HEADS. In the civil war which began in 1642, the adherents of Charles I. were called Cavaliers, and the friends of the parliament Round-heads. The term, it is said, arose from those persons who had a round bowl or dish put upon their heads, and their hair cut to the edge of the bowl; see *Cavaliers*.

ROUND TABLE, see under *Garter* and *Liberals*, 1887.

ROUNDWAY DOWN (near Devizes, Wiltshire). Here the royalists defeated the parliamentarians with great slaughter, 13 July, 1643.

ROVEREDO (Austrian Tyrol) was held by the Venetians from 1416 till 1609, when it was acquired by Austria. It was taken by Bonaparte and the French, 4 Sept. 1796, after a brilliant victory.

ROWING, see *Boat Races*, *Doggett*, and *University*.

On 16 Oct. 1873, Mr. Reginald Herbert undertook to row on the Thames, from Maidenhead to Westminster bridge (47 miles 3 furlongs), in twelve hours, for 1000*l*. He did it in 10h. 2m. 19 sec.

ROWLAND HILL MEMORIAL FUND. See *Mansion House*. Mr. W. D. Keyworth was chosen to make a bust of sir Rowland Hill for Westminster abbey, March, 1881. The establishment of a benevolent fund for the widows and orphans of postmen was proposed. A statue of him at the Royal Exchange uncovered by the prince of Wales, 17 June, 1882.

ROXBURGHE CLUB was instituted in 1812 by carl Spencer, for the republication of rare books, or unpublished MSS., in memory of John duke of Roxburghe.

ROYAL AGRICULTURAL, ASTRONOMICAL, GEOGRAPHICAL, HORTICULTURAL, &c.; see under *Agriculture, Astronomy, Geography, Horticulture,* &c.

ROYAL ACADEMY. A society of artists met in St. Peter's-court, St. Martin's-lane, about 1739, which Hogarth established as the society of Incorporated Artists, who held their first exhibition at the Society of Arts, Adelphi, 21 April, 1760. From this sprang the Royal Academy, in consequence of a dispute between the directors and the fellows. On 10 Dec. 1768, the institution of the present Royal Academy was completed under the patronage of George III.; and sir Joshua Reynolds, knighted on the occasion, was appointed its first president. *Leigh.* The first exhibition of the academicians (at Pall-Mall) was on 26 April, 1769, when 136 works appeared. In 1771 the king granted them apartments in old Somerset-house, and afterwards, in 1780, in new Somerset-house, where they remained till 1838, when they removed to the National Gallery. Among the professors have been Johnson, Gibbon, Goldsmith, Macaulay, and Hallam. Turner, the painter, gave funds to the academy for the award of a medal triennially for landscape-painting, which was awarded to Mr. N. O. Lupton in 1857. A commission of inquiry into the affairs of the academy, appointed in 1862, recommended various changes in July, 1863, which were carried into effect. The hundredth anniversary of the foundation of the academy was celebrated 10 Dec. 1868. The Royal Academy held its first exhibition in the new building, 3 May, 1869. The annual exhibition of pictures by the old masters, with some British, began 3 Jan. 1870. The money received has been devoted to the establishment of a professorship of chemistry and a laboratory, &c. In 1874 the exhibition included many of Landseer's pictures.

Sir Francis Chantrey, sculptor, died 25 Nov. 1841. At the death of his wife Jan. 1875, in conformity with his will, about 3000*l.* a year accrued to the Academy for the purchase of works of art for the nation, and other purposes.

The court of appeal upholds Mr. Justice North's decision that the works of sculpture purchased must be finished in marble or bronze, and not models, 4 June, 1889.

The gallery containing the sculptures of John Gibson, bequeathed by him, was opened free, 27 Nov. 1876.

The number of the works of art exhibited in 1789 was about 620, in 1889, 2196, including sculptures.

PRESIDENTS.
1768. Sir Joshua Reynolds.
1792. Benjamin West.
1805. James Wyatt.
1806. Benjamin West.
1820. Sir Thomas Lawrence.
1830. Sir Martin A. Shee.
1850. Sir Charles Eastlake, died 23 Dec. 1865.
1866. Sir Edwin Landseer elected; declines, 24 Jan.
" Sir Francis Grant, Feb. 1; died 5 Oct. 1878.
1878. Sir Frederick Leighton, 13 Nov.

ROYAL ACADEMY OF MUSIC was established in 1823, mainly by the exertions of lord Burghersh (afterwards earl of Westmoreland, who died 16 Oct. 1859), and was incorporated by charter 23 June, 1830. The first concert took place 8 Dec. 1828. Its reconstruction was proposed in 1866, and since effected. Sir George Macfarren principal, 1876; died, 31 Oct. 1887; succeeded by Dr. A. C. Mackenzie, Feb. 1888.

ROYAL ADELAIDE, see *Wrecks,* 1850.

ROYAL ASSENT. If the king assent to a public bill, the clerk of the parliament declares in Norman French, "*Le roy le veult*," the king wills it so to be. If the king refuses his assent, it is in the gentle language of "*Le roy s'avisera,*" the king will consider it. *Hale.* By the statute 33 Hen. VIII., 1541, the king may give his assent by letters-patent. *Blackstone's Com.*

ROYAL BOUNTY, a fund from which sums are granted to female relatives of officers killed or mortally wounded during service.

ROYAL CHARTER, see *Wrecks,* 1859.

ROYAL EXCHANGE (Cambium Regis), London. The foundation of the original edifice was laid by sir Thomas Gresham, 7 June, 1566, on the site of the ancient Tun prison. Queen Elizabeth opened it on 23 Jan. 1571, and her herald named it the *Royal* Exchange. *Hume.* It was totally destroyed by the great fire, Sept. 1666. Charles II. laid the foundation-stone of the next edifice, 23 Oct. 1667, which was completed by Mr. Hawkesmore, a pupil of sir Christopher Wren, in about three years; it was repaired and beautified in 1769. This also was burnt, 10 Jan. 1838. The new Royal Exchange, erected under the direction of Mr. Tite, was opened by the queen, 28 Oct. 1844.—The ROYAL EXCHANGE, Dublin, commenced 1769, opened 1779.

ROYAL GEORGE, a man-of-war of 108 guns, lost off Spithead. While keeled over to repair a pipe, a sudden gust of wind washed the sea into her ports, and she went down. The rear-admiral Kempenfeldt, the crew, many marines, women, and Jews, in all about 600 persons, were drowned, 29 Aug. 1782. By the use of the diving-bell, the ship, embedded in the deep, was surveyed in May, 1817, *et seq.* Portions of the vessel and its cargo were brought up in 1839-42, under the superintendence of sir Charles Pasley, when gunpowder was ignited by the agency of electricity.

ROYAL HUMANE SOCIETY (London), see *Humane Society.*

ROYAL INSTITUTION OF GREAT BRITAIN, the earliest of the kind in London, was founded 9 March, 1799, by count Rumford, sir Joseph Banks, earls Spencer and Morton, and several other noblemen and gentlemen. It received the immediate patronage of George III., and was incorporated 13 Jan. 1800, by royal charter, as " The Royal Institution of Great Britain, for the diffusing knowledge, and facilitating the general introduction of useful mechanical inventions and improvements, and for teaching, by courses of philosophical lectures and experiments, the application of science to the common purposes of life." It was enlarged and extended by an act of parliament in 1810; the original plan, as drawn up by count Rumford, in 1799, having been considerably modified. The members are elected by ballot, and pay ten guineas on admission, and five guineas annually, or a composition of sixty guineas. " The Royal Institution, its Founder, and its first Professors," by Dr. Bence Jones, hon. sec., published 1871.

The House (in Albemarle-street, Piccadilly) was purchased in June, 1799, and the present front was added by subscription in 1838. The Lecture theatre was erected in 1803, under the superintendence of Mr. T. Webster.

The Laboratory established in 1800: was rebuilt, with the modern improvements, 1872.

The LIBRARY was commenced in 1803, by the munificent subscriptions of the proprietors of the institution. It now (1889) comprises about 50,000 volumes. Classified catalogues (by W. Harris) were published in 1809 and 1821; new ones (by B. Vincent) in 1857 and 1882.

The MUSEUM contains original philosophical apparatus of Young, Cavendish, Davy, Faraday, and De la Rue.

The first LECTURE was delivered 4 March, 1801, by Dr. Garnett, he being the first professor of natural philosophy and chemistry.

In Aug. he was succeeded by Dr. Thomas Young, so celebrated for his researches in optics, resulting in the discovery of the interference of light, and the establishment of the theory of undulation. His "Lectures on Natural Philosophy and the Mechanical Arts," first published in 1807, are still considered a text-book of physical science. His works on antiquarian literature (hieroglyphic inscriptions, &c.) are highly esteemed.

In Feb. 1801, Mr. (afterwards sir *Humphry*) *Davy* was engaged as assistant lecturer and director of the laboratory, and on 31 May, 1802, he was appointed professor of chemistry. His lectures were eminently successful, and his discoveries in chemistry and electricity have immortalised his name, and conferred honour on the institution. By him the alkaline metals potassium and sodium, were discovered in 1807; the nature of chlorine was determined in 1810, and the safety-lamp invented in 1815.

William Thomas Brande succeeded sir Humphry Davy as professor of chemistry in 1813, and held that office till his resignation in 1852, since which time, till his death (Feb. 1866), he was hon. professor. From 1816 to 1850 he delivered, in the laboratory of this institution, his celebrated chemical lectures to students.

In 1813 *Michael Faraday* (born 22 Sept. 1791), on the recommendation of sir H. Davy, was engaged as assistant in the laboratory, and in 1825 as its director; in 1827 he became one of the permanent lecturers of the institution. In 1820 he commenced those researches in electricity and magnetism which form an era in the history of science. In 1823-4 he discovered the condensability of chlorine and other gases; in 1831 he obtained electricity from the magnet; in 1845 he exhibited the two-fold magnetism of matter, comprehending all known substances, the magnetism of gases, flame, &c.; in 1850 he published his researches on atmospheric magnetism: died, 25 Aug. 1867.

John Tyndall, F.R.S., professor of natural philosophy, July, 1853, hon. professor, 9 May, 1887, is eminent for his researches on magnetism, heat, glaciers, &c.

Lord Rayleigh, F.R.S., professor of natural philosophy, 9 May, 1887; is eminent for his researches on sound, light, &c.

Edward Frankland, F.R.S., professor of chemistry 1863-8, is eminent for his discoveries in organic chemistry.

In 1804, sir J. St. Aubyn and other gentlemen proposed to form a SCHOOL OF MINES at this institution; but the plan, although warmly supported by the members, was withdrawn for want of encouragement by the government and by mining proprietors.

The WEEKLY EVENING MEETINGS, on the Fridays, from January to June, as now arranged, commenced in 1826. Discourses (of which abstracts are printed) are given at these meetings by the professors of the institution, and other eminent scientific men.

ENDOWMENTS. In 1833, John Fuller, esq., of Rosehill, endowed two professorships, of chemistry and physiology; the former bestowed on Mr. Faraday for life; succeeded by Dr. Wm. Odling, 1868-73; by Dr. John Hall Gladstone, 1874; by James Dewar, 1877. The latter on Dr. Roget for three years, to be filled up afterwards by triennial election.—The Fullerian professors of physiology have been P. M. Roget, R. E. Grant, T. R. Jones, W. B. Carpenter, W. W. Gull, T. W. Jones, T. H. Huxley (*twice*), R. Owen, J. Marshall, Michael Foster, Wm. Rutherford, Alfred H. Garrod, and E. A. Schäfer (1878-81), J. G. McKendrick, 1881-4; A. Gamgee, 1884; C. J. Romanes, 1888.—In 1828, Mrs. Acton gave 1000*l*. to be invested for paying every seven years 100 guineas for the best essay on the beneficence of the Almighty, as illustrative of a department of science; which have been awarded—in 1844 to Mr. G. Fownes; in 1851 to Mr. T. Wharton Jones; in 1858 no award was made; in 1865 to Mr. George Warington; in 1872 to Rev. George Henslow and B. Thompson Lowne; in 1879, to Mr. G. S. Boulger; in 1886, to Prof. (aft. sir) G. G. Stokes, Pres. R.S.

The "Fund for the Promotion of Experimental Research" was founded on 6 July, 1863, by sir Henry Holland, Professor Faraday, sir R. I. Murchison, Dr. Bence Jones, and others.

The *first officers* were sir Joseph Banks, *president*, till the charter was granted, afterwards the earl of Winchilsea; Mr. (afterwards sir Thomas) Bernard, *treasurer*; rev. Dr. Samuel Glasse, *secretary*.—Algernon duke of Northumberland, K.G., elected *president*, 1842; succeeded by sir Henry Holland, in 1865 (died 27 Oct. 1873); by Algernon George, duke of Northumberland, K.G., 1873. W. Pole, esq., *treasurer*, elected 1849; succeeded by Wm. Spottiswoode, esq., in 1865; by George Busk, esq., 1873; by sir Henry Pollock, esq., 1886; by sir James Crichton Browne, 1889. The rev. John Barlow, *secretary*, elected 1842; succeeded by Henry Bence Jones, M.D., 1860; by Wm. Spottiswoode, 1873; by Warren de la Rue, 1879; by sir Wm. Bowman, Bart., 1882; by sir Frederick Bramwell, Bart., 1885. *Librarians*: Wm. Harris, 1803-23; S. Weller Singer, 1826-35; Wm. Mason, 1835-48; Benjamin Vincent, 1849-89 (hon. librarian, 1889); Henry Young, 1889.

ROYAL MARRIAGE ACT, &c., see *Marriage Act*; *Military* and *Naval Asylums*; *Navy*, and *Prerogative.*

ROYAL NAVAL COLLEGE, see *Naval*.

ROYAL SOCIETY (London). In 1645 several learned men met in London to discuss philosophical questions and report experiments; the *Novum Organon* of Bacon, published in 1620, having given great impulse to such pursuits. Some of them (Drs. Wilkins, Wallis, &c.), about 1648-9, removed to Oxford, and with Dr. (afterwards bishop) Seth Ward, the hon. Robert Boyle, Dr. (afterwards sir) W. Petty, and several doctors of divinity and physic, frequently assembled in the apartments of Dr. Wilkins, in Wadham college, Oxford. They formed what has been called the Philosophical Society of Oxford, which only lasted till 1690. The members were, about 1658, called to various parts of the kingdom, on account of their respective professions; and the majority coming to London, constantly attended the lectures at Gresham college, and met occasionally till the death of Oliver Cromwell, 3 Sept. 1658; see *Societies*.

The society was organised in 1660, and constituted by Charles II. a body politic and corporate, by the appellation of "The President, Council, and Fellowship of the Royal Society of London, for improving Natural Knowledge," 22 April, 1662.

Evelyn records the first anniversary meeting, St. Andrew's-day, 30 Nov. 1663.

The *Philosophical Transactions* begin 6 March, 1664-5.

In 1668 Newton invented his reflecting telescope (now in the possession of the society), and on 28 April, 1686, presented to the society the MS. of his *Principia*, which the council ordered to be printed. This was done under the superintendence and at the expense of Halley the astronomer, at that time clerk to the society.

The society met for some years at Gresham College, and afterwards at Arundel House (1666), where it came into possession of a valuable library, presented by Mr. Howard, grandson of its collector, the earl of Arundel. After various changes the fellows returned to Gresham College, where they remained till their removal to Crane-court, in a house purchased by themselves, 8 Nov. 1710.

The Bakerian lecture was established by Henry Baker, 1774.

The first Copley medal was awarded to Stephen Gray in 1731; the royal medal to John Dalton, 1826; the Rumford medal (instituted in 1797) to count Rumford himself in 1800.

The society remove to apartments granted them in Somerset-house, 1780; to apartments in Burlington-house, Piccadilly, 1857.

Parliament votes annually 4000*l*. to the Royal Society for scientific purposes.

Regulations made by which only fifteen fellows are to be annually elected, who pay ten pounds on admission, and four pounds annually, or a composition of sixty pounds, March, 1847. In consequence, the number of fellows was reduced from 839 in 1847, to 626 in 1866; to 567 in 1875; to 552 in 1877; to 523 in 1888.

The entrance fee abolished, and the annual payment reduced to 3*l*., announced, Nov. 1878.

The "Royal Society Scientific Fund" was founded in imitation of the "Literary Fund" in 1859; see *Scientific Fund*.

The Davy Medal (*which see*) first awarded, Nov. 1877.

ROYAL SOCIETY.

PRESIDENTS.

1660. Sir Robert Moray.	1768. James West.
1663. Lord Brouncker.	1772. James Burrow.
1677. Sir Joseph Williamson	,, Sir John Pringle.
1680. Sir Christopher Wren.	1778. Sir Joseph Banks.
1682. Sir John Hoskyns.	1820. Dr. W. H. Wollaston.
1683. Sir Cyril Wyche.	,, Sir Humphry Davy.
1684. Samuel Pepys, author of Diary.	1827. Davies Gilbert.
	1830. Duke of Sussex.
1686. John, earl of Carbery.	1838. Marquis of Northampton.
1689. Thomas, earl of Pembroke.	1848. Earl of Rosse.
1690. Sir Robert Southwell.	1854. Lord Wrottesley.
1695. Chas. Montague (afts. earl of Halifax).	1858. Sir Benj. C. Brodie.
	1861. Maj.-gen. sir Edward Sabine.
1698. John, lord Somers.	
1703. Sir Isaac Newton (M.P. for Cambridge University, 1688–1705).	1871. Sir G. B. Airy.
	1873. Dr., afterwards sir, Joseph Dalton Hooker.
1727. Sir Hans Sloane.	1878. Wm. Spottiswoode, died 27 June, 1883.
1741. Martin Folkes.	
1752. George, earl of Macclesfield.	1883. T. H. Huxley, 5 July.
	1885. Sir G. G. Stokes, 30 Nov. (M.P., 1887), Bart., 1889.
1764. James, earl of Morton.	
1768. James Burrow.	

ROYAL SOCIETY OF EDINBURGH, incorporated 29 March, 1783, arose out of the Philosophical Society of Edinburgh, founded in 1739. It received a second charter in 1811.

ROYAL SOCIETY OF LITERATURE was founded under the auspices of king George IV. in 1823, and chartered 13 Sept. 1826.

ROYAL STYLE, see *Style, Royal.*

ROYAL UNIVERSITY OF IRELAND, see *University.*

RUBICON, a small river flowing into the Adriatic sea, separated Cisalpine Gaul from Italy proper. Roman generals were forbidden to pass this river at the head of an army. Julius Cæsar did so, Jan. 49 B.C., and thereby began a revolt and deadly civil war.

RUBIDIUM, an alkaline metal, discovered by Bunsen by means of the spectrum analysis, and made known in 1861.

RUBRICS, directions in church offices, often printed in red. New ones for the English service agreed to by convocation, 4 July, 1879.

RUBY MINES OF BURMAH, Tavernier (middle of the 17th century) describes it as a place where rubies and other precious stones are largely obtained, in a country difficult of access. Similar accounts were given by Father Giuseppe d'Amato, about 1830. The largest stones were royal property. Mr. Bredemeyer had charge of these and other mines in 1868. Revenue about 1855, from 12,500*l.* to 15,000*l.* per annum. These mines are now British property (see under *Burmah*, 1885), and for the use of them a revenue is paid by the Shan tribes, 1887. An agreement respecting them made between the Indian Government and Messrs. Streeter & Co. of London, announced May, 1887; suspended July, 1887. Working licences issued to persons on the spot, 1887. Lease for seven years to the Streeter Syndicate signed at the India office, 22 Feb. 1839; proposed formation of a company headed by Messrs. Rothschild, March, 1889.

RUFFLES became fashionable about 1520; and went out about 1790.

RUGBY SCHOOL (Warwickshire), was founded in 1567 by Lawrence Sheriff, a London tradesman; its arrangements were affected by the Public Schools act 1868. Dr. Thomas Arnold, the historian, entered on the duties of head-master here in August, 1828, and under him the school greatly prospered. He died 12 June, 1842. See *New Rugby.*

Dr. H. Hayman, one of his successors, was opposed by the masters of the school, and after much dissension and discussion, was dismissed by the trustees, Dec. 1873, and Dr. Jex Blake elected in his room, Feb. 1874. Vice-Chancellor Malins decided against Dr. Hayman in his attempt to set aside his dismissal, but expressed his own opinion on "the grievous hardship of Dr. Hayman's case," 21 March, 1874. Succeeded by Rev. J. Percival, Nov. 1886.

Mr. Disraeli, the premier, presented Dr. Hayman to the living of Aldingham, Lancashire, April, 1874.

RUGEN, an island in the Baltic, has frequently changed masters, having been held by the Danes, Swedes, and French. It was transferred to Prussia in 1815.

RUHMKORFF'S INDUCTION COIL, see *Induction.*

"RULE, BRITANNIA." Nearly all the words are by James Thomson; the music, ascribed to Dr. Arne, is said by Schœlcher (in his life of Handel) to have been taken from an air in Handel's "Occasional Oratorio" composed 1746, but the song and music were really printed in Dr. Arne's masque of "Alfred," 1740. *Grove.*

RULE-OF-THE-ROAD, see *Seas.*

RULING MACHINES, used for ruling paper with faint lines, for merchants' account-books, &c. They were invented by an ingenious Dutchman, resident in London, in 1782, and were subsequently greatly improved by Woodmason, Payne, Brown, and others. They were improved in Scotland in 1803. An invention has lately rendered account-books perfect by the numbering of the pages with types, instead of the numbers being written by a pen, so that a page cannot be torn out from them without being discovered. The late Herr F. A. Nobert devised a ruling machine in 1845 for the production of microscopical test plates, diffraction gratings, and micrometers, specimens of which were exhibited in 1851. The test plates contain bands of lines in a graduated series of fineness from $\frac{1}{1000}$ to $\frac{1}{10000}$ of a Paris line.

RUM (French *rhum*), ardent spirit distilled from sugar lees and molasses, deriving its peculiar flavour from a volatile oil. Rum is principally made in the West Indies. The duty (since 1858) on colonial rum imported into the United Kingdom is 8*s.* 2*d.* per gallon. The duty on rum to be employed as methylated spirits was reduced in 1863.

Imported.	Gallons.	Imported.	Gallons.
1848	6,858,981	1881	4,816,887
1851	4,745,244	1882	7,305,673
1857	6,515,683	1883	5,979,498
1863	7,194,738	1884	7,376,472
1871	7,526,890	1885	6,877,581
1877	7,920,150	1886	5,100,010
1879	6,946,657	1887	6,362,070
1880	6,107,661		

RUMFORD MEDAL, see *Royal Society.*

RUMP PARLIAMENT, see *Pride's Purge.*

RUNES. Alphabetic characters, probably of Phœnician origin, but popularly ascribed to the god Odin, cut or scratched on stone monuments, weapons, ornaments, implements, &c., which have been hypothetically dated from 1000 B.C. to 1000 A.D.: principally found in Scandinavia and England, and sometimes in Western Europe. Professor George

Stephens, of Copenhagen, in his "Old Northern Runic Monuments in Scandinavia and England" (1866-84), has given the results of forty years' studies.

RUNNY-MEDE (council-mead), near Egham, Surrey. Here king John granted Magna Charta, 15 June, 1215.

RUPERT'S LAND (N. America), or *Red River Settlement*, formerly the territories of the Hudson's bay company, was made a bishopric in 1849. See *Hudson's Bay*, *Canada*, and *Manitoba*.

RUPTURE SOCIETY, London, established 1804; see *Truss*.

RUSKIN MUSEUM, see *Sheffield*.

RUSSELL ADMINISTRATIONS,* see *Palmerston Administration*, &c.

FIRST ADMINISTRATION (formed on the resignation of sir Robert Peel), July, 1846.
First lord of the treasury, lord John Russell.
Lord chancellor, lord Cottenham (succeeded by lord Truro).
Lord president of the council, marquis of Lansdowne.
Privy seal, earl of Minto.
Chancellor of the exchequer, Mr. (aft. sir Charles) Wood.
Foreign, home, and colonial secretaries, viscount Palmerston, sir George Grey, and earl Grey.
Boards of control and trade, sir John Hobhouse (aft. lord Broughton), and earl of Clarendon (succeeded by Mr. Labouchere).
Admiralty, the earl of Auckland (succeeded by sir Francis Thornhill Baring).
Duchy of Lancaster, lord Campbell (succeeded by the earl of Carlisle, late viscount Morpeth).
Secretary at war, Mr. Fox Maule.
Postmaster, marquis of Clanricarde.
Paymaster-general, T. B. Macaulay.
Lord John Russell and his colleagues resigned their offices, 21 Feb. 1851; but were induced (after the failure of lord Stanley's party to form an administration) to return to power, 3 March following.

SECOND ADMINISTRATION (or continuation of his first), March, 1851.
First lord of the treasury, lord John Russell.
President of the council, marquis of Lansdowne.
Lord privy seal, earl of Minto.
Chancellor of the exchequer, sir Charles Wood.
Home, foreign, and colonial secretaries, sir George Grey, viscount Palmerston (succeeded by earl Granville, 22 Dec.), and earl Grey.
Lord chancellor, lord Truro.
First lord of the admiralty, sir Francis T. Baring.
Board of control, lord Broughton.
Board of trade, Mr. Labouchere.
Secretary at war, Mr. Fox Maule (aft. lord Panmure, and earl of Dalhousie).
Postmaster-general, marquis of Clanricarde.
Paymaster-general, earl Granville.
Lord Seymour, earl of Carlisle, &c.
This ministry resigned 21 Feb. 1852; see *Derby Administration*.

---

* Lord John Russell, third son of John, duke of Bedford, was born 19 Aug. 1792; M.P. for Tavistock, 1813; for London, 1841-61; was paymaster of the forces, 1830-34; secretary for home department, 1835-9; for the colonies, 1839-41; first minister, July 1846 to March 1852; secretary for foreign affairs, Dec. 1852 to Feb. 1853; president of the council, June 1854 to Feb. 1855; secretary for the colonies, March to Nov. 1855; secretary for foreign affairs, June 1859 to Oct. 1865, when he succeeded lord Palmerston as premier; created a peer, as earl Russell, 30 July, 1861. His motion for reform in parliament was negatived in 1822; adopted 1 March, 1831; he introduced the registration bill and a new marriage bill in 1836; introduced and withdrew a reform bill, 1860; died, 28 May, 1878.

THIRD ADMINISTRATION. (On the decease of lord Palmerston, 18 Oct. 1865, earl Russell received her Majesty's commands to reconstruct the administration.)
First lord of the treasury, John, earl Russell.
Lord chancellor, Robert, lord Cranworth.
Postmaster-general, John, lord Stanley of Alderley.
President of the poor-law board, Chas. Pelham Villiers.
Lord president of the council, George, earl Granville.
Lord privy seal, George, duke of Argyll.
Chancellor of the exchequer, Wm. E. Gladstone.
Secretaries—foreign affairs, George, earl of Clarendon; *colonies*, Edward Cardwell; *home*, sir George Grey; *war*, George, earl de Grey and Ripon, succeeded by Spencer, marquis of Hartington, Feb. 1866; *India*, sir Charles Wood, resigned (created viscount Halifax); succeeded by earl De Grey, Feb. 1866.
First lord of the admiralty, Edward, duke of Somerset.
President of the board of trade, Thos. Milner Gibson.
Chancellor of the duchy of Lancaster, George J. Goschen.
Secretary for Ireland, Chichester Fortescue.
This ministry resigned, 26 June, 1866, in consequence of a minority on 19 June (see under *Reform*, and *Derby Administrations*).

RUSSELL INSTITUTION (Great Coram-street, London), was founded in 1808 by sir Samuel Romilly, Francis Horner, Dr. Mason Good, Henry Hallam, sir James Scarlett (aft. lord Abinger), and others. The building comprises a library, news room, billiard room, &c.

RUSSELL TRIAL. William, lord Russell's trial for complicity in the Rye-house plot was marked by a most touching scene. When he requested to have some one near him to take notes to help his memory, he was answered, that any of his attendants might assist him; upon which he said, "My WIFE is here, and will do it for me." He was beheaded in Lincoln's-Inn-Fields, 21 July, 1683. Lady Russell survived him forty years, dying 29 Sept. 1723, in her eighty-seventh year. His attainder was reversed, 1 Will. III. 1689.

RUSSIA, the eastern part of ancient Sarmatia. The name is generally derived from the Roxolani, a Slavonic tribe. Ruric, a Varangian chief, appears to have been the first to establish a government, 862. His descendants ruled amid many vicissitudes till 1598. The progress of the Russian power under Peter the Great and Catherine II. is unequalled for rapidity in the history of the world. The established religion of Russia is the Greek church, with toleration of other sects, even Mahometans. By an imperial ukase, in 1802, six universities were established, viz., at St. Petersburg, Moscow, Wilna, Dorpat (in Livonia), Charcov, and Kasan; but literature made little progress till the present century, the native publications being very few, and the best books being translations. The Russian language, though not devoid of elegance, is, to a foreigner, of very difficult pronunciation: the number of letters and diphthongs is forty-two. The population in 1867, 82,159,630; in 1872, about 85,685,945; in 1877 (estimated), 86,952,347; in 1885, 108,843,192. By the first Russian budget (1862), the estimated revenue was 34,500,000*l.*; expenditure, 37,850,000*l.* Besides about 500 cathedrals, about 35,000 churches (Greek church, *which see*).

	A.D.
Russia invaded by the Huns	376
Ruric the Norman or Varangian, arrives at Novgorod (or New City), and becomes grand duke [anniversary kept 20 Sept. 1862]	862
Oleg successively invades the Greek empire	907
Baptism of Olga, widow of duke Igor, at Constantinople, about	955
Vladimir the Great marries Anne, sister of the emperor Basil II., and is baptized	988
The Golden Horde of Tartars conquer a large part of Russia about	1223

RUSSIA.

The grand duke Jnrie killed in battle	1237
Alexander Newski defeats the invading Danes	1241
The Tartars establish the empire of the khan of Kaptschak, and exercise great influence in Russia	1242
He is made grand duke of Russia by the Tartars	1252
Moscow made the capital	1300
Tartar war, 1380; Moscow burnt	1383
Tamerlane invades Russia, but retires	1395
Accession of Ivan III. the Great—able and despotic, founds the present monarchy	1462
Ivan introduces fire-arms and cannon into Russia	1475
Great invasion of the Tartars; consternation of Ivan	1479
His general Svenigorod annihilates their power	1481
War with Poland	1506-23
The English "Russian company" established	1553
Richard Chancellor sent to open the trade	1554
Discovery of Siberia	
The royal body-guard (the Strelitz) established	1568
Ivan solicits the hand of queen Elizabeth of England	1579
Murder of Feodor I., last of the race of Ruric, which had governed Russia for 700 years	1598
The imposition of Demetrius (see *Impostors*).— Matins of Moscow	29 May, 1606
Michael Fedorovitz, of the house of Romanoff, ascends the throne	1613
Finland ceded to Sweden	1617
Russian victories in Poland	1654
Subjugation of the Cossacks	1671
Reign of Ivan and Peter I. or the Great	1682
Peter sole sovereign	1689
He visits Holland and England, and works in the dockyard at Deptford	1697
Recalled by a conspiracy of the Strelitz, which he cruelly revenges; 2000 tortured and slain; he beheads many with his own hand	1698
The Russians begin their new year from 1 Jan. (but retain the old style)	1700
War with Sweden; Peter totally defeated by Charles XII. at Narva	30 Nov., "
Peter founds St. Petersburg as a new capital, 27 May,	1703
The Strelitz abolished	1704
Charles XII. totally defeated by Peter at Pultowa, and flees to Turkey	8 July, 1709
14,000 Swedish prisoners sent to Siberia	"
War with Turkey: Peter and his army cross the Pruth, and are surrounded by the Turks; they escape by the energy of the empress Catherine, who obtains a truce	June, 1711
Esthonia, Livonia, and a large part of Finland added to the empire	1715
Peter visits Germany, Holland, and France	"
The Jesuits expelled	1718
Conspiracy and mysterious death of prince Alexis	7 July, "
Peter II. (last of the Romanoffs) deposed, and the crown given to Anne of Courland	1730
Elizabeth, daughter of Peter I., reigns, in prejudice of Ivan VI., an infant, who is imprisoned for life	1741
Peter III. dethroned and murdered, succeeded by Catherine his wife	1762
Ivan VI., the rightful heir, till now immured, put to death	1764
Treaty of Kutschouc Kainardji; independence of the Crimea and freedom of Black sea	July, 1774
Rebellion of the Cossacks, 1774; suppressed	1775
Successful invasions of the Crimea	1769-84
Dismemberment of Poland; commenced by Catherine (see *Poland*), 1772; completed	1795
Catherine gives her subjects a new code of laws; abolishes torture in punishing criminals; and dies	1796
Unsuccessful war with Persia	"
Russian treaty with Austria and England	1798
Suwarrow, with an army joins the Austrians, and checks the French in Italy	1799
Mental derangement of Paul, 1800; murdered,	24 March, 1801
Alexander I. makes peace with England	May, "
He joins the coalition against France	11 April, 1805
Allies defeated at Austerlitz	2 Dec., "
Treaty of Tilsit with France	7 July, 1807
Russians defeated by the Turks, near Silistria,	26 Sept. 1809
War with France	June, 1812
The Russians defeated at Smolensko, 17 Aug.; and at the Borodino	7 Sept., "
Moscow burnt by the Russians, 14 Sept.; retreat of the French begins	15 Oct. 1812
Alexander present at the battle of Leipsic, Oct. 1813; entered Paris	March, 1814
He visits England	June, "
Forms the Holy Alliance	1815
The grand duke Constantine renounces the right of succession	26 Jan. 1822
Death of Alexander, 1 Dec.; Pestal's conspiracy against Nicholas I.; insurrection of troops at Moscow; suppressed	26-29 Dec. 1825
Nicholas crowned at Moscow	3 Sept. 1826
War against Persia	28 Sept. "
Nicholas visits England; invested with the order of the Garter	9 July, 1827
Peace between Russia and Persia	22 Feb. 1828
War between Russia and the Ottoman Porte declared (see *Turkey and Battles*)	26 April, "
Peace of Adrianople	14 Sept. 1829
The war for the independence of Poland against Russia (see *Poland*)	29 Nov. 1830
Failure of the expedition against Khiva	Jan. 1840
Treaty of London (see *Syria*)	15 July, "
The emperor Nicholas arrives in London	1 June, 1844
The grand duke Constantine arrives at Portsmouth in the *Ingermanland*, of 74 guns	9 June, 1846
[For the participation of Russia in the Hungarian war of 1848-9, see *Hungary*.]	
Russia demands the expulsion of the Hungarian and Polish refugees from Turkey (see *Turkey*)	5 Nov. 1849
They are sent to Konieh, in Asia Minor	Jan. 1850
Conspiracy against the emperor detected	6 Jan. "
Harbour of Sebastopol completed	Feb. "
The emperor decrees seven men in each thousand of the population of Western Russia to be enrolled in the army, giving a total increase of 180,000 soldiers	Aug. "
St. Petersburg and Moscow railway begun	1851
The czar visits Vienna	8 May, 1852
Concentrates forces on frontiers of Turkey	Feb. 1853
Origin of the Russo-Turkish war (*which see*, and *Holy Places*)	March, "
Conference between the emperors of Russia and Austria at Olmutz	24 Sept. "
And king of Prussia at Warsaw	2 Oct. "
Interview of Mr. J. Sturge and other quakers with the czar to obtain peace	Feb. 1854
The northern provinces put in a state of siege,	5 March, "
The czar issues a manifesto to his subjects; he will combat only for the faith and Christianity,	23 April, "
Death of the czar Nicholas, and accession of Alexander II.; no change of policy	2 March, 1855
Most extensive levy ordered by the czar (at Nicolaieff)	3 Nov. "
He visits his army at Sebastopol	10 Nov. "
Death of prince Ivan Paskiewitsch, aged 74	1 Feb. 1856
Treaty of peace at Paris	30 March, "
Alexander Gortschakoff foreign minister and chancellor	29 April, "
Amnesty granted to the Poles, 27 May; five political offenders, &c.; Alexander II. crowned at Moscow	7 Sept. "
Manifesto on account of the English and French interference in the affairs of Naples	2 Sept. "
St. Petersburg and Warsaw railway begun by government, 1851; ceded to Great Russian railway company (about 335 miles, the half completed)	"
Grand duke Constantine visits France and England,	April, 1857
The czar meets the emperor Napoleon at Stuttgardt, 25 Sept.; and the emperor of Austria at Weimar,	1 Oct "
Partial emancipation of the serfs on the imperial domains	2 July, 1858
A Russian naval station established at Villa Franca, on the Mediterranean, creates some political excitement	Aug. "
New commercial treaty with Great Britain	12 Jan. 1859
Russia reproves the warlike movements of the German confederation during the Italian war, 27 May,	"
The czar protests against the recognition of the sovereignty of peoples	13 Feb. 1860
Fruitless meetings of the emperors of Russia and Austria and the regent of Prussia at Warsaw	20-25 Oct. "

Treaty with China for enlargement of commerce . 1 Jan.	1861
Decree for the total emancipation of the serfs (23,000,000) throughout the empire in two years (19 Feb.) . 3 March,	,,
Demonstrations and repression in Poland (*which see*) Feb.-April,	,,
Disturbances in South Russia, caused by an impostor asserting himself to be a descendant of Peter III.; many peasants shot or flogged May and June,	,,
Inundations at Kiev, Moscow; 615 houses under water . May,	,,
Death of prince Michael Gortschakoff, governor of Poland . 14 May,	,,
Student riots at the university of St. Petersburg, which is closed, 6-9 Oct.; reopened . 24 Oct.	,,
The nobles sign a petition for a political constitution Nov.	,,
Increased privileges granted to the Jews . 26 Jan.	1862
Death of Nesselrode, the chancellor of the empire, 20 March,	,,
Alarming increase of fires at St. Petersburg and Moscow; the government suppresses various educational institutions . June,	,,
Russia recognises the kingdom of Italy . 10 July,	,,
1000th anniversary of the foundation of the Russian monarchy at Novgorod, celebrated 20 Sept.	,,
Re-organisation of the departments of justice decreed; juries to be employed in trials, &c. 14 Oct.	,,
Trade tax bill introduced, admitting foreigners to merchants' guilds, &c. . 26 Nov.	,,
Insurrection in Poland . 22-24 Jan.	1863
[For events, see *Poland*.]	
Termination of serfdom . 3 March,	,,
Provincial institutions established throughout Russia . 13 Jan.	1864
Great victory over the Oubykhs in the Caucasus, 31 March; emigration of the Caucasian tribes into Turkey, April; submission of the Abigas; the war declared to be at an end . 2 June,	,,
The czarowitch betrothed to the princess Dagmar of Denmark . 28 Sept.	,,
Serfdom abolished in the Trans-Caucasian provinces; new judicial system promulgated . Dec.	,,
The Russian nobles request the emperor to establish two houses of representatives (declined) 24 Jan.	1865
New province, "Turkestan," in central Asia, created 14 Feb.	,,
The czarowitch Nicholas dies at Nice . 24 April,	,,
Industrial exhibition at Moscow closes . 16 July,	,,
Censorship of the press relaxed; law begins, 13 Sept.	,,
Rupture with the pope, on account of Russian severity to Polish clergy . Jan. and Feb.	1866
Assembly of the nobility; short, stormy session March,	,,
Inauguration of trial by jury in Russia . 8 Aug.	,,
Karakozow attempts to assassinate the czar, 16 April; after long investigation into the origin of the plot, he is executed . 15 Sept.	,,
War with Bokhara; conflicts with varying results; Russians advance in May, *et seq.*; ended . Nov.	,,
Marriage of prince Alexander, heir to the crown, to princess Dagmar of Denmark . 9 Nov.	,,
Emancipation of many state serfs in Poland, 11 Nov.	,,
Three decrees for abolishing the remains of Polish nationality . 1 Jan.	1867
Congress of Slavonian deputies at Moscow 5 May,	,,
Russian America sold to the United States for 7,000,000 dollars, by treaty, 13 March; ratified 15 May,	,,
Amnesty in favour of the Poles . 29 May,	,,
The czar visits Paris (*which see*) . June,	,,
Escapes assassination by Berezowski, a Pole, 6 June,	,,
Decree for the use of the Russian language in the Baltic provinces . 7 July,	,,
A Romanist college to replace the authority of the pope, established at St. Petersburg . 2 Aug.	,,
The separate interior government in Poland suppressed . 29 Feb.	1868
Samarcand taken by Kaufmann . 26 May,	,,
Amnesty for political offences granted . 6 June,	,,
Polish language interdicted in public places in Poland . July,	,,
The *Government Messenger*, official journal, published at St. Petersburg . 13 Jan.	1869
Socialist secret conspiracy among the students, headed by Sergius Netschajew, detected; the informer assassinated . Jan.	1870
Burlingame, Chinese envoy, arrives . 2 Feb.	,,
Dies at St. Petersburg . 22 Feb.	,,
Russia neutral in the Franco-Prussian war July,	,,
Said to be arming, 20 Sept.; contradicted 27 Sept.	,,
Fruitless visit of M. Thiers at St. Petersburg on behalf of the French government . 27 Sept.	,,
Diplomatic circular of prince Gortschakoff, foreign minister, repudiating the clauses of the treaty of 30 March, 1856, respecting the Black Sea, 31 Oct.; received by earl Granville, 9 Nov., who replies, maintaining the force of the treaty . 10 Nov.	,,
Vigorous protest of British and Austrian governments . 16 Nov.	,,
Decree for forming military reserves, about 16 Nov.	,,
Conciliatory despatch from prince Gortschakoff to earl Granville, agreeing to a conference for revision of the treaty of 1856 . 21 Nov.	,,
Prussian government expresses surprise at Gortschakoff's circular, and proposes a conference about 26 Nov.	,,
Firm courteous despatch from earl Granville, consenting to a conference which shall "assemble without any foregone conclusion" . 28 Nov.	,,
The other powers agree to a conference . 7 Dec.	,,
Re-organisation of the army ordered . Jan.	1871
The conference meets in London . 17 Jan.	,,
The Black Sea clauses abrogated (see *Black Sea*), by treaty, signed . 13 March,	,,
Schamyl, the Circassian chief, dies about April,	,,
The grand duke Wladimir visits England . June,	,,
Military exercises, sham battles round St. Petersburg, 30,000 engaged; emperor present, 15-23 Aug.	,,
Trial of persons implicated in a socialist conspiracy (at St. Petersburg); many condemned to imprisonment . Sept.	,,
Electric telegraph between St. Petersburg and Nagasaki, Japan, completed . Nov.	,,
200th anniversary of the birth of Peter the Great, 30 May, 1672 (O.S.), solemnly observed by the court and nation . 11 June,	1872
Peter the Great ironclad (incomplete) launched at St. Petersburg . Aug.	,,
Great Russian Encyclopædia undertaken by prof. Beresina . autumn,	,,
Reconnoitring expedition to Khiva; defeat of gen. Markosoff announced . Dec.	,,
Diplomatic visit of count Schouvaloff to London respecting this; presented to the queen; Russian concessions reported satisfactory . 13 Jan.	1873
Expeditions against Khiva start . March,	,,
The emperor of Germany warmly received at St. Petersburg . 27 April,	,,
The Shah of Persia visits St. Petersburg 22-31 May,	,,
Khiva surrenders, 10 June; a rebellion suppressed, July,	,,
Jumuden Turcomans defeated at Tschamlyr 25, 27 July,	,,
New treaty with Bokhara, published . Dec.	,,
Marriage of the grand duchess Marie with the duke of Edinburgh . 23 Jan.	1874
Visit of the emperor of Austria at St. Petersburg, 13 Feb.; the czar in proposing his health, says, "In the friendship which binds us and also the emperor William and the queen Victoria, I see a most sure guarantee of peace" . 15 Feb.	,,
The czar visits England . 13-21 May,	,,
Count Schouvaloff succeeds Brunnow as ambassador in London . autumn,	,,
New law for organization of the army . Sept.	,,
Son born to the duke of Edinburgh and grand-duchess Marie . 15 Oct.	,,
Visit of the empress and the czarewitch to England 15 Oct.-24 Nov.	,,
Mitrophania, mother abbess, of Serpouchow, Moscow, prosecuted for fabricating commercial bills; convicted, and sentenced to 14 years' exile, Nov.	,,
International telegraphic conference at St. Petersburg . 1-19 July,	1875
Expedition (with scientific men) to Krasnovodsk, Central Asia, spoken of . Aug.	,,
War with Khokand (*which see*) . 4 Sept.-Oct.	,,
Commercial panic through failure of Dr. Strousberg, a German railway speculator, at Moscow, Prague, and Berlin . Nov.	,,

At a dinner of "Knights of St. George," the czar declares that the three emperors are united to maintain peace . . . . . 8 Dec. 1875
Baltic provinces (formerly a provincial federation with a governor), incorporated with the empire under the ministry of the interior, on the death of the governor Bagration . . . 29 Jan. 1876
Khokand, formally annexed (as Ferghana) 29 Feb. ,,
Prosecution of a sect "White Doves" (Skoptzi) April, ,,
Warlike enthusiasm: Russian volunteers in the Servian army . . . . . July-Sept. ,,
Depression through Servian defeats . . Oct. ,,
Pacific declaration of the czar to lord Aug. Loftus 2 Nov. ,,
The czar, in an address at Moscow, says that if sufficient guarantees are not given by Turkey, he will act independently . . . 10 Nov. ,,
Dr. Strousberg and others tried for fraud, &c., Nov.; he is sentenced to banishment from Russia 14 Nov. ,,
Enthusiasm for Bulgarians; partial mobilisation of the army ordered . . . about 14 Nov. ,,
Internal loan of 10 million roubles . 19 Nov. ,,
Great enthusiasm for Bulgarians; war declared, and begun . . . . . . 24 April, 1877
See *Turkey*; and *Russo-Turkish War*, 1877.
The czar warmly received at Moscow, 4 May; and St. Petersburg . . . . . 7 May, ,,
Great trial of Nihilists for revolutionary propagandism, began about . . . . 31 Oct. ,,
Russian loan of 15,000,000l. at 5 per cent. announced 12 Nov. ,,
The czar at St. Petersburg; celebrates centenary anniversary of birth of Alexander I. 23 Dec. ,,
Ill-feeling against Bulgarians . . . Dec. ,,
Nihilist trial ended; about 160 sentenced to hard labour; about 90 acquitted, . about 9 Feb. 1878
Treaty of peace with Turkey signed at San Stefano; Europe dissatisfied . . . . 3 March, ,,
Vera Zasulitch (or Sassnlitch), a young woman, who acknowledged firing at gen. Trepoff, prefect of St. Petersburg (5 Feb.), for severity to prisoners, acquitted by jury . . . . . 12 April, ,,
Reported spread of Nihilism in Kieff, Moscow, &c. April, ,,
Public depression: feeling against Bulgarians; desire to get quit of the Eastern question May-June, ,,
Conference at Berlin (*which see*) meets 13 June; treaty signed . . . . . 13 July, ,,
Gen. Kaufmann's advance on the Oxus to occupy Balkh; reported . . . . . Aug. ,,
Nihilists tried and condemned at Odessa; riots ensued . . . . . . 5 Aug. ,,
General disaffection to the government; general De Mesentzoff, chief of police, assassinated in the street in St. Petersburg . . . 16 Aug. ,,
New 5 per cent. loan (300,000,000 roubles) issued on bonds . . . . . 29, 30, 31 Aug. ,,
Ukase decreeing state offences to be punished by military law . . . . . end of Aug. ,,
Gen. Drentelen made chief of police . 6 Oct. ,,
Students at a college in St. Petersburg present an address to the czarewitch complaining of grievances, 11 Dec.; they are attacked and punished by the police and cossacks, 12 Dec.; they issue an address soon after . . . . . Dec. ,,
Prince Demetrius Krapotkine, governor, assassinated while returning from a ball at Kharkoff, 21 or 22 Feb. 1879
Attempted assassination of Drentelen, 25 March; and of the czar by Alexander Solovieff, a schoolmaster, with a revolver . . . . . 14 April, ,,
The poll tax abolished by ukase . . April, ,,
Riots at Rostoff on the Don suppressed by military, 14 April, ,,
Ukase establishing martial law in the provinces of St. Petersburg, Moscow, Kieff, Odessa, and Warsaw, dated . . . . . 17 April, ,,
"Land and Liberty," a Nihilist newspaper, freely yet surreptitiously circulated . . April, ,,
Solovieff condemned, 7 June; executed . 9 June ,,
Discontent at the small results of the war . July, ,,
Trials, convictions, and executions of Nihilists at Kieff and Odessa . . . . May-Aug. ,,
Gen. Lazareff, commander of expedition against the Tekké Turkomans, dies at Tchat about 13 Aug. ,,

Gen. Lomakine succeeds in command; severe battle at Geok Tepe or Dengli Tepé; Russians said to be victorious, yet retreat with heavy loss 28 Aug. (O.S.), 9 Sept. 1879
Tergukasoff succeeds Lomakine in command, 25 Sept. ,,
Leon Mirsky condemned to death for attempted assassination of gen. Drentelen, chief of police 27, 28 Nov. ,,
Count Schouvaloff, ambassador at London, resigns, 27 Nov. ,,
Attempted assassination of the czar, by undermining railway train near Moscow; none hurt; baggage carriages destroyed . . . 1 Dec. ,,
The newspaper *Golos* suspended for 6 months, 4 Dec. ,,
Proclamation of the executive revolutionary committee justifying the attempted assassination on 1 Dec. . . . . . . 4 Dec. ,,
Plot to blow up the Winter Palace, St. Petersburg, discovered . . . . . 12 Dec. ,,
"Will of the People" revolutionary paper freely circulated . . . . . Nov. Dec. ,,
Explosion in a guard-room filled with dynamite and gun-cotton under the dining-room of the Winter Palace, St. Petersburg: the czar and family escape through being a little late for dinner; 11 soldiers killed; 47 wounded; between 6.0 and 7.0 P.M., 17 Feb. 1880
Hartmann, owner of a house near the explosion, arrested at Paris . . . about 20 Feb. ,,
Panic at St. Petersburg; ukase issued; appointing supreme executive commission, gen. Loris Melikoff, president, with extensive powers; virtual dictator . . . . . . 24 Feb. ,,
Extradition of Hartmann requested by Russia; declined . . . . . . March, ,,
Twenty-fifth anniversary of the czar's accession celebrated at St. Petersburg . . . 2 March, ,,
Hippolyte Molodzoff (Mladetsky, or Wladitsky, or Mlodecki), a converted Jew, fires at gen. Loris Melikoff, 4 March; hanged . . 5 March, ,,
Hartmann expelled from France; goes to England; Prince Orloff, ambassador, quits France, about 6 March, ,,
Nihilist trials at St. Petersburg; sentences to death and imprisonment (Dr. Weimar and others); commuted . . . . . . May, ,,
Death of the empress after a long illness, 3 June, ,,
21 extreme Nihilists convicted at Kieff (capital sentences remitted) . . . . about 7 Aug. ,,
Ukase of 24 Feb. superseded; Melikoff, who had governed well, appointed minister of the interior, with charge of the police . . 18 Aug. ,,
Count Loris Melikoff's scheme for administrative reform sanctioned by the czar; announced 3 Oct.; put into action . . . 25 Oct. *et seq.* ,,
"*Russia*," new national daily paper, published Oct. ,,
Great Nihilist trial at St. Petersburg for assassinations, explosion at Winter Palace, &c.; sentences, Kviatofski and 4 others condemned to death: 8 men and 3 women to imprisonment . 10 Nov. ,,
Kviatofski and Priessnakoff hanged . 16 Nov. ,,
Gen. Skobeleff's expedition into Central Asia, 24 Dec. ,,
Severe conflicts with the Tekké Turkomans, 14 Jan. 1881
Geok Tepé besieged; taken . . 24 Jan. ,,
Assassination of the czar Alexander II. by explosion of a bomb; assassin himself killed; Risakoff seized . . . . . 2 P.M. 13 March, ,,
A mine for explosion discovered in the middle of St. Petersburg . . . . about 15 March, ,,
Circular of the new czar Alexander III. to foreign powers; he will aim at moral and material development of Russia, and a pacific foreign policy 16 March, ,,
Manifesto from the Nihilist executive committee to the czar offering peace, if an amnesty with a legislative assembly to be elected by universal suffrage, free press, &c., be granted . . 22 March, ,,
Sophie Peroffskaja, and other Nihilists, arrested 23 March, ,,
The czar's magnificent funeral at St. Petersburg; the prince and princess of Wales present, 27 March, ,,
A representative council for St. Petersburg elected about 31 March, ,,
Trial of Risakoff, Sophie Peroffskaja, Jelaboff, Jessie or Hessie Helfmann, Kibaichick, and Michailoff (four men and two women), all condemned to death . . . . . 8, 9 April, ,,

The Tekkés submit; maraudings cease; object of Skobeleff's expedition accomplished; announced . . . . 9 April, 1881
Risakoff and others hanged; Hellmann (enceinte) reprieved . . . . 15 April, "
Treaty of peace with China announced . April, "
Nihilist manifesto styling the assassins "martyrs," &c. . . . . 16 April, "
Changes in ministerial offices; tendency to reduce autocracy of the czar announced . about 4 May, "
Ukase supplementary to that of 19 Feb. 1861, for emancipating serfs, remitting payments to many peasant proprietors; announced . early May, "
Reactionary proclamations in favour of autocracy (29 April), 11 May; resignation of count Loris Melikoff and other liberal ministers soon after, about 13 May, "
General Ignatieff, chief minister, issues manifesto, declaring for suppression of rebellion, and promising reforms; manifesto from Nihilists offering peace if reforms be granted . . . 23 May, "
The czar, closely guarded, living in close seclusion; continued policy of repression . . . June, "
The czar well received at Moscow, &c., 30 July; the czar meets the emperor of Germany at Dantzic 3 Sept.; stringent decree respecting public order 21 Sept. "
Treaty with Persia signed . . . 22 Dec. "
Nihilist trials at St. Petersburg; 10 sentenced to death, 28 Feb.; commuted to penal servitude (except Suchanoff, to be shot) . March, 1882
Gen. Strelnikoff, public prosecutor, assassinated at Odessa by two students, 30 March; executed 3 April, "
Retirement of the chancellor and foreign minister, Gortschakoff (his policy war-like); succeeded by his assistant De Giers . . about 9 April, "
Mine discovered under Moscow cathedral; 80 workmen arrested . . . . about 15 April, "
General Kaufmann died, aged 64 . . 16 May, "
Decree for the gradual abolition of the poll tax (imposed by Peter the Great) . beginning June, "
Ignatieff resigns; succeeded by count Tolstoi about 12 June, "
Death of general Scobeleff, the hero of Plevna, aged 39 . . . . 7 July, "
General Tchernaïeff appointed to command in Central Asia . . . . "
Successful exhibition of Russian arts and manufactures . . . . . . summer, "
Revival of the Russian navy determined on . . "
Tranquillity restored; great festivities through the visit of the duke and duchess of Edinburgh Jan.—Feb. 1883
Death of prince Gortschakoff, aged 85 . 11 March, "
Arrest of 200 persons at St. Petersburg about 20 March, "
Trial of Nihilists at St. Petersburg; some sentenced to death (remitted), others to imprisonment 19 April, "
The emperor and empress crowned with great ceremony at Moscow . . . . 27 May, "
Patriotic and pacific manifesto, and amnesty, 27 May; and popular festival . . 2 June, "
Poll tax abolished for the poorest, reduced for others (1 Jan. 1884) on . . . 8 June, "
The czar and the kings of Denmark and Greece breakfast with Mr. Gladstone on board the Pembroke Castle, Copenhagen . . 18 Sept. "
Reported discovery of a great conspiracy at St. Petersburg; many arrests . about 27 Sept. "
Government projects for re-modelling the communes . . . . . . published Oct. "
Grand funeral of Tourgénieff at St. Petersburg 9 Oct. "
Foundation of memorial church at the place where Alexander II. was assassinated at St. Petersburg laid by the czar . . . . . 16 Oct. "
63 Nihilists sentenced to Siberia . 19 Oct. "
Lieut. Sudeikin, chief of secret police, and his nephew, M. Sadovsky, assassinated at St. Petersburg; attributed to Nihilists aided by Jablonsky, a subordinate, whose life he had saved night of 28-29 Dec. "
37 students at Moscow arrested announced 9 Jan. 1884
Loyal address of the nobles to the czar, advocating union of nobles and peasantry . . 25 Jan. "
Surrender of Merv to Russia, effected by general Komaroff . . . . announced 14 Feb. "

Proposals for state loan not taken up, Nov. 1883; another loan at 6 per cent, offered in open market about 3 Dec. 1883; taken up . . April, 1884
Convention with Persia for cession of Snaklus (threatening to Afghanistan) reported 6 May, "
The majority of the czarewitch (aged 16) declared 18 May, "
Death of general Todleben, born 1818 . 1 July, "
Alleged dynamite conspiracy against the czar at Warsaw . . . . 8 Sept. "
Maria Wassilieona Kaliouchnaia, at Odessa, sentenced to 20 years' hard labour for attempt to shoot colonel Katensky . . . about 11 Sept. "
The czar meets the emperors of Germany and Austria at Skiernievice, near Warsaw 15, 16 Sept. "
The letters of "Stepniak" and others expose the cruel, dishonest, and unscrupulous conduct of government officials in prohibiting the diffusion of knowledge and literature; proposed united opposition of the nobility and peasantry Sept.-Oct. "
The circulation of many religious books prohibited "
14 Nihilists (including 6 officers and 3 women, one, Mary F. Figner) convicted by secret court martial; 8 sentenced to death at St. Petersburg, 11 Oct.; two men executed . . . . 18 Oct. "
The Nihilist journal, Narodnaia Volia, reappears about 27 Oct. "
Sir Robert Morier, British ambassador at St. Petersburg . . . . "
Great discontent among workmen and peasantry Jan. 1885
Mission of M. Lessar, engineer-diplomatist to London respecting central Asian boundaries . Feb. "
Ship canal from St. Petersburg to Cronstadt completed, Feb.; opened . . . 27 May, "
Russians advance to about 90 miles from Herat, and hold Zulfikar pass . . . Feb. "
Three courses before them: to retire; to remain and negotiate; to make war . . 1 March, "
Arrangement that no further advance on the "debated or debatable ground" be made by Russians or Afghans (since termed a "solemn covenant") . . . . 16 or 17 March, "
Gen. Komaroff attacks the Afghans at Aktapa, on the river Kushk, alleging provocation; hundreds of Afghans killed, others perish from exposure, and the rest retire from their camp; 53 Russians killed and wounded, 30 March; his statements controverted by sir Peter Lumsden, 14 April; British government announce agreement to arbitration (by Denmark) . . . 4 May et seq. "
The Russian general Komaroff, near the Kushk and Murgbab rivers, commands the Afghans to retire; on their refusal, attacks them at Aktapa (or Aktepe or Pul-i-khusti), near Penjdeh; defeats them with much slaughter, and captures artillery and stores; many Afghans perish in the retreat through exposure, 30 March; sir Peter Lumsden reports the attack on the Afghans to have been unprovoked . . about 21 April "
The British government prepares for war with great energy; strongly supported by the colonies and Indian princes . . . . . . "
British government statement: new agreement with Russia; arbitration respecting light on March 30 accepted 4 May; Denmark accepts work of arbitration . . . . May, "
Agreement on delimitation settled by earl Granville and earl of Kimberley, with MM. de Staal and Lessar; approval reported . 30 May, "
Cordial meeting of the czar and the emperor of Austria at Kremsier in Moravia . 25, 26 Aug. "
The Afghan boundary question settled 10 Sept. "
Discovery of plot against the czar; arrest of military officers and others . . April, 1886
Tchesmé ironclad launched by the czar at Sebastopol (other vessels constructing) 18 May, "
Russia violates treaty of Berlin by declaring Batoum not to be a free port . . July, "
Honours and income of the younger members of the imperial family much diminished, announced July, "
Russian interference in Bulgaria (which see) Sept.-Dec. "
Plot against the czar; students with dynamite and other explosives, detected 13 March; 200 arrested . . . . . . March, 1887
Three plotters executed 31 March; seven political offenders sentenced to death, the rest to various

RUSSIA. 783 RUSSIA.

terms of imprisonment, 1 May; more arrests about 18 May; five executed . . 16 May, 1887
Prince Nicholas, the czarewitch, made chief Ataman (Hetman) of all the Cossacks at Novo-Tcherkask . . . . 18 May, ,,
N. Katkoff, journalist and politician, editor of the *Moscow Gazette*, Russophile, died, aged about 69, 1 Aug. ,,
Statement in the *Cologne Gazette* of the existence of forged letters purporting to come from prince Bismarck (see *Germany*) . . . Nov. ,,
Baron Hirsch's present of 2,000,000l. for the establishment of primary Jewish schools in Russia, accepted by the czar; the money to be paid into the bank of England, trustees, barons Rothschild and Henry de Worms, announced Nov.; said to be premature . . . Dec. ,,
Movement of troops on the Galician border causes excitement in Berlin and Vienna . Nov.-Dec. ,,
The *Invalide Russe*, a government organ, declares that Russia desires peace but is prepared for war, 15 Dec. ,,
The stringent restrictions on the studies of the universities lead to much insubordination among the students, and severe punishment; the universities of Moscow, St. Petersburg, Odessa, and many other academical institutions closed; nearly all the undergraduate class in a state of rebellion . . . . . Nov.-Dec. ,,
Lord Randolph Churchill visits Russia; received by the czar . . . . . 26 Dec. ,,
Reported conspiracy; many arrests about 9 Jan. 1888
Reported surplus in the budget, yet a loan asked for; unsuccessful at Paris and Berlin . Jan. ,,
Moscow and other universities re-opened . Feb. ,,
For prince Ferdinand's position (see *Bulgaria*) Feb.-March, ,,
The highest courts of law decide against the claim of prince Hohenlohe to inherit the vast Wittgenstein estates in Lithuania, as a foreigner (in accordance with the Ukase, 14 March, 1887), March, ,,
Attempted assassination of the czar by lieut. Timofeieff (mad?) . . . . . May, ,,
Visit of the emperor of Germany to the czar at Peterhof. . . . . 19-23 July, ,,
Ninth centenary of the introduction of christianity celebrated at Kieff . . . 27 July, ,,
Central Asian (or Transcaspian) railway opened; promoted by general Anhenkoff . . May, ,,
Near Borki station in S. Russia, the engine of the imperial train (with the czar) ran off the line with four carriages (weak rails); 21 persons killed, the czar slightly injured . . . 29 Oct. ,,
Agreement for 20,000,000l. loan signed at St. Petersburg, 18 Nov.; chiefly taken up by the French Dec. ,,
The grand council disapproves of the administrative changes proposed by count Tolstoi substituting centralization for local self-government which, however, are approved by the czar (1883); the *Zemstvo*, established about 1864, being virtually abolished, ... Feb. 1889
Loan of 700,000,000 francs concluded with the Rothschilds and other bankers for the conversion of five per cent loans into four per cent . Feb. ,,
Captain Atchinoff, with a company of S. Cossacks (145 men with muskets and guns, also priests, women and children), evading French and Italian cruisers, landed at Tadjourah, in the bay of Obock, near the French settlement, on the Red Sea, on 18 Jan., professing to combine missionary and commercial enterprise in Abyssinia. He took possession of a fort at Sagallo, and hoisted the Russian flag. After useless negotiation, the French admiral Olry on 18 Feb. bombarded the fort, killing 6 Russians; the party then surrendered and were eventually conveyed to Russia. The French government virtually apologised for the precipitate conduct of the admiral . Feb. ,,
Alleged discovery of a dynamite conspiracy, especially in the south, originating in Zurich (discredited) . . . . . March, ,,
Death of count Tolstoi, minister of the interior, 7 May, ,,
Second four per cent loan announced, completing the financial scheme . . . 13 May, 1889

The czarewitch, aged 21, appointed to military and political office . . . . . 18 May, 1889
Marriage of the archduke Paul and the princess Alexandra of Greece . . . 16 June, ,,

SOVEREIGNS OF RUSSIA.
DUKES OF KIOW or KIEF.
850? Ruric.
879. Oleg.
913. Igor I.
945. Olga, widow; regent.
955. Swiatoslaw I.—victorious.
973. Jaropalk I.
980. Vladimir, Wladimir, the Great.
1015. Swiatopalk.
1018. Jaraslaw, or Jaroslaf I.
1054. Isiaslaw I.
1073. Swiatoslaw II.
1078. Wsewolod I.
1093. Swiatopalk II.
1113. Vladimir II.
1125. Mitislaw.
1132. Jaropalk II.
1138. { Wiatschelaw.
1139. { Wsewolod II.
1146. { Isiaslaw II. and Igor II.
1153. { Rostislaw.
1149. Jurie or George I.; the city of Moscow was built by this duke.

GRAND-DUKES AT WLADIMIR.
1157. { Andrew I. until 1175; first grand-duke.
1175. { Michael I.
1177. Wsewolod III.
1213. { Jurie or George II.
1217-18. { Constantine.
1238. Jaraslaw II.; succeeded by his son,
1245. Alexander-Nevski or Newski, the Saint.
1263. Jaraslaw III.
1270. Vasali or Basil I.
1275. Dmitri or Demetrius I.
1281. Andrew II.
1294. Daniel-Alexandrovitz.
1303. Jurie or George III.; deposed.
1305. Michael III.
1320. Vasali or Basil II.
1325. Jurie or George III; restored.
1327. Alexander II.
[The dates are doubtful, owing to the difficulty that occurs at every step in early Russian annals.]

GRAND-DUKES OF MOSCOW.
1328. Ivan or John I.
1340. Simeon, the proud.
1353. Ivan or John II.
1359. Demetrius II. prince of Susdal.
1362. Demetrius III. Donskoi.
1389. Vasali or Basil III. Temnoi.
1425. Vasali or Basil IV.

CZARS OF MUSCOVY.
1462. Ivan (Basilovitz) or John III.; took the title of czar, 1432.
1505. Vasali or Basil V. obtained the title of emperor from Maximilian I.
1533. Ivan IV. the terrible; a tyrant.
1584. Feodor or Theodor I.; and his son, Demetrius, murdered by his successor
1598. Boris-Godonof, who usurped the throne.
1605. Feodor II., murdered.
1606. Demetrius, the Impostor, a young Polish monk; pretended to be the murdered prince Demetrius; put to death.
,, Vasali-Chouiski, or Zouinski.
1610. Ladislaus of Poland; retired 1613.
1613. Michael-Feodorovitz, of the house of Romanoff, descended from the czar Ivan-Basilovitz.
1645. Alexis, son; styled the father of his country.
1676. Feodor or Theodor II.
1682. { Ivan V. and
{ Peter I. brothers of the preceding.

EMPERORS AND EMPRESSES.
1689. Peter I. the Great, alone; took the title of emperor 22 Oct. 1721; founded St. Petersburg.
1725. Catherine I. his widow; at first the wife of a Swedish dragoon, said to have been killed on the day of marriage.

1727. Peter II. son of Alexis-Petrovitz, and grandson of Peter the Great: deposed.
1730. Anne, duchess of Courland, daughter of the czar Ivan.
1740. Ivan VI. an infant, grand-nephew to Peter the Great; immured in a dungeon for 18 years; murdered in 1764.
1741. Elizabeth, daughter of Peter the Great, reigned during Ivan's captivity.
1762. Peter III. son of Anne and of Charles-Frederick, duke of Holstein-Gottorp: deposed, and died soon after, supposed to have been murdered.
,, Catherine II. his consort: a great sovereign; extended the Russian territories on all sides; died 17 Nov. 1796.
1796. Paul, her son, murdered, 24 March, 1801.
1801. Alexander I., son (who, after many adverse battles, and a forced alliance with France, at length aided in the overthrow of Napoleon Bonaparte), died 1 Dec. 1825.
1825. Nicholas I. brother; died 2 March, 1855.
1855. Alexander II. son, born 29 April 1818; married 28 April, 1841, Mary princess of Hesse (she died 3 June, 1880); said to have married (morganatic), princess Dolgorouki, 19 (31) July; marriage announced, Oct. 1880; assassinated at St. Petersburg, 2 P.M., 13 March, 1881.
1881. Alexander III., born 10 March, 1845; married Mary (formerly Dagmar), princess of Denmark, 9 Nov. 1866.

Heir: Nicholas, son, born 18 May, 1868.

RUSSIA COMPANY, see *Russia*, 1553-4. See *America*.

RUSSO-TURKISH WAR.* The Russian and French governments having each taken a side in the dispute between the Greek and Latin churches as to the exclusive possession of the *Holy Places* (*which see*) in Palestine, the Porte advised the formation of a mixed commission, which decided in favour of the Greeks, and a firman was promulgated accordingly, 9 March, 1853: to this decision the French acceded, although dissatisfied.

The Russians make further claims, and prince Menschikoff (who arrived at Constantinople 28 Feb. 1853), by various notes (between 22 March and 18 May), demands that a convention should be signed by the sultan granting to the czar such a protectorate over the Greek Christians in Turkey, as the sultan considered inimical to his own authority . . . . 22 March-18 May, 1853
Menschikoff's ultimatum rejected; he quits Constantinople . . . . . 21 May, ,,
The sultan issues a hatti-scherif confirming all the rights and privileges of the Greek Christians, and appeals to his allies . . . 6 June, ,,
The English and French fleets anchor in Besika Bay 13 June, ,,
The Russians, under gen. Luders, cross the Pruth and enter Moldavia . . . 2 July, ,,
Circular of count Nesselrode in justification, 2 July; lord Clarendon's reply . . . 16 July, ,,

---

* In 1844, when the czar was in England, he conversed with the duke of Wellington and lord Aberdeen (whom he had known many years) respecting the dissolution of the Turkish empire; and on his return he embodied his views in a memorandum drawn up by count Nesselrode, which was transmitted to London, but kept secret till March, 1854. In January and February of that year the czar had several conversations on the subject with the British envoy at St. Petersburg, sir G. H. Seymour, in one of which (Jan. 14) he compared Turkey to a "sick man" in a state of decrepitude, on the point of death, and made proposals to the British government as to the disposal of his property. He stated frankly that he would not permit the British to establish themselves at Constantinople; but said in another conversation, he would not object to their possessing Egypt. The purport of these conversations was conveyed in despatches to lord John Russell, who replied that the British government declined to make any provision for the contingency of the fall of Turkey. The czar made similar proposals to the French government with the same result.

The conference of representatives of England, France, Austria, and Prussia meet at Vienna, agree to a note, 31 July; accepted by the czar, 10 Aug.; the sultan requires modifications, 19 Aug.; which the czar rejects . . . 7 Sept. 1853
Two English and two French ships enter the Dardanelles . . . . . 14 Sept. ,,
The sultan (with consent of a great national council) declares war against Russia . . 5 Oct. ,,
The Turkish fortress at Issakteocha fires on a Russian flotilla (the first act of war) . . 23 Oct. ,,
The Turks cross the Danube at Widdin and occupy Kalafat . . . . 28 Oct.-3 Nov. ,,
Russia declares war against Turkey . 1 Nov. ,,
English and French fleets enter Bosphorus 2 Nov. ,,
Russians defeated at Oltenitza . . 4 Nov. ,,
Turks (in Asia) defeated at Bayandur, Atskur, and Achaltzik . . . 14, 18, 26 Nov. ,,
Turkish fleet destroyed at Sinope . 30 Nov. ,,
Collective note from the four powers requiring to know on what terms the Porte will negotiate for peace . . . . . . 5 Dec. ,,
Contests at Kalafat . . 31 Dec. 1853-9 Jan. 1854
At the request of the Porte (5 Dec.), the allied fleets enter the Black Sea . . . 4 Jan. ,,
Russians defeated at Citate . . 6 Jan. ,,
Reply of the Porte to the note of Dec. 5, containing four points as bases of negotiation: viz., 1. The promptest possible evacuation of the principalities. 2. Revision of the treaties. 3. Maintenance of religious privileges to the communities of all confessions. 4. A definitive settlement of the convention respecting the Holy Places (dated 31 Dec.),—approved by the four powers 13 Jan. ,,
Vienna conferences close . . 16 Jan. ,,
Kalafat invested by the Russians . 28-31 Jan. ,,
Proposal in a letter from the emperor of the French to the czar (29 Jan.) declined . . 9 Feb. ,,
Turkish flotilla at Rustchuk destroyed by the Russians under Schilders . . 15 Feb. ,,
Ultimatum of England and France sent to St. Petersburg . . . . . 27 Feb. ,,
The czar "did not judge it suitable to give an answer" . . . . . 19 March, ,,
Baltic fleet sails, under sir C. Napier . 11 March, ,,
Treaty between England, France, and Turkey, 12 March, ,,
Russians under Gortschakoff pass the Danube and occupy the Dobrudscha; severe conflicts; the Turks retire . . . 23, 24 March, ,,
France and England declare war against Russia, 27, 28 March, ,,
Rupture between Turkey and Greece 28 March, ,,
Gen. Canrobert and French troops arrive at Gallipoli, soon after followed by the English, 31 March, ,,
Russians defeated by the Turks at Karakal 30 May, ,,
English vessel *Furious*, with a flag of truce, fired on at Odessa . . . . . 8 April, ,,
Four powers sign a protocol at Vienna guaranteeing the integrity of Turkey and civil and religious rights of her Christian subjects . 10 April, ,,
Russians defeated at Kostelli by Mustapha Pacha, 10 April, ,,
Offensive and defensive alliance between England and France . . . . 10 April, ,,
Treaty between Austria and Prussia . 20 April, ,,
Bombardment of Odessa by allied fleet 22 April, ,,
Russians, under gen. Schilders, assault Kalafat; repulsed; the blockade raised . 19-21 April, ,,
The *Tiger* steamer run aground near Odessa, captured by the Russians . . . 12 May, ,,
Russians defeated at Turtukal . . 13 May, ,,
Siege of Silistria begun . . . 17 May, ,,
Allied armies disembark at Varna . 29 May, ,,
Mouths of the Danube blockaded by allied fleets, 1 June, ,,
Russians repulsed at Silistria; Paskiewitsch and many officers wounded . . . 5 June, ,,
Turks defeated at Ozurgheti (in Asia) . 16 June, ,,
Severe conflict before Silistria; the siege raised, 18-26 June, ,,
Batteries at the Sulina mouths destroyed by capt. Parker . . . . 26, 27 June, ,,
Captain Parker killed . . . 8 July, ,,
Russians defeated at Giurgevo . . 7 July, ,,
10,000 French troops embark at Boulogne for the Baltic . . . . . 15 July, ,,

RUSSO-TURKISH WAR.

Turks defeated at Bayazid in Armenia, 29, 30 July; and near Kars . . . . . . 5 Aug.	1854
Surrender of Bomarsund . . . . 16 Aug.	,,
[In July and August the allied armies and fleets in the east suffered severely from cholera.]	
The Russians defeated by Schamyl in Georgia, about 28 Aug.	,,
They evacuate the principalities . Aug.-20 Sept.	,,
By virtue of a treaty with Turkey (June 14) the Austrians, under count Coronini, enter Bucharest, 6 Sept.	,,
Allies sail from Varna, 3 Sept. and land at Old Fort, near Eupatoria* . . . . . . 14 Sept.	,,
Skirmish at the Bulganac . . . . 19 Sept.	,,
Battle of the Alma (see *Alma*) . . . 20 Sept.	,,
Russians sink part of their fleet at Sebastopol, 23 Sept.	,,
Allies occupy Balaklava . . . . 26 Sept.	,,
Death of marshal St. Arnaud . . . 29 Sept.	,,
General Canrobert, his successor . . 24 Nov.	,,
Siege of Sebastopol commenced—grand attack (without success) . . . . . 17 Oct.	,,
Battle of Balaklava—charge of the light cavalry, with severe loss . . . . . 25 Oct.	,,
Sortie from Sebastopol repulsed by generals Evans and Bosquet . . . . . . 26 Oct.	,,
Russian attack at Inkerman; defeated . 5 Nov.	,,
Miss Nightingale and nurses arrive at Scutari, 6 Nov.	,,
Great tempest in the Black Sea, loss of the *Prince* and store vessels . . . . 14-16 Nov.	,,
Treaty of alliance between England, France, Austria, and Prussia—a commission to meet at Vienna; signed . . . . 2 Dec.	,,
Russian sortie . . . . . . 20 Dec.	,,
Omar Pacha arrives in the Crimea (followed by the Turkish army from Varna) . . . 5 Jan.	1855
Sardinia joins England and France . . 26 Jan.	,,
Great sufferings in the camp from cold and sickness, Jan. & Feb.	,,
Russians defeated by the Turks at Eupatoria, 17 Feb.	,,
Death of emperor Nicholas; accession of Alexander II. (no change of policy) . . 2 March,	,,
Sortie from the Malakhoff tower . . 22 March,	,,
Capture of Russian rifle-pits . . . 19 April,	,,
Arrival of Sardinian contingent . . . 8 May,	,,
Resignation of gen. Canrobert, succeeded by gen. Pelissier . . . . . . 16 May,	,,
Desperate night combats . . . 22-24 May,	,,
Expedition into the sea of Azoff (under sir E. Lyons and sir G. Brown); destruction of Kertch and large amount of stores . . 24 May-3 June,	,,
Taganrog bombarded . . . . 3 June,	,,
Massacre of an English boat's crew with flag of truce at Hango . . . . . . 5 June,	,,
Russians evacuate Anapa . . . 5 June,	,,
The White Works and Mamelon Vert taken, 6, 7 June,	,,
Unsuccessful attack on the Malakhoff tower and Redan . . . . . . 18 June,	,,
Death of lord Raglan; succeeded by general Simpson, 28 June,	,,
Russians invest Kars in Armenia, defended by gen. Williams . . . . . . 15 July,	,,
Bombardment of Sweaborg . . . 9 Aug.	,,
Defeat of the Russians at the Tchernaya . 16 Aug.	,,
Ambuscade on the glacis of the Malakhoff taken; Russian sortie repulsed . . . 18 Aug.	,,
The French take the Malakhoff (*which see*) by assault; the English assault the Redan without success; the Russians retire from Sebastopol to the North Forts, and the allies enter the city; the Russians destroy or sink the remainder of their fleet, 8 Sept. &c.	,,
Tanan and Fanagoria captured . . 24 Sept.	,,
The Russians assaulting Kars are defeated with great loss . . . . . . 29 Sept.	,,
Russian cavalry defeated (50 killed, 105 prisoners) at Koughil, near Eupatoria, by the French, 29 Sept.	,,
Kinburn taken . . . . . 17 Oct.	,,
Russians blow up Oczakoff . . . 18 Oct.	,,
Large stores of corn destroyed near Gheisk, in the sea of Azoff . . . . . 4 Nov.	,,

* 40,000 men, a large number of horses, and a powerful artillery, were landed in one day.

Defeat of the Russians, and passage of the Ingour by the Turks under Omar Pacha . . 6 Nov.	1855
The czar visits his army near Sebastopol . 10 Nov.	,,
Sir Wm. Codrington takes the command in room of gen. Simpson . . . . . 14 Nov.	,,
Explosion of 100,000 lb. of powder in the French siege-train at Inkerman, with great loss of life, 15 Nov.	,,
Sweden joins the allies by a treaty . 21 Nov.	,,
Capitulation of Kars to gen. Mouravieff, after a gallant defence by gen. Williams . . 26 Nov.	,,
Death of admiral Brust . . . . 27 Nov.	,,
Russian attack on the French posts at Daidar repulsed . . . . 8 Dec.	,,
Proposals of peace from Austria, with the consent of the allies, sent to St. Petersburg . 12 Dec.	,,
Centre dock at Sebastopol blown up by the English, 2 Jan.	1856
Council of war at Paris . . . 11 Jan.	,,
Protocol signed accepting the Austrian propositions as a basis of negotiation for peace . . 1 Feb.	,,
Destruction of Sebastopol docks . . 1 Feb.	,,
Report of Sir John M'Neill and col. Tulloch on state of the army before Sebastopol, published 5 Feb.	,,
Peace conferences open at Paris, an armistice till 31 March agreed on . . . . 25 Feb.	,,
Suspension of hostilities . . . . 29 Feb.	,,
Treaty of peace concluded at Paris . 30 March,	,,
Proclamation of peace in the Crimea, 2 April; in London . . . . . . 29 April,	,,
The Crimea evacuated . . . . 9 July,*	,,

RUSSO-TURKISH WAR, 1877. For the insurrections, Servian war, and the negotiations, see *Turkey*.

The czar addresses the army near Kischeneff, saying that "he has done everything in his power to avoid war, and patience is exhausted;" the Russian embassy quits Constantinople . . 23 April	1877
War declared; the czar's manifesto says that he is compelled, by the haughty obstinacy of the Porte, to proceed to more decisive acts; a justificatory circular to foreign powers sent out by prince Gortschakoff; the Russians enter the Turkish dominions in Roumania and Armenia . 24 April,	,,
The sultan's circular protests against the war, and refers to his reforms and the treaty of Paris 25 April,	,,
[Russian generals-in-chief in Bulgaria, grand duke Nicholas; in Armenia, grand duke Michael; Turkish generals: Abdul-Kerim in Europe; Mukhtar Pasha, in Asia Minor.]	
Russians defeated at Tchuruk Sou, near Batoum 26 April,	,,
The Russians, under the grand duke Michael and Loris Melikoff, advance into Armenia, defeat Turks and occupy Bayazid (deserted) 29, 30 April,	,,
The Turks stop the passage of the Danube, and blockade the Black Sea . . . 3 May.	,,
The earl of Derby replies to the Russian circular; he refers to the treaty of 1856 as broken; does not consider that the war will benefit the Christians, and asserts that Russia has separated herself from European concert; the British government gives neither concurrence nor approval to the war 1 May,	,,
Kalafat occupied by Roumanians . . 3 May,	,,
Russians defeated in attacking Batoum . 4 May,	,,
The *Lufti-Djelil*, Turkish monitor, with 300 men, blown up near Ibraila, or Braila, on the Danube (said to be by Russian shells) . . 11 May,	,,
Much artillery firing down the river . May,	,,
Sukhum Khaleh, Russian fortress in the Caucasus, captured by Turks . . . . 14 May,	,,
Ardahan, near Kars, Armenia, stormed by Melikoff 17 May,	,,
Insurrection in the Caucasus supported by the sultan . . . . 18 May, *et seq.*	,,

* The English lost: killed in action and died of wounds about 3500; died of cholera, 4244; of other diseases nearly 16,000; total loss nearly 24,000 (including 270 officers); 2873 were disabled. The war added to the national debt 41,041,000*l*. The French lost about 63,500 men; the Russians about half a million. The army suffered greatly by sickness; see *Scutari*, *Times*, and *Nightingale*.

RUSSO-TURKISH WAR.

Explosion of Turkish monitor *Dar-Matoin*, by lieuts. T. Daubassoff and Sheshlakoff, with torpedoes . . . . 26 May, 1877
Neutrality of the Suez Canal assured: correspondence . . . . . . May-June, ,,
Kars invested by Russians . . . 3 June, ,,
The czar arrives at Plojesto (Ployesto) in Roumania 6 June ,,
Turks defeated at Tahir, or Taghir, Armenia 16 June ,,
Turks victors at Zewin Dooz, Eshek-Khalian, Delibaba, and other places; Russians retreating 20 June, ,,
Turks successful in Montenegro; country reported subdued . . . . . 12-20 June, ,,
Russians cross Lower Danube by bridges at Galatz and Braila; 6 hours' conflict ensues; Turks retire, 22 June; Russians occupy Matchin, 23 June, and Hirsova . . . . 25, 26 June, ,,
The grand duke Nicholas crosses the Danube at Simnitza by 708 pontoons, and enters Bulgaria; the Turks retire after severe conflicts; 289 Russians said to be killed . . . 27 June, ,,
The czar in his proclamation to Bulgarians encourages Christians and warns Mahometans 28 June, ,,
The Simnitza bridge destroyed by a storm or by Turks . . . . . about 30 June, ,,
The British fleet arrives at Besika bay . 3 July, ,,
Biela, Bulgaria, taken by Russians about 5 July, ,,
Plevna, Bulgaria, occupied by Russians 6 July, ,,
Tirnova, ancient capital of Bulgaria, captured by Russians under gen. Gourko . . 6, 7 July, ,,
Bayazid re-occupied by Turks . . 12 July, ,,
Russians compelled to retire from Kars by Mukhtar Pasha . . . . . . 13 July, ,,
The invasion of Armenia considered a failure July, ,,
Gourko crosses the Balkans and enters Roumelia, 13 July; (this movement censured), several skirmishes . . . . . 14, 15, 20 July, ,,
Nicopolis (Nikopol) surrenders (after severe conflicts, 12-14 July); capture of 2 pashas, 6000 men, 2 monitors, and 40 guns . . 15, 16 July, ,,
The Turkish commander Abdul-Kerim replaced by Mehemet Ali (Jules Détroit, of French extraction); Russians retreating . . . July, ,,
Suleiman Pasha brought from Montenegro to the Schipka Passes . . . . about 21 July, ,,
Aziz Pasha (able and popular) killed in a rash conflict at Esirje, near Rasgrad . 26 or 28 July, ,,
Russians severely defeated; Plevna retaken by Osman Pasha, 19, 20 July; Russians again defeated . . . . . . 30, 31 July, ,,
Hostilities revive in Montenegro; the Turkish fortress Niksich besieged . . . . July, ,,
The Roumanian army joins the Russians 9 Aug. ,,
Severe conflicts between Russians and Suleiman Pasha; the Turks eventually victors: Eski Saghra and Yeni Sagra, July; Kezanlik and Kalofer, 30 July, *et seq*. . . . . . ,,
Russians under Gourko expelled from Roumelia; retreat to Schipka passes . . about 11 Aug. ,,
Russians in the Schipka Passes relieved by Radetzky 21 Aug. ,,
Russians defeated at Karn Silar, near Osman Bazar, 14 Aug.; in the valley of the Lom, by Mehemet Ali . . . . . . about 22-24 Aug. ,,
Russians defeated by Mukhtar Pasha at Kurukdara, or Kizil Tepe, between Kars and Alexandropol 24, 25 Aug. ,,
Desperate fruitless attempts of Suleiman Pasha to gain the Schipka Pass held by Gourko and Radetzky; great slaughter . . 20-27 Aug. ,,
Severe twelve hours' battle in valley of the Lom, near Szedina; Karahassankoi taken and re-taken six times; Russians (under the Czarewitch) retire in good order . . . . . 30 Aug. ,,
Prince Charles with Roumanians crosses the Danube . . . . . about 31 Aug. ,,
Further successes of Mehemet Ali on the Lom at Katzelevo, Ablava, &c. . . . 4-6 Sept. ,,
Lovatz or Luftcha (important) captured by Prince Imeritinsky and Russians after a sharp conflict 3 Sept. ,,
Niksich (left by Turks) captured by Montenegrines 7 Sept. ,,
Sanguinary conflicts at Plevna, greatly strengthened by Osman Pasha; artillery duel . 7-10 Sept. ,,

Fierce assault by Russians and Roumanians; they gain the strong Gravitza redoubt (with others, which are re-taken); the czar present; Russian loss about 20,000 . . . . . 11, 12 Sept. 1877
Fort St. Nicholas in Schipka Pass taken by Suleiman Pasha and quickly lost; much bloodshed 17 Sept. ,,
Mehemet Ali repulsed in his attack on positions at Tchercovna, fifteen miles from Biela . 21 Sept. ,,
Siege of Plevna; Chefket Pasha enters with reinforcements after several skirmishes 22 Sept. ,,
Montenegrine successes continued . Sept. ,,
Battles of the Yagni; severe conflicts; Russians repulsed near Ardahan, Asia about 27, 30 Sept. ,,
Russian losses, killed, wounded, and missing, 47,400 reported . . . . up to 20 Sept. ,,
Mehemet Ali retires to Kara Lom about 25 Sept. ,,
Gen. Todleben made chief of staff before Plevna 28 Sept. ,,
Mehemet Ali replaced by Suleiman Pasha; Raouf Pasha sent to Schipka . . . . 2, 3 Oct. ,,
Battles near Kars; army of granddukee Michael attacks Turks under Mukhtar Pasha; severely defeated . . . . . . 2-4 Oct. ,,
Turkish monitor in the Danube exploded by torpedoes . . . . . . 8 Oct. ,,
Relief and supplies received by Turks at Plevna about 9 Oct. ,,
Battle of Aladja Dagh before Kars; Russians, under grand duke Michael, and generals Loris Melikoff, Lazareff, and Heimann, totally defeat Ahmed Mukhtar, taking 10,000 prisoners . 14, 15 Oct. ,,
Gravitza battery, near Plevna, captured by Roumanians, is quickly re-taken . . 19-20 Oct. ,,
Suleiman and his army said to be retreating from Kadikoi to Rasgrad . . . . 22 Oct. ,,
Battle at Gornij Dubnik, near Plevna; Russians under Gourko said to be victorious; losses about equal (2,500) . . . . . . 24 Oct. ,,
Russians said to be defeated near Kars Ourgan, Armenia . . . . . . 24 Oct. ,,
Battle of Sofia Road, near Plevna; Turkish position at Teliche captured . . . . 28 Oct. ,,
Mukhtar Pasha defeated by Heimann and Tergukasoff at Deve-Boyun, Armenia, after nine hours' conflict . . . . 4 Nov. ,,
Russians severely defeated at Azizi, before Erzeroum, by Mukhtar Pasha . . . 9 Nov. ,,
Change in Turkish generals: Suleiman ordered to command the army of Roumelia, replaced by Azli Pasha; Mehemet Ali organises army to relieve Plevna . . . . . early in Nov. ,,
Russian attack on Plevna repulsed . . 12 Nov. ,,
Turks thrice repulsed near Plevna . 15 Nov. ,,
Kars taken by storm; the Russians climbed steep rocks; fierce conflict from 8 p.m. to 8 a.m.; 300 guns and 10,000 prisoners taken; about 5000 Turks killed and wounded; Russian loss about 2,500; the grand-duke Michael present 17-18 Nov. ,,
Russians said to be severely repulsed at Orchanié, 16 Nov. ,,
Plevna said to be thoroughly invested (30 miles round, with 120,000 men) . . . Nov. ,,
Osman Pasha, invited to surrender at Plevna, refuses . . . . . . about 16 Nov. ,,
Rahova on the Danube taken by Roumanians, 21 Nov. ,,
Entropol (fortified) near Plevna taken by Russians, 24 Nov. ,,
Indecisive fighting in the valley of the Lom between the czarewitch and Mehemet Ali; Russians said to be defeated . . . . . 30 Nov. ,,
Turks capture Elena with guns and prisoners, after sharp conflict . . . . . 4 Dec. ,,
Skirmishing on the Lom . . . 4-6 Dec. ,,
Osman Pasha endeavours to break out of Plevna, about 7 p.m. 9 Dec.; six hours' fierce conflict; surrounded; unconditional surrender; said to be 30,000 prisoners, 128 officers, 100 guns; great slaughter on both sides . . . 10 Dec. ,,
The Servians declare war against Turkey, 12 Dec.; cross the frontier and capture villages 15 Dec. *et seq*. ,,
Turkish circular note to the great powers, requesting mediation, 12 Dec.; merely acknowledged; action declined . . . . about 12 Dec. ,,
Montenegrines successful . . . Dec. ,,
Suleiman made general of the army of Roumelia; and Todleben of that of Rustchuk, about 19 Dec. ,,

| RUSSO-TURKISH WAR. | 787 | RYSWICK. |

Suleiman retires on the quadrilateral; visits Constantinople; armies concentrating near Adrianople . . . . about 20 Dec. 1877
Servians said to have taken Ak Palanka after 3 hours' fight . . . . 24 Dec. ,,
Erzeroum, Armenia, nearly invested; brave resistance by Mukhtar Pasha . . about 24 Dec. ,,
Many Turkish wounded prisoners perish from cold during removal . . . . . . Dec. ,,
Turkish steamer with 875 men, said to be captured in Black Sea . . . . . about 25 Dec. ,,
Alleged Russian losses, 80,435 men; Turkish much more, and 80,000 prisoners . . . Dec. ,,
Mukhtar Pasha recalled to Constantinople, about 29 Dec. ,,
The sultan requests mediation of England; the British government only convey to Russia the sultan's desire to make peace; Russia declines mediation . . . . . . 26—31 Dec. ,,
Servians advancing successfully . end of Dec. ,,
Gourko crosses the Balkans and advances on Sofia; Turks defeated in an engagement, 31 Dec. ,,
Col. Baker gallantly protects the retreating Turkish army, defeating the Russians . . . . 1 Jan. 1878
Sofia taken by Russians after an engagement, 3 Jan. ,,
Russians said to be defeated near Erzeroum, about 5 Jan. ,,
Servians defeated; Kurschumli reoccupied by Turks . . . . . . 6, 7 Jan. ,,
Gen. Radetzky crosses the Balkans; the Trojan pass taken about 9 Jan.; the Turkish army (about 32,000) and cannon taken by Skobeleff and Radetzky, after conflicts, 8, 9, 10 Jan. (see *Senova*); Gourko advances towards Adrianople . 11 Jan. ,,
Nisch taken by the Servians; Antivari by the Montenegrines . . . . . about 10 Jan. ,,
Russians advance successfully; Turkish envoys proceed to treat for peace . about 16-18 Jan. ,,
Gourko advances toward Philippopolis; totally defeats Suleiman Pasha, who retreats to the sea, losing many prisoners and much cannon, 16, 17 Jan. ,,
Adrianople abandoned; occupied by Russians, 19, 20 Jan. ,,
Suleiman with remains of his army at Karala on the Ægean transporting his troops, about 21 Jan. ,,
Servians occupy nearly all Old Servia . 29 Jan. ,,
Russian attack on Batoum defeated . . 30 Jan. ,,
After much delay, an armistice signed at Adrianople, 31 Jan. ,,
Russian losses announced 89,879 men . Feb. ,,
Continued advance of Russians towards Constantinople; great panic; flight of many Turks; many deaths and great sufferings . . Jan., Feb. ,,
Part of British fleet ordered to Constantinople to protect British life and property, 8 Feb.; enters Dardanelles without permission of the Porte, 13 Feb. ,,
Erzeroum evacuated by Turks . . 17-21 Feb. ,,
Rustchuk occupied by Russians . 20 Feb. ,,
Treaty of peace signed at San Stefano (see *Stefano*), 3 March; ratified at St. Petersburg . 17 March, ,,
The war lasted 322 days, 12 April, 1877, to 3 March, ,,
Long negotiation respecting a European congress, March-May, 1878
Grand duke Nicholas in Roumelia replaced by gen. Todleben, who assumes command . 30 April, ,,
Conference at Berlin, meets 13 June; treaty signed (see *Berlin*), 13 July; ratified . . 3 Aug. ,,
Grand review of about 80,000 Russians near Constantinople . . . . . . 17 Aug. ,,
40,000 Russians have sailed for home . 12 Sept. ,,
Definitive treaty of peace with Turkey signed at Constantinople . . . . . 8 Feb. 1879
Estimated cost of the war to Russia, 120,000,000*l*.

RUSTCHUK, Turkish town on the Danube, one of the "quadrilateral" fortresses lost to Turkey with Bulgaria by treaty of Berlin, 13 July, 1878.

RUTHENIUM, a rare metal, discovered in an ore of platinum by M. Claus, in 1845.

RUTHERFURD'S ACT, Lord (13 & 14 Vict. c. 36), for simplifying law proceedings in Scotland, passed 1850.

RUTHVEN, Raid of, a term applied to the seizure of the person of James VI. of Scotland by William Ruthven, earl of Gowrie, and other nobles, in 1582, to compel the king to dismiss his favourites, Arran and Lennox. Ostensibly for this, Gowrie was judicially put to death by his two opponents in 1584.

RUTLAND, Statute of, 10 or 12 Edw. I. 1282 or 1284.

RYE-HOUSE PLOT, a plot (some think pretended) to secure the succession of the duke of Monmouth to the throne in preference to the duke of York (afterwards James II.), a Roman catholic. Some of the conspirators are said to have projected the assassination of the king, Charles II., and his brother. This design is said to have been frustrated by the king's house at Newmarket accidentally taking fire, which hastened the royal party away eight days before the plot was to take effect, 22 March, 1683; see *Newmarket*. The plot was discovered 12 June following. Lord William Russell on 21 July, and Algernon Sidney on 7 Dec. following, suffered death for being concerned in this conspiracy. The name was derived from the conspirators' place of meeting, the Rye-house at Broxbourne, Hertfordshire.

RYSWICK (Holland), where the celebrated peace was concluded between England, France, Spain, and Holland, signed, by their representatives, 20 Sept., and by the emperor of Germany, 30 Oct. 1697.

S.

SAALFIELD.

SAALFIELD (Saxony, N. Germany). Here the Prussians, under prince Louis of Prussia, were defeated and their leader slain by the French under Lannes, 10 Oct. 1806.

SAARBRÜCK, the Roman *Augusti Muri* or *Saræ pons*, an open town on the left bank of the Saar, in Rhenish Prussia, founded in the tenth century, long subject to the bishops of Metz, afterwards ruled by counts (about 1237), and by the house of Nassau about 1380. It was captured by the French and retaken by the Germans 1676, reunited to France 1794-1814, and ceded to Prussia, 1815. On 2 Aug. 1870, it was bombarded by the French under Frossard (between 11 and 1 in the daytime), and the Prussians in small force were dislodged, and the town occupied by the French general Bataille. The mitrailleuses were said to be very effective. The emperor Napoleon, who was present with his son, said in a telegram to the empress, "Louis has gone through his baptism of fire. He has not been in the least startled. We stood in the foremost rank, and the rifle balls were dropping at our feet, and Louis picked up one that fell near him. His bearing was such as to draw tears from the soldiers' eyes." On the 6 Aug. the Prussian generals Goeben and Von Steinmetz, with the first army, recaptured Saarbruck, after a sanguinary conflict at the village of Spicheren. The heights taken by the French on the 2nd are in Germany, those taken by the Germans on the 6th are in France, and both battles were fought between Saarbruck and the town of Forbach, which was captured and has given a name to the second conflict. The loss was great on both sides. The French general François was killed, and the 2nd corps under Frossard nearly destroyed. The French retreated to Metz. They were greatly superior in numbers at the beginning of the fight, but were badly commanded.

SABBATARIANS. Traces exist of Sabbatarii, or Sabbathaires, among the sects of the 16th century on the continent. Upon the publication of the "Book of Sports" in 1618, a violent controversy arose among English divines on two points: first, whether the Sabbath of the fourth commandment was in force among Christians; and secondly, whether, and on what ground, the first day of the week were entitled to be distinguished and observed as "the Sabbath." In 1628, Theophilus Brabourne, a clergyman, published the first work in favour of the Seventh-day or Saturday, as the true Christian Sabbath. He and several others suffered great persecution for this opinion; but after the restoration there were three or four congregations observing the last day of the week for public worship in London, and seven or eight in the country parts of England. In 1851 there were three Sabbatarian or Seventh-day Baptist congregations in England; but in America (especially in the New England states) they are more numerous.—Joseph Davis suffered imprisonment in 1670. He and his son bequeathed property to maintain the sect; and litigation respecting its disposal was settled by vice-chancellor Stuart in conformity with their intentions in June, 1870. Very few Sabbatarians then remained.

SACRAMENT.

SABBATH: ordained by God. *Gen.* ii.; *Exod.* xx. 8; *Isaiah* lviii. 13. Jews observe the seventh day in commemoration of the creation of the world, and of their redemption from the bondage of the Egyptians; Christians observe the first day of the week in commemoration of the resurrection of Christ from the dead, and the redemption of man; see *Sunday*.

SABBATH SCHOOLS, see *Sunday Schools*.

SABBATICAL YEAR: a Jewish institution, 1491 B.C. *Exodus* xxiii. During every seventh year the very ground had rest, and was not tilled; and every forty-ninth year all debts were forgiven, slaves set at liberty, and estates, &c., that were before sold or mortgaged, returned to their original families, &c.

SABELLIANISM, from Sabellius (of Ptolemais in Egypt), who flourished in the 3rd century, and who taught that there was but *one* person in the Godhead, the other persons of the Trinity being but different names of the same person. This doctrine was condemned at a council at Rome, 260.

SABINES, from whom the Romans, under Romulus, took away their daughters by force, having invited them to some public sports or shows on purpose. When the Sabines determined to revenge this affront, the women became mediators to their fathers in behalf of their husbands, the Romans, and a lasting peace was made between them, 750 B.C. After many conflicts, the Sabines became a part of the Roman people, about 266 B.C. One of the ecclesiastical provinces is still called Terra Sabina; chief town, Magliano.

SACCHARINE, see *Benzole*.

SACCHAROMETER, an instrument for determining the amount of sugar in solutions. Soleil, an optician, of Paris, in 1847 made use of rotary polarised light for this purpose in a saccharometer, since improved by Dubosq.

SACHEVEREL RIOTS, see *Riots*, 1710.

SACKVILLE INCIDENT, see *United States*, Oct. 1888.

SACRAMENT (from *sacramentum*, an oath, obligation, also mystery). The Christian sacraments are baptism and the Lord's supper. The council of Trent, in 1547, affirmed the doctrine of the schoolmen that there are *seven* sacraments: baptism, the Lord's supper, confirmation, penance, holy orders, matrimony, and extreme unction. The name was given to the Lord's supper by the Latin fathers. The wine was restricted to the clergy about the beginning of the 12th century. Communion in one kind only was authoritatively sanctioned by the council of Constance, 15 June, 1415. Henry VII. of Germany was poisoned by a priest by the consecrated wafer, 24 Aug. 1313. The sacramental wine was poisoned by the gravedigger of the church at Zürich, by which sacrilegious deed a number of persons lost their lives, 4 Sept. 1776. In 1614 members of both houses of parliament were ordered to take the sacrament, as a guard against the introduction of Roman Catholics. In 1673 the test act

was passed; repealed in 1828; see *Transubstantiation*.

"Society of the Blessed Sacrament" (English churchmen), London, founded, 1860; "Confraternity of the Blessed Sacrament," founded 1862; the two united, 1867.

SACRAMENTARIANS, followers of Zwingli (1487-1531), who differed from the Romanists and Lutherans in regard to the sacrament.

SACRAMENTO, ST., a Portuguese settlement in S. America, claimed by Spain in 1680, but relinquished in 1713; several times seized; ceded in 1777; acquired by Brazil in 1825.

SACRED BAND, see *Thebes*.

SACRED BOOKS OF THE EAST. The publication of translations of the sacred books of the religion of the Brahmans, Buddhists, and Mohammedans, and of the followers of Khung-fu-tze and Lao-tze, edited by professor Max Müller, began in 1879. Thirty volumes have been published, 1889.

SACRED HARMONIC SOCIETY, see *Music*.

SACRED HEART OF JESUS; a form of devotion said to have been instituted in England in the seventeenth century, and much promoted by Marguerite Marie Alacoque, an enthusiastic French nun, who asserted that Christ had appeared to her, and taken out her heart, placed it in his own, glowing in flame, and then returned it. She died in 1690. Her book "Dévotion au Cœur de Jesus," published in 1698, much advocated by father Joseph Gallifet about 1726; and introduced into France, by request 1765
A pilgrimage from England, specially blessed by the pope, and headed by the duke of Norfolk, went to the shrine of Marguerite, at Paray-le-Monial, and returned . . . . 1-6 Sept. 1873
The R.C. diocese of Salford dedicated to the Sacred Heart, 4 Sept. 1873: and a church at Moutmartre, near Paris, founded for the same purpose, ... 16 June, 1875
The pope dedicated the universal church to "the Sacred Heart" . . . . 15 June, ,,

SACRED WARS.—I. Declared by the Amphictyons against Cirrha, near Delphi, for robbery and outrage to the visitors to the oracle, 595 B.C. Cirrha was razed to the ground, 586.—II. Between the Phocians and Delphians for the possession of the temple at Delphi, 448, 447.—III. The Phocians, on being fined for cultivating the sacred lands, seized the temple, 357. They were conquered by Philip of Macedon, and their cities depopulated, 346. See *Crusades*.

SACRIFICE was offered to God by Abel, 3875 B.C. Sacrifices to the gods were introduced into Greece by Phoroneus, king of Argos, 1773 B.C. Human sacrifices seem to have originated with the Chaldeans, from whom the custom passed into other Eastern nations. All sacrifices to the true God were to cease with the sacrifice of Christ, 33 A.D. *Heb.* x. 12-14. Pagan sacrifices were forbidden by the emperor Constantius II. 341.

SACRILEGE. In 1835, the punishment (formerly death) was made transportation for life. By 23 & 24 Vict. c. 96, s. 50 (1861), breaking into a place of worship and stealing therefrom was made punishable with penal servitude for life.

SACRIPORTUS (Latium, Italy). Here Sylla defeated the younger Marius and Papirius Carbo with great slaughter, B.C. 82, and became dictator, 81.

SADDLES. In the earlier ages the Romans used neither saddles nor stirrups. Saddles were in use in the 3rd century, and are mentioned as made of leather in 304, and were known in England about 600. Side-saddles for ladies were introduced by Anne, queen of Richard II. in 1388. *Stow.*

SADDUCEES, a Jewish sect, said to have been founded by Sadoc, a scholar of Antigonus, about 200 B.C., who, misinterpreting his master's doctrine, taught that there was neither heaven nor hell, angel nor spirit; that the soul was mortal, and that there was no resurrection of the body from the dead. The Sadducees rejected the oral law, maintained by the Pharisees. See *Matt.* xxii. 23; *Acts* xxiii. 8.

SADLER'S WELLS (N. London), so called after Mr. Sadler, who built an orchestra to entertain the invalids who used the waters medicinally, 1683. In time the orchestra was enclosed, and the building became a place for dramatic performances. The theatre was opened in 1765. Eighteen persons were trampled to death at this theatre, on a false alarm of fire, 18 Oct. 1807; see under *Theatres*. The theatre put up to auction and not sold, 31 Aug. 1875; and 30 July, 1878. Opened for miscellaneous entertainments, 6 Jan. 1877. Taken by Mrs. Bateman, Sept. 1878; partly rebuilt; opened as New Sadler's Wells on 9 Oct. 1879, with the opera "Rob Roy." Miss Isabella Bateman became manager after her mother's death, 13 Jan. 1881, but did not succeed. The house was opened with Shakspeare's "Twelfth Night," by Roze de Vane, 12 April, 1884.

SADOWA, see *Königgrätz*.

SAFES. A National Safe Company, London, opened vaults for storage of valuables, 1876.

SAFETY LAMP. One was invented in 1815 by sir Humphry Davy, to prevent accidents which happen in coal and other mines. The safety-lamp is founded on the principle that flame, in passing through iron-wire meshes, loses so much of its heat as to be incapable of igniting inflammable gases. The father of all safety-lamps was Dr. Reid Clanny, of Sunderland, whose invention and improvements are authenticated in the *Transactions of the Society of Arts* for 1817. The "Geordy," constructed by George Stephenson, the engineer, in 1815, is said to be the safest. A miner's electric light, by MM. Dumas and Benoit, was exhibited in Paris on 8 Sept. 1862. On 14 Aug. 1867, safety-lamps were rigidly tested by several mining engineers, and serious doubts thrown upon their complete efficacy. Col. Shakespear's safety lamp (light extinguished by opening) exhibited at Royal Institution, &c., May, 1879. Messrs. Fleuss and Foster's new safety mining lamp approved, Jan. 1884.

Mr. J. Wilson-Swan's electric safety lamp, weighing 6¾ lb, exhibited at Aberdeen meeting of British Association, Sept. 1885.
Mr. Charles D. Aria's safety lamp reported successful; the supply of mineral oil is isolated from the burner, 1889.

SAFFRON (*saffran*, French; *saffrano*, Italian), the flower of crocus, was first brought to England in the reign of Edward III. by a pilgrim, about 1339, probably from Arabia, as the word is from the Arabic *saphar*. *Miller*. It was cultivated in England in 1582.

SAGE (*Sauge*, French; *Salvia*, Latin), a wholesome herb, comfortable to the brain and nerves. *Mortimer*. A species of this garden plant grew early in England, and some varieties were imported. The Mexican sage, *Salvia mexicana*, was brought from Mexico, 1724. The blue African sage, *Salvia africana*, and the golden African sage, *Salvia aurea*.

were brought to England from the Cape of Good Hope in 1731.

SAGUNTUM, or ZACYNTHUS, now Murviedro, in Valentia, E. Spain, renowned for the dreadful siege it sustained, 219 B.C. The citizens, after performing incredible acts of valour for eight months, chose to be buried in the ruins of their city rather than surrender to Hannibal. They burnt themselves, with their houses, and the conqueror became master of a pile of ashes, 218 B.C.

SAHARA, a great sandy desert, North Africa, south of Barbary States. A project for making an inland sea here was entertained in 1883.

SAIGON, French colony in Cochin China, founded in 1860, after a defeat of the Chinese, 17 Feb. 1859.

SAILORS' HOME, in Well-street, London Docks, established by Mr. George Green, 1830; opened, 1835; enlarged, 1865. In one year it admitted 5444 boarders, who, besides home, had evening instruction, the use of a savings' bank, &c. The establishment is self-supporting, aided by subscriptions. Similar institutions have since been established. *Sailors' orphan girls' school and home*, Hampstead, established 1829.

SAINT. For names with this prefix, see the names themselves throughout the book.

ST. JAMES'S GAZETTE, anti-radical evening paper, edited by Fred. Greenwood, formerly editor of *Pall Mall Gazette*, first appeared, 31 May, 1880. Price 2d., reduced to 1d. 2 Jan. 1882.

SAKYA MUNI, see *Buddhism*.

SALADO, a river, S. Spain; see *Tarifa*.

SALADS, are stated to have been in use in the middle ages; lettuces are said to have been introduced into England from the Low Countries, 1520-47.

SALAMANCA (W. Spain), taken from the Saracens 861. The university was founded 1240, and the cathedral built 1513. Near here the British and allies, commanded by lord Wellington, totally defeated the French army under marshal Marmont, 22 July, 1812. The loss of the victors was most severe, amounting to killed, wounded, and missing, to nearly 6000 men. Marmont left in the victor's hands 7141 prisoners, 11 pieces of cannon, 6 stands of colours, and 2 eagles. This victory was followed by the capture of Madrid.

SALAMIS (near Athens). In a great sea-fight here, 20 Oct. 480 B.C., Themistocles, the Greek commander, with only 310 sail, defeated the fleet of Xerxes, king of Persia; which consisted of 2000 sail.—Near Salamis, in Cyprus, the Greeks defeated the Persian fleet, 449 B.C.; and Demetrius Poliorcetes defeated the fleet of Ptolemy and his allies, 306 B.C.

SALASSI, a turbulent Alpine tribe, were thoroughly subdued by Terentius Varro, 25 B.C., and a Roman colony established in their territories (now Aosta).

SALDANHA BAY, S. Atlantic Ocean; northward of the Cape of Good Hope. Here on 17 Aug. 1796, a Dutch squadron, under admiral Lucas, was captured by vice-admiral sir George Keith Elphinstone, without resistance; sir George was created lord Keith.

SALE OF FOOD AND DRUGS ACT, passed 11 Aug. 1875; repeals all adulteration acts, and makes new arrangements.

SALENCKEMEN on the Danube. Here a victory was gained by the imperialists, under prince Louis of Baden, over the Turks, commanded by the grand vizier Mustapha Kiuprigli, 19 Aug. 1691.

SALERNO (Salernum, S. Italy), an ancient Roman colony. Its university, with a celebrated school of medicine, reputed to be the oldest in Europe, was founded by Robert Guiscard the Norman, who seized Salerno in 1077. Salerno suffered much in the wars of the middle ages.

SALFORD, near Manchester.
An incendiary explosion at the barracks caused one death; Fenians suspected . . . 14 Jan. 1881

SALIQUE or SALIC LAW, by which females are excluded from inheriting the crown of France, is said to have been instituted by Pharamond, 424, and ratified in a council of state by Clovis I., the real founder of the French monarchy, in 511. *Hénault*. This law, introduced into Spain by the Bourbons 1700, was formally abolished by decree 29 March, 1830; and on the death of Ferdinand VII. his daughter succeeded as Isabella II., 29 Sept. 1833; see *Spain*. By this law also Hanover was separated from England, when queen Victoria ascended the English throne, 1837.

SALISBURY (Wilts), founded in the beginning of the 13th century, on the removal of the cathedral hither from Old Sarum. National councils or parliaments were repeatedly held at Salisbury, particularly in 1296, by Edward I.; in 1328, by Edward III.; and in 1384. Henry Stafford, duke of Buckingham, was executed here by order of Richard III., in 1483.—On SALISBURY PLAIN is Stonehenge (*which see*). This plain was estimated at 500,000 acres. On it were so many cross roads, and so few houses to take directions from, that Thomas, earl of Pembroke, planted a tree at each milestone from Salisbury to Shaftesbury, for the traveller's guide. The autumn military manœuvres took place on Salisbury Plain, Aug., Sept. 1872; see under *Army*.—The first seat of the BISHOPRIC was at Sherborne, St. Aldhelm being prelate, 705. Herman removed the seat to Old Sarum, about 1072; and the see was removed to Salisbury by a papal bull, in 1217. It has yielded to the church of Rome one saint and two cardinals. The building of the cathedral commenced 28 April, 1220, and was completed in 1258. This edifice is reckoned one of our finest ecclesiastical erections. Its spire, the loftiest in the kingdom, was considered in danger in April, 1864, and subscriptions were begun for its immediate repair. The choir was re-opened, after restoration by sir G. G. Scott, 1 Nov. 1876. The bishopric is valued in the king's books at 1367*l*. 11*s*. 8*d*. Present income 5000*l*.

RECENT BISHOPS.
1797. John Fisher, died 2 July, 1825.
1825. Thomas Burgess, died 19 Feb. 1837.
1837. Edmund Denison, died 6 March, 1854.
1854. Walter Kerr Hamilton, died 1869.
1869. George Moberly, elected 9 Sept., died 6 July, 1885.
1885. John Wordsworth, Aug.

SALISBURY ADMINISTRATIONS.—Mr. Gladstone resigned in consequence of a defeat in the house of commons on the Budget Bill (264—252), 8-9 June, and was succeeded by the marquis of Salisbury, whose ministry received the seals, 24 June, 1885. In consequence of Mr. Jesse Collings's amendment on the address (respecting allotments for labourers) being carried (329—250), 26-27 Jan., resigned, 27 Jan. 1888.

Prime Minister and Foreign Secretary—Robert Arthur Talbot Gascoigne-Cecil, marquis of Salisbury.*

* He was born 3 Feb. 1830; lord Cranborne, on the

SALISBURY ADMINISTRATIONS. 791   SALT-PETRE.

First lord of the treasury—Sir Stafford Northcote (earl of Iddesleigh).
Lord chancellor—Sir Hardinge Giffard (lord Halsbury).
Lord president of the council—Gathorne Gathorne-Hardy, viscount Cranbrook.
Lord privy seal—Dudley Francis Stuart Ryder, earl of Harrowby.
Secretaries: home—Sir Richard Assheton Cross.
  the colonies— Col. Frederick Arthur Stanley.
  India—Lord Randolph Henry Spencer-Churchill.
  war—William Henry Smith; G. Gathorne Hardy, viscount Cranbrook, about 23 Jan. 1886.
  Scotland—Charles Henry, duke of Richmond, about 14 Aug. 1885.
First lord of the admiralty—Lord George Francis Hamilton.
Chancellor of the exchequer—Sir Michael Edward Hicks-Beach.
Lord lieutenant of Ireland—Henry H. M. Herbert, earl of Carnarvon; resigned Jan. 1886.
Lord Chancellor of Ireland—Edward Gibson (lord Ashbourne).
President of board of trade—Charles Henry Gordon-Lennox, duke of Richmond; Edw. Stanhope, about 17 Aug. 1885.
Postmaster-general—Lord John Manners.
Vice-president of the council—Edward Stanhope.
  The above form the cabinet.
Chancellor of duchy of Lancaster—Henry Chaplin.
President of local government board—Arthur J. Balfour.
Chief secretary for Ireland—Sir William Hart-Dyke, resigned; W. H. Smith, about 23 Jan. 1886.
First commissioner of works—David Robert Plunket.
Attorney-general—Sir R. E. Webster.
Solicitor-general—John E. Gorst.

SECOND ADMINISTRATION (26 July, 1886)—
Prime minister and first lord of the treasury foreign secretary (Jan. 1887)—Robert Arthur Talbot Gascoigne-Cecil, marquis of Salisbury.
First lord of the treasury—Wm. Henry Smith, 3 Jan. 1887.
Lord chancellor—Hardinge Stanley Giffard, lord Halsbury.
Lord president of the council—Gathorne Gathorne-Hardy, viscount Cranbrook.
Chancellor of the exchequer—Lord Randolph Henry Spencer Churchill; resigned 22 Dec. 1886;* George Joachim Göschen, 3 Jan. 1887.
Secretaries: home—Henry Matthews (R.C.).
  foreign—Stafford Henry Northcote, earl of Iddesleigh (died 12 Jan. 1887) ; marquis of Salisbury, Jan. 1887.
  the colonies—Edward Stanhope ; sir Henry Thurstan Holland, ; baron Knutsford, Feb. 1888 (Jan. 1887).
  India—Sir Richard Cross (viscount Cross).
  war—William Henry Smith; Edward Stanhope, 6 Jan. 1887.
First lord of the admiralty—Lord George Francis Hamilton.
Lord chancellor of Ireland—Edward Gibson, lord Ashbourne.
Chief secretary for Ireland—Sir Michael Edward Hicks-Beach ; resigns, but remains in the cabinet (retires Jan. 1888); succeeded by Arthur J. Balfour, 5 March, 1887.
Chancellor of the duchy of Lancaster—Lord John Manners, duke of Rutland, 4 March, 1888.
President of the board of trade—Sir Frederick Stanley lord Stanley of Preston); succeeded by sir M. E. Hicks-Beach, 15 Feb. 1888.
  The above form the Cabinet.
Lord privy seal—George Henry Cadogan (earl Cadogan); succeeded by Laurence Dundas, earl of Zetland, 30 May, 1889.
Lord lieutenant of Ireland — Charles Stewart Vane Tempest Stewart, marquis of Londonderry.
Secretary for Scotland—Arthur J. Balfour; succeeded by Schomberg Henry Kerr, marquis of Lothian, 8 March, 1887.
President of local government board—C. T. Ritchie.

death of his brother, 1865 ; succeeded his father as marquis in 1868; M.P. for Stamford, 1853-68; secretary for India, July, 1866, to March, 1867; and Feb. 1874 to April, 1878: for foreign affairs, April, 1878, to May, 1880 ; special ambassador to Constantinople, Nov. 1876; chancellor of the University of Oxford, 1869.

 * The marquis of Hartington and the liberal unionists declined to form part of a coalition ministry, 30 Dec. 1886.

Postmaster-general—Henry Cecil Raikes.
First commissioner of works—David Robert Plunket.
Attorney-general—Sir Richard Everard Webster, Q.C.
Solicitor-general—Sir Edward Clarke, Q.C.

SALISBURY'S ACT, see *Artisans*.

SALLEE, a port of Morocco, long a haunt for pirates, destroyed by the British in 1632, and about 300 captives released.

SALLENTINI, allies of the Samnites, the only Italian tribe not subject to Rome, were overcome in war in 267 and 266 B.C., and Brundisium, their port, taken.

SALMON FISHERIES. The laws relating to them were consolidated and amended in 1861, and the report of a commission of inquiry (including sir Wm. Jardine) was published, in Feb. 1862. An act restricting the capture of salmon at certain times, passed in 1863, was amended in 1869-1870, and 1873. During the "salmon fence," 14 Sept. to 1 Feb., it is unlawful to catch fish of the salmon kind. A salmon-fishery congress opened at South Kensington, 7 June, 1867. Salmon eggs sent to New Zealand, Jan. 1878.

SALMON OVA, packed in boxes with moss, charcoal, and ice, to retard development—a plan suggested and proved practicable by Mr. F. H. Moscrop in 1863—adopted successfully by Mr. J. A. Youl, who sent ova to Australia in the " Norfolk," . 1864
Salmon disease, in rivers, announced, 1879; commission of inquiry appointed, Mr. F. Buckland and others . . . . Jan. 1880
Very great increase in the number of salmon caught, 1883

SALONICA, see *Thessalonica*.

SALT (chloride of sodium, a compound of the gas chlorine and the metal sodium) is procured from the rocks in the earth, from salt-springs, and from sea-water. The famous salt-mines of Wielitzka, near Cracow in Poland, have been worked 600 years. The salt-works in Cheshire, called the WICHES (Nantwich, Northwich, and Middlewich), were of great importance in the time of the Saxon heptarchy. The salt-mines of Staffordshire were discovered about 1670. Salt duties were first exacted in 1702; they were renewed in 1732; reduced in 1823; and in that year were ordered to cease in 1825. During the French war the duty reached to 30*l*. per ton. For the salt-tax in France see *Gabelle*. The government salt monopoly in India was abolished in May, 1863, by sir C. Trevelyan. Since 1797 salt has been largely employed in the manufacture of chloride of lime or bleaching powder (by obtaining its chlorine), and soap (by obtaining its soda). On this are based the chemical works of Cheshire, Lancashire, and other places. See under *Alkalies*.

Much distress in the salt districts of Cheshire through the subsidence of land, 1887-8. The proprietors of the Cheshire salt mines combined to form a "trust" or syndicate in the autumn of 1888; central office, Northwich ; the trade being nearly ruined by great competition, first meeting 27 Sept. 1888.
Great advance in the price of salt Oct. 1888.
A " salt museum " presented to the town of Northwich by Mr. Brunner, M.P., March, 1889.

SALTAIRE, see *Alpaca*.

SALT LAKE, see *Mormonites*.

SALT-PETRE (from *sal petræ*, salt of the rock), or Nitre, is a compound of nitric acid and potash (nitrogen, oxygen, and potassium), and hence is called nitrate of potash. It is the explosive ingredient in gunpowder, many detonating powders, and lucifer matches. Boyle in the 17th century demonstrated that salt-petre was composed of aqua fortis (nitric acid) and potash; the discoveries of Lavoisier (1777) and Davy (1807) showed

its real composition. Its manufacture in England began about 1625. During the French revolutionary war, the manufacture was greatly increased by the researches of Berthollet.

SALUTE AT SEA. It is a received maxim at sea, that he who returns the salute always fires fewer guns than he receives, which is done even between the ships of princes of equal dignity; but the Swedes and Danes return the compliment without regarding how many guns are fired to them. The English claim the right of being saluted first in all places, as sovereigns of the seas; the Venetians claimed this honour within their gulf, &c. The admiralty issued a code of rules for salutes, Dec. 1876. See *Flag*, and *Naval Salute*.

SALVADOR, SAN, one of the Bahamas, and the first point of land discovered in the West Indies or America by Columbus. It was previously called Guanahani, or Cat's Isle, and Columbus (in acknowledgment to God for his deliverance) named it San Salvador, 11 Oct. 1492. The capital, San Salvador, was destroyed by an earthquake, 16 April 1854, and is now abandoned.

SALVADOR, SAN, one of the republics of Central America, with a constitution established 24 Jan. 1859. General Barrios elected president 1 Feb. 1860, was compelled to flee in Oct. 1863; when Francis Dueñas became provisional president; his formal election took place April, 1865. The ex-president, Gerard Barrios, was surrendered by Nicaragua, tried and shot, Aug. 1865. A re-attempted revolution failed; Zaldivar fled; general Gonzales president, 1 Feb. 1872; R. Zaldivar, May, 1876; Gen. Menendez, June, 1885; re-elected 1 March 1887 for four years. Population, 1886, 651,130. The capital, San Salvador, was nearly destroyed by an earthquake, 19 March, 1873, about 50 persons perished. The convulsion began 5 March and thus gave timely warning. A rebellion suppressed, 6—10 Sept. 1887.

"SALVATION ARMY," a name assumed by a body of persons terming themselves the "Christian Mission" (formed 1865), to deal with the lowest classes; Mr. William Booth, was general.
A great "Hosanna" meeting to celebrate the formation of the 104th corps at Northampton, was held at the headquarters (with prayers, addresses, and singing), 272, Whitechapel-road, 30 June, 1879.
17th anniversary kept at the Alexandra Palace,
              3 July, 1882
Gen. Booth set forth his principles in the *Contemporary Review* for August, 1882; he upholds the gospel, opposes sectarianism, and requires from his soldiers implicit obedience, aiming at the reformation of drunkards and other reprobates."
His army much annoyed by a "skeleton army;" he checks processions . . . . . Feb. 1883
The Eagle Tavern and Grecian Theatre, City Road, London, purchased; occupied, early 12 Aug.; devoted, 14 Sept. 1882; conditions of sale not kept, ordered to quit . . . . . . 6 July, "
Indian contingent (major Tucker and others), land at Bombay; fined; imprisoned on non-payment,
              28 Sept. "
Their "invasion" opposed by the authorities in Switzerland, Jan. *et seq.*; severely opposed, June; Miss Booth imprisoned at Neufchâtel, Sept.; acquitted, 1 Oct.; expelled . . . 11 Oct. "
Great fighting between Salvation and Skeleton armies at Gravesend (and other places) 15 Oct. "
"553 army brigades in the United Kingdom; 182 abroad."—*Gen. Booth* . . . April, 1884

* The army has officers of various grades; headquarters, 101, Queen Victoria Street, London; publishing offices, &c., Paternoster Square; official gazette, the *War Cry*, price ½d., in various languages, of which millions are sold. The propagandism is very vigorous.

West-end centre building founded . . 14 June, 1884
Severe rioting at Worthing; the army attacked by the Skeleton army, 18-20 Aug.; a man wounded by a revolver fired by Mr. G. Head, 7 Sept.; rioting at Brighton . . . . 7 Sept. "
International congress in London 28 May-4 June, 1886
General Booth appeals to the army for a subscription of 5,000*l*. . . . . . 20 Aug. "
Another appeal . . . . . Dec. 1887
He reports "advance of the army" throughout the world with varying success, opposition and indifference; about 100,000*l*. received in . . 1887
Celebration of the 23rd anniversary of the organization of the army at the Alexandra Palace 9 July, 1888
Severe decree against the army in Berne, 2 Sept.; unconstitutional persecution, Aug.-Sept. 1884, continued 1888-9

SALZBACH (Baden). Here the French general Turenne was killed, at the commencement of a battle, 27 July, 1675.

SALZBURG, an ancient city of Germany, was annexed to Austria, 1805; to Bavaria, 1809; to Austria again 1815. It was the birthplace of Mozart, 1756. The meetings of the emperors of Austria and France here, 18 Aug. 1867, and the emperors of Austria and Germany, 6 Sept. 1871, which caused some anxiety, were reported to be in favour of peace.

SAMAJ, or SOMAJ, see *Deism*.

SAMANIDE DYNASTY, began with Ismail Samani, who overcame the army of the Safferides, and established himself in the government of Persia, 902; his descendants ruled till 999.

SAMARCAND (in Tartary) was conquered by the Mahometans, 707; by Genghis Khan, 1220, and by Timur, or Tamerlane, who ruled here in great splendour. Samarcand was occupied by the Russians under Kaufmann 26 May, 1868, after a conflict on the previous day. The garrison left, resisted a fierce siege till relieved by Kaufmann, 13-20 June, 1868.

SAMARITANS. Samaria was built by Omri, 925 B.C.; and became the capital of the kingdom of Israel. On the breaking up of that kingdom (721 B.C.), the conqueror Shalmaneser placed natives of other countries at Samaria. The descendants of these mixed races were abominable to the Jews, and much more so in consequence of the rival temple built on Mount Gerizim by Sanballat the Samaritan, 332 B.C., which was destroyed by John Hyrcanus, 130 B.C.; see *John* iv. & viii. 48, and *Luke* x. 33. The Samaritan Pentateuch (of uncertain origin) was published in his Polyglot by Morinus, 1632.

SAMNITES, a warlike people of S. Italy, who strenuously resisted the Roman power, and were not subjugated till after three sanguinary wars, from 343 to 292 B.C. Their brave leader, Caius Pontius, who spared the Romans at Caudium, 320, having been taken prisoner, was basely put to death, 292. They did not acquire the right of citizenship till 88 B.C.

SAMOAN ISLES (or Navigators), (nine inhabited), near the Fiji islands; christianized by rev. John Williams, 1830. King Malietoa succeeded, 8 Nov. 1880. The isles have a political constitution; their parliament voted annexation to New Zealand, March, 1885.
King Malietoa deposed for alleged robbery and insult by Germans, and replaced by Tamatese, the British and French consuls protest, announced 8 Sept.; deposed and exiled by the Germans Sept. 1887
Insurrection against Tamatese, Malietoa or Mataafa said to be released, his supporters victorious in a battle proclaim him king 12 Sept; continued success . . . . . . Oct. 1888

Victory of king Mataafa, after a fierce battle 29 Nov. 1888
A party of Germans land, attacked by Mataafa's forces; 16 killed and the rest rescued 18 Dec. „
Difficulties regarding Samoa have arisen between the German, British, and United States governments . . . . Jan. 1889
The Germans declare war against Mataafa; 31 Jan. „
Prince Bismarck yields to United States claims Feb. „
Cessation of hostilities reported . 5 March, „
By a great storm three German and three American war vessels were driven ashore at Apia on the Island of Upola and destroyed; about 50 Americans and 96 Germans drowned; H.M.S. *Calliope* escaped by steaming out 15, 16 March, 1889
[Capt. Kane of the *Calliope* was thanked by the admiralty for his skill and seamanship.]
Conference on Samoan affairs at Berlin; plenipotentiaries: England, sir Edward Malet; Germany, count H. Bismarck; United States, Mr. John Kasson; first met 29 April; closing conference, agreement signed subject to legislative ratification 14 June, „
Peace between the rival chiefs reported 6 July, „

SAMOS, an island on the W. coast of Asia Minor. Colonised by Ionians about 1043 B.C. The city was founded about 986. Polycrates, ruler of Samos (532-22 B.C.), was one of the most able, fortunate, and treacherous of the Greek tyrants, and possessed a powerful fleet. He patronised Pythagoras (born here) and Anacreon. Samos was taken by the Athenians, 440; and, with Greece, became subject to Rome, 146. It was taken by the Venetians, A.D. 1125, who here made velvet (*samet*), and became subject to the Turks, about 1459.
It was made a principality by sultan Mahmoud in 1832; present prince, Constantine Adossides, born 23 Feb. 1822; appointed 4 March, 1879.

SAMPFORD COURTENAY (Devon). Here John, lord Russell, defeated the Cornish and Devonshire catholic rebels, the middle of Aug. 1549.

SANCTION, see *Pragmatic*.

SANCTUARIES, see *Asylums*. Privileged places for the safety of offenders are said to have been granted by king Lucius to churches and their precincts. St. John's of Beverley was thus privileged in the time of the Saxons. St. Burian's, in Cornwall, was privileged by Athelstan, 935; Westminster, by Edward the Confessor; St. Martin's-le-Grand, 1529. Being much abused, the privilege of sanctuary was limited by the pope in 1503 (at the request of Henry VII.), and much reduced in 1540. In London, persons were secure from arrest in certain localities: these were the Minories, Salisbury - court, Whitefriars, Fulwood's - rents, Mitre-court, Baldwin's-gardens, the Savoy, Clink, Deadman's-place, Montague-close, and the Mint. This security was abolished 1697, but lasted in some degree till the reign of George II. (1727).

SANDALS, see *Shoes*.

SAND-BLAST. Gen. B. C. Tilghman, of Philadelphia, has invented a method of cutting stone or hard metal by a jet of quartz sand impelled by compressed air or steam. A hole of 1¼ inch diameter and 1½ inch deep was bored through a block of corundum, nearly as hard as diamond, in 25 minutes. The invention was submitted to the Franklin Institute, Philadelphia, 15 Feb. 1871. It may be employed in the arts, for etching, &c.; for this purpose a company was at work, 1874.

SANDEMANIANS, see *Glasites*.

SANDHURST, ROYAL MILITARY COLLEGE, founded, first at High Wycombe, in 1799; removed to Great Marlow in 1802, and to Sandhurst in 1812. It consists of the staff college and cadets' college. Competitive examination for entrance into the latter began in Feb. 1858. A wing of the college was destroyed by fire, 21 Jan. 1868.

SANDWICH (*Portus Rutupensis*, Kent). It suffered by Danish invaders in 851, 993, and 1014, but was rebuilt by Canute, and became prosperous; it became chief of the cinque ports about 1066. It contributed 22 ships and 504 mariners to Edward III.'s French expedition. It was taken and plundered by the French under Brézé in Aug. 1457. Flemish silk and woollen manufactories were settled here by Elizabeth in 1561. Disfranchised 1885.

SANDWICH ISLANDS or HAWAII ARCHIPELAGO, a group in the Pacific Ocean, discovered by captain Cook in 1778. In *Owhyhee* or *Hawaii*, one of these islands, he fell a victim to the sudden resentment of the natives, 14 Feb. 1779. The king and queen visited London in 1824, and died there in July. These people have made great progress in civilisation, and embraced Christianity before any missionaries were settled among them. Population in 1884, 80,578. Numbers of native population said to be stationary. King Kaméhaméha IV. married Miss Emma Rooker, 1856. She came to England in 1865; landing at Southampton, 13 July, and visited our queen, 9 Sept. An English bishopric was established at Honolulu in 1861, for which Dr. Thomas Staley was consecrated, 18 Aug. 1862.
The king died; Kaméhaméha V. king . Nov. 1863
The duke of Edinburgh warmly received at Honolulu . . . . 21 July, 1869
Bishop Staley resigns, Aug. 1870; bishop Alfred Willis consecrated . . . . 2 Feb. 1872
Kaméhaméha V. died, unmarried . 11 Dec. „
Wm. C. Lunalilo crowned, 8 Jan. 1873; died, 3 Feb. 1874
Reciprocity treaty concluded between Hawaii and the United States 1875
David Kalakaua (born 16 Nov. 1836), elected king, in opposition to queen Emma 12 Feb.; visits the president at Washington 12 Dec. 1876; visits Europe; at Rome, 1 July; received by the queen at Windsor, 12 July, 1881; crowned . 12 Feb. 1883
Queen Kapiolani arrives at Liverpool to be present at the royal jubilee service 2 June; arrives in London . . . . . . 8 June, 1887
Revolution against a corrupt ministry 25 June; the ministry deposed 30 June; the king powerless appeals to the foreign representatives, who recommend the formation of a new constitution; the king signs a new constitution 7 July; new ministry formed . . . . . 10 July, „

SAN FRANCISCO (California). The centenary of its foundation by Franciscan monks, 8 Oct. 1776, was celebrated in 1876; owes its present prosperity to the gold discovery in 1847; see *California*.

SANHEDRIM. An ancient Jewish council of the highest jurisdiction, of seventy, or, as some say, seventy-three members, usually considered to be that established by Moses, *Num.* xi. 16,—1490 B.C. It was yet in being at the time of Jesus Christ, *John* xviii. 31. A Jewish Sanhedrim was summoned by the emperor Napoleon I., 23 July, 1806. A meeting of Jewish deputies was held 18 Sept, and the Sanhedrim assembled, 9 March, 1807.

SANITARY INSTITUTE OF GREAT BRITAIN, founded 13 July, 1876; president, the duke of Northumberland. Congress at Leamington, 3 Oct. 1877; at Stafford, 2 Oct. 1878; at Croydon, 21 Oct. 1879; opened a School of Hygiene in London, Nov. 1879. Congress at Glasgow, 27 Sept. 1883; at Dublin, 30 Sept. 1884; at Leicester, 22 Sept. 1885; York, 21 Sept. 1886; Bolton, 20 Sept.

1887; incorporated Aug. 1888. See under *Sanitation*.

SANITATION, the preservation of health. Strict cleanliness is enjoined in the law of Moses, 1490 B.C. Great attention has been paid to the public health in France since 1802. Tardieu published his "Dictionnaire de Hygiène," 1852-54. To Dr. Southwood Smith is mainly attributable the honour of commencing the agitation on the subject of public health in England about 1832; his "Philosophy of Health" having excited much attention. Since 1838 he has published numerous sanitary reports, having been much employed by the government. Professors of hygiene are now appointed.

Investigations of the Poor Law Commissioners and consequent disclosures and the reports of the registrar-general lead to legislation, 1834 *et seq.*	
Nuisances Removal act passed (repealed)	1845-1860
Baths and Washhouses act	1846-1847
Public Health act (subsequent Supplemental acts).	1848
Common Lodging Houses act	1851-1853
Labouring Classes Lodging Houses act	1851
Smoke Nuisance Abatement act	1853
Diseases Prevention act	1855
Public Health act passed	"
Metropolitan Interments acts	1850-1855
Labouring Classes Dwelling-house act passed March,	1866
New Sanitary act (stringent) passed Aug. 1866; amended	1868, 1870
Public Health act passed	10 Aug. 1872
National health society founded	1873
International sanitary congress at Vienna, closed 1 Aug.	1874
Public Health act for Ireland passed	7 Aug. "
Sanitary Laws Amendment act passed	7 Aug. "
New Consolidated Public Health act passed	1875
Parkes "museum of hygiene," instituted 1876, at University college, London ; incorporated and removed to Margaret-street, Cavendish-square, 1882; opened by the duke of Albany 26 May, 1883; incorporated with the Sanitary Institute of Great Britain	Aug. 1888
Sanitary Assurance Association, formed by sir Joseph Fayrer, Drs. Andrew Clark, Corfield, Tyndall, and others ; constituted	14 Dec. 1880
London Sanitary Protection Association, founded by sir Wm. W. Gull, professor Huxley, and others	1881
International sanitary exhibition, royal Albert hall, 16 July—13 Aug.	"
International sanitary congress at Washington, U.S.A., opened, Jan. 1881 ; at Geneva	1882
National health society's exhibition opened 2 June,	1883
International health exhibition, 1884; proposals adopted, Nov. 1883 ; opened by the duke of Cambridge, 8 May; closed, 30 Oct. ; conferences held about 12 June; the juries inaugurated by the prince of Wales, 17 June; admitted, 4,153,390; medals awarded (242 gold, 5096 silver, and others), 27 Oct. 1884 ; estimated surplus, 19,000*l.*	Feb. 1885
5th International sanitary conference at the Hague, 21 Aug.	1884
International Sanitary Conference at Rome, 28 states represented	20 May-13 June, 1885
Stated result of fifty years' sanitation saving of about 502,000 lives ; death rate reduced from above 22 to 19 per thousand	Nov. 1886
Great International Hygienic Congress opened at Vienna by crown prince Rudolph 26 Sept.-1 Oct. 1887; next to be at London	1891
The College of State Medicine for the training of persons officially employed in matters relating to public health inaugurated; address by Mr. Brudenell Carter	2 May 1888

SANITAS (health), a new antiseptic and disinfectant, invented by Mr. C. T. Kingzett, about 1875.
Having discovered that the salubrity of the air surrounding certain trees, such as the *Eucalyptus globulus* and pines, is due to their volatile oils producing peroxide of hydrogen and camphoric acid, he devised a method for procuring these re-agents by the decomposition of common turpentine, and in 1877 they were manufactured and sold as "Sanitas."

SAN JUAN ISLAND, see *Juan*.

SAN SALVADOR, see *Salvador*.

SANSCULOTTES, a term of reproach applied to the leaders of the French republicans about 1790, on account of their negligence in dress, and afterwards assumed by them with pride. The complementary days of their new calendar were named by the Mountain party *Sansculottides*.

SANSKRIT, the language of the Brahmans of India, spoken at the time of Solomon, has been much studied of late years. Sir Wm. Jones, who published a translation of the poem Sakuntalá, in 1783, discovered that a complete literature had been preserved in India, comprising sacred books (the Vedas), history and philosophy, lyric and dramatic poetry. Texts and translations of many works have been published by the aid of the East India Company, the Oriental Translation Fund, and private liberality. The professorship of Sanskrit at Oxford was founded by colonel Boden. The first professor, H. H. Wilson, appointed in 1832, translated part of the Rig-veda Sanhitá, the sacred hymns of the Brahmins, and several poems, &c. Professor Monier Williams (elected 1860) published an English and Sanskrit dictionary, 1851. Professor Max Müller published his history of Sanskrit Literature in 1859, and has edited the original text of the Vedas. Philologists have discovered an intimate connection between the Sanskrit, Persian, Greek, Latin, Teutonic, Slavonian, Celtic, and Scandinavian languages.

SAN STEFANO, see *Stefano*.

SANTA CRUZ (Teneriffe, Canary Isles). Here admiral Blake, by daring bravery, entirely destroyed sixteen Spanish ships, secured with great nautical skill, and protected by the castle and forts on the shore, 20 April, 1657. *Clarendon.* In an unsuccessful attack made upon Santa Cruz by Nelson, several officers and 141 men were killed, and the admiral lost his right arm, 24 July, 1797.* See under *Virgin Isles*.

SANTA FE DE BOGOTÁ, see *New Granada*.

SANTA HERMANDAD, see *Hermandad*.

SANTIAGO DE COMPOSTELLA (N.W. Spain), was sacked by the Moors in 995, and held by them till it was taken by Ferdinand III. in 1235. The order of Santiago, or St. James, was founded about 1170 to protect pilgrims to the shrine of St. James the Greater (Acts, xii. 2), said to be buried in the cathedral. The town was taken by the French in 1809, and held till 1814.—SANTIAGO, the capital of Chili, S. America, founded by Valdiña in 1541, has suffered much by earthquakes, especially in 1822 and 1829.
About seven o'clock in the evening of 8 Dec. 1863, the feast of the Immaculate Conception of the Virgin Mary, and the last day of a series of religious celebrations in the "month of Mary," the church of the Campania, when brilliantly illuminated in a dangerous manner, was burnt down, the fire beginning amidst the combustible ornaments, and above 2000 persons, principally women, perished ; the means of egress being utterly insufficient.

* Captain Fremantle, the friend of Nelson, and his companion in most of his brilliant achievements, was wounded in the arm immediately before Nelson had received *his* wound in the same limb. The following note, addressed to the lady of Captain Fremantle (who was on board with her husband at the time he wrote), has been preserved, as being the first letter written by the hero with his left hand :—"MY DEAR MRS. FREMANTLE,—Tell me how Tom is, I hope he has saved his arm. *Mine is cut off;* but, thank God ! I am as well as I hope he is. Ever yours, "HORATIO NELSON."

On 20 Dec. the government ordered the church to be razed to the ground, and much public indignation was excited against the fanatical priesthood.

SAPPERS AND MINERS, a name given in 1812 to the non-commissioned officers and privates of the corps of Royal Engineers. *Brande.*

SAPPHIC VERSE, invented by Sappho, the lyric poetess of Mitylene. She was equally celebrated for her poetry, beauty, and a hopeless passion for Phaon, a youth of her native country, on which last account it is said she threw herself into the sea from Mount Leucas, and was drowned, about 590 B.C. The Lesbians, after her death, paid her divine honours, and called her the tenth muse. Some consider the story fabulous.

SAPPHIRE, a precious stone of an azure colour, and transparent; in hardness it exceeds the ruby, and is next to the diamond. One was placed in the Jewish high priest's breast-plate, 1491. Thamas Kouli Khan is said to have possessed a sapphire valued at 300,000*l.*, 1733. Artificial sapphires were made in 1857 by M. Gandin. Equal parts of alum and sulphate of potash were heated in a crucible.

SARABAND. A stately dance invented by Sarabanda, a dancer of Seville, in the 16th century.

SARACENS, a warlike people of Arabia, were employed as mercenaries by the emperor Valens, 376, against the invading Goths, whom they repelled from Constantinople, 378. They frequently troubled the eastern empire in the 6th century, and in the seventh, became ardent followers of Mahomet, see *Mahometans*. In 712 they conquered Spain, and under Abderrahman, established the caliphate of Cordova 755. The Moors became supreme in the 11th century.

SARAGOSSA (N.E. Spain), anciently Cæsarea Augusta, founded 27 B.C., was taken by the Goths, 470; by the Arabs, 712; by Alfonso of Spain, 1118. Here Philip V. was defeated by the archduke Charles, 20 Aug. 1710. On 17 Dec. 1778, 400 of the inhabitants perished in a fire at the theatre. Saragossa, after successfully resisting the French in 1808, was taken by them after a most heroic defence by general Palafox, 20 Feb. 1809. The inhabitants, of both sexes, resisted until worn out by fighting, famine, and pestilence.

SARAH SANDS, see *Wrecks*, 1857.

SARAKHS, see *Russia*, 1884.

SARATOGA (New York State, N. America). Here general Burgoyne, commander of a body of the British army, after a severe engagement with the Americans at Germanstown, in which he was victorious, 3, 4 Oct., being surrounded, surrendered all his army (5791 men) to the American general Gates, 17 Oct. 1777. This was the greatest check the British suffered in the war.

SARAWAK, see *Borneo*.

SARDINIA, an island in the Mediterranean, successively possessed by the Phœnicians, Greeks, Carthaginians (about 500 B.C.), Romans (238), Vandals (A.D. 456), Saracens (720-40), Genoese (1022), Pisans (1165), Arugonese (1352), and Spaniards. From settlers belonging to these various nations the present inhabitants derive their origin. Victor Amadeus, duke of Savoy, acquired Sardinia in 1720, with the title of king; see *Savoy*. Population of the Sardinian dominions in 1858, 5,194,807; of Sardinia alone, 1887, 723,833. The king of Sardinia was recognised as king of Italy by his parliament in Feb. 1861; see *Italy*.

Conquered by the English naval forces, under sir John Leake and gen. Stanhope	1708
Ceded to the emperor Charles VI.	1714
Recovered by the Spaniards . . . 22 Aug.	1717
Ceded to the duke of Savoy with the title of *king*, as an equivalent for Sicily	1720
Victor Amadeus abdicates in favour of his son .	1730
Attempting to recover his throne, he is taken, and dies in prison	1732
The court kept at Turin, till Piedmont is overrun by the French	1792
Charles Emmanuel resigns to his brother, duke of Aosta . . . . . 4 June,	1802
Piedmont annexed to Italy . . . 26 May,	1805
The king resides in Sardinia . . .	1798-1814
Piedmont restored to its sovereign, with Genoa added . . . . . . Dec.	
King Charles-Albert promulgates a new code .	1837
Cavour establishes the newspaper "Il Risorgimento" ("the Revival") . . .	1847
The king grants a constitution, and openly espouses the cause of Italian regeneration against Austria, 23 March,	1848
Defeats the Austrians at Goito; and takes Peschiera 30 May,	,,
Incorporation of Lombardy with Sardinia 28 June, and Venice . . . . 4 July,	,,
Sardinian army defeated by Radetzky . 25 July,	,,
Sardinians at Milan capitulate to Radetzky 5 Aug.	,,
Armistice signed . . . . 9 Aug.	,,
Hostilities resumed . . . . 12 March,	1849
Radetzky defeats a division of the Sardinians, and occupies Mortara . . . 21 March,	,,
Complete defeat of the Sardinians by the Austrians at Novara . . . . 23 March,	,,
Charles-Albert abdicates in favour of his son, Victor-Emmanuel . . . 23 March,	,,
The Austrians occupy Novara, &c. . . 25 March,	,,
Another armistice . . . . 26 March,	,,
Death of Charles-Albert, at Oporto . 28 July,	,,
Treaty of Milan between Austria and Sardinia, signed . . . . . 6 Aug.	,,
Adoption of the Siccardi law, which abolishes ecclesiastical jurisdictions . . 9 April,	1850
Arrest of the bishop of Turin . . 4 May,	,,
He is released from the citadel . . 2 June,	,,
Cavour minister of foreign affairs . .	1851
Bill for suppression of convents and support of clergy by the state passed . . 2 March,	1855
Convention with England and France signed; a contingent of 15,000 troops to be supplied against Russia . . . . 10 April,	,,
10,000 troops under general La Marmora arrive in the Crimea . . . . 8 May,	,,
Who distinguish themselves in the battle of the Tchernaya . . . . 16 Aug.	,,
The king visits London, &c. . . 30 Nov. &c.	,,
Important note on Italy from count Cavour to England . . . . 16 April,	1856
Rupture with Austria; subsequent war (see *Austria*, 1857, *et seq.*)	
Cavour declares in favour of free trade . June,	1857
Prince Napoleon Jerome marries princess Clotilde (see *Italy*) . . . . 30 Jan.	1859
Preliminaries of peace signed at Villa Franca, 11 July; count Cavour resigns, 13 July; Rattazzi administration formed . . . 19 July,	,,
The emperor Napoleon's letter to Victor-Emmanuel advocating the formation of an Italian confederation: the latter declares it to be impracticable, and maintains his engagements with the Italians, 20 Oct.	,,
Treaty of peace signed at Zurich . . Nov.	,,
Garibaldi retires into private life . . 17 Nov.	,,
Count Cavour returns to office . . 16 Jan.	1860
The Sardinian government refers the question of annexation of Tuscany, &c., to the vote of the people . . . . . 29 Feb.	,,
Annexation of Savoy and Nice proposed by the French government; the Sardinian government refer it to the vote of the people . 25 Feb.	,,
Annexation to Sardinia voted almost unanimously by Æmilia, 14 March; by Tuscany, 15 March; accepted by Victor-Emmanuel . 18-20 March,	,,

Treaty ceding Savoy and Nice to France, signed 24 March, 1860
Prussia protests against the Italian annexations 27 March, ,,
New Sardinian parliament opens . . . 2 April, ,,
Annexation to France almost unanimously voted for by Nice, 15 April; by Savoy . 22 April, ,,
The government professes disapproval of Garibaldi's expedition to Sicily (*which see*) . . 18 May, ,,
The chambers ratify treaty of cession of Savoy and Nice . . . . 29 May, ,,
The Sardinian troops enter the papal territories (see *Italy*, and *Rome*) . . . . 11 Sept. ,,
Victor-Emmanuel enters the kingdom of Naples 15 Oct. ,,
Naples and Sicily vote for annexation to Sardinia 21 Oct. ,,
Railway from Sassari to the sea opened 9 April, 1872
[For the disputes, and war with Austria, and the events of 1859-61, see *Austria*, *France*, *Rome*, *Sicily*, and *Naples*.]

[For later history see *Italy*.]

KINGS OF SARDINIA. See *Savoy*.
1720. Victor-Amadeus I. king (as duke II.); resigned, in 1730, in favour of his son; died in 1732.
1730. Charles-Emmanuel I. (III. of Savoy), son.
1773. Victor-Amadeus II., son.
1796. Charles-Emmanuel II., son; resigned his crown in favour of his brother
1802. Victor-Emmanuel I., brother; 4 June.
1805. [Sardinia merged in the kingdom of Italy, of which the emperor Napoleon was crowned king, 26 May, 1805.]
1814. Victor-Emmanuel restored; resigned in March, 1821; and died in 1824.
1821. Charles-Felix.
1831. Charles-Albert; abdicated in favour of his son, 23 March, 1849. Died at Oporto, 28 July, 1849.
1849. Victor-Emmanuel II., son; born 14 March, 1820; died, 9 Jan. 1878.
Humbert, king of Italy; born, 14 March 1844. See *Italy*, end.

SARDIS, see under *Seven Churches*.

SARMATIA, the ancient name for the country in Asia and Europe between the Caspian Sea and the Vistula, including Russia and Poland. The Sarmatæ or Sauromatæ troubled the early Roman empire by incursions. After subduing the Scythians they were subjugated by the Goths, in the 3rd and 4th centuries. They joined the Huns and other barbarians in invading Western Europe in the 5th century.

SARNO (S. Italy). Near this river, Teias, king of the Goths, was defeated and slain by Justinian's general Narses, March, 553.

SARUM, OLD (Wiltshire), an ancient British town, the origin of Salisbury (*which see*). Although completely decayed, it returned two members to parliament till 1832.

SASSANIDES, descendants of Artaxerxes or Ardishir, whose father, Babek, was the son of Sassan. He revolted against Artabanus, the king of Parthia; defeated him on the plain of Hormuz, 226; and re-established the Persian monarchy. This dynasty was expelled by the Mahometans, 652; see *Persia*.

SATAN, see *Devil Worship*.

SATELLITES, see *Planets*, *Jupiter*, *Mars*, *Saturn*.

SATIRE. About a century after the introduction of comedy, satire made its appearance at Rome in the writings of Lucilius, called the inventor of it, 116 B.C. *Liry*. The Satires of Horace (35 B.C.), Juvenal (about A.D 100), and Persius (about A.D. 60), are the most celebrated in ancient times, and those of Churchill (1761) and Pope (1729), in modern times. Butler's "Hudibras," satirizing the presbyterians, first appeared in 1663. *Satire Menippée*, a celebrated satirical pamphlet, partly in verse and partly in prose, attacking the policy of the court of Spain and the league, written in the style of the biting satires of the cynic philosopher Menippus. The first part, "Catholicon d'Espagne," by Leroy, appeared in 1593; the second, "Abrégé des Etats de la Ligue," by Gillot. Pithou, Rapin, and Passerat, appeared in 1594. *Bouillet*.

SATRAPIES, divisions of the Persian empire, formed by Darius Hystaspes about 516 B.C.

SATTARA (W. India) was long a flourishing state, founded by Sevajee about 1646; subjugated by the Mahrattas about 1749; conquered by the British, 1818; ruled by a rajah under the protection of the company. The last rajah died without issue in 1848; when the country was annexed.

SATURDAY (the last, or seventh day of the week; the Jewish Sabbath; see *Sabbath*). It was so called from an idol worshipped on this day by the Saxons, and according to Verstegan, was named by them Saterne's day. *Pardon*. It is more probably from Saturn, *dies Saturni*. *Saturday Review*, an independent literary weekly journal, was first published, 3 Nov. 1855. See *Hospital*.

SATURN, the planet, ascertained to be about 900 millions of miles distant from the sun, and its diameter to be about 77,230 miles. One of the eight satellites was discovered by Huyghens (25 March, 1655); four by Cassini (1672-84); two by sir William Herschel (1789), and one by Bond and Lassells (1848). The ring was observed by Galileo, about 1610; its annular form determined by Huyghens, about 1655; and discovered to be two-fold by Messrs. Ball, 13 Oct. 1665; an inner ring was detected in 1850 by Dawes in England (29 Nov.), and by Bond in America.

SATURNALIA, festivals in honour of Saturn, father of the gods, were instituted long before the foundation of Rome, in commemoration of the freedom and equality which prevailed on the earth in his golden reign. Some, however, suppose that the Saturnalia were first observed at Rome in the reign of Tullus Hostilius (673-640 B.C.), after a victory obtained over the Sabines: whilst others suppose that Janus first instituted them in gratitude to Saturn, from whom he had learned agriculture. Others assert that they were first celebrated after a victory obtained over the Latins by the dictator Posthumius, when he dedicated a temple to Saturn, 497 B.C. During these festivals no business was allowed, amusements were encouraged, and distinctions ceased. *Lenglet*.

SAVAGE CLUB, instituted by various literary men, in 1857, facetiously terming themselves "savages," on account of their freedom from conventionalism. On some occasions they gave a war-whoop. *Sala*. Mr. W. E. Gladstone was present at the 22nd anniversary, 14 June, 1879, and the prince of Wales has been a visitor (1882).

SAVANDROOG (Mysore, S. India), a strong fortress, was captured by the British without loss, 21 Dec. 1791.

SAVINGS' BANKS. The first of these was instituted at Berne, in Switzerland, in 1787, by the name of *caisse de domestiques*, being intended for servants only; another was set up in Basel, in 1792, open to all depositors. The rev. Joseph Smith, of Wendover, began a Benevolent Institution in 1799; and in 1803-4, a "charitable bank" was instituted at Tottenham by Miss Priscilla Wakefield. The rev.

Henry Duncan established a parish bank at Ruthwell in 1810. One was opened in Edinburgh in 1814. The benefit clubs, among artisans, having accumulated stocks of money for their progressive purposes, a plan was adopted to identify these funds with the public debt of the country, and an extra rate of interest was held out as an inducement; hence were formed savings' banks to receive small sums, returnable with interest on demand.

Rt. hon. Geo. Rose developed the system, and brought it under parliamentary control, 1816.
In 1840 there were 550 banks; 766,354 depositors; amount, 22,060,904*l*.
Acts to consolidate and amend previous laws relating to savings' banks were passed in 1828 and 1847; extended to Scotland in 1835; again consolidated and amended in 1863, 1880 and 1887.
On 20 Nov. 1851, the number of savings' banks in Great Britain and Ireland was 574, besides above 20,000 friendly societies and charitable institutions. The depositors (in the banks) were 1,092,581, while the societies embraced a vast but unknown number of persons : the amount of deposits was 32,893,511*l*.
Amount of computed capital of savings' banks in the United Kingdom :—1853, 33,362,260*l*.; 1860, 41,258,368*l*.; 1870, 37,958,549*l*.—1871, England, 31,413,000*l*.; Wales, 1,066,543*l*.; Scotland, 4,119,735*l*.; Ireland, 2,220,383*l*.; total, 38,819,663*l*. In 1877, England, 34,750,747*l*.; Wales, 1,189,254*l*.; Scotland, 6,026,802*l*.; Ireland, 2,271,833*l*.; total, 44,238,686*l*. In 1883, England, 34,441,787*l*.; Wales, 1,103,201*l*.; Scotland, 7,359,586*l*.; Ireland, 2,082,549*l*.; total, 44,987,123*l*. In 1887, England, 35,595,889*l*.; Wales, 915,171*l*.; Scotland, 8,638,334*l*.; Ireland, 2,062,808*l*.; total, 47,262,222*l*.

1877.	Received by Trustees.	Paid.
England	£6,590,428	£7,031,233
Wales	178,760	224,434
Scotland	2,090,480	1,927,283
Ireland	504,463	472,185
	9,363,631	9,655,135

1887.	Received by Trustees.	Paid.
England	£5,871,807	£7,756,255
Wales	122,814	183,641
Scotland	2,472,590	2,340,033
Ireland	409,350	428,673
	9,876,561	10,708,602

For *Post-Office Savings' Banks*, established in 1861, see under Post Office.
Savings' Banks Investment acts, passed March, 1866, and Aug. 1869.
449 old Savings' Banks in the United Kingdom, 1,506,714 accounts, deposits, 43,797,805*l*., 1880.
New Savings' Bank Act, 43 & 44 Vict. c. 36, passed, 1880, came into effect, interest to depositors reduced to 2*l*. 15*s*. per cent. 1 Nov. 1880.
407 savings banks in the United Kingdom, 1884.

CLASSIFICATION OF THE FIRST 20,000 DEPOSITORS.

Domestic servants	7245
Persons in trade, mechanics, &c.	7473
Labourers and porters	672
Miners	1454
Friendly and charitable societies	58
Persons not classed, viz., widows, teachers, sailors, &c.	3098

SAVONA (a manufacturing town, N. Italy, long held by the Genoese) was captured by the king of Sardinia in 1746; by the French in 1809, and annexed; restored to Sardinia at the peace. Pope Pius VII. was kept here by Napoleon I., 1809-12. Soap is said to have been invented here, and hence its French name *saron*.

SAVOY, the ancient *Sapaudia* or *Sabaudia*, formerly a province in N. Italy, east of Piedmont. It became a Roman province about 118 B.C. The Alemanni seized it in A.D. 395, and the Franks in 490. It shared the revolutions of Switzerland till about 1048, when Conrad, emperor of Germany, gave it to Humbert, with the title of count. Count Thomas acquired Piedmont in the 13th century. Amadeus, count of Savoy, having entered his dominions, solicited Sigismund to erect them into a duchy, which he did at Cambray, 19 Feb. 1416. Victor-Amadeus, duke of Savoy, obtained the kingdom of Sicily from Spain, by a treaty, in 1713, but afterwards exchanged it with the emperor for the island of Sardinia, with the title of king, 1720. The French subdued Savoy in 1792, and made it a department of France, under the name of Mont Blanc, in 1800. It was restored to the king of Sardinia in 1814; but with Nice annexed to France in 1860, in accordance with a vote by universal suffrage, 23 April, 1860. Savoy was visited by the emperor and empress of the French in August, 1860. The annexation was censured in England.

DUKES OF SAVOY.
1391. Count Amadeus VIII. is made duke in 1416; he was named pope, as Felix V. He abdicated as duke of Savoy, 1439: renounced the tiara, 1449; died in 1451.
1439. Louis.
1465. Amadeus IX.
1472. Philibert I.
1482. Charles I.
1489. Charles II
1496. Philip II.
1497. Philibert II.
1504. Charles III.
1553. Emmanuel-Philibert.
1580. Charles-Emmanuel I.
1630. Victor-Amadeus I.
1637. Francis-Hyacinthe.
1638. Charles-Emmanuel II.
1675. Victor-Amadeus II. became king of Sicily, 1713 exchanged for Sardinia (*which see*) in 1720.

SAVOY PALACE (London), was built by Peter of Savoy, uncle of Eleanor, queen of Henry III., in 1245, on land granted to him. He gave it to the fraternity of Mountjoy (Monte Jovis), from whom it was purchased by queen Eleanor for her son Edmund. Here resided John, king of France, when a prisoner, 1357 *et seq*. The Savoy was burnt by Wat Tyler and his followers, 1381. It was restored as an hospital of St. John the Baptist by Henry VII. about 1505. The fruitless CONFERENCE of bishops and eminent puritans for the revision of the liturgy was held at the Savoy, April-July, 1661. The hospital was dissolved in 1702, and the buildings (then used as a military prison) removed for Waterloo-bridge and its approaches, 1817-19. The ancient *Chapel* (which once possessed the privilege of sanctuary), after several restorations, was destroyed by fire, 7 July, 1864, and was rebuilt at the queen's expense, and re-opened 26 Nov. 1865. The privilege of sanctuary, much abused, was abolished by parliament, 1697.

Savoy Theatre, erected for Mr. D'Oyly Carte by Mr. C. J. Phipps, opened 10 Oct. 1881; lit by Swan's incandescent electric light successfully (1194 lamps); 1000th performance of "Patience," by Sir A. Sullivan, libretto by W. G. Gilbert, 28 Dec. 1881. See *Operas*.

SAW. Invented by Dædalus. *Pliny*. Invented by Talus. *Apollodorus*. Talus, it is said, having found the jaw-bone of a snake, employed it to cut through a piece of wood, and then formed an instrument of iron like it. Saw-mills were erected in Madeira in 1420 ; at Breslau in 1427. Norway had the first saw-mill in 1530. The bishop of Ely, ambassador from Mary of England to the court of Rome, describes a saw-mill there, 1555. The attempts to introduce saw-mills in England were violently opposed, and one erected by a Dutchman in 1663 was forced to be abandoned. Saw-mills were erected near London about 1770. The excellent saw-machinery in Woolwich dockyard is based upon the invention of the elder Brunel,

1806-13. The circular saw was introduced into England about 1790. The *saw-gin* for separating cotton wool from the pod, invented by Eli Whitney, an American, in 1793, led to the immense growth of cotton in the southern states of the Union. Powis and James's band-saw was patented in 1858.

SAXE-ALTENBURG (formerly Hildburghausen), a duchy in central Germany. The dukes are descended from Ernest the Pious, duke of Saxony. Ernest, the first duke, died in 1715. The duke, Ernest, born 16 Sept. 1826; succeeded his father, George, 3 Aug. 1853; he entered into alliance with Prussia, 18 Aug. 1866. Heir, brother, Maurice, born 24 Oct. 1829.

SAXE-COBURG AND GOTHA (central Germany), capitals Gotha and Coburg. The reigning family is descended from John Ernest (son of Ernest the Pious, duke of Saxony), who died in 1729.

DUKES.

1826. Ernest I. duke of Saxe-Saalfeld-Coburg; born, 2 Jan. 1784; married Louisa, heiress of Augustus, duke of Saxe-Gotha, and became by convention duke of Saxe-Coburg-Gotha, 12 Nov. 1826; died, 29 Jan. 1844.
[His brother, Leopold, married the princess Charlotte of England, 2 May, 1816; became king of the Belgians, 12 July, 1831; and Ferdinand, the son of his brother Ferdinand, married Maria da Gloria, queen of Portugal, 9 April, 1836.]
1844. Ernest II. son (brother of Albert, prince consort of Great Britain); born 21 June, 1818; married Alexandrina, duchess of Baden, 3 May, 1842; no issue. He entered into alliance with Prussia, 18 Aug. 1866. Published Memoirs, vol. i., 9 Nov. 1887.
Heir (presumptive): Prince Alfred of England, duke of Edinburgh; born, 6 Aug. 1844 (in whose favour the prince of Wales resigned his rights, 19 April, 1863.)

SAXE-MEININGEN (a duchy in central Germany). The dukes are descended from Ernest the Pious, duke of Saxony. The first duke, Bernard (1680), died in 1706. Bernard (duke, 24 Dec. 1803, died 3 Dec. 1882), abdicated in favour of his son George II., 20 Sept. 1866, who professed his adhesion to the Prussian policy; he was born, 2 April, 1826. Heir, his son, Bernard, born 1 April, 1851. By a fire at Meiningen, about 3000 persons became houseless, 6 Sept. 1874.

SAXE-WEIMAR-EISENACH (central Germany). The grand-dukes are descended from John Frederic, the Protestant elector of Saxony, who was deprived by the emperor in 1548; see *Saxony*. The houses of Saxe-Coburg-Gotha, Saxe-Gotha, Hilburghausen, and Saxe-Meiningen also sprang from him. They are all termed the senior or *Ernestine* branch of the old family.—Saxe-Weimar became a grand duchy in 1815. The dukes have greatly favoured literature and their capital Weimar has been called the Athens of Germany.

GRAND-DUKES.

1815. Charles Augustus.
1828. Charles Frederic; died, 8 July, 1853.
1853. Charles Alexander; born, 24 June, 1818. He entered into alliance with Prussia, 18 Aug. 1866.
Heir: Charles Augustus: born, 31 July, 1844.

SAXONY, a kingdom in N. Germany. The Saxons were a fierce warlike race, the terror of the inhabitants of the later western empire, frequently attacked France, and conquered Britain (*which see*). After a long series of sanguinary conflicts they were completely subdued by Charlemagne, who instituted many fiefs and bishoprics in their country. Witikind, their great leader, who claimed descent from Woden, professed Christianity about 785. From him descended the first of Wettin (the houses Ascania intervened fr became a duchy, 880; kingdom, 1806. It w king being on the side of 1866 the king took t army fought in the b The Prussians entered between Prussia and (subjecting the Saxon king returned to Dresd 4 Sept. 1831; modified, and 1874. Populati 2,556,244; 1880, 2,972 Octocentenary of the ho Dresden with great ma many branches of the were represented; th Alfred of Edinburgh f senting Portugal and Austria and Russia included church serv formances, historical 12,000 costumed char about 150,000*l.* to the palace.

E
1423. Frederic I., first el
1428. Frederic II.
[His sons Ernest an
1464. Ernest.
1486. Frederick III.
1525. John.

1532. John Frederic; dep V.; succeeded b
1548. Maurice (of the All
1553. Augustus.
1586. Christian I.
1591. Christian II.
1611. John George I.
1656. John George II.
1680. John George III.
1691. John George IV.
1694. Frederic Augustus
1733. Frederic Augustus
1763. Frederic Augustus

1806. Frederic Augustus alliance with Fr of 1814.
1827. Anthony Clement.
1836. Frederic Augustus 9 Aug. 1854.
1854. John, brother (bor golden wedding 29 Oct. 1873.
1873. Albert; born, 23 1853, Caroline o *Heir*: George, bro

SCANDALUM statute relating to a writing, done to high as peers, judges, minis the state, and other g the circulation of the news, or horrible mes or discord between the scandal to their perso This law was first enac

SCANDINAVIA Norway, and great pa whence proceeded the conquered Normandy England (1066). The or Vikings. They sei and, it is thought, visi America, about the

"Scandinavian Society" has been formed at Stockholm; see *Sweden*, Dec. 1864.

SCARLET, or kermes dye, was known in the East in the earliest ages; cochineal dye, 1518. Kepler, a Fleming, established the first dye-house for scarlet in England, at Bow, 1643. The art of dyeing red was improved by Brewer, 1667. *Beckmann*.

SCARLET FEVER, was very prevalent in the metropolis from August, 1887, to Feb. 1888. Patients admitted into the hospitals, April, 1887—March, 1888, 7614. Arrangements for the crisis were made by the Metropolitan Asylums Board.

SCEPTICS, the sect of philosophers founded by Pyrrho, about 334 B.C. He gave ten reasons for continual suspense of judgment; he doubted of everything, never made any conclusions, and when he had carefully examined the subject, and investigated all its parts, he concluded by still doubting of its evidence. He advocated apathy and unchangeable repose. These doctrines were held by Bayle (died 1706).

SCEPTRE, a more ancient emblem of royalty than the crown. In the earlier ages the sceptres of kings were long walking-staves; afterwards carved and made shorter. Tarquin the elder was the first who assumed the sceptre among the Romans, about 468 B.C. The French sceptre of the first race of kings was a golden rod, A D. 481. *Le Gendre*.

SCHAFFHAUSEN (N. Switzerland), a fishing village in the 8th century, became an imperial city in the 13th; was subjected to Austria, 1330; independent, 1415; became a Swiss canton, 1501.

SCHAUMBURG LIPPE (Germany), was formed into a county by Adolphus, of Sondersleben, 1033. In 1640, on the death of count Otho IV., his mother, Elizabeth, transferred the domains to Philip of Lippe, from whom descended the reigning prince (the title assumed in 1807). Adolphus, born 1 Aug. 1817, succeeded his father, 21 Nov. 1860. Heir, son, George, born 10 Oct. 1846. Population of the principality, 1882, 35,753 ; 1885, 37,204.

SCHELDT TOLLS were imposed by the treaty of Munster (or Westphalia), 1648. The tolls were abolished for a compensation, 1867. The house of commons voted 175,650*l*. for the British portion, on 9 March, 1864. The Scheldt was declared free on 3 Aug. with much rejoicing at Antwerp and Brussels.

SCHIEHALLIEN, a mountain in Perthshire, where Dr. Neville Maskelyne, the astronomer-royal, made his observations with a plumb-line, 24 Oct. 1774, from which Hutton calculated that the density of the earth is five times greater than water.

SCHIPKA PASSES, on the Balkans, Turkey. Through these the Russian general Gourko entered Roumelia. After his retreat, they were fortified, and desperately, but on the whole unsuccessfully, assailed by the Turks under Suleiman Pasha, with great slaughter on both sides, 20-27 Aug. He took and lost fort St. Nicholas, 17 Sept. 1877. The Russians re-entered Roumelia, Jan. 1878.

SCHISM, see *Heresy*, and *Popes*.

SCHISM ACT, 13 Anne, c. 7, introduced by lord Bolingbroke, 1713; repealed by 5 Geo. I. c. 4, in 1719. By it teachers were required to declare their conformity to the established church.

SCHLESWIG, see *Holstein, Denmark*, and *Gastein*.

SCHOOL BOARD, see *Education*.

SCHOOLMEN or SCHOLASTIC PHILOSOPHY, began in the schools founded by Charlemagne, 800-14; and prevailed in Europe from the 9th to the 15th centuries; see *Doctors*.

SCHOOLS. Charity schools were introduced into London to prevent the seduction of the infant poor into Roman catholic seminaries, 3 James II. 1687. *Rapin*. Charter schools were instituted in Ireland, 1733. *Scully*. In England there were, in 1847, 13,642 schools (exclusively of Sunday schools) for the education of the poor; and the number of children was 998,431. The parochial and endowed schools of Scotland were (exclusively of Sunday schools) 4836 ; and the number of children, 181,467. The schools in Wales were 841, and the number of children, 38,164; in Ireland, 13,327 schools, and 774,000 children. In 1851 there were 2310 schools in connection with the Education Committee actually inspected in England and Scotland. They included: 1713 church of England schools in England and Wales; 282 protestant dissenting schools in England and Wales; 98 Roman catholic schools in Great Britain; and 217 presbyterian schools in Scotland, whereof 91 were of the free church: the whole affording accommodation for 299,425 scholars; see *Education, Design, Ascham*, &c.

SCHOOL SHIPS, see *Chichester*. *Cornwall*, off Purfleet, established 1859, accommodates between 250 and 300 vagrants (1878).

SCHWARZBURG (the seat of two principalities, N. Germany). Gunther, count of Schwarzburg, whose family dates from the 12th century, was elected emperor of Germany in 1349. From the two sons of count Gunther, who died 1552, sprang the present rulers.

SCHWARZBURG-RUDOLSTADT
(a principality, 1697).
1807. Albert (28 June), born 20 April, 1798; died 26 Nov. 1869.
1869. George (born 23 Nov. 1838), 26 Nov.

SCHWARZBURG-SONDERSHAUSEN
(a principality, 1710).
1835. Gunther (19 Aug.), born 24 Sept. 1801; abdicated.
1880. Charles, son (born 7 Aug. 1830), 17 July.

SCHWEIDNITZ, Prussia, often besieged and taken in the thirty years' and seven years' wars. Near it Frederick II. defeated the Austrians under marshal Daun, 16 May, 1762.

SCHWEIZ, a Swiss canton, which with Uri and Unterwalden renounced subjection to Austria, 7 Nov. 1307. The name Switzerland, for all the country, dates from about 1440.

SCIENCE, see *Education, Chemistry*, and other branches.

Science and Art Department began as the Normal School of Design, 1 Jan. 1837, with a grant of 1,500*l*. See under *Design*. The grant in 1885-6 was 391,573*l*.; 1888-9, 445,303*l*.

The 56th report states that in 1888 the department supported 1,952 schools, and 6,579 classes were examined in elementary science, with 112,808 pupils; the South Kensington museum is in the charge of the department.

SCIENTIFIC APPARATUS. The International Loan Exhibition, at South Kensington, consisting of about 17,000 objects, many of great historical interest, from all countries except America, was opened (by the queen,) 13 May, and closed 30 Dec. 1876. Conferences were held, 16 May —2 June, and many free lectures given by eminent persons. Reopened 30 June, 1877.

SCIENTIFIC ASSOCIATION, for promotion of research; proposed at the meeting of the American Association at Philadelphia, Sept. 1884. Mrs. Elizabeth Thompson promised liberal support.

SCIENTIFIC FRONTIER (in reference to Afghanistan), a term used by Lord Beaconsfield, 9 Nov. 1878.

SCIENTIFIC INDUSTRY, SOCIETY FOR PROMOTING, established at Manchester, in 1873. It proposed setting up a library and museum, the delivery of lectures, and the publication of reports.

SCIENTIFIC RELIEF FUND. In 1859, several fellows of the Royal Society (Messrs. Gassiot, Wheatstone, Miller, Tyndall, and others) commenced the collection of subscriptions with the view of establishing a permanent fund to be expended in aiding necessitous men of science and their families, in imitation of the "Literary Fund." In the spring of 1860, 3365*l*. had been subscribed; in Jan. 1865, 5320*l*.; in 1867, 6052*l*.; in 1877, 6428*l*.; and many cases had been relieved.

SCIENTIFIC SOCIETIES' HOUSE COMPANY proposed March, 1873.

SCIENTIFIC SURVEYING EXPEDITION, see *Deep Sea*.

SCILLY ISLES (the Cassiterides or Tin-islands). They held commerce with the Phœnicians; and are mentioned by Strabo. They were conquered by Athelstan, 936; and given to the monks. They were granted by Elizabeth to the Godolphin family, by whom they were fortified; the works were strengthened in 1649 by the royalists, from whom they were taken by Blake, 1651. Mr. Augustus Smith, the owner, and termed the king of these isles, after a long paternal rule, died in Aug. 1872.

A British squadron under sir Cloudesley Shovel were wrecked here, when returning from an expedition against Toulon; he mistook rocks for land, and struck upon them. His ship, the *Association*, in which were persons of rank, and 800 brave men, went instantly to the bottom. The *Eagle*, captain Hancock, and the *Romney* and *Firebrand*, were also lost; the rest of the fleet escaped, 22 Oct. 1707. Sir Cloudesley's body was conveyed to London, and buried in Westminster abbey, where a monument was erected to his memory.

SCINDE, see *Sinde*.

SCIO MASSACRE, 11 April, 1822, see *Chios*.

SCLAVONIA, see *Slavonia*.

SCONE (near Perth). The Scotch coronation chair was brought from Scone to Westminster abbey by Edward I. in 1296. Here Charles II. was crowned, 1 Jan. 1651.

SCOPTZI, see *White Doves*.

SCORE, MUSICAL, was written by the monk Hucbald, who wrote "Enchiridion Musicae;" he died 930. Specimens written in the 13th century exist in the British Museum.

SCOTTISH - IRISH CONVENTION, see *United States*, May, 1889.

SCOTISTS. Those who adopted the doctrines of John Duns Scotus (who died 8 Nov. 1308) on divine grace, freewill, the origin of the moral law, the Conception of the Virgin Mary, &c., strongly opposed by the Thomists, disciples of St. Thomas Aquinas, who died 7 March, 1274.

SCOTLAND, see *Caledonia*. At the death of queen Elizabeth, 24 March, 1603, James VI. of Scotland, as the most immediate heir, was called to the throne of England, and proclaimed king of Great Britain, 24 Oct. 1604. Each country had a separate parliament till 1707, when the kingdoms were united; see *England*.

Camelon, capital of the Picts, taken by Kenneth II. and every living creature put to the sword or destroyed. The Norwegians occupy Caithness 9th century.	843
Scotland ravaged by Athelstan	933
The feudal system established by Malcolm II.	1004
Invaded by Canute	1031
Divided into baronies	1032
The Danes driven out of Scotland	1040
Duncan I. is murdered by his kinsman Macbeth, by whom the crown is seized	"
Malcolm III., aided by Edward the Confessor, defeats the usurper at Dunsinane, 1054; Macbeth killed by Macduff	1056 or 1057
The Saxon-English language introduced into Scotland by fugitives from England escaping from the Normans	1080
Siege of Alnwick: Malcolm III. killed	1093
Reign of David I., a legislator	1124-53
Scotland invaded by Hacho, king of Norway, with 160 ships and 20,000 men; the invaders are defeated by Alexander III., who now recovers the Western isles	1263
Death of Margaret of Norway, heiress to the throne, 7 Oct.	1290
John Balliol and Robert Bruce contend for the throne, 1291; Edward I. of England, as umpire, decides in favour of John . Nov.	1292
John Balliol, king of Scotland, appears to a summons, and defends his own cause in Westminster hall against the earl of Fife	1293
Edward, wishing to annex Scotland to England, dethrones John, ravages the country, destroys the muniments of Scottish history, and seizes the prophetic stone (see *Coronation*)	1296
William Wallace defeats the English at Cambus Kenneth, and expels them, 1297; is defeated at Falkirk, 22 July, 1298; taken by the English, and executed at Smithfield . 23 Aug.	1305
Robert Bruce, crowned, 1306; he defeats the English 1307; and takes Inverness, 1313; defeats the English at Bannockburn . 24 June,	1314
Edward Balliol gains the throne for a little time by his victory at Dupplin, 11 Aug. 1332; and by the victory at Halidon-hill . 19 July,	1333
David II. taken prisoner at the battle of Durham (and detained in captivity 11 years)	1346
Battle of Chevy Chase, between Hotspur Percy and earl Douglas (see *Otterburn*) . 10 Aug.	1388
Murder of duke of Rothesay, heir of Robert III., by starvation . 3 April,	1401
The Scots defeated at Homildon-hill . 14 Sept.	1402
James I. captured by the English near Flamborough head on his passage to France . 30 March,	1406
St. Andrews university founded by bishop William Turnbull	1451
University of Aberdeen founded	1494
James IV. invades England, slain at Flodden Field, and his army cut to pieces . 9 Sept.	1513
James V. banishes the Douglases	1528
He establishes the court of session	1532
Order of St. Andrew, or the Thistle, is revived	1540
Mary, the queen of Scots, born 7 Dec.; succeeds her father, James V., who dies . 14 Dec.	"
The regent, cardinal Beaton, persecutes the reformers, 1539, 1546; he is assassinated at St. Andrews . 29 May,	1546
The Scots defeated at Pinkie . 10 Sept.	1547
Mary marries the dauphin of France . April,	1558
The parliament abolishes the jurisdiction of the pope in Scotland . 24 Aug.	1560
Francis II. dies, leaving Mary a widow . Dec.	"
The Reformation in Scotland, by John Knox, and others, during the minority of Mary, between 1550 &	"
Mary, after an absence of thirteen years, arrives at Leith from France . 21 Aug.	1561
Upon an inquisition, which was officially taken, by order of queen Elizabeth, only 58 Scotsmen were found in London. *Stow.*	1562
Mary marries her cousin, Henry Stuart, lord Darnley . 29 July,	1565
David Rizzio, her confidential secretary, murdered by Darnley in her presence . 9 March,	1566
Lord Darnley blown up by gunpowder, in his house (Mary accused of conniving at his death), 10 Feb.	1567

James Hepburn, earl of Bothwell, carries off the queen, who marries him . . . 15 May,	1567
Mary made prisoner at Carberry hill by her nobles, 15 June,	,,
Resigns her crown to her infant son James VI.; the earl of Murray appointed regent . 22 July,	,,
Mary escapes from prison, and collects a large army, which is defeated by the regent Murray, at the battle of Langside, 13 May; enters England, 16 May,	1568
The regent Murray murdered . . . 23 Jan.	1570
The earl of Lennox appointed regent . 12 July,	,,
The earl of Lennox murdered, 4 Sept.; the earl of Mar chosen regent . . . . Sept.	1571
Death of the reformer John Knox . 24 Nov.	1572
(His funeral in Edinburgh is attended by most of the nobility, and by the regent Morton, who exclaims, "There lies he who never feared the face of man !"	
The university of Edinburgh founded . . .	1582
The Raid of Ruthven (see *Ruthven*) . .	,,
Mary having taken refuge in England, 16 May, 1568, is after a long captivity, beheaded at Fotheringay castle (see *Fotheringay*) . . . 8 Feb.	1587
Gowrie's conspiracy fails . . . . 5 Aug.	1600
Union of the crown of Scotland with that of England by the accession of James VI. . 24 March,	1603
James proclaimed "king of Great Britain, France, and Ireland" . . . . 24 Oct.	1604
Charles I. attempts in vain to introduce the English liturgy; tumult at Edinburgh . 23 July,	1637
Solemn league and covenant subscribed 1 March,	1638
A Scotch army enters England . . .	1640
Charles joins the Scotch army, 1646; betrayed into the hands of the English parliament . 30 Jan.	1647
Marquis of Montrose defeated at Philiphaugh, 13 Sept. 1645; executed at Edinburgh . 21 May,	1650
Charles II. crowned at Scone, 1 Jan.; defeated at Worcester . . . . . 22 Aug.	1651
Scotland united to the English commonwealth by Oliver Cromwell . . . . Sept.	,,
Charles II. revives episcopacy in Scotland . .	1661
Argyll beheaded . . . . 27 May,	,,
Scottish hospital, London, incorporated . .	1665
The Covenanters defeated on the Pentland hills	1666
Abp. Sharpe murdered near St. Andrews, by John Balfour of Burley and others . . 3 May,	1679
The Covenanters defeat Claverhouse at Drumclog 1 June; are routed at Bothwell bridge 22 June,	,,
Richard Cameron's declaration for religious liberty 22 June,	1680
Resolution of a convention in favour of William III.; re-establishment of presbytery . . 14 March,	1689
The "claim of right" accepted by William and Mary . . . . . . 11 May,	,,
Insurrection of Claverhouse: killed at Killiecrankie, 27 July,	,,
Massacre of the Macdonalds at Glencoe 13 Feb.	1692
Parish schools established by the parliament. .	1697
Legislative union of Scotland with England 1 May,	1707
Insurrection under the earl of Mar in favour of the son of James II. (see *Pretender*) . .	1715
The rebels defeated at Preston, 12 Nov.; and at Dumblane (or Sheriffmuir) . . 13 Nov.	,,
Captain Porteous killed by a mob in Edinburgh (see *Porteous*) . . . . 7 Sept.	1736
Prince Charles Edward proclaimed at Perth, 4 Sept.; at Edinburgh, 16 Sept.; with the Highlanders defeats sir John Cope at Prestonpans, 21 Sept.; takes Carlisle, 15 Nov.; arrives at Manchester, 28 Nov.; at Derby, 4 Dec.; retreats to Glasgow . . . . . 25 Dec.	1745
Defeats general Hawley at Falkirk, 17 Jan.; is totally defeated at Culloden . . 16 April,	1746
The Highland dress prohibited by parliament, 12 Aug.	,,
Lords Kilmarnock and Balmerino executed for high treason on Tower-hill . . . 18 Aug.	,,
Simon Fraser, lord Lovat, aged 80, executed 9 April heritable jurisdictions abolished by parliament .	1747
Thomson, the poet, dies . . . 27 Aug.	1748
The Old Pretender, "Chevalier de St. George," dies at Rome . . . . . 30 Dec.	1765
Prince Charles Edward Louis Casimir, the Young Pretender, dies at Rome . . . 31 Jan.	1788
Death of Robert Burns . . . 21 July,	1796
Scott's "Lay of the Last Minstrel" published .	1806
Cardinal Henry duke of York (last of the Stuarts) dies . . . . . . 31 Aug.	1807
The Court of Session is formed into two divisions .	1807
Royal Caledonian asylum, London, founded . .	1813
Scott's "Waverley" published . . .	1814
The establishment of a jury court under a lord chief commissioner	1815
Visit of George IV. to Scotland . . Aug.	1822
Sir Walter Scott dies. . . . 21 Sept.	1832
Seven ministers of the presbytery of Strathbogie are deposed by the General Assembly of the Church of Scotland for obeying the civil in preference to the ecclesiastical law. (Their deposition was formally protested against by the minority of ministers and elders, headed by Dr. Cook) . . 28 May,	1841
The General Assembly condemn patronage as a grievance to the cause of true religion that ought to be abolished . . . . 23 May,	1842
Visit of the queen, prince Albert, and the court; she landed at Granton pier . . 1-13 Sept.	,,
Secession of the non-intrusion ministers of the church of Scotland (about 400) at the General Assembly (see *Free Church*) . . . 18 May,	1843
Death of Jeffrey . . . . 26 Jan.	1850
National Association for vindication of Scottish rights formed . . . . Nov.	1853
Act for better government of the universities passed Aug.	1858
Salmon Fisheries act passed . . July,	1864
The queen's visit to the borders, Kelso, Melrose, &c. 21-24 Aug.	1867
Scotch reform bill introduced into the commons, 17 Feb., passed . . . . 13 July,	1868
Procedure in court of session and justiciary and other courts amended . . . July,	,,
Scotch Reform act passed . . . 13 July,	,,
Land Registers and Titles to Land act passed July,	,,
Commission appointed to inquire into the administration of justice . . . . Oct.	,,
Municipal elections amendment act passed, 9 Aug.	1870
Act to unite counties for sheriffs' duties passed 9 Aug.	,,
Robert Chambers, author and publisher, died aged 69 17 March,	1871
Scott centenary celebrated in Edinburgh, &c. (Scott born 15 Aug. 1771) . . . 9 Aug.	,,
Scotch Education Act passed . . 10 Aug.	1872
Return of owners of land and heritages, 1872-3 (a kind of Domesday book), published by government . . . . . April,	1874
Patronage in the established church (see 1842) abolished by act passed . . . 7 Aug.	,,
Scottish Church Disestablishment Association: first annual meeting . . . . 8 March,	1875
Visit of the queen to Edinburgh; the Scottish national monument, by J. Steell, to prince Albert, unveiled by her . . . 17 Aug.	1876
Romanist hierarchy revived by the pope: archbishopric of Glasgow, bishopric of Dunkeld, &c. 4 March; the Scotch protestant bishops protest against this . . . . 13 April,	1878
Public Parks Act passed . . . 18 March,	,,
Marriage Notice Act passed . . 8 Aug.	,,
Education Act amended, by act . . 16 Aug.	,,
Visit of Mr. Gladstone to Mid-Lothian, Edinburgh, Glasgow, &c., many speeches . 24—29 Nov.	1879
About 40,000 Scottish volunteers reviewed in the Queen's Park, Edinburgh, by the queen 25 Aug.	1881
Agitation respecting rents in Aberdeen, Banff, &c. Sept.-Oct.	,,
Farmers' alliance founded at Aberdeen by delegates from above 4000 farmers . . 1 Dec.	,,
Movement for home rule (*which see*) began 4 April,	1882
Old Scottish regimental colours deposited in St. Giles's cathedral, Edinburgh, by the duke of Cambridge . . . . 13 Nov.	1883
Death of Walter, duke of Buccleuch, aged 78; munificent patron of public works, agriculture, science, literature, and art . . 15 April,	1884
Agitation for the dis-establishment of the church (see *Church of Scotland*) . . autumn,	1885
Secretary for Scotland Act passed . 14 Aug.	,,
Charles Henry, duke of Richmond, appointed secretary Aug. 1885; succeeded by G. O. Trevelyan about 6 Feb.; by Arthur J. Balfour 26 July, 1886; by Schomberg H., marquis of Lothian 8 March,	1887
Local government bill for Scotland introduced into the commons by the lord advocate J. P. B. Robertson, 8 April; read 1st time in the lords 25 July,	1889

3 F

Scotch universities bill, giving more freedom to teaching and increasing state grant read second time . . . . 20 June, 1889
New national portrait gallery for Scotland in Edinburgh, opened by the marquis of Lothian 15 July, ,,
The local government and universities bills passed Aug. ,,

See *Edinburgh.*

KINGS OF SCOTLAND.
BEFORE CHRIST.

[The early accounts of the kings are in a great measure fabulous. The series of kings is carried as far back as Alexander the Great.]

330. Fergus I. ; ruled 25 years ; lost in the Irish Sea.
[Fergus, a brave prince, came from Ireland with an army of Scots, and was chosen king. Having defeated the Britons and slain their king Coilus, the kingdom of the Scots was entailed upon his posterity for ever. He went to Ireland, and, having settled his affairs there, was drowned on his return, launching from the shore, near the harbour, called *Carrick-Fergus* to this day, 3699 A.M. *Anderson.*]

AFTER CHRIST.

357. Eugenius I., son of Fincormachus ; slain in battle by Maximus, the Roman general, and the Picts.
⁎ With this battle ended the kingdom of the Scots, after having existed from the coronation of Fergus I., a period of 706 years ; the royal family fled to Denmark. *Boece; Buchanan.*
(Interregnum of 27 years.)
404. Fergus II. (l.) great grandson of Eugenius, and 40th king ; slain in battle with the Romans.
420. Eugenius II. or Evenus : reigned 31 years.
451. Dongardus or Domangard, brother : defeated and drowned.
457. Constantine I., brother ; assassinated.
479. Congallus I. nephew ; just and prudent.
501. Goranus, brother ; murdered. *Boece.* Died while Donald of Athol was conspiring to take his life.
535. Eugenius III. nephew; "none excelled him in justice."
558. Congallus II. brother.
569. Kinnatellus, brother; resigned for
570. Aidanus or Aldan, son of Goranus.
605. Kenneth, son of Congallus II.
606. Eugenius IV. son of Aidanus.
621. Ferchard or Ferquhard I. son ; confined for misdeeds to his palace, where he laid violent hands upon himself. *Scott.*
632. Donald IV. brother ; drowned in Loch Tay.
646. Ferchard II. son of Ferchard I. ; "most execrable."
664. Malduinus, son of Donald IV. ; strangled by his wife for his supposed infidelity, for which crime she was immediately afterwards burnt.
684. Eugenius V. brother.
688. Eugenius VI. son of Ferchard II.
698. Amberkeletus, nephew; fell by an arrow from an unknown hand.
699. Eugenius VII. brother ; some ruffians designing the king's murder, entered his chamber, and, he being absent, stabbed his queen, Spontana, to death. *Scott.*
715. Mordachus, son of Amberkeletus.
730. Etfinus, son of Eugenius VII.
761. Eugenius VIII. son of Mordachus ; sensual and tyrannous ; put to death by his nobles.
764. Fergus III. son of Etfinus ; killed by his jealous queen, who afterwards stabbed herself to escape a death of torture.
767. Solvathius, son of Eugenius VIII.
787. Achaius : just and wise.
819. Congallus III. ; a peaceful reign.
824. Dongal or Dougal, son of Solvathius ; drowned.
831. Alpine, son of Achaius ; beheaded by the Picts.
834. Kenneth II. son; surnamed Mac Alpine; defeated the Picts, slew their king, and united them and the Scots under one sceptre, and became the first sole monarch of all Scotland, 843.
854. Donald V. brother ; dethroned ; committed suicide.
858. Constantine II. son of Kenneth II. ; taken in battle by the Danes and beheaded.
874. Eth or Ethus, surnamed Lightfoot ; died of grief in prison ; confined for sensuality and crime.
876. Gregory the Great ; brave and just.
893. Donald VI. son of Constantine II. ; excellent.
904. Constantine III. son of Ethus ; became a monk, and resigned in favour of
944. Malcolm I. son of Donald VI. ; murdered.
953. Indulfus or Gondulph ; killed by the Danes in an ambuscade.
961. Duff or Duffus, son of Malcolm ; murdered by Donald, the governor of Forres castle.
965. Cullen or Culenus, son of Indulfus ; avenged the murder of his predecessor ; assassinated.
970. Kenneth III. brother of Duffus ; murdered by Fenella, the lady of Fettercairn.
994. Constantine IV. son of Cullen ; slain.
995. Kenneth IV. or Grimus, the Grim, son of Duffus ; routed and slain in battle by Malcolm, the rightful heir to the crown, who succeeded.
1003. Malcolm II. son of Kenneth III. ; assassinated on his way to Glamis ; the assassins in their flight crossing a frozen lake were drowned.
1033. Duncan I. grandson ; assassinated by his cousin.
1039. Macbeth, usurper; slain by Macduff, the thane of Fife.
⁎ Historians so differ up to this reign, in the number of the kings, the dates of succession, and the circumstances narrated, that no account can be taken as precisely accurate.
1057. Malcolm III. (Canmore), son of Duncan ; killed while besieging Alnwick castle.
1093. Donald VII. (Donald Bane), brother ; usurper; fled to the Hebrides.
1094. Duncan II. natural son of Malcolm ; murdered.
,, Donald VII. again ; deposed.
1098. Edgar, son of Malcolm (Henry I. of England married his sister Maud).
1107. Alexander I. the Fierce, brother.
1124. David I. brother ; married Matilda, daughter of Waltheof, earl of Northumberland.
1153. Malcolm IV. grandson.
1165. William the Lion ; brother.
1214. Alexander II. son ; married Joan, daughter of John, king of England.
1249. Alexander III. married Margaret, daughter of Henry III. of England ; dislocated his neck, when hunting near Kinghorn.
1285. Margaret, the "Maiden of Norway," grand-daughter of Alexander, "recognised by the states of Scotland, though a female, an infant, and a foreigner ;" died on her passage to Scotland.
A competition for the vacant throne ; Edward I. of England decides in favour of
1292. John Balliol, who afterwards surrendered his crown, and died in exile.
[Interregnum.]
1306. Robert (Bruce) I. a great prince.
1329. David (Bruce) II. son ; Edward Balliol disputed the throne with him.
1332. David II. again ; a prisoner in England, 1346-57 (Edward Balliol king, 1332-4.)
1371. Robert (Stuart) II. nephew ; died 19 April.
1390. Robert (John Stuart) III. son ; died 4 April.
1406. James I. second son ; imprisoned 18 years in England; set at liberty in 1423 ; conspired against, and murdered at Perth, 21 Feb.
1437. James II. son ; killed at the siege of Roxburgh castle by a cannon bursting, 3 Aug.
1460. James III. son ; killed in a revolt of his subjects at Bannockburn-field, 11 June.
1488. James IV. son ; married Margaret Tudor, daughter of Henry VII. of England ; killed at the battle of Flodden, 9 Sept.
1513. James V. son ; succeeded when little more than a year old ; a sovereign possessing many virtues ; died 14 Dec.
1542. Mary, daughter; born, 7 Dec. 1542 succeeded 14 Dec. ; see *Annals,* above.
1567. James VI. son ; succeeded to the throne of England, and the kingdoms were united, 1603.

See *England.*

SCOTT CENTENARY, celebrated in London and throughout Scotland, 9 Aug. 1871. Sir Walter Scott was born 15 Aug. 1771.

SCOTTISH CORPORATION (charitable), established 1665. The old hall, Crane-court, Fleet-street, built by Wren, burnt 14 Nov. 1877 ; new hall inaugurated 21 July, 1880.

SCOURERS, see *Mohocks.*

SCOURING OF THE WHITE HORSE, see *Ashdown.*

SCREW, was known to the Greeks. The pumping-screw of Archimedes, or screw-cylinder for raising water, invented about 236 B.C., is still in use. It is stated that with the assistance of the screw, one man can press down or raise up as much as 150 men can do without it.—The SCREW-PROPELLER consists of two or more twisted blades, like the vanes of a windmill, set on an axis, running parallel with the keel of a vessel, and revolving beneath the water at the stern. It is driven by a steam-engine. The principle was shown by Hooke in 1681, and since by Du Quet, Bernouilli, and others. Patents for propellers were taken out by Joseph Braunah in 1784; by Wm. Lyttelton in 1794; and by Edward Shorter in 1799. But these led to no useful result. In 1836 patents were obtained by Francis Pettit Smith (knighted July, 1871; died, 12 Feb. 1874) and captain John Ericson (died, aged 86, March, 1889); and to them the successful application of the screw-propeller must be attributed. The first vessels with the screw were the *Archimedes*, built on the Thames in 1838 by H. Wimshurst, and the *Rattler*, built in the United States (1844), and tried in England in 1845. Double screw-propellers are now employed. A new form of screw-propeller invented by col. W. H. Mallory, of U. S. A. army, was tried on the Thames and reported successful, Aug. 1878.

SCRIBLERUS CLUB, a literary club, founded by Swift in 1714, included amongst its members, Bolingbroke, Pope, Gay, and Arbuthnot.

SCRIPTURE KNOWLEDGE INSTITUTION, Bristol, was founded by George Müller, a Prussian (born in 1805). He came to Bristol as a minister of the "Brethren" in 1832, and on 5 March, 1834, founded this institution, the objects of which are: 1. Assistance of schools giving instruction on scriptural principles; 2. Circulation of the scriptures; 3. Assistance to missions; 4. Circulation of tracts; 5. Provision for destitute orphans, see *Orphan-houses*. Without application, Mr. Müller, since he began, up to 1868, had received by voluntary contribution, 430,000*l.*

SCROFULA, see *King's-evil*.

SCRUTIN (French for ballot). In *scrutin de liste* the voter writes on his paper as many names as there are persons to be elected, for instance for the whole department. In *scrutin d'arrondissement*, the members are elected separately. The adoption of one of these modes was much discussed in France in 1875. The conservatives prefer the latter, the radicals the former. See *France*, Nov. 1875. The *scrutin de liste* was adopted in the elections of 1848, 1849, 1871, and 1875.

1. Bardoux's bill for adopting the *scrutin de liste* (warmly advocated by M. Gambetta), was passed by the chamber of deputies (243-235), 18 May, 1881; rejected by the senate (148-114), 9 June, 1881; again rejected, Jan. 1882.
2. Welbeck Rousseau's bill for the *scrutin de liste* passed by the deputies (412-99), 24 March, finally passed, 8 June, 1885.
The bill for the restoration of the *scrutin d'arrondissement* passed by the chamber 11 Feb. and senate 13 Feb. 1889.
The *scrutin de liste* was adopted by the Italian chamber, 14 Feb. 1882.

SCULLABOGUE, see *Massacres*, 1798.

SCULPTURE is said to have begun with the Egyptians. Bezaleel and Aholiab built the tabernacle in the wilderness, and made all the vessels and ornaments, 1491 B.C., and their skill is recorded as the gift of God. *Exod.* xxxi. 3. Dipœnus and Scyllis, statuaries at Crete, established a school at Sicyon. Pliny speaks of them as being the first who sculptured marble and polished it; all statues before their time being of wood, 568 B.C. Alexander gave Lysippus the sole right of making his statues, 326 B.C. He left no less than 600 pieces, some of which were so highly valued in the age of Augustus, that they sold for their weight in gold. Sculpture did not flourish among the Romans, and in the middle ages with some fine exceptions, was generally degraded. With the revival of painting, it revived also; and Donato di Bardi, born at Florence, A.D. 1383, was the earliest professor among the moderns. An institute of sculptors was established in 1861. See *Royal Academy*.

EMINENT SCULPTORS.

Pheidon flourished	B.C. 869
Myron	480
Phidias (the greatest)	442
Praxiteles	363
Lysippus	328
Chares	288
Michael Angelo Buonarotti	A.D. 1474-1564
Benvenuto Cellini	1500-1570
Giovanni L. Bernini	1598-1680
Caius Gabriel Cibber	1630-1700
Francis Bird	1667-1731
John Henry Danneker	1758-1741
Louis Roubiliac (statue of sir I. Newton)	died 1762
Peter Scheemakers	1691-1769
John M. Rysbrack	1693-1770
John Bacon	1740-1799
Thomas Banks	1735-1805
Joseph Nollekens	1737-1823
Antonio Canova	1757-1822
John Flaxman	1754-1826
J. C. F. Rossi	1762-1839
Peter Turnerelli	1774-1837
William Pitts	1790-1840
Francis Chantrey	1781-1841
Albert Thorwaldsen	1770-1844
Sir Richard Westmacott	1775-1856
Christian Rauch	1777-1857
Thos. Campbell	1790-1858
M. Cortes Wyatt	1777-1862
John E. Jones	1806-1862
John Thomas	1813-1862
Wm. Behnes	1790-1864
C. Kiss	1802-1865
John Gibson	1751-1866
Edw. Hodges Baily	1788-1867
Richd. Westmacott	1799-1872
Hiram Powers	1805 1873
John Henry Foley	1818-1874
Alfred Geo. Stevens	1817-1875
Matthew Noble	1820-1876
Thos. Woolner	1825
Joseph Edgar Boehm	1834
Mary Thornycroft	1814
Hamo Thornycroft	1852
Alfred Gilbert	1852

SCUTAGE or ESCUAGE. The service of the shield (scutum) is either uncertain or certain. Escuage uncertain is where the tenant by his tenure is bound to follow his lord; and is called Castleward, where the tenant is bound to defend a castle. Escuage certain is where the tenant is set at a certain sum of money to be paid in lieu of such uncertain services. The first tax levied in England to pay an army, 5 Hen. II. 1159. *Cowel*.

SCUTARI, Asiatic Turkey, opposite Constantinople, of which it is a suburb. It was anciently called *Chrysopolis*, golden city, in consequence, it is said, of the Persians having established a treasury here when they attempted the conquest of Greece. Near here Constantine finally defeated Licinius, 323. The hospital was occupied by the sick and wounded of the Anglo-French army, in 1854-5, whose sufferings were much alleviated by the kind exertions of Miss Florence Nightingale and a band of nurses under her, aided by a large fund of money (15,000*l.*)

subscribed by the public and placed in the care of the proprietors of the *Times* newspaper; see *Times*. Explosion of powder magazine by lightning, about 150 killed, 8 June, 1883.

SCYTHIA, situate in the most northern parts of Europe and Asia. The boundaries were unknown to the ancients. The Scythians made several irruptions upon the more southern provinces of Asia, especially 624 B.C., when they remained in possession of Asia Minor for twenty-eight years, and at different periods extended their conquests in Europe, penetrating as far as Egypt; see *Tartary*.

SEA. Lieut. Maury first published his "Physical Geography of the Sea" in 1854, and other important works since; he died Feb. 1873; see *Deep Sea*.

SEA BIRDS' PRESERVATION ACT, passed 24 June, 1869.

SEA FIGHTS, see *Naval Battles*.

SEA FISHERIES, see *Fisheries*.

SEAHAM, see under *Coal, Accidents*, 1880.

SEAL FISHERY ACT, passed 14 June, 1875.

SEALS or SIGNETS. Engraved gems were used as such by the Egyptians, Jews, Assyrians, and Greeks; see *Exod*. xxviii. 14. Ahab's seal was used by Jezebel, 899 B.C. (1 *Kings* xxi. 8.) The Romans in the time of the Tarquins (about 600 B.C.) had gemmed rings. They sealed rooms, granaries, bags of money, &c. The German emperor, Frederick I. (A.D. 1152) had seals of gold, silver, and tin. Impressions of the seals of Saxon kings are extant; and the English great seal is attributed to Edward the Confessor (1041-66). "A seal with armorial bearings before the 11th century, is certainly false." *Fosbroke*. The most ancient English seal with arms on it is said to be that of Richard I. or John. White and coloured waxes were used. Our present sealing-wax, containing shellac, did not come into general use in Germany and England until about 1556. Red wafers for seals came into use about 1624; but were not used for public seals till the 18th century. A seal acquired by the British Museum made of black hematite, thought to be Hittite, found at Yuzgat in Asia Minor, announced Nov. 1886. *Seal Society*, for publication of fac-similes of ancient seals, was established in 1883.—For SEALED LETTERS, see *Great Seal* and *Lettres de Cachet*.

SEAMEN. In consequence of the great loss of life by wrecks of merchant vessels, attributed to bad ships and overloading, a commission of inquiry was agreed to by parliament on the motion of Mr. S. Plimsoll (who published "Our Seamen: an Appeal"), 4 March, 1873. The duke of Edinburgh was on the commission; the duke of Somerset, chairman. Mr. Plimsoll has been censured for exaggeration.

The report issued in September tended to justify the public apprehensions, but suggested no remedy. The report presented to parliament, 2 July, 1874, condemned the present insurance system, and recommended increased responsibility of owners and others, and strengthening the powers of the Board of Trade for investigation.
The Merchant Shipping Survey Bill was rejected (173–170) . . . . 24 June, 1874
After much excitement, an Act was passed to give further powers to the Board of Trade to stop unseaworthy ships . . . . . . 13 Aug. 1875
Another Merchant Shipping Act (*which see*) passed 15 Aug. 1876
Strong circular issued by the Board of Trade (Mr. Chamberlain); deaths of the employed in ships asserted to be 1 in 60; in coal mines 1 in 315; present system stated to be ineffectual Jan. 1884

SEAS, SOVEREIGNTY OF THE. The claim of England to rule the British seas is of very ancient date. Arthur is said to have assumed it, and Alfred afterwards supported this right. It was maintained by Selden, and measures were taken by government in consequence, 8 Chas. I. 1633. The Dutch, after the death of Charles I., made some attempts to obtain it, but were roughly treated by Blake and other admirals. Russia and other powers of the north armed to avoid search, 1780; again, 1800; see *Armed Neutrality* and *Flag*. The international rule of the road at sea was settled in 1862'; (new rules were issued in 1879 and 19 Aug. 1884), yet near Great Britain alone there have been 13,000 collisions in six years. Mr. Wm. Stirling Lacon proposed to reduce the rules from 749 words to 144, for simplicity and security. His form had been nine times before parliament, 1873. Revised rules issued by the admiralty in a "Fleet Circular," Nov. 1885.

SEASONS. The four natural divisions of the year.

In the north temperate regions in 1884 the spring quarter began 20 March, 5 a.m., the summer, 21 June 1 a.m., the autumn, 22 Sept. 3 p.m., the winter, 21 Dec. 10 a.m. See Lapland seasons under *Year*.
James Thomson's "Seasons" published: "Winter," 1726; "Summer," 1727; "Spring," 1728; "Autumn," 1730
Haydn's "Seasons" first performed, 1801.

SEATS BILL, see under *Reform*.

SEBASTIAN, ST. (N. Spain), was taken by the French, under the duke of Berwick, in 1719 It was besieged by the British and allied army under Wellington. After a most heavy bombardment, by which the whole town was laid nearly in ruins, it was stormed by general Graham (afterwards lord Lynedoch), and taken 31 Aug. 1813.—On 5 May, 1836, the fortified works, through the centre of which ran the high road to Hernani, were carried by the English auxiliary legion under general Evans, after very hard fighting. The British naval squadron, off St. Sebastian, under lord John Hay, lent very opportune aid to the victors in this contest.—A vigorous assault was made on the lines of general De Lacy Evans, at St. Sebastian, by the Carlists, 1 Oct. 1836. Both parties fought with bravery. The Carlists were repulsed, after suffering severely. The loss of the Anglo-Spanish force was 376 men and 37 officers, killed and wounded General De Lacy Evans was slightly wounded. See under *Leagues*. The queen regent of Spain meets queen Victoria here, 27 March, 1889.

SEBASTOPOL or SEVASTOPOL, a town and once a naval arsenal, at S.W. point of the Crimea formerly the little village of Aktiar. The buildings were commenced in 1784, by Catherine II. after the conquest of the country. The town is built in the shape of an amphitheatre on the rise of a large hill flattened on its summit, according to a plan laid down before 1794, which has been since adhered to The fortifications and harbour were constructed by an English engineer, colonel Upton, and his sons, since 1830. The population in 1834 was 15,000. This place underwent eleven months' siege, by the English and French in 1854 and 1855. Immediately after the battle of the Alma, 20 Sept. 1854, the allied army marched to Sebastopol, and took up its position on the plateau between it and Balaklava, and the grand attack and bombardment commenced 17 Oct. 1854, without success.* After many sanguinary

* In consequence of the sufferings and disasters of the army in the winter of 1854-5, the Sebastopol Inquiry Committee was appointed, and the Aberdeen administration resigned, Feb. 1855. The committee sat from

encounters by day and night, and repeated bombardments, a grand assault was made on 8 Sept. 1855, upon the Malakhoff tower and the Redans, the most important fortifications to the south of the town. The French succeeded in capturing and retaining the Malakhoff. The attacks of the English on the great Redan and of the French upon the little Redan were successful, but the assailants were compelled to retire after a desperate struggle with great loss of life. The French lost 1646 killed, of whom 5 were generals, 24 superior and 116 inferior officers, 4500 wounded, and 1400 missing. The English lost 385 killed (29 being commissioned and 42 non-commissioned officers), 1886 wounded, and 176 missing. In the night the Russians abandoned the southern and principal part of the town and fortifications, after destroying as much as possible, and crossed to the northern forts. They also sank or burnt the remainder of their fleet. The allies found a very great amount of stores when they entered the place, 9 Sept. The works were utterly destroyed in April, 1856, and the town was restored to the Russians in July; gen. Todleben, the able defender, died 1 July, 1884, and was buried here. See *Russo-Turkish War*.

SECEDERS; SECESSION CHURCH, see *Burghers*.

SECONDARY OF LONDON, an ancient office, resembling that of under-sheriff in counties. The place was purchaseable till early in the present century, when it was bought up by the corporation.

SECRET SOCIETIES, *Assassins, Fenians, Ribbonism, Vehmic Tribunal, Rosicrucians, Illuminati, Carbonari, Mary-Anne, Nihilists*.

SECRETARIES OF STATE. The earliest authentic record of a secretary of state is in the reign of Henry III., when John Maunsell is described as "*Secretarius Noster*," 1253. *Rymer*. Towards the close of Henry VIII.'s reign, two secretaries were appointed; and upon the union with Scotland, Anne added a third as secretary for Scotch affairs; this appointment was afterwards laid aside; but in the reign of George III. the number was again increased to three, one for the American department. In 1782 this last was abolished by act of Parliament; and the secretaries were appointed for home, foreign, and colonial affairs. When there were but two secretaries, one held the *portefeuille* of the Northern department, comprising the Low Countries, Germany, Denmark, Sweden, Poland, Russia, &c.; the other, of the Southern department, including France, Switzerland, Italy, Spain, Portugal, and Turkey; the affairs of Ireland belonging to the elder secretary; both secretaries then equally directed the home affairs. *Beatson*. There are now six secretaries—home, foreign, colonial, war, (in 1858) India, and (in 1885) Scotland, all in the cabinet. Secretary of State for Scotland act passed 14 Aug. 1885, amended 1887. See *Administrations*, and separate articles.

SECTS, RELIGIOUS, see under *Worship*, and their respective titles.

1 March to 15 May, lord Aberdeen being the last person examined. Its report was presented 18 June. Mr. Roebuck, the chairman, moved on 17 July that the house should pass a vote of severe reprehension on every member of the Aberdeen administration. On 19 July his motion was lost by a majority of 107 against it. In 1855 the government sent sir John M'Neill and col. Tulloch to inquire into the state of the armies in the Crimea Their report was presented to parliament in Feb. 1856. A commission was appointed to consider the statements in the report (which were very unfavourable to many officers), but the substance of the report was unshaken.

SECULAR GAMES (*Ludi Sæculares*), very ancient Roman games, celebrated on important occasions. Horace wrote his "Carmen Sæculare" for their celebration in the reign of the emperor Augustus (17). They took place again in the reign of Claudius (47), of Domitian (88), and for the last time, of Philip (248), believed to be 2000 years after the foundation of the city.

SECULARISM, a name given to the principles advocated by G. J. and Austin Holyoake, about 1846, and since by Mr. Bradlaugh.

Its central idea is free, not lawless thought, and it considers scepticism to be scrutiny. It advocates liberty of action without injury to others. It is not against Christianity, but independent of it. Its standard is utilitarian; it is the religion of the present life only; teaching men to seek morality in nature, and happiness in duty. Mr. Austin Holyoake and other secularists repudiated atheism; Mr. Bradlaugh and others profess it.

SECURITY FROM VIOLENCE ACT, passed in 1863, appointed whipping as part of the punishment for attempts at garotting.

SEDAN, an ancient fortified city in the valley of the Meuse, N.E of France, the seat of a principality long held by the dukes of Bouillon. On 6 July, 1641, a victory was gained at La Marfée, near Sedan, by the count of Soissons and the troops of Bouillon and other French princes, over the royal army supporting Richelieu; but the count was slain on 23 June, 1642. The duke was arrested in the midst of his army, and was made to cede Sedan to the crown. The protestant university was abolished after the revocation of the edict of Nantes, 22 Oct. 1685. Around this place a series of desperate conflicts on 29, 30, and 31 Aug. between the French army of the north, under marshal MacMahon (about 150,000 men), and the greater part of the three German armies under the king and crown-prince of Prussia and the crown-prince of Saxony (about 250,000 men) was brought to a close on 1 Sept. 1870.

The battle began with attacks on the French right and left about 5 a.m., and was very severe at 2 p.m. At 4 p.m. the Germans remained masters of the field, and the crown-prince of Prussia announced a complete victory, the chief part of the French army retreating into Sedan.

The emperor Napoleon was present during the battle, and, it is said, stood at Iges, near Sedan, exposed for four hours to the German grenades. The impossibility of further resistance was then evident. The Germans had contracted their circle close round Sedan; their formidable artillery held all the heights, from which they could at pleasure wholly destroy the town and the army, and only 2000 men were in a condition to respond to their commander's call, and to make a supreme effort to break through the enemy with the emperor and escape to Montmédy.

At first general de Wimpffen (called to the command when MacMahon was wounded) indignantly rejected the terms offered by the victor, and the emperor had a fruitless interview with count Bismarck to endeavour to mitigate them.

On 2 Sept. the emperor wrote in autograph to the king of Prussia, "Mon frère, n'ayant pu mourir à la tête de mes troupes, je dépose mon épée au pied de votre majesté. NAPOLEON." A capitulation of Sedan and the whole army therein was signed by generals Von Moltke and De Wimpffen at the château of Bellevue, near Frenois, at 11.30 a.m., and at 2 p.m. an interview took place between the king and the emperor, who was downcast but dignified.

The conflict was principally carried on by the artillery, in which (according to the emperor) the Germans had the advantage, not only in number (600 to 500), but also in weight, range, and precision. The carnage was awful, and the field the next day was a mass of shattered bones, torn flesh, and coloured rags.

About 25,000 French prisoners were taken in the battle, and 83,000 surrendered the next day, together with

70 mitrailleuses, 400 field-pieces, and 150 fortress guns. About 14,000 French wounded were found lying in the neighbourhood, and about 3000 escaped into Belgium and laid down their arms. The great army of the north had ceased to exist. Among the killed was lieut.-col. Pemberton, a correspondent of the *Times*, who had approached too near the conflict.
The French emperor and his suite arrived at Wilhelmshöhe, a castle near Cassel appointed for his residence, (formerly inhabited by his uncle Jerome, when king of Westphalia), in the evening of 5 Sept.
On 1 Sept. the village of Bazeilles was stormed by the Bavarians and burnt, it was said, because the inhabitants fired on the ambulances; many women and children perished. The French denied the provocation. The place had been previously twice bombarded and stormed by the maddened combatants.
In a letter dated 12 May, 1872, the emperor Napoleon took upon himself the whole responsibility of the surrender of Sedan.

SEDAN CHAIRS (so called from Sedan), were first seen in England in 1581. One used in the reign of James I., by the duke of Buckingham, caused great indignation, and the people exclaimed that he was employing his fellow-creatures to do the service of beasts. Sedan chairs came into London in 1634, when sir Francis Duncomb obtained the sole privilege to use, let, and hire a number of such covered chairs for fourteen years. They came into very general use in 1649.

SEDGMOOR (Somersetshire), where the duke of Monmouth (natural son of Charles II. by Lucy Walters), who had risen in rebellion on the accession of James II., was completely defeated by the royal army, 6 July, 1685. The duke was made a prisoner in the disguise of a peasant, at the bottom of a ditch, overcome with hunger and fatigue. He was tried and beheaded on 15 July following.

SEDITION. Sedition acts were passed in the reign of George III. The proclamation against seditious writings was published May, 1792. The celebrated Sedition bill passed Dec. 1795. Seditious societies were suppressed by act, June, 1797. The Seditious Meetings and Assemblies' bill passed 31 March, 1817. In Ireland, during the Roman Catholic and Repeal agitation, acts or proclamations against sedition and seditious meetings were published from time to time until 1848.

SEEDS. An act was passed to prevent the adulteration of seeds (a common practice), 11 Aug. 1869; amended in 1878.

SEEKERS, see *Quakers.*

SEGEDIN, or SZEGEDIN, Hungary. Here was concluded a treaty between Ladislaus IV. and Amurath II., 12 July, 1444. It was treacherously annulled at the instigation of cardinal Julian, who with Ladislaus perished in the fatal battle of Varna, 10 Nov. 1444. See *Varna.*

SEICENTO, see under *Italian.*

SEIDLICE (Poland), where a battle was fought 10 April, 1831, between the Poles and Russians. The Poles obtained the victory after a bloody conflict, taking 4000 prisoners and several pieces of cannon; but this success was soon followed by fatal reverses.

SEISMOMETER (from *seismos*, Greek for earthquake), an apparatus for measuring the violence of the shocks. One is described by Mr. Robert Mallet in his work on earthquakes, published in 1858. Many described by Prof. J. A. Ewing, 1880-8.

SELA, see *Petra.*

SELBORNE SOCIETY, for the preservation of birds, plants, and pleasant places, originated in the Selborne league (afterwards society) formed by Mr. and Mrs. G. A. Musgrave in Nov. 1885. It has included the plumage league since Jan. 1886, (see under *Birds*).

SELDEN SOCIETY, founded 29 Jan. 1887, for the study of English legal history, and publication of ancient MSS. and books, by lords justice Fry, Coleridge, and Lindley, and other eminent lawyers. John Selden, legal antiquary, born 16 Dec. 1584, died 30 Nov. 1654.

SELECT-MEN, the earliest officers of the townships formed by the first colonists of New England about 1635.

SELECTION, NATURAL, see *Species.*

SELENIUM, a grayish-white elementary substance (chemically resembling sulphur), discovered in the stone riolite by Berzelius, in 1817.
The variation in its resistance to the electric current when subjected to light was observed by Mr. Willoughby Smith in 1873, and utilised in the photophone (*which see*). Dr. C. Wm. Siemens constructed a "*selenium eye.*"

SELEUCIA (Syria), made the capital of the Syrian monarchy by its builder, Seleucus Nicator, 312 B.C. On the fall of the Seleucidæ, it became a republic, 65 B.C. It was taken by Trajan, A.D. 116; several times given up and retaken; subjugated by the Saracens, and united with Ctesiphon, 636.

SELEUCIDES, ERA OF THE, dates from the reign of Seleucus Nicator. It was used in Syria for many years, and frequently by the Jews until the 15th century, and by some Arabians. Opinions vary as to its commencement. To reduce it to our era (supposing it to begin 1 Sept. 312 B.C.), subtract 311 years 4 months.

SELF-DENYING ORDINANCE, which ordained that no member of parliament should hold any civil or military office or command conferred by either or both of the houses, or by authority derived from them, after much discussion, was passed 3 April, 1645, by the influence of Cromwell, who thus removed the earl of Essex and other Presbyterians out of his way. A somewhat similar ordinance was adopted by the parliament at Melbourne in Australia, in 1858. The name was given to an arrangement made respecting British naval promotions and retirements in 1870.

SELLASIA (Laconia). Here the Spartans under Cleomenes were defeated by Antigonus Doson and the Achæans, 221 B.C.

SELSEY, see *Chichester.*

SEMAPHORE, see *Telegraphs.*

SEMATOLOGY (Greek *sēma*, a sign), the science of signs, a term proposed by B. H. Smart, who died 1872.

SEMINARA (Naples). Near here Gonsalvo de Cordova, the great captain, was defeated by the French, in 1495; but defeated them, 21 April, 1503.

SEMINCAS, see *Simancas.*

SEMPACH (Switzerland). Here the Swiss gained a great victory over Leopold, duke of Austria, 9 July, 1386, under Arnold von Winckelried; the duke and Arnold were slain, and the liberty of Switzerland was established. The day is still commemorated. Especially on 5 July, 1886.

SEMPER EADEM ("Always the same"), one of the mottoes of queen Elizabeth, was adopted by queen Mary and queen Anne, 13 Dec. 1702.

SEMPERINGHAM, see *Gilbertines*.

SENATE (*Senatus*). In the ancient republics the government was divided between the *senatus* (from *senis*, old; in Greek, *gerousia*, from *gerōn*, old), an assembly of elders, and the popular assembly (*comitia*, Latin; *ecclesia*, Greek), the king being merely the executive. The Roman senate, said to have originally been composed of 100 members, was raised to 300 by Tarquinius Priscus; to about 600 by Sylla, about 81 B.C.; and to 900 by Julius Cæsar. It was reformed and reduced to 600 by Augustus; and gradually lost its power and dignity under the emperors. The mere form existed in the reign of Justinian. A second senate, formed at Constantinople by Constantine, retained its office till the 9th century. S.P.Q.R. on the Roman standard stood for "Senatus Populusque Romanus," "the Roman senate and people." A *senatus consultum* was a law enacted by the senate.

The French senate was created by the constitution of the year 8, promulgated 24 Dec. 1799, to watch over the administration of the laws. The number of senators was raised gradually from 60 to 137. The senate was replaced by the chamber of peers in 1814; re-established by Napoleon III. 14 Jan. 1852; and abolished, 5 Sept. 1870. Its re-establishment was proposed in 1873. Establishment of a senate of 300 voted; 225 to be elected for 9 years by the departments; 75 (for life) by national assembly, 22 Feb. 1875.

The 75 elected, 9-21 Dec., 1875.

The congress of 13 Aug. 1884, ordered the gradual abolition of life senators as vacancies occurred; new senators were to be elected for 9 years by the departments; enacted, 5 Nov.; bill passed by the deputies and senate, 4-9 Dec. 1884. See *France*.

SENEFFE (Belgium). Near here was fought a severe but indecisive battle between the Dutch, under the prince of Orange (afterwards our William III.), and the French, led by the great Condé, 11 Aug. 1674.

SENEGAL, French colonies on the river of that name in Senegambia, W. Africa, settled about 1626; several times taken by the British, but recovered by the French, to whom they were finally restored in 1814.

SENESCHAL, a high officer of the French royal household. In the reign of Philip I. 1059, the office was esteemed the highest place of trust.

SENLAC, see *Hastings*.

SENONES (see *Gauls*), defeated by Camillus, 367 B.C. They defeated Metellus the consul at Arretium, 284, but were almost exterminated by Dolabella, 283. They invaded Greece in 279; were defeated by Antigonus Gonatas, 278; and sued for peace.

SENOVA, near Schipka, in the Balkans. Here Suleiman Pasha and the Turks were defeated by the Russian general Skobeleff, 9 Jan. 1878. This victory virtually closed the war, and opened the road to Adrianople. About 26,000 Turks and 283 officers were made prisoners, with 40 Krupp guns. About 8000 Turks and 2000 Russians were killed or wounded.

SENTINUM (central Italy). The site of a great victory of the Romans over the Samnites and Gauls, whose general, Gellius Egnatius, was slain, 295 B.C.

SEPARATISTS, a term applied to the Irish National Party, headed by Mr. Parnell, about 1883. In 1884 it vehemently attacked earl Spenser and the Irish executive.—The name is also assumed by a small Christian sect in Dublin, and some other places; originated by John Walker, a classical scholar, somewhat resembling the Glasites (Prov. xviii. 1); he died 25 Oct. 1833, aged 66.

SEPHARDIM, the name given to the descendants of the highly civilised Jews of Spain and Portugal, who fled from the persecutions of the Inquisition, 1492-1505. The Jews interpret Sepharad, in *Obadiah* 20, as Spain.

SEPOYS (a corruption of *sipāhī*, Hindostanee for a soldier), the term applied to the native troops in India. Under able generals they greatly aided in establishing British rule in India. For their mutinies, see *Vellore*, 1806; *Madras*, 1809; and *India*, 1857.

SEPTEMBER, the seventh Roman month reckoned from March (from *septimus*, seventh). It became the ninth month when January and February were added to the year by Numa; 731 B.C. The Roman senate would have given this month the name of Tiberius, but the emperor opposed it; the emperor Domitian gave it his own name Germanicus; the senate under Antoninus Pius gave it that of Antoninus; Commodus gave it his surname, Herculeus; and the emperor Tacitus his own name, Tacitus.—"September 4 government," see *France*, Sept. 1870.

SEPTEMBRIZERS. In the French revolution a dreadful massacre took place in Paris, 2-5 Sept. 1792. The prisons were broken open, and the prisoners butchered, among them an ex-bishop, and nearly 100 non-juring priests. Some accounts state the number of persons slain at 1200, others at 4000. The agents in this slaughter were named Septembrizers.

SEPTENNALISTS, the party in France who support the septennate or seven years' government of marshal MacMahon, enacted by the assembly, 19, 20 Nov. 1873. See *France*, 1874.

SEPTENNATE, in the German constitution, is the stipulation that every German fit for the duty is liable to serve for seven years in the Imperial army 4 May, 1871.

SEPTENNIAL PARLIAMENTS. Edward I. held but one parliament every two years. In the 4th Edward III. it was enacted, "that a parliament should be holden every year once." This continued to be the statute-law till 16th Charles I. 1641, when an act was passed for holding parliaments once in three years at least; repealed in 1664. The Triennial act was re-enacted in 1694. Triennial parliaments thence continued till the 2 Geo. I. 1716, when, in consequence of the allegation that "a popish faction were designing to renew the rebellion in this kingdom, and the report of an invasion from abroad," it was enacted that "the then parliament should continue for seven years." This *Septennial act*, entitled "an act for enlarging the continuance of parliaments" (1715 in the statutes, 4to, given as 1 Geo. I. stat. 2, c. 38), was passed 7 May, 1716; see *Parliaments*. Several unsuccessful motions have been made for its repeal; one in May, 1837.

SEPTIMANIA, a Roman province, S. France; see *Languedoc*.

SEPTUAGESIMA SUNDAY; see *Quadragesima Sunday*, and *Week*. Septuagesima is the season between Epiphany and Lent.

SEPTUAGINT VERSION OF THE BIBLE,

made from Hebrew into Greek, 277 B.C. Seventy-two translators were shut up in thirty-six cells; each pair translated the whole; and on subsequent comparison the thirty-six copies did not vary by a word or letter. *Justin Martyr.* St. Jerome affirms that they translated only the Pentateuch; others say they translated the whole. Ptolemy Philadelphus gave the Jews about a million sterling for a copy of the Old Testament, and seventy translators half a million more for the translation. *Josephus.* Finished in seventy-two days. *Hewlett.* The above statements are merely *traditional;* see *Bible,* and *Alexandrian Codex.*

SEQUESTRATION of Benefices Act passed 13 July, 1871.

SERAING, Belgium, on the Meuse, near Liege, formerly the site of a palace of the prince bishops of Liege; now containing great iron works, established in 1817, by John Cockerill, an Englishman. His father, who had works at Liege, died in 1813. Nearly the whole town has been built by Cockerill.

SERAJEVO, capital of Bosnia and Herzegovina, with about 50,000 inhabitants, was founded in 1465, by two nobles. It was taken by Mathias, king of Hungary, in 1480, and by prince Eugene, of Savoy, in 1698. In pursuance of the treaty of Berlin, 13 July, 1878, the Austrians entered Serajevo, after a sharp conflict with the Bosnians, and bombardment of the city, 19 Aug. 1878. By a fire 8, 9 Aug. 1879 above 20,000 persons were rendered homeless.

SERAPHINE, a free-reed musical instrument, a precursor of Debaine's harmonium, brought out by John Green in London, 1833.

SERAPIS, TEMPLE OF (near Naples), was exhumed in 1750. The investigations of Lyell and Babbage into the history of the sinking and burying of this temple were of great geological interest.

SERASKIER, the Turkish minister of war.

SERFS, see *Slavery* (note), and *Russia*, 1861, 1863.

SERINGAPATAM (S. India), the capital of Hyder Ali, sovereign of Mysore (*which see*). The battle of Seringapatam, called also the battle of Arikera, in which the British defeated Tippoo Sahib, was fought 15 May, 1791. The redoubts were stormed, and Tippoo was reduced by lord Cornwallis, 6 Feb. 1792. After this capture, preliminaries of peace were signed, and Tippoo agreed to cede one half of Mysore, and to pay 33,000,000 of rupees (about 3,300,000*l.* sterling) to England, and to give up to lord Cornwallis his two eldest sons as hostages.—In a new war the Madras army, under general Harris, arrived before Seringapatam, 5 April, 1799; it was joined by the Bombay army 14 April; and the place was stormed and carried by major-general Baird, 4 May, same year. In this engagement Tippoo was killed. See *Mysore.*

SERJEANTS-AT-LAW are pleaders from among whom the judges are ordinarily chosen, and who are called serjeants of the coif. The judges call them brothers; see *Coif.* Their exclusive rights of addressing court of common pleas suspended, 1834; restored, 1840; abolished, 1846. By the Supreme Court of Judicature Act, judges on their appointment need not be made serjeants, 1873. See *Inns of Court.*

SERPENT, an ancient wind instrument, parent of the Cornet family. A "contra serpent" was shown in the Exhibition, 1851, made by Jordan, of Liverpool. The "serpentcleid" was produced by Bencham in Jullien's orchestra about 1840.

SERPENTINE, see *Hyde Park.*

SERVANTS. An act levying a duty on male servants was passed in 1777, which was augmented in 1781, *et seq.* A tax on female servants, imposed in 1785, was repealed in 1792. The tax on servants yielded in 1830 about 250,000*l.* per annum; in 1840 the revenue from it had fallen to 201,482*l.*; in 1850 it produced about the same sum. The licence duty for male servants is now 15s. each. It produced in the year 1876-7, 167,004*l.*; 1877-8, 154,641*l.*; 1878-9, 146,661*l.*; 1883-4, 139,631*l.*; 1887-8, 136,287*l.* The law respecting servants was amended by the Master and Servants' act passed in 1867.

SERVIA, an independent kingdom, south of Hungary. The Servians or Serbs are of Slavonic origin. They embraced Christianity about 640. The emperor Manuel subjugated them in 1150; but they recovered their independence in 1180, and were ruled by princes. The country was subdued by the sultan Mahomet II. in 1459. Population in 1854, 985,000; 1873, 1,338,505; 1887, 2,013,691. Belgrade is the capital (*which see*).

The sultan Amurath I. defeated the combined Christian army of Servians, Hungarians, Albanians, &c., and was himself killed by a wounded Servian soldier in the plain of Cossova, or Kossova	15 June, 1389
A Servian rebellion quelled	1737
The Servians aid Austria by free companies	1788-90
Again rebel, and capture Belgrade	1806
Kara George, chosen leader, 1801; aided by the Russians, establishes a government	1807-11
The Turks break a treaty, and Kara George flees	1814
Their governor Milosch rebels	March, 1815
Kara George returning, is executed	1816
Alexander Milosch 1. Obrenovitch recognised as hereditary prince by the sultan	15 Aug. 1829
Milosch becoming despotic, made to abdicate, and a new constitution established	13 June, 1839
His son and successor Milan soon dies, whose brother Michael also retires; Alexander, son of Kara George, chosen prince	14 Sept. 1842
Alexander becoming unpopular, made to abdicate by the national party; Alexander Milosch re-elected prince	1858
Plot against Milosch frustrated, 11 July; the Servian assembly meets	13 July, 1860
Milosch dies; succeeded by his son Michael Obrenovitch, (born 4 Sept. 1825)	26 Sept. "
Rising movement to render Servia independent of Turkey	March, 1861
Disputes between the Servians and the Turkish garrison at Belgrade, which lead to bloodshed; the city bombarded, 15 June; submits 17 June; the Turkish pacha dismissed	19 June, 1862
A conference of the representatives of the great powers at Constantinople, Aug.; the Porte agrees to liberal concessions to the Servians, which their prince accepts	7 Oct. "
Servians demand withdrawal of Turkish garrisons from Belgrade and other fortresses	5 Oct. 1866
Which are evacuated, March; prince Michael, at Constantinople, thanks the sultan	30 March, 1867
Prince Michael assassinated in Belgrade	10 June, 1868
Milan IV. grand-nephew of prince Michael, chosen his successor, 22 June; 14 of the murderers were executed	28 July, "
Constitution affirming the hereditary rights of the Obrenovitch family	1869
Prince Karageorgevitch accused of complicity with murder; imprisoned at Pesth, Jan.; acquitted,	May, 1871
The regents surrender the government to prince Milan at Belgrade	22 Aug. 1872
Excitement through insurrection in Herzegovina, new ministry hostile to Turkey, formed, about 31 Aug.; resign; announced, 4 Oct.; peace ministry formed	9 Oct. 1875

SERVIA.

Ristitch, premier, opposed to Turkey . . July,	1876
See *Turkey*, for the war declared . . 1 July,	,,
Milan proclaimed king by Tchernayeff and the army at Deligrad; not approved . . . 16 Sept.	,,
Peace with Turkey ratified . . . 4 March,	1877
[Servian losses in the war, about 8000 killed, 20,000 wounded.]	
Servians again declare war and enter Turkey (see *Russo-Turkish war*) . . . 14, 15 Dec.	,,
Sultan deposes prince Milan . . . 22 Dec.	,,
Servia declared independent, with new frontiers, by treaty of San Stefano, 3 March, and of Berlin . . . . 13 July,	1878
Execution of Markovitch and other rioters end of May,	,,
Proclamation of peace and national independence at Belgrade . . . . . 22 Aug.	,,
The ministry re-modelled by Ristitch, about 15 Oct.	,,
Resignation of Ristitch (virtual dictator) announced 25 Oct.	1880
Milan proclaimed king by the Assembly about 6 March,	1882
[Married Natalie Keschko (born 1859), 17 Oct. 1875.]	
Escaped assassination by mad. Markovitch 23 Oct.	,,
Resignation of the Pirochanitz ministry, 27 Sept.; succeeded by Nicolas Christitch . . 3 Oct.	1883
New military organization leads to insurrection in S.E. Servia; soon suppressed . . announced 5-10 Nov.	,,
Insurgents defeated . . . about 10 Nov.	,,
18 members of the Radical committee arrested Nov.	,,
General tranquillity reported . . . 13 Nov.	,,
18 rebel leaders executed, about 19 Nov.; many others reprieved . . . . . Dec.	,,
Rebels enter Bulgaria; disputes with that country ensue; prospect of war . . . June,	1884
M. Garachanine, premier . . . 23 Oct.	,,
Dispute settled by arrangement . about 10 Nov.	,,
Political dissensions: Panslavist agitation by M. Ristitch . . . . . . Sept.	1885
Military movements consequent upon the *coup d'état* in Roumelia . . . . . Oct.	,,
Declaration of war against Bulgaria (*which see*) 13 Nov.	,,
Invasion: success followed by disastrous retreat 14-24 Nov.	,,
Royal decree calling out the army . 11 Feb.	1886
Peace between Servia and Bulgaria signed at Bucharest 3 March; ratified by the sultan 13 March,	,,
M. Ristitch fails to form a new ministry about 3 April,	,,
M. Garachanine resigns; succeeded by M. Ristitch (pro-Russian) about 13 June, 1887; by colonel Gruics . . . . . . 1 Jan.	1888
Strong independent speech of the king 13 Dec.	1887
New ministry under M. Nicolas Christitch 26-27 April,	1888
The king demands a divorce from the queen for disagreements; he favours Austria, she Russia; she refused the deed of terms offered; she gives up the crown prince and goes to Paris 18 July, Queen Natalie protests against the divorce 20 Aug. & 30 Oct.; the divorce decreed by the metropolitan Theodosius, abp. of Belgrade (authority questionable) . . . . . . Oct.	,,
A royal commission recommends universal suffrage, all electors eligible to the Skuptschina, independence of the church, all religions free and protected, liberty of the press, &c. . 24 Oct.	,,
The king proclaims coming constitutional changes 26 Oct.	,,
Elections of the chambers annulled by the king as not free . . . . . . 28 Nov.	,,
New elections give majority to the radicals, headed by M. Ristitch, against the progressists under M. Christitch, the minister . . . 16 Dec.	,,
The Skuptschina opened . . . 30 Dec.	,,
The king informs a deputation desiring changes in the proposed constitution that the deputies must accept it unaltered; otherwise he will set it aside and rule absolutely . . . 1 Jan.	1889
The new constitution passed (494-73) 2 Jan.; the session closed . . . . . 3 Jan.	,,
An amnesty proclaimed for political offences Jan.	,,
The Christitch ministry resigns; but continues after others fail . . . . 8 Jan. *et seq.*	,,
The formation of a radical ministry stopped by the king on suspicion of conspiracy . 13 Feb.	1889
Abdication of the king; his son Alexander proclaimed; liberal regency-M. Ristitch, gen. Bolimarkovitch, and gen. Protitch; radical cabinet headed by M. Taushanovitch . . 6 March,	,,
The Servians celebrate with mourning the quincentenary of the battle of Cossova . 27 June,	,,
The king founds a monument in memory of the slain. The king was anointed by the metropolitan Michael in the church of Zitcha, near Kruljevo . . . . . . 2 July,	,,

HEREDITARY PRINCES.

1829. Milosch (Obrenovitch) I., recognised by Turkey, 15 Aug. 1833; abdicates 13 June, 1839.
1839. Michael II., son; dies 1840.
1840. Michael III., brother; abdicates 1842.
1842. Alexander (Kara-Georgevitch), son of Kara George; chosen, 14 Sept.; deposed 23 Dec. 1858; died 3 May, 1885.
1858. Milosch (Obrenovitch), re-elected, 23 Dec.; dies, 1860.
1860. Michael III., son; succeeds, 26 Sept.; assassinated, 10 June, 1868.
1868. Milan (Obrenovitch) IV., grand-nephew, born, 22 Aug. 1854; married to Nata'ie Keschko, 17 Oct. 1875; again proclaimed, 2 July, 1858; he abdicated 6 March, 1889.
1889. Alexander, son, born 14 Aug. 1876.

SERVILE WARS insurrections of slaves against their masters. Two were quelled in Sicily, after much slaughter, 132, 99 B.C.; see *Spartans*.

SESSION COURTS in England were appointed to be held quarterly in 1413, and the times for holding them regulated in 1831; see *Quarter Sessions*, and *Court of Session*. The *kirk session* in Scotland consists of the minister and elders of each parish. They superintend religious worship and discipline, dispense money collected for the poor, &c.

SESTUS, on the Thracian Chersoneus; see *Hellespont*. Near Sestus was the western end of Xerxes' bridge, across the Hellespont, 480 B.C. Sestus was retaken from the Persians by the Athenians, 478, and held by them till 404, giving them the command of the trade of the Euxine.

SETTLED ESTATES ACT 40 & 41 Vict. c. 18, consolidates and amends the law relating to their leases, sales, &c. (passed 28 June, 1877). Other acts passed, 1882 and 1884.

SETTLEMENT, ACT OF, for securing the succession to the British throne, to the exclusion of Roman catholics, was passed in 1689. This name is also given to the statute by which the crown, after the death of William III. and queen Anne, without issue, was limited to Sophia, electress of Hanover, grand-daughter of James I., and her heirs being protestants, 1702. The Irish act of settlement, passed in 1662, was repealed in 1689; see *Hanover*.

SETTLEMENT, LAW OF, of the poor, the subject of many statutes since 1535, was somewhat changed by the poor law act of 1834.

SEVEN BISHOPS, see *Bishops*, 1688.

SEVEN BROTHERS, martyrs at Rome, under Antoninus; their feast is kept 10 July.

SEVEN CHURCHES OF ASIA, to the angels (ministers) of which the apostle John was commanded to write the epistles contained in the 2nd and 3rd chapters of his Revelation, viz., Ephesus, Smyrna, Pergamos, Thyatira, Sardis, Philadelphia, and Laodicea, 96.

1. *Ephesus* (*which see*). Paul founded the church here, 57. In 59, he was in great danger from a tumult created by Demetrius; to the elders of this church he delivered

his warning address, 60 (Acts xix. xx.). Ephesus was in a ruinous state even in the time of Justinian (527), and still remains so.
2. *Smyrna.* An ancient Greek city, claiming to be the birth-place of Homer; was destroyed by the Lydians; about 627 B.C. rebuilt by Antigonus and Lysimachus. Its first bishop, Polycarp, was martyred here about 169. It has been frequently captured. It was sacked by Tamerlane in 1402; and finally taken by the Turks, 1424. It is now the chief city of Asia Minor, and the seat of the Levant trade. Earthquake, above 2000 perish, 12 May, 1875. Great fire; about 700 houses destroyed, 18 July, 1882.
3. *Pergamos.* Capital of the kingdom of the same name, founded by Philetærus, whom Lysimachus, one of Alexander's generals, had made governor, 283 B.C. He was succeeded by Eumenes I., 263; Attalus (who took the title of king), 241; Eumenes II. (who collected a great library), 197; Attalus II., 159; Attalus III., 138. He bequeathed his kingdom to the Romans, 133. It revolted, was subdued, and made the Roman province, Asia. Pergamos is still an important place, called Bergamo. Parchment is said to have been invented here. The explorations of the ancient citadel, instituted by the German government in 1878, resulted in the discovery of Greek marble statuary, which has been deposited in the museum at Berlin.
4. *Thyatira.* Now a mean town of 2000 houses, called Ak-hissar, "White Castle."
5. *Sardis.* Formerly the capital of Lydia, the kingdom of Crœsus (560 B.C.); taken by Cyrus, 548; burnt by the Greeks, 499; it flourished under the Roman empire; was taken by the Turks; and destroyed by Tamerlane about 1462; it is now a miserable village, named Sart.
6. *Philadelphia* was built by Attalus (III.) Philadelphus, king of Pergamos (159-138 B.C.); was taken by Bajazet I., A.D. 1390. It is now called Allah Shehr, "The city of God," and is a miserable town of 3000 houses.
7. *Laodicea.* In Phrygia, near Lydia; has suffered much from earthquakes. It is now a deserted place, called Eske-hissar, "The old castle."

SEVEN DAYS' WAR, see *Army*, 1871.

SEVEN SAGES, see *Greece*, 590 B.C.

SEVEN-SHILLING PIECES in gold were authorised to be issued 29 Nov. 1797.

SEVEN SLEEPERS. According to an early legend seven youths, in 251, commanded to worship a statue set up in Ephesus by the emperor Decius, refused, and fled to a cavern in the mountain, where they were enclosed, and slept, according to Durandus, for 300 years. Other writers give shorter periods, and various accounts of the incidents which accompanied the awakening. A festival in their honour is kept by the Roman church on 27 July.

SEVEN WEEKS' WAR, see *Prussia*, 1866.

SEVEN WONDERS, see *Wonders*.

SEVEN YEARS' WAR, the conflict maintained by Frederick II. of Prussia against Austria, Russia, and France, from 1756 to 1763; see *Battles*. He gained Silesia; see *Hubertsburg*.

SEVENTH-DAY BAPTISTS, see article *Sabbatarians*, &c.

SEVERN, see under *Tunnels*.

SEVERNDROOG, see *Savandroog*.

SEVERUS'S WALL, see *Roman Walls*.

SEVILLE (S.W. Spain), the *Hispalis* of the Phœnicians, and the *Julia* of the Romans, was the capital until Philip II finally established his court at Madrid, 1563. It opened its gates to the Saracens in 712, and was taken from them by the Christians in 1247, after an obstinate siege. The peace of Seville between England, France, and Spain, and also a defensive alliance to which Holland acceded, signed 9 Nov. 1729. In the peninsular war, Seville surrendered to the French, 1 Feb. 1810; and was taken by assault by the British and Spaniards, after the battle of Salamanca, 27 Aug. 1812. It was besieged but not taken by Espartero, July, 1843. Visit of Prince of Wales, 20 April, 1876.

SÈVRES, see *Porcelain*.

SEWERS, see *Cloaca Maxima*. An act was passed in 1847 enforcing the conveyance of the sewage of houses in London into the public sewers. The commissioners of sewers in London were superseded by the metropolitan commissioners of sewers, nominated by the government. They abolished the large brick sewers, introducing pipe drains, and turned the contents of 30,000 cesspools into the river Thames. The necessity for purifying the defiled river led to the construction of a new system of drainage, under the superintendence of the Metropolitan Board of Works (*which see*). The main drainage (the plan of Mr. J. W. Bazalgette) consists of the Northern High-level, Middle-level, and Low-level, and Southern High-level and Low-level. On 14 March, 1865, the works were said to be completed, except the low-level sewer on the north side, which was waiting for the completion of the Thames embankment, &c. On 4 April, 1865, the prince of Wales started the engines which commenced lifting the waters of the southern outfall, at Crossness Point, near Erith.* The main drainage works of the metropolis (82 miles), were finally completed Aug. 1875. The sewage is carried 14 miles down the river. Total cost, 4,500,000*l*. See *Carbolic Acid*.

Royal commission on the Metropolitan Sewage discharge (lord Bramwell, sir John Coode, prof. A. W. Williamson and others), appointed 22 June, 1882; reports on the great contamination of the Thames at the outfalls, and need of change; approves of the combination of chemical precipitation with filtration through earth, June and Dec. 1884.

Mr. Wm. Webster's method of decomposing London sewage by electricity set up at Crossness; reported successful on inspection, March, 1889.

SEWING-MACHINE. It is said that Thomas Saint patented one for boots and shoes in 1790. Similar inventions are ascribed to Duncan (1804); Adams and Dodge (American, 1818); Thimonnier (French, 1834); and Walter Hunt (1834). The first really practical sewing-machine was the invention of Elias Howe, an American mechanic, of Cambridge, in Massachusetts, about 1841, who died at Brooklyn, 2 Oct. 1867, aged 47. It is now known under an improved form as Thomas's shuttle machine, by whom it was introduced into England in 1846. Many improvements have been since made.

SEXAGESIMA SUNDAY, see *Quadragesima Sunday*, and *Week*.

SEXTANT, an instrument used like a quadrant, containing sixty degrees, or the sixth part of a circle, invented by Tycho Brahe, at Augsburg, in 1550. The Arabian astronomers are said to have had a sextant of fifty-nine feet nine inches radius, about 995.

---

* *The utilisation of disinfected sewage* as manure is now much advocated. Great success is said to have been attained at Edinburgh, Carlisle, Croydon, and other places. Much hot controversy has arisen respecting this disposal of the London sewage. On 15 Nov. 1864, the Metropolitan board accepted a contract for its disposal from Messrs. Hope and Napier. Sewage Utilisation acts were passed in 1865 and 1867, and the Metropolitan Sewage and Essex Reclamation acts were passed in June, 1865. The sewage farm, near Barking, Essex, was reported to be flourishing in 1868: good grass and corn crops raised.

SEYCHELLES ISLES (Indian Ocean), settled by the French about 1768; captured by the British, 1794; ceded to them, 1815.

SFAXEES, see *Tunis*.

SHAFTESBURY'S ACT, LORD, 18 & 19 Vict. c. 86 (1855), relates to religious worship.

SHAFTESBURY MEMORIALS, relating to the earl of Shaftesbury, celebrated for his lifelong exertions to ameliorate the condition of the working classes, the poor and destitute, women and children. He died 1 Oct. 1885, aged 84. A large sum was subscribed for two statues and a national convalescent home, Oct. 1885. A statue uncovered in Westminster Abbey by the baroness Burdett Coutts, 1 Oct. 1888.

SHAFTESBURY PARK ESTATE, near Wandsworth, London, S.W., a model village, and termed "a workman's city;" built here for clerks, artizans, and labourers, by a company, was opened by the earl of Shaftesbury, 3 Nov. 1873, and 18 July, 1874.

SHAKERS, an English sect, now chiefly found in America, arose in the time of Charles I., and derived its name from their voluntary convulsion. It existed for a short time only, but was revived by James Wardley in 1747, and still more by Ann Lee (or Standless), expelled quakers, about 1757. The sect emigrated to America, May, 1772, and settled near Albany, New York, 1774. They denounce marriage as sinful, regard celibacy as holy, oppose war, disown baptism and the Lord's supper, and use dancing as part of their worship. *Marsden*. One of their elders, Fred. W. Evans, lectured in London, Aug. 1871.

Above a hundred of them settled in the New Forest, near Lymington, Hampshire, on property obtained for them by a Miss Wood; not paying the interest of a mortgage they were ejected in severe weather, and suffered much; end of Dec. 1874. They are called Girlingites, from Mrs. Girling, a leader among them, who died 18 Sept. 1886. The community then gradually dispersed.
Goods seized for debt, about 27 July; expelled, 22 Aug.; permitted to remain in the neighbourhood, Oct. 1878.
Miss Wood was confined as a lunatic, 27 Feb. 1875.
20 men and 40 women half-starved in the New Forest; will not work for hire, Jan. 1884.

SHAKSPEARE'S PLAYS. William Shakspeare was born at Stratford-upon-Avon, Warwickshire, 23 April, 1564, and died on his birthday, 1616. The first collected edition of his works is dated 1623 [a facsimile of this edition was published, 1862-5];* the second, 1632;* the third, 1664; the fourth, 1685; all in folio. Critical editions of the text, edited by Alexander Dyce, were published in 1857 and 1864-6; Boydell's edition, with numerous plates, was published in nine vols., folio, in 1802. Ayscough's Index to Shakspeare was published in 1790; Twiss's Index, in 1805, and Mrs. Cowden Clarke's Concordance, 1847; "Key to Shakspeare," 1879; Shakspeare-Lexicon, by Alexander Schmidt, 1874-5.

SHAKSPEARE'S GLOBE THEATRE, London, built by him and others, 1594, situated near the spot still called

* In 1849, Mr. J. P. Collier, editor of an edition of Shakspeare, purchased a copy of the second folio, on which was written in pencil, a number of corrections, supposed to have been made soon after the time of publication. At first he thought little of these marks; but in 1853 he was induced to publish "Notes and Emendations" derived from this volume. Much controversy ensued as to the authenticity of these corrections; and in 1859 it was generally agreed that they were of modern date, and consequently of little value. Mr. Collier died aged 94, 17 Sept. 1883.

Bankside. Shakspeare was himself part proprietor; here some of his plays were first produced, and he himself performed in them. It was of a horse-shoe form, partly covered with thatch. After it was licensed, the thatch took fire, through the negligent discharge of a piece of ordinance, and the whole building was consumed, 29 June, 1613. The house was crowded to excess, to witness the play of *Henry VIII.*, but the audience escaped unhurt; see *Globe*.

SHAKSPEARE'S JUBILEE, projected by David Garrick, was celebrated at Stratford-upon-Avon, 6-8 Sept. 1769. A similar festival was kept 23 April, 1836. The tercentenary of Shakspeare's birth was celebrated, with many festivities, at Stratford-upon-Avon, 23-29 April, 1864.

SHAKSPEARE'S HOUSE. In 1847, a number of persons of distinction interested themselves for the preservation of the house in which Shakspeare was born, then actually put up for sale: they held a meeting at the Thatched-House tavern, London, 26 Aug. in that year, and took measures for promoting a subscription set on foot by the Shakspearian Club at Stratford-upon-Avon; and a committee was appointed to carry out their object. In the end Shakspeare's house was sold at the Auction Mart in the city of London, where it was "knocked down" to the United Committee of London and Stratford for the large sum of 3000l. 16 Sept. 1847. In 1856, a learned oriental scholar, John Shakspeare (no relation of the poet), gave 2500l. to purchase the adjoining house, that it might be pulled down, in order to ensure the poet's house from the risk of fire.

SHAKSPEARE FUND, established in Oct. 1861, to purchase Shakspeare's garden, birth-place estate, and to erect and endow a public library and museum at Stratford-upon-Avon. The catalogue of the library and museum was published, Feb. 1868.

SHAKSPEARE MEMORIAL ASSOCIATION established 1875; eleventh annual meeting at Stratford-upon-Avon 28 April, 1886. A monument surmounted by a statue of Shakspeare, including statues of Shakspearian characters, executed by lord Ronald Gower, presented by him to the association, set up at Stratford-upon-Avon, unveiled by lady Hodgson (the mayoress) 10 Oct. 1888.

Bronze statue of Shakspeare (presented by Mr. William Knighton) erected in the boulevard Haussmann Paris, unveiled 14 Oct. 1888.

The hon. Ignatius Donnelly, an American, reports his discovery of a cryptogram of Francis Bacon in the text of one of the plays in the folio of 1623, and thereon asserts his belief that Bacon was the author of the Shakspeare plays, autumn 1887. His book entitled "The Great Cryptogram: Francis Bacon's cipher in the so-called Shakspeare Plays" was published in 1888.

The SHAKSPEARE LIBRARY, at Birmingham, was founded in 1864, and formally opened, 23 April, 1868; burnt 11 Jan. 1879.

SHAKSPEARE FORGERIES, see *Ireland*.
SHAKSPEARE GALLERY, see *Boydell*.
SHAKSPEARE MEMORIAL THEATRE, Stratford (capable of holding 800); foundation laid by lord Leigh, 23 April, 1877; opened with ceremonies, 23 April 1879.
SHAKSPEARE SOCIETY, issued 20 volumes, 1841-53.
NEW SHAKSPEARE SOCIETY issues works, 1874, *et seq*.
SHAKSPEARIAN SHOW at the Royal Albert Hall, 30 May, 1884.

SHAMROCK. It is said that the shamrock used by the Irish was adopted by Patrick M'Alpine, since called St. Patrick, as a simile of the Trinity, about 432.

SHANGHAI, or SHANGHAE (China), captured by the British, 19 June, 1842; by the Taeping rebels, 7 Sept. 1853; retaken by the imperialists, 1855. The rebels were defeated near Shanghai by the English and French, allies of the emperor, 1 March, 1862; see *China*.

SHARPSBURG (Maryland), see *Antietam*.

SHAWLS, of oriental origin, were introduced into Paris after the return of Napoleon Bonaparte from Egypt, 1801. The manufacture was introduced by Barrow and Watson, in 1784, at Norwich.

SHEEP. 812 SHERIFF.

It began at Paisley and Edinburgh about 1805. *Ure.*

SHEEP were exported from England to Spain, and, the breed being thereby improved, produced the fine Spanish wool, which proved detrimental to our woollen manufacture, 1467. *Anderson.* Their exportation was prohibited on pain of fine and imprisonment, 1522. The number of sheep in the United Kingdom has been variously stated—by some at 43,000,000, by others at 49,000,000, and by more at 60,000,000, in 1840. In 1851 there were imported into England 201,859 sheep and lambs; in 1858, 184,482; in 1864, 496,243. See under *Cattle.* In Aug. and Sept. 1862, many sheep in Wiltshire died of smallpox; and on Sept. 11, government declared its intention of enforcing the act for the prevention of contagion. The evil soon abated. In April, 1866, when the disease reappeared, the preventive regulations were re-issued.

Mortality amongst sheep through flukes, &c., April, 1880
In 1868, 341,155; in 1871, 916,799; 1874, 758,915; 1875, 985,052; 1876, 1,041,329; 1877, 874,055; 1878, 892,125; 1879, 944,888; 1880, 941,121; 1881, 935,144; 1882, 1,124,391; 1883, 1,116,115; 1885, 373,078; 1887, 295,961. For number in Great Britain, see under *Cattle.*

SHEEPSHANKS' DONATIONS. On 2 Feb. 1857, Mr. John Sheepshanks, by a deed of gift, presented to the nation his valuable collection of paintings and drawings, valued at 60,000*l*. In accordance with the donor's directions, the pictures were placed in the South Kensington Museum. The collection is rich in the works of Mulready, Landseer, and Leslie. He died 5 Oct. 1863.—On 2 Dec. 1858, the trustees of his brother, the late rev. Richard Sheepshanks, presented 10,000*l*. stock to Trinity college, Cambridge, for the promotion of the study of astronomy, meteorology, and magnetism.

SHEERNESS (N. Kent), a royal dockyard, planned by Charles II. in 1663, was taken by the Dutch, under De Ruyter, 9 June, 1667. Improved since 1815; new fortifications still in progress.
The old dock church burned; 3 persons killed,
26 Nov. 1881

SHEFFIELD, on the river *Sheaf,* West Riding, Yorkshire; renowned for cutlery, plated goods, &c. Sheffield thwytles are mentioned by Chaucer, in the time of Edward III. Sheffield in the time of the Conqueror was obtained by Roger de Buisli, and has since been held by the Lovetots, Nevils, Talbots, and Howards. See *Population.*

St. Peter's church built temp. Henry I.
Hospital and almshouses erected by the earl of
  Malmesbury 1616
Cutlers' company incorporated 1624
The castle (built in the 13th century) was taken by
  the parliamentarians, and demolished . . 1648
Cutlers' hall built 1726
Plate assay office established 1773
Made a borough by the Reform act . . . 1832
Wesley college opened 1838
Sheffield and Manchester railway opened . . 1845
Athenæum and Mechanics' Institution opened . 1849
John A. Roebuck (grandson of Dr. Roebuck of
  Sheffield), M.P. for Sheffield . . May, 1849-68
Embankment of the Bradfield water reservoir broke
  down, and flooded Sheffield and the country 12 or
  14 miles round; about 250 lives were lost; many
  buildings and much property destroyed; estimated loss, 327,000*l*. . . . . 11 March, 1854
52,751*l*. collected for the sufferers by . 29 April, „
The Surrey music hall burnt . . 25 March, 1865
House of Fearnehough, a non-unionist saw-grinder,
  blown up, attributed to unionists (no deaths),
8 Oct. 1866

Great excitement; meetings held; subscriptions made; a Sheffield manufacturers' protection society formed; and rewards offered, 12 Oct, &c. 1866
A commission (headed by Mr. Overend) to enquire
  into trade outrages met . . . 3 June-8 July, 1867
[Several murders and outrages (including the above)
  confessed to by Crookes, Hallam, and others,
  instigated and paid by Wm. Broadhead, secretary
  to the saw-grinders' union; indemnity granted.]
A meeting of workmen expresses abhorrence, 8 July, „
Mr. Roebuck loses his election (through opposing
  rattening) . . . . Nov. 1868
Great loss of life and property by storm of wind
16 Dec. 1873
Mr. Roebuck re-elected M.P. . . . Feb. 1874
Five board schools opened by the abp. of York,
  Mr. Roebuck, Mr. Forster, and others, 18 Aug. „
Prince and princess of Wales open Firth park, the
  gift of Mark Firth, the mayor; most enthusiastically received . . . . . . 16 Aug. 1875
Public museum and hall opened . . 6 Sept. „
Eighteenth Church Congress held here, 1-4 Oct. 1878
Great distress through stoppage of work, winter, 1878-9
Institution for the blind, endowed by Mr. Daniel
  Holy; opened . . . . . . 24 Sept. 1879
Firth College, built by Mr. Mark Firth, for 20,000*l*.;
  endowed by the town; inaugurated by prince
  Leopold . . . . 20 Oct. „
Death of Mr. Roebuck, M.P. for Sheffield, 30 Nov. „
Ruskin Museum of Art, &c. founded by Mr. John
  Ruskin, by gifts of historical sculpture, paintings,
  books, &c. 1881
New corn exchange, built by the duke of Norfolk,
  cost 55,000*l*., opened . . . . 13 Dec. „
Ruskin Society formed . . . . . Feb. 1882
Great conservative demonstration (marquis of Salisbury and others) . . . . . 22 July, 1884
Returns five M.P's. by act passed . . 25 June, 1885
Technical school opened . . . . 1 Feb. 1886
Explosion at Don steel works, Brightside, while
  casting a gun; 9 killed . . . . 6 Sept. 1887
Severe epidemic of small pox March 1887,-April, 1888

SHELBURNE ADMINISTRATION, formed at the death of the marquis of Rockingham, July, 1782; terminated April, 1783; the "Coalition" administration followed.
The earl of Shelburne* (afterwards marquis of Lansdowne), *first lord of the treasury.*
William Pitt, *chancellor of the exchequer.*
Lord (afterwards earl) Camden, *president of the council.*
Duke of Grafton, *privy seal.*
Thomas, lord Grantham, and Thomas Townshend (afterwards lord Sydney), *secretaries.*
Viscount Keppel, *admiralty.*
Duke of Richmond, *ordnance.*
Lord Thurlow, *lord chancellor.*
Henry Dundas, Isaac Barré, sir George Yonge, &c.

SHELLEY SOCIETY, founded by Dr. F. J. Furnivall, and Messrs. H. Sweet, W. M. Rossetti, Todhunter, and others, 1885.

SHELLS, see *Bombs.*

SHERIFF, or *shire-reeve,* governor of a shire or county. London had its sheriffs prior to William I.'s reign, but some say that sheriffs were first nominated for every county in England by William in 1079. According to other historians, Henry Cornhill and Richard Reynere were the first sheriffs of London, 1 Rich. I., 1189. The nomination of sheriffs, according to the present mode, took place in 1461. *Stow.* Anciently sheriffs were hereditary in Scotland, and in some English counties, as Westmoreland. The sheriffs of Dublin (first called bailiffs) were appointed in 1308, and obtained the name of sheriff by an incorporation of Edward VI. 1548. Thirty-five sheriffs were fined, and eleven excused in one year, rather than serve the

* William Petty, earl of Shelburne, born 1737; secretary of state under lord Chatham, July, 1766; premier, 1782-3; created f.rst marquis of Lansdowne, 1784; died, 7 May, 1805.

-office for London, 1734; see *Bailiffs*. The high sheriffs of the counties of England and Wales, except Middlesex and Lancaster, are nominated on the morrow of St. Martin, Nov. 12. This somewhat vice-regal office, of Saxon origin, has gradually lost much of its importance. The sheriffs' act passed. 1887

SHERIFFMUIR, see *Dumblane*.

SHERIFF'S FUND, see *Prisons*.

SHETLAND ISLES, see *Orkneys*.

SHIBBOLETH, the word by which the followers of Jephthah tested their opponents the Ephraimites, on passing the Jordan, about 1143 B.C. *Judges* xii. The term is now applied to any party watchword or dogma.

SHIITES, the Mahometan sect predominating in Persia; see *Mahometanism*.

SHILLING. The value of the ancient Saxon coin of this name was fivepence, but it was reduced to fourpence about a century before the conquest. After the conquest the French *solidus* of twelve pence, in use among the Normans, was called *shilling*. The true English shilling was first coined, some say, in small numbers, by Henry VII., 1504. *Ruding*. A peculiar shilling, value nine pence, but to be current at twelve, was struck in Ireland, 1560; and a large but very base coinage in England for the service of Ireland, 1598. Milled shillings were coined 13 Chas. II. 1662; see *Coins*.

SHILOH, see *Pittsburg*.

SHIP-BUILDING. The first ship (probably a galley) was brought from Egypt to Greece, by Danaus, 1485 B.C. *Blair*. The first double-decked ship was built by the Tyrians, 786 B.C. *Lenglet*. The first double-decked one built in England was of 1000 tons burthen, by order of Henry VII., was called the *Great Harry*, and cost 14,000l. *Stow*. Port-holes and other improvements were invented by Descharges, a French builder at Brest, in the reign of Louis XII., about 1500. Ship-building was first treated as a science by Hoste, 1696. A 74-gun ship was put upon the stocks at Van Diemen's Land, to be sheathed with India-rubber, 1829. Iron is now greatly used in ship-building.

A prehistoric ship cut out of solid oak, 48 feet long, 4 feet 4 inches wide, and 2 feet deep, was found by the Brigg gas company while excavating near the river Ancholme in Lincolnshire, April, 1885. Mr. Justice Chitty decided 5 July, 1886, that the ship was the property of the owner of the land, Mr. Elwes.

See *Navy, Steam, Carrack*, &c.

SHIPKA, see *Schipka*.

SHIP-MONEY was first levied about 1007, to form a navy to oppose the Danes. This impost, levied by Charles I. in 1634-6, was much opposed, and led to the revolution. He assessed London in seven ships, of 4000 tons, and 1560 men; Yorkshire in two ships, of 600 tons or 12,000l.; Bristol in one ship of 100 tons; Lancashire in one ship, of 400 tons. Among others, John Hampden refused to pay the tax; he was tried in the Exchequer in 1636. The judges declared the tax legal, 12 June, 1637. Ship-money was included in the grievances complained of in 1641. The five judges, who had given an opinion in its favour, were imprisoned. Hampden received a wound in a skirmish with prince Rupert, at Chalgrove, 18 June, and died 24 June, 1643.

SHIPPING, BRITISH. Shipping was first registered in the river Thames in 1786; and throughout the empire in 1787. In the middle of the 18th century, the shipping of England was but half-a-million of tons—less than London now. In 1830, the number of ships in the British empire was 22,785. The merchant shipping act of 1854 was amended in 1867; see *Merchant Shipping Act, Navy,* and *Navigation Acts*.

Shipwrights' Company International Exhibition, opened at Fishmongers' Hall, London, by the duke of Edinburgh . . . . 2 May, 1882
Chamber of Shipping of the United Kingdom was established in 1878, mainly by H. J. Atkinson, M.P., the first president. Meetings are held for discussing matters relative to shipping and to disseminate information. It holds annual meetings: 1878, Hull; 1879, Liverpool; 1880, London; 1881, Cardiff; 1882, London; 1883, Sunderland; 1884, London; 1885, Belfast; 1886, London; 1887, Newcastle-on-Tyne; 1888 and 1889, London. The chamber has an office at Whittington-avenue, Leadenhall-street, London.
A general meeting of shipowners at Newcastle-on-Tyne to form a defence association against seamens' strikes; committee appointed 14 June, 1839

NUMBER OF VESSELS REGISTERED IN THE BRITISH EMPIRE ON JAN. 1, 1840.

Country.	Vessels.	Tonnage.	Seamen.
England	15,830	1,983,522	114,593
Scotland	3,318	378,194	25,909
Ireland	1,889	169,289	11,288
Guernsey, Jersey, and Man	633	39,630	4,473
British Plantations	6,075	497,798	35,020
Total	27,745	3,068,433	191,283

The following are the numbers of the Registered Sailing and Steam Vessels (exclusive of River Steamers) of the United Kingdom, engaged in the home and foreign trade:—

	1849.		1861.		1871.		1877.		1887.	
	Vessels*	Tonnage.	Vessels†	Tonnage.	Vessels‡	Tonnage.	Vessels§	Tonnage.	Vessels‖	Tonnage.
Sailing	17,807	2,988,021	19,288	3,918,511	19,650	4,343,558	17,101	4,138,149	12,694	3,114,430
Steamers	414	108,321	997	441,184	2,557	1,290,003	3,218	1,977,489	5,029	4,009,324
Total	18,221	3,096,342	20,285	4,359,695	22,207	5,633,561	20,319	6,115,638	17,723	7,123,754

* Men employed—sailing vessels, 144,165; steamers, 8,446; total, 152,611.
† ,, ,, ,, ,, 144,949; ,, 27,008; ,, 171,957.
‡ ,, ,, ,, ,, 141,035; ,, 58,703; ,, 199,738.
§ ,, ,, ,, ,, 123,563; ,, 72,999; ,, 196,562.
‖ ,, ,, ,, ,, 81,442; ,, 121,101; ,, 202,543.

SHIP-RAILWAY, see under *Mexico*.

SHIPWRECKS, see *Wrecks*.

SHIRES, see *Counties*.

SHIRTS are said to have been first generally worn in the west of Europe early in the 8th century. *Du Fresnoy*. Woollen shirts were commonly worn in England until about 1253, when linen, but of a coarse kind (fine coming at this period from abroad), was first manufactured in England by Flemish artisans. *Stow*.

SHODDY, a kind of soft woollen goods, manufactured from old woollen rags, or the refuse, to which new wool is added, is stated to have been first manufactured about 1813, at Batley, near Dewsbury, Yorkshire.

SHOEBLACK SOCIETY Brigades (Blue, Red, and Yellow) were established at various times, especially in 1851, by the Ragged School Union (*which see*), founded 1844. In 1855, 108 boys had cleaned 544,800 pairs of boots and shoes, and thus earned 2270*l*.; of which 1235*l*. had been paid to the boys, 519*l*. to their bank, and 516*l*. to the society. The brigades earned 4548*l*. in 1859; 11,031*l*. in 1871; 10,936*l*. (in nine districts) in 1886. There were eleven shoeblack societies in the metropolis in 1888.

SHOEBURYNESS (Essex). Some ground here, purchased in 1842 and 1855, by an act of parliament in 1862 was set apart as "ranges for the use and practice of artillery," and a school for gunnery was established; see *Cannon*, note. Experiments with Mr. Whitworth's projectiles on 12 Nov. 1862, showed their great improvement in form and material. Shells were sent through 5½ inch plate and the wood-work behind it. It was objected, that they might not do this with ships in motion. The National Volunteer Artillery Association began their annual meetings here in July, 1865.

During shell experiments with a new sensitive fuse, col. Francis Lyon (the inventor), col. Fox-Strangways, capt. Francis M. Goold-Adams, and four others were killed, 26 Feb. 1885.

SHOES, among the Jews were made of leather, linen, rush, or wood. Moons were worn as ornaments in their shoes by Jewish women. *Isaiah* iii. 18. Pythagoras would have his disciples wear shoes made of the bark of trees; probably that they might not wear what were made of the skins of animals, as they refrained from the use of everything that had life. The Romans wore an ivory crescent on their shoes; and Caligula enriched his with precious stones. In England, about 1462, the people wore the beaks or points of their shoes so long that they encumbered themselves in walking, and were forced to tie them up to their knees; the fine gentlemen fastened theirs with chains of silver or silver gilt, and others with laces. This was prohibited, on the forfeiture of 20*s*. and on pain of being cursed by the clergy, 7 Edw. IV. 1467; see *Dress*. Shoes, as at present worn, were introduced about 1633. The buckle was not used till 1668. *Stow; Mortimer*. The buckle-makers petitioned against the use of *shoe-strings* in 1791. A strike of London shoemakers respecting wages, April, 1884.

SHOOTING STARS, see under *Meteors*.

SHOP HOURS' REGULATION ACT (Sir John Lubbock's), for the protection of young persons, passed, 1886.

SHOP-TAX enacted in 1785; caused so great a commotion, particularly in London, that it was deemed expedient to repeal it in 1789. The statute whereby *shoplifting* was made a felony, without benefit of clergy, was passed 10 & 11 Will. III. 1699. This statute has been some time repealed.

SHORE, JANE, the mistress of Edward IV. and afterwards of lord Hastings. She did public penance in 1483, and was afterwards confined in Ludgate; but upon the petition of Thomas Hymore, who agreed to marry her, king Richard III., in 1484, restored her to liberty; and sir Thomas More mentions having seen her. *Harleian MSS*.

SHORT-HAND, see *Stenography*.

"SHORT - LIVED" ADMINISTRATION—that of William Pulteney, earl of Bath, lord Carlisle, lord Winchelsea, and lord Granville, existed from 10 Feb. to 12 Feb. 1746.

SHOT. In early times various missiles were shot from cannon. Bolts are mentioned in 1413; and in 1418 Henry V. ordered his clerk of the ordnance to get 7000 stone shot made at the quarries at Maidstone. Since then chain, grape, and canister shot have been invented, as well as shells; all of which are described in Scoffern's work on "Projectile Weapons of War, and Explosive Compounds," 1858; see *Bombs* and *Cannon*.

SHREWSBURY ADMINISTRATION. Charles, duke of Shrewsbury, was made lord treasurer, 29 July, 1714, two days before the death of queen Anne. His patent was revoked soon after the accession of George I., 29 Oct. following, when the earl of Halifax became first lord of the treasury; see *Halifax*. The office of lord treasurer has been executed by commissioners ever since.

SHREWSBURY (Shropshire), arose after the ruin of the Roman town Uriconium (see *Wroxeter*), and became one of the chief cities of the kingdom, having a mint till the reign of Henry III. Here Richard II. held a parliament in 1397.—On 23 July, 1403, was fought a sanguinary *battle* at Hateley field, near Shrewsbury, between the army of Henry IV. and that of the nobles, led by Percy (surnamed Hotspur), son of the earl of Northumberland, who had conspired to dethrone Henry. Henry was seen in the thickest of the fight, with his son, afterwards Henry V. The death of Hotspur by an unknown hand gave the victory to the king. *Hume*.—Shrewsbury grammar school was founded by Edward VI. in 1551, endowed by Elizabeth, and opened 1562. Its arrangements were modified by the public school act, 1868.

SHROPSHIRE, BATTLE OF, in which the Britons were completely subjugated, and Caractacus, the renowned king of the Silures, became, through the treachery of the queen of the Brigantes, a prisoner to the Romans, 50.

SHROVE TUESDAY, the day before Ash-Wednesday, the first day of the Lent Fast; see *Carnival*.

SIAM, a kingdom in India, bordering on the Burmese empire. Siam was governed by two kings, one inferior, till Jan. 1887, when the second king being dead, the dignity was abolished. Siam was re-discovered by the Portuguese in 1511, and a trade established, in which the Dutch joined about 1604. A British ship arrived about 1613. In 1683, a Cephalonian Greek, Constantine Phaulcon, became foreign minister of Siam, and opened a communication with France; Louis XIV. sent an embassy in 1685 with a view of converting the king, without effect. After several ineffectual attempts, sir John Bowring suc-

ceeded in obtaining a treaty of friendship and commerce between England and Siam, which was signed 30 April, 1855, and ratified 5 April, 1856. Two ambassadors from Siam arrived in Oct. 1857, and had an audience with the queen; they brought with them magnificent presents, which they delivered crawling, on 16 Nov. They visited Paris in June, 1861. By a treaty with France, the French protectorate over Cambodia was recognised; signed 15 July, ratified 24 Oct. 1867. The king Khoulalonkorn, born 21 Sept. 1853, has reigned since 1 Oct. 1868; the king was entertained at Calcutta, 7-12 Jan. 1872; a political constitution was decreed, 8 May, 1874. Queen Victoria receives the order of the White Elephant from the Siamese minister at Windsor, 2 July, 1880. Population of Siam (1885) about 6,300,000.

King: Khoulalonkorn (born 21 Sept. 1853); succeeded his father Mongkout, 1 Oct. 1868.

Various changes and political reforms were begun by the king, 16 Nov. 1873. On 9 Oct., 1874, he invited astronomers to Bangkok to view the eclipse of 5 April, 1875. Death of the able ex-regent Somdetch Chau, 19 Jan. 1883.

Telegraphic communication with France opened, 14 July, 1883.

Gradual abolition of slavery nearly completed Aug. 1886.

SIAMESE TWINS. Two persons born about 1811, enjoying all the faculties and powers usually possessed by separate and distinct individuals, although united together by a short cartilaginous band at the pit of the stomach. They were named Chang and Eng, and were first discovered on the banks of the Siam river by an American, Mr. Robert Hunter, by whom they were taken to New York, where they were exhibited. Captain Coffin brought them to England. After having been exhibited for several years in Britain, they went to America, where they settled on a farm, and married two sisters. In 1865 they were in North Carolina in declining health. Their exhibition in London began again 8 Feb. 1869. Their death in America, within two hours of each other, took place 16, 17 Jan. 1874.

SIBERIA (N. Asia). In 1580 the conquest was begun by the Cossacks under Jermak Timofejew. In 1710 Peter the Great began to send prisoners thither. An insurrection broke out among the Poles in Siberia in June, 1866, and was soon suppressed. University founded, 1886.

SIBYLS, Sibyllæ, women believed to be inspired, who flourished in different parts of the world. Plato speaks of one, others of two, Pliny of three, Ælian of four, and Varro of ten. An Erythrean sibyl is said to have offered to Tarquin II. nine books containing the Roman destinies, demanding for them 300 pieces of gold. He denied her; whereupon the sibyl threw three of them into the fire, and asked the same price for the other six, which being still denied, she burnt three more, and again demanded the same sum for those that remained; when Tarquin conferring with the pontiffs was advised to buy them. Two magistrates were created to consult them on all occasions, 531 B.C.; see *Quindecemvirs.*

SICILIAN VESPERS, the term given to the massacre of the French (who had conquered Sicily, 1266), commenced at Palermo, 30 March, 1282.

On Easter Monday conspirators assembled at Palermo; and while the French were engaged in festivities, a Sicilian bride passed by with her train. One Drochet, a Frenchman, used her rudely, under pretence of searching for arms. A young Sicilian stabbed him with his own sword; and a tumult ensuing, 200 French were instantly murdered. The populace ran through the city, crying out, "Let the French die!" and, without distinction of rank, age, or sex, slaughtered all of that nation they could find, to the number of about 8000. Even the churches proved no sanctuary, and the massacre became general throughout the island.

SICILY (anciently *Trinacria,* three-cornered). The early inhabitants were the Sicani, or Siculi, a people of Spain, and Etruscans, who came from Italy about 1291 B.C. A second colony, under Siculus, arrived eighty years before the destruction of Troy, 1284 B.C. The Phœnicians and Greeks settled some colonies here (735-582). It is supposed that Sicily was separated from Italy by an earthquake, and that the straits of the Charybdis were thus formed. Its government has frequently been united with and separated from that of Naples (*which see*); the two now form part of the kingdom of Italy. Population of Sicily in 1856, 2,231,020; 1871, 2,565,323; 1875, 2,698,672; 1887, 3,192,108.

Syracuse founded. *Eusebius* . . . about B.C.	732
Gela founded. *Thucydides.* . . . 680 or	713
Agrigentum founded	582
Phalaris, tyrant of Agrigentum, put to death. See *Brazen Bull*	549
Law of Petalism instituted	460
Athenian expedition fails	413
War with Carthage	409
Dionysius becomes master of Syracuse, makes peace with the Carthaginians and reigns .	406-367
Dionysius II. sells Plato for a slave, who is ransomed by his friends	360
Dionysius expelled by Timoleon . . .	343
Who governs well; and dies . . .	337
Agathocles usurps sovereign power at Syracuse, 317; defeated at Himera by the Carthaginians, 310; poisoned	289
Pyrrhus, king of Epirus, invades Sicily; expels the Carthaginians from most of their settlements, but returns to Italy	278-277
The Romans enter Sicily (see *Punic Wars*) .	264
Agrigentum taken by the Romans . .	262
Palermo besieged by the Romans . .	254
Archimedes flourishes . . . . about	236
Hiero II. defeated by the Romans, 263; becomes their ally, and reigns till . . .	216
The Romans take Syracuse, and make all Sicily a province; Archimedes slain . . .	212
The Carthaginians lose half their possessions, 241; all the remainder	..
The Servile wars; much slaughter . . 135, 134,	132
Tyrannical government of Verres (for which he was accused by Cicero)	73-71
Sicily held by Sextus Pompeius, son of the great Pompey, 42; defeated; expelled . .	36
Invaded by the Vandals, A.D. 440; by the Goths, 493; taken for the Greek emperors by Belisarius, A.D.	535
Conquered by the Saracens . . .	832-78
The Greeks and Arabs driven out by a Norman prince, Roger I., son of Tancred, 1058; who takes the title of count of Sicily . . .	1061-1093
Roger II., son of the above-named, unites Sicily with Naples, and is crowned king of the Two Sicilies	1131
Charles of Anjou, brother of St. Louis, king of France, conquers Naples and Sicily, deposes the Norman princes, and makes himself king .	1266
The French massacred (see *Sicilian Vespers*) .	1282
Sicily seized by a fleet sent by the kings of Aragon; Naples remains to the house of Anjou .	..
Alphonso, king of Aragon, takes possession of Naples	1435
The kingdom of Naples and Sicily united to the Spanish monarchy under Ferdinand the Catholic	1501
Victor, duke of Savoy, by the treaty of Utrecht, made king of Sicily	1713
Which he gives up to the emperor Charles VI., and becomes king of Sardinia . . .	1720
Charles, son of the king of Spain, becomes king of the Two Sicilies	1735
The throne of Spain becoming vacant, Charles, who is heir, vacates the throne of the Two Sicilies, in favour of his third son Ferdinand, agreeably to treaty	1759
Dreadful earthquake at Messina, in Sicily, which destroys 40,000 persons . . .	1783
The French conquer Naples (*which see*); Ferdinand IV. retires to Sicily	1806
Political disturbances	1810

| SICILY. | 816 | SIEGES. |

New constitution granted, under British auspices . 1812
The French expelled; kingdom of Two Sicilies re-established; Ferdinand returns to Naples; abolishes the constitution 1815
Revolution at Palermo suppressed 1820
The great towns in Sicily rise and demand the constitution; a provisional government proclaimed
    12 Jan. 1848
The king nominates his brother, the count of Aquila, viceroy, 17 Jan.; promises a new constitution
    29 Jan. ,,
The Sicilian parliament decrees the exclusion of the Bourbon family, 13 April; and invites the duke of Genoa to the throne . . . . 11 July, ,,
Messina bombarded and taken by the Neapolitans
    7 Sept. ,,
Catania taken by assault, 6 April; Syracuse surrenders 23 April; and Palermo . . 15 May, 1849
Insurrections suppressed at Palermo, Messina, and Catania, 4 April et seq.; the rebels retire into the interior . . . . . 21 April et seq. 1860
Garibaldi and his followers (2200 men) embark at Genoa, 5 May; and land at Marsala, 11 May; he abandons his ships; and assumes the dictatorship in the name of the king of Sardinia . 14 May, ,,
He defeats the royal troops at Calatafimi, 15 May; storms Palermo, 27 May; which is bombarded by the royal fleet, 28 May; an armistice agreed to
    31 May, ,,
A provisional government formed at Palermo, 3 June; which is evacuated by the Neapolitans
    6 June, ,,
Garibaldi defeats the Neapolitans at Melazzo,
    20, 21 July, ,,
Convention signed, by which the Neapolitans agree to evacuate Sicily (retaining the citadel of Messina) . . . . . . 30 July, ,,
New Sicilian constitution proclaimed . 3 Aug. ,,
Garibaldi embarks for Calabria (see *Naples*)
    19 Aug. ,,
Professor Saffi (late of Oxford), a short time dictator . . . . Sept. ,,
The Sicilians by universal suffrage vote for annexation to Sardinia (432,054 against 667) 21 Oct. ,,
Victor-Emmanuel visits Sicily . . 1 Dec. ,,
Citadel of Messina blockaded, 28 Feb.; surrenders to general Cialdini . . . 13 March, 1861
King Victor-Emmanuel warmly received at Messina
    May, 1862
Imprudent speeches of Garibaldi at Marsala, 19 July; he enters Catania, and establishes a provisional government, 19 Aug.; embarks for Italy
    24 Aug. ,,
Sicily placed under blockade; removed in Sept.; tranquil . . . . Oct. ,,
Insurrection in Palermo, attributed to the priests and brigands, 16 Sept.; suppressed with bloodshed by Italian troops . . 21-26 Sept. 1866
Revival of brigandage and murder . . Aug. 1872
Martial law established in some places . Sept. 1874
Aliano, a brigand, tried at Potenza, for numerous murders, and other crimes . . . Nov. ,,
Capraro, great brigand, killed during capture
    about 2 Oct. 1875

Mr. Forester Rose carried off by brigands, 3 Nov.; ransomed for about 4000l. . . . Nov. 1876
Leone and other brigands surrounded and shot
    1 June, 1877
Five chief brigands surrender; abatement of brigandage announced . . about 6 Nov. ,,
Successful visit of the king and queen; arrive at Palermo . . . . . . 4 Jan. 1880
Explosion in sulphur mine at Gessolungo, near Caltanissetta, about 30 killed . 12 Nov. 1881
Violent cyclone in Catania, about 27 killed; 200,000l. damage . . . . . . 7 Oct. 1884

SICK CHILDREN, HOSPITAL FOR, Great Ormond-street, London; established 1851. The princess of Wales laid the foundation of new buildings, 11 July, 1872. A branch has been set up at Highgate.

"SICK MAN," an epithet applied to Turkey, by the czar Nicholas, 14 Jan. 1854; see *Russo-Turkish War*, note.

SICYON, an ancient Grecian kingdom in the Peloponnesus, founded, it is said, about 2080 B.C. Its people took part in the wars in Greece, usually supporting Sparta. In 252 it became a republic and joined the Achæan league formed by Aratus. It was the country of the sculptors Polycletes (436) and Lysippus (328 B.C.).

SIDEROSTAT (from *sidus*, Latin for a star), an apparatus constructed by M. Leon Foucault, shortly before his death, 11 Feb. 1868, for observing the light of the stars in precisely the same way in which the light of the sun may be studied in the camera obscura. It consists of a mirror moved by clockwork, and a fixed objective glass for concentrating the rays into a focus.

SIDON or ZIDON (Syria), a city of Phœnicia, to the north of Tyre. It was conquered by Cyrus about 537 B.C.; and surrendered to Alexander, 332 B.C.; see *Phœnicia*. The town was taken from the pacha of Egypt by the troops of the sultan and of his allies, assisted by some ships of the British squadron, under commodore Charles Napier, 27 Sept. 1840; see *Syria*, and *Turkey*.

SIEGES. Azoth, which was besieged by Psammetichus the Powerful, held out for nineteen years. *Usher*. It held out for twenty-nine years. *Herodotus*. This was the longest siege recorded in the annals of antiquity. The siege of Troy was the most celebrated, and occupied ten years, 1184 B.C. The following are the most memorable sieges since the 12th century; for details of many of them see separate articles.

Acre, 1192, 1799, 1832, 1840.
Algesiras, 1341.
Algiers, 1681 (*Bomb vessels first used by a French engineer named Renan*); 1816.
Alkmaer, 1573.
Almeida, 27 Aug. 1810.
Amiens, 1597.
Ancona, 1174, 1799, 1860.
Antwerp, 1576, 1583, 1585, 1746, 1832.
Arras, 1640.
Azoff, 1736.
Badajoz, 11 March, 1811; 6 April, 1812.
Bagdad, 1258.
Barcelona, 1697, 1714.
Belgrade, 1439, 1456, 1521, 1688, 1717, 1739, 1789.
Belle-Isle, 1761.
Bergen-op-Zoom, 1622, 1747, 1814.
Berwick, 1333, 1481.
Bethune, 1710.

Bilbao by Carlists, 1874.
Bois-le-Duc, 1603, 1794.
Bologna, 1512, 1796, 1799.
Bommel: *the invention of the covered way*, 1794.
Bonn, 1672, 1689, 1703.
Bouchain, 1711.
Boulogne, 1544.
Breda, 1625.
Brescia, 1238, 1512, 1849.
Breslau, 1807.
Brisac, 1638, 1704.
Brussels, 1695, 1746.
Bomarsund, 1854.
Buda, 1541, 2 Sept. 1686.
Burgos, 1812, 1813.
Cadiz, 1812.
Calais 1347 (*British historians affirm that cannon were used at Cressy, 1346, and here in 1347. First used here in 1388. RYMER'S FŒD.*), 1558, 1596.

Calvi, 1794.
Candia: *the largest cannon then known in Europe, used here by the Turks*, 1667.
Carthagena, 1706-7, 1740, 1873-4.
Chalus, 1199.
Charleroi, 1693.
Charleston, U.S., 1864-5.
Chartres, 1568.
Cherbourg, 1758.
Ciudad Rodrigo, 1810, 1812.
Colchester, 1648.
Comorn, 1849.
Compiègne (*Joan of Arc*), 1430.
Condé, 1676, 1793; 1794.
Coni, 1691, 1744.
Constantinople, 1453.
Copenhagen, 1658, 1801, 1807.
Corfu, 1716.
Courtray, 1646.
Cracow, 1702.
Cremona, 1702.

Dantzic, 1734, 1793, 1807, 1813, 1814.
Delhi, 1857.
Douay, 1710.
Dresden, 1756, 1813.
Drogheda, 1649.
Dublin, 1500.
Dunkirk, 1646, 1793.
Famagosta, 1571.
Flushing, 15 Aug. 1809.
Frederickshald; *Charles XII. killed*, 1718.
Gaeta, 1435, 1734, 1860-1.
Genoa, 1747, 1800.
Gerona, 1809.
Ghent, 1708.
Gibraltar, 1734, 1779, 1782-3.
Glatz, 1742, 1807.
Gottingen, 1760.
Graves, 1674.
Grenada, 1491, 1492.
Groningen, 1594.
Haerlem, 1572, 1573.
Harfleur, 1415.
Heidelberg, 1688.
Herat, 1838.
Humaitá, 1868.
Ismail, 1790.
Kars, 1855.
Khartoum, 1884.
Kehl, 1733, 1796.
Landau, 1702 *et seq.*, 1792.
Landrecy, 1712, 1794.
Laon, 988, 991.
Leipsic, 1757 *et seq.*, 1813.
Leith, 1560.
Lerida, 1647, 1707, 1810.
Leyden, 1574.
Liege, 1408, 1688, 1702.
Lille, 1708, 1792.
Limerick, 1651, 1691.
Londonderry, 1689.
Louisbourg, 1758.
Luxemburg, 1795.
Lyons, 1793.
Maestricht, 1579, 1673; *Vauban first came into notice*; 1676, 1748.
Magdala, 1868.
Magdeburg, 1631, 1806.
Malaga, 1487.
Malta, 1565, 1798, 1800.

Mantua, 1797, 1799.
Marseilles, 1524.
Menin, 1706.
Mentz, 1689, 1793.
Messina, 1282, 1719, 1848, 1861.
Metz, 1552-3, 1870.
Mons, 1691, 1709, 1792.
Montargis, 1426.
Montanban, 1621.
Montevideo, Jan. 1807.
Mothe: *the French, taught by a Mr. Muller, first practised the art of throwing shells*, 1634.
Namur, 1692, 1746, 1794.
Naples, 1435, 1504, 1557, 1792, 1799, 1806.
Newark, 1644-5.
New Orleans, 1814.
Nice, 1706.
Novogorod, 1478.
Nieuport, 1600.
Olivenza, 1801, 1811.
Olmutz, 1758.
Orleans, 1428, 1563.
Ostend, 1601, 1798.
Oudenarde, 1706.
Padua, 1509.
Pampeluna, 1813.
Paris, 1420, 1594, 1870, 1871.
Parma, 1248.
Pavia, 1524, 1655.
Perpignan, 1542, 1642.
Phalsburg, 1814, 1815, 1870.
Philipsburg, 1644, 1676, 1688, *first experiment of firing artillery à ricochet*, 1734, 1799.
Plevna, 1877.
Pondicherry, 1748, 1793.
Prague, 1741-1744.
Quebec, 1759-60.
Quesnoy, 1793-1794.
Rheims, 1359.
Rhodes, 1521.
Richmond, U.S., 1864-5.
Riga, 1700, 1710.
Rochelle, 1573, 1627.
Rome, 1527, 1798, 1849.
Romorantin: *artillery first used in sieges* (VOLTAIRE), 1356.
Rouen, 1419, 1449, 1591.

Roxburgh, 1460.
St. Sebastian, 1813.
Saragossa, 1710, 1808, 1809; *the two last dreadful*.
Sebastopol, 1854-5.
Schweidnitz: *first experiment to reduce a fortress by springing globes of compression*, 1757-1762.
Scio (see *Greece*), 1822.
Seringapatam, 1799.
Seville, 1247-8.
Silistria, 1854.
Smolensko, 1632, 1812.
Soissons, 1870.
St. Quentin, 1557.
Stralsund: *the method of throwing red-hot balls first practised with certainty*, 1715.
Strasburg, 1870.
Tarragona, 1811.
Temeswar, 1716.
Thérouenne, 1513.
Thionville, 1792.
Thorn, 1703.
Tortosa, 1811.
Toulon, 1707, 1793.
Toulouse, 1217.
Tournay, 1340, 1513, 1583, 1667, 1709 (*this was the best defence ever drawn from counter mines*), 1792.
Treves, 1635, 1673, 1765.
Tunis, 1270, 1535.
Turin, 1640, 1706.
Valencia, 1705, 1707, 1712.
Valenciennes, 1677, 1793, 1794.
Vannes, 1342.
Venice, 1879.
Venloo, 1702.
Verdun, 1792.
Vicksburg, U.S., 1863.
Vienna, 1529, 1683.
Wakefield, 1460.
Warsaw, 1831.
Xativa, 1246.
Xeres, 1262.
York, 1644.
Ypres, 1648.
Zurich, 1544.
Zutphen, 1586.

SIENNA (formerly Sena Julia), Italy, in the middle ages a powerful republic rivalling Florence and Pisa, weakened through intestine quarrels, was subjugated by the emperor Charles V., and given to his son in 1555, who ceded it to Cosmo of Tuscany, 1557. It was incorporated with France, 1808-14.

SIERRA LEONE (W. Africa), discovered in 1460. In 1786, London swarmed with free negroes living in idleness and want; and 400 of them, with sixty whites, mostly women of bad character and in ill-health, were sent out to Sierra Leone, at the charge of government to form a settlement, 9 Dec. 1786. Capital, Freetown. The settlement was attacked by the French, Sept. 1794; by the natives, Feb. 1802. Sir Charles Macarthy, governor of the colony, was defeated and killed by the Ashantee chief, 21 Jan. 1824.—16 & 17 Vict. c. 16, relates to the government, &c., of this colony. It was made a bishopric in 1852; see *Ashantees* and *West Africa*.

Robarrie, the stronghold of the insurgent Yonnie tribe, captured by sir Francis De Winton, 21 Nov. 1887
Further towns and strongholds captured with great slaughter of the natives; the king was captured and the rebellion suppressed Nov-Dec. "
The Gambia territory isolated and made an independent colony . . . . 22 Dec. 1888
Largoh, capital of the chief Mackiah captured by the British under governor Hay; 700 prisoners liberated; announced . . . 14 Feb. 1889

SIGNALS are alluded to by Polybius. Elizabeth had instructions drawn up for the admiral and general of the expedition to Cadiz, to be announced to the fleet in a certain latitude; this is said to have been the first set of signals given to the commanders of the English fleet. A system for the navy was invented by the duke of York, afterwards James II. 1665. *Guthrie*; see *Fog-signals*.

SIGNBOARDS were used by the Greeks and Romans. A "History of Signboards," by Jacob Larwood and John Hotten, was published in 1866.

SIGNETS, see *Seals*.

SIGN MANUAL, ROYAL, a stamp, imitating the royal signature, employed when the sovereign was so ill as to be unable to write: in the case of Henry VIII. 1547; James I. 1625; and George IV., 29 May, 1830. *Rosse.*

SIKHS, originally a Hindu religious sect (about 1500) a people of N. India, invaded the Mogul empire, 1703-8; see *Punjab*, and *India*, 1849.

SIKKIM, a small Himalayan State, joining Tibet, allied to the Indian government since 1814. By a treaty in 1861 free trade and passage through the country were secured.

The erection of a fort by the Rajah under the influence of Tibetans in contravention of the treaty, led to a military demonstration; 1,000 troops sent ostensibly to repair the road to

Tibet, Jan.; the rajah proving contumacious, the viceroy intervened ineffectually, March; about 2,000 men concentrated at Pedong, March; Lingtu fort quickly captured; flight of the Tibetans, 20 March; destruction of the fort ordered 21 March; slight skirmishes with the Tibetans, 24 killed, May; col. Graham defeats the attacking Tibetans, who are said to have lost 200 men . . . . . 23 May, 1888
Troops ordered to return to Darjeeling 17 June, ,,
Return to Sikkim on appearance of Tibetan aggression . . . . . . July, ,,
The Tibetans defeated at Jelapla pass; about 400 killed and wounded, 25 Sept.; col. Graham's advance suspended and the expedition recalled, Sept. ,,
Reported failure of the negotiations with China, 10 Jan. 1889

SILCHESTER, Hants. Here are the remains of the Roman town Calleva (built on the site of the British Caer Segeint or Segont); including walls of excellent masonry, a basilica and forum, private dwellings, &c. Many discoveries have been made during excavations made under the patronage of the duke of Wellington, since 1863. Coins of Claudius I. and later emperors have been found.

SILESIA, formerly a province of Poland, was invaded by John of Bohemia, 1325, and ceded to him, 1355. It was taken by the king of Hungary, 1478, and added to the Austrian dominion, 1526. It was conquered and lost several times during the Seven years' war by Frederick of Prussia, but was retained by him at the peace in 1763. The emperor William was most enthusiastically received during his visit, Sept. 1875.

SILICON or **SILICIUM** (from *silex*, flint), a non-metallic element, next to oxygen the most abundant substance in the earth, as it enters into the constitution of many earths, metallic oxides, and a great number of minerals. The mode of procuring pure silicon was discovered by Berzelius in 1823. *Gmelin*. See *Water-glass*, and *Ransome's Stone*.

SILISTRIA, a strong military town in Bulgaria, European Turkey. It was taken by the Russians, 30 June, 1829, and held some years by them as a pledge for the payment of a large sum by the Porte; but was eventually returned. In 1854 it was again besieged by the Russians, 30,000 strong, under prince Paskiewitch, and many assaults were made. The Russian general was compelled to retire in consequence of a dangerous contusion. On 2 June, Mussa Pacha, the brave and skilful commander of the garrison, was killed. On 9 June, the Russians stormed two forts, which were retaken. A grand assault took place on 13 June, under prince Gortschakoff and general Schilders, which was vigorously repelled. On the 15th, the garrison assumed the offensive, crossed the river, defeated the Russians, and destroyed the siege works. The siege was thus raised, and the Russians commenced their retreat as Omar Pacha was drawing near. The garrison was ably assisted by two British officers, capt. Butler and lieut. Nasmyth, the former of whom, after being wounded, died of exhaustion. They were highly praised by Omar Pacha and lord Hardinge, and lieutenant Nasmyth was made a major.

SILK. Wrought silk was brought from Persia to Greece, 325 B.C. Known at Rome in Tiberius's time, when a law passed in the senate prohibiting the use of plate of massive gold, and also forbidding men to debase themselves by wearing silk, fit only for women. Heliogabalus first wore a garment of silk, A.D. 220. Silk was at first of the same value with gold, weight for weight, and was thought to grow in the same manner as cotton on trees. Silk-worms were brought from India to Europe in the 6th century. Charlemagne sent Offa, king of Mercia, a present of two silken vests, 780. The manufacture was encouraged by Roger, king of Sicily, at Palermo, 1146, when the Sicilians not only bred the silk-worms, but spun and wove the silk. The manufacture spread into Italy and Spain, and also into the south of France, a little before the reign of Francis I. about 1510; and Henry IV. propagated mulberry-trees and silk-worms throughout the kingdom, about 1600. In England, silk mantles were worn by some noblemen's ladies at a ball at Kenilworth castle, 1286. Silk was worn by the English clergy in 1534. Manufactured in England in 1604; and broad silk wove from raw silk in 1620. Brought to perfection by the French refugees in London at Spitalfields, 1688. A silk-throwing mill was made in England, and fixed up at Derby, by sir Thomas Lombe, merchant of London, modelled from the original mill then in the king of Sardinia's dominions, about 1714. He obtained a patent in 1718, and died 3 Jan. 1739. Six new species of silk-worm were rearing in France, 1861.*

SILKWORM DISEASE. In 1853 the annual produce of sericulture in South France was estimated at about 4,680,000*l*. Soon after a disease broke out in the worms, which reduced the value of the silk crop to about one-third that amount. In 1858 a commission was appointed to inquire into the nature of the disease, then termed *pébrine*; and M. Quatrefages, in 1869, proved that it is hereditary, contagious, and infectious. M. Filippi discovered in the blood of the deceased worms a multitude of cylindrical corpuscles, since named *panhistophyton*, which Pasteur, who took up the study in 1865, has demonstrated to be parasitical, and the cause of the disease. He has since devised a way by which, it is hoped, the organic germs may be got rid of, and the disease extirpated.

SILOTVOR, a new explosive invented by M. Rouckteshell, who asked 50,000*l*. for the patent, 1887.

SILURES, a British tribe, occupying the counties of Monmouth and Hereford, was subdued by the Roman general Ostorius Scapula, 50; see *Shropshire*. From this tribe is derived the geological term "Silurian strata," among the lowest of the palæozoic or primary series, from their occurrence in the above-mentioned counties. *Murchison's* "*Siluria*" was published 1849.

SILVER exists in most parts of the world, and is found mixed with other ores in various mines in Great Britain. The silver mines of South America are far the richest. A mine was discovered in the district of La Paz in 1660, which was so rich that the silver of it was often cut out with a chisel. In 1749, one mass of silver weighing 370 lbs. was sent to Spain. From a mine in Norway, a piece of silver was dug, and sent to the Royal Museum at Copenhagen, weighing 560 lbs., and worth 1680*l*. In England silver-plate and vessels were first used by Wilfrid, a Northumbrian bishop, a lofty and ambitious man, 709. *Tyrrell*. Silver knives, spoons, and cups, were great luxuries in 1300; see *Mirrors*. The act of 1816 restricted the use of silver as legal tender to 40s. In 1855, 561,906 oz., in 1857, 532,866 oz., in 1865, 724,856 oz., in 1870, 784,562 oz.; in 1876, 483,422 oz.; in 1882, 372,544 oz.; in 1887, 320,345 oz. were obtained from mines in Britain. Pattinson's process for obtaining silver

* In 1858, M. Guérin-Méneville introduced into France a Chinese worm termed the *Cynthia Bombyx*, which feeds on the *Ailanthus glandulosa*, a hardy tree of the oak kind. The cynthia yields a silk-like substance termed *Allantine*. It was brought to Turin by Fantoni in 1856.

from lead ore was introduced in 1829. See *Bullion, Coins, Goldsmiths, Mirrors, Plate, India*, 1876, *United States*, 1878.

Fall in price of silver through introduction of gold coinage in Germany, and increased produce from South American mines . . . . spring, 1876
The report of a commission on the subject was issued in . . . . July, „
Another commission appointed, see under *Currency*, 7 Sept. 1886
Average price in London, 1845-9, 59*d.* and a fraction per oz.; 1850-72, 61*d.*; 1871, 60$\frac{1}{16}$*d.*; 1875, 56$\frac{1}{4}$*d.*; 1880, 52$\frac{1}{4}$*d.*; 1883, 50$\frac{9}{16}$*d.*; price 49$\frac{1}{2}$*d.* 7 May, 1885; 1886, 46$\frac{1}{16}$*d.*; 1887, 44$\frac{3}{4}$*d.*; 1888, 43$\frac{1}{16}$*d.*; 1889, Jan–March, 42$\frac{1}{16}$*d.*; 3 April, 42$\frac{1}{4}$*d.*; 7 May, 42$\frac{1}{2}$*d.*; June, 42$\frac{1}{8}$*d.*; 22 July, 42$\frac{1}{16}$*d.*

SILVER BOOK (Codex Argenteus), see under *Bible*.

SIMANCAS (Castile, Spain). Near it Ramirez II. of Leon, and Fernando of Castile, gained a great victory over Abderahman, the Moorish king of Cordova, 6 Aug. 938.

SIMLA CASE, see *India*, 1866.

SIMNEL CONSPIRACY, see *Rebellions*, 1486.

SIMONASAKI, see *Japan*, 1864.

SIMONIANS, a sect named after the founder, Simon Magus, the first heretic, about 41. A sect of social reformers called ST. SIMONIANS sprang up in France in 1819, and attracted considerable attention; the doctrines were advocated in England, particularly by Dr. Prati, who lectured upon them in London, 24 Jan. 1834. St. Simon died in 1825, and his follower, Père Enfantin, died 1 Sept. 1864.

SIMONY (trading in church offices), derives its name from Simon desiring to purchase the gift of the Holy Spirit (*Acts* viii. 18, 19). It is forbidden in England by the canon law, and by statute 31 Eliz. c. 6, "for the avoiding of simony and corruption in presentations, collations, and donations of and to benefices," &c., 1588-9; and by statute of 12 Anne 2, stat. 12 (1713). The rev. James John Merest was convicted of simony, 26-29 Nov. 1869, and deprived.

The bishop of Peterborough (Dr. Magee), moved for a committee on the laws relating to simony; appointed . . . . 21 April, 1874

SIMPLON, a mountain road, leading from Switzerland into Italy, constructed by Napoleon in 1801-7. It winds up passes, crosses cataracts, and passes by galleries through solid rock, and has eight principal bridges. The number of workmen employed at one time varied from 30,000 to 40,000.

SINAI, MOUNT. Here the ten commandments were promulgated, 1491 B.C. *Exod. xx.* After much investigation and discussion by many persons, Dr. Beke stated that he had discovered the true Sinai, Feb. 1874.

SINALUNGA or ASINALUNGA (near Sienna, Italy). Here Garibaldi, when about to enter the papal territory, was seized and conveyed to Alessandria, 23 Sept. 1867; see *Italy*.

SINDE (N. W. India), was traversed by the Greeks under Alexander, about 326 B.C.; conquered by the Persian Mahometans in the 8th century A.D.; tributary to the Ghazneyide dynasty in the 11th century; conquered by Nadir Shah, 1739; reverted to the empire of Delhi after his death, 1747; after various changes of rulers, Sinde was conquered by the English, and annexed, March, 1843.

SINGAPORE, see *Straits Settlements*.

SINGING, see *Music*, and *Hymns*.

SINKAT, see under *Soudan*, 1884.

SINKING FUND. First projected by sir Robert Walpole to redeem the debt to the bank of England; act passed in 1716. The act establishing the sinking fund of Mr. Pitt, devised by Dr. Price, was passed in March, 1786. A then estimated surplus of 900,000*l.* in the revenue was augmented by new taxes to make up the sum of 1,000,000*l.* which was to be invariably applied to the reduction of the national debt. The fallacy of the scheme was shown by Dr. Hamilton in 1813. In July, 1828, the sinking fund was limited to one-fourth of the actual surplus of revenue.

A new sinking fund was established by Act passed 2 Aug. 1875. The annual charge of the national debt of the year ending 31 March, 1877 to be 27,700,000*l.*; subsequent years to be 28,000,000*l.*

SINOPE, an important Greek colony on the Euxine, after resisting several attacks was conquered by Mithridates IV., king of Pontus, and made his capital. It was the birth-place of Diogenes, the cynic philosopher. On 30 Nov. 1853, a Turkish fleet of seven frigates, three corvettes, and two smaller vessels, was attacked by a Russian fleet of six sail of the line, two sailing vessels, and three steamers, under admiral Nachimoff, and totally destroyed, except one vessel, which conveyed the tidings to Constantinople. Four thousand lives were lost by fire or drowning, and Osman Pacha, the Turkish admiral, died at Sebastopol of his wounds. In consequence of this act (considered treacherous) the Anglo-French fleet entered the Black Sea, 3 Jan. 1854.

SION COLLEGE AND HOSPITAL, situated on the site of a nunnery, which, having fallen to decay, was purchased by William Elsynge, a citizen and mercer, and converted into a college and hospital, called from his name Elsynge Spital. In 1340 he changed it to an Austin priory, which was afterwards granted by Henry VIII. to sir John Williams, master of the jewel-office, who, with sir Roland Hayward, inhabited it till its destruction by fire. In 1623, Dr. Thomas White having bequeathed 3000*l.* towards purchasing and building a college and alms-house on the ancient site, his executors erected the present college. It is held by two charters of incorporation, 6 Chas. I. 1630 and 16 Chas. II. 1664. It contains a valuable library (easily accessible to the public), and an almshouse for ten men and ten women. New buildings erected on the Thames Embankment; memorial stone laid 21 April, 1885; opened by the prince of Wales, 15 Dec. 1886.

SIRENE, an instrument for determining the velocity of aërial vibrations corresponding to the different pitches of musical sounds, was invented by baron Cagniard de la Tour of Paris in 1819. The principle was shown in an apparatus exhibited by Robert Hooke before the Royal Society, 27 July, 1681.

SISTERHOODS in the English church were begun by Lydia Priscilla Sellon about 1846, in Devonshire; she died, Nov. 1876.

SISTERS OF CHARITY, an order for the service of the sick poor, was founded by Vincent de Paul, in 1634. Their establishment in London began in 1834.

SIX ACTS, a term given to certain acts, also named "Gagging Acts," 60 Geo. III. & 1 Geo. IV.

cc. 1, 2, 4, 6, 8, 9, passed in 1819-1820 to suppress seditious meetings and publications.

SIX ARTICLES, see *Articles*.

SIX CLERKS, officers of the court of chancery, who were anciently *clerici* or *clergy*. They were to conform to the laws of celibacy, and forfeit their places if they married; but when the constitution of the court began to alter, a law was made to permit them to marry; statute 24 & 25 Hen. VIII. 1533. The six clerks continued for many years officers of the chancery court, and held their offices in Chancery-lane, London, where proceedings by bill and answer were transacted and filed, and certain patents issued. *Law Dict.* The six clerks were discontinued by 5 & 6 Vict. c. 103, 1841.

SIXTEEN (*seize*), a large French political club, in the reigns of Henry III. and IV., sixteen members of which took charge of the sixteen quarters of Paris. They at first supported the catholic league, and attempted to overthrow Henry III. in 1587, but vacillating in their policy, and committing many crimes, their power was annihilated by Mayenne in 1591, and several of them were executed.

SKALITZ (Bohemia), was stormed by the Prussian general Steinmetz, 28 June, 1866; whereby the junction of the divisions of the Prussians was greatly facilitated.

SKATING (with blunt skates) is said to have been practised in prehistoric times by northern nations. See *Rinks*.

Mentioned by the Danish historian Saxo Grammaticus . . . . about 1134
William FitzStephens speaks of it in London, about 1180
Figures of skates in Olaus Magnus's history, printed 1555
Blade-skates, probably introduced from Holland, about 1660, were seen in St. James's-park by Evelyn and Pepys . . . . 1 Dec. 1662
Robert Jones's "Art of Skating," published . . 1772
An Edinburgh club established 1744
London Skating club, 1830; Oxford club . . . 1838
Severe frost, much skating . . . . . . Jan. 1880
International skating contest at Vienna . . Jan. 1882

SKIERNIEVICE, Poland; see *Russia*, 15, 16 Sept. 1884.

SKINS. The raw skins of cattle were usually suspended on stakes and made use of instead of kettles to boil meat, in the north of England and in Scotland, 1 Edw. III. 1327. *Leland*.

SKUPTSCHINA, the Servian legislative assembly.

SKYE, ISLE OF, N.W. Scotland. See *Crofters*.

SLADE PROFESSORSHIP OF FINE ART, Cambridge, established in pursuance of the will of Felix Slade, 24 June, 1869, sir Matthew Digby Wyatt, the first professor, 1869-73; Sidney Colvin, 1873-1885; Mr. J. H. Middleton, 1886.

SLATE. Fifteen persons were killed by the fall of a mass of rock and rubble at the Delaboll slate quarries, Cornwall, 21 April, 1869.

Great strike at lord Penrhyn's slate quarries Bethesda, Wales, in Sept.-Oct.; end . . Nov. 1874

SLAUGHTER HOUSES ACT for the metropolis, passed 7 Aug. 1874.

SLAVERY. The traffic in men came from Chaldæa into Egypt, Arabia, and all over the East. In Greece, in the time of Homer, all prisoners of war were treated as slaves. The Lacedæmonian youths, trained up in the practice of deceiving and butchering slaves, were from time to time let loose upon them to show their proficiency; and once, for amusement only, murdered, it is said, 3000 in one night, see *Helots*. Alexander, when he razed Thebes, sold the whole people for slaves, 335 B.C. There were 400,000 slaves in Attica, 317 B.C. In Rome slaves were often chained to the gate of a great man's house, to give admittance to the guests invited to the feast. By one of the laws of the XII. Tables, creditors could seize their insolvent debtors, and keep them in their houses, till by their services or labour they had discharged the sum they owed. C. Pollio threw such slaves as gave him the slightest offence into his fish-ponds, to fatten his lampreys, 42 B.C. Cæcilius Isidorus left to his heir 4116 slaves, 12 B.C. The first Janissaries were Christian slaves, 1329.

Slavery abolished in the French colonies by the agency of M. Schœlcher 1848
Serfdom was abolished by Frederick I. of Prussia in 1702; by Christian VII. of Denmark in 1766; by Joseph II. emperor of Germany, in his hereditary states in 1781; by Nicholas I. of Russia in the imperial domains in 1842; and by his successor, Alexander II. throughout his empire, 3 March, 1861.
Slavery ceased in the Dutch West Indies on 1 July, 1863.
It was decreed in Brazil in 1867 that all children born to slaves henceforth were to be free, and all slaves were to be free in 20 years from that time. In Nov. slaves of the state became free when made soldiers. Slavery was ordered to be abolished gradually (*Rio Branco*), 27 Sept. 1871.
The law nullified by the planters; liberal agitation increases; stronger emancipation bill of Senor Dantas rejected by the assembly; ministerial crisis . . . . Aug. Sept. 1884
Slavery abolished in Porto Rico . 23 March, 1873
Immediate suppression of slavery in the colonies of St. Thomas, &c. by Portugal, announced, Feb. 1876
Gradual emancipation in Cuba; bill passed in Spanish senate, 24 Dec. 1879; by deputies, 21 Jan. promulgated, 18 Feb. 1880; total abolition by decree . . . . 6 Oct. 1886
Slavery to be abolished in Egypt . end of July, 1881
Bill for the gradual abolition of slavery in Brazil passed, Sept. 1885; its total abolition voted by the chambers . . . . 10, 14 May, 1888

SLAVERY IN ENGLAND. Laws respecting the sale of slaves were made by Alfred. The English peasantry were commonly sold for slaves in Saxon and Norman times; children were sold in Bristol market like cattle for exportation. Many were sent to Ireland and to Scotland. Under the Normans the vassals (termed villeins, of and pertaining to the *vill*) were devisable as chattels during the feudal times.

Severe statutes were passed in the reign of Richard II., 1377 and 1385; the rebellion of Wat Tyler, 1381, arose partly out of the evils of serfdom.
A statute was enacted by Edward VI. that a runaway, or any one who lived idly for three days, should be brought before two justices of the peace, and marked V with a hot iron on the breast, and adjudged the slave of him who bought him for two years. He was to take the slave and give him bread, water, or small drink, and refuse meat, and cause him to work by beating, chaining, or otherwise; and, if within that space, he absented himself fourteen days, was to be marked on the forehead or cheek, by a hot iron, with an S, and be his master's slave for ever; second desertion was made felony. It was lawful to put a ring of iron round his neck, arm, or leg. A child might be put apprentice, and, on running away, become a slave to his master 1547
Queen Elizabeth ordered her bondsmen in the western counties to be made free at easy rates . 1574
Serfdom was finally extinguished in 1660, when tenures in capite, knights' service, &c., were abolished.

A slave named Somerset, brought to England, was, because of his ill state, turned adrift by his master. By the charity of Mr. Granville Sharp he was restored to health, when his master again claimed him. A suit was the consequence, which established, by decision of the Court of King's Bench, in favour of Somerset, that slavery could not exist in Great Britain
          22 June, 1772
Act for the abolition of slavery throughout the British colonies, and for the promotion of industry among the manumitted slaves, and for compensation to the persons hitherto entitled to the services of such slaves by the grant from parliament of 20,000,000l. sterling, passed
          28 Aug. 1833
Slavery terminated in the British possessions ;
770,280 slaves became free . . . 1 Aug. 1834
Slavery was abolished in the East Indies 1 Aug. 1838
British and Foreign anti-slavery society established,1839
In 1853 John Anderson, a runaway slave, killed Septimus Digges, a planter of Missouri, who attempted to arrest him, and escaped to Canada. The American government claimed him as a murderer. The Canadian judges deciding that the law required his surrender, Mr. Edwin James, Q.C. (15 Jan.), obtained a writ of habeas corpus for his appearance before the court of queen's bench. Anderson was discharged on technical grounds . . . . . . 16 Feb. 1861
Circular from the Admiralty concerning the surrendering fugitive slaves on board British ships to their owners, dated 31 July; much censured by the public, Sept., Oct. ; withdrawn Nov. 1875
A revised circular issued near end of Dec., 1875; met with much adverse criticism . . Jan. 1876
Government commission appointed (the duke of Somerset, chief justice Cockburn, sir Henry S. Maine, and others), Feb. ; report unfavourable to the circulars ; published . . . 13 June, ,,
New admiralty instructions : fugitive slaves to be received and not given up; action left to captain's discretion ; breach of international faith and comity to be avoided ; issued . 10 Aug. ,,
Jubilee meeting to celebrate the abolition of slavery in the British colonies at Guildhall, London, the prince of Wales in the chair . . 1 Aug. 1884

SLAVERY IN UNITED STATES. Before the war of independence all the states contained slaves. In 1783 the statement in the Massachusetts Bill of Rights, "All men are born free and equal," was declared in the supreme court at Boston to bar slave-holding in that state. Slaves in the United States in 1790, 697,897; in 1810, 1,191,364; in 1820, 2,009,031; in 1850, 3,204,313; in 1860, 4,002,996. In 1870, 4,889,193, free coloured persons.

Congress passes unanimously the celebrated ordinance "for the government of the territory to the N.W. of the Ohio," which contained an "unalterable" article, forbidding slavery or involuntary servitude in the said state, 13 July, 1787; after 1800, several of the states prayed, without effect, to be relieved from this prohibition.
Louisiana purchased, which was considered by many as fatal to the constitution . . . 1803
The enormous increase in the growth of cotton in the southern states (see *Cotton*) led to a corresponding increase in the demand for slave labour.
The *Missouri Compromise* (drawn up by Henry Clay, by which slavery was permitted in that state, but was prohibited in all that part of it to the north of 36° 30' N. lat.), carried Feb. 1820
Contest between the slave-holders and their opponents at the annexation of Texas ; a similar division to that of Missouri obtained 25 Dec. 1845
Another compromise effected ; California admitted as a free state : but the Fugitive Slave act passed (*which see*) 1850
The Missouri compromise was abrogated by the admission of Nebraska and Kansas as slaveholding states ; civil war ensued (see *Kansas*) . 1854
Dred Scot's case (see *United States*) . . 1857
John Brown's attempt to create a slave rebellion in Virginia failed (see *United States*) . Nov. 1859

Abraham Lincoln, the anti-slavery candidate, elected president of the United States 4 Nov. 1860
Secession of South Carolina (see *United States*), Dec. ,,
Slavery abolished in the district of Colombia
          16 April, 1864
President Lincoln proclaims the abolition of slavery in the southern states, if they have not returned to the union on 1 Jan. 1863 22 Sept. ,,
The total abolition of slavery in the United States officially announced . . . . 18 Dec. ,,
Mr. William Lloyd Garrison, a fervent champion for emancipation, entertained at St. James's-hall, London (he started the *Liberator* in 1831, and had suffered much for his zeal) . . 29 June, 1867
A negro judge present in a court at New Orleans,
          18 Sept. ,,
Negro equality with the whites completely recognised . . . . Feb. 1870

See *United States*, 1860-5.

SLAVE TRADE. The slave trade from Congou and Angola was begun by the Portuguese in 1481. The commerce in man has brutalised a tract fifteen degrees on each side of the equator, and forty degrees wide, or of 4,000,000 of square miles; and men and women have been bred for sale to the Christian nations during the last 250 years, and war carried on to make prisoners for the Christian market. The Abbé Raynal computed (1777) that, at the time of his writing, 9,000,000 of slaves had been consumed by the Europeans. The slave-trade is now approaching extinction.

In 1768 the slaves taken from Africa amounted to 104,100. In 1786 the annual number was about 100,000.
In 1807 it was shown by documents, produced by government, that since 1792 upwards of 3,500,000 Africans had been torn from their country, and had either perished on the passage or been sold in the West Indies.
SLAVE TRADE OF ENGLAND : begun by sir John Hawkins. His first expedition, with the object of procuring negroes on the coast of Africa, and conveying them for sale at the West Indies, took place in Oct. 1562 ; see *Guinea*, and *Assiento*.
England employed 130 ships and carried off 42,000 slaves, 1786.
Thos. Clarkson, at a spot in Wadesmill, Hertford, devotes his life to the abolition of the slave-trade, June, 1785.
The "Society for the Suppression of the Slave Trade," founded by Clarkson, Wilberforce, and Dillwyn, 1787.
Slave-trade question debated in parliament, 1787.
The debate for its abolition ; two days, April, 1791.
Mr. Wilberforce's motion lost by a majority of 88 to 83,
          3 April, 1798.
The question introduced under the auspices of Lord Grenville and Mr. Fox, then ministers, 31 March, 1806.
The trade abolished by parliament, 25 March, 1807.
Thomas Clarkson, died, aged 85, Sept. 1846.
An obelisk as a memorial of Thos. Clarkson, erected by Mr. Arthur Giles Puller, at Wadesmill, inaugurated 9 Oct. 1879.
A statue unveiled at Wisbeach, Cambridge, 11 Nov. 1881.
FOREIGN COUNTRIES : the trade was abolished by Austria in 1782 ; by the French convention in 1794 ; by the United States in 1808.
The allies at Vienna declared against it, Feb. 1815.
Napoleon, in the hundred days, abolished the trade, 29 March, 1815.
Treaty for its repression with Spain, 1817 ; with the Netherlands, May, 1818 ; with Brazil, Nov. 1826 ; prohibition, 1831 ; not effected till 1852.
Its revival was proposed in the congress of the United States of America, 14 Dec. 1856, and negatived by 183 votes to 58.
In June, 1857, the French government gave permission to M. Regis to convey *free* negroes from Africa to Guadaloupe and Martinido, French colonies.
This having led to abuses and consequent troubles (see *Charles et Georges*), was eventually given up in Jan. 1859.
It is said that about 40,000 slaves were landed at Cuba in 1860.
A treaty between Great Britain and the United States for the abolition of the slave trade, was signed 7 April ; ratified 20 May, 1862.

The Spanish government denounce the slave trade as piracy, Nov. 1865.
Sir Samuel Baker headed an expedition to put down slave-trading on the Nile (see *Egypt*), Jan. 1870; reported to be partially successful, 30 June, 1873. He published "Ismailia," a history of the expedition, 1874. He estimates that at least 50,000 are captured and sold as slaves, Nov. 1874.
A species of slave trade has lately risen in the South Seas; the natives being enticed on board certain British vessels and shipped to Queensland, Australia, and the Fiji isles; the subject was brought before parliament (see *Melanesia*), 1871-2.
The ship *Carl* (owner, Dr. James P. Murray; master, Joseph Armstrong) left Melbourne for South Sea isles; it anchored off Malokolo, Solomon's and Bougainville isles and kidnapped many natives as labourers for the Fiji isles; while about 20 miles from land, the prisoners rose and attempted to set fire to the ship; were fired on; about 50 killed and 20 wounded were cast into the sea. At Melbourne Murray gave evidence, and Armstrong was committed for trial, 16 Aug.; the master and mate sentenced to death, Nov. 1872.
Sir Bartle Frere went to Zanzibar on a mission to suppress the East African slave trade; see *Zanzibar*, 1872-3.
An act of parliament for consolidating with amendments the acts for carrying into effect treaties for the more effectual suppression of the slave trade (36 & 37 Vict. c. 88), was passed, 5 Aug. 1873.
Several African kings and chiefs, at Cape Coast Castle, agreed to give up slave trade, at an interview with governor Strahan, 3 Nov. 1874.
The slave-trade on the Gold Coast abolished, by proclamation of governor Strahan, 17 Dec. 1874.
Convention with Egypt forbidding the traffic, 4 Aug. 1877; col. Gordon's efforts in the Soudan reported successful, 1879.
Slave trade prohibited at West African conference, 7 Jan. 1885.
Slave trade in East Africa checked by British cruisers, 1886.
United action of England and Germany and other powers to check the maritime slave-trade and importation of arms on the east coast of Africa, which is to be blockaded for that purpose from Suakim to Zanzibar, Oct.-Nov.; proclamation of the commencement of the blockade, 2 Dec. 1888. See *Zanzibar*.
Mr. Sydney Buxton's resolution for urgent suppression of the slave trade passed in the house of commons, 26 March, 1889.
Slave trade reported nearly extinct in Egypt, and few slaves there, May, 1889.

SLAVONIA or **SCLAVONIA**, a province of Austria, derives its name from the Slavos, a Sarmatian people who replaced the Avars in Pannonia early in the 9th century. In 864 Cyril and Methodius, Greek missionaries, preached here, and adapted the Greek alphabet to the Slavonian language; the letters of which have since been a little altered. The country, after having been held at times by the Greeks, Turks, and Hungarians, and the cause of sanguinary conflicts, was ceded finally to Hungary in 1699, at the peace of Carlowitz. Deputies from the Slavonian provinces of Austria were entertained at Moscow and St. Petersburg, May, 1867. The Croatian-Slavonian diet, at Agram, was dissolved, May, 1867. It protested against incorporation with Hungary. The Slavonian family of languages includes Russian, Polish, Servian, Bohemian, Bulgarian, Wendic, Slovak, and Polabic. For the war, see *Turkey*, 1875-6.
Estimated number of Slavs in Europe in 1875: 90,365,633; Russians and Ruthenians, 66,129,590; Serbo-Croats, 5,940,539; Bulgarians, 5,123,952; Slovenes, 1,260,000; Slovaks,2,221,830; Czechs, 4,815,154; Poles,9,492,162.
Lord Ilchester's bequest to promote the study of Slavonian literature at Oxford; lectures first given, May, 1876.
Agitation against the Germans in Slavonic provinces of Austria, Aug. Sept. 1883.

SLEEP, see *Seven Sleepers*. M. Chauffat, awoke after a nineteen days' sleep at the Alexandra Palace, 28 Nov. 1888; many similar cases are reported.

SLESWIG, see *Holstein*.

SLIDING-SCALE, see *Corn Laws*.

SLING. In *Judges* xx. 16, is mentioned the skill of the Benjamite slingers (about 1406 B.C.), and with a sling David slew Goliath 1063 B.C. (1 *Sam.* xvii.) The natives of the Balearic isles (Majorca, Minorca, and Iviça) were celebrated slingers, and served as mercenaries in the Carthaginian and Roman armies. Slings are said to have been used by the Huguenots at the siege of Sancerre, in 1672, to economise their powder.

SLOANE'S MUSEUM, see *British Museum*.

SLOUGH, near Eton, Bucks, Mrs. Ann Reville, a butcher's wife, was barbarously murdered early in evening, 11 April, 1881. Alfred Payne, a lad, was tried and acquitted, same month.

SLOYD ASSOCIATION OF GREAT BRITAIN AND IRELAND, its object to promote the training of the eye and hand; first meeting held in London, the earl of Meath in the chair, 5 Dec. 1888. The "Sloyd" system is reported successful in Scandinavia.

SLUYS (Holland), near which Edward III. gained a signal naval victory over the French. The English had the wind of the enemy, and the sun at their backs, and began this sanguinary action. Two hundred and thirty French ships were taken; thousands of Frenchmen were killed, with two of their admirals; the loss of the English was inconsiderable: 24 June, 1340.

SMALCALD (Hesse), TREATY OF, entered into between the elector of Brandenburg and the other princes of Germany in favour of Protestantism, 31 Dec. 1530; see *Protestants*. The emperor, apprehensive that the kings of France and England would join this league, signed the treaty of Passau, 31 July, 1532, allowing liberty of conscience.

SMALLPOX, *variola* (diminutive of *varus*, a pimple), a highly contagious disease, supposed to have been introduced into Europe from the East by the Saracens. Rhazes, an Arabian, described it accurately, about 900. From Europe it was carried to America, soon after its discovery, and raged there with great severity, destroying the Indians by thousands. In 1694, queen Mary of England died of small pox, as did in 1711 and 1712 the emperor of Germany, the dauphin and dauphiness of France and their son, in 1730 the emperor of Russia, in 1741 the queen of Sweden, and in 1774 Louis XV. of France. It is stated that in the middle of the last century two millions perished by it in Russia. In London in 1723 one out of fourteen deaths was caused by small pox, and in France in 1754 the rate was one in ten. For the attempts to alleviate this scourge, see *Inoculation*, introduced into England in 1722, and *Vaccination*, announced by Dr. Jenner in 1798. *Smallpox Hospital*, established 1746. Smallpox raged in parts of London, and thousands died, 1870-1; a temporary hospital was established at Hampstead (*which see*). The Anti-Vaccination society has been active, and many parents have been fined for opposing the vaccination of their children, 1870-6. In Sept. and Oct. 1862, a great many sheep died of smallpox in the West of England, till successful preventive measures were resorted to. Many cases in London, 1876-8; deaths principally of unvaccinated persons.
Smallpox prevalent in London, 88 deaths 1—7 May; 103 deaths 15—21 May; diminishing July, 1881.

Deaths, June, 1880—June, 1881, 1532 deaths, 637 not vaccinated; in N.E. London, May, deaths, about 36 a week, June, 1884; deaths decreasing reported, 24 July; reappears, but subsides, Dec. 1884.
Severe epidemic of smallpox at Sheffield and neighbourhood, March, 1887; still prevalent, Jan. 1888; disappearing, April, 1888.

See Vaccination.

SMALL TENEMENTS ACTS (59 Geo. III. c. 12, 1819); 1850 (13 & 14 Vict. c. 99), provided for owners paying rates of houses instead of the occupiers. This was annulled by the new Reform act, 30 & 31 Vict. c. 102, s. 7 (1867).

SMECTYMNUUS, the initials of certain nonconformist writers against episcopacy in the seventeenth century: Stephen Marshall, Edmund Calamy, Thomas Young, Matthew Newcomen, William Spurstow. They were answered by bishop Hall in his "Divine Right of Episcopacy," 1640.

SMITH'S CHARITY (FOR POOR KIN). Alderman Henry Smith, by will dated 26 April, 1647, left 1000*l*. for relief of captives held by Turkish pirates, and 1000*l*. for his poor kinsmen.

The former object having become obsolete, an act was passed in 1772 to divert all the property to the poor kinsmen. In 1868 these were 412 in number. The value of the property is now 17,000*l*. a year (1889). The master of the rolls decided in Dec. 1877, that the funds should be applied to general charitable purposes. On appeal, the decision was in favour of the "poor Smiths," 12 Feb. 1878.

SMITHFIELD, WEST, in the heart of London, was once a favourite walk of the London citizens, outside the city walls. Sir W. Wallace was executed here, 23 Aug. 1305. On 15 June, 1381, Wat Tyler was met by Richard II. at this place, and was stabbed by Walworth the mayor. Many tournaments were also held here. In the reign of Mary (1553-8), many persons perished by fire; and Bartholomew Leggatt, an Arian, was burnt here, 18 March, 1612.—Bartholomew fair was held here till 1853.—This place is mentioned as the site of a cattle market as far back as 1150. The space devoted to this purpose was enlarged from about three acres to four and a half, and in 1834 to six and a quarter. The ancient regulations were called the "statutes of Smithfield." In one day there were sometimes assembled 4000 beasts and 30,000 sheep. The annual amount of the sales was about 7,000,000*l*.

Sold here 226,132 beasts, 1,593,270 sheep and lambs, 26,356 calves, 33,531 pigs. (About 160 salesmen) 1846
The contracted space of the market, the slaughtering places adjoining, and many other nuisances, gave ground to much dissatisfaction, and after investigation, an act was passed appointing metropolitan market commissioners with powers to provide a new market, slaughtering places, &c.; and to close the market at Smithfield . 1 Aug. 1851
Smithfield was used as a cattle market for the last time on 11 June; and the new market in Copenhagen-fields was opened on 13 June (see *Metropolitan Market*) 1855
A dead-meat and poultry market ordered to be erected in Smithfield, and Newgate market to cease 1861
A tender for its erection, from designs by Horace Jones, accepted from Messrs. Browne and Robinson for 134,460*l*. . . . . . Nov. 1866
The market inaugurated by the lord mayor Lawrence, 24 Nov.; opened to the public . 1 Dec. 1868
New poultry market, inaugurated by lord mayor Cotton . . . . 30 Nov. 1875
New central fruit and vegetable market determined on . . . . 14 July, 1879
The *Smithfield Club*, to promote improvements in the breed of cattle, was established 17 Dec. 1798; first president, Francis, duke of Bedford; first secretary,

Arthur Young. The members established an annual cattle show, held first in Dolphin-yard, Smithfield, Dec. 1799; next in Barbican, 1805; in Goswell-street, 1806; removed to Baker-street, 1839; and to the new Agricultural hall, Liverpool-road, Islington, 1862.
The show, suspended in Dec. 1866, on account of the cattle plague, was partially resumed Dec. 1867; wholly, Dec. 1868.
Three of the highest prizes were awarded to the queen; 110,000 visitors, 10-14 Dec. 1883.

SMITHSONIAN INSTITUTION, "for the increase and diffusion of knowledge among men," a handsome building at Washington, U.S., was founded in 1846, by means of a legacy of above 100,000*l*. bequeathed for the purpose to the United States government by James Smithson, illegitimate son of sir Hugh Smithson, who became duke of Northumberland in 1766. It publishes and freely distributes scientific memoirs and reports. The library was burnt on 25 Jan. 1865. Professor Joseph Henry, the first secretary, died, 13 May, 1878; succeeded by Mr. Spencer F. Baird, died, 19 Aug. 1887; succeeded by Professor S. P. Langley.

SMOKE NUISANCE. An act was passed in 1853 to abate this nuisance, proceeding from chimney shafts and steamers above London bridge. In 1856 another act, obtained for its further application to steamers below London bridge, and to potteries and glass-houses previously exempted, came into operation, 1 Jan. 1858; enactments have been made for all the kingdom.
Meeting at Mansion-house for the abatement of smoke in London, 7 Jan. 1881.
An exhibition of appliances for this purpose in the Royal Albert Hall, opened 30 Nov. 1881; closed 14 Feb. 1882; opened at Manchester, 17 March, 1882.
National Smoke Abatement Institution founded, and Mr. R. E. W. Coles appointed smoke inspector, autumn, 1882.
Smoke abatement fund opened, 1883.
The Thompson smoke consuming furnace tried successfully on the Thames, 15 July, 1886.
Messrs. Ashworth and Kneen patent a furnace which saves about 35 per cent. of coal and consumes smoke, autumn, 1887.

SMOLENSKO (Russia). The French in most sanguinary engagements here were three times repulsed, but ultimately succeeded in entering Smolensko, and found the city, which had been bombarded, burning and partly in ruins, 16, 17 Aug. 1812. Barclay de Tolly, the Russian commander-in-chief, incurred the displeasure of the emperor Alexander because he retreated after the battle, and Kutusoff succeeded to the command.

SMUGGLERS. The customs duties, instituted to enable the king to afford protection to trade against pirates, afterwards became a branch of public revenue, and gave rise to much smuggling. The Smugglers' act was passed in 1736, and its severity mitigated in 1781 and 1784. A revision of these statutes took place 1826 and 1835.

SMYRNA, see *Seven Churches*.

SNEEZING. The custom of saying "God bless you" to the sneezer originated, according to Strada, among the ancients, who, through an opinion of the danger attending it, after sneezing made a short prayer to the gods, as "Jupiter, help me." The custom is mentioned by Homer, the Jewish rabbis, and others, and is found among savages. Polydore Vergil says it took its rise at the time of the plague, 558, when the infected fell down dead sneezing, though seemingly in good health.

SNIDER GUN, see under *Firearms*.

SNUFF-TAKING took its rise in England

from the captures made of vast quantities of snuff by sir George Rooke's expedition to Vigo in 1702, and the practice soon became general. In 1839 there were imported 1,622,493 lbs. of snuff, of which 196,305 lbs. were entered for home consumption; the duty was 88,263*l*. ; see *Tobacco*. In 1853, 2,573,925 lbs. of snuff and cigars, in 1861, 2,110,430 lbs. ; in 1871, 3,852,236 lbs. ; 1877, 3,762,831 lbs.; 1883, 3,121,174 lbs.; 1887, 3,595,071 lbs. were imported.

SOANE MUSEUM, &c. No. 13, Lincoln's-inn-fields, was gradually formed by sir John Soane, the architect, who died in 1837, after making arrangements for its being open to the public by an act passed in 1833. It contains Egyptian and other antiquities, valuable paintings, rare books, &c. 150*l*. are distributed annually to distressed architects or their widows and children.

One of two sealed closets in the museum was opened 29 Nov. 1886; chiefly private legal documents discovered.

SOAP is a salt, a compound of a fatty acid with an alkali, soda or potash. The Hebrew *bôrith*, translated soap, is merely a general term for cleansing substances. *Job* ix. 30; *Jer.* ii. 22. Pliny declares soap to be an invention of the Gauls, though he prefers the German to the Gallic soap. Nausicaa and her attendants, Homer tells us, washed clothes by treading upon them with their feet in pits of water. *Odyssey*, book vi. The Romans used fuller's earth. *Savon*, the French word for soap, is ascribed to its having been manufactured at Savona, near Genoa. The manufacture of soap began in London in 1524, before which time it was supplied by Bristol at one penny per pound. The duty upon soap, imposed in 1711, after several reductions from 3*d*. per pound, was totally repealed in 1853. It then produced, according to the chancellor of the exchequer, Mr. Gladstone, about 1,126,000*l*. annually.

SOBRAON (N.W. India). The British army, 35,000 strong, under sir Hugh (afterwards viscount) Gough, attacked the Sikh force on the Sutlej, 10 Feb. 1846. The enemy was dislodged after a dreadful contest, and all their batteries taken; and in attempting the passage of the river by a floating bridge in their rear, the weight of the masses that crowded upon it caused it to break down, and thousands of Sikhs were killed, wounded, or drowned. The British loss was 2338 men.

SOCIALISM was warmly advocated in London, 24 Jan. 1834, by the celebrated Robert Owen. He had, beginning at New Lanark, in Scotland, about 1801, established a settlement at New Harmony in America in 1824. He died 17 Nov. 1858, aged 90. The French socialists, termed *Communists*, became a powerful political body in that country, were implicated in the revolution of 1848, and made an insurrection at Paris, 1871. See *France*, *Germany*, 1878 *et seq.*, *Positive Philosophy*, and *Working-men* (who, in Great Britain, have received by legislation nearly all they require).

The Rev. Charles Kingsley, Mr. Thomas Hughes, and others, endeavoured to set up *Christian Socialism*, about 1855-60
P. J. Proudhon, an eminent socialist, to whom is ascribed the saying "*la propriété c'est le vol*"; died 20 Jan. 1865
Communist manifesto issued by Carl Marx, 1848; (he died 14 March, 1883).
Social democratic party organised by Ferdinand Lassalle 1863
International workmen's association formed . 1864
"Gotha programme" (exalting labour) . . 1875

A grand congress of socialists met at Ghent, Sept. 1877
Socialism said to be increasing in Germany . ,,
Stringent bill to repress it passed in the parliament; socialists expelled from Germany by decree, Nov. many papers suppressed, Nov., Dec., 1878. Expulsions renewed . . . . . autumn, 1880
Illegal meeting of socialists permitted in Dod-street, Limehouse, London . . . 27 Sept. 1885
Social democratic federation holds meetings which tend to riots, see *Riots* . . 8 and 21 Feb. 1886
Peaceable meetings held in Trafalgar-square 29 Aug. and 21 Nov. ,,
Their proposal for a procession on 9 Nov. forbidden, Oct. ,,
About the end of 1886 they began "church parades" disturbing the service at several churches; ineffectually at St. Paul's cathedral . 27 Feb. 1887
The general council of the social democratic federation issues a manifesto exhorting to constant organized agitation for adequate relief works &c., to be provided by the government and local authorities; see *Hyde Park* and *Riots*, 13 Nov. ,,
Mr. William Morris, poet, author of the "Earthly Paradise," Mr. H. M. Hyndman, Mr. H. H. Champion, and Mr. John Burns became leaders of the "socialist league" formed in 1886.
A kind of state socialism instituted in Germany; see under *Working Men* 1889

SOCIAL SCIENCE. The National Association for the Promotion of Social Science originated in a meeting at lord Brougham's in May, 1857. Its object was to promote improvements in the administration of law, in education, in public health, and in social economy. It held annual meetings, and published its proceedings.

Mr. Wm. Ellis and Mr. John Stuart Mill began to promote the study . . . . about 1823
Birmingham, meeting opened . . . 12 Oct. 1857
Liverpool . . . . 11 Oct. 1858
Bradford . . . . 10 Oct. 1859
Glasgow . . . . 24 Sept. 1860
Dublin . . . . 14 Aug. 1861
London . . . . 6 June, 1862
Edinburgh . . . . 7 Oct. 1863
York . . . . 22 Sept. 1864
Sheffield . . . . 4 Oct. 1865
Manchester . . . . . . 2 Oct. 1866
Belfast . . . . 18 Sept. 1867
Birmingham . . . . . . 30 Sept. 1868
Bristol . . . . 29 Sept. 1869
Newcastle-on-Tyne . . . . 21 Sept. 1870
Leeds . . . . 4 Oct. 1871
Plymouth . . . . . . 11 Sept. 1872
Norwich . . . . 1 Oct. 1873
Glasgow . . . . 30 Sept. 1874
Brighton . . . . 6 Oct. 1875
Liverpool . . . . 11 Oct. 1876
Aberdeen . . . . 19 Sept. 1877
Cheltenham . . . . . . 23 Oct. 1878
Manchester . . . . . . 1 Oct. 1879
Edinburgh . . . . 5 Oct. 1880
Dublin . . . . 3 Oct. 1881
Nottingham . . . . . . 20 Sept. 1882
Huddersfield . . . . . . 3 Oct. 1883
Birmingham (the last congress) . . 17 Sept. 1884

SOCIAL WARS, see *Athens*, and *Marsi*.

SOCIETIES AND INSTITUTIONS, LITERARY AND SCIENTIFIC, in Great Britain. Further details of many of these will be found under their respective heads. All in the list below are in London, except otherwise stated. An act was passed 11 Aug. 1854, "to afford facilities for the establishment of institutions for the promotion of literature and science," by grants of land, &c.; and for their regulation. The Royal and London Institutions were exempted from the operation of the act.

The "Year-Book of Scientific and Learned Societies first appeared in 1884
Royal Society . . . . . Charter 1662
Christian Knowledge Society 1698

SOCIETIES.

Society of Antiquaries . . . (Charter 1751)	1717
Society of Dilettanti	1734
Society of Arts . . . (Charter 1847)	1753
Medical Society of London	1773
Bath and West of England Society . . .	1777
Gaelic Society of London	,,
Manchester Literary and Philosophical Society .	1781
Royal Society of Edinburgh (Charter 1783)	1782
Highland Society	1785
Royal Irish Academy . . . Charter	1786
Linnean Society . . . (Charter 1802)	1788
Newcastle Literary and Philosophical Society .	1793
Royal Institution (Act of parliament, 1810) Charter	1800
Glasgow Philosophical Society . . .	1802
Royal Horticultural Society . . (Charter 1809)	1804
Royal Medical and Chirurgical Society (Charter 1834)	1805
London Institution	,,
Geological Society . . . (Charter 1826)	1807
Russell Institution	1808
Swedenborg Society	1810
Liverpool Literary and Philosophical Society .	1812
Roxburghe Club	,,
Institution of Civil Engineers (Charter 1828)	1818
Leeds Literary and Philosophical Society .	,,
Egyptian Society	1819
Cambridge Philosophical Society . (Charter 1832)	,,
Hunterian Society	,,
Royal Astronomical Society . (Charter 1831)	1820
Medico-Botanical Society	1821
Royal Scottish Society of Arts . . .	,,
Hull Literary and Philosophical Society . .	1822
Yorkshire Philosophical Society . . .	,,
Sheffield Literary and Philosophical Society .	,,
Royal Society of Literature . (Charter 1826)	1823
Royal Asiatic Society . . (Charter 1824)	,,
Bannatyne Club, Edinburgh . . .	,,
Mechanics' Institution, London . . .	,,
Athenæum Club	1824
Western Literary Institution . . .	1825
Eastern Literary Institution . . .	,,
Zoological Society . . . (Charter 1829)	1826
Incorporated Law Society . (Charter 1831)	1827
Society for Diffusion of Useful Knowledge . .	1828
Ashmolean Society, Oxford . . .	,,
Maitland Club, Glasgow	,,
Royal Geographical Society . . .	1830
Royal United Service Institution (Charter 1860)	1831
Royal Dublin Society	,,
Harveian Society	,,
British Association	,,
Marylebone Literary Institution . . .	1832
British Medical Association . . .	,,
Entomological Society	1833
Statistical Society	1834
Westminster Literary Institution . .	,,
Surtees Society, Durham	,,
Royal Institute of British Architects (Charter 1837)	,,
Leicester Literary and Philosophical Society .	1835
Abbotsford Club, Edinburgh . . .	1835-7
Numismatic Society	1836
Ornithological Society	1837
Electrical Society	1837-8
Etching Club	1838
English Historical Society . . .	1838-56
Royal Agricultural Society (Charter 1840) .	1838
Camden Society	,,
Microscopical Society (Royal, 1866) . .	1839
Ecclesiological Society	,,
Spalding Club, Aberdeen	,,
Royal Botanical Society of London . .	,,
Parker Society	1840-55
Percy Society	1840-52
Irish Archæological Society, Dublin . .	1840
London Library	,,
Shakespeare Society	,,
Chemical Society	1841
Pharmaceutical Society	,,
Wodrow Society, Edinburgh . . .	1841-7
Philological Society	1842
Ælfric Society	1843-56
Chetham Society, Manchester . . .	1843
Spottiswoode Society, Edinburgh . . .	,,
British Archæological Association . .	,,
Royal Archæological Institute . . .	,,
Sydenham Society	,,
Ethnological Society	,,
Law Amendment Society	,,
Handel Society	1844
Syro-Egyptian Society	,,
Ray Society	,,
Caxton Society	1844-54
Celtic Society, Dublin	1845-53
Pathological Society	1846
Sussex Archæological Society, Lewes . .	,,
Cambrian Archæological Association . .	,,
Cavendish Society	,,
Hakluyt Society	,,
Palæontographical Society . . .	1847
Institute of Mechanical Engineers (Birmingham)	,,
Institute of Actuaries	1848
Arundel Society	,,
(British, now Royal) Meteorological Society (Charter 1866)	1850
Epidemiological Society	,,
North of England Institute of Mining Engineers, Newcastle	1851
Photographic Society	1852
Philobiblon Society	1853
Juridical Society	1855
Odontological Society	1856
Genealogical Society	1857
National Association for Social Science . .	,,
Horological Institute	1858
Society for the Encouragement of Fine Arts .	,,
Institution of Naval Architects . . .	1860
Clinical Society	1861
Anthropological Society	1863
Early English Text Society; began to publish .	1864
Victoria Institute . . . 24 May,	1865
London Mathematical Society . . .	,,
Aeronautical Society . . . 12 Jan.	1866
Dialectic Society	1867
Chaucer Society	,,
Holbein Society	1868
Royal Historical Society	,,
Colonial Institute (Royal Charter, 1882) .	,,
Iron and Steel Institute	1869
Harleian Society	,,
Amateur Mechanical Society . . .	,,
Christian Evidence Society . . .	1871
Biblical Archæology Society . . .	,,
Anthropological Institute (which see) . .	,,
Institution of Electrical Engineers (late Society of Telegraph Engineers)	,,
Marine Engineers' Institution . . .	1872
Society for Organization of Academical Study .	,,
London Anthropological Society (extinct) .	1873-5
Palæographical Society	1873
English Dialectic Society	,,
(New) Shakspeare Society . . .	,,
Physical Society	1874
Musical Association	,,
Public Analysts	,,
Psychological Society	1875
Education Society	,,
Royal Aquarium Society	,,
Mineralogical Society	1876
Sanitary Institute of Great Britain . .	,,
Philosophical Society (Birmingham) . .	,,
Library Association	1877
Index Society	,,
Institute of Chemistry of Great Britain . .	,,
Zetetical Society	1878
Folk-Lore Society	,,
Astrological Society	1879
Carlyle Society	,,
Hellenic Society	,,
Society for promoting Hellenic Studies . .	,,
Rabelais Club	,,
Willoughby Society	,,
Institute of Bankers	,,
Balloon Society	1880
Aristotelian Society	,,
Wordsworth Society	,,
Topographical Society of London . .	,,
Ascham Society	,,
Chemical Industry Society . . .	1881
Browning Society	,,
Society for Psychical Research . . .	1882
Wycliffe Society	,,
Seal Society	1883
Marine Biological Association . . .	1884
Society of Authors	,,
Pipe Roll Society	,,
Middlesex County Record Society . .	,,

Society of Medallists 1885
Bacon Society . . . . ,,
Selborne Society . . . . ,,
Shelley Society . . . . ,,
Goethe Society 1886
Selden Society 1887
Neurological Society . . . . ,,
Anatomical Society . . . . ,,

SOCIETY ISLANDS, Pacific Ocean, discovered by De Quiros in 1606; re-discovered by capt. Wallis, 1767, who gave Otaheite or Tahiti the name of King George's Island. Capt. Cook, who visited them in 1769 and 1777, named them Society Islands in honour of the Royal Society. See *Otaheite*.

SOCINIANS, persons who accept the opinions of Faustus Socinus (died 1562), and his nephew Lælius (died 1604), Siennese noblemen. They held — 1. That the Eternal Father was the one only God, and that Jesus Christ was not otherwise God than by his superiority to all other creatures; 2. That Christ was not a mediator; 3. That hell will endure for a time, after which the soul and body will be destroyed; 4. That it is unlawful for princes to make war. *Hook*. The Socinians established a church at Rakow, in Poland, and made proselytes in Transylvania, 1563. They were expelled from Poland in 1658. The Rakovian catechism was published in 1574; see *Unitarians*.

SOCOTRA, (*Dioscoridis insula*), an island in the Indian ocean, belonging to the imam of Muscat, 120 miles E. of cape Guardafui, Eastern Africa. In the summer of 1878, it was said to have been given up to the British; formally annexed, Nov. 1886.

SODIUM, a remarkable metal, first obtained in 1807 by sir Humphry Davy, from soda, which was formerly confounded with potash, but proved to be a distinct substance by Duhamel in 1736). This metal, like potassium, was obtained by the agency of the electric battery. In consequence of Deville's improved processes, sodium manufactured by Bell Brothers, of Newcastle, at 10s. a pound (1868). It is an important agent in the modern production of aluminium. Common salt (chloride of sodium) is a compound of sodium and chlorine. Mr. H. Y. Castner's (of New York) new process for the enlarged production of sodium, and through sodium of aluminium and magnesium, announced in June, 1887. His works were set up at Oldbury, near Birmingham; the price of sodium in 1889 was about 4s. 4d. a pound. See *Alkalies* and *Aluminium*.

SODOM AND GOMORRAH (Palestine), with their inhabitants, were destroyed by fire from heaven 1898 B.C., *Gen.* xix.

SODOR, said to be derived from Sodor-eys, or south isles (the Æbrides or Hebrides), in distinction from Orkneys, the north isles. The southern or western isles were made an episcopal diocese by Magnus, king of Norway, 1098, and joined to the isle of Man about 1113. See *Man*.

SOFIA, a manufacturing town in Bulgaria; founded by Justinian on the ruins of the ancient Sardica; became the capital of the new principality. A palace and other buildings were in course of erection, Aug. 1881. It contains 30 mosques and 10 churches.

SOFFARIDES DYNASTY reigned in Persia, 872-902.

SOFTAS, Mahometan students devoted to the Koran only. See *Turkey*, May, 1876.

SOHO BAZAAR AND THEATRE, see *Bazaars* and *Theatres*.

SOISSONS (France), capital of the Gallic Suessiones, was subdued by Julius Cæsar, 57 B.C. It was held by Syagrius, after his father Ægidius, till his defeat by Clovis, A.D. 486. Several councils have been held at Soissons (in 744, 1092, 1122). Its academy was established in 1674. During the Franco-Prussian war, Soissons, after three weeks' investment and four days' bombardment, surrendered to the Germans under the grand-duke of Mecklenburg, 16 Oct. 1870. 99 officers, 4633 men, 128 guns, &c., were said to be taken. The Germans thus obtained a second line of railway from Châlons to Paris.

SOLAR SYSTEM, nearly as now accepted, is said to have been taught by Pythagoras of Samos, about 529 B.C. He placed the sun in the centre, and all the planets moving in elliptical orbits round it—a doctrine superseded by the Ptolemaic system (*which see*). The system of Pythagoras, revived by Copernicus (1543), is called the Copernican system. Its truth was demonstrated by sir Isaac Newton in 1687. See *Planets*.

SOLDIERS' DAUGHTERS' HOME was established at Hampstead, near London, in Aug. 1857, by the surplus of the money collected by the central association in aid of the wives and families of soldiers in active service during the Crimean war, and opened by the prince consort, 18 June, 1858. It has been much indebted to the exertions of major Powys.

SOLEBAY or SOUTHWOLD BAY (Suffolk), where a fierce naval battle was fought between the fleets of England and France on one side, and the Dutch on the other, the former commanded by the duke of York, afterwards James II., 28 May, 1672. The English lost four ships, and the Dutch three; but the enemy fled, and were pursued to their coasts. The earl of Sandwich was blown up, and thousands were killed and wounded.

SOL-FA SYSTEM, see *Music*.

SOLFERINO (in Lombardy), the site of the chief struggle on the great battle of 24 June, 1859, between the allied French and Sardinian army commanded by their respective sovereigns, and the Austrians under general Hess; the emperor being present. The Austrians, after their defeat at Magenta, gradually retreated across the Mincio, and took up a position in the celebrated quadrilateral, and were expected there to await the attack. But the advance of Garibaldi on one side, and of prince Napoleon and the Tuscans on the other, induced them to recross the Mincio and take the offensive, on 23 June. The conflict began early on the 24th, and lasted fifteen hours. At first the Austrians had the advantage; but the successful attack of the French on Cavriana and Solferino changed the fortune of the day, and the Austrians, after desperate encounters, were compelled to retreat. The French attribute the victory to the skill and bravery of their emperor and the generals MacMahon and Niel; the Austrians, to the destruction of their reserve by the rifled cannon of their adversaries. The Sardinians maintained a fearful contest of fifteen hours at San Martino, it is said against double their number. Loss of the Austrians, 630 officers, and 19,311 soldiers; of the allies, 8 generals, 936 officers, and 17,305 soldiers killed and wounded. .This battle closed the war; pre-

liminaries of peace being signed at Villa Franca, 12 July. On 24 June, 1870, on the site of the battle, three ossuaries, containing the bones of thousands of the slain, were solemnly consecrated in the presence of representatives of Austria, France, and Italy.

SOLICITOR, see *Attorney*. By the Supreme Judicature Act, attorneys in future are to be styled solicitors; an act for regulating their examination was passed, 23 July, 1877.

SOLICITOR-GENERAL, the legal officer next in rank, and deputy to the attorney-general, whom he frequently succeeds.

1839.	Sir Thomas Wilde (afterwards lord Truro), 5 Dec.
1841.	Sir William Follett (second time), 6 Sept.
1844.	Sir Frederick Thesiger (since lord Chelmsford), 17 April.
1845.	Sir Fitzroy Kelly, 17 July.
1846.	Sir John Jervis, 4 July.
,,	Sir David Dundas, 18 July.
1848.	Sir John Romilly, April 4, aft. lord Romilly.
1850.	Sir Alex. J. E. Cockburn, 11 July.
1851.	Sir W. Page Wood, 28 March, aft. lord Hatherley.
1852.	Sir Fitzroy Kelly, Feb.
,,	Sir Richard Bethell, Dec., aft. lord Westbury.
1856.	Rt. Hon. James Stuart Wortley, Nov.
1857.	Sir Henry Keating, May.
1858.	Sir Hugh M. Cairns, 26 Feb., aft. earl Cairns.
1859.	Sir Henry Keating, 18 June.
,,	Sir William Atherton, Dec.
1861.	Sir Roundell Palmer, 27 June, aft. lord Selborne.
1863.	Sir Robert Porrett Collier, 2 Oct.
1866.	Sir William Bovill, 13 July.
,,	Sir John Burgess Karslake, 29 Nov.
1867.	Sir Charles Jasper Selwyn, July.
1868.	Sir Wm. Baliol Brett, Feb. (made judge, Sept.)
,,	Sir Richard Baggallay, 14 Sept.
,,	Sir John Duke Coleridge, 12 Dec., aft. ld. Coleridge.
1871.	Sir George Jessel, Nov.
1873.	Sir Henry James, 26 Sept.
,,	Sir Wm. Vernon Harcourt, Nov.
1874.	Sir Richard Baggallay, Feb.
1875.	Sir Hardinge Stanley Giffard, 25 Nov.
1880.	Sir Farrer Herschell, 3 May.
1885.	John E. Gorst, June.
1886.	Sir Horace Davey, 15 Feb.
,,	Sir Edward Clarke, 26 July.

SOLICITORS' ACT, passed 24 Dec. 1888.

SOLICITORS' REMUNERATION ACT, 44 & 45 Vict. c. 44; passed in 1881.

SOLIFIDIANS (from *solus*, only, and *fides*, faith) a name given to the Antinomians (*which see*).

SOLOMON'S TEMPLE, see *Temple*.

SOLWAY MOSS (Cumberland, bordering on Scotland). On 13 Nov. 1771, it swelled, owing to heavy rains. Upwards of 400 acres rose to such a height above the level of the ground, that at last it rolled forward like a torrent above a mile, sweeping along with it houses, trees, &c. It covered 600 acres at Netherby, and destroyed about 30 small villages. Near Solway Moss the Scots were defeated by the English, 25 Nov. 1542.

SOMAJ, see *Deism*.

SOMBRERO (West Indies). On this desert isle, Robert Jeffery, a British man-of-war's man, was put ashore by his commander, the hon. captain W. Lake, for having tapped a barrel of beer when the ship was on short allowance. After sustaining life for eight days on a few limpets and rain-water, he was saved by an American vessel, 13 Dec. 1807; and returned to England. Sir Francis Burdett advocated his cause in parliament, and he received 600*l.* as a compensation from captain Lake, who was tried by a court-martial, and dismissed the service, 10 Feb. 1810.

SOMERSET-HOUSE (London), formerly a palace, founded on the site of several churches and other buildings levelled in 1549, by the protector Somerset, whose residence fell to the crown after his execution, 22 Jan. 1552. Here resided at times queen Elizabeth, Anne of Denmark, and Catherine, queen of Charles II. Old Somerset-house, a mixture of Grecian and Gothic, was demolished in 1775, and the present edifice, from a design by sir William Chambers, was erected for public offices. The Royal Academy of Arts first assembled in the apartments given to the members by the king, 17 Jan. 1771. The Royal Society met here, 1780-1857; and apartments here were also held by the Society of Antiquaries and the Geological Society; all three now at Burlington House. Large suites of government buildings were erected in 1774. The Navy-office, Pipe-office, Victualling and other offices, were removed here in 1788, and various government departments since. The east wing forming the King's College (see *King's College*) was completed in 1833. By an act passed in 1854, the offices of the duchy of Cornwall were transferred to Pimlico.

CHIEF OFFICES AT SOMERSET HOUSE.

Probate and Divorce Division of high court of Justice and Registry Offices.	Stamp Offices, &c.
	Excise and Tax-Offices.
	Legacies and Succession Duty Offices.
Appeals Registry Office.	
Register of Births, Deaths, and Marriages.	Inland Revenue Offices.
	Bank Returns Office.
Exchequer and Audit Department.	Laboratory Department.
	Solicitors' Offices.
Property and Income Tax Offices.	Companies' Register Offices, &c., &c.

SOMERSET THE BLACK, see *Slavery in England*.

SOMERS-TOWN, a populous district in St. Pancras parish, N. London: named after earl Somers, whose family acquired the property about 1695. The building began about 1786; and many French refugees settled in it. Much of the district has been occupied by the railway companies.

SOMNATH GATES, the gates of an ancient Hindoo temple at Guzerat, which was destroyed by Mahmoud of Ghuznee in 1025. The priests wished to preserve the idol; but Mahmoud broke it to pieces and found it filled with diamonds, &c. He carried the gates to Ghuznee. When that city was taken by general Nott, 6 Sept. 1842, lord Ellenborough ordered the gates to be restored after an exile of 800 years, and issued a proclamation much censured at the time. The gates are made of sandal wood, and are described and figured in the *Archæologia* of the Society of Antiquaries, vol. xxx.

SOMORROSTRO, see *Spain*, 1874.

SONATA (Italian, sound-piece), the highest form of instrumental music, consisting of three or four movements, intending to express diverse kinds of human feelings.

It was developed from the *suite*, varied dance music (Tartini, 1624, and others). The form fixed by Corelli (1653-1713), was adopted and modified by Scarlatti, the Bachs, Handel, Mozart, Haydn, and culminated in the master-pieces of Beethoven (1770-1827). Fine sonatas have been composed by Dussek, M. Clementi, Weber, Schubert, Mendelssohn, Schumann, Wm. Sterndale Bennett, Chopin, Liszt, and Rubenstein.

SONDERBUND, see *Switzerland*, 1846.

SONNET, a poem in fourteen lines, with rhymes adjusted by rules, was invented, it is said,

by Guido d'Arezzo, about 1024. The most celebrated sonnets are those by Petrarch (about 1327), Shakspeare (1609), Milton (about 1650), and Wordsworth (1820).

SONNITES, the orthodox Mahometans who now possess the Turkish empire; see *Mahometanism*.

SONS OF THE CLERGY, see *Clergy*.

SONTAY, see *Tonquin*, Dec. 1883.

SONTHALS, a tribe of Northern India, brought to Bengal about 1830, where they prospered, till, partly from the instigation of a fanatic, and partly from the exactions of money-lenders, they broke out into rebellion in July, 1855, and committed fearful outrages. They were quite subdued early in 1856, and many were removed to the newly-conquered province of Pegu.

SOOLOO, see *Sulu*.

SOPHIA, ST. (in Constantinople). The first church was dedicated to St. Sophia (holy wisdom) by Constantius II., 360; this having been destroyed, the second, the present edifice, was founded by Justinian, 531, and dedicated 537. Since the Mahometan conquest in 1453, it has been used as an imperial mosque. Its length is 269 feet, and its breadth 243 feet. Six of its pillars are of green jasper, from the temple of Diana, at Ephesus; and of porphyry, from the temple of the Sun, at Rome. Four minarets were added by Selim II., who reigned in 1566. The interior of the dome is beautifully ornamented with mosaic work.

SOPHIA, see *Sofia*.

SOPHISTS, teachers of youth in Athens, who were censured by Socrates, and consequently were instrumental in causing his judicial murder, 399 B.C. The controversy against them was carried on by Plato and his disciples.

SORBONNE, a society of ecclesiastics at Paris, founded by Robert de Sorbonne in 1252. The members lived in common, and devoted themselves to study and gratuitous teaching. They soon attained a European reputation as a faculty of theology, their judgment being frequently appealed to, from the 14th to the 17th centuries. The influence of the Sorbonne was declining when the society was broken up in 1789. The buildings are now devoted to education. The new Sorbonne Buildings are to be opened on 5 Aug. 1889.

SORCERERS AND MAGICIANS. A law was enacted against their seductions, 33 Hen. VIII. 1541; and another statute equally severe was passed, 5 Eliz. 1563. The pretension to sorcery was made capital, 1 James I. 1603; see *Witchcraft*.

SORGHUM, see under *Sugar*.

SOUDAN or **SOUJAH**, the title of the lieutenant-generals of the caliphs, which they bore in their provinces and armies. The officers afterwards made themselves sovereigns. Saladin, general of the forces of Noureddin, king of Damascus, was the first that took upon him this title in Egypt, 1165, after having killed the caliph Caym.

SOUDAN or **NIGRITIA**, a region of Central Africa, partly subjected to the Khedive of Egypt since 1874, capital Khartoum. It was well governed, by col. Gordon, till 1879. See *Egypt*.

Insurrection headed by Sheik Mahomed Ahmed of Dongola, declaring himself to be a prophet (Mahdi or Muhdi, foretold by Moslem prophets), July, 1881

Defeated ; retires up the Blue Nile Nile with increased army . .
Defeats the Egyptians . .
Surrounds and massacres 6000 F Yussuf Pasha, 14 June ; occupi defeated at Bara, 19 Aug.; at I repulsed at Obeid, 8, 14 Sep Egyptians, 15 Sept.-24 Oct.; re Bara, 4 Nov.; Col. Stewart

The Mahdi captures Bara and Obe repulsed . . . .
Col. Hicks pasha with an army st dofan ; arrives at Berber, 1 March the Mahdi with great loss ; the

The Mahdi defeated at Khartoum
The Sennaar chiefs submit ; annou
Hicks marches up the Nile, 9 Sc Duem . . . .
Surprise and defeat of Egyptian Tokar, near Suakin ; about 150 l the brave and able British consu
Battle of El-Obeid, or Kashgal ; co into a defile ; about 11,000 men a whelming multitudes, they for resist till nearly all are killed Hicks, col. Farquhar, and c officers, only two said to have es desertion of some of Hicks' tro gains cannon and much ammuni
Egyptian force concentrated at I col. Coetlogon . . .
General rising throughout the coun government sends gunboats to and Red Sea ports, about 23 N Suakin forts, 26 Nov.—1 Dec. ; tians surrounded and 682 killed (
V. Baker pasha sent to Suakin with

Khartoum garrison strengthened
Osman ' Digma, a ruined slave-de for the Mahdi . . .
General (Chinese) Gordon sent to report) 18 Jan., starts 19 J governor-general of the Soudan

Sinkat closely besieged . .
Tokar besieged by rebels; surre Baker pasha with 3500 men defe loses about 2250 men (demora remnant retreats to Trinkitat, . by H.M.S. *Ranger*, 5, 6 Feb.; ordered to be sent to adm. He 6 Feb.; Baker pasha recalled ; in state of siege ; adm. Hewett l 7-9 Feb. ; desperate sortie of the by Tewfik bey, from Sinkat, all and children prisoners, town tak Reinforcements sent to Suakin
General Gordon arrives at Berber, slastically received as a delivere proclaims the Mahdi sultan of K sion of half the taxes, and with the slave trade, releases debts . . . .
Restoration of the former sultar proposed ; Kassala besieged by Os
The Black troops at Suakin muti announced . . . .
Battle of El-Teb, near where Bt defeated, 4 Feb. After fruitl negotiation, gen. Gerald Grahs 4000 men (consisting of 10th ar Gordon Highlanders, the Black shire and Yorkshire battalions, 11 a.m., advanced on the rebel who, after a most desperate, h were totally defeated with the lo men, at 2.30 p.m.; the British M. M. Slade, lieuts. F. H. Prol man, and Frank Royds, and quar Wilkins and 24 men killed, an

Tokar surrendered, and the rel

Osman Digna at Tamanieh . .
Several Arab sheikhs come into Su

SOUDAN.

Osman Digma disregards gen. Graham's proclamation, about 8 March. Osman Digma disdainfully rejects British proposals, and proclaims death to infidels	about 10 March, 1884
Battle of Tamanieb. The British advance to capture Osman Digma's camp at Tamasi, near El-Teb, 7.20 a.m.; the British were massed in oblong squares, one square broken into by a violent onslaught of hidden Arabs, who creep under and capture the Gatling and other guns, desperate hand to hand conflict; the British driven back; no panic; col. Wood with 700 cavalry charges the Arabs in flank, and drives them back, the infantry rally and recover the guns, the other square perfectly successful; the camp taken, 12.30 p.m. The British loss, killed, capts. H. G. V. Ford, Walker, and Aitken; lieuts. Montresor, Almack, and Houston Stewart, and 86 men, 111 wounded, and 19 missing; 2000 of the enemy killed out of above 10,000. The Black Watch and Naval Brigade suffered much	13 March, "
Osman Digma's camp with stores captured on 4 Feb.; burnt	14 March, "
Gordon defeats rebels and brings off garrison of Halfyeh	about 15 March, "
Through cowardice and treachery Gordon's troops (1500) defeated by about 60 rebels with great slaughter	16 March, "
Reward of 5000 dollars offered for capture of Osman Digma, alive or dead, 15 March; countermanded from home	17 March, "
Troops march to Handoub wells	18 March, "
Friendly sheikhs coming in	20 March, "
Hassan and Said pashas, Turko-Egyptian generals, tried and shot	23 March, "
The Mahdi rejects Gordon's offers; announced	23 March, "
General Graham advances on Tamanieb; slight skirmish; the Arabs flee; Osman Digma's villages burnt	27 March, "
Three regiments at Suakin, embark for home, &c.	29 March, "
March to Berber reported safe	29 March, "
Gordon contending with the rebels, with varying success; Kassala closely besieged, announced	30 March, "
Khartoum said to be closely invested; the rebels frequently defeated	April, "
General Gordon, col. Stewart, and Mr. Power, the *Times* correspondent, the only British there	8 April, "
The Mahdi said to have been twice defeated by the Jagalla tribes; reported	9 April, "
Egyptian troops arrive at Suakin	10 April, "
Adm. Hewett's mission well received by Ras Aloola	about 13 April, "
The Marines depart	about 15 April, "
Shendy closely besieged; 51 fugitives from it killed by Arabs; announced	19 April, "
Berber said to be closely invested	20 April, "
Reported evacuation of Berber; troops withdrawn to Korosko; announced	26 April, "
The whole country in insurrection; Egyptian troops joining the Mahdi	April, "
The government declining to send help, Gordon writes to sir Evelyn Baring, "I shall hold on here as long as I can, and if I can suppress the rebellion, I will do so. If I cannot, I shall retire to the equator."	
Col. Stewart and Mr. Power decide to remain with him	May, "
Subscriptions proposed to support Gordon	May, "
Adm. Hewett well received by the king of Abyssinia at Adowa; treaty signed	about 26 May, "
Fruitless attacks on Suakin checked by Marines,	27, 28, 31 May, 2, 4, 10 June, "
Gordon said to have been opposed by government in all his propositions	April, May, "
Highly successful sally from Khartoum; major Chermside made governor of Suakin; refugees from Korosko arrive at Assouan; reported rise of another Mahdi	28 May, "
The Mudir of Dongola said to have defeated the rebels	May, "
Advance of Egyptian troops	May, "
Fall of Berber announced	10 June, "
Assouan fortified	June, "
Rebels defeated at Debbeh with great loss,	29-30 June, 1884
Advance of the Mahdi said to be checked by another Mahdi; announced	2 July, "
Assouan occupied by the British	12 July, "
Additional troops sent to Alexandria from Malta,	July, "
Gordon dominant and successful at Khartoum; reported	22 July, "
Continued desertion of Egyptian troops, announced July; Gordon reports Khartoum and Sennaar holding out	2 Aug. "
Mudir of Dongola said to have greatly helped Gordon	July, Aug. "
Gen. Gordon repulses severe attack, 10 Aug.; defeats rebels	12 Aug. "
Osman Digma, near Suakin, frequently defeated,	Aug. "
Preparation for the expedition to relieve Khartoum, gen. Earle commander; British troops arrive at Wady Halfa	23 Aug. et seq.
The expedition to ascend the Nile in about 800 flat-bottomed boats, navigated by Canadian Indians (*voyageurs*); Sarras	Sept. Oct. "
Defeat of the Mahdi's troops by the Mudir of Dongola at Ambikol	8 Sept "
Gen. Earle to be at Wady Halfa; col. Stewart and lord Airlie at Dongola; col. Maurice at Assiout	Sept "
Another defeat of Mahdi's troops reported	15 Sept. "
Telegrams from Gordon requiring assistance	Sept. "
Friendly tribes defeat rebels, and relieve Suakin,	about 17 Sept. "
Victories of Gordon on 24 July and 30 Aug., and raising of the siege of Khartoum reported,	20 Sept. "
British army in Egypt, 13,559	about 22 Sept. "
Lord John Hay arrives with the fleet at Alexandria,	24 Sept. "
Several camel corps start from Woolwich for the Soudan	about 25 Sept. "
Mr. Power's journal of the siege of Khartoum, from April to 31 July published in the *Times*,	29 Sept. "
Lord Wolseley arrives at Wady Halfa	5 Oct. "
Shendy taken	6 Oct. "
Col. J. D. Stewart, with Mr. Power and M. Herbin, and about 40 men in a steamer, wrecked near Wady Garna, fifth cataract; land; massacred by Arabs offering guidance; announced	about 6 Oct. "
Gordon defeats rebels and returns to Khartoum; announced	1 Nov. "
Lord Wolseley arrives at Dongola	3 Nov. "
Attacks on Suakin repulsed	3, 4 Nov. "
Gordon reports all well at Khartoum	4 Nov. "
Rebels often repulsed	Nov. "
Above 200 whalers on the Nile conveying troops, &c.	15 Nov. "
Two steamers disabled by rebels near Khartoum; announced	18 Nov. "
Lord Wolseley's proclamation to the soldiers and sailors issued	1 Dec. "
Two hours' attack of the rebels on Suakin without effect, 3 Dec.; rebels defeated with loss	8 Dec. "
Lord Wolseley arrives at Korti	15 Dec. "
Successful sally of the garrison of Kassala,	26 Dec. "
Forward movement of the army	28 Dec. "
Rapid marches of gen. sir Herbert Stewart	Dec. "
Successful march in the desert	Jan. 1885.
Gen. Earle proceeding up the Nile, and gen. Stewart crossing the desert with troops, towards Metammeh	Jan. "
Near Abu Klea wells, about 120 miles from Khartoum, gen. Stewart, with 1500 men, defeats about 10,000 Arabs, who retire after a fierce conflict within the square, leaving about 800 dead. The British lose 9 officers (col. Fred. Gus. Burnaby, majors Atherton, Carmichael, and Gough, capts. Law and Darley, lieuts. Pigott, Delisle, and Wolfe), and 65 men killed, with 85 wounded	17 Jan. "
Gen. Stewart, marching towards Metammeh, is severely wounded by hidden sharpshooters; 12 killed, including correspondents of the *Morning Post* and *Standard*, Thos. St. Leger Herbert, and John A. Cameron; sir Charles Wilson takes command	19 Jan. "
At Gubat, near Metammeh, fierce Arab onset on	

SOUDAN.

the British square is repulsed with very heavy loss . . . . 19 Jan. 1885
Message from gen. Gordon received, dated 29 Dec.: "Khartoum is all right; could hold out for a year" . . . . . . about 19 Jan. ,,
Communications opened with Khartoum . 24 Jan. ,,
Gen. Earle with army marches to Handoub for Berber . . . . 24 Jan. ,,
Successful skirmishes of gen. Earle . . Jan. ,,
Gen. Stewart succeeded by sir Redvers Buller Jan. ,,
Surrender of Khartoum; Gordon and his faithful followers killed . . . . early 26 Jan. ,,
Sir Charles Wilson sails up the Nile . 28 Jan. ,,
Reconnaissances of gen. Fremantle; heavy Arab loss, about 30 Jan.; Handoub captured and burnt by a party which is intercepted by Arabs, and lose 12 men . . . . 2 Feb. ,,
The Italian flag hoisted beside Egyptian at Massowah, (*which see*) . . . . . . 6 Feb. ,,
Sir Charles Wilson and party, within 800 yards of Khartoum, fired upon; retreats; his steamer is wrecked by treachery of Arab pilots; lands on an island; is rescued from peril by the daring courage of lord Charles Beresford in face of batteries; arrives at Korti . . . . . 9 Feb. ,,
Victory at Kirbekan: the Arabs on a ridge, surrounded by gen. Earle's column (the Black Watch and Staffordshire regiments), many killed; gen. Earle and lieut.-cols. Eyre and Coveney, and nine others killed; attack well planned and gallantly executed; gen. Brackenbury takes the command . . . . . . 10 Feb. ,,
Gen. Buller retreats from Gubat to Abu-Klea wells, 13-15 Feb. ,,
Death of sir H. Stewart at Gakdul . . 16 Feb. ,,
Railway between Suakin and Berber ordered to be constructed . . . . . . Feb. ,,
Near Abu Klea, Arabs demoralised by skilful feat of major Wardrop, who takes the heights after much skirmishing; Arabs flee . . . 17 Feb. ,,
Sir Evelyn Wood arrives at Gakdul . 17 Feb. ,,
Gen. Gerald Graham, with Coldstream and Grenadier Guards and others, start for the Soudan; farewell given by the queen and prince of Wales,
19-21 Feb. ,,
Osman Digma massing his forces near Suakin, about 21 Feb. ,,
Rebels' attack on Kassala garrison defeated with great loss; announced . . . 22 Feb. ,,
Gen. Brackenbury's column reaches Gakdul, 26 Feb. ,,
Gen. Buller's column marches to Korti 1 March, ,,
Gen. Graham's staff and 15th Sikh regiment arrive at Suakin . . . . . . 4 March, ,,
Successful sally from Kassala announced 4 March, ,,
The queen's address of thanks read to the army at Korti by lord Wolseley . . . 7 March, ,,
The 17th Bengal Infantry and the Royal Engineers balloon corps arrive at Suakin . 7 March, ,,
Arab raids on Suakin camp; sentries killed 11 March, ,,
The bulk of lord Wolseley's army at Korti, 12 March, ,,
Gen. Graham arrives at Suakin with 5th Lancers, 12, 13 March, ,,
The last of the desert troops arrive at Korti, 16 March, ,,
Gen. Graham calls on Osman Digma to surrender, to avoid bloodshed . . . about 16 March, ,,
Battle of Hasheen: Graham, with part of his army, starts at daybreak; several of Osman Digma's positions on the hills taken after conflicts: about 21 British killed . 20 March, ,,
Gen. McNeil's brigade unexpectedly attacked by about 4500 Arabs, about 6 miles from Suakin; they are repulsed with heavy loss (about 1500), after a severe fight; British loss about 100 killed, including lieuts. Swinton, Seymour, and Newman, capt. Romilly and others . 22 March, ,,
Manifesto of the Mahdi claiming the caliphate published . . . . . . March, ,,
Fever at Korti; evacuated by the army, about 23 March, ,,
Arab attacks repulsed by the guards . 24 March, ,,
Attacks on British convoy repulsed 24-26 March, ,,
The last Egyptian troops leave Suakin 26 March, ,,
Zebehr Pasha arrested at request of lord Wolseley, 14 March; sent to Gibraltar . 29 March, ,,
[Released under conditions, 3 Aug. 1887.]

New South Wales contingent arrives at Suakin 29, 30 March, 1885
Graham advances; finds Tamai deserted; burns it and returns to Suakin . . . 2, 3 April, ,,
The railway to Berber constructing under military protection . . . . . . April, ,,
Handoub (deserted) occupied by the British 8 April, ,,
Successful raid of capt. Briggs, capturing prisoners, cattle, &c. . . . . . 15 April, ,,
Numerous night attacks . . . April, ,,
Rebellion against the Mahdi; his troops said to be defeated near Kordofan . . . April, ,,
Lord Wolseley arrives at Suakin . . 2 May, ,,
Takool burnt and cattle captured by gen. Graham; organised force of Arabs dispersed midnight, 5-6 May, ,,
Proposed armed defence of line from Assouan to Wady Halfa announced . . 11 May, ,,
General Graham with British troops, and the Indian (part) and New South Wales contingents, quit Suakin . . . . 17 May *et seq.* ,,
Major-gen. sir G. Greaves assumes command at Suakin, 18 May; leaves . . . 15 June, ,,
Handoub evacuated by the British, 22 May; occupied by the Arabs, many of whom join Osman Digma . . . . . . June, ,,
Dongola evacuated . . . . 15 June, ,,
Sir. F. Stephenson, commander-in-chief 6 July, ,,
Lord Wolseley arrives in London . 13 July, ,,
Repulse of attack on Kassala, about 3,000 of the rebels killed; the garrison capture much cattle in a sortie . . . . . 15, 16 June, ,,
Reported death of the Mahdi by small pox, 20, 21, or 22 June, ,,
Olivier Pain sent by the Irish in Paris to join the Mahdi at El Obeid, July, 1884; reported death, time uncertain; Selikovitch, an interpreter dismissed by the British, asserts without any evidence that Pain was executed by order of col. Kitchener in April, 1885; no British investigation; much excitement in Paris caused by M. Rochefort, ... Aug.-Sept. ,,
Sennaar surprised and taken . . 16 Aug. ,,
Rebels defeated and stores captured near Suakin, 19 Aug. ,,
Major Chermside sent to relieve Kassala . Aug. ,,
Khalifa Abdulla El Taashi reported successor of the Mahdi . . . . . . autumn, ,,
Successful skirmish of the hussars and Egyptians with Arabs near Giniss; fighting on the Nile; announced . . . . . 3 Dec. ,,
Advance of rebels northward; two battalions sent from Britain . . . . about 10 Dec. ,,
Attack of 3,000 Arabs on Mograkeh, near Kosheh, repulsed . . . . . . 12 Dec. ,,
6,000 Arabs defeated at Giniss, near Kosheh, 3½ hours' fight; one officer (lieut. Soltau) killed; 19 Egyptians killed and wounded; about 600 Arabs killed . . . . . . 30 Dec. ,,
Attack on Suakin repulsed . . 11 Feb. 1886
Osman Digma and the rebels active, about 2 March, ,,
Rebels defeated by friendly Arabs and the British, 13 March, ,,
Sir C. Warren appointed governor at Suakin, about 16 Jan.; [made commissioner of police, London]; gen. Dixon left in command . . March, ,,
Country south of Wady Halfa abandoned by the Egyptians, announced . . . April, ,,
General Watson nominated governor of the Red Sea territories about 14 April; arrives 8 May, ,,
British evacuation of Suakin completed 16 May, ,,
Fighting near Sheik Barghut; victory of friendly Arabs who take prisoners and recover captives, about 28 May, ,,
Major Kitchener succeeds general Watson, Aug.; arrives . . . . . . 7 Sept. ,,
By judicious advice of gen. Watson and col. Kitchener, the Arabs combine to overthrow Osman Digma; after serious losses he quits his stronghold at Tamai, which, with all its military stores is captured, with much slaughter of his followers . . . . . 7 Oct. ,,
Emin Bey (Austrian physician), an associate of gen. Gordon, holding Wadelai with black troops; news brought by Dr. Junker . . Nov. ,,
Retreat of the rebels on British advance, 3 Dec. ,,
Mr. H. M. Stanley starts from London for the

relief of Emin Pasha with a small armament, 21 Jan. 1887; after successful progress, checked by the want of supplies, arrives at Aruwimi, 9 June; his murder falsely announced 21 July; said to have left Aruwimi with 380 men, 2 June; letter from him received at Manchester dated 19 June, stating all well, 5 Sept.; letter from Emin Bey, 17 April, received . . . . 24 Sept. 1887
[Another dated 2 Nov. 1887, received April, 1888.]
Messengers from the new Mahdi with arrogant message, received and dismissed by the khedive, 19 April. ,,
Col. Chermside, with the Egyptians, defeats the Dervishes at Sarras, near Wady Halfa, after stubborn resistance; about 190 killed, 29 April, ,,
Great defeat of the Dervishes announced about 29 Aug. ,,
Successful skirmish of col. Wodehouse with the Dervishes . . . . . . 24 Oct. ,,
Arab attack on Wady Halfa repulsed, 25 Oct.; reinforcements sent . . . . 27 Oct. ,,
Expedition of the hon. Montague Kerr to Emin Pasha's station at Wadelai, starts . . Nov. ,,
[He is struck down by fever; returns to Europe; dies in France, 23 April, 1888.]
Osman Digma defeated with great loss by the friendly tribes . . . . 29 Dec. ,,
Unsuccessful attacks on Suakin Dec. 1887.–3 Jan. 1888
His camp at Handoub captured and his followers dispersed; they return and retake the camp; the friendly tribes forced to retreat, col. Kitchener and major Mc Murdo wounded . . 17 Jan. ,,
Colonel Kitchener leaves for Cairo; succeeded by col. Shakspear . . . . 19 Jan. ,,
A band of Dervishes dispersed after fierce conflict near Suakin, col. Tapp killed . . 4 March, ,,
Return of col. Kitchener to Suakin . 15 March, ,,
Affairs quiet; Osman Digma's followers dispersing April, ,,
Col. Kitchener leaves for England . 26 May, ,,
Defeat of the Dervishes near Wady Halfa about 20 July, ,,
Rumoured appearance of a "White Pasha," conjectured to be Emin Pasha or Mr. Stanley, with an army in s. Soudan . . July, ,,
The Dervishes severely defeated in an attack on Fort Khornoussa . . . midnight, 27 Aug. ,,
Attempted raid of Osman Digma checked 12 Sept. ,,
Lt. col. Holled Smith succeeds col. Kitchener as governor-general and commandant at Suakin, 13 Sept. ,,
Continued investment of Suakin by Arabs (Dervishes) with guns, &c.; severe night attacks; reinforcements ordered . . 22 Sept., Oct. ,,
Assassination of major Barttelot, near river Aruwimi, on his way to relieve Mr. Stanley and Emin Pasha by his carriers, 19 July; his successor in command, James Sligo Jameson, died 17 Aug.; failure of the expedition attributed to Tippoo Tib, who engaged to support it Sept. ,,
German expedition for the relief of Emin Pasha organized; supported by prince Hohenlohe Langenburg and other nobles . . Sept. ,,
Mr. Stanley reported well in Nov. 1887 . Nov. ,,
A sharp attack on Suakin vigorously repulsed, 30 Oct. ,,
General Grenfell with reinforcements arrives at Suakin . . . . . . 5 Nov. ,,
Defeat of the nominal Mahdi by the sultan of Wadai's people; gen. Grenfell 'reconnoitres; the enemy very strong; the Mahdi afterwards captures Wadai, and the sultan flees . Nov. ,,
More British troops sent to Suakin . . Dec. ,,
Letter from Osman Digma reporting capture of Emin Pasha and possibly of Mr. Stanley (discredited) . . . . . about 13 Dec. ,,
The enemy's redoubts stormed by the black brigade under gen. Grenfell: great slaughter, slight British loss; total flight of the enemy with loss of about 400; 7.30 a.m. . 20 Dec. ,,
General Grenfell and part of his army leave Suakin, 4 Jan. 1889
Handoub abandoned and burnt . . 11 Feb. ,,
Suakin declared open to commerce . . 20 Feb. ,,
Dr. Carl Peters, with 100 soldiers, &c., starts to relieve Emin Pasha (not successful July) 26 Feb. ,,
Graphic letter from Mr. H. M. Stanley, dated 28 Aug. 1888; published in *Times*, 3 April, 1889;

narrates his movements from Yambura since July 1887; suffers by conflicts with natives, by disease and starvation, and many deaths in a horrible wilderness; many desertions of his men; meets Emin Pasha on lake Nyanza and stays with him 29 April–25 May, 1888. Meets with Mr. Bonny and 71 men, the remains of 257 of mayor Barttelot's party, 17 Aug. Mr. Stanley, with 190 men out of 389, prepare to recross Africa.
The Dervishes repulsed with loss after their attack on Haliab, 19 April; again repulsed, 29, 30 April; again repulsed, and an outpost captured . . . . . 2 June, 1889
Letters reporting meeting of Mr. H. M. Stanley and Tippoo Tib, dated Ujiji, 10 March; news received by mail steamer Kinsembo confirming the account of the sufferings of the parties of Mr. Stanley and major Barttelot . . 29 June, ,,
Colonel Wodehouse, with three Egyptian black battalions, &c., defeats about 3,500 Dervishes at Arguin near Wady Halfa, they lose about, 500 killed, Egyptian loss about 70 killed and wounded . . . . . 2 July, ,,
The Dervishes repulsed with the loss of about 100 men, 4 July; they break up their camp, 7 July; which is occupied by the British 8 July ,,
Reinforcements from Malta; which is proclaimed to the natives by gen. Grenfell, 10 July [see ADDENDA] . . . . . . ,,

SOULAGES COLLECTION. About 1827, M. Soulages of Toulouse, collected 790 specimens of Italian art and workmanship, &c. These were bought for 11,000*l*. by 73 English gentlemen, with the view of first exhibiting them to the public, and afterwards selling them to the government (who gradually purchased them between 1858 and 1865). They formed part of the "Art Treasures" exhibited at Manchester in 1857.

SOUND, see *Acoustics*.

SOUND DUTIES. Till the year 1857 no merchant ship was allowed to pass the Sound (a narrow channel separating Zealand from Sweden) without clearing at Elsinore and paying toll. These duties had their origin in an agreement between the king of Denmark and the Hanse towns (1348), by which the former undertook to maintain lighthouses, &c., along the Cattegat, and the latter to pay duty for the same. The first treaty with England in relation to this was in 1450; other countries followed. In 1855 the United States determined to pay the dues no more; and in the same year the Danish government proposed that these dues should be capitalised; which was eventually agreed to, the sum being 30,476,325 rix-dollars. In Aug. 1857, the British government paid 10,126,855 rix-dollars (1,125,206*l*.) to the Danes as their proportion.—The passage of the Sound was effected, in defiance of strong fortresses, by sir Hyde Parker and lord Nelson, 31 March, 1801; see *Baltic Expedition*.

SOUNDINGS AT SEA. Captain Ross, of H.M.S. *Œdipus*, in 1840, took extraordinary soundings at sea. One taken 900 miles west of St. Helena, extended to the depth of 5000 fathoms. In the latitude 33° S. and longitude 9° W. about 300 miles from the Cape of Good Hope, 2266 fathoms were sounded; the weight employed amounted to 450 lbs. On 13 July, 1857, lieut. Joseph Dayman, in the North Atlantic Ocean, lat. 51° 9′ N., long. 40° 2′ W., in sounding, found a bottom at 2424 fathoms. The deepest sounding known (3875 faths.) was taken by the *Challenger*, capt. Nares, 24 March, 1873, in the North Atlantic, north of St. Thomas's.

SOUTH AFRICAN ASSOCIATION, established July, 1851, to promote the commercial and social interests of the South African colonies.

SOUTH AFRICAN CONFEDERATION: to comprise the three British colonies—Cape Town, Natal, and West Griqua Land (1873)—and the two Dutch republics, Orange River free state, and the South African or Trans-Vaal republic (1852). The formation was proposed by the earl of Carnarvon, colonial secretary, in a despatch to sir Henry Barkly, governor of Cape Town, 4 May, 1875, and advocated by the historian, J. A. Froude, on a visit. It was much opposed at the Cape. See *Cape*. A conference of delegates in London was opened, 5 Aug. 1876.
The South Africa Act "for the union under one government of such of the South African colonies and states as may agree thereto," was passed 10 Aug. 1877.

SOUTH AFRICAN REPUBLIC, name assumed by the Boers in the Transvaal (*which see*) in 1880-1, and adopted by treaty in Feb. 1884.

SOUTH AMERICA, see *America*.

SOUTHAMPTON, a seaport (S. England), a county of itself, near the Roman Clausentum and the Saxon Hamtune. It frequently suffered by Danish incursions: Canute, when king, occasionally resided here. The charter was granted by Henry I. and confirmed by Richard I. and John; and the free grammar school was founded by Edward VI. On 17 July, 1861, a monument to Dr. Isaac Watts, a native, was uncovered; and on 15 Oct. 1862, the Hartley institution was opened by lord Palmerston. The prince of Wales laid the foundation of the parish church of St. Mary, built as a memorial of Samuel Wilberforce, bishop of Winchester, 12 Aug. 1878; consecrated 19 June, 1879. The British Association met here 1846 and 1882.

SOUTH AUSTRALIA was visited by capt. Sturt in 1830, and explored shortly after by capt. Parker and Mr. Kent, the former of whom was killed by the natives. The boundaries of the province were fixed by 4 & 5 Will. IV. c. 95 (1834); and it was occupied 26 Dec. 1836, by capt. Hindmarsh, the first governor. It was colonised according to Mr. E. Gibbon Wakefield's scheme, which was carried out by the South Australian Colonisation Association. The colony for several years underwent severe trials through the great influx of emigrants, land-jobbing, building speculations, &c., which produced almost universal bankruptcy in 1839. In five years after, the energy of the colonists had overcome their difficulties, and the prosperity of the colony appeared fully established. In 1842 the highly productive Burra Burra copper mines were discovered, and large fortunes were suddenly realised; but in 1851 the discovery of gold in New South Wales and Victoria almost paralysed this province by drawing off a large part of the labouring population. Very little gold was found in South Australia; but a reaction took place in favour of the copper mines and agriculture, &c. Before the discovery of gold, little trade existed between Adelaide (the capital of South Australia) and Melbourne; but in 1852 gold was transmitted from the latter to the former to the amount of 2,215,167*l*. principally for breadstuffs, farm produce, &c. The bishopric of Adelaide was founded in 1847. Discovery of alluvial gold at Tatulpa, Waukaringa, Oct.; favourable report Dec. 1886. Sir Dominic Daly, appointed governor in Nov. 1861, died 19 Feb. 1868; succeeded by sir James Ferguson, Dec. 1868; by Anthony Musgrave, Jan 1873; by Wm. Wellington Cairns, Jan. 1877; Sir W. F. D. Jervois, June, 1877; sir W. Robinson, Nov. 1882;

the earl of Kintore, 1855, 85,821; in 1865, in 1877, 225,677; in 313,065.
See *Adelaide*. 1887, revenue, 2,145,133*l*. Imports, 5,330,780*l*.
Resignation of the ministry the hon. J. A. Cockburn

SOUTHCOTT, J, in 1750, came from E followers at one period sands, the low and i dupes. In 1792 she woman spoken of in a disease favoured the the mother of the pro Dec. 1814. In 1851 t congregations, profess Her successor, Mrs. aged 103 (?).

SOUTH-EASTE London to Folkestone, Dover, 7 Feb. 1844.

SOUTHERN CO see *Confederates*.

SOUTHERN CO Ocean was first trave and explored by Walli by Cook in 1773 and tinent little more is bound, and contains a covered in the first ins on 27 Feb. 1831, in lat extending east and we Enderby Land, after equipped him for the discovered Graham's situated in lat. 67° 1' Messrs. Enderby equi in search of the sout connection with some when capt. Balleny h 1839, discovered the S., long. 165° E., an Land, in lat. 65° 10' S. a French expedition, u D'Urville, and an Am command of commodo our knowledge in res southern continent, a by the expedition whi 1839, under the com Clark Ross, who disco and subsequently pe 78° 11'. Antarctic ex gentine republic and t objects collected to be under lieut. Booc, 1881

SOUTH KEN near Brompton old tures presented by M Mrs. Ellison, and t the great painter, as w and art, educational animal, vegetable, and opened on 22 June, 18 works of art, of immen was opened here in th in November. In Jul (aft. sir) Henry Cole, exertions in organizin moting its objects.

Mr. John Forster, biographer of Dickens, bequeathed his library of books, MSS., paintings, and drawings to this museum. He died 1 Feb. . 1876
Scientific Apparatus Loan Exhibition (*which see*) opened 13 May, closed . . . . 30 Dec. ,,
Mr. John Jones bequeaths a collection of works of art, &c.; estimated value, 500,000*l*. announced, Jan. 1882

SOUTH-SEA BUBBLE commenced with the establishment of the South-sea company in 1710, which was at first unwisely and afterwards dishonestly managed. It exploded in 1720, ruining thousands of families; and the directors' estates, to the value of 2,014,000*l*., were seized in 1721 and sold. Mr. Knight, the cashier, absconded with 100,000*l*.; but he compounded the fraud for 10,000*l*. and returned to England in 1743. Almost all the wealthy persons in the kingdom had become speculators; the artifices of the directors having raised the shares, originally 100*l*., to the price of 1000*l*. A parliamentary inquiry took place in Nov. 1720, and Aislabie, chancellor of the exchequer, and several members of parliament were expelled the house in 1721; see *Law's Bubble*.

SOUTHWARK (S. London), was governed by its own bailiffs till 1327. The city, however, found great inconvenience from the number of malefactors who escaped thither, in order to be out of the reach and cognizance of the city magistrates; and a grant was made of Southwark to the city of London by the crown, for a small annuity. In Edward VI.'s reign it was formed into a city ward, and was named Bridge Ward Without, 1550.—*Southwark bridge* was designed by John Rennie, and built by a company, 1815-19, at an expense of 800,000*l*. It consists of three great cast-iron arches, resting on massive stone piers and abutments; the distance between the abutments is 708 feet; the centre arch is 240 feet span, the two others 210 feet each; and the total weight of iron 5308 tons. The bridge was freed from toll on 8 Nov. 1864, the company receiving a compensation from the city. An act for the payment of dividends to shareholders was passed in 1872.—*Southwark park* was opened, 19 June, 1869. By the Seats Act (1885), Southwark sends three members to parliament.

SOUTHWELL, Nottinghamshire, an ancient Saxon town, where a church was founded by Paulinus, archbishop of York, 627; made collegiate before the conquest, refounded by Henry VIII., and made a bishopric by Henry VIII., 1541; dissolved by Edward VI. Collegiate church restored by Elizabeth, 1586. Near here Charles I. surrendered himself to the Scotch army in 1646. The Bishoprics act, authorising the establishment of a see at Southwell, was passed, 16 Aug. 1878. Constituted (to consist of the counties of Derby and Nottingham), 2 Feb. 1884. The restored minster re-opened as cathedral, 2 Feb. 1888.

FIRST BISHOP.
George Ridding, consecrated 1 May, 1884.

SOUTHWOLD, see *Solebay*.

SOVEREIGN, an ancient and modern British gold coin. In 1489 22½ pieces, in value 20*s*., " to be called the sovereign," were ordered to be coined out of a pound of gold. *Ruding*. In 1542 sovereigns were coined in value 20*s*., which afterwards, in 1550 and 1552 (4 & 6 Ed. VI.), passed for 24*s*. and 30*s*. "Sovereigns" of the new coinage were directed to pass for 20*s*. 1 July, and half-sovereigns for 10*s*. 10 Oct. 1817; see *Coin*, and *Gold*. By the Coinage act, 1870, the weight of the sovereign is fixed at 123·27447 grains troy; specific gravity,

17·57; (916·67, gold being 1000); half-sovereigns, 61·63723 grains. The *dragon* sovereigns were reissued in 1871.

SPA-FIELDS (N. London). Here about 30,000 persons assembled to vote an address from the distressed manufacturers to the prince regent, 15 Nov. 1816. A second meeting, 2 Dec. following, terminated in an alarming riot; the shops of several gunsmiths were attacked for arms by the rioters; and in the shop of Mr. Beckwith, on Snowhill, Mr. Platt was wounded, and much injury was done before the tumult was suppressed. For this riot, Cashman, a seaman, was hanged, 12 March, 1817. Watson, the ringleader, escaped to America.
Spafields Chapel, a dome building, originally a place of entertainment named the Pantheon, erected, 1770, was after several changes purchased by the countess of Huntingdon and used as a place of worship for her "connection," (see *Whitefieldites*). This chapel was pulled down in . . . 1887

SPAHIS, Turkish cavalry. African horsemen, under this name, were incorporated by the French in Algeria in 1834; three regiments of them came to France in 1863.

SPAIN (the ancient Iberia and Hispania). The first settlers are supposed to have been the progeny of Tubal, fifth son of Japheth. The Phœnicians and Carthaginians (360 B.C.) successively planted colonies on the coasts; and the Romans conquered the whole country, 206 B.C. Population of Spain in 1857, 15,464,078; of the colonies, 6,333,887; 1883, total 25,022,880; in 1887, 17,358,404. Revenue: 1822, about 6,000,000*l*.; 1850, 12,722,200*l*. 1860, 18,921,000; 1871, about 26,000,000*l*.; 1883-4, 32,095,075*l*.

	B.C.
The Carthaginians, enriched by the mines of Spain (480 B.C. *et seq.*) form settlements	360
New Carthage (Carthagena) founded by Hasdrubal	242
Hamilcar extends their dominions in Spain .	238-233
At his death, Hannibal, his son, takes the command, 221; prepares for war, 220; takes Saguntum, 219; crosses the Alps, and enters Italy . .	218
The Romans carry the war into Spain; two Scipios defeated and slain by Hasdrubal . . .	212
Pub. Cornelius Scipio Africanus takes New Carthage, 210; drives the Carthaginians out of Spain, 207; and annexes it	205
Celtiberian and Numantine war	153-133
Viriathus, general of the Celtiberians and Lusitanians, subdued all West Spain, 145; makes peace with the consul Fabius Servilianus, 142; assassinated by order of the Romans . . .	140
Insurrection of Sertorius, 78; subdued by Pompey, and assassinated	72
Julius Cæsar quells an insurrection in Spain . .	67
Pompey governs Spain	60-50
Revolt through the rapacity of Crassus . . .	43-47
Era of Spain: conquest by Augustus begun, 1 Jan.	38
The Vandals, Alani, and Suevi wrest Spain from the Romans . . . . A.D.	409
Adolphus founds the kingdom of the Visigoths .	414
The Vandals pass over to Africa	427
Theodoric I. vanquishes the Suevi	452
Assassinated by his brother Euric, who becomes master of all Spain	466
Recared I. expels the Franks	587
He abjures Arianism, and rules ably . . till	601
Wamba's wise administration; he prepared a fleet for defence against the Saracens . . .	672-677
The Arabs invited into Spain against king Roderic.	709
His defeat and death at Xeres	711
Establishment of the Saracens at Cordova . .	,,
Victorious progress of Musa and Tarik . . .	712-13
Emirs rule at Cordova; Pelayo, of Gothic blood, rules in Asturias and Leon	718
The Saracens defeated at Tours by Charles Martel,	732 or 733
Abderahman the first king at Cordova . . .	755
Invasion of Charlemagne	777-78
Sancho Iñigo, count of Navarre, &c. . . .	873

3 U

SPAIN.

Sancho of Navarre becomes king of Castile	1026
The kingdom of Aragon commenced under Raimirez I.	1035
Leon and Asturias united to Castile	1037
Portugal taken from the Saracens by Henry of Besançon (see *Portugal*)	1095
The Saracens, beset on all sides by the Christians, call in the aid of the Moors from Africa, who seize the dominions they came to protect, and subdue the Saracens	1091 *et seq.*
Exploits of the Cid Rodrigo; dies	about 1099
Dynasty of the Almoravides at Cordova	1094-1144
The Moors defeated in several battles by Alfonso of Leon	1144
Dynasty of the Almohades at Cordova	1144-1225
Cordova, Toledo, Seville, &c., taken by Ferdinand of Castile and Leon	1233-48
The kingdom of Granada begun by the Moors, last refuge from the power of the Christians	1238
The crown of Navarre passes to the royal family of France	1274
200,000 Moors arrive to assist the king of Granada	1327
They are defeated at Tarifa by Alfonso XI. of Castile with great slaughter	1340
Reign of Pedro the Cruel	1350
His alliance with Edward the Black Prince	1363
Defeated at Montiel and treacherously slain	1369
Ferdinand II. of Aragon marries Isabella of Castile, 18 Oct. 1469; and nearly the whole Christian dominions of Spain are united in one monarchy	1479
Establishment of the Inquisition	1480-4
Persecution of the Jews	1492-8
Granada taken after a two years' siege; and the power of the Moors is finally extirpated by Ferdinand	1492
Jews expelled	,,
Columbus is sent from Spain to explore the western ocean	17 April, ,,
Mahometans persecuted and expelled	1499-1502
Death of Columbus	20 May, 1506
Ferdinand conquers great part of Navarre	1512
Accession of the house of Austria to the throne of Spain; Charles I. of Spain	1516
Able administration of Ximenes; ungratefully used, 1516; his death	1517
Charles elected emperor of Germany	1519
Insurrection in Castile	1520-21
Philip of Spain marries Mary of England	25 July, 1554
Charles abdicates and retires from the world	1556
War with France; victory at St. Quentin	10 Aug. 1557
Philip II. commences his bloody persecution of the protestants	1561
The Escurial begun building	1563
Revolt of the Moriscoes, 1567; suppressed	1570
Naval victory of Lepanto over the Turks	7 Oct. 1571
Portugal united to Spain by conquest	1580
The Spanish Armada destroyed; see *Armada*.	1588
Philip III. banishes the Moors (900,000)	1598-1610
Ministry of the duke of Lerma	1598-1618
Ministry of Olivarez	1621-43
Philip IV. loses Portugal	1640
Death of Charles II., last of the house of Austria; accession of Philip V. of the house of Bourbon	1700
War of the Succession	1702-13
Gibraltar taken by the English	1704
Siege of Barcelona	1713
Able government of cardinal Alberoni; he re-established the authority of the king, reformed many abuses; and raised Spain to the rank of a first power, 1715-20; ordered to quit Spain	1720
Charles, son of Philip V., conquers Naples	1735
Charles III. king of the Two Sicilies, succeeds to the crown of Spain	1759
War with England, 1762-3; and	1796
Battle of Cape St. Vincent	14 Feb. 1797
Spanish treasure-ships, valued at 3,000,000 dollars, seized by the English	Oct. 1804
Battle of Trafalgar (see *Trafalgar*)	21 Oct. 1805
Sway of Godoy, prince of the peace	1806
The French enter Spain; a Spanish army sent to the Baltic	1807
Conspiracy of the prince of Asturias against his father	25 July, ,,
Treaty of Fontainebleau	27 Oct. ,,
The French take Madrid	March, 1808
The prince of peace dismissed	18 March, ,,
Abdication of Charles IV. in favour of Ferdinand, 19 March; and at Bayonne, in favour of his "friend and ally" Napoleon, when Ferdinand relinquished the crown	1 May, 1808
Revolution: the French massacred at Madrid,	2 May, ,,
The province of Asturias rises *en masse*	3 May, ,,
Napoleon assembles the notables at Bayonne	25 May, ,,
Joseph Bonaparte enters Madrid as king of Spain,	12 July; retires 29 July, ,,
Battle of Vimiera; French defeated	21 Aug. ,,
Supreme Junta installed	Sept. ,,
Madrid taken by the French, and Joseph restored	2 Dec. ,,
Napoleon enters Madrid	4 Dec. ,,
The royal family of Spain imprisoned in the palace of Chambery in Savoy	5 Dec. ,,
The French defeated at Corunna, 16 Jan.; take Ferrol, 27 Jan.; Saragossa, 21 Feb.; Oporto, 29 Feb.; Cordova and Seville, Nov.; Gerona,	12 Dec. 1809
Ney takes Ciudad Rodrigo	10 July, 1810
The Spanish cortes meet	24 Sept. ,,
Wellington defeats Massena at Fuentes de Onoro,	5 May, 1811
Soult defeated at Albuera	16 May, ,,
Constitution of the cortes (democratic)	8 May, 1812
Wellington takes Ciudad Rodrigo, 19 Jan.; storms Badajoz, 6 April; defeats Marmont at Salamanca,	22 July, ,,
He occupies Madrid, and totally defeats the French at Vittoria, 21 June; defeats Soult in the Pyrenees, 28 July; takes St. Sebastian, 31 Aug.; and enters France	8 Oct. 1813
Ferdinand VII. restored (constitution set aside),	14 May, 1814
Slave trade abolished for a compensation	1817
Insurrection at Valencia repressed	1819
Spanish revolution begun by Riego	Jan. 1820
Ferdinand swears to the constitution of the cortes,	8 March, ,,
The cortes remove the king to Seville, and thence to Cadiz	March, 1823
The French enter Spain, 7 April; and invest Cadiz,	25 June, ,,
Battle of the Trocadero	31 Aug. ,,
Despotism resumed; the cortes dissolved; executions of liberals	Oct. ,,
Riego put to death	7 Nov. ,,
The French evacuate Cadiz	21 Sept. 1828
Cadiz made a free port	24 Feb. 1829
Salique law abolished, 29 March; Carlist and Christina parties formed	1830
Queen of Spain appointed regent during the king's indisposition; change in the ministry, 25 Oct. 1832
Don Carlos declares himself legitimate successor to the king	29 April, 1833
Death of Ferdinand VII.; his queen assumes the title of governing queen until Isabella II., her infant daughter, attains her majority	29 Sept. ,,
Constitution termed "Estatuto Real" granted by advice of Martinez de la Rosa	,,
The royalist volunteers disarmed with some bloodshed at Madrid	27 Oct. ,,
Queen Christina marries Ferdinand Muñoz (afterwards duke of Rianzarés)	28 Dec. ,,
The quadruple treaty establishes the right of Isabella to the throne	22 April, 1834
Don Carlos suddenly appears in Spain	10 July, ,,
The peers vote his exclusion	30 Aug. ,,
Mendizabal, prime minister; Mina and Espartero commanded the royalists; the rebel leader, Zumalacarregui, killed near Bilbao	June, 1835
Sir De Lacy Evans and others raise a British legion for the queen of Spain	,,
They defeat the Carlists at St. Sebastian	1 Oct. 1836
Espartero gains the battle of Bilbao	25 Dec. ,,
General Evans takes Irun	17 May, 1837
Constituent cortes proclaimed	,,
Dissolution of the monasteries	,,
The Carlists under Maroto desert Don Carlos and conclude a treaty of peace with Espartero, at Vergara	31 Aug. 1839
Don Carlos seeks refuge in France	13 Sept. ,,
Surrender of Morello	28 May, 1840
Cabrera, the Carlist general, unable to maintain the war, enters France	7 July, ,,
The British auxiliaries evacuate St. Sebastian and Passages	25 Aug. ,,

Revolutionary movement at Madrid: the authorities triumphant . . . . 1 Sept.	1840
Dismissal of the ministry, and dissolution of the cortes . . . . 9 Sept.	,,
Espartero, minister, makes his triumphal entry into Madrid . . . . 3 Oct.	,,
The queen regent appoints a new ministry, who are nominated by Espartero, 5 Oct.; she abdicates and leaves the kingdom; visits France and Sicily; returns to France . . . . . 12 Oct.	,,
Espartero, duke of Victory, expels the papal nuncio 29 Dec.	,,
The Spanish cortes declare Espartero regent during the queen's minority . . . . 12 April,	1841
Queen Christina's protest . . . . 19 July,	,,
Insurrection in favour of Christina commenced at Pampeluna by general O'Donnell and Concha, 2 Oct.	,,
Don Diego Leon attacks the palace at Madrid; his followers repulsed, and numbers slain by the queen's guards, 7 Oct.; he is shot at Madrid, 15 Oct.	,,
Zurbano captures Bilbao . . . . 21 Oct.	,,
Rodil, constitutional general, enters Vittoria, 21 Oct.	,,
Montes de Oca shot . . . . . 21 Oct.	,,
General O'Donnell takes refuge in the French territory . . . . 21 Oct.	,,
Espartero decrees the suspension of queen Christina's pension . . . . . 26 Oct.	,,
Fueros of the Basque provinces abolished 29 Oct.	,,
Borio and Gobernado, implicated in the Christina plot, put to death at Madrid . . 9 Nov.	,,
Espartero enters Madrid . . . . 23 Nov.	,,
General pardon of all persons not yet tried, concerned in the events of October . 13 Dec.	,,
The effective strength of the army fixed at 130,000 men . . . . 28 June,	1842
An insurrection at Barcelona; the national guard joins the populace, 13 Nov.; battle in the streets between the national guard and the troops: the latter lose 500 in killed and wounded, and retreat to the citadel . . . . . 15 Nov.	,,
Barcelona blockaded, 26 Nov.; Espartero arrives before it, 29 Nov.; its bombardment and surrender . . . . . . 3, 4 Dec.	,,
The disturbances at Malaga . . . 25 May,	1843
The revolutionary junta is re-established at Barcelona . . . . 11 June,	,,
[Corunna, Seville, Burgos, Santiago, and numerous other towns, shortly afterwards "pronounce" against the regent Espartero.]	
Arrival of general Narvaez at Madrid, which surrenders . . . . . . 15 July,	,,
Espartero bombards Seville . . . 21 July,	,,
The siege is raised . . . . . 27 July,	,,
[The revolution is completely successful, and Espartero flees to Cadiz, and embarks on board her Majesty's ship Malabar.]	
The new government deprives Espartero of his titles and rank, 16 Aug.; he arrives in London, 23 Aug.	,,
Reaction suppressed at Madrid . . . Aug.	,,
Isabella II. 13 years old, is declared by the cortes to be of age; Narvaez (friend of the queen-mother), lieutenant-general . . . . . 8 Nov.	,,
The queen-mother returns to Spain . 23 March,	1844
Zurbano's insurrection, 12 Nov. 1844; he is shot, 21 Jan.	1845
Don Carlos relinquishes his right to the crown in favour of his son . . . . 18 May,	,,
Reactionary constitution	,,
England removed from "favoured nation" clause (treaty of Utrecht, 1713)	,,
Narvaez and his ministry resign, 12 Feb.; return to power, 17 March; again resign . 28 March,	1846
Escape of Don Carlos from France . . 14 Sept.	,,
Marriage of the queen to her cousin, Don Francisco d'Assiz, duke of Cadiz, and marriage also of the infanta Louisa to the duc de Montpensier, 10 Oct.	,,
[The Spanish marriages disturb the friendly relations of the French and English governments.]	
Amnesty granted to political offenders . 18 Oct.	,,
Two shots fired at the queen by an assassin, La Riva, 4 May,	1847
He suffers "death by the cord" . . 23 June,	,,
Espartero restored . . . . . 3 Sept.	,,
Sir Henry Lytton Bulwer, British envoy, ordered to quit Spain in 48 hours . . 17 May,	1848

Narvaez dismissed and recalled . . .	1849
Diplomatic relations with England restored, 18 April,	1850
The queen of Spain delivered of a male child, which lives but ten minutes . . . . 12 July,	,,
The American expeditions under Lopez against Cuba (see Cuba, and the United States) . 1850,	1851
Resignation of Narvaez . . . . 10 Jan.	,,
The infante don Henrique permitted to return to Spain . . . . 2 Feb.	,,
Madrid-Aranjuez railway opened . . 9 Feb.	,,
Law respecting the public debt (which has since excluded Spain from the European money-markets) . . . . 1 Aug.	,,
Death of Godoy, prince of the peace . 4 Oct.	,,
The queen pardons the prisoners taken in the attempt upon Cuba . . . . 11 Dec.	,,
Her majesty gives birth to a princess . 20 Dec.	,,
Attempt made on the life of the queen; she is slightly wounded by the dagger of Merino, a Franciscan . . . . . . 2 Feb.	1852
Gen. Castaños, duke of Baylen, renowned in the French war, dies, aged 95 . . . 23 Sept.	,,
Narvaez exiled to Vienna . . . . Jan.	1853
Ministerial changes—Lersundi forms a cabinet, 11 April; resigns: Sartorius's cabinet . Sept.	,,
Birth and death of a princess . . . 5 Jan.	1854
General O'Donnell, Concha, and others banished, 17 Jan.	,,
Disturbances at Saragossa, &c. . . . Feb.	,,
Don Francisco (father of the king consort), marries an "unfortunate" woman . . March,	,,
Military insurrection, under O'Donnell, near Madrid, 28 June,	,,
The movement headed by Espartero; Barcelona and Madrid pronounce against the government; barricades in Madrid . . . 1-17 July,	,,
Triumph of the insurrection; resignation of the ministry; the queen sends for Espartero, 19 July,	,,
Peace restored: the degraded generals reinstated, &c.; Espartero forms an administration, 31 July,	,,
The queen mother impeached; she quits Spain 28 Aug.	,,
Ministerial crisis; Espartero resigns, but resumes office . . . . . . 21-30 Nov.	,,
New constitution of the cortes . . 13 Jan.	1855
The cortes vote that all power proceeds from the people; they permit liberty of belief, but not of worship . . . . Feb.	,,
Don Carlos dies . . . . . 10 March,	,,
Insurrection of Valencia . . . 6 April,	1856
Resignation of Espartero; new cabinet formed, headed by marshal O'Donnell; insurrection in Madrid, 14 July; O'Donnell and the government troops subdue the insurgents; the national guard suppressed . . . . . 15-16 July,	,,
Insurrection at Barcelona and Saragossa quelled by O'Donnell, as dictator . . . 15-23 July,	,,
O'Donnell compelled to resign; Narvaez becomes minister . . . . . . 12 Oct.	,,
Amnesty granted to political offenders . 19 Oct.	,,
Espartero resigns as senator . . . 1 Feb.	1857
Insurrection in Andalusia; quickly suppressed; cruel military executions; 98 insurgents shot (24 at Seville) . . . . . June and July,	,,
Ministerial changes; Armero minister . 26 Oct.	,,
Birth of the prince royal . . . . 28 Nov.	,,
Isturitz, minister, 14 Jan.; O'Donnell, minister, 1 July,	,,
Cessation of state of siege at Barcelona, &c. 20 Sept.	1858
Joint French and Spanish expedition against Cochin China announced . . . . . 1 Dec.	,,
War with Morocco (which see) . . Nov.-Dec.	1859
An association for reforming the tariff, &c. formed .	,,
O'Donnell commands the army in Africa; indecisive conflicts reported; battle at Castillejos; a Spanish "Balaklava" charge . . . . 1 Jan.	1860
The Moors defeated near Tetuan, which surrenders 4 Feb.	,,
An ineffectual truce . . . . 16-23 Feb.	,,
The Moors defeated at Guad-el-ras . 23 March,	,,
Treaty of peace signed; 400,000,000 reals to be paid by Moors, and Tetuan to be held till paid 26 Mar.	,,
General Ortega, governor of the Balearic Isles, lands near Tortosa, in Valencia, with 3000 men, and proclaims the comte de Montemolin king, as Charles VI.; his troops resist, and he is compelled to flee,	,,

SPAIN.

with the comte and others, 3 April; Ortega shot 19 April, 1860
The comte de Montemolin and his brother Ferdinand arrested at Tortosa, 21 April; renounce their claim to the throne . . . 23 April, „
An amnesty proclaimed . . . . 2 May, „
Their brother Juan asserts his right, 5 June; and they, when at Cologne, annul their renunciation, 28 June, „
The emperor Napoleon's proposal to admit Spain as a first-class power is opposed by England, and given up . . . . Aug. „
The comte de Montemolin and his wife die at Trieste 14 Jan. 1861
The annexation of St. Domingo to Spain ratified; slavery not to be re-established . . 19 May, „
Insurrection at Loja suppressed . . . July, „
The queen said to be governed by the nun Patrocinio Dec. „
Intervention in Mexico (see Mexico) . 8 Dec. „
Much church property in course of sale . April, 1862
José Alhama and Manuel Matamoras, protestant propagandists, sentenced to 10 years' imprisonment . . . . 14 Oct. „
Don Juan de Bourbon renounces his right to the throne . . . . 8 Jan. 1863
Resignation of the premier, marshal O'Donnell, 26 Feb.; marquis de Miraflores minister 4 March, „
Insurrection in St. Domingo; war ensues (see Domingo) . . . . 1 Sept. „
Empress of France visits the queen . . Oct. „
Rupture with Peru (which see) . . April, 1864
General Prim exiled for conspiracy . . 13 Aug. „
Arrazola ministry, Jan.; Mon forms a ministry, 1 March; resigns, 13 Sept.; Narvaez forms a cabinet Sept. „
Queen Christina returns to Spain . . 26 Sept. „
English government recognises the insurrection at St. Domingo; Narvaez advises abandonment of the contest; the queen refuses; the ministry resign; but resume office . . 14-18 Dec. „
Peace with Peru, which has to pay a heavy indemnity 27 Jan. 1865
The queen orders the sale of crown lands, giving up three-fourths to the nation . . 20 Feb. „
Student riots at Madrid; several persons killed, 10 April, „
[Bravo Murillo accused of cruelty on this occasion.]
Decree relinquishing St. Domingo . . 5 May, „
Suppression of a conspiracy at Valencia to re-unite Spain and Portugal . . . . 10 June, „
Resignation of Narvaez, 19 June; O'Donnell forms a liberal cabinet . . . . . 22 June, „
Kingdom of Italy recognised by Spain . 26 June, „
Father Claret dismissed from court . . 20 July, „
Dispute with Chili; M. Tavira's settlement (20 May) disavowed by the government . 25 July, „
Emperor Napoleon visits the queen at St. Sebastian, 9 Sept.; she visits him at Biarritz, 11 Sept. „
Disturbances at Saragossa suppressed . . 3 Oct. „
Admiral Pareja, at Valparaiso, insults the Chilian government, 18 Sept.; which declares war, 25 Sept.; Pareja declares a blockade . . Oct. „
The Chilian captain Williams captures the Spanish vessel Covadonga (Pareja commits suicide) 26 Nov. „
Intervention fruitless . . . . . Dec. „
Claret returns to court . . . . 25 Dec. „
New cortes elected; the great Progresista party still abstains from action in public affairs; queen opens cortes . . . . . 27 Dec. „
Military insurrection at Aranjuez, headed by gen. Prim, 3 Jan.; martial law in Madrid, 4 Jan.; Concha and Zabala march against rebels, 4 Jan.; &c.; riots at Barcelona, 9, 10 Jan.; state of siege in New Castile, Catalonia, and Aragon 6-12 Jan. 1866
Prim enters Portugal and lays down arms; the insurrection ends . . . . . 20 Jan. „
Queen Victoria, British sloop, seized by a guardacosta . . . . 15 Jan. „
Admiral Mendez bombards Valparaiso, destroying much property, 31 March; he is repulsed at Callao with loss . . . . . . 2 May, „
The queen declares the campaign in the Pacific ended, 1 June, „
Great military revolt in favour of Prim at Madrid; about 1200 men, headed by non-commissioned officers, with cannon, quelled summarily by marshals O'Donnell and Narvaez, with much bloodshed; 200 prisoners shot, 22 June; 21 sergeants shot . . . . 26 June, 1866
Military revolts at Barcelona and at various other places . . . . 23 June, „
Resignation of O'Donnell as minister, succeeded by Narvaez and Bravo, who adopt severe measures against the liberals . . . . . July, „
The queen said to be subject to the influence of the "bleeding nun," Patrocinio, and the priests, July, „
Freedom of the press abolished, and writers transported to the colonies; a "reign of terror," Aug.-Sept. „
British screw steamer Tornado, com. E. Collier, seized by Spaniards (charged with aiding Chili), and carried to Cadiz . . . 21-22 Aug. „
33 persons condemned to death, many of whom had fled . . . . 23 Sept. „
Re-establishment of tranquillity declared at Madrid 3 Oct. „
Public instruction placed under the clergy Oct. „
Reform of the municipal institutions decreed on account of revolutionary proceedings . 3 Oct. „
Crew of Tornado detained as prisoners, 31 Oct. the case referred to law . . . . Nov. „
King and queen visit Lisbon . . . 11 Dec. „
Taxes for 1867 received in advance . . Dec. „
The queen dismissed the cortes (and imprisoned many eminent deputies for petitioning against it) 30 Dec. „
O'Donnell and his colleagues residing in Paris Jan. 1867
Decision in Tornado case—the ship a prize and the crew prisoners of war, 18 Dec. 1866; lord Stanley protests against the proceedings . . 8 Feb. „
Decree for making secret publication of journals and pamphlets penal . . . . 16 Feb. „
The Tornado prisoners released . . . Feb. „
State of siege raised . . . . 7 March, „
Queen Victoria sloop declared by Spain to have been wrongfully seized and reparation to be made, 21 April, „
Amnesty to revolters of June 1866 . 25 April, „
Son of duchess of Montpensier born . 1 May, „
Attempted insurrection in different parts (attributed to Prim) failed through want of organisation, about 15 Aug. „
Insurrectionary movements reported in Catalonia and Aragon . . . . . July, Aug. „
State of siege proclaimed . . . 17 Aug. „
Insurrection suppressed; amnesty . . Sept. „
Death of marshal O'Donnell, duke of Tetuan 5 Nov. „
Martial law annulled . . . . 16 Nov. „
Parliament opened by the queen in person 27 Dec. „
An armament bill adopted by the chamber of deputies . . . . . . 22 Jan. 1868
Proposed settlement with national creditors at 20 per cent. of the debt . . . . . Jan. „
General amnesty proclaimed . . . 23 Jan. „
Death of marshal Narvaez, duke of Valencia (aged 67) 21 April, „
New ministry formed by Gonzalez Bravo Murillo, 24 April, „
Marriage of princess Isabella, the queen's eldest daughter, to the count of Girgenti, brother of ex-king of Naples . . . . . 13 May, „
Law enacted abolishing normal schools and subjecting education to the priests . . 2 June, „
Ministerial changes . . . . 16 June, „
Duke and duchess of Montpensier arrested and exiled . . . . 6 July, „
Marshal Serrano, general Dulce, and others exiled about 10 July, „
Insurrection begins in the fleet, 18 Sept.; joined by the garrison and city of Cadiz, 19 Sept.; accepted by nearly all Spain . . . 19-30 Sept. „
Prim arrives at Cadiz, 17 Sept.; announces a provisional government . . . . 19 Sept. „
The ministers resign, 19, 20 Sept.; José Concha becomes president of the council, 22 Sept.; Bravo Murillo and his colleagues flee to Bayonne 23 Sept. „
[Royalist leaders: José Concha, marquis de Havana, Manuel Concha, marquis de Duero, at Madrid; the marquis de Pezuela at Barcelona; Eusebio de Calonge in the north; Pavia y Lacy, marquis de Novaliches in Andalusia.]
Novaliches, the royalist general, defeated at Alcolea by Serrano, 27 Sept.; surrenders . 28 Sept. „

The queen flies to Bayonne and thence to Pau, and protests . . . . . . 29, 30 Sept.	1868
The deposition of the queen declared at Madrid, 29 Sept.	,,
A national guard organised . . . 30 Sept.	,,
Don Juan, son of Don Carlos, renounces his hereditary rights in favour of his son, Carlos, 3 Oct.	,,
Serrano enters Madrid, 3 Oct. ; Serrano, Prim, and Olozaga constitute a provisional government 5 Oct.	,,
Prim enthusiastically received at Madrid 7 Oct.	,,
The education law of 2 June annulled ; the Jesuits and other religious orders suppressed ; the laws expelling the Jews abrogated ; freedom of religious worship decreed . . about 12, 13 Oct.	,,
All the local juntas dissolved by manifesto of the provisional government . . . 30 Oct.	,,
The provisional government recognised by the United States, 13 Oct. ; by England, France, and Prussia, 25 Oct. ; by Austria, Sweden, and Belgium about 31 Oct.	,,
Manifesto of the government declaring for universal suffrage, and free press and education 26 Oct.	,,
Prim created a marshal . . about 6 Nov.	,,
The queen arrives at Paris . . 6 Nov.	,,
The joint electoral committee at Madrid declare in favour of a limited monarchy . . 14 Nov.	,,
Decree for formation of a citizen force of the Volunteers of Freedom . . . . 18 Nov.	,,
Loan of 20,000,000l. proposed by Figuerea, minister of finance ; 4,000,000l. said to be undertaken by Rothschilds ; about 2,000,000 subscribed in Spain . . . . . about 25 Nov.	,,
Insurrection against the provisional government breaks out at Cadiz, 5 Dec. ; murderous conflicts, 6 Dec. ; the city invested ; surrenders ; entry of general Caballero de Roda, general of the army of Andalusia . . . . . 12 Dec.	,,
Peaceful elections for constituent cortes, 19, 20 Dec.	,,
Manifesto of the duc de Montpensier, justifying his recent entry into Spain . . dated 19 Dec.	,,
Violent insurrection at Malaga suppressed with much slaughter . . . . 31 Dec.	,,
Election of members for the cortes . 17 Jan.	1869
The Spanish envoy at Rome not received 23 Jan.	,,
Gutierez de Castro, civil governor of Burgos, murdered in the presence of priests while taking an inventory of the artistic treasures of the cathedral 24 Jan.	,,
Insurrection in Cuba increasing . . Feb.	,,
Meeting of the cortes, 11 Feb. ; Rivero elected president . . . . . 13 Feb.	,,
The provisional government resign ; Serrano reappointed head of the government with same ministry . . . . . 25, 26 Feb.	,,
Riots at Xeres on account of conscription, 16 March.	,,
Spanish Protestant religious service at Madrid 28 March,	,,
Insurrection in Cuba fomented by Americans April,	,,
61st anniversary of the Madrid revolution and massacre of the French (1808) . . 2 May,	,,
The cortes vote for a monarchy (214 to 71), 21 May,	,,
The new constitution promulgated . 6 June,	,,
Marshal Serrano elected regent by the cortes, 15 June ; sworn . . . . 18 June,	,,
New ministry under Prim . . about 18 June,	,,
Carlist risings in La Mancha and at Cindad Real, suppressed . . . . . July-Aug.	,,
United States' overtures respecting Cuba indignantly rejected . . . about 18 Sept.	,,
Candidature of the duke of Genoa discussed Sept., Oct.	,,
Republican risings at Tarragona, Barcelona, and other places, suppressed with bloodshed, Sept. ; republicans defeated near Reus, 4 Oct. ; Saragossa cannonaded, 8 Oct. ; Valencia surrendered, 16 Oct. ; tranquillity generally restored . 20 Oct.	,,
Warm discussions respecting the election of a king ; Topete, minister of marine, resigns . 2 Nov.	,,
General Dulce dies . . . . 23 Nov.	,,
Powerful republican speech of Castelar in the cortes about 18 Dec.	,,
Resignation of Prim and the ministry on the Italian government opposing the nomination of the duke of Genoa as king of Spain . . . 4 Jan.	1870
Prim resumes office with Topete and Rivero 10 Jan.	,,
Majority in the assembly for Prim against the combined unionists and liberals . . 5 April,	,,
Conscription riots at Barcelona ; soon suppressed 7, 8 April,	1870
The duc de Montpensier, after great provocation, kills don Enrique de Bourbon, brother of the exking, in a duel, 12 March ; tried, condemned, and fined . . . . . . 12 April,	,,
The offered crown declined by Espartero . May,	,,
Bill for gradual abolition of slavery in the colonies presented to the cortes . . . 28 May,	,,
Two Englishmen of Gibraltar seized by brigands : ransomed for 5200l. ; brigands afterwards attacked by the Spanish civil guard ; several of them killed, and part of the ransom recovered . June,	,,
Rojo Arias carries a resolution requiring an absolute majority in the cortes for any proposed sovereign (179 out of 336) ; this excludes all present candidates . . . . . June,	,,
Isabella II. abdicates in favour of her son Alfonso, 25 June,	,,
Prince Leopold of Hohenzollern Sigmaringen nominated king, accepted by the regent and ministry, 6 July ; this justified by the government in a circular, 7 July ; on the strong opposition of France he resigns . . . . . 12 July,	,,
Neutrality in the war announced . . 27 July,	,,
Renewed agitation for a republic . about 9 Aug.	,,
Amnesty for all political offences since 29 Sept. 1868, published . . . . . 10 Aug.	,,
Irruption of Carlists into Navarre, 27 Aug. ; defeated 28 Aug.	,,
The Basque provinces put into a state of siege, 28 Aug.	,,
The French republic warmly recognised . Sept.	,,
Ministerial crisis . . . . 15 Sept.	,,
Claret, the ex-queen's confessor, dies . 4 Oct.	,,
Amadeus, duke of Aosta (born 30 May, 1845), accepts the candidature for the crown . . 9 Oct.	,,
Elected by the cortes by 191 votes : (63 for a republic ; 27 for the duc de Montpensier) 16 Nov.	,,
Proclaimed king . . . . 17 Nov.	,,
The ex-queen, on behalf of her son Alfonso, protests against the election . . . 21 Nov.	,,
The duke accepts the crown from a deputation of the cortes at Florence, and says " that his honesty should rise above the struggle of parties, and that he had no other object than the peace and prosperity of the nation" . . . . 4 Dec.	,,
Stormy session in the cortes respecting arrangements for the new king, 19 Dec. ; Rivero, the president, resigns . . . . . 25 Dec.	,,
Prim fired at and wounded in his carriage by six men, who escaped ; great indignation at Madrid, 27 Dec. ; Topete rejoins the ministry ; vote of confidence in it . . . . . 28 Dec.	,,
Prim dies in the evening (aged 56) ; the king received by Topete at Cartagena . . . 30 Dec.	,,
Funeral of Prim . . . . . 31 Dec.	,,
The king enters Madrid, visits the body of Prim, and takes the oath . . . . 2 Jan.	1871
New ministry under Serrano . . 5 Jan.	,,
Warm reception of the queen at Madrid 19 March,	,,
New cortes opened ; the king's speech much applauded . . . . . 3 April,	,,
Del Castillo and other Alfonsists recognise the king . . . . . . April,	,,
Olozaga elected president of the cortes 4 April,	,,
The Tornado difficulty settled (Aug. Nov. 1866) compensation to be paid by the Spanish government . . . . . . May,	,,
Ministerial crisis through financial affairs ; settled by the king . . . . . June,	,,
Marshal Serrano fails in forming a cabinet, 23 July ; a ministry formed by Zorrilla . . 24 July,	,,
The king visits the provinces ; warmly received, 1 Sept. et seq. ; welcomed by Espartero at Logroño. 30 Sept.	,,
Cortes opened, 1 Oct. ; Sagasta elected president in opposition to Rivero (123-113), 3 Oct. ; the Zorrilla ministry resigns, 4 Oct. ; Malcampo forms a ministry . . . . . 5 Oct.	,,
Republican meeting at Madrid ; strong resolutions passed . . . . . . 15 Oct.	,,
Defeat of the ministry in the cortes ; dissolution, 24, 25 Nov.	,,
Angulo, the finance minister, proposes to tax the foreign national creditors 18 per cent. . 27 Nov.	,,
Suicide of the count of Girgenti . . 27 Nov.	,,
Ministry formed under Sagasta . . 21 Dec.	,,

Espartero, duke of Victory, made prince of Vergara, Jan. 1872
Resignation of Sagasta and the ministry for a trifling defeat; refused by the king; dissolution of the cortes; much excitement; troops under arms . . . . . . 25, 26 Jan. „
Ministry reconstituted by Sagasta and Topete, 20 Feb. „
Union of the opposition against the ministry, who determine to support the throne, about 8 March, „
Elections; majority of about 100 for ministers; Madrid elects for the opposition . 4-6 April, „
Insurrection of Carlists incited by priests in Navarre, Leon, &c.; manifesto of don Carlos, duke of Madrid; Diaz de Rada, his general about 20 April, „
The new cortes opened; the king says, "I will never impose myself on the Spanish people, but neither will I allow myself to be accused of deserting the post which I occupy by their will" . 24 April, „
Navarre, &c., in state of siege . . 25 April, „
Marshal Serrano enters Navarre with an army; don Carlos, calling himself Carlos VII., crosses the frontiers near Véra, and takes the command, Rada retiring, 2 May; totally defeated at Oroquieta (*which see*) . . . . . 4 May, „
The Carlists surrender by hundreds, or disperse, 8, 9, 20, 21 May, „
Reported small defeats at Oñate, &c. . 13, 20 May, „
Resignation of the Sagasta ministry . . 22 May, „
Band of Carlists defeated near Gerona, about 22 May, „
New ministry (supported by Serrano), adm. Topete president . . . . . . 25 May, „
Serrano offers amnesty to Carlists who surrender, 25 May; it is accepted, 27 May; he is censured, but exonerated by the cortes, 8 June; he assumes the presidency of the ministry . . 4 June, „
Carlism increases; the ministry propose martial law; the king opposes it; the ministry resign, 12 June, „
Ruiz Zorrilla (who had just retired from political life) becomes president of a new ministry, 14 June, „
Letter of the duc de Montpensier advocating the rights of prince Alfonso, 17 April; published, June, „
Dissolution of the cortes . . . 29 June, „
Don Carlos calls on Catalonia, Arragon, and Valencia, to rise, promising to restore their ancient liberties . . . . . . 16 July, „
Attempted assassination of the king and queen by about 15 men; one assassin killed, two taken; a little after midnight of . . . 18-19 July, „
The king's popular visit to the provinces, travelling nearly 2000 miles . . 26 July-24 Aug. „
Elections for the cortes; highly favourable to the Zorrilla ministry . . . 25 Aug. *et seq.* „
The cortes opened by the king with a fine speech, 15 Sept. „
Republican rising at Ferrol; red flag displayed; 1500 men under Montojo and Bozas, 11 Oct.; town captured by the captain-general of Galicia, 13 Oct. „
The insurgents disperse or surrender; about 500 prisoners . . . . . . 17 Oct. „
Impeachment of the Sagasta ministry for financial corruption proposed in the cortes; much agitation, end of Oct. „
The country disturbed by Carlists and republicans, Nov.-Dec. „
Gen. Hidalgo appointed to a military command; the artillery officers resigned; punished . Nov. „
Outbreak in Madrid suppressed . . 11 Dec. „
Changes in the ministry announced . 20 Dec. „
Bill for abolition of slavery in Porto Rico, for compensation, brought into congress . 24 Dec. „
Carlist bands defeated and several generals killed, Jan. 1873
King Amadeus' message to the cortes, announcing his abdication; he states that he sees Spain in a continual struggle, the era of peace more distant; he sought for remedies within the law, and did not find them; his efforts were sterile. The two chambers combine as the sovereign cortes of Spain, and vote for a republic (126-32) . 11 Feb. „
Reported success of the Carlists; agitation for the duc de Montpensier among the Orleanists in France . . . . 12 Feb. „
New ministry under Figueras . . 12 Feb. „
King Amadeus arrives at Lisbon . . 13 Feb. „

Irruption of Carlists; they hold part of Catalonia; demonstrations in favour of a federal republic, 22, 23 Feb. 1873
Ministry reconstituted; Figueras chief, 24, 25 Feb. „
Powerful circular to European powers from Castelar, foreign minister . . . . . 27 Feb. „
Appointment of a permanent committee of the cortes . . . . 22 March, „
Great dissensions between the radicals and republicans; fighting with Carlists in the provinces, early in March, „
Slavery in Porto Rico abolished . . 23 March, „
Proclamation of the government calling for volunteers against the Carlists . . 25 March, „
Mutinous spirit in the army . . . April, „
The Carlists beaten in several encounters; don Alfonso de Bourbon re-enters France 23 April, „
The old "monarchical volunteers" take possession of the bull-ring at Madrid; are disarmed and dispersed by the government troops; the "permanent committee" dissolved by the government, which assumes supreme power . . 26 April, „
Serrano and Sagasta have left Spain . 29 April, „
More defeats of the Carlists; Madrid tranquil, 29, 30 April-4 May, „
Elections for the cortes commence; monarchists abstain from voting . . . . 10 May, „
Mr. Bradlaugh, the English republican, entertained at Madrid . . . . . . 24 May, „
More Carlist defeats reported; their alleged cruelties denied by the Carlist committee . May, June, „
The Intransigentes or Irreconcilables (extreme republicans) very powerful . . . June, „
The new cortes opened; a speech by Figueras, 1 June, „
The federal republic voted by the cortes (210-2) and proclaimed, 8 June; Pi y Margall, president of a new ministry, rejected; Figueras and his ministry resume office . . . . . 9 June, „
Carlists besieging Irun . . . . 7 June, „
Ministerial crisis renewed, 10 June; Pi y Margall becomes minister; Figueras quits Spain, 11 June, „
Carlists defeat Castañon near Murieta . 26 June, „
Cadiz, Seville, Malaga, and Valencia very insubordinate . . . . . . 29 June, „
The Intransigentes withdraw from the cortes, 1 July, „
Defeat and death of Calvinety by Carlists; insurrection at Alcoy, promoted by Internationalists; the mayor and others killed, announced, 11 July „
Don Carlos (as Carlos VII.) enters Spain, "to save the country" . . . . . 13 July, „
Desperate fighting at Igualada, Catalonia 17, 18 July, „
Four prevailing parties:—1. The government, highly democratic; 2. The Intransigentes, or irreconcilables: extremely democratic; 3. The International, or communists; 4. The legitimists, Carlists.
Murcia and Valencia proclaim themselves federal cantons . . . . . . 18 July, „
Pi y Margall compelled to resign; Salmeron forms a ministry opposed to the Intransigentes, 18 July, „
Igualada taken by the Carlists under Don Alfonso, 19 July, „
The government determine to put down insurrection . . . . 24 July, „
Don Carlos enters Biscay . . . 31 July, „
Carlists hold chief of N. Spain . . . Aug. „
Insurgents repulsed in their attack on Almeria; beaten in fights at Seville, 28-30 July; gen. Pavia warmly received . . . . 31 July, „
Cadiz surrenders to him . . . 4 Aug. „
Troops attack Valencia, 26 July; it surrenders, 8 Aug. „
New constitution printed, 27 July; discussed, Aug. [118 Articles: includes separation of church and state; free religious worship; nobility abolished; 15 states in and near peninsula; 2 in the Antilles; cortes (senate and congress) to have legislative power; one deputy to 50,000 souls; cortes to be renewed in 2 years; members to be paid; executive: president and ministry; president elected for 4 years.]
Bombardment of Malaga stopped by the British and German admirals . . . . 1 Aug. „
Alleged Carlist victories at Elgueta, &c. 5-10 Aug. „
Reported total defeat of the insurgents at Chinchilla, while marching on Madrid . 10 Aug. „

Cartagena, held by Intransigentes, besieged, 22 Aug.	1873
The *Deerhound*, English yacht, conveying stores to Carlists, seized by the Spaniards, 11½ miles off Biarritz; crew imprisoned, and captain sent to Ferrol . . . . 13 Aug.	,,
Capt. Werner, of German ship, *Friedrich Karl*, captures *Almansa* and *Vittoria*, Spanish ironclads, held by rebels, gives them up to adm. Yelverton, who prepares for action against Intransigentes, claiming them, and sends them to Gibraltar unmolested . . . . 1 Sept.	,,
Carlists defeat republicans at Arrichulegui, near Renteria, many killed . . . . . 21 Aug.	,,
They take Estella after a conflict at Dicastillo, 25 Aug.	,,
Castelar elected president of the cortes . 26 Aug.	,,
The ministry propose abolition of capital punishment in the army, defeated in the cortes; resign 5 Sept.	,,
Castelar heads a ministry; proposes calling out 150,000 men, to end the war . . 7, 8 Sept.	,,
Carlists successful; yet do not advance . 5-8 Sept.	,,
Salmeron elected president of the cortes . 9 Sept.	,,
Castelar made virtually dictator . . 15 Sept.	,,
Ferdinand Muñoz, duke of Rianzarés, husband of queen Christina, dies at Havre . . 12 Sept.	,,
The *Deerhound* and crew given up; announced about 18 Sept.	,,
Reported victories of Loma over Carlists 18 Sept.	,,
Speech of Castelar, the cortes to be closed 2 Jan. 1874 . . . . 18 Sept.	,,
Carlist attack on Telosa repulsed by Loma, 19 Sept.	,,
The cortes prorogued . . . . . 21 Sept.	,,
The Carlist Merendon killed and his band dispersed about 26 Sept.	,,
The *Vittoria* and *Almansa* given up to the Spanish government . . . . . 26 Sept.	,,
Carlists in Navarre defeated by Moriones, 27 Sept.	,,
The Intransigentes' ironclads, *Mendez Nuñez* and *Numancia*, bombarding Alicante, repulsed 28 Sept.	,,
Combination of parties to support Castelar, about 6 Oct.	,,
Battle at Maneru, near Puenta de la Reyna, in Navarre, between republicans, under Moriones, and Carlists, under Ollo; both claim a victory; advantage with Carlists . . . . 6 Oct.	,,
Carlists said to be repulsed at La Junquera, in Catalonia . . . . . . about 8 Oct.	,,
Battle of Escembrera bay; the Intransigentes' ships attempt to break blockade of Cartagena; repulsed by admiral Lobo . . . . . 11 Oct.	,,
Many Carlists escape into France . about Oct.	,,
Lobo declines to fight, and retires, pursued by the Intransigentes, 13 Oct.; justifies himself at Madrid . . . . 22 Oct.	,,
Collision of the Intransigentes' vessels *Numancia* and *Fernando del Católico*, the latter sunk and 66 drowned . . . . 18 Oct.	,,
Unsuccessful sortie at Cartagena . . 21 Oct.	,,
Tristany, with 2,500 Carlists, defeated by Salamanca 25 Oct.	,,
Death of Rios Rosas, statesman . . 3 Nov.	,,
The *Murillo* (see *Wrecks*, 1873), captured; condemned to be sold by the British court of admiralty . . . . Nov.	,,
Indecisive conflicts at Monte Jurre and Monjardin, victories claimed by Carlists . . 7, 8, 9 Nov.	,,
Cartagena bombarded . . 26 Nov. *et seq.*	,,
Reported victory of Moriones near Telosa, 7 Dec.	,,
Lopez Dominguez becomes commander before Cartagena . . . . 13 Dec.	,,
Tetuan, insurgent vessel, at Cartagena, blew up (? purposely) . . . . . . 30 Dec.	,,
Pronunciamento:—Meeting of the cortes; speech of Castelar; vote of confidence in him lost by 70; he resigns; Salmeron attempts to form a ministry, 2-3 Jan.; Pavia, captain-general of Madrid, forcibly dissolves the cortes . . . 3 Jan.	1874
Marshal Serrano made president of a new ministry, including Topete; the national guard of Madrid disarming . . . . 4 Jan.	,,
Insurrection at Saragossa, suppressed with bloodshed . . . . 4 Jan.	,,
The new government issue a moderate manifesto, 9, 10 Jan.	,,
Cartagena captured by Lopez Dominguez, 12 Jan.	,,
Insurrection at Barcelona quelled . 12, 13 Jan.	,,
Numancia ironclad, with Intransigentes leaders and convicts, escapes; they land at Mers el Kebir, near Oran, on the African coast; are interned by the French . . . . . . 12 Jan.	1874
Blockade of the coast of Spain announced 31 Jan.	,,
The Carlists besiege Bilbao Moriones defeated at Somorrostro . . . . 25 Feb.	,,
Marshal Serrano resigns presidency of the ministry, and becomes chief of the executive, succeeded by Zabala; Serrano proceeds to Bilbao, 28 Feb. *et seq.*	,,
Serrano assumes command . about 8 March,	,,
The blockade of the coast (31 Jan.) raised 2 March,	,,
Asserted victory of the Carlists at San Felice, Burgos . . . . 15 March,	,,
Three days' conflict at Somorrostro, near Bilbao; the Carlists defeated, but retain their positions (about 2000 killed and wounded on both sides) 25, 26, 27 March,	,,
Armistice for three days . . . 28 March,	,,
General Manuel da Concha joins Serrano at Santander . . . . . . about 8 April,	,,
Great national effort to relieve Bilbao; union of parties; hostilities resumed . 20 April.	,,
After several days' conflict, Carlists retreat; marshal Concha enters Bilbao, which is much injured by long bombardment . . . . . 2 May,	,,
A battle at Prats de Llusanés, indecisive 6 May,	,,
New ministry formed under Zabala . 13 May,	,,
Carlists repulsed in severe attack at Ramales, about 20 May,	,,
Carlists defeated at Gondesa . about 6 June,	,,
Republicans repulsed before Estella . 25-27 June,	,,
Concha killed (succeeded by Zabala) . 27 June,	,,
Carlists accused of butchering prisoners, June and July,	,,
Alleged Carlist victories at Peña Mura (or Plata), near Abarzuza . . . . . 25-27 June,	,,
Schmidt, a German correspondent, shot as a spy by Carlists . . . . . . about 28 June,	,,
German intervention for killing of captain Schmidt by Carlists . . . . July,	,,
Carlists hold Navarre, Guipuscoa, Biscay, and Alava . . . . July,	,,
The Carlists capture Cuenca (about 80 miles from Madrid) . . . . 13 July,	,,
Don Carlos's manifesto promising constitutional government . . . . . . 16 July,	,,
Massacre of 86 republican prisoners by Carlists under Saballo at Valfogona . . 17 July,	,,
All Spain placed under martial law; levy of 125,000 men . . . . 18 July,	,,
Government circular to foreign courts respecting Carlist atrocities . . . . . 29 July,	,,
The government appeals to the French government respecting French assistance to Carlists; justificatory reply . . . . 3 Aug.	,,
The British Mediterranean squadron under admiral Drummond sails from Malta for Barcelona, 4 Aug.	,,
Don Carlos appeals to the chief powers not to intervene; justifies Dorregaray's severities, and the execution of Schmidt . . . . . 6 Aug.	,,
Moriones' alleged defeat of Mendiri and Carlists at Otelza . . . . 12 Aug.	,,
Duty of 5d. a ton on imported iron granted to Bilbao for repairs . . . . . 13 Aug.	,,
Serrano's government recognised by Great Britain, Germany, France; and other powers (not by Russia) . . . . . . about 14 Aug.	,,
Letter of sympathy and encouragement from the comte de Chambord to don Carlos . Aug.	,,
185 prisoners of war at Olot said to be shot by Carlists . . . . Aug.	,,
Puycerda vigorously besieged by Carlists, Aug.-Sept.	,,
Zabala resigns; ministry formed under Sagasta, 4 Sept.	,,
Carlists fire on German gunboats *Nautilus* and *Albatross* near San Sebastian; the Germans fire shells into the town . . . about 5 Sept.	,,
Lopez Dominguez said to have defeated Carlists five times, and relieved Puycerda . about 6 Sept.	,,
Carlists fire on German and Austrian ambassadors on the road to Madrid . . . 6 Sept.	,,
Carlists defeated by Lopez Pinto near Mora, about 9 Sept.; by Moriones at Barascoam near Tafalla, about 25 Sept.	,,
The ruthless Carlist general Dorregaray retires to	

Bayonne; said to have been superseded by Mendiri . . . . Oct. 1874
Pavia superseded by Jovellar in Valencia, early in Oct. „
Note sent to French government complaining of neglect respecting the Carlists on the frontiers, early in Oct. „
Carlists said to have been defeated at Fortuna, in Murcia, 11 Oct.; and at Villa Fortuna, 30 Oct. „
Carlists begin to bombard Irun, 4 Nov.; repulsed, 10 Nov. „
Serrano commander of the army in the north, Nov. „
Prince Alfonso issues a manifesto in reply to address, declaring himself to be "a true Spaniard, catholic, and liberal" . . . . 1 Dec. „
The army at Murviedro pronounces in favour of Alfonso; he is proclaimed king by gen. Martinez Campos, 29 Dec.; recognised by the other armies and the navy, 30 Dec.; proclaimed by gen. Primo da Rivera at Madrid; Antonio Canovas del Castillo head of a royal ministry . . 31 Dec. „
The president marshal Serrano withdraws to France, 1 Jan. 1875
Proclamation of Carlos against Alfonso . 6 Jan. „
Alfonso XII. recognised throughout Spain; well received at Barcelona, 9 Jan.; enters Madrid, 14 Jan. „
Orders of knighthood re-established; payments to clergy to be renewed . . . . Jan. „
Increased barbarities of the Carlists reported, Jan. „
Alfonso reviews 30,000 troops near Tafalla, 22 Jan.; issues proclamation to northern provinces, promising amnesty, and respect to local rights, 22 Jan. „
Serrano returns to Madrid . . . Feb. „
Carlists surprise and defeat royalists at Lucar, 3 Feb. „
Carlists retreat from Pampeluna; entered by the king, 6 Feb.; he exchanges decorations with Espartero at Logroño . . . 9 Feb. „
Resignation of generals Moriones, Loma, and Blanco; Concha sent for from Cuba . Feb. „
Serrano received by the king . . 8 March, „
Cabrera, an old Carlist general (see 1840) publishes an address, declaring for Alfonso XII., 11 March, „
Several professors seized and exiled for liberal opinions . . . . March, April, „
Eight prisoners shot by Carlist general Mendiri, in reprisal . . . . . 7 April, „
Papal nuncio received by the king . 3 May, „
Aguirre, Carlist general, joins the royalists, about 9 May, „
Jovellar, commander of royal army, about 7 June, „
Martinez Campos said to have taken fortress of Miraveti . . . . . 24 June, „
Vigorous action of the government troops; Carlists expelled from Castile; stringent measures ordered against those who favour them . July, „
Carlists defeated by Quesada and others 31 July, „
Strong citadel at Urgel surrendered by Carlists to Campos, after a gallant defence; the bishop and the brave general Lizarraga captured, 26 Aug. „
New conscription ordered, 12 Aug; reported successful . . . . . . Sept. „
Resignation of "conciliation ministry," 11 Sept; liberal cabinet headed by gen. Jovellar, 12 Sept. „
The papal nuncio issues a circular against toleration, about 13 Sept. „
Dorregaray said to be nominated to the chief command; declaration from don Carlos stating that his mission is "to quell the revolution, and that it will die" . . . . . Sept. „
Bombardment of San Sebastian, 28 Sept.-2 Oct.; resumed, 11 Oct. „
The government declare the civil war at an end, and purpose summoning the cortes to assist the king in re-organising the country, early in Oct. „
Reported defection of Mendiri from the Carlists, and trial of Dorregaray and Caballi for misconduct; and Carlist successes . . Oct. „
Reported interference of United States respecting Cuba . . . . . . Nov. „
Alleged victories of Quesada, near Pennacerada, 4, 5, Nov. „
Correspondence of ministry with the pope respecting ecclesiastical affairs . . . Nov. „
Letter from Don Carlos to the king proposing a truce, and offering help if war occurs with the United States (not answered) . . 9 Nov. „

Formation of a new constitutional party under Sagasta . . . . . . Nov. 1875
New proclamation of don Carlos to encourage his supporters . . . . . 23 Nov. „
Serrano and Sagasta greet the king on his birthday, 28 Nov. „
Ministry reconstructed under Canovas del Castillo, 27 Nov. „
Cortes elected, 364 nominal ministerialists out of 406, Jan. 1876
Cortes opened by the king . . 15 Feb. „
Carlists defeated at Estella, Vera, and Tolosa, by Quesada and Moriones . . . Feb. „
The king assumes command; Estella surrenders to Primo da Rivera: severe loss . 18 Feb. „
Reported letter from the pope recommending Carlos to retire from the contest . . 22 Feb. „
Many Carlists submit or flee into France, 24-26 Feb. „
Don Carlos with general Lizarraga and five battalions surrender to the governor of Bayonne, at St. Jean Pied de Port, 27 Feb.; he lands with some officers at Folkestone, and proceeds to London . . . . . 4 March, „
Triumphal entry of Alfonso XII. into Madrid, 20 March, „
Draft of new constitution submitted to the cortes, 28 March, „
The pope opposes moderate religious toleration in Art. 11 of the constitution . . April, „
The Jews (expelled in 1492) petition for re-admission April, „
The prince of Wales at Madrid by invitation, 25-30 April, „
Outbreaks in the Basque provinces reported; martial law . . . . about 27 May, „
Long debate in the cortes; confidence in ministry voted (211-26); the constitution passed; cortes adjourns . . . . about 21 July, „
Queen Isabella received by the king at Santander; declares that "her share in public affairs is at an end " . . . . . . 31 July, „
Repression of public worship of protestants by authority . . . . . . Sept. „
Ex-queen Isabella quietly received at Madrid, 13 Oct. „
Alleged federalist conspiracy of Ruiz Zorrilla and Salmeron; about 140 arrests . . 23 Oct. „
State of siege in Old Castile raised . 1 Feb. 1877
Treaty favoured nation clause in regard to England abrogated . . . . . . „
Royal progress in the provinces; the king well received . . . . . . March, „
General amnesty to Carlists and others surrendering . . . . . . April, „
Meeting of the new cortes; cheerful royal speech, 25 April, „
The cortes suddenly closed . . 11 July, „
New tariff passed; customs duties raised in respect to Great Britain, France, and United States, 17 July, „
The ex-queen, after visiting her son, disapproves of his proposed marriage, and associates with don Carlos in Paris, who is privately forbidden to remain, and goes to England; she is forbidden to return to Spain; her pension stopped, end of Dec. „
The king married to his cousin Mercedes, daughter of the duc de Montpensier . . 23 Jan. 1878
End of the insurrection in Cuba announced, 21 Feb. „
Death of queen Mercedes, deeply lamented, 26 June, „
Budget receipts, 30,025,208l., expendit. 30,127,114l. announced . . . . . . Aug. „
Death of the queen dowager Christina . 21 Aug. „
The king fired at (not injured) by Juan Oliva Moncasi, a member of the International Society, aged 23 . . . . 25 Oct. „
Moncasi executed . . . . 4 Jan. 1879
Espartero, duque de Victoria, dies . 8 Jan. „
Castillo ministry (1874) resigns; marshal Campos forms a ministry . . . . 3 March, „
The cortes dissolved, 16 March; to meet, 1 June, „
Heavy rains, 14 Oct.; consequent disastrous inundations in the provinces of Malaga, Almeria, Granada, Seville, and especially in Murcia and Alicante; about 1000 persons perish; about 10,000 houseless . . . . 15-17 Oct. „
Fresh storms and inundations; 21 persons drowned at Vera, in Almeria . . . 29, 30 Oct. „
The king married to the archduchess Maria Christina of Austria . . . . 29 Nov. „

Vines attacked by phylloxera in Malaga, &c. Nov. 1879
Resignation of the Campos ministry; Canovas del Castillo forms a cabinet . . . 9 Dec. ,,
Attempted assassination of the king and queen by Francisco Otero y Gonzalez by shooting, 30 Dec. ,,
Promulgation of law for gradually abolishing slavery in Cuba . . . . 18 Feb. 1880
Manifesto from 279 senators and deputies claiming liberty of religion, the press, &c., and education, universal suffrage, &c. . . . 6 April, ,,
Otero executed . . . . 14 April, ,,
Resignation of ministry; Sagasta forms a ministry (liberal), 8 Feb.; the chambers adjourned, 9 Feb. 1881
Calderon centenary, Madrid, begins . 23 May, ,,
Conference of advanced radicals at Biarritz to organize the party . . . . 13 June, ,,
Permission said to be given to about 60,000 Russian Jews to come to Spain . . June, ,,
Don Carlos expelled from France for expressing sympathy with legitimists (goes to London) 17 July, ,,
Elections; majority for the ministry . . Aug. ,,
The cortes opened by the king . 20 Sept. ,,
Consolidation of the National debt (60,000,000l.) proposed, Sept.; law published . 10 Dec. ,,
The king invested with the order of the Garter, 7 Oct. ,,
The kings of Spain and Portugal open a new railway between Madrid and Lisbon . 8 Oct. ,,
Great agitation against the free trade policy of the minister Camacho, in Catalonia, &c. (see Barcelona) . . . . . . ,,
Treaty with France passed by the cortes (237-65), 22 April, 1882
Continued disputes with England respecting tariff, Aug. et seq. ,,
"Dynastic Left," a new party formed by marshal Serrano and others, constituted (dividing the liberals) . . . . . 27 Oct. ,,
Gen. Maceo and five Cuban insurgent leaders surrendered at Gibraltar to the Spaniards (they had escaped from Cadiz, 20 Aug.); they petition queen Victoria to ask for their release; application made for inquiry; gen. Baynes, colonial secretary at Gibraltar, and Mr Blair, the chief inspector of police, dismissed for exceeding their authority, announced . . . 4 Dec. ,,
The "Dynastic Left" in cortes pronounce in favour of advanced liberalism . . . 15 Dec. ,,
Majority for government in elections for councils general . . . . . 17 Dec. ,,
Resignation of the ministry . . 6 Jan. 1883
New cabinet formed by Sagasta . . 8 Jan. ,,
Socialist and anarchist disturbances in Seville, &c. Feb. ,,
A secret society, entitled the "Black Hand (Mano Negra)," reported; arrests, 28 Feb.; total suppression reported . . . . 4 March, ,,
Release of two Cuban refugees; Maceo retained, March, ,,
The king and queen of Portugal at Madrid, 22 May, ,,
Temporary republican military insurrection at Badajoz, said to be planned by Ruiz Zorrilla, on the approach of troops; mutineers enter Portugal, and are disarmed . . . 4, 5, 6 Aug. ,,
Brief military outbreaks near Logroño and at Barcelona, 8 Aug.; Seo-de-Urgel . . 9 Aug. ,,
Spain reported tranquil . . . 13 Aug. ,,
The king's military tour, Valencia, Barcelona, Saragossa, &c. well received . . 17 Aug. et seq. ,,
He visits Vienna, 10 Sept.; Berlin, Homberg, and Brussels . . . . . 27 Sept. ,,
The king honourably received by president Grévy, but hissed and reviled by the Paris mob (on account of his having been made a colonel of Uhlans by the emperor William); behaved with dignity and courage . . 29, 30 Sept.; 1 Oct. ,,
Resignation of Sagasta and his ministry; succeeded by Posada Herrera and others . 11-13 Oct. ,,
The crown prince of Germany arrives at Madrid, 23 Nov. ,,
Amnesty granted to insurgent soldiers announced, 27 Nov. ,,
Treaty for new commercial tariff signed . 1 Dec. ,,
The king opens the cortes, with speech promising important reforms . . . . 15 Dec. ,,
Treaty with England condemned by the council of state; freetraders indignant . . Jan. 1884
Government defeated in the cortes (221-126) 17 Jan. ,,

Ministry resigned; Canovas del Castillo (conservative) forms a ministry . . 18 Jan. 1884
Dissolution of the cortes . . . 31 March, ,,
Suspected military insurrection; about 25 persons arrested, about 17 March; 7 of 15 condemned; Black Hand conspirators garrotted at Xeres, 14 June; Commander Fernandez and lieut. Telles shot as rebels . . . . 28 June, ,,
Fall of the Alcudia railway bridge near Badajoz, great loss of life (said to be 90); believed to be due to criminal work of republicans . 26 April, ,,
New cortes (three-fourths conservative) meets, 20 May; business begun . . . 10 June, ,,
Sir Robert Morier, British envoy, 1881; succeeded by sir Francis Clare Ford . . . ,,
Last section of the Great Asturian railway opened by the king . . . . 15 Aug. ,,
Indiscreet speech of Sen. Pidal y. Mon, minister of instruction, causes revival of agitation in favour of the Pope; resented by Italy; apology made . . . . Aug. Sept. ,,
Speech of professor Moraytor against clericals; university students at Madrid forbidden to attend his lectures by Sen. Pidal, resist; conflict with the police; many wounded, 20 Nov.; professors and students expelled from the university; many liberal newspapers suspended; other universities agitated . . . . . Nov. ,,
Passive resistance of the students . 1 Dec. et seq. ,,
Much sufferings by Earthquakes, which see, 25-31 Dec. ,,
National subscription proclaimed by the king, 3 Jan. 1885
The king visits the afflicted districts, 11-23 Jan.; liberal subscriptions in London . 11 Jan. ,,
Protocol restoring Great Britain to position of most "favoured nation" in regard to commerce (lost since 1845); wine duties modified; signed at Madrid, 21 Dec. 1884; gazetted . 6 Feb. ,,
Commercial treaty with England ratified by the deputies, 11 March; by the senate, 28 March; by the king . . . . . 1 April, ,,
Failure of the negotiations for the treaty announced, 18 May, ,,
Break out of cholera in Valencia (see Cholera), May, ,,
The ministers resign on account of the king's intention to visit Valencia; he gives in; they resume office . . . . 20, 21 June, ,,
Riots at Madrid through the Germans occupying Yap, a Caroline isle; the German legation attacked, 4, 5 Sept.; quiet restored 6 Sept.; Spanish note of apology sent to Berlin about 26 Sept.; mediation of the pope accepted (see Caroline Islands) . . . about 26 Sept. ,,
British legation insulted by claim of taxes, about 29, 30 Sept. ,,
Attempted military insurrection at Cartagena, 1 Nov.; suppressed . . about 4, 5 Nov. ,,
Death of king Alfonso XII., 25 Nov.; resignation of Canovas del Castillo; ministry formed by senor Sagasta . . . . 26, 27 Nov. ,,
Death of marshal Serrano . . . 26 Nov. ,,
Amnesty granted to press and political offenders, 10 Dec. ,,
Manifesto of the Spanish bishops to their dioceses, declaring the distinction to be observed between religion and politics, and the submission of the church to any lawful form of government, monarchical or republican . . 6 Jan. 1886
50 soldiers at Cartagena mutiny; most escape to a ship, 10, 11 Jan.; general Fajardo wounded; dies 27 Jan.; ringleader of mutiny shot, 3 March, ,,
Suspected intrigue of Zorilla and his followers, Jan. ,,
The duke of Seville sentenced to eight years' imprisonment, &c., for insulting, &c., the queen regent . . . . about 27 Feb. ,,
Assassination of the bishop of Madrid (see Madrid), 19 April, ,,
The commercial treaty with England (till 1892) again accepted by the cortes, May; ratified, 24 July; royal assent, 29 July; comes into operation . . . . . 15 Aug. ,,
Destructive cyclone at Madrid (which see), 12 May, ,,
Don Carlos protests against recognition of Alphonso XIII. . . . . . 20 May, ,,
Revolt of 300 of Madrid garrison under brigadier Villacampa; unsupported, quickly suppressed;

three officers killed, 19 Sept.; capital punishment of insurgents commuted . . . Oct. 1886
Republican manifesto of the duke of Seville issued at Tarbes . . . . . . about 30 Sept. „
Changes in M. Sagasta's cabinet . . 10 Oct. „
Solemn commemoration of the death of king Alphonso XII. . . . . . 25, 26 Nov. „
Attempted assassination by a Frenchman of marshal Bazaine . . . . . 18 April, 1887
The regent queen Christina visits the N. provinces; well received . . . . Aug. „
The Philippine exhibition at Madrid; the queen distributes the prizes . . . . 17 Oct. „
Opening of the cortes; the infant king enthroned; speech of the queen regent; the country prosperous and quiet . . . . . 1 Dec. „
Sir Francis Clare Ford, British envoy, &c., nominated ambassador; received by the queen regent . . . . 21 Jan. 1888
Rioting at the Rio Tinto mines suppressed with bloodshed . . . . . . 4, 5 Feb. „
Trial by jury introduced by the senate . 27 Feb. „
Ruiz Zorrilla's revolutionary manifesto issued, demanding a *plébiscité* for the form of national government . . . . . . 4 March, „
Resignation of the ministry . . 13 June, „
Senor Sagasta forms a new ministry . 14 June, „
Republican outbreak at Saragossa against conservatives; senor Canovas del Castillo attacked, 20 Oct.; outbreak at Seville, 7 Nov.; outbreak at Madrid . . . . . . 11 Nov. „
Resignation of the ministry, 9 Dec.; reconstituted by senor Sagasta . . . . . 10 Dec. „
Amnesty to political offenders and mutinous soldiers decreed . . . . . 23 Jan. 1889
The queen regent meets queen Victoria at San Sebastian . . . . . . 27 March, „
Long debate in the chamber, victory of ministers (227–65) . . . . 22 May, „
Trial by jury first put in force (at Madrid), 29 May, „
Parliamentary deadlock, the session closed by the queen regent . . . . . . 2 June, „
Powerful speech by senor Sagasta to his supporters, 12 June; the cortes reopened . . 14 June, „
Victory of senor Sagasta over senor Canovas del Castillo and the combined conservatives and dissentient liberals, reported . . 14 July, „

SOVEREIGNS OF SPAIN.
GOTHIC SOVEREIGNS.
411. Ataulfo; murdered by his soldiers.
415. Sigerico; reigned a few days only.
„ Valia, or Wallia.
420. Theodoric I.; killed in a battle, which he gained, against Attila.
451. Thorismund, or Torrismund; assassinated.
452. Theodoric II.; assassinated by
466. Euric, the first monarch of all Spain.
483. Alaric II.; killed in battle.
506. Gesalric; his bastard son.
511. Amalric, or Amalaric; legitimate son of Alaric.
531. Theudis, or Theodat; assassinated by a madman.
548. Theudisela, or Theodisele; murdered.
549. Agila; taken prisoner, and put to death.
554. Atanagildo.
567. Liuva, or Levua I.
568. Leuvigildo; associated on the throne with Liuva, in 568; and sole king in 572.
586. Recaredo I.
601. Liuva II.; assassinated.
603. Vitericus; also murdered.
610. Gundemar.
612. Sisibnt, or Sisebuth, or Sisebert.
621. Recaredo II.
„ Suintila; dethroned.
631. Sisenando.
636. Chintella.
640. Tulga, or Tulca.
642. Cindasuinto; died in 652.
649. Recesuinto; associated; in 653 became sole king.
672. Vamba, or Wamba; dethroned, and died in a monastery.
680. Ervigius, or Ervigio.
687. Egica, or Egiza.
698. Vitiza, or Witiza, associated; in 701 sole king.
711. Rodrigo, or Roderic; slain in battle.
[Six independent SUEVIC kings reigned 409-469; and

Two VANDALIC kings: Gunderic 409-425; his successor Genseric with his whole nation passed over to Africa.]

MAHOMETAN SPAIN.
CORDOVA.
Emirs. The *first,* Abdelasis: the *last,* Yussuf-el-Tchri: A.D. 714-755.
Kings. The *first,* Abderahman I.; the *last,* Abu Ali; 755-1238.
GRANADA.
Kings. The *first,* Mohammed I.; the *last,* Abdalla; 1238-1492.

CHRISTIAN SPAIN.
KINGS OF ASTURIAS AND LEON.
718. Pelagius, or Pelayo; overthrew the Moors, and checked their conquests.
737. Favila; killed in hunting.
739. Alfonso the Catholic.
757. Froila; murdered his brother Samaran, in revenge for which he was murdered by his brother, and successor,
768. Aurelius or Aurelio.
774. Mauregato, the Usurper.
788. Veremundo (Bermuda) I.
791. Alfonso II., the Chaste.
842. Ramiro I.: he put 70,000 Saracens to the sword in one battle. *Rabbe.*
850. Ordoño II.
866. Alfonso III., surnamed the Great; relinquished his crown to his son,
910. Garcias.
914. Ordoño II.
923. Froila II.
925. Alfonso IV., the Monk; abdicated.
930. Ramiro II., killed in battle.
950. Ordoño III.
955. Ordoño IV.
956. Sancho I., the Fat; poisoned with an apple.
967. Ramiro III.
983. Veremundo II. (Bermuda), the Gouty.
999. Alfonso V.; killed in a siege.
1027. Veremundo III. (Bermuda); killed.

KINGS OF NAVARRE.
873. Sancho Iñigo. *Count.*
885. Garcia I., king.
905. Sancho Garcias; a renowned warrior.
924. Garcias II., surnamed the Trembler.
970. Sancho II., surnamed the Great (king of Castile through his wife).
1035. Garcias III.
1054. Sancho III.
1076. Sancho IV., Ramirez, king of Aragon.
1094. Peter of Aragon.
1104. Alfonso I., of Aragon.
1134. Garcias IV., Ramirez.
1150. Sancho V., surnamed the Wise.
1194. Sancho VI., surnamed the Infirm.
1234. Theobald I., count of Champagne.
1253. Theobald II.
1270. Henry Crassus.
1274. Joanna; married to Philip the Fair of France, 1285.
1305. Louis Hutin of France.
1316. John; lived but a few days.
„ Philip V., the Long, of France.
1322. Charles I., the IV. of France.
1328. Joanna II., and Philip, count d'Evreux.
1343. Joanna alone.
1349. Charles II., of the Bad.
1387. Charles III., or the Noble.
1425. Blanche and her husband John II., afterwards king of Aragon.
1479. Eleanor.
„ Francis Phœbus de Foix.
1483. Catherine and John d'Albret.
1512. Navarre conquered by Ferdinand the Catholic, and united with Castile.

KINGS OF LEON AND CASTILE.
1035. Ferdinand the Great.
1065. Sancho II., the Strong, son of Ferdinand; Alfonso in Leon and Asturias, and Garcias in Galicia.
1072. Alfonso VI., the Valiant, king of Leon.
1109. Uraca and Alfonso VII.
1126. Alfonso VII., Raymond.
1157. Alfonso VIII., surnamed the Beloved.
1158. Alfonso VIII., the Noble.
[Leon is separated from Castile under Ferdinand II., 1157-88.]

SPAIN.

- 1188. Alfonso IX., of Leon.
- 1214. Henry I.
- 1217. Ferdinand III., the Saint and the Holy. By him Leon and Castile were permanently united.
- 1252. Alfonso X., the Wise (the Alphonsine Tables were drawn up under his direction).
- 1284. Sancho IV., the Great and the Brave.
- 1295. Ferdinand IV.
- 1312. Alfonso XI.
- 1350. Peter the Cruel: deposed; reinstated by Edward the Black Prince of England; slain by his natural brother and successor,
- 1369. Henry II., the Gracious; poisoned by a monk.
- 1379. John I.: he united Biscay to Castile.
- 1390. Henry III., the Sickly.
- 1406. John II., son of Henry.
- 1454. Henry IV., the Impotent.
- 1474. Isabella, sister (had married Ferdinand of Aragon, 18 Oct. 1469).
- 1504. Joanna (daughter of Ferdinand and Isabella), and Philip I. of Austria. On her mother's death Joanna succeeded, jointly with her husband Philip; but Philip dying in 1506, and Joanna becoming imbecile, her father Ferdinand continued the reign; and thus perpetuated the union of Castile with Aragon.

KINGS OF ARAGON.

- 1035. Ramiro I.
- 1065. Sancho Ramirez (IV. of Navarre).
- 1094. Peter of Navarre.
- 1104. Alfonso I., the Warrior, king of Navarre.
- 1134. Ramiro II., the Monk.
- 1137. Petronilla, and Raymond, count of Barcelona.
- 1163. Alfonso II.
- 1196. Peter II.
- 1213. James I.; succeeded by his son,
- 1276. Peter III.; conquered *Sicily (which see)* in 1282.
- 1285. Alfonso III., the Beneficent.
- 1291. James II., surnamed the Just.
- 1327. Alfonso IV.
- 1336. Peter IV., the Ceremonious.
- 1387. John I.
- 1395. Martin.
- 1410. [Interregnum.]
- 1412. Ferdinand the Just, king of Sicily.
- 1416. Alfonso V., the Wise.
- 1458. John II., king of Navarre, brother of Alfonso; died 1479.
- 1479. Ferdinand II., the Catholic, the next heir; by marriage with Isabella of Castile (*styled the Catholic kings*), the kingdoms were united.

SPAIN.

- 1512. Ferdinand V. (of Castile), the Catholic; having conquered Granada and Navarre, became king of all Spain.
- 1516. Charles I., grandson, son of Joanna of Castile and Philip of Austria (emperor of Germany, as Charles V., in 1519); resigned both crowns, and retired to a monastery.
- 1556. Philip II., son, king of Naples and Sicily; a merciless bigot: married Mary, queen-regnant of England; died covered with ulcers.
- 1598. Philip III., son, drove the Moors from Granada and the adjacent provinces.
- 1621. Philip IV., son: wars with the Dutch and French; lost Portugal in 1640.
- 1665. Charles II., son; last of the Austrian line; nominated, by will, as his successor
- 1700. Philip V., duke of Anjou, grandson of Louis XIV. of France: hence arose the "war of the Succession," terminated by the treaty of Utrecht in 1713; resigned.
- 1724. Louis I., son; reigned only a few months.
- ,, Philip V. again.
- 1746. Ferdinand VI., the Wise, son; liberal and beneficent.
- 1759. Charles III., brother, king of the Two Sicilies, which he gave to his third son, Ferdinand.
- 1788. Charles IV., son; the influence of Godoy, prince of the Peace, reached to almost royal authority in this reign; Charles abdicated in favour of his son in 1808, and died in 1819.
- 1808. Ferdinand VII., whom Napoleon of France also forced to resign.
- ,, Joseph Bonaparte, brother of Napoleon; forced to abdicate.
- 1813. Ferdinand VII. restored; married Maria Christina of Naples, 11 Dec. 1829; died 29 Sept. 1833; succeeded by
- 1833. Isabella II., daughter (born, 10 Oct. 1830); declared of age, 8 Nov. 1843; married her cousin, Don Francis d'Assisi, 10 Oct. 1846; deposed 30 Sept. 1868; separated from her husband, March, 1870; and abdicated, 25 June, 1870, in favour of her son, Alfonso, prince of Asturias (born, 28 Nov. 1857).
- 1870. Amadeo I. (duke of Aosta, son of Victor-Emanuel II. king of Italy); born, 30 May, 1845; married Maria Victoria of Pozzo della Cisterna, 30 May, 1867; accepted the crown offered him by the cortes, 4 Dec. 1870; abdicated 11 Feb. 1873.

REPUBLIC founded, 11 Feb. 1873. Very unsettled, 1873-4.

KINGS.

- 1874. Alfonso XII. son of Isabella II. (born 28 Nov. 1857); proclaimed 30 Dec. 1874; married 1st, his cousin Mercedes, daughter of the duc de Montpensier (born 24 June, 1860), 23 Jan. 1878; she died 26 June, 1878; 2nd, archduchess Maria Christina of Austria (born 21 July, 1858), 29 Nov. 1879. He died 25 Nov. 1885.

Maria *Mercedes* Isabella, born 11 Sept. 1880; replaced by her brother, 1885.

- 1886. Alphonso (Leon &c.) XIII., born 17 May.

CARLIST LEGITIMIST PRETENDERS.

(See above 1833 *et seq.*)

Carlos V., brother of Ferdinand VII., born 29 March, 1788; died, 10 March, 1855.
Carlos VI., his son (conde de Montemolin), died 14 Jan. 1861.
Carlos VII. (son of don Juan, brother of Carlos VI., who renounced his right, 8 Jan. 1863); born, 30 March, 1848; see above 1873-6.

SPALATO (Dalmatia), the ancient Spalatum, and Salona. At his palace here, Diocletian spent his last nine years, and died July, 313. R. Adam published the "Antiquities of Diocletian's Palace," 1764.

SPANISH AMERICA, ARMADA, &c., see *America, Armada,* and *Eras.*

SPANISH EXHIBITION of Arts and Industries, Earl's Court, Kensington, London, W., chairman, the duke of Wellington, a grandee of Spain.

The exhibition, although unfinished, was informally opened with a fine display of pictures, 1 June, 1889.

SPANISH GRANDEES, the higher nobility, at one time almost equal to the kings of Castile and Aragon, and often setting their authority at defiance, were restrained on the union of the crowns by the marriage of Ferdinand and Isabella in 1474, who compelled several to relinquish the royal fortresses and domains which they held. Charles V. reduced the grandees to sixteen families (Medina-Sidonia, Albuquerque, &c.), dividing them into three classes.

SPANISH LANGUAGE (Lengua Castellana), is a dialect of Latin largely intermingled with Arabic, which was the legal language till the 14th century. Spanish did not become general till the 16th century.

EMINENT SPANISH AUTHORS.

	Born	Died
Garcilasso de la Vega	1503	1536
Boscan	1496	1543
Jorge de Montemayor	1520	1562
Las Casas	1474	1566
Ercilla	1533	1595
Cervantes (author of Don Quixote)	1547	1616
Mariana	1536	1623
Herrera	1565	1625
Gongora	1561	1627
Alarcon y Mendoza		1634
Lope de Vega	1568	1635
Quevedo	1570	1647

Gabriel Tellez	1585	1648
Calderon	1601	1682
Solis	1610	1686
Feyjoo	1701	1765
Yriarte	1750	1798
Leandro F. Moratin	1760	1828
José de Larra	1809	1837
Manuel Breton de los Herreros	1796	1873
José Zorilla	1818	
Antonio Canovas del Castillo	1830	

SPANISH REFORMED CHURCH, constituted at Gibraltar, 25 April, 1868. By permission of general Prim its missionaries entered Spain soon after the revolution, in Sept. following.

SPANISH SUCCESSION AND MARRIAGES, see *Spain*, 1700, and 10 Oct. 1846.

SPARTA, the capital of Laconia, or Lacedæmon, the most considerable republic of the Peloponnesus, and the rival of Athens. Though without walls, it resisted the attacks of its enemies by the valour of its citizens for eight centuries. Lelex is supposed to have been the first king. From Lacedæmon the fourth king, and his wife Sparta, who are also spoken of as the founders of the city, it obtained names. The Lacedæmonians were a nation of soldiers, and cultivated neither the arts, sciences, commerce, nor agriculture. The early history is traditional.

Sparta founded. *Pausanias*.	B.C.	1490
Tyndarus marries Leda; Helen born		1388
Helen stolen by Theseus, king of Athens, but recovered by her brothers		1228
The princes of Greece demand Helen in marriage; she makes choice of Menelaus of Mycenæ		1216
Paris, son of Priam, king of Troy, carries off Helen		1204
The Trojan war		1194
After a war of ten years, and a disastrous voyage of nearly eight, Menelaus and Helen return to Sparta		1176
The kingdom seized by the Heraclidæ		1104
Establishment of two kings, Eurysthenes and Procles, by their father Aristodemus		1100
Rule of Lycurgus, who establishes the senate, and enacts a code of laws. *Eusebius*. (Mythical)		884-850
Charilaus declares war against Polymnestor, king of Arcadia		848
Alcamenes, known by his apophthegms, makes war upon the Messenians		813
Nicander succeeds his father, Charilaus; war with the Argives		800
Theopompus introduces the Ephori, about		757
War declared against the Messenians, and Amphia taken		743
The progeny of the Partheniæ, the sons of Virgins		733
Battle of Ithome; Messenians beaten		730
Ithome taken; the Messenians become vassals to Sparta, and the war of nineteen years ends		724
Conspiracy of the Partheniæ with the Helots to take Sparta		707
The Partheniæ colonise Tarentum		706
The Messenians revolt, and league with Elis, Argos, and Arcadia, against the Lacedæmonians. [This war lasted fourteen years.]		685
Carnian festivals instituted		675
The Messenians settle in Sicily		669
War with the Argives, and celebrated battle between 300 select heroes of each nation		547
War with Athens		505
The Spartans resist the king of Persia		491
The states of Greece unite against the Persians		482
Leonidas, at the head of 300 Spartans, withstands the Persian arms at the defile of Thermopylæ (see *Thermopylæ*)		480
Persians defeated by Pausanias, king of Sparta, at Platæa		479
He is put to death for treason; the Grecian armies choose an Athenian general		472
An earthquake at Sparta destroys 30,000 persons; rebellion of the Helots		466
Sparta joins Macedon against Athens		454
Platæa taken by the Spartans		428
The Spartans, under Agis, enter Attica, and lay waste the country		426
Agis (king 427) gains a great victory over the Argives and the Mantineans		418
The Lacedæmonian fleet, under Mindarus, defeated at Cyzicum, and Mindarus slain		410
The Spartans, defeated by land and at sea, sue for peace, which is denied by the Athenians		409
Reign of Pausanias		408
The Athenians defeated at Ægospotami by Lysander		405
Athens taken by him; end of Peloponnesian war		404
Agesilaus (king 398) enters Lydia		396
The Athenians, Thebans, Argives, and Corinthians enter into a league against the Spartans, which begins the Corinthian war		395
Agesilaus defeats the allies at Coronea		394
The Lacedæmonian fleet, under Lysander, defeated by Conon, the Athenian commander, near Cnidos; Lysander killed in an engagement		,,
Peace of Antalcidas		387
The Thebans drive the Spartans from Cadmea		378
The Spartans lose the dominion of the seas; their fleet totally destroyed by Timotheus		376
The Spartans defeated at Leuctra		371
Epaminondas, heading 50,000 Thebans, appears before Sparta		369
Battle of Mantinea; the Thebans victors 27 June,		362
Philip of Macedon overcomes Sparta		344
Pyrrhus defeated before Sparta		294
Agis IV. endeavours to revive laws of Lycurgus		244
Leonidas II. vacates the throne, and flies		243
Recalled; becomes sole sovereign; Agis killed		241
Reign of Cleomenes III. the son of Leonidas		236
He re-establishes most of the laws of Lycurgus		225
Antigonus defeats Cleomenes, and enters Sparta		222
Cleomenes retires to Egypt		,,
The Spartans murder the Ephori		221
Machanidas ascends the throne, and abolishes the Ephori		210
He is defeated and slain by Philopœmen, prætor of the Achæan league		207
Cruel government of Nabis		,,
The Romans besiege Sparta; Nabis sues for peace		197
The Ætolians seize Sparta; Nabis assassinated		192
The laws of Lycurgus abolished		188
Sparta, under the protection or rather subjugation of Rome, retains its authority for a short time		147
Taken by Alaric	A.D.	396
Taken by Mahomet II.		1460
Burnt by Sigismund Malatesta		1463
Rebuilt at Misitra; it is now called Sparta, and is part of the kingdom of Greece.		

SPARTACUS'S INSURRECTION (or Servile War). Spartacus was a noble Thracian, who served in an auxiliary corps of the Roman army. Having deserted and been apprehended, he was reduced to slavery and made a gladiator. With some companions he made his escape, collected a body of slaves and gladiators, 73 B.C.; ravaged southern Italy; and defeated the Roman forces under the consuls sent against him. Knowing the impossibility of successfully resisting the republic, he endeavoured to conduct his forces into Sicily, but was defeated and slain by Crassus, 71 B.C.

"SPASMODIC SCHOOL" of poetry, a name sarcastically given to Alex. Smith, Sydney Dobell (died in Aug. 1874), Gerald Massey, and others (precursors of Morris, Algernon Swinburne, and Rossetti, sarcastically termed the "fleshly school"), ridiculed by professor Aytoun in his "Firmilian," published 1854.

SPEAKERS OF THE HOUSE OF COMMONS. Peter de Montford, afterwards killed at the battle of Evesham, was the first speaker, 45 Hen. III., 1260; Sir Thos. Hungerford is said to have been the first named "Speaker," 1372; but sir Peter de la Mare is supposed to have been the first regular speaker, 50 Edw. III., 1376. The king refused his assent to the choice of sir Edward Seymour, as speaker, 6 March, 1678; and serjeant William Gregory was chosen in his room. Sir John Trevor was expelled the chair and the house for taking a gratuity after the act for the

benefit of orphans had passed, 12 March, 1694-5; a deputy speaker was appointed Aug. 1853.

RECENT SPEAKERS.

1789. Henry Addington (aft. viscount Sidmouth), 5 June.
1801. Sir John Mitford (aft. baron Redesdale), 15 Feb.
1802. Charles Abbot (aft. lord Colchester), 10 Feb.
1817. Charles Manners Sutton (afterwards viscount Canterbury), 2 June.
1835. James Abercromby (afterwards baron Dunfermline), 19 Feb.
1839. Charles Shaw Lefevre (afterwards viscount Eversley), 27 May.
1857. John Evelyn Denison, 30 April (afterwards viscount Ossington).
1872. Sir Henry Wm. Bonverie Brand (afterwards viscount Hampden), 9 Feb.-25 Feb. 1884
1884. Arthur Wellesley Peel, 26 Feb.

SPEAKER'S COMMENTARY, a name given to an edition of the Bible with a revised text and a commentary by several bishops and other theologians edited by F. C. Cook. The undertaking originated, it is said, chiefly with Mr. John Evelyn Denison, speaker of the house of commons, with the view of opposing the interpretations of Dr. Colenso, and was announced in Nov. 1863. The publication, begun in 1871, was completed in 1881. The Apocrypha published in 1888.

SPEAKING-TRUMPET, used by ships at sea. One is said to have been used by Alexander, 335 B.C. One was constructed from Kircher's description by Saland, 1652 ; philosophically explained and brought into notice by Morland, 1670.

SPECIAL COMMISSION ACT, passed 13 Aug. 1888. A commission constituted to try certain charges and allegations against certain members of parliament. See *Parnellites* and *Ireland*, 1888.

SPECIAL CONSTABLES are sworn in for the preservation of the public peace when disturbances are feared. The laws relative to their appointment were amended in 1831 and 1835. Louis Napoleon, afterwards emperor, aided as a special constable in London, 10 April, 1848; see *Chartists*, and *London*, Dec. 1867. Instructions for their organisation were issued, 13 Jan. 1868. On 28 Jan. 52,974 in the metropolis, and 113,674 in the United Kingdom. had been sworn in. Their services were not required, and they were honourably dismissed by an order issued 31 March, 1868.

Special constables were sworn in in relation to the disturbances in Trafalgar Square (see *Riots*) 17 Nov. et seq. : 1,500 held Trafalgar Square, Sunday, 20 Nov. 1887; served till 18 Jan. 1888, and thanked.

SPECIES. Much controversy among naturalists arose in consequence of the publication, in 1859, of Mr. Charles Darwin's "Origin of Species," in which he suggests that all the various species of animals were not created at one time, but have been gradually developed by what he terms "natural selection," and the struggle for life in which the strong overcome the weak.

"This preservation of favourable individual differences and variations, and the destruction of those which are injurious, I have called *natural selection*, or the survival of the fittest."—*Darwin*.

The idea was put forth by Lamarck in his "*Philosophie Zoologique*," 1809. Similar views appear in the "Vestiges of Creation," 1844. Mr. Darwin says, that he infers "from analogy that probably all the organic beings which have ever lived on the earth have descended from some one primordial form, into which life was first breathed by the Creator." See *Development* and *Evolution*.

Charles Darwin was born 12 Feb. 1809; and died 19 April, 1882.

Statue of Darwin by J. E. Boehm, paid for by universal subscription, received at the British Museum of Natural History by the prince of Wales, and uncovered by professor Huxley, 9 June, 1885.

His Life and Letters edited by his son Francis Darwin, published Nov. 1887.

SPECIFIC GRAVITIES. See under *Weights*.

SPECTACLES, unknown to the ancients, are generally supposed to have been invented by Alexander de Spina, a monk of Florence, in Italy, about 1285. According to Dr. Plott, they were invented by Roger Bacon, about 1280. Manni attributes them to Salvino, who died 1317. On his tomb at Florence is the inscription, "Qui giace Salvino degli Armati, inventore degli occhiali : Dio gli perdoni le peccata" ("Here lies Salvino degli Armati, inventor of spectacles : May God pardon his sins").

SPECTATOR. The first number of this periodical appeared on 1 March, 1711; the last was No. 635, 20 Dec. 1714. The papers by Addison have one of the letters C L I O at the end. The most of the other papers are by sir Richard Steele, a few by Hughes, Budgell, Eusden, Miss Shepherd, and others.—The *Spectator* newspaper (philosophical, whig), begun 5 July, 1828.

SPECTRUM, the term given to the image of the sun or any other luminous body formed on a wall or screen, by a beam of light received through a small hole or slit, and refracted by a prism. The colours thus produced are red, orange, yellow, green, blue, indigo, and violet. The phenomena were first explained by Newton, whose "Optics" was published in 1704. Several of these colours are considered to be compounds of three primary ones : by Mayer (1775), red, yellow, and blue ;—by Dr. Thos. Young (1801), red, green, and violet ;—by Prof. Clerk Maxwell (1860), red, green, and blue. As the colour of a flame varies according to the substance producing it or introduced into it, so the spectrum varies. This led to the invention of a method of chemical analysis by professors Bunsen and Kirchhoff (1850), by which they discovered two new metals, and drew conclusions as to the nature of the atmosphere of the sun and stars, and of the light of the nebulæ, by comparing the spectrum with that produced by flames into which iron, sodium, and other substances have been introduced. For the invisible rays of the spectrum, see *Calorescence*, *Fluorescence*, and *Bolometer*.

Fraunhofer's Lines. In 1802 Dr. Wollaston observed several dark lines in the solar spectrum ; in 1815 Joseph Fraunhofer not only observed them, but constructed a map of them, giving 590 lines or dark bands. By the researches of Brewster and others the number observed is now above 2000.

Mr. Fox Talbot observed the orange line of strontium in the spectrum in 1826; and sir David Brewster observed other lines, 1833-42-3. In 1862-3 Mr. William Huggins analysed the light of the fixed stars and of the nebulæ; and in 1865 Dr. Bence Jones, by means of spectrum analyses, detected the presence of minute quantities of metals in the living body, introduced only a few minutes previously.

A spectroscopic society in Italy published a journal early in 1872.

H. Schellen's "Spectralanalyse" published 1870; new edition 1883.

Sir H. Roscoe's "Spectrum Analysis" published 1867-85.

Lecoq de Boisbaudran's "Spectres Lumineux" . . 1874

Oxygen detected in the solar spectrum by Mr. Draper 1877

The experiments of professor Dewar and others have shown that the spectra of various gases are affected by temperature and pressure 1883-9.

SPECULATIVE SOCIETY, Edinburgh (which had included among its members David Hume), celebrated its hundredth anniversary on 14 Oct. 1863; see *Philosophy*.

"SPELLING-BEES," meetings to test the proficiency in correct spelling; introduced into London from the United States of America; the first at Holloway, London, N., in the autumn of 1875. Geographical, musical, and other bees followed, and all soon ceased.

SPELLING REFORM. A resolution in favour of it was adopted by the London School Board, in 1877; a conference and public meeting were held at the Society of Arts, 29 May, 1877.
A Spelling Reform Association formed; Dr. Temple, bishop of Exeter, Robert Lowe, E. B. Tylor, and Max Müller were among the members, 1879; another association formed in the United States; professor F. A. March, president, . . . 1887
Mr. T. B. Sprague's article on a Marriage and Mortality Table, in the Journal of the Institute of Actuaries, is printed according to phonetic spelling July, 1879

SPHERES. The celestial and terrestrial spheres and sun-dials are said to have been invented by Anaximander, 552 B.C.; and the armillary sphere by Eratosthenes, about 225 B.C. The planetarium was constructed by Archimedes before 212 B.C. Pythagoras maintained that the motions of the twelve spheres must produce delightful sounds, inaudible to mortals, which he called the music of the spheres.

SPHYGMOGRAPH (from the Greek, *sphygmos*, a pulsation), an instrument for investigating disease, by showing the state of the pulse, invented by M. E. J. Marey, of Paris, and described by him in 1863.

SPICES. Imported into Great Britain: cinnamon and other spices, exclusive of pepper; 1846, 1,910,584 lbs.; 1856, 4,154,167 lbs.; 1867, 12,831,953 lbs.; 1877, 17,186,572 lbs.; 1879, 19,340,817 lbs.; 1883, 24,344,895 lbs.; 1887, 23,783,960 lbs.

SPICHEREN, see *Saarbruck*.

SPINET, a clavichord or keyed instrument, used, in the 17th century, a modification of the virginals, *which see*. Bull, Gibbons, Purcell, and especially Domenico Scarlatti composed for this instrument.

SPINNING was ascribed by the ancients to Minerva, the goddess of wisdom. Arcas, king of Arcadia, taught his subjects the art about 1500 B.C. Tradition reports that Lucretia with her maids was found spinning, when her husband Collatinus paid a visit to her from the camp, that the wife of Tarquin was an excellent spinner, and that a garment made by her, worn by Servius Tullius, was preserved in the temple of Fortune. Till 1767, the spinning of cotton was performed by the hand spinning-wheel, when Hargreaves, an ingenious mechanic, near Blackburn, made a spinning jenny, with eight spindles, and also erected the first carding machine, with cylinders. Arkwright's machine for spinning by water was an extension of the principle of Hargreaves; but he also applied a large and small roller to expand the thread, for which he took out a patent in 1769. At first he worked his machinery by horses; but in 1771 he built a mill on the stream of the Derwent, at Cromford. In 1774-9, Crompton invented the mule (*which see*).

SPIRES (in Bavaria). The emperors held many diets at Spires since 1309, and it was the seat of the imperial chamber till 1688, when the city was burned by the French, and not rebuilt till after the peace of Ryswick, in 1697. The diet to condemn the reformers was held at Spires, called there by the emperor Charles V. 1529; see *Protestants*.

SPIRIT-LEVEL. The invention is ascribed to J. Melchisedec Thevenot, who died 1692.

SPIRIT-MOTOR, Mr. Yarrow explained to the Institute of Naval Architects his method of employing vaporised spirit instead of steam in the propulsion of steam launches thus dispensing with the use of a boiler, &c., March, 1888. Petroleum is used as fuel.

SPIRITS, see *Distillation*. In all nations spirituous liquors have been considered as a proper subject of heavy taxation for the support of the state; see *Alcohol, Brandy, Methylated Spirits*, &c
In 1840 England made about ten millions of gallons of spirits, Scotland about seven millions of gallons, and Ireland about nine millions of gallons.
In 1851 the number of gallons on which duty was paid for home consumption was 23,976,596. The total amount paid was 6,017,218*l*., of which 3,758,186*l*. were paid by England, 1,252,297*l*. by Scotland, and 1,006,735*l*. by Ireland.
The total duty on home consumption paid in 1853 was 6,760,422*l*.
In 1858, 9,195,154*l*. were paid as duty on 27,370,93 gallons.
In 1855, *methylated* spirits of wine, for use in the arts and sciences, were made duty free.
In 1859, 27,657,721 gallons of spirits were distilled in the United Kingdom. The uniform duty of 8s. per gallon was paid on 24,254,403 gallons for home consumption producing 9,701,764*l*. In the year 1865-6 the tax produced about 13,955,000*l*., being the largest sum then ever raised by indirect taxation. In 1871-2, 16,798,344*l* (customs and excise); in 1875-6, 21,295,663*l*; in 1877-8 20,675,928*l*.; in 1883-4, 18,435,957*l*.; and in 1887-8 17,252,550*l*.
In 1861 an act was passed repealing wholly or in part 26 previous acts, and embodying all regulations for the guidance of manufacturers and dealers in spirits.
In 1870, about 80,000,000*l*. spent in spirits; 58,000,000*l* by working classes.
Proof spirits distilled in the United Kingdom in 1873 36,479,648 gallons (England, 9,531,058; Scotland 16,421,701; Ireland, 10,596,889); in 1874, 35,352,23 gallons; duty paid, 10*s*. a gallon.

SPIRITS ACT (43 & 44 Vict. c. 24), passed 26 Aug. 1880, consolidated and amended the law relating to the manufacture and sale of spirits.

SPIRITUALISM or SPIRIT-RAPPING
Spiritual manifestations (so called) began, it is said in America about 1848, and attracted attention in this country about 1851, in the shape of rapping table-turning, &c. Many inquisitive or credulous persons visited Mr. Daniel Dunglas Hume or Home and Mr. Forster, noted "spiritual mediums." Mr Home, secretary of the Spiritual Atheneum, Sloane street, Chelsea, published, in 1863, "Incidents of my Life," in which he states that the only benefit he derived from the "gift" was the convincing many unbelievers of the certainty of a life to come the *Trials*, April, May, 1868. The "Spiritual Magazine" began Jan. 1860; the "Spiritualist," 9 Nov. 1869. The London Dialectical society published a report on spiritualism in Nov. 1871. Mr W. Crookes, in 1871, investigated the phenomena and ascribed them to "psychic force" ("Quarterly Journal of Science," July and Oct. 1871). Miss Kate Fox, said to be the earliest American medium (about 1852) was married to Mr. H. D. Jencken, in London, Dec. 1872.
The impostures of the Davenport brothers exposed in 1865.
In 1874 Messrs. Maskelyne and Cooke, and Dr. Lynn exhibited tricks by which they said they demonstrated the imposture of spiritualism.
Spiritualism discussed by a section of the British Association at Glasgow (supported by Messrs. Wm. Crookes A. Russel Wallace, and other eminent men), without result, 12 Sept. 1876.

20 spiritualist journals publishing, 1876. Dr. Henry Slade, a medium, and Geoffrey Simmons, his assistant, charged at Bow-street by prof. E. Ray Lankester and others, with "unlawfully using certain subtle and crafty means and devices to deceive"; dealt with under Vagrant Act; 2, 10, 20 Oct.; Simmons discharged, Slade sentenced to 3 months' imprisonment with hard labour, 31 Oct. 1876; appeal to sessions; sentence quashed for a technical error, 29 Jan. 1877. Wm. Lawrence sentenced to 3 months' imprisonment for receiving money as a "medium," 16 Jan. 1877.

See Trials, 1881.

SPITALFIELDS (East London), so named from the priory of St. Mary Spittle, dissolved 1534. Here the French protestant refugees settled and established the silk manufacture in 1685. In consequence of commercial changes the weavers endured much distress about 1829.

SPITHEAD, a roadstead near the Spit, a sandbank between Portsmouth and the Isle of Wight. See *Naval Reviews*, under *Navy of England*.

SPITZBERGEN, an archipelago in the Arctic ocean, discovered in 1553 by sir Hugh Willoughby, who called it Greenland, supposing it to be a part of the western continent. In 1595 it was visited by Barents and Cornelius, two Dutchmen, who pretended to be the original discoverers, and called it Spitzbergen, or sharp mountains, from the many sharp pointed and rocky mountains with which it abounds; see *Phipps*.

SPITZCAP, see *Majuba*.

SPONTANEOUS COMBUSTION of the human body, declared by most chemists to be impossible, although many cases have been recorded. The case of the countess of Görlitz, 1847, disproved by confession of her murderer, March, 1850.

SPONTANEOUS GENERATION. The origin of the germs of infusorial animalcules developed during putrefaction, &c., has been warmly debated by naturalists. Spallanzani (about 1766), and especially M. Pasteur and others assert that these germs are really endowed with organic life existing in the atmosphere. Needham (about 1747), and especially M. Pouchet and his friends in our day, assert that these germs are spontaneously formed out of organic molecules.—Pouchet's "*Hétérogénie*" appeared in 1859. Bastian's "Beginnings of Life," 1872. The researches of professor Tyndall, supporting Pasteur, and opposing Bastian, were published 1876-8.

"Spontaneous generation" (also termed *generatio œquivoca* and *epigenesis*), has been still further disproved by the laborious microscopic investigations of the Rev. W. H. Dallinger, 1875-8. He found germs to stand a much greater heat than perfect animals.

SPORTING NEWSPAPERS: Bell's Life in London, began 1820; Sporting Life, 16 March, 1859; Sporting Gazette, 1862; Sporting Times, 1865; Sportsman, Aug. 1865; The Field, 1853; Illustrated Sporting and Dramatic News, 1874; Referee, 1877.

SPORTS. The *first* "Book of Sports," under the title of "The King's Majestie's Declaration to his Subjects concerning Lawful Sports to be used" on Sundays after evening prayers, was published by king James I., 24 May, 1618. The *second* "Book of Sports," with a ratification by his majesty Charles I., is dated 18 Oct. 1633. On the publication of the first "Book of Sports," there arose a long and violent controversy among English divines on certain points; see *Sabbatarians, Sunday*, &c.—The book was ordered to be burnt by the hangman, and the sports were suppressed by the parliament. The sportsman's annual exhibition, at the Agricultural Hall, London, began in 1882.

SPOTTSYLVANIA (Virginia), see *United States*, May, 1864.

SPRINGFIELD (Missouri), near which was fought the desperate battle of Wilson's Creek, in which the federals had the advantage over the confederates, but lost their brave general, Nathaniel Lyon, 10 Aug. 1861.

SPURS. Anciently the difference between the knight and esquire was, that the knight wore gilt spurs (*eques auratus*), and the esquire silver ones. Two sorts of spurs seem to have been in use at the time of the Conquest, one called a pryck, having only a single point, the other a number of points of considerable size. Spurs nearly of the present kind came into use about 1400; see *Plating*.

SPURS, BATTLE OF. Henry VIII. of England, the emperor Maximilian, and the Swiss, in 1513, entered into an offensive alliance against France. Henry VIII. landed at Calais in the month of July, and soon formed an army of 30,000 men. He was joined by the emperor with a good corps of horse and some foot, the emperor as a *mercenary* to the king of England, who allowed him a hundred ducats a day for his table! They invested Terouenne with an army of 50,000 men; and the duc de Longueville, marching to its relief, was signally defeated on the 16th of August, at Guinegate. This battle was called the battle of Spurs, because the French used their *spurs* more than they did their *swords*. The English king laid siege to Tournay, which submitted in a few days. *Hénault*. See *Courtrai*, for another "battle of spurs."

S. S., see *Collar*.

STABAT MATER, a Latin hymn, by Jacopone, 14th century, sung during Passion week in Catholic churches. Rossini's music to this hymn (1842) is often performed.

STADE DUES. At a castle near the town of Stade, in Hanover, certain dues on goods were charged by the Hanoverian government. The British government settled these dues in 1844. They were resisted by the Americans in 1855, and were abolished in June, 1861. Great Britain paid 160,000*l*. as her share of the compensation (3,000,000*l*.).

STADTHOLDER, see *Holland*.

STAFF COLLEGE (Sandhurst), for providing an education to qualify military officers for the duties of the staff. The foundation stone was laid by the duke of Cambridge on 14 Dec. 1859.

STAGE COACHES, so called from the stages or inns at which the coaches stopped to refresh and change horses. *Bailey*. The stage-coach duty act passed in 1785. These coaches were made subject to salutary provisions for the safety of passengers, in 1810; to mileage duties, 1815. The acts were consolidated in 1832, and amended in 1833 and 1842. See *Mail Coaches*, &c.

STAGYRITE, properly Stagirite, see *Aristotelian*.

STAMFORD BRIDGE (York). In 1066 Tostig, brother of Harold II., rebelled against his brother, and joined the invading army of Harold Hardrada, king of Norway. They defeated the northern earls and took York, but were defeated at Stamford-bridge by Harold, 25 Sept., and were both slain. The loss by this victory no doubt led to his defeat at Hastings, 14 Oct. following.

STAMP-DUTIES. By 22 & 23 Charles II. (1670-1) duties were imposed on certain legal documents. In 1694 a duty was imposed upon paper, vellum, and parchment. The stamp-duty on newspapers was commenced in 1711, and every year added to the list of articles upon which stamp-duty was made payable.

Stamp act, which led to the American war, passed 22 March, 1765; repealed in 1766
Stamp duties in Ireland commenced 1774
Stamps on notes and bills of exchange in . . 1782
The stamp-duties produced in England, in 1800, a revenue of 3,126,535£.
Many alterations made in 1853 and 1857. In June, 1855, the stamp-duty on newspapers as such was totally abolished; the stamp on them being henceforth for postal purposes.
In July and Aug. 1854, 19,115,800 newspaper stamps were issued; in the same months, 1855, only 6,870,000.
Drafts on bankers to be stamped 1858
Additional stamp duties were enacted in 1860 (on leases, bills of exchange, dock warrants, extracts from registers of births, &c.); in 1861 (on leases, licences to house-agents, &c.).
Stamp-duties reduced in 1864, 1865.
All fees payable in the superior courts of law, after 31 Dec. 1865, are to be collected by stamps, by an act passed in June, 1865. Also in Public Record office 1868
144,623,014 inland revenue penny stamps sold, besides other stamps 1869
By the Stamp acts, 10 Aug. 1870, newspaper stamps were abolished after . . . . . 1 Oct. 1870
New stamp duties imposed; came into effect 1 Jan., 1871
1d. receipt and postage stamps used for each other after . . . . 1 June, 1881
Stamp-duties imposed on foreign or colonial share certificates, bonds, &c. by Customs Act, 1888.

AMOUNT OF STAMP DUTIES RECEIVED IN THE UNITED KINGDOM.*

1840	£6,726,817	1881	£11,933,114
1845	7,710,683	1882	12,348,175
1850	6,558,332	1883*	11,691,025
1855	6,805,605	1884	11,681,431
1860 (to 31 Mar.)	8,040,091	1885	11,886,185
1865	9,542,645	1886	11,600,614
1870	9,288,553	1887	11,780,333
1876	11,023,374	1888	13,056,950
1880	11,306,914		

* Fee and patent stamps now omitted.

STANDARD for gold and silver in England fixed by law, 1300. Standard gold is 22 parts out of 24 of pure gold, the other two parts or carats being silver or copper. The standard of silver is 11 oz. 2 dwts. of fine silver alloyed with 18 dwts. of copper, or 37 parts out of 40 pure silver, and three parts copper. In 1300 these 12 oz. of silver were coined into 20 shillings; in 1412 they were coined into 30 shillings; and in 1527 into 45 shillings. In 1545 Henry VIII. coined 6 oz. of silver and 6 oz. of alloy into 48 shillings; and the next year he coined 4 oz. of silver and 8 oz. of alloy into the same sum. Elizabeth, in 1560, restored the old standard in 60 shillings; and in 1601 in 62 shillings. The average proportions of silver to gold at the royal mint are 15¼ to 1. The standard of plate and silver manufactures was affirmed, 6 Geo. I. 1719 *et seq.*; see *Gold, Goldsmiths, Silver, Coinage,* and *Currency.*

STANDARD, BATTLE OF THE, see *Northallerton.*

STANDARD MEASURES. In the reign of Edgar a law was made to prevent frauds arising from the diversity of measures, and for the establishment of a legal standard measure to be used in every part of his dominions. The standard vessels made by order of the king were deposited in the city of Winchester, and hence originated the well-known term of "Winchester measure" of the time of Henry VII. (1487). The bushel so made is still preserved in the museum of that city. Henry I. also, to prevent frauds in the measurement of cloth, ordered a standard yard of the length of his own arm to be made and deposited at Winchester, with the standard measures of king Edgar. The Guildhall contains the standard measures of succeeding sovereigns. *Camden.*— The standard weights and measures were settled by parliament in 1824. The pound troy was to be 5760 grains, and the pound avoirdupois 7000 grains. The "Standard yard of 1760," in the custody of the clerk of the house of commons, was declared to be the Imperial Standard yard and the unit of measures of extension. This standard having been destroyed by the fire in 1834, a new commission was appointed to reconstruct it, and researches for this purpose, in conformity with the act, which directed the comparison of the standard with a pendulum vibrating seconds of time in the latitude of London, were begun by Francis Baily (died in 1844), continued by the rev. R. Sheepshanks till his death in 1855, and completed by G. B. Airy, astronomer royal. In 1855 was passed "an act for legalising and preserving the lost standards of weights and measures." The parliamentary copies of the standard pound and yard are deposited at the Royal Observatory, Greenwich. The standard weights and measures act was passed Aug. 1866. The Standard Commission published reports, 1866 *et seq.*

"**STANDARD,**" conservative newspaper; begun, morning, 1827; evening, 29 June, 1857.

STANDARDS, see *Banners, Flags,* &c. The practice in the army of using a cross on standards and shields is due to the asserted miraculous appearance of a cross to Constantine, previously to his battle with Maxentius; Eusebius says that he received this statement from the emperor himself, 312. The standard was named LABARUM. For the celebrated French standard, see *Auriflamme.*— STANDARD OF MAHOMET; on this ensign no infidel dared look. Christians have been massacred by the Turkish populace for looking on it.—The British IMPERIAL STANDARD was first hoisted on the Tower of London, and on Bedford Tower, Dublin, and displayed by the Foot Guards, on the union of the kingdoms, 1 Jan. 1801.

STANFORD COURT, Worcestershire, the ancient mansion of sir Francis Winnington, burnt 5-7 Dec. 1832; valuable portraits, books, MSS. &c., destroyed.

STANHOPE ADMINISTRATION was formed by James (afterwards earl) Stanhope and the earl of Sunderland, 15 April, 1717. Stanhope was premier and chancellor of the exchequer; lord (afterwards earl) Cowper, lord chancellor; earl of Sunderland and Joseph Addison, secretaries of state, &c. In March, 1718, Addison resigned, and the earl of Sunderland became premier.

STANHOPE DEMONSTRATOR, see *Logic.*

STANNARY COURTS of Devon and Cornwall for the administration of justice among the tin miners, whose privileges were confirmed by 33 Edw. I. 1305. They were regulated by parliament in 1641, and at many times since. A "Stannaries act" was passed in 1869; another act in 1887.

STAPLE (literally that which is fixed). The chief English staple commodities which were traded in by privileged merchants, and on which customs were levied, were wool, skins, leather, tin, lead,

and sometimes cloth, butter, and cheese; certain towns were appointed for the collection of the duties; statutes relating to the staple were passed by Edward III., Richard II., and Henry VI. Edward III.'s "ordinacio stapularum" (ordinance of the staple) was enacted in 1353.

STARCH is a sediment produced at the bottom of vessels wherein wheat has been steeped in water: it is soft and friable, easily broken into powder, and is used to stiffen and clear linen, with blue; its powder is employed to powder the hair. The art of starching linen was brought into England by Mrs. Dingbein, a Flemish woman, 1 Mary, 1553. *Stow.* Patents for obtaining starch from other substances have been taken out: from potatoes by Samuel Newton and others in 1707; from the horse-chestnut by Wm. Murray in 1796; from rice by Thomas Wickham in 1823; from various matters by Orlando Jones in 1839-40.

STAR-CHAMBER, COURT OF. So called haply from its roof being garnished with stars. *Coke.* This court of justice was called Star-Chamber, not from the *stars* on its roof (which were obliterated even before the reign of queen Elizabeth), but from the *Starra*, or Jewish covenants, deposited there by order of Richard I. No *star* was allowed to be valid except found in those repositories, and here they remained till the banishment of the Jews by Edward I. The court was instituted or revived, 3 Hen. VII. 1486, for trials by a committee of the privy council, which was in violation of Magna Charta; as it dealt with civil and criminal causes unfettered by the rules of law. In Charles I.'s reign it exercised its power upon several bold innovators, who gloried in their sufferings, and contributed to render government odious and contemptible. It was abolished in 1640. There were in this court from 26 to 42 judges, the lord chancellor having the casting voice. The judicial committee of the privy council is the Star-chamber revived under another name.

STAR OF INDIA, a new order of knighthood for India, instituted by letters patent 23 Feb., gazetted 25 June, 1861, and enlarged in 1866. It comprised the sovereign, the grand master, 25 knights (Europeans and natives), and extra or honorary knights, such as the prince consort, the prince of Wales, &c. The queen invested several knights on 1 Nov. 1861. The prince of Wales held a grand chapter at Calcutta, 1 Jan. 1876.

STARS, THE FIXED. They were classed into constellations, it is supposed, about 1200 B.C. Hicetas, of Syracuse, taught that the sun and the stars were motionless, and that the earth moved round them, about 344 B.C. (this is mentioned by Cicero, and perhaps gave the first hint of this system to Copernicus). Job, Hesiod, and Homer mention several of the constellations. The Royal Library at Paris contains a Chinese chart of the heavens, made about 600 B.C., in which 1460 stars are correctly inserted. The aberration of the stars was discovered by Dr. Bradley, 1727; see *Astronomy*, and *Solar System*. Maps of the stars were published by the Society for the Diffusion of Useful Knowledge in 1839, and a set of Celestial Maps, issued under the superintendence of the Royal Prussian Academy, was completed in 1859.

Bessel discovered the annual parallax of star 61 Cygni (hence he calculated its distance from the earth to be about 60 billions of miles) 12 Feb. 1841
Struve made it 40 billions [supported by Brünnow and R. S. Ball] 1853
The calculations of T. Henderson (at the Cape) 1832 supported by D. Gill and others showed that probably a Centauri, is the star nearest to the earth 1883-4

STARVATION: Deaths attributed to it in the metropolitan districts, 1873, 107; 1875, 46; 1879, 80; 1888, 29. See *Abstinence.*

STATE MEDICINE, see under *Sanitation*, 2 May, 1888.

STATE PAPER OFFICE was founded in 1578, now merged into the Public Record Office. In 1856 the British government began the publication of Calendars of State Papers, invaluable to future historians.

STATES-GENERAL OF FRANCE. An ancient assembly of France, first met, it is said, in 1302 to consider the exactions of the pope. Previous to the Revolution, it had not met since 1614. The states consisted of three orders, the clergy, nobility, and commons. They were convened by Louis XVI., and assembled at Versailles, 5 May, 1789 (308 ecclesiastics, 285 nobles, and 621 deputies or *tiers état*, third estate). A contest arose whether the three orders should make three distinct houses, or but one assembly. The commons insisted upon the latter, and assuming the title of the National Assembly, declared that they were competent to proceed to business, without the concurrence of the two other orders, if they refused to join them. The nobility and clergy found it expedient to concede the point, and they all met in one hall; see *National Assembly*. Centenary, see *France*, 5 May, 1889.

STATES OF THE CHURCH, see *Pope*, and *Rome.*

STATIONERS. Books and papers were formerly sold only at stalls; hence the dealers were called stationers. The company of stationers of London is of great antiquity, and existed long before printing was invented, yet it was not incorporated until 3 Philip & Mary, 1557. Their old dwelling was in Paternoster-row.

STATISTICS, the science of the state, political knowledge, is said to have been founded by sir Wm. Petty, who died in 1687. The term is said to have been invented by professor Achenwall of Göttingen in 1749. The first statistical society in England was formed at Manchester in 1833; the Royal Statistical Society of London, which publishes a quarterly journal, was established 15 March, 1834, for the purpose of procuring, arranging, and publishing "facts calculated to illustrate the condition and prospects of society." Jubilee kept, 22, 23, 24 June, 1885; incorporated, 1887. Similar societies have been established on the continent. International Statistical Institute constituted in 1885, met at Rome, 12-16 April, 1887. International Statistical Congresses are now held occasionally. The 1st at Brussels, chiefly through the agency of M. Quetelet, in 1853; 2nd at Paris, 1855; 3rd at Vienna, 1857; 4th at London, under the presidency of the prince consort, 16-21 July, 1860; 5th at Berlin; 6th at Florence; 7th at the Hague; 8th at St. Petersburg, was opened 22 Aug. 1872; 9th at Pesth. 31 Aug. 1876. The eminent statistician, Dr. Wm. Farr, died 14 April, 1883. *Statistical Abstracts* have been published annually by the government for many years.

STATUES, see *Sculpture*, &c. Phidias, whose statue of Jupiter passed for one of the wonders of the world, was the greatest statuary among the ancients, 440 B.C. He had previously made a statue of Minerva at the request of Pericles, which was placed in the Parthenon. It was made of ivory and gold, and measured 39 feet in height. Acilius raised a golden statue to his father, the first that

STATUES.

appeared in Italy. Lysippus invented the art of taking likenesses in plaster moulds, from which he afterwards cast models in wax, 326 B.C. Michael Angelo was the greatest artist among the moderns. The first equestrian statue erected in Great Britain was that of Charles I. in 1678.* By 17 & 18 Vict. c. 10 (10 July, 1854), public statues were placed under the control and protection of the Board of Works. The following are the chief public statues in London:—

Achilles, Hyde-park, in honour of the duke of Wellington, by the ladies of Great Britain	18 June,	1822
Albert, prince consort, Royal Exchange, 1850 ; Horticultural Society gardens, 1863; Holborn circus,		1873
Anne, queen, St. Paul's Churchyard, 1712 ; replaced,		1886
Barry, sir Charles, Westminster		1865
Bedford, duke of, Russell-square		1809
Bentinck, lord George, Cavendish-square	after	1848
Burns †, Thames embankment	26 July,	1884
Byron, lord, Hamilton-place, Hyde-park,	24 May,	1880
Canning, Geo., New Palace-yard, Westminster		1832
Carlyle, Thos., embankment, Chelsea	Oct.	1882
Cartwright, major, Burton-crescent		1831
Charles I., Charing-cross		1678
Charles II., Soho-square		***
Clyde, lord, Waterloo-place		1868
Cobden, Richard, Camden-town	June,	1868
Cumberland, duke of, Cavendish-square		1770
Derby, Edward, earl of, Parliament-square		1874
Disraeli, Benj., lord Beaconsfield, Parliament-square	19 April,	1883
Elizabeth, queen, St. Dunstan's, Fleet-street		1586
Faraday, Michael, Royal Institution		1876
Fox, Charles James, Bloomsbury-square		1816
Franklin, sir John, Waterloo-place		1866
George I., Grosvenor-square		1726
George III., Somerset-house		1788
George III., Cockspur-street		1836
Gordon, gen. C. G., Trafalgar-square	25 Sept.	1888
Havelock, sir Henry, Trafalgar-square		1861
Herbert, lord, Pall Mall	3 June,	1867
Hill, Rowland, Royal Exchange		1882
Howard, John ; first erected in St. Paul's		1796
James II., Whitehall		1687
Jenner, Edward, Trafalgar-square, 1858 ; removed to Kensington-gardens		1864
Lawrence, lord, Waterloo-place (a new statue since)	April,	1885
Macgregor, sir James, Chelsea hospital		1863
Mill, John Stuart, Thames Embankment,	26 Jan.	1872
Myddelton, sir Hugh, Islington-green		1862
Napier, gen. sir Chas. J., Trafalgar-square		1856
Nelson, lord, Trafalgar-square [the lions at the base, designed by sir E. Landseer, were uncovered 31 Jan. 1867]		1843
Outram, sir James, Thames embankment	17 Aug.	1871
Palmerston, viscount, Parliament-street	29 Jan.	1876
Peabody, George, Royal Exchange		1869
Peel, sir Robert, Cheapside, 1855 ; near Westminster abbey, 1868 ; Parliament-square		1877
Pitt, William, Hanover-square		1831
Prince of Wales, Temple-bar site		1880
Queen Victoria, Royal Exchange, 1845 ; Temple-bar site		,,
Raikes, Robert, Thames embankment	3 July,	,,
Richard Cœur de Lion, near Westminster abbey		1860
Shakespeare, &c., Leicester-square		1874
Stephenson, Robert, Euston-road, near L. & N. W. station		1871
Tyndale, Wm., Thames embankment		1884
Wellington, duke of, Royal Exchange		1844
Wellington, duke of, arch, Hyde-park-corner, 1846 ; equestrian statue, height 27 feet, weight 40 tons		

STEAM

designed by Matthew C 1846 ; taken down, 24 Aldershot camp
Wellington, duke of, nev figures of four Waterloo sir J. E. Boehm, facing I 13 Nov. ; unveiled by tl William III., St. James's-s William IV., King William York, duke of, Waterloo-p

STATUTES, see *A Merton*, &c. Statute L_e in 1863-1876-1883-1887 Civil Procedure act, 44 Aug. 1881. " Statutes 1878)," in 18 volumes,

STATUTORY D 6 Will. IV. c. 62 (1835), permitted to make decl_e judges, &c.; commenci and sincerely declare tl times abused.
Mr. Alexander Chaffers h against the character o Travers Twiss, was pros drew during the examin ceased : but Chaffers wa magistrate, and by the ment

STEAM CARRIA invented by the earl o successful in 1860. It the rate of 8 miles an h_o per mile. His lordship in two days; see *Road*

STEAM ENGINE Hero of Alexandria, in I various methods of em₁ and to him is ascribed th a toy, possesses the proj he flourished about 284 pears to have foreseen power; see *Railways*, &c.
Solomon de Caus, a Frenc work which Arago on ins to have contained the g_e The marquis of Worcester in his " Century of Inve Papin's *digester* invented Captain Savery's engine water.
Papin's engine exhibited t [He is said to have made destroyed by boatmen c Thomas Newcomen, of Da constructed " the first s (used for nearly a cent amendment).
[He died in London whi a patent, 1729.]
First idea of *steam naviga* obtained by Jonathan H Watt's invention of perf_e separate vessel from the His first patent, 1769 ; his factories, and his patent

[He and Mr Symington are said to have constructed a small steamboat which travelled at about 4 miles an hour soon after.]	
W. Symington made a passage on the Forth and Clyde canal	1790
First steam-engine erected in Dublin by Henry Jackson	1791
First experiment with steam navigation on the Thames	1801
Trevethick's high-pressure engine	"
Woolf's double-cylinder expansion engine constructed	1804
Manufactories warmed by steam	1806
Fulton's steamboat *Clermont* on the Seine, 9 Aug. 1803; at New York, 1806; started a steamboat on the river Hudson, America	1807
Steam power to convey coals on a railway employed by Blenkinsop	1811
Comet, built by Henry Bell, sailed on the Clyde [John Robertson, who made the engine, died 20 Nov. 1858, aged 86]	18 Jan. 1812
[The *Comet* sailed from Glasgow to Greenock three times a week; fares, 3s. and 4s.; speed, 7½ miles an hour.]	
Steam applied to printing in the *Times* office (see *Printing machines*)	1814
There were five steam-vessels in Scotland (*Parl. Returns*)	"
First steam-vessel on the Thames, brought by Mr. Dodd from Glasgow	"
First steamer built in England (*Parl. Returns*)	1815
Rising Sun, a steamer built by lord Cochrane, crossed the Atlantic	1818
The *Savannah* steamer, of 350 tons, came from New York to Liverpool in 26 days	15 July, 1819
First steamer in Ireland	1820
Steamboats established between Dover and Calais and London and Leith	1821
Steam-gun, invented by Perkins	1824
Steam-jet applied by George Stephenson, 1814; by Timothy Hackworth, about	1825
Captain Johnson obtained 10,000l. for making the first steam voyage to India, in the *Enterprise*, which sailed from Falmouth	16 Aug. "
The locomotive steam-carriages on railways at Liverpool	Oct. 1829
The railway opened (see *Liverpool*)	1830
Capt. Ericsson's screw steamer, "*Francis Bogden*," speed 10 miles an hour, constructed: see *Screw-Propeller*	1837
The *Sirius* sailed from Queenstown 4 April; arrived at New York	21 April, 1838
The *Great Western* sails from Bristol to New York, being her first voyage	8-23 April, "
War-steamers built in England	"
War-steamers built at Birkenhead, named the *Nemesis* and *Phlegethon*, carrying each two thirty-two pounders, sent by government to China	1840
Hall's method of economising fuel introduced about	"
The Cunard steamers began to sail *	5 July, "
[Sir Sam. Cunard died 28 April, 1865, aged 78.]	
The Peninsular Company was formed in 1837; became the Peninsular and Oriental Steam Navigation Company in	1840
[They possessed 53 steamers and a fleet of tugs, Dec. 1866.]	
The *Great Britain* sailed from the Mersey 26 July, [She arrived at New York 10 Aug. During her second voyage, she ran aground in Dundrum bay, Ireland, 22 Sept. 1846. Her passengers were landed; and she was extricated with little injury, after long-continued and strenuous efforts, by I. Brunel, jun. and Bremner, 27 Aug. 1847.]	1845
The Collins steamers began	1850
Inman Company: began by Wm. Inman, first vessel *City of Glasgow*, 1850; the company became the Liverpool, New York, and Philadelphia company,	

* Since then many great steamers have been wrecked or burnt: viz, *Governor Fenner*, 19 Feb., 1841; *President*, March, 1841; *Ocean Monarch*, Aug. 1848; *St. George*, 22 Dec. 1852; *George Canning*, 1 Jan. 1855; *Pacific*, 1856; *Austria*, 13 Sept., 1858; *Indian*, 21 Nov., 1859; *Hungarian*, Feb., 1860; *Anglo-Saxon*, 27 April, 1863; *City of Boston*, Feb., 1870; *Germania*, 21 Dec., 1872; *Atlantic*, April, 1873; *Ville de Havre*, 22 Nov., 1873; *Cashmere*, 5 July, 1877; *Eten*, 15 July, 1877, &c.

1857; *City of Richmond*, sailed from Liverpool 6 p.m. 15 July, arrived at New York 12.30 p.m. 24 July, 1873. (Apparent time 7 days, 19 hours, 45 minutes; average 365 miles a day, 15 knots an hour.)	
The *Purifc* crosses the Atlantic in 9 days, 19 hours, 25 minutes, arriving at Holyhead	20 May, 1851
Manchester Steam-Users Association established about	1855
Steam packets leave Galway for America	1858
The merits of an attacking vessel termed a *steam-ram*, advocated by sir G. Sartorius, discussed	1859-60
Giffard's valuable steam-injector invented	about 1859
An iron-plated frigate, *La Gloire*, completed in France (see *Navy, French*)	1860
The *Warrior*, an iron-plated vessel, launched 29 Dec.	"
The *Far East*, a vessel with two screws, launched at Millwall	31 Oct. 1863
A *cigar ship*, a steam yacht, designed by Mr. Winan, built by Hepworth, launched on the Thames	19 Feb. 1866
Trial trip of the *Nautilus*, with a hydraulic propeller worked by steam, Ruthven's patent; no paddle or screw required	24 March, "
Successful trial trip of the *Water-witch*, a government hydraulic propeller iron-clad gun-vessel (Ruthven's patent), on the Thames	19 Oct. "
Mr. Ruthven patented his system in 1849, and exhibited his machinery at the International Exhibition in 1851. His object is to increase speed and save fuel. In the *Water-witch* a steam-engine gives the power of absorbing and expelling the water, and no screw or paddle is required. The water-wheel is 14½ feet in diameter.	
Trial trip of H.M. gun-boat *Thistle*; explosion of boiler, 8 killed	3 Nov. 1869
Channel Steamers: "Twin-ship" *Castalia*, steamer (two hulls, separated by 26 feet), 290 feet long; invented by capt. W. T. Dicey, for the English Channel steam company, to prevent sea-sickness when crossing the Channel; (really a single ship, with the middle part of her bottom raised out of the water throughout her whole length); launched, 2 June; tried in calm weather; reported successful but slow, 2 Aug. 1875; successful, June, 1876; sold Nov. 1876.	
Bessemer, saloon steamer, designed by Mr. Bessemer and E. J. Reed; built by the Earles company; launched at Hull, 24 Sept. 1874; first voyage from Hull to Gravesend, 5 March, 1875; sailed to Calais, 10 April, 1875. [Success doubtful, 1876.] Modified by E. J. Reed; trial near Hull, reported successful, 26 March, 1877.	
Express, twin steamer; built by A. Leslie, of Newcastle; sailed from the Tyne to Coquet Island, 22½ miles, in 1h. 22m., reported satisfactory, 13 March, 1878.	
Folkestone, twin steamer, launched at Hull, 23 March, 1878.	
Pizarro, steamer (the first built of Siemens-Martin steel), 340 feet long by 40 feet broad, 3400 tons, launched at Napier's yard, Govan, near Glasgow, 5 Aug. 1879.	
Livadia, a turbot-shaped steam yacht (broad and flat), built by Elder & Co. of Glasgow for the czar of Russia, launched on the Clyde, 7 July, 1880.	
Faraday, steam-ship (for laying electric cables, 360 feet long, 52 feet wide, 36 feet deep, 5000 tons register; to carry 6000 tons dead weight); next in size to *Great Eastern*; built for Messrs. Siemens by Messrs. Mitchell, at Newcastle; launched (much employed, 1881)	17 Feb. 1874
Orient, steamer, built by Elders of Glasgow, for Australian traffic; length, 460 feet; breadth, 46 feet; depth, 37⅜ feet; sailed from Greenock to West India Dock, London	10-12 Sept. 1879
Servia, Cunard royal mail steamer, 530 feet long, 52 feet broad, 44 feet depth; gross tonnage, 8500 tons; 5 decks and promenade; next in size to *Great Eastern*; launched in the Clyde,	1 March, 1881
Servia, sailed from America to Liverpool (by long route) in 7 days, 8 hours, 15 min. quickest passage hitherto made	26 Jan. 1882
City of Rome, mail steamer, length 586 feet, breadth 52 feet, left the Clyde	28 Sept. 1881
Alaska, Guion mail steamer crossed the Atlantic, 6 days, 22 hours	31 May-6 June, 1882
The Guion steamer *Arizona*, left Queenstown at 2.10 p.m. Sept. 11, and reached Sandy Hook at 6.20 p.m. on the 18th, which, including the difference in time, 4 hours, 27 min., makes the passage 7 days, 8 hours, 12 min. On the return passage she made the voyage in 7 days, 7 hours, 48 min.	
The Guion steamer *Alaska* arrived at Sandy Hook on Sunday, in 7 days, 17 min.	31 July, "

Black Star Line of steamers between Grimsby and America 1882
Victoria, steamer (jubilee of the P. and O. company), built by Messrs. Caird & Co.; length 465 feet, breadth 52 feet, depth 37 feet; sailed from Greenock to Southampton . . 16 July, 1887
Mr. Thomas Lishman's steam generator said to economize fuel without producing smoke, employed at Elswick Works, Newcastle, and other places ,,
Arcadia (P. and O. steamer), arrived at Albert Docks . . . . . 18 May, 1888
Etruria, Cunard line, sailed from Roches Point, Cork, to New York in 6 days, 1 hr., 47 minutes 2 June, ,,
Parisian, boat of the Allan line, said to have crossed the Atlantic from land to land in 4 days, 17 hours and 10 minutes . . . Aug. ,,
City of New York, length 560 feet, breadth 63½ feet, first voyage across Atlantic . . 1 Aug. ,,
Steam vessels belonging to the British empire in 1814, 6; in 1815, 10; in 1820, 43; in 1825, 168; in 1830, 315; in 1835, 545; in 1845, 1001; in 1850, 1187; in 1864, 2490; in 1871, 3382; in 1875, 4170; in 1877, 4564; in 1879, 5027; in 1883, 6260; in 1887, 6663.

See *Navy*, and *Shipping*.

LARGE STEAM VESSELS OF ENGLAND.

	Long.	Broad.
Great Western	236 feet	35 feet
Duke of Wellington	240 feet	60 feet
British Queen	275 feet	61 feet
Great Britain	322 feet	51 feet
Himalaya	370 feet	43 feet
Persia	390 feet	45 feet
Servia	530 feet	52 feet
GREAT EASTERN, for a short time (1857-8) called *Leviathan*	692 feet	83 feet

Horse Power: — Paddles, 1000; screw, 1600; *Weight* of ship, 12,000 tons; ordinary light draught, 12,000 tons; said to have cost 732,000*l*.
She was designed by Mr. I. K. Brunel (who died 15 Sept. 1859), and built by Messrs. Scott Russell and Co., at Millwall; launching lasted from 3 Nov. 1857, to 31 Jan. 1858.
The capital subscribed having been all expended, a new company was formed to fit her for sea.
On 7 Sept. 1859, she left her moorings at Deptford for Portland-roads. On the voyage an explosion took place (off Hastings), through some neglect in regard to the casing of one of the funnels, when ten firemen were killed and many persons seriously injured. After repairs she sailed to Holyhead, arriving there 10 Oct.; she endured the storm of 25-26 Oct. well; and proceeded to Southampton for the winter, 4 Nov.
She was fitted up to convey 5000 persons from London to Australia, a distance of 22,500 miles, with accommodation for 800 1st class passengers, 2000 2nd class, and 1200 3rd class. Her able captain (Harrison) was drowned in the Solent 22 Jan. 1860, deeply regretted. She sailed for New York 17 June, under command of captain Vine Hall, and arrived there 28 June. After being exhibited she left New York 16 Aug. and returned to England 26 Aug.
Owing to a lawsuit in April, the ship came into the hands of sheriff's officers; but was released and sailed for New York on 1 May, 1861. On 12 Sept. she suffered much loss through a violent gale.
In 1862 she performed several voyages to and from New York; but in Aug. ran on a rock near Long Island and injured her bottom.
She was repaired and arrived at Liverpool 17 Jan. 1863, and sailed to New York (16-27 May).
She was bought by Glass, Elliot, and Co. in March or April, 1864, and was chartered to convey the Atlantic telegraph cable; sailed from Sheerness 15 July; and returned 19 Aug. 1865; see under *Electric Telegraph*.
She sailed for New York, prepared for 2000 passengers, 26 March, and returned with 191. She was seized by the seamen, claiming their wages, May, 1867; and the case was carried into Chancery in July.
At the meeting of the shareholders 10 Feb. 1868, no dividend was declared.
She conveyed the French Atlantic telegraph cable, successfully laid . . . . . Oct. 1869
Arrived at Bombay with Bombay and Suez cable, 27 Feb.; returned to Sheerness . June, 1870
Sailed with the fourth Atlantic telegraph cable 8 June; which was completely laid . 3 July, 1873
Sailed with the fifth Atlantic telegraph cable: laid . . . . . Aug., Sept. 1874
Put up for sale at 30,000*l*.; not bought 19 Oct. 1881
(John Scott Russell died, aged 74) . 8 June, 1882
Proposed to be employed as a coal hulk in Gibraltar Bay . . . . . April, 1884
Sold by auction to Mr. Frederick de Mattos for 26,200*l*. for the London traders (limited) 28 Oct. 1885
The ship reported in good condition . 20 April, 1886
Sold to Mr. Worsley for 26,000*l*. . . ,,
In the Mersey . . . . 12 May-12 Oct. ,,
Largely visited; drink licence refused . April, 1887
Sold to Mr. Craik for 21,000*l*. . . 20 Oct. ,,
In the Clyde, sold to Messrs. Henry Bath, metal brokers, for 16,500*l*. . . . Dec. ,,
Messrs. Henry Bath and Sons cause the vessel to be moved to the Mersey, where she is beached 25 Aug. 1888
Total receipts of the sale at Liverpool 58,000*l*. 24 Nov. ,,

STEAM GUN; suggested by Wm. Murdoch, 1803. One patented by Messrs. Perkins, in 1824, was ineffectual.
In Oct. 1870, Mr. H. Bessemer proposed the application of steam power to artillery.

STEAM HAMMER, invented by Mr. James Nasmyth in 1838, and patented by him 18 June, 1842. Its main feature is the absolutely direct manner by which the elastic power of steam is employed to lift up and let fall the mass of iron constituting the hammer, which is attached direct to the end of a piston-rod passing through the bottom of an inverted steam cylinder placed immediately over the anvil.
In 1842, Mr. Nasmyth applied his steam-hammer o driving piles, which has importantly assisted in the execution of great public works. Owing to its vast range of power, forged iron-work can now by its means be executed on a scale, and for a variety of purposes, with an ease and perfection not previously possible. Parts of gigantic marine steam-engines, anchors, and Armstrong guns, as well as the most minute details of machinery, as in Enfield rifles, are executed by the steam-hammer.
A steam-hammer, said to be the then largest in the world, completed at Woolwich; the falling portion weighs 40 tons, and when used with top steam (51 tons) has the force of 91 tons, April, 1874. One at Schneider's works, Creuzot, France; weight between 75 and 80 tons, Dec. 1877.

STEAM-MAN. A figure constructed to drag a phaeton received this name in New York in March, 1868.

STEAM NAVIGATION, see under *Steam*.

STEAM-PLOUGHS were patented by G. Callaway and R. A. Purkes, 1849; H. Cowing, 1850; and others. John Fowler's of 1854 is much approved.

STEAM-RAM (to be used in naval warfare), was invented by Mr. James Nasmyth in 1836, and communicated to the Admiralty in 1845. Steam-rams built by Mr. James Laird of Birkenhead for the Confederates in N. America, were stopped and eventually bought by the British government, 1864.

STEAM-WHISTLES and **STEAM-TRUMPETS**, used in factories to summon or dismiss workmen, prohibited by an act passed Aug. 1872.

STEARINE (from *stear*, suet), that part of oils and fats which is solid at common temperature. The nature of these substances was first made known by Chevreul, in 1823, who showed that they were compounds of peculiar acids, with a base termed *glycerine;* of these compounds the chief are stearine, margarine, and elaine; see *Candles*.

STEEL, metal, a compound of iron and carbon, exists in nature, and has been fabricated from the

earliest times. It was certainly used by the Egyptians, Assyrians, and Greeks. It now largely replaces cast iron in ship building, &c.

Reaumur discovered the direct process of making steel by immersing malleable iron in a bath of cast iron 1722

A manufactory for cast steel is said to have been set up by Benjamin Huntsman at Handsworth, near Sheffield 1740

The manufacture of shear steel began in Sheffield, about 1800

German steel was made at Newcastle previously by Mr. Crawley.

The inventions of Mushat (1800), Lucas (1804), and Heath (1839), were important steps in this manufacture ; see *Engraving.*

Relpe patented his "puddled steel" . . . 1850

Mr. H. Bessemer made steel by passing cold air through liquid iron, 1856. By this method 20 tons of crude iron have been couverted into cast steel in 23 minutes.*

Tungsten steel was made in Germany, 1859 ; and M. Freny made steel by bringing red-hot iron in contact with carbonate of ammonia . . . 1861

M. Alfred Krupp exhibited an ingot of steel weighing 4500 lbs. in 1851, and one weighing 20 tons in 1862 (about 15,000 men are employed at his works at Essen, 1887)

The subject much investigated by M. Caron, 1861-5 ; much attention was excited by cutlery made from a metallic sand, brought from Taranaki or New Plymouth, in New Zealand 1860

A steel bridge, in connection with the exhibition, constructed at Paris by M. Joret . . . 1866

Mr. John Heaton published his process . 1867-8

Dr. Siemens, by means of his "regenerative gas furnaces," produced excellent steel, cheaply, in large masses . . . . . 1876, *et seq.*

Cutlers' Company, London, opened an exhibition, 1 May, 1879

Messrs. Bolchow, Vaughan & Co. of Middlesborough, by Thomas and Gilchrist's process, convert Cleveland iron ore into Bessemer steel, by lining the furnace with radial bricks of magnesian limestone and adding cold basic material, phosphorus being thereby removed.

The process reported successful . . . Oct. 1880

Mr. J. S. Jeans published his important work, "Steel : its History, Manufacture, Properties, and Uses" . . . . Feb. ,,

The *Garfield*, a steel sailing ship, 2,220 tons, 292 ft. length, 24 ft. 9 in. depth, 41 ft. breadth, launched at Belfast . . . . 7 Jan. 1882

Umbria, Cunard liner, above 8,000 tons, 520 ft. long, 57 ft. 3 in. broad, 41 ft. deep, launched on the Clyde . . . . Sept. 1884

Mr. B. H. Thwaite, of Liverpool, and Mr. A. Stewart, of Bradford, introduce an improved "rapid" process for the manufacture of steel, announced Oct. 1887

See under *Steam.*

STEEL PENS. "Iron pens" are mentioned by Chamberlayne in 1685. Steel pens, made long before, began to come into use about 1820, when the first gross of three-slit pens was sold wholesale for 7*l.* 4*s.* In 1830 the price was 8*s.*, and in 1832, 6*s.* A better pen is now sold for 6*d.* a gross. Birmingham in 1858 produced about 1000 million pens per annum. Women and children are principally employed in the manufacture. Perry, Mitchell, and Gillott are eminent makers. Joseph Gillott, originally a mechanic, made a large fortune by steel-pen making. He died 5 Jan. 1872, aged 72.

STEEL-YARD. An ancient instrument, the same that is translated *balance* in the Pentateuch. The *Statera Romana*, or Roman steel-yard, is mentioned in 315 B.C.—The STEEL-YARD or STILL-YARD COMPANY, London merchants, who had the steel-yard in Thames-street assigned to them by Henry III., about 1232, were Flemings and Germans, and the only exporters, for many years after, of the staple commodities of England. *Anderson.* The company lost its privileges, finally, in 1578 ; and the merchants were expelled from England in 1597.

STEENKIRK, see *Enghien.*

STEFANO, SAN, a small village on the sea of Marmora, S.W. of Constantinople ; here the grand duke Nicholas established his head quarters, 24 Feb. ; and here was signed a treaty of peace with Turkey, 3 March, 1878, much modified by the treaty of Berlin, signed 13 July, following. The Russians quitted San Stefano, 22 Sept. 1878. It established independence of Montenegro, Servia, and Roumania : constituted Bulgaria a tributary principality ; required a heavy indemnity from Turkey for Russia, who was to gain a port on the Black Sea and Kars ; to exchange the Dobrudscha for Bessarabia ; to obtain rights for Christians ; to open the Bosphorus and Dardanelles in peace and war ; &c.

STELLA-LAND, see *Trans-vaal* and *Bechuana-land.*

STENOCHROMY, see *Printing in Colours.*

STENOGRAPHY (from *stenos*, narrow), the art of short-hand, said to have been practised by the ancients. Its improvement is attributed to the poet Ennius, to Tyro, Cicero's freedman, and still more to Seneca. The *Ars Scribendi Characteris*, written about 1412, is the oldest system extant. Dr. Timothy Bright's "Characterie, or the Arte of Shorte, Swifte, and Secrete Writing," published in 1588, is the first English work on short-hand. Peter Bales, the famous penman, published on stenography in 1590; and John Willis published his "*Stenographie*" in 1602. There are now numerous systems : John Byrom's (1767), T. Gurney's (1710), "Brachygraphy," based on Mason's (1750), "a Shorthand Dictionary" (1777), Taylor's (1786), Mavor's (1789), Pitman's (phonographic), (1837) ; A. M. Bell's Stenophonography (1852) ; J. D. Everett's (1877) ; Pocknell's Legible Shorthand (1881) ; J. M. Sloan's (1882). See *Phonography.*

The Shorthand Society met . . . 1 Nov. 1881

Sig. A. Michela's stenographic machine for the graphic representation of phonetic sounds (about 200 words per minute); like a harmonium with a key-board, exhibited at the Turin exhibition of 1884, successfully adopted by the Italian Senate.

International Shorthand Congress at the Geological Museum, London, S.W. (482 systems noticed) 26 Sept.-1 Oct. 1887

STEPHEN'S CHAPEL, ST. (Westminster), built by king Stephen, about 1135. It was rebuilt by Edward III. in 1347, and by him made a collegiate church, to which a dean and twelve secular priests were appointed. Soon after its surrender to Edward VI., about 1548, it was applied to the use of Parliament; see *Parliament.* It was destroyed by fire, 16 Oct. 1834. The Society of Antiquaries published memorials of it about 1810; and Mr. Mackenzie's work appeared in 1844. The restoration of the beautiful crypt was complete in Jan. 1870.

STEPNEY, a parish, E. London, the Stebenhide of Domesday book. Edward I. summoned a parliament here, 1299. Stepney suffered severely by the plague, 1625 and 1665. Stepney-green was restored and opened as a park by the Metropolitan Board of Works, Aug. 1872.

STEREOCHROMY, a mode of painting in which water-glass (an alkaline solution of flint, silex) serves as the connecting medium between the

---

* For this invention he had received by royalties 1,057,748*l.* up to 1879; also many foreign honours; knighted June, 1379.

colour and the substratum. Its invention is ascribed to Von-Fuchs, who died at Munich on 5 March, 1856. Fine specimens of this art by Kaulbach and Echter exist in the Museum at Berlin, and also at Munich.

STEREOMETER, by which is compassed the art of taking the contents of vessels of liquids by gauging, invented about 1350. *Anderson.* M. Say's stereometer, for determining the specific gravity of liquids, porous bodies, and powders as well as solids, was described in 1797.

STEREOSCOPE (from *stereos*, solid, and *skopein*, to see), an optical instrument for representing in apparent relief natural objects, &c., by uniting into one image two plane representations of these objects as seen by each eye separately. The first stereoscope by reflection was constructed and exhibited by professor Charles Wheatstone in 1838, who had announced its principle in 1833. Since 1854 stereoscopes have been greatly improved.

STEREOTYPE, a cast from a page of movable printing-types, so named by the Parisian printer, Didot, 1798. It is said that stereotyping was known in 1711. It was practised by Wm. Ged of Edinburgh, about 1730.. Some of Ged's plates are at the Royal Institution, London. A Mr. James attempted to introduce Ged's process in London, but failed, about 1735.* *Nichols.* Stereotype printing was in use in Holland, in the last century; and a quarto Bible and a Dutch folio Bible were printed there. *Phillips.* It was revived in London by Wilson in 1804. Since 1850 the durability of stereotypes has been greatly increased by electrotyping them with copper or silver. Stereotyping used for printing the *Times*, 1856, *et seq.*

In the library of the Royal Institution is an edition of Sallust, with this imprint: "Edinburgi, Gulielmus Ged, auri faber Edinensis, non typis mobilibus, ut vulgo fieri solet, sed tabellis seu laminis fusis, excudebat. 1744." (Printed at Edinburgh by William Ged of Edinburgh, goldsmith, not with moveable types, as is commonly done, but with cast tablets or plates.)

STERLING (money). Ducange says (1733), "Esterlingus, sterlingus, are English words relating to money, and hence familiar to other nations, and applied to the weight, quality, and kind of money." "Denarius Angliæ, qui vocatur sterlingus," stat. Edw. I. (The penny of England, which is called sterling.) Camden derives the word from *easterling* or *esterling*, observing that the money brought from Germany, in the reign of Richard I., was the most esteemed on account of its purity, being called in old deeds "*nummi easterling.*" Others derive the word from the Easterlings, the first moneyers in England.

STETHOSCOPE. In 1816 Laënnec, of Paris, by rolling a quire of paper into a kind of cylinder, and applying one end to the patient's chest and the other to his own ear, perceived the action of the heart in a much more distinct manner than by the immediate application of the ear. This led to his inventing the stethoscope, or "breast-explorer," the principle of which, now termed "auscultation," was known by Hippocrates (357 B.C.), and by Robert Hooke, 1681.

STETTIN (Pomerania), an ancient city, formerly held by the Sidini and Venedes, was taken by Boleslas of Poland in 1121. After being conquered by the Swedes, Russians, and French, it was awarded to Prussia in 1814.

Visited by emperor William during military manœuvres, 12 Sept. 1887.

* It was hotly opposed by the journeymen printers.

STEWARD OF ENGLAND, LORD HIGH. The first grand officer of the crown. This office was established prior to the reign of Edward the Confessor, and was formerly annexed to the lordship of Hinckley, Leicestershire, belonging to the family of Montfort, earls of Leicester, who were, in right thereof, lord high stewards of England; but Simon de Montfort, the last earl of this family, having raised a rebellion against his sovereign, Henry III., was attainted, and his estate forfeited to the king, who abolished the office, 1265. It is now revived only *pro hâc vice*, at a coronation, or the trial of a peer. The first afterwards appointed was Thomas, second son of Henry IV. The first for the trial of a peer was Edward, earl of Devon, on the arraignment of the earl of Huntingdon, in 1400. The last was lord Denman at the trial of the earl of Cardigan, 16 Feb. 1841. The duke of Hamilton was lord high steward at the coronations of William IV. 1831, and Victoria, 1838.

STEWARD OF THE HOUSEHOLD, LORD (an ancient office), has the sole direction of the king's house below-stairs; he has no formal grant of his office, but receives his charge from the sovereign in person, who, delivering to him a white wand, the symbol of his office, says, "*Seneschal, tenez le bâton de notre maison.*" This officer has been called lord steward since 1540; previously to the 31st of Henry VIII. he was styled grand master of the household. His function as a judge was abolished in 1849.

STICKLESTADT (Norway). Here Olaf II., aided by the Swedes, was defeated in his endeavours to recover his kingdom from Canute, king of Denmark, and slain, 29 July, 1030. He was afterwards sainted, on account of his zeal for Christianity.

STIPENDIARY MAGISTRATES, see *Magistrates.*

STIRLING (S. Scotland). The strong castle was taken by Edward I. of England, 1304. Here James II. stabbed the earl of Douglas, 13 Feb. 1452, and here James VI. was crowned, 24 July, 1567. Stirling surrendered to Monk, 14 Aug. 1651. The statue of king Robert Bruce unveiled, 24 Nov. 1877. A gigantic bronze statue of sir William Wallace unveiled at the National Wallace Monument 25 June, 1887.

STIRRUPS were unknown to the ancients. Gracchus fitted the highways with stones to enable the horsemen to mount. Warriors had projections on their spears for the same purpose. Stirrups were used in the 5th century, but were not common even in the 12th.

STOCKACH, a town in Baden, near which the Austrians, under the archduke Charles, defeated the French, 25 March, 1799; and Moreau defeated Kray, 3 May, 1800.

STOCKHOLM, capital of Sweden (built on *holmen*, or islands), was fortified by Berger Jarl about 1254. Here the Swedish nobility were massacred by Christian II. in 1520; see *Sweden.*

Peace of Stockholm, between the king of Great Britain and the queen of Sweden, by which the former acquired the duchies of Bremen and Verden as elector of Brunswick . . . 20 Nov. 1719
Treaty of Stockholm, between Sweden and Russia, in favour of the duke of Holstein-Gottorp, 24 March, 1724
Another between England and Sweden . 3 March, 1813
And one between England, France, and Sweden, 21 Nov. 1855

STOCKINGS of silk are said to have been first worn by Henry II. of France, 1547. In 1560 queen

Elizabeth was presented with a pair of knit black silk stockings, by her silk-woman, Mrs. Montague, and she never wore cloth ones any more. *Howell.* He adds, "Henry VIII. wore ordinary cloth hose, except there came from Spain, by great chance, a pair of silk stockings; for Spain very early abounded with silk." Edward VI. was presented with a pair of Spanish silk stockings by his merchant, sir Thomas Gresham; and the present was then much taken notice of. *Idem.* Others relate that William Rider, a London apprentice, seeing at the house of an Italian merchant a pair of knit worsted stockings from Mantua, made a pair like them, the first made in England, which he presented to the earl of Pembroke, 1564. *Stow.* The art of weaving stockings in a *frame* was invented in England by the rev. Mr. Lee, of Cambridge, in 1589, twenty-five years after he had learnt to knit them with wires or needles. Cotton stockings were first made in 1730; see *Cotton. Digitated stockings* (like gloves), introduced 1882.

STOCKPORT (in Cheshire) has become eminent on account of the cotton trade. Heaton Norris, in Lancashire, is united to it by a bridge over the river. Here the Manchester blanketeers were dispersed, 11 March, 1817; and here was a serious religious riot, when two Roman catholic chapels were destroyed, and the houses of many Roman catholics gutted, and their furniture and other contents smashed or burnt, 29 June, 1852.

STOCKS, in which drunkards were placed. The last in London was removed from St. Clement Danes, Strand, 4 Aug. 1826.

STOCKS. The public funding system originated in Venice, about 1173, and was introduced into Florence in 1340. The English funding system may be said to have had its rise in 1690. See *Panics.*

"*Bulls*" are persons who buy stock and thus cause the market to rise; "*Bears*" those who sell and cause it to fall.

Act to prevent *stock-jobbing* passed March, 1734; repealed 1860

Stockbrokers' rents to the city of London abolished 1884; came into effect . . . . . Sept. 1886

The foundation of the Stock Exchange, in Capel-court, the residence of the lord mayor, sir Wm. Capel, in 1504, was laid on 18 May, 1801. It was stated on the first stone that the public debt was then 552,730,924*l.* Members, 1864, about 1100; above 2000 in 1878

The memorable Stock Exchange hoax, for which admiral lord Cochrane (afterwards lord Dundonald), Johnstone, and others, were convicted, 22 Feb. 1814. Lord Cochrane was in consequence expelled the house of commons. His innocence was afterwards proved, and he was restored to his rank by king William IV., and to the honours belonging to it by queen Victoria.

Stock-exchange coffee-house destroyed by fire, 11 Feb. 1816

Royal Commission (lord Penzance, justice Blackburn, Mr. Spencer Walpole, and others) to examine into the constitution and management of the London stock exchange, agreed to, 20 March, 1877; report issued; the majority recommend incorporation and other changes; signed 31 July, 1878

The number of stock-holders in 1840 amounted to 337,481.

Three per cent. annuities created 1726

Three per cent. consols created 1731

Three per cent. reduced 1746

Three per cent annuities, payable at the South Sea-house 1751

Three-and-a-half per cent. annuities created . . 1758

Long annuities 1761

Four per cent consols 1762

Five per cent. annuities . . . . 1797 and 1802

Five per cents. reduced to four 1822

Old four per cents. reduced to three-and-a-half in 1824

Further reductions made in 1825, 1830, 1834, 1841, and 1844: the maximum being now three per cent.

Further reductions proposed by Mr. Göschen (2¾ to 2½ in 15 years under specified conditions) 9 March; new threes all converted or paid off 6 April, 1888

Messrs. Thomas and Co., bankrupts, for above 8,000*l.*, suspected frauds . . . 31 Jan. 1884

Three per cents. convertible into 2¾, and 2½ per cent. by Act of 2 Sept., 1884.

The local loans stock exchangeable for the three per cents. consols created by the National Debt and Local Loans Act passed . . 12 July, 1887

By a return of the average price of the public funds by the Commissioners for the reduction of the national debt, it appears that *Consols* (*i.e.*, consolidated annuities, paying 3 per cent. per annum) averaged in the year—

1749	£100	0	0	1815	£58	13	9
1780	63	13	6	1820	68	12	0
1785	68	6	6	1825	90	0	8
1790	71	2	6	1830	89	15	7
1795	74	8	6	1840	89	17	6
1798	59	10	0	1845	93		6
1800	66	3	3	1848	86	15	0
1805	58	14	0	1850	96	10	0
1810	67	16	3	1852 (Dec. 101*l.* 10*s.*)	99	12	6

The price of £100 stock varied in

1853,	from	£101	to	£90¾
1854,	,,	96	,,	85½
1855,	,,	93⅜	,,	86½
1856,	,,	96⅝	,,	87½
1857,	,,	95⅞	,,	86½
1858,	,,	98⅞	,,	94
1859,	,,	97¾	,,	89
1861,	,,	94½	,,	89⅝
1862,	,,	94⅞	,,	90⅝
1863,	,,	94	,,	90
1864,	,,	91⅞	,,	87½
1865,	,,	87⅞	,,	86¼
1866,	average	88	June	86¼
1867,	,,	93	,,	94⅞
1868,	,,	93⅞	June	94⅝
1869,	,,	92⅞	,,	92⅝
1870,	,,	92⅜	,,	92¾
1871,	,,	92⅞	,,	92
1872,	,,	92⅞	,,	92⅜
1873,	,,	92⅞	,,	92½
1874,	,,	92⅜	,,	92⅛
1875,	average	93¾	,,	93
1876,	,,	95	,,	94½
1877,	,,	95⅜	,,	94⅞
1878,	,,	95$\frac{1}{16}$	,,	95⅝
1879,	,,	97⅞	,,	97⅝
1880,	,,	98½	,,	98⅜
1881,	,,	100	,,	100⅜
1882,	,,	100¼	,,	100½
1883,	,,	101$\frac{3}{16}$	,,	100¼

1884, highest 102⅝; lowest, 31 Dec. 98$\frac{11}{16}$.

1885, average . . 99⅜

1886, ,, 100¼; 13 May, (highest price recorded) 103¼.

1887, average . . . 101½

New Consols (2¾)

1888, 9 June . . 99⅜

1889, 2 Jan. 99¼; 28 June 98⅛.

"During the greatest crisis ever developed in the history of the world the funds remain day after day without a fractional movement." *Times*, 11 Oct. 1870.

Purchase of stock for 10*l.* legalised, 1880.

H. C. Burdett's "Official Intelligence of British, American, and Foreign Securities," published under the sanction of the Stock Exchange Committee, 1882 *et seq.*

STOICS, disciples of Zeno, the philosopher (about 290 B.C.); obtained the name because they listened to his instructions in a porch (Greek, *stoa*) at Athens. Zeno taught, that man's supreme happiness consisted in living agreeably to nature and reason, and that God was the soul of the world. *Stanley.*

STOKE, EAST (near Newark, Nottinghamshire). Near here, on 16 June, 1487, the adherents of Lambert Simnel, who personated Edward, earl of Warwick, and claimed the crown, were defeated by Henry VII. John de la Pole, the earl of Lincoln, and most of the leaders, were slain. Simnel was afterwards employed in the king's household.

STONE. Stone buildings erected in England by Benedict Biscop about 670. A stone bridge built at Bow, in the 11th or 12th centuries, is accounted the first; but a bridge exists at Crowland, which is said to have been built in 860; see *Bridges.* The first stone building in Ireland was probably a round tower; see *Building.* Stone china-ware was made by Wedgwood in 1762. *Artificial stone* for statues was manufactured by a Neapolitan, and introduced

into England, 1776. Stone paper was made in 1776; see *Ransome's Artificial Stone*, and *Lithotomy*. For stone implements, see *Flints*, and *Piano-forte*. An orchestra composed of wind instruments made of terra-cotta appeared in London in 1874.

STONEHENGE (on Salisbury Plain, Wiltshire) is said to have been erected on the counsel of Merlin, by Aurelius Ambrosius, in memory of 460 Britons, who were murdered by Hengist the Saxon about 450. *Geoffrey of Monmouth.* Erected as a sepulchral monument of Ambrosius, 500. *Polydore Vergil.* An ancient temple of the Britons, in which the Druids officiated. *Dr. Stukeley.* The Britons are said to have held annual meetings at Abury and Stonehenge, when laws were made and justice administered. The cursus near Stonehenge was discovered by Dr. Stukeley, 6 Aug. 1723. The origin and object of these remains are still very obscure. See W. M. Flinders Petrie's "Stonehenge: Plans, Description, and Theories." 1880.
The thorough preservation of Stonehenge strongly advocated Aug. 1886.

STONEWALL BRIGADE, see *United States*, 1862, note.

STORM-WARNINGS, see under *Meteorology*.

STORMS, see *Meteorology*, *Cyclones*, and *Waterspouts*. The following are recorded:—

In London a storm raged which destroyed 1500 houses, 944.
In several parts of England, the sky being very dark, the wind coming from the S.W.; many churches were destroyed; and in London 500 houses fell, 5 Oct. 1091.
On the coast of Calais, when Hugh de Beauvais and several thousand foreigners, on their voyage to assist king John against the barons, perished, 1215. *Holinshed.*
It thundered 15 days successively, with tempests of rain and wind, 1233.
Storm with violent lightnings; one flash passed through a chamber where Edward I. and his queen were conversing, did them no damage, but killed two of their attendants, 1285. *Hoveden.*
Violent storm of hail near Chartres, in France, which fell on the army of Edward III. then on its march. The hail was so large that the army and horses suffered very much, and Edward was obliged to conclude a peace, 1339. *Matt. Paris.*
When Richard II.'s queen came from Bohemia, on her setting foot on shore an awful storm arose, and her ship and a number of others were dashed to pieces in the harbour, Jan. 1382. *Holinshed.*
Richard's second queen also brought a storm with her to the English coasts, in which the king's baggage was lost, and many ships cast away, 1396. *Holinshed.*
Hurricane, throughout Europe, which did very considerable damage, on 3 Sept. 1658, the day that Cromwell died. *Mortimer.*
Storm on east coast of England: 200 colliers and coasters lost, with most of their crews, 1696.
The "Great Storm," one of the most terrible that ever raged in England. The devastation on land was immense; and in the harbours and on the coasts the loss in shipping and in lives was still greater, 26-27 Nov. 1703. The loss sustained in London alone was calculated at 2,000,000*l.* sterling. The number of persons drowned in the floods of the Severn and Thames, and lost on the coast of Holland, and in ships blown from their anchors and never heard of afterwards, is thought to have been 8000. Twelve men-of-war, with more than 1800 men on board, were lost within sight of their own shore. Trees were torn up by the roots, 17,000 of them in Kent alone. The Eddystone light-house was destroyed, and in it the ingenious contriver of it, Winstanley, and the persons who were with him. The Bishop of Bath and Wells and his lady were killed in bed in their palace in Somersetshire. Multitudes of cattle were also lost: in one level 15,000 sheep were drowned.
Snow-storm in Sweden, when 7000 Swedes, it is said,

perished upon the mountains, in their march to attack Drontheim, 1719.
One in India, when many hundreds of vessels were cast away, a fleet of Indiamen greatly damaged, and some ships lost, and 30,000 persons perished, 11 Oct. 1737.
Dreadful hurricane at the Havannah: many public edifices and 4048 houses were destroyed, and 1000 inhabitants perished, 25 Oct. 1768.
Awful storm in the north of England, in which many vessels were destroyed, and four Dublin packets foundered, 29 Oct. 1775.
One at Surat, in the East Indies; destroyed 7000 of the inhabitants, 22 April, 1782.
One hundred and thirty-one villages and farms laid waste in France, 1785.
One general throughout Great Britain: several hundred sail of shipping destroyed or damaged, 6 Oct. 1794.
One which did vast damage in London, and throughout almost the whole of England, 8 Nov. 1800.
A tremendous storm throughout Great Britain and Ireland, by which immense damage was done, and many ships wrecked, 16-17 Dec. 1814.
An awful gale, by which a great number of vessels were lost, and much damage was done to the shipping in general on the English coast, 31 Aug. 1816.
Dreadful hurricane, ravaged the Leeward Islands, from the 20th to the 22nd Sept. 1819. At the island of St. Thomas alone, 104 vessels were lost.
Great storm along the coast from Durham to Cornwall: many vessels lost, Nov. 1821.
In Ireland, particularly in the vicinity of Dublin, many houses were thrown down, and vast numbers unroofed, 12 Dec. 1822.
Awful storm on the coast of England: many vessels lost, and 13 driven ashore and wrecked in Plymouth alone, 12-13 Jan. 1828.
At Gibraltar, where more than 100 vessels were destroyed, 18 Feb. 1828.
Dreadful storm at the Cape of Good Hope, where immense property was lost, 16 July, 1831.
A hurricane visited London and its neighbourhood, which did great damage to the buildings, but without the destruction of human life, though many serious accidents occurred, 28 Oct. 1838.
Awful hurricane on west coast of England, and in Ireland. The storm raged through Cheshire, Staffordshire, and Warwickshire; 20 persons were killed in Liverpool, by the falling of buildings, and 100 were drowned in the neighbourhood; the coasts and harbours were covered with wrecks, the value of two of the vessels lost being nearly half-a-million sterling. In Limerick, Galway, Athlone, and other places, more than 200 houses were blown down, and as many more were burnt, the winds spreading the fires. Dublin suffered dreadfully; London and its neighbourhood scarcely sustained any damage, 6-7 Jan. 1839.
[The winter of 1852-3 (Dec. and Jan.) was one of storms, many of which were very destructive.]
Great storm in the Black Sea, 13-16 Nov. 1854, causing much loss of life, shipping, and stores sent for the allied armies in the Crimea.
Great storm on N. coast of Europe, &c, 31 Dec. 1854.
Great storm on N.E. coast of Scotland; 42 fishermen lost, 23 Nov. 1857.
Dreadful storm on the night 25-26 Oct.; the Royal Charter totally lost, and many other vessels; another storm, 31 Oct. and 1 Nov. 1859.
Great storm in the channel, causing much loss of life and property, 1 Jan. 1860.
Dreadful gales, doing much mischief, 26, 27, 28 Feb.; 28 May; and 2 June, 1860.
Great storm; part of the Crystal Palace blown down; Chichester cathedral steeple fell, 20-21 Feb. 1861.
Great storm on British coasts, 143 wrecks, 28 May, 1861.
Storm on the north-east; 50 wrecks, 13-14 Nov. 1861.
At Market Laverton, &c.; much damage to crops by hail, 2 Sept. 1862.
Storm on British coasts; many wrecks, 19, 20 Oct. 1862.
There were severe gales, doing much damage, and loss of life, 19 Jan. &c. 1863; and 14 Jan. &c. 1865 (see under *Wrecks*).
Dreadful hurricane in the Indian Ocean, &c. (see *Cyclone*, *Calcutta*), 5 Oct. 1864.
Hurricane at Lisbon, causes much damage, worst for many years, 13 Dec. 1864.
Severe gales; many vessels and lives lost (see *Wrecks*), 6-11 Jan. 1866; 2-4 Dec. 1867; 22 Jan. and 31 Jan. and 1 Feb. 1868; 11-12 Sept. 1869.

STORMS.

Severe storm; much damage; barometer very low, 24 Jan. 1872.
After several days' intense heat, violent storms, and deluges of rain in midland and southern counties; several persons killed, 24-26 June, 1872.
Very stormy in July and August, 1872.
Violent gale; much destruction (wind, greatest velocity 57 miles an hour), 8 Dec. 1872.
Awful storms in Scotland, and N. England; loss of life, and much damage, 22, 23 July; in Lancashire and Yorkshire, 16 Dec. 1873.
Awful storm, N. E. London; several persons killed; churches and buildings fired; railways flooded, 11 July, 1874.
Violent gales, with destruction of life and property, 21 Oct.; Nov. 29; 7, 8, 10, 11 Dec. 1874.
Much destruction by typhoon at Macao, Hong Kong, &c., 22 Sept. 1874.
Severe snowstorms in Scotland, several lives lost, 1, 3 Jan. 1875.
Destructive storms at Buda-Pesth, about 200 killed, 26 June, 1875.
On coast of Texas: Galveston, Indianapolis, and other places much injured; villages washed away by the sea; great loss of life, 15-18 Sept. 1875.
Severe snowstorm, south England; destruction of life and property; telegraph wires broken, 12 March, 1875.
Severe storms; great loss of shipping, 11-13 Nov.; 2, 3, and 22-24 Dec. 1876.
Most violent gale; great destruction of property on land and shipping throughout England, with loss of life, 14, 15 Oct. 1877.
Again; much damage on S.E. coast, &c., 24, 25 Nov. 1877.
Storm and heavy rain in London; inundations, 10, 11 April, 1878.
Many thunderstorms, destroying life and property in England, Aug. 1878.
At Kew and neighbourhood, 2, 3 Aug.; in Cheshire and Wales, 16, 17 Aug. 1879.
Violent gale; Tay bridge (*which see*) blown down, 28 Dec. 1879.
Destructive tornadoes, &c., western states North America; great loss of life and property, about 18 April, 1880.
Many thunderstorms in England, July, 1880.
Severe storms in England, with much destruction by inundations, 27, 28 Oct. 1880.
Severe snowstorm; railways and other traffic largely stopped; great loss of life at sea, 17-21 Jan. 1881.
Violent hurricane in England: great destruction of life and property: houses thrown down or unroofed; large trees torn up by the roots; telegraph wires and poles blown down; about 130 wrecks (105 British), &c., 14-19 Oct. 1881.
Many wrecks on south and west coasts of England with much loss of life, 19-20 Oct. 1881.
Great destruction of life and property by gales, 26, 27 Nov. 1881.
Lighthouse, Calf Rock, in Bantry Bay destroyed, 27 Nov. 1881.
Six men left on the rock got off, 9 Dec. 1881.
By a typhoon in Haifong, &c., China, about 300,000 persons perished, 8 Oct. 1881.
Destructive gales in England, &c.; many wrecks and loss of life by sea and land, 17-21 Dec. 1881.
Severe gale; much destruction in England and Scotland, 6 Jan.; another, 29 April, 1882.
Tornado in Iowa, &c., Grinnell and other towns nearly destroyed; great loss of life, about 16 June, *et seq.*, 1882.
Violent gales with damage, 22, 23 Aug.; 24 Oct. 1882; 26, 27, 28 Jan., 10 Feb., 6 March, 1883.
Tornadoes in southern states, U.S.A., about 150 killed, April, 1883.
Violent gale in British channel, &c.; many wrecks, 1-2 Sept. 1883.
Destructive gale on the Scotch and Irish coasts, 26 Sept. 1883.
Another with great loss of life and damage in London and other parts of Britain, morning, 12 Dec. 1883.
Violent S.W. gales; destruction of life and property; 23-24 Jan. 1884; very severe; many disasters, 26, 27 Jan. 1884.
Tornadoes in southern states, U.S.A.; about 600 killed, about 18 Feb. 1884.
Storm in Catania, Sicily (see *Sicily*), 7 Oct. 1884.
Destructive snowstorms in Piedmont (see *Italy*), 16 Jan. *et seq.* 1885.
Heavy storms on the Labrador coast, about 80 craft wrecked and about 300 lives lost 12-15 Oct. 1885.
Storm off Colon, Panama, 15 vessels wrecked, 50 lives lost 2 Dec. 1885.
Heavy snowstorm, N.E. England, &c.; locomotion stopped 1, 2, 3 March, 1886.
Destructive hurricane at Madrid, 32 lives lost, 320 wounded 12 May, 1886.
Destructive tornadoes in S. Ohio, Indiana, Illinois, &c., U.S.A. 12-15 May. 1880.
Violent storm N.E. France, much damage at Rheims, Nancy, &c. 10 Aug. 1886.
Hurricane at St. Vincent; great loss of life and property 16 Aug. 1886.
Violent gale in Texas, &c., causing inundation, above 250 persons drowned, 12 Oct. 1886.
Severe gale; very destructive on sea and land (see *Wrecks*) 15-16 Oct. 1886.
Destructive gale and storm, especially in S. & W. England; many wrecks and loss of life 8, 9 Dec. 1886 (see under *Lifeboat*).
Destructive snowstorm, specially E. and S. England; many wrecks; telegraphic and railway communications stopped; trees blown down, &c., 26-27 Dec. 1886.
Destructive hurricane at Bordeaux and S. France with loss of life 16 Aug. 1887.
Violent thunderstorm in London with destruction of property, several persons killed, about 5.30 p.m.; lasted about 4 hours 17 Aug.; many storms throughout the country, 17 Aug. *et seq.* 1887.
W. gale; destruction of life and property in France, the Channel, and S. England 30 Oct., another gale on the W. coast, destruction at Holyhead, Liverpool and in the Bristol channel 31 Oct.-1 Nov.; another gale on the S.E. coast, 3 Nov. 1837.
Snowstorm (blizzard) in N.W. of United States; about 235 persons perish and much cattle 11-13 Jan.; —another in New York 26 Jan. 1888.
Cyclone in Illinois, U.S.A.; great destruction of life and property 19 Feb. 1888.
Violent gale; several wrecks and loss of life, 9-11 March, 1888.
A destructive blizzard from the N.W. desolated the eastern coast of United States; communication between New York, Philadelphia and Boston suspended; many wrecks; great loss of life (about 400) and property; food at famine prices 11-13 March, 1888.
Town of Ninnescah in Kansas destroyed by a gale 27 March, 1888.
Great storm and a tidal wave, much destruction, near Wellington, New Zealand 28 March, 1888.
Destructive hurricane in Dacca, N.E. India; about 69 persons killed 7 April, 1888.
Great storm in Ontario and Quebec, many persons killed by lightning and fright; estimated loss in Quebec, 1,500,000 dollars 16 Aug. 1888.
Destructive cyclone in the West Indies (Cuba, &c.), 4 Sept. 1888.
Destructive gale; Scotland, N. England and Ireland; many shipwrecks; Forth bridge damaged, 15-16 Nov. 1888.
Severe storm on the N. American E. coast; more than 50 vessels wrecked and about 45 lives lost 25 Nov. 1888.
Tornado in eastern states U.S., especially in Pennsylvania; great destruction and loss of life in about 200 miles, especially at Pittsburg (14 killed) and at Reading (24 killed), through collapse of a silk-mill; suspension-bridge, Niagara, wrecked 9 Jan. 1889.
Destructive gales over Britain; wrecks and loss of life 2, 3, 8 Feb. 1889.
Violent hurricane in the Pacific (see *Samoan Isles*) 15, 16 March, 1889.
Destructive storm on the east coast of the United States 10 May, 1889.
Great storm in South Germany, especially in Austria, Bohemia, &c., great loss of life and property, 17 May; in Switzerland 3-4 June, 1889.
Destructive storm. Flintshire, Cheshire and Lancashire; heavy rain and large hail causing floods, crops much injured, buildings struck and fired 2 June, 1889.

See *United States* and *Pennsylvania*, 1889.

STORTHING, the Norwegian parliament, said to have been first held at Bergen by Haco V. in 1223.

STOVES. The ancients used stoves which concealed the fire, as the German stoves yet do. They lighted the fire also in a large tube in the middle of the room, the roof being open. Apartments were warmed by portable braziers. Stoves on this old principle, improved, continue in use in many houses and public establishments in England, and generally on the continent. Dr. Franklin and count Rumford (who invented a stove) pointed out the waste of fuel in our open fires; and Dr. Neil Arnott patented his "improvements in the production and agency of heat," 14 Nov. 1821. Dr. C. William Siemens described his smokeless stove in "*Nature*" for 11 Nov. 1880. See *Chimneys*, and *Cottager's Stove*.

Mr. T. Pridgin Teale publishes his inventions, in which he revives the principles of count Rumford with additions, 1885-6.

STOWMARKET EXPLOSION, see *Gun-Cotton*, 1871.

STRAIGHT-OUT DEMOCRATS, a party, which advocated limiting the powers of a government to police purposes arose in the United States of America in 1872, and nominated Charles O'Connor for the presidency. A state convention was convoked to meet at Harrisburg, 16 Oct. 1872.

STRAITS SETTLEMENTS, including Malacca, Penang or Prince of Wales island, and Singapore, secured to Great Britain in 1824, were made a separate dependency in 1853, and placed under the governor-general of India. They were separated from India, and constituted an independent settlement by an act passed 10 Aug. 1866, which took effect April, 1867. Governor, sir Harry St. George Ord, 1867; sir Andrew Clarke, 1873; sir William F. D. Jervois, Oct. 1875; sir W. C. F. Robinson, 1877; sir Frederick A. Weld, 1880; sir C. G. Smith, Aug. 1887.

Singapore, the capital, founded by sir T. Stamford Raffles in 1819, who compiled the constitution, laws, &c.
Traders complained to Sir H. Ord, governor, who said they must submit to their risks . . . 1872
Sir Andrew Clarke made a treaty establishing Abdullah as sultan in place of Ismail, and a British resident as his adviser, with plenary powers at Perak . . . . . . Jan. 1874
Mr. J. W. Birch, the resident, issues a proclamation, 1 Nov.; is suddenly attacked and killed,
 . . . . . . 2 Nov. 1875
The Malays rise, and besiege the residency, which is relieved by Capt. Innes, 6 Nov. He is killed in attacking a stockade . . . . 15 Nov. ,,
The Malays thoroughly defeated by troops from Hong Kong and Calcutta, under Gen. Colborne,
 . . . . 7 and 22 Dec. ,,
Kinti taken; Ismail retreats . . . 17 Dec. ,,
British power supreme at Perak . . . 27 Dec. ,,
Major Hawkins killed in an ambuscade; the village burnt . . . . 4 Jan. 1876
Ismail surrenders, about 21 March; Birch's assassin hanged . . . . 20 May, ,,
Great prosperity of the settlement reported, Aug. 1884

STRALSUND (Pomerania), a strongly fortified Hanse-town, built about 1230. It resisted a fierce siege by Wallenstein in 1628; was taken by Frederick William, of Brandenburg, in 1678; restored to the Swedes, 1679; re-captured by the Prussians and their allies, Dec. 1715. It surrendered to the French under Brune, 20 Aug. 1807; was awarded to Prussia, 1815.

STRAND (London). Houses were first built upon the Strand about 1353, at which period it was the court end of the town, or formed the communication between the two cities of London and Westminster, being then open to the Thames and to the fields. Somerset and other palaces were erected 1547-1605.—*Stow*. The Strand bridge was commenced 11 Oct. 1811; see *Waterloo bridge*. The Strand improvements were commenced in 1829. Strand returns one M.P. by act passed in 1885.

STRANGERS in house of commons; see *Parliament*, May, 1875.

STRASBURG, the Roman *Argentoratum*, the capital of Alsace. Here Julian defeated the Alemanni, 357, who captured it, 455. It was annexed to Germany, 870. Louis XIV. seized it 28 Sept. 1681, and retained it by the treaty of Ryswick, 1697. The citadel and fortifications, which he constructed have been so much augmented that Strasburg may be considered one of the strongest places in Europe. It was confirmed to France by the peace of Ryswick in 1697, but captured by the Germans, 28 Sept. 1870 and retained at the peace, May, 1871. The cathedral, an epitome of Gothic art, was founded by Clovis, and reconstructed by Pepin and Charlemagne. After destruction by lightning, 1007, it was principally rebuilt by Erwin de Steinbach and his son in the 14th century. The lofty tower was completed in 1439. The celebrated astronomical clock after a long stoppage, was repaired by M. Schwilgué, and inaugurated 1 Jan. 1843.

An attempt at insurrection in the city was made by prince Louis Napoleon (afterwards president of the French republic, and emperor), aided by two officers and some privates . . . 30 Oct. 1836
It was instantly suppressed by their arrest, and the prince was shipped off to America by the French government.
Strasburg invested by the Germans, principally from Baden, during the Franco-Prussian war 10 Aug. 1870
Gen. von Werder assumed the command of the besiegers, and the bombardment began 14 Aug., and a vigorous sally was repulsed . 16 Aug. ,,
Gen. Ulrich, the commander, declared that he would not surrender except upon a heap of ashes; but after a heroic resistance, and when a breach had been made and an assault was impending, notice was given, and the place surrendered at 2 A.M.; at 8 A.M. 17,150 men and 400 officers laid down their arms . . . 27 Sept. ,,
The German loss was said to be 906 men, of whom 43 were officers . . . . . 28 Sept. ,,
The Germans entered Strasburg on the anniversary of its surrender to the French in 1681 by a surprise . . . . 30 Sept. ,,
Ulrich received the grand cross of the legion of honour . . . . Oct. ,,
The invaluable library was destroyed and the cathedral much injured. About 400 houses were destroyed, and 8000 persons rendered homeless.
Visit of the emperor of Germany well received; but "France is still there" . . . 19 Sept. 1877

STRATFORD - UPON - AVON (Warwickshire), see *Shakspeare*.

STRATHCLUYD, a kingdom formed by the Britons, who retired northward after the Saxon conquest, about 560. It extended from the Clyde to Cumberland. The Britons in it submitted to Edward the Elder, in 924.

STRATHCLYDE CASE, see *Wrecks*, 1876

STRATHFIELD-SAYE, in Hampshire, is which is situate the estate bought of lord River by the nation for 263,000*l.*, and presented to the duke of Wellington, 1817. An act to provide suitable residence for his grace and his heirs was passed 11 July, 1815.

STRATHMORE ESTATES. Miss Bowes of Durham, the then richest heiress in Europe whose fortune was 1,040,000*l.*, with vast additions on her mother's death, and immense estates on the

demise of her uncle, married the earl of Strathmore, 25 Feb. 1766. Having, after the earl's death, married Mr. Stoney, she was forcibly carried off by him and other armed men, 10 Nov. 1786. She was brought up to the King's Bench by *habeas corpus* and released, and he committed to prison, 23 Nov. The lady recovered her estates, which she had assigned to her husband under the influence of terror, in May, 1788.

STRATTON-HILL, Battle of, in Cornwall, 16 May, 1643, between the royal army under sir Ralph Hopton, and the forces of the parliament under the earl of Stamford. The victory was gained over the parliamentarians, who lost numbers in killed and wounded.

STRAWBERRY, see *Fruits*.

STRAWBERRY-HILL, Surrey, the Gothic villa of Horace Walpole, constructed 1750, at Twickenham, near London. In April and May, 1842, his collection of pictures and articles of taste and virtu were sold by auction for 29,615*l*. 8*s*. 9*d*. The villa was enlarged by Mr. Chichester Fortescue, created lord Carlingford, and the countess of Waldegrave, daughter of John Braham, the singer. She died 5 July, 1879. The place bought by baron H. de Stern, July, 1883.

STREET MUSIC. An act was passed in 1864 for the better regulation of street music in the metropolitan police districts.

STREET RAILWAYS, see *Tramways*.

STRELITZ, the imperial guard of Russia, established by Ivan IV. about 1568. Becoming frequently seditious, it was suppressed by Peter the Great; great numbers were put to death, many by the czar's own hand, 1698-1704.

STRIKES, see under *Agriculture, Preston, London*, 1859-61; *Newcastle, Trials*, Aug. 1867; and *Railways*.

The tailors of London struck for increase of wages; they yield	April, 1834
The strike of the calico printers of Glasgow	,,
Staffordshire potters' strike; obtained an advance after much loss	Nov. 1834-March, 1835
The strike of the amalgamated engineers took place	1852
Strike of the London cabmen	27-30 July, 1853
Builders' strike	Aug.-Oct. 1859
A strike among the silk-workers at Coventry came to an end	30 Aug. 1860
An unsuccessful attempt to get up a strike in the building trade began	23 March, 1861
A strike of the puddlers in the iron trade occurred in the spring of (see *Iron*, and *Railways*)	1865
Strike of London west-end tailors (about 2000), lasted	22 April-Oct. 1867
Great strike of colliers near St. Helens, April, 1867; about 40,000 men on strike	April, 1868
Colliery strike at Thorncliffe, near Sheffield; dreadful riots and devastation	21 Jan. 1870
Strike of 10,000 miners at Le Creuzot, Burgundy, the property of M. Schneider; soon over	Jan. 1871
Engineers' strike at Newcastle (see *Newcastle*)	May-Oct. ,,
Strike of builders employed by Messrs. Brass and Jackson & Shaw, for a 9 hours' day, at 9*d*. an hour, 1 June; after negotiation led to a lock-out by the masters, beginning	19 June, 1872
The lock-out of the masons ceased, the carpenters going on, 9 July; arrangements were made, and strike ceased	about 27 Aug. ,,
Strike of London journeymen bakers, 23 Sept.-9 Oct.	,,
Strike of firewood cutters	Sept. ,,
Lock-out of miners in Wales for their excessive demands	Oct. ,,
Strike of London gas-stokers (see *Gas*)	2 Dec. ,,
Strike of about 60,000 colliers in S. Wales, refusing to submit to 10 per cent. reduction in wages, 1 Jan. Strike ended	about 25 March, 1873
Powerful speech of earl Fitzwilliam to his colliers of Low Stubbin after a strike	5 June, 1873
Strike of about 50,000 miners, South Wales, 2 Jan.; led to a lock-out, 1 Feb.; given up; gradual return of men to work end of	May, 1875
Strike of Warwickshire miners	May-Aug. ,,
Strikes at Oldham and Dundee	July-August ,,
Strike of earl Fitzwilliam's colliers on account of the compulsory use of safety lamps; he closes his mines and rejects their submission	Dec. ,,
Erith, strike of workmen of Eastons and Anderson, engineers, in opposition to piece-work, 18 Dec.; supported by amalgamated engineers, Dec., 1875; on trial for conspiracy, the men plead guilty; no sentence passed	14 July, 1876
Strike of 1600 miners against 15 per cent. reduction of wages, Bolton	24 Aug. ,,
"Operative Spinners' Association" of N. and N.E. Lancashire propose to set aside the "standard list of prices" after 1 Nov. The masters thereupon announced a lock-out of about 80,000 men (after 23 Nov.), 26 Oct. The association submits	18 Nov. ,,
Strike of Doulton's bricklayers respecting employment of others on terra-cotta work (settled) Oct.	
Great strike and lock-out of about 10,000 shipwrights, &c., on the Clyde, May; closed, Oct.; the arbitrator, lord Moncrieff, decided against the men	Nov. 1877
Northumberland miners (about 12,000), began, 29 May; over about	12 June, ,,
Great railway strike, see *United States*	July, ,,
Bolton cotton workers' strike, about 1 Sept.; closed by agreement	,,
Railway strike on Great Southern and Western line, Ireland, about	14-22 Sept. ,,
181 strikes, result mostly against workmen	,,
Lock-out of about 8000 miners in Northumberland, about 15 Dec. 1877; closed	Feb. 1878
Strike of masons of London (employed on the law courts, &c.), demanding increased pay and less working hours, 31 July; some firms yield, about 20 Sept.; Germans and others engaged, Oct.—Dec. 1877. Strike ends (cost about 60,000*l*.)	14 March, ,,
Strike and lock-out of cotton spinners in N. and N.E. Lancashire (about 120,000 men); masters required reduction of 10 per cent. on wages; began about 18 April; ended by the men submitting to arrangements	about 17 June, ,,
Partial strike and lock-out of labourers in Kent and Sussex	Oct. Dec. ,,
Cotton strike at Oldham, at reduction of wages 5 per cent., 25 Nov.; submission	28 Dec. ,,
277 strikes in the year	,,
Midland railway; sudden strike of goods guards	3-20 Jan. 1879
London engineers, 18 firms, against reduction of wages, began about 7 Feb.; closed	4 Oct. ,,
Durham coal miners, against reduction of wages, began 5 April; stoppage of Cleveland and other iron works; about 70,000 men unemployed, April; settled by arbitration	about 16 May, ,,
Bristol builders' 2 months' strike ends	30 July, ,,
Strike of cotton-workers at Blackburn, 15 May *et seq*.	
Strike of Lancashire miners; about 40,000 out, 12 Jan.; rioting with loss of life near Bolton, 25-28 Jan.; strike reported over	21 Feb. 1881
Strike in the potteries, 70 firms and 30,000 men, begun	about 25 Nov. ,,
The men agree to arbitration	6 Dec. ,,
Ironworkers' strike at Hopton and Darlington,	2 Feb.-9 June, 1882
Strike of Staffordshire colliers, about 8000, 12 May, ends	3 Sept. 1883
Great strike of South Staffordshire ironworkers at reduction of wages	about 5 July, ,,
Many submit, about 17 July; strike closed,	24 July, ,,
Cotton weavers on strike, opposition to the reduction of wages, in the N.W. districts, about 18,500, 18 Dec. 1883; men yield under conditions, about 8 Feb. 1884
Strike in the cotton trade; mass meeting at Burnley reject the masters' terms	16 July, ,,
Determined to maintain the strike against reduction of wages	24 July, ,,
End of Barnsley coal miners' long strike	23 Dec. ,,

Strike of about 2000 miners in west Cumberland,
16 March, 1885
Strike of about half the colliers in S. and W. Yorkshire . . . . . 1 April–May, ,,
Chorley, Lancashire, about 3,000 cotton weavers
16 July, ,,
Cotton weavers on strike at Oldham (25,000 out) against 10 per cent. reduction, 20 July, *et seq.*; compromise 5 per cent. accepted for three months about 16 Oct. ,,
Strike of 4,700 men at Elswick Iron Works, Newcastle; ascribed to two managers, 2 Sept.; closed
17 Sept. ,,
Close of engineers' strike (2½ years) at Sunderland; cost above 200,000*l.* . . . . Nov. ,,
Strike of shipwrights in the Tyne and Wear about
6 Jan.–24 Feb. 1886
Increase of strikes in France, Belgium, Germany, and United States . . . March, ,,
Shropshire ironworks strike (twenty weeks) ends; masters yield . . . . 14 July, ,,
Northumberland miners' strike about 30 Jan; terms arranged at a conference, and work resumed, twelve weeks . . . 23–28 May, 1887
Strike (wrought nail trade) in South Staffordshire of about 15,000 operatives . . 12 Sept. ,,
Strike of engineers at Bolton respecting wages, overtime, &c. 14 May; intimidation and boycotting of men at work; strike closes by conciliation . . . . 27 Oct. ,,
Shoemakers' strike at Northampton; about 20,000 out 3 Dec.; closed by arbitration, about 24 Dec. ,,
Strike of engineers at Blackburn, 21 weeks, closed by compromise . . . 12 March, 1888
Strike of match-girls at Bryant and May's factory (see *Lucifers*) . . . 5 July, ,,
Colliery strikes begin 22 Oct.; about 30,000 miners on strike in S. W. Yorkshire and the Midland counties 24 Oct.; the colliers' demands, 10 per cent. increase generally, acceded to, the owners gradually yield . . . 27–31 Oct. ,,
End of strike of 60,000 coal miners in S. Wales, 7½ per cent. increase wages granted . 2 April, 1889
Strike of coal miners in Westphalin (*which see*) May, ,,
Strikes in Silesia, Bohemia and Belgium, May, June, ,,
Temporary strikes of seamen and firemen in the steamers in the ports of Glasgow (ended 27 June), Leith, Aberdeen (ended), and Dundee for an advance of wages, end of May; gradually collapsing, end of June, *et seq.*; Liverpool May–July, ,,

STROME CASE, see *Trials*, 1883.

STRONTIUM. The native carbonate of strontia was discovered at Strontian, in Argyleshire, in 1787. Sir Humphry Davy first obtained from it the metal strontium in 1808.

STRYCHNIA, a poisonous vegetable alkaloid, discovered in 1818 by Pelletier and Caventou in the seeds of the strychnos ignatia and nux vomica, and also in the upas poison. Half a grain blown into the throat of a rabbit occasions death in four minutes; its operation is accompanied by lock-jaw. Much attention was given to strychnia in 1856, during the trial of William Palmer, who was executed for the murder of Cook, 14 June, 1856.

STUART (properly STEWART), HOUSE OF, see under *Scotland, England;* and *Pretenders.*
A collection of portraits and relics of the house of Stuart was exhibited in the New Gallery, Regent Street, autumn, 1888. The surplus receipts amounting to about 1,800*l.* were judiciously distributed.

STUCCO WORK was known to the ancients, and was much prized by them, particularly by the Romans, who excelled in it.—*Lenglet.* It was revived by D'Udine, about 1550; and in Italy, France, and England in the 18th century.

STUD Company, to improve the breed of British horses, held its first annual meeting, 20 Sept. 1873.

STUHM (W. Prussia). Here Gustavus Adolphus of Sweden defeated the Poles, 1628.

STUNDISTS, a pu said to be descendants o from the Greek church some were cruelly perse santry of Vossncassensk i of the ringleaders were 1879.

STURGES BOUR c. 69 (1818), relates to p

STUTTGART (Wü in 1229, was made his ro 1320; enlarged by Ulric the state, 1482. It has the last and present ce meeting here, 1 Aug. 18

STYLE, see *New S*

STYLE ROYAL, se and *Titles.* The *styles* are given in the later ed ology of History." The giving power to add to of India," after much c received royal assent 27 28 April; announced in Aug. 1876.

STYLITES, see *M*

STYRIA (Austria), and Pannonia, was held Ostrogoths, and Avars. magne, and divided an counts, among whom t 876, was the most pow margrave about 1030; a made duke. At his deat to the duchy of Austri by Bela IV. of Hungary Bohemia; after whose d feld, in 1278, it reverted was annexed to his posse

SUAKIN, a seaport an island off its W. coast Under the rule of col Gordon, R.E., Suakin h nable fortress and comm

SUBMARINE BO

SUBMARINE L. Siebe and Gorman, ha especially at Cherbourg. was exhibited, 1871.

SUBMARINE TE *graph* (under *Electricity*

SUBSCRIPTION *scription Act.*

SUBSIDIES to th formerly granted in ki 30,000 sacks were voted of the war with France, dies were raised upon James I. 1624; but they the redress of grievances last) were granted to Ch

SUBWAY, see *Tun*

SUCCESSION AC

* England granted subsi ral wars, particularly in the .n France, and against Bon

SUCCESSION, WAR OF (1702-1713), distinguished by the achievements of the duke of Marlborough and the earl of Peterborough, and their unprofitable results, arose on the question whether an Austrian prince or a French prince should succeed to the throne of Spain. The British court opposed Louis, and Marlborough was victorious; but the allies withdrew one after another, and the French prince succeeded; see *Spain*, and *Utrecht*.

SUCCESSION DUTY ACT (16 & 17 Vict. c. 51), after much discussion, was passed 4 Aug. 1853. By this act the legacy duty was extended to real estate, and was made payable on succession to both landed and personal property. Received year 1887-8, 830,503*l*. Additional duties imposed by customs, &c., acts of 1888 and 1889.

SUDBURY, in Suffolk, was disfranchised for bribery in 1844.

SUEVI, a warlike Gothic tribe, which, with the Alani and the Visigoths, entered Spain about 408, were overcome by the latter, and absorbed into their kingdom about 584.

SUEZ CANAL. The caliph Omar about 640 opposed cutting the isthmus. A plan for a canal between the head of the Red Sea and the bay of Pelusium was brought forward by M. Ferdinand de Lesseps in 1852. He undertook to cut a canal through 90 miles of sand, to run on moles into the Mediterranean; to deepen the shallow waters; to create ports to receive the ships from India and Australia, and to adapt the canal to irrigation. The consent of the Egyptian, Turkish, Russian, French, and Austrian governments was gradually obtained, but not that of the British. A company was formed for the purpose, and the work commenced in 1858 by Mr. Daniel Lange (knighted 1870). The cost was estimated at 8,000,000*l*. Engineer, M. L. Monteit.

M. de Delacour, a French engineer, after viewing the works which were "employing 25,000 men in the desert," expressed his conviction that they would be completed in four or five years .	7 Nov. 1862
The waters of the Mediterranean admitted into a narrow channel communicating with Lake Timsah .	Dec. "
The new town Timsah named Ismaila	4 March, 1863
The works visited by the Sultan and by Mr. Hawkshaw .	"
The company compelled by the Egyptian government to give up employment of compulsory labour; litigation ensued .	Aug. "
M. de Lesseps reported that a vessel containing 30 persons had been tugged along the canal the whole distance between the two seas .	Feb. 1865
Delegates from the British chambers of commerce visited the works, and reported that the success of the scheme was only an affair of time and money .	17 April, "
The flood gates of the smaller Suez canal were opened, the fresh water of the Nile admitted; a coal vessel passed from the Mediterranean to the Red Sea .	15 Aug. "
The *Primo*, 80 tons burden, passed through the canal from the Mediterranean into the Red Sea,	17 Feb. 1867
A loan raised in France .	"
French and English vessels enter the canal	Nov. 1868
Mr. John Fowler, the engineer, reported the canal as suitable for steamers and mail traffic, but not for vessels requiring tugs .	5 Feb. 1869
Water of the Mediterranean admitted to the salt lakes .	18 March, "
The works visited by the prince and princess of Wales .	23 March, "
The canal successfully opened in the presence of the emperor of Austria, the empress of the French, the viceroy of Egypt, and others .	17 Nov. "
M. de Lesseps entertained in London .	4 July, 1870
Traffic in 1870-1 doubled .	1872-3
Charges upon vessels passing through the canal increased 50 per cent.; the British appeal for a national conference .	April, 1873
International conference on Suez dues met at Constantinople; 21 sittings; report dated 18 Dec. Proposals of the sultan accepted by European powers .	Dec. "
M. de Lesseps protests; the lords of the admiralty informed (by D. A. Lange) that the canal will be closed unless the old dues are paid, 22 April; he gives way about .	26 April, 1874
Col. Stokes, after a survey, reported to the earl of Derby that the canal generally was in a satisfactory state .	20 April, "
British government authorise Messrs. Rothschild to buy for 4,080,000*l*. the Khedive's shares (176,602 shares of 20*l*. out of 400,000) in the canal: (5 per cent. to be paid till 1 July, 1894, after which dividends will be received) .	Nov. 1875
M. de Lesseps in a circular says he regards "as a fortunate circumstance the powerful union between English and French capitalists for the purely industrial and necessarily peaceful working of the universal maritime canal." .	29 Nov. "
The subject discussed in the commons, 14 Feb.; money (4,080,000*l*.) voted, 21 Feb.; act passed	15 Aug. 1876
Neutrality of the canal claimed by Great Britain	May, June, 1877
Freedom of the canal secured by settlement of Egypt .	1882-3
Receipts about 5,000,000 francs, 1870; 60,523,815 francs .	1882
Second canal determined on by British shipowners; syndicate appointed .	10 May, 1883
Arrangements made by the government for the construction of the canal and advancement of capital, to be virtually under control of De Lesseps' company, announced, 11 July; great dissatisfaction and opposition in England, 12 July; the proposed convention withdrawn by the government,	23 July, "
Sir Stafford Northcote's resolution against De Lesseps' monopoly negatived (284-185)	31 July, "
De Lesseps visits London; agrees with the steam shipowners to enlarge the present canal, or create a new one, giving additional power and influence in the direction of the company, and to reduce dues, &c.	30 Nov. "
The agreement approved by the British government, 25 Feb.; the shareholders at Paris protest against it, but ratify it (2608-556) .	29 May, "
International commission sits at Paris; English and French schemes discussed, April—May, 1885; parts of these schemes incorporated in treaty, May, 1885; last sitting .	13 June, 1886
The widening of the present canal decided on, after investigation by commission, Dec. 1884; plans adopted by the commission 9 Feb. 1885; arrangements with the Egyptian government completed	27 Dec. "
Convention signed at Paris for England and France neutralising the canal and placing it under a joint commission .	24 Oct. 1887
Adhesion of the other powers announced July; ratified by the sultan 25 Oct.; by the powers	29 Oct. and 22 Dec. 1888

Traffic passed through canal:

Year.	No. of Ships.	Gross Tonnage.	Gross Receipts.
1870	486	435,911	£255,488
1871	765	761,467	464,091
1872	1,082	1,439,169	758,659
1873	1,173	2,085,073	971,882
1874	1,264	2,423,672	1,029,492
1875	1,494	2,940,709	1,204,387
1876	1,457	3,072,107	1,229,157
1877	1,663	3,418,950	1,337,617
1878	1,593	3,291,535	1,272,435
1879	1,477	3,236,942	1,214,443
Total 10 years.	12,454	23,105,535	£9,737,651

Traffic passed through canal—*continued.*

Year.	No. of Ships.	Gross Tonnage.	Gross Receipts.
1880	2,026	4,344,519	1,672,836
1881	2,727	5,794,401	2,187,047
1882	3,198	7,122,125	2,536,343
1883	3,307	8,051,307	2,645,506
1884	3,284	8,319,967	2,480,000
1885	3,624	8,985,411	2,601,998
1886	3,100	8,783,313	2,241,095
1887	3,137	8,430,043	2,314,494
1888	3,444		2,680,000

Mr. Gladstone said that the country had gained from the canal, 4,700,000*l*. . . . April, 1881

SUFFRAGAN BISHOPS. Power to appoint them was given by parliament in 1534 to Henry VIII. as head of the church; see *Bishops* and *Supremacy*.

SUGAR* (*Saccharum officinarum*) is supposed to have been known to the ancient Jews. Found in the East Indies by Nearchus, admiral of Alexander, 325 B.C.—*Strabo*. An oriental nation in alliance with Pompey used the juice of the cane as a common beverage.—*Lucan*. It was prescribed as a medicine by Galen, 2nd century. Brought into Europe from Asia, A.D. 625;—in large quantities, 1150. Attempted to be cultivated in Italy; not succeeding, the Portuguese and Spaniards carried it to America about 1510.

The sugar-cane transported from Syria to Cyprus about 1148; from Madeira about 1420; and to the West Indies . . . . . . about 1506
It is not known at what date sugar was introduced into England, but it seems to have been prior to the reign of Henry VIII. Mr. Whittaker, in the History of Whalley, p. 109, quotes an instance in 1497
A manuscript letter from sir Edward Wotton to lord Cobham, dated Calais, advertises him that sir Edward had taken up for his lordship twenty-five sugar-loaves at six shillings a loaf, "whiche is eighte pence a pounde" . . . 6 March, 1546
Sugar first taxed (by James II.) 1685
Duties on free and slave-grown sugars equalized, Aug. 1846
Duties reduced and regulated . . . . Sept. 1848
Duty increased (war) 1855
Reduced, 1857, 1864; modified, 1867; greatly reduced, 1 Aug. 1870; further reduced, May, 1873; abolished from . . . . . 1 May, 1874
Sugar industries committee recommend a protective duty on the import of sugar from certain countries . . . . Aug. 1880
Sugar-refining was made known to Europeans by a Venetian, 1503, and was first practised in England in 1659, though some say we had the art a few years earlier. The invaluable vacuum-pan was invented by Howard, 1812. Dr. Scoffern's processes were patented in 1848-50, but not adopted in Britain.
Sugar manufactured from *sorghum* in United States Dec. 1882; success reported . . March, 1888
Manufacturers and colonies protest strongly against French and German bounties on beet sugar 1882-9
International Conference on Sugar Bounties, representatives from Germany, France, Austria and others, not United Sta H. de Worms chosen p tocol with a convent bounties and recommen abolition
The mission of baron de reported successful .
Final meeting, another p signed .
Finally signed for Great I Hungary, Italy, Russia Netherlands, declined Denmark and Sweden International commission enforce the convention Report adopted and sign to be referred to th

Bill for the adoption of th the commons May; def

A secret process of refinin to have been invented of New York announces organizing the New Yor company to carry out t collapsed and occasione and England by credu affair being an impostur It caused a temporary Mrs. Friend, then a v were arrested in Michig William E. Howard, on sentenced to imprisonm

For *Saechari*
RAW SUGAR IMPORTED INT
7,284,290 cwts.; 1860
10,250,524 cwts.; 1871,
16,264,711 cwts.; 1877,
17,734,223 cwts.; in 1
1887, 18,010,366 cwts.

See

SUICIDE (from s slayer of himself. The Jewish history are the and Saul, 1055 B.C. Th phers deemed it a crim hand apart from the res of Tarquin I., the Rom selves disgraced by bein sewers, destroyed them mitted suicide, 46 B.C church, in the 6th cent commemoration should for such as committed s tical law continued til was admitted into the s authority of parliamen land and goods. Till r was directed to be bu stake to be driven throu sing the barbarous cust is now usually buried out a religious ceren published "Suicides; were 7,572 suicides in I

MEMORABLE REC
Gen. Pichegru
Miss Champante

* Three instances of sel sopher Empedocles threw Etna; a Frenchman thr crater of Vesuvius; and into the furnace of a forge relates that an unaccount the Milesian virgins, from vented by the tears and r decree being issued that t who did self-murder shou streets, a stop was soon p

---

* Sugar, long considered a neutral substance, without congeners, has of late years become the head of a numerous family, viz.: Cane-sugar (*sucrose*, from the sugar-cane; boiled with dilute acids it becomes *glucose*); Fruit-sugar (from many recent fruits); Grape-sugar (*glucose*, from dried fruits and altered starch); sugar of milk; *Melitose* (from eucalyptus, by Berthelot in 1856); *sorbin* (from the berries of the mountain ash, by Pelouze); *inosite* (from muscular tissue, Scherer); *dulcose* (by Laurent); *mannite* (from manna, obtained from the fraxinus ornus, a kind of ash); *quercite* (from acorns); to these have been added *mycose*, by M. Mitscherlich, and *melezitose* and *trehalose*, by M. Berthelot.

erland . 31 May, 1810
merchant . . . . ,,
of the Marr family
. . . 15 Dec. 1811
. . . . 9 Dec. 1814
. . 1 June, 1815
. . . 6 July, ,,
. . . 13 Feb. ,,
. . . 2 Nov. 1818
. . . 8 Oct. 1820
. . . 23 June, 1821
. . . 12 Aug. 1822
. . . 26 Jan. 1825
ee *Prussic Acid*),
4 July, 1828
. . . 3 Jan. 1830
. . . 7 Feb. ,,
. . 13 Jan. 1832
. . . 13 June, ,,
. . 24 July, 1840
. . . 27 April, 1841
. . . 1 May, ,,
. . 20 March, 1842
. . 8 June, ,,
. . . 15 Feb. 1845
" Wellington's De-
. . . 25 Dec. ,,
. . 18 March, 1846
. . 22 June, ,,
. . . 2 Nov. 1847
. . . 12 July, 1850
ic theatre, 13 July, ,,
. . 20 Jan. 1853
. . 27 Dec. ,,
self off Shakspere's
. . 16 Aug. 1854
Allgemeine Zeitung,
. . . 3 Nov. 1855
ord of the treasury),
ad Heath. (He was
ormous frauds upon
. . 16 Feb. 1856
w himself from the
l's . 14 March, ,,
chairman of Great
. . 15 May, ,,
of *The Old Red Sand-*
rk) . . 23 Dec. ,,
ian army (14 March),
f the Indian navy.
mental depression
gainst Persia: see
. . 17 March, 1857
Harwich, brother of
. . 23 Oct. ,,
ung chemist, at the
. . 19 June, 1858
nity College, Dublin,
July, ,,
e diocese of Exeter,
27 Aug. 1860
. . . 8 Oct. 1861
. . 29 April, 1865
New Zealand, and
. . 30 April, ,,
the suppression of
to England, 9 May, 1867
off Clifton Suspen-
. . 11 May, ,,
is wife, at Brighton,
12 July, ,,
the north tower of
. . 18 Feb. 1868
. . 13 April, ,,
es; the "leviathan
. 9 Feb. 1869
olar . . 25 Feb. ,,
. . 3 April, ,,
ich banker, 15 July;
19 July, 1870
complished French
erly a correspondent
. . 19 July, ,,
ars manager of the
25 Aug. ,,
inent chemist, pro-
ospital . 6 Oct. ,,
. . 31 Jan. 1871

Sir James Shaw Willes, justice of common pleas (overwrought mind) . . . . 2 Oct. 1872
Earl Delawarr (insane) . . . . 22 April, 1873
Rev. Arthur Holmes, dean of Clare College, Cambridge, a great scholar; (overwrought mind) 17 April, 1875
George Lord Lyttelton, eminent scholar; temporary insanity; 18 April; died . . 19 April, 1876
Abdul Aziz, sultan of Turkey, deposed 29 May; said to have committed suicide (see *Turkey*, 1881), 4 June, ,,
Dr. Sam. Butcher, bishop of Meath; insane, 29 July, ,,
Harriet Mary, dowager countess Howe; insane through grief . . . . . . 29 Jan. 1877
Raphael Brandon, architect . . . . 8 Oct. ,,
J. W. Stevens, insane; threw himself from whispering gallery, St. Paul's . . . 10 Jan. ,,
E. M. Ward, *genre* painter; insane . . . 15 Jan. 1879
Isaac Fletcher, M.P., F.R.S. . . . 3 April, ,,
Rev. W. Gunson, able tutor of Christ's College, Cambridge (insane) . . . . 30 Sept. 1881
Carl Engel (musical archæologist) . . 18 Nov. 1882
Dr. William Whitfield Edwards, surgeon at Hounslow . . . . 27 Dec. ,,
Count Wimpffen, Austrian ambassador at Paris, 30 Dec. ,,
Morris Simeon Oppenheim, barrister . . 3 Jan. 1883
Joseph Dimsdale, Gutter Lane, E.C. . 13 Jan. ,,
Sir John Savage, formerly mayor of Belfast, 15 June, ,,
Rev. Alexr. Taylor, preacher of Gray's Inn 11 April, 1884
H. T. Edwards, dean of Bangor . . 24 May, ,,
The eighth earl of Shaftesbury (insane) in a cab in Regent-street . . . . . 13 April, 1886
Fred Archer, celebrated jockey (insane) 8 Nov. ,,
Louis II. king of Bavaria . . . . 13 June, ,,
Nagayori Asana, Japanese prince, law student (melancholia) at south Kensington . 24 Dec. ,,
John K. Cross, formerly M.P. and under secretary for India (1883–5) . . . . 20 March, 1887
Dr. Ridley of Tullamore gaol (see under *Ireland*,) 20 July, 1888
Archduke Rodolph, crown prince of Austria, 30 Jan. 1889
Richard Pigott (see *Ireland*) . . . 1 March, ,,
M. Denfert-Rochereau, manager of the Comptoir d'Escompte (see *France*) . . . 5 March, ,,

INQUESTS ON SUICIDES IN ENGLAND AND WALES.

	Males.	Females.	Total.
1856	919	395	1314
1858	909	366	1275
1860	961	396	1357
1861	961	363	1324
1862	938	346	1284
1863	1048	337	1385
1864	978	359	1337
1865	1028	369	1397
1866	973	387	1360
1867	985	371	1356
1868	1138	408	1546
1869	1165	397	1562
1870	1135	382	1517
1871	1073	391	1464
1872	1057	398	1455
1873	1099	382	1481
1874	1106	383	1549
1875	1170	407	1577
1876	1270	443	1713
1877	1253	383	1636
1878	1279	430	1709
1879	1461	480	1941
1880	1450	480	1930
1881	1440	478	1918
1882	1388	502	1890
1883	1437	507	1944
1884	1537	482	2019
1885	1504	484	1988
1886	1663	559	2222
1887	1672	555	2227

SUITORS' FUND (in the court of chancery), in 1862 amounted to 1,290,000*l*. As this money has no specific owner, a proposal was made by government to apply it to the building of new law-courts, payment of all legal claims being guaranteed, which was directed by the "Courts of Laws Fees" act, passed 20 Aug. 1867.

SULPHUR has been known from the earliest times. Basil Valentine mentions its production from green vitriol. Sulphuric acid (vitriol), produced by him from burning sulphur, was introduced into England about 1720. Sulphur has been the object of research of many eminent chemists during the present century, and many discoveries have been made, such as its allotropic condition, &c. It is the inflammable constituent in gunpowder, and a deleterious ingredient in coal gas. The sulphur mines of Sicily have been wrought since the 16th century, but the exportation was inconsiderable till about 1820; in 1838 the trade increased so much that Great Britain alone imported 38,654 tons. In that year the Neapolitan government was induced to grant a monopoly of the trade to a French company; but a firm remonstrance from the British government led to a discontinuance of this impolitic restriction in 1841, which, however, gave a great and lasting impetus to the British sulphur manufacture. In 1871, only 937,049 tons were imported into the United Kingdom.

SULTAN, or ruler, a Turkish title, from the Arabic, given to the grand signior or emperor of Turkey. It was first given to the Turkish princes, Angrolipez and Musgad, about 1055.—*Vattier.* It was first given, according to others, to the emperor Mahmoud, in the 4th century of the Hegira.
For the wreck of H.M.S. *Sultan* (see *Navy of England*) 1889

SULU, Sooloo or Soluk Archipelago, a group of above 60 islands in the Malay Archipelago. The Spanish under colonel Arolas, the governor, defeated the rebels at Maiburg, and burnt the town, announced 1 May, 1887.

SUMATRA, an island in the Indian ocean, called Java Minor by Marco Polo, and visited by Nicolo di Conti prior to 1449. Mainly on account of the pepper trade, the Dutch formed a settlement at Padang about 1649, and the British at Bencoolen about 1685. The Dutch possessions with Java were acquired by the British in 1811; but were restored in 1816. In 1824 the Dutch acquired all the British settlements in Sumatra, in exchange for Malacca and some possessions in India. Restrictions on their progress in Sumatra were removed by treaty Feb. 1872. Severe fighting between the Dutch and the Achinese natives with varying results, mostly in favour of the Dutch. April 1873 to 1879. Dutch successful in war, peace announced, Aug. 1879. New war; great victory of the Dutch, 13 Sept. 1882. Sumatra suffered much by the volcanic eruptions and earthquakes of 26-27 Aug. 1883. See *Java.*

SUMMARY JURISDICTION ACT, 42 & 43 Vict. c. 49, 11 Aug. 1879. It amends the law respecting the jurisdiction of magistrates, in regard to fines, imprisonments, &c. It came into operation 1 Jan. 1880. Amended 1881 and 1884.

SUMPTUARY LAWS restrain excess in dress, furniture, eating, &c. The laws of Lycurgus were severe against luxury, probably about 881 B.C. Those of Zaleucus ordained that no sober woman should go attended by more than one maid in the street, or wear gold or embroidered apparel, 450 B.C. —*Diog. Laert.* The *Lex Orchia* among the Romans (181 B.C.) limited the guests at feasts, and the number and quality of the dishes at an entertainment; and it also enforced that during supper, which was the chief meal among the Romans, the doors of every house should be left open. The English sumptuary laws, chiefly of the reigns of Edward III. and Henry VIII., were repealed in 1856; see *Dress.*

SUN.* Pythagoras taught that the sun was one of the twelve spheres, about 529 B.C. The relative distances of the sun and moon were first calculated geometrically by Aristarchus, who also maintained the stability of the sun, about 280 B.C. Numerous theories were ventured during fifteen centuries, and astronomy lay neglected till about A.D. 1200, when it was brought into Europe by the Moors of Barbary and Spain. The Copernican system was made known in 1530; see *Copernican System,* and *Solar System,* Galileo and Newton maintained that the sun was an igneous globe. The transit of Mercury was observed by Gassendi. For recent discoveries, see *Eclipses, Spectrum,* and *Venus.*

By the observations of Dr. Halley on the spot which darkened the sun's disc in July and August, 1676, he established the certainty of its motion round its own axis.
Parallax of the sun, Dr. Halley 1702
Solar spots were observed by Fabricius and Harriot in 1610. A macula three times the size of the earth passed the sun's centre, 21 April, 1766, and frequently since.
Dr. Wilson observed the motion of a spot . . 1769
Herschel measured two spots, whose length together exceeded 50,000 miles . . . 19 April, 1779
Schwabe discovered that a cycle of changes (from maximum to minimum and minimum to maximum) in the number of spots occurs in 11 years, confirmed by Wolf and others . . . 1826-51
Mr. Warren de la Rue took two photographs at the time of total obscuration . . 18 July, 1860
Mr. James Nasmyth discovers the lenticular-shaped objects on the sun (termed by him "willow-leaves," by Stone "rice-grains") . 28 Aug. „
Red flames, or protuberances, during an eclipse of the sun, observed by capt. Stannyan, 1706; by Halley, 1715; by F. Baily (hence termed "Baily's beads,") 1842.
Determined by M. Janssen to be due to the accumulated hydrogen of the photosphere, at the solar eclipse (see *Eclipses*) . . . 18 Aug. 1868
Mouchot constructed a solar boiler for distillation, &c. . . . . Oct. 1860
Mr. Ericsson proposed condensation of the sun's rays and their employment as a motive power, Oct. 1868
The observations of the eclipse of 22 Dec. 1870 and 12 Dec. 1871 led to the opinion that an unknown substance (represented in the spectrum by line 1474) existed in the sun.
"Solar physics" especially studied by Messrs. Warren de la Rue, Balfour Stewart, &c. . 1865 6
Apparatus for cooking by the *condensed solar rays* in the Paris exhibition 1878
Solar eclipse well observed in the United States; the corona much brighter than in 1871; 29, 30 July, „
M. Mouchot at Algiers, by a mirror, collected solar rays, and boiled water, drove an engine, &c., March, 1880; see under *Heat.*
Intensely red sunsets and after-glow, and very red sun-rises, seen in England and other parts of the globe, Nov. and Dec. 1883; attributed by Dr. Meldrum, Dr. Norman Lockyer and others, to the volcanic dust projected by the eruptions of

* The estimated diameter is 840,000 miles, and the distance from the earth, till lately given as 95,000,000 miles, has been recently corrected to 94,000,000, by the result of the experiments and calculations of MM. Fizeau and Foucault (1864). "The error corrected corresponds to the apparent breadth of a human hair at 125 feet, or of a sovereign 8 miles off."—*Herschel.* Distance computed by sir G. B. Airy from results of the observation of transit of Venus (Dec. 1874), 93,321,000 miles, Oct. 1877; 92,600,000, June, 1878. From the transit of 1882 by professor Harkness (an American), 92,385,000 miles, Oct. ber, 1888. The sun is now described as consisting of a solid or liquid nucleus, surrounded by a luminous envelope (photosphere) over which is a dense atmosphere, containing the vapours of various metals and other elements; see *Spectrum.*

Krakatoa (see *Java*, Aug. 1883), Dec. 1883; other causes, such as cosmic dust, were suggested. Similar sunsets in the autumn . 1884 and 1885
Interesting photographs of the sun's corona exhibited by Dr. Huggins at the Royal Institution,
. . . . 20 Feb. 1885
Eclipse of 19 Aug. 1887 not well observed through unfavourable weather, except at Moscow and other places in Russia and Germany.

SUNCION, TREATY OF, between general Urquiza, director of the Argentine confederation, and C. A. Lopez, president of the republic of Paraguay, recognising the independence of Paraguay, 14 July, 1852.

SUNDA ISLES, include Java and Sumatra (*which see*).

SUNDAY was the day on which, anciently, divine adoration was paid to the Sun. Among Christians it is commonly called *Dies Dominica*, or Lord's day, on account of our Saviour's appearance on that day, after his resurrection. The first civil law that was issued for the observance of this day, combined it with that of the seventh-day Sabbath and other festivals (*Eusebius, Life of Constantine*), and it was followed by several imperial edicts, in favour of this day, which are extant in the body of Roman law, the earliest being that of Constantine the Great, dated 7 March, 321. See *Sabbath, Sabbatarians, Sports, Book of,* &c.—For SUNDAY LETTER, see *Dominical Letter*.

The council of Orleans prohibited country labour . 538
The Sabbath-day was ordained to be kept holy in England, from Saturday at three in the afternoon to Monday at break-of-day, 4th Canon, Edgar . 960
Act of parliament, levying one shilling on every person absent from church on Sundays, 3 James I. 1606
James I. authorised certain sports after divine service on Sundays (see *Sports*) 1618
Act restraining amusements, 1 Charles I. . . 1625
Act restraining the performance of servile works, and the sale of goods except milk at certain hours and meat in public-houses, and works of necessity and charity, on forfeiture of five shillings, 29 Charles II. 1676
The Sunday act (of bishop Porteus) 21 Geo. III. c. 49, passed 1781
Lord Robert Grosvenor (aft. lord Ebury), introduced a bill to suppress Sunday trading. (It met with much opposition and was withdrawn), April-July, 1855
The Jews released from the compulsory observance of Sunday . . . . . began 28 May, 1871
Sunday act (1676) amended . . . 17 Aug. ,,
Opening of public museums and galleries on Sunday often proposed in parliament; negatived (271-68), 19 May, 1874; (229-87) . 8 June, 1877
"Sunday Society" established to promote the movement, 1875. Annual meeting; Dr. A. P. Stanley, the dean of Westminster, professors Tyndall and Huxley, &c., present . 12 May, ,,
The Brighton Aquarium Company fined for opening on Sunday, 27 April; much agitation; petitions to government for and against, May; an act was passed to enable the Home Secretary to remit the penalties, 13 Aug., 1875; the company again fined . . . . 28 April, ,,
Grosvenor gallery and other collections opened on Sundays, summer 1878
Act for closing public-houses in Ireland on Sundays, passed . . . . 16 Aug. ,,
Free libraries opened on Sundays at Manchester and other places . . . . Sept. ,,
Proposed opening of museums and galleries in London, negatived in the lords (67-59), 5 May, 1879; (34-41), 22 Feb. 1880; (91-67) 8 May, 1883; assented to (76-62) . . . . . 19 March, 1886
Opening of Guildhall library on Sundays, negatived by the common council . . . 16 Oct. 1879
Welsh Sunday Closing Act passed 1881
Alexandra Palace religious services on Sundays for a time . . . . Sept.-Oct. ,,
Jubilee memorial to the queen signed by 1,132,608

women of England, requesting the prohibition of the sale of intoxicating liquors on Sundays, given in . . . . 30 Dec. 1887
Protest of the bishops in convocation against increasing desecration of the Lord's day by the upper classes . . . . . . 2 March, 1888
Closing of public houses in England on Sunday frequently negatived; Sunday closing bill read second time in the commons . . 27 March, 1887

SUNDAY LECTURE SOCIETY was founded 25 Nov. 1869. It began its proceedings by a lecture delivered by Dr. W. B. Carpenter at St. George's-hall, Regent-street, 16 Jan. 1870. Its success was reported at the first annual meeting, 7 July, 1870. See *Recreative Religionists*.

SUNDAY NEWSPAPERS, see *Newspapers*.

SUNDAY SCHOOLS. Cardinal Sr. Charles Borromeo introduced Sunday instruction of children at Milan, about 1580; in the next century his example was followed in England by the rev. Joseph Alleine; by rev. David Blair, at Brechin, about 1760; by the rev. Theophilus Lindsey, at Catterick, Yorkshire, about 1763; and more especially organised by Robert Raikes, an eminent printer of Gloucester, conjointly with rev. Thos. Stock, 1780. Ludweek Hacker set up a Sabbath school at Ephrata, Pennsylvania, between 1740 and 1747.

Sunday-school buildings exempted from rates . 1869
Church of England Sunday-school Institute . . 1843
Sunday-school union was founded in 1802; it supported 4204 schools 1879
Monument in memory of twelve originators of Sunday-schools, Essex-street, Strand (names inscribed, 1st., cardinal Borromeo, Milan, 1580; last, rev. Thomas Stock and Robert Raikes, Gloucester, 1780); inaugurated by Henry Richard, M.P., the Italian ambassador, and others 26 June, 1880
National centenary celebration of the establishment of Sunday-schools, in London, &c., promoted by the royal family, archbishop of Canterbury, the lord mayor, and others . 27 June—3 July, ,,
Grand reception of scholars at Lambeth palace-gardens by the archbishop; prince and princess of Wales, &c., present . . . . . 3 July, ,,
See *Education*, and *Sabbath Schools*.

SUNDERLAND, seaport, N.E. Durham, anciently South Wearmo', made a borough by Reform Bill, 1832. Returns two members (1885). The magnificent bridge over the Wear, designed by Wilson, 236 feet in span, was built 1793-6.

On 16 June, 1883, 186 children were crushed to death against a doorway whilst rushing down from a gallery in Victoria Hall to obtain toys given away by Fay, a conjuror, at the close of his performances. Great distress of the unemployed, Sept. *et seq.* 1884.

SUNDERLAND ADMINISTRATION, formed in 1718, arose out of a modification of the Stanhope ministry. After various changes, it was broken up in 1721.
Charles, earl of Sunderland, *first lord of the treasury*.
Earl Cowper, *lord chancellor*.
Earl Stanhope and Mr. Craggs, *secretaries*.
Mr. Aislabie, *chancellor of the exchequer*, &c.

SUNDERLAND LIBRARY, see under *Libraries*.

SUN DIALS, see *Dials*.

SUNNITES, or SONNITES (*which see*).

SUNSHINE RECORDER, a sphere of glass so disposed as to char a marked piece of paper, by concentrating the sun's rays. The instrument (invented by Mr. J. F. Campbell in 1857), in its present form was devised by prof. G. G. Stokes, and made by Mr. R. J. Lecky (1880). A more delicate form of instrument for recording photometrically the duration and intensity of sunshine has

3 K

SUPERANNUATION ACTS.

been invented by Mr. J. B. Jordan, 1884; much improved, April, 1888.

SUPERANNUATION ACTS for the Civil Service were passed in April, 1859, and Aug. 1866.

SUPPER, see *Lord's Supper*.

SUPREMACY over the church was claimed by pope Gelasius I. as bishop of Rome, 494. On 15 Jan. 1535, Henry VIII. by virtue of the act 26 Hen. VIII. c. 1, formally assumed the style of "on earth supreme head of the church of England," which was retained by Edward VI., Mary I. (for a time), but was refused by Elizabeth, and has never been revived by succeeding sovereigns. The bishop of Rochester (Fisher) and the ex-lord chancellor (sir Thomas More) and many others were beheaded for denying the king's supremacy in 1535; and in 1578, John Nelson, a priest, and Thomas Sherwood, a young layman, were executed at Tyburn for the same offence. The "act of Supremacy," repealed by 1 & 2 Phil. and Mary, c. 8 (1554), was re-enacted 1 Eliz. c. 1 (1559).

SUPREME COURT OF JUDICATURE was constituted by the Judicature Act 36 & 37 Vict. c. 66, passed 5 Aug. 1873, to come into operation 1 Nov. 1874. In 1874 this was deferred to 1 Nov. 1875.

The existing courts were to be united into one Supreme Court, divided into the High Court of Justice and the Court of Appeal. The High Court to consist of the lord chancellor, the two lord chief justices, the vice-chancellors, and the other judges: (hereafter the court to consist of 21 judges.)

Five divisions : 1. Chancery, 2. Queen's Bench, 3. Common Pleas, 4. Exchequer, and 5. Probate, Divorce, and Admiralty; subject to alteration.

The Court of Appeal to consist of five ex-officio judges (viz., lord chancellor, two lord chief justices, lord chief baron, master of the rolls), and such others as may be appointed (§§ 20, 21, 22).

Appeals to the house of lords or the judicial committee of the privy council to be discontinued.

Law and equity to be concurrently administered: law terms abolished; and sittings in vacation provided for. See under *Terms*.

The act passed 11 Aug., 1875, suspended §§ 20, 21, and 55, converted the proposed court of appeal into an intermediate court till 1 Nov., 1876. (See below).

The Supreme Court of Judicature (comprising the High Court of Justice, Chancery division, Queen's Bench, Common Pleas, and Exchequer subdivisions, Probate, Divorce, and Admiralty division (*all which see*) began . . . . . 2 Nov. 1875

After one term, it was said in the *Times*, "Its operation has tended to economise judicial power and to prevent delay of justice" . . . 29 Nov. ,,

By the Appellate Jurisdiction Act (1876) the house of lords retains its powers as a court of ultimate appeal; the court to consist of the lord chancellor, two lords of appeal (to be created peers for life, with 6000*l.* salary) and any peers who are or have been lawyers. Act to come into operation . . . . 1 Nov. 1876

The court may sit during prorogation of parliament. The statute relating to the judicial committee of the privy council and to the intermediate court of appeal is amended . . . . . . ,,

By this act also the Queen's Bench, Common Pleas, and Exchequer divisions of the Supreme Court are converted into 15 courts of first instance or primary courts.

Additional judge for chancery division appointed.

Style of ordinary judges:—of the court of appeal to be, "lord justices of the appeal;" other judges, "justices of the high court;" by act passed 24 April, 1877

An amendment act (42 & 43 Vict. c. 78), relating to offices, fees, &c., passed . . . 15 Aug. 1879

At a meeting of the judges it was resolved to recommend the abolition of the exchequer and common pleas, and their consolidation into one, termed the "Queen's bench division," under the lord chief

justice of England, 30 ...

Carried into effect; old ... cature act carried out f... Further changes made by 68, passed 27 Aug. 1881. rolls was made a judg... chief justice of Englan... powers of the chief jus... the chief baron of the e... New code of rules of p... July; came into force 2 Amendment act passed

SUPREME CO... TURE FOR IRE... passed 14 Aug. 1877. 23 May, 1887, by which the exchequer and ch... pleas are to be abolished

COURT OF APPEAL : *ex-o...* lord chief justice of Ir... chief justice of common exchequer. *Ordinary* appeal.

HIGH COURT OF JUSTICE : cellor, master of the r... land judges.

Queen's Bench division : judges.

Common Pleas division : judges.

Exchequer division : lord *Probate and Matrimonial* See under *Chancery* and

SURAT (E. Indies India company obtaine... presidency of their aff... was at Surat; and the... lished under captain ... Mogul had here an off miral. An attack of ... on the British factory, Oxenden, 1664. The ... in 1670 and 1702, and East India company, i... ment, which dispossess... and, soon after, the p confirmed to them by ... was vested in the Bri... fourth part of Surat ... April, 1889.

SURGEONS. Bar... in one company in 1540 person using any shavin... occupy any surgery, let... excepting only. the dr... the surgeons and barbe... tinct corporations. Peer... charters in 1745, 1800. ... the "Royal College of S and 1859. Since that p... other important regul... promote their utility an... son is legally entitled to cities of London and W miles of the former, who college. The college ... re-modelled in 1836, a 1837. The premises we museum began with the... and the library was fo... Emily Dowson, the firs to act, was invested wi... the Irish college of surg *tomy*, *Physic*, and *Med...* Royal college of surgeo... 1796; Edinburgh .

SURGERY. It was not until the age of Hippocrates that diseases were made a separate study from philosophy, &c., about 410 B.C. Hippocrates mentions the *ambe*, the ancient instrument with which they reduced dislocated bones. Celsus flourished about A.D. 17; Galen, 170; Aëtius, 500; Paulus Ægineta, in 640. The Arabians revived surgery about 900; and in the 16th century a new era in the science began; between these periods surgery was confined to ignorant priests and barbers. Anatomy was cultivated under Vesalius, the father of modern surgery, in 1538. Surgeons and doctors were exempted from bearing arms or serving on juries, 1513, at which period there were only thirteen in London; see *Physic*.

SURGICAL AID SOCIETY, founded 1862; supplies the poor with instruments, waterbeds, &c.

SURINAM (Dutch Guiana), discovered by Columbus, 1498. The factories established by the English in 1640 were occupied by the Portuguese, 1643; by the Dutch, 1654; taken by the British, 1799, 1804; and restored to the Dutch, 1802, 1814.

SURNAMES were introduced into England by the Normans, and were adopted by the nobility about 1100. The old Normans used *Fitz*, which signifies son, as Fitz-herbert. The Irish used O, for grandson, O'Neal, O'Donnell. The Scottish Highlanders used Mac, as Macdonald, son of Donald. The northern nations added the word son to the father's name, as Williamson. Many of the most common surnames, such as Johnson, Wilson, Dyson, Nicholson, &c., were taken by Brabanters and other Flemings, who were naturalised in the reign of Henry VI., 1435. M. A. Lower's "Dictionary of English Surnames" was published in 1860.

SURPLICES were first worn by the Jewish priests, and are said to have been first used in churches in the fourth century, and encouraged by pope Adrian, 786. "Every minister saying public prayers shall wear a comely surplice with sleeves," Canon 58. The garb prescribed by stat. 2 Edw. VI. 1547; again 1 Eliz. 1558; and 13 & 14 Chas. II. 1662; see *Ritualism*.

SURREY CHAPEL, Blackfriars-road, was built for Calvinistic dissenters in 1783; the rev. Rowland Hill, their minister, who died in 1833, was buried in a vault here. The congregation under the rev. Newman Hall removed to Christ Church, in Westminster-road, July, 1876. See *Lincoln Tower*.

SURREY ZOOLOGICAL GARDENS (near London) were established in 1831, by Mr. Edward Cross, who brought hither the menagerie formerly at Exeter change. Various picture models have been exhibited here since 1837, viz., Vesuvius, Iceland, &c., accompanied by fireworks. In 1856, a company which had taken the gardens, erected a large yet elegant building for concerts; the architect being Mr. Horace Jones, on 19 Oct. 1856, when the hall contained about 9000 persons, attending to hear the rev. C. H. Spurgeon, seven were killed and thirty seriously injured, by a false alarm of fire. It was burnt 11 June, 1861; see *Fires*. In 1862 the hall was temporarily taken for the reception of the patients of St. Thomas's hospital.

SURTEES SOCIETY for publishing MSS. relating to the northern counties, established 1834; 84 volumes have been published, 1889.

SURVEY ACT, passed 12 May, 1870. See *Ordnance Survey*.

SURVEYORS, INSTITUTION OF, London, founded in 1868, to promote the "knowledge which constitutes the profession of a surveyor." Incorporated as "The Surveyors' Institution" in 1881. The number of members, 1,200 in 1886.

SUSA, or **SHUSHAN,** capital of Susiana, a province of Persia, was taken by Alexander the Great, 331 B.C.

SUSPENDING POWER, see *Dispensing Power*.

SUSPENSION BRIDGES are ancient in China. The Hungerford (or Charing-cross) suspension bridge, opened May 1, 1845, was removed to Clifton and opened there, 8 Dec. 1864. Parliament empowered the commissioners of woods to erect (among other improvements there) a suspension bridge at Battersea, Sept. 1846; and many bridges of similar construction have been erected in various parts of the kingdom. Lambeth and Westminster suspension bridge was opened 10 Nov. 1862; see *Menai Strait, Hungerford, Clifton*, &c.

SUSPENSORY BILL, the name given to "a bill to prevent for a limited time [to 1 Aug. 1869] new appointments in the church of Ireland; and to restrain, for the same period, in certain respects, the proceedings of the Ecclesiastical Commissioners for Ireland." This bill was introduced into the commons by Mr. Gladstone, 14 May, and passed through committee, 5 June; rejected by the lords (192 to 97), 30 June, 3 A.M., 1868.

SUSSEX, see *Britain*.

SUTLEJ, a river in N.W. India, the ancient Hyphasis or Hypana, on the banks of which were fought the desperate battles of Aliwal, 28 Jan., and Sobraon, 10 Feb. 1846 (*which see*).

SUTTEE, the burning of widows. This custom began in India from one of the wives of "Bramah, the Son of God," sacrificing herself at his death, that she might attend him in heaven. Seventeen widows have burnt themselves on the funeral pile of a rajah; and in Bengal alone, 700 have thus perished in a year. The English government, after long discouraging suttees, by the agency of lord William Bentinck, formally abolished them, 7 Dec. 1829; but they have since occasionally taken place. The wife of the son of the rajah of Beygoon thus perished, June, 1864, and several wives of sir Jung Bahadoor, minister of Nepaul, 1 March, 1877. About 20,000,000 women in enforced widowhood; much profligacy, 1885. Legislative interference with the Hindoo marriage laws declared by lord Dufferin, viceroy, to be ineffectual and unnecessary; moral influence progressing (see Brahmo Somaj, under *Deism*) announced Oct. 1886

SUWANOW, or **(SUWOROFF),** a group of small uninhabited isles in the Pacific, about 450 miles NNW. of the Samoan isles, annexed by Great Britain, 1889.

SWABIA, a province in S. Germany; was conquered by Clovis, and incorporated into the kingdom of the Franks, 496. After various changes of rulers, it was made a duchy by the emperor Conrad I., in 912, for Erchanger; according to some, in 916, for Burckhardt. The duchy became hereditary in the house of Hohenstaufen in 1080. Frederick III. became emperor of Rome, commonly styled of Germany, as Frederick I. (usually styled Barbarossa, red beard), in 1152. Conradin his descendant, was defeated at the battle of Tagliacozzo (*which see*), in 1268, and beheaded shortly after. The breaking up of the duchy gave rise to many of the small German

states; part of Swabia is included in Würtemberg and Switzerland. Swabia was made a circle of the empire in 1387 and 1500. A league, composed of Swabian cities and states, about 1254, was the germ of the great Swabian league, formed for the preservation of the peace of Germany, under the auspices of the emperor Frederick, in 1488.

SWAN RIVER SETTLEMENT, see *Western Australia*.

SWANSEA, Glamorganshire, an ancient Welsh town; seat of the copper trade since 1719. New dock opened by the prince of Wales, 18 Oct. 1831.

SWAT, or **SVAT**, a river, N.W. India. The Akhond, Abdul Ghafur, originally an austere Mahometan fanatic, about 1822, gradually obtained temporal power over the tribes in the hills near Afghanistan, dying in high reputation, about 1878.

SWEABORG, a strong fortress in Finland, the Gibraltar of the north, 3½ miles south of Helsingfors; it is situated on seven rocky islands; the fortifications were commenced by the Swedes in 1748, and completed after Finland was united to Russia in 1809. On 6 Aug. 1855, the English and French fleet anchored off Sweaborg, and bombarded it by mortar and gun-boats from the 9th to the 11th, causing the destruction of nearly all the principal buildings, including the dockyard and arsenal. Few casualties and no loss of life ensued in the allied squadron, but this success was not followed up.

SWEARING ON THE GOSPELS, first used about 528, and introduced in judicial proceedings about 600.—*Rapin*. PROFANE SWEARING made punishable by fine; a labourer or servant forfeiting 1s., others 2s. for the first offence; for the second offence, 4s.; the third offence, 6s.; 6 Will. III., 1695; see *Oaths*.

SWEATING SICKNESS, see *Plague*.

SWEATING SYSTEM, a term applied, especially in the east end of London, to the practice carried on by large tradesmen of entrusting orders to middlemen termed "sweaters," who employ men, women, and children (principally foreigners) to make up clothes, boots, and furniture in their own houses at excessively low wages with many evil consequences. Lord Dunraven's motion for a select committee of inquiry was carried in the lords, 28 Feb.; archbishop of Canterbury, earl of Derby, and others appointed 9 March, 1888. Painfully distressing evidence was obtained. The origin of the evil is attributed to the great competition in producing extreme cheapness. The new and foreign workmen are termed "greeners." It is stated that about 5s. are sometimes paid for a week of days of 14 hours, May. First session of committee closed, 27 July; report issued, Sept. 1888. The sufferings of the Cradley Heath chainmakers, nailmakers, and others, were disclosed to the committee March, 1889

SWEDEN (N. Europe). The ancient inhabitants were the Fins, now the modern inhabitants of Finland, who retired to their present territory on the appearance of the Scandinavians or Goths, who have ever since been masters of Sweden; see *Scandinavia*. The internal state of this kingdom is little known previous to the 11th century. By the union of Calmar in 1397, Sweden became a province of Denmark, and was not wholly rescued from this subjection till 1521, when Gustavus Vasa recovered the kingdom from the Danish yoke. He became king in 1523, and his descendants ruled till 1809. The government of Sweden is a limited monarchy. The diet consists of four orders, the nobles, the clergy, the peasants, and the burghers,

and meet every three years. The king is, as in Britain, the head of the executive. There are two universities, Upsal and Lund; and Sweden can boast, among its great men, Linnæus, Celsius, Scheele, Bergman, Berzelius, Thorwaldsen, and Andersen. Population (31 Dec. 1887) of Sweden, 4,734,901; of Norway (1875), 1,806,900.

Odin said to arrive in the north, and died	B.C.
His son Skiold reigns	40
The Skioldungs reign till Olaf the infant is baptized, and introduces Christianity among his people, about A.D.	1000
Waldemar I. of Denmark subdues Rugen, and destroys the pagan temples	1168
Stockholm founded	1260
Magnus Ladulas establishes a regular form of government	1279
The crown of Sweden, which had been hereditary, is made elective; and Steenchel Magnus, surnamed Smeek, or the foolish, king of Norway, is elected	1319
Waldemar lays Gothland waste	1361
Albert of Mecklenburg reigns	1363
Treaty or union of Calmar (*which see*), by which Sweden is united to Denmark and Norway, under Margaret	1397
University of Upsal founded	1476
Christian II. of Denmark, "the Nero of the North," massacres the Swedish nobility	1520
The Swedes delivered from the Danish yoke by the valour of Gustavus Vasa	1521
Gustavus Vasa raised to the throne	1523
He introduces Lutheranism and religious liberty	1527
Makes the crown hereditary	1544
Gustavus Adolphus heads the protestant cause in Germany	1628
He takes Magdeburg and Munich, 1630; slain at Lutzen 16 Nov.	1632
Rugen ceded to Sweden by Denmark	1648
Abdication of Christina 16 June,	1654
Charles X. overruns Poland	1655
Arts and sciences begin to flourish	1660
University of Lund founded	1666
Charles XII. "the Madman of the North," begins his reign; he makes himself absolute; abolishes the senate, 1699; and defeats the Russians at Narva 30 Nov.	1700
Battle of Pultowa, where Charles is defeated by the czar of Russia (see *Pultowa*) 8 July,	1709
He escapes to Bender, where, after three years' protection, he is made a prisoner by the Turks	1713
He is restored; and after ruinous wars, and fighting numerous battles, is killed at the siege of Frederickshald 11 Dec.	1718
Queen Ulrica abolishes despotism	1719
Bremen and Verden ceded to Hanover Nov.	
Royal Academy founded by Linnæus	1741
Conspiracy of counts of Brahe and Horne, who are beheaded	1756
The Hats and Caps (French and Russian parties), 1738-57; put down by Gustavus III.	1770
Despotism re-established	1772
Order of the Sword instituted	"
Assassination of Gustavus III. by count Ankerstrom, at a ball, 16 March; he expired 29 March,	1792
The regicide was scourged with whips of iron thongs three successive days; his right hand was cut off, then his head, and his body impaled, 18 May,	"
Gustavus IV. dethroned and the government assumed by his uncle the duke of Sudermania (Charles XIII.) 13 March,	1809
Representative constitution established 7 June,	"
Sweden cedes Finland to Russia 17 Sept.	"
Marshal Bernadotte, the prince of Ponte Corvo (one of Bonaparte's generals), chosen the crown prince of Sweden 21 Aug.	1810
Gustavus IV. arrived in London 12 Nov.	"
Swedish Pomerania seized by Napoleon 9 Jan.	1812
Alliance with England 12 July,	"
Sweden joins the grand alliance against Napoleon, 13 March,	1813
Norway is ceded to Sweden by the treaty of Kiel, 14 Jan.; carried into effect Nov.	1814
Bernadotte king, as Charles John XIV. 5 Feb.	1818
Canals and roads constructed	1822

Treaty of navigation between Great Britain and Sweden . . . . 19 May,	1826
Death of Charles John ; his son Oscar I. king, 8 Mar.	1844
Alliance with England and France . 21 Nov.	1855
Banishment decreed against catholic converts from Lutheranism . . . . Oct.	1857
Demonstration in favour of Italy . . 17 Dec.	1859
Increased religious toleration . . . May,	1860
The king visits England and France . . Ang.	1861
He is warmly received in Denmark . 17 July,	1862
Treaty of commerce with Italy, signed . 14 June,	,,
Demonstration in favour of Poland . . April,	1863
Inauguration of free trade . . . 1 Jan.	1864
Sweden protests against the occupation of Sleswig by the allies . . . . . . 22 Jan.	,,
Excitement throughout the country ; March : preparation for war ; (no result) . . . April,	,,
Foundation of a "National Scandinavian Society" at Stockholm to obtain by legal means a confederation of the three kingdoms for military and foreign affairs, reserving independent interior administration . . . . Dec.	,,
New constitution passed by the chambers, 4-8 Dec.	,,
Commercial treaty with France approved . Feb.	1866
Severe famine in North Sweden . Oct.-Dec.	1867
Resignation of ministers, 9 April ; new ministry under M. Wachtmeister . . . 4 June,	1868
Princess Louisa was married to Frederic, crownprince of Sweden . . . . 28 July,	1869
Neutrality in the Franco-Prussian war was proclaimed . . . . 4 Aug.	1870
The queen dies . . . . . 13 March,	1871
Prince Oscar visits England ; lays foundation of a Scandinavian church at Rotherhithe . 27 July,	,,
Re-organization of the army proposed, Aug. ; negatived . . . . Oct.	,,
Death of king Charles XV. . . . 18 Sept.	1872
The diet opened by king Oscar II. . . 20 Jan.	1873
The king and queen crowned . . 12 May,	,,
Ministry under baron de Geer . . 11 May,	1875
The king and queen visit Copenhagen and Berlin ; warmly received . . . . 26-28 May,	,,
Ministry under Dr. Forssell . . . 19 April,	1880
The king with the queen at Bournemouth for his health . . . . May,	1881
Ministry of count Posse defeated on the army bill, resigns . . . . 25 May,	1883
M. Thyselius appointed premier . 13 June,	,,
The crown prince made viceroy of Norway 19 March,	1884
M. O. R. Themptander appointed premier 16 May,	,,
The king visits Britain, July, Aug. 1884 ; at Constantinople . . . . . . 9 April,	1885
New ministry formed under baron Bildt, 6 Feb.	1888
Prince Oscar married to Miss Munck at Bournemouth, England ; his mother present 15 March,	,,
The king visits England . . . early June,	,,

KINGS OF SWEDEN (*previously Kings of Upsal*).

1001.	Olaf Schotkonung, or Olif Schœtkonung the Infant, is styled king, 1015.
1026.	Edmund Colbrenner.
1051.	Edmund Slemme.
1056.	Stenkill.
1066.	Halstan.
1090.	Ingo I. the Good.
1112.	Philip.
1118.	Ingo II.
1129.	Swerker or Snercher I.
1155.	St. Eric IX.
1161.	Charles VII. ; made prisoner by his successor.
1167.	Canute, son of Eric I.
1199.	Swerker or Suercher II. ; killed in battle.
1210.	Eric X.
1216.	John I.
1222.	Eric XI. the Stammerer.
1250.	Birger Jarl, regent.
,,	Waldemar I.
1275.	Magnus I. Ladulæs.
1290.	Birger II.
1319.	Magnus II. Smœk ; dethroned.
1350.	Eric XII.
1359.	Magnus restored ; deposed 1363.
1363.	Albert of Mecklenburg : his tyranny causes a revolt of his subjects, who invite Margaret of Denmark to the throne.
1389.	Margaret, queen of *Sweden and Norway* now also of *Denmark*, and Eric XIII.

1397.	[Union of Calmar, by which the three kingdoms are united under one sovereign.]
1412.	Eric XIII. governs alone ; deposed.
1440.	Christopher III.
1448.	Charles VIII. Canuteson, king of Sweden only.
1471.	[Interregnum.] Sten Sture, *Protector*.
1483.	John II. (I. of Denmark).
1502.	[Interregnum.]
1503.	Swante Sture, *Protector*.
1512.	Sten Sture, *Protector*.
1520.	Christiern, or Christian II., of Denmark, styled the "Nero of the North ;" deposed for his cruelties.
1523.	Gustavus I. Vasa ; by whose valour the Swedes are delivered from the Danish yoke.
1560.	Eric XIV., son ; dethroned and slain by
1569.	John III., brother.
1592.	Sigismund III., king of Poland, son ; disputes for the succession continued the whole of this reign.
1604.	Charles IX. brother of John III.
1611.	Gustavus II. Adolphus, the Great, son ; fell at the battle of Lutzen, 16 Nov. 1632.
1632.	[Interregnum.]
1633.	Christina, daughter of Gustavus. Resigned the crown to her cousin, 16 June, 1654 ; died at Rome in 1689.
1654.	Charles X. Gustavus, son of John Casimir, count palatine of the Rhine
1660.	Charles XI., son ; the arts and sciences flourished in this reign.
1697.	Charles XII., son ; styled the "Alexander," and the "Madman of the North ;" killed at Frederickshald, 11 Dec. 1718.
1718.	Ulrica Eleanora, sister, and her consort, Frederick I. Landgrave of Hesse Cassel. Ulrica relinquishes the crown, and in
1741.	Frederick reigned alone.
1751.	Adolphus Frederick of *Holstein Gottorp*, descended from the family of Vasa.
1771.	Gustavus III. Adolphus, son ; assassinated by count Ankerström at a masked ball, 16 March ; died 29 March, 1792.
1792.	Gustavus IV. Adolphus, son ; dethroned, and the government assumed by his uncle, the duke of Sudermania.
1809.	Charles XIII. duke of Sudermania. [Treaty of Kiel (1814) by which Norway falls under the sovereignty of Sweden.]
1818.	Charles (John) XIV. *Bernadotte*, the French prince of Ponte Corvo ; died 8 March, 1844.
1844.	Oscar I., son ; born 4 July, 1799 ; died 8 July, 1859.
1859.	Charles XV., son ; born 3 May, 1826 ; died 18 Sept. 1872 : a poet ; brave and impulsive ; much beloved.
1872.	Oscar II., brother ; born 21 Jan. 1829 ; married princess Sophia of Nassau, 6 June, 1857.

Heir: Gustavus, son, born 16 June, 1858 ; married to Victoria of Baden, 20 Sept. 1881.

SWEDENBORGIANS, or New Jerusalem Church, are those who adopt the theological teachings of Emanuel Swedenborg (born at Stockholm, 29 Jan. 1688 ; died in London, 29 March, 1772).

He claimed to have had his spiritual sight opened, and to have been introduced into heaven and hell by the Lord that he might disclose their true nature and the science of correspondences by which the internal sense of Scripture, which is the Word as it exists in the heavens, may be known to men : this he did in the *Arcana Cœlestia* and other works.

His disciples first meet as an organized body in London in 1788.

There were 70 churches in Great Britain in 1879.

Their belief is that the sole deity is centred in Jesus Christ, in whom is a trinity of essentials ; that salvation is effected by faith and works combined ; that as man's soul is a spiritual body he will never resume the material body ; that the Last Judgment was effected in the spiritual world during Swedenborg's lifetime ; and that the Lord's Second Coming has taken place through the revelation of a new system of truth from the inner sense of Scripture.

The Swedenborg Society instituted, 1810.
The Missionary and Tract Society of the New Church, 1821.
Centenary of the establishment of the New Jerusalem church celebrated in London, 13 Aug. 1883.

SWEET-BAY, *Laurus nobilis*, was brought to these realms from Italy before 1548. *Laurus indica*, or Royal Bay, was brought from Madeira in 1665. The Sweet-Fern bush, *Comptonia asplenifolia*, came from America, 1714. *Laurus aggregata*, or the Glaucous Laurel, came from China in 1806.

SWIMMING. Leander is said to have swum across the Hellespont, between Sestos and Abydos, about one mile; and Lord Byron, and lieut. Ekenhead did the same, 3 May, 1810. On 24 Aug., 1872, Mr. Johnson, styled the "hero of London-bridge," and swimming champion of the world, attempted to swim from Dover to Calais, but was prevented by cold. He was said to have swum seven miles in about sixty-five minutes.

Public swimming bath on the Thames opened, 6 July, 1875
Capt. Matt. Webb swam from Blackwall to Gravesend, 20 miles, in 4 hours 53 minutes, 3 July; and from Dover to Calais (22½ miles) in 23¾ hours, 24-25, Aug. 1875; drowned while attempting to cross the rapids of Niagara . . . 24 July, 1882
Agnes Beckwith, aged 14, swam from London bridge to Greenwich, 5 miles, in 1 h. 8 min. 1 Sept. 1875
Emily Parker, aged 15, swam from London bridge to Blackwall, 7 miles, in 1 h. 35 min. . 4 Sept. ,,
Mr. Cavill swam from Dover to Calais in 12 hours 20, 21 Aug. 1877
Miss Beckwith swam 30 continuous hours 7, 8 May, 1880
Taylor wins the amateur swimming championship of Great Britain at Birmingham . 19 Aug. 1882

Boyton's apparatus, see under *Life Boat*.

SWING. Between 1830 and 1833 many haystacks and barns were fired in the rural districts of England, and attributed to an imaginary person named "Swing." Many persons were caught and punished. The probable cause was disputes between the farmers and their deluded labourers.

SWISS GUARDS, Royal, in France, formed in 1616; massacred while defending the Tuileries, 10 Aug. 1792; re-organised Sept. 1815; defeated during the insurrection, 28 July, 1830; dismissed by Charles X. Aug. 1830.

SWITHIN'S DAY, ST., 15 July. St. Swithin lived in the 9th century; and, having been the preceptor to king Ethelwulf, was made bishop of Winchester in 852, and died 2 July, 862. The tradition states that it rained forty days in consequence of the proposed removal of his remains from the churchyard to the cathedral.

SWITZERLAND, the ancient Helvetia, was conquered by the Romans, 15 B.C.; and was successively subject to the Burgundians, Germans, and Franks. The canton of Schweitz was peopled by the Cimbrians, who, leaving their original habitation in Scandinavia, invaded Italy, and were defeated by the Roman general Marius; and fled into Helvetia, about 100 B.C. This canton has given name to the whole confederacy.—The present national council is elected every third year, at the rate of one member for 2000 persons. The revised federal constitution was voted 19 April, 1874.—Population, Dec. 1860, 2,507,170; 1870, 2,669,147; 1880, 2,846,102; June 1887, 2,957,527.
"The Swiss Confederation," by Sir F. O. Adams and C. D. Cunningham; published by Macmillan & Co. 1889

SWISS CONFEDERATION OF 1815.

Uri, 1307		Schaffhausen
Schweitz	first confederation.	Appenzell
Unterwalden		St. Gall
Zurich		Glaris
Bern		Zug
Lucerne		Freiburg

Solothurn		Tessins
Basle		Pays de Vaud
Grisons		Valais
Aargau		Neufchatel
Thurgau		Geneva

The Helvetians invading Gaul, severely defeated by Julius Cæsar . . . . B.C. 58
The Helvetians converted to Christianity by Irish missionaries . . . . A.D. 612
Helvetia ravaged by the Huns 909
Becomes subject to Germany 1032
Friburg built by Berthold IV. 1179
Berne built 1191
Tyranny of Gesler, heroism of William Tell, and revolt (demonstrated to be mythical), dated . 1306
Confederation against Austria; declaration of Swiss independence . . . . 4 Nov. 1307
A malignant fever carries off, in the canton of Basle, 1100 persons 1314
Form of government made perpetual . . . 1315
Leopold of Austria defeated at Morgarten, 15 Nov. 1335
Lucerne joins the confederacy 1335
The canton of Zurich joins and becomes head of the league 1350
Berne, Glaris, and Zug join 1351
Leopold II. of Austria defeated and slain at Sempach, 9 July, 1386
The Austrians defeated at Näfels, 9 April, 1388; make peace 1389
The Grisons league (see *Cadilee*) 1400
Second league of the Grisons 1424
The third league of the Grisons 1436
Battle of St. Jacobs on the Birs, near Basle (1600 Swiss resist 30,000 French, and are all killed, the enemy losing 10,000) . . . . . 26 Aug. 1444
The Swiss defeat Charles the Bold at Granson, 5 March; and at Morat . . . . . 22 June, 1476
And aid the duke of Lorraine at Nancy, where Charles is slain . . . . 5 Jan. 1477
Swiss soldiers first enter into the pay of France, under Louis XI. 1480
Fribourg and Soleure join; confederation formed . 1481
Maximilian I. emperor, acknowledges Swiss independence 1499
Schaffhausen and Basle join the union . . . 1501
The Swiss invade Milan and defeat the French at Novara . . . . 6 June, 1513
Defeated by them at Marignano . 13, 14 Sept. 1515
The Swiss confederacy acknowledged by France and other powers 1516
The Reformation begins at Basle; the bishop compelled to retire 1519
The Reformation adopted by some cantons; battle of Cappel, Zwingli killed and reformers defeated, 12 Oct. 1531
The Grison leagues join the Swiss confederacy as allies 1544
Appenzel joins the other Cantons ? 1597
Charles Emanuel of Savoy attempts Geneva by surprise, scales the walls, and penetrates the town, but in the end is defeated 1602
[This circumstance gave rise to an annual festival commemorative of their escape from tyranny.]
Independence of Switzerland recognised by the treaty of Westphalia (see *Westphalia*) . . 1648
Peace of Aargau, end of religious war . . Aug. 1712
[From this period until the French revolution the cantons enjoyed tranquillity, disturbed only by the changes arising out of their various constitutions.]
Alliance with France . . . . . 25 May, 1777
Strife in Geneva, between the aristocratic and democratic parties; France interferes 1781
1000 fugitive Genevese seek an asylum in Ireland (see *Geneva*) 1782
Swiss guards ordered to quit France . . . 1792
Helvetic confederation dissolved; its subjugation by France 1798
Helvetian republic formed 1799–1802
Switzerland the seat of war 1799–1802
The number of cantons increased to 19; the federal government restored; and a landamman appointed by France . . . . 12 May, ,,
Uri, Schweitz, and Underwald separate from the republic . . . . 13 July, ,,
Switzerland joins France with 6000 men 24 Aug. 1811
The allies entered Switzerland in the spring of . 1814

SWITZERLAND. 871 SYDNEY.

The number of cantons increased to 22, and the independence and neutrality of Switzerland secured by the treaty of Vienna . . . 1815
Revision of the constitution of the cantons . 1839
Law to make education independent of the clergy . 1830
leads to dissensions between the catholics and protestants 1840-4
Dispute about the convents of Aargau, 1844; to put education into the hands of the Jesuits, &c.; opposition of the protestant cantons . . . 1846
Lucerne, Uri, Schweitz, Unterwalden, Freiburg, Zug, and Valais (Roman catholic cantons), form a separate league (Sonderbund) to support education by the Jesuits, &c. . . . . . . ,,
Insurrection at Geneva against Jesuit teaching; a temporary provisional government established, 7 Oct. ,,
The diet declares the Sonderbund illegal, and dissolves it, 20 July; the seven cantons protest, 22 July; the diet orders the expulsion of the Jesuits, 3 Sept.; communal assemblies held to resist it, 26 Sept.; 3, 10 Oct.; appeal to arms 21 Oct. 1847
The diet prepares to repress the Sonderbund, 4 Nov.; Friburg surrenders, 14 Nov.; civil war; the Sonderbund defended by gen. H. Dufour, near Lucerne, 23 Nov.; end of the Sonderbund; it submits to the expulsion of the Jesuits, and the secularisation of monastic property . 29 Nov. ,,
New federal constitution . . . 12 Sept. 1848
Dispute about Neufchâtel (*which see*) . . 1857
Declaration of neutrality in the coming Italian war, 14 March, 1859
Mutiny and punishment of the Swiss mercenary troops at Naples; the confederation forbid foreign enlistment . . . . . July and Aug. ,,
Swiss government protests against the annexation of Savoy to France . . . . 15 March, 1860
150 Swiss attempt to enter Savoy; stopped by Genevese government . . . 30 March, ,,
M. Thorel, a Swiss, obtains a prize at the national shooting match at Wimbledon . . July, ,,
The government forbid the Swiss to enlist in foreign service without permission . . 30 July, ,,
Proposed European congress to preserve Swiss neutrality, put off . . . . July, ,,
Glarus destroyed by fire . . . 3 May, 1861
French troops occupy Vallée des Dappes, 28 Oct.; the Swiss announce the violation of their territory, 5 Nov. ,,
Treaty of France settles the question of the Vallée des Dappes by mutual cession of territory; no military works to be constructed on territory ceded; signed . . . . 8 Dec. 1862
Serious election riots at Geneva, with bloodshed, 22 Aug.; federal troops arrive . 23 Aug. 1864
Federal troops quit Geneva . . 11 Jan. 1865
International Social Science Congress meets at Berne . . . . 28 Aug. ,,
Revision of the constitution; deliberations begin 23 Oct. ,,
Nearly all the revised articles of the federal constitution rejected by the vote of the Swiss burgesses 14 Jan. 1866
J. J. Stehlen elected president . 1 July, 1867
Workmen's international congress at Lausanne, 2-7 Sept. ,,
Meeting of the federal assembly . 6-25 July, 1868
Queen Victoria visits Lucerne . Aug. Sept. ,,
International peace and liberty congress, at Geneva, 9-12 Sept. 1867; at Berne, 22-26 Sept. ,,
Neutrality in the Franco-Prussian War proclaimed, July, ,,
New constitution adopted by Zurich . 18 April, 1869
The French army under Clinchant (84,000), crosses the frontiers and is disarmed . . 1 Feb. 1871
The French soldiers interned at Zurich, and oppose German demonstrations . . 9-12 Mar. ,,
Extraordinary session of the federal assembly to revise the constitution . . . 6 Nov. ,,
Plebiscite respecting a new constitution, re-organizing the army, and promoting uniform education, &c. rejected by majority of 4967 out of 509,921 . . . . . . 12 May, 1872
M. Favre engaged to construct a tunnel through St. Gothard in 8 years, for 2,000,000*l.* . 8 Aug. ,,
The papal nuncio, Mermillod, expelled . 16 Jan. 1873
Revised federal constitution voted (321,370 for, 177,800 against) . . . . . 19 April, 1874
Swiss national catholic church constituted June, 1874
19 Catholic priests deprived for refusal to take constitutional oath . . . . 5 Sept. ,,
International postal congress at Berne, 15 Sept.; protocol signed (see *postal convention*) 9 Oct. ,,
Civil marriage law and registration adopted by universal suffrage (212,854—204,700) . 23 May, 1875
President of the national council for three years, J. Philippin, elected . . . . 6 June, 1877
Continued deficit in revenue, announced 16 March, 1878
Death of James Fazy, eminent statesman, 6 Nov. ,,
National voting for St. Gothard, railway and tunnel (161,000 majority) . . . . 19 Jan. 1879
Suicide of Herr Anderwert, the president elect, 27 Dec. 1880
Opening of St. Gothard railway from Milan to Lucerne . . . . . . 20, 21 May, 1882
Invasion of the salvation army (*which see*), autumn, 1884, much resisted at Berne, Geneva, &c. Jan. *et seq.* 1883
The watch-tool making village, Vallorbes, almost destroyed by fire . . . . 7 April, ,,
National exhibition at Zurich . 1 May—27 Dec. ,,
M. Schenck elected president . . Dec. 1884
Village of Mulligan, Aargau, destroyed by fire, 23 April, 1885
Fifth centenary of the battle of Sempach (9 July, 1386) celebrated . . . . . 5 July, 1886
Grand funeral of Mr. Hertenstein, the president at Berne, who died after a surgical operation, 30 Nov.; vice-president Bernard Hammer elected president . . . . . 13 Dec. 1888
The German government protests against the expulsion of its police officer, Wohlgemuth, from Switzerland, May; the great powers protest against the asylum given to political criminals; the Swiss propose new legal measures, June; the Swiss government repels the charge, but prepares legal measures for redress, June, 1889
The Swiss government in a reply note to Berlin, stands firm . . . . . 14 July, ,,

SWORDS were formed of iron taken from a mountain by the Chinese, 1879 B.C.—*Univ. Hist.* The Roman swords were from 20 to 30 inches long. The broadsword and scimitar are of modern adoption. Damascus steel swords were most prized; the next the sword of Ferrara steel. The Scotch Highlanders, from the artificer Andrea di Ferrara, called their swords *Andrew Ferraras*. The large sword shown at Dumbarton castle as Wallace's is asserted to be one of Edward IVth's (1872). The broadsword was forbidden to be worn in Edinburgh in 1724.

SYBARIS, a Greek colony in S. Italy, founded about 720 B.C.; destroyed by the Crotonians about 510 B.C. The people were greatly addicted to luxury; hence the term Sybarite.
Archæological investigations disclosed evidences of the existence of a great city and civilization anterior to the Greek invasion . . . 1888

SYCAMORE, or SYCOMORE TREE, In Mrs. Jameson's "Memoirs of Female Sovereigns" we are told that Mary queen of Scots brought over from France a little sycamore tree, which she planted in the garden at Holyrood, and that from this have sprung all the beautiful groves of sycamore now to be seen in Scotland.

SYDNEY, capital of New South Wales; founded by governor Phillip, on a cove on Port Jackson, 26 Jan. 1788, as a British settlement for the colony of convicts originally intended for Botany bay. It was named after lord Sydney, secretary for the colonies. Population 1888, 357,856. See *Australia, New South Wales, Convicts.*

A legislative council first held . 13 July, 1829
Sydney erected into a bishopric (afterwards an archbishopric) 1836
Lit with gas, the first place so lit in Australia, May, 1841
Bishop of Australia made bishop of Sydney and metropolitan 1847
University founded 1852

Roman Catholic cathedral burnt, and valuable property destroyed . . . . . 29 June, 1865
Visited by the duke of Edinburgh . . Feb. 1868
At Port Jackson he narrowly escaped assassination; O'Farrell, a Fenian, who shot him in the back on 12 March, was convicted on 31 March, and executed 21 April, ,,
The duke sailed for England 4 April, and arrived 26 June, ,,
New cathedral consecrated . . . . 30 Nov. ,,
Foundation of capt. Cook's monument laid by the duke of Edinburgh . . . 28 March, 1869
A conference of delegates from the Australian colonies met here for customs, postal and railway purposes, without effect . . . . Jan. 1873
Exhibitions opened here, April, 1873, and 11 April, 1874
Captain Cook's statue uncovered . . 2 Feb. 1878
International exhibition opened by the governor, lord A. Loftus . . . . 17 Sept. 1879
Direct railway to Melbourne completed . June, 1883
Canon Barry consecrated bishop of Sydney and metropolitan 1 Jan. 1884; resigns, . . Dec. 1888
Meetings of loyalists opposing the home rule delegates. . . . . . summer 1889
Death at Sydney of Mr. J. B. Watson (aged 64) termed the Australian "Quartz Reef King," said to have left to his family about 30,000,000*l*. the results of gold digging at Bendigo, Victoria, and other places and of railway and other speculations . . . . . about 12 July, ,,

SYLLABUS OF ERRORS in modern times. 80 paragraphs divided into 10 chapters, issued by pope Pius IX., with an encyclical letter, 8 Dec. 1864. It condemned heresy, modern philosophy, and liberalism in politics; was forbidden to be read in French churches, and was generally opposed, but was adopted by the council at Rome 1870.

SYMPHONIES. Short pieces of instrumental music between songs in operas; early in the 17th century. These were gradually developed by the great masters, such as Lulli, into independent pieces; of these the symphonies of Corelli, Handel, Mozart, Haydn, and Beethoven are eminent examples.

SYMPHONION, an improved form of the musical box capable of performing many more tunes, invented by Mr. Ellis Parr, 1887.

SYMPIESOMETER, a species of barometer invented by Adie of Edinburgh in 1819.

SYNAGOGUE (literally an assembly), a congregation of the Jews, and the place where such assembly is held for religious purposes. When these meetings were first held is uncertain; some refer them to the times after the Babylonish captivity. In Jerusalem were 480 synagogues. In 1851 there were in London 10 synagogues, in England and Wales, 53. A magnificent synagogue was consecrated at Berlin, 5 Sept. 1866; see *Jews*.

SYNDICATE, originally a body of syndics, officers of a government or any ruling body; the term is now frequently used as synonymous with a company or body of trustees, 1888. See *Trusts*.

SYNOD. The first general synods were called by emperors, and afterwards by Christian princes; but the pope ultimately usurped this power, one of his legates usually presiding; see *Councils*. The first national synod held in England was at Hertford, 673; the last was held by cardinal Pole in 1555. Made unlawful to hold synods but by royal authority, 25 Henry VIII. 1533; see *Dort*, and *Thurles*.

SYNONYM, a word having the same or nearly the same meaning as another, as valour, courage. Books of Greek and Latin synonyms were early compiled. G. Crabbe's dictionary appeared, 1816; Dr. P. M. Roget's excellent "Thesaurus of English Words and Phrases," 1852.

SYPHILIS, a disease said to have been introduced into Europe at the siege of Naples, 1495; but was probably known to the ancients.

SYRACUSE, S. E. Sicily, founded by Archias, 734 B.C.; 732 B.C. *Eusebius*; 749 B.C. *Univ. Hist.*; see *Sicily*.

Gelon becomes supreme . . . . . B.C.	485
Succeeded by Hiero	478
Republic established	467
Becomes predominant in Sicily . . .	453
Athenian expedition against Syracuse, under Niclas	415
Gylippus the Lacedæmonian succours Syracuse; defeats Niclas	413
Government of Dionysius the elder, 406: he receives Plato well	389
Dionysius, the younger, succeeds . . .	367
Opposed by Dion, 361; who is banished, and Plato, who endeavoured to reconcile them, is sold for a slave	360
Dion returns with a Greek army and fleet, and expels Dionysius, 356; rules Syracuse, 355; assassinated by Calippus	353
Dionysius recovers his authority, 347; but is banished to Corinth by Timoleon, 343; who governs well till his death	337
Agathocles usurps power, 317; defeated at Himera	310
He is poisoned by Hicetas, and the republic restored	289
Hiero, prætor of Syracuse, 275; elected king, 270; rules in peace till his death, 216; Hieronymus, his grandson, succeeds, 216; murdered . .	214
Syracuse declares against Rome, 215; besieged by Marcellus, 214, and taken; Archimedes, the illustrious mathematician, slain	212
Syracuse taken by the Saracens . . . A.D.	669
Retaken by count Roger, the Norman . .	1088
Destroyed by earthquakes in 1542, Jan. 1693; and nearly destroyed . . . . . 6 Aug.	1757
In the insurrection, Syracuse surrendered to the Neapolitan troops . . . . 8 April,	1849

SYREN, see *Sirene*.

SYRIA. The capital was originally Damascus; but after the battle of Ipsus, Seleucus founded Antioch.

Alliance of David king of Israel and Hiram king of Syria . . . . B.C.	1049
Syria conquered by David	1040
Liberated by Rezin	980
Benhadad, king of Syria, makes war on the Jews	898
Benhadad II. reigns . . . . . about	830
Syria subjugated by Tiglath-pileser, king of Assyria	740
Syria conquered by Cyrus	537
And by Alexander	333
Seleucus Nicator enters Babylon . . .	312
Æra of the Seleucidæ (*which see*)	
Great battle of Ipsus; death of Antigonus, defeated by Ptolemy, Seleucus, and Lysimachus . .	301
The city of Antioch founded	299
Antiochus, son of Seleucus, falling in love with his father's queen, Stratonice, he pines away nearly to death; but the secret being discovered, she is divorced by the father, and married by the son .	297
Battle of Cyropedium; Lysimachus slain by Seleucus	281
Seleucus foully assassinated by Cerauunus; Antiochus I. king	280
Antiochus I. (*Soter*, or Saviour,) defeats the Gauls .	275
Antiochus II. surnamed by the Milesians *Theos* (God) king	261
Poisoned by Laodice	246
Seleucus II. (king, 246) makes a treaty of alliance with Smyrna and Magnesia	243
Seleucus III. *Ceraunus* (or Thunder), king . .	226
Antiochus III. the Great (king, 223), conquers Palestine, but is totally defeated at Raphia . .	217
Again conquers Palestine, 198; but gives it to Ptolemy	193
Enters Greece, 192; defeated by the Romans at Thermopylæ, 191; and at Magnesia . .	190
Makes peace with the Romans, giving up to them Asia Minor	188
Seleucus Philopator, king.	187
Antiochus IV. king, who assumes the title of *Theos-Epiphanes*, or the Illustrious God . . .	175

SYRIA.

He sends Apollonius into Judea; Jerusalem is taken; the temple pillaged; 40,000 inhabitants destroyed, and 40,000 more sold as slaves . B.C.	168
Antiochus V. Eupator (king, 164), murdered by Demetrius Soter, who seizes the throne . . .	162
Demetrius is defeated and slain by his successor Alexander Bala, 150; who is also defeated and slain by Demetrius Nicator	146
Antiochus VI. Sidetes (son of Demetrius Soter) rules during the captivity of his brother Demetrius Nicator (after slaying the usurper Trypho) .	137
Antiochus grants peace to the Jews, and placates the Romans, 133; invades Parthia, 129; and is defeated and slain	128
Demetrius Nicator restored	,,
Cleopatra, the queen, murders her son Seleucus with her own hand	124
Her son Antiochus VII. Grypus (king, 125), whom she attempts to poison; but he compels his mother to swallow the deadly draught herself .	123
Reign of Antiochus VIII. Cyzicenus at Damascus, and of Grypus at Antioch	111
Seleucus, king	95
Antiochus IX. Eusebes, king	94
Dethroned by Philip	85
Tigranes, king of Armenia, acquires Syria . .	83
Antiochus X. Asiaticus, solicits the aid of the Romans	75
Defeat of Tigranes by Lucullus, 69; he submits to Pompey, who enters Syria, and dethrones Antiochus Asiaticus	65
Syria made a Roman province	63
Syria invaded by the Parthians . . . A.D.	162
By the Persians	256
Violent earthquakes	341
Invaded by the Saracens, 497, 502, 529; by the Persians	607
Conquered by the Saracens	638
Conquest of Syria by the Fatimite caliphs . .	970
Revolt of the emirs of Damascus . . .	1067
The emirs of Aleppo revolt	1068
The crusades commence (see *Crusades*) . .	1095
Desolated by the Crusades (which see) . .	1096-1272
Noureddin conquers Syria	1166
Saladin dethrones the Fatimite dynasty . .	1171
The Tartars overrun all Syria	1259
The sultans of Egypt expel the Crusaders . .	1291
Syria overrun by Tamerlane	1400
Syria and Egypt conquered by the Turks . .	1516-17
Syria continued in possession of the Turks till the invasion by the French, 1799; Bonaparte overruns the country, Gaza and Jaffa taken March,	1799
Siege of Acre begun by the French, 16 March; raised 20 May,	,,
Bonaparte returns to France from Egypt 23 Aug.	,,
Egypt and Syria evacuated by the French army, 10 Sept.	1801
Mehemet Ali attacks and captures Acre, and overruns the whole of Syria	1831
Ibrahim Pacha, his son, defeats the army of the grand signior at Konieh . . . 21 Dec.	1832
Numerous battles and conflicts follow with various success; the European powers intervene, and peace is made . . . . . 6 May,	1833
The war renewed, May; Ibrahim defeats the Turks at Nezib . . . . . . 24 June,	1839
The Turkish fleet deserts to Mehemet Ali, and arrives at Alexandria . . . 14 July,	,,
The five powers unite to support the Porte July,	,,
Death of lady Hester Stanhope . . 23 June,	1840
Treaty of London (not signed by offended France), 15 July,	,,
Capture of Sidon (see *Sidon*) . . . 27 Sept.	,,
Fall of Beyrout (see *Beyrout*) . . . 10 Oct.	,,
Fall of Acre (see *Acre*) . . . . 3 Nov.	,,
Long negotiations; the sultan grants hereditary rights to Mehemet, who gives up Syria . Jan.	1841
The Druses said to have destroyed 151 Christian villages and killed 1000 persons (see *Druses*), 29 May to 1 July,	1860
The Mahometans massacre Christians at Damascus: about 3300 slain; many saved by Abd-el-Kader, 9 July, &c.	,,
The English and French government intervene; a convention signed at Paris; 12,000 men to be sent by France . . . . . . 3 Aug.	,,
Vigour of Fuad Pacha; he punishes the Mahometans implicated in the massacres at Damascus very severely; 167 of all ranks, including the governor, executed . . . 20 Aug., *et seq.*	,,
4000 French soldiers, under general Hautpoul, land at Beyrout . . . . . . 22 Aug.	,,
Lord Dufferin, the British commissioner in Syria, arrives at Damascus . . . . 6 Sept.	,,
The French and Turks advance against Lebanon; 14 emirs surrendered . . . . Oct.	,,
Pacification of the country effected . . Nov.	,,
The French occupation ceases . . 5 June,	1861
Prince of Wales visits Syria . . . April,	1862
Insurrection of Joseph Karam, Maronite, in Lebanon; suppressed . . . . March,	1866
Another suppressed; Karam flies to Algeria, 31 Jan.	1867
Midhat Pasha appointed governor-general to inaugurate reforms, Nov. 1878; experiences great difficulty, Oct.; resigns, but continues, Oct. 1879-June,	1880
Hamed Pasha, governor of Smyrna, and Midhat Pasha change places . . . . Aug.	,,
Midhat Pasha, charged with complicity in the murder of the sultan Abdul Aziz, surrenders (see *Turkey*, 1881) . . . about 17 May,	1881

SYSTON, see under *Libraries*.

SZEGEDIN (Hungary), on the Theiss at its junction with the Maros, the seat of revolutionary government, 1849. Rebuilt under superintendence of Ludwig Tisza. Grand festival, the emperor present, 16 Oct. 1883. See *Inundations*, 1879 and 1887.

T.

TABERNACLE, the Holy Place of the Israelites, till the erection of Solomon's temple, was constructed by Divine direction, 1491 B.C. The tabernacle set up at Shiloh by Joshua, 1444 B.C. was replaced by the temple erected by Solomon, 1004 B.C. The chapel erected for George Whitefield in Moorfields in 1741, being of a temporary nature, received the name of Tabernacle, which was afterwards given to their chapels by the Calvinistic Methodists. Whitefield's Tabernacle in Tottenham-court-road was erected in 1756, and enlarged in 1760. His lease expired in 1828; and the chapel was opened by the Independents in 1830. A large metropolitan tabernacle, erected for the ministrations of Mr. C. H. Spurgeon, a Baptist, near the "Elephant and Castle," Kennington-road, Surrey, was opened on 31 March, 1861.

TABINET, see *Poplin*.

TABLES, see *Decemvirs*.

TABLET, Roman Catholic weekly paper, established 1840.

TABLE TURNING. This delusion, which came from America, and was popular in 1853, was attributed by Faraday and others to involuntary mechanical action. See *Spirit-Rapping*.

TABOR, in Bohemia, was founded by Ziska in 1420, and became a chief seat of the Hussites; see *Hussites*.

TADMOR, see *Palmyra*.

TAEPINGS, see *China*, 1851, note.

TAFFETY, an early species of silken manufacture, more prized formerly than now, woven very smooth and glossy. It was worn by our elder queens, and was first made in England by John Tyce, of Shoreditch, London, 41 Eliz. 1598. —*Stow's Chron.*

TAGLIACOZZO, in the Abruzzi mountains, S. Italy, where, on 23 Aug. 1268, Charles of Anjou, the usurping king of Naples, defeated and made prisoner the rightful monarch, young Conradin (the last of the Hohenstaufens, and grandson of the emperor Frederick II.), who had been invited into Italy by the Ghibelline or Imperial party; their opponents, the Guelfs, or papal party, supporting Charles. Conradin was beheaded, 29 Oct. following.

TAGLIAMENTO, a river in Lombardy, N. Italy, near which the Austrians, under the archduke Charles, were defeated by Bonaparte, 16 March, 1797.

TAHERITES, a dynasty of Persia, 813-872.

TAHITI. The French abbreviated name for Otaheite; see *Otaheite*.

TAILLEBOURG (W. France). Near here Henry III. of England was defeated and nearly captured by Louis IX. of France, 20 July, 1242.

TAKU FORTS, China, taken by the allies, 21 Aug. 1860.

TALAVERA DE LA REYNA (central Spain), was taken from the Mahometans by Ordoño, king of Leon, 913. Here a battle was fought 27, 28 July, 1809, between the united British and Spanish armies under sir Arthur Wellesley, and the French army commanded by marshals Victor and Sebastiani. After a conflict on the 27th, both armies remained on the field during the night, and the French at break of day renewed the attack, and were again repulsed by the British with great slaughter. At noon Victor charged the whole British line, was repulsed at all points, and retreated with a heavy loss. As Soult, Ney, and Mortier were in the rear, the British retired after the victory.

TALBOTYPE, see *Photography*.

"TALISMAN" affair, see *Peru*, 1874-6.

TALKING-MACHINE, see *Automatons*.

TALLY OFFICE in the Exchequer took its name from the French word *tailler*, to cut. A tally is a piece of wood written upon both sides, containing an acquittance for money received; which, being cloven asunder by an officer of the exchequer, one part, called the stock, was delivered to the person who paid, or lent, money to the government; and the other part, called the counter-stock, or counter-foil, remained in the office, to be kept till called for, and joined with the stock. This manner of striking tallies is very ancient.—*Beatson*. The practice was ordered to be discontinued in 1782. See *Exchequer*. On 16 Oct. 1834, the houses of parliament were burnt down by too many of these tallies being used in heating the stoves in the house of lords.

TALMUD (from *lamad*, to teach), the compendium of ancient Jewish oral or unwritten law, as distinguished from the Pentateuch, or written law; its origin is coeval with the return from the Babylonish captivity, 536 B.C. Its compilation in Hebrew was begun by the Scribes, and by their successors the work was carried on till 220 B.C. It is composed in prose and poetry, and contains two elements, legal and legendary. The morality resembles that of the New Testament, and the philosophy is rather Platonic than Aristotelian.
The Mischna, comprising the work of the rabbis, termed Thanaim, was compiled by Jehuda Hanassi, in the middle of the second century, A.D., and forms the Jerusalem Talmud, written at Tiberias, in Palestine, about 230. The Babylonian Talmud contains also the Gemera or Ghemara, the work of the rabbis termed Amoraim, criticisms and comments on the Mischna. The part named *Halacha*, is dogmatic, legal, and doctrinal; the *Agada*, is illustrative, narrative, and legendary.
After being almost universally condemned, and the MSS. often burnt, the defence of the Talmud was undertaken by the German reformer Reuchlin, in the 16th century, and between 1520 and 1523, the "Talmud Babylonicum," in 12 vols. fol., and the "Talmud Hierosolytanum," in one vol. fol., were printed at Venice. A discourse on the Talmud was given at the Royal Institution, 15 May, 1868, by Mr. Emanuel Deutsch, whose article in the "Quarterly Review," Oct. 1867, had attracted much attention.
Vol. I. of the first English translation of the Jerusalem Talmud by Dr. Moïse Schwab, appeared in 1885; had published part of a French translation.

TAMANIEB, or **TAMASI**, battle of, 13 March, 1884; see *Soudan*.

TAMATAVE, see *Madagascar*, 1883.

TAMMANY FRAUDS, see *New York*, 1871.

TANAGRA (Bœotia). Here the Spartans ated the Athenians 457 B.C., but were defeated hem in 456 and in 426, when Agis II. headed Spartans and Nicias the Athenians.

ANCRED'S CHARITIES. Valuable extions for students at Cambridge are maintained Christopher Tancred's endowment, 1721; established by chancery, 1757.

ANDY ARREST. James Napper Tandy osed a plan of reform in 1791. In the French edition against Ireland he acted as a general, . 1798. After its failure he fled to Hamburg, was there delivered up to the English, 24 Nov.; which Bonaparte declared war upon Hamburg, ct. 1799. Tandy was liberated after the peace miens in 1802.

ANGIER (Morocco, N. W. Africa), besieged rince Ferdinand of Portugal, who was beaten taken prisoner, 1437. It was conquered by nso V. of Portugal in 1471, and given as a dower rincess Catherine, on her marriage with Charles of England, 1662; who, in 1683, caused the ks to be blown up, and the place abandoned. giers afterwards became a piratical station.

ANISTRY (in Ireland), the equal division of ls, after the decease of the owner, amongst his , legitimate or illegitimate. If one of the sons , his son did not inherit, but a new division was e by the tanist or chief. Abolished 1604. ics.

ANJORE (W. India). About 1678, Vencajee, ahratta chief, brother of the great Sevajee, e himself rajah. In 1749 a British expedition avoured to restore a deposed rajah without ess; the reigning prince bought them off by the ion of territories. Much intervention ensued. 1799 the company obtained possession of the itry, engaging to support the rajah with nominal iority. The last is said to have died in 1855.

ANNENBERG (E. Prussia). Here Ladis- V. Jagellon of Poland defeated the Teutonic ;hts with great slaughter, the grand master being ng the slain, 15 July, 1410. The order never vered from this calamity.

A-NING leather with the bark of trees was practised. Tan was introduced into Great ain from Holland by William III. for raising ge trees about 1689. It was discontinued until it 1719, when bananas were first brought into land. Great improvements have been recently e in tanning by means of chemical knowledge.

ANTALUM, a rare metal, discovered in an rican mineral by Hatchett, in 1801, and named im columbium; and in a Swedish mineral by berg, who gave it its present name. Wollaston ted out the identity of the two metals in 1809; Berzelius prepared pure metallic tantalum in . In 1846 Rose discovered that tantalum was y a mixture of three metals, which he named alum, niobium, and pelopium.—*Gmelin.*

ANZIMAT, see *Turkey,* 1839-44.

APESTRY. An art of weaving borrowed i the Saracens, and hence its original workers in ace were called *Sarazinois.* The invention of stry hangings belongs [the date is not mened] to the Netherlands.—*Guicciardini.* Manured in France under Henry IV. by artists ted from Flanders, 1606. The art was brought England by William Sheldon; and the first iufactory of it was established at Mortlake by Francis Crane, 17 James I. 1619.—*Salmon.*

Under Louis XIV. the art of tapestry was much improved in France; see *Gobelin Tapestry.* Very early instances of making tapestry are mentioned by the ancient poets, and also in Scripture; so that the Saracens' manufacture is a revival of the art. For the tapestry said to have been wrought by Matilda, queen of England, see *Bayeux Tapestry.*
Tapestry manufactory established at Windsor by Mr. H. Henry, supported by the royal family, and others; exhibition opened in the town-hall, 6 December, 1878.
Manufacture revived by Messrs. Trollope of London, 1882-3

TAPIR, the American water-hog, a pachydermatous animal. The first born in England at Zoological Gardens, London, 12 Feb. 1882.

TAR. The chemist Becher first proposed to make tar from pit-coal—the earl of Dundonald's patent, 1781. The mineral tar was discovered at Coalbrookdale, Shropshire, 1779; and in Scotland, Oct. 1792. Tar-water was first recommended for its medicinal virtues by the good Dr. Berkeley, bishop of Cloyne, about 1744. From benzole, discovered in coal-tar, many brilliant dyes are now produced; see *Aniline.*

TARA, a hill in Meath, Ireland, where the early kings of Ireland were inaugurated. Near here, on 26 May, 1798, the royalist troops, 400 strong, defeated the insurgent Irish (4000 men), 500 killed. On 15 Aug. 1843, Daniel O'Connell held a monster meeting here (250,000 persons said to have been assembled).

TARBES (S. France, near the Pyrenees), capital of Bigorre, the property of the English kings in the middle ages. The French, under Soult, were forced from their position at Tarbes, with considerable loss, by the British army commanded by Wellington, 20 March, 1814. See *Toulouse.*

TARENTUM (now *Taranto,* S. Italy), was founded by the Greek Phalantus, B.C. 708. The people of Tarentum assisted by Pyrrhus, king of Epirus, supported a war which had been undertaken B.C. 281 by the Romans, to avenge the insults the Tarentines had offered to their ships when near their harbours; it was terminated after ten years; 300,000 prisoners were taken, and Tarentum became subject to Rome. Except the citadel, Tarentum was captured by the Carthaginians, 212, but recovered by Fabius, 209 B.C. Tarentum has shared in the revolutions of Southern Italy, and only ruins remain.

TARGUMS or EXPLANATIONS, names given to certain ancient Chaldee paraphrases of the Old Testament. The most remarkable are those of Onkelos, Jonathan-ben-Uzziel, and Joseph the Blind. The Targum of Onkelos is referred by some writers to the first century A.D.

TARIFA (S. Spain), the ancient Joza and Julia Traducta, where Muza landed when invading Spain, 712. It was taken from the Moors by Sancho IV. of Castile, 1291 or 1292; and was relieved, when besieged by them, after a great victory over the kings of Morocco and Granada, by Alfonso XI. of Castile and Alfonso IV. of Portugal, 28 or 30 Oct. 1340. The conflict is called the battle of Salado, having been fought on the banks of that river. Tarifa was taken by the French in 1823.

TARIFF (said to have been derived from Tarifa, where duties were formerly collected), a book of duties charged on goods exported or imported. Our tariff in 1840 comprised 1042 articles; the number was reduced (by sir Robert Peel) in 1845 and 1847. It comprised 439 articles in 1857; this number was greatly reduced in 1860.

TARPEIAN ROCK (Rome), owed its name to the tradition that Tarpeia, daughter of the keeper of the Roman citadel, was here crushed to death by the shields cast on her by the Sabines, whom she treacherously admitted, having bargained for the gift of what they wore on their left arms, meaning their bracelets; about 750 B.C.

TARRAGONA (N.E. Spain), occupied as a naval station by the British before their capture of Gibraltar in 1704. It was stormed and sacked by the French under Suchet, 29 Jan. 1811, and the inhabitants put to the sword.

TARTAN or **HIGHLAND PLAID**, the dress of the Scottish Highlanders, said to have been derived from the ancient Gauls, or Celtæ, the *Galli non braccati*.

TARTARIC ACID is said to have been the first discovery of the eminent chemist, Scheele, who procured it in a separate state by boiling tar with lime, and in decomposing the tartrate of lime thus formed by means of sulphuric acid, about 1770. In 1859 baron Liebig formed tartaric acid from other sources.

TARTARY (Asia). The Tatars, or Tartars, or Mongols, or Moguls, were known in antiquity as Scythians. During the decline of the Roman empire, these tribes began to seek more fertile regions; and the first who reached the frontier of Italy were the Huns, the ancestors of the modern Mongols. The first acknowledged sovereign of this vast country was the famous Genghis Khan. His empire, by the conquest of China, Persia, and all central Asia (1206-27), became one of the most formidable ever established; but it was split into parts in a few reigns. Timur, or Tamerlane, again conquered Persia, broke the power of the Turks in Asia Minor (1370-1400), and founded the Mogul dynasty in India, which began with Baber in 1525, and formed the most splendid court in Asia till the close of the 18th century; see *Golden Horde*. The Calmucks, a branch of the Tartars, expelled from China, settled on the banks of the Volga in 1672, but returned in 1771, and thousands perished on the journey.

TASIMETER, see *Micro-tasimeter*.

TASMANIA, the name now given to the British settlement in Van Diemen's Land (*which see*).

TATTERSALL'S, see *Races*.

TAUNTON (Somerset), was taken by Perkin Warbeck, Sept. 1497; and here he was surrendered to Henry VII. 5 Oct. following. The duke of Monmouth was proclaimed king at Taunton, 20 June, 1685; and it was the scene of the "bloody assize" held by Jeffreys upon the rebels in August.

TAVERNS may be traced to the 13th century. "In the raigne of king Edward the Third, *only three taverns* were allowed in London: one in Chepe, one in Walbrok, and the other in Lombard-street."—*Spelman*. The *Boar's Head*, in East-cheap, existed in the reign of Henry IV., and was the rendezvous of prince Henry and his dissolute companions. Shakspeare mentions it as the residence of Mrs. Quickly, and the scene of Falstaff's merriment.—*Shakspeare*, "Henry IV." The *White Hart*, Bishopsgate, established in 1480, was rebuilt in 1829. Taverns were licensed in 1752.

Taverns were restricted by 7 Edward VI. 1552-3, to 40 in London, 3 in York, 4 in Norwich, 3 in Westminster, 6 in Bristol, 3 in Lincoln, 4 in Hull, 3 in Shrewsbury, 4 in Exeter, 3 in Salisbury, 4 in Gloucester, 4 in Chester, 3 in Hereford, 3 in Worcester, 3 in Southampton, 4 in Canterbury, 3 in Ipswich, 3 in Winchester, 3 in Oxford, 4 in Cambridge, 3 in C Tyne.

TAXES were levie legislator, 540 B.C. Th an Attic talent of silv Darius, the son of Hy assessment, which wa subjects styled him, by Trader, 480 B.C.—D' first introduced into E and he raised them a kind, as in wool, leath country, continued till 1377.—*Camden*; see

TAXES ON KNOWLI Duty, *Newspaper Stam* exertions in repealing sented to Mr. T. Miln sessed taxes now inclu *property* and *income t* Act, 43 & 44 Vict. c. below). Mr. Stephen tion and Taxes in Er Receipts from general t

Assessed Taxes.

1800	£3,468,1
1805	4,508,7
1810	6,233,1
1815	6,524,7
1820	6,311,3
1825	5,176,7
1830	5,013,4
1835	3,733,9
1840	3,866,4

Assessed Tax

1851 (to Jan. 5)	.
1855 (year ending March	
1860 ,, ,,	
1865 ,, ,,	.
1866 ,, ,,	
1867 ,, ,,	
1868 ,, ,,	
1869 ,, ,,	
1870 ,, ,,	
1871	{ Land tax and l
1872	{ see L
1873	.
1874	.
1875	.
1876	.
1877	.
1878	.
1879	.
1880	.
1883	.
1884	.
1886	.
1888	.

TAY BRIDGE a across the Tay; act pa 1871; Mr. De Bergue ceeded by Messrs. Hopl borough. Engineer, much injured by a g 30 Aug.; tried, 25 S 1878. Length, 10,61 spans, some above 90 said to be 350,000*l*. construction.

The bridge was partly d N. British mail-train w of about 3,000 feet was persons perished; abou 46 bodies were recovered Liberal collections were loss of relatives. After the Board of Trade i in the report, stated " badly designed, badly maintained"

. . 30 Oct. 1880
ldge approved, May, 1881
. . . . Jan. 1882
. . . . Dec. 1885
. . 20 June. 1887

r in the Crimea. On
he allied army at this
Russians under prince
lsed with the loss of
d 600 prisoners. The
erne by two French
Herbillon. The loss of
200 of these were from
ich behaved with great
nd of general La Mar-
Read, and the Sardinian
killed. The object of
ebastopol, then closely
French.

pe by the Dutch, 1610.
en used in England on
1657, and sold for 6*l*.
Price of inferior kinds,
n 1871, 1*s*. 10*d*. For

rst "cup of tea."
25 Sept. 1660
every gallon of tea
) . . . . . . ,,
nport it 1669
by lord Ossory and
: and being admired
ported from thence,
ings per pound, till
ok up the trade.—

. 1715
20*s*.; of green, 12*s*.
. . . . 1728
erica, 1767: this tax
f 17 chests at New
Dec. 1773, and ulti-
ar (see *Boston*).
nd . . about 1768
gn-boards fixed up,
. . . . Aug. 1779
he duty on tea from
ndows in lieu, June, 1784
sloe, liquorice, and
mixed with Chinese
he *House of Commons*, 1818
ole civilised world,
about 22,000,000 of
nsumption in Great
idence in *House of*
. . . . 1830
the abolition of the
ast India Company
. . . 19 Aug. 1834
the duty was 96 and
r pound . . . 1836
port of tea in 1850
d the amount was
. . . . in 1852
1855 . . and 1856
) . . . April, 1857
ed from 2*s*. 2½*d*. to
per pound, 1 June, 1865
. . . . 1869
. . . . 1871
1875-6; 4,002,210*l*.
513,311*l*. . . 1887-8

TO ENGLAND.

30 . . .	lb 30,544,404
35 . . .	44,360,550
40 . . .	38,068,555
45 . . .	44,193,433
50 *govt. retns.*	90,512,384
56 . . .	86,200,414
58 . . .	75,432,535
61 . . .	96,577,383
64 . . .	124,359,243

1866	lb 139,610,044	1877	lb 187,515,284
1867	128,028,726	1878	204,872,899
1868	154,845,863	1879	184,076,472
1869	139,223,298	1880	206,971,570
1870	141,020,767	1881	209,801,522
1871	169,898,303	1882	210,663,133
1872	184,927,128	1883	222,262,431
1873	163,765,269	1884	213,877,759
1874	162,782,810	1885	212,143,820
1875	197,505,316	1886	230,669,292
1876	185,536,371	1887	221,841,490

The importation of tea grown in India has very greatly increased.

TEACHERS, NATIONAL UNION OF ELEMENTARY (about 20,000 certificated and 30,000 pupil teachers), held their fourth annual conference, April 1874. The *Teachers' Association* held their 3rd annual conference at University College, London, 9 Jan. 1878. The Teachers' Guild held its first public meeting, Mr. Mundella in the chair, 23 Jan. 1884.

TEACHING, see *Apostles* and *University*.

"TEARLESS VICTORY," was won by Archidamus III., king of Sparta, over the Arcadians and Argives, without losing a man, 367 B.C.

TEA-ROOM MEETING of members of the house of commons, 8 April, 1867. See *Reform*, 1867.

TEB, Battle of, 29 Feb. 1884. See *Soudan*.

TECHNICAL EDUCATION, see *Education*. Polytechnic schools in Darmstadt established 1830; in Hanover 1835; the trade association of the grand duchy of Hesse, 1836; Berlin working mens' union, 1843; Wurtemburg workmen's school, 1848; Society for promoting the interests of the working classes at Amsterdam, 1854. The first real practical technical school in England was formed in the Chester Diocesan Training College, by the rev. Arthur Rigg, principal, 1839-69.

Central Institution of City and Guilds Institute, South Kensington; foundation laid by the prince of Wales . . . . . . 18 July, 1881
A royal commission (Mr. B. Samuelson, prof. H. E. Roscoe (since knighted) and others) to inquire as to technical instruction in foreign countries Aug. ,,
Technical education reported highly successful in Britain; much aided by the London city companies, (see *Companies*) 1883 *et seq*.
Technical schools (Scotland) act passed 1887
Technical instruction bill introduced in Parliament; dropped . . . . . . 10 July, 1888
Great meeting at the Mansion House to promote technical education in the metropolis, 27 March, 1889

TE DEUM, a song of praise used by the Romish and English churches, beginning "*Te Deum Laudamus*—We praise thee, O God," supposed to be the composition of Augustin and Ambrose, about 390. The original music is very ancient.

TEETOTALER, a term applied to an abstainer from all fermented liquors, originated with Richard Turner, an artisan of Preston, who, contending for the principle at a temperance meeting about Sept. 1833, asserted "that nothing but *te-te-total* will do." The word was immediately adopted. He died 27 Oct. 1846. These facts are taken from the "Staunch Teetotaler," edited by Joseph Livesey, of Preston (an originator of the movement in 1832, he died, aged 90, 2 Sept. 1884), Jan. 1867. See *Encratites*, *Good Templars*, *Temperance*, and *United Kingdom*.

TEFLIS, see *Tiflis*.

TEGYRA, Bœotia. Here Pelopidas defeated the Spartans, 375 B.C.

TEHERAN became capital of Persia about 1795.

TELEGRAPHS (from the Greek, *tele*, afar, and *grapho*, I write). Æschylus, in his Agamemnon (B.C. 500), describes the communication of intelligence by burning torches as signals. Polybius, the Greek historian (who died about 122 B.C.), calls the different instruments used by the ancients for communicating information, *pyreiæ*, because the signals were always made by fire. In 1663, a plan was suggested by the marquis of Worcester, and a telegraph was suggested by Dr. Hooke, 1684. M. Amontons is also said to have been the inventor of telegraphs about this period. James II., while duke of York, originated a set of navy signals, which were systematised by Kempenfeldt in 1780; and a dictionary was compiled by sir Home Popham. M. Chappe then invented the telegraph first used by the French in 1792, and two were erected over the Admiralty-office, London, 1796. The semaphore was erected there 1816. The naval signals by telegraph enabled 400 previously concerted sentences to be transmitted from ship to ship, by varying the combinations of two revolving crosses. Baron Reuter's telegraph agency founded at Aix la Chapelle, 1851. Acts relating to telegraphs were passed in 1863 and 1866. The telegraph act, passed 31 July, 1868, enabled the postmaster-general to purchase existing electric telegraphs (not less than 1s. for a telegram, 20 words). Mr. Scudamore was appointed director, Jan. 1872. The principle of a 6d. telegram adopted by the Commons, 29 March, 1883, and enacted to come into operation 1 Oct. 1883; deferred; bill introduced by Mr. Shaw-Lefevre 30 March; act passed 14 Aug.; came into operation 1 Oct. 1885. Great destruction of telegraph posts and wires by gale and snowstorm; London streets blocked by fallen wires 26-27 Dec. 1886. The Society of Telegraph Engineers founded 1871; held first general meeting, 28 Feb. 1872, Chas. Wm. Siemens, president; incorporated 1883. Present title "Institution of Electrical Engineers" (1889). See *Electric Telegraph*, under *Electricity*, and *Telegraphs*, under *Post Office*, 1869, *et seq*. The *Telegraphic Journal* began 15 Nov. 1873.

TELEKOUPHONON, or speaking telegraph, consisted of piping of gutta percha, caoutchouc, glass, or earthenware, with a terminal mouthpiece of ivory, bone, wood, or metal. It was used for dockyards and large establishments. It was described by Mr. Francis Whishaw at the meeting of the British Association at Swansea, August, 1848.

TEL-EL-KEBIR, Egypt, the site of the entrenched camp of the rebel general, Arabi Pasha, his force being about 17,500 regular infantry, 2,500 cavalry, 6000 Bedouins and other irregulars, and 70 guns; captured by the British 13 Sept. 1882.

Sir Garnet Wolseley broke up his camp at Ismailia on the night of 12 Sept. and began his advance at 1.30 a.m., his force being about 11,000 infantry, 2000 cavalry, and 40 guns; the troops marched rapidly in the dark, each regiment endeavouring to be first. At daybreak they arrived at the camp. The surprised Egyptians filled the trenches and fought well under cover; but when the British scaled the parapets, they at first resisted bravely, but afterwards fled, being hotly pursued by the British cavalry, leaving all their guns, ammunition, &c. in the hands of the victors. Thousands were killed or made prisoners. Arabi Pasha fled towards Cairo. Among our killed were majors Colville, Underwood, and Somervell, and lieut. McNeill. The British general's masterly plans of the campaign were thus successfully carried out by his efficient staff and gallant army, which included many young soldiers. The Irish and Highland regiments and the Guards being specially distinguished. Arabi Pasha's army was completely broken up, and the British entered Cairo the next day, 14 Sept. British killed about 52,

and 380 wounded; Egyptian killed and wounded about 1500. The Highlanders bore the brunt of the action.

TELEMETER, &c., an instrument for determining the distance between a gun and the object fired at. Lieut. von Ehrenberg and major Montaudon, in Baden, constructed a telemeter the size of a watch, by which the distance is determined and shown on a dial by the action of sound, 1878-85. *Teletopometer*, another apparatus for ascertaining the distance from point to point, invented by Dr. Luigi Cerebotani, was announced in Sept. 1885; two telescopes are employed.

TELEPATHY, "the supersensory transference of thoughts and feelings from one mind to another"; the principal subject of "Phantasms of the Living," edited by Messrs. Edmund Gurney, Frederic Myers and Frank Podmore, and issued by the society for psychical research about 30 Oct. 1886.

TELEPHONE (from Greek, *tele*, afar, *phone*, voice, sound), a name now given to apparatus for transmitting articulate and musical sounds, by means of wire, vibrating rods, threads, or magneto-electricity. See *Electrophone*, in article *Electricity*, *Phonograph*, *Microphone*, *Phonopore*.

Robert Hooke conveyed sounds to a distance by distended wire	1667
Wheatstone conveyed the sounds of a musical-box from a cellar to upper rooms by means of a deal rod (termed "Enchanted Lyre")	1831
Page produced galvanic musical tones by magnetising and demagnetising an iron bar	1837
The principle advanced by De la Rive	1843
Professor Pepper lectured on Wheatstone's telephone before the queen at the Polytechnic, 10 May	1855
Philip Reis exhibited a partially articulate electric telephone at Frankfort	25 April 1861
Cromwell Varley produced a musical one, 1870; played on at the Queen's theatre, Long Acre	12 Feb. 1877
Elisha Gray improved Reis's telephone, and is said to have anticipated prof. Bell's discovery	1873
Professor A. Graham Bell's articulating telephone produced: (he employs a thin disk of iron vibrating in front of a permanent magnet, surrounded by a coil of insulated copper wire; the sound or voice causes the vibration of the disk, thereby generating a current of electricity which, sent round a similar coil on a distant magnet, sets vibrating another disk, and thus the sound is reproduced; sound is converted into electricity and electricity reconverted into sound;) experiments at Boston and Salem, United States (13 miles apart); speech, music, singing, laughing, &c., distinctly heard	12 Feb. 1877
This telephone exhibited by Mr. W. H. Preece before the British Association, Plymouth, 23 Aug. 1877; before the queen at Osborne, Isle of Wight	14, 15 Jan. 1878
Debates in the House of Commons, reported by it for *Daily News* (unsuccessful)	22 Jan. "
Telephone company established	summer "
Edison's carbon "loud speaking" telephone; conversation heard between London and Norwich; 115 miles of wire	11 Nov. "
Mr. Frederick Allen Gower improves Bell's telephone; shown at Royal Institution, London	20, 21 March, 1879
Telephone Exchange (Edison's system), Lombard-street; ten offices connected; private conversation between two persons in either a loud or low tone carried on; successfully tried	6 Sept. "
The Bell and Edison companies become the United Telephone Company; announced	26 July, 1880
The telephone tried by lord Elphinstone in his coalmines near Carberry, Scotland	Sept. "
Telephone communication established between Liverpool and Manchester; exchange of messages between the mayors	9 Nov. "
20,000 Gower-Bell telephones said to have been ordered by the post office	Dec. "
The attorney-general applies for injunction against the Telephone company and the Edison telephone	

company; case deferred; the companies directed to keep accounts, 20 Jan. 1880; decision that the Telephone company is an infringement of the electric telegraph monopoly bought by the act of 1868, 20 Dec. 1880; legal arrangements with the company . . . . 11 April, 1881
The postmaster-general now grants licences . . ,,
Professor Dolbear of Tuft's college, Massachusetts announced a new system, with improved telephone receiver (an articulating air condenser), different to Bell's and Edison's . . Aug. ,,
Opera at Royal Comedy theatre, Panton street, London, heard at Bristol hotel, Burlington Gardens . . . . . 21 Dec. ,,
National Telephone company 2nd annual meeting, report gross revenue 30 June, 1881, 15,050l.; 30 June, 1882, 26,996l.; dividend 6 per cent. announced . . . . . Aug. 1882
Telephonic communications between Brighton and London established . . . . 21 Dec. ,,
The system largely developed in Europe and America in . . . . . . ,,
United Telephone company v. Harrison, Cox, Walker & Co., for infringements of patents (Gordon, Bell and Edison); verdict for plaintiffs on appeal . . . . . 6 Feb. 1883
Distinct communication between New York and Chicago 1000 miles (by steel wire coated with copper) reported . . . . 24 March, ,,
Sermons at churches and chapels transmitted at Bradford . . . . . . Aug. ,,
The Post office makes large concessions to the companies . . . . . Sept. 1884
Successful experiments between Uxbridge and Liverpool (200 miles) . . . 9 July, 1885
Simple mechanical telephone of Messrs. A. A. Knudson and T. G. Ellsworth of New York announced . . . . . . Aug. ,,
Telephonic communication between Brussels and Paris opened by means of Dr. Cornelius Herz's micro-telephone . . . . 2 Feb. 1887
A telephone palace at Stockholm with excellent arrangements . . . . Feb. ,,
Communication by telephone between Paris and Marseilles opened . . . 6 Aug. 1888
Proposed amalgamation of the United Telephone Company with other companies opposed by the postmaster-general in regard to their licences from government . . . . June, 1889

TELEPHOTOGRAPHY, a process for transmitting to a distance images of objects by the agency of electricity and selenium, was invented by Mr. Shelford Bidwell, early in 1881.

TELERADIPHONE, an arrangement of apparatus in which M. Mercadier has adapted prof. Graham Bell's photophone to telegraphy, announced Jan. 1882.

TELESCOPES. Their principle was described by Roger Bacon about 1250, and Leonard Digges (who died about 1573) is said to have arranged glasses so that he could see very distant objects.

Telescopes constructed by John Lipperhey and Zacharias Jansen, spectacle-makers of Middleburg, and James Metius of Alkmaer . about 1608
Galileo (from a description of the above) constructed telescopes (May, 1609), gradually increasing in power, till he discovered Jupiter's satellites, &c., Jan. 1610
The telescope explained by Kepler . . . 1611
Huyghens greatly improved the telescope; discovered the ring and satellites of Saturn, &c. 1655-6
Telescopes improved by Gregory, about . . 1663
Reflecting telescope invented by Newton . . 1668
Achromatic telescopes made by Chester More Hall, about 1723; re-invented by John Dollond . 1758
Sir Wm. Herschel (originally an organist at Bath) greatly improves telescopes, and discovers the planet Uranus (which see), 21 March, 1781, and a volcanic mountain in the moon, in 1783; he completes his forty-feet focal length telescope in 1789, and he discovers two other volcanic mountains; he lays before the Royal Society a catalogue of 5000 nebulæ and clusters of stars . . 1802

A telescope made in London for the observatory of Madrid, which cost 11,000l., in 1802
Telescopes improved by Guinand and Frannhofer, 1805-14
The great telescope taken down, and one of twenty-feet focal length erected by sir John Herschel (who afterwards took it to the Cape of Good Hope, and made with it his observations) . 1822
The earl of Rosse erected at Parsonstown, in Ireland, a telescope (at a cost exceeding 20,000l.) 6 feet in diameter, and 54 feet in length; it is moved with ease 1828-45
Mr. Lassell constructed a telescope by which he discovered the satellite of Neptune, 1846; and the eight satellites of Saturn 1848
One of gigantic size, 85 feet in length (very imperfect), completed at Wandsworth by the rev. John Craig 1852
Magnificent equatorial telescopes set up at the national observatories at Greenwich and Paris . 1860
M. Foucault exhibits at Paris a reflecting telescope, the mirror 31½ inches in diameter; the focal length 17½ feet 1862
Mr. R. S. Newall's telescope (with object glass 25 inches diameter; tube nearly 30 feet), set up at Gateshead by Cookes of York . . . 1870
One at United States Observatory, Washington; object-glass, 26 inches diameter, 33 feet length.
Mr. A. Ainslie Common's reflecting telescope; speculum 37½ inches diameter; length, 20 feet; said to be the most powerful in existence; Ealing, Middlesex; completed . . . Sept. 1879
The largest refracting telescope yet made; by Howard Grubb at Dublin (for Vienna); approved by the commissioners . . . 16 March, 1881
A very large refracting telescope by Messrs. Clark of America was set up in the observatory at Mount Hamilton, California, named after Mr. Lick (who left money for its foundation) . . 1883

TELL, WILLIAM. The popular stories respecting him were demonstrated to be mythical by Professor Kopp of Lucerne, 1872.

TELLERS, see under *Exchequer*.

TELLURIUM, a rare metal, in its natural state containing small quantities of iron and gold, was discovered by Müller of Reichenstein, in 1782, and named by Klaproth.

TELODYNAMIC TRANSMITTER, invented by M. Hirn, is an arrangement of waterwheels, endless wires, and pulleys, for conveying and using the power of water-falls at a distance, and has been much used since 1850. The apparatus was shown at Paris in 1862.

TELPHERAGE, an application of electrical motion, invented by professor Fleeming Jenkin, aided by professors Ayrton and Perry, for conveying heavy goods, 2d. a ton per mile, 4 miles an hour, shown at Millwall, 1884.
A Telpherage company was formed. A Telpher line at the estate of lord Hampden at Glynde near Lewes, opened . . . . . 17 Nov. 1885

TEMESWAR (Hungary), capital of the Banat, often besieged by the Turks. On 10 Aug. 1849, Haynau totally defeated the Hungarians besieging this town, and virtually ended the war.

TEMNOGRAPH, an instrument designed to plot to any accurate scale a section of the ground over which it travels. It works by frictional motion governed by two pendulous weights. Invented by A. M. Rymer-Jones in 1879.

TEMPERANCE SOCIETIES originated with Mr. Calhoun, who, while he was secretary of war in America, in order to counteract the habitual use of ardent spirits among the people, prohibited them altogether in the United States' army, 1818. See *Teetotaler*, and *Permissive Bill*.

TEMPERED GLASS.

The first public temperance society in America was projected in 1825, and formed . . 13 Feb. 1826
Many temperance societies immediately afterwards formed in America, England, and Scotland.
British and foreign temperance society formed, 29 June, 1831
The "Rechabites" (see Jer. xxxv.) began . about 1838
In Ireland, the rev. Dr. Edgar, of Belfast, published upon temperance in 1829-31; and father Mathew, a Roman catholic clergyman, affirmed that he had made more than a million of converts to temperance 1841
Father Mathew arrived in America in July, 1849; was not so successful there; he died, aged 66, 8 Dec. 1856
In England, the National temperance society, formed 1843
London temperance league 1851
The United Kingdom alliance for the legislative suppression of the sale of intoxicating liquors, 1 June, 1853
Mr. J. B. Gough lectures in London, &c. . . . "
United Kingdom Band of Hope Union formed, 1855 ; 11,400 societies with 1,414,900 members . . 1888
The National union for suppression of intemperance by means of "few houses, shorter hours, and better provisions," established end of . . 1871
Church of England temperance society inaugurated by the archbishop of Canterbury and others at Lambeth . . . . 18 Feb. 1873
A Temperance hospital, where no alcoholic drinks are to be given for disease, was opened . 6 Oct. "
British Women's temperance association inaugurated at Newcastle-on-Tyne . . . April 1876
Mr. J. B. Gough lectures in London, Sept. 1878; Oct. 1879
London Temperance Hospital, Hampstead-road, London, building (21,000l. out of 30,000l. subscribed) . . . . Sept. "
International exhibition of objects connected with temperance opened at the Agricultural hall, Islington . . . . 22 Aug. 1881
The Green and Blue Ribbon Armies of persons advocating temperance were prominent in . . 1882
A Yellow Army of moderate drinkers proposed (gen. Hicks) . . . . about Sept. "
National Temperance Jubilee at the Crystal Palace; above 50,000 present . . . . . 5 Sept. "
International temperance conferences: Brussels, 1880; London 1882; Antwerp . . . 1885
Mr. J. B. Gough dies in Philadelphia, aged 69, about 17 Feb. 1886
British and colonial congress in London, bishop of London president . . . . 14-16 July, "
"National Prohibition Party," Mr. Alex. Gustafson, in the Christian Commonwealth, strongly urges the total abolition of alcohol . April, 1887

TEMPERED GLASS, see Glass.

TEMPLARS. The military order of "soldiers of the Temple," to protect pilgrims, was founded about 1118 by Baldwin II., king of Jerusalem, confirmed by pope Honorius II., 1128. The Templars were numerous in several countries, and came to England before 1185. Their wealth having excited the cupidity of the French kings, the order was suppressed by the council of Vienne, and part of its revenues was bestowed upon other orders about 1312. Numbers of the order were tried, condemned, and burned alive or hanged in 1308-10, and it suffered much persecution throughout Europe; 68 knights were burnt at Paris, 1310. Pope Clement V. abolished the order, April, 1312. The grand master Molay was burnt alive at Paris, 18 March, 1314. Their property in England was given to the Hospitallers, and the head of the order in England died in the Tower. See Good Templars.

TEMPLE (London), the dwelling of the Knights Templars, consecrated by Heraclius, patriarch of Jerusalem, 1185, at the suppression of the order, was purchased by the professors of the common law, and converted into inns, 1311, afterwards called the Inner and Middle Temple. Essex house, also a part of the house of the Templars,

TENERIFFE.

was called the Outer Temple, because it wa situated without Temple-bar.
The Temple hall was built in 15;
St. Mary's, or the Temple Church, situated in the Inner Temple, is a Gothic stone building, erected by the Templars in 1240, and is remarkable for its circular vestibule, and for the tombs of the crusaders, who were buried here. The church was recased with stone by Mr. Smirke in . . 182
The Middle Temple new library was opened by the prince of Wales, 31 Oct. 1861; he becomes treasurer of the Middle Temple . . . Nov. 181
New Inner Temple, all opened by princess Louisa, 14 May, 187
Anniversary of consecration, celebrated by Mr. E. J. Hopkins . . . . . . 10 Feb. 188
TEMPLE BAR, erected outside the gates; ordered to be rebuilt 27 June, 1669; erected by sir C. Wren; completed March 1672-3; cost 1397l. 10s.; room above contained books of Child and Co. for 200 years; reported dangerous March, 1868; began to sink 30 July; shored up 186
Its removal voted by the common council, 27 Sept. 18, 6; the removal began 2 Jan., 1878; last stones removed . . . . 13 June, 18;
The stones, &c., given to sir H. B. Meux to be erected at Theobald's Park, near Cheshunt, June, 1887; the bar set up . . . . . Nov. 188
The memorial to mark the site (including statues of the queen and prince of Wales); cost about 11,550l.; inaugurated by prince Leopold, 8 Nov. 188
"Temple" at Paris, formerly an asylum for debtors, and a prison during the republic, was made the site of a market in 1809, and rebuilt in 1864.
The "City Temple," a dissenters' chapel (minister, Dr. Parker), Holborn Viaduct, was opened, 19 May, 187

TEMPLES originated in the sepulchres bui for the dead.—Eusebius. The Egyptians were th first who erected temples to the gods.—Herodotus The first erected in Greece is ascribed to Deucalion —Apollonius.

The temple of Jerusalem built by Solomon, 1012 B.C. consecrated 1004; pillaged by Shishak, 971; repaire by Joash, 856; profaned by Ahaz, 740; restored b Hezekiah, 726; pillaged and fired by Nebuchadnezza 588, 587; rebuilt, 536; pillaged by Antiochus, 170 rebuilt by Herod, 18; destroyed by Titus, A.D. 70.
The temple of Apollo, at Delphi, first a cottage wit boughs, built of stone by Trophonius, about 1200 B.C. burnt by the Pisistratidæ, 548; a new temple raised b the family of the Alcmæonidæ, about 513.
Temple of Diana at Ephesus, built seven times; planne by Ctesiphon, 544 B.C.; fired by Eratostratus c Herostratus, to perpetuate his name, 356 B.C.; to r build it employed 220 years; destroyed by the Goth A.D. 260.
The temple of Piety was built by Acilius, on the spo where once a woman had fed with her milk her age father, whom the senate had imprisoned, and exclude from all aliments.—Val. Max.
Temple of Theseus, built 480 B.C. is at this day the mo perfect ancient edifice in the world.
Most of the heathen temples were destroyed throughou the Roman empire by Constantine the Great and Theo dosius, 331-392. See separate articles.

TENANT, see Rent. Bills to amend the posi tion of Irish tenants in relation to their landlord were brought into parliament by Mr. Sharma Crawford, 1835, sir Joseph Napier, 1852, Mr. Card well, 1860, Mr. Chichester Fortescue, 1866, Lor Naas, 1867. The Irish land bill settling the ques tion passed 8 July, 1870. See Ulster. For th Tenants' Defence League (Ireland), see Addenda.

TENASSERIM (N.E. India), ceded by Bur mah to the British, 24 Feb. 1826.

TENERIFFE (Canaries, N.W. coast of Africa) The peak of Teneriffe, 15,396 feet above the level o the sea, was ascended in 1856 by professor C. Piazz Smyth for astronomical observations. An earth quake in this island destroyed several towns an many thousands of people in 1704. See Santa Cru

TEN MINUTES' BILL, see *Reform.*

TENNESSEE, a southern state of North America, was settled about 1760, and admitted into the union 1 June, 1796. An ordinance of secession 'om the union was passed—it is asserted illegally —on 6 May, 1861. On 23 Feb. 1862, the federal general Nelson entered Nashville, and in March, Andrew Johnson (afterwards the president of the United States) was made military governor over a large part of Tennessee. In Sept. 1863, Rosencrans expelled the confederate government. The representatives of Tennessee wer re-admitted to the congress, July, 1866. Population, 1880, 1,542,359; capital, Nashville.

TENNIS. This game, brought from France, became fashionable in England in the reign of Charles II. 1660-85; see *Jeu de Paume.* "Lawn Tennis" became fashionable in 1877, replacing croquet. Julian Marshall's "Annals of Tennis" published June, 1878.
A National Lawn Tennis Association started Jan. 1888

TEN TABLES, see *Decemvirs.*

TENTERDEN'S ACT, LORD, 2 & 3 Will. IV. c. 71, for shortening the time of prescription in certain 'cases (such as rights of way, and use of light), passed 1 Aug. 1832.

TEN THOUSAND, see *Retreat.*

TENTHS, see *Tithes.*

TENURES, the mode in which land is held. Military tenures in England were abolished in 1660. Lyttelton's book on Tenures is dated 1481.

TERBIUM, a metal sometimes found with yttrium (*which see*).

TERCEIRA, see *Azores.*

TERMS OF LAW AND VACATIONS. They were instituted in England from the Norman usage, the long vacation being suited to the time of the vintage in France, 14 Will. I. 1079.—*Glanvills de Leg. Anglic.* They were gradually formed.—*Spelman.* The terms were fixed by statute 11 Geo. IV. and 1 Will. IV. 22 July, 1830: *Hilary Term* to begin 11 Jan. and end 31 Jan.; *Easter,* 15 April, to end 8 May; *Trinity,* 22 May, to end 12 June; *Michaelmas,* 2 Nov. to end 25 Nov. This act was amended 1 Will. IV. 15 Nov. 1830. Now law terms (now sittings) were appointed under the Supreme Court of Judicature Act, passed 5 Aug. 1873.
Michaelmas sittings: 2 Nov. to 21 Dec.
Hilary: 11 Jan. to Wednesday in Passion week.
Easter: Thursday in Easter week to Friday before Whit-Sunday.
Trinity: Tuesday after Whit-Sunday to 8 Aug.
The new *legal vacations* ordered to be as follows:—
Christmas: 24 Dec. to 6 Jan. *Easter:* Good Friday to Easter-Tuesday. *Whitsun:* Saturday before Whit-Sunday to Whit-Tuesday. *Long vacation:* 10 Aug. to 24 Oct.

TERNOVA, see *Tirnova.*

TERRITORIAL WATERS JURISDICTION ACT, passed, 16 Aug. 1878. It regulates the law relating to the trial of offences committed on the sea within a certain distance of her majesty's dominions.

TERROR, see *Reign of.*

TEST ACT, directing all officers, civil and military, under government, to receive the sacrament according to the forms of the church of England, and to take the oaths against transubstantiation, &c.; enacted 29 March, 1673. The Test and Corporation acts were repealed, 9 May, 1828. See *University Tests.*

TESTAMENT, see *Bibles,* and *Wills.*

TESTER, *testone,* a silver coin struck in France by Louis XII. 1513; and also in Scotland in the time of Francis II. and of Mary, queen of Scots, 1559. It was so called from the head of the king, stamped upon it. In England the tester was of 12*d.* value in the reign of Henry VIII., afterwards of 6*d.* (still called a tester).

TESTRI (N. France). Pepin d'Heristal, invited by malcontents, here defeated and captured Thierry III., king of Austrasia, and established himself as duke, 687.

TETTENHALL (Staffordshire). It was probably at this place, then named Teotenheal, that the Danes were defeated by the Saxon king, Edward the Elder, 6 Aug. 910.

TETUAN (Morocco) was entered by the Spaniards 6 Feb. 1860, after gaining a decisive victory on 4 Feb. The general O'Donnell, was made a grandee of the first class.

TEUTOBERG FOREST (the Teutobergiensis saltus, *Tacitus*), probably situate between Detmold and Paderborn, where Hermann, or Arminius, and the Germans defeated the Romans under Varus, with very great slaughter, A.D. 9. Varus and many of his officers preferred suicide to captivity. This defeat was regarded at Rome as a national calamity, and Augustus, in agony, cried, "Varus, give me my legions!"

TEUTONES, a people of Germany, who with the Cimbri made incursions upon Gaul, and cut to pieces two Roman armies, 113 and 105 B.C. They were at last defeated by the consul Marius at Aix, and a great number made prisoners, 102 B.C. (see *Cimbri*), with whom authors commonly join the Teutones. The appellation came to be applied to the German nation in general (hence *Deutsche*).

TEUTONIC ORDER, military knights established in the Holy Land about 1191, through the humanity of the Germans (Teutones) to the sick and wounded of the Christian army in the Holy Land, under Guy of Lusignan, before Acre. The order was confirmed by a bull of pope Cœlestine III. On their return from Germany, the knights were invited to subdue and christianise the country now called Prussia and its neighbourhood, which they gradually accomplished. Their territories were invaded, and their army was defeated, with great slaughter, near Tannenberg, in East Prussia, by Jagellon, duke of Lithuania, 15 July, 1410, when the grand master and many of the knights were slain. A large part of their possessions was incorporated into Poland in 1466, and into Brandenburg about 1521. In 1525, the grand master was made a prince of the empire, and the order much weakened. Its remaining possessions were seized by Napoleon I. in 1809. See *Prussia,* &c.

TEWKESBURY (Gloucestershire), where Edward IV. gained a decisive victory over the Lancastrians, 4 May, 1471. Queen Margaret, the consort of Henry VI., was taken prisoner and her son killed. The queen was conveyed to the Tower of London, where king Henry expired soon after this fatal engagement; being, as is generally supposed, murdered by the duke of Gloucester, afterwards Richard III. The queen was ransomed in 1475 by the French king, Louis XI., for 50,000 crowns. See *Roses.*
The *abbey,* founded by Robert Fitz-Hamon, cousin of William I., completed and consecrated 1123; grand y

3 L

altered, 14th century; a monastery destroyed by Henry VIII.; the abbey spared; restored by G. G. Scott, 1877-9.

TEXAS (N. America) was settled by the French, 1687, who were expelled soon after. It revolted from Mexico in 1835; was helped by the Americans in 1836. Its independence was acknowledged in 1840. Its proposed annexation led to war between Mexico and the United States. It was admitted into the Union by the latter in 1846; seceded from it in 1861; submitted in 1865; re-admitted to state rights, March, 1870. The coast was desolated by a great storm, 15-18 Sept. 1875. Population 1880, 1,591,749; capital, Austin. See *Storms*.

Great fire at Galveston, above 700 residences burnt, loss about 800,000*l*. . . . . . 13 Nov. 1885
About 1,000 Mexicans entered Rio Grande and caused disturbances, soon quelled, . . . Sept. 1888

TEXEL (at the mouth of the Zuyder Zee, Holland). Its vicinity has been the scene of memorable naval engagements. An engagement between the English under Blake, Dean, and Monk, and the Dutch under Van Tromp and De Ruyter, in which the latter were worsted and admiral Van Tromp was killed, 31 July, 1653. Again, in the mouth of the Texel a sharp indecisive action took place between the allied English and French fleets under prince Rupert and comte d'Estrées, and the Dutch fleet under De Ruyter, 11 Aug. 1673. The Dutch fleet was vanquished by admiral Duncan on 11 Oct. 1797; see *Camperdown*. The Dutch fleet of 12 ships of war and thirteen Indiamen surrendered to admiral Mitchell, who, entering the Texel, possessed himself of them without firing a shot, 30 Aug. 1799.

THALLIUM, a metal, occurring in the sulphuric acid manufacture, discovered by Mr. Wm. Crookes, by means of the spectrum analysis, March, 1861.

THAMES (London), the Roman Tamesis or Tamesa, Saxon Temesc, Temesa, rises in four springs, at Ullen farm, near Coates, Gloucestershire. The head of the river in Wiltshire is about 170 miles from London bridge, and its whole course from source to mouth about 220 miles. See *London* and *London-bridge*.

The river rose so high at Westminster that the lawyers were brought out of the hall in boats. . 1235
It rose to a great height, 1736, 1747, 1762 . 1791
The conservation of the Thames was given to the mayors of London 1489
The Thames was made navigable to Oxford . . 1624
It ebbed and flowed twice in three hours, 1658; again, three times in four hours, 22 March, 1682; again, twice in three hours . . 24 Nov. 1777
An act of parliament gave the conservation of the Thames to the corporation of London; twelve conservators were to be appointed—three by the government 1857
In consequence of the great contamination of the Thames by the influx of the sewage of London, and the bad odours emanating from it in the summer of 1858, an act was passed empowering the Metropolitan Board of Works (*which see*) to undertake its purification by constructing new drainage 1858
The Thames Angling Preservation Society (established about 1838) is revived in . . . 1863
Mr. Leach, engineer of the conservators, reported that "the river is dreadfully mismanaged from its source to its mouth" . . 23 July, ,,
The Thames navigation acts, appointing five more conservators, &c., and prohibiting pollution by sewage, &c., passed . . . . Aug. 1866
The powers of the act extended up to Staines . 1867
New bye-laws to protect the fish in the Upper Thames passed by the conservators. . 14 June, 1869
Highest tide known for many years; river overflowed from Gravesend to its tidal limit; great damage and distress in Blackfriars and Lambeth; Woolwich arsenal flooded and suffered; river said to have risen above 29 feet . . 15 Nov.;
The lord mayor and others (with carriages and horses) cross by ferry from Rotherhithe to Wapping . . . . . . 1 Nov.
Thames SteamFerry; first pile of a landing-place at Wapping struck by Lord Mayor Stone, 11 Oct., 1875; first steam ferry boat, *Jessie May*, launched . . . . . . 26 Feb.
In consequence of the wreck of the saloon steamer *Princess Alice*, by collision with the *Bywell Castle*, 3 Sept., a committee appointed by the Board of Trade to inquire into matters connected with safety of navigation, &c., in the river. Sept.
Floods on the south side, through heavy rains and high tides, 2, 3, Jan. 1877; during severe frost, 18, 19 Jan.
Very high tide, 19 Feb.; another, very destructive, Charing Cross pier carried away . . 28 Oct.
Appointment of committee to inquire into the acts for preserving the Thames for recreation agreed to . . . . 11 March,
Thames Preservation Act passed . . 14 Aug.
Greenwich great steam-ferry formally opened 13 Feb. 1888; one between North and South Woolwich (free) formally opened by lord Rosebery 23 March,
THAMES TUNNEL. One proposed, 1799; shaft sunk, 1804. The present one proposed by I. K. Brunel to form a communication between Rotherhithe and Wapping, 1823. The bill received the royal assent . . 24 June,
The shaft was begun, and the first brick laid by Mr. Smith, 2 March; the excavation commenced, 1 April; the first horizontal excavation in Dec.
At a distance of 544 feet from the shaft, the first irruption took place . . . 18 May,
The second irruption, by which six workmen perished . . . . . . 12 Jan.
The tunnel was opened throughout for foot-passengers, 25 March, 1843. [The length of the tunnel is 1300 feet; its width is 35 feet; height, 20 feet; clear width of each archway, including foot-path, about 14 feet; thickness of earth between the crown of the tunnel and the bed of the river, about 15 feet.]
The Thames Tunnel Company was dissolved in The tunnel, transferred to the East London railway company, was closed . . . 21 July,
The *Tower subway*, an iron tube tunnel beneath the Thames, constructed by Messrs. Barlow, was begun 16 Feb. 1869, and privately opened, April, 1870. It was said to have cost only 16,000*l*.
A *tubular Thames tunnel*, chiefly for workmen, between North and South Woolwich, begun 23 Aug.,
THAMES EMBANKMENT: recommended by sir Christopher Wren, 1666, and by Wm. Paterson, founder of the bank of England, about 1694. The corporation embanked a mile in 1767. It was further recommended by Gwynne, 1767; by sir Frederick Eden, 1798; by sir Frederick Trench, 1824; by James Walker; by the duke of Newcastle, 1844; and by John Martin the painter, 1856. In 1860, the Metropolitan Board of Works recommended that the north bank of the Thames should be embanked, whereby the bed of the river would be improved; a low-level sewer could be easily constructed beneath a broad roadway; docks to be constructed within the embankment wall; the expense to be defrayed by the city duties on coal, and by means provided by government. The principle of this recommendation was approved by parliament, and a committee was appointed, which sat for the first time, 30 April,
An act for "embanking the *North* side of the Thames from Westminster bridge to Blackfriars bridge, and for making new streets in and near thereto," passed 7 Aug.; the work begun in Nov.
First stone of the northern (Victoria) embankment laid by Mr. Thwaites near Whitehall stairs, 20 July, 1864; the footway opened to the public, 30 July, 1868; the roadway opened by the prince of Wales . . . . . 13 July,
The proposal to build public offices upon the reclaimed land negatived by the house of commons, July,

"*Cleopatra's Needle*" (see *Obelisk*), set up on the
  embankment . . . . 12 Sept. 1878
Mr. J. W. Bazalgette presented a report, with a
  plan for embanking the *South* side of the Thames,
  6 Nov. 1862; act for carrying it out passed,
                                           28 July, 1863
Southern (*Albert*) *Embankment*. First stone laid by
  Mr. (aft. sir Wm.) Tite, 28 July, 1866; partially
  opened . . . . 24 Nov. 1869
Chelsea (*Victoria*) *Embankment.* Authorised by
  parliament, 13 July, 1868; commenced 5 Aug.
  1871, opened by the duke of Edinburgh 9 May, 1874
Savoy theatre opened . . . . . 10 Oct. 1881
Avenue theatre opened . . . . 11 March, 1882
Thames Mystery. See *London*, 1873.

THANE, a Saxon title of nobility, abolished in
England at the conquest, upon the introduction
of the feudal system, and in Scotland by king Malcolm III., when the title of earl was adopted, 1057.

THANET (Kent) was the first permanent
settlement of the Saxons, about 449. The Danes
held a part of it, 853-865, and ravaged it 980, 988
et seq.

THANKSGIVINGS, special national, were
offered up at St. Paul's cathedral for the defeat of
Spanish Armada, queen Elizabeth present, 8 Sept.
and 24th Nov. 1588; for Marlborough's victories,
12 Nov. 1702, and 7 Sept. 1704; for George III.'s
recovery from illness, 23 April, 1789; for Duncan's
and other naval victories, 19 Dec. 1797; and for
the recovery of the prince of Wales, 27 Feb. 1872.

THAPSUS (N. Africa). Near here Julius
Cæsar totally defeated the army of the party which
supported the policy of Pompey, Feb. 46 B.C. The
suicide of Cato followed soon after.

THEATINES, a religious order, the first who
assumed the title of regular clerks, founded by
Caraffa, bishop of Theate, or Chieti, in Naples
(afterwards pope Paul IV.), 1524, to repress heresy.
They first established themselves in France, according to Hénault, in Paris, 1644. The Theatines
vainly endeavoured to revive among the clergy the
poverty of the apostles.

THEATRES. That of Bacchus, at Athens,
built by Philos, 420 B.C., is said to have been the
first erected. Marcellus' theatre at Rome was
begun by Cæsar, and dedicated by Augustus, 12
B.C. Theatres were erected in most cities of Italy.
Most of the inhabitants of Pompeii were assembled
at a theatre on the night of 24 Aug. 79, when an
eruption of Vesurius covered the city. Scenes were
introduced into theatres, painted by Balthazar
Sienna, A.D. 1533. See *Drama*, *Plays*, &c.

THEATRES IN ENGLAND. The first royal
licence for a theatre in England was in 1574, to
master Burbage and four others, servants of the
earl of Leicester, to act plays at the Globe, Bankside. The Blackfriars, the first public theatre in
London, was built in 1576. The London theatres
in Elizabeth's reign were the Shoreditch and the
Curtain near it, Bankside, Whitefriars, Rose, Hope,
Swan, Red Bull, Cockpit or Phœnix, Drury Lane,
and several others. Shakespeare and his fellow
actors erected the Globe theatre on Bankside, 1594.
The prices of admission are said to have been—
gallery, 2*d.*; lords' rooms, 1*s.*; see *Drama*, *Drury
Lane*, and other theatres. The theatres were closed
by parliament, 1642-60.

The first play-bill was dated 8 April, 1663, and
issued from Drury-lane; it runs thus: "By his
Majestie his company of Comedians at the New
Theatre in Drury-lane, will be acted a comedy
called the *Humorous Lieutenant.*" After detailing
the characters, it concludes thus: "The play will
begin at three o'clock exactly." . . 8 April, 1663

Lincoln's-inn theatre (the duke's theatre) opened by
  sir Wm. Davenant's patent, 25 April, 1662;
  rebuilt 1695
Acts for licensing plays and play-houses (placing
  them under the lord chamberlain) 10 Geo. II.
  c. 28 1737
Act for regulating theatres (6 & 7 Vict. c. 68).
                                           22 Aug. 1843
      See *Trials*, 1843.
Marionettes or Puppets produced at the Adelaide
  Gallery 1852
Several of the theatres first opened on Sunday
  evenings for religious worship, and filled . Jan. 1860
Lord Chamberlain warned managers against inde-
  cent dances and scanty dresses 28 Jan. 1869 and
                                           21 Dec. 1874
Introduction of the *queue*, as at French theatres,
  by Mr. D'Oyly Carte, at the Savoy . 29 Dec. 1882
The employment of children under ten years of
  age forbidden in theatres by the Home Secretary
                                         about 5 Dec. 1886
Theatres in Great Britain, 166; in London, 33,
  summer of 1868; 45, Jan. 1876; 57, capable of
  holding 126,100 persons, June, 1878; 43, Jan.
  1885; 41, Jan. 1889

DRURY LANE.
Killigrew's patent . . . . . 25 April, 1662
Opened . . . . 8 April, 1663
Nell Gwynn performed 1666
Theatre burnt down with 60 houses . . . Jan. 1672
Rebuilt by sir C. Wren, and opened . 26 March, 1674
Cibber, Wilkes, Booth 1712
Garrick's *debut* here 1742
Garrick and Lacy's tenure (revival of Shakspeare) . 1747
Theatrical fund founded by Mr. Garrick, 1766; in-
  corporated 775
Interior rebuilt by Adams; opened . . 23 Sept.   ,,
Garrick's farewell . . . . . . 10 June, 1777
Sheridan's management . . . . ,,
Mrs. Siddons' *debut* as a *star* . . . 10 Oct. 1782
Mr. Kemble's *début* as *Hamlet* . . . 30 Sept. 1783
The theatre rebuilt on a large scale, and re-opened,
                                           12 March, 1794
Charles Kemble's first appearance (as *Malcolm* in
  Macbeth) . . . . 21 April,   ,,
Dowton's first appearance (as *Sheva* in the *Jew*),
                                             11 Oct. 1796
Hatfield fired at George III. . . . . 11 May, 1800
The theatre burnt . . . . 24 Feb. 1809
Rebuilt by Wyatt, and re-opened with a prologue
  by lord Byron . . . . 10 Oct. 1812
Edmund Kean's appearance (as *Shylock*) . 26 Jan. 1814
Mr. Elliston, lessee . . . . . . 3 Oct. 1819
Madame Vestris's first appearance . 19 Feb. 1820
Real water introduced in the *Cataract of the Ganges*,
                                             27 Oct. 1823
Mr. Price, lessee . . . . July, 1826
Ellen Tree's appearance (as *Violante*) . 23 Sept.   ,,
Charles Kean's appearance (as *Norval*) . 1 Oct. 1827
Mrs. Nisbet's first appearance (as the *Widow Cheerly*)
                                              9 Oct. 1829
Mr. Alexander Lee's and captain Polhill's manage-
  ment 1830
Mr. Alfred Bunn, lessee 1831
Mr. Forrest's first appearance (as *Spartacus*),
                                             17 Oct. 1836
Mr. Hammond's management 1839
German operas commenced here . . 15 March, 1841
Mr. Macready's management . . . . . . ,,
Mr. Bunn, again lessee 1843
Miss Clara Webster burnt on the stage, 14 Dec.;
  and died . . . . 16 Dec. 1844
Mr. Anderson's management 1849
Mr. Macready's farewell . . . . 26 Feb. 1851
Mr. Bunn, lessee and manager 1852
Mr. E. T. Smith 1853-9
English opera (Mr. Harrison and Miss Pyne) . . 1858
Italian opera, part of 1859-78
Opened by Mr. E. T. Smith . . . 15 Oct. 1860
Suddenly closed . . . . . . 20 April, 1861
Mr. G. V. Brooke appears (as *Othello*) . 27 Oct.   ,,
  [Drowned in the *London*: see *Wrecks*, 11 Jan. 1866.]
Mr. Falconer . . . . Dec. 1862-1865
Messrs. Falconer and Chatterton, managers, Jan. 1866
Re-opened with Halliday's *King of Scots*, 26 Sept. ,,
Re-opened with *Antony and Cleopatra* . 26 Sept. 1873
Balfe's posthumous *Talisman* produced . 11 June, 1874

3 L 2

THEATRES. 894 THEATRES.

Balfe's statue uncovered	25 Sept. 1874
Salvini as *Othello* 1 April; as *Hamlet*	31 May, 1875
Wagner's *Lohengrin*	12 June, ,,
Boucicault's new drama the *Shaughraun* produced	4 Sept. ,,
Manager and lessee, F. B. Chatterton	1876-78
Re-opened with *Richard III.*	23 Sept. 1876
Mr. Wills's *Charles II.*	24 Sept. 1877
Theatre suddenly closed; strike of actors, &c.	4 Feb. 1879
Saxe-Meiningen Court Company (Germans), *Julius Cæsar*	30 May et seq. 1881
Mad. Ristori as *Lady Macbeth*	July, 1882
Mr. Augustus Harris, lessee and manager	Sept. 1879-89
Carl Rosa's Opera Company	part of 1883-5
Re-opens the House (*Le Nozze de Figaro*)	31 May, 1886
Re-opens with the *The Spanish Armada* by Messrs. H. Hamilton and A. Harris	22 Sept. 1888

COVENT GARDEN.

The theatre opened by Rich	7 Dec. 1732
Beef-steak Society, founded by Rich and Lambert	1735
Theatrical fund instituted 1760; incorporated	1764
Mr. Harris's tenure	1767
Lewis's first appearance (as *Belcour*)	15 Sept. 1773
Miss Reay killed by Mr. Hackman, coming from the house	7 April, 1779
Jack Johnstone's first appearance in Irish characters	3 Oct. 1783
Munden's appearance	2 Dec. 1790
Fawcett's first appearance (as *Caleb*)	21 Sept. 1791
G. F. Cooke's appearance (as *Richard III.*)	31 Oct. 1800
Braham's appearance	9 Dec. 1801
Mr. Kemble's management	1802
Appearance of Master Betty, the *Infant Roscius*	1 Dec. 1804
Lewis's last appearance (as the *Copper Captain*)	28 May, 1808
Theatre burnt down	20 Sept. ,,
Rebuilt by R. Smirke, R.A., and re-opened with *Macbeth*	18 Sept. 1809
The O. P. Riot (*which see*)	18 Sept. to 10 Dec. ,,
Horses first introduced; in *Bluebeard*	18 Feb. 1811
The farewell benefit of Mrs. Siddons (immense house)	29 June, 1812
Mrs. Siddons performed once afterwards, in June, 1819, for Mr. and Mrs. C. Kemble's benefit.	
Miss Stephens' first appearance (as *Mandane*)	7 Sept. 1813
Miss Foote's appearance here (as *Amanthis*)	26 May, 1814
Miss O'Neill's appearance (as *Juliet*)	6 Oct. ,,
Miss Kelly fired at by George Barnet, in the house	7 Feb. 1816
Mr. Macready's first appearance (as *Orestes*)	16 Sept. ,,
Mr. J. P. Kemble's farewell (as *Coriolanus*)	23 June, 1817
Henry Harris's management	1818
Charles Kemble's management	1823
Miss Fanny Kemble's appearance (as *Juliet*), 5 Oct. 1829	
Mr. Fawcett's farewell	21 May, 1830
Charles Young's farewell	30 May, 1832
Mr. Macready's management	1837
Madame Vestris's management	1839
Miss Adelaide Kemble's appearance (as *Norma*)	2 Nov. 1841
Charles Kemble again	10 Sept. 1842
Mr. Laurent's management	26 Dec. 1844
Opened by F. Gye for Italian opera	6 April, 1847
Destroyed by fire (during a *bal masqué*, conducted by Anderson the Wizard)	5 March, 1856
New theatre (by Barry) opened by Mr. F. Gye (*Les Huguenots*)	15 May, 1858
English opera (Miss Pyne and Mr. Harrison), Oct. 1859	
All principal actors perform parts of plays for the benefit of the Dramatic College	29 March, 1860
Balfe's *Bianca* brought out	6 Dec. ,,
Italian opera (Mr. Gye)	April, 1861
Last appearance of Grisi	3 Aug. ,,
English opera (Pyne and Harrison)	31 Oct. ,,
Italian opera (Mr. Gye)	April, 1862
English opera (Pyne and Harrison)	25 Aug. ,,
Italian opera (Mr. Gye)	7 April, 1863
Gounod's *Faust*	July, ,,
English opera (Pyne and Harrison)	12 Oct. ,,
Italian opera (Mr. Gye)	April, 1864

English opera, &c. (Opera Compa[ny])	
Italian opera (Mr. Gye)	
Becomes the property of a compa[ny] manager	
Reopened (Mr. Gye) April, 1866; a[gain]	
Opened by Mr. Mapleson's company	
Opera season (Gye and Mapleson)	
Mr. Dion Boucicault lessee and mana[ger]	
Italian opera	
Mr. F. Gye, many years lessee, died, accident with gun	
A. & S. Gatti, managers	
Mr. Lionel Gye, lessee	
"Royal English opera" under Mr. [ ] short season	
Sig. Salvini's company, *Othello*, &c.	
Grand International cirque	
William Holland, lessee and manager	
Mr. Mapleson, with Italian opera	J[an.]
Grand demonstration to Madame [ ]	
Revival of Italian opera, signor B[ ] ductor	
Italian opera, opened under Mr. Ma[pleson] (*Traviata* performed)	
Donizetti's *La Favorita* performed	
Donizetti's *Lucrezia Borgia* perfor[med] successful season; closed	
Italian opera season opens, Mr. A. H[arris]	

HER MAJESTY'S THEATRE, OR ITAL[IAN].

Opera-house opened. *Pennant.* (Se[e])	
The theatre was enlarged	
Burnt down	
Rebuilt, and reopened	
Exterior improved by Mr. Nash	
The *rilievo* by Mr. Bubb	
Madame Rachel's appearance	
Mr. Lumley's management	
Jenny Lind's first appearance	
Association formed for conducting fi[nances] of the house	
Jullien's concerts	
Festive performances on the marriag[e of] princess royal	
Macfarren's *Robin Hood* brought out	
[Not opened in 1861.]	
Italian opera (Mr. Mapleson)	
Burnt down; great loss	
Rebuilt—its affairs in Chancery	
Sold for 31,000l.	
[Lease to earl Dudley, till 1891.]	
Opened for Italian opera by Mr. Map[leson]	
Carl Rosa's company, Wagner's operas	
Carl Rosa, Wagner's *Lohengrin*	
Sig. Rossi as *Lear*.	
Opened by M. Carillon (Cargill); Go[ ] performance stopped by strike o[f] panty, carpenters, &c., riot	
Mr. Mayer, lessee; appearance of [ ] Bernhardt in *Fedora*, &c.	
French opera	
Promenade concerts inaugurated by [ ] son 20 Aug.; by Mr. Van Biene	
Italian opera season begins (under [ ])	
The establishment of a company " [ ] Theatre (limited)," with a capital [ ] restore the theatre to its orig[inal] proposed by lord Hay, Mr. Henry [ ] others	

HAYMARKET.

Built	
Opened by French comedians	
Fielding's Mogul company	
A French company prohibited from audience	
Mr. Foote's patent	
The Bottle-conjuror's dupery (see B[ ])	
The theatre rebuilt	
Mr. Colman's tenure	
Miss Farren's appearance here (after[wards] of Derby)"	

THEATRES.

oyal visit great crowd—16 persons killed and
many wounded . . . . . 3 Feb. 1794
r. Elliston's *debut* here . . . 24 June, 1796
irst appearance of Mr. Mathews (as *Lingo*) 16 May, 1803
r. Morris's management 1805
ppearance of Mr. Liston (as *Sheepface*) . 8 June,
he tailors' riot . . . . . 15 Aug. ,,
ppearance of Mr Young (as *Hamlet*) . 22 June, 1807
f Miss F. Kelly (as *Floretta*) . . 12 June, 1810
resent theatre rebuilt by Nash; opened . 4 July, 1821
iss Paton's (Mrs. Wood) appearance (as *Susannah*),
 3 Aug. 1822
r. Webster's management . . . 12 June, 1837
r. Charles Kean's appearance here . . . 1839
r. Webster's management (16 years) terminated
with his farewell appearance . . 14 March, 1853
irst appearance of *Our American Cousin* (said to be
by Tom Taylor, and to have been acted 800 times
in America), Mr. Sothern, *Lord Dundreary* (played
496 nights) . . . . . 11 Nov. 1861
r. Buckstone's management 1853-76
r. John S. Clarke 1878
e-opened; pit removed, and other changes; temporary riot . . . . . 31 Jan. 1880
r. & Mrs. Bancroft 1879-85
'and closing performance . . . 20 July, 1885
pened by Messrs. Russell and Bashford 26 Sept. ,,
terior re-constructed and re-opened by Mr. Beer-
bohm Tree, lessee . . . . . Sept. 1887-9

LYCEUM, FORMERLY ENGLISH OPERA-HOUSE.

ilt by Dr. Arnold 1794-5
inor experiments with gas-lighting 1803-4
pened as the Lyceum in 1809
ppearance of Mr. Wrench (as *Belour*) . 7 Oct. ,,
e-opened with an address by Miss Kelly 15 June, 1816
ouse destroyed by fire . . . . 16 Feb. 1830
ebuilt, and re-opened . . . . 14 July, 1834
questrian performances . . . . 16 Jan. 1844
rs. Keeley's management . . . . 8 April, ,,
adame Vestris and Mr. C. Mathews' management,
 Oct. 1847-56
etirement of Mr. C. Mathews . . March, 1855
ppearance of Madame Ristori . . . June, 1856
iken by Mr. Gye for Italian opera for forty nights,
 14 April, 1857
pened for English opera by Miss Louisa Pyne and
Mr. Harrison . . . . . 21 Sept. ,,
alfe's opera, *Rose of Castile*, produced . . Oct. ,,
r. G. Webster and Mr. Falconer, July, 1858; closed,
 April, 1859
pened by Madame Celeste Nov. 1859, and Oct. 1860
e " Savage Club " perform before the queen and
prince . . . . . . 7 March, ,,
alian opera . . . . . . 8 June, 1861
r. Falconer, manager (English comedy) 19 Aug. ,,
ep o'Day brought out . . . . 9 Nov. ,,
r. Fechter . . . . . 10 Jan. *et seq.* 1863
apanese troupe . . . . . Spring, 1868
ord Lytton's *Rightful Heir* brought out . 3 Oct. ,,
r. H. Irving as *Hamlet* (long run) . . 31 Oct. 1874
 " *Macbeth* . . . 25 Sept. 1875
 " *Othello* . . . 14 Feb. 1876
nnyson's *Queen Mary* performed . . 19 April, ,,
r. H. L. Bateman, lessee and manager . . 1873-6
rs. Bateman, ditto 1876-8
r. H. Irving, lessee . . . . Sept. 1878-89
e-opens with *Hamlet* . . . . 30 Dec. 1878
r. Chippendale's benefit (68 years on the stage),
 24 Feb. 1879
'uch Ado about Nothing; grand scenery . 11 Oct. 1882
r. Irving's company visit United States . . 1883-9
iss M. Anderson and American actors . 1 Sept. 1883
iust, adapted by W. G. Wills, 19 Dec. 1885; 250th
performance . . . . . 22 Nov. 1886
iss Mary Anderson, autumn season . 10 Sept. 1887
evival of *Macbeth* with new rendering by Mr.
Irving and Miss E. Terry . . . 29 Dec. 1888
is company performs the *Bells* before the queen
at Sandringham . . . . . 26 April, 1889
Ir. Mayer with Italian opera and French plays:
Verdi's *Otello*, 5 July; Madame Sarah Bernhardt
in *Léna* . . . . . . 9 July ,,

ADELPHI THEATRE.

ormerly called the *Sans Pareil*, opened under the
management of Mr. and Miss Scott . 27 Nov. 1806
mler Rodwell and Jones, who gave it the present
name 1820-21

Terry and Yates 1825
Messrs. Mathews and Yates' management join
(*Mathews at Home*) 1828
New front 1840
Madame Celeste's management . . 30 Sept. 1844
Rebuilt and opened, with improved arrangements,
 27 Dec. 1858
Colleen Bawn represented . . . 10 Sept. 1860
[Immense run; above 360 nights.]
Miss Bateman appears as *Leah*, 1 Oct. 1863, to
 11 June, 1864
Messrs. F. B. Chatterton and Mr. B. Webster,
lessees 1844-73
Messrs. Gatti, lessees and managers . . 1873-89

ST. JAMES'S, LATE PRINCE'S.

This theatre was built by and opened under the
management of Mr. Braham . . 14 Dec. 1835
German operas performed here under the manage-
ment of Mr. Bunn 1840
Mr. Mitchell's tenure; performance of French plays,
 22 Jan. 1844
German plays 1852
Mrs. Seymour's tenure . . . 22 Oct. 1854-5
French plays 1857
Neapolitan buffo-opera . . . . . Nov. ,,
Italian plays 1858
French operas . . . . . . Jan. 1859
French plays . . . . . . May, ,,
English comedy, under Mr. F. Chatterton, manager,
 Oct. ,,
French plays . . . . . 28 May, 1860
English plays . . . . . 12 Aug. ,,
Mr. Wigan, manager 1860-2
French plays . . . . May, 1868, April, 1869
French plays 1871-3
The Iron Master . . . . . 17 April, 1884
Messrs. Hare & Kendal, lessees and managers . 1885
Mr. Rutland Barrington 1889

PRINCESS'S THEATRE, OXFORD STREET.

First opened for concerts . . . . Sept. 1840
Sold for 16,400*l*. . . . . . 9 Sept. 1841
Opened for plays by Mr. J. Maddox . 26 Dec. 1842
Mr. Bartley's farewell here . . . 18 Dec. 1852
Mr. Charles Kean's management, 1850; closed,
 29 Aug. 1859
Mr. A. Harris's management; opened . 29 Sept. ,,
Zouave Crimean company . . . 23 July, 1860
Mr. Fechter appears (as *Hamlet*) . 20 March, 1861
Mr. Harris, lessee 1860-1
Mr. Lindus, manager . . . . 20 Oct. 1862
Mr. G. Vining, lessee and manager . May, 1863-66
Mr. F. B. Chatterton, lessee 1872-78
Carl Rosa's Opera company 1875
Mr. Walter Gooch, lessee and manager . . 1878-81
Closed for rebuilding, 19 May; rebuilt; opened (1st
appearance of Edwin Booth) . . 6 Nov. 1880
G. R. Sims' *Lights o' London* . . . Sept. 1881
Mr. Wilson Barrett, lessee and manager . Aug. 1883
Claudian, by Herman and Wills . 6 Dec. ,,
Miss G. Hawthorne, lessee . . . Jan. 1888-9
Mr. Wilson Barrett closes his season, going to
America for a year . . . . 18 May, 1889

OLYMPIC.

Erected by the late Mr. Astley, and opened with
horsemanship . . . . . 18 Sept. 1806
Here the celebrated Elliston (1813), and afterwards
Madame Vestris, had managements; the latter
until 1839
Mr. George Wild's tenure 1840
Miss Davenport's tenure . . . 11 Nov. 1844
Mr. Watts's management 1848
The theatre destroyed by fire . . 29 March, 1849
Rebuilt and opened—Mr. Watts resumes his man-
agement . . . . . . 26 Dec. ,,
Mr. William Farren's management . . . 1850
Lessee and manager, Mr. A. Wigan . 17 Oct. 1853-7
Messrs. Robson and Emden's management,
 Aug. 1857-62
Mr. Horace Wigan, manager . . . 1864-68
Lessee, Mr. B. Webster 1868
Lessee and manager, Miss Ada Cavendish . 1873
Mr. Wills's *Buckingham* produced . . Dec. 1875
Mr. Henry Neville 1873-78
Mrs. A. Conover, lessee 1883
Mr. J. Pitt-Hardacre 1889

SAVOY THEATRE, see under *Savoy*. Opened 10 Oct. 1881.

STRAND THEATRE.

First opened—Mr. Rayner and Mrs. Waylett	1831
Mr. William Farren's management	1849
Lessee, Mr. F. Allcroft; manager, Mr. T. Payne	1855
Lessee, Miss Swanborough	1858-61
Mr. Swanborough, sen. . . . . Dec.	1862
Mrs. Swanborough, 1865-88; she died (aged 84) 6 Jan.	1889
Rebuilt; re-opened . . . . 18 Nov.	1882
Mr. J. S. Clarke, lessee . . . . Jan.	1888
Re-opens, Mr. C. Wyndham and Mr. Wm. Duke, managers . . . . 6 Feb.	1889
Mr. Arthur Rousbey's opera company perform *Figaro* . . . . 14 March,	,,

ASTLEY'S AMPHITHEATRE.

Built by Philip Astley, and opened	1773
Destroyed by fire, with numerous adjacent houses, 17 Sept.	1794
Rebuilt	1795
Burnt again, with forty houses . . 1 Sept.	1803
Ducrow's management	1825
Again destroyed by fire . . . 8 June,	1841
Rebuilt and re-opened by Mr. Batty . 17 April,	1843
Lessee and manager, Mr. W. Cooke	1855-60
Mr. W. Cooke's farewell benefit . . 30 Jan.	1860
A man killed by a lion . . . . Jan.	1861
Opened by Mr. Batty . . . . 6 Dec.	,,
Opened by Mr. Boucicault, as the THEATRE ROYAL, WESTMINSTER . . . . 26 Dec.	1862
Horsemanship and opera (under Mr. E. T. Smith), June,	1865
Sold by auction	1868

SURREY THEATRE (FORMERLY CIRCUS).

[Originally devoted to equestrian exercises, under Mr. Hughes]

Mr. Hughes] . . . . 4 Nov.	1782
Opened for performances . . 4 Nov.	1783
Destroyed by fire . . . . 12 Aug.	1805
Mr. Elliston's management	1809
Mr. Elliston again . . . . 4 June,	1827
Mr. Davidge's tenure	1833
Mr. Shepherd and Mr. Anderson, managers, 12 Sept.	1863-5
Destroyed by fire, 31 Jan.; rebuilt and opened, 26 Dec.	1865
Used for melodramas, pantomimes, &c. at low prices	1889

VICTORIA (FORMERLY COBURG).

[The erection was commenced under the patronage of the late princess Charlotte and the prince Leopold of Saxe-Coburg]

pold of Saxe-Coburg]	1816
The house was opened	1818
Messrs. Egerton and Abbott had the management in	1833
Mr. Osbaldiston's tenure	1840
Alarm of fire, sixteen persons killed . 27 Dec.	1858
Now *Victoria Hall*, used for popular lectures, concerts, &c.	1889

SADLER'S WELLS.

Opened as an orchestra	1683
Present house opened	1765
Eighteen persons trampled to death on a false alarm of fire . . . . 15 Oct.	1807
Management of Mrs. Warner and Mr. Phelps, 20 May,	1844-59
Management of Mr. Josephs . . 25 March,	1861
Re-opened by Mr. Phelps . . . 7 Sept.	,,
Lessee, Miss C. Lucette . . . 27 Sept.	1862
Miss Marriott, manager . 5 Sept. 1863—20 May,	1864
Miss C. Lucette, for opera	1865
Miss Marriott, legitimate drama (with intervals)	1865-8
Miss Hazlewood, Miss Marriott, and others .	1868-73
Opened by Mrs. Bateman as New Sadler's Wells, 9 Oct.	1879
Mrs. Bateman dies (Miss I. Bateman succeeds), 13 Jan.	1881
Opened by Miss Roze de Vane . . 12 April,	1884
Closed and re-opened occasionally; opened by Mr. J. A. Cave . . . . Oct.	1887

OTHER THEATRES.

Queen's Theatre, Tottenham-court-road	1828
Garrick Theatre, Goodman's-fields	1830
City Theatre, Norton-Folgate	1837
Miss Kelly's Theatre (since named *Soho* and *New Royalty*)	1840
Marylebone, opened	1842

Standard Theatre, built ; rebuilt	
Pavilion Theatre burnt	
Alhambra, Leicester-squ: 7 Dec. 1882; and re-ope	
New Royalty (Soho)	
Holborn Theatre (afterwa: the *Duke's*), opened, 16	
Royal Amphitheatre (for opened	
New East London, opene:	
"New Queen's Theatre," opened by Alfred Wigan	
St. George's Opera-house by Mr. German Reed	
The Globe, Strand, opene:	
The Gaiety, Strand, opene	
Charing Cross, opened	
Vaudeville, opened	
Opera Comique, 299, St Déjazet)	
Court Theatre, Chelsea, o:	
Royal Alexandra Theatr town, opened, 31 May,	
Criterion, Regent's Circu Spiers and Pond, 21 M 1883; re-opened	
National Opera House (w	
Charing Cross re-opened ; "Imperial theatre," at W	
Holborn theatre reopened theatre "	
H.M.S. Pinafore, by W. Sullivan, much perform of *Penzance*, by the sa:	
Savoy Theatre opened (w:	
Avenue Theatre, Thames	
Prince's Theatre, Coven: opened	
New Alhambra Theatre o:	
Empire Theatre, formerly	
Mr. Terry's new theatre, :	
Grand Theatre, Islington burnt	
New Court Theatre opene	
Shaftesbury Theatre, Lon	
Lyric Theatre, London	
Garrick Theatre, Charin , Mr. Hare	

DUBLIN

Werburg-street, commenc	
Orange-street, now Smock	
Aungier-street (*Victor*)	
Ditto, management of Mr.	
Crow-street Music-hall	
Rainsford-street Theatre	
Smock-alley Theatre, rebu	
Fishamble-street Music-ha	
Capel-street Theatre	
Crow-street, Theatre Roya	
Peter-street, Theatre Roya	
Hawkin's-street, Theatre	
Destroyed by fire	
Queen's Theatre, Brunswi	

EDINBURG

Theatre of Music	
Allan Ramsay's	
The Caledonian Theatre	
Adelphi Theatre burnt do	
Royal Theatre burnt down	

FIRST OR LA

Quin's first appearance	
Macklin at Lincoln's-Inn-fi	
Garrick's at Goodman's-fie	
Miss Farren (afterwards co pears at Liverpool	
Garrick's last appearance	
Mrs. Robinson, *Perdita*; he	
Braham's first appearance	
Madame Storace, her first	

THEATRES.

Incledon's first appearance	1790
Miss Mellon, her first appearance as *Lydia Languish*,	31 Jan. 1795
Master Betty (*Infant Roscius*) début in London, enthusiastically received	1 Dec. 1804
Liston's first appearance in London	1 June, 1805
Miss F. M. Kelly's first appearance	1807
Romeo Coates appears as *Lothario*	10 April, 1811
Mrs. Jordan's last appearance, as *Lady Teazle*,	1 June, 1814
Miss O'Neill, as *Juliet*	6 Oct. ,,
Mr. Macready's first appearance at Bath, as *Romeo*,	29 Dec. ,,
Booth's first appearance	12 Feb. 1817
W. Farren's first appearance	1818
Munden's last appearance	May, 1824
Fanny Kemble's first appearance	5 Oct. 1829
Edmund Kean's last appearance, as *Othello*,	25 March, 1833
Liston's last appearance	31 May, 1838
Adelaide Kemble's first appearance	2 Nov. 1841
Jenny Lind's first appearance	4 May, 1847
Mrs. Glover's farewell	12 July, 1850
Mr. Bartley's farewell	18 Dec. 1852
Mr. W. Farren's farewell	1855
Clara Novello's farewell	21 Nov. 1860
Adelina Patti's first appearance at Covent Garden,	14 May, 1861
Miss Bateman appears as *Leah*	1 Oct. 1863
Her farewell at H.M.'s theatre	22 Dec. 1865
Madlle. Nillson's first appearance at H.M.'s theatre as *Violetta*	8 June, 1867
Miss Kate Terry's last appearance (*Juliet* at the New Adelphi)	31 Aug. ,,
Madlle. Kellogg's *début* at Drury-lane	2 Nov. ,,
Mr. Sandmann's *début*	17 Feb. 1868
Mr. Paul Bedford's farewell at New Queen's theatre,	16 May, ,,
Madlle. Marimon's *début*, as *Amina*	6 May, 1871
Mario's farewell in *La Favorita* at Italian opera,	19 July, ,,
Miss Isabella Bateman's *début*	12 Sept. ,,
Mr. and Mrs. Alfred Wigan's last appearance (at Drury Lane)	6 July, 1872
Mr. H. Irving first appears as *Hamlet*, 31 Oct. 1874, 200th performance	29 June 1875
Our Boys by H. J. Byron, 1st time 16 Jan. 1875 (at the Vaudeville); 1350th, 1 April; and last	18 April, 1879
Mr. Byron's *The Girls*, 1st performance	19 April, ,,

MEMORANDA.

David Garrick died	1779
Charles Macklin died	1797
Mr. Palmer died on the stage at Liverpool, 2 Aug. 1798
Lannister retired from the stage	1815
John P. Kemble died	1823
Talma died in Paris	1826
Weber came to London	Feb. ,,
The Brunswick theatre fell, owing to the weight of a newly-erected roof, and numbers of persons were wounded and some killed	29 Feb. 1828
Sarah Siddons died	1831
Edmund Kean died	1833
Charles Mathews died	28 June, 1835
Madame Malibran died at Manchester	23 Sept. 1836
Paganini died	27 May, 1840
President steamer, about 13 March, 1841
Elton lost in the *Pegasus*	18 July, 1843
Theatres' Registry Act passed	22 Aug. ,,
Madlle. Mars died at Paris	23 March, 1847
Madame Catalini died at Paris	13 June, 1849
W. C. Macready retired	26 April, 1851
Alexander Lee died	9 Oct. ,,
Mrs. Warner died	5 Sept. 1854
Charles Kemble died	12 Nov. ,,
John Braham died	17 Feb. 1856
Madame Vestris died	8 Aug. ,,
Madlle. Rachel died	4 Jan. 1858
Mrs. Nisbet (lady Boothby) died	16 Jan. ,,
Louis Lablache (buffo singer) died	23 Jan. ,,
John Pritt Harley died	22 Aug. ,,
Flexmore, celebrated clown, died	20 Aug. 1860
Mrs. Yates died	30 Oct. ,,
Alfred Bunn died	20 Dec. ,,
William Farren died	25 Sept. 1861
Mr. Vandenhoff died	4 Oct. ,,
M. Tree (Mrs. Bradshaw) died	Feb. 1862

THEFT.

Subscription testimonial (value 2000*l.*) presented to C. J. Kean: Mr. Gladstone in the chair, 22 March, 1862
Sheridan Knowles died	30 Nov. ,,
Mrs. Wood (Miss Paton) died	21 July, 1864
Mr. F. Robson died	11 Aug. ,,
Madame Pasta died, aged 66	1 April, 1865
Charles J. Kean died	23 Jan. 1868
Robert Keeley died, aged 74	3 Feb. 1869
Madame Grisi died	25 Nov. ,,
Wm. Brough, burlesque-writer, died, aged 44, 13 Mar. 1870
Paul Bedford died	11 Jan. 1871
T. W. Robertson, dramatist, died	3 Feb. ,,
Lady Wrixon Becher (Miss O'Neill, *Juliet*), died	29 Oct. 1872
William C. Macready died	27 April, 1873
Wm. Hy. West Betty (the *Infant Roscius*) died, aged 82	Aug. 1874
Charles James Mathews died	24 June, 1878
Alfred Wigan died	29 Nov. ,,
Frederick Gye, died (accidentally shot), nearly 30 years lessee and manager of Royal Italian Opera, Covent Garden	5 Dec. ,,
Wm. H. Schofield Payne, "King of Pantomime" (aged 70), died	18 Dec. ,,
Mrs. Wybrow Rousby died	19 April, 1879
J. B. Buckstone died	31 Oct. ,,
Mrs. Charles Kean (Miss Ellen Tree), died 20 Aug. 1880
Countess of Essex, formerly Miss Stephens, died,	22 Feb. 1882
Benjamin Nottingham Webster died	8 July, ,,
Miss Francis M. Kelly, aged 92, died	6 Dec. ,,
Grand dinner to Mr. H. Irving	4 July, 1883
Miss Mary Anderson's *début*	1 Sept. ,,
Sig. Giuseppe Mario, aged 75, died	11 Dec. ,,
H. J. Byron, author, died	11 April, 1884
Mr. Frederick Balsir Chatterton, lessee of Drury Lane, &c. died	18 Feb. 1886
Jenny Lind (Madame Lind Goldschmidt) died, aged 67	2 Nov. 1887
Mrs. Swanborough dies	6 Jan. 1889
Mrs. Dallas, known as Miss Glyn, dies, aged 66	18 May, ,,

THEATRICAL FUNDS. The Theatrical fund of Covent Garden was established in 1760, incorporated 1774; that of Drury Lane by Garrick 1766; incorporated 1775. They grant pensions to members and their families. The General Theatrical fund was established in 1839, incorporated 1853.

The *Theatrical Mission and Institute* for the benefit of theatrical employed, started in 1876. The princess Christian inaugurated for them "Macready" house, Covent Garden 30 Nov. 1887.

THEBAN LEGION, according to tradition, was composed of Christians, and submitted to martyrdom rather than attack their brethren during the persecution of the emperor Maximin, or sacrifice to the gods, about A.D. 286. Their leader Maurice was canonised.

THEBES or **LUXOR,** in Egypt, called also Hecatompylos on account of its hundred gates, and Diospolis, as being sacred to Jupiter. In the time of its splendour (1600-800 B.C.) it is said to have extended about thirty-three miles. Thebes was ruined by Cambyses, king of Persia, 525 B.C., and by the foundation of Alexandria, 332 B.C.; it rebelled and was taken by Ptolemy Lathyrus, 86 B.C., and few traces of it were seen in the age of Juvenal; see *Memnoneium*. After centuries of neglect, it has been greatly visited since the explorations of Belzoni, 1817.—THEBES, N. Greece (the capital of the country successively called Aonia, Messapia, Ogygia, Hyantis, and Bœotia) was called Cadmeis, from Cadmus, its founder, 1493 B.C. It became a republic about 1120 B.C., and flourished under Epaminondas 378-362 B.C. The "sacred band" formed by him, 377 B.C., was revived in 1877. Thebes' seven gates are mentioned by Homer. See *Bœotia* and *Greece*.

THEFT was punished by heavy fines among

the Jews; by death at Athens, by the laws of Draco; see *Draco*. The Anglo-Saxons nominally punished theft with death, if above 12d. value; but the criminal could redeem his life by a ransom. In the 9th of Henry I. this power of redemption was taken away, 1108. The punishment of theft was very severe in England, till mitigated by Peel's acts 9 & 10 Geo. IV. 1829. The laws respecting theft were consolidated in 1862.

THEINE, see *Cafeine*.

THEISTS (*Theos*, God), a name given to deists about 1660.—*Dean Martin*. See *Deism, Unitarians*, and *Voysey*.

THELLUSSON'S WILL, a most singular document. Mr. Peter Isaac Thellusson, a Genevese and an affluent merchant of London, left 100,000l. to his widow and children; and the remainder of his property, more than 600,000l., he left to trustees, to accumulate during the lives of his three sons, and the lives of their sons; then the estates, directed to be purchased with the produce of the accumulated fund, were to be conveyed to the eldest lineal male descendant of his three sons, with the benefit of survivorship. Should no heir then exist, the whole was to be applied, by the agency of the sinking fund, to the discharge of the national debt. It is said that Mr. Thellusson held much property in trust, and that he desired a sufficient interval of time to elapse for the appearance of just claimants. He died 21 July, 1797. His will incurred much public censure, and was contested by the heirs-at-law, but finally established by a decision of the house of lords, 25 June, 1805. The last surviving grandson died in Feb. 1856. A dispute then arose whether the eldest male descendant or the male descendant of the eldest son should inherit the property. The question was decided on appeal by the house of lords (9 June, 1859), in favour of the latter, lord Rendlesham and Charles S. Thellusson confirming the decision of the Master of the Rolls in 1858. In consequence of the legal expenses the property is said not to exceed greatly its value in the testator's lifetime. On 28 July, 1800, the Thellusson act was passed, restraining testators from devising their property for purposes of accumulation for longer than 21 years after death; any other direction to be void.

THEOCRACY, government by God, existed among the Israelites till Saul was made king, about 1095 B.C. (*Sam*. viii. 7.)

THEODOLITE, an instrument for measuring horizontal angles, used in surveying, consists of a telescope and a divided circle. It was probably first constructed in the 17th century. Jesse Ramsden, in 1787, completed the great theodolite employed in the trigonometrical survey of England and Wales by general Roy.

THEODOSIAN CODE, see *Codes*.

"THEOLOGIA GERMANICA," or "Teutsche Theologey" (printed 1528; Latin and French editions, 1558), a German mystical work, written about the 14th century. In it the "good man," disgusted with the corruptions in church and state, is led to seek for God in the temple of the heart. Luther is said to have placed the work next to the Bible and St. Augustin.

THEOLOGY (from the Greek *Theos*, God), the science which treats of the nature and attributes of God, of his relations to man, and of the manner in which they may be discovered. It is generally divided into two heads. 1. *Inspired*, including the

Holy Scriptures, their interpretation, &c. 2. *Natural;* which lord Bacon calls the first part of philosophy. — Butler's "Analogy of Religion" (1736) and Paley's "Natural Theology" (1802) are eminent books on the latter subject.—Abelard (died 1142) wrote "Theologia Christiania." The "Summa Totius Theologiæ" by Thomas Aquinas (born about 1224), a standard Roman catholic work, was printed with commentaries, &c., in 1596.

THEOPHILANTHROPISTS (lovers of God and man), a sect formed in France in 1796; and headed by one of the five directors, Lepaux, in 1797; was dissolved in 1802.

THEOSOPHISTS, followers of Paracelsus in the 16th century.

The *Theosophical Society* was founded in America by Madame Blavatsky, aided by colonel Olcott, about 1875-6. Aims at universal brotherhood and the study of Eastern philosophy. It has a station in London, and many branches in India and other parts. Mrs. Anna Kingsford, M.D., president in 1883, died 22 Feb. 1888.

THERMIDOR REVOLUTION. On the 9th Thermidor of the 2nd year (27 July, 1794), the Convention deposed Robespierre, and on the next day he and twenty-two of his partisans were executed.

THERMO-ELECTRICITY, see under *Electricity*, and *Heat*.

THERMOMETER. Freezing point: *Fah.* 32°; *R*. 0°; *C*. 0°. Boiling point: *Fah.* 212°, *R.* 80°, *C.* 100°.

Invented by Galileo, before 1597. *Libri*.
Invented by Drebbel of Alcmaer, 1609. *Boerhaave*.
Invented by Paulo Sarpi, 1609. *Fulgentio*.
Invented by Sanctorio in 1610. *Borelli*.
Fahrenheit's thermometer invented about 1726; Réaumur's and Celsius's (the latter now termed centigrade) soon after. [Fahrenheit's scale is usually employed in England, and Réaumur's and the centigrade on the continent.]
The mode of construction by substituting quicksilver for spirits was invented some years subsequently. Halley proposed it in 1697.
Mr. L. M. Casella issued a minimum thermometer in Sept. 1861. It registers degrees of cold by means of mercury.
Negretti and Zambra's registering minimum thermometers, adapted for deep sea purposes, made known early in 1874.

THERMOPHONE, in which sonorous vibrations are produced by the expansion of heated bodies connected with an electro-magnet. The apparatus was constructed by Theodor Wiesendanger, and described by him in October, 1878.

THERMOPYLÆ (Doris, N. Greece). Leonidas, at the head of 300 Spartans and 700 Thespians, at the defile of Thermopylæ, withstood the whole force of the Persians during three days, 7, 8, 9 Aug. 480 B.C., when Ephialtes, a Trachinian, perfidiously leading the enemy by a secret path up the mountains, brought them to the rear of the Greeks, who, thus placed between two assailants, perished gloriously on heaps of their slaughtered foes. One Greek only returned home, and he was received with reproaches for having fled.* Here Antiochus the Great, king of Syria, was defeated by the Romans, 191 B.C.

THERMUM, THERMUS, or THERMA (Greece), a strong city, the Acropolis of Ætolia, N.

---

* The distich, in the Greek Anthology, by Simonides their contemporary, is thus translated by Bowles:—

"Go, tell the Spartans, thou that passest by,
That here, obedient to their laws, we lie."

tured and ravaged by Philip V. B and 206 B.C., on account of its Romans.

US (treasury), a title given in the centuries to large collections of small y and archæology. The most cele-

quitatum Græcorum," by J. Grono-	
L.	1697-1702
quitatum Romanorum," by J. G.	
l. fol.	1694
qnitatum et Historicum Italiæ, G. Grævius and P. Burmannus.	
. . . .	1725
quitatum Sacrarum," by B. Ugo-	
ol.	1744-69

, a city of Bœotia, N. Greece. 700 erished with Leonidas at Thermo- I.C. It suffered through the jealousy who destroyed its walls in 372 B.C.

)NICA (now Salonica), a city in Greece, originally Therme, but reder, and said to have been named Thessalonica, daughter of Philip, Here Paul preached, 53; and to the addressed two epistles in 54. In seditions, a frightful massacre of :ock place in 390, by order of the sius. Thessalonica partook of the Eastern empire. Thessalonica was iracens, with great slaughter, 30 he Normans of Sicily, 15 Aug. 1185; us changes was taken from the e Turks under Amurath, 1430.
a Christian girl, said to be an unwilling metanism, was rescued from the Turks he American consul's, 5 May; riots eu-·; the German and French consuls, onlin, were murdered; the Western ued; reparation was ordered by the l murderers were executed 16 May; ere imprisoned; and 40,000l. said to be llies of the victims, Aug. 1876.

Γ (N. Greece), the seat of many of described by the poets. The first we have any certain knowledge was Deucalion, from whom his subjects lenists, a name afterwards extended From Thessaly came the Achæans, he Dorians, the Hellenes, &c. The kable events in the early history e the deluge of Deucalion, 1548 B.C., ion of the Argonauts, 1263 B.C.; ly. Thessaly long aimed at neu- ian affairs, but became involved rs, the tyrants of Pheræ;—Lyco- t B.C.; his son Jason, 374, assassi- xander, the most eminent, defied bes; assassinated 359. Philip of defeat (353 B.C.), gained a victory , 352; and subjugated the country he Romans gave a nominal freedom r their victory at Cynoscephalæ, included in the kingdom of Greece 24 May, signed 2 July, and occu- ·pt. 1881. Railway from Volo to by the king, 4 May, 1884. See 33.

D (Norfolk), said to have been the us, and an important Saxon town, from 1075 to 1091, when the see Norwich. It was made a suffragan ry VIII.; the power given him 1534.

TIBET (central Asia), is said to

have been a kingdom 313 B.C., conquered by Genghis Khan 1206, and gradually subdued by and annexed to China, 1255-1720. Buddhism became the dominant religion about 905; and the Lamas have absolute power in religious and temporal affairs. Thibet was visited by Marco Polo, 1278; by Jesuits about 1661-2; Bogle and Hamilton, 1774; and Thomas Manning, 1810. An astronomical survey was carried on surreptitiously by two pundits of semi-Thibet origin, under the superintendence of capt. Montgomerie, 1865-7. War with Nepaul, May; peace, June, 1884. Hon. Colman Macaulay's expedition to Lachen valley, to promote commerce; well received, announced 30 Nov. 1884.
A mission to Tibet, including Mr. Macaulay with scientific assistance, organised in India; scheme suspended July, 1886. See Sikkim.

THIEVES' ISLAND, see *Ladrones*.

THIEVES' SYNOD, at Ephesus, 349 or 449, where the doctrines of Eutyches respecting Christ's incarnation were approved, received the name because his opponents were silenced or excluded.

THIMBLES are said to have been found at Herculaneum, and long ago used by the Chinese. The bi-centenary of their invention in Europe by Nicolas van Beuschoten was celebrated at Amsterdam, Dec. 1884. The art of making them was brought to England by John Lofting, a mechanic, from Holland, who set up a workshop at Islington, near London, and practised the manufacture in various metals with profit and success, about 1695.
A *Thimble League* patronised by the queen 1886; the object being to provide employment for distressed needlewomen; there was a sale of the work at lady Winchilsea's house, 23, Eunismore Gardens, 24-25 Oct. 1888.

THIONVILLE, the ancient *Theodonis villa*, a fortified city on the Moselle, N. E. France. It was the occasional residence of Charlemagne and his successors, and on the extinction of his race it was successively held by private lords, the counts of Luxemburg, the dukes of Burgundy, the house of Austria, and the kings of Spain. It was taken by the duke of Guise, 23 June, 1558, after an obstinate defence, and returned to Philip II. by the peace of Château Cambresis. It successfully resisted the marquis de Feuquières in 1637; but was taken after four months' siege by the duc d'Enghien, 10 Aug. 1643, and remained with France. It successfully resisted the Austrians in 1792, and the Prussians in 1814. It was invested by the Germans in Aug. 1870, and after bombardment, being in flames, surrendered 24 Nov. following.

THIRTY-NINE ARTICLES, see *Articles*.

THIRTY TYRANTS, a term applied to the governors of Athens, in 404 B.C., who were expelled by Thrasybulus, 403; and also to the numerous aspirants to the imperial throne of Rome during the reigns of Gallienus and Aurelian, A.D. 259-274.

THIRTY YEARS' WAR, in Germany, between the catholics and protestants. It began in Bohemia in 1618, and ended with the peace of Westphalia in 1648. It is renowned for the victories of Wallenstein and Gustavus Adolphus of Sweden, and for its history by Schiller, published 1790-93. See *Battles*, 1618-48.

THISTLE,[*] ORDER OF THE, SCOTLAND,

[*] Some Scottish historians make the origin of this order very ancient. The abbot Justinian says it was instituted by Achaius I. of Scotland, 809, when that

founded by James V. 1540. It consisted originally of himself, as sovereign, and twelve knights, in imitation of Christ and his twelve apostles. In 1542, James died, and the order was discontinued, about the time of the Reformation. The order was renewed by James VII. of Scotland and II. of England, by making eight knights, 29 May, 1687; increased to twelve by queen Anne in 1703; to sixteen by George IV. in 1827. The original knights of 1687 were

George, duke of Gordon.
John, marquis of Athol.
James, earl of Arran, afterwards duke of Hamilton; killed in a duel, 1712.
Alexander, earl of Moray.
James, earl of Perth; attainted.
Kenneth, earl of Seaforth; attainted.
George, earl of Dumbarton.
John, earl of Melfort; attainted.

THISTLEWOOD'S CONSPIRACY, see *Cato-street Conspiracy*.

THOMAS'S HOSPITAL, ST. (Southwark), was founded as an almshouse by Richard, prior of Bermondsey, in 1213, and surrendered to Henry VIII. in 1538. In 1551 the mayor and citizens of London, having purchased of Edward VI. the manor of Southwark, including this hospital, repaired and enlarged it, and admitted into it 260 poor, sick, and helpless objects; upon which the king, in 1553, incorporated it, together with Bethlehem, St. Bartholomew's, &c. It was rebuilt in 1693. In 1862, the site was sold to the South-eastern railway company, and the patients were removed to the Surrey music hall. The foundation stone of the new hospital, erected at Stangate, near the Surrey side of Westminster-bridge, was laid by the queen, 13 May, 1868; and the new hospital was opened by her majesty, 21 June, 1871.

The appointment of a paid resident treasurer, instead of an honorary one, and other changes recommended by committees, were negatived by the general committee, Nov. 1877.
Establishment of wards for paying-patients, settled 20 Nov. 1878

THOMAS, ST., see *Virgin Isles*.

THOMISTS, see *Scotists*.

THOMITES or TOMITES, a body of enthusiasts who assembled at Boughton, near Canterbury. An insane Cornish publican named John Nicholls, called Thom, or Tom, assumed the name of sir W. Courtenay, knight of Malta and king of Jerusalem, came into Kent, was an unsuccessful candidate for parliament, and incited the rabble against the Poor Law act. On 31 May, 1838, a farmer of the neighbourhood, whose servant had joined the crowd which attended Thom, sent a constable to fetch him back; but on his arrival on the ground he was shot dead by Thom. The military were then called out, and lieut. Bennett proceeded to take the murderer into custody; but Thom advanced, and, firing a pistol, killed the lieutenant on the spot. One of the soldiers fired at Thom, and laid him dead by the side of lieut. Bennett. The people then attacked the military, who were compelled to fire, and eight more persons were killed before the mob dispersed.

THORACIC DUCT, discovered first in a horse, by Eustachius, about 1563; in the human body, by Ol. Rudbec, a Swedish anatomist. Thomas Bartholine, of Copenhagen, and Dr. Jolliffe, of England, also discovered it about 1654. See *Lacteals*.

THORINUM, a very rare metal (a heavy gray powder), discovered by Berzelius in 1828.

THORN (on the Vistula, Poland) was founded by the Teutonic Knights in 1231. Here they acknowledged themselves to be vassals of Poland in 1466. Thorn was taken by Charles XII. of Sweden in 1703. Many protestants were slain here (after a religious riot) at the instigation of the Jesuits, 7 Dec. 1724. Thorn was acquired by the Prussians in 1793; taken by the French in 1806; restored to Prussia at the peace in 1815.

THOROUGH. The name given by Thos. Wentworth, earl of Strafford, to his unsuccessful scheme for making Charles I. an absolute monarch. He was attainted and beheaded, 12 May, 1641.

THORPE, see *Railway Accidents*, 1874.

THOUGHT READING. In 1881 Mr. W. Irving Bishop professed to be able to read a person's thoughts by touching some part of the skin. On June 11 in the presence of Mr. G. J. Romanes, professor E. Ray Lankester, Mr. F. Galton, and others he was successful with some persons, and failed with others (*Nature*, No. 608).

In 1883 he was challenged by Mr. Labouchere, M.P., to operate under certain conditions, at St. James's Hall on 12 June, but virtually declined the tests. Other experiments by Mr. Bishop, 3, 4 June, 1884; success doubted.
Mr. Bishop sentenced to pay 10,000l. damages to Mr Maskelyne for libel in *Truth* (23 July, 1884), 15 Jan. appeal disallowed, 28 Jan.; damages reduced to 500l. 2 July, 1885. He died of catalepsy at New York, 1 May, 1889.
Experiments by Mr. Stuart Cumberland reported successful on the prince of Wales and others, 19 July, 1884.

THRACE (now *Roumelia*, in Turkey) derived its name from Thrax, the son of Mars.—*Aspin*. The Thracians were a warlike people, and therefore Mars was said to have been born and to have had his residence among them.—*Euripides*. See *Odrysæ*.

	B.C.
Byzantium, the capital, founded by the Megarians, about	675
Invasion of Darius I. 513; Thrace subdued by Megabazus	508
Xerxes marches against Greece through Thrace, and retreats	480
Other Greek colonies established	450-400
Wars between Macedon and the Odrysæ (*which see*)	429-343
Philip II. acquires Amphipolis, 358; and gradually all the Greek colonies	357-341
Death of Alexander; Thrace allotted to Lysimachus, 323; who builds Lysimachia	309
Lysimachus defeated and slain by Seleucus at Corupedion	281
Thrace overrun by the Gauls	279
Lysimachia and the chief towns seized by the fleet of Ptolemy Euergetes	247
Recovered by Philip V. of Macedon	205-200
Lost by him to the Romans	196
Seized by Antiochus III. of Syria, who is defeated at Magnesia, 190; and surrenders Thrace	188
Perseus defeated in his attempt to regain Thrace,	171-163
The Thracian kings rule nominally under the Romans	148 *et seq*.

	A.D.
Rebellion of Vologæsus quelled	14
Rhœmetalces II. last king	38
Thrace made a Roman province, about	47
Invaded by the Goths	255
Settled by Sarmatians	334-376
Ravaged by Alaric, 395; by Attila	447

monarch made an alliance with Charlemagne, and then took for his device the thistle. It is stated that the king Hungus, the Pict, had a dream, in which St. Andrew made a midnight visit, and promised him a sure victory over his foes, the Northumbrians; and that the next day St. Andrew's Cross (x) appeared in the air, and the Northumbrians were defeated. On this story, it is said, Achaius framed the order more than 700 years before James V.

conquered by the Turks, who made Adrianople their capital 1341-53
Constantinople captured by Mahomet II., 29 May, 1453

THRASHING-MACHINES. The flail was the only instrument formerly in use for thrashing corn. The Romans used a machine called the *tribulum*, a sledge loaded with stones or iron, drawn over the corn-sheaves by horses. The first machine attempted in modern times was invented by Michael Menzies, at Edinburgh, about 1732; Andrew Meikle invented a machine in 1776. Many improvements have been since made, and steam is employed. An act for the prevention of accidents by these machines was passed in 1879.

THRASYMENE or TRASIMENE (N. Italy). A most bloody engagement took place near the Trasimene lake between the Carthaginians under Hannibal and the Romans under Flaminius, 217 B.C. No less than 15,000 Romans were left dead on the field of battle, and 10,000 taken prisoners; or, according to Livy, 6000; or Polybius, 15,000. The loss of Hannibal was about 1500 men. About 10,000 Romans made their escape, all covered with wounds.—*Livy; Polybius.* On the same day, an earthquake occurred, which desolated several cities in Italy.

THREATENING LETTERS. Sending letters, whether anonymously written, or with a fictitious name, demanding money, or threatening to kill a person, or fire his house, was made punishable as a felony, without benefit of clergy, by the Black Act, in 1722. Persons extorting money by threatening to accuse others of such offences as are subjected to death, or other infamous punishments, were to be adjudged imprisonment, whipping, or transportation, by 30 Geo. II., 1756, and other acts; the latest 24 & 25 Vict. cc. 96, 97 (1861).

THREE DENOMINATIONS, see *Denominations*.

THREE CHOIRS (Gloucester, Worcester, and Hereford). Festivals held in 1724, if not earlier, at Gloucester, for the performance of cathedral music on a grand scale for charitable purposes, still continued.

THREE F.'S, see F.

THREE ACRES AND A COW, see *Land*, 885.

THRIFT, see under *National*.

THROAT AND EAR DISEASES, a hospital for them opened near Gray's-inn-road, March, 1874; foundation of a new building laid by madame Adelina Patti, marchesa de Caux, 16 Sept. 1875.

THUGS, organised secret fanatical murderers in India, who considered their victims to be sacrifices to their goddess Kali or Bhowain. The English commenced suppressing them about 1810, but did not succeed till about 1830, when a plan for the purpose was adopted by lord Wm. Bentinck.

THUMB-SCREW, an instrument used in the first stages of torture by the Spanish inquisition. In Great Britain, rev. Wm. Carstares, a presbyterian minister, was the last who suffered by it, before the Scotch privy council, to make him divulge secrets entrusted to him, which he firmly resisted. After the revolution in 1688, the thumb-screw was presented to him by the council. King William expressed a desire to see it, and tried it on, bidding the doctor to turn the screw; but, at the third turn, he cried out "Hold—*hold!* doctor: another turn would make *me* confess anything."

THUNDERER, see *Navy of England*, 1872, 1876, 1879.

THUNDERING LEGION. During a contest with the invading Marcomanni, the prayers of some Christians in a Roman legion are said to have been followed by a storm of thunder, lightning, and rain, which tended greatly to discomfit the enemy; and hence the legion received the name, 174.

THURII or THURIUM, a Greek city, S. Italy, founded after the fall of Sybaris, about 452 B.C. It suffered from the incursions of the Lucanians, by whom the Thurians were severely defeated, 390 B.C. It became eventually a dependent ally of Rome; was ravaged by the troops of Hannibal, 204; was established as a colony by the Romans, 194; and was captured by Spartacus in the Servile war, who levied upon it heavy contributions, 72.

THURINGIA, an early Gothic kingdom in central Germany, was overrun by Attila and the Huns, 451; the last king, Hermanfried, was defeated and slain by Thierry, king of the Franks, who annexed it to his dominions, 530. It formed two duchies, 630-717, and 849-919; a margraviate, 960-1090; landgraviate and county, 1130-1247; and was, after various changes and many conflicts, absorbed into Saxony in the 15th century. In 1815 it was surrendered to Prussia.

THURLES (S. Ireland). Here was held a synod of the Roman catholic archbishops, bishops, inferior clergy, and religious orders, under the direction of archbishop Cullen, the Roman catholic primate, 22 Aug. 1850. It condemned the Queen's Colleges, and recommended the foundation of a Roman catholic university, 10 Sept. following. The acts were forwarded to Rome for approval of the pope, Pius IX., and published, 1 Jan. 1852.

THUROT'S INVASION. Thurot, an Irish commodore in the French service, became a terror to all the merchant-ships of this kingdom. He had the command of a small armament, and landed 1000 men at Carrickfergus in Ireland, and plundered the town. He reached the Isle of Man, and was overtaken by captain Elliot, with three frigates, who engaged his little squadron, which was taken, and the commodore killed, 28 Feb. 1760. Thurot's true name was O'Farrell. His grandfather had followed the fortunes of James II.; but his mother being of a family of some dignity in France, he assumed her name.—*Burns.*

THURSDAY, the fifth day of the week, named from Thor, the most valiant son of Odin, a deified hero worshipped by the northern nations, particularly by the Scandinavians and Celts. His authority was said to extend over the winds, seasons, thunder and lightning, &c. Thursday is in Latin *dies Jovis*, or Jupiter's day.

THYATIRA (Asia Minor), the place assigned for the battle at which the rebel Procopius was defeated by the army of the emperor Valens, 366. See *Seven Churches.*

THYMBRA (Asia Minor). Here Cyrus the Great defeated the confederate army aiding Crœsus, and obtained supremacy in Asia, B.C. 548.

TIARA, head ornament of the ancient Persians. The name is given to the triple crown of the pope (anciently called *regnum*), indicative of his civil rank, as the keys are of his ecclesiastical jurisdiction. The right to wear a crown is said to have been granted to the bishops of Rome by Constantine

the Great, and by Clovis, founder of the French monarchy. Their ancient tiara was a high round cap. Pope Damasus II. first caused himself to be crowned with a tiara, 1048. "Boniface VIII. encompassed the tiara with a crown; Benedict XII. added a second; and John XXIII. a third."
—*Rees.*

TIBER (central Italy), the river on whose banks Rome was built. In the flourishing times of the city the navigation of the river was enormous. Livy states that the Tiber was frozen over, 398 B.C. A commission was appointed to dredge the bed of the river near Rome. Dec. 1871. Garibaldi's scheme for improving the river, making a new port, &c., laid before the Italian parliament, 25 May, 1875; works begun, March, 1877.

TIBERIAS, a city in Palestine, built by Herod Antipas, and named after the emperor Tiberius, 39. Near it Guy de Lusignan, king of Jerusalem, and the crusaders, were defeated by Saladin, 3, 4 July, 1187; and Jerusalem fell into his hands.

TIBET, see *Thibet.*

TIBUR (now Tivoli), a Latin town more ancient than Rome, and frequently at war with it. The Tiburtines were defeated 335 B.C., and the subjection of all Latium followed; for which Furius Camillus obtained a triumph and an equestrian statue in the forum.

TICHBORNE CASE, see *Trials*, 1871-4. Dr. Kenealy, the claimant's counsel, elected M.P. for Stoke, moves for a royal commission to inquire into the trial; rejected, 433 to 3 (Dr. Kenealy, Mr. Whalley, and the O'Gorman); 26 April, 1875. See *Englishman.*

TICINO or **TESSIN**, a Swiss canton south of the Alps, conquered by the Swiss early in the 16th century; made a separate canton in 1815. It suffered by internal disputes 1839 and 1841.

TICINUS, a river, N. Italy. Here Hannibal defeated the Romans, 218 B.C.

TICKETS OF LEAVE, see *Transportation,* and *Crime.*

TICONDEROGA (N. America). The French fortress here was unsuccessfully besieged by Abercromby in July, 1758; taken 26 July, 1759. The Americans took it 10 May, 1775, but retired July, 1777. The British retired from it shortly after.

TIDES. Homer is the earliest profane author who speaks of the tides. Posidonius of Apamea accounted for the tides from the motion of the moon, about 79 B.C.: and Cæsar speaks of them in his fourth book of the Gallic war. The theory of the tides was first satisfactorily explained by Kepler, 1598; but the honour of a complete explanation of them was reserved for sir Isaac Newton, about 1683; see *Thames.* Sir Wm. Thomson, at the Royal Institution, 9 April, 1875, described a valuable tide-calculating machine.

TIEN-TSIN, see *China*, June, 1858-Jan. 1861, and 1870.

TIERRA DEL FUEGO, see under *Missions.*

TIERRA DEL FUEGO (*The Land of Fire*)—A group of five large islands, and many smaller ones, the extreme S.W. of South America, misnamed by Magellan from the fires seen on the coast 1520. Recent discoveries have shown that the country is not so inhospitable and the natives not so degraded as was formerly supposed.

TIERS-ETAT, see *States-General.*

TIFLIS (Asiatic Russia), built about 469 by Vakhtang; became the capital of Georgia. It was taken by Genghis Khan in the 12th century; by Mustapha Pacha, 1576; by the Persians, 1796; and by the Russians, 1801, who have made it the capital of their Trans-Caucasian possessions.

TIGRANO-CERTA, capital of Armenia, built by Tigranes the Great, and taken by Lucullus and the Romans, after a great victory, B.C. 69.

TIGRIS, a river forming the eastern boundary of Mesopotamia, celebrated for the cities founded on its banks: Nineveh, Seleucia, Ctesiphon, and Bagdad. It was explored by an English steamer in 1838. Colonel Chesney, in 1850, published an account of his survey in 1836-7.

TILBURY (Essex). The camp formed here in 1588 to resist the Spanish invasion was visited by queen Elizabeth.

TILES are said to have been first made in England about 1246. They were taxed in 1784. The number of tiles taxed in England in 1820 was 81,924,626; and in 1830, 97,318,264. The tax was repealed in 1833.

TILSIT (on the Niemen), on which river, on a raft, the emperors of France and Russia met, 25 June, 1807. By a treaty concluded between France and Russia, signed 7 July, Napoleon restored to the Prussian monarch one-half of his territories, and Russia recognised the Confederation of the Rhine, and the elevation of Napoleon's three brothers, Joseph, Louis, and Jerome, to the thrones of Naples, Holland, and Westphalia.

TILTS, see *Tournaments.*

TIMBER. The annual demand of timber for the royal navy, in war, was 60,000 loads, or 40,000 full-grown trees, a ton each, of which 35 will stand on an acre; in peace, 32,000 tons, or 48,000 loads. A 74 gun ship consumed 3000 loads, or 2000 tons of trees, the produce of 57 acres in a century. —*Allnutt.* Iron is now largely used in preference to timber. In 1843 we imported 1,317,645 loads of timber (cut and uncut); in 1857, 2,495,904 loads; in 1866, 3,638,344 loads; in 1871, 4,497,136 loads; in 1875, 5,092,394 loads; in 1877, 6,788,789 loads; in 1883, 6,609,942 loads; in 1887, 5,653,791 loads. In 1866, we imported 53,458 tons of mahogany; in 1871, 29,256 tons; in 1875, 80,705 tons; in 1877, 53,600 tons; in 1883, 50,158 tons; in 1887, 37,650 tons. The duties on timber were modified in 1851.

TIMBER BENDING. Apparatus was invented for this purpose by Mr. T. Blanchard, of Boston, U.S., for which a medal was awarded at the Paris Exhibition of 1855. A company was formed for its application in this country in 1856.

TIMBUCTOO (N. Africa), a city built by Mansa Suleiman, a Mahometan, about 1214, and frequently subjugated by the sovereigns of Morocco. Since 1727 it has been partially independent.

TIME. See *Hour, Day, Month, Year, Geodesy, Dials, Clocks and Watches.*

TIMES NEWSPAPER. On 1 Jan. 1785, Mr. John Walter published the first number of the *Daily Universal Register*, price 2½d., printed on the logographic system (invented by Henry Johnson, a compositor), in which types containing syllables and words were employed instead of single letters. On 1 Jan. 1788, the paper was named the *Times.*

In 1803, when Mr. John Walter gave up the paper to his son John, the circulation was about 1000; that of the *Morning Post* being 4500.

Mr. John Walter (1) died 16 Nov. 1812.

Dr. Stoddart (satirised as Dr. Slop by Moore the poet) became editor in 1812, but five years after retired and set up in opposition the *New Times*, an unprofitable speculation. Thomas Barnes became next editor. He died 7 May, 1841, and was succeeded by his assistant John Thaddeus Delane (son of W. F. A. Delane, financial manager) who retired in 1877, and died 22 Nov. 1879.

On 28 Nov. 1814, the *Times* was first printed by steam power (the invention of F. König), 1200 per hour, afterwards increased to 2000 and 4000.

It is asserted that the *Times* was termed the "*Thunderer*" in consequence of an article by Edward Sterling in which are the words, "We thundered forth articles on reform, &c." when Barnes was editor.

On 19 Jan. 1829, the first double number appeared.

In July, 1834, an attack of Mr. O'Connell in the house of commons on the correctness of the reports of the debates in the *Times* was signally defeated.

Shortly after began the convenient summary of the debates, written in the first instance by Mr. Horace Twiss.

In 1841 the *Times* was instrumental in detecting and exposing a scheme organised by Allan George Bogle and others, to defraud by forgery all the influential bankers of Europe. This brought on the proprietors an action for libel (in the case Bogle *v.* Lawson). The jury found the charge to be true, giving a verdict of one farthing damages, but the judges refused costs. Subscriptions were set on foot at the Mansion-house and in all parts of Europe to reimburse the proprietors for the immense outlay in defending the action. This they firmly declined; and the money was expended in establishing *Times Scholarships* at Oxford and Cambridge, and at Christ's Hospital, and other schools; a marble tablet also, commemorating the event, was set up in the Royal Exchange and at the *Times* office. These were the greatest honours ever conceded to a newspaper.

In Oct. 1845, the *Times* express was for the first time conveyed to India overland, by the agency of lieut. Waghorn.

Of the number of the *Times* containing the life of the duke of Wellington for 19 Nov. 1852, 70,000 were sold—the ordinary number being then 36,000; the circulation is stated to vary from 50,000 to 60,000 (1868).

The *Times* (a slip) announcing permission to relax restriction of issue of bank-notes, published 24 Oct. 1847.

Mr. John Walter (2) died 28 July, 1847; Mr. John Walter (3) born in 1818.

In 1854, the proprietors sent Mr. W. H. Russell as their special correspondent to the seat of war in the Crimea; in 1857 to India.

Times Fund.—On the 12th of Oct. 1854, sir Robert Peel originated by a letter in the *Times* a subscription for the sick and wounded in the Crimean war, and in less than a fortnight 15,000*l.* were sent to the *Times* office to be thus appropriated. Mr. MacDonald was sent out by the proprietors as special commissioner to administer the fund, from which large quantities of food and clothing were supplied to the sufferers, with inestimable advantage; see *Scutari*, and *Nightingale*.

In Dec. 1858, the *Times* drew attention to the state of the houseless poor of London; and in a few days 8000*l.* were subscribed for their relief.

In 1851, 13,000,000 copies were sold; in 1857, 16,100,000; in 1859, 16,000,000; in 1860, 16,670,000.

The *Times* of 21 June, 1861, contained 4076 advertisements (about 1810 it contained 150 advertisements).

Stereotypes from papier-mâché moulds introduced, 1856; much improved 1860.

The "Walter press" invented by John Cameron MacDonald (aft. Manager) & Joseph Calverley, prints about 15,000 an hour, perfected, 1862-71.

A list of the contents, inserted over the first leader, appeared first, 3 Feb. 1869.

3½ pages tables of metropolitan charities appeared 11 Feb. 1869.

Special train for conveying the *Times*, North-Western Railway, began to run, 4.55 a.m., 16 Feb. 1875.

Annual summaries, 1851-75, reprinted, price 1*s.* (type set-up by composing-machines).

12,000 perfect sheets per hour printed by "Walter Press," Jan. 1876.

Weekly issue, price 2*d.*, began, 5 Jan. 1877.

The Rapieff electric lamp adopted in the machine-room, Nov. 1878.

Mr. Palmer's "Index to the *Times*" begun 1867; now printing for *Times* before 1846 and continuing 1889.

Summary of the *Times* published daily, ½*d.* about 26 July, 1883; stopped, Oct. 1884.

Death of Thomas Chenery, six years editor, long correspondent, 11 Feb.; succeeded by G. E. Buckle, Feb. 1884.

The *Times* consisted of 24 pages 21, 26 June, 1861; 14 June, 1884; 5 times in 1886; 3 times in 1887; 6 times in 1888; 11, 18, 25 May, 1, 22, 29 June, 1889.

Death of Chas. Ross, aged 84, 63 years a parliamentary reporter and 30 years a chief, 6 Dec. 1884.

Edwin Murray (watch dealer) *r. Times*, libel case, farthing damages, 26-27 Oct. 1886.

Articles "Parnellism and Crime," published 7, 10, 14 March; article on Mr. Dillon, 2 May, declared by the commons not to be a breach of privilege, 4-6 May, 1887.

Centenary of the publication of the *Times*; special leader 2 Jan. 1888.

O'Donnell *v.* Walter and another (*see* under *Parnellites*) verdict for the defendant 2-5 July, 1888.

No. 31,725 (5 April, 1886) published as a book at Leipsic with German notes by Dr. F. Landmann, Oct. 1888.

For the trial by the special commission see under *Parnellites*.

Rev. lord Sidney G. Osborne (S.G.O.), long a philanthropic writer to the *Times*, dies 9 May, 1889.

TIN. The Phœnicians traded with England for more than 1100 years before the Christian era. Under the Saxons, our tin mines appear to have been neglected; but under the Normans, they produced considerable revenues to the earls of Cornwall, particularly to Richard, brother of Henry III. A charter and various immunities were granted by Edmund, earl Richard's brother, who framed the Stannary Laws (*which see*), laying a duty on the tin. Edward III. confirmed the tinners in their privileges, and erected Cornwall into a dukedom, with which he invested his son, Edward the Black Prince, 1337. Since that time the heirs-apparent to the crown of England, if eldest sons, have enjoyed it successively. Tin mines were discovered in Germany, which lessened the value of those in England, till then the only tin mines in Europe, 1240.—*Anderson.* Discovered in Barbary, 1640; in India, 1740; in New Spain, 1782. In 1857, 9783 tons; in 1860, 10,462 tons; in 1864, 10,108 tons; in 1865, 10,039 tons; in 1870, 10,200 tons; in 1874, 9942 tons; in 1876, 8500 tons; in 1879, 9532 tons; 1882, 9158 tons; in 1884, 9,574 tons; in 1887, 9,282 tons of metallic tin were procured from British mines. Of tin plates we exported in value, in 1847, 484,184*l.*; in 1854, 1,075,531*l.*; in 1860, 1,500,812*l.*; in 1864, 1,263,246*l.*; in 1866, 1,896,192*l.*; in 1871, 2,900,625*l.*; in 1873, 3,953,042*l.*; in 1877, 3,033,126*l.*; in 1879, 3,507,977*l.*; in 1883, 4,705,403*l.*; in 1887, 4,792,854*l.*

TINCHEBRAY (N. W. France), where a battle was fought between Henry I. of England and his brother Robert duke of Normandy. England and Normandy were reunited under Henry, at the decease of William Rufus, who had already possessed himself of Normandy by a mortgage from his brother Robert, at his setting out for Palestine. Robert, on his return, recovered Normandy by an accommodation with Henry; but having afterwards quarrelled, Robert was defeated in the battle of Tinchebray, 28 Sept. 1106, and Normandy was annexed to the crown of England.—*Hénault.*

TIPPERMUIR (near Perth). Here the marquis of Montrose defeated the covenanters under lord Elcho, 1 Sept. 1644.

TIRNOVA on the Jantra a tributary of the Danube, capital of the ancient kingdom of Bulgaria. It was occupied without resistance by general Gourko, 6, 7 July, 1877, and made the Russian head-quarters.

TIRYNS, an ancient city of Greece, S.E. of Argos, with massive cyclopæan remains. Excavations of Dr. Schliemann in 1884 led to the discovery of what he termed "the Prehistoric Palace of the kings of Tiryns." His book on Tiryns was published in 1886. As Byzantine remains are also found some of his conclusions are disputed by eminent antiquaries.

TITANIUM, a rare metal, discovered by Gregor in menaccanite, a Cornish mineral, in 1791, and in 1794 by Klaproth.

TITHES or **TENTHS**, were commanded to be given to the tribe of Levi, 1490 B.C. (*Lev.* xxvii. 30). Abraham returning from his victory over the kings (*Gen.* xiv.), gave tithes of the spoil to Melchisedek, king of Salem, priest of the most high God (1913 B.C.) For the first 800 years of the Christian church they were given purely as alms, and were voluntary.—*Wickliffe.* "I will not put the title of the clergy to tithes upon any divine right, though such a right certainly commenced, and I believe as certainly censed, with the Jewish theocracy."—*Blackstone.* They were established in France by Charlemagne, about 800, and abolished 1789. Tenths were confirmed in the Lateran councils, 1215.—*Rainalda.* The payment of tithes appears to have been claimed by Augustin, the first archbishop of Canterbury, and to have been allowed by Ethelbert, king of Kent, under the term "God's fee," about 600.

The first mention of them in any English written law is a constitutional decree made in a synod strongly enjoining tithes, 786.
Offa, king of Mercia, gave unto the church the tithes of all his kingdom, to expiate the death of Ethelbert, king of the East Angles, whom he had caused to be basely murdered, 794.
Tithes were first granted to the English clergy in a general assembly held by Ethelwold, 844. *Henry.*
In England, in 1545, tithes were fixed at the rate of 2s. 9d. in the pound on rent; since then, many acts have been passed respecting them.
The Tithe Commutation act, passed 13 Aug. 1836. It was amended in 1837, 1840, 1846, 1860, and 1878.
A *rector* is entitled to all the tithes; a *vicar* to a small part only, frequently to none.
Several acts relating to tithes in Ireland have been passed in 1832-47, altering and improving the tithe system.
Tithe redemption trust appointed, 1846.
Agitation against "extraordinary tithes," 11 Aug. *et seq.* 1881.
An Anti-Extraordinary Association existed in 1882.
Extraordinary Tithe Redemption Act passed 1886.
Riotous opposition to tithes in Wales, Aug.; anti-tithe league formed Sept. 1886; riots (see *Wales*) 1887.
Tithe Bill brought in; dropped Aug. 1887.

TITHING. The number or company of ten men with their families knit together in a society, all of them being bound to the king for the peaceable and good behaviour of each of their society; of these companies there was one chief person, who, from his office, was called (toothingman) tithingman; but now he is nothing but a constable, formerly called the headborough. *Cowel.*

TITLES ROYAL. Henry IV. had the title of "Grace" and "My liege," 1399. Henry VI., "Excellent Grace," 1422. Edward IV., "Most High and Mighty Prince," 1461. Henry VII., "Highness," 1485; Henry VIII. the same title, and sometimes "Grace," 1509 *et seq.* Francis I. of France addressed Henry as "Your Majesty" at their interview in 1520; see *Field of the Cloth of Gold.* Henry VIII. was the first and last king who was styled "Dread Sovereign." James I. coupled to "Majesty" the present "Sacred," or "Most Excellent Majesty." "Majesty" was the style of the emperors of Germany; the first king to whom it was given was Louis XI. of France, about 1463.

TITLES TO LAND CONSOLIDATION ACT (Scotland), passed 31 July, 1868, and amended in 1869.

TIVOLI, see *Tibur*.

TOBACCO,* *Nicotiana tabacum*, received its name from Tabacco, a province of Yucatan, New Spain; some say from the island of Tobago, one of the Caribbees; others from Tobasco, in the Gulf of Florida. It is said to have been first observed at St. Domingo, in Cuba, 1492; and to have been used freely by the Spaniards in Yucatan in 1520. Tobacco was either first brought to England in 1565, by sir John Hawkins; or by sir Walter Raleigh and sir Francis Drake, in 1586. It was manufactured only for exportation for some years. *Stow's Chron.* The Pied Bull inn, at Islington, is said to have been the first house in England where tobacco was smoked. In 1584 a proclamation was issued against it. James I. published "A Counterblaste against Tobacco," and the star-chamber ordered the duties to be 6s. 10d. per pound, 1614. Its cultivation was prohibited in England by Charles II., 1684. Act laying a duty on the importation was passed 1684. The cultivation was allowed in Ireland, 1779. The tax was increased and put under the excise, 1789. *Anderson; Ashe.* Various statutes have passed relative to tobacco. Act to revive the act prohibiting the culture of tobacco in Ireland passed 2 Will. IV., Aug. 1831. Act directing that tobacco grown in Ireland be purchased in order to its being destroyed, 24 March, 1832. The quantity consumed in England in 1791 was nine millions and a half of pounds, and in 1829 about fifteen millions of pounds. We imported in 1850, 35,166,358 lbs., and 1,557,558 lbs. manufactured (cigars and snuff); in 1855, 36,820,846 lbs., and 2,651,544 lbs. manufactured; in 1860, 48,936,471 lbs., and 2,110,430 lbs. manufactured; in 1864, 61,042,667 lbs., and 6,578,707 lbs., manufactured; in 1866, 54,374,800 lbs., and 3,171,906 lbs. manufactured; in 1871, 73,042,305 lbs., and 3,852,236 manufactured; in 1876, 76,814,974 lbs., and 3,818,682 lbs. manufactured; in 1879, 38,861,220 lbs., and 3,591,558 lbs. manufactured; in 1883, 56,475,199 lbs., and 3,121,174 lbs. manufactured; in 1887, 72,178,994 lbs. and 3,595,071 manufactured. The tobacco duties were modified in 1863; raised April, 1878. 2d. a lb. extra duty on cigars added, April, 1879. Net customs duties paid for tobacco and snuff in the year 1875-6, 7,744,977l.; 1877-8, 8,006,836l.; 1883-4, 8,991,205l.; 1886-7, 9,367,186l.; 1887-8, 8,713,944l.
Permission to grow tobacco in England with conditions granted by the Board of Trade, April, 1886.
Tobacco successfully cultivated by Messrs. James Carter and Co., near Bromley, Essex, Sept. 1886; and by others in 1887.
Duty per lb on unmanufactured tobacco reduced from 3s. 6d. to 3s. 2d.; cigars 5s.; snuff 3s. 9d. or 4s. 6d. 1887.

TOBAGO (West Indies), discovered by Columbus in 1498; settled by the Dutch 1642. Taken by the English, 1672; retaken, 1674. In 1748, it was declared a neutral island; but in 1763 it was ceded

---
* *British Anti-Tobacco Crusade*, originated by the late Thos. Reynolds in 1853. 60,000 of its publications had been circulated gratuitously in 1876.

to the English. Tobago was taken by the French under De Grasse in 1781, and confirmed to them in 1783. Again taken by the English, 14 April, 1793, but restored at the peace of Amiens, 6 Oct. 1802. The island was once more taken by the British under general Grinfield, 1 July, 1803, and was confirmed to them by the peace of Paris, in 1814. Population in 1887, 19,937. Tobago is one of the Windward isles.
United with Trinidad by parliament in 1887.

- **TOBITSCHAU** (Moravia). In a sharp action here, on 15 July, 1866, the Austrians were defeated by the army of the crown prince of Prussia with the loss of 500 killed and wounded and 500 prisoners, and seventeen guns.

TOISON D'OR or GOLDEN FLEECE (*which see*).

TOKENS, BANK, silver pieces issued by the Bank of England, of the value of 5s., 1 Jan. 1798. The Spanish dollar had a small profile of George III. stamped on the neck of the Spanish king. They were raised to the value of 5s. 6d. 14 Nov. 1811. Bank tokens were also current in Ireland, where those issued by the bank passed for 6s. and lesser sums until 1817. They were called in on the revision of the coinage. Tradesmen were permitted to issue tokens as small coins from 1648 till 16 Aug. 1672, when their circulation was prohibited by royal proclamation. These tokens are figured and described in a work by Wm. Boyne, 1858.

TOKIO, the name given to Jeddo, the capital of Japan, about 1869. See *Jeddo*.

TOLBIAC (now ZULPICH), near the Rhine, where Clovis totally defeated the Allemanni, 496.

TOLEDO, the ancient Toletum (Central Spain), made capital of the Visigothic kingdom by Athanasild, 554; taken by the Saracens, 712. Toledo was taken after the war begun 1081, by Alfonso I. of Castile, 25 May, 1085. In 1088 the archbishop was made primate of Spain. The university was founded in 1499. Toledo sword-blades have been famed since the 15th century.
The alcazar, ancient Moorish palace, used by the emperor Charles V., destroyed by fire, 9-10 Jan. 1887.

TOLENTINO (Italy, formerly in the Papal states), where a treaty was made between the pope and the French, 19 Feb. 1797. Here Joachim Murat, having resumed arms against the allies, was defeated by the Austrians, 3 May, 1815, taken prisoner, and shot.

TOLERATION ACT, passed in 1689, to relieve Protestant dissenters from the church of England. Their liberties were, however, greatly endangered in the latter days of queen Anne, who died on the day that the Schism bill was to become a law, 1 Aug. 1714.
The toleration granted was somewhat limited. It exempted persons who took the new oath of allegiance and supremacy, and made also a declaration against popery, from the penalties incurred by absenting themselves from church and holding unlawful conventicles; and it allowed the quakers to substitute an affirmation for an oath, but did not relax the provisions of the Test act (*which see*). The party spirit of the times checked the king in his liberal measures.

TOLLS were first paid by vessels passing the Stade on the Elbe, 1109. They were first demanded by the Danes of vessels passing the Sound, 1341; see *Stade*, and *Sound*. Tollbars in England originated in 1267, on the grant of a penny for every waggon that passed through a certain manor; and the first regular toll was collected a few years after for mending the road in London between St. Giles's and Temple-bar. Gathered for repairing the highways of Holborn-inn-lane and Martin's-lane (now Aldersgate-street), 1346. Toll-gate or *turnpikes* were set up in 1663. In 1827, 27 turnpikes near London were removed by parliament; 81 turnpikes and toll-bars ceased on the north of London on 1 July, 1864; and 61 on the south side, ceased on 31 Oct. 1865; and many others on the Essex and Middlesex roads ceased on 31 Oct. 1866; the remainder on the north of London ceased 1 July, 1872. The tolls on the Commercial roads, London, E., were abolished 5 Aug. 1871. The tolls on Waterloo and other metropolitan bridges abolished, 1878-9. The high road from Brighton to London free from toll, 31 Oct. 1881. See *Wales*, 1843 and 1889.

TOLOSA. On the plain named las Navas de Tolosa, near the Sierra Morena, S. Spain, Alfonso, king of Castile, aided by the kings of Arragon and Navarre, gained a great victory over the Moors, 16 July, 1212. This conflict is sometimes termed the battle of Muradal.

TONGA ISLES, Pacific Ocean. The king, George I., concluded a treaty with Germany, 1 Nov. 1876; with Great Britain, 29 Nov. 1879.

TONIC SOL FA SYSTEM. See *Music*.

TONK, Rajpootana, India. The nawab and his minister, for a massacre of Hindoo chiefs, 1 Aug. 1867; were deposed by the British. In 1872 he demanded investigation, and his case came before parliament without any issue.

TONNAGE. The Tonnage Act of 1694 established the Bank of England (*which see*). See *Tunnage*.

TONOMETER, a delicate apparatus (consisting of 52 forks) for tuning musical instruments, by marking the number of vibrations, was invented by H. Scheibler of Crefeld, and described in his "Tonmesser," 1834. It received little notice till M. Kœnig removed some of the difficulties opposed to its successful use, and exhibited it at the International Exhibition of 1862.

TONQUIN, S.E. Asia, the delta of the river Songkoi, a province of Annam, subject to China. Here a French missionary bishop, Melchior, was murdered with great barbarity 27 July, 1858: the abbé Neron was also murdered, 3 Nov. 1860; see *Annam*.

Successful attack and death of lieut. Garnier . .	1873
Naomdink captured by the French announced,	
	11 April, 1883
Lin-Yang-Fu declares war against French aggressors, 8 May; a new expedition voted for 15 May,	"
Commander ft. T. Rivière (French), and 32 others besieged by the Black Flags* at Hanoi; captured and killed in a sortie . . . . . 20 May,	"
[He was buried at the Madeleine, Paris, 30 Jan. 1885.]	
Gen. Bouet arrives 7 June; fortifies Hanoi 16 June,	"
China firmly opposed to French aggression; Tu Duc, emperor of Annam, opposed to the French.	
Successful French sortie from Nam Din; much slaughter . . . . 19 July,	"
Proclamation of capt. Morel Beaulien offering protection to the people, deserted by Annam, announced . . . . 20 July,	"
The Black Flags severely defeated . 7 Aug.	"
French advance, under gen. Bouet, checked at Cachao . . . . 15 Aug.	"
Bombardment and capture of the Hué forts, great slaughter of natives . . . . 18-20 Aug.	"

* The Black Flags originated with Li-Hung-Chang, an able leader of the Canton rebels, who about 1863 with his followers took refuge in Tonquin, where he was at first tolerated by the emperor of Annam, but afterwards, being strengthened by many adherents, established an independent despotic government. He strenuously opposed the French.

TONQUIN.

Armistice granted, submission of the Annamite government; treaty signed, recognising French protectorate, ceding province of Bin Hnam, &c. 25 Aug. 1883
The Black Flags defeated at Phokhai by gen. Bouet with great loss, the French suffer severely 1-2 Sept. ,,
Negotiations of Jules Ferry and Mandarin Tseng respecting the protectorate of Tonquin . Sept. ,,
Disbandment of the Annamite troops yellow flags opposed to the French . . about 15 Sept. ,,
Gen. Bouet replaced by adm. Courbet as commander of the French forces . . announced 20 Sept. ,,
Admiral Courbet begins actual occupation of Tonquin . . . . . about 3 Nov. ,,
Ninh-Binh and Knang Yen occupied by the French without resistance . . announced 4 Nov. ,,
The Black Flags repulsed in a violent attack on the French gun-boat *Carabine* and on Haidznong, 17 Nov. ,,
The Yellow book on Tonquin, published . 5 Dec. ,,
The French take forts on the Red river opposite Sontay . . . . . about 16 Dec. ,,
Sontay captured, the Black Flags retire, alleged French loss, about 77 killed, 231 wounded 16, 17 Dec. ,,
Sontay fortified and left . . . . Dec. ,,
The unarmed native Tonquinese suffer on all sides by the war . . . . . Aug.-Dec. ,,
Namdinh attacked by pirates, houses burnt, people killed . . . . . 1, 2 Jan. 1884
Arrival of Chinese troops to defend Hainan against the French . . . . about 20 Jan. ,,
Gen. Millot (successor in command to adm. Courbet) captures Bacninh, after hard fighting Chinese flee, 25 French killed . . . . 12 March, ,,
Gen. Brière de L'Isle captures citadel of Thai-Nguyen . . . . . 22 March, ,,
Rainy season . . . . March—Oct. ,,
Honghoa fired by the Chinese and quitted about 9 April, ,,
Treaty signed by capt. Fournier and Li-hung-Chang at Tientsin ; French protectorate of Tonquin and Annam recognised . . 11 May, ,,
The Chinese garrison of Langson resist capt. Dugenne and a French column (700), (unauthorised), advancing to occupy it ; 10 killed ; a violation of the treaty of 11 May . . . 23 June, ,,
The French appeal to Pekin for indemnity ; the Chinese deny the ratification of the treaty about 1 July ; but order the evacuation of Langson and other places, announced . . 18 July, ,,
Gen. Millot resigns, succeeded by gen. Brière de l'Isle . . . . . . 30 Aug. ,,
Fighting resumed . . . . . Oct. ,,
Chinese regulars, attacks, repulsed with great loss ; French suffer little (at Kep) ; gen. Négrier in command . . . . . 6-8 Oct. ,,
Victory of col. Donnier, great Chinese loss ; 20 French killed . . . . 10, 11 Oct. ,,
Chinese hold strong camps with reinforcements ; their attacks repulsed at Tuguen Quan-hung with great loss . . . . . 13 Oct. ,,
Fighting : the Black Flag defeated about 20 Nov. ,,
Chinese pirates said to be severely defeated, announced . . . . . . Dec. ,,
Gen. Négrier defeats 12,000 Chinese E. of Chu, announced . . . . . 6 Jan. 1885
Dong Song camp captured by the French after severe conflict . . . . . 5 Feb. ,,
Several forts captured . . . 10-25 Jan. ,,
Severe conflict with about 10,000 Chinese, who are compelled to retreat 12 Feb.; the French flag placed on the captured citadel of Langson 13 Feb. ,,
Mutiny on the *Bayard* on account of deficient rations, &c.; 12 sailors shot ; announced end of Jan. ,,
39 French killed and many wounded 9-12 Feb. ,,
Chinese 18 days' siege of Thuyen-Quan raised after 18 desperate assaults . . . 2 March, ,,
The Chinese defeated by col. Duchesne, 4-7 March, ,,
French attack Dong-dang, successful 22 March, ,,
Heavy Chinese attack on French positions ; gen. Négrier wounded, compelled to retreat ; Langson evacuated . . . . . 28 March, ,,
Preliminaries of peace signed at Pekin ; Tonquin to be abandoned by the Chinese, &c. . 5 April, ,,
Luh Vinh Phuoc, chief of the Black Flags, rewarded for his services by the Chinese government . . . . . . April, 1885
The Chinese troops retiring . . . May, ,,
Reported massacre of christians . . Aug. ,,
The Black Flag Bands very troublesome Oct. ; defeated by Négrier . . . Dec. ,,
Reported massacre of 700 christians ; and destruction of 30 villages . . . . Aug. 1886
Renewed warfare : French successes . Nov. ,,
M. Paul Bert, French resident, appointed 21 Jan. ; dies 11 Nov. 1886 ; succeeded by M. Bihourd Jan. 1887
Much fighting ; insurgents defeated by the French Jan. ,,
Col. Bosc captured Muong losing 9 men 19 April, 1890
Establishment of the civil native guard for suppression of piracy, and other organizations reported . . . . . . Sept. ,,
Renewed fighting by pirates ; defeated by gen. Borgnis des Bordes with French loss 17 Jan. 1892
Surrender of Doivan, chief of the Bac Ninh pirates ; country reported quiet . . 16 March, ,,

TONSURE, the clerical crown, adopted, it is said, in imitation of St. Peter, or of Christ's crown of thorns, was disapproved of in the fourth century as pertaining only to penitents, and not made essential till the end of the fifth or beginning of the sixth century.

TONTINES, loans given for life annuities with benefit of survivorship, invented by Laurence Tonti, a Neapolitan. They were first set on foot at Paris to reconcile the people to cardinal Mazarin's government, by amusing them with the hope of becoming suddenly rich, 1653. *Voltaire*. Tonti died in the Bastile after seven years' imprisonment. Mr. Jennings was an original subscriber for a 100*l*. share in a tontine company; and being the last survivor of the shareholders, his share produced him 3000*l*. per annum. He died aged 103 years 19 June, 1798, worth 2,115,244*l*.; see *Alexandre Park.*
By the termination of a tontine begun by M. Lafarge in 1791 to diminish the national debt the French government received 1,218,000 francs Dec. 1888.

TÖPLITZ (Bohemia). Here were signed, in 1813, two treaties—one between Austria, Russia and Prussia, 9 Sept.; and one between Great Britain and Austria, 3 Oct.

TOPOGRAPHICAL SOCIETY OF LONDON was founded 1879; inaugurated at the Mansion-house, 28 Oct. 1880.

TORBANEHILL MINERAL. Mr. Gillespie, of Torbanehill, granted a lease of all the coal in the estate to Messrs. Russell. In the course of working, the lessees extructed a combustible mineral of considerable value as a source of coalgas, and realised a large profit in the sale of it as gas-coal. The lessor then denied that the mineral was coal, and disputed the right of the lessees to work it. At the trial in 1853 there was a great array of scientific men and practical gas engineers, and the evidence was most conflicting. One side maintained the mineral to be coal, the other that it was a bituminous schist. The judge set aside the scientific evidence, and the jury pronounced it to be coal. The authorities in Prussia have since pronounced it *not* to be coal. *Percy*.

TORDESILLAS (near Valladolid). Here was signed, 7 June, 1494, a treaty modifying the boundary line which pope Alexander VI. had assigned, in May, 1493, in his division of the new world between Spain and Portugal.

TORGAU.

TORGAU (Saxony, N. Germany), the site of a battle between Frederick II. of Prussia and the Austrians, in which the former obtained a signal victory ; the Austrian general, count Daun, being

wounded, 3 Nov. 1760. He had, in 1757, obtained a great victory over the Prussian king. Torgau was taken by the allies in 1814; and given to Prussia, 1815.

TORIES, a term given to a political party about 1678; see *Whig*. Dr. Johnson defines a Tory as one who adheres to the ancient constitution of the state, and the apostolical hierarchy of the Church of England. The Tories long maintained the doctrines of "divine hereditary indefeasible right, lineal succession, passive obedience, prerogative," &c. *Bolingbroke*; see *Conservatives*. For the chief Tory administrations, see *Pitt, Perceval, Liverpool, Wellington, Peel, Derby*, and *Disraeli*. For TORY DEMOCRACY see *Fourth Party*.

TORNADOS. See *Storms*.

TORONTO, the capital of Canada West, founded in 1794 as York; it received its present name in 1834. It was made a bishopric in 1839. Population 1885, 118,403.
Opera-house burnt, 8 Feb. 1883.
Industrial exhibition opened by marquis of Lorne, 12 Sept. 1883; another opened by lord Lansdowne, 6 Sept. 1887.
Dynamite cartridges found under the parliament-house; much excitement, 30 April, 1884.

TORPEDO SHELLS, a name given to explosives placed under ships, an invention ascribed to David Bushnell, an American, in 1777. His attempt to destroy H.M.S. *Cerberus* failed. The action of Fulton's torpedoes was successful in Britain 1805; but their use was declined by the government. Torpedo shells ignited by electricity were successfully employed in the war in the United States, 1861-5. On 4 Oct. 1865, Messrs. M'Kay & Beardslee tried them at Chatham before the duke of Somerset and others. An old vessel, the Terpsichore, was speedily sunk. Torpedoes, made by professor (aft. sir Frederick) Abel, of Woolwich, were tried in May, 1866. A torpedo invented by Mr. Wightman and an Austrian, tried and reported successful at Sheerness; an old hulk was sunk, 8 Oct. 1870. Torpedoes to be ignited from a distance by an electric battery are now made at Woolwich. A Turkish monitor in the Danube was blown up by a torpedo (see *Russo-Turkish war, II.*), 26 May, 1877. Whitehead's fish torpedoes, projected by compressed air from a boat; very destructive if skilfully directed; described Nov. 1884.
The new torpedo boat *Peacemaker* invented by prof. J. H. L. Tuck announced . . . Aug. 1886
Nordenfelt's submarine torpedo boat tried in Southampton Water (see under *Boats*) . 19, 20 Dec. 1887
Several severe accidents with torpedo boats July, 1888
Mr. A. Lége's torpedo, based upon the principle of a flying kite, announced . . 16 March, 1889
See under *Cannon* 1889.

TORRES STRAIT, dividing Australia from Papua or New Guinea, was discovered by Torres, a Spaniard, in June, 1606.

TORRES VEDRAS (a city of Portugal). Near here Wellington, retreating from the French, took up a strong position, called the *Lines of Torres Vedras*, 10 Oct. 1810.

TORTOLA, see *Virgin Isles*.

TORTURE was only permitted by the Romans in the examination of slaves. It was applied to heretics by the Roman catholic clergy, and was used in England so late as 1640 (when Archer, who took part in an attack on Laud's palace, was racked), and in Scotland until 1690. The trial by torture was abolished in Portugal, 1776; in France,

by Louis XVI., in 1789; and in Sweden by Gustavus III., 1786. General Picton was convicted of allowing the torture to be applied to Louisa Calderon, in Trinidad, in accordance with the old law of the island, at his trials, 21 Feb. 1806, and 11 June, 1808.

TOTAL ABSTINENCE, see *Teetotaller*.

TOTNES (Devon): thought to be the Roman *Ad Durium Amnem*. It was held by Judhael de Totneis, who built the castle about 1085. It was disfranchised for gross corruption and bribery, by the Reform act, 15 Aug. 1867.

TOUGHENED GLASS, see *Glass*.

TOUL, the Roman *Tulli Leucorum*, a fortified town on the Moselle, N.E. France, one of the most ancient in the empire. The city and diocese acquired great privileges from Charles the Simple, 925, when it was united with the German empire. It was reunited with France, 1552. The fortifications, begun in 1238, were rebuilt and enlarged in 1700, according to the plans of Vauban. After a vigorous resistance to the Germans, commencing 14 Aug. 1870, Toul surrendered with its garrison of 3000 men, 23 Sept., when the town was burning in twenty-three places. The Germans thus acquired an uninterrupted railway communication to Paris.

TOULON, the ancient *Telo Martius* (S. France), an important military port. It was taken by the constable of Bourbon, 1524, and by the emperor Charles V. in 1536. In 1707 it was bombarded by the allies, both by land and sea, by which almost the whole town was reduced to a heap of ruins, and several ships burned; but the allies were at last obliged to raise the siege. It surrendered 27 Aug. 1793, to the British admiral, lord Hood, who took possession both of the town and shipping, in the name of Louis XVII., under a stipulation to assist in restoring the French constitution of 1789. A conflict took place between the English and French forces, when the latter were repulsed, 15 Nov. 1793. Toulon was retaken by Bonaparte, 19 Dec., when great cruelties were exercised towards such of the inhabitants as were supposed to be favourable to the British.—A naval battle off this port was fought 11 Feb. 1744, between the English under Mathews and Lestock, against the fleets of France and Spain: in this engagement the brave captain Cornewall fell. The victory was lost by a misunderstanding between the English admirals. Mathews was afterwards dismissed for misconduct. See *Cholera*, 1884.

TOULOUSE, the ancient TOLOSA (S. France), founded about 615 B.C.; was the capital of the Visigothic kings in A.D. 419; and was taken by Clovis in 508. The dukes of Aquitaine reigned here, 631-761. A university was established here, 1229, and a parliament, 1302. The inquisition was established here to extirpate heretics, 1229. The troubadours, or rhetoricians of Toulouse, had their origin about 850, and consisted of a fraternity of poets, whose art was extended throughout Europe, and gave rise to the Italian and French poetry; see *Troubadours*. The allied British and Spanish army entered this city on 12 April, immediately after the BATTLE OF TOULOUSE, fought between the British Peninsular army under lord Wellington, and the French led by marshal Soult, 10 April, 1814. The French were forced to retreat, after twelve hours' fighting. Neither of the commanders knew that Napoleon had abdicated the throne of France.

TOULOUSE. The county was created out of the kingdom of Aquitaine by Charlemagne, in 778.

It enjoyed great prosperity till the dreadful war of the Albigenses (*which see*), when the count Raymond VI. was expelled, and Simon de Montfort became count. At his death, in 1218, Raymond VII. obtained his inheritance. His daughter Jane and her husband, Alphonso (brother of Louis IX. of France), dying without issue, the county of Toulouse was united to the French monarchy in 1271. A large part of Toulouse destroyed by an inundation of the Garonne; St. Cyprien like a sepulchre; 23 June, 1875.

TOURAINE, the garden of France, was conquered by the Visigoths about 480. It was ceded to Geoffroy count of Anjou, 1044, and thus became the property of the Plantagenet kings of England. It was seized by Philip Augustus in 1203, and was made a duchy by John, 1360. It was finally united to the crown on the death of the duke of Anjou, 1584.

TOURNAMENTS, or JOUSTS, were martial sports of the ancient cavaliers. Tournament is derived from the French word *tourner*, "to turn round." Tournaments were frequent about 890; and were regulated by the emperor Henry I., about 919. Tournaments were introduced into England early in the 12th century; prohibited by Henry II., but revived by Richard I., his son. Solemn tournaments were held by Edward III., 25 Sept. 1329, in London; and 19 Jan. 1344, at Windsor; and by Richard II. in Smithfield, London, 10 Oct. 1319; and also by Henry VIII., in May 1513. The Lateran council published an article against their continuance in 1136. Henry II. of France, in a tilt with the comte de Montgomerie, had his eye struck out, an accident which caused the king's death in a few days, 29 June, 1559. Tournaments were then abolished in France.—A magnificent feast and tournament, under the auspices of Archibald, earl of Eglintoun, took place at Eglintoun castle, 29 Aug. 1839, and the following week: many of the visitors (among whom was the late emperor of the French) assumed the characters of ancient knights, lady Seymour, aft. duchess of Somerset, being the "Queen of Beauty." She died 14 Dec. 1884. Among the festivities at the marriage of prince Humbert, at Turin, was a tournament, 24 April, 1868. Tournaments held at the Agricultural hall, London, N. (for benefit of soldiers' widows, &c.), 21 June *et seq*. 1880; (8th) 11 June, 1887; (9th) 14 June, 1888; (10th) 20 June, 1889. Amount received by the charities 1880-8 about 21,000*l*. The "Royal Military Tournament," as an institution for development of skill in arms in the army, was organised Oct. 1883.

TOURNAY (S. Belgium) was very flourishing till it was ravaged by the barbarians in the 5th century. It has sustained many sieges. Taken by the allies in 1709, and ceded to the house of Austria by the treaty of Utrecht; but the Dutch were allowed to place a garrison in it, as one of the barrier towns. It was taken by the French under general La Bourdonnaye, 8 Nov. 1792. Several battles were fought near Tournay in May, 1793, and May, 1794.

TOURNIQUET (from *tourner*, to turn), an instrument for stopping the flow of blood into a limb, by tightening the bandage employed in amputations, is said to have been invented by Morelli at the siege of Besançon, 1674. J. L. Petit, in France, invented the screw tourniquet in 1718.

TOURS, an ancient city, central France, near which Charles Martel gained a great victory over the Saracens, and saved Europe, 10 Oct. 732, and from which he acquire fying *hammer*. This co of Poitiers. When Pa mans, M. Crémieux at the French governmen together with the repre 18 Sept., 1870. On Gambetta, minister of war (who escaped from In consequence of the Loire near Orleans, Bordeaux, 11 Dec.

TOWERS. That read, built in the plai B.C.; see *Babel*. Th Athens, built 550 B.C. *Pharos*), 280 B.C. Th were the only structu arrival of the English, in the maritime tow These towers are tall drical, but narrowing t lateral holes to admit conical roofs. Fifty-si 50 to 130 feet high; se

TOWER OF LO Julius Cæsar founded is very doubtful. A r more than what is no which appears to hav William the Conquero 1078, and completed who, in 1098, surround deep ditch. Several s tions to it, and king E In 1638, the old Whi under king Charles II., 1680-5, and a great ings made to it. He office, and various oth peculiar interest. Here of illustrious persons, Henry VI., 1471; king 1485; sir Thomas Ove and 280,000 stand of fire, 30 Oct. 1841. Th Tower were complete *Tower-Subways*, see : constables of the Tower lington, lord Comberm Sir George Pollock, Oct. 1872; sir Wm. March, 1875; sir Char 20 Nov. 1880; sir W. 1881; gen. sir R. J. D 1886; lord Napier of M The menagerie, long here, Gardens, 1831; the stat Record Office, 1857. Opened free to the public 3 April, 1875. Lanthorne Tower rebuilt The White Tower and oth explosion of dynamite hurt, about 2 p.m. 24 J and Harry Burton app for trial, 27 March, 188 Tower Bridge act passed the bridge laid by the

TOWNLEY MA Museum, were purchas

TOWTON (Yorks) battle was fought, 29 houses of York (Edward VI.), to the latter of

whose side more than 37,000 fell. Edward issued orders to give no quarter, and the most merciless slaughter ensued. Henry and his queen, Margaret, fled to Scotland; and Edward IV. was settled on the throne.

TOXOPHILITES (from *toxon*, a bow, and *philos*, a lover), a society established by sir Aston Lever in 1781. The Toxophilites formed a division of the Artillery Company about 1784-1803. In 1834 they took grounds in the inner circle of Regent's-park, and built the archery lodge. They possess a very curious piece of plate, given by Catherine, queen of Charles II., to be shot for by the Finsbury archers, of whom the Toxophilites are the representatives.

TOYNBEE HALL, see under *University Teaching*.

TRACT SOCIETIES. The Society for Promoting Christian Knowledge was founded in 1698; the Religious Tract Society, London, in 1799; and other similar societies since.

TRACTARIANISM, a term applied to certain opinions on church matters propounded in the "Tracts for the Times," of which ninety numbers were published, 1833-41. The principal writers were the revs. Dr. E. Pusey, J. H. Newman, J. Keble, J. Froude, and I. Williams—all of the university of Oxford; see *Puseyism*. The tracts (specially No. 90) were condemned by the authorities at Oxford, 15 March, 1841.

TRACTION-ENGINES were used on common roads in London in 1860, but afterwards restricted. In Aug. 1862 one of Bray's traction-engines conveyed through the city a mass of iron which would have required 29 horses; see *Road-steamers*, and *Railways*.

TRADE OF GREAT BRITAIN, see *Exports* and *Imports*. In 1861 the value of the two amounted to 377,017,522*l*.; in 1871 to 614,590,180*l*.; in 1875 to 655,551,900*l*.; in 1877, to 646,705,702*l*.; in 1879, 611,775,239*l*.; in 1881, 694,105,264*l*.; in 1883, 732,328,649*l*.; in 1887, 642,930,725*l*. See *Commerce*.

Trade with the United States doubled in value in ten years. 1877, 77,805,000*l*.; 1878, 89,070,000*l*.
Royal commission for enquiry into causes of depression of trade, 31 Aug. 1885. Earls of Iddesleigh and Dunraven, Mr. G. Sclater Booth, prof. Bonamy Price, and twenty others. First meeting 7 Oct. 1885; final report issued Feb. 1887. The majority refer to over-production, rise in value of gold, and in regard to agriculture, fall of prices, as probable causes; improved condition of the working classes noted, Jan. 1887.

TRADE AND PLANTATIONS, BOARD OF. Cromwell seems to have given the first notions of a board of trade: in 1655 he appointed his son Richard, with many lords of his council, judges, and gentlemen, and about twenty merchants of London, York, Newcastle, Yarmouth, Dover, &c., to meet and consider by what means the trade and navigation of the republic might be best promoted. *Thomas's Notes of the Rolls*. Charles II., on his restoration, established a council of trade for keeping a control over the whole commerce of the nation, 1660; he afterwards instituted a board of trade and plantations which was remodelled by William III. This board was abolished in 1782; and a new council for the affairs of trade on its present plan was appointed, 2 Sept. 1786.
The parliamentary recommendation in 1880 to appoint a "minister of trade and commerce," was dropped by Mr. Gladstone in March, 1881.
Board of trade journal of tariffs &c. published, 15 Sept. 1886.

TRADE CONGRESSES, see *Working men*.

TRADE MARKS REGISTRATION ACT, passed 13 Aug. 1875. The registration office, Quality-court, Chancery-lane (Mr. H. Reader Lack, registrar), was opened 1 Jan. 1876; a similar act passed in the United States, 1881. See *Merchandise Marks Act*.

TRADES' MUSEUMS. The formation of one was undertaken in 1853, jointly by the commissioners of the Great Exhibition of 1851, and the Society of Arts. The animal department was opened 17 May, 1855, when a paper on the mutual relations of trade and manufactures was read by professor E. Solly. The contents of this museum were removed to the South Kensington Museum, which was opened 24 June, 1857. The French "Conservatoire des Arts et Métiers," was established 1795.

TRADES' UNIONS. The steam engine makers' society, Manchester, established in 1824. By 6 Geo. IV. c. 129 (1825), the combination laws were repealed, and other provisions made. As trades' unions formed for maintaining the rate of wages, &c., are not recognised by law, a commission (including lord Elcho, Thomas Hughes, and others, with sir Wm. Erle as chairman) was appointed to inquire into their constitution, 14 Feb. 1867, and an act to facilitate their proceedings was passed 5 April following. Their reports were issued during the year, disclosing the existence of murderous practices, with great intimidation; see *Sheffield*, and *Manchester*. An act to protect union funds from embezzlement was passed in 1869. A trade union act passed 29 June, 1871, amended by act passed 30 June, 1876. To counteract the influence of trades' unions, the National Federation of Employers was formed Dec. 1873; see *Employers*, and *Working men*.

207 trades unions in England in 1885.
Trades Union Congress opened at Liverpool, 18 Jan. 1875, 1876; at Leicester, 17 Sept. 1877; at Bristol, 9 Sept. 1878; at Edinburgh, 15 Sept. 1879; Dublin, 13 Sept. 1880; London, 12 Sept. 1881; Manchester, 18 Sept. 1882; Nottingham [134 unions, 552,091 members], 10 Sept. 1883; Aberdeen, 8 Sept. 1884; Southport, 7 Sept. 1885; Hull, 6 Sept. 1886; Swansea, 5 Sept. 1887; Bradford, 3 Sept. 1888.

TRAFALGAR (Cape S. Spain), off which a great naval victory was gained by the British, under Nelson, over the combined fleets of France and Spain, commanded by admiral Villeneuve and two Spanish admirals, 21 Oct. 1805. The enemy's force was eighteen French and fifteen Spanish vessels, all of the line: that of the British, twenty-seven ships. After a protracted fight, Villeneuve and the other admirals were taken, and nineteen of their ships captured, sunk, or destroyed. Nelson was killed, and admiral Collingwood succeeded to the command. Nelson's ship was the *Victory*; and his last signal was, "England expects every man will do his duty;" see *Nelson*. TRAFALGAR-SQUARE, London, begun 1829; completed 1845. An act passed in 1844, declaring that the square is Crown property, the charge of it placed in the hands of the Commissioners of Woods and Forests and under police regulations. In 1851, the charge was transferred to the Commissioners of Works. The right of preventing public meetings in the square by the executive affirmed by the Commons (316—224), 2 March, 1888. Grand Hotel opened by Lord Mayor, 29 May, 1880. See *Riots*.

TRAFFIC in the metropolis is now regulated by the Metropolitan Streets act, passed 20 Aug. 1867.

3 M 2

TRAGEDY, see *Drama*.

TRAINING SCHOOLS, begun by the National Society, 1811. One was founded at Battersea in 1840, by sir J. Kay Shuttleworth, and Mr. E. C. Tufnell; the latter, who was then in the Poor Law Commission, devoting a year's salary towards the expenses. Mr. Mann stated, in 1855, that there were about forty of these schools in different parts of the country.
Finsbury training college established about 1883.

TRAINING SHIPS, see *Marine Society* and *Chichester*.

TRAJAN'S COLUMN (in Rome), erected 114, by the Roman senate and people, to commemorate his victories, and executed by Apollodorus. It was built in the square called the *Forum Trajanum*; it is of the Tuscan order, and from its base, exclusive of the statue and pedestal, is 127½ feet high.

TRAM-ROADS: as Mr. Benjamin Outram, father of sir James, the Indian general, in 1800, made improvements in the system of railways for common vehicles in the north of England, the name is ascribed to him, but it is said to have existed in Derbyshire before, a coal waggon having been called a tram. The iron tram-road from Croydon to Wandsworth was completed on 24 July, 1801. Street railways or tramways for omnibuses drawn by horses, previously established by Mr. Train in New York, were opened by him at Birkenhead, Cheshire, 30 Aug. 1860, and at Bayswater, London, 23 March, 1861. (See *Ireland*, 1868.) A street railway bill was rejected by the house of commons in April, 1861. Several of these railways existed for a time in various parts of the metropolis in 1861, but were all taken up in 1862. An act to facilitate the construction of tramways passed 9 Aug. 1870. Tramways from Brixton to Kennington, and from Whitechapel to Bow, were opened 9 May, 1870; and others since. Their introduction into the city was much recommended but opposed, March-May, 1873. Dividend of the North Metropolitan tramways company, 8 per cent. Aug. 1876. The use of steam locomotives proposed: approved in Paris, July, 1876.
Elevated street railways erected in New York, 1877-8.
233 miles of tramways constructed in England and Wales, 1870-80.
Steam cable tramway on Highgate Hill, N. London (the first in Europe), opened 29 May, 1884.
Steam employed by the North London Tramways Company, 1 April, 1885. See under *Air*.
886 miles of tramways in the united kingdom in 1887.
An international tramway congress opened at Brussels, 5 Sept. 1888.

TRANQUEBAR (East Indies), the Danish settlement here, founded in 1618, was purchased by the English in 1845.

TRANSCASPIAN RAILWAY, see under *Railways*, 1888.

TRANSFIGURATION. The change of Christ's appearance on Mount Tabor, in the presence of Peter, James, and John, A.D. 32 (*Matt.* xvii.). The feast of the Transfiguration, kept on 6 Aug., was instituted in the East before 700, and seems to have been observed in the West as early as 450. Pope Calixtus III. in 1456 issued a bull making it a "feast of obligation" to be generally observed in honour of the defeat of the Turks at Belgrade in that year.

TRANSFORMATION PRINTS. A method of printing one picture over another, the former being easily effaced, patented by Mr. Andrew Reid of Newcastle-on-Tyne, and 1885.

TRANSFUSION OF BLOOD, see
TRANSIT, see *Venus*.

TRANSLATION TO HEAVEN. The lation of Enoch to heaven at the age of 365 3017 B.C. The prophet Elijah was transl heaven in a chariot of fire, 896 B.C.—The pos of translation to the abode of eternal life ha maintained by some extravagant enthusiasts Irish house of commons expelled Mr. Asgil his seat, for his book asserting the possib translation to the other world without death,

TRANSPADANE REPUBLIC, com Lombardy and part of the Venetian territori established by Bonaparte after his victory a 10 May, 1796. With the Cispadane repu merged into the Cisalpine republic, Oct. 179;

TRANSPORTATION, see *Banis* Judges were given the power of sentencing of to transportation "into any of his majesty's nions in North America," by 18 Charles I (1666), and by 4 Geo. I. c. 11 (1718). Tran tion ceased in 1775, but was revived in 1786 reception of convicts was successfully refused Cape of Good Hope (in 1849) and by the Aus colonies (1864). Transportation, even to Australia, where labour is wanted, ceased few years, through the fierce opposition eastern colonies. In consequence of the di then experienced in transporting felons, 1 Vict. c. 99 was passed to provide other punis namely, penal servitude, empowering her r to grant pardon to offenders under certain tions, and licences to others to be at large licences being liable to be revoked if nec and many have been. These licences are "tickets of leave." The system is said t originated in Australia under the superinte of captain Maconochie. It was much in Oct. and Nov. 1862, on account of violent being traced to *ticket-of-leavers ;* and was m by the Penal Servitude Act, 1864; and th vention of Crimes Acts, 1871 and 1879. It considered successful. See *Crime*.

John Eyre, esq., a man of fortune, was sentenced transportation for stealing a few quires of pap
—*Phillips* . . . . 1 No
The Rev. Dr. Halloran, tutor to the earl of Chesfield, was transported for forging a frank (t postage) . . . . 9 Sep
The first transportation of felons to Botany Bay w in May, 1787; where governor Phillip arriv with about 800 on 20 Jan. 1788; convicts we afterwards sent to Van Diemen's Land, Norfo Island, &c.
Returning from transportation was punishable wi death until 5 Will. IV. c. 67, Aug. 1834, when act was passed making the offence punishable transportation for life.
A shipment of convicts to West Australia (whi had already received 10,000) in 1867.

TRANSUBSTANTIATION, the doc the "real presence." That the bread and v the Eucharist are changed into the very fle blood of Christ by the consecration, was broa the days of Gregory III. (731), and accep Amalarius and Radbertus (about 830), but r by Rabanus Maurus, Johannes Scotus E Berengarius, Wicliffe, and others. In the I council, held at Rome by Innocent III., th "Transubstantiation" was used to expre doctrine, which was decreed to be incontrove and all who opposed it were condemned as h

This was confirmed by the council of Trent, 18 Jan. 1562. John Huss, Jerome of Prague, and other martyrs of the reformation, suffered for denying this dogma, which is renounced by the church of England (28th article), and by all protestant dissenters. The declaration against transubstantiation, invocation of the saints, and the sacrifice of the mass, on taking any civil office, was abolished by an act passed 25 July, 1867; see *Sacrament*.

Luther maintained the doctrine of *con-substantiation*, viz., that after consecration the body and blood of Christ are substantially present in the bread and wine. He was opposed by Bucer, Carlstadt, Zwingle, and others (termed sacramentarians), who asserted that the Lord's supper is only a commemorative rite.

TRANSVAAL REPUBLIC (South Africa), founded by Dutch Boers (farmers) in 1848, after several years' severe conflict with the natives. Its independence was declared 17 Jan. 1852; and its constitution proclaimed 13 Feb. 1858; capital Pretoria. President for four years, T. F. Burgers, 27 May, 1872. Population about 38,000 Boers, 5000 English settlers, 770,000 blacks (1881). Total population in 1886, 370,848.

War with the Kaffirs begun; Cetywayo, king; Secocoeni (siekakuni), an eminent chief . July, 1876
Republican government blamed; its troops defeated; Sir Theophilus Shepstone sent to mediate Sept. ,,
Dutch boers assisted by the Amazwasies, a warlike tribe, who check Kaffirs . . . Sept. ,,
Severe dispatch of the earl of Carnarvon, censuring Burgers for aggression on Kaffirs . Oct. ,,
Secocoeni threatening Leydenburg . Nov. ,,
Schlickman, the Dutch general, killed in an attack 17 Nov. ,,
Sir T. Shepstone well received; a desire expressed for federation, Feb.; opposition to it March, 1877
Anarchy in the Traxsvaal; annexation of the Transvaal (for protection) to the British dominions proclaimed by sir T. Shepstone, 12 April; he is sworn in as administrator . . 30 May, ,,
Conflict with Secocoeni (disapproved); some volunteers killed . . . . 17 June, 1878
Sir Wm. Owen Lanyon made governor of the Transvaal . . . . March, 1879
Great opposition to the British rule; appeased after much discussion . . 12 April, ,,
Sir G. Wolseley appointed governor of Natal, &c., May et seq.
His stronghold captured by col. Baker Russell (under sir Garnet Wolseley), with British and native troops . . . . 28 Nov. ,,
Secocoeni surrenders . . . 2 Dec. ,,
The Transvaal declared a crown colony Dec. ,,
The Boers meet and claim independence; Bok, Kruger, and Pretorius arrested for signing a document issued by the Boer committee Dec. 1879, and Jan. 1880
The Boers seize Heidelberg, 16 Dec.; establish the South African republic, Paul Kruger president 17 Dec. ,,
A party of Boers stop at Bronker's Spruit about 250 British troops of the 94th regiment, who resist; some killed or wounded; others disarmed and dismissed . . . . 20 Dec. ,,
Potchefstrom seized by Boers, who retire when the place is shelled; col. Bellairs besieged in it 27 Dec. et seq.
Capt. J. M. Elliot said to be treacherously killed while fording the Vaal . . 29 Dec. ,,
The South African Republic proclaimed by a triumvirate; Kruger, Joubert, and Pretorius 30 Dec. ,,
Troops sent from Britain, &c., Dec., 1880, and Jan. 1881
Sir George P. Colley (appointed governor of Natal 1880) takes command in the war . Jan. ,,
Gen. Colley's attack on Laing's Nek, a pass, repulsed with heavy loss; col. Bonar Millet Deane, majors Ruscombe Poole and Wm. Hunt Hingeston killed . . . . 28 Jan. ,,
Severe conflict on the Ingogo river; the British 12 hours under fire; repulsed with heavy loss, 8 Feb. ,,
Sir Evelyn Wood arrives with reinforcements and joins gen. Colley . . . 17 Feb. ,,
The Orange Free State proclaim neutrality and mediation . . . . about 22 Feb. 1881
Gen. Colley marches in the night to Majuba hill (*which see*); defeated and killed after a desperate conflict . . . . 26-27 Feb. ,,
Gen. sir F. Roberts sent to Africa . 28 Feb. ,,
Armistice proposed by the Boers; accepted for 6-14 March; armistice extended, 14 March; Boers agree to British terms, 21, 22 March; peace proclaimed; the Boers disperse; gen. Roberts recalled 24 March, ,,
Potchefstrom surrenders with honours of war, 21 March; given up as occupied by mistake April ,,
Vote of censure on the Government policy in the Commons negatived (314-205) . 25, 26 July, ,,
Commissioners to carry out treaty of peace appointed 5 April, agree to convention ceding virtually all the territory to "The TRANSVAAL STATE" on 8 August, subject to suzerainty of the Queen, and a British resident; with debt of about 420,867*l*., &c.; independence of the Swazies guaranteed; signed by Royal commissioners and Martin W. Pretorius and Peter J. Joubert, (Stephen J. P. Kruger not present), 3 Aug.; effected . . . . . 8 Aug. ,,
Meeting of the Volksraad, 21 Sept.; treaty confirmed, 25 Oct. ,,
Mr. G. Hudson appointed first British resident, Nov. ,,
Departure of the British troops . about 28 Dec. ,,
Fighting with the natives . . . Feb. 1882
Secocoeni killed by a rival chief . . Aug. ,,
War with the insubordinate chief Mapoch . Oct. ,,
Renewed troubles with the natives . Sept.-Oct. ,,
Fighting with the natives, who are repulsed, under their chief Mapoch . . 16-17 Nov. ,,
Again defeated . . . . Jan. 1883
Combination of chiefs against the Boers announced, March, ,,
Negotiations for peace begun by Mapoch announced, 5 April, ,,
Paul Krüger, president . 9 May, 1883—30 April, 1888
Peace concluded . . . . July, 1883
Transvaal deputies, Paul Krüger and others received by lord Derby . . . 7 Nov. ,,
Definite proposals submitted to the government, 22 Dec.; amended boundary lines accepted, 2 Feb.; convention signed, the republic to be styled the "South African Republic" under British suzerainty . . . 27 Feb. ,,
The convention adopted by the Transvaal assembly, 8 Aug. ,,
The filibustering settlers of Goshen and Stella-land, break the convention; seize and annex Montsioa's lands in Bechuana-land; sanctioned by a proclamation; withdrawn on remonstrance, Sept., Oct. 1884
Sir H. Robinson's ultimatum from Cape Town, requiring protection of the frontiers . about 14 Oct. ,,
Joubert resigns his presidency . about 21 Oct. ,,
Short war with the natives, refusing to pay taxes;
Mamusa taken; battle . . . 2 Dec. 1885
Defensive treaty with the Orange Free State, about 13 March, 1889

TRANSYLVANIA, an Austrian province, was part of the ancient Dacia (*which see*). In 1526, John Zapoly rendered himself independent of the emperor Ferdinand I. by the aid of the Turks. His successors ruled with much difficulty till Jan. 1699, when the emperor Leopold I., by the treaty of Carlowitz, finally incorporated Transylvania into the Austrian dominions. The Transylvanian deputies did not take their seat in the Austrian parliament till 20 Oct. 1863. A decree for the convocation of the Transylvanian diet was issued 12 Sept. 1865. The inhabitants are about 1,100,000 ignorant Roumans, 1,500,000 Saxon colonists, and 550,000 Magyars, the last being the ruling class. The union of Transylvania with Hungary in 1848, which has caused much discontent, was ratified by the Transylvanian diet, 25 Dec. 1866.

Serious agrarian riots at Föeblvar suppressed with bloodshed, 27 June, 1888.

PRINCES OF TRANSYLVANIA.
1526. John Zapoly.
1540. John Sigismund.
1571. Stephen Zapoly I. Bathori.
1576. Christopher Bathori.
1581. Sigismund Bathori.
1602. Emperor Rodolph.
1605. Stephen II. Bottskai.
1607. Sigismund Ragotzski.
1608. Gabriel I. Bathori.
1613. Gabriel II. (Bethlem Gabor).
1631. George I. Ragotzski.
1648. George II. Ragotzski.
1660. John Kemin.
1662. Michael I. Abaffi.
1690-99. Michael II. Abaffi.

TRAPPISTS. The first abbey of La Trappe in Normandy was founded, in 1140, by Rotrou, comte de Perche. The present order of Trappists owes its origin to the learned Jean le Bouthillier de la Rancé (editor of *Anacreon* when aged 14), who renounced the world, and sold all his property, giving the proceeds to the abbey of La Trappe, to which he retired in 1662, to live there in great austerity. After several efforts he succeeded in reforming the monks, and in establishing a new rule, which commands silence, prayer, reading, and manual labour, and which forbids study, wine, fish, &c. Rancé was born in 1620, and died in 1700. The Trappists' new building was consecrated in Aug. 1833.

A number of these monks, driven from France in the revolution of 1790, were received by Mr. Weld, of Lulworth, Dorsetshire, who gave them some land to cultivate and a habitation, where they remained till 1815. This order was charged with rebellion and conspiracy in France, and sixty-four English and Irish Trappists were shipped by the French government at Paimbœuf, 19 Nov., and were landed from the *Hebe*, French frigate, at Cork, 30 Nov. 1831. They established themselves at Mount Melleray, county of Waterford.

TRASIMENE, see *Thrasymene*.

TRAUTENAU (Bohemia). On 27 June, 1866, the first corps of the army of the crown-prince of Prussia seized Trautenau, but was defeated and repulsed by the Austrians under Gablenz; on the 28th, the Prussians defeated the Austrians with great loss.

TRAVELLERS' CLUB (Pall-mall), established in 1815. A member must have "travelled out of the British islands to a distance of at least 500 miles from London, in a direct line."

TRAVELLING IN ENGLAND. In 1707 it took in summer one day, in winter nearly two days, to travel from London to Oxford (55 miles). In 1817 the journey was accomplished in six or seven hours. By the Great Western Railway express (63 miles) it is done in 1¼ hour. In 1828, a gentleman travelled from Newcastle to London (273 miles) inside the best coach in 35 hours, at an expense of 6*d*. 15*s*. 3*d*. or 6*d*. per mile (including dinner, &c.). In 1857, the charge of the Great Northern railway (275¼ miles) first-class express (6 hours) was 50*s*. 9*d*.

TRAWLING. Deep-sea fishing with a boat (sometimes driven by steam) having a very large net attached to it, and thereby catching the fish which mostly live at the bottom of the sea; principally practised on the N.E. coast of Britain.

Commissions reported in 1864 and since, that trawling was not injurious to the supply of fish as suggested; but another commission, with scientific advice, reported in Feb. 1885, that there was some ground for the fishermen's complaints.

TREAD-MILL, an invention of the Chinese, to raise water for the irrigation of the fields. The complicated tread-mill introduced into the prisons of Great Britain is the invention of Mr. (afterwards sir William) Cubitt, of Ipswich. It was erected at Brixton gaol, 1817, and soon afterwards in other large prisons.

TREASON, see *High Treason*. PETTY TREASON (a term abolished in 1828, defined by the statute of 25 Edw. III. 1352) was a wife's murder of her husband; a servant's murder of his master; and an ecclesiastical person's murder of his prelate or other superior.

TREASON-FELONY. By the Crown and Government Security Act, 11 Vict. c. 12 (1848), certain treasons heretofore punishable with death were mitigated to felonies, and subjected to transportation or imprisonment. The Fenians in Ireland were tried under this act; see *Trials*, 1865.

TREASURER OF ENGLAND, LORD HIGH, the third great officer of the crown, a lord by virtue of his office, having the custody of the king's treasure, governing the upper court of exchequer, and formerly sitting judicially among the barons. The first lord high treasurer in England was Odo, earl of Kent, in the reign of William I. This great trust is now confided to a commission, and is vested in five persons, called "lords commissioners for executing the office of lord high treasurer," and of these the chancellor of the exchequer is usually one; the first lord being usually the premier; see *Administrations*, for a succession of these officers. Sir Stafford Northcote (aft. Earl of Iddesleigh) was first lord of the treasury and not premier, 24 June, 1885, as was Mr. W. H. Smith, 26 July, 1886; see *Salisbury Administrations*. A third lord of the treasury (Mr. Stansfeld) was appointed, Dec. 1868, succeeded by Mr. W. E. Gladstone, Dec. 1869.

The first of this rank in IRELAND was John de St. John, Henry III. 1217; the last, William, duke of Devonshire, 1766; vice-treasurers were appointed till 1789; then commissioners till 1816, when the revenues of Great Britain and Ireland were united.

The *first* lord high treasurer of SCOTLAND was sir Walter Ogilvie, appointed by James I. in 1420; the *last*, in 1641, John, earl of Traquair, afterwards commissioners were appointed.

TREASURER OF THE CHAMBER, formerly an officer of great consideration, and always a member of the privy council. He discharged the bills of all the king's tradesmen, and had his office in Cleveland-row, in the vicinity of the royal palace. His duties were transferred and the office suppressed at the same time with the offices of master of the great wardrobe and cofferer of the household in 1782. *Beatson*.

TREATIES. The first formal and written treaty made in England with any foreign nation was entered into at Kingston between Henry III. and the dauphin of France (then in England and leagued with the barons), 11 Sept. 1217. The first commercial treaty was with Guy, earl of Flanders, 2 Edw. 1274: the second with Portugal and Spain, 1308. *Anderson*. The chief treaties of the nations of Europe will be found described in their respective places: the following forms an index; see *Coalitions, Commerce, Leagues*, &c. Hertslet's "Commercial Treaties," 16 vol. 1820-85.

TREATIES.

Aix, peace	7 Aug. 1743
Adrianople, peace	14 Sept. 1829
Aix-la-Chapelle	2 May, 1668
Aix-la-Chapelle, peace	1748
Ackermann, peace	4 Sept. 1826
Allahabad (Bahar, &c., ceded to E. I. Company)	1765
Alt Radstadt, peace	24 Sept. 1706
America, peace	3 Sept. 1783
Amiens, peace	25 Mar. 1802
Ancon (Chili and Peru)	20 Oct. 1883
Anglo-Spanish convention,	29 July, 1886
Anglo-Turkish convention,	4 June, 1878
Antwerp, truce	9 April, 1609
Armed Neutrality, convention,	16 Dec. 1800
Arms	22 Sept. 1435
Arras	1482
Augsburg, league of	1686
Austria with England, convention; the latter agrees to accept 2,500,000l. as a composition for claims on Austria, amounting to 30,000,000l. sterling	1824
Baden, peace	Sept. 1714
Bagnalo (Venice, Naples, &c.)	1484
Balta Liman	1838 and 1849
Barcelona (France and Spain)	1493
Barrier treaty	15 Nov. 1715
Barwalde (France and Sweden)	1631
Basel, peace (France and Spain)	22 July, 1795
Bassein (Great Britain and Mahrattas)	1802
Bayonne	5 May, 1808
Belgrade, peace	18 Sept. 1739
Berlin, peace	28 June, 1742
Berlin, decree	29 Nov. 1806
Berlin convention	5 Nov. 1808
Berlin, peace (Prussia & Saxony)	21 Oct. 1866
Berlin treaty (Russia, Turkey, &c.)	13 July, 1878
Beyars	31 Aug. 1839
Broda, peace	25 July, 1667
Bretigny, peace	8 May, 1360
Bucharest, 28 May, 1812; (Servia and Bulgaria)	3 March, 1886
Cambray, league	10 Dec. 1508
Cambray, peace	5 Aug. 1529
Campo Formio	17 Oct. 1797
Canton	29 Aug. 1842
Capua, convention	20 May, 1815
Carlowitz, peace	26 Jan. 1699
Carlsbad, congress of	1 Aug. 1819
Château-Cambresis, peace	1559
Chaumont	1 Mar. 1814
Chefoo, convention	17 Sept. 1876
Chunar, India	1781
Cintra, convention	22 Aug. 1808
Closterseven, convention 8 Sept. 1757	
Coalition, first, against France	26 June, 1792
Coalition, second	22 June, 1799
Coalition, third	8 Sept. 1805
Coalition, fourth	6 Oct. 1806
Coalition, fifth	9 April, 1809
Coalition, sixth	1 March, 1813
Commerce (Great Britain and Turkey)	16 Nov. 1839
Commerce (Great Britain and the Two Sicilies)	25 June, 1845
Concordat, with France, 15 July, 1801	
Conflans	1465
Constantinople, peace, 16 April, 1712	
Constantinople	8 July, 1833
Constantinople	8 May, 1854
Constantinople (Russia and Turkey, definitive)	8 Feb. 1879
Constantinople (settling boundaries of Greece)	24 May and 2 July, 1881
Copenhagen, peace	27 May, 1660
Copenhagen (composition for Sound dues)	14 March, 1857
Crecy	1544
Dover	1670
Dresden, peace	25 Dec. 1745
Egypt, viceroy and admiral Codrington, convention	6 Aug. 1828
Eliot convention	April, 1835
England, convention with Austria, Russia, Prussia, and Turkey, for settlement of the East	15 July, 1840
England and United States, convention	13 Nov. 1826
Evora Monte	26 May, 1834
Family Compact	15 Aug. 1761
Fommanah (Ashantee war)	13 Feb. 1874
Fontainebleau, peace	2 Sept. 1679
Fontainebleau	8 Nov. 1785
Fontainebleau, concordat 25 Jan. 1813	
France and England, convention respecting the slave trade	29 May, 1845
France and Italy, convention respecting the occupation of Rome	15 Sept. 1864
Frankfort (peace between Germany and France)	10 May, 1871
French commercial treaty,	23 Jan. 1860
Friedwald	5 Oct. 1551
Fuessen, peace	23 April, 1745
Gandamak (with Afghanistan),	26 May, 1879
Gastein convention	14 Aug. 1865
Ghent, pacification	8 Nov. 1576
Ghent, peace (America)	24 Dec. 1814
Golden Bull	1356
Grand alliance	12 May, 1689
Hague	21 May, 1659
Hague	7 May, 1669
Halle	1610
Hamburg, peace	2 May, 1762
Hanover	3 Sept. 1725
Hanover and England	22 July, 1834
Holy alliance	26 Sept. 1815
Hubertsburg, peace	15 Feb. 1763
Hué (France and Annam)	25 Aug. 1883
"Interim"	15 May, 1548
Japan and Great Britain 26 Aug. 1858	
Jay's treaty	19 Nov. 1794
Kaynardji, or Koutschouc-Kaynardji	21 July, 1774
Kiel	14 Jan. 1814
Laybach, congress	6 May, 1821
League, holy	1576
Leipsic, alliance	April, 1631
Leoben, peace	1797
Lisbon, peace	13 Feb. 1668
London (settlement of Greece)	6 July, 1829
London (separating Belgium from Holland)	15 Nov. 1831
London (convention respecting Belgium)	19 April, 1839
London (Turkey and Egypt)	15 July, 1840
London (succession to crown of Denmark)	1852
London (neutrality of Luxemburg settled)	11 May, 1867
Lubeck, peace	22 May, 1629
Luneville, peace	9 Feb. 1801
Madrid, concord	1526
Methuen treaty	1703
Milan decree	17 Dec. 1807
Milan (Austria and Sardinia)	6 Aug. 1849
Munster, peace	24 Oct. 1648
Nankin, peace	29 Aug. 1842
Nantes, edict	13 April, 1598
Naumberg	1554
Nice	1538
Nimeguen, peace	10 Aug. 1678
Noyon	16 Aug. 1516
Nuremberg	2 Aug. 1532
Nystadt	30 Aug. 1721
Oliva, peace	3 May, 1660
Paris, peace (Paris)	10 Feb. 1763
Paris	20 June, 1784
Paris	15 May, 1796
Paris, peace (Sweden)	6 Jan. 1810
Paris	11 April, 1814
Paris	10 June, 1817
Paris	11 April, 1856
Paris (settlement of Neufchâtel affair)	26 May, 1857
Partition, first	11 Oct. 1698
Partition, second	1700
Passarowitz, peace	13 Mar. 1718
Passau	12 Aug. 1552
Pekin, peace, 24 Aug. 1860 ;	5 April, 1885
Persia, peace	3 March, 1857
Petersburg, St., peace	5 May, 1762
Petersburg, St.	5 Aug. 1772
Petersburg, St.	28 April, 1805
Peterswald, convention	8 July, 1813
Pilnitz, convention	20 July, 1791
Poland, partition	25 Nov. 1795
Pragmatic sanction	1438
Pragmatic sanction	17 April, 1713
Prague, peace	30 May, 1635
Prague (peace between Austria and Prussia)	23 Aug. 1866
Presburg, peace	26 Dec. 1805
Pretoria (see Transvaal)	3 Aug. 1881
Public good, league for the	1464
Pyrenees, peace	7 Nov. 1659
Quadruple alliance	2 Aug. 1718
Radstadt, peace	6 March, 1714
Radstadt, congress	9 Dec. 1797
Ratisbon, peace	13 Oct. 1630
Ratisbon	1 Aug. 1806
Reichenbach, treaties	June, 1813
Religion, peace of	1555
Rhine, confederation	1 Aug. 1806
Ryswick, peace	20 Sept. 1697
St. Cloud, convention	3 July, 1815
St. Germains, peace	1570
St. Germain-en-Laye, peace	29 June, 1679
St. Ildefonzo, alliance	19 Aug. 1796
San Stefano (peace between Russia & Turkey), see Berlin	3 March, 1878
Sjöröd, peace	1613
Sistowa, peace	4 Aug. 1791
Smalcald, league	31 Dec. 1529
Spain, pacification	22 April, 1834
Spain, convention, satisfying British claims	26 June, 1826
Stettin, peace	13 Dec. 1570
Stockholm, peace	20 Nov. 1719
Stockholm	24 March, 1724
Stockholm	3 March, 1813
Stockholm, treaty of (Sweden and allies)	21 Nov. 1856
Suncion	15 July, 1852
Temeswar, truce	7 Sept. 1664
Teschen, peace	12 May, 1779
Teusin, peace	18 May, 1595
Tien-Tsin, China, peace 26 June, 1858 ;	11 May, 1884
Tilsit, peace	7 July, 1807
Tolentino	19 Feb. 1793
Töplitz	9 Sept. 1813
Triple alliance	28 Jan. 1668
Triple alliance	4 Jan. 1717
Triple alliance (Austria, Germany, and Italy)	13 March, 1887
Troppeau, congress	20 Oct. 1820
Troyes	21 May, 1420
Turin (cession of Savoy and Nice)	24 March, 1860
Turkmanchay, peace	22 Feb. 1828
Ulm, peace	3 July, 1620
Unkiarskelessi	8 July, 1833
Utrecht, union	22 Jan. 1579
Utrecht, peace	11 April, 1713
Valençay	8 Dec. 1813
Verona, congress	25 Oct. 1822
Versailles, peace	20 Jan. 1783
Vienna	30 April, 1725
Vienna, alliance	16 March, 1731
Vienna, peace	18 Nov. 1738

Vienna, peace	14 Oct. 1809	Villa Franca (*prelim.*)	12 July, 1859	Washi
Vienna, convention	28 Sept. 1814	Vossem, peace	16 Jan. 1673	
Vienna, 25 March; 31 May;		Warsaw, alliance	31 March, 1653	Westn
	9 June, 1815	Warsaw	24 Feb. 1768	Westn
Vienna (Austria and Prussia), commercial	19 Feb. 1853	Washington, reciprocity treaty between Great Britain and the		Westp Wilna,
Vienna	30 Oct. 1864	United States, respecting New-		Wurm
Vienna (Austria & Great Britain, commercial)	16 Dec. 1865	foundland fishery, commerce, &c.	2 July, 1854	Wurtz Zurich
Vienna (peace between Austria and Italy)	3 Oct. 1866	Washington (settling Alabama claims, &c.)	8 May, 1871	Zurich Sard

TREBIA, now *Trebbia*, a river in North Italy, near which Hannibal defeated the Roman consul Sempronius, 218 B.C.; and Suvarrow, after a struggle, defeated the French marshal Macdonald and compelled him to retreat, 17-19 June, 1799.

TREBIZOND, a port of Asia Minor in the Black Sea, was colonised by the Greeks, and became subject to the kings of Pontus. It enjoyed self-government under the Roman empire, and when the Latins took Constantinople in 1204, it became the seat of an empire which endured till 1461, when it was conquered by the Turks under Mahomet I.

EMPERORS.

1204.	Alexis I. Comnenus.	1332.	Manuel II.
1222.	Andronicus I.	,,	Basil.
1235.	John I.	1340.	Irene.
1238.	Manuel I., great captain.	1341.	Anna.
1263.	Andronicus II.	1343.	John III.
1266.	George.	1344.	Michael.
1280.	John II.	1349.	Alexis III.
1285.	Theodora.	1390.	Manuel III.
,,	John II.	1417.	Alexis IV.
1297.	Alexis II.	1446.	John IV. (Calo-Joannes)
1330.	Andronicus III.	1458-61.	David.

TRECENTO, see *Italian*.

TREES in London. Many were planted by John Evelyn in the Mall, St. James's, &c. He recommended this in his "Fumifugium," published 1661. The planting of rows of trees in suburban roads began in 1875.

TREES OF LIBERTY were planted in Paris and other parts of France during the revolutionary eras, 1790 and 1848. These trees were cut down in Paris in Jan. 1850, when riots ensued, put down by the military. The celebrated tree *Férrier*, planted in 1789 near the National Library, Paris, was felled early in 1884.

TRENT (the ancient Tridentum), in the Tyrol, belongs to Austria. The council held here is reckoned in the Roman catholic church as the 18th general council. Its decisions have been implicitly received as the standard of faith, morals, and discipline in that church. It first sat 13 Dec. 1545, and continued (with interruptions) under popes Paul III., Julius III., and Pius IV. to 4 Dec. 1563; its last sitting (the 25th). A jubilee in relation to this council was celebrated in June, 1863. Trent was several times taken during the French war.

At this council was decreed, with anathemas: the canon of scripture (including the apocrypha), and the church its sole interpreter; the traditions to be equal with scripture; the seven sacraments (baptism, confirmation, the Lord's supper, penance, extreme unction, orders, and matrimony); transubstantiation; purgatory; indulgences; celibacy of the clergy; auricular confession, &c.

TRENT STEAMER, see *United States*, Nov.-Dec. 1861.

TREVECCA, see *Cheshunt*.

TRÉVES, or **TRIER**, the Roman Treviri, in Rhenish Prussia, was a prosperous city of the Gauls 12 B.C. The emperor Gallienus held his court here A.D. 255. The church of St. Simeon dates from the 4th century. Tréves was made an electorate in the 14th century, and becan in 1585. Councils hel bishopric is said to hav 7th century and to b After various changes Prussia, June 1815. I occasioned by miricles by a "Holy Coat."

"*TRIA JUNCTA* in one), the motto of order of the Bath, sig charity;" see *Bath*.

TRIAL AT BAR, or a plurality of judges Bristol after the riots in trial, 1844; and arra claimant of the Tichbo April, 1873. See *Juri*

TRIALS. Regulati were made by Lothaire about 673 to 680. Alfr begun trial by jury; bu such trials before his made for more speedy sizes Act," 1876. See

	REMARK
King Charles I.	20 Jan.;
Oates's Popish Plot: Edw 27 Nov.; Wm. Ireland a	
—— Robt. Green and oth bread and other Jesu Langhorne, counsellor,	
Sir George Wakeman, th quitted	
Viscount Stafford: convic	
Rye House Plot: convicte 13 July; Algernon Sidn	
The Seven Bishops; acqu	
Captain Porteous, for mur	
Jenny Diver, for felony, e:	
William Duell, executed fo who came to life when tion at Surgeons' Hall	
Lords Kilmarnock and Ba	
Mary Hamilton, for marry wives	
Lord Lovatt, 80 years o beheaded	
Freney, the celebrated Ir dered himself	
Amy Hutchinson, burnt a her husband	
Miss Blandy, the murder	
Ann Williams, for the n burnt alive	
Eugene Aram, for mur	
Earl Ferrers, for the mur cuted	
Mr. MacNaughten, at Stra Miss Knox	
Ann Bedingfield, for the r burnt alive	
Mr. Wilkes, alderman of poem ("Essay on Woma Murderers of captain Gl mate, and passengers, on *Sandwich*, at sea	

Elizabeth Brownrigg, for the murder of one of her
  female apprentices; hanged . . 12 Sept. 1767
Lord Baltimore, the libertine, and his female accom-
  plices, for rape . . . . 28 March, 1768
Great cause between the families of Hamilton and
  Douglas . . . . . 27 Feb. 1769
Great Valencia cause in the house of peers, in Ireland
  . . . . . . 18 March, 1772
Cause of Somerset the slave (see *Slavery*) 22 June
Elizabeth Herring, for the murder of her husband;
  hanged, and afterwards burnt at Tyburn 13 Sept. 1773
Messrs. Perreau brothers, bankers, forgery; hanged
  . . . . . . 17 Jan. 1776
Duchess of Kingston, for marrying two husbands;
  guilty (see *Kingston*) . . . 15 April, "
Dr. Dodd, for forging a bond of 4200l. in the name
  of the earl of Chesterfield, 22 Feb. (see Forgery;)
  executed . . . . . 27 June, 1777
Admiral Keppel, by court-martial; honourably acquitted . . . . . 11 Feb. 1779
Mr. Hackman, for the murder of Miss Reay, when
  coming out of the theatre-royal, Covent-garden
  . . . . . . 16 April, "
Lord George Gordon, on a charge of high treason;
  acquitted . . . . . 5 Feb. 1781
Mr. Woodfall, the celebrated printer, for a libel on
  lord Loughborough, afterwards lord chancellor
  . . . . . . 10 Nov. "
Lord George Gordon, for a libel on the queen of
  France; guilty . . . . 28 Jan. 1788
Mr. Warren Hastings: a trial which lasted seven
  years and three months (see *Hastings, Trial of*),
  commenced . . . . . 13 Feb. "
The printer of *the Times* newspaper, for libels on
  the prince of Wales, and dukes of York and Clarence; fined 200l. and imprisoned one year, 3 Feb. 1790
Renwick Williams, called the *Monster*, for stabbing
  women in London . . . 8 July, "
Barrington, the pickpocket, most extraordinary
  adept; transported . . . 22 Sept. "
Thomas Paine, political writer and deist, for libels
  in the *Rights of Man*; guilty . 18 Dec. 1792
Louis XVI. of France (see *France*) . 1792-3
Archibald Hamilton Rowan, for libel; imprisoned
  and fined . . . . . 29 Jan. 1794
Mr. Purefoy, for the murder of colonel Roper in a
  duel; acquitted . . . . 14 Aug. "
Mr. Robert Watt and Downie, at Edinburgh, for
  treason . . . . . 3 Sept. "
Messrs. Hardy, Horne Tooke, Thelwall, and Joyce,
  for high treason; acquitted . . 29 Oct. "
Earl of Abingdon, for his libel on Mr. Serman;
  guilty . . . . . 6 Dec. "
Major Semple, *alias* Lisle, for felony . 18 Feb. 1795
Redhead Yorke, at York, libel . . 27 Nov. "
Lord Westmeath v. Bradshaw, for *crim. con.*: dam-
  ages, 10,000l. . . . . 4 March, 1796
Lord Valentia v. Mr. Gawler, for adultery, damages,
  2000l. . . . . . 16 June, "
Daniel Isaac Eaton, for libels on kingly government;
  guilty . . . . . 8 July, "
Sir Godfrey Webster v. lord Holland, for adultery;
  damages, 6000l. . . . . 27 Feb. 1797
Parker, the mutineer at the Nore, called admiral
  Parker (see *Mutinies*) . . . 27 June, "
Boddington v. Boddington, for *crim. con.*; damages,
  10,000l. . . . . . 5 Sept. "
William Orr at Carrickfergus, for high treason;
  executed . . . . . 12 Oct. "
Mrs. Phepoe, *alias* Benson, murderess . 9 Dec. "
The murderers of col. St. George and Mr. Uniacke,
  at Cork . . . . . 15 April, 1798
Arthur O'Conner and O'Coigley, at Maidstone, for
  treason; latter hanged . . . 21 May, "
Sir Edward Crosbie and others for high treason;
  hanged . . . . . 1 June, "
Beauchamp Bagenal Harvey, at Wexford, for high
  treason . . . . . 21 June, "
Two Messrs. Sheares, at Dublin, for high treason;
  executed . . . . . 12 July, "
Theobald Woulfe Tone, by court-martial (he committed suicide, died on the 19th) . 10 Nov. "
Sir Harry Brown Hayes, for carrying off Miss Pike
  of Cork . . . . . 13 April, 1800
Hatfield, for shooting at George III.; see *Hatfield*
  . . . . . . 26 June, "
Mr. Tighe of Westmeath v. Jones, for *crim. con.*;
  damages, 10,000l. . . . . 2 Dec. "

Mutineers at Bantry Bay, hanged; see *Bantry Bay*
  . . . . . . 8 Jan. 1802
Governor Wall, for cruelty and murder, twenty years
  before (tried under 33 Hen. VIII. c. 23)(see *Goree*)
  . . . . . . 20 Jan. "
Crawley, for the murder of two females in Peter's-
  row, Dublin . . . . 6 March, "
Colonel Despard and his associates, for high treason;
  hanged on the top of Horsemonger-lane gaol (see
  Despard) . . . . . 7 Feb. 1803
M. Peltier, for libel on Bonaparte, first consul of
  France, in *l'Ambigue*; guilty . . 21 Feb. "
Robert Aslett, cashier at the bank of England, for
  embezzlement and frauds; the loss to the bank,
  320,000l.: found *not guilty*, on account of the in-
  validity of the bills . . . 18 July, "
Robert Emmett, at Dublin, for high treason; exe-
  cuted next day . . . . 19 Sept. "
Krenan, one of the murderers of lord Kilwarden;
  hanged . . . . . 2 Oct. "
Mr. Smith for the murder of the supposed *Hammer-
  smith Ghost* . . . . 13 Jan. 1804
Lockhart and Laudon Gordon for carrying off Mrs.
  Lee . . . . . . 6 March, "
Rev. C. Massy v. marquis of Headfort, for *crim.
  con.*; damages, 10,000l. . . 27 July, "
William Cooper, the *Hackney Monster*, for offences
  against females . . . . 17 April, 1805
General Picton, for applying the torture to Louisa
  Calderon, to extort confession, at Trinidad, tried
  (under 42 Geo. III. c. 85) in the court of King's
  Bench; guilty [new trial, same verdict, 11 June,
  1808] . . . . . 24 Feb. 1806
Mr. Patch, for the murder of his partner, Mr.
  Bligh . . . . . 6 April, "
Lord Melville, impeached by the house of com-
  mons; acquitted . . . 12 June, "
Hamilton Rowan, in Dublin; pleaded the King's
  pardon . . . . . 1 July, "
The Warrington gang, for unnatural offences;
  executed . . . . . 23 Aug. "
Palm, the bookseller, by a French military com-
  mission at Brennan . . . 26 Aug. "
Judge Johnson, for a libel on the earl of Hard-
  wicke; guilty . . . . 23 Nov. "
Lord Cloncurry v. Sir John B. Piers, for *crim. con.*;
  damages, 20,000l. . . . . 19 Feb. 1807
Holloway and Haggerty, the murderers of Mr.
  Steele: thirty persons were crushed to death at
  their execution, at the Old Bailey . 20 Feb. "
Sir Home Popham, by court-martial; repri-
  manded . . . . . 7 March, "
Knight v. Dr. Wolcot, *alias* Peter Pindar, for *crim.
  con.* . . . . . 27 June, "
Lieut. Berry, of H.M.S. *Hazard*; for an unnatural
  offence . . . . . 2 Oct. "
Lord Elgin v. Ferguson, for *crim. con.*; damages,
  10,000l. . . . . . 22 Dec. "
Simmons, the murderer of the Boreham family, at
  Hoddesdon . . . . 4 March, 1808
Sir Arthur Paget, for *crim. con.* with Lady Borrington . . . . . 14 July, "
Major Campbell, for killing Captain Boyd in a duel;
  hanged . . . . . 4 Aug. "
Peter Finnerty and others, for a libel on the duke
  of York . . . . . 9 Nov. "
The duke of York, by inquiry in the house of
  commons, on charges preferred against him by
  colonel Wardle, from 26 Jan. to 20 March . 1809
Wellesley v. Lord Paget, for *crim. con.*; damages,
  20,000l. . . . . . 12 May, "
The king v. Valentine Jones, for breach of duty as
  commissary-general . . . 26 May, "
Wright v. colonel Wardle, for Mrs. Mary Ann
  Clarke's furniture . . . 1 June, "
The earl of Leicester v. *Morning Herald*, for a libel;
  damages 1000l. . . . . 29 June, "
William Cobbett, for a libel on the German legion
  convicted . . . . 9 July, "
Hon. captain Lake, for putting Robert Jeffery, a
  British seaman, on shore at Sombrero; dismissed
  the service (see *Sombrero*) . . 10 Feb. 1810
Mr. Perry for libels in the *Morning Chronicle*; ac-
  quitted . . . . . 24 Feb. "
The Vere-street gang, for unnatural offences;
  guilty . . . . . 20 Sept. "
Peter Finnerty, for a libel on lord Castlereagh;
  . . . . . . 31 Jan. 1811

TRIALS.

The king v. Messrs. John and Leigh Hunt, for libels; guilty . . . . . . 22 Feb. 1811
Ensign Hepburn, and White the drummer; both were executed . . . . . 7 March, ,,
Walter Cox, in Dublin, for libels; he stood in the pillory . . . . . . 12 March, ,,
The king v. W. Cobbett, for libels; convicted . . . . . . 15 June, ,,
Lord Louth, in Dublin; sentenced to imprisonment and fine, for oppressive conduct as a magistrate . . . . . . 19 June, ,,
The Berkeley cause, before the house of peers, concluded . . . . . 28 June, ,,
Dr. Sheridan, physician, on a charge of sedition; acquitted . . . . . 21 Nov. ,,
Gale Jones, for seditious and blasphemous libels; convicted . . . . . 26 Nov. ,,
William Cundell and John Smith, for high treason (see *High Treason*) . . . 6 Feb. 1812
Daniel Isaac Eaton, on a charge of blasphemy; convicted . . . . . 6 March, ,,
Bellingham, for the murder of Mr. Perceval, prime minister . . . . . 15 May, ,,
The king v. Mr. Lovell, of the *Statesman*, for libel; guilty . . . . . 19 Nov. ,,
Messrs. John and Leigh Hunt, for libels in the *Examiner*; convicted . . . . 9 Dec. ,,
Marquis of Sligo, for concealing a sea-deserter . . . . . . 16 Dec. ,,
The murderers of Mr. Horsfall; at York; executed . . . . . . 7 Jan. 1813
Mr. Hugh Fitzpatrick, for publishing Scully's *History of the Penal Laws* . . 6 Feb. ,,
The divorce cause against the duke of Hamilton for adultery . . . . 11 April, ,,
Mr. John Magee, in Dublin, for libels in the *Evening Post*; guilty . . . 26 July, ,,
Nicholson, the murderer of Mr. and Mrs. Bonar; hanged . . . . . 21 Aug. ,,
Tuite, murder of Mr. Goulding; executed 7 Oct. ,,
The celebrated Mary Ann Clark, for a libel on the right hon. Wm. Vesey Fitzgerald, afterwards lord Fitzgerald . . . . . 7 Feb. 1814
Lord Cochrane, Cochrane Johnstone, Berenger, Butt, and others, for frauds in the public funds, 22 Feb.; convicted (see *Stocks*) . 8, 9 June, ,,
Admiral Bradley, at Winchester, for frauds in ship letters . . . . . 18 Aug. ,,
Colonel Quentin, of the 10th Hussars, by court-martial . . . . . 1 Nov. ,,
Sir John Henry Mildmay, bart., for *crim. con.* with the countess of Rosebery; damages, 15,000*l.* . . . . . 5 Dec. ,,
George Barnett, for shooting at Miss Kelly, of Covent Garden theatre . . 8 April, 1816
Captain Hutchinson, sir Robert Wilson, and Mr. Bruce, in Paris, for aiding the escape of count Lavalette (see *Lavalette*) . . . 24 April, ,,
"Captain Grant," the famous Irish robber at Maryborough . . . . . 16 Aug. ,,
Vaughan, a police officer, Mackay, and Browne, for conspiracy to induce men to commit felonies to obtain the reward; convicted . . 21 Aug. ,,
Colonel Stanhope, by court-martial, at Cambray, in France . . . . . 23 Sept. ,,
Cashman, a seaman, for the Spafields riots and outrages on Snowhill; convicted and hanged (see *Spafields*) . . . . . 20 Jan. 1817
Count Maubreuil, at Paris, for robbing the queen of Westphalia . . . . 2 May, ,,
Mr. R. J. Butt, for a libel on lord chief-justice Ellenborough . . . . 23 May, ,,
Mr. Wooler, for libels on the government and ministers . . . . . 6 June, ,,
Thistlewood, Dr. Watson, Hooper, and others, for treason . . . . . 9 June, ,,
The murderers of the Lynch family at Wildgooselodge, Ireland . . . . 19 July, ,,
Mr. Roger O'Connor, on a charge of robbing the mail; acquitted . . . . 5 Aug. ,,
Brandreth, Turner, and others, at Derby, for high treason . . . . . 15 Oct. ,,
Hone, the bookseller, for parodies; three trials before Lord Ellenborough; extemporaneous and successful defence . . 18, 19, 20 Dec. ,,
Mr. Dick, for abduction and rape of Miss Crockatt . . . . . 21 March, 1818
Appeal of murder case; Ashford, the brother of Mary Ashford, against Abraham Thornton, accused of her murder (see *Appeal*) and acquitted 16 April, 1818
Rev. Dr. O'Halloran, for forging a frank (see *Transportation*) . . . . . 9 Sept. ,,
Robert Johnston, at Edinburgh; his dreadful execution . . . . . 30 Dec. ,,
Sir Manasseh Lopez, for bribery at Grampound (see *Bribery*) . . . . 18 March, 1819
Mosely, Woolfe, and other merchants, for conspiracy and fraud . . . . 20 April, ,,
Carlile, for the publication of Paine's *Age of Reason*, &c. . . . . 15 Oct. ,,
John Scanlan, at Limerick, for murder of Ellen Hanly . . . . . 14 March, 1820
Sir Francis Burdett, at Leicester, for a seditious libel . . . . . 23 March, ,,
Henry Hunt, and others, for their conduct at the Manchester meeting; convicted (see *Manchester Reform Meeting*) . . . . 27 March, ,,
Sir Charles Wolseley and rev. Mr. Harrison, for sedition; guilty . . . . 10 April, ,,
Thistlewood, Ings, Brunt, Davidson, and Tidd, for conspiracy to murder the king's ministers; commenced (see *Cato-street*) . . 17 April, ,,
Louvel, in France, for the murder of the duke de Berri . . . . . 7 June, ,,
Lord Glerawley v. John Burn, for *crim. con.* . . . . . 18 June, ,,
Major Curtwright and others at Warwick, for sedition . . . . . 3 Aug. ,,
"Little Waddington," for a seditious libel; acquitted . . . . . 19 Sept. ,,
Lieutenant-colonel French, 6th dragoon guards, by court-martial . . . . 19 Sept. ,,
Caroline, queen of England, before the house of lords, for adultery, commenced 16 Aug.; it terminated (see *Queen Caroline's Trial*) . 10 Nov. ,,
The female murderers of Miss Thompson, in Dublin; hanged . . . . 1 May, 1821
David Haggart, an extraordinary robber, and a man of singularly eventful life, at Edinburgh, for the murder of a turnkey . . . 9 June, ,,
Samuel D. Hayward, the favourite man of fashion, for burglary . . . . 8 Oct. ,,
The murderers of Mrs. Torrance, in Ireland, convicted and hanged . . . 17 Dec. ,,
Cussen, Leahy, and others, for the abduction of Miss Gould . . . . 29 July, 1822
Barthelemi, in Paris, for the abduction of Elizabeth Florence . . . . 23 Sept. ,,
Cuthbert v. Browne, singular action for deceit . . . . . 28 Jan. 1823
The famous "Bottle Conspirators," in Ireland, by *ex-officio* . . . . 23 Feb. ,,
The extraordinary "earl of Portsmouth's case" commenced . . . . 18 March, ,,
Probert, Hunt, and Thurtell, murderers of Mr. Weare; Probert turned king's evidence; afterwards hanged for horse-stealing (see *Executions*) . . . . . 5 Jan. 1824
Mr. Henry Fauntleroy, banker of London, for forgery; hanged . . . . 30 Oct. ,,
Foote v. Hayne, for breach of promise of marriage; damages, 3000*l.* . . 22 Dec. ,,
Mr. Henry Savary, a banker's son at Bristol, for forgery . . . . . 4 April, 1825
O'Keefe and Bourke, murderers of the Franks family . . . . . 18 Aug. ,,
The case of Mr. Wellesley Pole, and the Misses Long; commenced . . . 9 Nov. ,-
Captain Bligh v. the hon. Wm. Wellesley Pole, for adultery . . . . 25 Nov. ,,
Fisher v. Stockdale, for libel in *Harriette Wilson* . . . . . 20 March, 1826
Edward Gibbon Wakefield, and others, for abduction of Miss Turner . . 24 March, 1827
Rev. Robert Taylor for blasphemy; found guilty . . . . . 24 Oct. ,,
Richard Gillan, for the murder of Maria Bagster, at Taunton . . . . 8 April, 1828
Mr. Montgomery, for forgery; he committed suicide in prison on the morning appointed for his execution . . . . . 4 July, ,,
Brinklett, for the death of lord Mount Sandford by a kick . . . . 16 July, ,,
William Corder, for murder of Maria Marten; executed . . . . . 6 Aug. ,,

TRIALS.

rchant, for forgery;
. . 28 Oct. 1328
Burking murders;
ame approver (see
. . 24 Dec. ,,
iers, for fraudulent
. . 21 March, 1829
ire to York minster
. . 31 March, ,,
rderers, at Glasgow;
. . 14 July, ,,
st, for murders of
. . 4 Aug. ,,
martial, at Ports-
. . 26 Aug. ,,
'orning Journal, for
on; convicted 10 Feb. 1830
ig out the tongues of
. . 4 March, ,,
use in the county of
. . 6 March, ,,
of Mr. Clayton in a
. . 2 April, ,,
William Malcolm;
. . 30 July, ,,
m, for killing Mr.
. . 24 Aug. ,,
of lieut. Crowther in
. . 8 Oct. ,,
anslaughter of Miss
. . 30 Oct. ,,
thers, ministers of
. . 21 Dec. ,,
inciting to a riot;
. . 10 Jan. 1831
n of proclamation;
. . 12 Feb. ,,
er of Mrs. Lloyd (see
. . 19 Feb. ,,
on of Miss Adams;
. . 26 May, ,,
ained the revolting
xplain"), for reviling
. . 6 July, ,,
bel; the jury could
. . 7 July, ,,
igham Baring, M.P.
. . 14 July, ,,
f age, for the murder
hanged at Maidstone
. . 1 Aug. ,,
ston v. lord Lorton;
. . 9 Nov. ,,
er of the Italian boy
. . 3 Dec. ,,
or shooting at Mr.
. . 17 Dec. ,,
of Mrs. Walsh, by
. . 6 Jan. 1832
rtial, at Bristol (see
. . 9 Jan. ,,
of Applevale, county
. . 28 Feb. ,,
murder of his wife
. . 26 March, ,,
rated Miss Aston) v.
. . 26 July, ,,
et of duty in the
. . 26 Oct. ,,
s church, for heresy
. . 13 March, 1833
ailor, for swindling;
. . 10 May, ,,
ly Hewley's charity,
tarians) . 23 Dec. ,,
, by court-martial, at
d; his colonel, lord
. . Jan. 1834
libels; guilty, 6 Feb. ,,
lebrated murderess,
. . 10 April, 1835
y; acquitted, 29 May, ,,
ting the life of the
sploding an infernal
. . 30 Jan. 1836
lbourne, in court of
, with the hon. Mrs.
it . . 22 June, ,,

Lord de Roos v. Cumming, for defamation, charging lord de Roos with cheating at cards; verdict in favour of Mr. Cumming . . . 10 Feb. 1837
James Greenacre and Sarah Gale, for the murder of Hannah Browne; Greenacre convicted and hanged; Gale transported . . . 10 April, ,,
Francis Hastings Medhurst, esq., for killing Mr. Joseph Alsop; guilty . . . 13 April, 1839
Bolam, for murder of Mr. Millie; verdict, manslaughter . . . . . 30 July, ,,
Rev. Mr. Stephens, at Chester, for inflammatory language . . . . . 15 Aug. ,,
John Frost, an ex-magistrate, and others, for high treason; guilty; sentence commuted to transportation (see Newport) . . . 31 Dec. ,,
Benjamin Courvoisier, for murder of lord William Russell; hanged . . . 18-20 June, 1840
Gould, for murder of Mr. Templeman; transported . . . . . 22 June, ,,
Edward Oxford, attempted the life of the queen; adjudged insane, and confined in Bethlehem (see Oxford) . . . . . 9, 10 July, ,,
Madame Lefarge, in France, for the murder of her husband; guilty . . . . 2 Sept. ,,
Prince Louis Napoleon, for his descent upon France (see France) . . . . . 6 Oct. ,,
Captain R. A. Reynolds, 11th hussars, by courtmartial; guilty; the sentence excited great popular displeasure against his colonel, lord Cardigan 20 Oct. ,,
Lord Cardigan before the house of peers, capitally charged for wounding captain Harvey Tucket in a duel; acquitted . . . 16 Feb. 1841
The Wallaces, brothers, merchants, for having wilfully caused the destruction of the ship Dryad at sea, to defraud the underwriters; transported . . . . . 4 March, ,,
Josiah Mister, for attempting the life of Mr. Mackreth; guilty . . . 23 March, ,,
Bartholomew Murray, at Chester, for the murder of Mrs. Cook . . . . . 5 April, ,,
Earl of Waldegrave and captain Duff, for an aggravated assault on a police constable; guilty; judgment, six months' imprisonment, and fines of 200l. and 20l. . . . . 3 May, ,,
Madame Lefarge again, for robbery of diamonds . . . . . 7 Aug. ,,
The great case, Allen Bogle v. Mr. Lawson, publisher of the Times newspaper, for an alleged libel, in stating the plaintiff to be connected with numerous bank forgers throughout Europe in their schemes to defraud Messrs. Glyn and Company, bankers of London, by means of fictitious letters of credit; damages, one farthing. This exposure, so honourable to the Times, led to the Times Testimonial . . . 16 Aug. ,,
Mr. MacLeod, at Utica, America, for taking part in the destruction of the Caroline, commenced; acquitted after a trial that lasted eight days, 4 Oct. ,,
Robert Blakesley, for murder of Mr. Burdon, of Eastcheap; hanged . . . 28 Oct. ,,
Mr. Beaumont Smith, for forgery of Exchequer bills to an immense amount; he pleaded guilty, and was sentenced to transportation for life 4 Dec. ,,
Sophia Darbon v. Rosser; breach of promise of marriage; damages, 1600l. . . . 8 Dec. ,,
Mr. John Levick and Antonio Mattei, principal and second in the duel in which lieut. Adams was killed at Malta; both acquitted . 10 March, 1842
Vivier, courier of the Morning Herald, at Boulogne, for conveying the Indian mail through France, for that journal, contrary to the French regulations . . . . . 13 April, ,,
Daniel Good, for murder of Jane Jones; the Roehampton murder; found guilty, and sentenced to be hanged . . . . . 13 May, ,,
John Francis, for attempting to assassinate the queen (see Francis) . . . 17 June, ,,
Thomas Cooper, for the murder of Daly, the policeman; hanged . . . . . 4 July, ,,
Nicholas Suisse, valet of the late marquis of Hertford, at the prosecution of that nobleman's executors, charged with enormous frauds; acquitted 6 July, ,,
M'Gill and others, for abduction of Miss Crellin; guilty . . . . . 8 Aug. ,,
Nicholas Suisse again, upon like charges, and again acquitted . . . . . 24 Aug. ,,

Benn, for pointing a pistol at the queen; 18 months' imprisonment . . . . . 25 Aug. 1842
The rioters in the provinces, under a special commission, at Stafford . . . . 1 Oct. ,,
The Cheshire rioters, under a special commission, before lord Abinger . . . . 6 Oct. ,,
The Lancashire rioters, also under a special commission . . . . . . 10 Oct. ,,
Alice Lowe, at the prosecution of lord Frankfort; acquitted . . . . . 31 Oct. ,,
Mr. Howard, attorney, v. sir William Gosset, serjeant-at-arms . . . . . 5 Dec. ,,
Mr. Egan, in Dublin, for the robbery of a bank parcel; acquitted . . . . 17 Jan. 1843
Rev. W. Bailey, LL.D., for forgery; guilty: transportation for life . . . . 1 Feb. ,,
Mac Naughten, for the murder of Mr. Drummond, secretary to sir Robert Peel: acquitted on the ground of insanity . . . . 4 March, ,,
The Rebeccaites, at Cardiff, under a special commission . . . . . . 27 Oct. ,,
Samuel Sidney Smith, for forgery; sentenced to transportation for life . . . . 29 Nov. ,,
Edward Dwyer, for the murder of his child at Southwark; guilty . . . . 1 Dec. ,,
Mr. Holt, of the *Age*; libel on the duke of Brunswick; guilty . . . . 29 Jan. 1844
Lieut. Grant, second to lieut. Munro, in his duel with col. Fawcett; acquitted . . 14 Feb. ,,
Fraser v. Bagley, for crim. con.; verdict for the defendant . . . . . 19 Feb. ,,
Lord William Paget v. earl of Cardigan, for crim. con.; verdict for defendant . . 26 Feb. ,,
Mary Furley, for the murder of her child in an agony of despair . . . 16 April, ,,
The will-forgers, William Henry Barber (since declared innocent), Joshua Fletcher, Georgiana Dorey, William Saunders, and Susannah his wife: all found guilty, 15 April; sentenced 22 April, ,,
[In 1848 Mr. Barber returned to England with a free pardon, and an acknowledgment of his innocence by his prosecutors: he was re-admitted to practise as an attorney; and on the 3rd of August, 1859, in conformity with the recommendation of a select committee of the house of commons, the sum of 5000l. was voted him " as a national acknowledgment of the wrong he had suffered from an erroneous prosecution."]
Crouch, for the murder of his wife; found guilty, 8 May; hanged . . . . 27 May, ,,
Messrs. O'Connell, sen., O'Connell, jun., Steele, Ray, Barrett, Grey, Duffy, and rev. Thomas Tierney, at Dublin, for political conspiracy: the trial commenced 15 Jan., and lasted twenty-four days: all the traversers were found guilty, 12 Feb. Proceedings on motions for a new trial, &c., extended the case into Easter term; and sentence was pronounced upon all but the clergyman, on whom judgment was remitted . . 30 May, ,,
Augustus Dalmas, for the murder of Sarah Macfarlane; guilty . . . . 14 June, ,,
Wm. Burton Newenham, for the abduction of Miss Wortham; guilty . . . . 17 June, ,,
Bellamy, for the murder of his wife by prussic acid; acquitted . . . . 21 Aug. ,,
John Tawell, for murder of Sarah Hart; hanged 13, 14 March, 1845
Thomas Henry Hocker, for murder of James Delarue . . . . . . 11 April, ,,
Joseph Connor, for murder of Mary Brothers, 16 May, ,,
The Spanish pirates, for murder of ten Englishmen at sea . . . . . . 26 July, ,,
Rev. Dr. Wetherall, for crim. con. with Mrs. Cooke, his own daughter . . . 16 Aug. ,,
Captain Johnson, of the ship *Tory*, for the murder of several of his crew . . . 5 Feb. 1846
Miss M. A. Smith v. earl Ferrers; breach of promise of marriage . . . . 18 Feb. ,,
Lieut. Hawkey, for the murder of Mr. Seton, in a duel; acquitted . . . 16 July, ,,
Richard Dunn, for perjury and attempted fraud on Miss A. Burdett Coutts . . . 27 Feb. 1847
Mitchell, the Irish confederate; transported for 14 years (see *Ireland*) . . . 26 May, 1848
Wm. Smith O'Brien, Meagher, and other confederates, sentenced to death; the sentence afterwards commuted to transportation (pardoned in 1856) . . . . . . 9 Oct. ,,

Bloomfield Rush, for murder of Messrs. Jermy, at Norwich; hanged . . . . 29 March, ,,
Gorham v. the bishop of Exeter; ecclesiastical case; judgment given in the court of Arches against the plaintiff . . . . 2 Aug. ,,
[The bishop had refused to institute the rev. Mr. Gorham into the living of Brampton-Speke, in Devonshire, alleging want of orthodoxy in the plaintiff, who denied that spiritual regeneration was conferred by baptism; the court held that the charge against the plaintiff of holding false doctrine was proved, and that the bishop was justified in his refusal. Mr. Gorham appealed to the Judicial Committee of the Privy Council, which pronounced its opinion (8 March, 1850) that "the doctrine held by Mr. Gorham was not contrary or repugnant to the declared doctrine of the church of England, and that Mr. Gorham ought not, by reason of the doctrine held by him, to have been refused admission to the vicarage of Brampton-Speke." This decision led to subsequent proceedings in the three courts of law, successively, for a rule to show cause why a prohibition should not issue, directed to the judge of the Arches court, and to the archbishop of Canterbury, against giving effect to the judgment of her majesty in council. The rule was refused in each court, and in the end Mr Gorham was instituted into the vicarage in question, 7 Aug. 1850.]
Manning and his wife, for murder of O'Connor; guilty: death . . . . 27 Oct. ,,
Walter Watts, lessee of the Olympic theatre, for forgery, &c. . . . . 10 May, ,,
Robert Pate, a retired lieutenant, for an assault on the queen . . . . . 11 July, ,,
The Sloanes, man and wife, for starving their servant, Jane Wilbred . . . 5 Feb. ,,
The Board of Customs v. the London Dock Company, on a charge of defrauding the revenue of duties; a trial of 11 days ended in a virtual acquittal . . . . . . 18 Feb. ,,
Sarah Chesham, for murder of husband, by poison: she had murdered several of her children and others by the same means; hanged . 6 March, ,,
Thomas Drory, for the murder of Jael Denny: hanged . . . . . . 7 March, ,,
Doyle v. Wright, concerning the personal custody of Miss Augusta Talbot, a Roman catholic ward of chancery, before the lord chancellor: protracted case . . . . . 22 March, ,,
The murderers of the rev. George Edward Hollest, of Frimley, Surrey; guilty . . 31 March, ,,
Achilli v. Newman, for libel; tried before lord chief justice Campbell in the Queen's Bench: verdict for the plaintiff, Nov. 1852; . 31 Jan. ,,
Miller v. ald. Salomons, M.P., for voting as a member without having taken the required oath; verdict against the defendant . . 19 April, ,,
The case "Bishop of London v. the rev. Mr. Gladstone:" judgment of the Arches court against the defendant . . . . 10 June, ,,
Lord Frankfort, for scandalous and defamatory libels; guilty . . . . 3 Dec. ,,
Richard Bourke Kirwan, for the murder of his wife; guilty . . . . . 10 Dec. ,,
Eliot Bower, for murder of Mr. Saville Morton, at Paris; acquitted . . . . 28 Dec. ,,
Henry Horler, for murder of his wife; hanged at the Old Bailey . . . . 15 Jan. ,,
James Barbour, for murder of Robinson; hanged at York . . . . . 15 Jan. ,,
George Sparkes and James Hitchcock, for the murder of William Blackmore at Exeter; guilty 19 March, ,,
Five Frenchmen (principal and seconds) for the murder of a sixth Frenchman in a duel at Egham; verdict, manslaughter . . 21 March, ,,
Moore and Walsh, for the murder of John Blackburn, at Stafford; hanged . . 21 March, ,,
Saunders, for murder of Mr. Toler; hanged at Chelmsford . . . . . 30 March, ,,
The Stackpole family, four in number; two of them females, and wives to the others, for the murder of their relative, also a Stackpole; hanged at Ennis . . . . . . 28 April, ,,
Case of Holy Cross Hospital, Winchester, decided against rev. earl of Guildford . . 1 Aug. ,,
Smyth v. Smyth, ended in the plaintiff being com-

TRIALS.

rging the will on which
. . . . 8, 9, 10 Aug. 1853
ting liability to church-
ouse of lords, against the
. . . . . 12 Aug. „
specting Madlle. Wagner ;
. . . . 22 Feb. 1854
yor of Rye, convicted of
. . . . 2 March, „
will case . . April, „
m of Miss E. Arbuthnot,
n Smithwick ; convicted
. . . . 28, 29 July, „
urdering her six children ;
. . . . . 9 Aug. „
Butler v. viscount Mount-
intiff, who thus came into
being proved illegitimate
. . . . . Aug. „
Perry and Greer; sen-
Hardinge 29 July-Aug. „
Belcher, captain McClure,
eir ships in the Arctic
. . . . . Oct. „
r murder of Charles Col-
cuted) . . . 4 Jan. 1855
herwise De Burgh (cruelty
d charges against lord
ised . . . . „
pwood (will set aside)
. . . . 3-10 April, „
er of Joseph Latham (or
April) . . 12 April, „
hief-trainer ; transported
. . . . 13 April, „
for cruelties in Birming-
. . . . . 3 Aug. „
iam Strahan, and Robert
r disposing of their cus-
the amount of 113,625l.) :
. . . . 27 Oct. „
ge of poisoning his wife ;
. . . . . 7 Nov. „
on decorations, &c., in
e ; decision against them)
. . . . . 5 Dec. „
council, partly for both
his own costs, 21 March,
. . . . . „
r murder of her child ;
l) . . . 6 March, 1856
of J. P. Cook by poison
. . . 14-27 May, „
ord on 14 June, in the pre-
is. If he had been ac-
been tried for the murder
.] . . . . „
his wife (executed 9 Aug.)
. . . . 19 July, „
nison, respecting the doc-
defendant deprived, and
rdict set aside by privy
. . . . 22 Oct. „
H. Attwell ; convicted of
. . . . 31 Oct. „
of Crystal Palace Com-
of about 28,000l.); trans-
s . . . . 1 Nov. „
ews, for libel ; verdict for
. . . . . 3 Dec. „
ester ; see *Gold Robbery*,
. . . . 14 Jan. 1857
rgeries (to the amount of
Northern Railway Com-
life . . . 16 Jan. „
called the Penman), Wm.
, convicted of extensive
ques . . 5 March, „
on charge of poisoning
Glasgow ; not proven
. . . 30 June-9 July, „
poisoning his mother, con-
. . . . 25 July, „
charge of murdering two
same year. His wife con-
appeared to be insane.]

James Spollen, on charge of murder of Mr. Little,
near Dublin ; acquitted . . . 7-11 Aug. 1857
W. Attwell and others, convicted of stealing the
countess of Ellesmere's jewels (value 15,000l.)
from the top of a cab . . . 15 Dec. „
Strevens v. Campion, for slander, in charging the
plaintiff with complicity in the murder of his
aunt, Mrs. Kelly ; damages 6d. . . 21 Dec. „
The directors of the British Bank, Humphry Brown,
Edw. Esdaile, H. D. Macleod, alderman R. H.
Kennedy, W. D. Owen, James Stapleton, and
Hugh Innes Cameron, for fraud (see under *Banks*) ;
convicted . . . . . 13-27 Feb. 1858
Rev. S. Smith and his wife, for murderous assault
on John Leech ; convicted . . 6-7 April, „
Edw. Anchmuty Glover, M.P., for false declaration
of qualification of M.P. . . . 9 April, „
Simon Bernard, as accessory to the conspiracy
against the life of the emperor Napoleon ; acquitted
. . . . . . 12-17 April, „
The earldom of Shrewsbury case ; earl Talbot's claim
allowed . . . . . 1 June, „
James Seal, for the murder of Sarah Guppy ; convicted (and executed) . . . 23 July, „
The Berkeley peerage case . . . 23 July, „
Patience Swynfen v. F. H. Swynfen ; a will case ;
the will affirmed . . . . 27 July, „
[The plaintiff was Patience Swynfen, widow of Henry
John Swynfen, son of the testator, Samuel Swynfen. Her husband died 15 June, 1854, and his
father on 16 July, following, having made a will
19 days before his death, devising the Swynfen
estate (worth about 60,000l.) to his son's wife,
but leaving a large amount of personal estate un-
disposed of. The defendant, F. H. Swynfen, son
of the testator's eldest half-brother, claimed the
estate as heir-at-law on the ground of the testator's
insanity. The issue was brought to trial in March,
1856 ; but proceedings were stayed by Mrs. Swynfen's counsel, sir F. Thesiger, entering into an
agreement with the opposite counsel, sir Alexander Cockburn, without her consent, and in defiance of her instructions. After various proceedings, the court of chancery ordered a new
trial. She gained her cause, mainly through the
energy of her counsel, Mr. Chas. R. Kennedy, to
whom she had promised to pay 20,000l. for his
extraordinary services. Mrs. Swynfen, however,
married a Mr. Broun, and repudiated Mr. Kennedy's claim. The latter, in an action against
her, obtained a verdict in his favour on 29 March,
1862, which was, on appeal, finally reversed in
Feb. 1864. Mrs. Swynfen was non-suited in an
action brought against her counsel (afterwards
lord Chelmsford and lord chancellor), in July,
1859, and June, 1860.]
Lemon Oliver, a stockbroker, convicted of extensive frauds . . . . . 10 Nov. „
Marchmont v. Marchmont ; a disgraceful divorce
case, begun . . . . . 30 Nov. „
W. H. Guernsey, for stealing Ionian despatches
from the Colonial Office ; acquitted . 15 Dec. „
Evans v. Evans and Rose, divorce case . Dec. „
Lieut.-col. Dickson v. earl of Wilton, for libel ; verdict for the plaintiff . . . 14 Feb. 1859
Black v. Elliott, 850 sheep poisoned by a sheep-
wash sold by defendant ; damages 140l. 23 Feb. „
Wagner, Bateman, and others, a gang of bank
forgers ; convicted . . . . 13 May, „
Earl of Shrewsbury v. Hope Scott, and others ; the
earl gains the Shrewsbury estates . 3 June, „
Thellusson will case decided (see *Thellusson*) 9 June, „
T. R. Marshall, E. A. Mortimer, and H. S. Eicke,
convicted of illegal sale of army commissions,
. . . . . . 29 June, „
Thomas Smethurst, a surgeon, for the murder by
poison of Isabella Bankes, whom he had married
during his wife's lifetime ; convicted 15-19 Aug. „
[He was reprieved on the ground of insufficient evidence ; but was tried and found guilty of bigamy,
16 Nov. 1859. On 11 Nov. 1862, he proved Miss
Bankes's will, and obtained her property.]
Oakley v. the Moulvie Ooddeen, "ambassador of
the king of Oude." Verdict for the defendant,
who seems to have fallen among bill-sharpers,
. . . . . . 17 Dec. „
David Hughes, an attorney, convicted of gross
frauds upon his clients . . . . Jan. 1860

Eugenia Plummer, aged 11 years, convicted of perjury against rev. Mr. Hatch . . . 14 May, 1860
Mr. W. H. Leatham, M.P., convicted of bribery at Wakefield . . . . . . 19 July, ,,
Thomas Hopley, a schoolmaster, convicted of manslaughter of Reginald Cancellor, by flogging, 23 July, ,,
Nottidge v. Prince (see *Agapemone*) . 25 July, ,,
Rev. J. Bonwell, of Stepney, degraded for immorality, 29 Aug. ,,
James Mullens, convicted for the murder of Mrs. Elmsley; by endeavouring to inculpate one Emn, he led to his own conviction . . 25 Oct. ,,
Miss Shedden v. Patrick. (The plaintiff ably pleaded her own cause when the case was opened; her object, to prove the legitimacy of her father, was not attained) . . . 9 Nov. *et seq.* ,,
Hooper v. Ward; disgraceful profligacy of a magistrate; verdict for plaintiff . . 19, 20 Dec. ,,
Constance Kent inquiry; trial refused, see *Road Murder* . . . . . . Jan. 1861
Thelwall v. hon. Major Yelverton. The plaintiff sued for expenses incurred by defendant's wife; the major denied the validity of his marriage with Miss Longworth, having since married the widow of professor Edward Forbes, the eminent naturalist. The court in Dublin supported the first marriage . . . 21 Feb. to 4 March, ,,
[Miss Longworth endeavoured to establish her marriage. On appeal, the Scotch court annulled the marriage, July, 1862, and this judgment was affirmed by the house of lords, 28 July, 1864, and again finally, 30 July, 1867. An attempt to set aside the judgment of the house of lords rejected by the court of session, 29 Oct. 1868.]
Brook v. Brook; see *Marriage with Wife's Sister*. The house of lords on appeal decided against the validity of such marriages, even when celebrated in a foreign country . . . 18 March, ,,
Reade v. Lacy; the dramatising a novel restrained, 17 April, ,,
Beamish v. Beamish; the lords on appeal decide that a clergyman cannot perform the ceremony of marriage for himself . . . 22 April, ,,
Emperor of Austria v. Day; verdict for plaintiff. The defendant had printed 100 millions florin notes on the bank of Hungary, for Louis Kossuth. The notes were ordered to be destroyed within one month, 6 May; judgment affirmed 12 June, ,,
Cardross case. John MacMillan, a free-church minister, was expelled for drunkenness and misconduct, May, 1858. The Glasgow synod and the general assembly of the free church affirmed the sentence. He appealed to the court of session, which set aside the decree (which involved temporalities), asserting that the assembly had only spiritual authority . . July, ,,
W. B. Turnbull v. Bird, secretary of protestant alliance; libel; verdict for defendant 8-10 July, ,,
J. C. Charlesworth, M.P., convicted of bribery at the Wakefield election . . . 20 July, ,,
Baron de Vidil; convicted of wounding his son; the latter refused to give evidence against his father, 23 Aug. ,,
Vincent Collucci: convicted of obtaining money on false pretences, from Miss F. Johnstone 23 Oct. ,,
John Curran, a Dublin cabman, convicted of a violent assault on Miss Jolly, who heroically defended herself . . . . 25-30 Oct. ,,
Patrick McCaffery; shot col. Crofton and capt. Hanham, at Preston; convicted . 13 Dec. ,,
Inquiry into sanity of Wm. Fred. Wyndham (on behalf of his relatives), with a view of annulling an injudicious marriage; trial lasted 34 days: 140 witnesses examined; verdict *sane* mind (see *Lunacy*) . . 16 Dec. 1861, and 30 Jan. 1862
[Each party adjudged to pay its own costs, March, 1862.]
Capt. Robertson, by court-martial; convicted of submitting to ungentlemanly conduct from his brother officers:—30 days' inquiry; ended, 24 March, ,,
[The court was much blamed by the public and the sentence was annulled.]
Mrs. A. C. Vyse for poisoning her two children; acquitted as insane . . . 9 July, ,,
Roupell v. Waite; during the trial, W. Roupell,

M.P., a witness, confessed himself guilty of forging a will, and other frauds . 18, 19 Aug. 1862
Jessie McLachlan: convicted for the murder of Jessie Macpherson, at Glasgow; she confessed to being accessory after the murder, which she imputed to Mr. Fleming, a gentleman 80 or 90 years old . . . . . . 17-20 Sept. ,,
[She was respited 27 Oct. 1862.]
Wm. Roupell, M.P., for forgery; convicted, on his own confession (released Sept. 1876) . 24 Sept. ,,
Catherine Wilson, convicted of poisoning Mrs. Soames in 1856 . . . . 25-27 Sept. ,,
27 indictments and 24 convictions for savage personal outrages in the streets of the metropolis during the month . . . . . Nov. ,,
Wm. Digby Seymour, M.P., v. Butterworth; libel; verdict for plaintiff, damages 40s. . 3 Dec. ,,
Hall v. Semple; verdict for plaintiff, who had been consigned to a lunatic asylum through his wife's getting the defendant to sign a certificate of lunacy with culpable negligence; damages 150l. 10 Dec. ,,
George Buncher, Wm. Burnett, Richd. Brewer, and James Griffiths, for forging bank-notes, printed on paper stolen from the paper-mill at Laverstoke; convicted . . . . 7-12 Jan. 1863
Clare v. The Queen; petition of right for infringement of a patent; verdict for defendant 2-6 Feb. ,,
Rev. John Campbell v. Spottiswoode (as printer of a libel in *Saturday Review*): verdict for plaintiff, 27 Feb. ,,
Queen on appeal of earl of Cardigan v. col. Calthorpe for libel, charging the earl with deserting his men at Balaclava, 25 Oct. 1855; verdict for defendant (who, however, admitted his error), 9, 10 June, ,,
Attorney-general v. Sillim and others, for having built the *Alexandra* for the Confederates, against the Enlistment act; verdict for defendants, 25 June, ,,
[Decision finally affirmed on appeal to the house of lords, 6 April, 1864.]
Col. Lothian Dickson v. viscount Combermere, earl of Wilton, and gen. Peel, for conspiracy to expel him from the army; verdict for defendants, 27 June, *et seq.*
Morrison (Zadkiel) v. sir Edward Belcher; libel; verdict, 20s. damages . . . 20 June, ,,
Richard Roupell v. Haws: arising out of Roupell forgeries; no verdict . . . 16-24 July, ,,
Woolley v. Pole, for Sun Fire Office; verdict for plaintiff, awarding him his claim for 29,000l. for his insurance of Campden-house; burnt 23 March, 1862 . . . . . . 29 Aug. ,,
George Victor Townley, for murder of Miss Goodman, through jealousy; convicted . 12 Dec. ,,
[He escaped execution through a certificate of insanity, too hastily signed; and committed suicide in prison, 12 Feb. 1865.]
Lieut.-col. Crawley, by court-martial at Aldershot, for alleged oppression and cruelty to sergeant-major John Lilley, in consequence of a court-martial at Mhow, in India; honourably acquitted, 17 Nov.-23 Dec. ,,
Franz Müller, for murder of Mr. Briggs in a railway carriage, 9 July; convicted . 27-29 Oct. 1864
Gedney v. Smith, a supposititious child detected and deprived of much property . 10 Nov. ,,
E. K. Kohl, for murder of Theodore Fuhrkop; convicted . . . . . 11, 12 Jan. 1865
Queen v. Wm. Rumble, for infringement of Foreign Enlistment act, in equipping the *Rappahannock* for the Confederate government; acquitted, 4 Feb. ,,
Woodgate v. Ridout (for *Morning Post*), for libel respecting the great will case of the earl of Egmont v. Darell; verdict for plaintiff, 1000l., 10 Feb. ,,
Bishop Colenso's appeal to privy council against decision of bishop of Capetown, deposing him, which is annulled . . . 21 March, ,,
Roberts, Jeffery, Casely, and others, for jewel robberies in London; convicted . . 13 April, ,,
J. W. Terry and Thos. Burch, for misdemeanor in connection with the Unity Bank; acquitted, April, ,,
Edw. Wm. Pritchard, M.D., for murder of his wife and her mother, by poisoning; guilty 3-7 July, ,,
Charlotte Winsor, a child-murderer, convicted on the evidence of an accomplice . . July, ,,

f legal irregularities in her trial, her
is long deferred, and her sentence was
o life-imprisonment, 23 May, 1866.]
it tried (see *Road Murder*) 21 July, 1865
ans for treason-felony: Thos. Clarke
cted and sentenced to 20 years' penal
8 Nov.-1 Dec.; O'Leary and others
O'Donovan Rossa (previously con-
nced to imprisonment for life, 13 Dec.;
cted at Cork . . . Dec. ,,
ood (or Ernest Southey), for murder
nd children: guilty . 20-21 Dec. ,,
; convicted at Dublin (see *Fenians*),
Jan. 1866
eerage: succession decided in favour
of Glenfalloch. . . 26 Jan. ,,
yves v. the attorney-general; an en-
rove the marriage of king George III.
h Wilmot, and that of his brother
e of Cumberland, with Olive Wilmot;
lded that the claim was not made out,
ve Serres, the alleged mother of Mrs.
not the legitimate daughter of the
mberland, and that the 82 documents
vidence were forged (Mrs. Ryves died
. . . . 13 June, ,,
iirwee prize case (Indian mutiny);
nirulty decide that 700,000l. are to be
ween the soldiers commanded by
ttelocke, Rose, Roberts, and others,
. . . . 30 June, ,,
o v. Gladstone and others, trustees of
hoprie fund (for withholding his
ewlict for plaintiff, with costs 6 Nov.
arpe (*Pall Mall Gazette*), for libel
tim with quackery); one farthing
ned by plaintiff . . 1 Dec. ,,
tinson, manager of joint stock bank,
f fraud . . . 9 et seq. Jan. 1867
ti free pardon, after investigation,

t; decision against prescriptive right
o claim a marriage-fee . 23 Jan. ,,
ebb, Lionel Holdsworth, and others,
f fraud (scuttling a ship, and claiming
. . . . 4 Feb. ,,
a Swede; convicted of murdering a
on superstition . 12 April, ,,
eerage; Wm. J. Campbell declared
eal to house of lords . 16 July, ,,
itt and others; a will case, disposing
of 400,000l.; verdict for defendants,
he will of Ann Thwaites, who is de-
msound mind, after a long trial, in
lay; judgment given . 6 Aug. ,,
uand, and others; appeal case, house
lecision affirming liability of share-
he company of Overend, Gurney, and
) . . . . 15 Aug. ,,
M. Lawrence, and John Anderson,
he operative tailors' association, con-
misdemeanor (organising the system
ng," or watching men on strike; and
g non-unionists; which began 24
. . . . 21 Aug. ,,
ricted of "picketing" . 22 Aug. ,,
s at Manchester, Allen, &c. (see
. . . . 30 Oct.-12 Nov. ,,
cer convicted of brutal murder of a
. . . . 6 Dec. ,,
ason v. Walter (for publication of an
l in the *Times*; viz., a correct report
in the house of lords, &c.); verdict
int, settling that such a report is
. . . . 18-20 Dec. ,,
med again, 25 Nov. 1868. Mr. Wa-
ly, 1875.]
ckonochie (for ritualistic practices);
of arches, 4 Dec. 1867, and 14 days;
ed; closed . . 18 Jan. 1868
mpson; similar case; begun 5 Feb.;
demning elevation of sacrament, use
and mixture of water with the wine in
nion service . . 28 March, ,,
lsworthy for fraudulent misrepresen-
dict for plaintiff, damages 35,000l.
18 Feb. ,,

Trial of Fenians for Clerkenwell outrage (see
Fenians), begun 20 April; all acquitted except
Michael Barrett . . . 20-27 April, 1868
Richard Burke (*alias* Geo. Berry, &c.), Theobald
Casey, and Henry Shaw (*alias* Mullody), Fenians,
for treason felony, at Old Bailey; Burke and
Shaw convicted, Casey acquitted 28-30 April, ,,
Mornington v. Wellesley, and Wellesley v. Mornington, a 29 years' suit in chancery, decided (costs
above 30,000l.); 22,000l. awarded to the countess
of Mornington . . . 7 May, ,,
Lyon v. Home (the spiritual medium). The plaintiff, a widow, sought to recover 60,000l. stock,
given to Home at the alleged command of her
deceased husband's spirit, between Oct. 1866 and
Feb. 1867: suit instituted 15 June, 1867; trial,
21 April to 1 May, 1868; verdict given for
plaintiff, by the vice-chancellor, sir G. M. Giffard,
22 May, ,,
[The judge, in concluding, said, regarding
spiritualism, that "the system, as presented
by the evidence, is mischievous nonsense;
well calculated on the one hand to delude
the vain, the weak, the foolish, and the
superstitious; and on the other to assist the
projects of the needy, and the adventurer."]
Esmonde will case, Dublin; Lady Esmonde
bequeathed property to support protestantism in
Ireland, by endowing a college, &c.; will disputed
by her family: no verdict by jury 3-13 June, ,,
[New trial: will affirmed, Aug. 1869.]
Thomas Edgeley, convicted of fraud against Leeds
Banking Company . . . 11-13 June, ,,
Risk Allah v. Whitehurst (for *Daily Telegraph*):
libel case; damages for plaintiff, 960l., 19 June, ,,
Attorney-general v. Dakin: appeal case; decision
that privilege of exemption from execution of
legal process does not extend to Hampton Court
palace . . . . 20 June, ,,
Madame Sarah Rachel Leverson convicted of con-
spiracy . . . . 25 Sept. ,,
[Writ of error: new trial refused, 11 May, 1869.]
Chorulord v. Lingo: female suffrage declared illegal
7-9 Nov. ,,
Baxter v. Langley: Sunday evening lectures
declared not illegal . . . 19 Nov. ,,
Martin v. Mackonochie: see *Church of England*,
. . . . 23 Dec. ,,
Phillips v. Eyre: verdict for defendant; see
Jamaica . . . . 20 Jan. 1869
Saurin v. Star and another (convent case; a sister
sued her mother superior, for ill-usage and ex-
pulsion); verdict for plaintiff, damages 500l.
3-26 Feb. ,,
[Case compromised, April, 1870.]
James Thos. Gambier, admiralty clerk, and Wm.
Rumble, engineer, convicted of fraud and seeking
bribes from contractors . . 9 April, ,,
Cooper v. Gordon: verdict for plaintiff; the vice-
chancellor decides that the majority of a congregation of dissenters may dismiss their minister
for any cause . . . 28 May, ,,
Major Frederick Beswick, constable of Birkenhead,
convicted of forgery . . 10 June, ,,
Farrer (president of the Amalgamated Carpenters'
Society) v. Close (the secretary), for misappro-
priation of money. In 1867 the justices dismissed
the charge because the society had illegal rules.
At the trial at the Queen's bench the court was
equally divided, and no verdict given . 3 July, ,,
Fanny F. M. Oliver convicted of murder of her
husband . . . . 20 July, ,,
Lyons v. Rev. N. Thomas and others, for abduction
of Esther Lyons, a Jewish girl, a proselyte;
damages 50l. . . . 31 July, ,,
Frederick Hinson convicted of murder of his para-
mour, Maria Death, and Wm. Douglas Boyd
. . . . 24 Nov. ,,
Rev. James John Merest, convicted of simony;
deprived . . . 26-29 Nov. ,,
Martin v. Mackonochie: before judicial committee
of privy council, defendant censured for evading
verdict, and condemned in costs . 4 Dec. ,,
Mrs. Kelly v. Rev. J. Kelly; judicial separation for
ill usage (not violence) decreed . 7 Dec. ,,
Messrs. Gurney and others, for conspiring to defraud; acquitted . . . 13-23 Dec. ,,

Smith v. Earl Brownlow; after long litigation decision against the enclosure of the common at Berkhampstead by lord of the manor   14 Jan. 1870
James Clifford, a retired artilleryman, convicted of "sweating" sovereigns by the voltaic battery,
    1 Feb.   ,,
Jacob Spinass, a Swiss, convicted of murder of Cecilia Akridge, an unfortunate   . . 3 March,   ,,
Dr. Kinglake convicted of bribery on behalf of his brother at Bridgewater   . . . . 26 March,   ,,
Wicklow peerage case: claim for an infant declared to be unfounded by House of Lords (remarkable evidence)   . . . . . 31 March,   ,,
Demetrius Pappa, a bank manager, sentenced to 5 years' penal servitude for embezzlement, 6 May,   ,,
Sir Charles Mordaunt v. lady Mordaunt, and others, for divorce: preliminary trial of her sanity (declared insane on 30 April, 1869), 16-25 Feb. 1870; appeal, 27 April, 1870; judgment affirmed 2 June,   ,,
Bishop Goss (R.C.) v. Hill and Whittaker: will case; Mr. Moreton's will, bequeathing the chief of his property to the bishop, set aside 16 June,   ,,
Phillips v. Eyre, for imprisonment during Jamaica rebellion ; verdict for defendant   . . 23 June,   ,,
Chelsea Murders: Walter Miller convicted of murder of Rev. Elias Huelin and Anne Boss, his housekeeper (8 or 9 May, 1870)   . . . 13, 14 July,   ,,
Michael Davitt and John Wilson, treason felony; see Fenians   . . . . . . 18 July,   ,,
John Jones or Owen, convicted of murder of Emanuel Marshall and family (7 persons, early 22 May, 1870), at Denham, near Uxbridge   . 22 July,   ,,
Shepherd v. Bennett (Arches); decision that defendant had retracted heresy; appeal to privy council,
    23 July,   ,,
Margaret Waters convicted of murder of John Cowen, infant; her sister and accomplice, Sarah Ellis, was convicted of fraud, 22 Sept. (baby farming case; see Infanticide)   . 21-23 Sept.   ,,
Rev. C. Voysey v. Noble: appeal to privy council judicial committee against condemnation for heresy   . . . . . . 10 Nov.   ,,
Eldy v. McGowan; verdict against an architect for refusing to give up the plans of a building he was about to erect   . . . . . . 16 Nov.   ,,
Catch v. Shaen: for libel on master of Lambeth workhouse; verdict for plaintiff, 600l. damages; execution stayed   . . . . . 15 Dec.   ,,
Diamond Robbery: London and Ryder's man made insensible and robbed of diamonds, 12 Jan.; Martha Torpey acquitted, 1 March; James Torpey pleaded guilty (sentenced to 8 years' penal servitude)   . . . . . . 1 May, 1871
E. Boulton, L. C. Hurt, F. W. Park, and others (frequently dressed as women) tried for a conspiracy; acquitted   . . . . . 9-15 May,   ,,

Tichborne v. Lushington: the plaintiff declared himself to be sir Roger Charles Tichborne, supposed to have been lost at sea; and claimed the baronetcy and estates, worth about 24,000l. a year.
Roger Charles Tichborne, son of sir James, born   . 1829
Educated in France till   . . . . about 1843
Entered the army   1849
Proposed marriage to his cousin Kate Doughty; declined   . . . . Jan. 1852
Sailed from Havre for Valparaiso (March), and arrived there   . . . . . . 19 June, 1853
Sailed from Rio Janeiro in the Bella, which foundered at sea   . . . . . 20 April, 1854
[A Chancery suit was instituted, and his death legally proved.]
His mother advertised for her son   . 19 May, 1865
The claimant (found by Gibbes and Cubitt in Australia) asserted that he and eight of the crew were saved from the wreck of the Bella; that he went to Australia, and lived there, roughly, 13 years under the name of Castro; married as Castro, Jan.; as Tichborne .   . . . 3 July, 1866
He set up his claim; and was accepted by the dowager lady Tichborne as her son at Paris   . Jan. 1867
[No others of the family accepted him; but sir Clifford Constable and some brother officers did.]*

* Mr. Guildford Onslow, who spent about 15,000l., in supporting the claimant, died 20 Aug. 1882.

His claim was resisted c minor), son of sir Alf chancery proceedings (began in the court of c justice Bovill .
The claimant was examin journed on 40th day, case for claimant closed
Trial resumed, 15 Jan.; tl D. Coleridge, spoke 26 jury expressed themselv ant was not sir Roger; declared nonsuited .
The law proceedings are s nearly 92,000l.
He was lodged in Newgat 7 March; indicted as Arthur Orton, for perju
The court of queen's benc admitted to bail, 23 Ap
The trial of the claiman begun before chief justi Mellor and Lush at h prosecution closed, 10 J

Lady Doughty, mother of

[Up to 27 June (47th day witnesses above 100 ha was not Tichborne; a Arthur Orton.]
The claimant forbidden to

Case for the defence clos adjourned from 31 O 27 Nov.; rebutting evi
Dr. Kenealy's summing-r Mr. Hawkins's reply .
[Mr. Whalley, M.P., fine 250l., 23 Jan.]
The chief-justice's summ Verdict: that the claimar he was Roger Charles duced Catherine N. E. he was not Arthur Ort imprisonment with har
[Longest trial .
New trial refused by the .
On appeal, sentence affir 10, 11 March, 1881; rel

Eltham Murder: E. W. Maria Clousen; acquitt
Hannah Newington, or F manslaughter of Frede mistress, and excited b
Capt. H. Hamilton Bear stranding the Agincoui primanded by the court
Robert Kelly: for murde stable and informer agr 12 July; acquitted (ext

Peek v. Gurney and other tiff's claim for loss incu tations in the company by master of rolls on ac verify the prospectus costs refused to defend
Mr. Pigott condemned to comments on a trial, in
Rev. John Selby Watson his wife in a fit of passi imprisoned for life .
Christiana Edmunds; c Brighton; she purchas returned poisoned ones thus caused death to or other persons; reprieve
The Queen v. the Lords repaying expenses for p of Lancaster; mandamu

* See Englishman.
† Charles Orton decla brother Arthur, at the Glo

Park-lane Murder: Margaret Dixblancs, a Belgian emigrant, murdered her mistress, madame Riel, on Sunday, 7 April; escaped; taken at Paris; confessed to killing her mistress in a quarrel; convicted, but recommended to mercy, 11-14 June; sentence commuted to penal servitude for life . . . . 21 June, 1872
Ellen Kettel: charged with poisoning her husband's first wife in order to marry him; acquitted, 24, 25 Oct. „
Chelsea Tragedy: Hermann Nagel and Paul May, young Prussians, came to London to avoid conscription; their money being spent, they agreed to commit suicide; after wounding May, Nagel shot himself dead, 21 Aug.; May recovered, and was indicted for murder, tried, and acquitted, 21 Nov. „
[He was convicted and punished for forgery at Berlin, Feb. 1873.]
Baker *v.* Loader: widow, to whom 107,000*l.* had been bequeathed; in ten years is reduced to poverty by imposition; she sues the widow of her friend Loader and solicitors; verdict of vice-chancellor Malins, ordering deeds to Loader to be cancelled; the solicitor to pay his own costs, 20 Nov. „
Mr. Hepworth Dixon *v.* Smith (*Pall-Mall Gazette*), for libel; damages, one farthing . 26-29 Nov. „
Mr. Guildford Onslow and Mr. G. H. Whalley, M.P.'s, fined for contempt of court in speeches respecting the Tichborne case, 20 Jan.; Mr. Skipworth, barrister, for same offence, condemned to three months' imprisonment and fined; the claimant made to give securities for 1000*l.*, for a similar offence . . . . 29 Jan. 1873
Parke *v.* Harvey Lewis, sir Joseph McKenna, and others: for misuse of a company's funds while directors; 10 days' trial; verdict for plaintiff, 30 Jan. „
Omagh Murder: (of Mr. Glass, 29 June, 1871); sub-inspector Montgomery tried; 12 days; strong evidence; jury not agreed . . 19 March, „
Broughton *v.* Knight: will of Mr. Knight set aside on account of unsound mind . 31 March, „
Andrews *v.* Salt: decision by lord-chancellor that a child shall be educated as a protestant by grandmother, not by Roman catholic uncle; confirmed on appeal . . . . . 6 May, „
Rev. O'Keeffe *v.* Cardinal Cullen (for libel, and virtually suspending him from his office); consideration of demurrer; judges (at Dublin) divided in opinions; three decide that the papal ordinance on which the cardinal relied was prohibited by the statutes of Elizabeth; demurrer set aside, 7 May; the trial begun 12 May; verdict for plaintiff; the jury gave one farthing damages, 27 May, „
[Mr. O'Keeffe submitted to the cardinal, May, 1876.]
Sub-inspector Montgomery, at his third trial for the brutal murder of Mr. Glass, at Newton-Stewart, Ireland, on 8 June, 1871; convicted and confessed, 28 July [executed, Aug. 26] „
Great jewellery frauds; Michael and Rebecca Goldsmid convicted . . . . . 8 July, „
Farrell *v.* Gordons: much property left to R. C. Church; will affirmed . . . 9 July, „
Todd *v.* Lyne (father Ignatius); son of the plaintiff rescued from convent (where he had taken vows) by chancery . . . . . 25 July, „
Bank Forgery: Austin Biron Bidwell, George Macdonnell, George Bidwell, and Edwin Noyes, Americans, forged bills for discounting at the Bank of England, West-Branch, and obtained 102,217*l.*; detected through not dating one bill; convicted; penal servitude for life [their plot to escape by bribing the warders failed] 18-26 Aug. „
Rev. John Berrington (after 30 years' swindling) sentenced to 15 years' penal servitude 22 Aug. „
Cheltenham Chronicle fined 150*l.* for commenting on trial of the Tichborne claimant . 23 Sept. „
Marshal Bazaine; see *France* . . 6 Oct. „
Gilbert *v.* Enoch (for *Pall Mall Gazette*) for libel in critique on "*The Wicked World,*" a play; verdict for defendant (both regarded harmless) 27 Nov. „
Capt. Charles S. Maunsell sentenced to a month's imprisonment with hard labour for assaulting the duke of Cambridge on 6 Jan. . 4 Feb. 1874
Miss Fairland gave her fortune to St. Mary's Dominican convent, Belfast; her trustees oppose the transfer; the master of the rolls affirms the gift, 24 Feb. 1874
Dr. Hayman *v.* the governing body of Rugby school; judgment for the defendants . 21 March, „
Jean Luie (Lindgren) and "capt." Brown convicted of perjury in the Tichborne case (7 years and 5 years' penal servitude) . . . 9, 10 April, „
Mordaunt case (see 1870), divorce court; 3 judges hold that insanity is no bar to suit for divorce; 2 judges hold that it is . . . 13 May, „
Callan, M.P., *r.* O'Reilly Dease; for libel (termed "wilful and malicious" by ch.-just. Whiteside), Dublin; damages one farthing . 2 July, „
E. Welby Pugin, convicted of libel against J. R. Herbert, R.A., 23 Sept.; not sentenced, 24 Sept., „
Epping forest case; decision against the enclosures of the lords of the manors as illegal; see *Commons,* 10 Nov. „
Frederick *v.* Attorney-General: col. Charles Edward Frederick declared heir to baronetcy; the validity of the marriage of his grandparents affirmed in divorce court . . . . . 18 Dec. „
Rubery *v.* baron Albert Grant and M. B. Sampson (long city editor of the *Times*) for libel; the article in *Times,* 18, 20 Nov. and 20 Dec. 1872, charged Rubery with connection with a fraud in a certain diamond mine in Colorado; 10 days' trial; Grant cleared; Sampson fined 500*l.* . . . 18 Jan. 1875
[By these articles the public were protected from a bad scheme.]
Alleged False Prospectus Case: (Canadian Oil-Works Corporation), Charlton *v.* sir John Hay, Mr. Eastwick, and others grossly deceived; 17 days' trial; jury divided; discharged; no verdict 24 Feb. „
[Oil-wells in Ontario, Canada, property of Prince's company got up to buy them, by Longbottom; scheme not accepted in the city; taken up at west-end; sir John Hay, Mr. M'Cullagh Torrens, Mr. Eastwick, and others induced to become directors; wells bought; company collapsed.]
Philpotts *v.* Boyd: see *Reredos;* settled by judicial committee of privy council . . . 24 Feb. „
Mordaunt *v.* Mordaunt and viscount Cole, (see above, May, 1874); divorce granted 11 March, „
Terry *r.* Brighton Aquarium Company, for opening on Sundays; verdict; penalty 200*l.*, (see *Sunday*), 27 April, „
Jackson *v.* Grand Junction Canal Company, (see *Gunpowder Explosion,* 2 Oct. 1874); company adjudged responsible for damages . 14 May, „
Keith Johnston *v.* Proprietors of *Athenæum,* for libel in criticism of an atlas; Edinburgh; damages, 1275*l.*; 24 March, new trial; damages reduced to 100*l.* . . . . 16 June, „
John Neave, Arthur Keen (or Murrell) and Annie Bolwell, convicted of coining and uttering false coin at railway stations . . 12, 13 July, „
Jenkins *v.* Rev. Flavel Cook (for excluding him from the communion for heresy (denying personality of Satan and eternal punishment); verdict for defendant in Court of Arches) . 16 July, „
Col. Valentine Baker sentenced to fine of 500*l.*, and 12 months' imprisonment for indecently assaulting Miss Dickenson in a railway carriage 2 Aug. „
Mrs. Gladstone *v.* capt. Gladstone (long case concluded); divorce granted . . . 6 Aug. „
Wm. Thompson Hunt convicted of manslaughter for administering strychnia to Mrs. Hudson (who died) and others, as a remedy for intoxication; 5 years' penal servitude . . . 25 Sept. „
Wm. Talley, a solicitor, for dissuading a person bound over to prosecute from fulfilling his engagement; sentence 1 year's imprisonment 25 Sept. „
Sugden and others *v.* St. Leonards, will case (lord St. Leonards' will missing; many codicils left); verdict for plaintiffs, affirming the lost will on his daughter's, Miss Sugden's, recollection of its provisions . . . . . 17-26 Nov. „
[Verdict affirmed on appeal, 14 March, 1876.]
Whitechapel Murder (which see).
Henry Wainwright for murder of Harriet Lane, and his brother Thomas as accessory before and after the fact; before chief justice Cockburn (nine days); Henry sentenced to death; Thomas, as accessory after fact, to 7 years' penal servitude 22 Nov.-1 Dec. „

Smith v. Union Bank of London (see *Drafts*); verdict for defendants . . . . 29 Nov. 1875
Rev. H. Keet v. Rev. G. E. Smith (see *Reverend*); appeal to privy council; verdict for the plaintiff 21 Jan. 1876
Persons representing the parish of Folkestone v. Rev. C. J. Ridsdale, vicar (for ritualistic practices); verdict for plaintiffs; the vicar to be admonished and pay costs . . . 3 Feb. ,,
Jenkins v. Rev. F. S. Cook, appeal from the dean of Arches to the privy council judicial committee; verdict for plaintiff; (Rev. F. Cook resigned) 16 Feb. ,,
Eupion Gas Company (1874); Queen v. Aspinall and others, directors, for fraud; long trial; verdict, Aspinall and another convicted of improperly obtaining settlement of quotation on Stock Exchange; acquitted of charge of fraud . 17 Feb. ,,
[The lord chief justice declared the company to be "a fiction and a sham from beginning to end;" sentence, Joseph Aspinall and Charles Knocker, 12 months' imprisonment, John Saunders Muir and William Whyte, 2 months' imprisonment, 1 July, 1876.]
W. K. Vance and Ellen Snee, conspiracy to murder (ostensibly herself); singular case; sentenced to imprisonment . . . . 1 June, ,,
Robert Buchanan, the poet, v. P. A. Taylor, M.P., proprietor of *Examiner*, libels in papers 27 Nov. and 1 Dec. (letter said to be by Mr. A. Swinburne, the poet); damages, 150*l*. . . 1 July, ,,
Twycross (representing many others) v. baron Albert Grant and others, to recover money paid for shares in Lisbon tramway company, promoted by defendant and others; long trial; able speech of Grant; verdict, 700*l*. damages . 13 July, ,,
[Judgment affirmed on appeal, 2 June, 1877.]
Buckhurst peerage, claimed by earl Delawarr and by his brother, Mortimer Sackville West; house of lords decide in favour of the earl . 18 July, ,,
Blackburn Murder; Wm. Fish convicted of murder and violation of Emily Mary Holland, aged 7 (28 March); pleaded temporary insanity . 28 July, ,,
Richard Banner Oakley, manager of Co-operative Credit Bank, convicted of obtaining money by false pretences; much credulity in victims; 5 years' penal servitude . . . 9-12 Aug. ,,
Will Frauds: Charles Howard (count von Howard, &c.), sentenced to 5 years' penal servitude for obtaining 380*l*. from John Harvey, for a pretended will, (other cases) . . . 26 Oct. ,,
Frederick Henry Vane v. sir Henry Ralph Vane (his nephew); verdict for defendant, maintaining his father's legitimacy; chancery division 25 Nov. ,,
Lewis v. Higgins, for alleged slander in speech as counsel; verdict for defendant, affirming privilege of counsel . . . . 4 Dec. ,,
Coe (stage manager, Haymarket, dismissed as accused of receiving payments from actors engaged) v. Sothern and Buckstone; verdict for plaintiff; damages, 1035*l*. . . . 13 Dec. ,,
Lord Longford v. Wellington Purdon; will giving property to the plaintiff's young son set aside by the testator, Cooke, having been under the undue influence of Rev. Wm. Lyster (plaintiff not blamed); 25 days' trial . . . Feb. 1877
Lynall Thomas v. the Queen (petition of right); for patent of cannon, &c.; verdict for plaintiff, with damages . . . . 10 March, ,,
Great Turf Frauds; forgery of cheques for 10,000*l*., &c.; about 13,000*l*. obtained; five sentenced to penal servitude; Henry Benson, 15 years; Wm. and Fred. Kerr and Chas. Bate, 10 years; Edwin Murray, accessory, 18 months 11-23 April, ,,
Cresswell and others v. Walrond; will of Bethell Walrond set aside by arrangement (he had bequeathed his property to strangers and dogs, had been cruel to his children, decorated his bed with skulls and hearse plumes, &c.) 13 June, ,,
Queen v. Charles Bradlaugh and Annie Besant, for publication of "Fruits of Philosophy," by Dr. Knowlton, which they defended, on grounds of humanity, in long speeches; verdict, the book calculated to deprave, but not intended, 18-21 June; sentence (through the defendants not submitting to the court), 6 months' imprisonment, 200*l*. fine for both, 28 June; appeal, on ground of legal informality, disallowed by queen's bench 16 Nov. 1877
Nathaniel Druscovitch, John Meiklejohn, and Wm. Palmer, police inspectors, and Edward Froggatt, solicitor, charged with conspiracy to defeat the ends of justice in respect to turf frauds (see *above*, 12-23 April); examination began, 12 July; Froggatt committed, 6 Sept.; chief inspector Clarke arrested, 8 Sept.; 28 days' examination; committed, 22 Sept.; trial began, 24 Oct.; all convicted except Clarke; sentence, 2 years' imprisonment with hard labour . 20 Nov. ,,
Wm. Swindlehurst, secretary, and Dr. John Baxter Langley, director of Artisans' Dwelling Company, and Edward Saffery, convicted of defrauding shareholders of about 24,312*l*.; officers sentenced to 18 months', Saffery 12 months' imprisonment . . . . 23-26 Oct. ,,
Thos. Hyslop (aged 19) and John Denham (aged 18) convicted of highway robbery at Blackheath 23 Oct. ,,
Penge Case: Louis A. E. Staunton, Patrick L. Staunton his brother, and Eliz. Ann, his wife, and her sister, Alice Rhodes, mistress of Louis: tried for murder by starvation of Harriet, wife of Louis (a woman of weak intellect, married for her property, and soon deserted), 19 Sept.; all convicted, 26 Sept.; respited, 13 Oct.; Alice Rhodes pardoned; the others sentenced to penal servitude for life; announced . . 30 Oct. ,,
Coote (solicitor) v. Kenealy; for payments; verdict for plaintiff . . . . 14 Nov. ,,
Forged Leases: Frederick Dimsdale, solicitor, Chas. Burrell Moore, clerk, and others; forged leases, and borrowed money on them (above 300,000*l*.); many lenders did not appear; pleaded guilty; sentence, Dimsdale, penal servitude for life; Moore, 7 years; others less . 16, 17 Jan. 1878
Rev. H. J. Dodwell fired at the master of the rolls, sir George Jessel, 22 Feb.; acquitted as insane 15 March, ,,
Madame Rachel (Levison, or Leverson), convicted of misdemeanour; obtained money and jewels from Mrs. Pearce, for "beautifying;" 5 years' penal servitude . . . 10, 11 April, ,,
Eugene Marie Chantrelle, Frenchman, convicted of murder of wife, at Edinburgh; much cruelty disclosed . . . . . 10 May, ,,
Will case, Dublin; Christopher Neville Bagot, made a fortune in Australia; made will, disinheriting his son as illegitimate; died, 23 May, 1877; trial, 23 days; painful disclosures; the will set aside (see *below*, 1879) . 20 May, ,,
Harrington v. Victoria Graving Dock Company; he claimed remainder of commission for obtaining an order from Great Eastern railway company; nonsuited; such commissions declared illegal by queen's bench . . . 4 June, ,,
Jas. T. Northcott, Geo. Thompson, Thos. G. Wood (of the Albion Life Insurance company); sentenced to 5 years' penal servitude for conspiracy, and obtaining money on false pretences; subordinates sentenced to less imprisonment 8 June, ,,
Charles Marvin, copying-clerk of foreign office, examined for copy of an Anglo-Russian agreement published in *Globe*, 14 June, 27 June; discharged 16 July, ,,
Taylor v. Gwyn; claim for Jermy estates (see Jermy murders by Rush, *Trials*, 1849); claim denied; trial set aside by statute of limitations 5 Aug. ,,
In re Agar Ellis; the husband's promise before marriage that his children should be brought up Romanists, permitted to be withdrawn by chancery . . . . . . 6 Aug. ,,
The Board of Works v. rev. F. G. Lee, of All Saints, Lambeth; queen's bench division decide that the incumbent of a church is not its owner, and therefore not responsible for keeping it in repair, 11 Nov. ,,
Annie Louisa lady Gooch (with Ann Walker); she tried to pass a child as her own and her husband's, committed for trial 30 Nov., indictment ignored, 11 Dec. ,,
Paul and others v. Summerhayes; appeal; sentence against plaintiffs affirmed (foxhunters may not trespass), queen's bench . . . ,,
Queen v. Bandmann (for assault on Mrs. Rousby), not guilty . . . . 19-20 Nov. ,,

TRIALS. 915 TRIALS.

Henry Sturt Marshall, asst. sec. of curates' augmentation fund, convicted of embezzling about 7,000*l*.; confessed . . . . . 24 Oct. 1878
Whistler *v.* Ruskin, for libellous criticism in "*Fors Clavigera*," one farthing damages . 25, 26 Nov. ,,
Hill and others *v.* managers of Metropolitan Asylums District 11 (days), verdict, that Hampstead small-pox hospital was a nuisance (verdict affirmed on appeal, 28 Jan. 1879) . . . . 29 Nov. ,,
Mr. Wybrow Robertson (manager of Westminster Aquarium) *v.* Labouchere, for libel in *Truth*, 27 Nov., verdict for defendant . . 20 Dec. ,,
Muir and others; court of session, decides that trustees who have invested in the "City of Glasgow bank," are responsible [affirmed on appeal to house of lords, 7 April, 1879] . . . 20 Dec. ,,
Stephen Gambrill for murder of Mr. Arthur Gillow (on 5 Dec. when defending agricultural machinery), at Wednesborough, near Sandwich, Kent, convicted . . . . 14-15 Jan. 1879
Long firm forgeries, Kettle and others convicted, sentenced to various terms of imprisonment, 16-17 Jan. ,,
City of Glasgow Bank directors and managers (see under *Banks*, note) convicted . 20 Jan.-1 Feb. ,,
Charles Peace (or John Ward), committed many burglaries in skilful manner, convicted of attempting life of policeman, 19 Nov.; convicted of murder of Arthur Dyson, at Bannercross near Sheffield, 29 Nov. 1876 . . . . 4 Feb. ,,
[He jumped from a moving railway train near Sheffield, and was nearly killed, 22 Jan.; confessed to murders, &c.; exonerated William Habron, convicted as an accomplice in a murder (therefore released, 18 March); executed at Leeds, 25 Feb.]
Dr. Julius r. Bishop of Oxford (for not prosecuting rev. T. T. Carter of Clewer for ritualistic practices), queen's bench, (verdict for plaintiff, set aside on appeal, 30 May, Mr. Carter resigned 24 March, 1880) . . . . . 8 March, ,,
Kentish Town murder, Thomas Perryman convicted of murder of his mother . . . 2 April, ,,
Queen *v.* Booker & Wyman (for libel in *Truth*, against Mr. Lambri), verdict against Wyman; long trial . . . . . . 30 April, ,,
Duke of Norfolk *v.* Arbuthnot, claiming ownership of Fitz-alan chapel in Arundel church, verdict for plaintiff, common pleas . . . 17 May, ,,
[Decision affirmed on appeal, 7 June, 1880.]
Bagot will case, appeal, new trial ordered 5 June, ,,
Shepherd *v.* Francis (for libel in a review in the "Athenæum"). damages, 150*l*. . . 16 June, ,,
The Queen *v.* sir Charles Reed; the queen's bench decide that the metropolitan school board have power to borrow money . . . 27 June, ,,
Sturla *v.* Freccia : Antonio Mangini, born 1735, consul here about 1771, died 1803; his daughter married Aquila Brown, 1792; after 8 years contest established her disputed legitimacy, 1811 : died intestate in London, aged 93, 1871, her property, after a trial, awarded to the Freccia family, 1876. The claim of Madame Sturla set aside by vice-chancellor . . . 24 June, ,,
Richmond murder, Katherine Webster, convicted of murder of Mrs. Julia Martha Thomas (see *Richmond*) . . . . . 8 July, ,,
Edmund Galley convicted of murder, by error, and transported; declared innocent by the house of commons . . . . . 25 July, ,,
Euston-square mystery, Hannah Dobbs, for murder of Matilda Hacker, acquitted . . 23 July, ,,
The mutilated remains of Matilda Hacker, eccentric, about 50 years old, were found in a coal-cellar, No. 4, Euston-square. Hannah Dobbs was maidservant there. She published her autobiography, in which she attacked her former master, Sewerin Bastendorff, who, after bringing an action for libel, was convicted of perjury . . Dec. ,,
(He was awarded by consent 500*l*. damages for the libel), ... 27 Jan. 1881
Rev. Christopher Newman Hall *v.* Mrs. Hall, and Mr. Richardson, long trial, divorce granted, 8 Aug. ,,
Jonathan Gaydon (or Geyden), for murder of Miss Mary White at Chingford, 21 June, 1857, confessed, retracted, convicted (reprieved) . 24 Oct. ,,
Adolphus Rosenberg, for libel against Mrs. Langtry and Mrs. West, in *Town Talk*, convicted, 18 months' imprisonment . . 25, 27 Oct. ,,

Tranmere baby-farming case (near Birkenhead), John and Catherine Barns, convicted of manslaughter; (they received illegitimate infants with premiums of 30*l*., &c.) . . . . 28, 29 Oct. 1879
Dr. Arthur H. Nowell *v.* George Williams (for placing him in a lunatic asylum), verdict for the defendant, medical men censured by the jury, 13 Nov. ,,
Phillips, surgeon, *v.* S. W. railway company, for injury, awarded 7000*l*. by justice Field; new trial, awarded 16,000*l*. by lord ch. justice Coleridge, common pleas, new trial refused 6 Dec. ,,
Smee *v.* Smee and corporation of Brighton, will set aside, Brighton loses a free library bequeathed, 5 Dec. ,,
Hilliard *v.* Rose & Todd, will affirmed, singular case, 12 Dec. ,,
Edward Froggatt (see above, 20 Nov. 1877), sentenced to 7 years' penal servitude for fraudulent conversion of trust property (8000*l*.) . 17 Dec. ,,
James Lewis Paine and Fanny Matthews, for murder of Miss Annie Maclean, aged 34, daughter of col. Maclean, C.B., a deformed lady of property, by starving, administering spirits, and ill-usage, committed 15 Dec.; Fanny Matthews acquitted 16 Feb. Paine sentenced to penal servitude for life . . . . . . 24 Feb. 1880
Railway commissioners, powers limited (see *Railways*, 1880) . . . . . 13 Jan. ,,
Martin *v.* Mackonochie, new action for deprivation, first movement, see *Public Worship* . 17 Jan. ,,
Alexander Schosser attempted to kill priests in the Italian chapel, Hatton-garden, 10 Jan., tried, sentenced to imprisonment for life . 10, 11 Feb. ,,
Wm. Henry Walter, forger by chemicals, &c., sentenced to 20 years' penal servitude . 23 March, ,,
Dr. Caleb Charles Whiteford sentenced to 2 months' imprisonment and fine of 50*l*. for forging letter to stop execution of Charles Shurety, 24 March, ,,
Great Western bank directors (Jerome Murch and others), for publishing false balance-sheets, acquitted . . . . 28 April—5 May, ,,
Lambri *v.* Labouchere, for libel in *Truth*, verdict for defendant . . . . . 15 May, ,,
Tichborne case, writ of error before court of appeal, granted 13 Jan., sentence affirmed . 24, 25 June, ,,
Northern Counties Insurance Company, James E. Crabtree, manager, Geo. Edw. Nesbitt, accountant, and four directors, sentenced to imprisonment for making and circulating false accounts, 22 July, ,,
Pleasance Louisa Ingle, nurse at Guy's hospital, convicted of manslaughter (she putting Louisa Morgan, a patient, into a cold bath and leaving her), 3 months' imprisonment . . 9 Aug. ,,
Henry Perry, for robbing Clarence Lewis in a Kensington railway carriage, and attempting to throw him out of the carriage, &c.; whipping and 20 years' penal servitude . . . 15 Sept. ,,
Thomas Wheeler for murder of Edward Anstee at Marshall's Wick farm, near St. Alban's, 22 Aug. convicted . . . . . 6, 8 Nov. ,,
Sergeant Wm. Marshman (by court-martial), for alleged fraudulent marking at the volunteer rifle meetings at Wimbledon, 1878, 1879, 1880, acquitted . . . . 13 Aug.—16 Sept. ,,
George Pavey convicted of murder of Ada Shepherd, aged ten (*Acton murder*), and Wm. Herbert, convicted of murder of Jane Messenger in Finsbury park . . . . . . 24 Nov. ,,
Mr. P. Callan, M.P., convicted of libel against Mr. A. M. Sullivan, M.P. (fine 50*l*.) . . 30 Nov. ,,
Debenham & Freebody *v.* Mellon, appeal, house of lords decide that a husband is not responsible for wife's debts if he allow her sufficient means, 27 Nov. ,,
Attorney-general *v.* Edison Telephone company, 29 Nov. *et seq.*, verdict against company, establishing monopoly bought by Government . 20 Dec. ,,
Trial of Charles Stewart Parnell, Thomas Sexton, Timothy Daniel Sullivan, John Dillon, Joseph Gillis Biggar, all M.P.'s, Thomas Brennan, Patrick Egan and Michael O'Sullivan, secretary, treasurer, and assist. secretary of the land league, Michael Boyton, Patrick Joseph Gordon, Matthew Harris, John W. Mally, John W. Walsh, and P. J. Sheridan, indicted for conspiracy to prevent tenants paying rent, &c. Queen's Bench, Dublin;

lord chief justice May retires, as having been alleged to have given an opinion on the case previously; trial began 28 Dec. 1880, jury disagreeing were discharged . . . 25 Jan. 1881
Jones and others (trustees) v. rev. John Turner Stannard, nonconformist minister, and others, to dismiss him for doctrine contrary to trust deed; verdict for plaintiffs, chancery division 1 Feb. ,,
Mary Annie Wilmot, nurse, attempt to poison Mrs. Booth (whose son and daughter had died under doubtful circumstances), at Sheffield, strong case, acquitted . . . . . 16 Feb. ,,
Hampstead small-pox hospital case (see above, 1878-9), on appeal, to the house of lords, preceding judgments reversed . . . 7 March, ,,
Dysart peerage legitimacy case, Wm. John Manners claims by an English marriage of lord Huntingtower, Albert Edwin Tollemache by a Scotch marriage, which is declared not proved, house of lords (painful details) . . . . 7 March, ,,
Clarke v. Bradlaugh, suit for penalty of 500l. for sitting and voting as M.P. without taking the oath, on July 2, 1880; verdict for plaintiff; appeal, sentence confirmed* . . 30, 31 March, ,,
Edward Levi Lawson v. Labouchere, M.P. for libels in *Truth*, seven days' trial, jury disagree, no verdict . . . . . . 28 March, ,,
Spiritualist case, Susan Wills Fletcher (wife of a spiritualist doctor in America, who was concerned in the case), convicted of obtaining by false pretences about 10,000l. (in jewellery, &c.), of Mrs. Hart-Davies, long trial, twelve m nths' imprisonment with hard labour . . . 12 April, ,,
Johann Most, convicted of libel against Alexander II. of Russia, and incitement to murder in the *Freiheit* for 19 March, 25 May; sentence affirmed on appeal, 18 June; 16 months' imprisonment with hard labour . . . 29 June, ,,
Saunders v. Richardson, 5 judges decide that parents must either pay board-school fees for child beforehand or apply for pecuniary help; coming without fee considered non-attendance 27 June, ,,
Bend Or libel, Barrow v. "Morning Post," for accusation of doctoring the horse, verdict for plaintiff, damages 1750l. . . . 27, 28 June, ,,
Big Ben libel, Stainbank (for Mears) v. sir E. C. Beckett, 27 June, verdict for plaintiff, 200l. damages . . . . . . 5 July, ,,
Percy Lefroy *alias* Mapleton committed for trial for murder of Mr. Fk. I. Gold on the London and Brighton railway (27 June), 21 July; convicted, 8 Nov.; confessed; executed . . 29 Nov. ,,
Notting Hill Fire, William Nash and Maria Wright, for murder of Elizabeth Jane Clark and others by fire, 30 May; he sentenced to death (reprieved), she acquitted . . . . 3, 4 Aug. ,,
Ledru Rolin Reynolds, adventurer, with many aliases, convicted of remarkable frauds connected with the silver mine company, two years' penal servitude . . . . . 15 Sept. ,,
Mabel Wilberforce, an adventuress, convicted of gross perjury in action against Mr. Philip; nine months' penal servitude . . . 24 Oct. ,,
Kate Dover, for murder of Chas. Skinner, artist, at Sheffield, convicted of manslaughter . 7 Feb. 1882
Dr. G. H. Lamson, for murder of Percy M. John (see *Wimbledon*); convicted, 8—14 March; executed . . . . . . 28 April ,,
Roderick Maclean, for shooting at the queen, acquitted as insane . . . 19 April, ,,
Esther Pay, for murder of Georgiana Moore (see *Pimlico*), acquitted . . . 27—29 April, ,,
Albert Young, for threatening to shoot at the queen, 10 years' penal servitude . 26 May, ,,
Mr. Thomas Scrutton v. Miss Helen Taylor, a libel concerning St. Paul's industrial school; damages 1000l. . . . . . . 30 June, ,,
Sir Henry Tyler, M.P., v. Wm. Jas. Ramsey, Geo. Wm. Foote, and Edwd. Wm. Whittle, also Chas. Bradlaugh, for blasphemous libel in the *Freethinker* (lord mayor, 11 July), committed for trial, 21 July, ,,

* Verdict affirmed (see *Barratry*), 22 July; Bradlaugh appeals, 12—14 Nov.; new trial granted, 2, 3 Dec. 1881; appeal allowed by lords justices, 22—24 Feb.; sentence confirmed, 30 March, 1882; sentence reversed by the lords, 9 April, 1883.

Next of Kin Fraud, J. F. Rogers, A. Mc.Kenzie, J. H. Shakspear, and W. Evans sentenced to imprisonment . . . . . 21 July, 1882
Thomas Walsh, for treason-felony (see *Fenians*), 7 years' penal servitude . . . 7—9 Aug. ,,
John Saunders, desperate ruffian, convicted of burglary and attempt to murder at Stamford-hill; penal servitude for life . . . 19 Oct. ,,
Charles Soutar, for stealing the body of the earl of Crawford; Edinburgh; 5 years' penal servitude, 23, 24 Oct. ,,
Wm. Meager Bartlet, a manager of mines, convicted of murder of illegitimate child, Exeter, 27 Oct. ,,
Charles Brookshaw, for threatening to kill the prince of Wales, 10 years' penal servitude, 21 Nov. ,,
St. Luke's Mystery, Franz Felix Stum, convicted of forgery of signature of Urban Napoleon Stanger, baker, who had disappeared; 10 years' penal servitude . . . . . 11 Dec. ,,
Plumstead Murder, Louisa Jane Taylor, convicted of poisoning Mary Ann Tregillis, aged 81, 15 Dec. ,,
Maxwell Heron, commander of H.M.S. *Clyde*, at Aberdeen sentenced by court-martial to dismissal for embezzlement and misconduct . 21 Dec. ,,
Richard Claude Belt (sculptor) v. Charles Lawes (sculptor), for libel in *Vanity Fair*, 20 Aug. 1881, *et seq.*; (charges of fraudulent imposture, &c.,) before Baron Huddleston, Exchequer division, 21 June, *et seq.*, 14 Nov., *et seq.*; verdict on 43rd day for plaintiff, damages 5000l. . 28 Dec. ,,
Goodacre v. Watson, to restrain deposition of pestilential refuse on building ground, as a nuisance at Fulham; injunction granted with costs, 22 Feb. 1883
Bethell v. Sir Percy Shelley, for infringement of the Theatre act, verdict for defendant, 1s. damages 23 Feb. ,,
G. W. Foote, editor, W. J. Ramsey, printer, and H. A. Kemp, publisher, sentenced to imprisonment for blasphemous libels in the *Freethinker*, 5 Mar. ,,
Clarke v. Bradlaugh, verdict for defendant on appeal to lords (see *above*, March, 1881) 9 April, ,,
C. Bradlaugh, for blasphemy in the *Freethinker*, 10 April, acquitted . . . 14 April, ,,
Bradlaugh v. Newdegate, for supporting an action by a common informer, verdict for plaintiff with costs . . . . . 23 April, ,,
Phœnix park murders (see under *Ireland*) , April, May, ,,
Belt v. Lawes: appeal for new trial, 24 May—9 June, ,,
Dynamite Plot (see *Birmingham*, *England*, and *London*, 1883), Thomas Gallagher, Henry Wilson, John Curtin, and Alfred Whitehead, for treason-felony, sentenced to penal servitude for life; William Ansburgh and Bernard Gallagher, acquitted . . . . . 11—14 June, ,,
Strome Ferry Case, Ten men were sentenced to four months' imprisonment for violently stopping the transmission of fish by Highland railway on Sunday, 3 June . . . . 23 July, ,,
Dynamite conspiracy, Timothy Featherstone, and three other Fenians, convicted at Liverpool, 7—9 Aug. ,,
Wm. Gouldstone convicted of murder of his five children at Walthamstow (on 8 Aug.), 14 Sept. ; respited as insane . . . 3 Oct. ,,
Bournemouth case. Mrs. Miller, the *Joy* breach of promise; conflicting evidence; damages for plaintiff, 2350l. . . . . 15 Nov. ,,
French *Date Coffee Co.*, Bellairs v. Haymen and others, promoters; misleading prospectus, verdict for plaintiff . . . . 22 Nov. ,,
London and River Plate Bank robbery, George Warden pleads guilty to robbery of securities (about 116,000l.), 26 Nov., and John Davis Walters convicted of receiving the same; both sentenced to 12 years' penal servitude . . . 27 Nov. ,,
Dobbs v. Grand Junction water works co.; on appeal the house of lords decides that houses are to be rated for water on the rated, not the gross value . . . . . 30 Nov. ,,
Patrick O'Donnell, convicted of murder of James Carey, the informer (see *Ireland*), 30 Nov., 1 Dec. ,,

TRIALS.

Priestman v. Thomas; *Whalley will case*; incredible incidents; verdict for plaintiff; a forged will; fraudulent compromise proposed by defendant, 15 days' trial . . . . . 4 Dec. 1883
Central News v. *Judy*, for libel respecting telegrams, verdict for defendant . . . 13 Dec. ,,
Belt v. Lawes, again; the judges decide for a new trial unless Mr. Belt accepts 500*l.* instead of 5,000*l.*; Belt accepts, defendant objects, 21 Dec. ,,
Wm. Wolff and Edwd. Bondurand, for plot to blow up German embassy, arrested in Westminster, 22 Nov. 1883; jury disagree, 14—19 Jan.; prisoners discharged . . 28 Jan. 1884
Bradlaugh v. Gosset; verdict for defendant (see *Parliament*) . . . . 9 Feb. ,,
Attorney-general v. Birkbeck, for contravention of the Bank act of 1844; verdict for the crown, 9 Feb. ,,
Liverpool poisoning case, Catherine Flanagin and Margaret Higgins, convicted of the murder of Thomas Higgins; other charges, 16 Feb.; executed . . . . . 3 March, ,,
Belt v. Lawes, appeal before Master of the Rolls and others, 3 March, sentence of the other court affirmed with costs . . . 17 March, ,,
London Financial Association v. Keik and others; case dismissed (see *Alexandra park*) 8 March, ,,
Earl v. countess of Euston, divorce sought on ground that she had a husband living when she married; as it was proved that this man had a wife living when he married her, and that thus she was free, divorce was refused . 4 April, ,,
Parks-place Club declared by the Queen's Bench to be a gaming-house; Mr. Jenks, the proprietor and others fined . . . 24 June, ,,
Mrs. Weldon v. Dr. Semple, for signing certificate of lunacy; ten days; verdict for plaintiff, 1000*l.* damages . . . . 28 July, ,,
Daley and Egan, Aug. 1884 (see *Dynamite*) . May, ,,
Thomas Henry Orrock, convicted of murder of policeman Cole (on 1 Dec. 1882); remarkable evidence . . . . 19, 20 Sept. ,,
Tichborne Claimant (see *above*, 1871—4) released on ticket-of-leave . . . 20 Oct. ,,
Mignonette Case (see *Wrecks*) . . 6 Nov. ,,
Miss Finney v. viscount Garmoyle; breach of promise of marriage; a verdict by consent for 10,000*l.* 20 Nov. ,,
Defence society for innocent prisoners; Morley Jervis sentenced to 2 years' penal servitude, Vernon Garland 15 months' and Charles Kemp 9 months', for fraud . . . 21 Nov. ,,
Adams v. Hon. B. Coleridge, for libel in a letter to Miss M. Coleridge; verdict of jury for plaintiff, 3,000*l.*; verdict by judge Manisty for defendant, the letter being privileged . . 21, 22 Nov. ,,
Whalley Will Case (see Dec. 1883), Charles Thomas and Thomas William Nash, convicted of forgery, 15 years' penal servitude, Edward Gunnell acquitted . . . . 24 Nov.—2 Dec. ,,
Mrs. Weldon v. Dr. Forbes Winslow, for treating her as a lunatic, 500*l.* awarded to plaintiff, 4th trial, 25—29 Nov. ,,
Eliz. Gibbons, for murder of husband; she asserted his suicide, 18-19 Dec.; life imprisonment, 31 Dec. ,,
Mr. Edmund Yates sentenced to 4 months' imprisonment, for libel against the earl of Lonsdale (in *The World*), July, 1883-April, 1884; appeal disallowed . . . . 16 Jan. 1885
Mr. Irving Bishop fined, 10,000*l.* for libel (reduced to 500*l.* on appeal) (see *Thought Reading*) 15 Jan. ,,
John Lee, footman, convicted of murder of Miss Emma A. W. Keyse, his mistress (at Babbicombe, near Torquay, 15 Nov.), 2-4 Feb.; when about to be hanged at Exeter, the drop failed three times, and Lee was removed and reprieved . 23 Feb. ,,
The earl of Durham's petition for annulling his marriage, on account of his wife's alleged insanity at the time of their union dismissed with costs by sir James Hannen, after 8 days' trial, 10 March, ,,
Mrs. Georgina Weldon sentenced to 6 months' imprisonment for libel on M. Jules Prudence Riviere . . . . . 30 March, ,,
James Lee, convicted of murder of Inspector Simmons at Romford (25 Jan.) . 28 April ,,
John Gilbert Cunningham and Harry Burton convicted of treason-felony (see under *Tower*), and

for complicity with criminal explosions (25 Feb. *et seq.*); sentenced to penal servitude for life, 11-18 May, 1885
Weldon v. Gounod for libel; 10,000*l.* awarded 7 May, ,,
Eugene Loraine, engraver, an accomplished swindler, and chief of a seminary of crime, convicted of attempted fraud by forgery, 22 May, ,,
Benj. Warburton's will; Warburton v. Childs, Hobson & Moss; testator declared insane and intestate; legacies lost by Royal Society and others; seven days' trial . . 23 June, ,,
Mrs. Lotinga v. Commercial Union Insurance Co. Policy of her husband Isaac for 2,000*l.* established; conflicting evidence respecting his death and temperance (14 days' trial) . 2 July, ,,
James Malcolm (otherwise capt. Macdonald) for bigamy (gross case), Emma Dash at Brighton, 4 April; doubtful identity; jury disagree 25 Sept.; second trial, 16 Oct.; convicted, seven years' penal servitude . . . 24 Oct. ,,
W. T. Stead, editor of *Pall Mall Gazette*, !(2) Sampson Jacques (assistant)(3), Bramwell Booth, of Salvation Army, (4) Rebecca Jarrett, and (5) Louise Mourey, connection with abduction of Eliza Armstrong, under 16, and indecent assault: (1) three months' imprisonment, (2) one month, (3) acquitted, (4) six months', (5), six months' with hard labour . . 23 Oct.-10 Nov. ,,
Mrs. Weldon v. sir Henry De Bathe for slander, 19 Nov.; 1,000*l.* damages awarded . 23 Nov. ,,
Anthony Benjamin Rudge, James Baker, and John Martin convicted for burglary at Netherby Hall, Cumberland, 28 Oct., and murder of police constable Byrnes at Plumpton, 29 Oct. (captured by railway servants) . . 18-20 Jan. 1886
John Magee, photographer, sentenced to seven years' penal servitude for threatening the prince of Wales . . . . . 15 Jan. ,,
Richard Belt, sculptor, sentenced to twelve months' imprisonment with hard labour for fraudulent sale of jewellery to sir Wm. Abdy; his brother Walter acquitted . 15 March, ,,
John Burns, Henry Hyde Champion, Henry Mayers Hyndman, and John Edward Williams, for seditious words; acquitted but censured, 6-10 April, ,,
Mrs. Adelaide Bartlett tried for the murder of her husband by chloroform; (Rev. George Dyson charged as an accessory before the fact discharged, 12 April); Mrs. Bartlett acquitted 12-17 April, ,,
Dr. Lyell, for heirs-at-law, v. Kennedy, agent for Anne Duncan, intestate; long litigation respecting property; verdict for plaintiff, 22 June, ,,
Crawford v. Crawford; divorce of Mrs. Crawford, decreed, 12 Feb.; confirmed; serious charges against sir Charles Dilke, denied by him but accepted by jury . . . 23 July, ,,
Diamond robbery with violence to Mr. Julius Tabak, the owner, 25 March; conviction and sentences: Adolphe Weiner, instigator, seven years' penal servitude; James Palmer, perpetrator ten years'; accomplices, Leon Weiner, Daniel Jacoby, and Samuel Scandland, each five years, ... 1-4 Nov. ,,
[Principal witness, Toussaint or Denancis, who was sentenced to 15 years' penal servitude in June for his joint action with Palmer, who escaped when Toussaint was taken.]
Mary Lena Sebright (formerly Scott) v. Arthur Sebright; a merely formal marriage contract entered into by the terrorised plaintiff annulled, 16 Nov. ,,
Adams v. lord Coleridge and his son, the hon. B. Coleridge, for libel in letters sent to an arbitrator (lord Monkswell), wrongly delivered; verdict for defendants with costs . . 17-25 Nov. ,,
Lord and lady Colin Campbell divorce, double suit (previous judicial separation); numerous charges on both sides not proved); suits for divorce dismissed . . . 27 Nov.-20 Dec. ,,
Miss Allcard v. Miss Skinner (superior of the "Sisters of the Poor", an Anglican convent, Rev. Henry Nihill, director), to recover property given as under undue influence; verdict for defendant, 31 Jan.; appeal rejected . 9 July, 1887
Thomas William Currell convicted for atrocious

murder of Lydia Green, at 8, Baches-street, Hoxton, 5 Feb. . . . 30 March–2 April, 1887
Mr. Dillon and other M.P's. for conspiracy; jury disagree (see *Ireland*) . . . 14–24 Feb. ,,
Col. Sandoval sentenced to one month's imprisonment and fined 500*l*. for fitting out vessel against Venezuela . . . . 21 March, ,,
Mr. James Davis, proprietor of the *Bat*, convicted for libel against Mr. Robert Peek; three months' imprisonment, and fine of 500*l*. . 30 March, ,,
Mr. Edward St. John Brenon *v.* Messrs. Ridgway, publishers of the "Black Pamphlet" (relating to Irish republican brotherhood &c.); 500*l*. awarded as damages . . . 3 May, ,,
Professor Caird *v.* Syme (a bookseller); after differing decisions of the courts, the house of lords, on appeal, decides against the publication of university lectures without the consent of the lecturers . . . . . . 13 June, ,,
Beyfus *v.* Jonas and others, charge of fraudulent conspiracy; thirteen days' trial; verdict for plaintiff, 40*s*. damages . . . 5 July, ,,
Samuel Taylor, driver, and Robert Davis, fireman, tried for manslaughter (see *Railway Accidents*, Doncaster) . . . . . 14 Oct. ,,
Police constable Endacott acquitted of perjury (see under *Police*) . . 31 Oct.–1 Nov. ,,
Joyce (the marquis's agent) *v.* the marquis of Clanricarde, for libel in a letter; verdict for plaintiff; damages 2,500*l*. . . . 6, 7 Dec. ,,
Long firm fraud; thirteen men convicted; sentenced to various terms of imprisonment . 21 Dec. ,,
Cunninghame Graham, M.P., and John Burns tried for assaulting police, &c., on 13 Nov. 1887 (see *Riots*); convicted of taking part in an unlawful assembly; six weeks' imprisonment without hard labour . . . 16–18 Jan. 1888
Dynamite conspiracy (see under *Dynamite*), Thomas Callan and Michael Harkins sentenced to fifteen years' penal servitude . . . 3 Feb. ,,
Slater *v.* Slater; a chancery forgery case; the court defrauded of about 4,000*l*., the property of Miss Rose Maud Maxwell, by the forgeries of William Bowden, a solicitor's clerk: the money ordered to be paid to her by the court of chancery; Bowden in Nebraska; John Francis Lidiard, a solicitor, his friend, ordered to repay the money to the court . . . 4 Feb. ,,
Marquis of Abergavenny *v.* bishop of Llandaff, after much litigation, verdict for the bishop who had refused to induct the Rev. Robert W. Gosse into a living, being ignorant of the Welsh language . . . . . 22 Feb. ,,
Major Borrowes fined 400*l*. and costs for assaulting his brother-in-law, lord Howard de Walden, 10 March, ,,
Major Templer honourably acquitted of charge of divulging secret information concerning military ballooning, &c. . . . . 9 April, ,,
Mr. Samuel Peters *v.* Mr. C. Bradlaugh, M.P., for libel respecting cheques given him by lord Salisbury and others for the relief of the unemployed; 300*l*. awarded to the plaintiff . 18 April, ,,
Warne & Co. *v.* Scebohm (see *Copyright*), 10 May, ,,
Hutt and another *v.* The governors of Haileybury college (see under *Haileybury*) . . 19 June, ,,
Wood *v.* Cox (see under *Races*) . 29 June, ,,
O'Donnell *v.* Walter and another (for libel in the *Times*); verdict for the defendants (see under *Parnellites*) . . . . 2–5 July, ,,
Trials respecting electric light patents (see under *Electricity*) 1886–8
George and Kelynge Greenway, bankers, of Warwick and Leamington, sentenced to imprisonment, &c., for frauds . . 31 July, 1888
Trial of Regent's Park murderer (see *Regent's Park*), July, ,,
R. P. B. Frost and his presumed wife, Annie Frost (clever and fascinating), who as Mrs Gordon Baillie and other names, had carried on a long series of frauds at home and abroad by means of fictitious cheques, convicted of cheating tradesmen of goods and money; he sentenced to eighteen months' imprisonment with hard labour, she to five years' penal servitude . . 24 Oct. ,,
Anthony Isidor Glika sentenced to ten years' penal servitude for defrauding his employers, Messrs. Vagliano Bros., and the Bank of England, of 71,500*l*., 27 June,–7 July; in a subsequent trial trial the Queen's Bench Division adjudged the bank to bear the loss . . . 2 Nov. 1888 [Sentence confirmed by court of appeal, 21 May, 1889.]
Mrs. Weldon *v.* M. Riviere and others; verdict for defendants . . . . . 15 Nov. ,,
Charles Richardson and Edgell, who had confessed to burglary at Edlingham vicarage, near Alnwick, on 7 Feb. 1879; sentenced to five years' penal servitude . . . . 24 Nov. ,, [Michael Brannagham and Peter Murphy, who had been wrongfully convicted for this crime, and attempt to murder, had been sentenced to penal servitude for life, April, 1879; each received 800*l*. as compensation, Dec. 1888; the police were acquitted of perjury, and doubts were thrown on the confession of Richardson and Edgell, Feb. 1889.]
Lyster, Burdett, and Clarke convicted of burglary and attempt to murder Mr. George Atkin at Muswell Hill; sentenced to penal servitude for life . . . . . . 7 March, ,,
Mrs. Sophia Irwin *v. Pall Mall Gazette* for libel; damages awarded, 1,000*l*. . . 4 April, 1889
Sir George Chetwynd *v.* the earl of Durham, for libels relating to racing transactions, the damages claimed, 20,000*l*. After some litigation and much discussion, the case was referred to the arbitration of the stewards of the jockey club, Mr. Jas. Lowther, M.P., the earl of March, and prince Soltikoff; they awarded sir George Chetwynd ¼*d*. damages, each person to pay his own costs . . . . . 29 June, ,, [Sir George Chetwynd, who was exonerated from the graver, but censured for the lighter charges, quitted the club, 5 July, 1889.]
W. O'Brien, M.P., *v.* the marquis of Salisbury for libel in a speech at Watford, 10 March; charging him with inciting to crime in a speech at Ballyneale near Clonmel, 30 Sept. 1888; damages claimed, 10,000*l*.; trial at Manchester; verdict for defendant . . . . 20 July, ,,
See *Executions*.

TRIBUNES OF THE PEOPLE (*Tribuni Plebis*), magistrates of Rome, first chosen from among the commons to represent them, 494 B.C., when the people, after a quarrel with the senators, had retired to Mons Sacer. The first two tribunes were C. Licinius and L. Albinus; but their number was soon after raised to five, and 37 years after to ten, which number remained fixed. The office was annual, and as the first had been created on the 4th of the ides of December, that day was chosen for the election. In A.D. 1347, Nicolo di Rienzi assumed absolute power in Rome as tribune of the people, and reformed many abuses; but committing extravagances, he lost his popularity and was compelled to abdicate. He returned to Rome and was assassinated, 8 Sept. 1354.

TRICHINIASIS, a fatal disease, occasioned by eating raw or underdone pork containing a minute worm named *Trichina spiralis*. Professor Owen discovered these worms in cysts, in human muscle, in 1832. The trichinae are thoroughly destroyed by proper cooking. The disease excited much attention in 1865, and was the subject of a lecture by Dr. Thudichum at the Society of Arts on 18 April, 1866.

TRICOLOR FLAG (red, white, and blue, white representing the ancient monarchy; red and blue, Paris) invented by La Fayette, adopted by France, 1789.

TRICOTEUSES (knitters), a name given to a number of French republican females, who zealously attended political meetings and executions in 1792, knitting at intervals.

TRIDENTINE, see *Trent*, and *Catechism*.

TRIENNIAL PARLIAMENTS. On 15 Feb. 1641, an act was passed providing for the meet-

ing of a parliament at least once in three years. This law was broken by the Long Parliament, and was repealed in 1664. Another triennial bill, passed in 1694, was repealed by the Septennial act, 1716; see *Parliaments*, and *Septennial Parliaments*.

TRIESTE, an Austrian port on the Adriatic, declared a free port by the emperor Charles VI., 1719, confirmed by Maria Theresa in 1750. It was held by the French in 1797 and 1805. Since the establishment of the overland mail to India, it has risen to great commercial importance. After various changes of rulers it was restored to Austria in 1814; see *Lloyd's*, note. The emperor and empress were warmly received here mid. Sept. 1882.

Cordial reception of the duke of Edinburgh and the Mediterranean fleet . . . 15 Sept. 1887

TRIGONOMETRICAL SURVEY, see *Ordnance*.

TRIMMER, a term applied to George Savile, earl of Halifax, and others who held similar political opinions, midway between those of the extreme Whigs and Tories, about the latter part of the 17th century. He assumed the title as an honour, asserting that it could be rightly given to the British constitution and church. Macaulay says that Halifax was a trimmer on principle, and not a renegade. He died in 1695.

TRINACRIA, a name of Sicily. The title "King of Trinacria," was temporarily assumed by Frederick II. (1302), and Frederick III. (1373).

TRINCOMALEE (Ceylon), was taken from the Dutch, by the English, in 1782; it was retaken by the French the same year; but was restored to the Dutch by the peace of 1783. It surrendered to the British, under colonel Stewart, 26 Aug. 1795, and was confirmed to England by the peace of Amiens, in 1802; see *Ceylon*. Of a series of actions off Trincomalee between sir Edward Hughes and the French admiral Suffren, one was fought 18 Feb. 1782, the enemy having eleven ships to nine; on 12 April following, they had eighteen ships to eleven, and on 6 July, same year, they had fifteen ships to twelve. In all these conflicts the French were defeated.

TRINIDAD, an island in the West Indies, discovered by Columbus in 1498, was taken from the Spaniards by sir Walter Raleigh in 1595; by the French from the English in 1676. Taken by the British, with four ships of the line, and a military force under command of sir Ralph Abercromby, to whom the island capitulated, 18 Feb. 1797; they captured two, and burnt three Spanish ships of war in the harbour. This possession was confirmed to England by the peace of Amiens in 1802. The insurrection of the negroes occurred 4 Jan. 1832. Population in 1861, 84,438; in 1881, 153,128; in 1887, 203,423. Governor, Hon. Arthur H. Gordon, 1866; James R. Longden, 1870; sir H. T. Irving, 1874; sir Sandford Freeling, 1880; sir Wm. Robinson, Aug. 1885. Trinidad united with Tobago by parliament in 1887.

Port of Spain nearly destroyed by fire 28 Jan. *et seq.* 1884
The Indian coolies at San Fernando forbidden to go in festival procession to cast their taboots (small shrines) on the last day of Mohurrum, disobey, and are fired upon by the police and soldiers; 12 killed, and many wounded 30 Oct. „
This course was justified, after due investigation, by sir Henry Norman, governor of Jamaica; blue book published . . . 14 April, 1885

TRINITY AND TRINITARIANS. Theophilus, bishop of Antioch, who flourished in the 2nd century, was the first who used the term Trinity, to express the three sacred persons in the Godhead. His "Defence of Christianity" was edited by Gesner, at Zurich, in 1546. *Watkins*. An order of the Trinity, termed Mathurins, was founded about 1198 by John de Matha and Felix de Valois. See *Crutched Friars*. The Trinity fraternity, originally of fifteen persons, was instituted at Rome by St. Philip Neri, in 1548. The act to exempt from penalties persons denying the doctrine of the Trinity (such as Unitarians and Swedenborgians) passed in 1813. *Trinitarian Bible Society* founded, 1831.

TRINITY COLLEGES, see *Cambridge*, and *Oxford*. Trinity College, Dublin, called the University: grant of the Augustine monastery of All Saints within the suburbs for erecting this college, conferred by queen Elizabeth, 1591. First stone laid by Thomas Smith, mayor of Dublin, 1 Jan. 1593. New charter, 1637. Made a barrack for soldiers, 1689. *Burns*. The principal or west front erected, 1759. Library erected, 1732. This college grants degrees upon examination without residence. The Roman Catholics desire exemption from mixed education and special privileges. Great changes were proposed by the Irish University bill, which was brought into parliament Feb. 1873, but withdrawn. Religious tests were abolished in the same year.

A proposal to establish a Roman catholic college within the university was negatived by the senate (74-7) . . . . 18 May, 1874
The church choral society incorporated as Trinity College, London 1875

TRINITY HOUSE, LONDON, founded by sir Thomas Spert, 1512, as an "association for piloting ships," was incorporated in 1514, and re-incorporated in 1604, 1660, and 1685. The present Trinity House was erected in 1795. By their charter the brethren of the Trinity House have the power of examining, licensing, and regulating pilots, and of erecting beacons and lighthouses, and of placing buoys in the channels and rivers. Spert, the first master, died 8 Sept. 1541.—TRINITY HOUSES, originally guilds or fraternities, founded at Deptford, Hull, and Newcastle, were incorporated by Henry VIII., 1536-41.

RECENT MASTERS.
William Pitt 1790
Earl Spencer 1806
Duke of Portland 1807
Earl Camden 1809
Earl of Liverpool 1815
Marquis Camden 1828
Duke of Clarence 1829
Marquis Camden 1831
Duke of Wellington 1836
The Prince Consort 1852
Viscount Palmerston . . . . 16 June, 1862
Duke of Edinburgh . . . . 15 March, 1866

TRINITY SUNDAY, the Sunday following Whitsunday. The festival of the Holy Trinity was instituted by pope Gregory IV. in 828, on his ascending the papal chair, and is observed by the Latin and protestant churches on the Sunday next following Pentecost or Whitsuntide, of which, originally, it was merely an octave. The observance of the festival was first enjoined in the council of Arles, 1260. It was appointed to be held on the present day by pope John XXI. in 1334.

TRINOBANTES, a British tribe which occupied Middlesex and Essex, and joined in opposing the invasion of Julius Cæsar, 54 B.C.; but soon submitted. They joined Boadicea and were defeated by Suetonius Paulinus near London, A.D. 61.

TRIPARTITE TREATY, name given to treaty of Paris, 1856.

TRIPLE ALLIANCE was ratified between the States-General and England against France, for the protection of the Spanish Netherlands; Sweden afterwards joining the league, it was known as the Triple Alliance, 23 Jan. 1668.—Another Triple Alliance was that between England, Holland, and France against Spain, Jan. 1717.—Another between Great Britain, Russia, and Austria, 28 Sept. 1795. Another between Germany, Austria, and Italy, said to have been proposed June, 1882, and adopted 1883, and signed 13 March, 1887.

TRIPOLI (three cities). I., in Syria, comprised three quarters built by the Tyrians, Sidonians, and Arabians; was taken by the Crusaders 1109, and made a county for Raymond of Toulouse. It was conquered by the Egyptians in 1832; restored to the Porte 1835; surrendered to the British 1841. II., a Turkish province, N. Africa, comprised the cities Sabrata, Œa (the present Tripoli, the capital), and Leptis (the ancient Tripolitana), after having been held by Greeks, Romans, Vandals, and Saracens, was conquered and annexed by the Turks 1551. Hamet Bey, pacha in 1741, made himself independent, and the government remained in his family till 1835, when Tripoli was restored to nominal subjugation to the sultan. Population (1884) about 1,000,000. Panic through fear of insurrection about 20 July, 1882.

TRIPOLITZA (Greece), was stormed by the Greeks, who committed dreadful cruelties, 5 Oct. 1821; retaken by the Egyptians, 30 June, 1825; given up to the Greeks, 1828.

TRIREMES, galleys with three banks of oars, are said to have been invented by the Corinthians, 784 or 700 B.C.

TRIUMPHS were granted by the Roman senate to generals of armies after they had won great victories. They were received into the city with great magnificence and public acclamations. There were the great, called *the* Triumph; and the less, the Ovation; see *Ovation*.

TRIUMVIRATES, ROMAN. In 60 B.C., Julius Cæsar, Pompey, and Crassus formed a coalition to rule the state. This lasted ten years, and the civil war ensued. The second triumvirate, 43 B.C., was formed by Octavius Cæsar, Mark Antony, and Lepidus, through whom the Romans totally lost their liberty. Lepidus was expelled in 36; Antony was subdued in 31, and Octavius made himself absolute; see *Rome*. In Feb. 1849, a triumvirate was appointed at Rome, consisting of Joseph Mazzini, Armellini, and Saffi, which resigned on 1 July, 1849, when the city was taken by the French.

TRIVIUM, see *Arts*.

TROCADERO, Paris, a mount on the right bank of the Seine, so named in memory of a fort near Cadiz, captured by the French while suppressing the insurrection in 1823. On this ground was erected the palace of the "Trocadéro," in connection with the international exhibition of 1878; see *Paris*.

TROPPAU, CONGRESS OF, in Austrian Silesia. The emperors Francis of Austria and Alexander of Russia met at Troppau, 20 Oct. 1820. The congress between them and the king of Prussia, against Naples, took place 10 Nov.; and the conference was transferred to Laybach, as nearer to Italy, 17 Dec. 1820; see *Laybach*.

TROUBADOURS AND TROUVÈRES (from *troubar, trouver*, to find or invent), the poets of the middle ages (from the 11th to the 15th century). The former flourished in the south of France and north of Spain, and used the Langue d'oc (that is, *oc* for *oui*, yes); the latter flourished in the north of France, and used the Langue d'oïl (that is, *oïl* for *oui*). The Troubadours produced romances, but excelled chiefly in lyric poetry; the Trouvères excelled in romances, several of which are extant; as, the *Brut d'Angleterre*, and the *Rou*, by Wace; the "Romance of the Rose," by Guillaume de Lorris and Jean de Meung. The Troubadours were usually accompanied by *Jongleurs*, who sang their masters' verses, with the accompaniment of the guitar. Histories of these French poets, and specimens of their works, have been published in France. These poets, although frequently very licentious, tended to promote civilisation during those warlike times.

TROY or ILIUM, capital of the Troas, Asia Minor; see *Homer*. Its history mythical.

Arrival of Scamander in Phrygia. *Blair*	B.C. 1546
Teucer succeeds his father	1502
Dardanus succeeds; builds Dardania	1480
Reign of Erichthonius	1449
Reign of Tros; from whom the people are called Trojans, and the city Troas	1374
Ilus, his son, reigns; the city called Ilium	1314
Reign of Laomedon	1260
Arrival of Hercules in Phrygia. Hesione delivered from the sea monster. *Blair; Usher*	1225
War of Hercules and Laomedon	1224
Reign of Priam or Podarces	"
Rape of Helen, by Alexander Paris, son of Priam, 20 years before the sacking of Troy. *Homer's Iliad*, book xxiv.	1204
Commencement of the invasion of the Greeks to recover Helen	1193
Troy taken and burnt in the night of the 11th of June, i.e., 23rd of the month Thargelion. *Parian Marbles.* 408 years before the first Olympiad. Apollodorus, Hales, and Clinton, 1183; others	1184
Mr. W. E. Gladstone dates the war	1316-1307
Æneas arrives in Italy. *Lenglet.*	1183

[Some time after the destruction of Troy, a new city was built with the same name, about thirty stadia distant from the old site. It was favoured by Alexander the Great in his Asiatic expedition, but never rose to much importance, and in the age of Strabo was nearly in ruins. *Priestley.*]

Dr. H. Schliemann, during his excavations at Hissarlik in the Troad, discovered the remains of a very ancient city with temples, which he named "Novum Ilium"	A.D. 1872-3
He published *Troy and its Remains* (trans. by Dr. P. Smith)	1875
His Trojan antiquities arranged at South Kensington Museum, for exhibition	Dec. 1877
Dr. Schliemann resumes excavations at Hissarlik; discovers Trojan houses and many antiquities, a dagger, earrings, bracelets, idols, shells, &c.,	30 Sept.-1 Dec. 1878
Again with professor Virchow and M. Burnouf, 1 March; makes fresh discoveries described in letter 5 June, 1879; desists investigation; published his book *Ilios*, 1880, and *Troja*	1883

TROY WEIGHT. The Romans introduced their ounce, our avoirdupois ounce, into Britain. The present ounce was brought from Grand Cairo into Europe, about the time of the Crusades, 1095, and was first adopted at Troyes, a city of France, whence the name. It is used to weigh gold, silver, and precious stones. The Troy weight, Scots, was established by James VI. (our James I.) in 1618; see *Standard*.

TROYES (Central France), where a treaty was concluded between England, France, and Burgundy, whereby it was stipulated that Henry V. should marry Catherine, daughter of Charles VI., be appointed regent of France, and, after the death of Charles, should inherit the crown. 21 May, 1420. Troyes was taken by the allied armies, 7 Feb.; re-

taken by Napoleon, 23 Feb.; and again taken by the allies, 4 March, 1814.

TRUCE OF GOD (*Frera* or *Treuga Dei*), a term given to a cessation of the private feuds and conflicts so general during the middle ages all over Europe, said to have been strongly advocated by the bishop of Aquitaine, in 1032. The clergy strenuously exerted their influence for the purpose. A synod at Roussillon, 1027, decreed that none should attack his enemy between Saturday evening (at nones) and Monday morning (at the hour of prime). Similar regulations were adopted in England, 1042 (sometimes Friday and Wednesday being chosen for the time). The truce of God was confirmed by many councils of the church, especially the Lateran Council, in 1179.

TRUCK SYSTEM of paying workmen's wages in goods (sold at "*tommy shops*") instead of money, was prohibited by parliament in 1831. By the Truck act a commission to inquire into its alleged prevalence was appointed; act passed 10 Aug. 1870; amended 1887.

TRUMPET. Some of the Greek historians ascribe the invention of the trumpet to the Tyrrhenians, and others to the Egyptians. It was in use in the time of Homer. First torches, then shells of fish, sounded like trumpets, were the signals in primitive wars. *Potter*. The Jewish feast of trumpets was appointed 1490 B.C. (*Lev.* xxiii. 24). Oda, king of Mercia, is said to have had trumpets sounded before him when travelling, about A.D. 790. The *speaking trumpet* is said to have been used by Alexander the Great in 335 B.C.; improved by Kircher in A.D. 1652; by Salland, 1654; and philosophically explained by Morland, 1671.

Trumpet blasts employed for railway signalling in Scotland 1887

TRUMPET-FLOWER. *Bignonia radicans*, was brought hither from North America, about 1640. The Trumpet Honeysuckle, *Lonicera sempervirens*, came from North America in 1656. The *Bignonia capensis* was brought to England from the Cape in 1823. The Large-flowered Trumpet-flower, or *Bignonia grandiflora*, was brought from China in 1800.

TRURO, W. Cornwall. The town was founded by Richard de Lucy, chief justice of England in the 12th century, and chartered by Reginald, earl of Cornwall, illegitimate son of Henry I. An act to provide for the foundation of a bishopric of Truro passed 11 Aug. 1876, and money sufficient for its endowment having been subscribed, the see was constituted by order in council, 9 Dec. same year. Act amended in 1887. Truro was made a city, Aug. 1877; absorbed into the county, 1885.

Foundation of new cathedral (St. Mary's) laid by the prince of Wales, 20 May, 1880; it includes part of the old parish church; the eastern part erected, consecrated and opened for public worship in the presence of the prince of Wales and the archbishop of Canterbury, 3 Nov. 1887; architect, Mr. Pearson; the first cathedral erected since St. Paul's, London.
See *Mansion House Fund*.

BISHOPS.
1877. Edward White Benson, consecrated, 25 April; trans. to Canterbury, Dec. 1882.
1883. George Howard Wilkinson, consecrated 25 April.

TRUSS. A transverse spring-truss for ruptures was patented by Robert Brand in 1771, and by many other persons since. The National Truss Society to assist indigent persons, was established in 1786; and many similar societies since.

TRUSTEES, see *Fraudulent*.
Trustees' act passed 1833

TRUSTS and COMBINES. Terms applied in the United States to the union of manufacturers and traders as corporate bodies for the purpose of creating and maintaining strict monopolies and thereby controlling the output and the prices of goods of all kinds and the wages of workmen, a system injurious to all classes of society.
In the autumn of 1888, legislation for the repression of the evil was urgently demanded. There is a petroleum trust, a cotton trust, a steel rail trust &c. (see *Corner*). The proprietors of the salt mines in Cheshire combined to form a "trust" in the autumn of 1888. Similar trusts have been projected and opposed.

TUAM (W. Ireland). St. Jarlath, the son of Loga, who lived about 501, is looked upon as the first founder of the cathedral of Tuam, though the abbey is said to have been founded in 487. The church was anciently called *Tuaim-da-Gualand*. In 1151, Edan O'Hoisin was the first archbishop, at least the first who received the pall, for some of his predecessors are sometimes called bishops of Connaught, and sometimes archbishops, by Irish historians. The see of Mayo was annexed to Tuam in 1559. Tuam is valued in the king's books, by an extent returned *anno* 28 Eliz., at 50*l*. sterling per annum. *Beatson*. It ceased to be archiepiscopal, conformably with the statute 3 & 4 Will. IV., 1833; and is now a bishopric only, to which Killala and Achonry, a joint see, has been added; see *Archbishops*. New protestant cathedral of St. Mary, consecrated by the bishop, the Hon. Dr. Charles B. Bernard, 9 Oct. 1878.

TÜBINGEN SCHOOL of rationalistic criticism was founded by professor F. C. Baur about 1835.

TUBMAN, see *Postman*.

TUBULAR BRIDGES. The Britannia Tubular Suspension Bridge, then the most wonderful enterprise in engineering in the world, was constructed, 1846-50 (Mr. R. Stephenson and Mr. Fairbairn, engineers); about a mile southward of the Menai Strait Suspension Bridge.*

On the Britannia rock, near the centre of the Menai Strait, the surface of which is about ten feet above low water level, is built a tower two hundred feet above high water (commenced building, May, 1846), and on which rest two lines of tubes or hollow girders strong enough to bear their weight and laden trains in addition, the ends resting on the abutments on each shore; each tube being more than a quarter of a mile in length. The height of the tube within is thirty feet at the Britannia tower, diminishing to twenty-three feet at the abutments. The lifting of these tubes to their places was a most gigantic operation, successfully performed,
                                      27 June, 1849
The first locomotive passed through   March, 1850
The Conway tubular bridge, a miniature copy of the Britannia (principal engineers, Mr. Robt. Stephenson and Mr. Fairbairn) erected . . . 1846-8
At Chepstow, a railway tubular bridge . . . 1852

* The Britannia tubular bridge was intended to supply the place of one of the finest bridges in the kingdom; and the railway, of which the tubular bridge forms a part, is in like manner a substitute for one of the finest mail-coach roads ever constructed. The road from London to Holyhead has been long regarded as the highway from the British metropolis to Dublin; and the late Mr. Telford was applied to by the government to perfect this route by the London and Holyhead mail-coach road, which he did by erecting a beautiful suspension bridge over the river Conway and over the Menai Strait; commenced in July, 1818, and finished in July, 1825.

A bridge or viaduct on the tubular principle (called the Albert viaduct) over the river Tamar at Plymouth, opened by the prince consort . 2 May, 1859 See *Victoria Railway Bridge* and *Tay Bridge.*

TUDELA (N. Spain). Near here marshal Lannes totally defeated the Spaniards, 23 Nov. 1808; see *Ebro.*

TUDOR SOVEREIGNS; see *England,* 1485-1603.

TUESDAY, in Latin *Dies Martis,* the day of Mars, the third day of the week, so called from *Tuisto, Tiw,* or *Tuesco,* a Saxon deity, worshipped on this day. Tuisto is mentioned by Tacitus; see *Week Days.*

TUGENDBUND ("league of Virtue"), formed in Prussia soon after the peace of Tilsit, June, 1807, ostensibly for relieving the sufferers by the late wars, and for the revival of morality and patriotism. Its head-quarters were at Königsberg. It excited the jealousy of Napoleon, who demanded its suppression in 1809. It was dissolved at the peace in 1815.

TUILERIES (Paris), the imperial palace of France, commenced by Catherine de Medicis, after the plans of Philibert de l'Orme, 1564; continued by Henry IV.; and finished by Louis XIV. This palace was stormed by the mob, 10 Aug. 1792; and ransacked in the revolutions of July, 1830, and Feb. 1848. Louis Napoleon made it his residence in 1851, and greatly renovated it. The restoration of the Tuileries (much injured by fire by the communists, May 1871) was determined on, Oct. 1872; not proceeded with. The ruins were sold for 32,200*l*. to M. Picard, 4 Dec. 1882.

TULCHAN BISHOPS; a mere nominal episcopacy set up in Scotland by the regent Morton, who, with other nobles, absorbed the larger portion of the revenue, 1572-3. *Tulchan* was a stuffed calf's skin set before a cow to facilitate milking.

TULIPS, indigenous in the east of Europe, came to England from Vienna about 1578. It is recorded in the register of Alkmaer in Holland, that in 1639, 120 tulips, with the offsets, sold for 90,000 florins: and that one, called the *Viceroy*, sold for 4203 guilders! The States stopped this ruinous traffic. The *tulip tree, Liriodendron tulipifera,* was brought to England from America, about 1663.

TUNBRIDGE WELLS (Kent). The springs were discovered, it is stated, by Dudley, lord North, who, when very ill, was restored to health by the use of the waters, 1606. The wells were visited by the queens of Charles I. and II., and by queen Anne, and soon became fashionable.
The town was incorporated by royal charter early in 1889

TUNGSTEN (also called wolfram and scheelium), a hard whitish brittle metal. From tungstate of lead, Scheele in 1781 obtained tungstic acid, whence the brothers De Luyart in 1786 obtained the metal. In 1859 it was employed in making a new kind of steel.

TUNIS (N. Africa) stands nearly on the site of Carthage. Tunis was besieged by Louis IX., of France, who died near it 25 Aug. 1270. It remained under African kings till taken by Barbarossa, for Solyman the Magnificent, 1531. Barbarossa was expelled by the emperor Charles V., when 10,000 Christian slaves were set at liberty, June, 1535. The country was recovered by the Turks under Selim II. 1575. The bey of Tunis was first appointed in 1574; Tunis was reduced by admiral Blake, on the bey refusing to deliver up the British captives,

1655. The Hussein dynasty was founded 1705. In July, 1856, the bey agreed to make constitutional reforms. He died 22 Sept. 1859; and his brother and successor Mohamed-es-Sadok took the oath of fidelity to the constitution. He died, and was succeeded by his brother Sidi Ali, 28 Oct. 1882. Tunis is now under French protection.

Insurrection, 18 April; ships of war sent to protect
Europeans . . . . May, 1880
Tunis decreed to be an integral part of the Turkish
empire . . . . 25 Oct. 1871
A dispute with France settled by submission of the
bey . . . . Jan. 1871
The bey, embarrassed by debt (5,000,000*l.*), places his
finances in hands of an international commission 1881
Disputes between France and Italy respecting railway concessions . . . . Aug. "
Dispute between a British subject here and a French
company respecting purchase of the Enfida estate,
decision left to the legal tribunals . . Feb. 1881
Dispute with France; predatory incursions of the
Kroumirs, nomadic shepherd tribes, on Algerian
territory, March; the bey appeals to Turkey, 11
April; and the Great Powers, 27 April: military
expedition sent from France; lands in Tabarka,
bombards fortress, and occupies Bizerta, 30 April, "
The Kroumirs said to be enclosed by the French;
the bey's army retreats . . . early May, "
Alleged battle with the Kroumirs . about 2 May, "
The French approach Tunis, alleging the object to
be to restrain warlike tribes and protect their
frontier . . . . 11 May, "
Treaty with France signed; it assures to France the
right to occupy the positions which the French
military authorities might deem necessary for the
maintenance of order and the security of the frontier and the coast, and to send a resident minister
to the capital. The French government guarantees to the bey the security of his person, his
states, and his dynasty, and the maintenance of
existing treaties with the European powers; while
the bey undertakes not to conclude any international convention without a previous understanding with the French government, and to prevent
the introduction of arms into Algeria through
Tunis. The financial system of the regency to be
regulated by France in concert with the bey,
12 May, "
Reported conflict between the French under gen.
Bréart and the Arabs; the French enter Mater,
18 May, "
The Sultan of Turkey protests against the treaty, May, "
M. Séguin, a news correspondent, murdered at Beja
by a fanatic (who is executed) . . 28 May, "
M. Brangard, inspector of telegraphs, and assistants,
murdered by Arabs, near Oran . about 5 June, "
M. Roustan, the consul, appointed French resident
minister (said to be virtual ruler, replacing bey),
French army returning home . . June, "
Mustapha Ben Ismail, the bey's chief minister, received by president Grévy, at Paris . 21 June, "
Insurrection at Sfax, revolt of great chief Ali Ben
Khalifa, announced . . . . . 30 June, "
Europeans attacked, nearly all flee to ships, alleged
massacres . . . . 31 July, "
Sfax bombarded by the French, 5 July, *et seq.*;
captured after severe conflict . . 16 July, "
Arabs revolting; anarchy reported . 20 July, "
Enfida case; decision against the English, Mr.
Levy . . . . Aug. "
Collapse of Bey's authority . about 15 Aug. "
Asserted conflict at Hammamet, the French repulsed about 31 Aug.; the French retreating about
8 Sept. "
Arrival of 2,000 French troops at Goletta 9 Sept. "
General Sabattier with troops at Zaghouan surrounded by Arabs . . . about 13 Sept. "
28,000 men sent to Tunis announced . 26 Sept. "
Alleged defeat of the Bey's troops under Ali Bey;
4 hours' conflict . . . . about 25 Sept. "
All Bey's army surrounded . about 4 Oct. *et seq.* "
Union of the French and Ali Bey's army, about
8 Oct. "
Tunis occupied by the French . . 10 Oct. "
Gen. Sabattier defeats the Arabs; six hours' conflict; 800 killed, French loss slight . 13 Oct. "

. . about 22 Oct. 1881
ine enter Kairwan,
. . . . 26 Oct. ,,
(11 May) confirmed
. . . 9 Nov. ,,
ir Gerid, by Gen.
. about 16 Nov. ,,
are of a large rebel
. about 17 Nov. ,,
ppressed; army of
announced 29 Nov. ,,
d . about 14 Dec. ,,
ochfort acquitted of
in . . 15 Dec. ,,
. about 29 Dec. ,,
. about 23 Feb. 1882
. about 1 April, ,,
. . . . May, ,,
over debt about
. . . July, ,,
. about 3 Oct. ,,
d; foreign consular
ulations) 1 Jan. 1884

NDAGE were ancient
of wine and pound of
;ported, and were the
They commenced in
re granted to the kings
lward IV. Charles I.
ing them on his own
granted to Charles II.
1660. By the act 27
er duties were repealed,
t of excise and customs

ge, are ancient. The
avigation was executed
Louis XIV., at Bezières
England was by Mr.
Bridgewater's canal,
766. Project of the
e report upon it, 1801.
:ojected by Mr. Brunel
passengers, 25 March,
Innumerable tunnels
. The railway tunnel
in the middle of 1829,
d once a week. On the
ailway there are eight
Watford, Kilsby, &c.),
336 yards. *Smiles.* It
er, that there were 80
ited Kingdom in 1865,
, at the average of 45*l*.
les.

iis, suggested by M.
. . . . about 1802
i the channel from
Messrs. J. F. Bate-
. . . 30 Aug. 1869
my years' study, ex-
867; his scheme re-
and Nov. 1873; a
s signed for France
n., 1875; engineers,
Lavally; monopoly
an for English com-
or; plan of boring
r. D. Brunton.
. . . Feb., 1876
begun 25 Feb.; 200
. . . 3 June, ,,
osed treaty between
. . . . Aug. ,,
d by G. Remington.

cession for prelimi-
renewed for 3 years
from 2 Aug. 1880

Experimental boring going on, April, 1881; 800
  metres from the coast . . . . . May, 1883
Meeting of Channel Tunnel Company 2 Feb.; of
  submarine Continental railway company 3 Feb. 1882
Channel Tunnel near Dover; about 1 mile exca-
  vated; visited by Mr. Gladstone and others
  . . . . 11 March, ,,
The Channel Tunnel disapproved of by sir G.
  Wolseley, and other officers, British and foreign
  . . . . March, *et seq.* ,,
The works stopped by government about 1 May;
  by order of Mr. Justice Kay . . . 6 July, ,,
Two channel tunnel bills discharged in the commons
  . . . . 16 Aug. ,,
Report of a commission on the channel tunnel (sir
  A. Alison, chairman) unfavourable on political
  grounds issued . . . . . . 11 Oct. ,,
The question referred to a committee of lords and
  commons 4, 6 April, which meets 24 April; decide
  against the tunnel (5-4) . . . about 10 July, 1883
The company resolutely determine to wait 17 Aug. ,,
Bill rejected by the commons (222-84) 14 May, 1884;
  (281-99) . . . . 12 May, 1885
Boring of the channel tunnel still continued, 2 Feb. 1887
The channel tunnel bill again rejected by the
  commons (153-107) . . . . 3 Aug. ,,
Sir E. Watkin's bill for experimental works
  opposed by the government and rejected in the
  commons (307-165) . . . . 27 June, 1888
Mersey tunnel, between Liverpool and Birkenhead,
  one mile long, projected 1866, execution frequently suspended, boring renewed by the energy
  of major Samuel Isaac, 1880, boring completed
  under his superintendence, 17 Jan. 1884 (he died,
  22 Nov. 1886); tunnel opened, 13 Feb. 1885; first
  passenger train run through, 22 Dec. 1885;
  formally opened by the prince of Wales, 20 Jan. 1886
The Severn tunnel near Bristol, constructed by W.
  C. Richardson, for the Gt. Western company's
  railway begun, March, 1873; official train passed
  through, 5 Sept. 1885; opened for traffic, 1 Sept.,
  for passengers . . . . . . 1 Dec. ,,
"Joseph II. mining adit," Schemnitz, begun 1782,
  after many delays, finished, 16,538 metres long,
  . . . . 5 Sept. 1878
Arlberg tunnel, Austria, 10,270 metres long; begun
  June, 1880; completed, and train passed through,
  . . . . 13 Nov. 1883
Subway for electric tramcars from the Monument
  to Stockwell; completed to Kennington, March, 1889

TURAN, see *Turkestan*.

TÜRCKHEIM, see *Türkheim*.

TURIN, the ancient Augusta Taurinorum in Piedmont, capital of the Sardinian States, and of the kingdom of Italy, till 1864, when it was superseded by Florence. Its importance dates from the permanent union of Savoy and Piedmont in 1416. The French besieged this city; but prince Eugène defeated their army, and compelled them to raise the siege, 7 Sept. 1706. In 1798, the French republican army took possession of Turin, seized all the strong places and arsenals of Piedmont, and obliged the king and his family to remove to the island of Sardinia. In 1799, the French were driven out by the Austrians and Russians; but the city and all Piedmont surrendered to the French, June 1800. In May 1814, it was restored to the king of Sardinia; see *Italy*, 1864. Here prince Humbert was married to his cousin Margherita amidst great rejoicing, 22 April, 1868. The monument to Cavour was inaugurated, 8 Nov. 1873. An exhibition opened by the king, 25 April, 1880. See *Treaties*, and *Italy*, 1884.

TURKESTAN, called by the Persians Turan, Independent Tartary, the original country of the Turks, in Central Asia, was reached by Alexander, 331 B.C. The Russians are gradually encroaching on this country; on 14 Feb. 1865, a new province, Turkestan, was created by decree, and gen. Kauffmann made governor, 26 July, 1867; died 16 May,

1882. The rule of the czar accepted by the chief tribes at Merv, (*which see*), announced 8 Feb. 1884.

TURKEY. The Turks were originally a tribe of Tartars; but, by incorporation with the peoples they have conquered, have become a mixed race. About 760, they obtained possession of a part of Armenia, expelled from them the Turcomania. They gradually extended their power; but in the 13th century, being harassed by other Tartar tribes, they returned to Asia Minor. The Turkish empire till 1878 comprehended the almost independent principalities of Moldavia and Wallachia, Servia, and Montenegro, the hereditary vice-royalty of Egypt, and Tunis. The Turkish quadrilateral fortresses were Shumla, Varna, Silistria, and Rustchuck. The population of the empire was estimated in 1887 at 32,978,100. (Immediate Possessions, 21,633,000, tributaries and protectorates, 11,345,100); in Europe, 8,987,000; Asia, 16,174,100; Africa, 7,817,000. By the treaty of Berlin (13 July, 1878) Turkey is said to have

	Square Miles.	Inhabitants.	Mohammedans.
Ceded to Roumania	5,935	246,000	142,000
„ Servia	4,326	264,000	75,000
„ Montenegro	1,549	40,000	9,000
„ Austria	15	2,000	—
„ Greece (?)	5,300	750,000	40,000
To be occupied and administered by Austria	28,125	1,061,000	513,000
Formed into the Principality of Bulgaria	24,404	1,773,000	681,500
Included in Eastern Roumelia	13,646	746,000	265,000

If we exclude the provinces "indefinitely" to be occupied by Austria, Bulgaria, and Eastern Roumelia, there remain to Turkey in Europe only 74,790 square miles, with 4,779,000 inhabitants, of whom 2,521,500 are Mohammedans. In Armenia Russia takes 10,000 square miles, with about 350,000 inhabitants. Cyprus, entrusted to the keeping of England, has an area of 3,584 square miles, and 186,173 inhabitants in 1881. Thessaly ceded to Greece by convention, 24 May; treaty signed, 2 July, 1881.

Alp Arslan and the Turks conquer Armenia and Georgia 1065-8
Asia Minor conquered, 1074-84; Jerusalem taken . 1076
Soliman Shah drowned in the Euphrates, while on the march; his son Ertoghul, granted territories near Angora, dies 1288
Othman, his son, emir of the sultan of Iconium, founded the Ottoman empire at Prusa, Bithynia, by policy and conquest, in 1299
Organisation of Janissaries by Orcan about . . 1330
Nicæa conquered, 1330; and the Morea . . . 1346
The Turks enter Thrace, and take Adrianople . . 1361
Amurath I. remodels the Janissaries 1362
Bajazet I. overruns provinces of the Eastern empire 1389 *et seq*.
He defeats Sigismund of Hungary at Nicopolis 28 Sept. 1396
He besieges Constantinople; but is interrupted by the approach of Tamerlane (or Timour), by whom he is defeated and made prisoner, at Ancyra, 28 July, 1402
Macedonia annexed 1430
Ladislas of Hungary defeated and slain at Varna by Amurath . . . . . . 10 Nov. 1444
Amurath defeats John Huniades at Kossova Oct. 1448
The Turks, invading Hungary, repelled by Huniades 1450
Constantinople taken by the Turks under Mahomet II., which ends the Eastern Roman empire, 29 May, 1453
Belgrade relieved by Huniades' victory over the Turks . . . . July, 1456
Greece subjected to the Turks (see *Greece*) . 1458-60
The Turks take Otranto, diffusing terror throughout Europe 1480
Selim I. raised to the throne by the Janissaries; murders his father, brothers, &c. . . . 1512

He takes the islands of the Archipelago . . . 1514
He overruns Syria 1515
Gains Egypt by defeat of Mamelukes . . Aug. 1516
Solyman takes Belgrade, Aug. 1521; and Rhodes. Dec. 1522
Defeats Hungarians at Mohatz . . . 29 Aug. 1526
Repulsed before Vienna . . . . . Oct. 1529
Peace with Austria 1533
Cyprus taken from the Venetians . . Aug. 1571
Great battle of Lepanto (*which see*) . . 7 Oct. „
Treaty of commerce with England 1576
Turks driven out of Persia by Shah Abbas . . 1585
Great fire in Constantinople 1606
War with the Cossacks, who take Azof . . . 1637
The Turks defeat the Persians and take the city of Bagdad 1638
Candia (Crete) taken from Venice, after a 25 years' siege 1669
Vienna besieged by Mahomet IV. but relieved by John of Poland . . . . . 12 Sept. 1683
Peace of Carlovitz . . . . . 26 Jan. 1699
Mustapha II. deposed by Janissaries . . . 1703
The Morea retaken by the Turks 1715
The Turks defeated at Peterwardein . . . 1716
They lose Belgrade; and their power declines . 1717
Peace of Erivan (with Persia) 1733
Belgrade taken from Austria; and Russia relinquishes Azof 1739
The Turks defeated at Kars 1744
Insurrection of Wahabees 1770
Great sea-fight in the channel of Scio; the Russian fleet defeats the Turkish 1770
The Crimea ceded to Russia . . . . Jan. 1774
Disastrous war with Russia and Austria, the Turks lose more than 200,000 men 1787-8
Cession of Oczacow 1792
War with the French, who invade Egypt . . 1798
Insurrection of Mamelukes at Cairo . . . 1800
War against Russia and England . 7 Jan. 1807
Passage and repassage of the Dardanelles effected by the British fleet, but with great loss; see *Dardanelles* . . . . . . 19 Feb. „
Murder of Hali Aga . . . . . 25 May, „
The Janissaries massacre the newly disciplined troops . . . . „
The Russians defeated at Silistria . . . . „
Treaty of Bucharest (*which see*) . . 28 May, 1812
A caravan consisting of 2000 souls, returning from Mecca, destroyed by a pestilential wind in the deserts of Arabia; 20 saved . . . 9 Aug. „
Subjugation of the Wahabees (*which see*) . 1818
Ali Pacha of Janina, in Greece, declares himself independent . . . . . . „
Insurrection in Moldavia and Wallachia, 6 March, 1821
Persecution of Christians, 6 March; the Greek patriarch put to death at Constantinople, 23 April, „
[For the events in connection with the independence of Greece, see *Greece*.]
Horrible massacre at Scio (see *Chios*) . 23 April, 1822
Sea-fight near Mitylene; Turks defeated . 6 Oct. „
New Mahometan army organised . . 29 May, 1826
Insurrection of the Janissaries at Constantinople; they are suppressed and massacred, 14-16 June, „
6000 houses burnt at Constantinople . 30 Aug. „
Battle of Navarino; the Turkish fleet destroyed by the fleets of England, France, and Russia (see *Navarino*) . . . . . 20 Oct. 1827
Banishment of 132 French, 120 English, and 85 Russian settlers from the empire . 5 Jan. 1828
War with Russia . . . . . 26 April, „
The czar Nicholas takes the field . . 20 May, „
Capitulation of Ibrahilow . . . . 19 June, „
Surrender of Anapa . . . . . 23 June, „
Eminences of Shumla taken by Russians, 20 July, „
The czar arrives before Varna . . . 5 Aug. „
Battle of Akhalzic . . . . . 24 Aug. „
Fortress of Bajazet taken . . . . 9 Sept. „
The sultan proceeds to the camp with the sacred standard . . . . . . 26 Sept. „
Dardanelles blockaded . . . . 1 Oct. „
Surrender of Varna . . . . . 11 Oct. „
Russians retreat from Shumla . . . 16 Oct. „
Surrender of the castle of the Morea to the French, 30 Oct. „
Siege of Silistria raised by Russians . 10 Nov. „
Victory of the Russians at Kuleftscha, near Shumla, 11 June, „

			Great Britain, France, and Austria guarantee integrity of Turkish empire . . . 15 April,	1856
. . 2 July,	1829		Austrians quit the principalities . . March,	1857
Russians, 20 Aug.;			Misunderstanding among the allied powers respecting Moldavian elections, which are annulled,	
. . 29 Aug.	,,		July,	,,
. 14 Sept.	,,		Death of Reschid Pacha . . . 7 Jan.	1858
ished by the men			Massacre of Christians at Jedda (which see),	
. . 22 Jan.	1830		15 June,	,,
ependence of Greece			Lord Stratford de Redcliffe, many years English	
25 April,	,,		ambassador at Constantinople, returned to England, Jan.; he is succeeded by sir H. Lytton Bulwer; accredited . . . 12 July,	,,
7 May,	,,		Indecisive conflicts in Montenegro between the natives and the Turks . . . July,	,,
mbassy destroyed,			Turkish financial reforms begun . . . Aug.	,,
2 Aug.	1831		The first Turkish railway opened (from Aidan to Smyrna) . . . . . 19 Sept.	,,
(Nischan) founded			Base coinage called in; a fictitious Turkish coinage begun at Birmingham suppressed . . Oct.	,,
19 Aug.	,,		The allied powers determine the Montenegrine boundaries . . . . . 8 Nov.	,,
hhim Pacha, son of			Prince Alexander Consa elected hospodar of both Moldavia and Wallachia . . 5 and 7 Feb.	1859
2 July,	1832		[The porte at first objects, but afterwards accedes to the double election.]	
sultan at Konieh,			Electric telegraph completed between Aden and Suez . . . . . . May,	,,
21 Dec.	,,		Great fire at Constantinople; 1000 houses destroyed 10-14 Sept.	,,
n eighty leagues of			Conspiracy against the sultan, 17 Sept.; his brother implicated; several condemned to die; reprieved,	
an asks the aid of			Sept. and Oct.	,,
. Jan.	1833		Great agitation for financial reform . . Oct.	,,
ple . 3 April,	,,		Alleged ill treatment of Christians in Turkey; proposed intervention of the great powers, 5 May; the Turkish government promises investigation and redress, 30 May; all the powers satisfied except Russia . . . . . June,	1860
re and defensive,				
8 July,	,,			
. 30 March,	1838			
land, concluded by			War between the Druses and Maronites in Lebanon; massacres (see Druses) . . . June,	,,
. 16 Aug.	,,		Massacre of Christians at Damascus (see Damascus, and Syria) . . . . 9-11 July,	,,
1840 in relation to			Convention on behalf of the Great Powers at Paris; armed intervention of the French agreed to,	
eing many reforms,			2 Aug.	,,
itions) 3 Nov. 1839;			Inundations at Galatz; loss about 175,000l.	
again 1844.			24 Feb.	1861
Turkey . June,	1849		Christians revolt in the Herzegovina, aided by the Montenegrins . . . . March,	,,
es to surrender the			Great need of financial reform: the British ambassador, sir H. Lytton Bulwer, proposes a scheme . . . . . . April,	,,
es on the joint demands				
. 16 Sept.	,,		Discussion respecting the French occupation of Syria; it ceases . . . . 5 June,	,,
igland) firmly resists			Death of the sultan, Abdul-Medjid; accession of Abdul-Aziz, his brother . . . 25 June,	,,
with the Porte.			Economical reforms begun; Fuad Pacha made president of the council . . . July,	,,
12 Nov.	,,		The late sultan's jewels sold in London . Aug.	,,
Parker, anchors in			Imperial order of knighthood (Osmaneh) to include civil as well as military persons, founded, Sept.	,,
. . 13 Nov.	,,		Imperial guard reorganised . . . Oct.	,,
tussia and the porte			Fuad Pacha made grand vizier . . 22 Nov.	,,
sending the refugees			He puts forth a budget; treaties of commerce with Sweden, Spain, &c. . . . March,	1862
. Jan.	1850		A Turkish loan (8,000,000l.) taken up in London,	
bellion . . Jan.	1851		May,	,,
g the Holy Places			Secularisation of the property of the mosques, (value about 3,000,000l.) said to be determined on,	
. 13 Feb.	1852		Oct.	,,
ded . . Aug.	,,		Insurgents in the Herzegovina submit; peace made with Montenegro . . . 23 Sept.	,,
Constantinople as			Dispute with Servia (which see) settled . 7 Oct.	,,
. ; his peremptory			Ministerial crisis through the sultan's attempt at reaction; Fuad Pacha and others resign, but resume office . . . . . 7 Jan.	1863
. 19 April,	1853			
ign minister; the				
Menschikoff quits			A new bank established . . . 28 Jan.	,,
. 21 May,	,,		Fuad Pacha becomes seraskier . . 12 Feb.	,,
g the rights of the			The sultan visits Egypt . . 7-17 April,	,,
. 6 June,	,,		Fuad Pacha made grand vizier . . 1 June,	,,
key . . 26 June,	,,		Exhibition of the produce of the empire opened in March; closed . . . . 26 July,	,,
h . . 2 July,	,,		Great immigration of the Caucasian tribes April,	1864
o be declared if the			Financial reforms; conversion and verification of the Turkish debt . . . . Aug.	1865
ed . . 26 Sept.	,,			
. . 5 Oct.	,,		Cholera rages at Constantinople, nearly 50,000 deaths, Aug.; cholera subsides, Sept.; great fire	
ot (see Loans, 1854) .	1854			
lbania, favoured by				
thens—Hellenic em-				
. . 27 Jan.	,,			
. 14 March,	,,			
urkey 28 March,	,,			
ith varied success.]				
central point of the				
. 25 April,	,,			
nents, after many				
which arrive at the				
e submits, and pro-				
e Greek volunteers				
. 25 and 26 May,	,,			
take the intrenched				
insurrection shortly				
18 June,	,,			
d (3 June), resumes				
1 July,	,,			
ad Austria 14 June,	,,			
principalities, which				
the Austrians, Sept.	,,			
. . Aug.	1855			
se of religion 18 Feb.	1856			
f Paris . 30 March,	,,			

there, about 2500 buildings (mosques, dwellings, &c.) destroyed . . . . . 6 Sept. 1865
Fuad Pacha proposes confiscation of the property of the mosques; opposition of the Sheikh-ul-Islam 21 Sept. „
Lord Lyons, ambassador at Constantinople . Oct. „
Revolt of the Maronites under Joseph Karam, 30 Dec. „
The grand vizier, Fuad Pacha, superseded by Mehemet Ruchdi . . . . 5 June, 1866
Revolution in Bucharest (see *Danubian principalities*).
Insurrection in Candia (*which see*) . . Aug. „
International conference respecting cholera at Constantinople . . . 13 Feb.-26 Sept. „
European Turkey very unsettled . . Jan. 1867
Maronite revolt, under Joseph Karam, suppressed; his flight, Jan. ; Turks leave . 28 March, „
Ministerial changes: Ali Pacha becomes grand-vizier; Fuad Pacha, foreign minister 11 Feb. „
The recommendation of the European powers to the sultan to give up Candia finally declined 31 Mar. „
Omar Pacha, commander-in-chief of the Turkish army . . . . . . April, „
Destruction of the dockyards in the Golden Horn by fire . . . . 2 April, „
The sultan, with his son and nephew, visits Paris, 1-12 July; arrives at Buckingham Palace, London, 12 July; entertained by the queen at Windsor, 13 July ; by the lord mayor, 18 July ; at a ball at New India House, 19 July ; gives 250*l*. to the poor of London, 22 July ; sails from Dover, 23 July ; at Vienna, 27 July-1 Aug. ; returns to Constantinople . . . . 7 Aug. „
The Sultan declines the proposition of Russia, for the suspension of hostilities in Crete, and an international commission . . . . 4 Sept. „
Ministerial crisis; Fuad Pacha resigns, but resumes his office . . . . . Jan. 1868
Meeting of the new council of state (including Jews and Christians), with legislative, but not executive, functions . . . . 18 May, „
Arrival of prince Napoleon Jerome at Constantinople . . . . . . 26 June, „
Arrests on account of a supposed plot against the sultan . . . . 30 Sept. „
Dispute with Greece for intervention in the Cretan insurrection ; see *Greece* . . . . Dec. „
Fuad Pacha dies . . . . . Feb. 1869
The prince and princess of Wales's visit April, „
Memorial of the porte to the European powers desiring the abolition of the consular jurisdictions termed "capitulations" . . . June, „
The khedive or viceroy of Egypt censured for assuming sovereign powers encroaching on those of the sultan . . . . . . Aug. „
System of compulsory education promulgated, Oct. „
Arrival of the empress of the French at Constantinople . . . . . . 15 Oct. „
Inauguration of the Suez canal . . 17 Nov. „
The khedive submits to the sultan . . Dec. „
Modification of the "capitulations" . April, 1870
Great fire at Pera ; British embassy and about 7900 houses destroyed; great loss of life . 5 June, „
Another fire at Constantinople; about 1500 houses burnt . . . . 11 July, „
Change in the cabinet; Mustapha Fazyl, finance minister . . . . . . 14 Aug. „
Reported treaty between Turkey and Greece to resist European aggression in the East . 21 Oct. „
Russia repudiates the treaty of Paris, 1856, 31 Oct. „
A note delivered to the ports (see *Russia*), 15 Nov. „
The sultan agrees to a conference on the Black Sea question alone . . . . about 3 Dec. „
Mustapha Fazyl, replaced by Mehemet Ruchdi about 15 Jan. 1871
The Black Sea question settled by the conference at London (see *Russia*) . . 13 March, „
Omar Pacha, general, dies . . 18 April, „
Insurrection in Yemen, subdued . . May, „
Great fires at Constantinople . . 7 June, „
Aali Pacha, grand vizier, an able statesman, dies 6 Sept. „
Mahmoud Pacha, grand vizier . . Sept. „
Tunis made an integral part of the empire, by decree . . . . 23 Oct. „

Political reforms inaugurated by the new ministry Nov. 1871
Important speech of the sultan to his council respecting the finances ; . . . 16 May, 1872
Mahmoud Pacha, grand vizier, having made enemies through dismissing foreign employés,&c., is dismissed and replaced by Midhat Pacha, about 30 July, „
Midhat Pacha, who favoured Austria, dismissed ; replaced by Mehemet Ruchdi . . 19 Oct. „
Essad Pacha, grand vizier, 15 Feb.; Mehemet Ruchdi again . . . . . April, 1873
The Roumelian railway connecting Constantinople, Adrianople, &c., opened . . . 17 June, „
The sultan's jewels, &c. (valued at 8,000,000*l*.) exhibited at Vienna . . . . . Aug. „
The shah of Persia arrives at Constantinople 19 Aug. „
Inability to raise a loan ; the sultan gives up a large sum ; great financial reforms proposed . Oct. „
Turkish aggressions on South Arabia checked by Great Britain . . . . . Nov. „
Great improvements in the army ; formation of reserves . . . . „
Hussein Avni, pacha ; made grand vizier . Feb. 1874
Improved financial arrangements reported April, „
The sultan ill ; he recognises his nephew Murad as successor . . . . about 5 Oct. „
Austria, Germany, and Russia inform Turkey that they consider they have the right to conclude separate treaties with Roumania . 20 Oct. „
Mésondivé or *Mesoudiyé*, Turkish ironclad, launched at Blackwall . . . . . 28 Oct. „
Turkish debt 3,000,000*l*. in 1854 ; 180,000,000*l*. „
Budget : estimated receipts, 21,711,764*l*.; expenditure, 26,299,178*l*. . . . June, 1875
Insurrection in Herzegovina (*which see*) ; great excitement in Bosnia, Servia, and Montenegro July-Aug. „
Mahmoud Pacha made grand vizier, with a strong ministry, about . . . . . 25 Aug. „
Decree (in consequence of the deficit of 5,000,000*l*. in the budget) that for 5 years half the interest on the debt be paid in cash and half in 5 per cent. bonds . . . . 6 Oct. „
Circular note remitting taxes and promising economical and commercial reform, 7 Oct. ; another stating object of the government to stop onerous loans, develop the resources of the empire, &c., 20 Oct. „
Remonstrances of British and Russian ambassadors with the government respecting expenditure and treatment of Christian subjects . Sept.-Nov. „
Raschid Pasha new foreign minister . Nov. „
Midhat Pasha, reformer, resigns . 4 Dec. „
Firman issued; ordering great reforms, equality of rights to Christians, &c. . . Dec. „
Note of Andrassy, Austrian minister, respecting reforms, 30 Dec. ; adopted by Germany and Russia, Jan. ; by Great Britain, 18 Jan. ; transmitted to the porte, about 7 Feb., agreed to . 10 Feb. 1876
Payment of April dividends deferred to July April 11 „
Insurrection in Bulgaria, promoted by foreign agitators, 1, 2 May ; quickly suppressed by troops sent 7 May ; about 65 villages burnt by the Bashi-bazouks, and other Turkish troops; several towns destroyed ; about 15,000 persons killed ; atrocious cruelties to women and children ; a few Turks killed by Bulgarians in self-defence (report by Mr. Schuyler, *see below*) . . . May, „
Riots at Constantinople ; the softas, fanatical students, and others, demand reforms ; their cry, "Turkey for the Turks ;" ministerial changes ; Mahmoud Pacha, the grand vizier, replaced by Mehemet Ruchdi; Europeans much alarmed 10 May *et seq.* „
British fleet arrives in Besika Bay . 26 May, „
Meeting at Berlin of ministers of Austria, Germany, and Russia ; they agree to a note to Turkey, requiring an armistice of two months, and other measures, 11, 12 May ; the note accepted by France and Italy, not by Great Britain, 19 May ; not presented through the revolution . 30 May, „
The grand vizier Mehemet Ruchdi, Hussein Avni, and Midhat Pacha, request the sultan to give up some of his treasure to save the nation from

ruin; he refuses and is deposed, 29 May; his nephew proclaimed as Murad V.; joyfully accepted by the people, and recognised by the western powers . . . . . 30 May, *et seq.* 1876
Manifesto recognising the danger of the empire through misgovernment, and promising amendment . . . . 2 June, „
Abdul-Aziz recognises Murad; said to have committed suicide by cutting arteries in the arm; said to be insane; (decided, by trial, to have been murdered; *see below*, June, 1881) . 4 June, „
Assassination of Hussein Avni, the war minister, Raschid Pacha, the foreign minister, and others, by Hassan, a disgraced Circassian officer, 15 June, who is hanged . . . . 17 June, „
Declaration of war by Servia, 1 July; by Montenegro . . . . 2 July, „
Tchernayeff and Servians enter Turkey; battle at Saitschar or Zaicar; Turks said to have the advantage . . . . 3 July, „
Severe conflict of Turks with Servians at Yavor, near Novi Bazar, 6 July; with Montenegrins at Nevesinje . . . . 27 July, „
League in aid of Turkish Christians formed in London . . . . 27 July, „
Mukhtar Pacha defeated by prince Nikita at Urba or Urbitza in Herzegovina . . . 28 July, „
Issue of paper money announced . . 28 July, „
Several days' conflict; the Turks enter Servia, and capture Gurgosavatz; Servians retreat 7 Aug. „
Turkish barbarities in Bulgaria reported by *Daily News'* correspondent, substantiated by report of Mr. Schuyler, the American commissioner from Constantinople, dated . . . . . 10 Aug. „
Asserted victory of prince Nikita at Medun, near Kutchi, about . . . . 14 Aug. „
Advance of the Turks under Abdul-Kerim Pacha upon Alexinatz; severe fighting, 9 Aug.
. . . . 19-30 Aug. „
Servia invites the mediation of the guaranteeing powers, about . . . . 24 Aug. „
Murad V. deposed on account of bad health; his brother Abdul-Hamid II. proclaimed 31 Aug. „
The great powers propose an immediate armistice, the restoration of the *status quo ante bellum*, payment of an indemnity by Servia, &c.; memorandum presented . . . . 3, 4 Sept. „
Servians said to be severely beaten before Alexinatz 1, 2 Sept.; continued indecisive fighting . „
Armistice till 25 Sept. agreed to about . 17 Sept. „
Prince Milan proclaimed king by the army at Deligrad; disapproved . . . . . 16 Sept. „
Report of Mr. Baring, the British commissioner in Bulgaria, published . . . . . . 19 Sept. „
[It establishes the facts "that a ferocious Mussulman soldiery, in revenge for a feeble and abortive insurrection, were let loose on the inhabitants of a large province; that the population were barbarously massacred, men, women, and children included; and that during the storm of savage fury crimes of all descriptions and outrages unmentionable were perpetrated on the inhabitants."—*Times*.]
Firm incisive despatch from Lord Derby to Sir H. Elliot, referring to Mr. Baring's report, proposing longer armistice, &c. . . . . . 21 Sept. „
The porte receives the propositions of the six great powers . . . . 26 Sept. „
Lord Derby informs the deputation from the city of London that, in regard to the Eastern question, the government is labouring for local self-government for the Turkish provinces in Europe, equal treatment of Mahometans and Christians, better administration for both, security for life and property, and effectual guarantees against repetition of outrages . . . . 27 Sept. „
Servia rejects the renewal of the armistice; Tchernayeff and army dominant; fighting renewed, 26, 27 Sept. „
Servian attacks on the Turks near Alexinatz severely repulsed . . . . 28, 29 Sept. „
In reply to the great powers the porte declines an armistice, opposes administrative autonomy to the provinces as impracticable, proposes a senate, and guarantees incisive reforms . . 2 Oct. „
Mukhtar Pacha said to defeat Montenegrines. 7 Oct. „
Montenegrine victory at Danilograd . 13 Oct. „

Turkey's proposal of an armistice for 6 months, 10 Oct.; declined by Russia, who proposes 4 to 6 weeks, longer being injurious to commerce, &c. . . . . 14 Oct. 1876.
Continued fighting, generally unfavourable to Servians . . . . 15-19 Oct. „
Alexinatz bombarded . . . . 16-19 Oct. „
Medun surrenders to Montenegrines . 20 Oct. „
Krevet taken by Turks . . . . 21 Oct. „
Result of fighting very favourable to Turks 19-24 Oct. „
Alleged conspiracy at Constantinople against the reform ministry; many arrests . about 23 Oct. „
Important Turkish successes in the valley of the Morava . . . . 19-24 Oct. „
Servians and Russians defeated; armies under Tchernayeff and Horvaritch divided, 19-24 Oct.;
Djunis taken by Turks; Deligrad untenable; severe Russian loss . . . . 29 Oct. „
Neutral despatch of lord Derby . dated 30 Oct. „
Alexinatz captured by Turks; Russian ultimatum given, demanding 6 weeks' armistice within 48 hours . . . . dated 31 Oct. „
Armistice for two months signed . . 1 Nov. „
Deligrad captured by Turks, now virtually masters of Servia . . . . 1 Nov. „
Pacific declaration of the czar to lord Aug. Loftus, 2 Nov. „
Deligrad evacuated by Turks; farewell address of Tchernayeff to officers, exhorting to constancy, 4 Nov. „
Czar's speech at Moscow; he will act independently if guarantees are not obtained . . 10 Nov. „
Marquis of Salisbury appointed special ambassador for conference at Constantinople; he arrives at Paris, 18 Nov.; Berlin, 20 Nov.; Vienna, 24 Nov.; Rome, 29 Nov.; Constantinople . 5 Dec. „
Alleged abortive conspiracy to restore Murad, about 8 Dec. „
Preliminary meetings of conference of representatives of six great powers begin (Great Britain, Russia, Austria, Germany, France, and Italy), 12 Dec. „
Ruchdi Pacha, grand vizier, replaced by Midhat Pacha, a reformer . . . . . 19 Dec. „
Armistice extended to Feb. 1877 . . „
New political constitution proclaimed: (chief provisions: indivisibility of the empire; the sultan supreme; individual liberty; freedom of all creeds, of the press, and of education; equal legal taxation; a senate and two chambers; general elections by ballot every fourth year; irremovable judges, &c.) . . . . 23 Dec. „
Opening of the conference . . . 23 Dec. „
Financial decree of 6 Oct. 1875, abrogated, 27 Dec. „
Armistice extended to 1 March . . 28 Dec. „
The great national council of Turkey rejects the propositions of the conference, 18 Jan.; it closes, 20 Jan.; chief ambassadors leave soon after 22 Jan. 1877
Negotiations for peace opened with Servia and Montenegro . . . . . . about 26 Jan. „
Midhat Pacha, the grand vizier, dismissed and banished; succeeded by Edhem Pacha (educated at Paris); reforms to go on . . . 5 Feb. „
Gortschakoff's circular to great powers, inquiring what they intend to do, signed 19 Jan.; published . . . . about 7 Feb. „
Protocols of the conference published in *Times*, &c. early in Feb. „
In Turkey "there is no aristocracy, no governing class; no organised democracy; no representative government," (marquis of Salisbury) 20 Feb. „
Peace with Servia signed . . . 1 March, „
First Turkish parliament opened: 30 senators, 90 deputies; speech from the sultan read, 19 March, „
Gen. Ignatieff visits Berlin, Paris, London, Vienna, &c. . . . . March, „
Protocol signed for six powers: principles—to wait for Turkish reforms and watch; conditional disarmament in Russia and Turkey (voidable under certain conditions) . . . . . 31 March, „
Protocol rejected by Turkey, 12 April; justificatory circular sent to the powers; Mr. Layard sent as temporary ambassador to Turkey . April, „
Insurrection of Mirdites or Miridites, April; armistice with Montenegro not renewed . 13 April, „
Arrival of Mr. Layard as ambassador, at Constanti-

nople; he affirms the neutrality of Great Britain, about 24 April, 1877
War declared by Russia (see *Russo-Turkish war, 1877*) . . . . . . 24 April, ,,
Riotous manifestation by the softas, soon subsides, 24 May, ,,
A *jihad* or holy war against Russia propounded by the sheikh-ul-Islam . . . about 28 May, ,,
Suleiman Pacha successful in Montenegro; relieves Nicksics, besieged . . . May, *et seq.* ,,
Miridite leaders captured . . . June, ,,
The parliament closed without a speech. 28 June, ,,
Safvet Pacha, foreign minister, replaced by Aarifi Pacha . . . . . about 18 July, ,,
Other ministerial changes . . . July, ,,
Protests against alleged Russian atrocities, July, —Aug. ,,
Bosnian revolt reported to be ended . Aug. ,,
Proclamation for increase of army by 150,000— Christians and others to serve . 26 Nov. ,,
Reported intrigues at Constantinople by peace and war parties . . . . . Nov. ,,
The sultan issues a rather vague proclamation of amnesty to Bulgaria . . about 27 Nov. ,,
Surrender of Plevna, 10 Dec.; circular note to the great powers requesting mediation . . 12 Dec. ,,
Parliament opened; the sultan's speech censures the war, and praises his generals and soldiers, 13 Dec. ,,
The ministry censured, resigns; still holds office; Suleiman dismissed; crisis at Constantinople, 5, 6, 7 Jan. 1878
Hamed Pacha, grand vizier . . 11 Jan. ,,
New ministry under Ahmed Nefik; grand vizierslip abolished . . . . . 4, 5 Feb. ,,
British fleet enter the Dardanelles without permission of the sultan . . . . 13 Feb. ,,
The parliament dissolved by the sultan . 14 Feb. ,,
Insurrection in Crete, Thessaly, Epirus, &c. (see *Greece*) . . . . Feb., March, ,,
Treaty of peace with Russia signed at San Stefano (see *Stefano*), 3 March; ratified at St. Petersburg, 17 March, ,,
Osman Pacha honourably received by the sultan, 24 March, ,,
Grand-duke Nicholas and the sultan exchange visits at Constantinople . . . 26 March, ,,
Ahmed Nefik replaced by Sadyk as prime minister, about 18 April, ,,
Insurrection near Rhodope, in Roumelia, against Russians going on; see *Rhodope* . April, ,,
Insurrection (said doubtfully to be in favour of the ex-sultan Murad) in Constantinople, suppressed; Ali Suavi, a softa and fanatical reformer, with others, killed . . . . 20 May, ,,
Public offices, &c., at Constantinople destroyed by fire; attributed to incendiaries . 22 May, ,,
Office of grand vizier revived for Mehemet Ruchdi, May; soon replaced by Safvet . 29 May, ,,
Secret agreement between the marquis of Salisbury and count Schouvaloff, Russian ambassador, 30 May, ,,
Secret British convention with Turkey (defensive alliance); if by the treaty of Berlin, Russia acquires Kars, Ardahan, or Batoum, Great Britain is to join the sultan in arms in defending his dominions, he engaging to reform his government; Cyprus to be held by Great Britain till Russia returns its acquisitions . . . 4 June, ,,
Cyprus ceded to Great Britain . 3 July, ,,
Berlin conference meets, 13 June; treaty signed (see *Berlin*) . . . . 13 July, ,,
A conspiracy against the sultan suppressed, about 10 July, ,,
A ministerial crisis ends; the vizier Safvet Pacha's policy approved by the sultan, who gives him a present; ratification of the treaty of Berlin announced . . . . . . 4 Aug. ,,
Trial of Suleiman Pacha for misconduct during the war begun . . . . . Aug. ,,
The Turks said to be grossly ill treated in Bulgaria, and other surrendered places . . Aug. ,,
Safvet Pacha's circular to foreign powers refusing to recognise Greek proposal for annexation of Candia, Thessaly, &c. . . . 8 Aug. ,,
Murder of Mehemet Ali Pacha at Ipek, near Scutari, by Albanian rioters . . . 6 Sept. ,,

Alleged conspiracies on behalf of the ex-sultan Murad; instigated by the ulemas, about 10 Sept. 1878
Albanian leader with 40,000 men said to be ruling from Janina to Montenegro . . 12 Sept. ,,
German circular to the powers on Turkish delays in carrying out the Berlin treaty . middle Sept. ,,
The sultan accepts the reforms proposed by the British government; announced . 24 Oct. ,,
Insurrectionary movements in Macedonia Oct. ,,
Midhat Pacha appointed governor-general of Syria, to inaugurate reforms . . about 11 Nov. ,,
Suleiman Pacha sentenced to degradation and imprisonment, 2 Dec.; absolved the sultan 4 Dec. ,,
New ministry; Kheredine Pacha (grand vizier); Caratheodori, and others . . 4 Dec. ,,
Macedonian insurrection ended . . 3 Jan. 1879
Definitive treaty of peace with Russia, signed 8 Feb. ,,
British fleet leaves the sea of Marmora March, ,,
Definitive treaty with Austria, published 26 May, ,,
Mahmoud Nedem, old statesman, returns to Constantinople on invitation . . . 30 June, ,,
Kheredine, Caratheodori, and others compelled to resign through opposition of the assembly of Ulemas (their policy said to be against the Khoran); succeeded by Aarifi Pacha 28, 29 July, ,,
The Russians evacuate Turkey . July, Aug. ,,
New ministry under Said Pacha . 18, 19 Oct. ,,
Pressure for reforms put upon the government by the British; admiral Hornby and the fleet enter Turkish waters; quit . . . early in Nov. ,,
Baker Pacha appointed inspector-general of gendarmerie in Asia Minor . announced 18 Nov. ,,
Great financial depression . . Nov. Dec. ,,
Official relations with Great Britain temporarily suspended on account of the imprisonment of Dr. Köller, a German missionary, and Ahmed Tewfik, who assisted him in translations . 31 Dec. ,,
Successful intervention of sir A. H. Layard, 1-10 Jan. 1880
Note of Savas Pacha to the Powers acknowledging corruptions in judicial affairs and promising efficient reforms (in *Times*) . . 30 Jan. ,,
Col. and Mrs. Synge (distributors of relief to Mussulmans) captured by Greek brigands, near Salonica, about 19 Feb.; released for 10,000*l.* about 24 March, ,,
Mr. Göschen sent as temporary ambassador; arrives at Constantinople . . 28 May, ,,
New ministry under Kadri Pacha . about 8 June, ,,
Identic note from European powers, 11 June; given in . . . . . 12 June, ,,
Osman Pacha, war minister, dismissed about 10 July, ,,
Naval demonstration by the European powers at Dulcigno, suggested by earl Granville July, ,,
Collective note of the Berlin conference presented 15 July, ,,
Madame Skobeleff, mother of the Russian general, robbed and murdered near Philippopolis by Ouzalis, a Russian . . . 18 July, ,,
Midhat Pacha, governor of Syria, and Hamed Pacha of Smyrna exchange offices . . Aug. ,,
Collective note from the powers urging cession of Dulcigno, &c., to Montenegro, and proposing to aid the prince in taking possession . 3 Aug. ,,
The ministry modified under Said Pacha, premier 12 Sept. ,,
A final note from the powers respecting cession of Dulcigno to Montenegro, delivered 15 Sept. ,,
Admiral Beauchamp Seymour, commander of combined fleet at Ragusa, sent to make a demonstration near Dulcigno . . . 20 Sept. ,,
The sultan refuses to surrender Dulcigno; the French decline to partake in attack on the town, about 27 Sept. ,,
Note from the sultan limiting his concessions and resisting coercion; presented . 3 Oct. ,,
Immediate cession of Dulcigno ordered by the sultan, about 23 Oct.; effected . . 26 Nov. ,,
The combined fleet disperses . . 4 Dec. ,,
Note from the sultan to the powers respecting the Greeks arming . . . . 14 Dec. ,,
Circular from the powers recommending arbitration, 24 Dec. 1880; declined by Turkey and Greece . . . . early in Jan 1881

Circular from Turkey proposing conference at Constantinople &c. . . . . about 15 Jan. 1881
Notes from the powers presented . . 21 Feb. ,,
Conference at Constantinople; agreement between Turkey and the powers; proposals referred to Athens . . . . 30 March, ,,
Mr. Henry Suter, engaged in mines, seized by brigands at Cassandra, in Salonica, about 8 April, ,,
Rebellion in Albania (which see) suppressed May, ,,
Midhat Pacha's palace surrounded by soldiers; he escapes and appeals to the powers . 17 May, ,,
The sultan protests against French invasion of Tunis (which see) . . . . . May, ,,
Midhat surrenders, claiming a fair trial about 17 May, ,,
Turkey protests against the Tunis treaty of 12 May May, ,,
Mr. Suter's release for 15,000l. ransom announced 23 May, ,,
Convention between Turkey and Greece arranged at Constantinople settling frontiers; Thessaly ceded by Turkey . . . . 24 May, ,,
Mr. Göschen leaves Constantinople; his mission successful; succeeded by lord Dufferin, 26 May; who arrives at Constantinople, . 15 June, ,,
Trial of Midhat Pacha and others for murder of the late sultan Abdul-Aziz; convicted; Mustapha Fahri Bey and Hadj Mehmed actual assassins; others, Mahmond and Nouri Pachas, the sultan's brothers-in-law, Midhat Pacha, and others accomplices . . . . 27, 28 June, ,,
Sentence; death to all except two subordinates to imprisonment . . . . . 29 June, ,,
Turco-Greek convention ceding Thessaly to Greece, signed at Constantinople . . 2 July, ,,
The trial of Midhat and others said to be a mockery; punishment commuted to exile on intercession of the British Government; announced 31 July, ,,
The captors of Mr. Suter taken in Greece, about 15 Aug. ,,
Turkish mission at Cairo . . . . 7-18 Oct. ,,
Continued negotiations at Constantinople respecting national debt . . . . Oct. et seq. ,,
The German vessel *Vulcan* laden with dynamite (said to belong to Russia) cargo unshipped near Constantinople . . . . about 8 Oct. ,,
Decree signed for a satisfactory settlement of the national debt . . . . . . 28 Dec. ,,
Capt. Selby, R.N., wounded by Albanians at Artaki, announced 16 Feb.; died . . . 20 Feb. 1892
Mehemet Ruchdi Pasha dies . . . 26 March, ,,
Russian-war indemnity convention ratified 6 May, ,,
The minister Said Pasha dismissed, succeeded by Abdurrahman Pasha, about 2 May; who resigns 7 July, ,,
Said Pasha reinstated . . . about 8 July, ,,
Sultan protests against bombardment of forts at Alexandria (see *Egypt*) . . about 11 July, ,,
Protracting negotiations respecting a military convention; agreed to . . . . 29 Aug. ,,
Alleged conspiracy of Fuad Pasha and others to dethrone the sultan . . . about 28 Nov. ,,
Said Pasha dismissed; Circassian guard dismissed 29 Nov. ,,
Frontier disputes with Montenegro . Nov. ,,
Said Pasha restored with honours, made grand Vizier 3 Dec. Fuad Pasha restored to favour 7 Dec. ,,
Excitement of the sultan through dread of assassination . . . . . about 13 Dec. ,,
Fight among the sultan's body guard, (Albanians and Negroes) about 30 killed or wounded 17 Jan. 1883
Turkish note to the powers against British Egyptian circular . . . . . about 23 Jan. ,,
Difficulties with the Greek church respecting political reforms; resignation of the Œcumenical Patriarch Yoachim II.; not accepted; conciliation proposed . . . 29 Dec.-3 Jan. 1884
Resignation maintained . . . . 9 Jan. ,,
Amicable settlement of dispute, announced April, ,,
The Imperial prince and princess of Austria hospitably entertained by the sultan . . April, ,,
Death of Midhat Pasha, great statesman and reformer in exile, aged 62 . . . . May, ,,
Circular to the six great powers announcing the stoppage of the post offices in Constantinople,

20 July, resisted; the Turkish arrangements fail, and are withdrawn . . . . Aug. 1884
Sir Edward Thornton appointed to succeed lord Dufferin . . . . Sept. ,,
Greek patriarch elected . . . . 13 Oct. ,,
Mutiny of troops at Monastir, for want of pay and clothing; settled by concession . about 21 Nov. ,,
Petitions to the sultan from Macedonia, respecting Turkish atrocities signed . . . 12 Oct. ,,
Hassan Fehmy Pasha sent to London to confer on the Egyptian question; his proposals not received, end of . . . . . . Jan. 1885
Turkey protests against Italian occupation of Massowah on the Red Sea . . about 23 Feb. ,,
New tariff with England signed . . 9 July, ,,
Sir H. D. Wolff arrives at Constantinople on a mission respecting Egypt, 22 Aug.; well received by the Sultan . . . . . 29 Aug. ,,
Revolution in Roumelia (which see), 18 Sept.; firm Turkish note to the powers about 22 Sept. ,,
Said Pasha, grand vizier, and other ministers dismissed; succeeded by Kiamil Pasha, 24 Sept. ,,
Conference of ambassadors, 4 Oct.; the ambassadors present a collective note condemning the revolution in Roumelia as breaking the treaty of Berlin, 14 Oct. ,,
Decree for Turkish commission to go with sir H. D. Wolff to Cairo, about 12 Oct.; convention signed . . . . . . 24 Oct. ,,
Turkey asks assistance of the powers to settle the Roumelian affair . . . . 19 Oct. ,,
Conference of ambassadors at Constantinople, 5 Nov.; collective declaration for maintenance of *status quo ante*, about 7 Nov.; division of opinion as to enforcement. . . . . ,,
Rustem Pasha succeeds Musurus Pasha (1856-85) as ambassador in London . . . Nov. ,,
The Sultan ratifies the treaty between Bulgaria and Servia . . . . 13 March, 1886
Sir Edward Thornton, British ambassador, received by the Sultan . . . . 11 March, ,,
Hobart Pasha, Turkish admiral, dies, aged 64, 19 June, ,,
Sir William White appointed British ambassador, Oct.; received . . . . . 2 Nov. ,,
Four English gentlemen captured near Smyrna by brigands who demand 3,000l. ransom, 24 Sept.; released by payment of a ransom of 750l. 26 Sept. 1887
Reported deficit of 1,000,000l. in the budget; increase of brigandage . . . . Nov. ,,
After the celebration of the feast of Mevlud, the Sultan delivers an optimist speech to the officials on the state of the empire . 27 Nov. ,,
Direct railway communication between London and Constantinople via Dover and Calais in 94 hours; first train from Vienna . 12-14 Aug. 1888
The government contracts a loan for 1,350,000l. from the "German" bank; consequent rupture with the Ottoman bank, its usual financial agent, Oct. ,,

See *Candia, Egypt, Greece, Montenegro*, and *Servia*.

TURKISH SULTANS.

1299. Othman, Osman, or Ottoman, founded the empire, retained the title emir, but ruled despotically.
1326. Orchan, son, took the title "sultan."
1360. Amurath (or Murad), I.: stabbed by a soldier, of which wound he died.
1389. Bajazet I., Ilderim, son; defeated by Tamerlane, and died imprisoned.
1403. Solyman, son: dethroned by his brother.
1410. Musa-Chelebi: strangled.
1413. Mahomet I., son of Bajazet.
1421. Amurath II., son.
1451. Mahomet II., son: took Constantinople, 1453.
1481. Bajazet II., son.
1512. Selim I., son.
1520. Solyman I. or II., the Magnificent, son.
1566. Selim II., son.
1574. Amurath III., son: killed his five brothers; their mother, in grief, stabbed herself.
1595. Mahomet III., son: strangled all his brothers, and drowned his father's wives.
1603. Ahmed (or Achmet) I., son.
1617. Mustapha I., brother: deposed by the Janissaries, and imprisoned.
1618. Osman II., nephew: strangled by Janissaries.

1622. Mustapha I. again: again deposed, sent to the Seven Towers, and strangled.
1623. Amurath IV., brother of Osman II.
1640. Ibrahim, brother: strangled by the Janissaries.
1648. Mahomet IV., son: deposed by
1687. Solyman II. or III., brother.
1691. Ahmed (or Achmet) II., son of Ibrahim, nephew.
1695. Mustapha II., eldest son of Mahomet IV.: deposed.
1703. Ahmed (or Achmet) III., brother: deposed, and died in prison in 1736.
1730. Mahmud I. (or Mahomet V.), son of Mustapha II.
1754. Osman III., brother.
1757. Mustapha III., brother.
1774. Abdul-Ahmed or Hamid I. (or Achmet IV.) brother.
1789. Selim III., son of Mustapha III.; deposed by the Janissaries.
1807. Mustapha IV., son of Abdul-Ahmed; deposed, and, with the late sultan Selim, murdered.
1808. Mahmud II., or Mahomet VI., brother.
1839. Abdul-Medjid (son), 2 July (born 23 April, 1823); died 25 June, 1861.
1861. Abdul-Aziz, brother, born 9 Feb. 1830, deposed 29 May; alleged suicide 4 June, 1876 (see 1881).
1876. Amurath V. (Murad) son of Abdul-Medjid, born 21 Sept. 1840; proclaimed 30 May; deposed for bad health, 31 Aug.
,, Abdul-Hamid II., brother, 31 Aug. born 22 Sept., 1842.
["He is not a tyrant; he is not dissolute; he is not a bigot or corrupt."—*Lord Beaconsfield*, 27 July, 1878.]
Son: Mehemed Selim, born 11 Jan. 1870.

TURKEY TRADE, commenced in the year 1550. The Turkey or Levant Company of London was instituted by charter of Elizabeth, in 1579.

TURKEYS AND GUINEA FOWLS, first brought to England about 1523, and to France in 1570. Turkeys are natives of America, and were consequently unknown to the ancients.

TÜRKHEIM (E. France). Here the elector of Brandenburg and the Imperialists were defeated by the French under Turenne, 5 Jan. 1675.

TURKISH BATHS, see *Baths*.

TURKISH COMPASSIONATE FUND, instituted by the *Daily Telegraph*, and supported by lady Burdett Coutts, the abp. of Canterbury, and others, to relieve sufferers by the war, Aug. 1877.

TURKOMANS, see *White Sheep*, and *Turkestan*.

TURNER'S ACT, 13 & 14 Vict. c. 35 (1850), relates to the court of chancery.

TURNER'S LEGACIES. Joseph M. W. Turner, a great landscape painter, was born in April, 1775, and died 19 Dec. 1851. He bequeathed to the nation all the pictures and drawings collected by him and deposited at his residence, 47, Queen Anne-street, London, on condition that a suitable gallery should be erected for them within ten years; and directed his funded property to be expended in founding an asylum at Twickenham for decayed artists. The will was disputed by his relatives, but a compromise was made. The oil-paintings (100 in number) and the drawings (1400) were obtained by the nation, and the engravings and some other property were transferred to the next of kin. The drawings were cleaned and mounted under the careful superintendence of Mr. Ruskin, and the pictures were sent to Marlborough-house for exhibition. In 1861, many of the pictures were removed from the South Kensington Museum to the National Gallery, others in 1869. The sketches, plates, &c., of *Turner's Liber Studiorum*, were sold for about 20,000*l*. 28 March, 1873.

TURNING, see *Lathe*. In our dockyards, blocks and other materials for our ships of war are now produced by an almost instantaneous process, from rough pieces of oak, by the machinery of Mr. (afterwards sir Mark Isambard) Brunel (died 1849); see *Blocks*.

TURNPIKES, see *Tolls*.

TURPENTINE TREE, *Pistacia Terebinthus*, came from Barbary, before 1656. Spirits of turpentine were first applied, with success, to the rot in sheep; one-third of the spirit diluted with two-thirds water, 1772.

TURRET SHIPS, see *Navy of England*.

TUSCAN ORDER OF ARCHITECTURE, a debased Doric, used in Tuscany for buildings in which strength is chiefly required. *Wotton*.

TUSCANY, formerly a grand duchy in Central Italy, the northern part of the ancient Etruria (*which see*). It formed part of the Lombard kingdom, after the conquest of which by Charlemagne, 774, it was made a marquisate for Boniface about 828. His descendant, the great countess Matilda, bequeathed the southern part of her domains to the pope (1115). In the northern part (then called Tuscia), the cities, Florence, Pisa, Sienna, Lucca, &c., gradually became flourishing republics. Florence became the chief under the government of the Medici family; see *Florence*. The duchy in that family began in 1531; and the grand-duchy in 1569. After the extinction of the Medicis in 1737, Tuscany was given by the treaty of Vienna (1738) to Francis, duke of Lorraine (married to Maria Theresa of Austria in 1736), who had ceded his hereditary estates to France. Population in 1882, 2,226,265.

The French enter Florence	28 March, 1799
The grand-duke is dispossessed, and his dominions given to Louis duke of Parma (of the royal house of Spain), with the title of king of Etruria	1801
Tuscany incorporated with the French empire	1807
The grand-duchy given to Eliza, sister of Napoleon	1808
Ferdinand III. restored	1814
Lucca united to Tuscany	1847
Leopold II. grants a free constitution	15 Feb. 1848
Insurrection at Florence; republic proclaimed; the grand-duke flies	11 Feb. 1849
He is restored by the Austrians	July, 1850
Rigorous imprisonment of the Madiai, husband and wife, converts to protestantism, for reading the Bible	May, 1852
The earls of Shaftesbury and Roden and others in vain intercede for them at Florence	Oct. ,,
They are released after the intervention of the British government	March, 1853
[An annuity was provided for them by subscription.]	
The Tuscan army demand alliance with the Sardinians; the grand-duke refuses, and departs to Bologna; the king of Sardinia is proclaimed dictator, and a provisional government formed	27 April, 1859
The king assumes the command of the army, but declines the dictatorship	30 April, ,,
The Sardinian commissary Buoncompagni invested with the powers of government	11 May, ,,
Prince Napoleon arrives at Leghorn, addresses the Tuscans, and erects his standard	23 May, ,,
The grand-duke Leopold II. abdicates in favour of his son Ferdinand	21 July, ,,
Tuscan constituent assembly meets	11 Aug. ,,
It declares against the house of Lorraine, and votes for annexation to Sardinia	Sept. ,,
Prince Eugene of Savoy-Carignan elected governor-general of central Italy; he declines: but recommends Buoncompagni, Nov.; who is accepted by the Tuscans	8 Dec. ,,
Annexation to Sardinia voted by universal suffrage, 11, 12 March; decreed	22 March, 1860
Prince Eugene appointed governor	26 March, ,,

Florence made the capital of Italy, by decree published . . . . 11 Dec. 1864
(See *Italy*, and *Florence*.)

SOVEREIGNS OF TUSCANY.

DUKES.
1531. Alexander I.
1537. Cosmo I.

GRAND-DUKES.
1569. Cosmo I., *Medici*.
1574. Francis I.
1587. Ferdinand I.
1608. Cosmo II.
1621. Ferdinand II.
1670. Cosmo III. (visited England, and wrote an account of his travels).
1723. John Gaston (last of the Medici).
1737. Francis II. (duke of *Lorraine*), became emperor of Germany in 1745.
1765. Leopold I. (emperor in 1790).
1790. Ferdinand III. (second son of Leopold I.); expelled by the French in 1800.

KINGS OF ETRURIA.
1801. Louis I., duke of Parma.
1803. Louis II.

GRAND-DUCHESS.
1808-14. Eliza Bonaparte (married to Bacciochi, made prince of Lucca).

GRAND-DUKES.
1814. Ferdinand III. restored.
1824. Leopold II., 18 June (born 3 Oct. 1797; abdicated, 21 July, 1859), died 29 Jan. 1870.
1859. Ferdinand IV., 21 July (born 10 June, 1835); protested against the annexation of his grand duchy, 26 March, 1860.
Son : Leopold Ferdinand, born 2 Dec. 1868.

TUSCULUM (now Frascati), a city of Latium (S. Italy). The Tusculans supported Tarquinius Superbus against the Romans, by whom they were totally defeated, 497 B.C. The Tusculans, on account of their friendship with Rome, suffered much from the other Latins, who took their city, 374, but were severely chastised for it. Here Cicero during his retirement wrote his "Tusculanæ Disputationes," about 46 B.C.

TWELFTH-DAY, the feast of the Epiphany, or manifestation of Christ to the Gentiles, 6 Jan. ; see *Epiphany*.

TWELVE TABLES, see *Decemvirs*.

TWINS, joined together, have been born frequently, but seldom lived long. Helen-Judith, joined Hungarian twins, were born in 1715, and died in 1723. Millie-Christine, negro twins, born in North Carolina in 1851, were wholly distinct in the upper part of the body, but one in the lower part of the spinal column and pelvis ; the four legs obeying nerves from a common centre. They sang and danced well, and were named the "Two-headed Nightingale." The will, understanding, and conscience were distinct. Exhibited in London 17 Feb. 1885. See *Siamese Twins*.

TWIN-SHIP, see under *Steam*.

"TWOPENNY TRASH," a term given to W. Cobbett's *Weekly Political Register*, after 2 Nov. 1816, when he reduced the price from 12½d. to 2d., the sale greatly increased.

TYBURN (W. London), at the west end of Oxford-road (now street), the chief place in London for the execution of malefactors till 1783. Pennant (who died 1798) remembered Oxford-street as "a deep, hollow road, and full of sloughs, with here and there a ragged house, the lurking-place of cut-throats."

In conformity with an act passed in 1697, a so-called "Tyburn ticket" was given to the prosecutor of a criminal executed at Tyburn. The ticket gave exemption from serving on juries and parochial offices. The act was repealed in 1818.

"TYBURNIA" (a N.W. suburb of London), was built between 1839 and 1850, on the green fields and nursery grounds in Paddington belonging to the see of London.

TYLER'S INSURRECTION, in opposition to the poll-tax imposed on all persons above 15, 5 Nov. 1380. One of the collectors, acting with indecent rudeness to Wat Tyler's daughter, was struck dead by the father, June, 1381. His neighbours took arms, and in a short time almost the whole of the population of the southern and eastern counties rose, extorting freedom from their lords, and plundering. On 12 June, 1381, they gathered upon Blackheath to the number of 100,000 men, and on 14 June murdered Simon of Sudbury, archbishop of Canterbury, and sir Robert Hales, the royal treasurer. The king, Richard II., invited Tyler to a parley, which took place on the 15th at Smithfield, where the latter addressed the king in a menacing manner, now and again lifting up his sword. On this the mayor, Walworth, stunned Tyler with a blow of his mace, and one of the king's knights dispatched him. Richard temporised with the multitude by promising a charter, and thus led them out of the city, when sir R. Knollys and a band of knights attacked and dispersed them with much slaughter. The insurrection in Norfolk and Suffolk was subdued by the bishop of Norwich, and 1500 of the rebels were executed.

TYNDALE MEMORIAL. A statue of William Tyndale, protestant martyr, translator of the new testament, published 1525, was set up on the Thames Embankment in 1883. Sculptor, Mr. J. E. Boehm.

TYNEMOUTH, Northumberland. Here are remains of a monastery built by king Edwin, 625; destroyed by the Danes; rebuilt by king Egfrid, 671-85; often ravaged by Danes, 795-993; refounded and made a castle, by Rob. de Mowbray, 1090; plundered by Scots, 1316 and 1389; fortified for Charles I., 1642; taken by Scots, 1644; finally ruined, 1665; and made a depot, 1783. The chapel has been restored. Tynemouth was made a borough, returning one member to parliament, 1832. An aquarium, winter-garden, &c., was opened, 27 Aug. 1878.

TYPE-COMPOSING MACHINES, see under *Printing*, 1842-72.

TYPE-FOUNDING, see under *Printing*, 1452, 1720.

TYPE-WRITERS. M. Foucault sent to the Paris exhibition of 1855, a writing-machine for the blind; and several were invented by Wheatstone. After successive improvements, Messrs. Remington, in America, in 1873, contracted to construct 25,000. The speed is said to have been raised to seventy-five words a minute.

The action of the type-writer somewhat resembles that of a pianoforte. Pressure upon a key marked with a letter raises a hammer with a type-cut letter, which presses upon paper ; provision is made for inking the type, shifting, &c.

The Hall type-writer exhibited in London, 1883.
Mr. E. Peacock's new compact and expeditious type writer exhibited in April, 1885.
T. G. and H. Daw's type-writer for reporters commended May, 1885.
Hammond type-writer 1886.
The "Simplex" type-writer (cost about 10s. 6d.) introduced into London by a company April, 1887.
A speed contest with the Remington type-writer at St. James's Hall ; several prizes awarded by the proprietors Messrs. Wyckoff & Co. Jan. 1889.

TYRANT. In early Greek history, the term was applied to any man who governed with irresponsible power. Solon objected to the term, and chose the name Archōn (ruler), 594 B.C. The earliest tyrants were those at Sicyon, beginning with Cleisthenes, in the 7th century B.C. Tyranny declined in Greece about 490 B.C., and revived after the close of the Peloponnesian war, 404 B.C.; see *Thirty Tyrants*.

TYRE (Phœnicia), a great city, said to have been first built by Agenor. Another city was built 1257 (about 2267, *Hales*) B.C. It was besieged by the Assyrians, who retired from before it, after a siege of upwards of five years, 713 B.C. Taken by Nebuchadnezzar, 572 B.C., and the city demolished, when the Tyrians removed to an opposite island, and built a new and magnificent city. It was taken by Alexander with much difficulty, after a siege of seven months, July, 332 B.C. He joined the island to the continent by a mole. *Strabo.* Tyre was captured by the Crusaders, 7 July, 1124; by the French, 3 April, 1799; and by the allied fleet, during the war against Mehemet Ali, 1841.

TYRE, ERA OF, began on 19 Oct. 125 B.C., with the month of Hyperberetæus. The months were the same as those used in the Grecian era, and the year is similar to the Julian year. To reduce this era to ours, subtract 124; and if the given year be less than 125, deduct it from 125, and the remainder will be the year before Christ.

TYROL, the eastern part of ancient Rhætia, now a province of the Austrian empire, was ceded to the house of Hapsburg in 1359 by Margaret, the heiress of the last count. It became an appanage of the younger (or Tyrol) branch of the imperial house, which came to the throne in the person of Maximilian II., in 1618. The French conquered the Tyrol in 1805, and united it to Bavaria; but in 1809 an insurrection broke out, headed by Andrew Hofer, an innkeeper, who drove the Bavarians out of the Tyrol, thoroughly defeated some French detachments, but laid down his arms at the treaty of Vienna. He was subsequently accused of corresponding with the Austrians, captured and sent to Mantua, and there shot by order of the French government, 20 Feb. 1810. The Austrian emperor ennobled his family in 1819, and erected his statue in Innsbruck in 1834. The Tyrolese riflemen were very effective in the Italian war in 1859. The Arlberg tunnel railway from Innsbruck to Bregenz inaugurated by the emperor 20 Sept. 1884.

TYRONE (near Ulster, N. Ireland), formerly the territories of the O'Neills, and the seat of the insurrection in 1641.

TYRRHENI, included the ancient Etruscans, and other tribes, said to have come from Lydia, Asia Minor.

U.

UBIQUITARIANS.

UBIQUITARIANS or **UBIQUARIANS**, a small German sect, originated by John Breutius about 1560, who asserted that the body of Christ was present everywhere (*ubique*).

UGANDA. A kingdom in Equatorial Africa, near the head of the Nile. The king Mtesa, who acted in a friendly manner towards Grant, Speke, Stanley, and other travellers, and missionaries, died 10 Oct. 1884. He was succeeded by his son Mwanga, who, suspicious of European interference, killed the missionary bishop Hannington for advancing by a new route, about 29 Oct. 1885. Severe persecution of native christians who show much constancy; many killed, June, *et seq.*, 1886. Mission still maintained by the Rev. E. C. Gordon, nephew of the late bishop, Oct. 1887.
Revolution with bloodshed; Mwanga deposed and replaced by his brother Klwewa (Oct.) whose attempts to revive his father's policy are frustrated by the Arab slave-dealers; much persecution ensues; the Europeans flee and their settlements are destroyed Nov. 1888. King Klwewa resists the Arabs, and is expelled, they set up his brother Kilema; civil war Nov. 1888.

UHLANS, the German lancers, very effective in the war in 1870.

UKRAINE (Polish for a frontier), a vast fertile plain in Russia, ceded to the Cossacks by Poland in 1672, and obtained by Russia in 1682. The country was divided, Poland having the west side of the Dnieper, and Russia the east. The whole country was assigned to Russia by the treaty of partition in 1795.

ULM, in Würtemberg, S. Germany, where a PEACE was signed, 3 July, 1620, by which Frederick V. lost Bohemia (having been driven from it previously). Ulm was taken by the French in 1796. After a battle between the French and Austrians, in which the latter, under general Mack, were defeated with dreadful loss by marshal Ney, Ulm surrendered with 28,000 men, the flower of the Austrian army, 17-20 Oct. 1805.

ULPHILAS'S BIBLE, see under *Bible*.

ULSTER, the N. division of Ireland. After the death of Strongbow, 1176, John de Courcy was made earl of Ulster; Hugh de Lacy was earl, 1243; and Walter de Burgh, 1264; whose descendant, Elizabeth, married Lionel, son of Edward III., 1352. He thus became earl of Ulster. In 1611, the British colonisation of the forfeited lands (termed the *Ulster settlements* or *plantations*) began, much land being granted to the corporation of London; see *Irish Society*. The consequent rebellion of the Irish chieftains, Roger More, Phelim O'Neale, McGuire, earl of Inniskillen, and others, broke out on 23 Oct. 1641 (see *Ireland*).—*Ulster King of Arms* appointed for Ireland, 1553.—By the ancient "Ulster tenant-right," the outgoing tenant of a farm received from his successor a sum of money for the privilege of occupancy. A modified form of this right was adopted in the Irish land act, passed 8 July, 1870.

ULTRAMONTANISTS (from *ultra montes*, beyond the mountains), a term originally applied in France to those who upheld the extreme authority of the pope in opposition to the freedom of the Gallican church, which had been secured by various bulls, and especially by the concordat of 15 July, 1801. Ultramontanists now are those who maintain the *official* infallibility of the bishop of Rome.

ULUNDI, Zululand, South Africa. On 4 July, 1879, the Zulus, commanded by their king, Cetywayo, who had refused the conditions of peace, were totally defeated near here by lord Chelmsford, after a severe conflict. Capt. Wyatt-Edgell, 17 Lancers, and 9 men were killed, and about 53 wounded. The British were attacked in the open country by the Zulus, who enveloped our hollow square and charged on all sides up to within 60 yards, when they broke and fled under the heavy fire. They were pursued and routed by cavalry. About 23,000 Zulus engaged, 1,500 killed. The British showed much firmness and the Zulus displayed great courage. The royal kraal at Ulundi and other military kraals were burnt.

UMBRELLA, described in early dictionaries as "a portable pent-house to carry in a person's hand to screen him from violent rain or heat." Umbrellas appear in the carvings at Persepolis. Niebuhr saw a great Arabian prince returning from a mosque, he and each of his family having a large umbrella carried by his side. Old chinaware shows the Chinese shaded by umbrellas. It is said that the first person who generally used an umbrella in the streets of London was the benevolent Jonas Hanway, who died in 1786.
John Macdonald, a footman, who wrote his own life, informs us that he had "a fine silk umbrella, which he brought from Spain; but he could not with any comfort to himself use it, the people calling out, 'Frenchman! why don't you get a coach?'" The hackney-coachmen and chairmen were clamorous against their rival. The footman says he "persisted for three months, till they took no further notice of this novelty. Foreigners began to use theirs; and then the English." 1778.
Mr. Samuel Fox, inventor of the hollow-steel paragon frame, strong, light, and elastic, having made a great fortune, especially at Lille in France, died 25 Feb. 1887. In 1885 Mr. Gladstone's political programme was termed his *umbrella*, by lord Rosebery.

UNCLAIMED MONEY, &c., a pamphlet with this title published by Mr. Edward Preston in 1886, describes six classes and recommends legislation to facilitate publication for the benefit of claimants.
1.—Dividends on government East India and Colonial stocks (government stocks 4 Jan. 1887, 537,815*l.*).
2.—Dividends of companies, surplus assets in bankruptcy, &c.
3.—Army and navy prize-money.
4.—Dormant funds in chancery (28 Feb. 1886, 77,677,531*l.*).
5.—Intestates' estates in the United Kingdom, India, and the colonies.
6.—Deposits in banks (including plate, jewellery, &c.).

"**UNCLE TOM'S CABIN**," a story by Mrs. H. Beecher-Stowe, published in portions in a newspaper in 1850; complete in March, 1852; setting forth the evils of negro slavery. The sale was enormous, and the translations numerous, and it greatly contributed to emancipation. The Rev. Josiah Henson, the original "Uncle Tom," was received by the queen at Buckingham palace, 2 March, 1877, and was much benefited by his visit to Britain; he died May, 1883, aged 93.

UNCTION, Extreme, see *Anointing.*

UNDULATORY THEORY of Light, supposes a progressive wave-like motion between the eye and the luminous body seen. It is said to have been suggested by Francisco Grimaldi about 1665, and was propounded by Robert Hooke and Huyghens, about 1672; opposed by Newton; but confirmed by Thomas Young by experiments in 1801, and is now generally adopted; see *Emission* and *Light.*

UNEMPLOYED, see under *Riots,* 1886-7, and *Mansion House Funds,* 1886.
A plan for providing work proposed by the bishops of London, Rochester and Bedford, cardinal Manning, Mr. Spurgeon and Mr. Reaney Nov. 1886. A conference of poor-law guardians at Exeter Hall declare that there is no exceptional distress in the country 8 Dec. 1886.
Disorderly demonstrations of so-called unemployed in London early Oct. 1887; conference at Memorial Hall, lord Herschel in the chair 5 Dec. 1887.
Deputation (not unanimous) to lord Salisbury recommending public works, inquiry, and registration, state-aided emigration and repression of alien pauper immigrants 1 Feb. 1888.
Lord mayor de Keyser, aided by the earl of Meath and rev. Harry Jones, puts forth a scheme for employment of the London poor in making open spaces, gardens and recreation grounds with due stipulations (20,000*l.* wanted) *Times* 22 Dec. 1887.
The Gardens and Pleasure Grounds Fund started (see under *Mansion House*) about 24 Dec. 1887.
The scheme in action reported partially successful Aug. 1888.

UNIFORMITARIANS, see *Continuity.*

UNIFORMITY ACTS. That of 2 & 3 Edward VI., 15 Jan. 1549, ordained that the order of divine worship, drawn up by Cranmer and others, "with the aid of the Holy Ghost," should be the only one used after 20 May. The penalties for refusing to use it were fine and imprisonment. This act was confirmed in 1552; repealed by Mary, 1554; and re-enacted by Elizabeth in 1559. The act of Uniformity, 14 Charles II. c. 4, was passed in 1662. It enjoined uniformity in matters of religion, and obliged all clergy to subscribe to the thirty-nine articles, and use the same form of worship, and same book of common prayer. Its enforcement on 24 Aug. 1662, termed Black Bartholomew's day, caused, it is said, upwards of 2000 ministers to quit the church of England. This day was commemorated by dissenters in 1862. The Act of Uniformity Amendment act, whereby shortened services were authorised, and other changes made, was passed 18 July, 1872. The *Uniformity of Process* act, which made many law changes, was passed 23 May, 1832.

UNIFORMS. Military uniforms were first used in France, "in a regular manner" by Louis XIV. about 1668. In England the uniform was soon afterwards adopted in the military service, but with little analogy to the modern dress. See under *Navy.*

UNIGENITUS, see *Bull.*

UNINFLAMMABLE SALTS. At the British Association, 15 Sept. 1859, MM. Versmann and Oppenheim announced their discovery that fabrics steeped in solutions of tungstate of soda, or sulphate or phosphate of ammonia, burn without flame.

UNION CHAPEL, Islington, rebuilt; opened, 5 Dec. 1877; was termed a "congregational cathedral." Rev. Dr. H. Allon, minister, 1852.

UNION of Calmar, 1397; of Utrecht, 1579.

UNION of England and Scotland by the accession of James VI. of Scotland as James I. of England, 24 March, 1603. The legislative union of the two kingdoms (as Great Britain) was attempted, but failed in 1604 and 1670; in the reign of Anne, commissioners were appointed, the articles discussed, and, notwithstanding a great opposition made by the Tories, every article in the union was approved by a great majority, first in the house of commons, and afterwards by the peers, 22 July, 1706; was ratified by the Scottish parliament, 16 Jan. 1707, and became law, 1 May, same year.

UNION of Great Britain and Ireland effected, 2 July, 1800.
Proposed in the Irish parliament . . 22 Jan. 1799
Rejected by the commons of Ireland, the votes being 105 for, to 106 against the union, 24 Jan. ,,
The English house of commons on the same question divided, 140, 141, and 149 for the union; against it, 15, 25, and 28 respectively . . . ,,
Lord Castlereagh detailed his plan of the union, in the Irish house of lords, founded on the resolutions of the British parliament thereon 5 Feb. 1800
Votes of the commons agreeing to it, 161 against 115, 17 Feb. ; and again, 152 against 108 21 Feb. ,,
The houses of lords and commons wait on the lord lieutenant with the articles of union, 27 March, ,,
The act passed in the British parliament 2 July, ,,
The imperial united standard first displayed at the tower of London, and upon Bedford Tower, Dublin Castle, on the act of legislative union becoming an operative law . . . . 1 Jan. 1801
For attempts to *dissolve* this union, see *Repeal, Ireland* 1886
National Union Club, Albemarle Street, London, established . . . . . 18 Jan. 1887

UNION JACK. The original flag of England was the banner of St. George, *i.e.,* white with a red cross, which, 12 April, 1606 (three years after James I. ascended the throne) was incorporated with the banner of Scotland, *i.e.,* blue with a white diagonal cross. This combination obtained the name of " Union Jack," in allusion to the union with Scotland, and the word Jack is considered a corruption of the word Jacobus, Jacques, or James. This arrangement continued until the union with Ireland, 1 Jan. 1801, when the banner of St. Patrick, *i.e.,* white with a diagonal red cross, was amalgamated with it, and forms the present Union flag.

UNION CHARGEABILITY ACT, providing for the better distribution of the charge for relieving the poor in unions, was passed in June, 1865. One object of the act is the improvement of the dwellings of agricultural labourers.

UNION RELIEF ACT, passed in 1862, continued in 1863, to enable boards of guardians of certain unions to obtain temporary aid to meet the extraordinary expenditure for relief occasioned by the distress in the cotton manufacturing districts.

UNION REPEAL ASSOCIATION, Ireland, see *Repeal of the Union.*

UNIONIST LIBERALS, opposed to Mr. Gladstone, see *Liberals,* 1886, *et seq.*

UNIONISTS. A Spanish political party, long headed by marshal Serrano. In 1869 they advocated the election of the duc de Montpensier as king. See *Progresistas* and *Spain.*

UNIONS, see *Poor,* and *Trades.*

UNION GÉNÉRALE, see *France,* Dec. 1882.

UNIT, a gold coin, value 20*s.*, issued by James I. in 1604.

UNITARIANS, termed Socinians from Lælius Socinus, who founded a sect in Italy about 1546. They profess to believe in and worship one only

self-existent God, in opposition to those who worship the Trinity in unity. They consider Christ to have been a mere man; and do not admit the need of an atonement or of the complete inspiration of the Scriptures. Michael Servetus printed a tract in disparagement of the doctrine of the Trinity. In 1553, proceeding to Naples through Geneva, Calvin induced the magistrates to arrest him on a charge of blasphemy and heresy. Servetus, refusing to retract his opinions, was condemned to the flames, which sentence was carried into execution, 27 May, 1553. Servetus is numbered among those anatomists who made the nearest approach to the doctrine of the circulation of the blood, before Harvey established that doctrine. Matthew Hamont was burnt at Norwich for asserting Christ not to be the Son of God, 1 June, 1579. The Unitarians were numerous in Transylvania in the 17th century; they came to England about 1700, and many of the original English presbyterian churches became Unitarians about 1730. They were not included in the Toleration act till 1813. There were 229 congregations in England in 1851. Their tenets resemble those of the Arians and Socinians (*which see*). The Unitarian marriage bill was passed, June, 1827. In Dec. 1833, by a decision of the vice-chancellors the Unitarians (as such) lost the possession of lady Hewley's charity; the decision was affirmed on appeal in 1842. *British and Foreign Unitarian Association* founded, to promote Unitarianism, 1825; meeting in London, 64th anniversary kept in London, 12 June, 1889. There were 320 Unitarian churches in the United Kingdom in Feb. 1884.

UNITED BRETHREN, see *Moravians*.

UNITED IRISHMEN, a political society which met secretly, to establish a republic, became active in 1795. Theobald Wolf Tone, the founder, was captured by sir John Warren in the *Hoche*, one of six frigates destined to support the rebellion, in Oct. 1798. He anticipated his punishment by suicide in prison Nov. 1798. *United Ireland* newspaper first published July, 1881. See under *Ireland*.

UNITED KINGDOM. England and Wales were united in 1283; Scotland to both in 1707; and the British realm was named the United Kingdom on the union of Ireland, 1 Jan. 1801; see *Union*.— The UNITED KINGDOM ALLIANCE, for the total suppression of liquor traffic, was founded, 1 June, 1853. See *Permissive Bill*. The subscribed manifesto of this alliance occupied a page of the *Times*, 11 Dec. 1871. United Kingdom Beneficent Association, founded 1863, grants annuities to poor persons of a better class.

UNITED PRESBYTERIAN CHURCH, in Scotland, was formed 13 May, 1847, see *Burghers*, and *Relief Church*.

UNITED PROVINCES (Holland, Zealand, Utrecht, Friesland, Groningen, Overyssell, and Guelderland), the deputies of which met at Utrecht, 23 Jan. 1579, and signed a treaty for their mutual defence; see *Holland*.

UNITED SERVICE INSTITUTION, ROYAL, Whitehall, London, was established in 1831. Its museum contains many remarkable military and naval relics. The lectures given are reported in its journal, which first appeared in 1857. The *United Service Gazette* first published 9 Feb. 1833.

UNITED STATES.

UNITED STATES OF AMERICA were so styled by the congress of the revolted British provinces, 9 Sept. 1776. Their flag was declared to be thirteen stripes, alternately red and white, and thirteen stars in a blue field, corresponding with the then number of states of the union, 20 June, 1777. There are now 42 states. The government of the United States is a pure democracy. Each of the states has a separate and independent legislature for the administration of its local affairs, but all are ruled in matters of imperial policy by two houses of legislature, the senate, elected for six years, and the house of representatives, elected for two years, to which delegates are sent from the different members of the confederacy. The president of the United States is elected every fourth year by the free voice of the people. He and his ministers have no seat in the legislative assemblies. The election of Abraham Lincoln as president on 4 Nov. 1860, was followed by the secession of eleven slaveholding states, and led to the great civil war, 1861-5; see *Confederates*, and below.

The thirteen states of the union at the declaration of Independence in 1776: the italics indicate the then slaveholding states; those with a * prefixed, *seceded* from the federal government in 1860 and 1861, and were subdued in 1865.

New Hampshire. | *Delaware*.
Massachusetts. | *Maryland*.
Rhode Island. | *Virginia*.
Connecticut. | *North Carolina*.
New York. | *South Carolina*.
New Jersey. | *Georgia*.
Pennsylvania. | See *separate articles*.

The following have been added:—
Vermont (from New York) 1791
Tennessee (from North Carolina) 1796
Kentucky (from Virginia) 1792
Columbia district (under the immediate government of congress) contains Washington, the seat of government 1790-1
Ohio (created) 1802
Louisiana (bought from France in 1803) . . 1812
Indiana (created) 1816
Mississippi (from Georgia) 1817
Illinois (created) 1818
Alabama (from Georgia) 1819
Maine (from Massachusetts) 1820
Missouri (from Louisiana) 1821
Arkansas 1836
Michigan 1837
Florida (ceded by Spain, 1820); made a state 1845
Texas . . . . ,,
Iowa 1846
Wisconsin 1848
California 1850
New Mexico (territory) 1850
Minnesota (territory, 1849); state . . . 1857
Oregon (territory, 1850), state 1859
Kansas (territory, 1854); state 1861
Utah (territory) 1850
Washington (territory 1853); state . . . 1889
Nevada (territory, 1861); state 1864
Colorado (territory, 1861); state 1876
Dakota (territory 1861); north and south state 1889
Arizona (territory) 1863
Idaho (territory) . . . . ,,
West Virginia (from Virginia); state . . . ,,
Montana (territory 1864); state 1889
Nebraska (territory, 1854); state 1867
Wyoming (territory) 1868
Alaska (territory) . . . . ,,

Electoral College in 1872, 366 members; 40 for New England, 95 for the southern States, 12 for the Pacific States, 84 for the middle States, and 135 for the western States.

POPULATION. See *Slavery in America*.

	Slaves.	Total.		Slaves.	Total.		Slaves.	Total.
1776	. . .	2,614,300	1840	. . .	17,069,453	1870	. . .	38,558,371
1800	896,849	5,309,756	1850	3,204,313	23,191,876	1880	. . .	50,497,057
1810	1,191,364	7,239,903	1860	3,952,801	31,445,980	1888	. . .	61,702,000
1830	2,009,050	12,858,670						

UNITED STATES.

The Census of 1880 thus classifies the population: Males, 25,518,820; females. 24,636,963. Native born, 43,475,840; foreign born, 6,679,043. Whites, 43,402,970; coloured, 6,580,793. The remaining 339,098 are composed of Indians not in tribal relations and under Government care, Chinese, and other Asiatics. The Chinese are estimated at 105,613.
The *senate* is composed of 2 members for each state, elected for 6 years. The *representatives* in congress were formerly elected for 2 years in the ratio of 1 in 93,423 persons (five slaves were counted as three persons); but this system ended with the abolition of slavery. In 1872 the number of representatives was raised from 233 to 283, to commence 3 March, 1873.

Revenue.— Dollars.
Total receipts, year ending 30 June, 1855, 65,003,930
ditto ditto 1859, 53,405,071
ditto ditto 1863, 688,082,128
ditto ditto 1866, 1,273,960,215
ditto ditto 1875, 284,020,771
ditto ditto 1877, 269,000,586
ditto ditto 1880, 333,526,610
ditto ditto 1884, 348,519,869
ditto ditto 1888, 379,266,072
ditto ditto 1889, 388,591,675

Expenditure—
Year ending 30 June, 1855 56,365,393
ditto 1859 66,346,226
ditto 1863 714,709,995
ditto 1866 1,141,072,666
ditto 1875 274,623,392
ditto 1877 238,660,008
ditto 1880 267,642,957
ditto 1884 244,126,244
ditto 1888 267,924,801
ditto 1889 300,064,795

Public Debt—
June, 1867, 2,515,615,936 dollars.
June, 1871, 2,292,030,835 dollars.
June, 1875, 2,237,813,048 dollars.
June, 1876, 2,176,947,758 dollars.
June, 1880, 2,120,415,370 dollars.
June, 1884, 1,830,528,923 dollars.
Dec. 1888, 1,690,975,251 dollars.

YEAR ENDING 30 JUNE.	VALUE OF IMPORTS.	EXPORTS.
1872	£114,502,161	£112,361,676
1875	106,600,905	109,013,805
1877	90,261,510	117,933,898
1880	133,590,660	164,789,270
1884	133,539,538	144,992,970
1888	$723,957,114	$683,862,104

ARMY.—That which achieved independence was disbanded at the end of the war. In 1789, a war department was established, and in 1790 the army consisted of 1216 men for the Indian frontier. In 1808, the militia was newly equipped. When war with Great Britain was declared on 18 June, 1812, 35,000 men were voted; and this army was disbanded at the peace in 1815. Armies were voted for the wars in 1833 and 1835, afterwards disbanded.
In 1855, Army, 11,658. Militia, 1,873,558. *Fleet,* 72 vessels (2300 guns).
In 1860, the United States Militia were 3,070,987. *Fleet,* 92 vessels (of all kinds); in Oct. 1862, 256 vessels of war.
Federal Army, 29 July, 1861, estimated at 660,971. In Dec. 1862, nearly 1,000,000 men. In April, 1865, about 1,500,000, at the end of the war, when the reduction began at once. Number of soldiers in 1867, 54,890; In July, 1871, 32,135; 1875, 27,525 men; in 1883, 25,478 men; in 1888, 26,270 men.
Fleet, in July, 1867, 261 vessels of all kinds, 2218 guns; Jan. 1871, 179 vessels, 1440 guns; 1875, 155 vessels, 1203 guns; 1884, 92 vessels; 1888, 66 vessels.
Railways, miles : 1839, 23; 1861, 31,286; 1873, 73,533; in 1884, 121,532; in 1888, 150,710.

Act of the British parliament, imposing new heavy duties on imports . . . . . 11 March, 1764
Obnoxious stamp-act passed . . 22 March, 1765
First American congress held at New York, June; the stamp-act resisted . . . . 1 Nov. ,,
Stamp-act repealed . . . . 18 March, 1766
British act, levying duties on tea, paper, painted glass, &c. . . . . . 14 June, 1767
Gen. Gage sent to Boston . . . Oct. 1768
840 chests of tea destroyed by the populace at Boston, and 17 chests at New York . 18 Dec. 1773
Boston port bill (port rights annulled) 25 March, 1774
Deputies from the states meet at Philadelphia, 5 Sept. ; Declaration of Rights issued 4 Nov. ,,
First action between the British and Americans, at Lexington; British retreat . . . 19 April, 1775
Act of perpetual union between the states 20 May, ,,
George Washington appointed commander-in-chief, May; battle of Bunker's-hill, the Americans retire after a severe conflict . . 17 June, ,,
America declared "free, sovereign, and independent" . . . . . . 4 July, 1776
General Howe takes Long Island, 27 Aug. ; new York, 15 Sept. ; victor at White Plains, 20 Oct. ; takes Rhode Island . . . . 8 Dec. ,,
The Hessians surrender to Washington . 25 Dec. ,,
La Fayette and other French officers join the Americans 1777
Washington defeated at Brandywine . 11 Sept. ,,
Lord Cornwallis takes Philadelphia . Sept. ,,
Burgoyne victor at Germantown, 3, 4, Oct. ; surrounded; capitulates at Saratoga . 17 Oct. ,,
A federal government adopted by congress 15 Nov. ,,
The states recognised by France . . 16 Dec. ,,
Alliance with France . . . . 6 Feb. 1778
The king's troops quit Philadelphia . June, ,,
Americans defeated at Brier's Creek . 3 March, 1779
Charleston surrenders to the British . 13 May, 1780
Cornwallis defeats Gates at Camden . 16 Aug. ,,
Major André hanged as a spy . . 2 Oct. ,,
[André (born 1751) was an adjutant-general in the British army, and was taken in disguise on his return from a secret expedition to the traitorous American general Arnold, 23 Sept. 1780. He was sentenced to execution as a spy by a court of general Washington's officers at Tappan, New York, and suffered death, 2 Oct. following. His remains were removed to England in a sarcophagus, 10 Aug. 1821, and interred in Westminster abbey. Impartial judges justify the severity of this punishment.]
American Academy of Arts and Sciences at Boston founded . . . . ,,
The federal government accepted by all the states, 1 March; congress assembles . 2 March, 1781
Cornwallis defeats Green at Guildford, 15 March;
Arnold defeats the Americans at Eutaw 8 Sept. ,,
Surrender of lord Cornwallis and his whole army of 7000 men to generals Washington and Rochambeau, at Yorktown . . . . . 19 Oct. ,,
Arrival of sir Guy Carleton to treat for peace, 5 May ; provisional articles signed at Paris by commissioners . . . . . . 30 Nov. 1782
Definitive treaty of peace signed at Paris, 3 Sept. 1783; ratified by congress . . 4 Jan. 1784
Samuel Seabury consecrated bishop of the episcopal church in America at Aberdeen . 14 Nov. ,,
John Adams, first American ambassador's first interview with the king of England . 1 June, 1785
The cotton plant introduced into Georgia . 1786
New constitution signed by a convention of states, 17 Sept. 1787
The same ratified . . . . 23 May, 1788
The quakers of Philadelphia emancipate their slaves, 1 Jan. ,,
New government organised, 4 March ; *George Washington, 1st president,* 6 April; present departments of state established . . . 27 July, 1789
Death of Benjamin Franklin . . 4 March, 1790
Bank instituted ; capital, 10,000,000 dollars, 7 June, 1791
City of Washington chosen the capital of the states, 8 July, 1792
Eli Whitney's invention of the cotton-gin gives an immense impetus to the growth of American cotton 1793
Re-election of general Washington as president, 4 March, 1793; resigns . . 17 Sept. 1796
John Adams, 2nd president . . 4 March, 1797
Washington dies ; universal sorrow . 14 Dec. 1799
The seat of government removed to Washington 1800
Thomas Jefferson, 3rd president . 4 March, 1801
Louisiana purchased from the French . 30 April, 1803
Discussion between England and America respecting the rights of neutrals 1807
American ports closed to the British, July; trade suspended . . . . . 9 Dec. 1807
Importation of slaves abolished . . 1 Jan. 1808

James Madison, 4th president . . . 4 March, 1809
War with Great Britain (New England States opposed to it, threatened to secede) . 18 June, 1812
Action between the American ship *Constitution*, and the British frigate *Guerrière*, an unequal contest, 19 Aug. „
Fort Détroit taken . . . . . 21 Aug. „
The British sloop *Frolic* taken by the American sloop *Wasp*, 18 Oct. ; the privateer *Defiance* also captured by the *Wasp* . . . . „
The ship *United States* of 54 guns, great calibre (commodore Decatur), captures the British frigate *Macedonia* . . . . . 25 Oct. „
Battles of Frenchtown (*which see*). . 22-24 Jan. 1813
The *Hornet* captures the British sloop of war *Peacock* 25 Feb. „
Fort Erie and Fort George abandoned by the British, 27 May, „
The American frigate *Chesapeake* captured by the *Shannon* frigate, captain Broke . 1 June, „
At Burlington Heights, Americans defeated, 6 June, „
H.M. sloop *Pelican* takes the sloop *Argus* 14 Aug. „
Buffalo town burnt by the British Dec. „
American frigate *Essex* taken by the *Phœbe* and *Cherub* . . . . . 29 March, 1814
The British defeat the Americans in a severe conflict, 2 July, „
[Several engagements with various success followed.]
The British, under Ross, defeat the Americans at Bladensburg ; the city of Washington taken and public edifices burnt . . . . 24 Aug. „
The British sloop of war *Avon* sunk by the American sloop *Wasp* . . . . . 8 Sept. „
The British squadron on Lake Champlain captured, 11 Sept. „
Attack on Baltimore by the British; general Ross killed . . . . . . 12 Sept. „
Treaty of peace with Great Britain, signed at Ghent, 24 Dec. „
The British repulsed at New Orleans . 8 Jan. 1815
The British ship *Endymion* captures the *President*, 15 Jan. „
The Ghent treaty ratified . . . 17 Feb. „
James Monroe, 5th president . . 4 March, 1817
Treaty with Canada respecting fisheries . . 1818
Centre foundation of the capitol of Washington laid, 24 Aug. „
The "Missouri Compromise" of Henry Clay, regarding slavery, passed . . . Feb. 1820
Spain cedes Florida to the American States 24 Oct. „
The States acknowledge the independence of South America . . . . . 8 March, 1822
Treaty with Columbia . . . . 3 Oct. 1824
John Quincey Adams, 6th president . 4 March, 1825
Death of the two ex-presidents, Adams and Jefferson, on the 50th anniversary of the independence of the American States . . . 4 July, 1826
Convention with Great Britain concerning indemnities for war 1812-14 . . . 13 Nov. „
American Tariff Bill imposing heavy duties on British goods . . . . 13 May, 1828
General Jackson, 7th president . . 4 March, 1829
Treaty between the United States and the Ottoman Porte . . . . . . 7 May, 1830
Ports re-opened to British commerce . 5 Oct. „
First railway made . . . . . „
New tariff laws . . . . 14 July, 1832
Commercial panic . . . . . „
Great fire at New York, 674 houses and many public edifices burnt ; loss estimated at 20,000,000 dollars . . . . . 16 Dec. 1835
National debt paid off 1836
Martin Van Buren, 8th president . 4 March, 1837
In the Canadian insurrection, many Americans assist the insurgents . . Oct. to Dec. „
The American steamboat *Caroline* is attacked and burnt by the British, near Schlosser, to the east of the Niagara, on the territory of the United States . . . . . 29 Dec. „
Proclamation of the president against American citizens aiding the Canadians . . 5 Jan. 1838
The *Great Western* steam-ship first sails from Bristol to New York . . . . 8-15 April „
American banks suspend cash payments . Oct. 1839
Alex. MacLeod, charged with aiding in the destruction of the *Caroline*; true bill found against him for murder and arson . . 6 Feb. 1841

The United States bank again suspends payment, 7 Feb. 1841
Gen. W. H. Harrison, 9th president . 4 March, „
Died . . . . . . 4 April, „
Mr. Fox, British minister, demands the release of Mr. MacLeod . . . . 12 March, „
John Tyler, 10th president . . . April. „
The case of MacLeod removed to supreme court at New York . . . . . 6 May, „
A party of British volunteers from Canada carry off col. Grogan . . . . . 9 Sept. „
Resignation of all the United States ministers, with the exception of Mr. Webster. . 11 Sept. „
President's proclamation against lawless attempts of American citizens to invade British possessions, and to suppress secret lodges, clubs, and associations . . . . . 25 Sept. „
Grogan restored to the Americans . 4 Oct. „
Trial of MacLeod at Utica, 4 Oct. ; acquitted, 12 Oct. „
Colossal statue of Washington placed in the capitol at Washington . . . . 1 Dec. „
Affair of the *Creole*; dispute with England Dec. „
[This American vessel was on her voyage to New Orleans with a cargo of slaves : they mutinied, murdered the owner, wounded the captain, and compelled the crew to take the ship to Nassau, New Providence, where the governor, considering them passengers, allowed them, against the protest of the American consul, to go at liberty.]
Announcement of lord Ashburton's mission to the United States . . . . 1 Jan. 1842
Arrest of Hogan, implicated in the *Caroline* affair, 2 Feb. „
Lord Ashburton arrives at New York . 1 April, „
Washington treaty, defining the boundaries between the United States and the British American possessions, and for suppressing the slave trade, and giving up fugitive criminals ; signed at Washington, by lord Ashburton and Mr. Webster, 9 Aug. „
The tariff bill is passed . . . 30 Aug. „
Lord Ashburton leaves the United States . 5 Sept. „
Death of Dr. Channing . . . 2 Oct. „
James Knox Polk, 11th president . . 4 March, 1845
War declared against the United States by Mexico, on account of the proposed annexation of Texas, 4 June, „
[Several actions are fought between the belligerents, adverse to Mexico.]
Resolution of the senate and house of representatives for terminating the joint occupancy of Oregon . . . . . 20 April, 1846
Annexation of New Mexico to the United States, after a protracted war . . 23 Aug. „
Mexicans defeated by Taylor at Palo Alto, 8, 9 May, „
Treaty fixing the north-west boundary of the U.S. at the 49th parallel of latitude, and giving the British possession of Vancouver's island, the free navigation of the Columbia river, &c., signed 12 June, „
Treaty with Columbia guaranteeing neutrality of the isthmus of Panama . . . „
The Mexicans defeated by general Taylor, at Bueno Vista . . . . . 22, 23 Feb. 1847
Vera Cruz taken by storm, 29 March ; the Mexicans everywhere worsted. Great battle of Sierra Gorda ; the Mexicans signally defeated by general Scott, 18 April, „
Treaty between Mexico and the United States, ratified . . . . . 19 May, 1848
Gen. Zachary Taylor, 12th president . 4 March, 1849
Riot at the theatre, New York, occasioned by the dispute between Mr. Forrest and Mr. Macready, 10 May, „
Proclamation of the president against the marauding expedition to Cuba . . 11 Aug. „
[Lopez, a Spanish adventurer, landed 600 men at Cuba ; after a short but obstinate struggle they took the town of Cardenas ; and soon after had a land engagement with some Spanish soldiers, in which many of them were killed or taken prisoners ; the others embarked with Lopez in the *Creole* steamer, and thus escaped from a Spanish war steamer, the *Pizarro*, May, 1850.]
The French ambassador dismissed from Washington, 14 Sept. „
Treaty with England for a transit way across Panamá (see *Bulwer*), 19 April ; ratified . 4 July, 1850

UNITED STATES.

President Zachary Taylor dies; death of M. Calhoun . . . . 31 March, 1850
Millard Fillmore, 13th president . . March, ,,
California admitted a state . . . 15 Aug. ,,
Fugitive slave bill passed . . . . Aug. ,,
President Fillmore issues a second proclamation against the promoters of a second expedition to Cuba, and the ship *Cleopatra*, freighted with military stores destined for that island, is seized, 25 April, 1851
Census of the United States taken, the population ascertained to amount to 23,347,884, in the whole union . . . . 16 June, ,,
Henry Clay, American statesman, dies . 29 June, ,,
Failure of the second expedition against Cuba by Lopez and his followers; they are all defeated and taken; 51 are shot by the Cuban authorities, Lopez is garotted, and the rest are sent prisoners to Spain, where, after some negotiation, they are mercifully set at liberty (see *Cuba*) Aug.-Sept. ,,
J. F. Cooper, American novelist, dies . 14 Sept. ,,
The president issues a proclamation against the sympathisers with the revolutionary movement in Mexico . . . . 22 Oct. ,,
Part of the capitol of Washington, and the whole of the library of the United States congress, destroyed by fire . . . . . 24 Dec. ,,
M. Kossuth, the Hungarian chief, arrives at Washington, on the invitation of the United States legislature . . . . 30 Dec. ,,
Publication of "Uncle Tom's Cabin," by Mrs. Stowe . . . . 20 March, 1852
The dispute with England relating to the Fisheries occurs about this time; Mr. Webster's note upon the subject . . . . . . 14 July, ,,
Lone Star Society (see *Lone Star*) . . Aug. ,,
The United States Ship *Crescent City* boarded at Havannah, and not allowed to land her mails or passengers . . . . . . 3 Oct. ,,
Death of the eminent statesman Daniel Webster in his 70th year . . . . . 24 Oct. ,,
Expedition to Japan . . . . . . ,,
Address to the women of America on slavery, adopted by the duchess of Sutherland and other ladies (signed afterwards by 576,000 English-women) . . . . . . 26 Nov. ,,
Gen. Franklin Pierce, 14th president . 4 March, 1853
Affair of Koszta at Smyrna (see *Koszta*) 21 June, ,,
Crystal palace opens at New York . . 14 July, ,,
Duel between M. Soulé (American minister at Madrid) and M. Turgot . . . 18 Dec. ,,
Great fire at New York—*Great Republic* clipper destroyed . . . . 26 Dec. ,,
Astor Library, New York, opened . 9 Jan. 1854
William Walker proclaims the republic of Sonora divided into two states—Sonora and Lower California . . . . 18 Jan. ,,
American steamer *Black Warrior* seized at Cuba, 28 Feb. ,,
The Spanish government remitted the fine, but considered the seizure legal . . . April, ,,
Commercial treaty concluded between Japan and United States by commodore Perry (sent there for the purpose) . . . . 23 March, ,,
Reciprocity treaty between Great Britain and United States (respecting Newfoundland fishery, international trade, &c.) concluded . 7 June, ,,
Captain Hollins in American sloop *Cyane*, bombards San Juan de Nicaragua . . . 13 July, ,,
Negotiation for the annexation of the Sandwich Islands . . . . Oct. ,,
Dreadful election riots in Kansas, March and April, 1855
Indian war: they are defeated . 25, 29 April, ,,
Dispute with British government on enlistment (see *Foreign Legion*) . . . . . July, ,,
Gen. Harney gains a victory over the Sioux Indians, 3 Sept. ,,
Senator Charles Sumner savagely assaulted by senator Preston Brooks in the senate-house for speaking against slavery . . . 2 May, 1856
Mr. Crampton, British envoy, dismissed, 28 May, ,,
John C. Fremont nominated the "Republican" candidate for the presidency . . . 17 June, ,,
Battle in Kansas; the slavers (under capt. Reid) defeat Brown and the abolitionists . 30 Aug. ,,
James Buchanan, elected 15th president . 4 Nov. ,,
The *Resolute* presented to queen Victoria (see *Franklin*) . . . . 12 Dec. ,,

Lord Napier appointed British envoy to United States (16 Jan.); warmly received 18 March, 1857
Central American question settled . March, ,,
Judgment given in the "Dred Scott" case in the supreme court. (He was claimed as a slave in a free state: 2 judges declared for his freedom, 5 against it, which causes great dissatisfaction throughout the free states) . . March, ,,
Disorganised state of Utah; troops march to support new governor . . . . May and June, ,,
Riots in Washington against Irish electors; and in New York on account of changes in the police arrangements . . . . . June, ,,
Insurrection in Kansas quelled . . July, ,,
Commercial panic in New York . . Aug. ,,
Outrage at Staaten Island; quarantine house burnt, 7 Sept. ,,
Dispute respecting right of search, settled May, 1858
Tranquillity restored in Utah . . June, ,,
Great rejoicing at the completion of the Atlantic telegraph (see *Electric Telegraph*) . Aug. ,,
A massacre of emigrants at Mountain Meadows, Utah (Mormons suspected) . . 18 Sept. ,,
Lieut. Moffat seizes the American slave ship *Echo* and takes her to Charleston . . . Sept. ,,
Death of W. H. Prescott, the historian . 28 Jan. 1859
Daniel Sickles, a government official, killed Philip Barton Key, for adultery with his wife; acquitted of murder . . . . . . 26 Feb. ,,
The American commodore Tatnall assists the English at the Chinese engagement on the river Peiho, saying, "Blood is thicker than water," 25 June, ,,
Gen. Ward, the United States envoy, goes to Pekin, but does not see the emperor . . July, ,,
Gen. Harney sends troops to San Juan Island, near Vancouver's Island, "to protect the American settlers;" moderation of the British, who have a naval force at hand; governor Douglas also sends troops . . . . . . 27 July, ,,
Insurrection at Harper's Ferry . . 16 Oct. ,,

[John Brown, called captain Brown and old Brown, was a prominent leader in the violent conflicts in Kansas, during the agitation respecting the question of its becoming a slave state. He was a monomaniac on the slavery question, and contended that all means for annihilating slavery were justifiable. He gathered together a band of desperate characters, who so much annoyed Missouri and other slave states, that a reward was offered for his head. He had arranged for the successful issue of the insurrection above mentioned, so far as to devise a provisional government and a new constitution. On 16 Oct. he and his band, aided by a mob, seized the arsenal at Harper's Ferry, a town on the borders of Virginia and Maryland, stopped the railway trains, and cut the telegraph wires; a conflict with the military ensued, when many of the insurgents were killed. Temporary panic in southern states.]

Gen. Harney superseded by gen. Scott at San Juan, who makes conciliatory overtures; accepted by governor Douglas . . . . Nov. ,,
Death of Washington Irving . . 28 Nov. ,,
John Brown captured and tried; executed 2 Dec. ,,
Great agitation in the congress, Nov. 1859; no speaker elected till . . . . 1 Feb. 1860
President Buchanan protests against a proposed inquiry into his acts . . . 28 March, ,,
Companions of John Brown executed . March, ,,
The national republican convention meet at Chicago; Abraham Lincoln chosen as candidate for the presidency . . . . 16 May, ,,
Japanese embassy received by the president at Washington . . . . . 17 May, ,,
Fresh disputes at San Juan, through gen. Harney, who is recalled . . . . . May, ,,
William Goodrich (Peter Parley) dies . May, ,,
The national democratic convention meet at Baltimore; a large number of delegates secede; the remainder nominate Stephen Douglas as president: the seceders nominate John Breckinridge, 18 June, ,,
The *Great Eastern* arrives at New York 23 June, ,,
The prince of Wales arrives at Detroit in the United States, 20 Sept.; visits Washington, 3 Oct.; Philadelphia, 9 Oct.; New York, 11 Oct.; Boston, 17 Oct.; embarks at Portland . 20 Oct. ,,

UNITED STATES.

Abraham Lincoln, the republican candidate, elected 16th president (see *Southern Confederacy*), 6 Nov. 1860 [303 electors are appointed to vote for a president; 152 to be a majority. The numbers were, for A. Lincoln, 180; John C. Breckinridge, 72; John Bell, 39; Stephen A. Douglas, 12.]
Intense excitement at Charleston, South Carolina, and in other southern states . . . Nov. „
South Carolina secedes from the union . 20 Dec. „
Major Anderson, of United States army, occupies Fort Sumter in Carolina . . . . 26 Dec. „
Delegates from South Carolina not received by the president . . . . . . 30 Dec. „
Vacillating policy of president Buchanan; the secretaries Cass, Cobb, Floyd, and Thompson resign, Dec. 1860–Jan. 1861
New York and other northern states protest against the secession; a general fast proclaimed; observed on . . . . . . 4 Jan. „
Vicksburg, Mississippi, fortified . . 12 Jan. „
Kansas admitted a state . . . 21 Jan. „
Secession (by convention) of Mississippi, 8 Jan.; Alabama, Florida, 11 Jan.; Georgia, 19 Jan.; Louisiana, 26 Jan. Texas (by legislature), 1 Feb. „
Jefferson Davis, elected by the six seceding states, 8 Feb.; is inaugurated president of the "southern confederacy," at Montgomery, Alabama, 18 Feb. „
New (Morrill) tariff bill passed (nearly prohibits commerce with England) . . . 2 March, „
President Davis prepares for war (100,000 men to be raised) . . . . . . March, „
Abm. Lincoln, inaugurated president at Washington, says, "the central idea of secession is the essence of anarchy" . . . 4 March, „
Southern commissioners not received by the president at Washington . . . 12 March, „
Gen. Winfield Scott, in a letter to president Lincoln, sets before him four courses: either, I., to surrender to slavery half the territory acquired or to be acquired; II., to blockade all revolted ports; III., to say to seceding states, "Wayward sisters, go in peace!" or IV., to conquer the south, which would require 300,000 men and afterwards a resident army [the letter became public Oct. 1862] March, „
(*Statement denied in* 1874.)
Great excitement at the operation of the new Morrill tariff, which begins . . . 1 April, „
The war begins: Major Anderson refuses to surrender Fort Sumter, Charleston, when summoned, 11 April; it is taken by the secessionists, after a bloodless conflict . . . . 13 April, „
President Lincoln summons the congress to meet on 4 July; issues a proclamation, calling on the states to furnish a contingent of 75,000 men, &c. 15 April, „
Massachusetts, New York, Pennsylvania, and other states zealously respond, with vigorous preparations for war; Kentucky, North Carolina, Virginia, Tennessee, and Missouri, decidedly refuse, asserting the proposed coercion to be wicked, illegal, and unconstitutional . . April, „
The mob in Baltimore, Maryland, attack some Massachusetts regiments on their way to Washington; several persons killed in the conflict, 19 April, „
President Davis issues letters of marque, 17 April; president Lincoln proclaims the blockade of the ports of seceding states . . . 19 April, „
U.S. Arsenal at Harper's Ferry, Virginia, fired by command, and 15,000 stand of arms destroyed, 18 April; 9 ships of war and naval stores in the navy yard, Norfolk, Va., burnt to prevent them falling into the hands of the southern confederates, who occupy the place . . 21 April, „
Virginia (except West Virginia) secedes by ordinance (the 8th state) . . . 25 April, „
Lincoln calls for 42,034 volunteers for three years, 3 May, and informs foreign powers of his intention to maintain the union by war . 4 May, „
The confederates under Beauregard and Johnston, in Virginia, threaten Washington, defended by the federals under generals Winfield Scott and George McClellan . . . . May, „
The British queen commands her subjects to be neutral in the ensuing war . . 13 May, „
The federals enter Virginia; Beauregard calls on the Virginians to rise and expel them 1 June, 1861
Formal *secession* of Arkansas, 6 May; North Carolina, 20 May; Tennessee (9th, 10th, and 11th), 8 June, „
Several British vessels seized while endeavouring to break the blockade; the southern privateer *Savannah* captured . . . June, „
Neutrality announced by the French emperor 10 June, „
Fast-day in confederate states . . 13 June, „
Missouri.—Gen. Lyon raises a federal army, and defeats the state troops, 17 June; the federals successful at Carthage, 5 July; Fremont takes command in West Missouri, 26 July; federals victorious at Athens, 5 Aug.; at Wilson's Creek (gen. Lyon killed), 10 Aug.; Fremont proclaims martial law, and freedom to slaves or rebels, 31 Aug.; Lexington surrenders to confederates, 20 Sept.; Fremont blamed, retires; succeeded by Hunter . . . . . 2 Nov. „
Virginia.—Federals defeated at Big Bethell, 10 June; occupy Harper's Ferry, evacuated by the confederates, 16 June; col. Pegrim and 600 confederates surrender at Beverley . 13 July, „
[Very many skirmishes, with various results.]
McClellan defeats confederates at Rich Mountain, 11 July; Paterson permits the junction of the confederates under Johnston and Beauregard near Manassas, 15 July; who are repulsed at Blackburn's Ford, near Centreville . 18 July, „
Battle of Bull Run (*which see*) or Manassas, Virginia; the federals, seized with panic, flee in utter disorder . . . . 21 July, „
Meeting of U. S. Congress, 4 July; a loan of 250 million dollars authorised . . 17 July, „
Meeting of confederate congress at Richmond, Virginia . . . . . 20 July, „
Passport system introduced into the northern states, and the liberty of the press greatly restricted . . . . . . Aug. „
The charges in the Morrill tariff greatly raised; the confederates prohibit exportation of cotton except by southern ports . . . Aug. „
Battle of Springfield or Wilson's Creek; confederates defeated . . . . 10 Aug. „
McClellan assumes command of the army of the Potomac . . . . . 20 Aug. „
Federal gen. Butler takes Fort Hatteras, N. Carolina (700 prisoners and 1000 stand of arms), 29 Aug. „
Fast-day in federal states . . 26 Sept. „
Garibaldi declines command in the federal army, Sept. „
Battle of Ball's Bluff; federals defeated and gen. Baker killed, near Leesburg, Virginia; hundreds drowned . . . . . 21 Oct. „
The federals and confederates enter Kentucky; the governor protests; many skirmishes, Sept.-Dec. „
Resignation of lieut.-gen. Scott, 31 Oct.; George McClellan made commander-in-chief of the federal army . . . . . 1 Nov. „
The federal general Sherman takes Port Royal forts, S. Carolina . . . . 7, 8 Nov. „
Capt. Wilkes, of federal war steamer *San Jacinto*, boards the Royal British mail packet *Trent*, and carries off Messrs. Mason and Slidell, confederate commissioners, and their secretaries, 8 Nov., and conveys them to Boston . 19 Nov. „
Great rejoicings in the northern states at the capture of Mason and Slidell . . Nov. „
McClellan reviews 70,000 men . . 20 Nov. „
Capt. Pegram, of confederate steamer *Nashville*, burns the federal ship *Harvey Birch*, 19 Nov., and brings the crew on to Southampton . 21 Nov. „
A secession ordinance passed by a party in Missouri, 2 Nov.; the same in Kentucky . 30 Nov. „
Dissensions increase between the republicans (abolitionists) and the democrats in New York, &c. Nov. „
Jefferson Davis elected president of confederate states for six years . . . 30 Nov. „
President Lincoln states that the federal armies comprise 660,971 men . . . 2 Dec. „
Meeting of congress, which votes thanks to capt. Wilkes, 2 Dec.; the foreign envoys at Washington protest against his act . . . 3 Dec. „
The federals commence sinking hulks filled with stones to block up Charleston harbour (S. Carolina) [much indignation in England] . 21 Dec. „

Banks at New York, &c., suspend cash payments, 30 Dec. 1861
A firm despatch from the British government arrives, 18 Dec. 1861; Mason, &c., surrendered, sail for Europe . . . . . . 1 Jan. 1862
Phelps' fruitless expedition to Ship Island, Mississippi Sound . . . . 3 Dec. 1861-Jan. ,,
Confederate general Zollicoffer defeated by Thomas and slain at Mill Springs or Somerset, Kentucky, 19 Jan. ,,
Tennessee.—The federals (Grant) take Fort Henry, 6 Feb.; Fort Donnelson, with 15,000 prisoners, 16 Feb.; and Nashville . . . 23 Feb. ,,
Confederates defeated at Pea Ridge, Arkansas, 6, 7, 8 March, ,,
Confederate iron-plated ship *Merrimac* destroys federal vessels *Cumberland* and *Congress* in Hampton roads, 8 March; is repulsed by federal iron-clad floating battery *Monitor* . . 9 March, ,,
McClellan and his army (100,000) cross the Potomac and find the confederate camp at Bull Run evacuated . . . . . . 10 March, ,,
McClellan resigns general command, and assumes that of the army of the Potomac only; Fremont that of the Mountain department; and Halleck that of the Mississippi . . . 11 March, ,,
Burnside's expedition sails, 11 Jan.; takes Roanoke, N. Carolina, 7, 8 Feb.; Newbern . 14 March, ,,
Capt. Wilson (British) boldly rescues his vessel, *Emily St. Pierre*, a merchantman, from the federals 21 March, ,,

[She was sailing from Calcutta to New Brunswick, and while attempting to inquire whether a blockade existed, was captured off Charleston bar by a federal ship of war. Her captain, and his cook and steward, were permitted to remain on board on her voyage to Philadelphia. On 21 March, Wilson with his two associates succeeded, by stratagem and courage, in recovering the command of the vessel, overcoming two U.S. officers and 13 sailors, and brought his into Liverpool. The owners of the ship gave him 2000 guineas, and the Liverpool merchants presented him with a magnificent testimonial of their admiration of his gallantry. The British government refused to restore the vessel when claimed by the Americans.]

Confederates defeated at Winchester . 23 March, ,,
General Burnside occupies Beaufort and Fort Macon 1 April, ,,
Slavery abolished in district of Columbia, 4 April, ,,
McClellan advances into Virginia, with the view of taking Richmond; he besieges York town, held by 30,000 confederates . . . . 5 April, ,,
Correspondents of English newspapers excluded from federal army . . . . . 5 April, ,,
Great battles of Shiloh or Pittsburg Landing, near Corinth, Tennessee; confederates victorious, but lose their able gen. Albert Johnston; they retire 6, 7 April, ,,
Treaty between Great Britain and the United States for the suppression of the slave trade, 7 April, ,,
Federals take Fort Pulaska on the Savannah, 11 April; and New Orleans . . 25-28 April, ,,
Yorktown evacuated by confederates . 3 May, ,,
The Seward-Lyons treaty between Great Britain and the United States, for suppression of the slave trade, signed 7 April; ratified . 20 May, ,,
Confederates repulsed at Williamsburg, 5 May; their naval depôt at Norfolk, Virginia, surrenders, 10 May; they burn the *Merrimac* . 11 May, ,,
Commodore Farragut with a flotilla ascends the Mississippi . . . . . . May, ,,
Little Rock, Arkansas, taken by federals . May, ,,
Stonewall Jackson defeats Banks at Winchester, 18 May, ,,
McClellan takes Hanover court-house . 27 May, ,,
Skirmishes in Virginia; success varying . May, ,,
Severe battles of Fair Oaks, before Richmond (indecisive) . . . . 31 May, 1 June, ,,
Beauregard and the confederates retreat from Corinth, Tennessee, 30 May; pursued by Halleck and the federals . . . . . June, ,,
Memphis, on the Mississippi, taken . 6 June, ,,
Federals defeated near Charleston . 16 June, ,,
Federal forces under Fremont, Banks, and McDowell, placed under Pope; Fremont resigns, 27 June, 1862
Federals suffer through several severe engagements in Virginia . . . . . 25-30 June, ,,
General Butler excites great indignation by his military rigour at New Orleans May and June, ,,
Seven days' conflict on the Chickahominy before Richmond; the confederate gen. Lee compels McClellan to abandon the siege and retreat 17 miles, taking up a position at Harrison's Landing, on James's river . . 25 June-1 July, ,,
The tariff still further raised . . . July, ,,
Many conflicts in Kentucky, Missouri, and Tennessee, through confederate guerilla parties. June and July, ,,
Lincoln visits and encourages the army of McClellan, and calls for 300,000 volunteers . . July, ,,
Lincoln's assent to a bill confiscating the property and emancipating the slaves of all rebels in arms after 60 days . . . . . 17 July, ,,
Halleck supersedes McClellan as commander-in-chief 26 July, ,,
Slow volunteering; many emigrations to Canada and Europe; habeas corpus suspended; the president ordains a draft if the volunteers are not ready by 15 Aug. . . . . . July, ,,
Public debt of United States estimated at 1,222,000,000 dollars . . . . 1 July, ,,
Pope takes command in Virginia . . 14 July, ,,
Lincoln's proclamation of confiscation of property of rebels . . . . . . 26 July, ,,
Fierce attack of Breckenridge (confederates) on Baton Rouge; the federals soon after retire, 5 Aug. ,,
Pope's troops ravage Virginia; Banks, his subordinate, defeated at Cedar Mountain by gen. Thos. "Stonewall" Jackson . . . . 9 Aug. ,,

[According to some accounts he obtained the name by promising Beauregard, at the battle of Bull Run, that his brigade should stand like a "stone wall;" others say that Beauregard gave the name himself.]

McClellan retreats from Harrison's Landing (said to have lost 70,000 men, killed, wounded, prisoners, and deserters) . . . . 16 Aug. ,,
The federals surprised, and Pope loses his baggage, 25 Aug. ,,
Jackson turns the flank of Pope's army, and attacks him at Groveton, 29 Aug.; and when reinforced by Lee, defeats him and McDowell at Bull Run, 30 Aug.; Pope retreats to Centreville . 1 Sept. ,,
The remains of Pope's army flee behind the lines of Washington, 2 Sept.; he is removed to the north-west to act against the Indian insurrection 3 Sept. ,,
McDowell superseded; charged with treachery, he claims a trial . . . . . . Sept. ,,
McClellan appointed commander-in-chief, saves Washington, and marches against the confederates under Lee, who have crossed the Potomac and entered Maryland . . . 5, 6 Sept. ,,
Severe conflicts at South Mountain Gap (or Middletown), 14-16 Sept.; confederates, after a great fight near Antietam Creek and Sharpsburg road, retreat . . . . 17 Sept. ,,
Harper's Ferry surrendered to Jackson, 15 Sept.; he crosses Potomac and joins Lee's army 17 Sept. ,,
Federal cause declining in the west; they lose Lexington, Aug.; and Munsfordville . 17 Sept. ,,
Thanksgiving-day in southern states, . 18 Sept. ,,
Rosencrans defeats the confederates at Iuka 19 Sept. ,,
Confederates re-enter Virginia laden with stores 22 Sept. ,,
Lincoln proclaims freedom to the slaves in the confederate states, on 1 Jan. 1863, if the states have not returned to the union . . 22 Sept. ,,
Secret convention of 16 governors of states at Altoona, Pennsylvania, approve Lincoln's policy 24 Sept. ,,
Draught of 40,000 men ordered in New York state by 17 Oct. . . . . . . Sept. ,,
Lincoln suspends habeas corpus writ, and authorises severe measures against disloyal persons 25-27 Sept. ,,
Desperate but indecisive conflicts near Corinth, Tennessee, 3-5 Oct.; and at Perrysville, Kentucky 8, 9 Oct. ,,
Confederate gen. Stuart crosses Upper Potomac, and enters Pennsylvania; enters Chambersburg

UNITED STATES.

and other places, carrying off horses, ammunition, &c.; rides round the federal army, and returns to his camp . . . . 10, 13 Oct. 1862
Gold at 29 premium at New York . . . Out. ,,
Great democratic meeting at New York, condemning the president's policy . . . . . 12 Oct. ,,
At New Orleans Butler compels all persons who refuse to take the oath of allegiance to send in their names and register their property to the provost marshal . . . . . . 12 Oct. ,,
McClellan's head-quarters at Harper's Ferry 17 Oct. ,,
Raid of confederate gen. Morgan in Kentucky; he carries off 80 federal waggons of ammunition, &c. 18 Oct. ,,
Ten confederate prisoners at Palmyra shot by order of gen. McNeil in consequence of the disappearance of Abraham Allsman . . . 18 Oct. ,,
Rosencrans supersedes Buell in the west . 30 Oct. ,,
Elections for next congress; great majority for the democratic (opposition) candidates in New York and several other states . . . . 4 Nov. ,,
McClellan, while advancing towards Richmond, is superseded by gen. Burnside, 5 Nov.; who advances towards Richmond . . . 7 Nov. ,,
M. Drouyn de Lhuys, on behalf of the French government, proposes joint mediation in the American conflict to Great Britain and Russia, 30 Oct.; declined by Gortschakoff, 8 Nov.; by earl Russell . . . . . . 13 Nov. ,,
The confederate steamer *Alabama*, capt. Semmes, captures many U.S. vessels, and excites much alarm at New York . . . . Oct.-Dec. ,,
President Davis threatens reprisals if general McNeil is not surrendered (see 18 Oct.) 17 Nov. ,,
Burnside summons Fredericksburg to surrender; confederate gen. Lee with about 80,000 men near 22 Nov. ,,
100,000 federal soldiers on the sick list . Nov. ,,
Great honour shown to McClellan; he is proposed as the next president . . . . . Nov. ,,
The federal government orders release of disaffected persons in prisons . . . . . 25 Nov. ,,
Annual session of U.S. congress; the president recommends compensated emancipation of all slaves in the loyal states before the year 1900 1 Dec. ,,
Battle of Fredericksburg (*which see*); Burnside crosses the Rappahannock, 10 Dec.; bombards Fredericksburg, 11 Dec.; a series of desperate attacks on the confederates; Burnside totally defeated, 13 Dec.; recrosses the river 15 Dec. ,,
Engagements in Tennessee with varying results, Dec. ,,
Discovery of frauds in the U.S. army financial accounts; public dissatisfaction with the government; secretaries Chase and Seward resign, but resume office . . . . Dec. ,,
Homestead and Pre-emption act (relating to settlement of free land) passed . . . . . ,,
Battles near Murfreesboro', or Stone River, between Rosencrans and the federals and Braxton Bragg and the confederates: begin 29 Dec.; severe but indecisive, 31 Dec.; battle continued, 1 Jan.; Bragg defeated, retreats . . . . 2 Jan. 1863
["There have been about 7000 battles and skirmishes since the commencement of the war."—*American Almanack*.]
President Lincoln proclaims the freedom of slaves in the rebel states, except in parts held by the U.S. army . . . . 2 Jan. ,,
Burnside superseded by Joseph Hooker in command of army of the Potomac . . 26 Jan. ,,
The French government's offer of mediation, 9 Jan. declined . . . . 6 Feb. ,,
The *George Griswold*, a vessel containing provisions and other relief for the distressed cotton workers in Lancashire, arrives . . . . 9 Feb. ,,
A conscription bill (for men between 18 and 45) passed . . . . 25 Feb. ,,
The congress authorises the suspension of the habeas corpus act, 3 March; and establishes a National Academy of Sciences at Washington 4 March, ,,
Confederate loan for 3,000,000l. well taken up in Europe . . . . March, ,,
Charleston, South Carolina, attacked by monitors and gunboats; the Keokuk, a monitor, sunk 7 April, ,,
Battle of Chancellorsville (*which see*); the federals under Hooker cross the Rappahannock, 28 April;

defeated (gen. Stonewall Jackson is mortally wounded), 2-4 May; Hooker recrosses the Rappahannock . . . . . . 5 May, 1863
Stonewall Jackson dies . . . 10 May, ,,
Grant's successful campaign in Tennessee; he defeats the confederates under Joseph Johnston at Jackson, 14 May; and under Pemberton at Champion Hills, 16 May; and invests Vicksburg, Mississippi, which is strongly fortified, 18 May, a dreadful assault on it repelled . 22 May, ,,
Great peace meeting at Norfolk . . 5 June, ,,
Confederate invasion under Lee; invade Maryland and Pennsylvania, and take various towns 14 June, *et seq.* ,,
The federal gen. Hooker superseded by George H. Meade . . . . . . 27 June, ,,
Meade advances against Lee; great battle of Gettysburg, indecisive; but the confederates evacuate Pennsylvania and Maryland 1-3 July, ,,
Vicksburg bombarded, 3 July; surrendered by Pemberton to Grant and Porter . 4 July, ,,
Port Hudson, a confederate fortress on the Mississippi, surrenders . . . . 8 July, ,,
Fierce riots at New York against the conscription; many negroes murdered, and much property destroyed . . . . . 13-16 July, ,,
The Sioux defeated, 7 Aug.; gen. Pope reports that the Indian war is ended . . . . Aug. ,,
New York rioters tried and convicted, 12 Aug.; conscription going on peaceably . 21 Aug. ,,
Siege of Charleston: defended by Beauregard—attacks with varied success, July; Fort Sumter bombarded and destroyed (and so-called Greek fire employed); attacks on the ruins repulsed 21, 22 Aug. ,,
Knoxville occupied by Burnside . 10 Sept. ,,
A Russian squadron warmly received at New York Sept. and Oct. ,,
Battles of Chickamauga, Tennessee; Rosencrans defeated by Bragg . . . . 19, 20 Sept. ,,
Mason, the confederate commissioner in England, protests against the mode of his reception, and quits . . . . 22 Sept. ,,
Confederates defeated at Blue-Springs, Tennessee 10 Oct. ,,
Lincoln calls for 300,000 volunteers . 17 Oct. ,,
Rosencrans' command of the federal army in Tennessee superseded by Grant, and Thomas, and Sherman . . . . . . 19 Oct. ,,
The steam rams *El Tousson* and *El Monassir*, built by Mr. Laird at Birkenhead, and suspected to be for the confederates, are placed under charge of a government vessel in the Mersey . 31 Oct. ,,
British consuls dismissed from southern states Oct. ,,
Meade captures a part of Lee's army on the N. side of the Rappahannock . . . . 7 Nov. ,,
The chief justices Lowrie, Woodward, and Thompson declare that the Conscription act is unconstitutional . . . . . 12 Nov. ,,
Longstreet defeats Burnside, and compels him to retire into Knoxville . . . 14-17 Nov. ,,
Sherman and Thomas defeat Bragg at Chattanooga 23, 24 Nov. ,,
Longstreet's attack on Knoxville, defended by Burnside, fails, and he retreats into Virginia 29 Nov. and 1 Dec. ,,
The confederate general Bragg superseded by Hardee . . . . 2 Dec. ,,
Lincoln's message to congress warlike; he proffers amnesty to all except heads of governments, &c., 4 Dec.; Davis's message, firm, but acknowledging reverses . . . . . 7 Dec. ,,
Gen. Joseph Johnston takes command of the confederate army in Georgia . . . 27 Dec. ,,
President Lincoln orders a draft of 500,000 men in 3 years . . . . 1 Feb. 1864
Federal expedition into Florida; defeated at Olustee . . . . 20 Feb. ,,
Failure of attack of Kilpatrick and Dahlgren on Richmond . . . . 27 Feb.-4 March, ,,
Ulysses Grant made commander-in-chief, succeeding Halleck . . . . . . 12 March, ,,
Confederate raids into the Western states March, ,,
Sherman's expedition against Mobile, 2 March, defeated by Kirby-Smith . . . 5 April, ,,
James E. Stuart, the celebrated confederate cavalry officer, killed . . . . . 11 May, ,,

Campaign in Virginia; the army of the Potomac crosses the Rapidan; advance of Lee (now supported by Longstreet), 2 May; severe battle in the "Wilderness" (near Chancellorsville), indecisive, 5, 6 May; battle of Spotsylvania; the federals remain on the field; much carnage	10-12 May, 1864
Sherman (in Georgia) beats the confederates at Resacca, 14 May, and at Dallas	28 May, "
Fugitive slave act repealed by the house of representatives	13 June, "
After a succession of attacks on both sides, Grant compels Lee to retire gradually, and by a flank movement marches to the other side of Richmond, and faces Petersburg, 15 June; where, having taken the first intrenchments after desperate assaults, he is repulsed with considerable loss	18 June, "
The confederate steamer *Alabama* (capt. Semmes) attacked and sunk by the U.S. corvette *Kearsage* (capt. Winslow) near Cherbourg, France, 19 June,	"
Mr. Chase, secretary to the U.S. treasury, resigns; succeeded by Mr. Fessenden	July, "
Part of Lee's army invades Maryland, 1 July; defeats Wallace near Monocracy river, 9 July; threatens Baltimore and Washington, and retreats	12, 13 July, "
Sherman's 3 battles at Atlanta (Georgia), 20, 22 July; victory remains with the federals	28 July, "
Confederates again invade Maryland and Pennsylvania, and destroy Chambersburg	30 July, "
Grant orders the explosion of a mine at Petersburg, whereby 250 confederates are killed: but the assault following is repulsed with great slaughter	30 July, "
The *Tallahassee* confederate steamer (built in London) destroys many U.S. merchantmen	July, Aug. "
Severe conflicts in the Shenandoah valley: the federals victors	Aug. "
The confederate flotilla near Mobile destroyed by Farragut, 5 Aug.; Fort Gaines taken	8 Aug. "
McClellan nominated for the presidency by the "Democratic" Chicago convention	1 Sept. "
Sherman occupies Atlanta; the confederate general Hood retires	2 Sept. "
Sherman orders the depopulation of Atlanta,	7 Sept. "
McClellan declares for maintaining the union; the democratic party divided	13 Sept. "
Sheridan (federal) defeats Early at Winchester, in the Shenandoah valley, but with very great loss	19 Sept. "
Longstreet replaces Early in the command of the confederates	Oct. "
Longstreet defeats the federals at Cedar Creek; Sheridan arrives, rallies his troops, and defeats the confederates	19 Oct. "
St. Alban's Raid.—Between 20 and 30 armed men enter St. Alban's, Vermont; rob the bank and carry off horses and stores; fire on and kill several persons, and flee to Canada, 19 Oct.; where 13 of them are arrested	21 Oct. "
Lincoln re-elected president; McClellan resigns his command in U.S. army	8 Nov. "
Sherman destroys Atlanta and begins his march through Georgia to Savannah	13 Nov. "
Hood's attack on Thomas (federal), at Franklin, repulsed with severe loss	30 Nov. "
Lincoln's message to congress considered "bold"	6 Dec. "
The St. Alban's raiders discharged by Judge Coursol; general Dix issues an intemperate order for reprisals (disannulled by the president)	14 Dec. "
Hood defeated by Thomas (federal) near Nashville	14-16 Dec. "
Sherman storms fort M'Allister, 13 Dec.; enters Savannah	21 Dec. "
Wilmington bombarded; the attack of general Butler and admiral Porter repulsed	24, 25 Dec. "
The St. Alban's raiders recaptured and committed for trial	27 Dec. *et seq.* "
The federal congress abolishes slavery in the United States	1 Feb. 1865
Fruitless meeting of president Lincoln and secretary Seward with the confederate secretary Stephens, and 2 commissioners to treat for peace at Fort Monroe	2, 3 Feb. "
The Canadian government surrenders Burley, a raider, to the federals	3 Feb. 18
Lee takes the general command of the confederate armies; he recommends enlistment of negroes	18 Feb. "
Wilmington captured by Schofield; Charleston evacuated by the confederates; retreat of Beauregard	22 Feb. "
The confederate congress decree the arming of the slaves	22 Feb. "
Abraham Lincoln and Andrew Johnson inaugurated as president and vice-president	4 March, "
A new stringent tariff comes into operation,	1 April, "
Three days' sanguinary conflict at Five Forks, began 31 March; Sheridan turns Lee's front, and totally defeats him, 1 April; Lee retreats,	2 April, "
Richmond and Petersburg evacuated by the confederates and occupied by Grant	2, 3 April, "
Sheridan overtakes and defeats Lee at Sailor's Creek, 6 April; Lee surrenders with the army of Northern Virginia to Grant, at Appomatox courthouse	9 April, "
Mobile evacuated by the confederates	12 April, "
The Union flag replaced at Fort Sumter, Charleston,	14 April, "
President Lincoln shot at Ford's Theatre, Washington, about 11 o'clock, p.m., 14 April, by Wilkes Booth, who escapes; Mr. Seward, the foreign secretary, and his son, wounded in his own house by an assassin about the same time; Lincoln dies at 7.30 a.m., 15 April; *Andrew Johnson*, vice-president, sworn in as 17th president,	15 April, "
The convention between Sherman and Johnston (favourable to confederates), 17 April, disavowed by the government, 21 April; Johnston surrenders on same terms as Lee	26 April, "
Wilkes Booth shot, and his accomplice Harrold captured, in a farmhouse	26 April, "
The confederate general Dick Taylor (near Mobile) surrenders	4 May, "
President Jefferson Davis captured at Irwinsville, Georgia; imprisoned	10 May, "
The confederate general Kirby Smith, in Texas, surrenders; end of the war	26 May, "
President Johnson proclaims the opening of the southern ports, 22 May; and an amnesty with certain exemptions	29 May "
Solemn fast observed for death of president Lincoln,	1 June, "
The armies on both sides rapidly disbanding; fierce riots at New York between whites and negroes,	June, "
[Registered loss of the Federals 359,496; of which officers 9,584.]	
Galveston, Texas, the last seaport held by the south, surrendered by Kirby-Smith	5 June, "
The British and French governments rescind their recognition of the confederates as belligerents,	2, 6 June, "
President Johnson, uniting with the democrats, and acting leniently towards the south; reorganisation of the state governments	June, "
Close of the long trial of the assassination conspirators, 29 June; execution of Payne, Atzerott, Harrold or Herold, and Mrs. Suratt	7 July, "
The president declines recognition of the emperor of Mexico	18 July, "
All southern prisoners of war to be released on parole on taking oath of allegiance	29 July, "
Federal debt declared 2,757,253,275 dollars,	31 July, "
The confederate privateer *Shenandoah* (captain Waddell) captures and destroys many federal vessels (about 30)	Aug. "
Pacific policy of president Johnson; he declares himself opposed to centralisation and in favour of state rights; and is bitterly opposed by the radicals	Sept. "
Correspondence between earl Russell and Mr. Adams (U.S. minister, London) respecting the *Alabama*, confederate privateer; proposal of a commission to whom claims for reparation shall be referred	7 April-18 Sept. "
Alex. Stephens and other southern officials pardoned	11 Oct. "

Great meeting of Fenians at Philadelphia; the Irish republic proclaimed . . . . 16-24 Oct. 1865
Much public discussion respecting equal negro suffrage . . . . . . July-Oct. „
The national debt stated to be £600,000,000l. Oct. „
General Robert Lee becomes president of Washington College, Virginia . . . 2 Oct. „
Several southern states pass ordinances annulling secession, abolishing slavery, and renouncing confederate debt . . . Sept. Oct. Nov. „
National thanksgiving for the peace . 2 Nov. „
Captain Waddell arrives at Liverpool, 6 Nov.; surrenders the *Shenandoah* to the British government, stating that he had not heard of the end of the war till 2 Aug.; he and his crew paroled, 8 Nov.; the vessel given up to the American consul . . . . 9 Nov. „
Capt. Wirz, after long military trial, executed for cruelty to the federal prisoners at Andersonville, 10 Nov. „
A negro convention at Charleston, appeals for justice and generosity . . . . 25 Nov. „
Ex-president Buchanan publishes his justification, Nov. „
Habeas corpus act restored in N. states 1 Dec. „
Close of correspondence between the British and U.S. governments respecting depredations of *Alabama*, *Shenandoah*, &c. The earl of Clarendon maintains that "no armed vessel departed during the war from a British port, to cruise against the commerce of the United States" . . 2 Dec. „
Congress and government protest against the French intervention in Mexico, Nov.; . 6, 16 Dec. „
Opening of 39th congress; president Johnson's message conciliatory and firm (he requires from the southern states—repeal of their act of secession, abolition of slavery, and repudiation of confederate debt) . . . . 4 Dec. „
The radical party, opposed to the president, and to clemency to the south, predominate in the congress, and move violent resolutions against restoration of southern states to the union . Dec. „
Estimated federal debt, 600,000,000l.; revenue, 80,000,000l. . . . . . . Dec. „
35 members for the southern states excluded from congress; the conservative party support the president in his endeavours to reconstruct the union; the radicals violently oppose his policy, requiring the south to undergo previously a severe probation; the president has restored state government to all the southern states except Texas and Florida . . . . 29 Dec. „
The radicals demand for the negroes, personal, civil, and political rights, equal to those of the whites; the president proposes gradual enfranchisement, in separate states . . Feb. 1866
The president vetoes the Freedmen's Bureau bill, 21 Feb.; and the bill for the civil rights of the blacks . . . . . . 27 March, „
The president fiercely opposed by the radicals; the conservatives and democrats unite to support him . . . . March, „
He proclaims the rebellion at an end 3 April, „
The Civil Rights bill passed in spite of the veto, 9 April, „
The veto on the admission of Colorado as a state, 15 May; set aside . . . . May, „
Fenian raids in Canada . . 31 May-7 June, „
The radical reconstruction clause termed the "constitutional amendment" (granting negro suffrage to be enforced by the different states; the whites and the blacks to be equal in the sight of the law, &c.), passed by the senate . 13 June, „
Death of general Winfield Scott, aged 80, 29 May; and of Lewis Cass, aged 83 . . . 17 June, „
Continued dissension between the president and the congress . . . . . . July, „
The representatives of Tennessee re-admitted to the congress (10 states still excluded) . July, „
The Atlantic telegraph completed (see *Electric Telegraph*) . . . . . . 27 July, „
The congress adjourns . . . . 28 July, „
Great meeting at Philadelphia of the National Union Convention, consisting of delegates (the moderate men of all the parties, in every state, north and south, now termed the conservative party), whose object is to establish the national union, restore the south to its rights, and vindicate the president's policy . . 14 Aug. 1866
Tour of the president; he visits Philadelphia, New York, Chicago, &c.; he is very enthusiastically received; and speaks warmly, and often injudiciously . . . . . 28 Aug.-18 Sept. „
Elections for congress go in favour of the republicans . . . . Oct. „
[They demand that three-fifths of the blacks in the south shall be entitled to vote; that where negro suffrage is not established, only whites shall count; and that all persons who have taken any part in the rebellion shall be disqualified to vote.]
Death of Martin Van Buren, ex-president Oct. „
Trial of Jefferson Davis deferred till spring Oct. „
Elections in all the states except Delaware and Maryland in favour of the radicals (about 2,200,000 to 1,800,000); two coloured deputies elected in Massachusetts . . . . Oct.-Nov. „
Government policy declared to be "dead" Nov. „
Meeting of congress; president's message; he declares that he adheres to his policy 3 Dec. „
Bills to provide territorial governments in southern states; and restriction of president's appointing powers proposed . . . . . 3 Dec. „
The president charged with being "silent and motionless;" congress absorbs all the power Dec. „
A bill admitting negroes to the suffrage in district of Columbia passed . . . . 13 Dec. „
Veto of president set aside . . . Jan. 1867
Supreme court decides that congress has not power to appoint military tribunals . . Jan. „
Impeachment of president by a judicial committee agreed to . . . . . . 7 Jan. „
Division among the radicals; Stevens successfully opposed by Ashley . . . . 29 Jan. „
Debt of the United States reported 2,543,000,000 dollars . . . . 1 Feb. „
Nebraska admitted as the 37th state, over president's veto . . . . . . 9 Feb. „
Bill for establishing military government in the southern states, divided into five districts, discussed . . . . . . 13-15 Feb. „
Modified and passed, 20 Feb.; vetoed by the president . . . . 28 Feb. „
Mr. Peabody gives 1,000,000 dollars to promote education in the south . . . Feb. „
40th congress opened . . . 4 March, „
Supplementary reconstruction bill for the south passed . . . . 20 March, „
Tenure of Office act passed . . March, „
Russian America purchased for 7,000,000 dollars; treaty ratified by the senate . . 9 April, „
"Protection" rife: taxation on British manufactures 80 per cent.; much smuggling; public debt not diminishing; many strikes amongst operatives . . . . April, „
Jefferson Davis released on bail, 13 May; proceeded to New York, and thence to Canada.
20 May, „
Supplementary reconstruction bill adopted over the president's veto . . . 15 July, „
Long trial of John H. Suratt, for complicity in assassination of president Lincoln; jury not agreed on verdict (discharged, 6 Nov. 1868), 10 Aug. „
Insubordination of gen. Sheridan, favoured by Edw. Stanton, secretary of war, who refuses to resign at the requisition of the president, 5 Aug.; suspended; succeeded by gen. Grant 12 Aug. „
General amnesty proclaimed by the president, 9 Sept. „
Removal of gen. Sheridan from the government of Louisiana, and of Sickles from N. Carolina, for insubordination to the president Aug.-Sept. „
National cemetery at Antietam (*which see*) dedicated in presence of the president . 17 Sept. „
Sir Fred. Bruce, British ambassador, died at Boston, 9 Sept. „
Russian America ceded . . . 8 Oct. „
Jefferson Davis's trial adjourned . . 26 Nov. „
Elections in the south give supremacy to the negroes; in the north, great majorities for the democrats . . . . . . Oct.-Nov. „
President's message, maintaining his principles on reconstruction . . . . . 3 Dec. „

UNITED STATES. 944 UNITED STATES.

Revenue of the states fallen off; public debt about 520,000,000*l*. . . . . . . Dec, 1867
Proposed impeachment of the president negatived in congress (108 to 57) . . . . 8 Dec. ,,
Treaty for purchase of Danish West Indies (St. Thomas and St. John), for 7,500,000 dollars, signed . . . . Dec. ,,
Great general storm of snow and sleet; many perish; many wrecks . . . . 11-15 Dec. ,,
President Johnson censured; and gen. Sheridan thanked by house of representatives (*see* Aug. 1867) . . . . 4 Jan. 1868
General Grant replaced by Stanton (by the senate), 14, 15 Jan. ,,
The house of representatives declare that there is no valid government in the south; and transfer the jurisdiction from president Johnson to Grant, as general of the army . . . . 21 Jan. ,,
Great commercial depression; Mr. Wells, the revenue commissioner, recommends " peace, retrenchment, and reform" . . . . . . Jan. ,,
The inland cotton tax repealed . about 1 Feb. ,,
Edward Thornton, new British ambassador, and Charles Dickens received by the president 7 Feb. ,,
Angry correspondence between the president and gen. Grant . . . . . 28 Jan.-14 Feb. ,,
President Johnson orders dismissal of Stanton, and appoints gen. Thomas secretary of war, 21 Feb.: declared illegal by the senate . 22 Feb. ,,
The impeachment of the president voted by house of representatives (126 to 47), 24 Feb.; reported at the bar of the senate by Thaddeus Stevens and Bingham . . . . 25 Feb. ,,
Nine articles of impeachment (for issuing order for removal of E. M. Stanton from war-office, and following proceedings) adopted by representatives (127 to 47) . . . . . 2 March, ,,
Bill of impeachment of Johnson sent up to the senate by the house of representatives, 4 March, ,,
Judicious speech of lord Stanley in the British house of commons on the *Alabama* claims, 6 March, ,,
Trial of president Johnson comes before the senate, 23 March, ,,
Impeachment opened by gen. Butler . 30 March, ,,
Mr. Dickens sails from New York, after most affectionate parting . . . . . 22 April, ,,
National republican convention at Chicago; announce their "platform"; approving the congress reconstruction policy; severely condemning president Johnson; denouncing repudiation of the debt; declaring for protection of naturalised citizens, &c., 20 May; and proposing general Ulysses Grant as the next president, and Mr. Colfax as vice-president . . . 21 May, ,,
The senate reject the 11th article of the impeachment . . . . 16 May, ,,
Reject 2nd and 3rd articles; and adjourn *sine die*; intense excitement among republicans, 26 May, ,,
Mr. Stanton resigns, 27 May; succeeded by gen. Schofield . . . . 30 May, ,,
Death of the ex-president James Buchanan, 1 June, ,,
Chinese embassy received by the president, 5 June, ,,
Bill for re-admitting North and South Carolina, Georgia, Louisiana, Florida, and Alabama, to representation in congress, passed by the senate, 11 June, ,,
Mr. Reverdy Johnson nominated ambassador to Great Britain . . . . . . 12 June, ,,
Arkansas re-admitted over the president's veto, 20 June, ,,
The democratic convention nominate Horatio Seymour for president, and Francis P. Blair for vice-president . . . . . . 4-7 July, ,,
General amnesty (with exceptions) issued 4 July, ,,
Wyoming territory organised . . . 22 July, ,,
Act for protection of naturalised citizens abroad passed . . . . 27 July, ,,
Thaddeus Stevens dies . . . . 12 Aug. ,,
Total debt declared, 2,641,002,572 dollars . Aug. ,,
General Ulysses Grant, elected 18*th president* 3 Nov. ,,
General Sheridan's victory over Insurgent Indians; a village burnt . . . . . 27 Nov. ,,
Any repudiation of debt renounced by the house of representatives (154 to 6) . . . 14 Dec. ,,
General pardon issued . . . . 25 Dec. ,,
Cornell university (*which see*) founded . . ,,

Convention respecting *Alabama* claims signed by lord Clarendon and Mr. Reverdy Johnson, 14 Jan. ,,
Prosecution of Jefferson Davis dropped; a *nolle prosequi* entered . . . . . 6 Feb. ,,
Indian war reported over . . . . Feb. ,,
Alabama treaty rejected by committee of senate, 18 Feb. ,,
Suffrage bill, abolishing all distinctions of race, colour, and property, passed . . 27 Feb. ,,
General Schenk's bill, declaring that all national obligations shall be paid in coin, passed 3 March, ,,
Adjournment of 40th congress; meeting of 41st congress; gen. Grant assumes office . 4 March, ,,
Schenk's bill for cash payments passed by senate, 15 March, ,,
Convention respecting *Alabama* claim rejected by the senate . . . . . . 13 April, ,,
John Lothrop Motley appointed minister at London, April, ,,
Naturalisation treaty with Great Britain ratified by senate . . . . 15 April, ,,
Great peace jubilee held at Boston; colossal concert (10,371 voices, 1094 instruments, with anvils, bells, &c.) began . . . . 15 June, ,,
Wm. Pitt Fessenden, financier, died . 8 Sept. ,,
Steam-boat, *Stonewall*, burnt on the Mississippi; about 200 persons perish . . . 27 Oct. ,,
Free-trade agitation prevalent . . Oct.—Dec. ,,
Adm. Charles Stewart, "old iron-side," aged 92, died 6 Nov. ,,
Correspondence respecting *Alabama* claims, &c., between lord Clarendon and Mr. Hamilton Fish (June—Oct. 1869), published . . . Dec. ,,
Renewal of the reciprocity treaty with Canada rejected by congress . . . . 13 Dec. ,,
U. S. corvette *Oneida* sunk by collision with British P. & O. steamer *Bombay*; 112 lives lost, 24 Jan. ,,
[Capt. Eyre, of the *Bombay*, severely censured for not waiting to give succour.]
Darien canal scheme approved by congress, Jan.; treaty signed . . . . . 26 Jan. ,,
Virginia (15 Jan.) and Mississippi re-admitted to congress . . . . 3 Feb. ,,
Prince Arthur presented to president Grant, 24 Jan.; attended Mr. Peabody's funeral . 8 Feb. ,,
Bill for purchase of St. Thomas's isle rejected by senate . . . . 23 March, ,,
Texas (15 Mar.) and Georgia re-admitted to congress, 20 April, ,,
By amendments of the constitution, negroes admitted to equal rights with whites . April, ,,
The tariff bill opposed by freetraders . May, ,,
Non-recognition of Cuba affirmed . June, ,,
Lincoln state (out of New Mexico) constituted, June, ,,
Strong opposition to Chinese immigration; citizenship refused by the senate . . 4 July, ,,
Admiral J. A. Dahlgren died . 12 or 13 July, ,,
Session of congress closed . . . 15 July, ,,
J. L. Motley, minister to Great Britain, recalled, July, ,,
New tariff bill passed (new rates take effect, 1 Jan. 1871) . . . . ,,
Admiral David Farragut died, aged 70 . 14 Aug. ,,
Strict neutrality in the Franco-Prussian war proclaimed . . . . Aug. ,,
Senator Oliver P. Morton accepts the embassy to Great Britain . . . . . . 23 Sept. ,,
Great loss of life and property through floods in Virginia and Maryland, end of . Sept.-2 Oct. ,,
Total public debt, the principal and interest, 2,346,913,652 dollars . . . . 1 Oct. ,,
Great reduction of the heavy internal taxation begins . . . . 1 Oct. ,,
Movement against the Mormons on account of their polygamy . . . . 1 Oct. ,,
Meeting of the southern convention at Cincinnati for political and commercial affairs . 4 Oct. ,,
General Robert Lee dies, aged 62 . . 12 Oct. ,,
President Grant issues a proclamation against Fenianism, and attacks on Cuba . . 13 Oct. ,,
Mr. Morton declines the embassy to Britain for party reasons . . . . about 25 Oct. ,,
The republican majority in the congress greatly reduced by the "fall" election (the first in which all races are duly represented) . . Nov. ,,

Gen. Cox, secretary of interior, dismissed; quarrel between him and the president . . Nov. 1870
Total debt, 2,334,308,494 dollars . . 1 Dec. ,,
Annual message of the president: he regrets failure of proposal for annexing St. Domingo; and of the non-settlement of the *Alabama* claims; and complains of Canadian aggression . 5 Dec. ,,
Population: 33,581,680 whites; 4,879,323 coloured; Indians, 25,733; Chinese, 63,196; Japanese, 55; total, 38,549,987 . . . . . Dec. ,,
Mr. Motley terms his recall "an outrage" 7 Dec. ,,
Gen. Robert Schenck appointed minister in London; accepts . . . . . 21 Dec. ,,
New tariff in operation . . . . 1 Jan. 1871
George Ticknor, historian, dies . . . 26 Jan. ,,
Statue of Abraham Lincoln in the capitol at Washington, unveiled . . . . . 25 Jan. ,,
42nd congress meets (senate, 47 republicans; 15 democrats) . . . . . 4 March, ,,
Proclamation against the Ku Klux in N. Carolina, 5 March, ,,
Commission to settle disputes with Great Britain respecting the *Alabama*, &c., fishery question, and the San Juan affair: for the British, the earl de Grey (since marquis of Ripon), sir Stafford Northcote, and others; for the Americans, secretary Fish, gen. Schenck, and others; announced 10 Feb.; meet at Washington, 27 Feb.; sign treaty, agreeing to arbitration at Geneva, &c. (see *Alabama*, and *San Juan*), 8 May; ratified, 26 May, ,,
General Schenck warmly received at Liverpool, 3 June, ,,
An American fleet, accompanied by English and French and German ships, arrives at Corea to conclude a treaty for protection of mariners; on attempting to explore the island the Europeans are assailed from masked batteries; the Corean forts are then attacked and destroyed; and negotiations renewed . . . . . June, ,,
Formation of the "new departure" democrat party advocating perfect freedom of all males irrespective of race and colour, full political restoration of the southern states, and free trade; about July, ,,
Chicago destroyed by fire; great exertions to relieve the sufferers; see *Chicago*; about 2000 lives lost by fires in N. W. forests . . 8-11 Oct. ,,
Col. Hodge, paymaster of the regular army, confesses great defalcations since 10 Sept. 1864; condemned to long imprisonment . . Nov. ,,
European and North American railway opened at Bangor, Maine, by lord Lisgar and gen. Grant, 18 Oct. ,,
Dispute between the U.S. foreign minister, Hamilton Fish, and the Russian envoy Katakazy (for undue interference); Katakazy dismissed Nov. ,,
Grand duke Alexis of Russia warmly received at New York . . . . . 18 Nov. ,,
Congress opened; president in his message refers to peace abroad and prosperity at home . 4 Dec. ,,
Formal meeting of the *Alabama* arbitration commission at Geneva (adjourned to 15 June) . 18 Dec. ,,
Gen. Halleck died . . . . . Jan. 1872.
General amnesty bill passed . . . 16 Jan. ,,
American case under the treaty of Washington; claims indirect damages by *Alabama* and other vessels; much excitement in England . Jan. ,,
Despatch from the British minister sent 2 Feb.; reply received (not divulged to parliament), 14 March; further correspondence (see *Alabama*), March, April, ,,
Formation of Yellowstone National Park (*which see*) authorised by congress . . . March, ,,
Horace Greeley, editor of the *New York Tribune*, nominated president by many republicans, 4 May, ,,
New tariff, reduced duties to begin from 1 Aug.; passed . . . . . . 4 June, ,,
General Grant nominated for re-election as president by the republicans at Pennsylvania . 6 June, ,,
Continued negotiations respecting the *Alabama* affair, May; nothing settled; congress adjourns to December . . . . . 10 June, ,,
Dispute with Spain respecting unjust imprisonment of Dr. Howard, an American citizen, in Cuba since 13 Dec. 1870; settled; Dr. Howard released . . . . . . June, ,,
nation of straight-out democrat party, about June, ,,

Great international musical peace jubilee at Boston, 17 June—4 July, 1872
Coalition between the democrats and the liberal republicans at Baltimore to support Greeley, 10 July, ,,
Trial of Edward S. Stokes for murder of James Fisk of the Erie Ring (see *New York*, 1872), 15 July, ,,
United States squadron at Southampton, England, visited by the prince of Wales . 13 Aug. ,,
Judge Barnard convicted of corruption, and removed from office and disqualified . . 19 Aug. ,,
The "straight-out democrats" nominate Charles O'Connor for president . . . Sept. ,,
Announcement of the award of the Geneva arbitration on the *Alabama*, &c. (about 3,229,166*l*.) Sept. ,,
Wm. Henry Seward, statesman, died . 10 Oct. ,,
The emperor of Germany, arbitrator in the San Juan difficulty, awards the island to the United States . . . . . . 23 Oct. ,,
Total debt of the States, 2,276,828,101 dollars, 1 Nov. ,,
Gen. Grant re-elected president (by 300 electoral votes; 68 for Greeley) . . . 5 Nov. ,,
Death of Horace Greeley, aged 61 . . 29 Nov. ,,
Sergeant William Bates walked from Gretna Green to London, carrying the American flag; warmly received everywhere (the feat originated in a wager); arrived 29 Nov.; rode through London to Guildhall . . . . . . 30 Nov. ,,
Gen. Grant in his message says that the results of the arbitration leave Great Britain and the United States without a shadow upon their friendly relations . . . . . . 2 Dec. ,,
Modoc Indians, near Oregon, defeat troops sent to expel them . . . . . 17 Jan. 1873
Visit of professor Tyndall; he lectures in Boston, Philadelphia, Washington, New York, &c., Sept. 1872—Feb. ,,
Vice-president Colfax accused of perjury . Feb. ,,
Civil war in Louisiana, fighting at New Orleans, Feb. ,,
The congress opened, great Credit Mobilier scandal, members accused of bribery . . March, ,,
Death of chief justice Chase . . . 7 May, ,,
General Canby and others massacred (see *Modocs*, 11 April; capt. Jack and others captured; end of the war . . . . . 1 June ,,
Hiram Powers, sculptor of "the Greek Slave," died at Florence . . . . 27 June, ,,
Steamer *Wawasset* takes fire on the Potomac; about 70 perish . . . . . . 8 Aug. ,,
Cash payments (in silver) resumed . 28 Oct. ,,
Great excitement through the execution of Americans taken in the *Virginius* (see *Cuba*) . Nov. ,,
Public debt (less money in treasury) 2,141,833,476 dollars (about 4*s*. gold per dollar) . 1 Nov. ,,
President Grant's message: (calm) . . 2 Dec. ,,
Great deficiency in the revenue (about 17,000,000*l*.) announced . . . . . . Dec. ,,
Alex. H. Stephens, the great confederate leader, returns to political life and the legislature Dec. ,,
Women's *whisky-war* in S. Ohio; endeavour to suppress the liquor traffic by prayers, singing, &c., opposite the shops, Feb.; in New York 27 Feb. 1874
Ex-president Fillmore died . . . 8 March, ,,
Charles Sumner, senator, died . . 11 March, ,,
Women's whisky-war resisted; subsides March, April, ,,
President Grant's veto of the currency bill for creating inconvertible paper money, advocated by the Butler party . . . . . 22 April, ,,
Total debt, 2,285,786,818·89 dollars . 1 Aug. ,,
Fierce white and black riots at Austin, Mississippi, quelled by the military (after loss of 15 lives) 12 Aug. ,,
Great excitement respecting the Beecher-Tilton scandal; the rev. H. Beecher, a great preacher, accused of adultery with Mrs. Tilton, July; acquitted by a committee of his church. 27 Aug. ,,
Pennsylvania Republican Convention choose governor John F. Hartranft for next president Aug. ,,
Insurrection of negroes at Trenton, Tennessee; suppressed; leaders hanged . . . Aug. ,,
Centenary of the meeting of delegates at Philadelphia celebrated . . . . . Sept. ,,
Insurrection of whites at New Orleans against R. D. Kellogg, the governor of Louisiana, whom

3 P

they depose, 15 Sept.; they submit to the president; and Kellogg is restored . . 18 Sept. 1874
Great fire at Fall River cotton mills, Mass., about 60 lives lost . . . . . 19 Sept. ,,
Reported massacre of whites by Indians in N.W. provinces . . . . . . Oct. ,,
The Republic, new government paper, started 4 Oct. ,,
Lincoln monument, Springfield, Illinois, inaugurated . . . . 15 Oct. ,,
Triennial convention of the episcopal church; canon passed against ritualism . . . 27 Oct. ,,
Majority for democratic party in elections for congress reported . . . . . 4 Nov. ,,
President Grant's message, moderate . 7 Dec. ,,
The senate passes a bill for the resumption of cash payment, 1 Jan., 1879 . . . . Dec. ,,
Disturbances in New Orleans: government troops eject conservative members from the legislative assembly as unduly elected . . . 4 Jan. 1875
New York, Boston, and other cities protest; the president's excuse in his message . . Jan. ,,
Senate rejects new reciprocity treaty with Canada 4 Feb. ,,
Colorado and New Mexico to be made states Feb. ,,
Civil rights (of negroes) bill passed . . Feb. ,,
The 44th congress comes into office, 4 March; (to meet on 6 Dec.). . . . . . . ,,
Centenary of battle of Lexington celebrated 19 April, ,,
Centenary of battle of Bunker's hill celebrated June, ,,
Trial of Tilton v. Beecher ends: jury disagreeing, discharged . . . . . 2 July, ,,
Andrew Johnson, ex-president, dies . 31 July, ,,
Democratic conventions of New York declare in favour of hard money and resumption of cash payments . . . . . . 16 Sept. ,,
John McCloskey, R. C. archbishop of New York, made the first North American cardinal, received in his church at Rome . . . 30 Sept. ,,
President Grant, in addressing the Tennessee army in Iowa, protests against Roman catholic aggression . . . . 30 Sept. ,,
Democratic inflationists defeated at elections for governor in Ohio and Iowa . about 12 Oct. ,,
Virginia city destroyed by fire (see *Nevada*) 26 Oct. ,,
State official elections give large majority for republicans . . . . . . about 2 Nov. ,,
President Grant's message; alludes to attacks on and defends unsectarian education; notices unsatisfactory state of Cuba, and hints at ultimate intervention . . . . . . 7 Dec. ,,
Centennial year begun with great demonstrations at Philadelphia, &c. . . . . 1 Jan. 1876
General Babcock, secretary to president, acquitted of complicity in "Whisky frauds;" (resigned) 24 Feb. ,,
Mr. Belknap, secretary at war, accused of selling official places; resigns; impeached by congress 2 March, ,,
General Schenck, minister in London, charged with complicity in "Emma Mine frauds;" resigns and proceeds to America; R. H. Dana, appointed in his room (opposed); John Walsh appointed next; John Walsh comes . . . March, et seq. ,,
Salary of next president proposed to be reduced from 50,000 to 25,000 dollars . . March, ,,
Increased opposition to Chinese immigration, March, ,,
Dana's appointment as minister to Britain rejected by the senate . . . . about 5 April, ,,
Lincoln monument, Washington; (erected by coloured people); unveiled . . . 14 April, ,,
Other scandals in government offices reported April, ,,
The president vetoes the bill for reduction of president's salary . . . . . 19 April, ,,
Issue of silver coin for small notes . . May, ,,
Dispute with Great Britain respecting the extradition of Winslow, an American forger March-May, ,,
Mr. Pierrepoint, attorney-general, nominated minister for London . . . . . 5 May, ,,
International exhibition opened (see *Philadelphia*) 10 May, ,,
Political conferences at Philadelphia urge reforms May, ,,
Governor Rutherford B. Hayes, of Ohio, nominated president, and Wm. A. Wheeler vice-president, by the republican convention, Cincinnati 16 June, ,,
The arrangements for surrendering fugitive criminals in the treaty of 1842 nullified by th of Winslow and Brent (see *Extradition*) .
General Custer and his army attack the I dians, fall into an ambuscade, and are r killed
Mr. Tilden nominated president by the de convention, St. Louis
Centenary of the foundation of the republi
Massacre of negro militiamen by whites burg, S. Carolina, 9 July; 53 whites ind murder .
Mr. Belknap's case in the senate: 35 guilty of official corruption; 25 not;
Death of gen. Braxton Bragg .
The president's proclamation against unlaw binations (of whites) in S. Carolina
He declines to receive a centennial add Irish home-rulers .
Election of electors for the president
International Exhibition at Philadelphi

President Grant's message; he declares toral system to have failed .
Election for president by delegates; M 184; Mr. Hayes, 185; (some votes ob
End of dispute with the British Govern nounced (see *Extradition*) .
Electoral tribunal (to settle the election dent) chosen in congress .
President in his message urges a speedy cash payments .
Mr. R. B. Hayes' election confirmed; Mr. Wheeler, vice-president, 2 March; sworn, inaugurated; in his message he profess tial devotion to the public good, 5 Mar forms an impartial ministry .
Gen. Grant visits Britain . . . 28 M
"Molly Maguire," murderous terrorist r Pennsylvanian coal-fields; subdued executed .
Strike of railway servants on Baltimore railway through reduced pay; violent West Virginia; reign of terror; success tance to the military; many killed and at Pittsburg; held by rioters; sheri cannon used 16
Strike extending to New York railways (no England) .
Mob (many foreign communists) beaten by at Chicago (15 killed, about 100 wounded) Gen. Sheridan sent to Pittsburg, 22 July; about 8,000,000l.; tranquillity restore

Death of Brigham Young .
General movement for the rights of labou the year.
President Hayes warmly received in the sou
Formation of a Cuban league on behalf gents, announced .
Opposition to the president in Ohio, an states; in elections .
The new congress opened (democratic ma the house of representatives; gaining senate); Sam. J. Randall, democrat, r speaker
Many suspicious failures of commercial co and others . . . . . . Se
Reduction of the federal army from 25,000 voted by congress, refused by senate O
Anti-resumption bill passed by house of r tatives .
President Hayes' message; recommends res of cash payments on 1 Jan. 1879; pacific the south; good treatment of the negroe
The government defeated in the senate by C and party; opposing civil service refor payments, &c.
Bland's "silver bill," making silver the instead of gold; (injurious to fundholde passed by senate, veto of the president payments in silver to be resumed 1 Jar dollar 412½ grains said to be 8 per cent. le than gold .
Committee appointed to investigate charge ruption against boards returning dele elect the president .

Gen. Butler secedes from the republicans, and joins a new "National party" connected with Kearney, a violent agitator from California; (they are popularly termed "Greenbackers," as contending for soft money, and opposing return to cash payments) . . . . Aug. et seq.	1878
Desire expressed for a new reciprocity treaty with Canada . . . . . . Aug.	,,
American association meet at St. Louis . 21 Aug.	,,
Many deaths by yellow fever in southern states . . . . . . Aug., Sept., Oct.	,,
Autumn elections (mostly on 5 Nov.) . .	,,
46th congress elected; 149 democrats, 130 republicans, 10 greenbackers . . . Nov.	,,
President's address to congress expresses gratitude "for countless blessings" . . . 2 Dec.	,,
Gold at par (1st time since 1862) . . 18 Dec.	,,
Resumption of cash payments; no great demand . . . . 2 Jan.	1879
Death of Caleb Cushing, U.S. minister at Madrid; aged about 79 . . . . . 11 Jan.	,,
Meeting of 46th congress . . . 4 March,	,,
Great emigration of negroes from the southern to the western states . . . March, April,	,,
1,000,000l. 5 per cents converted into 4 per cents at par . . . . . . April,	,,
Mr. John Walsh, minister in London, resigns, July; leaves England (succeeded by James Russell Lowell the poet] . . . . . 19 Aug.	,,
"Knights of Labour," a secret society for protection and advancement of workmen, active in the middle states	,,
Largest grain crops for many years . autumn,	,,
Public debt, 2,027,202,452 dollars . . 1 Oct.	,,
Elections specially favour republicans . Oct.	,,
Much distress of freed negroes in Kansas, &c. 1 Jan.	1880
The republican convention at Chicago choose gen. Garfield and Mr. Arthur as president and vice-president, 9 June; the democratic convention at Cincinnati choose gen. Winfield Scott Hancock and Wm. H. English . . . . 24 June,	,,
Gen. Garfield sets forth his proposed policy in a letter; says, "We legislate for the people of the United States, not for the whole world;" proposes a check for Chinese immigration, &c. . 12 July,	,,
10,000 office holders said to be liable to change Aug.	,,
Public debt reduced to 1,915,594,813 dollars 1 Oct.	,,
Gen. Garfield elected president; Mr. Chester A. Arthur vice-president (213-156) . . 2 Nov.	,,
Dispute between the president and senator Conkling respecting appointment of collector of customs at New York; Conkling resigns . May,	1881
Assassination of president Garfield by Charles Jules Guiteau, a lawyer of Chicago, at railway station, Washington; two pistol shots; ball enters the body . . . . . . 2 July,	,,
Destructive forest fires in Michigan; about 500 persons perish; 10,000 homeless . . 5 Sept.	,,
General Garfield, after much suffering, died 19 Sept.	,,
Queen Victoria's message to Mrs. Garfield: "Words cannot express the deep sympathy I feel with you at this terrible moment. May God support and comfort you, as He alone can" . 20 Sept.	,,
After lying in state at Washington the general is buried at Cleveland, in Ohio . . 23 Sept.	,,
Part mourning in Great Britain . 21—28 Sept.	,,
54,000 dollars collected for Mrs. Garfield up to . . . . 30 Sept.	,,
Centenary of the capture of Yorktown celebrated (English flag saluted) . . 16 Sept. et seq.	,,
Mr. Blaine's letter to the European powers asserting the treaty respecting neutrality at Panama in 1846 to be sufficient, and protesting against their interference . . . . . 25 Oct.	,,
The hon. Sackville West, the new British minister, warmly received at Washington . . 4 Nov.	,,
Guiteau's trial begins . . . . 14 Nov.	,,
Meeting of Congress . . . . 5 Dec.	,,
Mr. Frelinghuysen succeeds Mr. Blaine as foreign minister . . . . . . 12 Dec.	,,
Guiteau in the prison van shot at by Wm. Jones; his head grazed, 19 Nov. 1881; verdict, guilty . . . . 25 Jan.	1882
Chinese immigration suspended for 20 years; bill passed by senate about 10 March; vetoed by president, March; by the president about . . . . 4 April,	,
Bill abolishing polygamy passed . . 23 March,	1882
Great floods in the west (see *Mississippi*) March,	,,
United States constitution translated into Chinese by Tsai Sih Yung, completed . . .	,,
Representatives pass immigration bill excluding Chinese for ten years . . . 17 April,	,,
Great strike of iron-workers (about 150,000) in Pennsylvania begun 1 June; going on 13 July,	,,
Meeting of masters at Pittsburg to organise resistance . . . . 7 June,	,,
Guiteau executed . . . . . 30 June,	,,
The Chinese exclusion act comes into operation . . . . 4 Aug.	,,
Act imposing a tax of 2s. per head (opposed by government) comes into operation . Aug.	,,
One of only two copies of a life of general Garfield presented to queen Victoria; the other to Mrs. Garfield	,,
End of the iron-workers' strike . about 12 Sept.	,,
Robert E. Lee steamer burned on the Mississippi; about 20 deaths . . . . . 29 Sept.	,,
Elections greatly in favour of the Democrats . . . . 7 Nov.	,,
Death of Thurlow Weed, politician and journalist, aged about 85 . . . . . 22 Nov.	,,
Meeting of Congress; president's address; comments on financial prosperity; recommends reduction of taxation and tariff . . 4 Dec.	,,
Civil service reform bill adopted by the senate . . . . 27 Dec.	,,
Immigration, 1881, about 719,000; 735,000 in	,,
Presidential succession bill passed . 9 Jan.	1883
National debt, net, 1,607,543,676 dollars 1 Jan.	,,
The marquis of Lorne visits Washington . 26 Jan.	,,
Reduction in internal revenue and revision of the tariff by the senate and congress . 3 March,	,,
Last sitting of the congress . . 4 March,	,,
Great East River bridge, connecting New York and Brooklyn, opened . . . . 24 May,	,,
Great strike of telegraph clerks in various states July, ends about 15 Aug.	,,
Visit of chief justice Coleridge; very warmly received . . . . . Sept.—Oct.	,,
Gen. Sheridan succeeds gen. Sherman in command of the United States army . . 31 Oct.	,,
Autumn elections; favour republicans . Nov.	,,
The new congress meets . . . 3 Dec.	,,
Death of Wendell Phillips, energetic abolitionist, aged 72 . . . . . . 4 Feb.	1884
Excitement concerning the wreck of the *Daniel Steinmann* (see *Wrecks*); investigation 8 April,	,,
Financial embarrassment of gen. Grant through endeavouring to support his son [relieved by government, 1885] . . . . May,	,,
Mr. James G. Blaine and gen. Logan nominated republican candidates for the presidency and vice-presidency at Chicago, 6 June; great dissatisfaction thereat . . . . June,	,,
Meetings at New York, and other cities, about . . . . 21 June,	,,
Colossal statue of Liberty, by Bartholdi, the gift of the French to the United States, delivered at Paris by M. Jules Ferry, 4 July [received at New York, 19 June, 1885]	,,
Mr. Grover Cleveland, governor of New York, and Mr. Thomas A. Hendricks, nominated democrat candidates for the presidency and vice-presidency at Chicago . . . . . 11, 12 July,	,,
Gen. Butler offers himself as people's candidate . . . . 19 Aug.	,,
Great strike of miners in Hocking valley, Ohio, on account of foreigners; rioting . 1 Sept. et seq.	,,
Governor Cleveland, president, and Mr. Hendricks, vice-president, elected (defeat of the republicans) . . . . 4 Nov.	,,
Roman Catholic plenary council at Baltimore (about 70 archbishops and bishops) opened 9 Nov.	,,
Cattle-men's convention at St. Louis (see under *Cattle*) . . . . . 18—22 Nov.	,,
About 56,000,000 acres appropriated by the Homestead act of 1862, up to 1880; announced Jan.	1885
Public indignation at the criminal explosions in London; stringent dynamite bill introduced in the senate by government . . . 26 Jan.	,,
Public debt, 1,409,128,325 dollars, announced . . . . 2 Feb.	,,
The Chinese expelled from California; indemnity	,,

UNITED STATES.

to be claimed by their government; announced . Feb. 1885
Memorial obelisk of George Washington, 555 feet high, at Washington, inaugurated . 21 Feb. ,,
President Cleveland installed amid great acclamations . . . . 4 March, ,,
A new ministry; secretary of state, Thomas F. Bayard . . . . 4 March, ,,
Mr. Edward J. Phelps appointed U.S. minister in London, March; arrives at Southampton 16 May, ,,
Currency crisis; the banks oppose the Bland Act, and the compulsory coinage of silver . July, ,,
Death of gen. Grant, 23 July; he lies in state at New York, 5, 6, 7 Aug.; funeral procession 6 miles long includes the family, president Cleveland, government officials, gen. Hancock, and others of U.S. army; gen. Johnson (confederate), soldiers, marines, &c. ; about 400 carriages; starts at 9 A.M.; arrival at the temporary tomb in Riverside Park on the Hudson 5 P.M. . 8 Aug. ,,
Murderous attacks on the Chinese workmen at Rock Springs in Wyoming territory 29 Aug.; quelled by government . . about 3 Sept. ,,
Violent action against Chinese capitalists and workmen in Washington territory; proclamation for its suppression by the president . 9 Nov. ,,
Death of gen. G. B. McClellan, com.-in-chief Nov. 1861, aged 59 . . . . . 28 Oct. ,,
Death of T. A. Hendricks, vice-president U.S., aged 66 . . . . . . 25 Nov. ,,
Gen. Sherman elected vice-president . 7 Dec. ,,
Wm. H. Vanderbilt, aged 64, "railway king," dies suddenly at New York; said to be worth about 50 million pounds . . . . . 8 Dec. ,,
Meeting of congress . . . . 8 Dec. ,,
Much money subscribed for promoting Irish Home Rule 1885-6
Great ovation of Jefferson Davis through the Southern States . . . . April, 1886
German socialist agitation, eight hours' movement; riots at Chicago; dynamite employed; mob dispersed by police after fighting, 4 May; riots at Milwaukee 5 May; 10 killed, 115 wounded; 25 arrests, about 6 May; Herr Most (anarchist) arrested at New York, 12 May; convicted of inciting to riot, May; sentenced to fine and imprisonment . . . . . 2 June, ,,
Gradual cessation of strikes in different states about 24 May, ,,
Chinese Indemnity Bill passed . . June, ,,
Large subscriptions to the Parnellite fund for elections, &c. . . . . June, et seq. ,,
The president promotes civil service reform; political action of officials checked . July, ,,
Election tour of Mr. James G. Blaine in Pennsylvania, &c.; strongly advocating Protection 16 Oct. ,,
Bartholdi Statue of Liberty, 150 feet high, set up at the harbour of New York, 305 feet above the sea level, on Bedloe Island, publicly dedicated by the president . . . . . . 28 Oct. ,,
Alien's Landlord's Bill (almost limiting holding of land and mines in "territories" to citizens) passed . . . . 2 Aug. ,,
Ex-president Arthur dies . . . 18 Nov. ,,
Great increase of speculation in railway stocks and trade . . . . . Nov-Dec. ,,
Mr. Henry George (see under Land) propagates his doctrines of Land Nationalisation; much opposed 1886-7
Edmunds' Canadian Fisheries Bill passed senate (46-1) . . . . . . 24 Jan. 1887
Fisheries Retaliation Bill passed . 3 March, ,,
American Exhibition (which see) opened in London 9 May, ,,
Seven socialists sentenced to death for murders during riots at Chicago, May, 20 Aug. 1886; ordered for execution . . . 14 Sept. ,,
Centenary of the adoption of the Federal constitution celebrated at Philadelphia; five mile procession illustrating the progress of trade and industry; fall of a great stand, many spectators injured, 15 Sept.; review of the army by the president, &c. . . . . . 17 Sept. ,,
After great efforts for remission of sentence four of the Chicago anarchists executed (two sentenced to life imprisonment, one committed suicide) 11 Nov. ,,

Mr. Barnum's menagerie at Bridgeport, Connecticut, burnt (see Menagerie) . . . 10 Nov. ,,
Mr. J. Chamberlain warmly received at New York; grand dinner at the chamber of commerce, 15 Nov. ,,
President Cleveland's message strongly urges fiscal reform, large reduction of protective duties and other taxation; surplus income 1886-7 above 11,000,000l. (annually increasing) 6 Dec.; approved by the Democrats, opposed by the Republicans, Dec. ,,
Naturalization of British emigrants increasing: strongly advocated by the British American newspaper to neutralize Irish influence (see George, St.) . . . . . . autumn ,,
The Knights of Labour order strikes of colliers and railway men; total on strike about 50,000, end of Dec.; end of railway strike reported 28 Dec. ,,
Snowstorm in the N.W. states; about 235 persons perish and many cattle . . 11-13 Jan. 188
Reform club at New York to support tariff reform; first banquet . . . . . 21 Jan. ,,
Treaty respecting fisheries signed at Washington (see Fisheries) . . . . . 15 Feb. ,,
Destructive blizzard (see Storms) . 11-13 March, ,,
Deadlock in the House of Representatives on the Direct Tax Bill; ended . . . 13 April, ,,
Mr. James G. Blaine announces positively his retirement from his candidature for the presidency 17 May, ,,
Mr. Cleveland nominated by acclamation for reelection as president by the Democratic convention at St. Louis, 6 June; gen. Benjamin Harrison (born 20 Aug. 1833) nominated candidate by the Republican convention at Chicago . 25 June, ,,
Lock-out of about 100,000 ironworkers near New York . . . . 30 June, ,,
President Cleveland at New York declares vigorously for reduced import duties and fiscal reform 5 July, ,,
American Tariff Bill passed lower House 21 July, ,,
Death of gen. Philip Henry Sheridan, commander-in-chief of the army, aged 57, 5 Aug.; succeeded by gen. John M. Schofield . . 14 Aug. ,,
Treaty with China to prohibit Chinese immigration for 20 years 14 March; bill passed . 20 Aug. ,,
The senate refuses to ratify the fisheries treaty 21 Aug. ,,
The president in a message censures this, but declares for a policy of retaliation against Canada 23 Aug. ,,
Retaliation Bill passed by the House . 8 Sept. ,,
Agitation against "Trusts and Combines" (which see) . . . . autumn, ,,
Chinese Exclusion Bill approved by president Cleveland . . . . . . Oct. ,,
Chinese Exclusion Act vigorously carried out at San Francisco and at other places middle Oct. ,,
Lord Sackville, British minister at Washington, dismissed by president Cleveland for conversations with a reporter, and for writing a private "reply to an alleged" naturalised Englishman in California respecting the presidential election 30 Oct.; lord Sackville admitted indiscretion but repudiated other charges . . 26 Oct. ,,
Gen. Benjamin Harrison elected president, Mr. Levi P. Morton, vice-president; great defeat of the Democrats (233-168) . . . 5 Nov. ,,
Resolution introduced into the House proposing negotiations for the annexation of Canada 13 Dec. ,,
The American Commonwealth, by professor James Bryce, M.P., an elaborate work published . ,,
Destructive tornado in the Eastern states (see Storms) . . . . . . 9 Jan. 188
Bill introduced in the House for stringent repression of immigration, especially labourers and criminals . . . . . . 19 Jan. ,,
New Tariff Bill passed by the senate . 22 Jan. ,,
The Anglo-American Extradition Treaty rejected by the senate (38-15) . . . 1 Feb. ,,
The senate and house pass the Nicaragua Canal Bill . . . . 7 Feb. ,,
Explosion at Park Central Hotel in Hartford, U.S.; about 40 persons killed . . . 18 Feb. ,,
Gen. Harrison assumes office; his cabinet formed; Mr. Blaine, secretary of state . . 4 March, ,,
Demonstrations and subscriptions in honour of Mr. Parnell at Philadelphia and other places (see Ireland) . . . . . . March, ,,

UNITED STATES. 949 UNIVERSITIES.

Storm at Samoa; three American war-vessels with loss of 4 officers and 46 men (see *Samoa*) 16 March, 1889
Oklahoma (*which see*) reserved lands (virgin soil) near Kansas, Arkansas, and Texas proclaimed open to settlers; thousands of farmers and others with their goods, cattle, &c., migrate thither; riotous proceedings with bloodshed precede and attend the entering . . . . 22 April, "
Sir Julian Pauncefote becomes British minister at Washington, Feb.; arrives . . . 23 April, "
Guthrie and two other towns founded . 23 April, "
Order maintained by the military and lynch law 24 April *et seq.* "
Many unsuccessful settlers return, reported April, "
Celebration at New York of the centenary of gen. Washington's inauguration as first president 29 April–1 May, "
Naval procession; 300 vessels sail round the harbour 29 April; military procession (65,000 men) 30 April, civic and industrial procession 1 May, "
A convention met at Columbia, Tennessee, and organised an American-Scottish-Irish Association to perpetuate race memories and history 8 May, "
Cyclone from Maryland to Connecticut, much damage . . . . . . 10 May, "
Mr. Robert T. Lincoln, son of Abraham, appointed minister to Great Britain, March; arrives in London . . . . . . 22 May, "
Dr. Patrick Henry Cronin, Irish nationalist, disappears 4 May; found murdered at Lake View, Chicago 22 May; several men arrested 29 May *et seq.* "
The coroner's jury declare the murder to be the result of a conspiracy of which Alexander Sullivan, P. O. Sullivan, Daniel Coughlin and Frank Woodruff (connected with the Clan-na-Gael) were the principals. Arthur Sullivan and others arrested 12 June; Alexander Sullivan released on high bail . . . . . 15 June, "
Martin Burke arrested at Winnipeg, Canada, indicted about 20 June. The grand jury at Chicago after 16 days investigation, presents an indictment against Martin Burke, John F. Beggs, Daniel Coughlin, Patrick O'Sullivan, Frank Woodruff, Patrick Cooney, and John Kunz, with others unknown, of conspiracy and of the murder of Patrick Henry Cronin . . 29 June, "
[The conspiracy is said to have originated in camp 20 of the Clan-na-Gael.]
About 6,000 persons perish by the overflow of the dam of a lake in Conemaugh valley (see *Pennsylvania*) . . . . . . 31 May, "
Destructive floods in the eastern states; 8 persons drowned at Harper's Ferry, Virginia, and 13 at Corning, New York; estimated loss at Washington, 1,000,000 dollars; floods subsiding end of May, and 1, 2 June, "
Message of sympathy from queen Victoria to the president . . . . . 8 June, "
Visit of American, civil, mechanical, mining and electrical engineers; well received in London, &c.; early June, "
Death of Simon Cameron, aged 90, war secretary during the civil war . . . 26 June, "
Great public meeting at Chicago impeaching the Clan-na-Gael as "an association of assassins," "existing under the protection of the United States, usurping the highest acts of government, in that it decrees death, exacts fealty, and levies war." . . . . . 2 July, "
A meeting of Irish-Americans at Chicago propose the formation of an "Irish-American Republican Association," to be settled in Lower California 5 July, 1889
Inundation in Mohawk Valley, New York; 14

persons drowned at Johnstown . . 9 July, 1889
Martin Burke (otherwise Frank Williams) at Winnepeg ordered for extradition 10 July; given up . . . . . . 3 Aug. "

PRESIDENTS OF THE UNITED STATES OF AMERICA.

1789 & 1793. General George Washington, elected first president. 6 April.
1797. John Adams. 4 March.
1801 & 1805. Thomas Jefferson. 4 March.
1809 & 1813. James Madison. 4 March.
1817 & 1821. James Monroe. 4 March.
1825. John Quincy Adams. 4 March.
1829 & 1833. General Andrew Jackson. 4 March.
1837. Martin Van Buren. 4 March.
1841. General William Henry Harrison. 4 March. Died 4 April, succeeded by
1841. John Tyler (formerly vice-president).
1845. James Knox Polk. 4 March.
1849. General Zachary Taylor. 4 March. Died 9 July, 1850, succeeded by the vice-president,
1850. Millard Fillmore.
1853. General Franklin Pierce. 4 March.
1857. James Buchanan. 4 March.
1861 & 1865. Abraham Lincoln. 4 March. Shot 14 April; died 15 April, 1865; succeeded by vice-president,
1865. Andrew Johnson. 15 April.
1869 & 1873. Ulysses S. Grant. 4 March.
1877. Rutherford Birchard Hayes. 4 March.
1881. Gen. James Abram Garfield. 4 March.
   Gen. Chester A. Arthur. 19 Sept.
1885. Grover Cleveland. 4 March.
1889. Gen. Benjamin Harrison. 4 March (grandson of the president of 1841).

UNIVERSALISTS, who believe in the final salvation of all men. This doctrine, declared in the Talmud, and ascribed to Origen, about 230, was advocated by other early fathers, but opposed by St. Augustin, about 420; and condemned by the 5th general council at Constantinople, May, June, 553. It was received by the Unitarians in the 17th century, and avowed by numerous clergymen of the church of England. James Relly, who published his "Union" in 1760, founded the sect of Universalists in Britain; and John Murray, in America, about 1770. The sect barely exists in Britain, but flourishes in America.

UNIVERSAL REVIEW, edited by Mr. Harry Quilter, devoted to fine art, literature, &c., first published 15 May, 1888.

UNIVERSAL SUFFRAGE (*Plebiscitum*), one of the six points of the charter (see *Chartists*), was adopted by the French in their constitution of 1791; and used in the election of their president in 1851, and of their emperor in 1852; and by the Italian States in voting for annexation to Sardinia in 1860, 1861, 1866, and 1870.

UNIVERSAL TIME, see under *Day*.

UNIVERSITIES. The most ancient in Europe are those of Bologna, Oxford, Cambridge, Paris, and Salamanca. In old Aberdeen was a monastery, in which youths were instructed in theology, the canon law, and the school philosophy, at least 200 years before the university and King's College were founded; see *Degrees*. The following dates are generally given:

Aberdeen founded	. 1494	Bordeaux 1472	Copenhagen . . . 1476
Abo, Finland . .	. 1640	Bourges 1465	Cordova, Spain . . 968
Adelaide, Australia .	. 1876	Breslau 1702	Corfu 1823
Andrews, St., Scotland .	. 1411	Bruges, French Flanders . 1665	Cracow, Poland, 700; revived . 1364
Angers, chiefly law .	. 1364	Brussels 1834	Dijon, France. . . . 1722
Anjou, 1349; enlarged .	"	Caen, Normandy, 1436; revived 1803	Dillingen, Swabia . . 1565
Athens . .	. 1836	Cambridge, began about 635 (?):	Dole, Burgundy . . 1422
Barcelona, revived .	. 1841	revived 1109	Dorpat 1632
Basle, Switzerland .	. 1460	Cambridge, New England, pro-	Douay, French Flanders . 1568
Berlin . .	. 1810	jected 1630	Dresden, Saxony . . 1694
Berne . .	. 1834	Christiania . . . 1811	Dublin (see *Trinity College*) . 1591
Besançon, Burgundy .	. 1676	Cologne, in Germany, refounded 1385	Dublin College (catholic) . 1851
Bologna, Italy . .	. 1116	Compostella, Spain . . 1517	Durham 1831
Bonn . .	1784, 1818	Coimbra, Portugal. . . 1279	Edinburgh, founded by James VI. 1582

Erfurt, Thuringia; enlarged	1390	Lyons, France	830, 1300	Queen's University (Ireland)	1850
Erlangen	1743	Madrid	1836	Rheims, 1145; enlarged	1548
Evora, Portugal	1533	Mantua	1625	Rome	1245
Florence, Italy, enlarged	1439	Marburg	1527	Rostock, Mecklenburg	1419
Frankfort-on-the-Oder	1506	Mechlin, Flanders	1440	Salamanca	1239
Franeker	1585	Melbourne, Victoria	1855	Salerno	1233
Fribourg, Germany	1460	Mentz	1477	Salzburg	1623
Geneva	1368	Milan	1565	Saragossa, Aragon	1474
Ghent	1816	Montpellier	1289	Seville	1504
Glasgow	1450	Moscow, 1754; again	1803	Sienna	1380
Göttingen	1735	Munich	1826	Siguenza, Spain	1517
Granada, Spain	1537	Munster	1491	Sorbonne, France	1253
Gripswald	1547	Nancy	1769	Strasbourg	1538
Groningen, Friesland	1614	Nantes	1460	Stutgardt	1775
Halle, Saxony	1694	Naples	1224	Sydney, N. S. W.	1852
Harvard, U.S.	1638	Orange	1365	Toledo, Spain	1499
Heidelberg	1386	Orleans, France	1305	Toulouse	1229
Helmstadt	1575	Oxford (see *Oxford*)	879	Troyes, Germany	1473
Ingolstadt, Bavaria	1573	Paderborn	1592	Tübingen, Würtemberg	1477
Irish new	1879	Padua, Italy	1228	Turin	1405
Jena, or Sala, Thuringia	1547	Palenza, 1209; removed to Salamanca	1249	Upsal, Sweden	1476
Kiel, Holstein	1665			Utrecht, Holland	1634
King's College, London (*which see*)	1829	Palermo	1447	Valence, Dauphiné	1454
		Paris, 792; renovated	1200	Valencia	1209
Königsberg, Prussia	1544	Parma	1482	Valladolid	1346
Leipsic, Saxony	1409	Pau	1722	Venice	1592
Leyden, Holland	1575	Pavia, 1360; enlarged	1599	Victoria, N. England	1880
Liége	1816	Perpignan	1349	Vienna	1365
Lima, in Peru	1614	Perugia, Italy	1307	Wales	1883
Lisbon, 1290; removed to Coimbra	1391	Petersburg, St., 1747; again	1819	Wittenburg	1502
		Pisa, 1343; enlarged	1552	Würtzburg	1403
London University (*which see*)	1826	Poitiers	1431	Wilna	1803
Louvaine, Flanders, 926; enlarged	1426	Prague	1348	Zurich	1832

UNIVERSITIES OF OXFORD AND CAMBRIDGE. Royal commission appointed to inquire into their income and property, in 1872; reported in Oct. 1874, that the united income for 1871, was 754,405*l*. 5*s*. 1½*d*.; see *Cambridge and Oxford*. The Universities Act passed, 10 Aug. 1877, appoints commissioners with power to make statutes and other provisions.

UNIVERSITY BOAT-RACE. The contest between the universities of Oxford and Cambridge, at first near Oxford, afterwards on the river Thames, began 10 June, 1829, and has been annual since 1856. In 1864, after 20 contests, the opposing parties were equal; but on 8 April, 1865, 24 March, 1866, 13 April, 1867, 4 April, 1868, and 17 March, 1869, Oxford won; the last time being the 9th in succession. Cambridge won, 6 April, 1870, 1 April, 1871, 23 March, 1872, 29 March, 1873, and 28 March, 1874. Oxford won, March 20, 1875; Cambridge won, 8 April, 1876. Dead heat; neither won, 24 March, 1877; Oxford won, 13 April, 1878; Cambridge won, 5 April, 1879; Oxford won on Monday, 22 March, 1880; Friday, 8 April, 1881; Saturday, 1 April, 1882; and Thursday, 15 March, 1883; Cambridge, Monday, 7 April, 1884; Oxford, Saturday, 28 March, 1885; Cambridge, Saturday, 3 April, 1886; 26 March, 1887; 24 March, 1888; 30 March, 1889. (E. T. Campbell killed at Cambridge, 24 Feb. 1888). In the international boat-race between the universities of Oxford and Harvard, Massachusetts, U.S., Oxford won, 27 Aug. 1869.

The Oxford crew rowed from Dover to Calais in 4¼ hours . . . . . 25 July, 1885

UNIVERSITY COLLEGE (London), see *London University*, and *Oxford*.

UNIVERSITY EDUCATION (Ireland) Act, 42 & 43 Vict. c. 85, passed 15 Aug. 1879. It provides for the dissolution of the "*Queen's University*," and the foundation of the "*Royal University of Ireland*," the charter of which was signed by the queen, 19 April, 1880.

UNIVERSITY ELECTIONS, see *Dodson's Act*.

UNIVERSITY TEACHING, Society for its Extension formed in London about 1875, and supported by Cambridge, Oxford, and London universities; great meeting for its support at the Mansion-house, 19 Feb. 1879. Courses of lectures given in various parts of London, Oct. 1879.

Proposed establishment of a settlement in east London, by university men of Oxford and Cambridge, to improve social intellectual condition May, 1884; at *Toynbee Hall*, Whitechapel, volunteer lectures on science, art, &c. given; also instruction in music, athletic sports &c.; and a social club formed.

Oxford House, at Bethnal Green; a kind of club for social intellectual improvement, opened by the archbishop of Canterbury . . . 18 Feb. 1888

UNIVERSITY TESTS (Religious). A bill for their abolition was rejected by the lords, 19 July, 1869, and 14 July, 1870; passed, and received royal assent, 16 June, 1871. A similar act for Trinity College, Dublin, was passed in May, 1873. In April, 1878, on trial it was affirmed, that an endowment with a religious test at Hertford college, Oxford, was valid.

UNKNOWN TONGUES, see *Irvingites*, note.

UNLEARNED PARLIAMENT, see *Parliament, 1404*.

UNSEAWORTHY SHIPS COMMISSION, see *Seamen* and *Merchant Shipping Act*.

UPSAL (Sweden). The Swedish rulers were kings of Upsal till 1001. The university was founded in 1476, by Sten Sture, the "protector," and opened 21 Sept. 1477. Celebration of foundation of university, Sept. 1877.

URANIUM, a brittle grey metal discovered by Klaproth in 1789, in the mineral pitch-blende. It has lately been employed in the manufacture of glass for certain philosophical purposes.

URANUS, a planet with eight satellites, was discovered by William Herschel, 13 March, 1781, first called Georgium Sidus, after George III.; next

Herschel; and, finally, Uranus. It is about twice as distant from the sun as the planet Saturn. The anniversary of its first revolution (in 84 years 7 days) since its discovery, was celebrated on 20 March, 1865. Its perturbations led to the discovery of Neptune, in 1846. Uranus has 8 satellites; 6 discovered by Herschel, 2 in 1787, 2 in 1790, 2 in 1794; and 1 by Lassell, and 1 by Struve, in 1847.

URBANISTS, see *Clementines*, and *Clare*.

URBINO, the ancient Urbinum Hortense, central Italy, capital of a duchy created for Malatesta, 1474. It was treacherously seized by Cæsar Borgia, 1502; captured by Julius II., 1503; and given to Borgia, 1504; given to Lorenzo de' Medici by Leo X. 1516; after many vicissitudes recovered by the duke Francesco, 1522; on the duke's resignation annexed to the papal states, 1631; annexed to Italy, 1860.

URGENCY, see *Parliament*, 1881.

URICONIUM, see *Wroxeter*.

URIM AND THUMMIM, LIGHT AND PERFECTION (*Exodus* xxviii. 30), words connected with the breastplate worn by the high priest when he entered into the holy place, with the view of obtaining an answer from God (1490 B.C.).

URSULINE NUNS (so called from St. Ursula), founded originally by St. Angela of Brescia), about 1537. Several communities existed in England; and some still exist in Ireland.

URUGUAY, BANDA ORIENTAL, a republic in South America, formerly part of the vice-royalty of Buenos Ayres; declared its independence, 25 Aug. 1825; recognised 4 Oct. 1828; constitution proclaimed 18 July, 1830. Population in 1886 (estimated) 632,250.

The president of the executive, G. A. Pereyra, elected in 1856; succeeded by B. P. Berro . . 1860
Civil war broke out in consequence of the invasion of the ex-president, general Venancio Florés,
26 June, 1863
The vice-president Aguirre became president,
1 March, 1864
He refused to modify his ministry according to the desire of general Florés, who marched towards the capital . . . . June, ,,
Florés became provisional president . . Feb. 1865
F. A. Vidal elected president . . 1 March, 1866
During an insurrection of the Blanco party (headed by Berro), at Montevideo, general Florés was assassinated; the troops remained faithful; insurrection soon suppressed, and Berro shot,
19 Feb. 1868
Gen. Lorenzo Battle elected president . 1 March, ,,
Blanco insurrection repressed, July, 1871; ended,
Jan. 1872
Revolution at Montevideo; Ellazio's government overthrown; Pedro Varela provisional president, about . . . . . . 15 Jan. 1875
Col. L. Latorre president . . 11 March, 1876
Dr. F. A. Vidal, president, died, 17 March 1880;
gen. Maximo Santas, president . 1 March, 1882
Insurrection by general Arredondo, 29 March;
reported defeat of government troops, 30 March, 1886
Flight of general Arredondo to Brazil, March-April, ,,
Insurgents completely defeated . . 2 April, ,,
Resignation of general Santas, 18 Nov.; general Maximo Tajes as president. . . 18 Nov. ,,

USEFUL KNOWLEDGE SOCIETY, see *Diffusion*.

USES, STATUTE OF, 27 Hen. VIII. c. 10 (1535-6); see *Charitable Uses*.

USHANT, an island near Brest, N.W. France,
near which two naval battles were fought between the British and French fleets.
(1.) On 27 July, 1778, after an indecisive action of three hours, the French, under cover of the night, withdrew into the harbour of Brest. Admiral Keppel commanded the English fleet; the count d'Orvilliers the French. The failure of a complete victory was attributed to admiral sir Hugh Palliser's non-compliance with the admiral's signals. Palliser preferred articles of accusation against his commander, who was tried and acquitted, and the charge against him declared to be "malicious and ill-founded."
(2.) Lord Howe with 25 ships signally defeated the French fleet (26 ships, under Villaret-Joyeuse), taking six ships of the line, and sinking one (the *Vengeur**), 1 June, 1794. While the two fleets were engaged in this action, a large fleet of merchantmen, on the safety of which the French nation depended for its means of prosecuting the war, got safely into Brest harbour, which gave occasion to the enemy to claim the laurels of the day, notwithstanding their loss in ships, and in killed and wounded, which was very great. The day was long termed in England the "glorious first of June."

USURY from a stranger was permitted to the Jews, but forbidden from their brethren, 1491 B.C. (*Exod.* xxii. 25., *Deut.* xxiii. 13.) This law was enforced by Nehemiah, 445 B.C. (*Neh.* v.) Usury was prohibited by the English parliament, 1341. Until the 15th century, no Christians were allowed to receive interest of money, and Jews were the only usurers, and therefore often banished and persecuted; see *Jews*. By the 37th of Henry VIII. the rate of interest was fixed at 10 per cent., 1545. This statute was repealed by Edward VI., but re-enacted 13 Eliz. 1570. For later legislation, see *Interest*.

UTAH, a western territory of North America, was organised 9 Sept. 1850; the capital, Salt Lake City, became the chief seat of the *Mormonites* (*which see*). Population in 1880, 143,963.

UTICA (N. Africa), an ancient Tyrian colony, an ally of Carthage, named in the treaty with the Romans 348 B.C. Here Cato the younger, after the defeat of the partisans of Pompey at Thapsus, committed suicide, 46 B.C. Utica flourished greatly after the fall of Carthage, and was made a Roman city by Augustus on account of its favouring Julius Cæsar. It suffered by the invasion of the Vandals, 439; and of the Saracens, about 700.

UTILITARIANISM, termed the "greatest happiness principle," the philosophy which proposes the attainment of the greatest happiness of the greatest number; a doctrine ascribed to Priestley by Bentham. The doctrine is found in the writings of Locke, Hartley, Hume, and Paley; but was chiefly propounded by Jeremy Bentham in his "Introduction to the Principles of Morals and Legislation," 1780-89, and by John Stuart Mill, who died 9 May, 1873. Mill founded a small "utilitarian society," in 1822. He took the name from an expression in Galt's "Annals of the Parish."

UTRAQUISTS, see *Calixtins*.

UTRECHT (the Roman *Trajectum ad Rhenum*) became the seat of an independent bishopric about

* Various French histories, on the authority of the French demagogue Barrère, state that the English had 36 ships of the line, and the French only 26, and that the crew of the *Vengeur* sang the *Marseillaise* while the ship sank, displaying the tricolor flag. All this was denied in 1802, and disproved by rear-admiral Griffith in Nov. 1838. The *Vengeur* surrendered to the British, who exerted themselves to save the crew. The French statement was accepted by Alison, and at first by Carlyle, but afterwards contradicted by both.

695. The last prelate, Henry of Bavaria, weary of his turbulent subjects, sold his temporal government to the emperor Charles V. in 1528. The union of the Seven United Provinces began here (see *United Provinces*); signed 23 Jan. 1579; 300th anniversary celebrated 23 Jan. 1879. The *treaty of Utrecht*, which terminated the wars of queen Anne, was signed by the ministers of Great Britain and France, and all the other allies, except the ministers of the empire, 11 April, 1713. This treaty secured the Protestant succession in England, the separation of the French and Spanish crowns, the destruction of the works of Dunkirk, the enlargement of the British colonies and plantations in America, and a full satisfaction for the claims of the allies. Utrecht surrendered to the Prussians, 9 May, 1787; was acquired by the French, 18 Jan. 1795, and restored at the peace, 1814.

UXBRIDGE (W. Middlesex). On 30 Jan. 1645, commissioners met here to discuss terms of peace between Charles I. and the parliament; they separated without effect, 22 Feb. The latter required absolute control of the army and navy, the abolition of the episcopacy, liturgy, &c. Uxbridge murder, see *Trials*, Dec. 1884.

V.

VACATIONS.

VACATIONS, see *Terms*.

VACCINATION (from *Variola Vaccina*, the cow-pox), discovered by Dr. Edward Jenner. He was born in 1749, and educated for the medical profession, partially under John Hunter. Having heard that milkmaids who had had the cow-pox never took the small-pox, he, about 1780, conceived the idea of vaccination. He made the first experiment by transferring to a healthy child on 14 May, 1796, the *pus* from the pustule of a milkmaid who had caught the cow-pox from the cows. He announced his success in a memoir published 1798, and vaccination, begun 21 Jan. 1799, soon became general, after much opposition. For this Dr. Jenner received 10,000*l*. from parliament, 2 June, 1802, and 20,000*l*. in 1807. The first national institution for vaccination, the Royal Jennerian Institution, was founded 19 Jan. 1803. The emperor Napoleon valued Dr. Jenner so highly, that he liberated Dr. Wickham, when a prisoner of war, at Jenner's request, and subsequently whole families of English, making it a point to refuse him nothing that he asked. Vaccination, although much opposed, was practised throughout all Europe previously to 1816. Dr. Jenner died suddenly, 26 Jan. 1823.

Royal Jennerian and London Vaccine Institution, founded	1802
The Vaccination act, 3 & 4 Vict. passed . 23 July,	1840
Mr. John Badcock, of Brighton, began to inoculate cows with small-pox to produce new lymph for vaccination . . . . about	"
An important blue-book, entitled "Papers on the History and Practice of Vaccination," edited by Mr. John Simon, was published by the board of health in	1857
A statue, subscribed for by all nations, was erected to Jenner's memory in Trafalgar-square 30 April,	1858
It was removed to Kensington in . . .	1862
Vaccination was made compulsory in England in 1853, and in Ireland and Scotland . .	1863
A statue was erected by the French at Boulogne, and inaugurated . . . . 11 Sept.	1865
These laws were consolidated and amended by 30 & 31 Vict. c. 84, 12 Aug. 1867 (see *Small-pox* and *Inoculation*), and amended in . . .	1871
Much opposition to vaccination; an anti-vaccination society formed, 1870-71; a parliamentary commission appointed . . . . 13 Feb.	"
A government bill respecting punishment for compulsory vaccination dropped . . Aug.	1880
Vaccination direct from the cow or calf advocated and practised in Brussels, &c. . 1879 *et seq.*	
Successful vaccination of 68,900 sheep by M. Pasteur of Paris . . . . up to 1 Oct.	1881
The Grocers' company of London offer prize of 1000*l*. for a plan for propagating vaccine contagium apart from the animal body . 30 May,	1883
Great anti-vaccination demonstration at Leicester (many persons had been fined) . . 23 March,	1885
London society for abolition of compulsory vaccination, held 7th annual meeting . . 11 May,	1887
Estimated: 750,000 infants vaccinated annually; 50 die of disease in consequence; stated Oct.	"
Royal commission of inquiry to be appointed, 5 April,	1889

VACUUM, is produced by reducing the pressure of the atmosphere, whereby its power of absorbing moisture is greatly increased, this power has been utilised by M. Emil Passburg, of Breslau, in his drying apparatus which has been successfully employed for drying grains by Messrs. Guinness, of Dublin since the spring of 1888.

VALENTINE'S DAY.

VADIMONIS LACUS, the Vadimonian lake, Umbria, central Italy, near which the Etruscans were totally defeated in two severe engagements by the Roman consuls: 1, by Fabius Maximus, 309 B.C.; 2, by Cornelius Dolabella, 283.

VAGRANTS. By law, after being whipped, a vagrant was to take an oath to return to the place where he was born, or had last dwelt for three years, 1530. A vagrant a second time convicted was to lose the upper part of the gristle of his right ear, 1535; a third time convicted, death. A vagabond to be branded with a V, and be a slave for two years, 1547. If he absconded and was caught, he was to be branded with S, and be a slave for life. Vagrants were punished by whipping, gaoling, boring the ears, and death for a second offence, 1572. The milder statutes were those of 17 Geo. II.; 32, 35, and 59 Geo. III. The present Vagrant Act (5 Geo. IV. c. 83) was passed in 1824. There were about 33,000 tramps in England and Wales in 1865. For vagrants in London, see under *Poor*.

VALDENSES, see *Waldenses*.

VALENÇAY, a château near Châteauroux, central France, where Napoleon I. imprisoned Ferdinand of Spain from 1808 to 1813. His kingdom was restored to Ferdinand by a treaty signed 8 Dec. 1813.

VALENCIA (E. Spain), the *Valentia Edetanorum* of the Romans, became the capital of a Moorish kingdom, 1000; annexed to Aragon 1238. Its university, founded, it is said, in the 13th century, was revived in the 15th. Valencia was taken by the earl of Peterborough in 1705, but submitted to the Bourbons after the unfortunate battle of Almanza, in 1707. It resisted the attempts made on it by marshal Moncey, but was taken from the Spaniards with a garrison of more than 16,000 men, and immense stores, by the French under Suchet, 9 Jan. 1812.

VALENCIENNES (N. France). This city (the Roman Valentianæ), after many changes, was taken by Louis XIV. in 1677, and annexed 1678. It was besieged from 23 May to 28 July, 1793, when the French garrison surrendered to the allies under the duke of York. It was retaken, together with Condé, by the French, 27-30 Aug. 1794; on capitulation, the garrison and 1100 emigrants were made prisoners, with immense stores.

VALENTIA, a Roman province, including the country between the walls of Severus and Adrian, was reconquered from the Picts and Scots by Theodosius, and named after Valentinian I. the reigning emperor, 368.

VALENTINE'S DAY (14 Feb.). Valentine is said to have been a bishop, who suffered martyrdom under Claudius II. at Rome; others say under Aurelian, in 271. 618,000 letters passed through the post-office on 14 Feb. 1856. 530,300 was the estimated number of valentines delivered in 1864; in 1870, 1,545,755. The origin of the ancient custom of "choosing a valentine" has been much controverted; see *Post*.

VALENTINIANS, followers of Valentine, a priest, who, on being disappointed of a bishopric, forsook the Christian faith, declaring there were thirty gods and goddesses, fifteen of each sex, which he called Æones, or Ages. He taught in the 2nd century, and published a gospel and psalms: his followers added other errors.

VALLADOLID (Spain), the Roman Pintia and the Moorish Belad Walíd: was recovered for the Christians by Ordoño II., the first king of Leon, 914-23. It became capital of Castile in the 15th century. It was taken by the French Jan. 1808; and captured by the English, 4 June, 1813. Here died Christopher Columbus, 20 May, 1506.

VALLOMBROSA (Central Italy). A Benedictine abbey was founded here by John Gualbert, about 1038. The monks were termed Vallambrosians.

VALMY (N.E. France). Here the French, commanded by Kellermann, defeated the Prussians, commanded by the duke of Brunswick, 20 Sept. 1792. The victory was of immense moral advantage to the republicans; and Kellermann was made duke of Valmy in 1808.

VALOIS, a county (N. France) given by Philip III. to his younger son Charles, whose son Philip became king as Philip IV. in 1328; see *France*.

VALOR ECCLESIASTICUS, a report of the annual value of church property, made by order in 1534, was published by the Record Commission in 1810-34.

VALPARAISO, principal port of Chili, South America, was bombarded by the Spanish admiral Mendez Nuñez, on 31 March, 1866, when much property was destroyed. It suffered by earthquakes in 1822, 1829, and 1851.

VALTELLINE (N. Italy), a district near the Rhætian Alps, seized by the Grison league, 1512, and ceded to it, 1530. At the instigation of Spain, the catholics rose and massacred the protestants, 19-21 July, 1620. After much contention between the French and Austrians, the neutrality of the Valtelline was assured in 1639. It was annexed to the Cisalpine republic in 1797; to Italy, 1807; to Austria, 1814; to Italy, 1860.

VALUATION OF PROPERTY ACT, to provide for the uniform assessment of rateable property in the metropolis, was passed 9 Aug. 1869.

VALVASOR (or "VAVASOR"). Camden holds that the "Vavasor" was next below a baron. Du Cange maintains that there were two sorts of vavasors: the greater, who held of the king, such as barons and counts; and the lesser, called "valvasini," who held of the former, such as vassals holding land under a nobleman himself a vassal.

VANADIUM (from *Vanadis*, the Scandinavian Venus), metal discovered by Sefström, in 1830, combined with iron ore. A similar metal, discovered in lead ore by Del Rio in 1801, and named *Erythronium*, was proved by Wöhler to be Vanadium. Vanadium was discovered in the copper-bearing beds in Cheshire, in 1865, by Mr. (aft. Sir) H. E. Roscoe, by whom its peculiarities were further studied, and published in 1867-8. It is useful in photography and dyeing.

VANCOUVER'S ISLAND, North Pacific ocean, near the main land. Settlements were made here by the English in 1781, which were seized by the Spaniards in 1789, but restored. By a treaty between the British government and that of the United States in 1846, this island was secured to the former. It has become of much greater importance since the discovery of gold in the neighbouring main land in 1858, and the consequent establishment of the colony of British Columbia (*which see*). Victoria, the capital, was founded in 1857. The island was united with British Columbia by act passed in Aug. 1866; and on 24 May, 1868, Victoria was declared the capital. Lord Dufferin, governor-general of Canada, was warmly received here, 15 Aug. 1876. See *Juan, San*. Chinese immigrants are virtually excluded by a poll-tax, 1878.

Vancouver nearly destroyed by fire, about 15 June; again . . . . 6 July, 1886
Wellington colliery explosion; 76 lives lost, Jan. 1888

VANCOUVER'S VOYAGE. Captain Vancouver served as a midshipman under captain Cook, and was appointed to command during a voyage of discovery, to ascertain the existence of any navigable communication between the North Pacific and North Atlantic oceans. He sailed 7 Jan. 1791, and returned 24 Sept. 1795. He compiled an account of this voyage of survey of the north-west coast of America, and died in 1798.

VANDALS, a Germanic race, attacked the Roman empire in the 3rd century, and began to ravage Germany and Gaul, 406-14; their kingdom in Spain was founded in 411; under Genseric they invaded and conquered the Roman territories in Africa, 429, and took Carthage, Oct. 439. They were subdued by Belisarius in 534. They were driven out by the Saracen Moors. The dukes of Mecklenburg style themselves princes of the Vandals.

VANDAL KINGS IN AFRICA.
429. Genseric (see *Mecklenburg*).
477. Hunneric, his son.
484. Gundamund.
496. Thrasimund.
523. Hilderic.
531. Gelimer.

VAN DIEMEN'S LAND (called Tasmania since 1853), was discovered by Abel Jansen Tasman, 24 Nov. 1642, and named after the governor of the Dutch East Indies.

Population, 1857, 81,492; 1865, 95,201 (only four remained of the aborigines); 1870, 99,328; 1880, 114,762; 1888, 146,149. Revenue, 1887-8, 594,976*l*.; expenditure, 668,759*l*.; imports, 1887, 1,449,371*l*.; exports, 1,596,817*l*.
Revenue 1888-9, 683,000*l*., expenditure 670,000*l*.
Visited by Furneaux, 1773; Cook 1777
Proved to be an island by Flinders, who explored Bass's Straits 1799
Taken possession of by lieut. Bower 1803
Arrival of col. Collins, the first governor, with convicts; Hobart Town founded 1804
Bishopric of Tasmania established 1842
Transportation abolished 1853
Col. Thos. Gore Brown, governor 1862
Visited by the duke of Edinburgh . . 7-18 Jan. 1868
Charles Ducane, governor . . . . Aug. 1868
Fred. Aloysius Weld, governor 1874
Gen. sir John Henry Lefroy, governor . 21 Aug. 1880
Sir George C. Strahan, governor . . . Dec. 1881
Discovery of gold at Mount Lyell . . July, 1886
Sir Robert Hamilton, governor . . . Nov. „

VANGUARD, see *Wrecks*, 1875.

VARANGIANS, or **VARAGIANS**, a name given to northern pirates, who invaded Flanders, about 813; France, about 840; Italy, 852. Their leader, Ruric, invited by the Novgorodians to help them, founded the Russian monarchy, 862.

VARENNES, a town in N.E. France, is celebrated for the arrest of Louis XVI., his queen, sister, and two children. They fled from the

Tuileries on 21 June, 1791; were taken here the next day, and conducted back to Paris, mainly through Drouet, the postmaster, who, at an intermediate town, recognised the king.

VARIABLE STARS. The variation of brightness in certain stars is said to have been first observed in a small star of Cetus, or the Whale, by Daniel Fabricius, 13 Aug. 1596. In Oct. of same year the star had vanished. Since then many similar variations have been observed by Goodricke, Herschel, and other astronomers; and Mr. Pogson has constructed a table of 38 variable stars. No satisfactory explanation has yet been given of the phenomena. *Eng. Cyc.*

VARNA, a fortified seaport in Bulgaria, formerly European Turkey. A great battle was fought near this place, 10 Nov. 1444, between the Turks under Amurath II. and the Hungarians under their king Ladislaus and John Hunniades. The latter were defeated with great slaughter: the king was killed, and Hunniades made prisoner, who had opposed the Christians breaking the truce for ten years, recently made at Szegedin. The emperor Nicholas of Russia arrived before Varna, the headquarters of his army, then besieging the place, 5 Aug. 1828. The Turkish garrison made a vigorous attack on the besiegers, 7 Aug.; and another on the 21st, but were repulsed. Varna surrendered, after a sanguinary conflict, to the Russian arms, 11 Oct. 1828. It was restored at the peace in 1829; its fortifications were dismantled, but have since been restored. The allied armies disembarked at Varna, 29 May, 1854, and sailed for the Crimea, 3 Sept. They suffered severely from cholera. In conformity with the treaty of Berlin, Varna was evacuated by the Turks, and occupied by Russians, autumn, 1878.

VASSALAGE, see *Feudal Laws*, and *Slavery*.

VASSAR COLLEGE (on the east bank of the Hudson, United States), for the higher education of women, was founded by Matthew Vassar in 1861.

VASSY (N.E. France). The massacre of the protestants at this place by the duke of Guise on 1 March, 1562, led to desolating civil wars.

VATICAN (Rome), the ancient Mons Vaticanus, a hill of Rome. The commencement of the palace is ascribed to Constantine, Liberius, and Symmachus. It became the residence of the pope at his return from Avignon, 1377. The palace is said to contain 7000 rooms, rich in works of art, ancient and modern. The library, founded by pope Nicholas V., 1448, is exceedingly rich in printed books and MSS.— Pistolesi's description of the Vatican, with numerous plates, was published 1829-38.—The phrase "Thunders of the Vatican" was first used by Voltaire, 1748. — The ancient Vatican Codex of the Old and New Testament in Greek was published at Rome in 1857. For "Vatican Decrees," see *Councils*.

VAUD, a Swiss canton, after having been successfully held by the Franks, the kings of Burgundy, emperors of Germany, dukes of Zähringen, and dukes of Savoy, was conquered by the Bernese, Jan. 1536, and annexed, 1554. Vaud, made independent in 1798, joined the confederation in 1815. A new constitution was obtained in 1830, after agitation.

VAUDOIS, see *Waldenses*.

VAUXHALL BRIDGE, constructed of iron under the direction of Mr. Walker, at an expense of 150,000l. (to be defrayed by a toll). The first stone was laid 9 May, 1811, by prince Charles, eldest son of the duke of Brunswick; and the bridge was opened on 4 June, 1816; freed from toll, 24 May, 1879.

VAUXHALL GARDENS (London), were so denominated from the manor of Vauxhall, Falkeshall, Fox-hall, or Faukeshall, said to have been the property of Fulke de Breauté about 1282. The tradition that this house or any other adjacent was the property of Guy Fawkes is erroneous. The premises were the property of Jane Vaux in 1615, and the mansion-house was then called Stockden's. From her it passed through various hands, till it became the property of Mr. Tyers in 1732. There is no certain account of the time when these premises were first opened for the entertainment of the public; but the New Spring Gardens at Vauxhall are mentioned by John Evelyn in his diary 2 July, 1661, Pepys 29 May, 1662, Wycherley 1672, and in the *Spectator* 1711, as a place of great resort. The gardens were opened for a "ridotto al fresco" 7 June, 1732, by Jonathan Tyers, who spared no pains or expense to maintain his success. The greatest season was in 1823, when 133,279 persons visited the gardens, and the receipts were 29,590l. The greatest number of persons in one night was 2 Aug. 1833, when 20,137 persons paid for admission. The number on the then *supposed last* night, 5 Sept. 1839, was 1089 persons. Vauxhall was sold by auction, 9 Sept. 1841, for 20,200l., and again 20 Aug. 1859. The last performances at Vauxhall took place on 25 July, 1859. The ground has been sold for building purposes. Six persons killed and many injured by fall of stack of wood at Buckley's sawmills, 25 Feb. 1880.

VAVASOR, see *Valvasor*.

VEDAS, the sacred books of the Hindoos, in Sanskrit, were probably written about 1000 B.C. Veda means knowledge. These books comprise hymns, prayers, and liturgical formulae. The edition by professor Max Müller, printed under the patronage of the East India Company, appeared in 1849-74. Four volumes of a translation by H. H. Wilson appeared in 1850-67.

Vol. V. & VI, edited by professor Cowell & W. F. Webster, completing the work, appeared in 1889.
In 1887 the Maharajah of Vizianagram proposed to bear the expense of a new edition of the text, edited by professor Max Müller.

VEGETABLES for the table were brought from Flanders about 1520; see *Gardening*.

VEGETARIAN SOCIETY, founded 1847, whose members restrict themselves to a vegetable diet, held their fifteenth anniversary in London, 4 Sept. 1862.

Meetings held at Manchester, 14 Oct. 1874 *et seq.*; 22 Oct. 1879; 36th meeting at Manchester, 17 Oct. 1883.
"Fraternia," a settlement of vegetarians, existed in California in 1880.

VEHMIC TRIBUNALS: *Vehmgerichte, Fehmgerichte*, or *Femgerichte*, secret tribunals established in Westphalia to maintain religion and the public peace, had their origin in the time of Charlemagne, and rose to importance in 1182, when Westphalia became subject to the archbishop of Cologne. Persons of the most exalted rank were subjected to their decisions, being frequently seized, tried, and executed. The emperors endeavoured to suppress them, but did not succeed till the 16th century. Their last court, it is said, was held in 1568. Sir W. Scott has described them in "Anne of Geierstein." A remnant of these tribunals was abolished by Jerome Bonaparte, king of Westphalia, in 1811.

VEII, an independent Latin city near Rome. Between the Romans and Veientes frequent wars occurred, till Veii was utterly destroyed, after ten years' siege, 396 B.C. The Roman family, the Fabii, who had seceded from Rome for political reasons, were surprised and destroyed at the river Cremera, by the Veientes, 477 B.C.

VELLORE (S.E. India) became the residence of the family of the dethroned sultan of Mysore, and was strongly garrisoned by English troops, 1799. The revolt of the sepoys, in which the family of the late Tippoo took an active part, took place 10 July, 1806. The insurgents were subdued by colonel Gillespie, and mostly put to the sword; about 800 sepoys were killed.

VELOCIPEDES. A machine of this kind was invented by Blanchard the aëronaut, and described in the *Journal de Paris*, 27 July, 1779; and one was invented by Nicéphore Niepce in 1818. The "dandy-horse" or "Draisena, a machine called a velocipede," was patented for the Baron von Drais, in Paris and London in 1818, and described in "Ackermann's Repository," Feb. 1819. These machines came again into use in 1861; and since 1867 have been very common under various forms, termed bicycles and tricycles; the chief inventor of which, James Starley, an ingenious mechanic of Albourne, Sussex, was buried at Coventry, June, 1881. The popular "Otto" bicycle, first patented in 1881, much improved since. Velocipede races took place at the Crystal Palace, 26 May, 1869, and frequently since. Mr. John Mayall and two friends travelled to Brighton on velocipedes, 17 Feb. 1869.

Mr. Stanton went from London to Bath, 106 miles, on a bicycle, in 8 h. 28 min. . . 17 Aug. 1874
Similar feats since performed. Ordinary speed with bicycles 8 (now 10) miles an hour; with tricycles 10 miles may be attained.—*Field*. Oct. ,,
A gentleman said to have travelled 1000 miles in Ireland and Wales; expenses 25*l*. . . ,,
Bicycle clubs formed in London, &c. . . 1875
Above 1500 velocipedes at a meeting at Hampton Court . . . . . 26 May, 1877
Middlesex magistrates decide that a bicycle is a carriage, and fine a rider for damage . 31 July, 1878
John Rankin went from Kilmarnock to London and back to Glasgow, with stoppages (112 miles one day) . . . 23 July-10 Aug. ,,
The Bicycle Union, the National Cyclists' Union, and the Cyclists' Touring club founded . . ,,
Six days' contest, Agricultural Hall, London, Mr. George Waller won prize-belt (100*l*.) and 105*l*., rode 1172 miles, 28 April-3 May. Mr. Waller again won, rode 1404 miles (6 days of 18 hours), 1-6 Sept. 1879
Ivan Zmertych, Hungarian, travelled on his velocipede from Ostend to Pesth (about 1200 miles), 10-30 June, 1880
Mr. Alfred Nixon, hon. sec. London tricycle club, on 'Premier' tricycle from John o' Groat's to Land's End in 13 days, 23 hours, 55 minutes, 16-30 Aug. 1882; Mr. E. Oxborrow did the reverse in a week, 1-8 June, 1885; Mr. H. R. Goodwin, on a bicycle, did the double journey, 1-16 June, 1885
F. J. Lees, of Sheffield, covers 20 miles within an hour with a bicycle . . 18 Aug. 1883
Switzerland crossed by bicycles and tricycles Aug.—Sept. ,,
17th annual exhibition of bicycles, &c., at the Floral Hall, Covent Garden . . 4 Feb. 1884
Mr. Alfred Nixon went from London to Edinburgh on a tricycle in three days . 28-31 Aug. ,,
Crypto-dynamic gearing invented by Mr. W. T. Shaw 1885
Annual congress of cyclists held at Colchester, 2 June, 1886
The cycling championship of Europe gained by Mr. E. Hall of Gainsborough at Berlin, 16 Aug. ,,
Mr. Thomas Stevens, on a bicycle, travelled 11,700 miles through America, across Europe to Asia, April, 1884,-Jan. 1887
Messrs. Wilkins' bicycle for travelling rough roads and up hills exhibited at Hanwell, Middlesex, 8 Sept. ,,
The Rev. Hugh Callan, of St. Andrews, Glasgow, travelled to Jerusalem, through Europe and Asia Minor, and back on a bicycle . . autumn, 1888
The use of bicycles, &c., regulated by local government act of 1888, part 1., sect. 84.

VELVET. The manufacture, long confined to Genoa, Lucca, and other places in Italy, was carried to France, and thence to England, about 1685. Velvet is mentioned by Joinville in 1272; and our king Richard II., in his will, directed his body to be clothed "in velveto," 1399. Jerome Lanyer in London patented his "velvet paper" in 1634.

VENAISSIN COMTAT, or COMTAT (S. France), after various changes, was ceded to pope Gregory X. 1274; and retained by his successors till 1791, when, with Avignon, it was re-united to France.

VENDÉE, see *La Vendée*.

VENDÉMIAIRE, 12, 13, 14 (3, 4, 5 Oct.), 1795, Barras and Napoleon Bonaparte suppress a royalist revolt against the convention.

VENDÔME COLUMN (132 feet 2 inches high), erected in the Place Vendôme, Paris, by Napoleon I. in 1806, to commemorate his successful campaign in Germany in 1805. On its side were bas-reliefs by Launay. It was pulled down by the communists "in the name of international fraternity," 16 May, 1871; restored by the national assembly, 31 Aug. 1874; statue of Napoleon I. on the top, replaced 28 Dec. 1875.

VENETI, maritime Gauls inhabiting Armorica, N.W. France. They rose against the Romans 57 B.C., and were quelled by Julius Cæsar, who defeated their fleet, 56, and cruelly exterminated an active commercial race.

VENETIA, see *Venice*.

VENEZUELA, the seat of a South American republic. When the Spaniards landed here in 1499, they observed some huts built upon piles, in an Indian village named Cora, in order to raise them above the stagnated water that covered the plain; and this induced them to give it the name of Venezuela, or Little Venice. This state in July, 1814, declared in congressional assembly the sovereignty of its people, which was recognised in 1818. It formed part of the republic of Columbia till it separated from the federal union, Nov. 1829. The population in 1881, 2,075,245; in 1886, 2,198,320; capital, Caracas.

Its independence was recognized by Spain . . 1845
General D. T. Monagas was elected president . . 1855
A new constitution promulgated . . Dec. 1858
A revolution; Don José Castro became president, March, 1858; compelled to resign in Aug. 1859; and Dr. Pedro Gual assumed the government, Aug. 1859
General José Paez elected president . . 8 Sept. 1861
He resigned; and Juan E. Falcon succeeded, 17 June, 1863
General Febres Cordero protested, and set up a rival government at Porto-Cabello . Oct. ,,
Marshal J. C. Falcon proclaimed president, 18 March, 1865
A revolution in Caracas; president Falcon fled, 22-26 June, ,,
The president Monagas dies, 18 Nov., and Pulgar becomes provisional president . . Dec. ,,
Caracas captured by general Guzman Blanco, after three days' conflict . . . 27 April, 1870

He is made president, virtually dictator	13 July, 1870
A rebel general, Salazar, tried and shot about 17 May,	1872
Blanco re-elected president . . . . 20 Feb.	1873
Severity towards the church for opposition to civil marriages; bishop of Merida expelled . 1 July,	1874
Renunciation of papal authority announced Sept.	1876
Gen. F. L. Alcantara president, elected . 27 Feb.	1877
Gen. A. Guzman Blanco, president, elected . .	1879
Dispute respecting territories containing gold mines; diplomatic relations broken off with Great Britain . . . . . Feb.	1888
Dr. J. Pablo Rojas Paul, president, elected 29 June,	,,
The dictatorship of Don G. Blanco (now envoy at Paris) set aside by the congress, about 10 June, (See *Colombia*; *Trials* 21 March 1887.)	1889

"**VENGEUR STORY**," see *Ushant*, note.

VENI, VIDI, VICI,—" I came, I saw, I conquered;" see *Zela*.

VENICE (N. Italy). The province of Venetia, held by the Veneti, of uncertain origin, was invaded by the Gauls about 350 B.C. The Veneti made an alliance with the Romans, 215 B.C., who founded Aquileia, 181, and gradually acquired the whole country. Under the empire, Venetia included Padua, Verona, and other important places. Population of the city of Venice in 1857, 118,173; in 1881, 129,445. New line of steamers for the east started from Venice by the Peninsular and Oriental Company, July, 1872.

Venice, founded by families from Aquileia and Padua fleeing from Attila . . . about A.D.	452
First doge (or duke) chosen, Anafesto Paululio . .	697
Bishopric founded	733
The doge Orso slain; an annual magistrate (maestro di militi, master of the militia) appointed . .	737
Diodato, son of Orso, made doge	742
Two doges reign: Maurizio Galbaio, and his son Giovanni	777
The Rialto made the seat of government . . .	811
Venice becomes independent of the eastern empire, and acquires the maritime cities of Dalmatia and Istria	597
Its navy and commerce increase . . . 1000-1100	
The Venetians aid at the capture of Tyre and acquire the third part, 1124; and ravage the Greek archipelago	1125
Bank of Venice established	1157
Ceremony of wedding the Adriatic instituted, about	1177
Zara captured by the Venetians . . 24 Nov.	1202
The Venetians aid the crusaders with men, horses, and ships	1202
Crete purchased	1204
Venice helps in the Latin conquest of Constantinople, and obtains power in the East . . 1204-5	
The four bronze horses by Lysippus, brought from Constantinople, placed at St. Mark's by the doge Pietro Ziani, who died	1229
The Venetians defeat the Genoese near Negropont,	1263
War with Genoa	1293
The Venetian fleet severely defeated by the Genoese in the Adriatic, 8 Sept. 1298; peace between them	1299
Louis of Hungary defeated at Zara . . 1 July,	1346
Severe contest with Genoa 1350-81	
The doge Marino Faliero, to avenge an insult, conspires against the republic; beheaded 17 April	1355
The Venetians lose Istria and Dalmatia . . .	1358
War with the Genoese, who defeat the Venetians at Pola, and advance against Venice, which is vigorously defended	1377
The Genoese fleet is captured at Chiozza . . .	1380
And peace concluded	1381
Venice flourishes under Antonio Vernieri . 1382-1400	
War with Padua; conquest of Padua and Verona .	1404
War against Milan; conquest of Brescia 1425; of Bergamo	1428
The city suffers from the plague	1447
War against Milan, 1430; conquest of Ravenna .	1454
War with the Turks; Venice loses many of its eastern possessions 1461-77	
The Venetians take Athens, 1466; and Cyprus . .	1475
Venice excommunicated, 1483; joins league against Naples, 1493; helps to overcome Charles VIII. of France	1495
Injured by the discovery of America (1492), and the passage to the Indies	1497
The Venetians nearly ruined by the league of Cambray formed against them	1508
They assist in defeating the Turks at Lepanto, 7 Oct.	1571
The Turks retake Cyprus	,,
Destructive fire at Venice	1577
The Rialto bridge and the Piazza di San Marco erected . . . . about	1592
Paul V.'s interdict on Venice (1606) contemptuously disregarded	1607
Naval victories over the Turks; at Scio, 1651; and in the Dardanelles	1655
The Turks take Candia, after 24 years' siege . .	1569
Venice recovers part of the Morea, 1683-99; loses it, 1715-30	
Venice occupied by Bonaparte, who, by the treaty of Campo Formio, gives part of its territory to Austria, and annexes the rest to the Cisalpine republic	1797
The whole of Venice annexed to the kingdom of Italy by the treaty of Presburg . . 26 Dec.	1805
All Venice transferred to the empire of Austria .	1814
Venice declared a free port . . . 24 Jan.	1830
Insurrection begins 22 March, 1848; the city, defended by Daniel Manin, surrenders to the Austrians after a long siege . . . 22 Aug.	1849
[During the Italian war in 1859, the country was much disorganised, and many persons emigrated in 1860-1.]	
Venetian deputies will not attend the Austrian parliament at Vienna . . . . . May,	1861
Venetia surrendered to France for Italy (by the treaty of Vienna, signed 3 Oct.), and transferred to Italy . . . . 17 Oct.	1866
Plebiscitum: 651,758 votes for annexation to Italy; 69 against . . . . 22 Oct.	,,
Result reported by Venetian deputies, and the iron crown given to the king at Turin . . 4 Nov.	,,
He enters Venice . . . . . 7 Nov.	,,
Master-piece of Titian (" Death of Peter Martyr ") destroyed at the burning of a chapel . 15 Aug.	1867
The remains of Daniel Manin (brought from Paris) buried in St. Mark's . . . . 23 March,	1868
His statue unveiled . . . . 22 March,	1875
The emperor of Austria and king of Italy at Venice 5-7 April,	,,
The bronze equestrian statue of Victor Emmanuel II. by Ferrari unveiled in the presence of the king and queen of Italy; great festivities . . 1 May,	1887
Art exhibition opened by the king . . 2 May,	,,
(Venice has had 122 doges; Anafesto, 697, to Luigi Manin, 1797.]	

VENLOO (Holland), surrendered to the allies, under Marlborough, 23 Sept. 1702; and to the French, under Pichegru, 26 Oct. 1794.

VENNER'S INSURRECTION, see *Anabaptists*, 1661.

VENTILATORS were invented by the rev. Dr. Hales, and described to the Royal Society of London, May, 1741; and the ventilator for the use of ships was announced by Mr. Triewald, in November, same year. The marquis of Chabannes' plan for warming and ventilating theatres and houses for audiences was applied to those of London about 1819. The systems of Dr. Reid (about 1834) and others followed, with much controversy. Dr. Arnott's work on this subject was published in 1838. A commission on warming and ventilation issued a report in 1859.

New air machine in the house of commons started 5 June, 1874

Mr. Tobin's plan, a horizontal tube from without communicating with vertical tube inside; successful at Leeds; described (in *Times*,) 12 April, 1875

VENTRILOQUISM (speaking from the belly), is evidently described in *Isaiah* xxix. 4 (about 712 B.C.). Among eminent ventriloquists were baron

Mengen and M. Saint Gille, about 1772 (whose experiments were examined by a commission of the French Academy); Thomas King (about 1716); Charles Mathews (1824); and M. Alexandre (1822).

VENUS, the Roman goddess of love and beauty (the Greek Aphrodité). The transit of the planet Venus over the sun was predicted by Kepler, but not observed. The first transit observed, was by the rev. Jeremiah Horrox, or Horrocks, and his friend, Wm. Crabtree, on 24 Nov. 1639, as predicted by Horrox in 1633. The astronomer-royal Maskelyne observed her transit at St. Helena, 6 June, 1761. Capt. Cook made his first voyage in the *Endeavour*, to Otaheite, to observe a transit of Venus, 3 June, 1769; see *Cook's Voyages.* The diurnal rotation of Venus was discovered by Cassini in 1667. See *Sun,* note. *Statues:* Venus de Medicis, found near Tivoli and removed to France, 1680; the Venus found at Milo or Melos, 1820, placed in the Louvre, Paris, 1834.

Halley suggested the observation of the transit as a means of estimating the distance of the earth from the sun, and devised a method for this purpose 1716
Another method was invented by Delisle about . 1743
Both plans were used in . . . . Dec. 1874
Expeditions for the accurate observation of the phenomena, on 8 Dec. astronomical day; ordinary day, 9 Dec. 1874, were sent to different parts of the globe by all the great powers, and favourable results have been reported 1875-6
The transit, on 6 Dec. 1882, was observed at Bath, Penzance, Cork, Cape Town, Washington, Melbourne, and many other places. The next transits will take place 8 June, 2004, and 6 June, 2012.

VERA CRUZ (Mexico), built about 1600; was taken by the Americans in 1847, and by the allies on 17 Dec. 1861, during the intervention; retaken by the liberals, under Juarez, 27 June, 1867.

VERCELLI, the ancient Vercellæ, Piedmont, near which Marius defeated the Cimbri, 101 B.C. It was the seat of a republic in the 13th and 14th centuries. It was taken by the Spaniards, 1630; French, 1704; and allies, 1706; and afterwards partook of the fortunes of Piedmont.

VERDEN (Hanover). Here Charlemagne massacred about 4500 Saxons, who had rebelled and relapsed into idolatry, 782.

VERDUN (the ancient Verodunum), a first-class fortress on the Meuse, N.E. France, made a magazine for his legions by Julius Cæsar. It was acquired by the Franks in the sixth century, and formed part of the dominions of Lothaire by the treaty of Verdun, 843, when the empire was divided between the sons of Louis I. It was taken and annexed to the empire by Otho I. about 939. It surrendered to France in 1552; and was formally ceded in 1648. It was taken and held by the Prussians 43 days, Sept.—Oct. 1792. Gen. Beaurepaire, the commandant, committed suicide before the surrender, and 14 ladies were executed on 28 May, 1794, for going to the king of Prussia to solicit his clemency for the town. Verdun surrendered to the Germans 8 Nov. 1870, after a brave defence; two vigorous sallies being made 28 Oct. Above 4000 men were captured, with a large number of arms and ammunition. It was the last place held by the Germans; and was given up 15, 16 Sept. 1873, and the troops retired.

VERGARA, N. SPAIN. Here the Carlist general, Maroto, made a treaty, termed "The pacification of Vergara," with Espartero, 31 Aug. 1839.

The monument to celebrate it was destroyed by the Carlists in Aug. 1873.

VERMANDOIS (N. France), a county given by Charlemagne to his second son Pepin, whose family held it till the 11th century; in 1156 it came, by marriage, to the counts of Flanders; and in 1185 it was seized by Philip II., and incorporated with the monarchy in 1215.

VERMONT, a northern state in North America, was settled by the French, 1724-31; and ceded to Great Britain in 1763. It was freed from the authority of New York, and admitted as a state of the union in 1791. Population 1880, 332,286; capital, Montpelier.

VERNEUIL (N.W. France), the site of a battle fought 17 Aug. 1424, between the Burgundians and English under the regent duke of Bedford, and the French, assisted by the Scots, commanded by the count de Narbonne, the earls of Douglas and Buchan, &c. The French at first were successful; but some Lombard auxiliaries, who had taken the English camp, commenced pillaging. Two thousand English archers came then fresh to the attack; and the French and Scots were totally defeated, and their leaders killed.

VERNON GALLERY. The inadequate manner in which modern British art was represented in the National Gallery was somewhat remedied in 1847 by the munificent present to the nation, by Mr. Robert Vernon, of a collection of 157 pictures, all but two being by first-rate British artists. They were first exhibited at Mr. Vernon's house in Pall-mall, next in the vaults beneath the National Gallery, afterwards at Marlborough House, and are now at the South Kensington Museum. In 1857, Mr. John Sheepshanks followed Mr. Vernon's example; see *Sheepshanks' Donations.*

VERONA (N. Italy) was founded by the Gauls or Etruscans; see *Campus Raudius.* The amphitheatre was built by Titus, A.D. 82. Verona has been the site of many conflicts. It was taken by Constantine 312; and on 27 Sept. 489 Theodoric defeated Odoacer, king of Italy. Verona was taken by Charlemagne 774. About 1260 Mastino della Scala was elected podestà, and his descendants (the Scaligeri) ruled, till subdued by the Visconti, dukes of Milan, 1387. Verona was conquered by the Venetians 1405, and held by them with some intermissions till its capture by the French general Massena, 3 June, 1796. Near to it Charles Albert of Sardinia defeated the Austrians 6 May, 1848. Verona is one of the four strong Austrian fortresses termed the Quadrangle, or Quadrilateral (*which see*), and here the emperor Francis Joseph, on 12 July, 1859, in an order of the day, announced to his army that he must yield to circumstances unfavourable to his policy, and thanked his people and army for their support. It was surrendered to the Italian government, 16 Oct. 1866; and the king was received by 70,000 persons in the amphitheatre, 18 Nov. 1866. Above 50,000 coins of Gallienus and other emperors, chiefly bronze, discovered near Verona, Jan. 1877.

VERSAILLES (near Paris) was a small village, in a forest thirty miles in circuit; where Louis XIII. built a hunting-seat about 1632. Louis XIV. between 1661 and 1687 enlarged it into a magnificent palace, which became the usual residence of the kings of France. By the treaty between Great Britain and the revolted colonies of British North America, signed at Paris, the latter power was admitted to be a sovereign and independent state, 3

Sept. 1783. On the same day a treaty was signed at Versailles between Great Britain, France, and Spain, by which Pondicherry and Carical, with other possessions in Bengal, were restored to France, and Trincomalee restored to the Dutch. Here was held the military festival of the royal guards 1 Oct. 1789, which was followed (on the 5th and 6th) by the attack of the mob, who massacred the guards and brought the king back to Paris. Versailles became the residence of Louis-Philippe in 1830. The historical gallery was opened in 1837. Versailles, with the troops there, surrendered to the Germans 19 Sept. 1870, and the crown prince of Prussia entered the next day; and on 26 Sept. he awarded the iron cross to above 30 soldiers at the foot of the statue of Louis XIV. The palace was converted into an hospital. The royal head-quarters were removed here from Ferrières 5 Oct. After the peace, Versailles became the seat of the French government (see *France*) March, 1871. Removed to Paris 27 Nov. 1879. The congress for the revision of the constitution met here 4—13 Aug. 1884. See *France*, 1889.

VERSE, see *Poetry, Hexameter, Elegy, Iambic*, &c. Surrey's translation of part of *Virgil's Æneid* into *blank verse* is the first English composition of the kind, omitting tragedy, extant in the English language (published in 1547). The verse previously used in our grave compositions was the stanza of eight lines, the *ottava rima* (as adopted with the addition of one line by Spenser in his *Faëry Queene*), who probably borrowed it from Ariosto and Tasso. Boccaccio introduced it into Italy in his *Teseide*, having copied it from the old French *chansons*. Trissino is said to have been the first introducer of blank verse among the moderns, about 1508. *Vossius*.

VERULAM, see *Alban's, St.*

VERVINS (N. France). Here was concluded the peace between Philip II. of Spain and Henry IV. of France, with mutual concessions, 2 May, 1598.

VESERONCE (S.E. France), near Vienne. Here Gondemar, king of the Burgundians, defeated and killed Clodomir, king of Orleans, and revenged the murder of his brother Sigismond and his family, 524. This conflict is called also the battle of Voiron.

VESPERS, see *Sicilian Vespers*. In the house of the French ambassador at Blackfriars, in London, a Jesuit was preaching to upwards of three hundred persons in an upper room, the floor of which gave way with the weight, when the whole congregation was precipitated to the street, and the preacher and more than a hundred of his auditory, chiefly persons of rank, were killed. This catastrophe, termed the *Fatal Vespers*, occurred 26 Oct. 1623. *Stow*.

VESTA. The planet Vesta (the ninth) was discovered by Dr. Olbers, of Bremen, on 29 March, 1807. She appears like a star of the sixth magnitude.

VESTALS, virgin priestesses, took care of the perpetual fire consecrated to Vesta. The mother of Romulus was a vestal. Numa is said to have appointed four, 710 B.C., and Tarquin added two. Minutia was buried alive for breaking her virgin vow, 337 B.C.; Sextilia, 273 B.C.; and Cornelia Maximiliann, A.D. 92; see *Chastity*. The order was abolished by Theodosius, 389.

"VESTIGES OF THE NATURAL HISTORY OF CREATION," a work which upholds the doctrine of progressive development as a hypothetic history of organic creation, ascribed to Robert Chambers, and other persons, first appeared in 1844, and occasioned much controversy. See *Origin of Species*.

VESUVIUS. By an eruption of Mount Vesuvius, the cities of Pompeii and Herculaneum (*which see*) were overwhelmed 24 Aug. 79 A.D., and more than 200,000 persons perished, among them Pliny the naturalist. Numerous other disastrous eruptions have occurred. Torre del Greco, with 4000 persons, was destroyed, 17 Dec. 1631. There was a dreadful eruption took place suddenly, 24 Nov. 1759, and another 8 Aug. 1767. The violent burst in 1767 was the 34th from the time of Titus. One in June, 1794, was most destructive: the lava flowed over 5000 acres of rich vineyards and cultivated land, and Torre del Greco was a second time burned; the top of the mountain fell in, and the crater is now nearly two miles in circumference. A great eruption in Oct. 1822, and others in May, 1855, May and June, 1858, caused great destruction. A series of violent eruptions causing much damage occurred in Dec. 1861, and in Feb. 1865. Torre del Greco was again destroyed in Dec. 1861. Another eruption began 12 Nov. 1867, and continued increasing in grandeur and danger, March, 1868. The phenomena were observed by professors Tyndall and Miller, sir John Lubbock, and other scientific men, in April, 1868. A great eruption began 8 Oct. 1868, and continued, causing much destruction, 19, 20 Nov. A severe eruption began 23 April and ended about 3 May, 1872; above 60 lives were lost. The mountain was disturbed in 1876; and another eruption began about 20 Sept. 1878; lava was spouted to the height of 300 feet: an eruption began 11 June, 1879; an intermittent eruption 2 May, 1885. Professor John Phillips' "Vesuvius" was published 1869.

VETERINARY COLLEGES. The Royal College of Veterinary Surgeons, at Red Lion Square London, which alone grants diplomas, was chartered in 1844. The Veterinary Surgeons act, 44 & 45 Vict. sec. 62; passed 27 Aug. 1881, deals only with this college. The Royal Veterinary College at Camden Town, London, N.W., was founded in 1791. There are veterinary colleges in Edinburgh and Glasgow.

VICE, an instrument of which Archytas of Tarentum, disciple of Pythagoras, is said to have been the inventor, along with the pulley and other implements, 420 B.C. *Society for the Suppression of Vice*, established 1802.

VICE-ADMIRALTY COURTS ACT, 1863, was extended and amended in 1867.

VICE-CHANCELLOR OF ENGLAND, an equity judge, appointed by parliament, first took his seat 5 May, 1813. A new court was erected for him about 1816 contiguous to Lincoln's-inn-hall. Two additional vice-chancellors were appointed under act 5 Vict. c. 5, 5 Oct. 1841. The office of vice-chancellor *of England* ceased in August, 1850, and a *third* vice-chancellor was appointed in 1851, when two more equity judges, styled *lords justices*, were appointed.

VICE-CHANCELLORS OF ENGLAND.
1813. Sir Thomas Plumer, 13 April.
1818. Sir John Leach, 13 Jan.
1827. Sir Anthony Hart, 4 May.
1827-50. Sir Lancelot Shadwell, 1 Nov. THE LAST.

VICE-CHANCELLORS.
1852. Sir John Stuart, sat last, 27 March, 1871.

VICENZA. 960 VICTORIA.

1853. Sir Wm. Page Wood, made a justice of appeal, 1868; lord chancellor, Dec. 1868.
1868. Sir Geo. Markham Giffard, died 1870.
1869. Sir Wm. M. James, Jan.; made a lord justice of appeal, June, 1870.
1871. Sir John Wickens, April; died, 23 Oct. 1873.
1866. Sir Richard Malins, resigned 1881; died 15 Jan. 1882.
1870. Sir James Bacon, the last
of the vice-chancellors, } now included in the
resigned 10 Nov. 1886. } chancery division.
1873. Sir Charles Hall, Nov.; died 12 Dec. 1883.

VICENZA (the ancient Vicentia, N. Italy) was the seat of a republic in the 12th century. It greatly suffered by the ravages of Alaric, 401, and Attila, 452. Having joined the Lombard league, it was sacked by Frederic II. 1236. After many changes it was subjected to Venice, and with it fell under the French domination, 1796; and was given to Austria in 1814. Having revolted, it was retaken by Radetzky, 11 June, 1848. It was annexed to the kingdom of Italy, Oct. 1866.

VICE-PRESIDENT OF THE BOARD OF TRADE. This office was abolished in 1867, and a secretary with a seat in parliament substituted.

VICKSBURG, see *United States,* 1863.

VICTORIA, formerly PORT PHILLIP, (Australia), situated between New South Wales and South Australia. In 1798, Bass, in his whale-boat expedition, visited Western Port, one of its harbours; and in 1802 Flinders sailed into Port Phillip Bay.
Population of the colony in 1836, 224; in 1841, 11,738; in 1846, 32,879; in 1851, 77,345; 31 Dec. 1852, about 200,000; in March 1857 there were 258,116 males and 145,403 females; in all 403,519. In 1859, in all 517,366; in 1861, 540,322; Dec. 1865, 626,639; in 1871, 729,654; 1877, 849,021; in 1881, 858,582; 1888, 1,090,869. Revenue, 1886–7, 6,733,867*l.*; expenditure, 6,665,863*l.*; imports, 1886, 18,530,575*l.*; exports, 11,795,321*l.* Revenue, 1888–9, 8,674,000*l.*; expenditure, 8,172,000*l.*
Colonel Collins lands with a party of convicts with the intention of founding a settlement at Port Phillip, but afterwards removed to Van Diemen's Land 1804
Messrs. Hume and Hovell, two stock-owners from New South Wales, explore part of the country, but do not discover its great advantages . 1824
Mr. Edward Henty (of a Sussex family), comes from Tasmania with cattle, sheep, shepherds, &c., and settles in Portland Bay; his brothers, Stephen George and John, follow soon . . 1832
Mr. John Batman enters between the heads of Port Phillip, and purchases a large tract of land from the aborigines for a few gewgaws and blankets; he shortly after, with fifteen associates from Hobarton, took possession of 600,000 acres in the present Geelong country . . May, 1835
The Launceston associates and Mr. John Pascoe Falkner ascend the Yarra-Yarra (or overflowing) river, and encamp on the site of Melbourne . „
The colonists (450 in number) possess 140,000 sheep, 2500 cattle, and 150 horses; sir R. Bourke, governor of New South Wales, visits the colony, determines the sites of towns, and causes the land to be surveyed and resold, setting aside many contending claims; he appoints captain Lonsdale chief-magistrate (see *Melbourne*) . 1837
The colony named Victoria 1839
Mr. C. J. Latrobe appointed lieutenant-governor under sir G. Gipps . . . . . . „
Its prosperity brings great numbers to it, and induces much speculation and consequent embarrassment and insolvency 1841-2
The province declared independent of New South Wales; a reward of 200*l.* offered for the discovery of gold in Victoria, which was soon after found near Melbourne, and was profitably worked Aug. 1851
7000 persons were at Ballarat, Oct.; 10,000 round Mount Alexander . . . . . Nov. „

From 30 Sept. to 31 Dec. 1851, 30,311 ounces of gold were obtained from Ballarat; and from 29 Oct. to 31 Dec. 94,524 ounces from Mount Alexander—total 124,835 ounces
The production was still very great . . . 1859
Immense immigration to Melbourne (see *Melbourne*) 1852
Sir Charles Hotham, governor . . June, 1854
A representative constitution granted . . 1855
Sir Henry Barkly appointed governor . . 1856
The parliament was opened . . 26 Nov. 1857
Four administrations had been formed in . 1857-1860
Exhibition of the products of the colony opened by the governor . . . . . 1 Oct. 1861
Sir Charles Darling appointed governor, May; arrives . . . . . . 10 Sept. 1863
Great opposition to reception of convicts in any part of Australia; a ship containing them sent back . . . . Oct. 1864
Important land act passed . . 22 March, 1865
The assembly passes the new government tariff, Jan., which is rejected by the legislative council; the governor raises money for the public service irregularly . . . . . . July. „
The crisis still continues; appeal to the queen proposed . . . . Oct. „
Parliament prorogued . . . . . Dec. „
Sir Charles Darling recalled . . 26 Feb. 1866
Ministerial difficulties: Mr. McCulloch becomes premier . . . . . . April, „
The assembly votes 20,000*l.* to lady Darling; sir Charles departs . . . . . May, „
New governor, sir John H. T. Manners Sutton, (viscount Canterbury in 1869) arrived 13 Aug. „
Intercolonial Exhibition opened . . 25 Oct. „
Vote of 20,000*l.* to lady Darling rejected by legislative council . . . . . 20 Aug. 1867
Ministerial crisis; dispute continues between the assembly and the council . . . Oct. „
Duke of Edinburgh arrives; great rejoicings 23 Nov. „
An address presented to him by Mr. Edward Henty, the first settler, and others . . „
Parliament dissolved . . . . 30 Dec. „
New parliament; ministry resigned because the governor objected to insertion of the Darling grant in the appropriation bill . 12 March, 1868
First woollen and paper manufactories established May, „
The M'Culloch ministry arrange the Darling affair July, „
The M'Pherson ministry announced . . Oct. 1869
Mr. M'Culloch forms a ministry including Mr. M'Pherson, April; is knighted . May, 1870
Mr. M'Culloch resigns . . . 14 June, „
The federation of the Australian colonies, proposed by Mr. Gavan Duffy in 1857, revived by him and discussed in the legislative assembly . June, „
Industrial Museum at Melbourne, opened 8 Sept. „
Mr. Duffy minister . . . . July, 1871
He resigns on a vote against him . . 29 May, 1872
Mr. Francis forms a ministry . . June, „
Payment (300*l.* a year) to M. P.'s begins . . „
Sir George Ferguson Bowen succeeds viscount Canterbury . . . . . . Feb. 1873
Ministerial crisis: Mr. Kerford premier; Mr. Service's budget; expenditure, 4,500,000*l.*; deficit, about 340,000*l.*; he proposes a moderate free-trade policy; reduction of taxation and a loan; rejected by the parliament; Mr. Kerford resigns, as sir Wm. Stowell, the acting governor, would not dissolve . . . . . . Aug. 1875
Mr. Graham Berry, premier; would continue protection and tax the richer colonists heavily (a financial *coup d'état*); defeated; resigns Oct. „
Sir James M'Culloch forms a coalition ministry, Oct.; proposing tax on income, land, and realised property . . . . . Nov. „
Passes his income-tax bill with a majority of 3 announced June, 1876
Dispute of government with Messrs. Stevensons, respecting their alleged undervaluing goods for payment of duties; their letters opened March-June, „
Elections; triumph of protectionists; sir James M'Culloch resigns; Mr. Berry again premier, May; a land-tax enacted . . . Oct. 1877
Legislative council rejects Mr. Berry's appropriations, defence, and exhibition bills, end of Oct. „
County court and other judges dismissed by the

govenor, supports
. . . Jan. 1878
; council; orders
its sole vote, about
13 Feb. ,,
ouse predominant
March-Aug. ,,
nted governor, Feb. 1879
rland . . Feb. ,,
pt.; which is with-
. . . Dec. ,,
eb.; elections give
l Feb.; his cabinet
under Mr. James
. . 3 March, 1880
, 24 June; dissolu-
; the ministry re-
. . 14 July, ,,
. . 28 July, ,,
ng of bush-rangers
lers and robberies
ured and sent to
. 27, 28 June, ,,
ourne, open 1 Oct. ,,
. . 11 Nov. ,,
in parliament lost;
dnistry . July, 1881
signs, March; sir
ds . . April, 1884
a confederation bill
about 30 June ,,
tually excluded. 1885
192,000*l*., 22 July,
24 July, 1888
an Gillies, formed
18 Feb. 1886
ith royal assent,
24, 25 Nov. 1887
orkmen and oppo-
. . autumn, 1888
. C. F. Robinson,

y reported), 4 June, 1889
d governor about
22 July, ,,

Kong. Vancouvers' Wrecks 1852, *British*

lony in Ambas bay, on
inally a Baptist mis-
19 July, 1884.
lermany by consul
oons 28 March, 1887
. new order of merit,
ntry of persons of all
, 5 Feb. 1856. It is
n cannon from Sebas-
d the honour on 62
Friday, 26 June, 1857;
1 army, 2 Aug. 1858.
Knighthood for ladies,
2.

TE, or PHILOSOPHI-
BRITAIN, established
oject being the attempt
ancies between Chris-

. London), was origi-
l, which enabled her
woods and forests to
royal park, with the
e same act, by the sale
of Sutherland. The
o purchased, contain-
parishes of St. John,
thnal-green; and St.
e park was completed
845. Lady (then Miss)
. handsome drinking
t its inauguration, 28

June, 1863. The park was visited by the queen,
2 April, 1873; and in memory of her reception, she
presented a clock and peal of bells to St. Mark's
church; recognition service, 21 May, 1874. See
Parks.

VICTORIA RAILWAY BRIDGE (tubu-
lar), over the St. Lawrence, Montreal, erected by
Mr. James Hodges, under the superintendence of
Mr. Robert Stephenson and Mr. A. M. Ross,
engineers, was begun 24 May, 1854, and formally
opened by the prince of Wales, 25 Aug. 1860. It
forms part of the Grand Trunk railway, which con-
nects Canada and the seaboard states of North
America. The length is about sixty yards less than
two English miles, and about 7¼ times longer than
Waterloo bridge, and ten times longer than new
Chelsea bridge; the height sixty feet between the
summer level of the river and the under surface of
the central tube. It is supported by 24 piers. The
cost was 1,700,000*l.* On 5 Jan. 1855, while constructing, the bridge was much injured by floating
ice, but the stonework remained firm.

VICTORIA REGIA, the magnificent water-
lily brought to this country from Guiana by sir
Robert Schomburgk, in 1838, and named after the
queen. Fine specimens are at the Botanic Gardens
at Kew, Regent's Park, &c. It was grown in the
open air in 1855, by Messrs. Weeks, of Chelsea.

VICTORIA STEAMER; sunk; see *Wrecks*,
24 May, 1881.

VICTORIA UNIVERSITY constituted; is
to consist of Owen's college, Manchester, and others;
the charter was granted in April; the first council
met, 14 July, 1880.

VICTORY, MAN-OF-WAR, of 100 guns, the
finest first-rate ship in the navy of England, was
lost in a violent tempest near the race of Alderney,
and its admiral, sir John Balchen, and 100 gentlemen's sons, and the whole crew, consisting of 1000
men, perished, 8 October, 1744.—The *Victory*, the
flag-ship of Nelson, at the battle of Trafalgar, 21
Oct. 1805, is kept in fine preservation at Portsmouth.

VICTUALLERS, an ancient trade in England. The Vintners' company of London was
founded 1437; their hall rebuilt in 1823.

None shall sell less than one full quart of the best
beer or ale for 1*d.* and two quarts of the smaller
sort for 1*d.* 1603
The power of *licensing* public-houses was granted
to sir Giles Mompesson and sir Francis Mitchel . 1621
The number in England then was about 13,000 ,,
In Great Britain about 76,000 public-houses . . 1790
England, 59,335; Scotland, 15,081; Ireland,
14,080; total, 88,496 in 1850
In England and Wales, 23,028 in 1889
Public-houses allowed to be opened on Sundays
from 1 o'clock till 3, and from 5 till 11 P.M . 1828
The prescribed time enlarged 1855
127,352 licences were issued for the sale of beer,
cider, and perry in the United Kingdom, produc-
ing a revenue of 304,688*l.*; and 93,936 licences
for the sale of spirits: revenue 560,557*l.* . . 1858
Licensed Victuallers' School established . . . 1803
Licensed Victuallers' Asylum established 22 Feb. 1827
Licensed Victuallers in the United Kingdom
99,465 1872
Between 100,000,000*l.* and 150,000,000*l.* said to be
invested in the liquor trade. The licensed victuallers actively opposed Mr. Bruce's licensing
bill, which was withdrawn . . summer of 1871
New licensing act, regulating hours of opening and
shutting, &c., passed and came into execution
10 Aug. 1872
[It caused much irritation, and was said to have conduced
to the fall of the Gladstone ministry, 1874.]

3 Q

Public-houses in Ireland closed on Sundays, by act passed . . . . . 16 Aug. 1878
Payment for licenses raised . . June, 1880

VICTUALLING OFFICE (London), for managing the victualling of the royal navy, was instituted Dec. 1663. The number of commissioners was five, afterwards seven, and then reduced to six. The various departments on Tower-hill, St. Katherine's, and Rotherhithe, were removed to Deptford in Aug. 1785, and the office to Somerset-house, 1783. In 1832 the office of commissioners was abolished, and the victualling-office made one of five departments under the lords of the admiralty.

VIENNA (the Roman *Vindobona*), was capital of the margraviate of Austria, 984; virtual capital of the German empire, 1273; since 1806, capital of the Austrian dominions only. Population in 1857, 476,222; 1872,901,000; 1880, 1,103,857; see *Austria*.
Vienna made an imperial city 1136
Walled and enlarged with the ransom paid for Richard I. of England, 40,000*l.* . . . 1194
Besieged by the Turks under Solyman the Magnificent, with an army of 300,000 men; but he was forced to raise the siege with the loss of 70,000 of his best troops 1529
Besieged by the Turks . . . July, 1683
The siege raised by John Sobieski, king of Poland, who defeats the Turkish army of 100,000, 12 Sept. ,,
Vienna taken by the French under prince Murat, 14 Nov. 1805, evacuated . . . 12 Jan. 1806
Captured by Napoleon I. . . . 13 May, 1809
Restored on the conclusion of peace . 14 Oct. ,,
Congress of sovereigns at Vienna . . Nov. 1814
Imperial Academy of Sciences founded . . 1846
The revolt in Hungary induces an insurrection in Vienna . . . . . 13 March, 1848
The emperor retires, 17 May; returns . Aug. ,,
A second insurrection : Count Latour, the war minister, is murdered . . . . 6 Oct. ,,
The emperor again takes flight . . . 7 Oct. ,,
Vienna is bombarded by Windischgrätz and Jellachich, 28 Oct.; its capitulation . 30 Oct. ,,
Conferences respecting the Russo-Turkish war held at Vienna* 1853-5
The fortifications demolished, and the city enlarged and beautified 1857-8
The imperial parliament (Reichsrath) assembles here . . . . . 31 May, 1860
The Prussians encamp near Vienna; state of siege proclaimed . . . . . July, 1866
Visited by the sultan . . . 27 July, 1867
New palace of the fine arts founded by the emperor about 18 Sept. 1868
The great international exhibition opened by the emperor; the prince of Wales and many dignitaries present . . . . 1 May, 1873

* A conference of the four great powers, England, France, Austria, and Prussia, was held 24 July, when a note was agreed on and transmitted for acceptance to St. Petersburg and Constantinople, 31 July. This note was accepted by the czar, 10 Aug., but the sultan required modifications, which were rejected by Russia, 7 Sept. The sultan's note (31 Dec.) contained four points :— 1. The promptest possible evacuation of the principalities. 2. Revision of the treaties. 3. Maintenance of religious privileges to the communities of all confessions. 4. A definite settlement of the convention respecting the holy places. It was approved by the four powers, and the conferences closed on 16 Jan. 1854.—A new conference of plenipotentiaries, from Great Britain (lord John Russell), France (M. Drouyn de l'Huys), Austria (count Buol), Turkey (Arif Effendi), and Russia (count Gortschakoff), took place, March, 1854. Two points, the protectorate of the principalities and the free navigation of the Danube, were agreed to; but the proposals of the powers as to the reduction of the Russian power in the Black Sea were rejected by the czar, and the conference closed, 5 June, 1854. The English and French envoys' assent to the Austrian propositions was not approved of by their governments, and they both resigned their official positions.

[The enormous building with annexes was designed by Mr. Scott Russell, most ably supported by the Austrian engineers; the grand central rotunda, 312 feet in diameter, with lofty dome, is an exaggerated Pantheon, suspended on iron girders in place of masonry, and dwarfs St. Peter's at Rome.]
Great financial failures; affect all Europe, 9 May, 1873
Visit of the czar, 1-7 June; of the shah of Persia, 30 July, ,,
Prizes to exhibitors presented by the archduke Albert . . . . . 18 Aug. ,,
Visit of Victor Emmanuel, king of Italy, 17-22 Sept.; of the emperor of Germany . 17-23 Oct. ,,
Waterworks inaugurated by the emperor 24 Oct. ,,
The exhibition closed . . . . 2 Nov. ,,
New bed of the Danube inaugurated . 30 May, 1876
Johann Zich throws a stone at Russian ambassador 19 Jan. 1882
International art exhibition opened . 1 April, ,,
The Ring theatre destroyed by fire, caused by the fall of a large spirit lamp, 447 persons perished out of about 2000, 8 Dec. 1881; [accusations of culpable negligence]; imprisonment decreed . . . . . 16 May, ,,
Riot of shoemakers and others suppressed by military . . . . . 7—8 Nov. ,,
International exhibition of graphic art, &c. 15 Sept.—1 Nov. 1883
Electric exhibition . . 16 Aug.—3 Nov. ,,
Bi-centenary of the siege raised by John Sobieski, king of Poland, celebrated . . 12 Sept. ,,
The imperial parliament meets in its new grand house early in . . . . . Dec. ,,
Much disaffection, see *Austria* . . . Jan. 1884
Awful storm; destruction of life and property 10 Dec. ,,
Joseph Pircher, a gilder, secretly climbs up the steeple of St. Stephen's cathedral and places a banner on the cross (432 German feet high) and descends safely . . . 17, 18 Aug. 1886
Anarchist conspiracy to burn Vienna on the nights of 3, 4 Oct.; detected; premises in the suburbs fired, 27 Sept.; 17 men arrested and houses searched, bombs, &c. discovered and police disguises; announced . . . 10 Oct. ,,
Great international hygienic congress opened by crown prince Rudolph . . 26 Sept. ,,
International art exhibition opened . 3 March, 1888
Grand monument of the empress queen Maria Theresa inaugurated in the presence of the emperor and empress . . . 13 May, ,,
National industrial exhibition opened in honour of the 40th year of the emperor's reign, 14 May; closed . . . . . 31 Oct. ,,
Grand funeral of Beethoven on the removal of his remains from Währing cemetery to the central cemetery at Simmering . . 22 June, ,,
Goldsmith's exhibition opened . 22 April, 1889
Strike of tram-car men, anti-semitic rioting suppressed by the military; close of strike, 20-24 April, ,,

TREATIES OF VIENNA.
1. The treaty between the emperor of Germany and the king of Spain, by which they confirmed to each other such parts of the Spanish dominions as they were respectively possessed of; and by a private treaty the emperor engaged to employ a force to procure the restoration of Gibraltar to Spain, and to use means for placing the Pretender on the throne of Great Britain. Spain guaranteed the Pragmatic Sanction 30 April, 1725.
2. Treaty of alliance between the emperor of Germany, Charles VI., George II., king of Great Britain, and the states of Holland, by which the Pragmatic Sanction was guaranteed, and the disputes as to the Spanish succession terminated. (Spain acceded to the treaty on the 22nd of July.) Signed 16 March, 1731.
3. Treaty of peace between the emperor Charles VI. of Germany and the king of France, Louis XV., by which the latter power agreed to guarantee the Pragmatic Sanction, and Lorraine was ceded to France. Signed 18 Nov. 1738; see *Pragmatic Sanction*.
4. Treaty between Napoleon I. of France and Francis (II. of Germany) I. of Austria, by which Austria ceded to France the Tyrol, Dalmatia, and other territories

which were shortly afterwards declared to be united to France under the title of the Illyrian Provinces, and engaged to adhere to the prohibitory system adopted towards England by France and Russia. 14 Oct. 1809.
5. Treaty between Great Britain, Austria, Russia, and Prussia, confirming the principles on which they had acted by the treaty of Chaumont, 1 Mar. 1814. Signed 25 March, 1815.
6. Treaty between the king of the Netherlands on the one part, and Great Britain, Russia, Austria, and Prussia on the other, agreeing to the enlargement of the Dutch territories, and vesting the sovereignty in the house of Orange. 31 May, 1815.
7. Treaty by which Denmark ceded Swedish Pomerania and Rugen to Prussia, in exchange for Lauenburg. 4 June, 1815.
8. Commercial treaty for twelve years between Austria and Prussia. Signed at Vienna, 19 Feb. 1853.
9. Treaty for the maintenance of Turkey, by the representatives of Great Britain, France, Austria, and Russia. Signed 9 April, 1854.
10. Treaty between Austria and Prussia and Denmark, by which Denmark ceded the duchies. 30 Oct. 1864.
11. Treaty of peace between Austria and Italy; Venetia given up to Italy. 3 Oct. 1866.

VIENNE, the ancient Vienna Allobrogum (S.E. France). Here the emperor Valentinian II. was put to death by Arbogastes, 15 May, 392, and a short reaction in favour of paganism followed. Vienne was capital of the kingdom of Burgundy in 432 and 879, and sometimes gave its name to the kingdom. A general council was held here in 1311. Vienne was annexed to the French monarchy, 1448.

VIGILANCE ASSOCIATION, see under *National*.

VIGILANCE MURDER ASSOCIATION, see *Ireland*, 1883.

VIGO (N. W. Spain) was attacked and burned by the English, under Drake and Norris in 1589. Sir George Rooke, with the combined English and Dutch fleets, attacked the French fleet and the Spanish galleons in the port of Vigo, when several men-of-war and galleons were taken, and many destroyed, and abundance of plate and other valuable effects fell into the hands of the conquerors, 12 Oct. 1702. Vigo was taken by lord Cobham in 1719, but relinquished after raising contributions. It was again taken by the British, 27 March, 1809.

VIKINGS. Scandinavian chiefs, Swedes, Danes, and Norsemen, who in the 4th century migrated—eastward, to the countries beyond the Baltic; westward and southward, chiefly to the British isles.

VILLA FRANCA. Near here, and Llerena, Spain, the British cavalry, under sir Stapleton Cotton, defeated the French cavalry under marshal Soult, 11 April, 1812.—VILLA FRANCA, a small port on the Mediterranean, near Genoa, was bought for a steam-packet station by a Russian company, about Aug. 1858, which caused some political

VILLAIN, or **VILLEIN**, see *Slavery in England*.

VILLE DE HAVRE, French Atlantic mail steamer, 5,100 tons, sailed from New York for Havre, 15 Nov. 1873; was run into by a Glasgow clipper, *Lochearn*, about 2 a.m., 22 Nov., and sank in twelve minutes; 226 out of 313 persons perished. The crew of the *Lochearn* rescued 87, who were conveyed to Cardiff by the American vessel *Tri-Mountain*, capt. Urquhart, arriving there 1 Dec. 1873 The *Lochearn*, beginning to sink, 28 Nov., was abandoned by her crew, who were rescued by the *British Queen*, and brought to Plymouth 7 Dec. ,, On judicial examination, the *Lochearn* was exonerated in England, but censured in France Jan. 1874

VILLETA (Paraguay, South America). Here Lopez and the Paraguayans were totally defeated by the Brazilians and their allies, 11 Dec. 1868. Lopez and 200 men fled; 3000 prisoners were made; and the war was considered to be ended.

VIMIERA (in Portugal), where the British and Spanish forces, under sir Arthur Wellesley, defeated the French, under marshal Junot, duke of Abrantes, 21 Aug. 1808. The attack, made with great bravery, was gallantly repulsed; it was repeated by Kellermann at the head of the French reserve, which was also repulsed. The French, charged with the bayonet, withdrew on all points in confusion, leaving many prisoners.

VINCENNES, a strong castle near Paris; a residence of the French kings from the 12th to the 14th centuries. Henry V. of England died at the Bois de Vincennes, 31 Aug. 1422. At the fosse of the castle, Louis duc d'Enghien was shot by order of Napoleon, after a hasty trial, early on the morning of 22 March, 1804.

VINCENT, CAPE ST. (S. W. Portugal). See *Cape St. Vincent*, and *Rodney's Victories*.

VINCENT, ST. (West Indies), long a neutral island; but at the peace of 1763, the French agreed that the right to it should be vested in the English. The latter soon after engaged in a war against the Caribs, on the windward side of the island, who were obliged to consent to a peace, by which they ceded a large tract of land to the British crown. In 1779 the Caribs greatly contributed to the reduction of this island by the French, who, however, restored it in 1783. In 1795 the French landed some troops, and again instigated the Caribs to an insurrection, which was not subdued for several months. The great eruption of the Souffriere mountain, after the lapse of nearly a century, occurred in 1812. Population in 1861, 31,755; in 1881, 40,548.
Great destruction of life and property by a hurricane . . . . . . 16 Aug. 1886

VINCENT DE PAUL, ST., CHARITABLE SOCIETY, founded in 1833, in France, by twelve young men. It extends its extremely beneficial operations into Britain. Its power excited the jealousy of the French government, which sup-

structed the South Gauls in tillage, vine-dressing, and commerce, about 600 B.C. Some think that vines are aborigines of Languedoc, Provence, and Sicily, and that they grew spontaneously on the Mediterranean shores of Italy, France, and Spain. The vine was carried into Champagne, and part of Germany, by the emperor Probus, about A.D. 279. The vine and sugar-cane were planted in Madeira in 1420. In the gardens of Hampton-court palace is an old and celebrated vine, said to surpass any known vine in Europe; see *Grapes*, and *Wine*. The Tokay vines were planted in 1350.

Vine Disease. In the spring of 1845, Mr. E. Tucker, of Margate, observed a fungus (since named *Oïdium Tuckeri*) on grapes in the hot-houses of Mr. Slater, of Margate. It is a whitish mildew, and totally destroys the fruit.
The spores of this *oïdium* were found in the vineries at Versailles in 1847. The disease soon reached the trellised vines, and in 1850 many lost all their produce.
In 1852, it spread over France, Italy, Spain, Syria, and in Zante and Cephalonia attacked the currants, reducing the crop to one-twelfth of the usual amount.
Through its ravages, the wine manufacture in Madeira ceased for several years.
Many attempts have been made to arrest the progress of this disease, but without much effect. Sulphur dust is the most efficacious remedy.
The disease had much abated in France, Portugal, and Madeira, in 1863. In 1862 Californian vines were introduced into the two latter.
New malady (microscopic insect, *phylloxera vastatrix*), in S. France, observed 1865
Remedy, sulphuret of carbon, recommended by M. Dumas . . . . Aug. 1873
Not successful; great destruction; 12,000*l.* offered for a remedy . . . . July, 1876
Phylloxera prevalent in Malaga and France; reported July, Aug. 1878; Portugal, Italy, Spain; Sept..-Nov. 1879; appears in Victoria, Australia, Nov. 1880
Phylloxera congress at Bordeaux . . 10—15 Oct. 1881
The phylloxera is said to be exterminated in Switzerland by fire . . . . Nov. 1882
Phylloxera ravaging vines on the Douro; consequent emigrations to Brazil . . . 7 Feb. 1884
Phylloxera checked in W. France; prosperous vintages 1883-4

VINEGAR. The ancients had several kinds, which they used for drink. The Roman soldiers were accustomed to take it in their marches. The Bible represents Boaz, a rich citizen of Bethlehem, as providing vinegar for his reapers (1312 B.C.), a custom still prevalent in Spain and Italy.

VINEGAR-HILL (near Enniscorthy, in Wexford, S. E. Ireland). Here the Irish rebels, headed by father John, a priest, encamped and committed many outrages on the surrounding country. They were gradually surrounded by the British troops, commanded by Lake, 21 June, 1798, and after a fierce struggle, with much slaughter, totally dispersed.

VINTNERS, see *Victuallers*.

VIOL AND VIOLIN. The lyre of the Greeks became our harp, and the viol of the middle ages became the violin. The violin is mentioned as early as 1200, in the legendary life of St. Christopher. It was introduced into England, some say, by Charles II. Straduarius (or Stradivarius) of Cremona, was a renowned violin-maker (1700 to 1722). The eminent violinist Paganini visited England, 1831; died at Nice. 27 May, 1840.

VIRGINALS; an early keyed instrument of the kind termed clavichords; used in the 16th and 17th centuries; played on by queen Elizabeth and Mary queen of Scots. According to Johnson, it owed its name to young women being the usual performers. Tallis, Morley, Purcell, Gibbons, and Bull composed for this instrument.

VIRGINIA, see *Rome*, 449 B.C.

VIRGINIA, the first British settlement in North America, was discovered by John Cabot in 1497, and was taken possession of and named by Raleigh, after the virgin-queen Elizabeth, 13 July, 1584. Vain attempts were made to settle it in 1585. Two expeditions were formed by patent in 1606, and others in 1610. In 1626 it reverted to the crown; and a more permanent colony was established soon afterwards. George Washington was delegate for Virginia in the congress of 1774. Eastern Virginia seceded from the Union, 25 April, 1861, but Western Virginia declared for the Union, 13 Feb. and elected a governor, 20 Feb. 1861. Virginia was a chief seat of the war. The state was readmitted to the congress, Jan.-Feb. 1870; see *United States*, and *Richmond*. Population in 1880, 1,512,565; capital, Richmond. Western Virginian, population, 618,457; capital, Wheeling.

VIRGINIA CITY, see *Nevada*.

VIRGIN ISLANDS (West Indies), an eastern group discovered by Columbus, (1494): Virgin Gorda, Tortola, Anegada, &c., and the Danish Isles, St. Thomas, Santa Cruz, and St. John.

Tortola settled by Dutch buccaneers about 1648;
expelled by the English (who have held it since) 1666
St. Thomas settled by Danes 1672, and St. John a few years after; held by the British 1801-2; 1807-15; proposed sale to the United States for 1,500,000*l.* to be made a "territory." Danish proclamation, 25 Oct. 1867; purchase declined by U. S. senate . . . . . 23 March, May, 1870
By a dreadful hurricane off St. Thomas, the Royal Mail steamers *Rhone* and *Wye* were entirely wrecked; the *Conway* and *Derwent*, and above 50 other vessels, driven ashore; about 1000 persons said to have perished . . . . . 29 Oct. 1867
Much suffering was occasioned in Tortola; houses blown down or unroofed, &c. (a report reached London that the isle was submerged).
Earthquake at St. Thomas's and other Isles; much damage; few lives lost . . . . . Nov. ,,
Santa Cruz. A negro insurrection, in which M. Fontaine, a planter, was killed; Fredrikstadt and 36 out of 50 sugar plantations were burnt, and about 3000 whites rendered homeless. During the suppression by col. Garde, the governor, about 200 negroes were killed . . . . . 1-5 Oct. 1878

VIRGINIUS, American blockade-runner, see *Cuba*, 1873.

VIRGIN MARY. The Assumption of the Virgin is a festival in the Greek and Latin churches, in honour of the miraculous ascent of Mary into heaven, according to their belief, 15 Aug. A.D. 45. The Presentation of the Virgin is a feast celebrated 21 Nov., said to have been instituted among the Greeks in the 11th century; its institution in the West is ascribed to pope Gregory XI. 1372; see *Annunciation*, and *Conception, Immaculate*.

VIRTUE, LEAGUE OF, see *Tugendbund*.

VISCONTI, the name of a noble Italian family, which ruled in Milan from about 1277 to 1447; the heiress of the family was married to Francesco Sforza, who became duke 1450.

VISCOUNT (*Vice Comes*), anciently the name of the deputy of an earl. The first viscount in England created by patent was John, lord Beaumont, whom Henry VI. created viscount Beaumont, giving him precedence above all barons, 10 Feb. 1440. *Ashmole.* This title is of older date in Ireland and France. John Barry, lord Barry, was made viscount Buttevant, in Ireland, 9 Rich. II. 1385. *Beatson.*

VISIBLE SPEECH, a term applied by Mr. Alex. Melville Bell to his "Universal Self-Interpreting Physiological Alphabet," comprising thirty symbols representing the conformations of the mouth when uttering sounds. He stated that about fifty different types would be required to print all known languages with these symbols. He expounded his system to the Society of Arts, London, 14 March, 1866; and published a book in 1867.

VISIGOTHS, separated from the Ostrogoths about 330; see *Goths*. The emperor Valens, about 369, admitted them into the Roman territories upon the condition of their serving when wanted in the Roman armies; and Theodosius the Great permitted them to form distinct corps commanded by their own officers. In 400, under Alaric, they invaded Italy, and in 410 took Rome. They founded their kingdom of Toulouse, 414; conquered the Alani, and extended their rule into Spain, 414; expelled the Romans in 468; and finally were themselves conquered by the Saracens under Muza, in 711, when their last king, Roderic, was defeated and slain; see *Spain* for a list of the Visigothic kings. Their rule in France ended with their defeat by Clovis at Vouglé, in 507.

VISITATIONS, see *Heralds*.

VITAL FORCE, defined by Humboldt "as an unknown cause preventing the elements from obeying their primitive affinities." This theory is now opposed by many physiologists, and animal motion is attributed to muscular and nervous irritability, illustrated by the researches of Galvani, Humboldt, sir Charles Bell, Marshall Hall, and others. The subject has been much discussed recently by Huxley and other eminent physiologists.

VITI ISLES, see *Fiji*.

VITTORIA (N. Spain), the site of a victory obtained by Wellington over the French army commanded by Joseph Bonaparte, king of Spain, and marshal Jourdan, 21 June, 1813. The hostile armies were nearly equal, from 70,000 to 75,000 each. After a long and fearful battle, the French were driven, towards evening, through the town of Vittoria, and in their retreat were thrown into irretrievable confusion. The British loss was 22 officers and 479 men killed; 167 officers and 2640 men wounded. Marshal Jourdan lost 151 pieces of cannon, 451 waggons of ammunition, all his baggage, provisions, cattle, and treasure, with his bâton as a marshal of France. Continuing the pursuit on the 25th, Wellington took Jourdan's only remaining gun.

VIVARIUM, see *Aquaricarium*.

VIVISECTION. Physiological experiments upon living animals having much increased, the societies for the prevention of cruelty to animals in Dresden and Paris in 1859 requested the opinion of a committee of eminent scientific men on the merits of the knowledge thus acquired. Their judgment was not unanimous. The London society took up the question in 1860; and printed a pamphlet by Mr. G. Macilwain against vivisection. In Aug. 1862 an international conference to discuss the question was held at the Crystal Palace, Sydenham. The subject was discussed in 1866, and a prize awarded by the London society. Sir Charles Bell's opinion of vivisection was, that it either obscured the subject it was meant to illustrate, or misled men into practical errors of the most serious character. Discussion revived in consequence of the prosecution of Dr. Schiff in Florence, who justified vivisection when chloroform or any other anæsthetic is used 1873-6

Rival societies: 1. Society for the abolition of vivisection, 1875; 2. International Association for total suppression of vivisection 1876
Commission (viscount Cardwell, professor Huxley and others) to inquire into the practice, appointed 23 June, 1875; report signed, 8 Jan.; published, March, 1876; a bill to regulate vivisection (cruelty to animals act) brought into parliament; strongly opposed by the medical profession in general, June, July; passed, 15 Aug. 1876. Vivisectors are to have a licence or certificate.
Resolution in favour of vivisection passed by the International Medical Congress, London 9 Aug. 1881
The prosecution of prof. Ferrier (who had experimented on the brains of monkeys under anæsthetics) and others failed . . . . Nov. "
Dr. Koch, of Berlin, demonstrates that tubercular disease can be propagated by organisms termed *bacilli* 1882
Mr. R. T. Reid's bill to prohibit vivisection, talked out . . . . 4 April, 1883
Report for 1883: Great Britain, 44 licences; 535 experiments; Ireland, 8 licences: 34 experiments; anæsthetics employed when required.
441 experiments in Great Britain in . . . 1884
Report for 1886 and 1887: Great Britain 64 licences. In 1888 55 licences and 1,069 experiments.
Instructed by Dr. Ferrier's vivisection experiments, Dr. Hughes Bennett localized in a man's brain a tumour, which was removed by Mr. Godlee 25 Nov. 1884

VIZIANAGRAM, a town in Madras presidency, formerly a kingdom, among the last bulwarks against the Mahomedan invasion, and a refuge for Hindoo learning. The sovereigns date from the 14th century. See *Vedas*.

VIZIER, GRAND, an officer of the Ottoman Porte, said to have been first appointed by Amurath I., about 1386. The office was abolished in 1838; but since been frequently revived and suppressed.

VLADIMIR (central Russia), a city founded in the 12th century, and the capital of a grand duchy from 1157 to about 1328.

VOCALION, a new musical instrument in which tones are produced from strings made to vibrate by currents of air, the joint invention of Mr. James Baillie Hamilton and Mr. John Farmer assisted by Mr. Hermann Smith, described and illustrated by Mr. Hamilton at the Royal Institution, 21 May, 1875, and tried successfully at Harrow, 23 March, 1882, and soon after at Westminster Abbey; and at other places.

VOIRON, see *Veserence*.

VOLAPÜK (from 'world' and 'speak'), universal commercial language invented by M. Schleyer, who taught it in Paris in Feb. 1886. The Philological Society of London advocated its use in diplomacy and science, in 1887. The roots chiefly borrowed from Romanic, Germanic, and especially English languages shortened. There is a Volapük Academy at Munich, and about 500,000 people are using or learning it.
Mr. C. E. Sprague's handbook of Volapük published . . . . Jan. 1888
Volapük reported successful and spreading in Europe and America
Mr. P. Hoinix publishes his "Anglo Franca" in opposition to Volapük . . . March, 1889

VOLCANOES. In different parts of the earth there are above 200 volcanoes which have been active in modern times; see *Etna, Vesuvius, New Zealand, Owhyhee,* and *Iceland*. In Mexico, a plain was filled up into a mountain more than a thousand feet in height by the burning lava from a volcano, in 1759. A volcano in the isle of Ferro broke out

13 Sept. 1777, which threw out an immense quantity of red water, that discoloured the sea for several leagues. A new volcano appeared in one of the Azore islands, 1 May, 1808.

VOLHYNIA, a Polish province, annexed to Russia 1793.

VOLSCI, an ancient Latin people, frequently at war with the Romans. From their capital, Corioli, Caius Martius (who defeated them about 490 B.C.) derived his name Coriolanus. The story of his banishment by his ungrateful countrymen; of his revenge on them by bringing the Volsci to the gates of Rome, yet afterwards sparing the city at the entreaties of his mother, Volumnia (487 B.C.), is considered by many as a poetical legend. The Volsci and their allies were totally defeated at Sutrium by the consul Valerius Corvus (346), and incorporated with the Roman people about 338.

VOLSINII, the inhabitants of an Etrurian city, who, after a sharp contest, were completely overcome by the Roman consul Titus Coruncanius, 280 B.C.

VOLTAIC PILE or BATTERY, was constructed by Galvani; see *Galvanism* in article *Electricity*. The principle was discovered by Alessandro Volta, of Como (born 1745), for thirty years professor of natural philosophy at Pavia, and announced by him to the Royal Society of London in 1793. The battery was first set up in 1800. Volta was made an Italian count and senator by Napoleon Bonaparte, and was otherwise greatly honoured. While young he invented the electrophorus, electric pistol, and hydrogen lamp. He died in 1826, aged 81. The form of the Voltaic battery has been greatly improved by the researches of modern philosophers. The nitric acid battery of sir W. R. Grove was constructed in 1839; Alfred Smee's battery in 1840; the carbon battery of professor Robert Bunsen in 1842. The first is very much used in this country; that of Bunsen on the continent, see *Copper-Zinc Couple*.

VOLTURNO, a river in S. Italy, near Capua, near to which Garibaldi and his followers held a strong position. This was furiously assailed by the royal troops on 1 Oct. 1860, who were finally repulsed after a desperate struggle, the fiercest in which Garibaldi had yet been engaged. He was aided greatly by a band of Piedmontese from Naples. On 2 Oct. general Bixio completed the victory by capturing 2500 fresh Neapolitan troops and dispersing others.

VOLUNTARY CONTRIBUTIONS. Public contributions for the support of the British government against the policy and designs of France amounted to two millions and a half sterling in 1798. About 200,000*l*. were transmitted to England from India in 1799. Sir Robert Peel, of Bury, among other contributions of equal amount, subscribed 10,000*l*. *Annual Register;* see *Patriotic Fund.* In 1862 nearly a million pounds were subscribed in the British empire for the relief of the Lancashire cotton spinners; see *Cotton* and *Mansion House*, where voluntary contributions for beneficent purposes are continually received.

VOLUNTEERS were enrolled in England for the American war, 1778, and especially in consequence of the threatened invasion of revolutionary France, 1793-4. Besides our large army, and 85,000 men voted for the sea, we subsidised 40,000 Germans, raised our militia to 100,000 men, and armed the citizens as volunteers; the yeomanry formed cavalry regiments. Between 1798 and 1804, when this force was of greatest amount, it numbered 410,000, of which 70,000 were Irish;[*] Yeomanry in 1883, 11,400. On 26 Oct. 1803, king George III. reviewed in Hyde Park 12,401 London volunteers, and on 28 Oct. 14,676 more. The English volunteers were, according to official accounts, 341,600 on 1 Jan. 1804; see *Naval Volunteers.* In May, 1859, in consequence of the prevalence of the fear of a French invasion, the formation of volunteer corps of riflemen commenced under the auspices of the government, and by the end of the year many thousands were enrolled in all parts of the kingdom. The volunteers were said to be "a force potentially the strongest defence of England," 19 April, 1870; see *Artillery Association*, and *Naval Artillery Volunteer Force.*

YEOMANRY were enrolled by lord Chatham in 1761. The present 49 regiments of cavalry (about 300 each), cost 80,000*l*. 1870
[The first Middlesex volunteers were formed in 1803 as the duke of Cumberland's sharpshooters. They retained their organisation as a rifle club, when other volunteers were disbanded. In 1835 they were permitted by the duchess of Kent to take the name of the Royal Victoria Rifle Club.]
Circular letter from col. Jonathan Peel, proposing organization of *National Volunteer Association* for promoting the practice of Rifle-shooting, 12 May, 1859. It was established in London, under the patronage of the queen and prince consort, Mr. Sidney (afterwards lord) Herbert, secretary at war, president, and the earl of Derby and other noblemen vice-presidents. (Annual subscription one guinea, or a composition for life of ten guineas) . . . . 16 Nov. 1859
2500 volunteer officers presented to the queen; a dinner followed, with the duke of Cambridge in the chair; and a ball . . . . 7 March, 1860
The queen reviews about 18,450 volunteers in Hyde-park . . . . 23 June, ,,
[Mr. Tower, of Wealdhall, Essex, aged 80, was present as a private; he had been present as an officer in a volunteer review in 1803.]
First meeting of the National Association for rifle-shooting held at Wimbledon; captain Edw. Ross (North York) obtained the queen's prize of 250*l*. and the gold medal and badge of the association 2-7 July, 1860
[M. Thorel, a Swiss, obtained a prize.]
Successful sham-fight at Bromley, Kent 14 July, ,,
Above 20,000 volunteers reviewed by the queen at Edinburgh . . . . 7 Aug. ,,
Above 10,000 Lancashire volunteers reviewed by the earl of Derby at Knowsley . . . 1 Sept. ,,
Lord Herbert stated that the association had a capital of 3000*l*. and an annual income of 1500*l*., 16 Feb. 1861
Volunteers in Britain estimated at about 160,000, May, ,,
Second meeting at Wimbledon; Mr. Jopling (S. Middlesex) gains the queen's prize and the association medal . . . . 4-10 July, ,,
Review of 11,504 volunteers at Wimbledon, 13 July; of 9000 at Warwick . . . . . . 24 July, ,,
Registered number of volunteers, 162,681 1 April, 1862

* The first regiment of Irish volunteers was formed at Dublin, under command of the duke of Leinster, 12 Oct. 1779. They armed generally to the amount of 20,000 men, and received the unanimous thanks of the houses of lords and commons in Ireland, for their patriotism and spirit, for coming forward and defending their country. At the period when the force appeared, Irish affairs bore a serious aspect; manufactures had decreased, and foreign trade had been hurt by a prohibition of the export of salted provisions and butter. No notice of the complaints of the people had been taken in the English parliament, when, owing to the alarm of an invasion, ministers allowed the nation to arm, and an immense force was soon raised. The Irish took this occasion to demand a free trade, and government saw there was no trifling with a country with arms in its hands. The Irish parliament unanimously addressed the king for a free trade, and it was granted, 1779.

20,000 volunteers reviewed by lord Clyde at Brighton . . . . . . 21 April, 1862
Third meeting at Wimbledon; Mr. Pixley (S. Victoria) gains the queen's prize, &c. 1-14 July, ,,
A commission recommends that an annual grant of either 20s., 30s., or 34s., be given to each volunteer according to circumstances . Oct. ,,
Fourth meeting at Wimbledon, 7 July, &c.; queen's prize, &c., won by sergeant Roberts (12th Shropshire) . . . . . . 14 July, 1863
An act to amend and consolidate the acts relating to the volunteer force of Great Britain was passed, 21 July, ,,
[Annual grant of 30s. to each volunteer authorised.]
22,000 volunteers reviewed by the prince of Wales in Hyde-park (great improvement noticed), 28 May, 1864
Fifth meeting at Wimbledon, 11 July, &c.; the queen's prize, &c., won by private John Wyatt (London rifle brigade) . . 23 July, ,,
Volunteers estimated at 165,000 in 1864.
Sixth meeting at Wimbledon, began 11 July; the queen's prize was won by private Sharman (4th West York), 18 July; the meeting ended with a review by the duke of Cambridge . 22 July, 1865
Seventh meeting at Wimbledon, began 9 July; queen's prize won by Angus Cameron (6th Inverness), 17 July; the value of about 7000l. distributed in prizes; and review by duke of Cambridge . . . . . . 21 July, 1866
The volunteers reviewed by the prince of Wales at Brighton, 2 April; at York, 11 Aug.; by duke of Cambridge at Hyde-park . . 23 June, ,,
Estimate of volunteers: 135,000 infantry, 27,000 artillery, and 4000 engineers.—*Times* . 9 Oct. ,,
About 1100 volunteers visit Brussels, headed by col. Loyd Lindsay; warmly received; first prize gained by Curtis, of the 11th Sussex rifles, 11-22 Oct. ,,
Parliamentary vote for volunteers, 361,009l.
6 June, 1867
Metropolitan and Berkshire volunteers reviewed in Windsor Great Park . . . 10 June, ,,
Eighth meeting at Wimbledon, began 8 July; Belgian Garde civique and volunteers (above 2000) received by prince of Wales, 13 July; resignation of lord Elcho, chairman of the council; succeeded by earl Spencer, 13 July; grand review by prince of Wales, the sultan, &c.; the queen's prize given to sergeant Lane (Bristol) by the princess of Teck, 20 July, ,,
Grand review in New Sefton park, Liverpool, 5 Oct. ,,
About 28,000 volunteers reviewed by the queen at Windsor . . . . . . 20 June, 1868
Review of regulars and volunteers at Edinburgh, 4 July, ,,
Ninth meeting at Wimbledon, 13 July; the queen's prize gained by lieut. Carslake (5th Somerset), 25 July, ,,
Lord Elcho re-elected chairman of the council (earl Spencer resigned) . . . . Feb. 1869
Memorial to government respecting the capitation grant; signed by noblemen and gentlemen, 19 Feb. ,,
Volunteers reported to number 170,000 . . ,,
Review of volunteers of southern and western counties at Portsmouth . . 26 April, ,,
Tenth meeting at Wimbledon 3 July; queen's prize gained by corporal Angus Cameron (6th Inverness), 2nd time, 13 July; grand review 24 July, 1869
Volunteers' act, 1863, amended . . 9 Aug. ,,
"*Army Service Corps*" to be composed of volunteers; established by royal warrant . 12 Nov. ,,
Eleventh meeting at Wimbledon, 11 July; queen's prize won by corporal Humphries (6th Surrey), 19 July, 1870
Letter from the lord mayor recommending the enlargement of the volunteer system, and its greater efficiency . . . . . . 22 Sept. ,,
Establishment of an extensive rifle range, drill ground, armoury, &c., for the London volunteers resolved on . . . . . . 3 Oct. ,,
Distribution of breech-loaders commenced . Nov. ,,
The volunteers recognised as part of the national army 1871
Lord Elcho (chairman) resigned; succeeded by the earl of Ducie . . . . . June, ,,

Twelfth meeting at Wimbledon, 8 July; queen's prize won by ensign A. P. Humphry, undergraduate (Cambridge university), aged 19 18 July, 1871
Vote for volunteer force, 1872-3, 473,200l. 24 June, 1872
Thirteenth meeting at Wimbledon, 8 July; queen's prize won by colour-sergeant Michie (London Scottish) . . . . . 16 July, ,,
The Elcho shield, the International trophy, and the Irish International trophy (all won by the English) placed in the custody of the lord mayor, 27 July, ,,
Some volunteers visit Ghent . . 14-21 Sept. ,,
Fourteenth meeting at Wimbledon, 7 July; queen's prize won by sergeant Robert Menzies (1st Edinburgh) . . . . . 15 July, 1873
Volunteers visit Havre; shoot for prizes; 50 obtain prizes, end of May; given . . 29 June, 1874
Fifteenth meeting at Wimbledon, 6 July; queen's prize won by private W. C. Atkinson (1st Durham)
14 July, ,,
An "efficient volunteer" defined by order in council (substitute for schemes of 27 July, 1863, and 15 Oct. 1872) . . . . . Aug. ,,
Resignation of earl of Ducie as chairman . April, 1875
Sixteenth meeting at Wimbledon, 12 July; queen's prize won by capt. George Pearse (15th Devon)
20 July, ,,
175,387 enrolled volunteers 1874; 181,080, . . ,,
30,000 volunteers reviewed by the prince of Wales in Hyde Park ("complete success."—*Times*.)
1 July, 1876
Seventeenth meeting at Wimbledon, 10-22 July; queen's prize won by sergeant Pullman, 2nd (South) Middlesex . . . 18 July, ,,
185,501 enrolled volunteers . . . . ,,
Eighteenth meeting at Wimbledon, 9-21 July; queen's prize won by private George Jamieson (a Scot), of 15th Lancashire corps (Liverpool)
17 July, 1877
Nineteenth meeting at Wimbledon, 8-20 July; queen's prize won by private Peter Ray (a Scot), 11th Stirling . . . . . 16 July, 1878
203,213 enrolled volunteers . . . Nov. ,,
Twentieth meeting at Wimbledon, 14-26 July; queen's prize won by corporal George Taylor, 47th Lancashire . . . . 22 July, 1879
International trophy won by England . 19 July, ,,
Standard of efficiency: 69 per cent. 1863; 85 per cent. 1868; 96 per cent. 1880
Earl Stanhope elected chairman in room of earl Wharncliffe . . . . . . May, ,,
Twenty-first meeting at Wimbledon, 12-24 July; Queen's prize won by Alexander Ferguson, private 1st Argyll . . . . . . 21 July, ,,
East York volunteer artillery corps resign on account of dismissal of col. Humphrey (through continued personal disagreements), 16 June; resignations said to be illegal . 29 June, ,,
Sergeant Wm. Marshman, tried by court-martial for alleged fraudulent marking at the rifle meetings, 1878, 1879, 1880, acquitted . 13 Aug.—16 Sept. ,,
Earl Stanhope, chairman, succeeded by earl Brownlow . . . . . . 4 May, 1881
Above 52,000 volunteers reviewed by the queen at Windsor, 9 July. ["A magnificent success; the crowning achievement of the volunteer movement."—*Times*, 11 July] . . . . ,,
About 40,000 Scotch volunteers reviewed by the queen, in Queen's-park, Edinburgh . 25 Aug. ,,
Twenty-second meeting at Wimbledon, 11-23 July; queen's prize won by private Thomas Beck, 3rd Devon . . . . . . 22 July, ,,
Twenty-third meeting at Wimbledon, 10-22 July; queen's prize won by sergeant Lawrence, 1st Dumbarton . . . . . 18 July, 1882
Enrolled volunteers, 207,336 . . 1 Nov. ,,
Twenty-fourth meeting at Wimbledon, 9-21 July; queen's prize won by sergeant Mackay, 1st Sutherland . . . . . . 17 July, 1883
International rifle match between British and Americans: won by British . 21 July, ,,
Twenty-fifth meeting at Wimbledon, 14-26 July; queen's prize won by private Gallant, 8th Middlesex . . . . . . 22 July, 1884
Volunteers exercised in camping out; sham conflicts in Berkshire and other counties . Aug. ,,
Volunteers Forces' Benevolent Association, inaugurated . . . . . . 6 July, 1885

Twenty-sixth meeting at Wimbledon, 13—25 July; queen's prize won by sergeant Bulmer, and Lincoln . . . . 21 July, 1885
Twenty-seventh meeting at Wimbledon, 12-24 July; queen's prize won by private Jackson, of 1st V. B. Lincoln (one of three ties) 21 July, 1886
Enrolled volunteers, 224,012, Nov. 1885; 226,752 Nov. ,,
28,000 volunteers reviewed by the queen at Buckingham palace; march past in 1½ hours . 2 July, 1887
Twenty-eighth meeting at Wimbledon, 11-23 July; queen's prize won by lieut. R. O. Warren, 1st Middlesex, (Victoria) rifles, Middlesex 19 July, ,,
Lord Wantage elected chairman, 1887; active in search of a site in place of Wimbledon . . 1888
Order issued for the formation of 95,000 volunteers into 19 brigades for immediate mobilisation for home defence . . . . . 3 July, ,,
Twenty-ninth meeting at Wimbledon, 9-21 July; queen's prize won by private Fulton, 13th Middlesex (queen's Westminsters) rifles, 17 July, ,,
Broadwood to be called Bisley common, chosen for 1890 . . . . . . 28 Feb. 1889
Estimated grant for 220,000 men, 742,700*l*. April, ,,
Thirtieth meeting at Wimbledon . . 8-20 July, ,,
Queen's prize won by sergeant Reid (1st Lanark Engineers) . . . . . . 16 July, ,,
Patriotic volunteer fund started by lord mayor Whitehead in the spring; he appeals for subscriptions for the full equipment of a citizen army, equal to that of the regulars. The prince of Wales 105*l*., 1 June; the queen 200*l*. 2 July; many others; amount received about 37,567*l*. 16 July, ,,

EASTER MONDAY REVIEWS AND SHAM FIGHTS.
Brighton . . . 21 April, 1862, and 5 April, 1863
Guildford . . . . . 28 March, 1864
Brighton . . . 17 April, 1865; and 2 April, 1866
Dover . . . . . . 22 April, 1867
Portsmouth (the most successful hitherto, 29,490 volunteers present) . . . . 13 April, 1868
Dover (bad weather) . . . . 29 March, 1869
Brighton, 18 April, 1870; (considered a failure) 10 April, 1871
——— Mock battle between sir Arthur Horsford (12,180 men, 22 guns) and gen. Lysons (11,082 men, 20 guns) . . . . . 1 April, 1872
Small reviews at Wimbledon and other places, 14 April, 1873; 6 April, 1874; 29 March, 1875; at Tring, &c., 17 April, 1876; at Dunstable, &c., 2 April, 1877; at Staines, &c., 22 April, 1878; at Dover, Reigate, Wimbledon, &c., 14 April, 1879; Brighton, battle, successful; 29 March, 1880; 18 April, 1881; Portsmouth, 20,000 ("Genuine success," *Times*), 10 April, 1882; Brighton (evolutions very successful), 26 March, 1883; Dover, Portsmouth, &c., (12-)14 April, 1884; Brighton and Dover, 6 April, 1885; at Dover, Portsmouth, Colchester &c., 26 April, 1886; successful military operations at Dover, Eastbourne, and Aldershot, 11 April, 1887; campaign operations and battles, invasions, &c. at Portsmouth, Dover, Eastbourne &c., 30, 31 March; battles: Invaders successful at Portsmouth . 2 April, 1888
Meetings for brigade drill, &c., Eastbourne, Portsmouth, Dover, Brighton, and other places, 22 April, 1889
ELCHO CHALLENGE SHIELD, shot for by teams, and kept by the winning nation :
Won by England: 1862, 1863, 1865, 1867, 1868, 1870, 1871, 1872, 1876, 1881 (July 22), 1882 (July 20), 1885 (July 23), 1887 (July 21).
Scotland: 1864, 1866, 1869, 1874, 1879 (July 24).

Ireland: 1873, 1875, 1877, 1878, 1880 (, 1883 (July 19), 1884 (July 24), 1886 (July (July 19), 1889 (July 18).
Volunteer Medical Staff Corps established, a

VOSSEM, PEACE OF, between Brandenburg and Louis XIV. of Franc engaged not to assist the Dutch agains signed 6 June, 1673.

VOTING PAPERS. See *Dodso* proposal to use them was negatived in on reform in 1867; adopted by the ball

VOUGLÉ or VOUILLÉ, S.W. Poitiers), where Alaric II., king of t was defeated and slain by Clovis, kin 507, who subdued the whole country fr to the Pyrenees. A peace followed Franks and Visigoths, who had been one hundred years in that part of Septimania. Clovis soon afterwards his capital.

VOYAGES. By order of Phara Egypt, some Phœnician pilots sailed down the Arabian Gulf, round what the Cape of Good Hope, entered the M by the Straits of Gibraltar, coasted alo of Africa, and at length arrived in E navigation of about three years, 604 B.C The first voyage round the world wa ship, part of a Spanish squadron whi under the command of Magellan (who the Philippine Islands in a skirmish) see *Circumnavigators*, and *North-Wes*

VOYSEY ESTABLISHMEN The Rev. Charles Voysey having been heresy (see *Church of England*, 1871), of services at St. George's hall, Langhan 1871. The fund for their maintenance w by Bp. Hinds of Norwich (retired), Si ring, and other eminent liberals. H congregation a "Theistic Church."

VULCAN, see *Planets*. The Gr phaistos answered to the Roman Vulca

VULCANITE (vulcanised india-termed *Ebonite*.

VULGATE (from *vulgatus*, publi applied to the Latin version of th which is authorised by the council of and which is attributed to St. Jerom The older version, called the Italic, is been made in the beginning of the 2nd critical edition was printed by order of p in 1590, which, being considered ina superseded by the edition of pope C 1592. The earliest printed vulgate is by Gutenburg and Fust, probably ab first dated (Fust and Schœffer) is 1462

W.

WACHT.

WACHT DES DEUTSCHEN VATERLAND ("Watch of the German Fatherland"). German national hymn, by Reichardt, first performed 2 Aug. 1825. Very popular during the war 1870-71.

WADHAM COLLEGE (Oxford). Founded by Nicholas Wadham, and Dorothy, his wife, in 1613. In this college, in the chambers of Dr. Wilkins (over the gateway), the founders of the Royal Society frequently met prior to 1658.

WAGER OF BATTLE, see *Appeal*.

WAGES IN ENGLAND. The wages of sundry workmen were first fixed by act of parliament 25 Edw. III. 1350. Haymakers had but one penny a day. Master carpenters, masons, tilers, and other coverers of houses, had not more than 3*d*. per day (about 9*d*. of our money); and their servants, 1½*d*. *Viner's Statutes.**

By the 23 Henry VI. the wages of a bailiff of husbandry was 23*s*. 4*d*. per annum, and clothing of the price of 5*s*. with meat and drink; chief hind, carter, or shepherd, 20*s*., clothing, 4*s*.; common servant of husbandry, 15*s*., clothing, 4*od*.; woman-servant, 10*s*., clothing, 4*s*. 1444

By the 11 Henry VII., a like rate of wages with a little advance: as, for instance, a free mason, master carpenter, rough mason, bricklayer, master tiler, plumber, glazier, carver or joiner, was allowed from Easter to Michaelmas to take 6*d*. a

WAHABEES.

day without meat and drink; or, with meat and drink, 4*d*.; from Michaelmas to Easter, to abate 1*d*. A master having under him six men was allowed a 1*d*. a day extra 1495

Agricultural labourers per week: Warwickshire, 3*s*. 6*d*. and 4*s*.; Devonshire, 5*s*.; Suffolk, 5*s*. and 6*s*.; wool-weavers, about 3*s*. and 4*s*. (Macaulay) about 1685

In 1866 the annual amount of wages paid in the United Kingdom was estimated by Mr. Gladstone at 250,000,000*l*.; by Mr. Bass at 350,000,000*l*.; and by professor Leone Levi at 418,300,000*l*., earned by 10,697,000 workers, ages 20 to 60.

In 1872-3 many trades struck for increase of wages, and frequently were successful; in 1877-9, unsuccessful.

In 1878 professor Levi estimated that 503,000,000*l*. were earned (by men, 390,000,000*l*.; by women, 113,000,000*l*.); after deducting for holidays, &c., 422,700,000*l*.

He says, that "In no other country are wages more liberal, but in no other country are they more wastefully used." See *Strikes*.

Payment of wages in public houses prohibited by act passed in 1883

	LABOURERS' WAGES PER WEEK.		CORN PER QUARTER.	
	s.	d.	s.	d.
1824	7	7	62	0
1837	8	0	55	10
1860	9	6	53	3
1869	11	0	48	2
1872	11	9	57	1

WAGES OF HARVEST-MEN IN ENGLAND AT DIFFERENT PERIODS.

Year.		s.	d.	Year.			s.	d.	Year.			s.	d.
In 1350	per diem	0	1	In 1716		per diem	0	9	In 1800		per diem	2	0
1460	,,	0	2	1740		,,	0	10	1811		,,	2	1½
1568	,,	0	4	1760		,,	1	0	1850		,,	3	0
1632	,,	0	6	1788		,,	1	4	1857		,,	5	0
1688	,,	0	8	1794		,,	1	6, Since then increased.					

WAGGONS were rare in the last century. They, with carts, &c., not excepting those used in agriculture, were taxed in 1783. The carriers' waggons are now nearly superseded by the railways.

WAGHORN'S NEW OVERLAND ROUTE TO INDIA. Lieut. Waghorn devoted a large portion of his life to connect India with England. On 31 Oct. 1845, he arrived in London, by a new route, with the Bombay mail of the 1st of that month. His despatches reached Suez on the 19th, and Alexandria on the 20th, whence he proceeded by steamboat to a place twelve miles nearer London than Trieste. He hurried through Austria, Baden, Bavaria, Prussia, and Belgium, and reached London at half-past four on the morning of the first-mentioned day. The authorities of the different countries through which he passed eagerly facilitated his movements. The ordinary express, *via* Marseilles, reached London 2 Nov. following. Mr. Waghorn subsequently addressed a letter to the *Times* newspaper, in which he stated that in a couple of years he would bring the Bombay mail to London in 21 days. He died 8 Jan. 1850. On 3 Feb. 1884, at a meeting at the Mansion-house,

* Mr. J. E. Thorold Rogers, "Six Centuries of Work and Wages," published in 1884.

London, it was determined to erect a national monument to his memory.

The Overland Mail, which had left Bombay on 1 Dec. 1845, arrived early on the 30th in London, by way of Marseilles and Paris. The speedy arrival was owing to the great exertions made by the French government to show that the route through France was shorter and better.

WAGNERISM, see under *Music*.

WAGRAM, a village near Vienna, where Napoleon I. totally defeated the archduke Charles, 5, 6 July, 1809. The slaughter on both sides was dreadful; 20,000 Austrians were taken by the French, and the defeated army retired to Moravia. An armistice was signed on the 12th; and on 24 Oct., by a treaty of peace, Austria ceded all her sea-coast to France; the kingdoms of Saxony and Bavaria were enlarged at her expense; part of Poland in Galicia was ceded to Russia; and Joseph Bonaparte was recognised as king of Spain.

WAHABEES OR **WAHABITES**, a warlike Mahometan reforming sect, considering themselves the only true followers of the prophet, established themselves in Arabia about 1750, under the rule of Abd-el-Wahab, who died 1787. His grandson, Saoud, in 1801, defeated an expedition headed by the caliph of Bagdad. In 1803 this sect seized

Mecca and Medina, and continued their conquests, although their chief was assassinated in the midst of his victories. His son, Abdallah, long resisted Mahommed Ali, pacha of Egypt, but in 1818 was defeated and taken prisoner by Ibrahim Pacha, who sent him to Constantinople, where he was put to death. The sect, now flourishing, is well described by Mr. W. Gifford Palgrave, in his "Journey and Residence in Arabia in 1862-3," published in 1865. It is influential in India, and is suspected of a tendency to insurrection.

WAHLSTATT, see *Katzbach*.

WAITS, the night minstrels who perform shortly before Christmas. The name was given to the musicians attached to the king's court. We find that a company of waits was established at Exeter in 1400 to "pipe the watch." The waits in London and Westminster were long officially recognised by the corporation.

WAKEFIELD (W. Yorkshire), an ancient town. Near it a battle was fought between the adherents of Margaret, the queen of Henry VI., and the duke of York, in which the latter was slain, and 3000 Yorkists fell upon the field, 31 Dec. 1460. The earl of Warwick supported the cause of the duke's son, the earl of March, afterwards Edward IV., and the civil war was continued. An art and industrial exhibition was opened at Wakefield, 30 Aug. 1865. The Bishoprics act, authorising the establishment of a see at Wakefield, was passed 16 Aug. 1878. The required funds subscribed Jan. 1888.
Bishopric founded by the queen, 17 May, 1888; the Rev. W. W. How (suffragan bishop of Bedford) appointed first bishop . . . . Feb. 1888

WAKES, the ancient parish festivals on the saint's day to commemorate the dedication of the church; regulated in 1536, but gradually became obsolete.

WALBROOK CHURCH (London), a masterpiece of sir Christopher Wren, completed in 1679. There was a church here in 1135, and a new church was erected in 1429.

WALCHEREN (an island at the mouth of the Scheldt, Holland). The unfortunate expedition of the British to this isle in 1809 consisted of 35 ships of the line, and 200 smaller vessels, principally transports, and 40,000 land forces, the latter under the command of the earl of Chatham, and the fleet under sir Richard Strachan. For a long time the destination of the expedition remained secret; but before 28 July, 1809, when it set sail, the French journals had announced that Walcheren was the point of attack. Flushing was invested in August; a dreadful bombardment followed, and the place was taken 15 Aug.; but no suggestion on the part of the naval commander, nor urging on the part of the officers, could induce the earl to vigorous action, until the period of probable success was gone, and necessity obliged him to return with as many of the troops as disease and an unhealthy climate had spared. The place was evacuated, 23 Dec. 1809. The house of commons instituted an inquiry, and lord Chatham resigned his post of master-general of the ordnance, to prevent greater disgrace; but the policy of ministers in planning the expedition was, nevertheless, approved. The following epigram, of which various readings exist, appeared at the time:—

"Lord Chatham [or *the warrior earl*] with [his] sabre drawn,
Stood waiting for sir Richard Strachan;
Sir Richard, longing [or *eager*] to be at 'em,
Stood waiting for the earl of Chatham."

WALDECK AND PYRMONT, united German principalities, established in 1682. The late reigning family claim descent from the Saxon hero, Witikind, who flourished about 772. Prince George Victor, born 14 Jan. 1831, succeeded his father, George, 15 May, 1845. Heir: Frederic, son, born 20 Jan. 1865. On 22 Oct. 1867, the states approved a treaty of annexation, and the administration was transferred to Prussia, 1 Jan. 1868.

WALDENSES (also called Valdenses, Vallenses, and Vaudois), a sect inhabiting the Cottian Alps, derives its name, according to some authors, from Peter de Waldo, of Lyons (1170). They had a translation of the Bible. The Waldenses settled in the valleys of Piedmont about 1375, but were frequently dreadfully persecuted, especially in the 17th century, when Charles I. of England interceded for them (1627-9) and Oliver Cromwell by threats (1655-6) obtained them some degree of toleration. All the Waldensian Barbes or pastors, save two, died in the great plague of 1630. Gilles and Gros went to Geneva and Lausanne for Swiss Calvinist ministers to fill the vacancies. The new ministers were no sooner inducted than they deposed the surviving Barbes and abolished all the distinctive teaching and usages of the community, substituting the Genevese model. They were permitted to have a church at Turin, Dec. 1853. In March, 1868, it was stated that there were in Italy 28 ordained Waldensian ministers, and 30 other teachers.

WALES, Cambria, Cymru, the land of the Cymry, called by the Romans *Britannia Secunda*. Welsh and Wales are corruptions of Teutonic epithets applied to foreigners, especially Gauls. After the Roman emperor Honorius gave up Britain, Vortigern was elected king of South Britain. He invited over the Saxons to defend his country against the Picts and Scots; but the Saxons perfidiously sent for reinforcements, consisting of Saxons, Danes, and Angles, by which they made themselves masters of South Britain. Many of the Britons retired to Wales, and defended themselves against the Saxons, in their inaccessible mountains, about 447. In this state Wales remained unconquered till Henry II. subdued South Wales in 1157; and in 1282 Edward I. entirely reduced the whole country, an end being put to its independence by the death of Llewelyn, the last prince.* In 1284 the queen gave birth to a son at Caernarvon, whom Edward styled prince of Wales, now title of the heir to the crown of Great Britain. Wales was united and incorporated with England by act of parliament, 1536; see *Britain* and *Bards*.

Ostorius Scapula, proprætor of Britain, defeats the
Cymry . . . . A.D. 50
The supreme authority in *Britannia Secunda* intrusted to Suetonius Paulinus, who caused desolating wars 58-61
Conquests by Julius Frontinus 70
The Silures totally defeated . . . . . . ,,
The Roman, Julius Agricola, commands in Britain . 78
Bran ab Llyr, the Blessed, dies about 80
The Druidical class gradually dissolved by the influence of Christianity in 300-400
The Britons defeat the Saxons 447-448
Vortigern king 448
The renowned Arthur elected king . . about 500

* The statute of Wales, enacted at Rhuddlan, 19 March, 1284 (or March, 1283), alleges that—"Divine Providence has now removed all obstacles, and transferred wholly and entirely to the king's dominion the land of Wales and its inhabitants, heretofore subject unto him in feudal right." The ancient laws were to be preserved in civil causes; but the law of inheritance was to be changed, and the English criminal law to be put in force. *Annals of England*.

Defeats Saxons . . . . . . about	527
Cadwallawn, king of Gwynedd, defeated and slain by the Saxons at Denisburn . . . about	634
Dyvnwal Moelmud, said to have come from Armorica, and to have established his authority west of the Tamar and Severn as king of the Cymry about	640
Reign of Roderic the Great	844
He unites the petty states into one principality; his death	877
Division of Wales—into north, south, and central (or Powys-land) .	,,
The Welsh princes submit to Alfred . . .	885
The Danes land in Anglesey	900
Laws enacted by Howel Dha, prince of all Wales, about	920
Athelstan subdues the Welsh	933
Civil wars at his death . . . . about	948
Great battle between the sons of Howel Dha and the sons of Idwal Voel ; the latter victorious	954
Edgar invades Wales . . . . . about	973
Devastations committed by Edwin, the son of Eineon	980
Danes invade Wales ; lay Anglesey waste, &c.	980-1000
The country reduced by Aedan, prince of North Wales .	1000
Aedan, the usurper, slain in battle by Llewelyn	1015
Part of Wales laid waste by the forces of Harold	1063
William I. claims feudal authority over Wales	1070
Rhys ab Owain kills king Bleddyn, 1073 ; defeated and slain	1077
Ravaging invasion of Hugh, earl of Chester .	1079-80
Invasion of the Irish and Scots	1080
William I. invades Wales	1081
Battle of Llechryd	1087
[In this conflict the sons of Bleddyn ab Cynvyn were slain by Rhys ab Tewdwr, the reigning prince.]	
Rhys ab Tewdwr slain ; S. Wales conquered by the English	1090
Invasion of the English under William II. .	1095-7
The settlement in Wales of a colony of Flemings	1106
Violent seizure of Nest, wife of Gerald de Windsor, by Owain, son of Cadwgan ab Bleddyn .	1108
Cardigan conquered by Strongbow . . .	1109
Cadwgan assassinated	1112
Gruffydd ab Rhys lays claim to the sovereignty	1113
Another body of Flemings settle in Pembrokeshire	,,
[The posterity of these settlers are still distinguished from the ancient British population by their language, manners, and customs.]	
Civil war in South Wales and Powysland leads to the subjugation of the country by the English ; Henry I. erects castles in Wales. . . .	1114 et seq.
Owain killed in battle with Gerald de Windsor	1116
Revolt of Owen Gwynedd on the death of Hen. I. ; part of South Wales laid waste . . .	1135
The English defeated in several battles . .	1136
Strongbow, earl of Pembroke, invested with the powers of a count palatine in Pembroke . .	1138
Henry II. invades Wales, receives a stout resistance from Owen Gwynedd, but subdues S. Wales . .	1157
Confederacy of the princes of Wales for the recovery of their independence	1164
Prince Madoc said to have emigrated to America about	1169
Anglesey devastated	1173
The crusades preached in Wales by Baldwin, archbishop of Canterbury	1188
The earl of Chester's inroad into North Wales .	1210
King John invades Wales, laying waste a great part of the principalities ; exacts tribute and allegiance	1211
The pope incites the Welsh to resist John . .	1212
Revolt of the Flemings	1220
Llewelyn, prince of North Wales, commits great ravages ; overcomes Henry III. . . .	1228
The earl of Pembroke and other nobles join Llewelyn against Henry III., 1233 ; a truce . . .	1234
Prince David ravages the marches, &c. . .	1244
Invasion of Henry III.	1245
Anglesey cruelly devastated by the English Sept.	,,
Llewelyn ap Griffith, the last prince . . .	1246
Welsh princes combine against the English .	1256
Great invasion of the English ; threatened extermination of the Welsh, compelled to retreat with loss	1257

Welsh offers of peace refused	1257-62
Llewelyn's incursions into English territory. .	1263
Reported conference between him and Simon de Montfort against the Plantagenets . . .	1265
Llewelyn does homage to Henry III. for a treaty Sept.	1267
Edward I. summons Llewelyn to Westminster ; on his refusal to come, deposes him, 1276 ; and invades Wales . . . . . . June,	1277
Llewelyn submits and obtains good terms 10 Nov.	,,
He marries Eleanor de Montfort . . 13 Oct.	,,
The sons of Grufydd treacherously drowned in the river Dee, by the earl Warrenne and Roger Mortimer ; great insurrection	1281
Hawarden castle taken by surprise by Llewelyn and his brother David, 21 March ; they destroy Flint and Rhuddlan castles. Fruitless negotiations Nov.	1282
Battle between Llewelyn and the English near Aber Edw : Llewelyn slain, after the battle, by Adam Frankton . . . . . . 11 Dec.	,,
Prince David surrenders, and is executed . .	1283
Wales finally subdued by Edward I. . . .	,,
The first English prince of Wales, son of Edward, born at Caernarvon castle (see *Princes of Wales*, p. 902) . . . . . . 25 April,	1284
Statute of Wales (see p. 900) enacted . 19 March,	,,
Many insurrections suppressed and the leaders executed	1287-1320
Great rebellion of Owain Glyndwr, or Owen Glendower (descendant of the last prince, Llewelyn), commences	1400
Radnor and other places taken by Owain Glyndwr	1401
Allies with the Scots and the Percies ; besieges Caernarvon	1402
And seizes Harlech castle	1404
Makes a treaty with France . . . 10 May,	,,
Harlech castle retaken by the English forces .	1407
Loses his allies by their defeat at Bramham moor 19 Feb.	1408
Ravages the English territories	1409
Refuses to ask for terms or submit ; dies 21 Sept.	1415
His son submits . . . . . . 24 Feb.	1416
Margaret of Anjou, queen of Henry VI., takes refuge in Harlech castle	1459
Town of Denbigh burnt	1460
The earl of Richmond, afterwards Henry VII., lands in Pembroke, and is aided by the Welsh Aug.	1485
Palatine jurisdictions in Wales abolished by Henry VIII.	1535
Monmouth made an English county ; counties of Brecknock, Denbigh, and Radnor formed .	,,
Act for "laws and justice to be administered in Wales in same form as in England," 27 Henry VIII	,,
Wales incorporated into England by parliament .	1536
Divided into twelve counties	1543
Dr. Ferrar, bishop of St. David's, burnt at the stake for heresy . . . . . . 30 March,	1555
Lewis Owain, a baron of the exchequer, attacked and murdered while on his assize tour . .	,,
The bible and prayer-book ordered to be translated into Welsh, and divine service to be performed in that language	1562
Welsh bible printed	1588
First congregation of dissenters assembled in Wales ; Vavasour Powel apprehended while preaching .	1620
Beaumaris castle garrisoned for king Charles I. .	1642
Powys castle taken by sir Thos. Myddelton Oct.	1644
Dr. Laud, formerly bishop of St. David's, beheaded on Tower hill . . . . . 10 Jan.	1645
Surrender of Hawarden castle to the parliament general Mytton	,,
Charles I. takes refuge in Denbigh . . .	,,
Rhuddlan castle surrenders	,,
Harlech castle surrenders to Cromwell's army under Mytton	1647
Battle of St. Fagan's ; the Welsh defeated by col. Horton, Cromwell's lieutenant . . 8 May,	1648
Beaumaris castle surrenders to Cromwell . .	,,
Pembroke castle taken ; Colonel Poyer shot, 25 Apr.*	1649

* At the commencement of the civil war, Pembroke castle was the only Welsh fortress in the possession of the parliament, and it was entrusted to the command of col. Laugharne. In 1648, he, and colonels Powel and Poyer, embraced the cause of the king, and made Pembroke their head-quarters ; after the defeat at

The lords marchers court suppressed . . . 1688
"Charitable society of Ancient Britons" and Welsh
 charity schools, established (now at Ashford) . 1715
Cymmrodorion Society (for charitable purposes),
 established 1751-81
The French land in Pembrokeshire, and are made
 prisoners . . . . Feb. 1797
Rebecca or "Becca" riots broke out against toll-
 gates. Feb.; an old woman, a toll-keeper, was
 murdered, 10 Sept.; many persons were tried and
 punished . . . . Oct. 1843
Cambrian Archæological Association founded . 1846
Subscriptions begun for a university in Wales Dec. 1863
A national unsectarian University college at
 Aberystwyth opened . . . . 9 Oct. 1872
Great strike of colliers in S. Wales, 1 Jan.; ends
 about . . . . 27 March, 1873
Cymmrodorion society, to promote literature and
 art, re-established 1877
Great distress in South Wales through decay of
 coal trade by strikes and commercial depression 1877-8
"Rebecca" riots; people of Rhayader on the Wye
 capture fish out of season illegally; and resist the
 water bailiffs . . . . . Dec. 1878-Jan. 1879
Welsh Sunday closing act 1881
A Cambrian academy of arts settled to be established at Llandudno . . . . Jan. 1882
A university college of South Wales and Monmouth-
 shire established at Cardiff; professors appointed
 6 Sept.; opened . . . . . . 4 Oct. 1883
North Wales university college, Bangor, opened,
 . . . . 18 Aug. 1884
The college at Aberystwith burnt; prof. Macpherson and three others perish; damage about
 50,000l. . . . . . . night, 8, 9 July, 1885
Proposed disestablishment of the church negatived
 in the commons (241–229) . . . 9 March, 1886
Anti-tithe league formed; intimidation of payers,
 . . . . Aug.-Sept. ,,
Tithe riots at Mochdre, Clwyd; many injured;
 suppressed by military and police . 16 June, 1887
Great destruction of forest on Slievenamon moun-
 tain caused through beacon fire . 21 June, ,,
Three weeks fire on Ruabon and Berwyn mountains;
 extinguished after much destruction of life and
 game . . . . 25 July, ,,
Inauguration of the national council of Wales at
 Aberystwith; disestablishment and disendow-
 ment of the church, home rule &c. advocated,
 Stuart Rendel, M.P. president, 7 Oct. 1887;
 annual meeting at Newtown . . 8 Oct. ,,
Formation of a Welsh land league advocated in
 America; this league issues a manifesto 24 Dec. ,,
A Welsh clergy defence association formed about
 . . . . Nov. ,,
Marquis of Avergavenny v. bishop of Llandaff;
 after much litigation, verdict for the bishop who
 had refused to induct the rev. Robert W. Gosse
 into a living, being ignorant of the Welsh
 language . . . . . . 22 Feb. 1888
Death of Henry Richard "M.P. for Wales," ardent
 nonconformist and peace advocate . 20 Aug. ,,
1,000 miles of road freed from toll in S. Wales by
 local government act . . . . 2 April, 1889
Mr. Dillwyn's motion for disestablishment of the
 church in Wales, rejected by the commons
 (284–231) . . . . . . 14 May, ,,
Visit of the queen.

SOVEREIGNS OF WALES.
630. Cadwallawn, king of Gwynedd.
634. Cadwaladyr, his son.
661. Idwal, son.
728. Rhodri, or Roderic; heroic defender.
755. Cynan and Howel, sons; incessant war.

St. Fagan's, they retired to the castle, followed by an army led by Cromwell. They capitulated, after having endured great sufferings from want of water. Laugharne, Powel, and Poyer were tried by a court-martial, and condemned to death; but Cromwell having been induced to spare the lives of two of them, it was ordered that they should draw lots for the favour, and three papers were folded up, on two of which were written the words, "Life given by God;" the third was left blank. The latter was drawn by colonel Poyer, who was shot in London accordingly on the above-mentioned day, after long imprisonment. *Pennant.*

816. Mervyn; son-in-law, and Essylt (wife).
844. Roderic the Great, son.

PRINCES OF OWYNEDD OR NORTH WALES AND FREQUENTLY
 OF ALL WALES.
877. Anarawd, son of Roderic.
915. Idwal Voel.
943. Howel Dha the Good, prince of all Wales.
948. Iefan and Iago; sons of Idwal.
972. Howel ap Iefan, the Bad.
984. Cadwallon, brother.
985. Meredith ap Owen ap Howel Dha.
992. Idwal ap Meyric ap Edwal Voel; able, brave.
998. Aedan, a usurper.
1015. Llewelyn ap Sitsyllt, good sovereign.
1023. Iago ap Idwal ap Meyric.
1039. Griffith ap Llewelyn ap Sitsyllt; killed.
1067. Bleddyn.
1073. Trahaern ap Caradoc.
1079. Griffith ap Cynan; able; warlike; generous.
1137. Owain Gwynedd; energetic, successful warrior.
1169. Howel, son.
 ,, David ap Owain Gwynedd, brother; married sister
 of Henry II.
1194. Llewelyn, the Great.
1240. David ap Llewelyn.
1246. Llewelyn ap Griffith, last prince of the blood; slain
 after battle, 11 Dec., 1282.
 ENGLISH PRINCES OF WALES.*
1284. Edward Plantagenet (afterwards king Edward II.)
 son of Edward I., born in Caernarvon Castle on
 the 25th April, 1284. It is asserted that immediately after his birth he was presented by his
 father to the Welsh chieftains as their future
 sovereign, the king holding up the royal infant
 in his arms, and saying, in the Welsh language,
 "Eich Dyn," literally in English, "This is your
 man," but signifying, "This is your countryman
 and king." See, however, "*Ich Dien.*"
1301. Edward of Carnarvon made prince of Wales and
 earl of Chester.
1343 Edward the Black Prince.
1376. Richard, his son (afterwards Richard II.).
1399. Henry (afterwards Henry V.), son of Henry IV.
1454. Edward, son of Henry VI.; slain at Tewkesbury,
 4 May, 1471.
1471. Edward (aft. Edward V.), son of Edward IV.
1483. Edward, son of Richard III.; died in 1484.
1489. Arthur, son of Henry VII.; died in 1502.
1503. Henry, his brother (afterwards Henry VIII.).
 Edward, his son (afterwards Edward VI.) was duke
 of Cornwall, and not prince of Wales.
1610. Henry Frederic, son of James I.; died 6 Nov. 1612.
1616. Charles, his brother (afterwards Charles I.).
 Charles, his son (afterwards Charles II.), never
 created prince of Wales.
1714. George Augustus (afterwards George II.).
1729. Frederic Lewis, his son; died 20 March, 1751.
1751. George, his son (afterwards George III.).
1762. George, his son (afterwards George IV.): born 12 Aug.
1841. Albert-Edward, son of queen Victoria: born 9 Nov.
 Baptized, king of Prussia a sponsor, 15 Jan. 1842.
 Travelled on the continent, and studied at Oxford
 and Edinburgh, in 1859.
 Visited Canada, with the dignity of a viceroy, and
 the United States, 1860.
 Entered the university of Cambridge in Jan.:
 attended the camp at the Curragh, Kildare, July
 to Sept.; opened New Middle Temple Library,
 31 Oct. 1861.
 Ordered to be prayed for as Albert-Edward,
 8 Jan.; visited the continent, Syria, and Egypt,
 March-June; Germany and Italy, Aug-Dec. 1862.
 Admitted to the house of peers, 5 Feb.; a privy
 councillor, 8 Dec. 1863.
 Married to princess Alexandra of Denmark, 10
 March, 1863.

* WALES, PRINCESS OF. This title was held, some authors say, during the early period of her life, by the princess Mary of England, eldest daughter of Henry VIII., and afterwards queen Mary I. She was created, they state, by her father princess of Wales, in order to conciliate the Welsh people and keep alive the name, and was the only princess of Wales in her own right: a rank she enjoyed until the birth of a son to Henry, who was afterwards Edward VI., born in 1537. This is denied by Banks.

Visited Denmark and Sweden, Sept.-Oct. 1864; Russia, Nov.-Dec. 1866.
Visited International Exhibition, Paris, May, 1867.
Visited Ireland; arrived at Dublin, 15 April, 1868.
Installed knight of St. Patrick, 18 April, 1868.
Opened Leeds Fine Arts Exhibition, 19 May, 1868.
With the Princess at Glasgow, laid foundation of new university, 8 Oct. 1868.
Sailed for the continent, 17 Nov.; called at Paris; arrived at Copenhagen, 29 Nov.; visited Berlin, Vienna, and arrived at Cairo, 3 Feb. 1869.
Examined the Suez canal, Feb.; arrived at Constantinople, 1 April; at Sebastopol, 13-17 April; at Athens, 19-24 April; landed at Dover, 13 May, 1869.
Inaugurated Victoria Embankment (Thames) 13 July, 1870.
Opened Workmen's International Exhibition, Islington, 16 July, 1870.
Attacked with typhoid fever, about 19 Nov.; greatest danger, 6-13 Dec.; amendment began 14 Dec., 1871.
Went to St. Paul's with the queen for thanksgiving, 27 Feb.; sailed for the continent, 11 March; visited the Pope, 27 March; opened new grammar school at Yarmouth, 6 June; the East London Museum, 24 June, 1872.
At the opening of the great exhibition at Vienna, 1 May, 1873.
At the duke of Edinburgh's wedding at St. Petersburg, 23 Jan.; visit to France; entertained by the duc de Rochefoucauld Bisaccia, duc d'Aumale, and others, about 17 Oct.; at Birmingham, 3 Nov. 1874.
Installed grand master of the freemasons of England, 28 April, 1875.
112,000*l.* voted for his visit to India [more than sufficient] July, 1875.
Sailed from Dover, 11 Oct.; warmly received at Athens, 18 Oct.; at Cairo, invested Mohammed Tewfik, the son of the Khedive, with the Star of India, 25 Oct. 1875.
Arrived at Bombay, 8 Nov.; Poonah 13 Nov.; Goa, 27 Nov.; Colombo, Ceylon, 1 Dec.; Madras, 13 Dec.; Calcutta, 23 Dec. 1875.
At Benares, 5 Jan.; Lucknow, 6 Jan.; Delhi, 11 Jan.; Lahore, 18 Jan.; Jummoo, Cashmere, 20 Jan.; Agra, 25 Jan.; Gwalior, 31 Jan.; in Nepaul, 12 Feb.; at Allahabad, 7 March; sailed from Bombay, 13 March; arrived in Malta, 6 April; Gibraltar, 15 April; Seville, 21 April; Madrid, 25 April; Lisbon, 1 May; London, with about 500 animals for the Zoological gardens, 11 May; banquet at Mansion house, 19 May; reviewed 30,000 volunteers in Hyde Park, 7 July. 1876.
President of the British commissioners at the Paris exhibition, 1878.
Presided at National Water Supply conference, 21 May; laid foundation of St. Mary's, Wilberforce memorial church, Southampton, 12 Aug. 1878.
Laid foundation of new hospital, Norwich, 27 June; opened new dock at Great Grimsby, 22 July, 1879.
Laid foundation of new cathedral at Truro, 20 April; opened new dock at Holyhead, 17 June, 1880.
Laid foundation of central Institution of City and Guilds of London Institute, South Kensington, 18 July, 1881.
Opens the Royal College of Music, 7 May, 1883.
Opens the International Fishery Exhibition, 12 May; closes it 31 Oct. 1883.
Inaugurated the juries at the Health Exhibition, 17 June, 1884.
Visits Newcastle and opens Armstrong park, museum, &c., 20, 21 Aug. 1884.
Visit to Dublin (enthusiastically received), 8 April; Cork, 15 April; Killarney, 16 April; Limerick (warmly received), 20 April; from Dublin to Belfast (warm reception), 23 April; Londonderry, 25 April; sailed from Larne, 27 April, 1885.
Opens art gallery, &c., at Birmingham, 27, 28 Nov. 1885.
Formally opens the Mersey tunnel, 20 Jan. 1886.
Kept his silver wedding, 10 March, 1888.
Opens the international exhibition at Glasgow, 8 May, 1888.
Founds a technical school at Blackburn, 9 May, 1888.
Visits Austria and Hungary, Sept.; Roumania, &c. 4 Oct.; returns to London, 22 Oct. 1888.
" Speeches and Addresses," 1863-1888; published 12 Jan. 1889.
Uncovers several Jubilee statues of the queen, &c. (*See Jubilee*), 1887-9.
Visits the universal exhibition at Paris, June, 1889.
Acts for the queen at the royal agricultural show (*see Windsor*), 24-29 June. 1889.
Receives and attends the Shah of Persia, 1 July, *et seq.*
Annual payment of 36,000*l.* to the prince as a provision to his family, voted by the commons 29 July, 1889.
Issue: Albert-Victor, born 8 Jan. 1864;
George-Frederick, born 3 June, 1865;
Louise Victoria, born 20 Feb. 1867. (Married to Alexander William George, duke of Fife, 27 July, 1889.)
Alexandra, born 6 July, 1868.
Maud, born 26 Nov. 1869.
Alexander John, born 7 April, died 8 April, 1871.

WALHALLA or **VALHALLA** (the Hall of Glory), a temple near Ratisbon, erected by Louis, king of Bavaria, to receive the statues and memorials of the great men of Germany, commenced 18 Oct. 1830, and inaugurated 18 Oct. 1842. The name is derived from the fabled meeting-place of Scandinavian heroes after death.

WALKERITES, see *Separatists*.

WALKING, see *Pedestrianism*.

WALKING-STICKS, a term satirically applied to candidates for the house of commons nominated by political associations, and subject to them in their parliamentary votes, 1878.

WALLACE MONUMENT, at Abbey Craig, near Stirling, was inaugurated 27 Aug. 1869, and soon after given into the charge of the magistrates of Stirling. It cost about 13,000*l.* The telescope there was presented by the Scotch inhabitants of Ipswich, 24 June, 1865.

WALLACHIA, see *Danubian Principalities*. On 23 Dec. 1861, the union of Wallachia and Moldavia, under the name of Roumania, was proclaimed at Jassy and Bucharest.

WALLER'S PLOT. Edmund Waller, the poet, and others, conspired to disarm the London militia and let in the royalists, May, 1643. The plan was detected and punished, June-July, 1643. Waller betrayed his confederates, and was suffered to emigrate.

WALLIS'S VOYAGE. Captain Wallis sailed from England on his voyage round the world, 26 July, 1766; and returned to England, 19 May, 1768.

WALLOON. This name was given to those inhabitants of the low countries who retained the ancient German language, and to those who adopted the Walloon language (based on the Gaulish), which though surviving as a patois, has been supplanted in France by the modern French. The language of the Walloon protestant refugees in 1556 was French.

A church was given to Walloon refugees by queen Elizabeth at Sandwich, and they still have one at Canterbury. The frontier line of Flemish and German towns may be traced from the north through Gravelines to Luxemburg; that of the Walloon towns from Calais to Metz.

WALLS, see *Roman Walls, China*.

WALNUT-TREE has long existed in Eng-

land.* The black walnut-tree (*Juglans nigra*) was brought to this country from North America before 1629.

WALPOLE'S ADMINISTRATIONS. Mr. Walpole (afterwards sir Robert, and earl of Oxford) was born in 1676; became secretary-at-war in 1708; was expelled the house of commons on a charge of misappropriating the public money, 1711; committed to the Tower, 17 Jan. 1712; became first lord of the treasury and chancellor of the exchequer in Oct. 1715. He resigned, on a disunion of the cabinet, in 1717, bringing in the sinking fund bill on the day of his resignation. On the earl of Sunderland retiring in 1721, he resumed his office, and held it till Feb. 1742. He died 18 March, 1745.

SECOND WALPOLE ADMINISTRATION (APRIL, 1721).
Sir Robert Walpole, *first lord of the treasury.*
Thomas, lord Parker, created earl of Macclesfield, *lord chancellor.*
Henry, lord Carleton (succeeded by William, duke of Devonshire), *lord president.*
Evelyn, duke of Kingston (succeeded by lord Trevor), *privy seal.*
James, earl of Berkeley, *first lord of the admiralty.*
Charles (viscount Townshend), and John, lord Carteret (the latter succeeded by the duke of Newcastle), *secretaries of state.*
Duke of Marlborough (succeeded by the earl of Cadogan), *ordnance.*
George Treby (succeeded by Henry Pelham), *secretary-at-war.*
Viscount Torrington, &c.

WALRUS. One placed in the Zoological Gardens in 1853 lived a few days only; another was placed there in the autumn of 1867, and died 25 Dec.

WALTZ, the popular German national dance, was introduced into England by baron Neuman and others in 1813. *Raikes.*

WANDEWASH (S. India). Here the French, under Lally, were severely defeated by colonel Eyre Coote, 22 Jan. 1760.

WANDSWORTH, near London. Here was organised a "presbytery," 20 Nov. 1572. In Garratt-lane, near this place, a mock election of a mayor of Garratt was formerly held, after every general election of parliament, to which Foote's dramatic piece, *The Mayor of Garratt* (1763), gave no small celebrity. The iron bridge here was opened 26 Sept. 1873.

Wandsworth returns one M.P. by act passed 25 June, 1885.

WAR, called by Erasmus "the malady of princes." Osymandyas of Egypt, the first warlike king, passed into Asia, and conquered Bactria, 2100 B.C. *Usher.* He is supposed by some to be the Osiris of the priests. It is computed that, up to the present time, no less than 6,860,000,000 of men have perished on the field of battle; see *Battles; Secretaries; Neutral Powers.* An international conference on "usages of war" began at Brussels, 27 July, 1874, and closed without important results. See *Brussels Conference.* In 1880, about 4,000,000 men in arms, annual cost, 500,000,000*l.*

FOREIGN WARS OF ENGLAND SINCE THE CONQUEST.

War with		Peace.	War with		Peace.	War with		Peace.
Scotland	. . 1068 .	. 1092	France	. . 1422 .	. 1471	Spain	. . 1588 .	. 1604
France	. . 1116 .	. 1118	Scotland	. . 1480 .	. 1486	Spain	. . 1624 .	. 1629
Scotland	. . 1138 .	. 1139	France	. . 1492 .	. 1492	France	. . 1627 .	. 1629
France	. . 1161 .	. 1186	France	. . 1512 .	. 1514	Holland	. . 1651 .	. 1654
France	. . 1194 .	. 1195	France	. . 1522 .	. 1527	Spain	. . 1655 .	. 1660
France	. . 1201 .	. 1216	Scotland	. . 1522 .	. 1542	France	. . 1666 .	. 1668
France	. . 1224 .	. 1234	Scotland	. . 1542 .	. 1546	Denmark	. . 1666 .	. 1668
France	. . 1294 .	. 1299	Scotland	. . 1547 .	. 1550	Holland	. . 1666 .	. 1668
Scotland	. . 1296 .	. 1323	France	. . 1549 .	. 1550	Algiers	. . 1669 .	. 1671
Scotland	. . 1327 .	. 1328	France	. . 1557 .	. 1559	Holland	. . 1672 .	. 1674
France	. . 1339 .	. 1360	Scotland	. . 1557 .	. 1560	France	. . 1689 .	. 1697
France	. . 1368 .	. 1420	France	. . 1562 .	. 1564	Peace of Ryswick, 20 Sept. 1697		

War of the *Succession,* commenced 4 May, 1702. Peace of Utrecht, 13 March, 1713.
War with Spain, 16 Dec. 1718. Peace concluded, 1721.
War; *Spanish War,* 23 Oct. 1739. Peace of Aix-la-Chapelle, 30 April, 1748.
War with France, 31 March, 1744. Closed also on 30 April, 1748.
War; the *Seven Years' War,* 9 June, 1756. Peace of Paris, 10 Feb. 1763.
War with Spain, 4 Jan. 1762. General peace, 10 Feb. 1763.
War with the United States of North America, 14 July, 1774. Peace of Paris, 30 Nov. 1782.
War with France, 6 Feb. 1778. Peace of Paris, 20 Jan. 1783.
War with Spain, 17 April, 1780. Closed same time, 20 Jan. 1783.
War with Holland, 21 Dec. 1780. Peace signed, 2 Sept. 1783.
War of the *Revolution,* 1 Feb. 1793. Peace of Amiens, 27 March, 1802.
War against *Bonaparte,* 29 April, 1803. Finally closed, 18 June, 1815.

* Near Welwyn, in Hertfordshire, there was the largest walnut-tree on record; it was felled in 1627, and from it were cut nineteen loads of planks; and as much was sold to a gunsmith in London as cost 10*l.* carriage; besides which there were thirty loads of roots and branches. When standing it covered 76 poles of ground; a space equal to 2299 square yards, statute measure.

War with America, 18 June, 1812. Peace of Ghent, 24 Dec. 1814.
War with Russia, 27 March, 1854. Peace of Paris, 31 March, 1856.
For the wars with India, China, Persia, Abyssinia, Afghanistan, and Zululand, see those countries respectively.

WAR AFFAIRS. On account of the war with Russia, the duke of Newcastle, previously colonial secretary, was appointed a secretary for war affairs, and a cabinet minister, 9 June, 1854; see *Secretaries.* War Office act, passed 20 June, 1870, appoints a financial secretary (who may sit in parliament) and other officers. An act for the protection of war department stores was passed in 1867. By the warrant abolishing purchase in the army, in 1871, Mr. Cardwell became virtually uncontrolled minister of war. For WAR OFFICE CHANGE, see under *Army* and *Admiralty.*

New war offices erected by virtue of the Public Offices site act, passed . . . . . 24 July, 1882
War *Exhibition* of trophies, &c., from Egypt, opened at Knightsbridge . . . . 14 Feb. 1883
Important changes in the war office announced; increased responsibilities of heads of departments, &c. . . . . . . Feb. 1888

WAR, GAME OF (German, *Kriegspiel*), based on the game of chess, was described in a pamphlet in 1780, and rules for it laid down by Domänenrathe von Reisswitz about 1820, and published by his son in 1824-8. Capt. (now sir) Evelyn Baring published a translation of works on the subject in 1872. A society (including von Moltke) was formed at Magdeburg to study it. Prince Arthur (now duke of Connaught) lectured on this game at Dover, 13 March, 1872.

WARBECK'S INSURRECTION. Perkin Warbeck, the son of a Florentine Jew, to whom Edward IV. had stood godfather, was persuaded by Margaret, duchess of Burgundy, sister to Richard III., to personate her nephew Richard, Edward V.'s brother, which he did first in Ireland, where he landed, 1492. The imposture was discovered by Henry VII. 1493. Some writers consider that Warbeck was not an impostor.

Warbeck attempted to land in Kent, with 600 men, 169 were taken prisoners, and executed, July, 1495.
Recommended by the king of France to James IV. of Scotland, who gave him his kinawoman, lord Huntley's daughter, in marriage, when he assumed the title of Richard IV. James IV. invaded England in his favour, 1496.
Left Scotland, and went to Bodmin, in Cornwall, where 3000 joined him, Sept. 1497.
On the approach of Henry took sanctuary at Beaulieu; surrendered; taken to London, Oct. 1497.
Said to have been set in the stocks at Westminster and Cheapside, and sent to the Tower, June, 1499.
Accused of plotting with the earl of Warwick to escape out of the Tower, by murdering the lieutenant, Aug.; the plot failed, and he was hanged at Tyburn, 23 Nov.; the earl beheaded, 28 Nov. 1499.

WARBURG (N. Germany). Here the French were defeated by the duke of Brunswick and the allies, 31 July, 1760.

WARDIAN CASES. In 1829, Mr. N. B. Ward, from observing a small fern and grass growing in a closed glass bottle, in which he had placed a chrysalis covered with moist earth, was led to construct his well-known *closely glazed* cases, which afford to plants light, heat, and moisture, and exclude deleterious gases, smoke, &c. They are particularly adapted for ferns. In 1833 they were first employed for the transmission of plants to Sydney, &c., with great success, and professor Faraday lectured on the subject in 1838.

WARDMOTES, meetings of the citizens of London in their wards, where they elect annually their common councilmen. The practice is said to have begun in 1386. They had previously assembled in Guildhall.

WARRANTS, GENERAL, do not specify the name of the accused. They were declared to be illegal by lord chief justice Pratt, 6 Dec. 1763, in relation to the seizure and committal of Mr. Wilkes for a libel on the king; see *North Briton*.

WARRIOR, see under *Navy of England*, 1860.

WARSAW, the metropolis of Poland. The diet was transferred to this city from Cracow in 1566, and it became the seat of government in 1689. Population in 1882, 406,261.

The Poles defeated in three days' battle by the Swedes . . . . . . 28-30 July,	1656
Alliance of Warsaw, between Austria and Poland, against Turkey, in pursuance of which, John Sobieski assisted in raising the siege of Vienna (September following), signed . 31 March,	1683
Warsaw surrenders to Charles XII. . . .	1703
Treaty of Warsaw between Russia and Poland, 24 Feb.	1768
The Russian garrison here expelled with the loss of 2000 killed and 500 wounded, and 36 pieces of cannon . . . . . . 17 April,	1794
The Poles defeated by the Russians at Maciejovice, 4 Oct.	,,
The king of Prussia besieges Warsaw, July; compelled to raise the siege, Sept.; it is taken by the Russians . . . . Nov.	,,
Suwarrow, the Russian general, after the siege and destruction of Warsaw, cruelly butchered 30,000 Poles, of all ages and conditions, in cold blood, 4 Nov.	,,
Warsaw constituted a duchy, and annexed to the house of Saxony . . . . . Aug.	1807
The duchy overrun by the Russians; Warsaw made the residence of a Russian viceroy . .	1813
The last Polish revolution commences at Warsaw, 29 Nov.	1830
Battle of Grochow, near Warsaw, in which the Russians were defeated, and forced to retreat with the loss of 7000 men . . . . 25 Feb.	1831
Battle of Warsaw, when, after two days' hard fighting, the city capitulated, and was taken possession of by the Russians; and great part of the Polish army retired towards Plock and Modlin, 6-8 Sept.	,,
The czar meets the emperor of Austria and the regent of Prussia; no result . . 20-25 Oct.	1860
Panic in a church; great loss of life . 25 Dec.	1881
Alexander III. visits Warsaw; great precautions, 8 Sept.	1884

(See *Poland*, 1861-5.)

WARTBURG, a castle in Saxony (N. Germany), where Luther was conveyed for safety after the diet of Worms, April, 1521, and where he translated the Bible into German.

WARWICK CASTLE (Warwickshire), the seat of the Beauchamps, Nevilles, Plantagenets, Dudleys, Riches, and Grevilles, successively, and frequently besieged; suffered much by fire, 3 Dec. 1871; some of the more ancient part was destroyed.

WASH-HOUSES, see *Baths*.

WASHING MACHINES. Several have been invented by Americans. At an hotel in New York hundreds of garments are washed in a few minutes, by steam, and dried by a centrifugal machine (1862). The ingenious machines of Messrs. Hornsby, of Norwich, appeared in the great exhibition of London, 1862.

WASHINGTON. A northern state of the American Union, first settled in 1845, organized as a Territory in 1853, as a State 1889; population in 1880, 75,116. Capital Olympia.

The flourishing town of Seattle was nearly destroyed by fire about 6 June, 1889; estimated loss about $15,000,000; few lives lost.
Ellensburg, a small town also nearly destroyed by fire, 4 July, 1889; estimated loss, $2,000,000.

WASHINGTON (in Columbia district, partly in Virginia and partly in Maryland, on the bank of the Potomac, N.E. Virginia), the capital of the United States, founded in 1791, and made the seat of government in 1800. Population, 1880, 147,293.

The house of representatives opened . 30 May,	1808
Washington was taken by the British forces under general Ross, after his victory at Bladensburg: its superb structures and national library burnt, 24 Aug.	1814
General Ross killed by some American riflemen, in a desperate engagement at Baltimore 12 Sept.	,,
Naval observatory founded	1842
Smithsonian institute (*which see*) founded .	1846
Part of the capitol and the whole of the library of the United States congress destroyed by fire, 24 Dec.	1851
The prince of Wales entertained by the president here . . . . Oct.	1860
Washington fortified in . . . . April,	1861
President Lincoln shot by Booth in Ford's theatre, 14 April; died . . . . . 15 April,	1865

Memorial obelisk to George Washington, 555 feet
high, inaugurated . . . . . 21 Feb. 1885
National theatre burnt down . . . 27 Feb ,,
See *United States.*

IMPORTANT TREATIES OF WASHINGTON.
Fixing N.W. boundary of British America and
United States, &c. . . . . . 12 June, 1846
" Reciprocity " treaty regulating trade with Canada,
7 June, 1854
Referring the *Alabama* claims and the San Juan
boundary question to arbitration; settling disputes respecting fisheries (see *Alabama* and *Juan*);
and laying down three rules; asserting that it is
the duty of a neutral state, which desires to remain at peace with belligerents, and to enjoy the
rights of neutrality, to abstain from taking any
part in the war by affording military aid to one
or both of the belligerents; and to take care that
no acts which would constitute such co-operation
in the war be committed by any one within its
territory . . . . . . 8 May, 1871

WASIUM (named from the royal house of
Wasa or Vasa), a supposed new metal, discovered by
F. Bahr, of Stockholm, in 1862. In Nov. 1863 Nickles
declared it to be a compound of didymium, yttrium,
and terbium.

WASTE LANDS. The inclosure of waste
lands and commons, in order to promote agriculture,
first began in England about the year 1547, and gave
rise to Ket's rebellion, 1549. Inclosures were again
promoted by the authority of parliament, 1785. The
waste lands in England were estimated in 1794 to
amount to 14 millions of acres, of which there were
taken into cultivation, 2,837,476 acres before June,
1801. In 1841, there were about 6,700,000 acres of
waste land, of which more than half was thought to
be capable of improvement; see *Agriculture.*

WATCH OF LONDON, at night, appointed
1253, proclaimed the hour with a bell before the introduction of public clocks. *Hardie.* The old watch
was discontinued, and a new police (on duty day
and night) commenced, 29 Sept. 1829; see *Police.*

WATCHES are said to have been first invented
at Nuremberg, 1477, although it is affirmed that
Robert, king of Scotland, had a watch about 1310.
Watches first used in astronomical observations by
Purbach 1500
Authors assert that the emperor Charles V. was
the first who had anything that might be called a
watch, though some call it a small table-clock . 1530
Watches first brought to England from Germany in 1577
A watch which belonged to queen Elizabeth is preserved in the library of the Royal Institution,
London.
Spring pocket-watches (watches properly so-called)
have had their invention ascribed to Dr. Hooke
by the English, and to M. Huyghens by the Dutch.
Dr. Derham, in his *Artificial Clockmaker*, says that
Dr. Hooke was the inventor; and he appears certainly to have produced what is called the pendulum
watch about 1658: manifest, among other evidences, from an inscription on one of the doublebalance watches presented to Charles II., "Rob.
Hooke, inven. 1658; T. Tomplon, fecit, 1675."
Repeating watches invented by Barlowe . . 1676
Harrison's first time-piece produced (see *Harrison*), 1735
Watches and clocks were taxed in . . . 1797
The tax was repealed in 1798. See *Clocks.*
Arrangements made at Kew observatory for testing
high class watches, and granting graduated certificates; fees, 1L 1s., 10s. 6d., &c.; announced
April, 1884

WATER. Thales of Miletus, founder of the
Ionic sect, considered water to be the original
principle of everything, about 594 B.C. *Stanley.*
Cavendish and Watt demonstrated that water is
composed of 8 parts of oxygen and 1 part of hydrogen 1781-4
Water was decomposed into oxygen and hydrogen

gases by Lavoisier, 1783; by the voltaic battery
by Nicholson and Carlisle, 1800; by the heat of
the oxy-hydrogen flame by W. R. Grove . . 1846
In freezing, water contracts till it is reduced to 42°
or 40° Fahr.; it then begins to expand till it becomes ice at 32°.
Water was first conveyed to London by leaden pipes,
21 Henry III. 1237. *Stow.* It took nearly fifty
years to complete it; the whole being finished,
and Cheapside conduit erected, only in . . 1285
The New River water brought to London from
Chadwell and Amwell in Hertfordshire, at an immense expense, by sir Hugh Myddelton, in . 1609-13
The city was supplied with its water by conveyances of wooden pipes in the streets and small
leaden ones to the houses, and the New River
Company was incorporated, 1620. So late as queen
Anne's time there were water-carriers at Aldgate-pump.
The water-works at Chelsea completed, and the
company incorporated 1722
London-bridge ancient water-works destroyed by
fire . . . . 29 Oct. 1779
An act to supply the metropolis with water, 15 & 16
Vict. c. 84, was passed, 1 July, 1852. This act was
amended by an act passed 21 Aug. 1871. The
companies were bound to provide a constant
supply when required; the owner or occupier of
the house to provide the prescribed fittings.
[The supply is now considered to be much improved
in quality and quantity.]
A company was formed to carry out Dr. Normandy's
patent for converting salt water into fresh, in
Jan. 1857
Commissioners for metropolitan water supply appointed, 27 April, 1867; report signed 9 June, 1869
London supplied by nine companies: the New River
(the best), East London, Chelsea, Grand Junction,
Southwark and Vauxhall, Kent, West Middlesex,
Lambeth, and South Essex; who deliver about
108,000,000 gallons daily, 1867; about 116,250,000
gallons 1877
New schemes for supplying London with water,
1867:—
1. Mr. Bateman; from the sources of the Severn.
2. Messrs. Hemans and Hassard; from the Cumberland lakes.
3. Mr. Telford Macneill; Thames water filtered
through Bagshot sand.
4. Mr. Bailey Denton; storage reservoirs near the
sources of the Thames.
5. Mr. Remington; from the Derbyshire and
Staffordshire hills.
The water from the first two sources analysed and
highly approved by professors Frankland and
Odling . . . . April, 1868
Water from the chalk districts softened by Homersham's process strongly recommended, Jan. 1871
. . . . Aug. 1878
Conference on the national water supply at Society of Arts (suggested by the prince of Wales,
president) . . . . . 21, 22 May, ,,
Letter from the prince of Wales to the earl of
Beaconsfield suggesting the appointment of a
commission on water supply, dated . 24 March, 1879
National Water Supply Exhibition, Alexandra Palace; opened . . . . . . 14 Aug. ,,
Government proposal to buy companies' works for
34,398,700l. (New River company, 9,146,000l.),
dropped . . . . . . April, 1880
Annual revenue, according to Mr. E. J. Smith's calculations, above 1,500,000l. 1881
Atkins' process for softening hard water an improvement upon Clarks' process, announced July, 1882
Water companies (regulation of powers) act, passed 1887
See *Artesian Wells* and *London Water.*

WATER-BED, CLOCKS, see *Beds, Clocks.*

WATER-COLOUR PAINTING was gradually raised from the hard dry style of the last
century to its present brilliancy, by the efforts of
Nicholson, Copley Fielding, Sandby, Varley, the
great Turner, Pyne, Cattermole, Prout, &c., within
the present century. The Water-Colour Society's
exhibition which began in 1805, was made Royal in
1881, the diplomas were to be signed by the queen

after Nov. 1882. The Institute of Painters in Water Colours, established about 1831 (made Royal in 1883), open new galleries in Piccadilly, and propose to give free instruction, 27 April, 1883.

WATERFORD (S. Ireland), built about 879, was totally destroyed by fire in 981. Rebuilt and considerably enlarged by Strongbow in 1171, and still further in the reign of Henry VII., who granted considerable privileges to the citizens. Richard II. landed and was crowned here in 1399; in 1690, James II. embarked from hence for France, after the battle of the Boyne; and William III. resided here twice, and confirmed its privileges. Memorable storm here, 18 April, 1792. The cathedral of Waterford, dedicated to the blessed Trinity, was first built by the Ostmen, and by Malchus, the first bishop of Waterford, after his return from England from his consecration, 1096. This see was united with that of Lismore in 1363. It was valued in the king's books, by an extent returned 29 Henry VIII., at 72l. 8s. 1d. Irish per annum. By stat. 3 & 4 Will. IV., c. 37 (the Irish Church Temporalities act), the see of Waterford and Lismore was united with the see of Cashel and Emly, 14 Aug. 1833. The interior of the cathedral, organ, &c., were destroyed by fire, 25 Oct. 1815.

Waterford returns three M.P.'s, by act passed 25 June, 1885

WATER-GLASS, a name given to a liquid mixture of sand (silex) and one of the alkalies (potash or soda). Glauber (*De Lithiase*) mentions a similar mixture in 1644. Dr. Von Fuchs, the modern inventor, gave an account of his process in 1825; and Mr. Frederick Ransome, of Ipswich, ignorant of Von Fuchs's discovery, patented a mode of preparing water-glass in 1845, which he has since greatly improved upon. In 1857, M. Kuhlmann, of Lille, published a pamphlet setting forth the advantageous employment of water-glass in hardening porous stone and in stereochromy (*which see*). It has been applied to the exterior of many buildings in France and England. The memoirs of Von Fuchs and Kuhlmann were translated and printed in England, in 1859, by direction of the prince consort.

WATERING STREETS. Mr. Cooper's plan for using solutions of chloride of lime or of sodium which dry slowly and attract moisture and ammonia and other gases, and combine them with the material of the road) was partially used in the parish of St. Mary-le-bone in 1868, and also in Liverpool, Boston, and other towns. The plan was ordered to be tried in Westminster in July, 1870.

WATERLOO, in Belgium, the site of the great battle, on Sunday, 18 June, 1815, between the French army, of 71,947 men and 246 guns, under Napoleon, and the allies, commanded by the duke of Wellington; the latter, with 67,661 men and 156 guns, resisted the various attacks of the enemy from about ten in the morning until fire in the afternoon. About that time, 16,000 Prussians reached the field of battle; and by seven, the force under Blucher amounted to above 50,000 men, with 104 guns. Wellington then moved forward his whole army. A total rout ensued, and the carnage was immense. Of the British (23,991), 93 officers and 1916 men were killed and 363 officers and 4560 men wounded—total, 6932; and the total loss of the allied army amounted to 4206 killed, 14,539 wounded, and 4231 missing, making 22,976 *hors de combat*. Napoleon, quitting the wreck of his army, returned to Paris; and, finding it impossible to raise another, abdicated. *P. Nicolas.*

Napoleon attributed his defeat to the failures of marshal Grouchy, Wellington said unjustly.
Proposed monument over the British officers and men who died of their wounds, 7 Jan. 1888.
By the side of the chapel of Waterloo, which was uninjured by shot or shell on 18 June, 1815, Marlborough cut off a large division of the French forces, 17 Aug. 1705. The conquerors on the same field are the only British commanders whose career brought them to dukedoms.

WATERLOO BRIDGE, LONDON. A bridge over this part of the Thames was repeatedly suggested during the last century, but no actual preparations to carry it into effect were made till 1806, when Mr. G. Dodd procured an act of parliament, and gave the present site, plan, and dimensions of the bridge; but, in consequence of some disagreement with the committee, he was superseded by Mr. John Rennie, who completed this noble structure. It was commenced 11 Oct. 1811, and opened 18 June, 1817, on the anniversary of the battle of Waterloo, when the prince regent, the duke of Wellington, and other distinguished personages, were present. Its length within the abutments is 1242 feet; its width within the balustrades is 42 feet; and the span of each arch, of which there are nine, is 120 feet. Bought for 475,000l. by metropolitan board of works; opened toll free, 5 Oct. 1878; lit by electric light from 10 Oct. 1879.

On Oct. 9, 1857, two youths, named Kilsby, found on one of the abutments of the bridge a carpet bag, containing human bones and flesh, which had been cut up, salted, and boiled, and some foreign clothes. No clue could be found respecting these remains, which were interred in Woking cemetery.

WATERLOO CUP, see *Dogs*.

WATER-MILLS, used for grinding corn, are said to have been invented by Belisarius, the general of Justinian, while besieged in Rome by the Goths, 555. The ancients parched their corn, and pounded it in mortars. Afterwards mills were invented, which were turned by men and beasts with great labour; yet Pliny mentions wheels turned by water. See *Telo-dynamic transmitter*.

WATERSPOUT. Two waterspouts fell on the Glatz mountains in Germany, and caused dreadful devastation to Hautenbach and many other villages; many persons perished, 13 July, 1827. A waterspout at Glanflesk, near Killarney, in Ireland, passed over a farm of Mr. John Macarthy, destroying farm-houses and other buildings; seventeen persons perished, 4 Aug. 1831. The estimated length of one seen near Calcutta, 27 Sept. 1853, was 1000 feet. It lasted ten minutes, and was absorbed upwards. One seen on 24 Sept. 1856, burst into heavy rain. The town of Miskolcz, Hungary, destroyed by a waterspout; great loss of life and property, 30 Aug. 1878. 61 persons said to have been killed by a waterspout in Algeria, Oct. 1881. A waterspout at Arequipa, Peru, caused immense damage, several persons drowned, 14 Feb.; one at Pachuca, Mexico, 30 deaths, 27 Sept. 1884; another near Lagos, very destructive, 6 or 7 June, 1885. Destructive waterspout at Swansea 4 Sept. 1886; another on Batcombe hills, Dorsetshire, greatly damaged the villages of Chatnole, Cerne, and Mintern, 7 June, 1889.

WATER TOFANA, see *Poisoning*.

WATLING-STREET, see *Roman Roads*.

WATTIGNIES (N. France). Here Jourdan and the French republicans defeated the Austrians under the prince of Coburg, and raised the siege of Maubeuge, 14-16 Oct. 1793.

WAT TYLER'S INSURRECTION, see *Tyler*.

WAVE PRINCIPLE (in accordance with which the curves of the hull of a ship should be adapted to the curves of a wave of the sea) formed the subject of experiments begun by Mr. John Scott Russell in 1832, with the view of increasing the speed of ships. Colonel Beaufoy is said to have spent 30,000*l*. in researches upon this matter. It was also taken up by the British Association, who have published reports of the investigations. The principle has been adopted by naval architects; see *Undulatory Theory*, and *Yacht*.

WAVERLEY NOVELS. The publication of the series began with "Waverley; or, 'Tis Sixty Years since," in 1814, and closed with "Tales of my Landlord," fourth series, in 1831. The authorship was acknowledged by sir Walter Scott, at a dinner, 23 Feb. 1827. The original MSS. of several of Scott's poems and novels were sold by auction by Christie and Manson for 1255 guineas, 6 July, 1867.

WAWZ or **WAWER** (Poland). The Poles under Skrzynecki attacked the Russians at Wawz, and after two days' hard fighting, all the Russian positions were carried by storm, and they retreated with the loss of 12,000 men and 2000 prisoners, 31 March, 1831. The loss of the Poles was small, but their triumph was soon followed by defeat and ruin.

WAX came into use for candles in the 12th century; and wax candles were esteemed a luxury in 1300, being but little used. In China, candles of vegetable wax have been in use for centuries; see *Candleberry*. The wax tree, *Ligustrum lucidum*, was brought from China before 1794.—SEALING-WAX was not brought into use in England until about 1556. Its use has been much superseded by the introduction of adhesive envelopes, about 1844.

WAXWORK.—Exhibition of models in wax were popular in the 17th and 18th centuries. The collection of wax figures exhibited by Mrs. Salmon at Aldgate, early in the last century, were removed to Fleet-street and shown there till 1812, when they were sold, it is said, for 50*l*. Madame Tussaud, a skilful modeller, exhibited her remarkable collection of models and casts of eminent persons with costumes and other interesting relics in the boulevard du Temple, Paris, 1785. In 1802 she exhibited her collection at the Lyceum, Strand, London, and afterwards at other places. The interest of the exhibition has been energetically sustained for many years at Baker-street, London, W., and latterly at Marylebone-road, by madame Tussaud and her family; she died 15 April, 1850, aged 90. Easter in 1889 the collection was purchased by a company, Mr. John Tussaud being engaged as manager.

WE. Sovereigns generally use *we* for *I*, which style began with king John, 1199. *Coke*. The German emperors and French kings used the plural about 1200.

WEALD of Kent and Sussex, the site of very large, ancient forests; St. Leonard's still remaining; near which, in the Wealden formation, Dr. G. A. Mantell discovered the remains of huge extinct animals, 1825 *et seq*. Mr. R. Furley published an exhaustive "History of the Weald of Kent," 1871-4.

WEATHER, see *Meteorology*.

WEAVING appears to have been practised in China more than a thousand years before it was known in Europe or Asia. The Egyptians ascribed the art to Isis; the Greeks to Minerva; and the Peruvians to the wife of Manco Capac. Our Saviour's vest, or coat, had not any seam, being woven from the top throughout, in one whole piece. The print of a frame for weaving such a vest may be seen in *Calmet's Dictionary*, under the word *Vestments*. Two weavers from Brabant settled at York, where they manufactured woollens, which, says king Edward, "may prove of great benefit to us and our subjects" (1331). Flemish dyers, cloth drapers, linen-makers, silk-throwsters, &c., settled at Canterbury, Norwich, Colchester, Southampton, and other places, on account of the duke of Alva's persecution, 1567; see *Loom*, and *Electric Loom*.

WEDDINGS. Silver weddings are celebrated after a union of 25 years; golden weddings after a union of 50 years; and diamond weddings after a union of 60 years, some apply it to 75 years. John, king of Saxony, celebrated his golden wedding, 10 Nov. 1872.

WEDDING-RINGS were used by the ancients, and put upon the wedding finger, from a supposed connection with a vein there with the heart. According to Pliny they were made of iron; in the time of Tertullian of gold. Wedding-rings are to be of standard gold, by statute, 1855; see *Adriatic*.

WEDGE-LIKE CHARACTERS, see *Cuneiform*.

WEDGWOOD WARE, pottery and porcelain produced by Mr. Josiah Wedgwood, of Staffordshire, in 1762. His potteries, termed Etruria, were founded in 1771. Previously to 1763, much earthenware was imported from France and Holland.

WEDNESDAY, the fourth day of the week, so called from the Saxon idol Woden or Odin, worshipped on this day. Woden was the reputed author of magic and the inventor of all the arts, and was thought to answer to the Mercury of the Greeks and Romans.

WEEDON INQUIRY (Northamptonshire). Commissioners were appointed to inquire into the accounts of Mr. Elliot, superintendent of the great military clothing establishment at this place, in July, 1858, and commenced sitting in September. Many of the statements were afterwards disputed, and caused much dissatisfaction.

WEEK, the space of seven days, supposed to be first used among the Jews, who observed the sabbath every seventh day. They had three sorts of weeks—the common one of seven days; the second of years, seven years; the third of seven times seven years, at the end of which was the jubilee. All the present English names are derived from the Saxon:—

Latin.		French.
Dies Solis,	Day of the Sun,	Dimanche.
Dies Lunæ,	Day of the Moon,	Lundi.
Dies Martis,	Day of Mars,	Mardi.
Dies Mercurii,	Day of Mercury,	Mercredi.
Dies Jovis,	Day of Jupiter,	Jeudi.
Dies Veneris,	Day of Venus,	Vendredi.
Dies Saturni,	Day of Saturn,	Samedi.
English.	*Saxon.*	*German.*
Sunday,	Sun's day,	Sonntag.
Monday,	Moon's day,	Montag.
Tuesday,	Tiw's day,	Dienstag.
Wednesday,	Woden's day,	Mittwoche.
Thursday,	Thor's day,	Donnerstag.
Friday,	Friga's day,	Freitag.
Saturday,	Saterne's day,	Samstag, or Sonnabend.

WEEKLY DISPATCH, liberal weekly Sunday paper, established 1801.

WEIGHTS AND MEASURES. These and the stamping of gold and silver money, are attributed to Pheidon, tyrant of Argos, 895 B.C.; see *Arun-*

delian Marbles. Weights were originally taken from grains of wheat, the lowest being still called a grain. *Chalmers*. See *Crith*.
Much information is given by Mr. H. W. Chisholm in his work "On the Science of Weighing and Measuring." 1877.
The Jews ascribed weights and measures to Cain; the Egyptians to Theuth, or Thoth; the Greeks, to Hermes (the Roman Mercury).
The basis of ancient measures was the natural proportions of the human body; the digit, or breadth of the middle part of the first joint of the fore finger, being the lowest unit of the scale.
The Egyptian cubit (six palms), under the Pharaohs, was about 18.24 English inches; the cubit of Ptolemy about 21.87 inches; he determined the length of a stadium, and of a degree.
The sacred cubit of the Jews (Newton), 24.7 inches.
Assyrian weights are described by Mr. Layard in his "Nineveh."
The standard measure was originally kept at Winchester by the law of king Edgar 972
Standards of weights and measures were provided for the whole kingdom of England by the sheriffs of London, 9 Rich. I. 1197
A public weighing-machine was set up in London, and all commodities ordered to be weighed by the city-officer, called the weigh-master, who was to do justice between buyer and seller, stat. 3 Edw. II. (Stow) 1309
Edward III. ordered that there should be "one weight, measure, and yard," throughout the kingdom 1353
First statute, directing the use of avoirdupois weight, of 24 Hen. VIII. 1532
Weights and measures ordered to be examined by the justices at quarter-sessions, 35 Geo. III. . . 1795
Again regulated 1800
Statute for establishing a uniformity of weights and measures, 1824, took effect throughout the United Kingdom . . . . 1 Jan. 1826
New acts relating thereto passed in 1834, 1835, 1855, and in 1859
16 & 17 Vict. c. 29, regulates the weights to be used in the sale of bullion, and adopts the use of the Troy ounce 1853
A commission (consisting of Mr. G. B. Airy, gen. E. Sabine, lord Rosse, Mr. T. Graham and others), appointed to examine the standards . 9 May, 1867
3rd report of the Standards commission states that errors exist in official standards, dated 24 July, 1868
A new Weights and Measures act passed to enforce uniformity in all markets in the United Kingdom, and abolish local measures, 8 Aug. 1878; came into operation . . . . 1 Jan. 1879
Specific gravities (unit, pure water): iridium, 22.38; platinum, 21.45; osmium, 21.4; gold, 19.32; lead, 11.35; silver, 10.51; copper, 8.94; iron, 7.87; tin, 7.29; zinc, 7.19; iodine, 4.95; carbon, 3.52; aluminium, 2.56; sulphur, 2; sodium, 0.97; lithium, 0.59; oxygen, 0.001431; nitrogen, 0.001257; hydrogen, 0.0000896, *Dr. O. J. Broch*. 1878
(See *Standard*; and *Metrical System*.)

WEIMAR, capital of the grand-duchy of Saxe Weimar (*which see*).

WEINSBERG, see *Guelphs*.

WEISSENBURG, see *Wissembourg*.

WELLINGTON, a town in New Zealand, North Island, settled in 1840, made a bishopric in 1858, became a seat of government, 24 Dec. 1864. Population in 1887, about 30,000.

WELLINGTON ADMINISTRATION, succeeded that of viscount Goderich, Jan. 1828. The duke resigned 16 Nov. 1830.
Duke of Wellington, *first lord of the treasury*.
Lord Lyndhurst, *lord chancellor*.
Henry Goulburn, *chancellor of the exchequer*.
Earl Bathurst, *president of the council*.
Lord Ellenborough, *privy seal*.
Mr. (afterwards sir) Robert Peel, earl Dudley, and Mr. Wm. Huskisson, *home, foreign*, and *colonial secretaries*.
Viscount Melville, *board of control*.

Mr. Charles Grant, *board of trade*.
Lord Palmerston, *secretary-at-war*.
J. C. Herries, *minister of the mint*.
Earl of Aberdeen, *duchy of Lancaster*.
Mr. Huskisson, earl Dudley, viscount Palmerston, and Mr. Grant quitted the ministry, and various changes followed in May and June same year.
The earl of Aberdeen and sir George Murray became, respectively, *foreign* and *colonial secretaries*.
Sir Henry Hardinge, *secretary-at-war*.
Mr. Vesey Fitzgerald (afterwards lord Fitzgerald), *India board*.
Lord Lowther, *first commissioner of land revenues*, &c., May and June, 1828.
Mr. Arbuthnot, Mr. Vesey Fitzgerald, &c.

WELLINGTON COLLEGE (Sandhurst), was erected by subscription in memory of the great duke of Wellington, for the support and education of orphan sons of commissioned officers. The first stone was laid by the queen on 2 June, 1856; and the building was opened by her majesty on 29 Jan. 1859. Out of the 150,000*l.* subscribed, 55,000*l.* were expended on the building, and the rest invested for the maintenance of the institution.
A controversy respecting its management; certain charges explained or rebutted . . Aug.-Oct. 1878
Proposal for royal commission of inquiry negatived in the commons . . . . 1 April, 1879
Commission appointed; lord Penzance, bishop of Exeter, Mr. R. Lowe (since lord Sherbrooke), col. Chesney, &c., June, 1879; report recommending greater economy and improvement of income,
Aug. 1880

WELLINGTONIA GIGANTEA, the largest tree in the world, a native of California, was discovered by W. Whitehead, June, 1850; a specimen first gathered by Mr. W. Lobb in 1853, and described by Dr. John Lindley. When full grown it is about 450 feet high, and 116 feet in circumference. The prince consort (5 June, 1861) and the queen (24 July, 1861) planted Wellingtonias at the new gardens of the Royal Horticultural Society. The trees did not live; the gardens were given up in 1887.

WELLINGTON'S VICTORIES, &c. For details see separate articles.
Arthur Wellesley was born, according to some authorities, in March or April (baptised 30 April); incorrectly said by others . . . . 1 May, 1769
Appointed to command in the Mahratta war in India, takes Poonah and Ahmednuggur, 12 Aug.; gains his first victory at Assaye, 23 Sept.; defeats Scindiah at Argaum, Nov.; and at Gawalghur
13 Dec. 1803
Becomes secretary for Ireland 1807
Takes the command in Portugal, defeats Junot at Vimeira . . . . 21 Aug. 1808
Defeats Victor at Talavera, 28 July; created viscount Wellington . . . . . 4 Sept. 1809
Repulses Massena at Busaco, 27 Sept.; and occupies the lines at Torres Vedras . . . 10 Oct. 1810
Defeats Massena at Fuentes de Oñoro, 5 May; takes Almeida . . . . 10 May, 1811
Passes the Douro and defeats Soult . 12 May, 1812
Storms Ciudad Rodrigo, 19 Jan.; and Badajos, 6 April; defeats Marmont at Salamanca, 22 July; enters Madrid . . . . . . 12 Aug. "
Defeats Joseph Bonaparte and Jourdan at Vittoria, 21 June; storms St. Sebastian, 31 Aug.; enters France . . . . 8 Oct. 1813
Defeats Soult at Orthez, 27 Feb.; and at Toulouse
10 April, 1814
Created duke of Wellington, with an annuity of 13,000*l.* and a grant of 300,000*l.* . . May, "
First appeared in the house of lords; his patents of creation as baron, earl, marquis, and duke being read at the same time . . . . 28 June, "
Commands the army in the Netherlands; repulses an attack of Ney at Quatre Bras, 16 June; defeats Napoleon at Waterloo, 18 June; invests Paris
7 July, 1815
Commands the army of occupation in France
July, 1815, till Nov. 1818

His assassination attempted by Cantillon, who escapes . . . . 10 Feb. 1818
Appointed master-general of the ordnance . . 1819
The Wellington shield and supporting columns designed by Stothard, commemorating all the above-mentioned victories, presented to the duke by the merchants and bankers of London. (It was manufactured by Green and Ward, and cost 11,000*l*.) . . . . 16 Feb. 1822
The duke appointed commander-in-chief, 22 Jan.; resigns . . . . 30 April, 1827
Becomes first minister . . . . . 8 Jan. 1828
Aids in carrying the Catholic Emancipation bill April, 1829
Asserts that no reform in parliament is needed, 2 Nov.; resigns . . . . . . 16 Nov. 1830
Transacts all the business of the country, after the resignation of lord Melbourne, till the arrival of sir R. Peel from Italy, Nov.; and becomes foreign secretary under sir R. Peel, Dec. 1834; resigns April, 1835
Again commander-in-chief . . . . 15 Aug. 1842
Dies at Walmer castle* . . . . 14 Sept. 1852
Removed to Chelsea hospital, where he lay in state 10 Nov. „
Removed to the Horse Guards . . 17 Nov. „
Public funeral at St. Paul's cathedral . 18 Nov. „
A multitude of all ranks, estimated at a million and a half of persons, were congregated in the line of route, a distance of three miles, to witness and share in the imposing spectacle.
The military consisted of the household regiments of horse and foot guards, the and battalion of the rifles, a battalion of the Royal Marines, the 33rd regiment, the 17th Lancers, and the 18th Light Dragoons, the regiment of Scots Greys; a body of Chelsea pensioners, and men of different arms of the Indian army.
The body was placed upon a sumptuous funeral car, drawn by twelve horses richly caparisoned, and the coffin was thus seen by the whole of the crowd.
The procession moved about seven o'clock, and it was three o'clock before the body was lowered into the vault beside the remains of Nelson, under the dome of St. Paul's cathedral.
Memorial by Marochetti erected by the present duke, his son, and tenants at Strathfieldsaye, July, 1866.

WELLINGTON MONUMENT, in St. Paul's.
A number of models exhibited in Westminster hall; none chosen, 1857.
The execution of the monument entrusted to Mr. A. Stevens, sculptor, and Mr. Penrose, architect. The stone sarcophagus was completed in 1858.
In Aug. 1870, above 17,000*l*. had been expended, and it was stated that 15,000*l*. more were required. Parliament had granted 20,000*l*. Fresh arrangements were made with Mr. Stevens. He died 1 May, 1875. Monument reported complete, 1 Feb.; uncovered, 20 April, 1878.

See Statues.

WELLS were dug by Abraham, 1892 B.C., and Isaac, 1804 (*Gen.* xxi. 30, and xxvi. 19). Danaus is said to have introduced well-digging into Greece from Egypt. Norton's "tube-well," patented Oct. 1867, is said to be the invention of Hiram J. Messenger, Stephen Brewer, and Byron Mudge, Americans of the state of New York. The apparatus consists of an iron tube perforated with holes at the lower end, and shod with a steel point, which readily enters the hardest soil when forcibly driven. It was used with great advantage during the civil war 1861-4; by the British in their campaign in Abyssinia in 1867-8; and by the Russians in Khiva, 1873.
Messrs. Meux, brewers, New Oxford-street, London, boring, found water beneath the greensand, about 1000 feet deep, April, 1877.

WELLS (Somerset). The cathedral church was built by Ina, king of the West Saxons, 704, and by him dedicated to St. Andrew. Other West Saxon kings endowed it, and it was erected into a

* His favourite old horse, Copenhagen, (born 1808, at Waterloo), died 1836.

bishopric in 909, during the reign of Edward the Elder. The present church was begun by Robert, 18th bishop of this see, and completed by his immediate successor. The first bishop was Ethelm or Adelmus (afterwards bishop of Canterbury). The see was united with Bath (*which see*) in 1088.

WELSH CHARITY SCHOOLS; established in Gray's-inn-road, London, 1715; removed to Ashford, near Staines, Middlesex, 1852.

WENDS, a branch of the Slavonic family which spread over Germany in the 6th century, and settled especially in the north-eastern parts.

WESLEYAN METHODISTS, a sect founded by John Wesley (born 1703, died 1791) and his brother Charles, who in 1727 with a few other students formed themselves into a small society for the purpose of mutual edification by religious exercises. From their strictness of life they were called *Methodists*, in 1729. John Wesley went to Georgia in America, in 1735, with a view of converting the Indians. On his return to England, in 1738, he commenced itinerant preaching, and gathered many followers. On finding many churches shut against him, he built spacious meeting-houses in London, Bristol, and other places. The Wesleyan Methodist society, as such, began in 1739. For some time he was united with George Whitefield; but differing with him respecting the doctrine of election, they separated in 1741; see *Whitefield*. Wesley was almost continually engaged in travelling through the United Kingdom. His two leading doctrines were the instantaneousness of conversion, and Christian perfection, or deliverance from all sin. His society was well organised, and he preserved his influence over it to the last. "His genius for government was not inferior to that of Richelieu." *Macaulay.*
The deed of declaration, establishing the conference, is dated 28 Feb. 1784. In 1851 there were 428 circuits in Great Britain, with between 13,000 and 14,000 local or lay preachers, and about 920 itinerant preachers, and 6579 chapels.

The *Conference*, the highest Wesleyan court, till lately, composed of 100 ministers, who meet annually. It was instituted by John Wesley in . 1784
At the centenary of the existence of Methodism 216,000*l*. were collected, to be expended on the objects of the society 1839
An œcumenical conference to be held in the autumn of 1881, settled . . . . . . 31 July, 1880
138th annual conference opened . . 19 July, 1881
Out of the original connection have seceded:—
 Chapels in 1851
New Connection (in 1796) 301
Primitive Methodists (1810) 2871
Bible Christians, or Bryanites (from Wm. O'Bryan) (1815) 403
Wesleyan Methodist Association (1834) . . 329
Wesleyan Methodist Reformers (1849) . . 2000
The last arose out of the publication of "Fly Sheets," advocating reform in the body (1844-8). The suspected authors and their friends were expelled. By these disruptions the main body is thought to have lost 100,000 members.—This sect in America numbered about a million in 1844, when a division took place on the slavery question.
The *United Methodist Free Churches*, an amalgamation of the Protestant Methodist (1828), Wesleyan Methodist Association (1834) and the Wesleyan Reform Association (1849) effected in . . 1857
Wesleyan Methodist church members in Great Britain in 1868, 342,580; in 1872, 346,580; in 1876, 372,538; 1878, 380,867 (1412 ministers); 1885, 413,163; March, 1889, 421,784.
Letter from Dr. Pusey requesting aid in opposing Coleridge's bill for admitting dissenters to the universities, read at the conference, but not received . . . . 13 Aug. 1863

The establishment of a high school for Wesleyans at Cambridge (to prepare for the university) proposed . . . . May 1872
The chapel in the City-road, London, founded by John Wesley, 1 April, 1877, was nearly destroyed by fire . . . . 7 Dec. 1879
Œcumenical Methodist conference (at City-road Chapel, London), of 400 delegates, ministers and laymen from all parts of the world (representing nearly 4,000,000) . . . . 6 Sept. et seq. 1881
Members in United Kingdom, 435,232 . . 1884
Conference at Newcastle-on-Tyne . . 21 July 1885
,, ,, Camborne, Cornwall . . 24 July 1888
,, ,, Sheffield (146th) . . 23 July 1889

WESSEX, see *Britain*.

WEST AFRICAN SETTLEMENTS—Sierra Leone, Gambia, &c. Governor, sir Arthur E. Kennedy, 1867; sir Garnet Wolseley, Aug. 1873; Cornelius H. Kortright, 1875; Dr. Samuel Rowe, 1876; capt. Arthur E. Havelock, 1881; sir Samuel Rowe, 1884. See *Ashantees*.
Turbulent chiefs subdued . . . . June, 1883
International conference at Berlin, on West African affairs.* Freedom of trade on the Congo; Rights of States occupying open territory; proposed by Germany, accepted by France, England, Portugal, Spain, Holland, Belgium, the United States, and Turkey . . . . . 8 Oct. 1884
Conference opened, prince Bismarck president 15 Nov. ,,
The conference declares free trade in the Congo valley and affirms British protectorate over the Niger, and recognises the International African Association . . . . . . Dec. ,,
Prohibits slave trade . . . . . 7 Jan. 1885
Approves rules for future annexations on the coast 1 Feb. ,,
Result of the conference embodied in a general act signed . . . . 26 Feb. ,,
International limitations on the lower Congo, settled 15 Feb. ,,

WESTERN AUSTRALIA, formerly SWAN RIVER SETTLEMENT, which was projected by colonel Peel in 1828. Regulations issued from the colonial office, and Captain Stirling, appointed lieutenant-governor, Jan. 17, 1829, arrived at the appointed site in August following. The three towns of Perth, Freemantle, and Guildford were founded same year. In March, 1830, fifty ships, with 2000 emigrants, with property amounting to 1,000,000l., had arrived before hardly any dwellings had been erected or land surveyed. The more energetic settlers left for home, or the neighbouring colonies, and the colony languished for twenty years for want of suitable inhabitants—the first settlers, from their previous habits and rank in life, proving unfit for the rough work of colonisation. In 1848, the colonists requested that convicts might be sent out to them, and in 1849 a band arrived, who were kindly received and well treated. The best results ensued. By 1853, 2000 had arrived, and the inhabitants of Perth had requested that 1000 should be sent out annually. The reception of convicts is to cease in after-years, in consequence of the energetic opposition of the other Australian colonies (1865).—The settlement of King George's Sound was founded in 1826 by the government of New South Wales. It was used as a military station for four years. In 1830, the home government ordered the settlement to be transferred to Swan River. Since the establishment of steam communication, the little town of Albany here, employed as a coaling station, has become a thriving sea-port. It possesses an excellent harbour, used by whalers. A journal called the *Freemantle Gazette* was published here in March, 1831. Bishopric of Perth founded 1857. Population of Western Australia in 1859, 14,837; Jan. 1862, 15,555; Dec. 1883, 31,233; Dec. 1888, 42,137; revenue 1887, 377,903l.; expenditure, 456,897l.; imports, 832,213l.; exports, 604,656l. Governor John Stephen Hampton, appointed 1861; sir Benjamin C. C. Pine, May, 1868; Frederick A. Weld, 1869; Wm. C. F. Robinson, 1874; major-gen. sir Harry St. George Ord, 1877; sir W. F. Robinson, 1880; sir Frederick Napier Broome, 1882.
New gold field at Perth discovered, May; gold discovered in n.w. Australia . . . (?) May, 1886
The legislative council petition for responsible self-government instead of being a crown colony, autumn, 1887; a bill granting this was passed by the house of lords, 16 July, but deferred by government in the commons . . . Aug. 1889

WESTERN CHURCH (called also the LATIN or ROMAN) broke off communion with the Greek or Eastern Church, 653; see *Greek Church*. Its history is mainly comprised in that of the popes and of the European kingdoms; see *Popes*. This church was disturbed by the Arian heresy about 345 and 500; by Pelagianism, about 409; by the introduction of image-worship about 600; by the injunction of the celibacy of the clergy and the rise of the monastic orders about 649; by the contests between the emperors and the popes respecting ecclesiastical investitures between 1073 and 1173; by the rise and progress of the Reformation in the 15th and 16th centuries; by the contests between the Jesuits and Jansenists in the 17th and 18th centuries; and by the progress of modern philosophy and rationalism, and by ultramontanism, in the 19th; see *Roman Catholics*.

WESTERN EMPIRE. The Roman empire was divided into Eastern and Western by Diocletian in 296; but was reunited under Constans in 340. It was again divided into Eastern and Western by Valentinian and Valens, the former having the Western portion or Rome, 364; see *Eastern Empire, Italy,* and *Rome*.

EMPERORS.

364. Valentinian, son of Gratian, takes the Western, and his brother Valens the Eastern empire.
367. Gratian, a youth, son of Valentinian, made a colleague in the government by his father.
375. Valentinian II., another son, also very young, is on the death of his father, associated with Gratian, who is assassinated by his general, Andragathius, in 383. Valentinian murdered by one of his officers, Arbogastes, in 392.
392. Eugenius, a usurper, assumes the imperial dignity; he and Arbogastes are defeated by
394. Theodosius the Great, who becomes sole emperor. [Andragathius threw himself into the sea, and Arbogastes died by his own hand.]
395. Honorius, son of Theodosius, reigns, on his father's death, in the West, and his brother Arcadius in the East. Honorius dies in 423.
423. Usurpation of John, the Notary, defeated and slain near Ravenna.
425. Valentinian III., son of the empress Placidia, daughter of Theodosius the Great: murdered at the instance of his successor
455. Maximus: he marries Eudoxia, widow of Valentinian, who, to avenge the death of her first husband and the guilt of her second, invites the African Vandals into Italy, and Rome is sacked. Maximus stoned to death.
455. Marcus Marcilius Avitus; forced to resign, and dies in his flight towards the Alps.
457. Julius Valerius Majorianus; murdered at the instance of his minister, Ricimer, who raises
461. Libius Severus to the throne, but holds the supreme power; Severus poisoned by Ricimer.
465. [Interregnum. Ricimer retains the authority, without assuming the title of emperor.]

---

* Mr. H. S'anley, at Berlin.

467. Anthemius, chosen by the joint suffrages of the senate and army; murdered by Ricimer, who dies soon after.
472. Flavius-Anicius Olybrius: slain by the Goths soon after his accession.
473. Glycerius: forced to abdicate by his successor.
474. Julius Nepos: deposed by his general, Orestes, and retires to Salona.
475. Romulus (called Augustulus, or Little Augustus), son of Orestes. Orestes is slain, and the emperor deposed by
476. Odoacer, king of the Heruli: takes Rome, assumes the style of king of Italy, and completes the fall of the Western empire.
See *Italy*, *Rome*, and *Germany*.

WEST HAM, S.W. Essex, (called London over the border) parish containing Plaistow, Stratford, &c., the population in 1841, 12,738; owing to the large increase of factories and other works rose to 99,142 in 1871, and 200,752 in 1881.
West Ham returns two M.P.'s by the act of 1885; and was incorporated by royal charter, July, 1886. West Ham is outside of the jurisdiction of the metropolitan board of works. The dreadful sanitary condition of 1855 gradually improved by the action of a new local board, now succeeded by a municipal corporation. Rateable value 79,000l. in 1856; nearly 700,000l. in 1886.

WESTERN ISLES OF SCOTLAND. Royal commission to inquire into extreme destitution appointed 20 March, 1883 (lord Napier and Ettrick, Mr. Donald Cameron, M.P., and others). See *Mansion House*.

WEST INDIES, islands discovered by Columbus, St. Salvador being the first land he made in the New World, and first seen by him in the night between the 11th and 12th Oct. 1492. The largest are Cuba, Hayti (or St. Domingo), Jamaica, Porto Rico, Trinidad, and Guadaloupe; see *the Islands* respectively.
A royal commission to inquire into their condition appointed in 1882, reported on their great need of important judicial and fiscal reforms April, 1884: Depressed condition through increased use of beet sugar; inadmissible remedies proposed by deputation to lord Derby, 28 Aug. 1884.

WEST INDIAN SETTLEMENTS, see *Jamaica*.

WESTMINSTER, so called on account of its western situation with regard to St. Paul's cathedral, or from there being formerly a monastery named East Minster, on the hill now called Great Tower-hill. This city joins London at Temple-bar. Formerly Westminster was called Thorney, or Thorney Island: and in ancient times Canute had a palace here, burnt in 1263. Westminster and London were one mile asunder in 1603, when the houses were thatched, and there were mud walls in the Strand. It is said that the great number of Scotsmen who came over after the accession of James I. occasioned the building of Westminster, and united it with London. *Howel's Londinopolis*; see *Parliament*, 1834-52, 1884. By the Seats act of 1885, Westminster returns one M.P.

Earl Grosvenor created marquis of Westminster, 1831; the marquis created duke . . . 1874
Westminster industrial exhibition, opened 24 May, closed . . . . . 9 Aug. 1879
Baroness Burdett Coutts lays foundation of New Town Hall, near Victoria Street, 29 March, 1882; opened . . . . . 19 July, 1883

WESTMINSTER ABBEY. Christopher Wren, in his survey of the present edifice, found nothing to countenance the belief that it was erected on the ruins of a pagan temple. The erection of the first abbey in the 7th century is ascribed to St. Sebert, king of Essex.

The church becoming ruinous, splendidly rebuilt by Edward the Confessor (1055-65) and filled with monks from Exeter (Pope Nicholas II. constituted it the place for the inauguration of the kings of England); dedicated . . . 28 Dec. 1065.
Re-built in a magnificent style by Henry III. 1220-69.
In the reigns of Edward II., Edward III., and Richard II. the great cloisters, abbot's house, and principal monastic buildings, erected . . 1300-1400
The western parts of the nave and aisles rebuilt between . . . . . 1340 and 1483
The west front and the great window built by Richard III. and Henry VII.; the latter commenced the chapel which bears his name; the first stone laid . . . . 24 Jan. 1502-3
The abbey dissolved and made a bishopric . . 1540
Made a collegiate church by Elizabeth . . 1560
Made a barrack for soldiers (*Mercurius Rusticus*), July, 1643
The great west window and the western towers rebuilt in the reigns of George I. and II. . . 1714-60
The choir injured by fire . . . 9 July, 1803
Mr. Wyatt commenced restoring the dilapidated parts at an expense of 42,000l. in . . . 1809
A fire, without any serious injury . 27 April, 1829
The evening services for the working classes, when a sermon was preached by the dean, Dr. Trench, commenced on . . . . 3 Jan. 1858
The 800th anniversary of the foundation celebrated, 28 Dec. 1865
7000l. voted by parliament to restore the chapter-house (G. Gilbert Scott employed), 1 May, 1866; re-opened . . . . . 29 April, 1872
Lectures in the Abbey on foreign missions; professor Max Müller, a layman, 3 Dec. 1873; principal Caird of Scotch church, 30 Nov. 1874; rev. Robert Moffat, father-in-law of Livingstone 30 Nov. 1875.
Sir Charles Lyell, sir Wm. Sterndale Bennett, and bishop Connop Thirlwall, buried in the Abbey, 1875; G. E. Street, 29 Dec. 1881; C. R. Darwin, 26 April, 1882.
Repairs connected with the principal entrance after designs by Gilbert Scott, completed at a cost of about 20,000l. . . . . . Nov. 1881
New Abbey gardens opened . . 12 April, 1882
New organ set up . . . . 28 April, 1884
Thanksgiving jubilee services for the queen (see *Jubilee*) . . . . 21, 22 June, 1887
Proposed transfer of the charge of restoring and maintaining the abbey to the ecclesiastical commissioners who are to advance 10,000l. March; legalised by act passed . . 28 June, 1888

WESTMINSTER AQUARIUM, see *Aquarium*.

WESTMINSTER BISHOPRIC AND DEANERY. At the dissolution of monasteries, Westminster abbey was valued at 3977l. per annum; king Henry VIII. in 1539 erected it into a deanery; and in 1540 into a bishopric, and appointed Thomas Thirlby prelate. He was translated to Norwich in 1550, and with him ended the bishopric of Westminster; Middlesex, his diocese, being restored to London. The dean presided until the accession of Mary, who restored the abbot. Elizabeth displaced the abbot, and erected the abbey into a collegiate church of a dean and twelve prebendaries, as it still continues. On the revival of the order of the Bath, in 1725, the dean of Westminster was appointed dean of that order, which honour has been continued. Dr. Nicholas Wiseman was created *archbishop of Westminster* by the pope Pius IX. 30 Sept. 1850; see *Papal Aggression*. Dr. Wiseman died 8 Feb. 1865; Henry Manning was consecrated his successor 8 June, following.

RECENT DEANS.
1793. Samuel Horsley; bishop of St. Asaph, 1802.
1802. William Vincent; died 21 Dec. 1815.
1815. John Ireland; died 21 Sept. 1842.
1842. Thomas Turton; bishop of Ely, 1845.
1845. Samuel Wilberforce; bishop of Oxford, 1845.

1845. William Buckland; died 14 Aug. 1856.
1856. Richard C. Trench; abp. of Dublin, 1 Jan. 1864.
1864. Arthur Penrhyn Stanley; died 18 July, 1881.
1881. George Granville Bradley; 14 Sept.

WESTMINSTER BRIDGES. The handsome old bridge was begun (after a design of M. Labelye), 13 Sept. 1738, the first stone laid 29 Jan. 1738-9; opened for passengers 18 Nov. 1750; cost 426,650*l*. It was built of Portland stone, and crossed the river where the breadth is 1223 feet.

Owing to the sinking of several of its piers, most of the balustrades on both sides were removed, to relieve the structure of its weight.
By 16 & 17 Vict. c. 46 the estates of its commissioners were transferred to her majesty's commissioners of works, who were empowered to remove the then existing bridge, and build a NEW BRIDGE (near the old one) . . . . 4 Aug. 1853
The contract required the completion of the works by . . . . 1 June, 1857
The works were suspended for a time, in consequence of the failure of Messrs. Mare the contractors. The government eventually undertook the building, which they entrusted to Mr. Thomas Page, the engineer. One half of the new bridge was opened for use early in 1860; the whole on 24 May, 1862

WESTMINSTER CONFESSION OF FAITH AND CATECHISMS were drawn up by the "Assembly of Divines" (partly consisting of laymen), who sat by authority of parliament in Henry VII.'s chapel, Westminster, from 1643 to 1647. These have ever since been the doctrinal standards of Scotch Presbyterians.

WESTMINSTER HALL (London), first built by William Rufus in 1097, for a banqueting-hall; and here in 1099, on his return from Normandy, "he kept his feast of Whitsuntide very royally." The hall became ruinous before the reign of Richard II., who repaired it in 1397, raised the walls, altered the windows, and added a new roof, as well as a stately porch and other buildings. In 1236 Henry III. on New-year's day caused 6000 poor persons to be entertained in this hall, and in the other rooms of his palace, as a celebration of queen Eleanor's coronation; and here Richard II. held his Christmas festival in 1397, when the number of the guests each day the feast lasted was 10,000. *Stow.* The courts of law were established here by king John. *Idem.* Westminster hall was stated to be the largest room in Europe unsupported by pillars (except a hall of justice at Padua); it is 270 feet in length, 74 feet broad. The hall underwent a general repair in 1802. Concurrently with the erection of the palace of Westminster, many improvements and alterations have lately been made in this magnificent hall. The Volunteer Rifle corps were drilled in the hall in the winter of 1859, and since. The courts of law removed to the new buildings in the Strand Jan. 1883. Restorations proposed by Mr. J. L. Pearson, R.A., July, 1884. The roof and windows greatly damaged by an explosion of dynamite (?) about 2 p.m. 24 Jan. 1885.

WESTMINSTER HOSPITAL, founded, 1719; chartered, 1836.

WESTMINSTER PALACE, see under *Palace of Westminster*, and *Parliament*.

WESTMINSTER REVIEW, liberal in religion and politics, first appeared, 1824, as the organ of the philosophic radicals, termed the Westminster school, friends of Jeremy Bentham. See *Utilitarianism.*

WESTMINSTER SCHOOL or ST. PETER'S COLLEGE, was founded by queen Elizabeth in 1560, for the education of forty boys, denominated the Queen's scholars, who are prepared for the university. It is situated within the abbey enclosure. Besides the scholars on the foundation, many of the nobility and gentry send their sons to Westminster for instruction. A proposal in 1860 to remove the school was disapproved of in 1861.

Westminster Schools, United, comprise Emanuel and St. Margaret's hospitals, and rev. James Palmer's and Emery Hill's school charities, which were abolished by the endowed school commissioners 27 June, 1873. New schools are to be erected.

WESTMINSTER, STATUTES OF, are 3 and 13 Edward I., 1275-90; see *Acts of Parliament.*

WESTMORELAND. This county and Cumberland were granted as a fief to Malcolm of Scotland by Edward the Elder in 945; but resumed by Henry III. in 1237. Neville, earl of Westmoreland, revolted against Elizabeth in 1569, and was attainted in 1570.

WESTPHALIA (Germany). This duchy belonged in former times to the dukes of Saxony, and afterwards became subject to the archbishop of Cologne. On the secularisation in 1802, it was made over to Hesse Darmstadt; and in 1814 was ceded for an equivalent to Prussia. The *kingdom of* Westphalia, one of the temporary kingdoms of Bonaparte, composed of conquests from Prussia, Hesse-Cassel, Hanover, and the smaller states to the west of the Elbe, was created by decree 18 Aug. 1806, and Jerome Bonaparte appointed king, 1 Dec. 1807. Hanover was annexed to it, 1 March, 1810. The kingdom was abolished in 1813, and the countries were restored to their former rulers.

Through strike of the coal miners for increased pay and shorter hours of labour, Herr Krupp, of Essen, had to stop his iron and steel works at several places for want of coal about 4 May. A conflict took place near Gladbeck between the troops and miners, and three miners were killed, 7 May; the owners stand firm; about 39,000 men on strike, 8 May; nearly 100,000 strikers out, 13 May; the government intervenes to effect a compromise, about 13 May; the emperor receives three delegates from miners, 14 May, and advises both parties to come to a compromise, about 15, 16 May; strike spreading to Silesia &c., 15 May; strikers in Westphalia about 110,000, in Silesia 10,000, 15 May—20 May; 40 members of the striking committee arrested 26 May; strike ends by a compromise, 31 May, 1889.

WESTPHALIA or MÜNSTER, PEACE OF; the treaties signed at Osnaburg 6 Aug., and at Münster 24 Oct. 1648, between France, the emperor, and Sweden; Spain continuing the war against France. By this peace (ending the thirty years' war) the principle of a balance of power in Europe was first recognised; Alsace given to France, and part of Pomerania and some other districts to Sweden; the Lower Palatinate restored to the elector palatine; the religious and political rights of the German states established; and the independence of the Swiss Confederation recognised by Germany.

WEST SAXONS, see *Wessex,* in *Britain.*

WEYMOUTH, Dorsetshire, was given by Henry I. to St. Swithin's, Winchester. Taken from Charles I., by the parliamentarians, 1644; visited and brought into note by George III., 1789. First Dorset industrial exhibition was opened here, 25 July, 1878.

WHALE-FISHERY, it is said, was first carried on by the Norwegians in the ninth century. *Lenglet.* Whales were killed at Newfoundland and Iceland, for their oil only, 1578; the use of their

fins and bones was not yet known, consequently (a writer adds) no stays were worn by the ladies. The English whale-fishing commenced at Spitzbergen in 1598; but the Dutch had been previously fishing there. The fishery was much promoted by an act of parliament passed in 1749. From 1800 to 2000 whales have been killed annually on the coast of Greenland, &c. The quantity of whale-oil imported in 1814 was 33,567 tuns; in 1826, when gas-light became general, 25,000 tuns; in 1840, about 22,000 tuns; in 1850, 21,360 tuns; in 1861, 19,176 tuns; in 1864, 14,701 tuns; in 1867, 15,945 tuns; in 1871, 24,679 tuns; in 1872 18,719 tuns; in 1878, 20,656 tuns; in 1883, 17,156 tuns; in 1887, 17,698 tuns. *A living whale* from Labrador, 9 feet 6 inches long, placed in the Westminster aquarium, 26 Sept., died 29 Sept. 1877. White whale (Beluga), arrived 28 May; died in latter part of June.

WHARNCLIFFE MEETINGS of public companies (held to give enlarged powers under certain prescribed conditions) are so called because the standing orders of the house of lords, under which they are held, were introduced by lord Wharncliffe, about 1846.

WHEAT. The Chinese ascribe to their emperor, Ching-Noung, who succeeded Fohi, the art of husbandry, and method of making bread from wheat, about 2000 years before the Christian era. Wheat was introduced into Britain in the 6th century, by Coll ap Coll Frewi. *Roberts.* The first wheat imported into England of which we have a note was in 1347. Various statutes have regulated the sales of wheat, and restrained its importation, in order to encourage its being raised at home. In 1862 attention was drawn to the probable utility of considering the pedigree of wheat. In 1871 it was estimated that 3,571,894 acres in the United Kingdom were devoted to wheat; in 1876, 3,124,342. See *Bread*, and *Corn Laws*. Greatest producers (in order), United States, Russia, France, Great Britain, &c. The wheat crop for Great Britain is said to have yielded 71,939,647 bushels in 1888.

IMPORTED INTO GREAT BRITAIN.

Wheat.	Flour.
1854, 2,656,455 qrs.	6,329,038 cwts.
1861, 29,955,532 ,,	6,152,938 ,,
1862, 41,033,503 ,,	7,207,113 ,,
1864, 23,196,714 cwts.	4,512,391 ,,
1866, 23,156,329 ,,	4,972,280 ,,
1868, 32,639,768 ,,	3,093,022 ,,
1871, 39,389,803 ,,	3,977,933 ,,
1872, 42,127,726 ,,	4,388,136 ,,
1874, 41,527,638 ,,	6,236,044 ,,
1877, 54,269,800 ,,	7,377,303 ,,
1878, 49,906,484 ,,	7,828,079 ,,
1879, 59,591,795 ,,	10,728,252 ,,
1880, 55,261,924 ,,	10,558,312 ,,
1881, 57,147,933 ,,	11,357,381 ,,
1882, 64,240,749 ,,	13,057,403 ,,
1883, 64,138,631 ,,	16,329,312 ,,
1884, 47,306,156 ,,	15,095,301 ,,
1885, 61,498,864 ,,	15,832,843 ,,
1886, 47,435,806 ,,	14,689,560 ,,
1887, 55,802,518 ,,	18,063,234 ,,

VALUE OF WHEAT IMPORTED INTO THE UNITED KINGDOM.

1854	£11,693,737	1866	£12,983,090
1855	9,679,578	1867	24,985,096
1856	12,716,349	1868	22,069,353
1857	9,563,099	1869	19,515,758
1858	9,050,467	1870	16,264,027
1859	8,713,532	1871	23,318,883
1860	16,554,083	1872	26,169,185
1861	19,051,464	1873	28,538,746
1862	23,203,800	1874	25,236,932
1863	12,015,006	1875	27,510,469
1864	10,674,654	1876	23,178,011
1865	9,775,616	1877	33,895,437

1878	£27,433,444	1883	£31,454,481
1879	31,468,171	1884	19,901,794
1880	30,621,711	1885	24,085,913
1881	31,531,535	1886	17,909,630
1882	34,259,126	1887	21,337,918

Average Annual Price per Quarter in England and Wales.

	s. d.		s. d.		s. d.		s. d.
1801	119 6	1840	66 4	1868	63 9	1876	46 2
1805	89 9	1845	50 10	1869	48 2	1877	56 9
1810	106 5	1850	40 3	1870	46 10	1878	46 5
1815	65 7	1855	74 8	1871	56 8	1879	43 10
1820	67 10	1860	53 3	1872	57 0	1880	44 2
1825	68 6	1865	41 10	1873	58 8	1881	45 4
1830	66 4	1866	49 11	1874	55 8	1882	45 1
1835	39 4	1867	64 5	1875	45 2	1883	41 7

WHEEL, BREAKING ON THE. A barbarous mode of death, of great antiquity, ordered by Francis I. for robbers, about 1535; see *Ravaillac*.

WHEEL-WORK, see *Spinning*, *Looms*, *Automaton*.

WHIGS. In the reign of Charles II. the name *Whig* was a term of reproach given by the court party to their antagonists for holding the principles of the "whigs," or fanatical covenanters in Scotland; and in return the name *Tory* was given to the court party, comparing them to the Tories, or popish robbers in Ireland. *Baker*. The distinction arose out of the discovery of the Meal-tub plot (*which see*) in 1678. Upon bringing up the meal plot before parliament, two parties were formed: the ones who doubted the plot styled those who believed in it *Whigs*; these styled their adversaries *Tories*. In time these names, given as marks of opprobrium, became honoured distinctions. *Hume*. The Whigs brought about the revolution of 1688-9, and established the protestant succession. They were chiefly instrumental in obtaining the abolition of the slave trade and slavery, the repeal of the Test and Corporation act, Catholic emancipation, parliamentary and municipal reform, the repeal of the corn laws, and similar measures. The Whig Club was established by Charles James Fox; one of its original members was the great Francis, duke of Bedford, who died in 1802. See *Liberals*. For the principal Whig ministries, see *Halifax*, *Walpole*, *Rockingham*, *Grenville*, *Grey*, *Melbourne*, *Russell*, *Palmerston*, and *Gladstone*.

WHIP, the popular title of the patronage secretary of the treasury, whose duty it is to collect members to make a house on important occasions, &c. Sir Wm. Hayter, the liberal "whip," 1850-8, received a testimonial for his energetic services, early in 1861. The right hon. Wm. P. Adam, an able whip, died governor of Madras, 24 May, 1881. It is the duty of both conservative and liberal whips to promote the interest of their party in every conceivable way.
The management of the house of commons by bribery is said to have begun with Clifford of the " Cabal " ministry, and continued by Whigs and Tories. Mr. Roberts (under Henry Pelham), is said to have paid members sums of 1,000*l.*, 500*l.*, &c., to each at the close of a session for their support. *Wraxall*.

WHISKY, the spirit distilled from malt and other corn in Scotland and Ireland, of which about eight millions of gallons have been distilled annually in the former, and upwards of nine millions of gallons in the latter. The duty upon this article once produced annually about three millions. The distillation of whisky is referred to the 16th century; but some authors state it to have been earlier; see *Distillation*. In 1855 the duties on spirits distilled in Scotland and Ireland were equalised with those distilled in England. *Women's Whisky War*, see *United States*, 1874.

WHIST, a game at cards, became general at the end of the 17th century.

Edmund Hoyle, who published his "Short Treatise" about 1742, died in 1769, aged 97; lord Peterborough introduced short whist early in the present century; the laws were revised in 1864
" Whist," a poem 1791
Laws by "Cavendish," compiled . . . about 1861
James Clay, M.P., an eminent player, died 26 Sept. 1871

WHITBY, N.R. Yorkshire. The monastery here, under St. Hilda, founded by king Oswy, 657, destroyed by the Danes 876, was restored by William de Percy about 1100. The Cholmleys established alum works here in 1615. Whitby was made a borough in 1832, and absorbed into the county in 1885.

WHITEBAIT DINNER, when the cabinet ministers met at the end of each session, is said to have begun at the end of the last century, through sir Robert Preston and Mr. George Rose inviting Mr. Pitt and his colleagues to dine at Dagenham, and afterwards at Greenwich. Another account dates its origin in 1721. The annual whitebait dinner, stopped by the Gladstone ministry, was revived by the Disraeli ministry, 1 Aug. 1874, and continued by the Gladstone, 1 Sept. 1880. No dinner, 1884. The whitebait (*clupea alba*) is a subject of controversy. Albert Günther, of the British Museum, in his Catalogue of Fishes, says the whitebait is "a purely nominal species," and that all the examples which he has examined were young herrings (1868).

At the inquiry in June, 1878, James Henry Cannon, fisherman, claimed the discovery of the fish for his grandfather, Richard, who named it 1780. It was mentioned in a letter in the life of lord Malmesbury, 2 July, 1763.

WHITEBOYS, a body of ruffians in Ireland, so called on account of their wearing linen frocks over their coats. They committed dreadful outrages in 1761, but were suppressed by a military force, and their ringleaders executed in 1762. They rose and were again suppressed in 1786-7. The insurrection act was passed on their account in 1822.

WHITECHAPEL, a parish in East London, was part of Stepney till 1329. The church, built in 1673, was replaced by one consecrated 2 Feb. 1877, which was burnt 26 Aug. 1880.
New Loan Art exhibition opened . . 4 April, 1882

WHITECHAPEL MURDERS, &c. Henry Wainwright, a brushmaker, murdered Harriet Lane, his mistress, on his premises, 215, Whitechapel-road, and buried the body, Sept. 1874.

While conveying the mutilated remains to be concealed in his cellars in Southwark, Wainwright and Alice Day were apprehended, through the courage and activity of Alfred Philip Stokes, 11 Sept. Day was discharged; Henry and his brother Thomas were committed for trial 13 Oct. 1875
Nine days' trial before chief justice Cockburn; Henry convicted of murder; Thomas as accessory after the fact (seven years' penal servitude), 22 Nov.-1 Dec. ; Henry executed . . 21 Dec. 1875
1232l. subscribed for Henry's family.
30l. awarded to Stokes.
Much excitement was caused by the murder and brutal mutilation of four unfortunate women at different times—Smith, 3 April ; Tabran, 7 Aug. ; Nichols, 31 Aug. ; Chapman, 7, 8 Sept. Coroners return open verdict. The evidence showed the murderer possessed surgical knowledge, his object being to get possession of certain organs.
Two more women murdered in a similar manner near Commercial Road and Aldgate; E. Watts or Stride and C. Conway or Eddowes between 1 and 2 A.M. 30 Sept. The lord mayor offers 500l. reward in relation to the murder near Aldgate;

Mary Jane Kelly's body found dreadfully mutilated in 26, Dorset Street, Spitalfields 9 Nov. 1888
Rose Milett or Davis (?) strangled at Poplar 28 Dec. ,,
Alice McKenzie found with throat cut, &c., in Castle Alley, Whitechapel . . 17 July, 1889

WHITE CROSS ARMY, the shorter title of the Church of England Purity Society, established by Miss Ellice Hopkins, supported by the bishops of Durham and Lichfield and other prelates, highly successful at Oxford, Edinburgh, Liverpool, and other places, 1884.

WHITE DOVES, a South Russian religious sect, said to be wealthy and superstitious, strongly advocating celibacy: under a chief named Koudrine. Members were tried for moral offences about April, 1876.

WHITEFIELDITES. George Whitefield, the founder of the "*Calvinistic Methodists*," born 1714, was the son of an innkeeper at Gloucester, where he received his first education. He was admitted a servitor at Oxford in 1732, became a companion of the Wesleys there, and aided them in establishing Methodism. He parted from them in 1741, on account of their rejection of the doctrine of election. He was the most eloquent preacher of his day. His first sermon was preached in 1736, and he commenced field preaching in 1739. He is said to have delivered 18,000 sermons during his career of 34 years. He visited America in 1737, 1739, and 1744. His followers are termed "the countess of Huntingdon's connexion," from his having become her chaplain in 1748, and from her energetic support of the sect, by establishing a college at Trevecca, 1767. See *Spafields*. There were 109 chapels of this connexion in 1851; but many of his followers have joined the Independents. He died 30 Sept. 1770, and the countess died 17 June 1791; see *Tabernacle*.

WHITE FLAG, see *Flag*.

WHITE FRIARS, see *Carmelites* and *Sanctuaries*.

WHITEHALL (London), built by Hubert de Burgh, earl of Kent, before the middle of the 13th century. It afterwards devolved, by bequest, to the Black Friars of Holborn, who sold it to the archbishop of York, whence it received the name of York-place, and continued to be the town residence of the archbishops till taken by Henry VIII. from cardinal Wolsey, in 1530. At this period it became the residence of the court. Queen Elizabeth, who died at Richmond in 1603, was brought from thence to Whitehall, by water, in a grand procession. It was on this occasion, Camden informs us, that the following quaint panegyric on her majesty was written:—

"The queen was brought by water to Whitehall,
At every stroke the oars did *tears* let fall.
More clung about the barge: fish under water
Wept out their *eyes of pearl*, and swam blind after.
I think the bargemen might, with easier thighs,
Have rowed her thither in her people's eyes:
For howsoe'er thus much my thoughts have scann'd,
She had come by *water*, had she come by *land*."

Whitehall was partly burnt 9-10 April, 1691; totally destroyed by fire, 4 Jan. 1697-8, except the banqueting-house, which had been added to the palace of Whitehall by James I., according to a design of Inigo Jones, in 1619. In the front of Whitehall Charles I. was beheaded 30 Jan. 1649. George I. converted the hall into a chapel 1723-4. The exterior of this edifice underwent repair between 1829 and 1833.

WHITE HATS, a party in the Low Countries formed about 1377, against Louis, count of Flanders. The struggle lasted till 1384, when it was settled by Philip, duke of Burgundy.

WHITE HOODS, see *Catechumens.*

WHITE HORSE, see *Ashdown.*

WHITE HOUSE (Washington), built of freestone, the residence of the president, gives name to the United States government, as St. James's palace does to that of Great Britain.

WHITE LEAGUE, formed in Louisiana and other southern states of North America, to resist the aggressions of the emancipated negroes and their friends, termed "carpet-baggers." See *New Orleans,* 1874.

WHITE PASHA, see *Soudan,* July, 1888.

WHITE PLAINS (N. America), where a battle was fought 28 Oct. 1776, between the revolted Americans and the British forces under sir William Howe. It terminated in the defeat of the Americans, who suffered considerable loss in killed, wounded, and prisoners.

WHITE ROSE, ORDER OF THE, includes men and women of many shades of opinion, agreeing on one point, that all authority comes from above, utterly independent of the will of the people. They regard the revolution of 1688 as a national crime, and Jacobitism as true loyalty. The order has no religious test, its sole object being to maintain the doctrine of the divine right of kings, and revive public interest in the sufferings of the house of Stuart. (Feb. 1888.)

WHITE SHEEP, a name given to the Turcomans who conquered Persia about 1468, and persecuted the Shiites, but were expelled by Ismail, who founded the Sophi dynasty in 1501.

WHITE TOWER, the keep or citadel in the Tower of London, a large, square, irregular building, erected in 1070 by abbot Gundulph, afterwards bishop of Rochester. It measures 116 feet by 96, and is 92 feet in height: the walls, which are 11 feet thick, having a winding staircase continued along two of the sides, like that in Dover Castle. It contains an extensive armoury. Within this tower is the ancient chapel of St. John, originally used by the English monarchs. The turret at the N.E. angle, the highest of the four by which the White Tower is surmounted, was used for astronomical purposes by Flamsteed previously to the erection of the royal observatory at Greenwich.

WHITSUNTIDE, a festival appointed to commemorate the descent of the Holy Ghost upon the apostles: the newly-baptized persons, or catechumens, are said to have worn white garments on Whitsunday. This feast is movable, being always exactly seven weeks after Easter. Rogation week (*which see*) is the week before Whitsunday. Whitsunday 1889, 9 June; 1890, 25 May; 1891, 17 May; 1892, 5 June; 1893, 21 May.

Whitsunday, a Scotch quarter-day, is always on 15 May, as settled by an act of 1693, but local usage varies.

WHITTINGTON'S CHARITIES. Sir Richard Whittington, a citizen and mercer of London, served the office of lord mayor three times, the last in 1419. Many false stories are connected with his name, and his munificent charities are little known. He founded his college, dedicated to the Holy Ghost and the Virgin Mary, in 1424; and his almshouses in 1429; the latter, originally built in London, now stand on Highgate-hill (built 1808) near the supposed site of the supposed famous stone which commemorated the legend of his return to London, after leaving it in despair.

WHITWORTH (aftd. sir) Joseph Wh neer (born 21 Dec. in a letter to the first l March, 1868, offered to annual value of 100*l*. further instruction of United Kingdom, select their intelligence and p practice of mechanics a a view to the promotion cal industry in this cou that means might be fo industry into closer rel at present obtains here. the lords of the commit March, 1868. In 1875, to support these scholar

WHO ? WHO ? *Derby's,* earl of, Feb. 1

"WHOLE DUT ship doubtfully attri Frewen, and Sterne; t to Dorothy, lady Pac published, 1659. Lo some to John Ischam.

WICKLIFFITES Wickliffe (born 1324), university of Oxford an Leicestershire. He was tion of the English (among the first who o pope, transubstantiatio &c. Wickliffe, protect ward's son and Rich persecuted by the chur tyrdom by a paralytic death, 31 Dec. 1384, in of Constance, in 1414, d terred and burnt, whic Lincoln, and his dust 1415. Wickliffe's Eng was commenced in 138C printed at Oxford in 18 in 1882 to publish his his death celebrated in See *Lollards.*

WIDOWS. The J brother to marry his wid M.C.). For the burning tee. Among the nume for the relief of widow musicians, instituted in men, founded in 1739; 1788 : a law society, for tlemen, 1817; and a soc —WIDOWERS were tax duke, 12*l.* 10*s.*; lower mon person, 1*s.*; 7 Wi

WIEN, see *Vienna.*

WIFE, see *Wives.*

WIG, see *Peruke.*

WIGAN (Lancashi manded by the earl o driven out of the town forces under sir John S defeated by colonel Ash tions of Wigan to the g more by a greatly su colonel Lilburne, 1651. sir Thomas Tildesley, a

pillar was erected to his memory in 1679. The colliers in the neighbourhood struck, and acting riotously 17, 18 April, 1868, were quelled by the military. Arrangements were soon after made with he employers. The prince and princess of Wales it their visit, 4 June, 1873, opened a new hospital, &c., and received a hearty welcome. See *Railway decidents*, 2 Aug. 1873.

WIGHT, ISLE OF, the Roman *Vecta* or *Victis*, was conquered by Vespasian in the reign of Claudius. It was conquered by the Saxons under Cerdic about 530; by the Danes, 787, and in 1001, when they held it for several years. It was invaded by the French, July, 1377, and has several times suffered from invasion by them. In 1442, Henry VI. alienated the Isle to Henry de Beauchamp, first premier earl of England and then duke of Warwick, and afterwards crowned him king of the Isle of Wight, with his own hands; but dying without heirs male, his regal title died with him. and the lordship of the isle returned to the crown. Charles I., after his flight from Hampton-court, was a prisoner in Carisbrook castle, in 1647. In the time of Charles II. timber was very plentiful. In this isle is the queen's marine residence, Osborne-house.

Prince Henry of Battenberg appointed governor Jan. 1889, officially received 29 July.

WILD BIRDS' PROTECTION ACTS, passed 10 Aug. 1872, 24 July, 1876, and 7 Sept. 1880.

WILDERNESS BATTLES, see *United States*, May, 1864.

WILHELMSHAFEN, at Hippens, bay of Jahde, Oldenburg, the first German military port, was inaugurated by William, king of Prussia, 17 June, 1869. Since 1871 it has become the Chatham of Germany. By explosion of a gun on the *Mars*, 8 men killed and 20 injured, 27 April, 1881.

WILKES'S NUMBER, 45, see *North Briton*, and also *Warrants, General*.

WILLIAMS' LIBRARY, see *Libraries*.

WILLIS'S ROOMS, see *Almack's*.

WILLOW-LEAVES, see *Sun*.

WILLS AND TESTAMENTS are of very high antiquity, see *Genesis* xlviii. The private will of Sennacherib, king of Assyria, 680 B.C., found at Nineveh, is translated in *Records of the Past*, vol. I. Solon introduced them at Athens, 578 B.C. There are regulations respecting wills in the Koran. Trebatius Testa the civilian, introduced codicils to wills at Rome, 31 B.C. The power of bequeathing lands by the last will and testament of the owner was confirmed to English subjects 1 Henry I. 1100; but with great restrictions and limitations respecting the feudal system, which were taken off by the statute of 32 Hen. VIII. 1541. *Blackstone's Commentaries*. The first will of a sovereign on record is stated (but in error) to be that of Richard II. 1399; Edward the Confessor made a will. 1066. Various laws have regulated the wills and testaments of British subjects. All previous statutes were repealed by the "Wills Act," 1 Will. IV. & 1 Vict. c. 26, 1837, and the laws with relation to wills amended.* The present

PROBATE COURT (*which see*) was established in 1857. An office for the reception of the wills of living persons was opened in Jan. 1861. See *Thellusson's Will*. In 1869 twenty probates of wills or letters of administration were stamped for personal property, each exceeding a quarter of a million; one had a stamp of 21,000*l*. The Wills Office, removed from Doctors' Commons to Somerset House, was opened 24 Oct. 1874.

The will of Peter the Great, described in the "*Mémoires de la Chevalière d'Eon*," as a "plan for compassing European supremacy," left for his successors, and deposited in the archives of the palace of Peterhoff near St. Petersburg. It advocated "approach as near as possible to Constantinople, and towards the Indies: wars with Turkey and Persia; possession of the shores of the Black Sea, and the Baltic;" &c. The existence of the will (denied by the czars), was first announced by M. Lesur in his "*Progrès de la Puissance Russe*," published at Paris in 1812. In 1863, Dr. Berkholz of Riga asserted that the will was a forgery, probably dictated by Napoleon I. Mr. W. J. Thoms, the antiquary, and others, contend for the genuineness of the will, June, 1878.

EXTRACTS FROM THE LAST WILL OF NAPOLEON I., EMPEROR OF FRANCE.†

[He died 5 May, 1821, eleven days after he had signed these documents. The original in French occupies about twenty-six pages in Peignot's "Testamens Remarquables," 1829.]

"This day, 24 April, 1821, at Longwood, in the island of St. Helena. This is my testament, or act of my last will : . . . .

"I leave to the comte de Montholon 2,000,000 francs as a proof of my satisfaction for the attentions he has paid to me for these six years, and to indemnify him for the losses which my residence in St. Helena has occasioned him. I leave to the comte Bertrand 500,000 francs. I leave to Marchand, my first valet-de-chambre, 400,000 francs ; the services he has performed for me are those of a friend. I desire that he may marry a widow, sister, or daughter of an officer or soldier of my old guard. To St. Denis, 100,000 francs. To Novarre, 100,000 francs. To Pijeron, 100,000 francs. To Archambaud, 50,000 francs. To Cuvier, 50,000 francs. To Chandelle, idem.

"To the Abbé Vignali, 100,000 francs. I desire that he may build his house near Ponte Novo de Rossino. To the comte Las Casas, 100,000 francs. To comte Lavalette, 100,000 francs. To the surgeon-in-chief, Larrey, 100,000 francs. He is the most virtuous man I have known. To general Brayer, 100,000 francs.

"To general Lefevre Desnouettes, 100,000 francs. To general Drouet, 100,000 francs. To general Cambronne, 100,000 francs. To the children of general Mnton Duvernais, 100,000 francs. To the children of the brave Labédoyère, 100,000 francs. To the children of general Girard, killed at Ligny, 100,000 francs. To the children of general Chartrand, 100,000 francs. To the children of the virtuous general Travost, 100,000 francs. To general Lallemand, the elder, 100,000 francs. To general Clausel, 100,000 francs. To Costa Bastilica, also 100,000 francs. To the baron de Meneville, 100,000 francs. To Arnault, author of *Marius*, 100,000 francs.

"To colonel Marbot, 100,000 francs : I request him to continue to write for the defence and glory of the French armies, and to confound the calumniators and the apostates. To the baron Bignon, 100,000 francs : I request him to write the history of French Diplomacy from 1792 to 1815. To Poggi de Talaro, 100,000 francs. To the surgeon Emmery, 100,000.

"These sums shall be taken from the six millions which I deposited on leaving Paris in 1815, and from the interest at the rate of 5 *per cent*. since July, 1815; the

written legibly and intelligibly, and signed by the testator, or by his direction, in the presence of two or more witnesses, who also must sign. A married woman may bequeath only her pin money or separate maintenance, without the consent of her husband.

† These documents, dated from 15-24 April, deposited since 1821 in England, have been given up to the authorities at Paris, at the request of the French Government.

---

* By this act the testator must be above 21, not a lunatic or idiot, not deaf and dumb, not drunk at the time of signing, not an outlawed or unpardoned felon. All kinds of property may be devised. The will must be

account of which shall be adjusted with the bankers by the counts Montholon and Bertrand and by Marchand.

"These legacies, in case of death, shall be paid to the widows and children, and in their default, shall revert to the capital. I institute the counts Montholon, Bertrand, and Marchand my testamentary executors. This present testament, written entirely by my own hand, is signed and sealed with my arms.

"NAPOLEON.

"24 April, 1821, Longwood."

The following are part of the eight *Codicils* to the preceding will of the emperor:—

"On the liquidation of my civil list of Italy—such as money, jewels, plate, linen, coffers, caskets of which the viceroy is the depository, and which belong to me, I dispose of two millions, which I leave to my most faithful servants. I hope that without their showing any cause, my son Eugene Napoleon will discharge them faithfully. He cannot forget the forty millions which I have given him in Italy, or by the right (*parage*) of his mother's inheritance.

"From the funds remitted in gold to the empress Maria Louisa, my very dear and well-beloved spouse, at Orleans, in 1814, there remain due to me two millions, which I dispose of by the present codicil, in order to recompense my most faithful servants, whom I beside recommend to the protection of my dear Maria Louisa. I leave 200,000 francs to count Montholon, 100,000 francs of which he shall pay into the chest of the treasurer (Las Casas) for the same purpose as the above, to be employed according to my dispositions in legacies of conscience.

"10,000 francs to the sub-officer Cantillon (died July, 1869), who has undergone a prosecution, being accused of a desire to assassinate lord Wellington, of which he has been declared innocent. Cantillon had as much right to assassinate that oligarch, as the latter had to send me to perish on the rock of St. Helena," &c. &c. &c.

LETTER TO M. LAFITTE.

"MONSIEUR LAFITTE,—I remitted to you in 1815, at the moment of my departure from Paris, a sum of nearly six millions, for which you gave me a double receipt. I have cancelled one of these receipts, and I have charged comte de Montholon to present to you the other receipt, in order that you may, after my death, deliver to him the said sum with interest at the rate of five *per cent.*, from the 1st of July, 1815, deducting the payments with which you have been charged in virtue of my order. I have also remitted to you a box containing my medallion. I beg you will deliver it to comte Montholon.

"This letter having no other object, I pray God, Monsieur Lafitte, that He may have you in His holy and worthy keeping.

"NAPOLEON.

"Longwood, in the island of St. Helena, 25 April, 1821."

The following WILL OF NAPOLEON III. was published in the *Times*, 30 April, 1873:—

"April 24, 1865.

"This is my will. I commend my son and my wife to the high constituted authorities of the state (aux grands corps de l'Etat), to the people, and the army. The empress Eugénie possesses all the qualities requisite for conducting the regency well, and my son displays a disposition and judgment which will render him worthy of his high destinies. Let him never forget the motto of the head of our family, 'Everything for the French people.' Let him fix in his mind the writings of the prisoner of St. Helena; let him study the emperor's deeds and correspondence; finally, let him remember, when circumstances so permit, that the cause of the peoples is the cause of France. Power is a heavy burden, because one cannot always do all the good one could wish, and because your contemporaries seldom render you justice, so that, in order to fulfil one's mission, one must have faith in, and consciousness of, one's duty. It is necessary to consider that from heaven on high those whom you have loved regard and protect you; it is the soul of my illustrious uncle that has always inspired and sustained me. The like will apply to my son, for he will always be worthy of his name. I leave to the empress Eugénie all my private property. It is my desire that on the majority of my son she shall inhabit the Elysée and Biarritz. I trust that my memory will be dear to her, and that after my death she will forget the griefs I may have caused her. With regard to my son, let him keep as a talisman the seal I used and which comes from preserve everything th peror, my uncle, and let and my soul remain wit faithful servants. I am my son will never aba Catholic, Apostolic, anc will always honour by hi with my hand at the pa April, 1865.

The WILL OF PRINCI with his own hand, and before he sailed for So while on a reconnoitring that he dies in the Cat for his country, his mot and his gratitude to the land, and to the Englis tality. He constitutes h legacies and memorial Pietri, baron Corvisart assigns to Victor, the Jerome, the task of cor and Napoleon III. Exe

WILLUGHBY study of birds; foun Francis Willughby *thologia*, published i

WILMINGTO by the confederates; federals in Dec. 186 assault on 15 Jan., a by the confederates, :

WILMINGTO succeeded that of sir

Earl of Wilmington, *fir*
Lord Hardwicke, *lord*
Earl of Harrington, *pre*
Earl Gower, *lord privy*
Mr. Sandys, *chancellor*
Lord Carteret and the state.
Earl of Winchilsea, *firs*
Duke of Argyll, *comma*
of the ordnance.
Mr. Henry Pelham, *pa*
With several of the ho
[On lord Wilmingt ham became prime formed the "Broa Pelham.]

WILMOT'S AC (1840) relates to sch

WIMBLEDON of London. See *I'o*
Percy Malcolm John, died suddenly at his 1881; his brother-in son suspected of p 2 Dec.; was convic confessed his guilt

WINCHESTE city, whose erection the Celtic Britons, w It was made the ca dom under Cerdic, Egbert, 827; it be 879-991. In the re gan to rival-it; an houses by Henry V1 kings resided at Win were held there. ority exist in the nat of quantity, as Win &c., the use of whicl

WINCHESTER SCHOOL. 989 WINDSOR.

ial measures. The cathedral church was
ided and endowed by Cynegils, or Kene-
ie first Christian king of the West Saxons.
g ruinous, the present fabric was begun
p Walkelyn, the 34th bishop, 1073. The
as first dedicated to St. Amphibalus, then
:ter, and afterwards to St. Swithin, once
:re. Dedicated to the Holy Trinity by Henry
t. Birinus was the first bishop of the West
his seat Dorchester, 636; Wina, in 660,
first bishop of Winchester. The see is
i the king's books at 2793*l*. 4*s*. 2*d*. annually.
ncome, 6,500*l*.

the Danes, 871-3; ravaged by Sweyn	1013
tufus buried here	1100
of Holy Cross, founded by bishop Henry	
	1132
use of "Noble Poverty," engrafted on the	
ross by cardinal Beaufort, revived in 1883.	
er school, founded by bishop William of	
im 1382-7; the 500th anniversary of the	
if the first stone of New College, 26 March,	
:lebrated 26 March, 1887.	
er several times taken and re-taken, 1641-3;	
y Cromwell and the castle dismantled	1645
I. began a palace here by Wren	1683
e Society of Natives founded	1699
er Cross restored	1866
dhall opened by lord-chancellor Selborne,	
11 May,	1873
iversary of the incorporation of the city,	
ted . . . . 3, 4 July,	1884

CENT BISHOPS. (Prelates of the Order of
the Garter.)
)wnlow North, died 12 July, 1820.
)rge Pretyman Tomline, died 1827.
arles Richard Sumner, resigned 1869; died, 15
Aug. 1874.
nuel Wilberforce, elected Nov.; killed, through
the fall of his horse, 19 July, 1873.
ward Harold Browne, translated from Ely, Aug.

CHESTER SCHOOL, the oldest of our
chools, "Seinte Marie College of Wyn-
" the charter of which is dated Oct. 1382,
nded in 1387 by William (Long) of Wyke-
shop of Winchester, who had established a
here in 1373. The ancient statutes were
in 1855; and still further altered by the
Schools act of 1868. In Nov.-Dec. 1872 there
ich published correspondence respecting the
—the excessive punishment of the boys by
fects.

NDING-UP ACTS (to facilitate the
g up the affairs of joint-stock companies
ire unable to meet their engagements) were
in 1848, 1849, 1857, and 1862.

DMILLS are of great antiquity, and
:o be of Roman or Saracen invention. They
d to have been originally introduced into
by the knights of St. John, who took the
om what they had seen in the crusades.
Windmills were first known in Spain,
, and Germany, in 1299. *Anderson*. Wind
ills were invented by a Dutchman, in 1633;
ine was erected near the Strand, in London.

DOWS. There were glass windows in
ii, A.D. 79, as is evident from its ruins. It
ain that windows of some kind were glazed
y as the 3rd century, if not before, though
hion was not introduced until it was done by
et Biscop, about 650. Windows of glass
used in private houses, but the glass was im-
1177. *Anderson*. In England, in 1851,
5000 houses had fifty windows and upwards in
about 275,000 had ten windows and up-

wards; and 725,000 had seven windows, or less
than seven.
Window-tax first enacted in order to defray the
expense of and deficiency in the re-coinage of silver 1695
The tax increased, 5 Feb. 1746-7; again in 1778;
and again on the commutation-tax for ten 1 Oct. 1784
The tax again increased in . 1797, 1802, and 1808
Reduced 1823
The revenue derived from windows was in 1840
about a million and a quarter sterling; and in
1850 (to April 5), 1,832,684*l*.
The tax repealed by act 14 & 15 Vict. c. 36 (which
act imposed a duty upon inhabited houses in lieu
thereof) . . . . 24 July, 1851

WINDSOR (Berkshire). The *Castle*, a residence of the British sovereigns, begun by William
the Conqueror, and enlarged by Henry I. about
1110. Edward III., who was born here, 13 Nov.
1312, caused the old building, with the exception of
three towers at the west end, to be taken down, and
re-erected the whole castle, under the direction of
William of Wykeham, 1356, and built St. George's
chapel. He assessed every county in England to
send him workmen. James I. of Scotland was imprisoned here, 1406-23. Several additions were
made by Henry VIII. Elizabeth made the grand
north terrace; and Charles II. repaired and beautified it, 1676-80.

The chapel repaired and opened	Oct.	1790
The castle repaired and enlarged, 1824-8; George		
IV. took possession . . . . 8 Dec.		1828
Royal stables built		1839
A serious fire in the prince of Wales's tower, owing		
to some defect in the heating apparatus,		
19 March,		1853
Our sovereigns have here entertained many royal		
personages, as the emperor and empress of the		
French, in . . . . . April,		1855
Here died the prince consort . . 14 Dec.		1861
The Albert memorial chapel, on the site of Wolsey		
chapel, was opened . . . 30 Nov.		1875

Windsor Forest, situated to the south and west of
the town of Windsor, was formerly 120 miles in
circumference; in 1607, it was 77½ miles round,
but it has since been reduced in its bounds to
about 56 miles. It was surveyed in 1789, and found
to contain 59,600 acres.
Virginia Water and the plantations about it were
taken out of the forest.
The marshes were drained and the trees planted for
William, duke of Cumberland, about 1746: and
much was done by George IV., who often resided
at the lodge.
On the south side is Windsor Great Park; it contains about 3800 acres.
The Little Park, on the north and east sides of the
castle, contains about 500 acres. The gardens are
elegant, and have been considerably improved by
the addition of the house and gardens of the duke
of St. Albans, purchased by the crown.

Cumberland Lodge partially destroyed by fire; pic-		
tures burnt . . . . . 14 Nov.		1869
Albert Institute, Windsor, opened by the prince of		
Wales . . . . . . 10 Jan.		1880
About 52,000 volunteers reviewed by the queen,		
9 July,		1881
Jubilee fêtes and illuminations; the queen uncovers		
a statue of herself near the castle; torchlight		
procession of the Eton boys . . 22 June,		1887
The queen being here her 70th birthday is kept with		
great enthusiasm . . . . 24 May,		1889
Royal Agricultural Society to meet here; the queen		
president		"
The Royal Agricultural Society held its jubilee		
show, the greatest one of the kind in the century		
in Windsor Great Park . . 24-29 June,		"
The prince of Wales acted on behalf of the queen,		
who was president for the year; her majesty		
visited the show . . . . 27, 28 June,		"
The weather was very fine during the week, and the		
show was reported to be a great success in atten-		
dance and receipts.		
Mr. Jacob Wilson, the hon. director of the show,		
knighted . . . . . . 30 June,		"

[A fund was started at the Mansion House, London, in aid of the expenses 24 June; 5,516*l.* had been received up to 1 Aug.]

The royal pavilion with its decorations was presented to the queen by Mr. Charlton Humphreys and Messrs. Shoolbred and accepted about 29 June, 1889

WINDSOR KNIGHTS, see *Poor Knights*.

WINDWARD ISLES (West Indies)—Barbadoes, St. Vincent, Grenada, Tobago, and St. Lucia, (*which see*). Governor, Rawson W. Rawson, 1868; J. Pope Hennessy, Feb. 1875; capt. Strahan, Nov. 1876; sir Henry Bulwer, April, 1880; William Robinson, 1881; Walter J. Sendall, May, 1885.

WINE. "Noah planted a vineyard, and drank of the wine," 2347 B.C. (*Gen.* ix. 20); see *Vine*. Ching-Noung, emperor of China, is said to have made rice wine, 1998 B.C. Christ changed water into wine at the marriage of Cana in Galilee, A.D. 30. *John* ii. 3-10.

Wine sold in England by apothecaries as a cordial in 1300, and so continued for some time after, although there is mention of "wine for the king" so early as John.	
The price regulated by statute, 5 Richard II.	1381
The price was twelve shillings the pipe in	1400
A hundred and fifty butts and pipes condemned, for being adulterated, to be staved and emptied into the channels of the streets, by Rainwell, mayor of London. *Stow's Chron.*	1427
An act for licensing sellers of wine in England passed . . . . . 25 April,	1661
By the Methuen treaty, Portuguese wines were highly favoured, and French wines discouraged by heavy duties	1703
Wine duties to be 2*s*. 9*d*. per gallon on Cape wine, and 5*s*. 6*d*. on all other wines	1831
In year ending 31 March, 1856, the customs duties on wines produced 1,856,120*l*.; in 1858, 1,733,729*l*.; 1867, 1,391,192*l*.; 1876, 1,755,710*l*; 1884, 1,268,842*l*.	
By the French treaty of commerce, 1860, the duty on wines was reduced from 5*s*. 9*d*. to 2*s*. 6*d*. and 1*s*. according to the alcoholic strength . Jan.	1860
Licences granted to refreshment houses by an act passed in	"
The Oporto Wine Company (a monopoly), established in 1756, and abolished	1865
Commission on the wine duties appointed by the commons . . . . . April,	1879
The ancient duties on wine paid to the corporation on its entering the port of London 4*s*. 9½*d*. per tun of 252 gallons amounted to 8,488*l*. lost, in	1885
The abolition of these dues was discussed in 1889; the city dues on coal were abolished by parliament 8 July,	1889
Additional import duties on wine imposed by customs	1888

WINE IMPORTED INTO UNITED KINGDOM.

	Gallons.		Gallons.
1800	3,307,460	1870	17,774,782
1815	4,306,528	1871	18,224,900
1830	6,879,558	1875	18,429,305
1839	9,909,056	1876	19,950,723
1845	8,469,776	1879	15,162,857
1850	9,304,312	1880	17,385,496
1854	10,875,855	1881	16,297,033
1857	10,336,485	1882	15,715,813
1859	8,195,513	1883	15,559,795
1861	11,052,436	1884	15,106,271
1864	15,451,593	1885	14,629,739
1868	16,953,429	1886	14,552,864
1869	17,184,330	1887	15,383,641

WINNIPEG, capital of the province of Manitoba, Canada, has recently risen to great importance. The population, which was 215 in 1870, had risen to 20,238 in 1886. A period of depression from 1882 to 1884 has been followed by great prosperity, especially since the suppression of Riel's rebellion in 1885. See *Canada*.

WINTER. Recen 1873, 1876, 1881. See

WINTER ASSIZ (11 Aug. 1876), gives to unite counties for t for more speedy trials

WIRE. The in ascribed to Rodolph Mills for this purpose berg in 1563. The fir erected at Mortlake in

WIRTEMBERG,

WISCONSIN, a was organised as a ter into the union, 29 May 1,315,497. Capital, M

WISSEMBOURG France, in the depart situate on the right b boundary of France an formerly an imperial ci by Louis XIV. in 1673 the treaty of Ryswick, sembourg, erected by the Austrians and re after Hoche's victory 1870, the crown - prin Lauter and gained a over the French (a par storming the lines, and Douay was mortally w soners were made. T both sides appear to ha German army, compos and Würtembergers, w against about 10,000 F perate bravery.

WITCHCRAFT. xxii. 18), 1491 B.C., suffer a witch to live. condemning witchcraft Endor, 1056 B.C. (1 Sa "Discoverie of Witchcr published 1584. Repri inson's historical "Ess lished in 1718. Pope I against witchcraft in 14 persons were burnt, an applied.

Many Templars burnt at 1 Joan of Arc burnt at Rou About five hundred witc months, 1515. Many burnt in the dioce 1524. A great number in France confessed to having 120 Nine hundred burnt in L One hundred and fifty-se and young, learned and l Grandier, the parish pries of having bewitched a v In Bretagne, twenty poor v 1654. Disturbances commenced America, at Massachus raged dreadfully in Pen At Salem, in New Englan the Puritans) for witch fifty confessed themsel pardoned, 1692. Maria Renata burnt at Wu At Kalisk, in Poland, n having bewitched and belonging to that palati

Five women condemned to death by the Brahmins, at Patna, for sorcery, and executed, 15 Dec. 1802.

WITCHCRAFT IN ENGLAND.
A statute enacted declaring all witchcraft and sorcery to be felony without benefit of clergy. 33 Hen. VIII. 1541. Again, 5 Eliz. 1562, and 1 James I. 1603. The 73rd canon of the church prohibits the clergy from casting out devils, 1603.
Barrington estimates the judicial murders for witchcraft in England in 200 years at 30,000.
Matthew Hopkins, the "*witch-finder*," causes the judicial murder of about 100 persons in Essex, Norfolk, and Suffolk, 1645-7.
Sir Matthew Hale burnt two persons for witchcraft in 1664.
Seventeen or eighteen persons burnt at St. Osyths, in Essex, about 1676.
Two pretended witches were executed at Northampton in 1705, and five others seven years afterwards.
In 1716, Mrs. Hicks, and her daughter, aged nine, were hanged at Huntingdon.
Northamptonshire and Huntingdon preserved the superstition about witchcraft later than other counties.
In Scotland, thousands of persons were burnt in the period of about a hundred years. Among the victims were persons of the highest rank, while all orders in the state concurred. James I. even caused a whole assize to be prosecuted for an acquittal. The king published his *Dæmonologie* in Edinburgh, 1597. The last sufferer in Scotland was at Dornoch in 1722.
The laws against witchcraft had lain dormant for many years, when an ignorant person attempting to revive them (by finding a bill against a poor old woman in Surrey for the practice of witchcraft), they were *repealed*, 10 Geo. II. 1736.
Credulity in witchcraft still abounds in the country districts of England. On 4 Sept. 1863, a poor old paralysed Frenchman died in consequence of having been ducked as a wizard at Castle Hedingham, Essex, and similar cases have since occurred.
Ann Turner, old ; killed as a witch by a half-insane man at Long Compton, Warwickshire, 17 Sept. 1875.

WITENA-MOT or **WITENA-GEMOT**, the assembling of the wise men, the great council of the Anglo-Saxons. A witena-mot was called in Winchester by Egbert, 800, and in London, 833, to consult on the proper means to repel the Danes ; see *Parliament*.

WITEPSK (in Russia), where a battle was fought between the French under marshal Victor, duke of Belluno, and the Russians commanded by general Wittgenstein. The French were defeated after a desperate engagement, with the loss of about 3000 men on both sides, 14 Nov. 1812.

WITNESSES. Two or more witnesses were required by the law of Moses, 1451 B.C. (*Deut.* xvii. 6), and by the early Christian Church in cases of discipline (2 *Cor.* xiii. 1), A.D. 60. The evidence of two witnesses required to attaint for high treason, 25 Edw. III. 1352. In civil actions between party and party, if a man be subpœnaed as a witness on a trial, he must appear in court on pain of 100*l*. to be forfeited to the king, and 10*l*., together with the damages equivalent to the loss sustained by the want of his evidence to the party aggrieved. Lord Ellenborough ruled that no witness is obliged to answer questions which may tend to degrade himself, 10 Dec. 1802. New act relating to the examination of witnesses passed 13 Geo. III. 1773. Act to enable courts of law to order the examination of witnesses upon interrogations and otherwise, 1 Will. IV. 30 March, 1831.

WIVES, see *Marriage*. By the Divorce and Matrimonial Causes Act, passed in 1857, the condition of married women has been much benefited. When ill-used they can obtain a divorce or judicial separation ; and while in the latter state any property they may acquire is secured to them personally, as if unmarried. By another act passed in 1857, they are enabled to dispose of reversionary interests in personal property or estates. An act to amend the law relating to the property of married women was passed 9 Aug. 1870. By it the separate earnings of a wife were secured to her own use, as well as personal and freehold property bequeathed to her. She may maintain an action at law, and acquires other rights. The husband is declared not liable for debts contracted by his wife prior to marriage, and she may be sued for them. This act was amended in 1874. Husband and wife may be jointly sued for her debts before marriage. By the Matrimonial Causes Act, 1878, a magistrate can grant judicial separation, with maintenance, to a wife suffering from her husband's ill-usage.
House of lords decide that the husband is not responsible for his wife's debts if he allow sufficient for dress, &c. *Debenham v. Mellon* . 27 Nov. 1880
Married Women's Property Act, 45 & 46 Vict. c. 75, passed 18 Aug. 1882, making their powers almost equal to those of single women, and increasing their responsibilities in regard to debt, &c., came into effect . . . . . 1 Jan. 1883
Provision made for deserted wives made by Act passed in 1886

WIVES' POISON or **WATER TOFANA,** see *Poisoning*.

WIZARD : WIZARD OF THE NORTH, a name given to sir Walter Scott, on account of his romances ; also to Mr. Anderson, the conjurer, who died 3 Feb. 1874, see *Covent Garden.*
Robert - Houdin's *Confidences d'un Prestidigitateur* published in 1859.
Herr Hermann, an eminent rich beneficent conjurer or prestidigitateur, died at Carlsbad aged 71, June, 1887. See *Automaton Figures.*
The feats of Maskelyne and Cooke in recent years are well known.

WŒRTH SUR SAUER, a town in the department of the Lower Rhine, N.E. France. After storming Wissembourg (*which see*) on 4 Aug. 1870, the crown-prince of Prussia, with the 3rd army (about 150,000) marched rapidly forward and surprised part of the French army under Marshal MacMahon, including the corps of Canrobert and part of that of Failly (about 47,000), and defeated it in a long, desperate, and sanguinary engagement near this place 6 Aug. The battle lasted from 9 a.m. till 4 p.m. The chief struggles occurred in the country round Reichshoffen and in the village of Fræschweiller ; the French are said to have charged the German line eleven times, each time breaking it, but always finding a fresh mass behind. The ridge on which Wœrth stands was not captured until the French were taken in flank by the Bavarians and Würtembergers. Nearly all MacMahon's staff were killed, and the marshal himself, unhorsed, fell fainting into a ditch, from which he was rescued by a soldier. He then, on foot, directed the retreat towards Saverne, to cover the passes of the Vosges. The victory is attributed to the very great numerical superiority of the Germans as well as to their excellent strategy. The French loss has been estimated at 5000 killed and wounded, and 5,000 prisoners, 2 eagles, 6 mitrailleuses, 35 cannon, and much baggage. The Germans are stated to have had above 8000 men put *hors de combat.* It was admitted that MacMahon had acted as an able and brave commander.

WOLVERHAMPTON (Staffordshire), an old town formerly named Hamton ; owes its present name to the foundation of a college here by Wulfruna, sister of king Edgar, and widow of Aldhelm, duke of Northampton, 996. The queen

was present at the inauguration of the prince consort's statue here, 30 Nov. 1866, and the church congress was opened here 1 Oct. 1867. Wolverhampton is eminent for its manufactures in metal. Statue of hon. C. P. Villiers (its M.P., 1835-85) was uncovered, 6 June, 1879; jubilee celebrated 10 Jan. 1885.
Wolverhampton returns three M.P.'s by act passed 25 June, 1885.

WOLVES were once very numerous in England. Their heads were demanded as a tribute, particularly 300 yearly from Wales, by king Edgar, 961, by which step they were falsely said to be totally destroyed. *Carte.* Edward I. issued his mandate for the destruction of wolves in several counties of England, 1289. Ireland was infested by wolves for many centuries after their extirpation in England; for there are accounts of some being found there so late as 1710, when the last presentment for killing wolves was made in the county of Cork. Wolves still infest France, in which kingdom 8384 wolves and cubs were killed in 1828-9. They were troublesome in the Vosges, Oct. 1875. 701 wolves killed in France in 1887.

WOMEN. The employment of women is regulated by the *Factory and Workshop Regulation Acts* (which see).
(See *Degrees, Female Medical School, Jubilee, Marriage,* and *Wives.*)
Mary Wollstonecraft's Vindication of the Rights of Women, published 1791
Great advances in the legal rights, position, and employment of women 1837-89
Women's hospitals founded: Soho 1842
J. S. Mill's Subjection of Women, published . . 1869
Female medical society and obstetrical college founded . . . . about 1864
Female suffrage for members of parliament was proposed by J. S. Mill, and negatived by 196 against 73 . . . . 20 May, 1867
Lily Maxwell, a shopkeeper at Manchester, voted for Jacob Bright . . . . . . 26 Nov. ,,
First annual meeting of the Manchester national society for women's suffrage . . . 30 Oct. 1868
Female suffrage decided to be illegal, by the court of common pleas . . . . 7, 9 Nov. 1868
Women's Club and Institute, Newman-street, London, W. opened . . . . . Jan. 1869
Women's Disabilities removal bill rejected by the commons (220 to 94) 12 May, 1870; (222-143) 1 May, 1872; (223-155) 30 April, 1873; withdrawn, 1874; (187-152) 7 April, 1875; (239-152) 26 April, 1876; hustled out, 6 June, 1877; (219-140) 19 June, 1878; (217-103) 7 March, 1879; (130-114) 6 July, 1883
Miss Garrett and Miss Davies elected members of the metropolitan school-board . . 29 Nov. 1873
Medical school for women opened (see *Physic*) Oct. 1874
Women's Protective and Provident League founded by Mrs. Paterson and others, Great Queen Street, (out of this has arisen several independent trades unions, book-binders, upholsterers, &c.) . . 1874
Miss Merington elected guardian of the poor for Kensington (the first case in London) . April, 1876
Women's Whisky War, see *United States,* 1874.
Women permitted to be registered under "Medical Act," by 39 & 40 Vict. c. 41 . . . . 11 Aug. ,,
Women's Education Union, president, the princess Louise, founded at the Society of Arts, in 1871, to promote the better education of women; said to be languishing in . . . . Oct. 1877
University of London: senate vote for granting degrees to women, 28 Feb.; convocation vote against it, 8 May, and July 1877; vote for a supplemental charter granting it (242-132), 15 Jan.; charter granted . . . . 28 March, 1878
Great meeting for female suffrage; St. James's Hall, 6 May, 1880
Women excluded from government employment in the United States, by order . about 27 Dec. 1881
Women to be admitted to examinations for honours at Oxford; by statute . . . 29 April, 1884
Female householders' suffrage (widows and spinsters), proposed by Mr. Woodall in the commons, 10 June; negatived (271-135) 12-13 June; in consequence Miss H. Müller refuses to pay queen's taxes, and her goods are distrained . 2 July, 1884
Women's suffrage bill; lords read 1st time, 3 July; negatived 10 July, 1884; again 28 July, 1885; read second time commons 18-19 Feb.; blocked March; negatived by the lords 16 March, 1886; again 13 Sept. 1887; 13 April, 1888; and 18 March, 1889
Female suffrage granted in Madras presidency announced 28 Sept. 1885
Enactments for the protection of women and girls formed part of the Criminal Law Amendment Act passed . . . . . . 14 Aug. ,,
Women's Suffrage Society annual meeting July, 1886
Many women's liberal associations (Unionist and Gladstonian) formed 1886-89
Miss A. F. Ramsay, of Girton, and Miss B. M. Hervey, of Newnham, obtain high university honours (see *Cambridge*) . . 18 June, 1887
International "council of women," advocating women's rights met at Washington, U.S. 25 March, 1888; a similar congress met at Paris 25 June, 1889
Women's hospital with female practitioners begun in Marylebone 1871; the new building in Euston Road founded by the princess of Wales 7 May, ,,
Mrs. Scharlieb made M.D. . . . . 16 May, ,,
Two ladies elected for the London County Council; this declared illegal, a bill to legalise it rejected by the lords . . . . . 20 May, ,,

WONDERS OF THE WORLD. 1. The pyramids of Egypt. 2. The mausoleum or tomb built for Mausolus, king of Caria, by Artemisia, his queen. 3. The temple of Diana, at Ephesus. 4. The walls and hanging gardens of the city of Babylon. 5. The vast brazen image of the sun at Rhodes, called the Colossus. 6. The ivory and gold statue of Jupiter Olympus. 7. The pharos or watch-tower, built by Ptolemy Philadelphus, king of Egypt; see *separate articles.*

WOOD-CUTS, see *Engraving on Wood.*

WOODITE, a combination of india-rubber, cork, and other substances for the coating of lifeboats and other vessels to defend them against collision and attacks of guns, &c.; invented by Mrs. A. M. Wood, recommended by sir E. J. Reed, July, 1886.

WOODS, FORESTS, &c., see *Forests.* The board of woods, forests, and land revenues was constituted in 1810. The oversight of works and public buildings was added to its duties in 1832, but transferred to a separate board of commissioners in 1851. In 1874 the annual revenue of the crown woods and forests was 487,695*l.*; 1882-3, 380,000*l.*, 1886, 492,624*l.*

WOOD'S HALF-PENCE, for circulation in Ireland and America, were coined by virtue of a patent, passed 1722. Against them, Dr. Jonathan Swift, by his letters signed M. B. Drapier published about 1723, raised such a spirit of opposition that the patent was withdrawn. Wood received a compensation, but was virtually banished the kingdom. The half-pence were assayed in England by sir Isaac Newton, and proved to be genuine, in 1724.

WOODHALL SPA, Lincolnshire, celebrated for mineral waters, especially containing iodine. On 22 May, 1888, Mr. E. Stanhope, M.P., sir Richard Webster, M.P., and others, inspected the pump-room, baths, hotel, and other buildings recently erected to promote the use of the waters by all classes of invalids.

WOOD PAVEMENT was laid down at Whitehall in 1839; and in Oxford-street, the Strand, and other streets. The principal part was soon taken up. In Nov. 1872, the improved wood pavement company put forth a prospectus; and

in May, 1876, wood had been largely laid down, and was said to be the best pavement in London.

Oxford-street was paved by Henson's street paving company, with a compound of wood, asphalt, felt, and Portland cement in 1876; with wood, 1878. Bond-street and many other streets paved with wood, 1879-81.

WOODSTOCK (Oxfordshire). In Woodstock, now Blenheim-park, originally stood a royal palace, in which king Ethelred held a parliament, and Alfred the Great translated *Boethius de Consolatione Philosophiæ*, 888. Henry I. beautified the palace; and here resided Rosamond, mistress of Henry II. 1154. In it were born Edmund, second son of Edward I., 1301, and Edward, eldest son of Edward III., 1330; and here the princess Elizabeth was confined by her sister Mary, 1554. A splendid mansion, built at the expense of the nation, for the duke of Marlborough, was erected here to commemorate his victory at Blenheim in 1704. At that time every trace of the ancient edifice was removed, and two elms were planted on its site; see *Blenheim*. Scott's romance, "Woodstock," was published, June, 1826. Marshall's "History of Woodstock," 1873.

WOOL. From the earliest times to the reign of queen Elizabeth the wool of Great Britain was not only superior to that of Spain, but accounted the finest in the universe; and even in the times of the Romans a manufacture of woollen cloths was established at Winchester for the use of the emperors. *Anderson.* In later times wool was manufactured in England, and is mentioned 1185, but not in any quantity until 1331, when the weaving of it was introduced by John Kempe and other artisans from Flanders. This was the real origin of our now unrivalled manufacture, 6 Edw. III. 1331. *Rymer's Fœdera.*

Duties on exported wool were levied by Edw. I.	1275
The exportation prohibited	1337
Staples of wool established in Ireland, at Dublin, Waterford, Cork, and Drogheda, 18 Edw. III.	1343
Sheep were first permitted to be sent to Spain, which has since injured our manufacture. *Stow.*	1467
First legislative prohibition of the export of wool from Ireland	1521
The exportation of English wool, and the importation of Irish wool into England, prohibited	1696
The export forbidden by act passed	1718
Bill to prevent the running of wool from Ireland to France	1738
The duty on wool imported from Ireland taken off	1739
Woolcombers' act, 35 Geo. III.	1794
The non-exportation law was repealed, 5 Geo. IV.	1824

In 1851 we imported 83,311,975 ℔. of wool and alpaca; in 1856, 116,211,392 ℔.; in 1859, 133,284,634 ℔.; in 1861, 147,172,841 ℔.; in 1864, 206,473,645 ℔.; in 1866, 239,358,689 ℔.; in 1871, 323,036,999 ℔.; in 1875, 365,065,578 ℔.; in 1877, 409,949,198 ℔.; in 1879, 417,110,099 ℔.; in 1881, 450,141,735 ℔.; in 1883, 495,946,779 ℔.; in 1887, 577,924,661 ℔.

Re-imported from Australia, in 1842, 12,979,856 ℔.; in 1856, 56,052,139 ℔.; in 1861, 68,506,222 ℔.; in 1866, 113,773,694 ℔.; in 1871, 182,710,567 ℔.; in 1875, 238,631,824 ℔.; in 1877, 281,247,190 ℔.; in 1879, 287,831,804 ℔.; in 1881, 329,665,855 ℔.; in

Cæsar, and are familiarly alluded to by him; see *Wearing.*

The Jews were forbidden to wear garments of woollen and linen together . . . . B.C.	1451
70 families of cloth-workers (from the Netherlands) settled in England by Edward III. *Rymer.* A.D.	1331
Worsted manufacture in Norfolk	1340
A kind of blankets were first made in England. (*Camden*)	about ,,
Woollens made at Kendal	1390
No cloth but of Wales or Ireland to be imported into England	1463
Medleys, or mixed broad-cloth, first made	1614
Manufacture of fine cloth began at Sedan, in France, under the patronage of Cardinal Mazarine .	1646
Broadcloth first dressed and dyed in England, by Brewer, from the Low Countries	1667
British and Irish woollens prohibited in France	1677
All persons obliged to be buried in woollens, and the persons directing the burial otherwise to forfeit 5*l.*, 29 Charles II.	1678
The manufacture of cloth greatly improved in England by Flemish settlers	1688
Injudiciously restrained in Ireland, 11 Will. III.	1698
The exportation from Ireland wholly prohibited, except to certain ports of England	1701
English manufacture encouraged by 10 Anne, 1712, and 2 Geo. I.	1715
Greater in Yorkshire in 1785 than in all England at the revolution. *Chalmers.*	
Value of woollen manufactures of all kinds exported in 1847, 6,896,038*l.*; in 1854, 9,120,759*l.*; in 1861, 11,118,692*l.*; in 1864, 18,569,089*l.*; in 1871, 2^,182,385*l.*; in 1875, 21,659,325*l.*; in 1877, 17,343,203*l.*; in 1879, 15,861,166*l.*; in 1881, 18,128,756*l.*; in 1883, 18,315,575*l.*; in 1887, 20,594,962*l.*	
International Woollen Exhibition at the Crystal Palace, Sydenham, opened by the duke of Connaught	2 June, 1881
Association for the encouragement of British woollen manufactures founded by the countess of Bective and about 200 other ladies	

WOOLSACK, the seat of the lord high chancellor of England in the house of lords, so called from its being a large square bag of wool, without back or arms, covered with red cloth. Wool was the staple commodity of England in the reign of Edward III., when the woolsack first came into use.

WOOLWICH (Kent), the most ancient military and naval arsenal in England. Its royal dockyard, where men-of-war were built in the reign of Henry VIII., was closed, 1 Oct. 1869. Here *Harry Grâce de Dieu* was built, 1512; and here she was burnt in 1552. The royal arsenal was formed about 1720, on the site of a rabbit-warren; it contains vast magazines of great guns, mortars, bombs, powder, and other warlike stores; a foundry, with many furnaces, for casting ordnance; and a great laboratory, where fireworks, cartridges, grenades, &c., are made for the public service. The Royal Military Academy was erected in the royal arsenal, but the institution was not completely formed until 19 Geo. II. 1745. Woolwich returns one M.P., by act of 1885.

The arsenal, storehouses, &c., burnt (loss of 200,000*l.*)
20 May, 1802

Free steam-ferry (between North and South Woolwich) inaugurated in great state by lord Rosebery 23 March, 1889

(*Woolwich Infant*, see *Cannon*, 1872.)

WORCESTER, successively an important British, Roman, and Saxon town, was burnt by the Danes (1041) for resisting the tribute called Danegelt. William I. built a castle, 1090. The city was frequently taken and retaken during the civil wars of the middle ages, and by Cromwell in 1651.—The BISHOPRIC was founded by Ethelred, king of the Mercians, 680, and taken from the see of Lichfield, of which it composed a part. The married priests of the cathedral were displaced, and monks settled in their stead, 964. The church was rebuilt by Wolstan, 25th bishop, 1030. The see has yielded to the church of Rome four saints, and to the English nation five lord chancellors and three lord treasurers. It is valued in the king's books at 1049*l*. 16*s*. 3¼*d*. per annum. Present income, 5000*l*.

The renovated cathedral opened . . 8 April, 1874
Much excitement through the refusal of the dean and chapter to permit the cathedral to be used as a concert room for the three choirs festival
Oct.-Nov. ,,
The festival held as strictly religious services
22, 23 Sept. 1875

RECENT BISHOPS.

1781. Richard Hurd, died 28 May, 1808.
1808. Folliott H. Cornwall, died 5 Sept. 1831.
1831. Robert James Carr, died 24 April, 1841.
1841. Henry Pepys, died 13 Nov. 1860.
1860. Henry Philpott (PRESENT bishop).

WORCESTER, BATTLE OF, 3 Sept. 1651, when the Scots army which came to England to reinstate Charles II. was defeated by Cromwell, who called it his *crowning mercy*. Charles with difficulty escaped to France. More than 2000 of the royalists were slain, and of 8000 prisoners most were sold as slaves to the American colonists; see *Boscobel*.

WORDSWORTH SOCIETY, formed "as a bond of union among those who are in sympathy with the general teaching and spirit of Wordsworth" and "to promote and extend the study of the poet's works," &c., was inaugurated at Grasmere, Westmoreland, 30 Sept. 1880. First President, Dr. Charles Wordsworth, bishop of St. Andrews. The society dissolved 7 July, 1886.

WORKHOUSES, see under *Poor*.

WORKING MEN. Since the great Exhibition of 1851, much has been done to benefit the labouring classes by organisation. See *Artisan*.

Working Men's Clubs considered to have begun with the Working Men's Mutual Improvement and Recreation Society, established in Lancaster by the instrumentality of the rev. H. Solly in . . 1860
The Westminster Working Men's Club, in Duck-lane, originated with Miss Adeline Cooper; opened in
Dec. ,,
The Working Men's Club and Institute Union established by lord Brougham and others, 4 June, 1862
The Working Men's Club and Lodging-house, Old Pye-street, Westminster, was opened 20 April, 1866
Working Men's Colleges, &c. The first, established in Sheffield, by working-men. The second, in London, by the rev. professor Frederick D. Maurice, as principal, in Oct. 1854 (died 1 April, 1872); a third in Cambridge; and, in 1855, a fourth at Oxford; all wholly for the working classes, and undertaking to impart such knowledge as each man feels he is most in want of. The colleges engage to find a teacher wherever 10 or 12 members agree to form a class, and also to have lectures given. There were eleven classes at the one in Bloomsbury, London, in 1856; Mr. Ruskin gave lessons in drawing. Some of these colleges have been found to be self-supporting.
A Working Women's College, begun at Queen's-square, Bloomsbury 1864
The two colleges amalgamated as the "New College for men and women," inaugural meeting 12 Oct. 1874
Working Women's College, Fitzroy-street, inaugurated . . . . . . 16 Oct. ,,
Act to establish councils of conciliation, to adjust differences between masters and workmen, passed
20 Aug. 1867
The Arbitration (Masters and Workmen) Act passed
6 Aug. 1872
Working Men's College, for South London, opened with a lecture by professor Huxley . 4 Jan. 1868
Workmen's International Exhibition proposed by the duke of Argyll, lord Elcho, and others, March, 1868; meeting for arrangements, 10 Jan. 1870, held in the Agricultural Hall, Islington (16 classes and a fine art department); opened by the prince of Wales, 16 July ; closed by Mr. Gladstone . . . . 31 Oct. 1870
National trades societies congress meet at Manchester, 1868; at Birmingham . . Aug. 1869
Demonstration of working men in Hyde park against certain clauses relating to masters and servants in the Criminal Law Amendment Act,
2 June, 1873
International Working Men's Association (termed the *International*) owes its origin to some German socialists in London, 1847, and was much promoted by the foreign visitors to the great exhibition in 1862. It was definitely organised, 28 Sept. 1864, George Odger first president. Its professed object is the complete emancipation of labour from the tyranny of capitalists. It has held congresses at Geneva, Sept. 1866; Lausanne, Sept. 1867; Brussels, 6-13 Sept. 1868; Basel, 6-11 Sept. 1869; Barcelona, June, 1870; at the Hague, when great dissensions arose between the "authoritarians," who consider a government needful, and the "anarchists," who deny it. One party including the council seceded from the trade portion, and adjourned to New York, 3-10 Sept. 1871
Four of its members were elected into the French national assembly . . . . Feb. 1871
The association took part in the communist insurrection at Paris . . . . . . Dec. ,,
It made a demonstration at New York . 18 Mar. 1872
It is said to have about 2,500,000 members in all countries, and to be allied with several secret societies, such as Fenians, the Mary Anne, &c.
A proposal from Spain that European governments should combine for its suppression, 9 Feb., was declined by Great Britain, 8 March. It was proscribed in France by the national assembly,
14 March, ,,
The British section met at McQueen's club-house, Parliament-street . . . . 21 July, ,,
One party took the name of International Association, and held annual congresses: Geneva, Sept. 1873; Brussels, 7 Sept. 1874; Berne, 1876; Verviers, 7 Sept. 1877. A congress of socialists met at Ghent (partly united the two divisions), Sept. 1877
International congress Paris assembled 2-12 Sept. ,,
Report of an alliance between conservative peers and the working men for the improvement of the condition of the latter, about 15 Oct. ; explained by Mr. Scott Russell (*Times*, 14 Nov. 1871), who issued a programme . . . . Jan. 1872
Workmen's Peace Association held its first annual meeting in London . . . . 20 Sept. 1871
A "Workman's city," Shaftesbury Park, Clapham, was inaugurated by the earl of Shaftesbury
3 Nov. 1872
Annual trade congress at Sheffield . 12-17 Jan. 1874
Alex. Macdonald and Thos. Burt, working-men, elected M.P.'s for Stafford and Morpeth . Feb. ,,
Royal commission on labour laws appointed (chief justice Cockburn, lord Winmarleigh, Messrs. Roebuck, T. Hughes, Alex. Macdonald and others) . . . . . March, ,,
Dwellings of working classes protected from railway bills by new standing orders . 30 July, ,,
Employers and Workmen Act passed . 13 Aug. 1875
Annual trade congress at Glasgow . 11-16 Oct. ,,
Church of England Working Men's Society founded at St. Alban's, Holborn . . . 5 Aug. 1877

Working-Lads' Institutes, London; meeting at the Mansion House to found them, 27 Oct.; first institute opened at Whitechapel . . 14 Nov. 1876
Workmen's Social Education League, founded June, 1879; professor J. R. Seeley, president, announced . . . . 10 June, 1879
Employers' Liability Act (to compensate workmen for injuries) passed . . . . . 7 Sept. 1880
International conference of workmen at Paris closes . . . . 29 Oct. 1883
International trades union congress at Paris; main objects, shorter hours, safety and comfort; British, most moderate 29 Oct. *et seq.* 1883; again 23 Aug. 1886; London, (79 English and 44 foreign delegates) . . . . 6 Nov. 1888
Workmen, &c., of the United Kingdom, about 9,000,000; average wages each 19*l.* per annum (1835); about 13,000,000, average wages each nearly 42*l.* per annum (1885). *R. Giffen*. . 19 Jan. 1886
Working Men's Jubilee Festival held at the Crystal Palace . . . . 25 June, 1878
Accounts of a new *International* formed to replace the old one, which had gradually disappeared, were published in the autumn of 1888. It was stated to have branches in the United States, and in various cities in Europe.
The German parliament, influenced by prince Bismarck, passed bills to compel the working classes, with the assistance of their employers and the state, to provide for sickness (1883), for accidents (1884), for old age and infirmity 24 May, 1889
International congress of workers at Paris 14 July, *et seq.* ,,
See *Co-operative Societies, Employers,* and *Trades-Unions.*

WORKS AND PUBLIC BUILDINGS, see *Woods.*

WORKSHOPS, see *Ateliers* and *Factories.*

WORKSHOP REGULATION ACT, supplement to Factory Acts, passed 21 Aug. 1867; amended, 1871.

WORLD, see *Creation,* and *Globe.* WORLD weekly newspaper began 8 July, 1874.

WORMS, a city on the Rhine, in Hesse-Darmstadt. The Roman city, Borbetomagus, was plundered by the Alemanni, 354, and by Attila, 451; rebuilt by Clovis I. about 475. Here Charlemagne resided in 806 B.C. Here was held the imperial diet before which Martin Luther was summoned, 4 April, 1521, and by which he was proscribed. Luther was met by 2000 persons on foot and on horseback, at the distance of a league from Worms. When Spalatin sent to warn him of his danger, he answered, "If there were as many devils in Worms as there are tiles upon the roofs of its houses, I would go on." He appeared before the emperor, the archduke Ferdinand, six electors, twenty-four dukes, seven margraves, thirty bishops and prelates, and many princes, counts, lords, and ambassadors, 17 April; acknowledged his writings and opinions, and left Worms, in fact, a conqueror. Yet, to save his life, he had to remain in seclusion under the protection of the elector of Saxony for about a year. The *edict* putting him under the ban of the empire was issued 26 May, 1521. Worms was burnt, by order of Louis XIV., 1689, the cathedral excepted; and was taken by the French, under Custine, 4 Oct. 1792. A memorial statue of Luther at Worms was uncovered, 25 June, 1868, in the presence of the king of Prussia and other sovereigns.

WORSHIP. The first worship mentioned is that of Abel, 3872 B.C. (*Gen.* iv.) "Men began to call on the name of the Lord," 3769 B.C. (*Gen.* iv.) The Jewish order of worship was set up by Moses, 1490 B.C. Solomon consecrated the temple, 1004 B.C. To the corruptions of the simple worship of the patriarchs all the Egyptian and Greek idolatries owed their origin. Athotes, son of Menes, king of Upper Egypt, is supposed to be the *Copt* of the Egyptians, and the *Tuth,* or *Hermes,* of the Greeks, the *Mercury* of the Latins, and the *Teutates* of the Celts or Gauls, 2112 B.C. *Usher.*

WORSHIP IN ENGLAND. The Druids were the priests here, at the invasion of the Romans (55 B.C.), who eventually introduced Christianity, which was almost extirpated by the victorious Saxons (455), who were pagans. The Roman catholic form of Christianity was introduced by Augustine, 596, and continued till the Reformation (*which see*). See *Hymns, Liturgies, Prayers, Public Worship, Ritualists.*

PLACES OF WORSHIP IN ENGLAND AND WALES IN 1851.

	Places of Worship.	Sittings.
Church of England	14,077	5,317,915
Wesleyan Methodists	6,579	2,194,298
Independents	3,244	1,067,760
Baptists	2,789	752,343
Roman Catholics	570	186,111
Society of Friends	371	91,559
Unitarians	229	68,554
Scottish Presbyterians	160	86,692
Latter day Saints (*Mormonites*)	222	30,783
Brethren (Plymouth)	132 (?)	18,529
Jews	53	8,438
New Church (Swedenborgians)	50	12,107
Moravians	32	9,305
Catholic and Apostolic Church (Irvingites)	32	7,437
Greek Church	3	291
Countess of Huntingdon's Connexion	109	35,210
Welsh Calvinistic Methodists	828	198,242
Various small bodies, some without names	546	105,557

June, 1884, total sittings in the metropolis (population 4,019,361), 1,388,792; Church of England, 677,645. See *Wesleyan Methodists,* note.
116 sects having 20,330 places of worship, Oct. 1871. *Certified Places of Worship,* 4 Nov. 1884, 23,341.

WORSTED, spun wool, obtained its name from having been first spun at a town called Worsted, in Norfolk, in which the inventor lived, and where manufactures of worsted are still extensively carried on, 14 Edw. III. 1340. *Anderson.* "A worsted-stocking knave" is a term of reproach or contempt used by Shakspeare.

WORTH, see *Warth.*

WORTHIES, NINE, a term long ago given to the following eminent men:—

Jews.	Died.
Joshua	B.C. 1426
David	1015
Judas Maccabæus	161
Heathens.	
Hector of Troy	1184
Alexander the Great	323
Julius Cæsar	44
Christians.	
King Arthur of Britain	A.D. 542
Charlemagne of France	814
Godfrey of Bouillon	1100

In some lists, Gideon and Samson are given, instead of Hector and Arthur. In Shakspeare's *Love's Labour's Lost,* act v. sc. 2, Hercules and Pompey appear as worthies.

WOTHLYTYPE, see under *Photography.*

WOUNDED IN BATTLE, see *Geneva Convention,* and *Aid to Sick and Wounded.*

WOUNDING. Malicious wounding of another was adjudged death by the English statutes. The Coventry Act was passed in 1671; see *Coventry Act.* By lord Ellenborough's Act, persons who stab or

cut with intent to murder, maim, or disfigure another were declared guilty of felony without benefit of clergy. Those guilty of maliciously shooting at another in any dwelling-house or other place, are also punishable under the same statute in the same degree, 43 Geo. III. 1802. This offence is met by some later statutes, particularly the act for consolidating and amending the acts relating to offences against the person, 9 Geo. IV., June, 1828. This last act is extended to Ireland by 10 Geo. IV., 1829. An act for the prevention of maliciously shooting, stabbing, &c., in Scotland, 6 Geo. IV., 1825; amended by 10 Geo. IV., 4 June, 1829, for the prevention and punishment of assaults on women and children.

WRECKS. The loss of merchant and other ships by wreck upon lee-shores, coasts, and disasters in the open sea, was estimated at Lloyd's, in 1800, to be about an average of 365 ships a year. In 1830, it appeared by *Lloyd's Lists* that 677 British vessels were totally lost, under various circumstances, in that year. The laws respecting wrecks were consolidated in 1846 and 1854. See *Seamen* (commission of inquiry).

British vessels wrecked in 1848, were, sailing vessels, 501; steamers, 13; tonnage, 96,920.

In 1851, there were wrecked 611 vessels, of which number 11 were steamers: the tonnage of the whole being 111,976.

The year 1852-3, particularly the winter months (Dec. and Jan.), was very remarkable for the number of dreadful shipwrecks and fires at sea: but a few of them are recorded. Wrecks in 25 years (1854-79), 49,322; lives lost, 18,319.

Many vessels were lost in the great storms, 25, 26 Oct. 1859; 28 May, 1861; 19, 20 Oct. 1861; and 13, 14 Nov. 1862; by a cyclone, India, 5 Oct. 1864; in the West Indies, Oct. 1867.

See under *Life Boat*.

WRECKS OF VESSELS ON BRITISH COASTS.

	Vessels.	Lives lost.
1852	1115	920
1853	832	689
1854	987	1549
1855	1141	469

	Vessels wrecked or suffering other casualties.	Vessels totally wrecked.	Lives lost.
1856	1153	—	521
1857	1143	384	532
1858	1170	354	340
1859	1416	—	1645
1860	1379	542	536
1861	1494	—	884
1862	1488	455	690
1863	1664	503	620
1864	1390	467	516
1865	1656	—	698
1866	1860	—	896
1867	2090	656	1333
1868	1747	—	824
1869	2114	—	933
1870	1502	411	774
1871	1575	398	626
1872	1958	419	590
1873	967 (Jan.-June)	—	—
1873-4	408	346	506
1874-5	3590	472	926
			(331 by *Schiller*.)
1875-6	3757	502	778
1876-7	4104	511	776
1877-8	3641	422	892*
1878-9	3002	397	490
1879-80	2519	355	231
1880-1	3575	705	984
1881-2	3660	606	1097
1882-3	3654	551	1020
1883-4	3647	473	661
1884-5	3764	—	478
1885-6	3596	1290	396
1886-7	4224	1582	645

* 318 in *Eurydice*.

REMARKABLE CASES OF BRITISH VESSELS WRECKED OR BURNT.

Mary Rose, 60 guns, going from Portsmouth to Spithead, upset in a squall; all on board perished, 20 July, 1545

Coronation, 90 guns, foundered off the Ramhead; crew saved: *Harwich*, 70 guns, wrecked on Mount Edgcumbe; crew perished . 1 Sept. 1691

Royal Sovereign, 100 guns; burnt in the Medway, 29 Jan. 1696

Stirling Castle, 70 guns; *Mary*, 70 guns; *Northumberland*, 70 guns, lost on the Goodwin; *Vanguard*, 70 guns, sunk at Chatham; *York*, 70 guns, lost near Harwich; all lost but four men; *Resolution*, 60 guns, coast of Sussex; *Newcastle*, 60 guns, at Spithead, 193 drowned; *Reserve*, 60 guns, at Yarmouth, 173 perished; in the night of 26 Nov. 1703

Association, 70 guns, and other vessels, lost with admiral sir C. Shovel, off the Scilly isles (*which see*) 22 Oct. 1707

Solebay, 32 guns, lost near Boston neck; crew perished . 25 Dec. 1709

Edgar, 70 guns, blew up at Spithead; all on board perished . 15 Oct. 1711

Wager; part of commodore Anson's South Sea expedition; wrecked on desolate island, lat. 47° S. 14 May 1741

Victory, 100 guns, near the Isle of Alderney; all perished . 5 Oct. 1744

Colchester, 50 guns, lost on Kentish Knock; 50 men perished . 21 Sept. ,,

Namur, 74 guns, foundered near Fort St. David, East Indies; all perished except 26 persons; *Pembroke*, 60 guns, near Porto Novo; 330 of her crew perished . 13 April, 1749

Prince George, 80 guns, burnt in lat. 48 N., on way to Gibraltar; about 400 perished . 13 April, 1758

Lichfield, 50 guns, lost on the coast of Barbary; 130 of the crew perished . 29 Nov. ,,

Tilbury, 60 guns, lost off Louisbourg; most of the crew perished . 25 Sept. 1759

Ramilies, 90 guns, lost on the Bolt-head; only 26 persons saved; *Conqueror*, lost on St. Nicholas's Island, Plymouth . 15 Feb. 1760

Duc d'Aquitaine, 64 guns, and *Sunderland*, 60 guns, lost off Pondicherry; all perished . 1 Jan. 1761

Raisonnable, 64 guns, lost at the attack of Martinique . 3 Feb. 1762

Repulse, 32 guns, foundered off Bermuda; crew perished . 1775

Thunderer, 74 guns; *Stirling Castle*, 64; *Defiance*, 64; *Phœnix*, 44; *La Blanche*, 32; *Laurel*, 28; *Shark*, 28; *Andromeda*, 28; *Deal Castle*, 24; *Penelope*, 24; *Scarborough*, 20; *Barbadoes*, 14; *Cameleon*, 14; *Endeavour*, 14; and *Victor*, 10 guns: all lost in the same storm, in the West Indies, in Oct. 1780

Gen. Parker, Indiaman, off Scheveling . 17 Feb. 1781

Grosvenor, Indiaman, coast of Caffraria . 4 Aug. 1782

Swan, sloop of war, off Waterford; 130 drowned, 4 Aug. ,,

Royal George; above 600 perished . 29 Aug. ,,

Centaur, 74 guns, foundered on her passage from Jamaica; capt. Inglefield and 11 of the crew saved 21 Sept. ,,

Ville de Paris, of 104 guns, one of admiral Rodney's prizes; the *Glorieux*, of 74 guns, lost in the West Indies . 5 Oct. ,,

Superb, 74 guns, wrecked in Tellicherry roads, East Indies . 5 Nov. 1783

Cato, 50 guns, admiral sir Hyde Parker, on the Malabar coast; crew perished . ,,

Count Belgioioso, Indiaman, off Dublin Bay; 147 souls perished . 13 March, ,,

Menai, ferry-boat, in the Menai Strait 60 drowned, 5 Dec. 1785

Halsewell, E. Indiaman; 386 persons perished, 6 Jan. 1786

Hartwell, Indiaman, with immense wealth on board 24 May, 1787

Charlemont Packet, from Holyhead to Dublin; 104 drowned . 22 Dec. 1790

Pandora, frigate on a reef; 100 perished . 28 Aug. 1791

Union, packet of Dover, lost off the port of Calais; a similar occurrence had not happened for 105 years before . 28 Jan. 1792

WRECKS.   997   WRECKS.

Winterton, E. Indiaman: many perished 20 Aug. 1792
Impetueux, 74 guns, burnt at Portsmouth 24 Aug. „
Scorpion, 74 guns, burnt at Leghorn . 20 Nov. 1793
Ardent, 64 guns, burnt off Corsica . . April, 1794
Boyne, by fire, at Spithead (see *Boyne*) . 4 May, 1795
Courageux, 74 guns, capt. B. Hallowell, near Gibraltar; crew, except 124, perished . 18 Dec. 1796
La Tribune, 36 guns, off Halifax; 300 souls perished 16 Nov. 1797
Proserpine frigate; in the Elbe; 15 lost . 1 Feb. 1798
Resistance, blown up in the straits of Banca, 24 July, „
Royal Charlotte, East Indiaman, blown up at Culpee, 1 Aug. „
H.M.S. *Lutine*, 32 guns, was wrecked off Vlieland, coast of Holland; only one saved, who died before reaching England * . . 9-10 Oct. 1799
Impregnable, 98 guns, wrecked between Langstone and Chichester . . . . 19 Oct. „
Nassau, 64 guns, on the Haak Bank; 100 perished, 25 Oct. „
Sceptre, 64 guns, wrecked in Table Bay, cape of Good Hope; 291 of the crew perished . 5 Nov. „
Ethalion, frigate, 38 guns, on the Penmarks, 24 Dec. „
Queen, transport, on Trefusis Point; 369 souls perished . . . . . 14 Jan. 1800
Mastiff, gunbrig, on the Cockle Sands . 19 Jan. „
Repulse, 64 guns, off Ushant . . 10 March, „
Queen Charlotte (which see), burnt; 673 perish 17 March „
Queen, W. Indiaman, by fire, off Brazil . 9 July, „
Brazen, sloop of war, off Newhaven; all lost except one man . . . . . . „
Invincible, 74 guns, near Yarmouth; capt. John Rennie, and the crew, except 126 souls, perished, 16 March, 1801
Margate, Margate-hoy, near Reculver; 23 persons perished . . . . . 10 Feb. 1802
Bangalore, E. Indiaman, Indian Sea . 12 April, „
Active, West Indiaman, in Margate Roads 10 Jan. 1803
Hindostan, East Indiaman, went to pieces on the Culvers . . . . . 11 Jan. „
La Déterminée, 24 guns, in Jersey Roads, many drowned . . . . . 26 March, „
Resistance, 36 guns, off Cape St. Vincent. 31 May, „
Lady Hobart, packet, on an island of ice 28 June, „
Seine, frigate, 44 guns, off Schelling . 31 July, „
Antelope, capt. Wilson, off Ebew Islands 9 Aug. „
Victory, Liverpool ship, at Liverpool; 27 drowned, 30 Sept. „
Circe, frigate, 32 guns, off Yarmouth . 16 Nov. „
Nautilus, E. Indiaman, on Ladrones . 18 Nov. „
Fanny, in Chinese Sea: 46 souls perish 29 Nov. „
Suffisante, sloop, 16 guns, off Cork . 25 Dec. „
Apollo, frigate, on coast of Portugal . 1 April, 1804
Cumberland Packet, on Antigua coast . 4 Sept. „
Romney, 50 guns on Haak Bank, Texel 19 Nov. „
Venerable, 74 guns, at Torbay; lost 8 men 24 Nov. „
Severn, on a rock, near Gronville . . 21 Dec. „
Doris, frigate, on the Diamond Rock, Quiberon Bay, 12 Jan. 1805
Abergavenny, East Indiaman, on the Bill of Portland; more than 300 persons perished 6 Feb. „
Naias, transport, on Newfoundland coast 23 Oct. „
Æneas, transport, off Newfoundland; 340 perished, 23 Oct. „
Aurora, transport, on the Goodwin Sands; 300 perished . . . . . 21 Dec. „
King George, packet, from Park-gate to Dublin, lost on the Hoyle bank; 125 persons, passengers and crew drowned . . . . 21 Sept. 1806

* *La Lutine* was a French ship captured by admiral Duncan. She contained much bullion and money, belonging to merchants; a great loss to the underwriters at Lloyd's. The Dutch government claimed the wreck, and granted one third of the salvage in 1801 to the bullion fishers. After much discussion, and occasional recoveries, the king of the Netherlands ceded to Great Britain (for Lloyd's) half the remainder of the wreck. A Dutch salvage company began operations in Aug. 1857. At the end of 1859, Lloyd's had received 22,162*l*. 6*s*. 7*d*. About 99,803*l*. recovered; about 1,175,000*l*. remaining. A chair and table at Lloyd's were made of the rudder recovered in 1859. *Martin's History of Lloyd's*.

Athénien, 64 guns, near Tunis; 347 souls perished, 27 Oct. 1806
Glasgow, packet, off Farm Island; several drowned, 17 Nov. „
Felix, 12 guns, near Santander; 79 souls lost 22 Jan. 1807
Blenheim, 74 guns, admiral sir T. Troubridge, and *Java*, 23 guns, foundered near island of Rodriguez, East Indies . . . . . 1 Feb. „
Ajax, 74 guns, by fire, off the island of Tenedos; 250 perished . . . . 14 Feb. „
Blanche, frigate, on the French coast; 45 men perished . . . . . 4 March, „
Ganges, East Indiaman, off the Cape of Good Hope, 29 May, „
Prince of Wales, Park-gate packet, and *Rochdale*, transport, on Dunleary point, near Dublin; nearly 300 souls perished . . . 19 Nov. „
Boreas, man-of-war, upon the Hannois rock in the Channel . . . . . 28 Nov. „
Anson, 44 guns, wrecked in Mount's Bay; 60 lives lost . . . . . . 29 Dec. „
Agatha, near Memel; lord Royston and others drowned . . . . . 7 April, 1808
Astrea, frigate, on Anagada coast . . 23 May, „
Frith, passage-boat, in the Frith of Dornoch; 40 persons drowned . . . 13 Aug. 1809
Foxhound, 18 guns, foundered on passage from Halifax; crew perished . . 31 Aug. „
Sirius, 36 guns, and *Magicienne*, 36 guns, wrecked when advancing to attack the French, off Isle of France . . . . . 23 Aug. 1810
Satellite, sloop of war, 16 guns, upset, and all on board perished . . . . 14 Dec. „
Minotaur, of 74 guns, wrecked on the Haak Bank; 360 persons perished . . . 22 Dec. „
Pandora, sloop of war, off Jutland; 30 persons perished . . . . . 13 Feb. 1811
Saldanha, frigate, on the Irish coast; 300 persons perished . . . . . 4 Dec. „
St. George, of 98, and *Defence*, of 74 guns, and the *Hero*, stranded on the coast of Jutland, adm. Reynolds and all the crews (about 2000 persons) perished, except 18 seamen . 24 Dec. „
Manilla, frigate, on the Haak Sand; 12 persons perished . . . . . 28 Jan. 1812
Atalante; H.M. frigate off Nova Scotia . 10 Nov. 1813
British Queen, packet, from Ostend to Margate, wrecked on the Goodwin Sands, and all on board perished . . . . . 17 Dec. 1814
Duchess of Wellington, at Calcutta, by fire 21 Jan. 1816
Seahorse, transport, near Tramore Bay; 365 persons, chiefly soldiers of the 59th regiment, and most of the crew, drowned . . . 30 Jan. „
Lord Melville and *Boadicea*, transports, with upwards of 200 of the 82nd regiment, with wives and children, lost near Kinsale; almost all perished, 31 Jan. „
Harpooner, transport, near Newfoundland; 200 persons drowned . . . . 10 Nov. „
William and Mary, packet, struck on the Willeys rocks, near the Holmes lighthouse, Bristol Channel; nearly 60 persons perished . 23 Oct. 1817
Queen Charlotte, East Indiaman, at Madras; all on board perished . . . . 24 Oct. 1818
Ariel, in the Persian Gulf; 79 souls perished, 18 March, 1820
Blendon Hall, on Inaccessible Island, many perished, 23 July, 1821
Earl of Moira, on the Burbo Bank, near Liverpool 40 drowned . . . . . 8 Aug. „
Juliana, East Indiaman, on the Kentish Knock; 40 drowned . . . . . 26 Dec. „
Thames, Indiaman, off Beachey Head; several drowned . . . . . 3 Feb. 1822
Drake, 10 guns, near Halifax; several drowned, 20 June, „
Ellesmere, steamer; 11 persons lost . 14 Dec. „
Alert, Dublin and Liverpool packet; 70 souls perished . . . . . 26 March, 1823
Robert, from Dublin to Liverpool; 60 souls perished, 16 May, „
Kent (*which see*); East Indiaman; burnt . March 1825
Fanny, in Jersey Roads; lord Harley and many drowned . . . . . 1 Jan. 1828
Venus, packet, from Waterford to Dublin, near Gorey; 9 persons drowned . 19 March, „
Newry, from Newry to Quebec, with 360 passengers;

cast away near Bardsy, about 40 persons were drowned . . . . . 16 April, 1830
Lady Sherbrooke, from Londonderry to Quebec; lost near Cape Ray; 273 souls perished; 32 only were saved . . . . . . 19 Aug. 1831
Experiment, from Hull to Quebec; wrecked near Calais . . . . . 15 April, 1832
Hibernia, burnt in W. long. 22°, S. lat. 4°; 150 persons (out of 232) perished . . 15 Feb. 1833
Earl of Wemyss, near Wells, Norfolk: the cabin filled, and 11 ladies and children were drowned; all on deck escaped . . . . 13 July, ,,
Amphitrite, ship with female convicts to New South Wales; lost on Boulogne Sands; out of 131 persons, 3 only were saved . . . 30 Aug. ,,
United Kingdom, W. Indiaman, with rich cargo; run down by the Queen of Scotland steamer off Northfleet, near Gravesend . . . 15 Oct. ,,
Waterwitch, steamer, on the coast of Wexford; 4 drowned . . . . . 18 Dec. ,,
Lady Munro, from Calcutta to Sydney; of 90 persons on board, not more than 20 were saved, 9 Jan. 1834
Cameleon, cutter, run down off Dover by the Castor frigate; 13 persons drowned . 27 Aug. ,,
Earl of Eldon; East Indiaman; burnt . 27 Sept. ,,
Killarney, steamer, off Cork; 29 persons perished, 26 Jan. 1838
Forfarshire, steamer, from Hull to Dundee; 38 persons drowned. Owing to the courage of Grace Darling and her father, 15 persons were saved (see Forfarshire) . . . . 6 Sept. ,,
Protector, E. Indiaman, at Bengal; of 178 persons on board, 170 perished . . . 21 Nov. ,,
Diligence, naval cutter, capt. sir J. Reid, bart., and 56 souls perish in the Irish channel . 7 Jan. 1839
William Huskisson, steamer, between Dublin and Liverpool; 93 passengers saved by capt. Clegg, of the Huddersfield . . . 11 Jan. 1840
Lord William Bentinck, off Bombay; 58 recruits, 20 officers, and 7 passengers perished; the Lord Castlereagh also wrecked, most of her crew and passengers lost . . . . 17 June, ,,
H.M.S. Fairy, captain Hewitt; sailed from Harwich on a surveying cruise, and was lost next day in a violent gale, off the coast of Norfolk . 13 Nov. ,,
City of Bristol, steam packet, 35 perished 18 Nov. ,,
Thames, steamer, captain Gray, from Dublin to Liverpool, wrecked off St. Ives; the captain and 55 persons perished . . . 4 Jan. 1841
Governor Fenner, from Liverpool for America; run down off Holyhead by the Nottingham steamer out of Dublin; 122 persons perished . 19 Feb. ,,
Amelia, from London to Liverpool; lost on the Herne Sand . . . . . 26 Feb. ,,
President, steamer, from New York to Liverpool, with many passengers on board; sailed on 11 March, encountered a terrific storm two days afterwards, and has never since been heard of, 13 March, ,,
[In this vessel were, Mr. Tyrone Power, the comedian; a son of the duke of Richmond, &c.]
William Browne, by striking on the ice; 16 passengers who had been received into the long boat were thrown overboard by the crew to lighten her 19 April, ,,
Isabella, from London to Quebec; struck by an iceberg . . . . . 9 May, ,,
Solway, steamer, on her passage between Belfast and Port Carlisle; crew saved . 25 Aug. ,,
Amanda, off Metis; 29 passengers and 12 of the crew lost . . . . . 26 Sept. ,,
James Cooke, of Limerick, coming from Sligo to Glasgow . . . . . 21 Nov. ,,
Abercrombie Robinson and Waterloo transports, in Table Bay, Cape of Good Hope: of 330 persons on board the latter vessel, 189, principally convicts, perished . . . 28 Aug. 1842
Spitfire, war-steamer, off Jamaica. . 10 Sept. ,,
Reliance, East Indiaman, from China to London, off Merlemont, near Boulogne; of 116 persons on board, seven only were saved . . 13 Nov. ,,
Hamilton, on the Gunfleet sands, near Harwich; 11 of the crew perished . . . 15 Nov. ,,
Conqueror, East Indiaman, homeward bound, near Boulogne; crew and passengers lost . 13 Jan. 1843

Jessie Logan, East Indiaman, on the Cornish coast; many lives lost . . . . 16 Jan. 1843
Solway, royal mail-steamer, near Corunna; 28 lives lost, and the mail . . . 7 April, ,,
Catherine, trader, blown up off the Isle of Pines; most of the crew were massacred by the natives, or afterwards drowned . . 12 April, ,,
Amelia Thompson, near Madras, part of crew saved 23 May, ,,
Albert, troop-ship, from Halifax, with the 64th regiment on board, which was miraculously saved 13 July, ,,
Pegasus, steam-packet, from Leith; off the Fern Islands; of 59 persons (including Mr. Elton, the actor), 7 only were saved . . 19 July, ,,
Phoenix, in a terrific snow-storm, off the coast of Newfoundland; many lives were lost 26 Nov. ,,
Elberfeldi, iron steam-ship, from Brielle 22 Feb. 1844
Manchester, steamer, from Hull to Hamburg, off the Vogel Sands, near Cuxhaven about 30 lives lost, 16 June, ,,
John Lloyd, by collision, in the Irish sea; several lives lost . . . . 25 Sept. 1845
Margaret, Hull and Hamburg steamer; many lives lost . . . . . 22 Oct. ,,
Tweed, steamer; off Yucatan - . . 12 Feb. 1846
Great Britain, iron steam-ship, grounded in Dundrum bay (see Great Britain). . 22 Sept. ,,
[Recovered by Brunel, &c., 27 Aug. 1847.]
Tweed, W. India mail-packet; 72 souls perished, 19 Feb. 1847
Exmouth, emigrant-ship, from Londonderry to Quebec; of 240 persons on board, nearly all were drowned . . . . 28 April, ,,
Carrick, brig; a gale in the St. Lawrence; 170 emigrants perished . . . 19 May, ,,
Avenger, H.M. steam-frigate; off N. coast of Africa; officers and crew (nearly 200) lost 20 Dec. ,,
Ocean Monarch (which see) . . 24 Aug. 1848
Forth, steamer; off Campeachy . 13 Jan. 1849
Caleb Grimshaw, emigrant-ship, fire; 400 persons miraculously escaped . . . 12 Nov. ,,
Royal Adelaide, steamer, wrecked on the Tongue Sands, off Margate, above 400 lives lost, 30 March, 1850
Orion, steam-ship, off Portpatrick (see Orion), 18 June, ,,
Rosalind, from Quebec; a number of the crew drowned . . . . . 9 Sept. ,,
Edmund, emigrant-ship, with nearly 200 passengers from Limerick to New York (of whom more than one-half perished), wrecked off the Western coast of Ireland . . . . 12 Nov. ,,
Amazon, W. India mail-steamer (see Amazon), 4 Jan. 1852
Birkenhead, troop-ship, iron paddle-wheeled, and of 556 horse-power, sailed from Queenstown, 7 Jan. 1852, for the Cape, having on board detachments of the 12th Lancers, 2nd, 6th, 12th, 43rd, 45th, and 60th Rifles, 73rd, 74th, and 91st regiments. It struck upon a pointed pinnacle rock off Simon's bay, South Africa, and of 638 persons only 184 were saved by the boats; 454 of the crew and soldiers perished . . . 26 Feb. ,,
Victoria, steam-packet, wrecked near Wings beacon off Gottenburg; many lives lost 8, 9 Nov. ,,
Lily, stranded and blown up by gunpowder, on the Calf-of-Man; by which more than 30 persons lost their lives . . . . 24 Dec. ,,
St. George, steam-ship, bound from Liverpool to New York, with 121 emigrant passengers (chiefly Irish), and a crew consisting of twenty-nine seamen (the captain inclusive), was destroyed by fire at sea. The crew and seventy of the passengers were saved by the American ship Orlando, and conveyed to Havre, in France; 51 supposed to have perished . . . . 24 Dec. ,,
Queen Victoria, steam-ship, bound from Liverpool, was wrecked off the Bailey lighthouse, near Dublin; mistook her course in a snow-storm: 67 lost out of 120 . . . . 15 Feb. 1853
Independence, on the coast of Lower California, and which afterwards took fire; 140 persons were drowned or burnt to death, a few escaping, who underwent the most dreadful additional sufferings on a barren shore . . . 16 Feb. ,,
Duke of Sutherland, steamer, from London to Aber-

deen; struck on the pier at Aberdeen, and the captain (Edward Howling) and 16 (of the crew and passengers) perished . . . 1 April, 1853
Rebecca, on west coast of Van Diemen's Land, capt. Shephard and many lives lost . . 29 April, ,,
William and Mary, an American emigrant ship, near the Bahamas. She struck on a sunken rock; about 170 persons perished . . . 3 May, ,,
Aurora, of Hull; sailed from New York, 26 April, and foundered; about 25 lives lost . 20 May, ,,
Bourneuf, Australian emigrant vessel; struck on a reef near Torres Straits; the captain (Bibby) and six lives lost . . . . . 3 Aug. ,,
Annie Jane, of Liverpool, an emigrant vessel, driven on shore on the Barra Islands, on west coast of Scotland; about 348 lives lost 29 Sept. ,,
Harwood, brig, by collision with the *Trident* steamer, near the Mouse light near the Nore; foundered; six of the crew perished . 5 Oct. ,,
Dalhousie, foundered off Beachey Head; the captain (Butterworth), the passengers, and all the crew (excepting one), about 60 persons in all, perished; the cargo was valued at above 100,000*l*. 19 Oct. ,,
Marshall, screw-steamer, in the North Sea, ran into the barque *Woodhouse*; about 48 persons supposed to have perished . . 28 Nov. ,,
Taylour, emigrant ship, driven on the rocks off Lambay Island, north of Howth; about 380 lives lost . . . . . . 20 Jan. 1854
Favourite, in the Channel, on her way from Bremen to Baltimore, came into violent contact with the American barque *Hesper*, off the Start, and immediately went down; 201 persons were drowned 29 April, ,,
Lady Nugent, troop-ship, sailed from Madras, 10 May, 1854; foundered in a hurricane; 350 rank and file of the Madras light infantry, officers, and crew, in all 400 souls, perished . . May, ,,
Forerunner, African mail-steamer, struck on a sunken rock off St. Lorenzo, Madeira, and went down directly afterwards, with the total loss of ship and mails, and 14 lives . . 25 Oct. ,,
Nile, iron screw-steamer, struck on the Godevry rock, St. Ives' Bay, and all perished . 30 Nov. ,,
City of Glasgow, a Glasgow steamer, with 480 persons on board, disappeared in . . . ,,
In the storm which raged in the Black Sea, 13-16 Nov. 1854, eleven transports were wrecked and six disabled. The new steamship *Prince* was lost with 144 lives, and a cargo worth 500,000*l*. indispensable to the army in the Crimea. The loss of life in the other vessels is estimated at 340 ,,
George Canning, Hamburg and New York packet, near the mouth of the Elbe; 96 lives lost, and *Stately*, English schooner, near Neuwiek, in a great storm . . . . . . 1 Jan. 1855
Mercury, screw-steamer, by collision with a French ship; passengers saved . . 11 Jan. ,,
Janet Boyd, bark, in a storm off Margate Sands; 28 lives lost . . . . . 20 Jan. ,,
Will o' the Wisp, screw-steamer, on the Burn Rock, off Lambay; 18 lives lost . . 9 Feb. ,,
Morna, steamer on rocks near the Isle of Man; 21 lives lost . . . . . 25 Feb. ,,
John, emigrant vessel, on the Muncles rocks off Falmouth; 200 lives lost . . 1 May, ,,
Pacific, Collins steamer, left Liverpool for New York, with 186 persons on board; never since heard of (supposed to have struck on an iceberg) 23 Jan. 1856
Josephine Willis, packet-ship, lost by collision with the screw-steamer *Mangerton*, in the Channel; about 70 lives lost . . . . 3 Feb. ,,
John Rutledge, from Liverpool to New York, ran on an iceberg and was wrecked; many lives lost 20 Feb. ,,
Many vessels and their crews totally lost 1-8 Jan. 1857†

---

* *Arctic*, U.S. mail steamer, by collision in a fog with the *Vesta*, French steamer, off Newfoundland; above 300 lives lost, 27 Sept. 1854.

† A large American vessel, *Northern Belle*, was wrecked near Broadstairs. The American government sent 21 silver medals and 270*l*. to be distributed among the heroic boatmen of the place, who saved the crew, 5-6 Jan. 1857.

Violet, royal mail-steamer, lost on the Goodwin; many persons perished . . . 5 Jan. 1857
Tyne, royal-steamer, stranded on her way to Southampton from the Brazils . . . 13 Jan ,,
St. Antrew, screw-steamer, totally wrecked near Latakia; loss about 145,000*l*. . 29 Jan. ,,
Charlemagne, Iron clipper, wrecked by the coast of Canton: passengers saved; loss, about 110,000*l*. 20 March, ,,
H.M.S. *Raleigh*, 50 guns, wrecked on south-east coast of Macao . . . . 14 April, ,,
Catherine Adamson, Australian vessel, wrecked 25 miles from Sydney, 20 lives lost about 3 June, ,,
Erin, P. & O. Co's steamer, wrecked on coast of Ceylon . . . . . . June, ,,
H.M.S. *Transit*, wrecked on a reef in the Straits of Banca . . . . . 10 July, ,,
Dunbar, clipper wrecked on the rocks near Sydney; 121 persons, and cargo valued at 22,000*l*., lost; one person only saved, who was on the rocks 30 hours . . . . . 20 Aug. ,,
Sarah Sands, an iron screw-steamer, sailed from Portsmouth to Calcutta, in Aug. 1857; 300 soldiers on board. On 11 Nov. the cargo (government stores) took fire. By the exertions of major Brett and captain Castle, the master of the vessel, who directed the soldiers and the crew, the flames were subdued, although a barrel of gunpowder exploded during the conflagration. A new danger then arose—the prevalence of a strong gale; water was shipped heavily where the port quarter had been blown out. Nevertheless, after a fearful struggle, the vessel arrived at the Mauritius, 21 Nov., without losing a single life 11-21 Nov. ,,
Windsor, emigrant-ship, struck on a reef near the Cape de Verde Islands . . . 1 Dec. ,,
Ava, Indian mail-steamer, with ladies and others from Lucknow on board, wrecked near Ceylon 16 Feb. 1858
Eastern City, burnt about the equator on her way to Melbourne; by great exertions all on board were saved . . . . . 23, 24 Aug. ,,
Austria, steam-emigrant ship, burnt in the middle of the Atlantic. Of 538 persons on board, only 67 were saved. The disaster due to carelessness 13 Sept. ,,
St. Paul, captain Pennard, from Hong Kong to Sydney, with 327 Chinese emigrants, wrecked on the Island of Russel, 30 Sept. 1858. The captain and eight of the crew left the island in search of assistance, and were picked up by the *Prince of Denmark* schooner. The French steamer *Styz* was despatched to the island, and brought away one Chinese, 25 Jan. 1859. All the rest had been massacred and devoured by the natives . ,,
Czar, steamer, wrecked off the Lizard; 14 lives lost 23 Jan. 1859*
Eastern Monarch, burnt at Spithead; out of 500, eight lives lost. The vessel contained invalid soldiers from India, who, with the crew, behaved admirably . . . . . 2 June, ,,
Alma, steamer, grounded on a reef near Aden, Red Sea, about 35 miles from Mocha; all persons saved; after 3½ days' exposure to the sun, without water, they were rescued by H.M.S. *Cyclops*; sir John Bowring, who was on board, lost valuable papers . . . . . 12 June, ,,
Admella, steamer, running between Melbourne and Adelaide, struck on a reef; of about 72 persons, only 23 were saved; many perished through exposure to cold . . . . 6 Aug. ,,
Royal Charter, screw-steamer, captain Taylor, totally wrecked off Moelfra, on the Anglesea coast; 446 lives lost. The vessel contained gold amounting in value to between 700,000*l*. and 800,000*l*.; much of this has been recovered night of 25-26 Oct. ,,
Indian, mail-steamer, wrecked off the coast of Newfoundland; out of 116, 27 lives lost 21 Nov. ,,
Blerrie Castle, sailed from London docks for Adelaide; lost in the Channel and all on board, 57 persons; last seen on . . . 25 Dec. ,,

---

* *Pomona*, an American ship, captain Merrihew; 419 persons on board, from Liverpool to New York; was wrecked on Blackwater Bank, through the master mistaking the Blackwater for the Tuskar light, only 24 persons saved, night of 27-28 April, 1859.

WRECKS.

Northerner, steamer, wrecked on a rock near Cape Mendorino, between San Francisco and Oregon; 38 lives lost . . . . . . 6 Jan. 1860
Endymion, sailing-vessel, burnt in the Mersey; loss above 20,000l. . . . . . 31 Jan. ,,
Dreadful gales; and many wrecks on the coast,* 15-19 Feb. ,,
On-line, steamer; lost through collision with the *Heroine*, of Bideford, abreast of Beachey Head; the captain and about 50 persons perished 19 Feb. ,,
Luna, American emigrant vessel, wrecked on rocks off Barfleur; about 100 lives lost . 19 Feb. ,,
Hungarian, new mail-steamer, wrecked off coast of Nova Scotia; all on board (205) lost on the night of 19-20 Feb. ,,
Nimrod, steamer, wrecked on rocks near St. David's Head; 40 lives lost . . . . 28 Feb. ,,
Malabar, iron ship, on her way to China, with lord Elgin and baron Gros: wrecked off Point de Galle, Ceylon. The ambassadors displayed much heroism; no lives lost. Of much specie sunk, a good deal was recovered . . . . . 22 May, ,,
Lady Elgin, an American steamer, sunk through collision with schooner *Augusta* on lake Michigan; of 385 persons on board, 287 were lost, including Mr. Herbert Ingram, M.P., founder of the "Illustrated London News," and his son; morning of 8 Sept. ,,
Arctic, Hull steamer, wrecked off Jutland; many persons saved by Mr. Earle, who lost his own life while endeavouring to save others. . 5 Oct. ,,
Connaught, steamer, burnt; crew saved through the gallantry of the crew of an American brig, 7 Oct. ,,
Juanita, wrecked through collision with an American vessel, *Joseph Fish*, 13 lives lost . 15 March, 1861
Canadian, steamer, struck on a field of ice in the straits of Belle-isle, and foundered in half an hour; 35 lives lost . . . . . 4 June, ,,
H.M.S. *Conqueror*, stranded on Rum Cay, near Bahamas, and lost [the captain and master were censured for neglect of duty] . 29 Dec. ,,
Harmony, lost with all hands off Plymouth 27 Feb. 1862
Ocean Monarch, 2195 tons, sailed from New York, 5 March, laden with provisions; foundered in a gale . . . . 9 March, ,,
Upwards of 60 merchantmen lost during gales in March, ,,
Mars, Waterford steamer, struck on a rock near Milford haven; about 50 lives lost. . April, ,,
Bencoolen, East Indiaman, 1400 tons; struck on sands near Bude haven, Cornwall; about 26 lives lost . . . . . . 19 Oct. ,,
Lotus, merchantman, off Chale Bay, in the great storm; crew all lost except two . 19 Oct. ,,
Many vessels lost during storm . 19 Oct. ,,
Colombo, East India mail steamer, in thick weather, wrecked on Minicoy Island; 440 miles from Point de Galle, Ceylon; no lives lost (the crew and passengers taken off by the *Ottawa* from Bombay, 30 Nov.) . . . . . . 19 Nov. ,,
Lifeguard, steamer, left Newcastle, with about 41 passengers; never since heard of; supposed to have foundered off Flamborough head 20 Dec. ,,
Orpheus, H.M.S. steamer, new vessel, 1700 tons; commander Burnett; wrecked on Manakau bar, W. coast New Zealand; 70 persons saved; about 190 perished . . . . . 7 Feb. 1863
Anglo-Saxon, mail steamer, captain Burgess, in dense fog, wrecked on reef off Cape Race, Newfoundland; about 237, out of 446, lives lost, 27 April, ,,
All Serene, Australian ship; gale in the Pacific; above 30 lives lost (the survivors suffered much till they reached the Fiji isles in a punt) 21 Feb. 1864
Many shipwrecks in consequence of the cyclone at Calcutta . . . . . . 5 Oct. ,,
H.M.S. *Racehorse*, off Chefoo Cape, Chinese coast; 99 lives lost . . . . . 4 Nov. ,,
The *Stanley*, *Friendship*, &c., in the gale off Tynemouth; and the *Dalhousie*, screw steamer, mouth of the Tay; same gale; 34 lives lost . 24 Nov. ,,

* American barque *Lima*, with emigrants, wrecked off Barfleur; above 100 lives lost, 17 Feb. 1860. On the same rock, on 25 Nov. 1120, was wrecked the *Blanche Nef*, containing the children of Henry I. and a large number of attendants; in all 363 persons perished.

H.M.S. *Bombay*, burnt off Flores Island, near Montendes; 92 lives lost . . . . 14 Dec. 1864
Lelia, cutter, off Great Orme's Head, during a gale; several lives lost; 7 persons drowned by upsetting of the life-boat . . . . 14 Jan. 1865
Eagle Speed, emigrant vessel, foundered near Calcutta; 265 coolies drowned; great cruelty and neglect imputed . . . . 24 Aug. ,,
Duncan Dunbar, wrecked on a reef at Las Rocas, S. America; no lives lost . . . 7 Oct. ,,
Samphire, mail-steamer; collision with an American barque; several lives lost . . . 13 Dec. ,,
Ibis, steamer, machinery damaged, off Ballycroneen bay; 15 lives lost; sailed from Cork . 18 Dec. ,,
London, steamer, on her way to Melbourne; foundered in Bay of Biscay; about 220 persons perished (including captain Martin, Dr. Woolley, principal of the university of Sydney, G. V. Brooke, the tragedian); about the same time the *Amalia* steamer went down with a cargo worth 200,000l.; no lives lost . . . 11 Jan. 1866
Many wrecks and much loss of life during gales, especially off Torbay . . . . 6-11 Jan. ,,
Spirit of the Ocean, steamer; wrecked on a rock near Dartmouth; all lost except 4 . 23 March, ,,
General Grant, on voyage from Melbourne to London, wrecked off Auckland Isles; only 13 out of about 100 saved. . . . . . . May, ,,
Amazon, H.M. screw sloop, and screw steamer *Osprey*, sunk by collision near Plymouth; several passengers and sailors drowned . 10 July, ,,
Bruiser, steamer, sunk by collision with the *Haswell*, off Aldborough; about 15 lives lost 19 Aug. ,,
Bhima, Indian steamer; foundered through collision with *Nana*, steamer, between Bombay and Suez; 19 lives lost . . . . . 11 Sept. ,,
H.M.S. *Berenice*, burnt in Persian Gulf; none perished . . . . . . 13 Oct. ,,
Ceres, near Carnsoe, Ireland; about 36 lives lost [captain Puscoe censured for neglecting to sound] 10 Nov. ,,
Many wrecks in the Channel . . 5, 6 Jan. 1867
James Crosfield, iron ship; wrecked off Langness, Isle of Man; all on board lost . . . 5 Jan. ,,
Singapore, Peninsular and Oriental steamer, struck on a sunken rock, and went down; no lives lost, 20 Aug. ,,
Rhone and *Wye*, Royal Mail steamers, totally lost, and about 50 other vessels driven ashore; great loss of life by a hurricane, off St. Thomas (see *Virgin Islands*) . . . . . 29 Oct. ,,
Hibernia, screw steamer; the shaft of screw propeller broke, 600 miles off coast of Ireland; many lives lost . . . . 24 or 25 Oct. or Nov. 1868
Many wrecks on the Cornish coast during a gale, 19-20 March, 1869
Italian, merchant steamer, struck on a rock near Finisterre; about 26 lives lost about 21 March, ,,
Carnatic, Peninsular and Oriental steamer, wrecked off Shadwan in the gulf of Suez; about 25 lives lost, 13 Sept. ,,
Oneida, American vessel, run down by collision with P. & O. steamer *Bombay* off Yokohama; about 115 lives lost (captain of *Bombay* suspended for 6 months) . . . . . 24 Jan. 1870
City of Boston, sailed from New York, long missing; a board stating that she was sinking found in Cornwall . . . . 11 Feb. ,,
Normandy, S. W. company's steamer, by collision with the steamer *Mary*, off the Isle of Wight, sunk; the captain, C. B. Harvey, and 33 others perish, 17 March, ,,
H.M.S. *Slaney*, wrecked by a typhoon near Hong Kong; about 42 lives lost . . . 9 May, ,,
H.M.S. *Captain*, iron-clad, sank in a squall off Finisterre (see *Navy of England*) . 7 Sept. ,,
Cambria, iron screw-steamer, lost in a storm off Inishtrahul Island, N.W. Ireland; about 170 lives lost . . . . . . 19 Oct. ,,
Queen of the Thames, magnificent vessel, sailed from London to Sydney by the Cape in 58 days; returning, was lost by striking on sands off Cape Agulhas, Africa; 4 lives and valuable cargo lost; the captain was censured . . 18 March, 1871
Cornwall, wrecked by collision with the *Himalaya* steamer off Hartlepool . . . 19 March, ,,
Megæra, government iron screw-steamer, sailed with about 400 on board for Australia, Feb. 1871;

WRECKS.

sprang a leak, 8 June; when it was discovered that her bottom was nearly worn away by corrosion; she was beached on St. Paul's Isle, in the Indian ocean, 16 June; huts were erected, and the crew settled, and stores landed; lieut. Jones was taken on board a Dutch vessel, 16 July; the Oberon brought provisions, 26 Aug.; the crew was carried off during a storm, the stores being left behind, by the *Malacca* . . . 3 Sept. 1871

[The vessel was reported unfit for service in 1867; capt. Thrupp was tried and acquitted of blame, 17 Nov.; sir Spencer Robinson and various admiralty officials were censured by a government commission, 6 March, 1872.]

Rangoon, Peninsular and Oriental steamer, valued at 78,000l., wrecked on Kadir rock, off Point de Galle; cargo lost; no lives lost . . 1 Nov. ,,
Norfolk Hero, fishing lugger, lost off Norfolk coast, 2 Dec. ,,
Delaware, large steamer; wrecked off Scilly rocks; only 2 out of 47 saved . . . . 20 Dec. ,,
Severe gales; many wrecks, and lives lost.
Kinsale, steamer, off Waterford; *Albion*, schooner, off Looe; *Dee*, schooner, &c. . . 22-23 Nov. 1872
Royal Adelaide, emigrant vessel; went ashore on Chesil beach, between Weymouth and Portland; 5 lost . . . . 25 Nov. ,,
Germania, mail packet; wrecked off La Rochelle; about 24 perished . . . . . 21 Dec. ,,
Northfleet, vessel laden with railway iron for Van Diemen's Land, and railway navigators, run into by a foreign steamer (probably the *Murillo*,* a Spanish vessel) off Dungeness, about 10.30 p.m.; about 300 lost . . . . . 22 Jan. 1873
Chembuco, iron ship; sunk in the Channel, 15 miles from Orme's head, by collision with the *Torch* steamer; 24 lost . . . . . 1 March, ,,
Byne, barque; wrecked off Mohlo bay, Cornwall; about 20 lost . . . . . 1 March, ,,
Atlantic, steamer, of White Star company, struck on Meagher rock, west of Sambro; said to have fallen short of coals steaming for Halifax; 442 (including capt. Williams) saved; about 560 lost, 1 April, 1873; many on the rigging perished through cold and want. The case was investigated, and the captain was suspended for two years . . . . 18 April, ,,
Eden, ship, with 150 tons of gunpowder, sailing for Valparaiso; set on fire by her mad captain, and blew up: (the crew in a boat were rescued by the *Juanita*) . . . . 7, 8 Nov. ,,
Nuypore, from Calcutta, took fire and ran into Kingstown harbour, doing much damage till it went to pieces; the captain of the *Echo* and some sailors were drowned . . . . . . 9 Nov. ,,
Lochearn lost, through collision with the *Ville de Havre* (which see), 22 Nov.; quitted by her crew 28 Nov. ,,
Ella, London and Hamburg steamer; crew, 32; left Thames 14 Dec., supposed to have foundered in a gale . . . . 16 Dec. ,,
Queen Elizabeth, Glasgow steamer from India; went ashore near Tarifa; about 20 perished; middle of March, 1874
Tacna, steamer, from Valparaiso; foundered; about 19 lost (see *Chili*) . . . . March, ,,
Liberia, British and African Steam-ship Co.; wrecked by collision with *Barton* steamer, off Scilly isles; probably all lost on board both vessels about 13 April, ,,
British Admiral, emigrant ship; wrecked on King's island, Bass's strait; about 80 out of 89 lost 23 May, ,,
Milbanke, iron steamer; laden with zinc from Carthagena; sunk through collision with *Hankow* steamer off Dungeness; 14 perish; 1.30 a.m. 28 July, ,,
Calcutta, ship, from Shields to Aden; took fire; nearly all lost . . . . about 11 Sept. ,,
Malvern, barque, from Sunderland; foundered off Singapore; all hands lost . . . 23 Sept. ,,
Kingsbridge, iron ship, sunk off the Lizards, by collision with the *Candahar*, iron ship; the master,

* This vessel was captured near Dover, 22 Sept. and condemned by the court of admiralty to be sold; (the officers severely censured); 4 Nov. 1873.

his wife and daughter, and 8 of the crew perish 14 Oct. 1874
Maja, iron ship, of London; new clipper; wrecked off the Hebrides in a gale; crew, about 24, lost 20 Oct. ,,
Chusan, from Glasgow for Shanghai; sunk in a gale off Ardrossan; about 7 lost . . . 20 Oct. ,,
Cutter of H.M.S. *Aurora* swamped in the Clyde; 15 lost . . . . 19 Nov. ,,
La Plata, steamer (capt. Dudden), 1600 tons; sailed from Gravesend with telegraph cable for Brazil, 26 Nov.; foundered in a gale in the Bay of Biscay; 17 escape out of 85 . . . . 29 Nov. ,,
Cospatrick, emigrant vessel (capt. Emslie), on her way to Auckland, New Zealand; took fire, midnight, 17-18 Nov.; only 5 or 6 (out of 476) escaped; picked up, 27 Nov.; arrived at St. Helena 6 Dec. ,,
Japan, Pacific Mail steamer, from Yokohama; took fire off Hong Kong; many lost about 17 Dec. ,,
Delphic, steamer; struck on sunken rock, west coast of Africa; nearly all lost . . . . . ,,
Scorpio, steamer, from Cardiff to Charente; not heard of, 30 Dec. . . . . . 4 Dec. ,,
Cortes, of London, foundered in Bay of Biscay; laden with coal for Aden; capt. E. King; about 25 lost . . . . 16 Dec. ,,
Hong Kong, steamer; wrecked on sunken rock near Aden; about 12 lost . . . . 22 Feb. 1875
Stuart Hahnemann, sailed from Bombay, 4 April; capsized; about 40 drowned; (some rescued by *Blandina*, Austrian barque, 27 April) . 14 April, ,,
Cadiz, London steamer; wrecked on Wizard Rock, Brest; about 62 lost . . . . . 8 May, ,,
Vicksburg, steamer, left Quebec, 27 May; struck on ice, 30 May; sank, 1 June; between 40 and 50 lost . . . . 1 June, ,,
Strathmore, emigrant vessel, wrecked in a fog near the Crozet isles, South Indian ocean, on way to New Zealand; 45 out of 89 lost . . 1 July, ,,
Boyne, mail steamer, from Brazil; ran on a rock during a fog, 15 miles off Ushant; 2 lives lost 13 Aug. ,,
Mistletoe, Mr. Heywood's pleasure yacht; sunk by collision with H.M.'s steamer, *Alberta* (the queen on board): in the Solent; near Isle of Wight; Miss Annie Peel and two others drowned 18 Aug. ,,

[Coroner's inquest on Nathaniel Turner; verdict, accidental death, with a note alleging error of navigating officers, 10 Sept.; another inquest, closed without verdict, 7 Dec. 1875; captain Welch, of the *Alberta*, was reprimanded; 3000l. paid to Mr. Heywood, and others compensated; announced, April, 1876.]

See under *Navy of England*.

H.M.S. *Vanguard*, double-screw iron-clad, 3774 tons; cost about 350,000l. (captain Dawkins) struck by ram of the *Iron Duke* during a fog off the coast of Wicklow; crew (about 400) saved; 50 m. past noon . . . . . 1 Sept. ,,
Pacific, steamer, from Victoria, British Columbia, to California; foundered off Cape Flattery; above 150 lost . . . . . about 4 Nov. ,,
Goliath, old man-of-war, fitted up as a training-ship for poor boys; burnt through a lamp falling on the dirty floor of the lamp-room; about a dozen lives lost out of about 500; the boys were highly commended for their courage and discipline under the command of captain Bourchier . 22 Dec. ,,
Many wrecks autumn and winter, 1875.†
Warspite, old training-ship of the Marine Society's boys, on the Thames between Woolwich and Charlton, burnt; no loss of life; good discipline shown . . . . 3 Jan. 1876

* *Schiller*, Hamburg mail steamer; wrecked in a fog, on rocks of the Scilly isles; about 331 drowned, 7 May, 1875
† *Deutschland*, fine Atlantic steamer, from Bremen to New York, during a gale, went on sandbank, the Kentish Knock, at mouth of the Thames; about 70 lost (many emigrants), 6 Dec. 1875. The *Liverpool*, tug steamer, saved a great many lives; on investigation, it was shown that there had been no delay in helping, and no robbery, 31 Dec. The captain censured for error in navigation, and want of judgment.

Strathclyde, Glasgow steamer, sunk by collision with Hamburg ship *Franconia*, in Dover bay, in daylight; about 17 lost; (verdict of manslaughter against Kuhn, captain of *Franconia**). 17 Feb. 1876

Edith, steamer, sunk by collision with the *Duchess of Sutherland* (both owned by the London and North Western Railway Company) off St. John's Point, Ireland; 2 lives lost. 8 Sept. ,,

Shannon, mail steamer; struck on a shoal, 80 miles S.S.W. of Port Royal, Jamaica; no lives lost, 8 Sept. ,,

Western Empire, in Gulf of Mexico; a leak sprung, 13 Sept.; vessel left (10 lost). 18 Sept. ,,

Great Queensland, with impure patent gunpowder, and ordinary gunpowder; 569 persons on board; sailed for Melbourne, 5 Aug.; supposed to have exploded (pieces of wreck found), near Finisterre after 12 Aug. ,,

[Verdict of wreck commission against owners, 21 July, 1877.]

St. Lawrence, troop-ship, capt. Hyde; ran aground in St. Helena's bay, Africa; no loss of life 8 Nov. ,,

Ambassador, steamer; sunk by collision with an American ship, *George Manson*, returning from Calcutta: lat. 58° 6′ N., lon. 73° 27′ E.; 73 lost (crew, 43) 25 Dec. ,,

Cairo, iron ship; bound for Australia; carried much gunpowder; (said to have been wrecked off Tristan or Gough island); disappeared about middle of Jan. 1877

Cashmere, steamer (British India Steam Navigation company); wrecked off Guardafui; 7 drowned 12 July, ,,

Eten, steam ship (English Pacific Steam Navigation company); wrecked about 70 miles N. of Valparaiso; about 100 (of 160) lost; many rescued by H.M.S. *Amethyst* 15 July, ,,

Avalanche, emigrant iron vessel; from London to New Zealand; above 100 on board; struck by *Forest* (of Windsor, Nova Scotia), 21 crew; both sank; about 12 lives saved; in channel, 15 miles S. by W. of Portland, 9.15 p.m. 11 Sept. ,,

Many losses by severe gale 14, 15 Oct. ,,

Knapton Hall, steamer; sank through collision with *Lochfyne*, to whose assistance she was coming; 9 perish 15 Oct. ,,

Atacama, steamer; wrecked 22 miles S. of Caldera, near Copiapo; about 104 lost; end of Nov. ,,

European, Clyde steamer, from Algoa Bay; wrecked off Ushant; diamonds, &c., lost; no lives 5 Dec. ,,

Mizpah, steamer; sunk by collision with unknown vessel, 15 miles S.W. of Beachy Head; above 6 lost; early 6 Dec. ,,

C. M. Palmer, steamer, of Newcastle; lost by collision with *Ludworth* steamer, near Harwich; about 14 lives lost; fog, 10 a.m.. 17 Feb. 1878

Eurydice, H.M.S., frigate; training ship; returning from Bermudas; founders off Dunnose headland, near Ventnor, Isle of Wight; through a squall; capt. A. S. Hare, lieut. Tabor, and about 300 men perish 24 March, ,,

[Raised with much skill and labour, and taken into Portsmouth, Aug.]

Childwall Hall, Hull steamer; wrecked near Cape St. Vincent, Portugal; about 14 lost 11 April,†

Princess Alice (*which see*), run into by the screw steamer, *Bywell Castle*, in the Thames, near Woolwich, and sunk; between 600 and 700 lost; about 7.40 p.m. 3 Sept. ,,

Fanny, coastguard cruiser; run down by National steamer *Helvetia*, off Tuskar, Irish channel; 17 lost 31 Oct. ,,

Much damage and loss of life by gales 8-10 Nov.‡

Mesopotamia, steamer, run ashore at Peniche, coast of Portugal; 8 perished 18 Dec.§

* Verdict quashed on appeal; 7 judges (against 6), decide against British jurisdiction, 13 Nov. 1876.

† The German ironclad, *Grosser Kurfürst*, sunk by collision with *König Wilhelm*; about 300 lost; 31 May, 1878.

‡ *Pomerania*, Hamburg-American mail steamer, sunk off Folkestone, by *Moel Eilian*, iron bark, of Carnarvon; 162 saved by boats; about 48 missing; a little after midnight, 25 Nov., 1878.

§ French steamer, *Byzantin*, sank (losing above 200 lives) by collision with English steamer, *Rinaldo*, in Dardanelles, during a fearful gale, 18 Dec. 1878.

Ava, British India Navigation Steam Company steamer, sank by collision with sailing ship *Brunhilda*, in the Bay of Bengal; capt. Dickenson and about 70 perish 24 April,* 1879

City of London, Aberdeen steamer; run down and sunk by the *Vesta*, in the Thames, near Barking Reach; no lives lost 13 Aug. ,,

Borussia, a Dominion steamer, left Liverpool 20 Nov.; sprang a leak in the Atlantic after leaving Corunna, 1 Dec.; went down; about 160 lost; 10 out of 184 saved by boats 2 Dec. ,,

Valentine foundered in a gale near Falmouth; about 16 lost 8 Feb. 1880

Many wrecks in the North Atlantic during terrific gale (see *Atalanta*) 12-16 Feb. ,,

Struthnairn, of Dundee: collision with *Edith Hough*, steamer, off Ushant; all lost 13 Feb. ,,

Hindoo, steamer, from New York; loaded with grain, which shifted; abandoned; three officers lost and much cattle 22 Feb. ,,

Vingoria, steamer; sprang a leak 70 miles N. of Bombay; captain and 65 persons perish: announced 1 March, ,,

Barita, British steamer, sunk in a fog by collision with an Australian mail steamer near Galatz; 16 perish 9 April, ,,

American, steamer (Union Steamship Company), capt. Maclean Wait, foundered off Cape Palmas; all passengers and crew escaped in boats: (picked up by vessels, and carried to Madeira, St. Paul de Loanda, the Canaries, &c.) 23 April, ,,

Hydaspes, sailing ship; sank by collision with *Centurion*, screw steamer, off Dungeness, in a fog; both blamed; no lives lost 17 July,†

James Harris, steamer, loaded with iron; sunk by collision with the *Andalusia*, steamer, off the Ferne Isles 14 April,‡ 1881

H.M.S. *Doterel* destroyed by explosion in the Straits of Magellan (see *Navy*) 26 April, ,,

Victoria, steamer, on the Thames, Canada; overloaded; upset; several hundreds drowned; between 600 and 700 on board 24 May, ,,

Ten fishing boats sunk off the Shetland Isles in a storm; about 58 lives lost 20 July, ,,

Teuton, Union Company's mail screw steamer, struck on a rock near Cape Agulhas, Cape of Good Hope; and foundered a few hours after; of above 200 persons, not many saved; capt. E. Manning and most of the officers lost 30 Aug. ,,

[Inquiry: attributed to the captain's imprudent navigation 19 Sept.]

Govino, British steamer; about 13 perished, 7 Oct. ,,

130 wrecks (105 British) with great loss of life and property by the gales 10-15 Oct. ,,

Corsica, steamer; stranded near mouth of the Tagus; 21 deaths 11 Oct. ,,

[The captain exonerated, 8 Nov.]

Cyprian, iron steamer, lost in Carnarvon bay; capt. Strachan and another drowned 14 Oct. ,,

———, Glasgow steamer, wrecked in the Irish sea; many lost about 20-22 Oct. ,,

Clan Macduff, steamer, capt. Webster; foundered off the Irish coast (over-loaded) 32 lives lost [captain censured] 21 Oct. ,,

Albion, steamer, wrecked on the Atlantic coast of Columbia; 32 lost 5 Nov. ,,

Crown, British steamer, stranded near Jutland; 7 drowned 15 Nov. ,,

Solway, channel steamer, capt. W. Fry; during a storm off the Skerries; greatly burned through ignition of naphtha oil flooding the decks through bursting of casks, about 14 burned, and 5 drowned, who escaped in a boat (the steamer got back to Kingston harbour); officers exonerated of blame 16 Nov. ,,

Culzean, iron steamer; capt. Pirnie, while being towed to be repaired during a gale, stranded on rocks in the sound of Java; crew of 17 lost 22 Nov. ,,

* *Arrogante*, French ironclad battery, sank off Hirères Isles; 47 drowned; 19 March, 1879.

† *Vera Cruz*, U.S. steamer; foundered through hurricane in N. Atlantic, 30 miles from shore; 11 out of 82 saved; 4 Sept. 1880.

‡ *Oncle Joseph*, French steamer, sunk by collision with *Ortigia*, Italian steamer, off Spezzia; about 50 out of 300 saved; 24 Nov. 1880.

Many wrecks with loss of life and property during a gale . . . . . 26-27 Nov. 1881
Kildare, barque, stranded off Aberdeen coast in gale . . . . . . Dec. ,,
Helenslea, barque, collision with *Catalonia*, Cunard steamer; 9 of the crew lost . . 25 Dec. ,,
Lanarkshire, screw steamer, stranded off Codling Bank, Wicklow; some of the crew lost 15 Jan. 1882
Bahama, steamer, foundered between Porto Rico and New York; 20 lives lost . . 4 Feb. ,,
Kosmos, steamer, sank off Kilia; captain and 20 of crew drowned . . . . . Feb. ,,
Livadia, steamer, from Shields, sunk off Yarmouth; 23 lives lost . . . . 29 Feb. ,,
Douro, royal mail steamer; collision with Spanish steamer, *Yurrac Bat*, both sunk; about 23 English and 36 Spanish lost, about 11 p.m. (captain of *Douro* blamed) . . . . 1 April, ,,
Norara, ship; on voyage from Newcastle to San Francisco, burned; 19 missing . . 13 April, ,,
Alexandroonos, Liverpool ship, wrecked off Swanage; crew all lost . . . early in May, ,,
Peru, iron steamer; foundered 30 miles S.W. Cape Race; about 10 men lost . . . 10 June, ,,
Escambia, British screw steamer, wrecked at Escambia, near San Francisco; crew (about 20) lost, unannounced . . . . 20 June, ,,
Alice, steam-tug, wrecked off Bondecao rocks, Northumberland; 16 lives lost . . 29 June, ,,
Fleurs Castle, steamer, run aground, near Cape Guardafui, N.E. Africa; several perished, 9 July, ,,
Ethiopia, African mail steamer, run on a reef 28 July, ,,
Armenian, Liverpool steamer, lost in the Baltic; crew about 23 perish, announced . . 23 Aug. ,,
Panoma, Glasgow iron ship, foundered off Yarmouth; about 20 perish, announced 9 Sept. ,,
Constantia and *City of Antwerp*, steamers, sunk by collision off the Eddystone; about 14 lives lost 16 Oct. ,,
Winton, lost off Ushant; 24 perish 16 Nov. ,,
Wearmouth, steamer, lost off Magdalen Island 21 Nov. ,,
Cambronne, steamer, sunk by collision with *Marion*, near Lundy . . . . 26 Nov. ,,
St. George, steamer; lost off Portreath, Cornish coast; 11 perish . . . . 29 Nov. ,,
Cedar Grove, steamer, lost off Cape Canto, Nova Scotia; 17 persons missing . about 30 Nov. ,,
Many wrecks, with loss of life . . Dec. ,,
Langrigg Hall, barque, wrecked off Wexford; 24 deaths . . . . . 15 Dec. ,,
35 wrecks during a storm off Newfoundland about 19 Dec. ,,
British Empire, ship, burnt off Alleppy; several persons perish . . . . . 5 Jan. 1883
City of Brussels, sunk by collision with the *Kirby Hall*, in the Mersey; 10 drowned . . 7 Jan.† ,,
Kenmure Castle, steamer, wrecked in Bay of Biscay; 30 drowned . . . . about 1 Feb. ,,
King Arthur, Hull steamer, sunk near the mouth of the Bosphorus; 14 lost . . 22 Feb. ,,
Wrecks through gales in North sea, 382 lives lost, 6 March, ,,
Navarre, Scotch steamer; sunk near Christiansand; about 45 lost . . . . 7 March, ,,
Dunstaffnage, Liverpool ship, wrecked off Aberdeen; 23 perished . . . 17 March, ,,
Wykeham, steamer, of Whitby, foundered near Lisbon; 22 drowned; sailed from Cardiff March, ,,
British Commerce, sunk by collision with *County of Aberdeen*, off Selsey Bill; 25 perish . 24 April, ,,
Grappler burnt near Bute Inlet (Vancouver Island) about 70 perish . . . . 3 May, ,,
H.M.S. *Lively* stranded on rocks off Stornoway 7 June, ,,
[Commander Parr dismissed, 28 June.]
Waitara, sunk by collision with *Hurunui* (New Zealand Steamship Co.) off Beachy Head; 25 perish . . . . . 22 June, ,,
Daphne, coasting steamer, heeled over, during launch in the Clyde; about 124 drowned 3 July, ,,

* *Asia*, N.W. transit service steamer, foundered between Ontario and Saule Sainte Marie; about 98 lost, 14 Sept. 1882.
† *Cimbria*, Hamburg steamer, sunk by collision with English steamer, *Sultan*, off coast of Holland, about 454 perish, 19 Jan. 1883.

79 wrecks on British coasts reported through violent gale . . . . 1-2 Sept. 1883
Holyhead, L. & N. W. railway's cattle steamer and German barque, *Alhambra*, sailing vessel, sunk by collision between Dublin and Holyhead; 15 deaths; midnight . . . 31 Oct. ,,
Iris, sunk off Cape Villano; about 35 perish; announced . . . . . 8 Nov. ,,
Auk, Liverpool steamer, at South Handen; 22 lives lost . . . . . 11 Dec. ,,
Simla, wrecked by collision with the *City of Lucknow*, both Glasgow Australian sailers, near the Needles, English channel; about 20 perish; 3 p.m. 25 Jan. 1884*
Very many wrecks . . . 23-27 Jan. ,,
Nokomis, barque, struck on Black Rock, Antrim; 16 perish . . . . . 26 Jan. ,,
Juno, iron ship, stranded in the Mersey by a gale; the crew (30) perish . . . 26, 27 Jan. ,,
State of Florida, Glasgow steamer, and *Ponema*, barque, sunk by collision in mid-ocean off Canada coast; about 123 perish . . 18 April,† ,,
Larham (capt. Lothian), English steamer, and *Gijon*, Cuban steamer, sunk by collision in a fog off Cape Finisterre; about 130 perish; many picked up by *Santo Domingo* . . night, 21 July, ,,
Dione, steamer, sunk by collision with *Camden*, steamer, near Gravesend; about 17 drowned; soon after midnight . . . 2-3 Aug. ,,
[capt. of the *Dione* punished for reckless navigation, Aug].
Wasp, H.M. gun-boat (see under *Navy*).
Little Beck, stranded near the mouth of the Maas; 14 drowned . . . . 26 Oct. ,,
Indus, P. & O. company's steamer wrecked on coast of Ceylon . . . . . 8 Nov. ,,
Durango, screw steamer, run down by *Luke Bruce*, iron barque, in the English channel; 20 lives lost 27 Nov. ,,
Pochard, steamer, foundered off Holyhead; crew lost . . . . . . 7 Dec. ,,
Mignonette, yacht; sailed from Southampton to Australia, 19 May; foundered in a storm about 1600 miles from the Cape; 3 men and a boy escaped in a boat, without provisions, 5 July; proposed killing of one by lot rejected by Brooks, boy (Richard Parker) killed by captain, and eaten, 20th day, *et seq.*; men picked up by German barque, *Montezuma*, 24th day, and carried to Falmouth; capt. Thos. Dudley, and Edwin Stephens, mate, tried for murder at Exeter; facts affirmed, 6 Nov.; affirmed by lord chief justice and other judges in Queen's bench, 4 Dec.; sentence of death passed, 9 Dec.; reprieved, 6 months' imprisonment without labour . . . . . 13 Dec. ,,
Admiral Moorsom, L. and N. W. R's steamer, sunk near Holyhead by collision with *Santa Clara* (American); capt. Weeks, and about 4 perish 15 Jan. 1885
Cheerful, Liverpool steamer, collision with H.M.S. *Hecla* in the Bristol channel, 13 lives lost in a fog, 4 a.m. . . . . 21 July, ,,
Yarra Yarra, Liverpool barque, 27 lives lost, announced . . . . . 11 Sept. ,,
Dolphin, steamer (Gen. Nav. St. Co.), sunk by collision with the *Brenda*, eight perish, 18 Sept. ,,
Merchantman, on Sand Heads; about 70 lives lost, Sept. ,,
Albula, British ship, wrecked during typhoon off Loochoo islands, 10 perish . . 14 Oct. ,,
Algoma, Canadian steamer, foundered in lake Superior; 45 lives lost . . . 7 Nov. ,,
Corinth, Union line steamer, sunk by collision with H.M.S. *Firebrand* . . March, 1886
Oregon, Cunard steamer, foundered (without loss of life), by collision with an unknown schooner near Long Island in America; schooner sunk with all on board . . . . 14 March, ,,

* *City of Columbus*, U.S. passenger ship; ran on reef, coast of Massachusetts; 29 lives saved; about 97 perish; alleged negligence; 18 Jan. 1884.
† *Daniel Steinmann*, White Cross steamer, struck on rock off Sambro' Isle, Nova Scotia; about 120 perish, about 3 April, 1884.
Senorine, French brig, wrecked off Great Bank, Newfoundland about 62 perish, 6 May, 1884.

Ly-ee-Moon, an iron steamer, Australasian steam navigation company, wrecked off Green Cape, between Melbourne and Sydney; 76 persons drowned . . . . . 30 March, 1886
Ferntower, British steamer, foundered near Saigon; about 50 lives lost . . . . 26 Aug. ,,
Malleny, Liverpool iron steamer, foundered on the Tuskar reef, Bristol channel; all hands lost in the gale (about 20) . . . . 15 Oct. ,,
Many vessels lost, many injured, and great loss of life during a severe gale . . . 14–16 Oct. ,,
Teviotdale, steamer of Glasgow, lost on the Carnarthen coast; 18 lives lost . . . 15 Oct. ,,
Keilawarra and *Helen Nicholl* collision (42 lives lost) off the coast of Queensland; announced 9 Dec. ,,
Sultan, British ironclad, and *Ville de Victoria*, French steamer, collision in Lisbon harbour; the latter vessel sunk; 35 lives lost . 23 Dec. ,,
Kapunda, emigrant ship for Australia, said to have foundered by collision with *Ada Melmore* off Brazil; about 298 perish, 3 a.m. 20 Jan., officers of the *Ada Melmore* censured . . 29 March, 1887
Victoria, London & Brighton company's steamer, during fog struck on rock at Point D'Ailly; no fog horn sounded, about 16 lives lost out of 90 passengers through panic and recklessness; the rest saved by skill and courage of the captain and officers . . . . . 13 April, ,,
Tasmania, P. & O. steamer wrecked on Monachi rocks, Corsica; 23 lives lost including captain Perrin . . . . . . 17 April, ,,
Volta, Eastern Telegraph company's steamer, wrecked off Myconos, Greece; 12 lives lost, 18 April, ,,
Benton, steamer, of Singapore, foundered by collision; about 150 lives lost, announced 28 April, ,,
Destruction of a Pearl fishing fleet, N.E. coast of Australia, with a loss of 550 lives, in a hurricane on 22 April; reported . . . 28 April, ,,
John Knox, British steamer, wrecked at St. John's; 27 lost . . . . . . 4 May, ,,
City of Montreal (cotton ship), Inman steamer, burnt 400 miles off Newfoundland on her way from New York to Liverpool . . 10 Aug. ,,
Monarch, pleasure yacht, founders near Ilfracombe; 11 lives lost . . . . . 26 Aug. ,,
Falls of Bruar, of Glasgow, sunk off Yarmouth; 24 lives lost . . . . . 2 Sept. ,,
Lydia, British schooner, lost in a hurricane in the North Atlantic; 15 lives lost . . Sept. ,,
H.M.S. *Wasp*, gunboat, disappeared since 7 Oct.; probably lost in a typhoon in the China sea on 17 Sept.* ,,
Lanoma, iron barque, wrecked near Weymouth; 12 lives lost . . . . . 8 March, 1888
City of Corinth sunk by collision with *Tasmania* near Dungeness . . . . 9 March, ,,
Smyrna, sailing vessel, loses 12 men by collision with the *Moto*, steamer, off Dorset coast, 28 April, ,,
Trerelyan, emigrant ship, sunk off Cape Agulhas, all on board lost . . . . 3 June, ,,
Star of Greece wrecked in Aldinga Bay, near Adelaide; 17 lives lost . . . 13 July,†
Earl of Wemyss and *Ardencaple*, Glasgow barques, collision, 16 lives lost . . . 8 Sept. ,,
Collision between *La France* (French) and *Sud America* (Italian) off the Canary Islands; about 87 lives lost . . . . . 13 Sept. ,,
Collision between Glasgow steamer *Neptune* and Russian steamer *Archangel* at Christiania; 18 lives lost . . . . . 19 Oct. ,,
Nor, Norwegian barque, and *Sormundham*, steamer from the Tyne; collision; 12 lives lost, 4 Nov. ,,

* *W. A. Scholten*, Dutch steamer, sunk by collision with *Rosa Mary* of Hartlepool, at anchor off Dover; about 130 persons perish, many saved by the crew of the *Ebro* of Sunderland. 19 Nov. 1887.
Alfred D. Snow, American vessel, wrecked off Waterford; 28 perish, 4 Jan. 1888.
† Collision between *Thingvalla* and *Geiser*, German steamers, off Sable Island, N. Atlantic; 105 lives in the *Geiser*, lost 14 Aug. 1888.

Steamer *Hartlepool* wrecked on a rock at Naalevig; 17 lives lost . . . . . 6 Dec.* 1881
British steamer, *The Priam*, wrecked near Cape Finisterre; about five lives lost . 12 Jan. 1889
Nereid, steamer, of Newcastle, collision with the Scotch ship *Killochan* off Dungeness; 23 lives lost . . . . . . 3 Feb. ,,
Collision of the *Largo Bay* with steamer *Glencoe* which founders off Beachy Head; all hands lost, 4 Feb. ,,
Wreck of the Grimsby fishing fleet; 73 lives lost, 9 Feb.†
German and American war vessels wrecked off Samoa (see *Storms*) . . . 16 March,‡
Cotopaxi, Pacific steamer, struck on unknown reef, Smyth's channel, straits of Magellan, and foundered; no lives lost . . . 15 April, ,,
Altimore, British steamer, struck on rocks off Fiji islands; about 12 persons drowned, 22 April, ,,
The *German Emperor*, screw steamer, ran into the *Beresford*, anchored off Dover, in a fog, and sank; nine missing . . . . 21 May, ,,
Gettysburg, barque, of Aberdeen, wrecked on a coral reef off Morant Cayes, 33 miles from Jamaica, with a crew of 16 hands, 30 March–1 April; by very great exertions, the captain and part of the crew succeeded in getting on the desolate isle, where they stayed, living on shell-fish, &c. On 22 April two men on a raft started for Jamaica and landed seven miles from Morant Bay, 24 April. On their reaching Kingston, H.M.S. *Forward* was sent off, and brought the captain and the rest of the crew to Kingston 27 April, whence they were conveyed to England having lost seven of their number, where they arrived . . . . . . 18 May, ,,
Isaac Houston, British schooner, foundered in a storm off Milwaukee; 16 lives lost; reported 14 June, ,

WRECK COMMISSION, a new court established to inquire into the causes of shipwrecks; first sat, 30 Oct. 1876, Mr. H. C. Rothery, president.

WREXHAM, S. E. Denbighshire, the Saxon Wrightesham, given to earl Warren by Edward I.; made a borough by the reform act, 1832. An exhibition of art treasures of North Wales, and the border counties, was opened here by the duke of Westminster, 22 July, 1876. Musical festival here 1883, *et seq*.

WRITING. Pictures are considered to be the first essay towards writing. The most ancient remains of writing are upon hard substances, such as stones and metals, used by the ancients for edicts, and matters of public notoriety. Athotes, or Hermes, is said to have written a history of the Egyptians, and to have been the author of the hieroglyphics, 2112 B.C. *Usher*. Writing is said to have been taught to the Latins by Europa, daughter of Agenor, king of Phœnicia, 1494 B.C. *Thucydides*. Cadmus, the founder of Cadmen, 1493 B.C., brought the Phœnician letters into Greece. *Vossius*. The

* *John Hanna*, steamer, laden with cotton, burnt on the Mississippi; about 20 persons perish, 24 Dec. 1888.
† The *Comtesse de Flandre* cut in half by collision with the *Princess Henriette*, both Belgian mail boats; the captain and 14 others killed, prince Napoleon Bonaparte escapes; about 1·45 p.m. 20 March, 1889.
‡ *Danmark*, Danish emigrant vessel sank in the Atlantic about 800 miles from Newfoundland; captain Murrell of the *Missouri*, Atlantic transport line, and his crew, with great energy rescued all on board (735), 6 April, 1889.
[He landed part on the Azores and part in Philadelphia.]
At the Mansion House, on 24 May, 1889, captain Murrell, in the presence of distinguished company, received from the lord mayor a silver salver with an inscription, and a purse of money (about 500*l*.) from the citizens of London; the officers and crew also received testimonials.

commandments were written on two tables of stone, 1491 B.C. *Usher.* The Greeks and Romans used wax table-books, and continued the use of them long after papyrus was known; see *Papyrus, Parchment, Paper.* Thos. Astle's "History of Writing" was first published in 1784; Natalis de Wailly's "Élémens de Paléographie," 1838; see *Diplomatics* and *Type-Writers.*[*]

The Palæographical Society was founded in 1873; Mr. Birch, of the British Museum, president.

WROXETER (in Shropshire), the Roman city *Uriconium.* Roman inscriptions, ruins, seals, and coins were found here in 1752. New discoveries having been made, a committee for further investigation met at Shrewsbury on 11 Nov. 1858. Excavations were commenced in Feb. 1859, which were continued till May. Large portions of the old town were discovered; also specimens of glass and pottery, personal ornaments and toys, household utensils and implements of trade, cinerary urns, and bones of man and of the smaller animals. A committee was formed in London in Aug. 1859, with the view of continuing these investigations, which were resumed in 1861, through the liberality of the late Beriah Botfield, M.P. The investigations, stopped through want of funds, were resumed for a short time in 1867. Mr. Thomas Wright published "Uriconium" in 1872.

WURSCHEN, see *Bautzen.*

WÜRTEMBERG, originally part of Swabia, was made a county for Ulric I., about 1265, and a duchy for Eberhard in 1494. The dukes were protestants until 1722, when the reigning prince became a Roman catholic. Würtemberg has been repeatedly traversed by armies, particularly since the great French revolution of 1793. Moreau made his celebrated retreat, 23 Oct. 1796. The political constitution is dated 25 Sept. 1819. Würtemberg opposed Prussia in the war, June, 1866, but made peace, 13 Aug. following; in Oct. 1867, joined the Zollverein (*which see*), but sent a contingent to Prussia in the war, 1870. Population of Würtemberg in 1871, 1,818,539; 1880, 1,971,118; 1885, 1,995,185.

DUKES.

1494. Eberhard I.
1496. Eberhard II.
1498. Ulric; deprived of his states by the emperor Charles V.; recovers them in 1534.
1550. Christopher the Pacific.
1568. Louis the Pious.

[*] "I would check the petty vanity of those who slight good penmanship, as below the notice of a scholar, by reminding them that Mr. Fox was distinguished by the clearness and firmness, Mr. Professor Porson by the correctness and elegance, and sir William Jones by the ease and beauty of the characters they respectively employed." *Dr. Parr.*

1593. Frederic I.
1608. John Frederic; joined the protestants in the Thirty years' war.
1628. Eberhard III.
1674. William Louis.
1677. Eberhard Louis; served under William III. in Ireland; and with the English armies on the continent.
1733. Charles Alexander.
1737. Charles Eugene.
1793. Louis Eugene (joins in the war against France).
1795. Frederic I., makes peace with France, 1796.
1797. Frederic II. marries the princess royal of England, 18 May; made *elector* of Germany, 1803; acquired additional territories, and the title of king in 1805.

KINGS.

1805. Frederic I. supplies a contingent to Napoleon's Russian army; yet joined the allies at Leipsic in 1813. Died in 1816.
1816. William I., 30 Oct.; son; born 27 Sept. 1781. He abolished serfdom in 1818; instituted representative government in 1819; entered into a concordat with Rome in 1857; was the oldest living sovereign, in 1862; died 25 June, 1864.
1864. Charles I., son; born 6 March, 1823; married princess Olga of Russia, 13 July, 1846. No issue.

Heir presumptive: William, born 25 Feb. 1848.

WÜRZBURG (in Bavaria), was formerly a bishopric, and its sovereign one of the greatest ecclesiastic princes of the empire. It was given as a principality to the elector of Bavaria in 1803; and by the treaty of Presburg, in 1805, was ceded to the archduke Ferdinand of Tuscany, whose electoral title was transferred from Salzburg to this place. In 1814 this duchy was again transferred to Bavaria, in exchange for the Tyrol, and the archduke Ferdinand was reinstated in his Tuscan dominions. Ministers from the second-rate German states met at Würzburg to promote union amongst them, 21-27 Nov. 1859. Near here the archduke Charles defeated the French under Jourdan, 3 Sept. 1796; and the Prussians defeated the Bavarians, 28 July, 1866.

WYATT'S INSURRECTION, see *Rebellions,* 1554.

WYCLIFFITES, see *Wickliffites.*

WYOMING, a western territory of the United States of America, constituted in 1868, capital, Cheyenne. Lynch Law has not long been superseded. Women have been enfranchised. It includes Yellowstone park (*which see*). The desolation of Wyoming, in Pennsylvania, by an incursion of Indians allied with the British, 3 July, 1778, forms the subject of Campbell's poem, "Gertrude of Wyoming" published 1809. Wyoming abounds in iron, coal, natural soda, mineral oil, &c. Population 1880, 20,789.

X.

XANTHIAN MARBLES.

XANTHIAN MARBLES, see *British Museum*.

XANTHICA, a military festival observed by the Macedonians in the month called Xanthicus (our April), instituted about 392 B.C.

XANTHUS, Lycia, Asia Minor, was taken by Harpagus for Cyrus, about 546 B.C., when the inhabitants buried themselves in the ruins. It was besieged by the Romans under Brutus 42 B.C. After a great struggle the inhabitants set fire to their city, destroyed their wives and children, and perished. The conqueror wished to spare them, and offered rewards to his soldiers if they brought any of the Xanthians into his presence, but only 150 were saved. *Plutarch*.

XENOPHON, see *Retreat of the Greeks*.

XERES DE LA FRONTERA (S.W. Spain), the *Asta Regia* of the Romans, and the seat of the wine-trade in Spain, of which the principal wine is that so well known in England as Sherry, an English corruption of Xeres. The British importations of this wine in 1850 reached to 3,826,785 gallons; and in the year ending 5 Jan. 1852, to 3,904,978 gallons. Xeres is a handsome and large town, of great antiquity. At the battle of Xeres, 26 July, 711, Roderic, the last Gothic sovereign of Spain, was defeated and slain by the Saracens, commanded by Tarik and Muza.

XYLOTECHNOGRAPHICA.

XERXES' CAMPAIGN. Xerxes crossed the Hellespont by a bridge of boats, and entered Greece in the spring of 480 B.C., with an army which, together with the numerous retinue of servants, eunuchs, and women that attended it, amounted (according to some historians) to 5,283,220 souls. Herodotus states the armament to have consisted of 3000 sail, conveying 1,700,000 foot, besides cavalry and the marines and attendants of the camp. This multitude was stopped at Thermopylæ (*which see*) by the valour of 300 Spartans under Leonidas, 7-9 Aug. 480 B.C. The fleet of Xerxes was defeated at Artemisium and Salamis, 20 Oct. 480 B.C.; and he hastened back to Persia, leaving behind Mardonius, the best of his generals, who, with an army of 300,000 men, was defeated and slain at Platæa, 22 Sept. 479 B.C. Xerxes was assassinated by Artabanus, 465 B.C.

XIMENA (S. Spain), the site of a battle between the Spanish army under the command of general Ballasteros, and the French corps commanded by general Regnier, 10 Sept. 1811. The Spaniards defeated their adversaries; the loss was great on both sides.

XYLOTECHNOGRAPHICA, a process for staining wood various colours, invented and patented by Mr. A. F. Brophy; announced early in 1875.

Y.

YACHT.

YACHT (from the Dutch *jaght*); a light vessel for pleasure or races.

YACHT RACES.—The *America*, an American yacht schooner, built on the wave principle, 171 tons; at Cowes regatta, in a match round the Isle of Wight, open to all comers, came in first by 8 miles, gaining the Royal Yacht's Squadron's International queen's cup worth 100l. . 22 Aug. 1851

Three American yachts, the *Henrietta*, *Vesta*, and *Fleetwing*, sailed from New York, 11 Dec. 1866, at 1 P.M. The *Henrietta* arrived at Cowes at 5.40 on 25 Dec., the quickest voyage ever made in a sailing vessel. Her rivals were only a few hours after her

In a contest off the Isle of Wight, between the American vessel *Sappho* and the English cutters *Aline*, *Cambria*, *Oimara*, and *Condor*, the *Oimara* won . . . . . . 25 Aug. 1868

In a triangular race between *Sappho* and *Cambria*, *Sappho* won, 10 May; no race, 14 May; won 17 May, 1870

In a yacht race off Staten Island, New York, for the squadron or queen's cup, the *Magic* won, *Cambria* being the 8th in 16 . . . . Aug. ,,

In a series of matches off Staten island between Mr. Ashbury's *Livonia*, and the vessels of the New York Club, she was beaten by the *Columbia*, 16, 18 Oct: by the *Dauntless*, 21 Oct. The two vessels were disabled by a gale in attempting the race . . . . . . 25 Oct. 1871

In consequence of the collision of Mr. Heywood's yacht, *Mistletoe*, with her majesty's steam yacht, *Alberta*, 18 Aug. 1875 (see under *Wrecks*), a letter was written on behalf of the queen to the marquis of Exeter, commodore of the Royal Victoria Yacht Club, desiring yachts not to be brought too near to her majesty's, whether from loyalty or curiosity . . . Sept. 1875

Yacht Racing Association formed as a court of appeal . . . . . . 17 Nov. ,,

Death of George Inman, of Lymington, head of the firm which built the *Alarm*, and many other swift sailing yachts . . . 20 Oct. 1883

Match between the British *Genesta* and the American *Puritan*; the *Puritan* won by 1¼ minutes . . . . . 16 Sept. 1885

Genesta beat the *Dauntless* in a race, 26-28 Sept. 1885; the *Mayflower* beat the *Galatea*, 11 Sept. 1886.

Ocean yacht race from New York to Roche's Point, Queenstown, Ireland, between *Coronet* and *Dauntless* (American), 12 March; *Coronet* arrives at Roche's Point, 0·50 a.m. 28 March; *Dauntless* arrives 6·45 p.m. . . . 28 March, 1887

Jubilee yacht race; twelve yachts start from Southend, 14 June; the *Genesta* (sir Richard Sutton) arrives at Dover at 5 a.m.; the *Sleuthhound* 11·45 p.m. 27 June; first prize 1,000gs.

Race between the Scotch yacht *Thistle* and American yacht *Volunteer* for American cup over the New York yacht club course; *Volunteer* wins first race 27 Sept.; second race 30 Sept. ,,

Yacht clubs:—Royal Yacht Squadron, Cowes, 1812; Royal Albert, 1864; Alfred, 1864; Barrow, 1871; Channel Islands, 1863; Cinque Ports, 1872; Clyde, 1856; Cork, 1720; Cornwall, 1871; Dartmouth, 1866; Dorset, 1875; R. Eastern, 1835; R. Forth, 1868; R. Harwich, 1843; R. Highland, 1881; R. Irish, 1846; R. London (Arundel, 1838), 1849; R. Mersey, 1844; R. Northern, 1824; R. Portsmouth, 1880; R. St. George, 1838; R. Southampton, 1875; R. Southern, 1843; R. Thames, 1823; R. Torbay, 1875; R. Ulster, 1867; R. Victoria, 1844; R. Welsh, 1847; R. Western of England, 1827; R. Yorkshire, 1847; and a few others.

YANKEE, from "Yengees," a corruption of

YEAR.

"English," the name originally given by the Massachusetts Indians to the colonists: applied solely to the New Englanders by the British soldiers in the American war (1775-81); afterwards by foreigners to all natives of the United States; and latterly by the confederates of the south to the federals of the north during the war 1861-64.

YARD. The word is derived from the Saxon *geard*, or *gyrd*, a rod or shoot, or from *gyrdan* to enclose, being anciently the circumference of the body, until Henry I. decreed that it should be the length of his arm; see *Standard Measures*.

YARMOUTH, GREAT (Norfolk), was a royal demesne in the reign of William I., as appears from Domesday Book, 1086. It obtained a charter from John. and one from Henry III. In 1348, a plague here carried off 7000 persons; and did much havoc again in 1579 and 1664.

Theatre built 1778
Nelson's pillar, a fluted column 140 feet in height, erected 1817
Suspension chain bridge over the Bure, built by Mr. R. Cory, at an expense of about 4000l.; owing to the weight of a vast number of persons who assembled on it to witness an exhibition on the water, it suddenly gave way, and seventy-nine lives (mostly children) were lost . 2 May, 1845
Yarmouth disfranchised for bribery and corruption by the Reform Act . . . Aug. 1867
The prince of Wales opened a new grammar school, 6 June, 1873
Aquarium and winter garden opened 5 Sept. 1876
New municipal buildings opened by the prince of Wales . . . . . 31 May, 1882
Returns one M.P. by Act of 1885.

YASHGAR, a country, Central Asia; Yakoob, its able despotic chief, was contending with China and Russia, 1875.

YEAR. The Egyptians, it is said, were the first who fixed the length of the year.

The Roman year introduced by Romulus, 738 B.C.; corrected by Numa, 713 B.C.; and again by Julius Cæsar, 45 B.C. (see *Calendar*).

The *solar* or astronomical year was found to comprise 365 days, 5 hours, 48 minutes, 51 seconds, and 6 decimals, 265 B.C.

The *lunar* year (twelve lunar months, or 354 days, 8 hours, 48 minutes) was in use amongst the Chaldæans, Persians, and Jews. Once in every three years was added another lunar month, so as to make the solar and the lunar year nearly agree. But though the months were lunar, the year was solar; that is, the first month was of thirty days, and the second of twenty-nine, and so alternately: and the month added triennially was called Ve-Adar or the second Adar. The Jews afterwards followed the Roman manner of computation.

The *sidereal* year, or return to the same star, is 365 days, 6 hours, 9 minutes, 11 seconds.

The Jews dated the beginning of the sacred year in March, and civil year in September; the Athenians began the year in June; the Macedonians on 24 Sept.; the Christians of Egypt and Ethiopia on 29 or 30 Aug.; and the Persians and Armenians on 11 Aug. Nearly all Christian nations now commence the year on 1 January.

In France, the Merovingian kings began the year with March; the Carlovingians sometimes began the year with Christmas, 25 Dec.; and sometimes with Easter, which, being a movable feast, led to much confusion. Charles IX. of France, in 1564, published an arrêt, the last article of which ordered the year for the time to

come to be constantly and universally begun, and written on and from 1 January.
The beginning of the year has been reckoned from the day celebrating the birth of Christ, 25 Dec.; his circumcision, 1 Jan.; his conception, 25 March; and his resurrection, Easter.
The English began their year on the 25th of December, until the time of William the Conqueror. This prince having been crowned on 1 Jan. gave occasion to the English to begin their year at that time, to make it agree with the then most remarkable period of their history. *Stow.* Until the act for altering the style, in 1752 (see *Style*), when the year was ordered to begin on Jan. 1, it did not legally and generally commence in England until 25th March. In Scotland, at that period, the year began on the 1st of January. This difference caused great practical inconveniences; and January, February, and part of March sometimes bore two dates, as we often find in old records, 1745-1746, or 1745-6, or 174$\frac{5}{6}$. Such a reckoning often led to chronological mistakes; for instance, we popularly say the "revolution of 1688," as that event was completed in February, 1688, according to the then mode of computation: but if the year were held to begin, as it does now, on the first of January, it would be the revolution of 1689.
The year in the northern regions of Siberia and Lapland is described in the following calendar, given by a traveller:—"23 *June*, snow melts. 1 *July*, snow gone. 9 *July*, fields quite green. 17 *July*, plants at full growth. 25 *July*, plants in flower. 2 *Aug.*, fruits ripe. 10 *Aug.*, plants shed their seed. 18 *Aug.*, snow." The snow continues upon the ground from 18th Aug. of one year to 23rd June of the year following, being 309 days out of 365; so that while the three seasons of spring, summer, and autumn are together only fifty-six days, or eight weeks, the winter is of forty-four weeks' duration in these countries.
See *New Style, Platonic Year, Sabbatical Year, Mahometanism, French Revolutionary Calendar*.

YEAR OF OUR LORD; see *Anno Domini*.

YEAR OF THE REIGN. From the year of William the Conqueror, 1066, the year of the sovereign's reign has been given to all public instruments. The king's patents, charters, proclamations, and all acts of parliament have since then been generally so dated. The same manner of dating is used in most of the European states for all similar documents and records; see List of Kings under *England*.

YEAR AND A DAY. A space of time in law, and in many cases establishes and fixes a right; as in an estray, on proclamation being made, if the owner does not claim it within the time, it is forfeited. The term arose in the Norman law, which enacted that a beast found on another's land, if unclaimed for a year and a day, belonged to the lord of the soil. It is otherwise a legal space of time.

YEAR-BOOKS contain reports in Norman-French of cases argued and decided in the courts of common law. The printed volumes extend from the beginning of the reign of Edward II. to nearly the end of the reign of Henry VIII., a period of about 220 years; but in this series there are many omissions. These books are the first in the long line of legal reports in which England is so rich, and may be considered as, to a great extent, the foundation of our unwritten law, "*Lex non scripta*." In 1863 *et seq.* various year-books of Edward I. (1292-1304) edited by Mr. A. J. Horwood, for the series of the Chronicles and Memorials, were published at the expense of the British government.

YEAST, a substance causing fermentation, was discovered by Cagniard de la Tour and Schwann, independently, in 1836, to be a vegetable cell or fungus.

YELLOW FEVER, an American pestilence, made its appearance at Philadelphia, where it committed great ravages, 1699. It appeared in several islands of the West Indies in 1732, 1739, and 1745. It raged with unparalleled violence at Philadelphia in Oct. 1762; and most awfully at New York in the beginning of Aug. 1791. This fever again spread great devastation at Philadelphia in July 1793; carrying off several thousand persons. *Hardie.* It again appeared in Oct. 1797; and spread its ravages over the northern coast of America, Sept 1798. It reappeared at Philadelphia in the summer of 1802; and broke out in Spain, in Sept. 1803. The yellow fever was very violent at Gibraltar in 1804 and 1814; in the Mauritius, July 1815; at Antigua, in Sept. 1816; and it raged with dreadful consequences at Cadiz, and the isle of St. Leon, in Sept. 1819. A malignant fever raged at Gibraltar in Sept. 1828, and did not terminate until the following year. Yellow fever raging in the southern of the United States, Sept. Oct. 1878; at Memphis, autumn, 1879; in Florida (specially in Jacksonville) and other southern states, autumn 1888. Mr. R. A. Proctor, the astronomer, died of it at New York on his way from Florida to England, 12 Sept. 1888; the epidemic abating Oct. 1888; 4,583 cases, and 396 deaths in Jacksonville to Nov. 17, 1888.

YELLOWSTONE NATIONAL PARK, about 3300 square miles, in territory of Wyoming.
It includes Yellowstone lake, about 330 square miles, with numerous geysers, volcanic and other grand natural phenomena, rugged mountains, forests, meadows, rivers, and much beautiful scenery. Its formation was authorised by congress in March, 1872. It was visited by president Arthur in 1883.

YELVERTON CASE, see *Trials*, 1861.

YENIKALE, see *Azoff*.

YEOMANRY, see under *Volunteers*.

YEOMEN OF THE GUARD, a peculiar body of foot guards to the king's person, instituted at the coronation of Henry VII. 30 Oct. 1485, which originally consisted of fifty men under a captain. They were called beef-eaters, a corruption of *buffitiers*, being attendants on the king's buffet or sideboard; see *Battle-Axe*. They were of a larger stature than other guards, being required to be over six feet in height, and were armed with arquebuses and other arms. The band was increased by Henry's successors to one hundred men, and seventy supernumerries; and when one of the hundred died, it was ordered that his place should be supplied out of the seventy. They were clad after the manner of king Henry VIII. *Ashmole's Instit.* This is said to have been the first permanent military band instituted in England. John earl of Oxford, was the first captain in 1486. *Beatson's Pol. Index.*

YERMUK (Syria). Near here the emperor Heraclius was totally defeated by the Saracens, after a fierce engagement, Nov. 636. Damascus was taken, and his army expelled from Syria.

YEW-TREE (*Taxus*). The origin of planting yew-trees in churchyards was (these latter being fenced) to secure the trees from cattle, and in this manner preserve them for the encouragement of archery. A general plantation of them for the use of archers was ordered by Richard III. 1483. *Stow's Chron.* Near Fountaines Abbey, Yorkshire, were seven yew-trees, called the Seven Sisters, supposed to have been planted before 1088; the circumference of the largest thirty-four feet seven inches round the trunk. In 1851 a yew-tree was said to be growing in the churchyard of Gresford, North Wales, whose circumference was nine yards nine inches, being the largest and oldest yew-tree in the British dominions; but tradition states that there are some yews in England older than the introduction of Christianity. The old yew-tree, mentioned

YEZIDIS. 1009 YORK.

in the survey taken of Richmond palace in 1649, is said to be still existing.

YEZIDIS, an eastern tribe, living near the Euphrates, visited by Mr. Layard in 1841: see *Devil Worship*.

YEZDEGIRD, or **PERSIAN ERA**, was formerly universally adopted in Persia, and is still used by the Parsees in India, and by the Arabs, in certain computations. This era began on the 26th June, 632, when Yezdegird was elected king of Persia. The year consisted of 365 days only, and therefore its commencement, like that of the old Egyptian and Armenian year, anticipated the Julian year by one day in every four years. This difference amounted to nearly 112 days in the year 1075, when it was reformed by Jelaledin, who ordered that in future the Persian year should receive an additional day whenever it should appear necessary to postpone the commencement of the following year, that it might occur on the day of the sun's passing the same degree of the ecliptic.

YNGLINGS (youths, or off-shoots), descendants of the Scandinavian hero Odin, ruled Sweden till 830, when the last of the pontiff kings, Olaf Tretelia, being expelled, led to the foundation of the Norwegian monarchy.

YOKE is spoken of as a type of servitude. The ceremony of making prisoners pass under it was practised by the Samnites towards the Romans, 321 B.C.; see *Caudine Forks*. This disgrace was afterwards inflicted by the Romans upon their vanquished enemies. *Dufresnoy*.

YOKOHAMA, see *Japan*.

YORK (N. England), a town of the Brigantes, named Evraue, settled by the Romans during the second campaign of Agricola, about 79, and named *Eboracum* or *Eburacum*, and became the metropolis of the north. See *Population*.

The emperor Severus died here	4 Feb. 211
Here Constantius Chlorus died, and his son Constantine the Great was proclaimed emperor,	25 July, 306
Abbey of St. Mary's, founded by Seward the Dane	1050
York burnt by the Danes, allies of Edgar Atheling, and all the Normans slain	1069
The city and many churches destroyed by fire,	3 June, 1137
Massacre and suicide of many Jews	1190
York received its charter from Richard II., and the mayor was made a lord	1389
The Guildhall erected	1446
Richard III. crowned again here	8 Sept. 1483
At a parliament held here Charles I. professed his intention to govern legally	13 June, 1642
York taken for the parliament, after the battle of Marston-moor	16 July, 1644
Injured during the civil war by Fairfax	April, ,,
The corporation built a mansion-house for the lord mayor	1728
The castle was built by Richard III., 1484, and was rebuilt as a gaol	1741
The York petition to parliament, to reduce the expenditure and redress grievances	Dec. 1779
Yorkshire Philosophical Society established	1822
First meeting of the British Association held here	27 Sept. 1831
British Association (and time)	1844
Population, 45,385	1861
Fall of the iron bridge over the Ouse; five persons killed	27 Sept. ,,
Social Science Association met here	22 Sept. 1864
Fine Arts and Industrial Exhibition opened	24 July, 1866
Visit of prince and princess of Wales	9-11 Aug. ,,
Meeting of the Church Congress	9 Oct. ,,
The provincial mayors gave a festival to the lord mayor of London, &c., at York	25 Sept. 1873
Permanent Fine Art Exhibition opened by the archbishop	7 May, 1879
British Association jubilee meeting 31 Aug.-8 Sept. 1881
Royal Agricultural Society's annual meeting,	16 July, 1883
Yorkshire Institute, memorial stone laid by the prince of Wales 18 July, 1883; opened by the marquis of Lorne	10 June, 1883
Yorkshire college of science opened 26 Oct. 1874; new building opened by the prince of Wales,	15 July, ,,
Population, 50,761, 3 April, 1871; 59,596, 4 April, 1881.

DUKES.

1385.	Edmund Plantagenet (fifth son of king Edward III.); created duke, 6 Aug.; died 1402.
1406.	Edward (his son), was degraded by Henry IV. in 1399, but restored in 1414; killed at Agincourt, 1415; succeeded by his nephew,
1415.	Richard (son of Richard, earl of Cambridge, who was beheaded for treason in 1415); became regent of France in 1435; quelled the rebellion in Ireland in 1449; claimed the throne, and was appointed protector in 1454; his office was annulled, and he began the civil war in 1455, and was slain after his defeat at Wakefield in 1460.
1460.	Edward (his son) afterwards king Edward IV.
1474.	Richard (his second son), said to have been murdered in the Tower, 1483.
1494.	Henry Tudor, afterwards Henry VIII.
1605.	Charles Stuart, afterwards Charles I.

DUKES OF YORK AND ALBANY.

1643.	James Stuart (his second son), afterwards James II.
1716.	Ernest (brother of George I.); died 1728.
1760.	Edward (brother of George III.); died 1767.
1784.	Frederic (son of George III.), born 16 Aug. 1763
	Marries princess Frederica of Prussia, 29 Sept. 1791
	Commands the British forces at Antwerp, 8 April, 1793
	Present at the siege of Valenciennes 23 May, ,,
	Defeated at Dunkirk . 7 Sept. ,,
	At Bois-le-Duc, 14 Sept.; and at Boxtel, 17 Sept. ,,
	Appointed commander-in-chief . 1794
	Defeated near Alkmaar, 19 Sept. and 6 Oct. 1799
	Accused by colonel Wardle of abuse of his patronage; he resigns . 27 Jan. 1809
	Becomes again commander-in-chief . 1811
	Strongly opposes the catholic claims . 1825
	Dies . 5 Jan. 1827
	See *Albany*.

YORK, ARCHBISHOPRIC OF. The most ancient metropolitan see in England, being, it is said, so made by king Lucius about 180, when Christianity was first partly established in England. The bishop Eborius was present at the council of Arles, 314. The see was overturned by the Saxons, and was revived by pope Gregory on their conversion, and Paulinus is said to have been consecrated archbishop, 21 July, 625. York and Durham were long the only two sees in the north of England, until Henry I. erected a bishopric at Carlisle, and Henry VIII. another at Chester. York was the metropolitan see of the Scottish bishops; but during the time of archbishop Nevil, 1464, they withdrew their obedience, and had archbishops of their own. Much dispute arose between the two English metropolitans about precedency, as by pope Gregory's institutions it was thought he meant, that whichever of them was first confirmed, should be superior: appeal was made to the court of Rome by both parties, and it was determined in favour of Canterbury. The archbishop of York was allowed to style himself primate of England, while the archbishop of Canterbury styles himself primate of *all* England. The province of York now contains the dioceses of York. Carlisle, Chester, Durham, Sodor and Man, Manchester, and Ripon (*which see*). York has yielded to the church of

Ionic eight saints and three cardinals, and to England twelve lord chancellors, two lord treasurers, and two lord presidents of the north. It is rated in the king's books, 39 Henry VIII. 1546, at 1609*l*. 19*s*. 2*d*. per annum. *Beatson.* Present income 10,000*l*.

ARCHBISHOPS.

1501. Thomas Savage, died, 3 Sept. 1507.
1508. Christopher Bainbrigg, poisoned at Rome, 14 July, 1514.
1514. Thomas Wolsey, died, 29 Nov. 1530.
1531. Edward Lee, died, 13 Sept. 1544.
1545. Robert Holgate, deprived, 23 March, 1554.
1555. Nicholas Heath, deprived.
1561. Thomas Young, died, 26 June, 1568.
1570. Edmund Grindal, translated to Canterbury, 10 Jan. 1576.
1577. Edwin Sands or Sandys, died, 10 July, 1588.
1589. John Piers, died, 28 Sept. 1594.
1595. Matthew Hutton, died, 16 Jan. 1606.
1606. Tobias Matthew, died, 29 March, 1628.
1628. George Mountaigne, died, 24 Oct. 1628.
,, Samuel Harsnet, died, 25 May, 1631.
1632. Richard Neyle, died, 31 Oct. 1640.
1641. John Williams, died, 25 March, 1650.
[See vacant ten years.]
1660. Accepted Frewen, died, 28 March, 1664.
1664. Richard Sterne, died, 18 June, 1683.
1683. John Dolben, died, 11 April, 1686.
[See vacant two years.]
1688. Thomas Lamplugh, died, 5 May, 1691.
1691. John Sharp, died, 2 Feb. 1714.
1714. Sir William Dawes, died, 30 April, 1724.
1724. Launcelot Blackburn, died, 23 March, 1743.
1743. Thomas Herring, translated to Canterbury, Oct. 1747.
1747. Matthew Hutton, translated to Canterbury, March, 1757.
1757. John Gilbert, died, 1761.
1761. Robert Hay Drummond, died, 10 Dec. 1776.
1777. William Markham, died, 3 Nov. 1807.
1808. Edward Venables Vernon, died, 5 Nov. 1847.
1847. Thomas Musgrave, died, 4 May, 1860.
1860. Charles T. Longley, translated to Canterbury (from Durham), 1862.
1862. William Thomson, translated from Gloucester.

YORK MINSTER (dedicated to St. Peter). The first Christian church erected here, which appears to have been preceded by a Roman temple, was built by Edwin, king of Northumbria, of wood, about 625, and of stone about 635. It was damaged by fire in 741, and was rebuilt by archbishop Albert, about 780. It was again destroyed by fire in the year 1069, and rebuilt by archbishop Thomas, of Bayeux. It was once more burnt down in 1137, with St. Mary's abbey, and 39 parish churches in York. Archbishop Roger built the choir, 1154-81; Walter Gray added the south transept in 1227; John de Romayne, the treasurer of the cathedral, built the north transept in 1260. His son, archbishop Romanus, laid the foundation of the nave in 1291. In 1330, William de Melton built the two western towers, which were finished by John de Birmingham in 1342. Archbishop Thoresby, in 1361, began to rebuild the choir, in accordance with the magnificence of the nave, and he also rebuilt the lantern tower. The minster was set on fire by Jonathan Martin, a lunatic, and the roof of the choir and its internal fittings destroyed, 2 Feb. 1829; the damage, estimated at 60,000*l*., was repaired in 1832 under sir Robert Smirke. An accidental fire broke out, and in one hour reduced the belfry to a shell, destroyed the roof of the nave, and much damaged the edifice, 20 May, 1840. This was restored by Sidney Smirke, at a cost of 23,000*l*., 1841.

YORK AND LANCASTER, WARS OF, see *Roses.*

YORK (Upper Canada), founded in 1794; since 1834 named Toronto. In the war between America and Great Britain, the United States' forces made several attacks upon the province of Upper Canada and succeeded in taking York, the seat of the government, 27 April, 1813; but it was soon afterwards again retaken by the British.

YORKSHIRE Exhibition of Arts and Manufactures, opened at Leeds, by the duke of Edinburgh, 13 May, 1875. The Yorkshire Registric Act passed 7 Aug. 1884.

YORK TOWN (Virginia, United States) Lord Cornwallis had taken possession of York town in Aug. 1781; but after sustaining a disastrous siege, he was obliged to surrender his army, consisting of about 7000 men, to the allied armies of France and America, under the command of generals Washington and count Rochambeau, 19 Oct. 178 This mischance was attributed to sir Henr Clinton, who had not given the garrison th necessary succour they expected; and it main led to the close of the war. The centenary w celebrated 16 Oct. 1881 *et seq.* On 19 Oct. th British flag was saluted generally. The town w strongly fortified by the confederates in the America civil war, but surrendered to M'Clellan, May, 186.

YOUNG ENGLAND, a name given to number of young tory gentlemen earnestly oppose to the repeal of the corn laws and other liber measures, and very desirous of reviving the o relations between the upper and lower class mixing in rural sports, &c., yet preserving the di distinctions (1842-6). Lord John Manners (Du) of Rutland. 1888), and the hon. G. Smythe, we eminent leaders, and their ideas were favoured I Mr. Disraeli (lord Beaconsfield) in his novel "Co1 ingsby," published 1844.

YOUNG ITALY, see *Italy*, 1831.

YOUNG IRELAND, see *Ireland, Young.*

YOUNG MEN'S CHRISTIAN ASSO CIATION, for improvement of young men l means of classes, meetings, &c., founded 184 Exeter-hall, Strand, was bought for the associa tion about July, 1880. It met there, 29 March, 188 The Young Men's Christian Institute bought th Polytechnic Institute, about Dec. 1881.

YTTRIUM, a rare metal. The earth ytt was discovered by professor Gadolin in a mineral Ytterby, in Sweden, 1794. The metal was fir obtained by Wöhler in 1828. It is of a dark gr colour, and brittle.

YUCATAN, Mexico, discovered by Hernand Cordova, 1517; conquered by Bernal Diaz, 152 declared for independence, 1813. Its ancient cit: are described in works by the American travel Stephens, 1838 and 1842.

YVRES (now IVRY, N. W. France), where battle was fought, 14 March, 1590, between Hen IV. of France, aided by his chief nobility, a the generals of the catholic league, over whom t king obtained a complete victory.

Z.

ZAGRAB.

ZAGRAB (Hungary). Here Andrew II. defeated the invader Charles Martel, to whom the pope had assigned his crown, 1292.

ZÄHRINGEN (Baden), the seat of dukes, ancestors of the grand dukes of Baden, descended from Herman I., margrave, 1074; see *Baden*.

ZAMA (near Carthage, N. Africa), the scene of the battle between the two greatest commanders in the world at the time, Hannibal and Scipio Africanus. The victory was won by Scipio, and was decisive of the fate of Carthage; it led to an ignominious peace the year after, which closed the second Punic war. The Romans lost about 2000 killed and wounded, while the Carthaginians lost in killed and prisoners more than 40,000; some historians make the loss greater; 202 B.C.

ZAMBESI, river of E. Africa, explored by Livingstone 1851-6, 1858-64. His book published, Nov. 1865.

ZAMORA (Spain). Here Alphonso the Great defeated the Moors, in 901.

ZANTE. One of the Ionian Islands (*which see*).

ZANZALEENS. This sect rose in Syria, under Zanzalee, 535; he taught that water baptism was of no efficacy, and that it was necessary to be baptized by fire, with the application of a red-hot iron. The sect was at one time very numerous.

ZANZIBAR or **ZANGUEBAR**, an island, east Africa, metropolis of the Imaum of Muscat, and chief market for ivory, gum, coral, and cloves, and also for slaves. At the death of the Seyyid (or lord), miscalled "imaum" and "sultan," of Muscat, 1856, his dominions were divided between his sons; see *Muscat*. Majid obtained Zanzibar, after a contest with his brother, Barghash Seyyid, who, however, succeeded at his death, 7 Oct. 1870. An expedition for the purpose of suppressing the slave trade was sent to Zanzibar, under the command of sir Bartle Frere, 20 Nov. 1872, arrived about 12 Jan. 1873. After some delay and negotiation by Dr. Kirke, a treaty was signed, abolishing the trade, 5 June, 1873. The contract for the mail to Zanzibar was censured as too expensive in July, 1873, and altered. The Seyyid Barghash visited England in 1875, arrived 9 June; received by the queen, 21 June; received freedom of London, 12 July; sailed for France, 15 July. He decreed confiscation of slaves brought to Zanzibar, 18 April, 1876. The sultan made knight of St. Michael and St. George, 14 Sept. 1883. Territorial disputes with the German East African company, May; settled, reported, Aug. 1885.

Treaty with Germany comes into force, 19 Aug. 1886. The Sultan's rights recognized by Anglo-German treaty . . . . 29 Oct. & 1 Nov. 1886
Rupture with Portugal respecting non-cession of territories (see *Mozambique*) . Feb.-March, 1887
Seyyid Barghash died; succeeded by his brother Seyyid Khalifah . . . . 26 March, 1888
Dispute with Italy respecting cession of territories by the late Sultan . . . . 6 June, „
A party of German men-of-war's men land at Bagamoyo and kill 100 natives, 23 Sept.; native rising along the coast . . . Sept. „
Collapse of the German settlement attributed to

ZEND-AVESTA.

the action of the Arab slave dealers; announced Oct. 1888
Lieut. Cooper captures a dhow but is killed; much regretted . . . . . 17 Oct. „
The universities' mission warned to retire from the mainland of Africa by government on account of operations against slave traders by England and Germany . . . . . . Oct. „
The coast blockaded by Germany and England, 2 Dec.; the Germans make war on the chiefs who burn Bagamoyo and retire . . 7 Dec. „
The Arab slave dealers attack some German stations and carry off the freed slaves; eight missionaries killed . . . 11-13 Jan. 1889
Mr. Brooks and 26 others, missionaries, murdered near Saadani . . . . 21 Jan. „
Captain Wissmann appointed imperial commissioner in east Africa, 21 Feb.; arrives with Dr. Peters, 31 March, „
The Germans defeat the Arabs at Bagamoyo, 6 March, „
German attack on Saadani . . . 22 March, „
German flag hoisted at Consulate; capt. Wissmann assumes command . . . . 5 April, „
Dr. Peters organizing his Emin Pasha relief expedition; men and camels engaged, March,- April, „
Captain Wissmann, aided by 200 German sailors, defeats Bushiri, and destroys his camp, with little loss; Bushiri's loss 80 killed and 20 prisoners, 8 May, „
Admiral Deinhard bombards Saadani, the natives flee, and capt. Wissmann burns Wingi; reported 7 June; captures Pangani . . . 8 July, „

ZARA, capital of Dalmatia, a Roman colony under Augustus. It revolted from Venice and was recaptured, 18 Nov. 1202; unsuccessfully besieged by the Turks 1572, 1577; given up to Austria, 1791.

ZE, ZOW, ZIERES, for *ye, you,* and *yours*. The letter z was retained in Scotland, and was commonly written for the letter y so late as the reign of queen Mary, up to which period many books in the Scottish language were printed in Edinburgh with these words, 1543.

ZEALAND, one of the 13 provinces which formed the League of Utrecht, 1579; see *Holland*, and *New Zealand*.

ZELA, N.E. Asia Minor, where Julius Cæsar defeated Pharnaces, king of Pontus, son of Mithridates. Cæsar, in announcing his victory, sent his famous despatch to the senate of Rome, in these words: "*Veni, vidi, vici,*"—"I came, I saw, I conquered" (perhaps the shortest despatch on record). This battle ended the war; Pharnaces escaped into Bosporus, where he was slain by his lieutenant, Asander; Pontus was made a Roman province, and Bosporus given to Mithridates of Pergamus, 47 B.C.

ZELL (Hanover), see *Denmark*, 1772.

ZEND-AVESTA, ancient sacred books of the Parsees; of which 3 out of 21 are extant. The age of these books is much disputed. Professor Max Müller says that the MSS. had been preserved by the Parsee priests at Bombay, where a colony of fire-worshippers had fled in the 10th century. Anquetil Duperron's French translation, from a modern Persian version, was published in 1771; edition by Eugene Burnouf, 1829-43.

ZENO or **ZENON**, see *Stoics*.

ZENOBIA, Queen of the East, see *Palmyra*.

ZENTA, in Hungary, the scene of a battle where the Germans, under prince Eugene, defeated the Turks, 11 Sept. 1697. This victory led to the peace of Carlowitz, ratified January, 1699.

ZETETICAL SOCIETY, established in 1878, to afford opportunities for the unrestricted discussion of a variety of questions.

ZETUNIUM. After defeating Samuel king of Bulgaria here, 29 July, 1014, the emperor Basil II. blinded his 15,000 prisoners, except one in a hundred, to whom he left one eye. The king died of grief.

ZIDON, see *Sidon*.

ZINC. The ore of zinc, calamine or spelter, known to the Greeks, who used it in the manufacture of brass. It is said to have been known in China also, and is noticed by European writers as early as 1231; though the method of extracting it from the ore was unknown for nearly five hundred years after. The metal zinc is mentioned by Paracelsus (died 1541). A mine of zinc was discovered on lord Ribblesdale's estate, Craven, Yorkshire, in 1809. Zincography was introduced in London shortly after lithography became known in England, in 1817; see *Lithography*. Zinc is much used in voltaic batteries; and its application in manufactures has greatly increased of late years; see *Photozincography*.

ZINC OBTAINED IN THE UNITED KINGDOM.

	tons.	value.
1875.	6,713	162,790*l*.
1880.	7,162	123,544*l*.
1882.	16,130	286,710*l*.

ZIRCONIUM, the metallic base of the earth Zirconia, which was discovered by Klaproth in 1789; from this Berzelius obtained the metal in 1824. Zirconia is found in the sand of the rivers of Ceylon. The metal exists in the form of a black powder.

ZIZYPHUS VULGARIS. A shrub brought from the south of Europe about 1640. The *Zizyphus Paliurus* shrub (Christ's Thorn) was brought from Africa before 1596; see *Flowers*.

ZODIAC. Its obliquity was discovered, its twelve signs named, and their situations assigned them by Anaximander, about 560 B.C. The Greeks and Arabians borrowed the zodiac from the Hindoos. *Sir W. Jones.* The zodiacal light was observed by Tycho Brahe, Descartes, and others, and named by Cassini, 1683.

ZOLLVEREIN (*Customs' Union*), the name given to the German commercial union, projected by Prussia 1818, and gradually joined by nearly all the German states except Austria. On 19 Feb. 1853, an important treaty of commerce and navigation, between Austria and Prussia, to last from Jan. 1854 to Dec. 1865, was signed, to which the other states of the Zollverein gave in their adhesion on 5 April, 1853. In Nov. 1861, Prussia threatened to withdraw unless certain changes were made. By the treaty of 8 July, 1867, between the North German confederation, and the southern states (Bavaria, Würtemberg, Baden, and Hesse), various changes were made, and by other treaties signed in Oct. these states agreed to send delegates to a customs parliament to be held at Berlin. A session of this parliament was opened by the king of Prussia, 27 April, and closed 23 May,

1868. Federal chancellor, the count von Bismarck. Imports, 1882, valued at 158,235,000*l*.; exports, 1882, 162,235,000*l*.

ZOOLOGY (from *zoön*, Greek for animal) is the division of biology which treats of animals; Aristotle (322-284 B.C.) the founder of the science. Systems of classification have been made by John Ray (1628-1705), Charles Linné (1707-78), G. Buffon (1707-88), and George Cuvier (1769-1832).

Linnæus divided the animal kingdom into six classes, —*Mammalia*, which includes all animals that suckle their young: *Aves*, birds; *Amphibia*, or amphibious animals; *Pisces*, fishes; *Insecta*, insects; *Vermes*, worms; 1741.

Cuvier (died in Paris, 13 May, 1832), in his great work, *Règne Animal*, published in 1816, distributed the animals into four great divisions, the *Vertebrata* (backboned); the *Mollusca* (soft-bodied); the *Articulata* (jointed); and the *Radiata* (the organs disposed round a centre).

In 1859, professor Owen made known a system of arranging the class *Mammalia* according to the nature of their brains.

The ZOOLOGICAL SOCIETY OF LONDON (originally the Zoological Club) was founded in 1826; the society was mainly founded by sir Stamford Raffles, sir H. Davy, and its gardens in the Regent's Park were opened in April, 1827; the society was chartered 27 March, 1829. 2072 animals in the gardens, 31 Dec. 1871; about 500 animals from India given by the prince of Wales, May, 1876.

Dr. James Murie was appointed by the society to be their first "anatomical prosector," 3 May, 1865.

New reptile house opened, 6 Aug. 1883.

On the demolition of Exeter 'Change, in 1829, the menagerie of Mr. Cross was temporarily lodged in the King's Mews, whence it was removed to the Surrey Zoological Gardens, 1832.

The Zoological Gardens of Dublin were opened, 1832.

Zoological Station for study, open to the public, established at Naples by professor Anton Dohrn, opened 1 Oct. 1873.

Wombwell's (latterly Edmonds') great collection of trained animals sold, 29, 30 July, 1884. Bought by Mr. R. T. Barnum, Jan. 1888.

See *Aquarium, Hippopotamus, Giraffe*, and *Acclimatization*, &c.

ZOOPRAXISCOPE, optical apparatus invented by Mr. Eadweard J. Muybridge to exhibit photographs of moving animals, about 1881. The apparatus was successfully employed at the Royal Institution (in the presence of the prince of Wales) 13 March, 1882, and again in March and May, 1889; also at the Royal Society and other places in the same year. His great work on the subject was published in 1887-9.

ZORNDORFF, Prussia, where a battle was fought between the Prussian and Russian armies; the former, commanded by the king of Prussia, obtained a victory over the forces of the czarina, whose loss amounted to 21,529 men, while that of the Prussians was about 11,000 : 25, 26 Aug. 1758.

ZOUAVES AND FOOT CHASSEURS. When the French established a regency at Algiers, in 1830, they hoped to find the employment of native troops advantageous, and selected the *Zooaouas*, a congregation of daring Arab tribes. In time, numbers of red republicans, and other enthusiastic Frenchmen, joined the regiments, adopting the costume, &c.: eventually the Africans disappeared from the ranks, and no more were added. Among their colonels were Lamoricière and Cavaignac. The French Zouaves formed an important part of the army in the Crimean war, 1854-5.*

---

* The Zouave organization and drill were introduced into the federal army in the great civil war in America, by Ephraim E. Ellsworth, early in 1861. He was assassinated on 24 May same year, at Alexandria, just after taking down a secession flag.

ZUG, the smallest canton of Switzerland, joined the confederation, 1352, and the Sonderbund, 1846.
Many persons killed by fall of about 27 houses into the lake of Geneva . . . . 5-7 July, 1887

ZUIDER ZEE, or SOUTH SEA, a gulf in the Netherlands, formerly a lake, united with the North Sea by inundations in the twelfth and thirteenth centuries. In 1875, the Dutch chamber voted 9,500,000*l.* to reclaim the submerged land by drainage, and to erect a dyke, 26 feet high above the water, and 25 miles long; thus adding 759 square miles to the country. The Dutch Texel fleet here surrendered to admiral Mitchell, 30 Aug. 1799.

ZUINGLIANS, the followers of the reformer, Ulric Zuingli, who at Zurich declaimed against the church of Rome, and effected the same separation for Switzerland from the papal dominion which Luther did for Saxony. He procured two assemblies to be called; by the first he was authorised to proceed, by the second, the ceremonies of the Romish church were abolished 1519. Zuingli died in arms, being slain in a skirmish against his popish opponents, 11 Oct. 1531. The Zuinglians were also called Sacramentarians.

ZULLICHAU (Prussia). Here the Russians, under Soltikow, severely defeated the Prussians under Wedel, 23 July, 1759.

ZULPICH, see *Tolbiac*.

ZULU CELIBATE MILITARY SYSTEM, founded by Godongwana, confirmed by Chaka and Dingaan; completed by Cetywayo.

ZULULAND, South-east Africa; near the British colony, Natal. In the last century, the Zulus were a peaceful pastoral people.

Godongwana, a chief, (termed Dingiswayo, "the Wanderer," from his early life,) began a military organisation by forming a celibate army; killed in battle and succeeded by his vigorous and merciless ally, Chaka, styled king, by whom Zulu supremacy was mainly established over the Fingoes and other tribes . . . . about 1812
Chaka assassinated; succeeded by his brother Dingaan, crafty, treacherous, and cruel; at first friendly with the British at Natal (*which see*); made treaty with capt. Allen Gardiner, 6 May, 1835
Massacres Retief, 70 Boers, and their servants (who had recovered his stolen cattle), 2 Feb., and about 600 afterwards; defeats the British and Dutch in several encounters; but is severely beaten by Andries Pretorius . . . Dec. 1838
Dingaan again defeated; killed by one of his chiefs; succeeded by his brother Umpanda, peaceful and crafty; who keeps peace with the English and Dutch . . . . . 1840, *et seq.*
Cetywayo (pronounced Ketchwāyo) his eldest son, kills his brothers; succeeds at his father's death; organizes still further his army, named by Frere "the celibate man-slaying war-machine" . Oct. 1872
Recognized on behalf of the British by Mr. Shepstone; crowned . . . . . 1 Sept. 1873
Opposes missionaries; organizes armed resistance to the British; when remonstrated with for outrages, defies them 1876
Sir Bartle Frere, governor of the Cape, requests help from England; 90th regiment and a battery sent . . . . . . Jan. 1878
Cetywayo refuses to give up leaders of a raid on British territory (in July); and tenders a fine; sir Bartle Frere, demands, as an ultimatum their surrender within 30 days . . . . Dec. ,,
The time (extended) having elapsed, 11 Jan., the British, under lord Chelmsford, cross the Tugela and enter Zululand . . . . 12 Jan. 1879
Col. Pearson defeats the Zulus and advances to Echowe (which he fortifies) . . 21 Jan. ,,
British camp at Isandula or Isandlwana, about 10 miles from Rorke's Drift (on the Tugela), surprised and attacked by about 15,000 Zulus: 5 companies of the 24th regiment, and many natives killed; with cols. Durnford and Pulleine, and other officers; total loss about 837; 2000 Zulus said to have been killed; (lieuts. Melville and Coghill said to have perished while preserving the colours) . . . . . . 22 Jan. 1879
Rorke's Drift severely attacked; successfully defended by lieuts. Chard and Bromhead 22 Jan. ,,
Zulus attack Inkanyana; defeated by col. Evelyn Wood . . . . . . 24 Jan. ,,
Reinforcements requested; troops rapidly sent off from England . . . . 19 Feb. *et seq.* ,,
Prince Louis Napoleon requesting to join the British, permitted to go as a guest; sails 27 Feb. ,,
Arrival of the *Tamar* with 800 men, &c., at Pietermaritzburg . . . . . 11 March, ,,
British convoy near Itombi river cut to pieces by Zulus; waggons and stores captured; capt. David Moriarty killed . . . . 12 March ,,
Cetywayo's brother Ohani, with 600 men, joins the British; announced . . . 18 March, ,,
Col. Evelyn Wood attacks the Zulus on the Zlobani mountains; suffers much loss, 28 March; gains victory at Kambula . . . . 29 March, ,,
British advance to relieve Echowe . 29 March, ,,
Zulus defeated at Ginghilovo . . . 2 April, ,,
Col. Pearson marches out of Echowe . 2, 3 April, ,,
Sir Garnet Wolseley appointed commander-in-chief, governor of Natal, &c., sails for the Cape May, ,,
British total loss; 1186 killed; 86 died of disease; announced . . . . . 27 May, ,,
Cetywayo said to have suppressed an insurrection, and retired to his kraal (or village) at Ulundi, May, ,,
Reconnoitring party, under capt. J. Brenton Carey, on Imbabani, near the Mozani river, surprised; prince Louis Napoleon (acting as commander) killed . . . . . 1 June, ,,
Ultimatum sent to Cetywayo, requiring restitution of cannon, and total submission; time expired, 12 June, ,,
Sir G. Wolseley arrives at the Cape . 23 June, ,,
Stafford House South African aid committee formed, June, ,,
Zulu raid on cattle; which are recovered 25 June, ,,
Sir Garnet Wolseley sworn in as high commissioner at Pietermaritzburg . . . 28 or 29 June, ,,
Cetywayo totally defeated at Ulundi (*which see*); 4 July, ,,
Sir G. Wolseley receives chiefs . 12 July, *et seq.* ,,
Lord Chelmsford resigns . . . . 15 July, ,,
Sentence upon capt. Carey, respecting death of prince Napoleon, quashed . . . 22 Aug. ,,
Pursuit of Cetywayo: captured by major Richard Marter . . . . . . 28 Aug. ,,
Meeting of Sir G. Wolseley with Zulu chiefs; settlement by treaty; Zululand to be divided into 13 independent districts; John Dunn to be a chief; lands reserved for the British; British residents in each district (to be eyes and ears); celibate military system abolished; no arms to be imported; ancient laws and liberties retained; [John Dunn, 20 years in Zululand; conformed to Zulu ways) . . . . . . 1 Sept. ,,
Sir G. Wolseley's despatch, announcing end of the war, dated . . . . . . 3 Sept. ,,
Cetywayo (dignified) arrives at Cape Town 15 Sept. ,,
His petition to the Queen for restitution declined, about 11 July, 1881
John Dunn energetically subdues a revolting chief about 30 July, ,,
Cost of Zulu war, 4,922,141*l.* . . . ,,
Sir Evelyn Wood visits Zululand and makes important changes . . . . . Sept. ,,
Reported fighting among the chiefs . . Nov. ,,
The country reported quiet by John Dunn . Dec. ,,
Cetywayo lands at Plymouth and proceeds to London . . . . . . 3 Aug. 1882
Visited Mr. Gladstone 9 Aug.; received by the Queen, 14 Aug.; by the prince of Wales 16 Aug. ,,
His restoration to part of his kingdom with restrictions, proposed by the British government Aug.; sails from Southampton . . . 1 Sept. ,,
Changes made in the territories previous to Cetywayo's return, announced . . . 29 Dec. ,,
Cetywayo's restoration accepted; proclaimed at Ulundi . . . . . . 29 Jan. 1883

ZULULAND.

Struggle between Cetywayo and chiefs, announced . . . . . 25 April, 1883
Cetywayo defeated by Oham and others with heavy loss, announced . . . . . 16 May, ,,
Mr. Fynn, British resident, resigns, announced June, ,,
Cetywayo is attacked at Ulundi, by Usibepu, 20 July; and said to be killed . . . 21 July, ,,
Usibepu said to be all-powerful, Cetywayo a living fugitive, announced . . . . 8 Aug. ,,
Great battle; Usibepu defeated by Cetywayo's supporters, announced . . . 16 Aug. ,,
Cetywayo demands a British enquiry into his treatment, announced . . . 20 Aug. ,,
Cetywayo surrenders to Mr. Osborn, and is taken to Durban, about 15 Oct.; at Ekowe . 5 Nov. ,,
Defeats of Usibepu by other chiefs . . Nov. ,,
Flight, and recapture of Cetywayo . 27, 28 Jan. 1884
Zibedu defeats Usutus . . . about 31 Jan. ,,
Cetywayo dies of heart disease . . 8 Feb. ,,
Much warfare . . . . . March-May, ,,
Dinizulu, son of Cetywayo, crowned king by the Boers, in presence of 10,000 people; grants an amnesty, and promises fidelity to the British 21 May, ,,
Usibepu, severely defeated by the Boers and Usutus, flies, announced . . . 14 June, ,,
A Boer republic established; Joubert, president Aug. ,,
British flag hoisted at St. Lucia's bay . Dec. ,,
Quietness in Zululand reported . . Jan. 1886
Proposed annexation of Zululand to Natal declined, Oct.; British protectorate over the Zulu territories planned by government . . Nov. ,,
Agreement with the Boer republic announced, 4 Nov. ,,
Annexation of Zululand as a British possession; the governor to rule by proclamation, May; proclaimed at Durban . . . 21 June, 1887
Troubles with Dinizulu announced 5 Nov.; his uncle Undabuko and others submit to sir Arthur Havelock, announced 7 Nov.; military preparations; Dinizulu submits, 13 Nov.; Usibepu reinstated in his lands . . . 15 Nov. ,,
The chiefs attacked by the police and military for stealing cattle . . . . 2 June, 1888
ulu rebels under Ishingana defeated after a severe conflict . . . . . . 2 July, ,,
Rebellion of Dinizulu announced . 11 July, ,,
Somkeli, the rebel chief, surrenders; announced 1 Aug. ,,
Dinizulu and about 1,000 rebels with cattle enter into the Transvaal territory, 10 Aug.; revolt ended; reported . . . . 29 Aug. ,,
Dinizulu surrenders conditionally to the Transvaal government . . . . . Sept. ,,
Surrender of Undabuko, 19 Sept; his trial began 27 Sept. ,,
Ishingana, rebel chief, surrenders . 12 Nov. ,,
Trial of Undabuko and Somkeli for treason, began 15 Nov. ,,
Dinizulu surrenders to the British . . Nov. ,,

ZWITTAU.

Somhlolo sentenced to five years' hard labour for high treason . . . . . 22 Nov. 1888
Several chiefs convicted of high treason and sentenced to imprisonment for five years, 1 Dec. ,,
Dinizulu sentenced to ten years', Undabuko to 15 years', and Ishingana to 12 years' imprisonment, 27 April, 1889

ZURICH was admitted a member and made head of the Swiss confederacy, 1351, and was the first town in Switzerland that separated from the church of Rome; see *Zuinglians*. A grave-digger at Zurich poisoned the sacramental wine, by which 8 persons lost their lives and many others were grievously injured, 4 Sept. 1776. The French, under Massena, after repelling an attack of the Austrians, retired from Zurich, 5 June, 1799. The Imperialists were defeated by Massena, the former losing 20,000 men in killed and wounded, 25, 26 Sept. 1799; see *Switzerland*. A new democratic constitution was adopted, 18 April, 1869.

On 24 June, 1859, the Austrians were defeated by the allied French and Sardinian army at Solferino. Preliminaries of peace were signed at Villa Franca by the emperors of Austria and France on 12 July following.

A conference between the representatives of the powers concerned having been appointed, the first meeting took place at Zurich, on 8 Aug.

After many delays a treaty was signed 10 Nov. Lombardy was ceded to Sardinia; the formation of an Italian Confederation, under the presidency of the pope, was determined on, and the rights of the ex-sovereigns of Tuscany, Modena, and Parma were reserved.

The formation of the kingdom of Italy in 1861 annulled the treaty of Zurich.

Swiss National exhibition, 1 May—27 Dec. 1883.

ZUTPHEN, in Holland. At a battle here 22 Sept. 1586, between the Spaniards and the Dutch, the amiable sir Philip Sidney, author of "Arcadia," was mortally wounded. He died 7 Oct. He was serving with the English auxiliaries, commanded by the earl of Leicester.

ZUYDER ZEE, see *Zuider Zee*.

ZUYPER SLUYS (Holland). Here sir Ralph Abercromby defeated an attack of the French under Brune; the latter suffered great loss, 9 Sept. 1799.

ZWITTAU, Moravia. Here the Prussians defeated the Austrians and captured provisions, 10 July, 1866.

INDEX.

[The references are to *articles* in the body of the work ; the italics refer to articles in this Index. The year given is A.D. when B.C. is not mentioned ; two dates after the name, thus, 1508-82, signify the year of the person's birth and death ; *b.*, born ; *d.*, died ; *fl.*, flourished ; *m.*, murdered ; *k.*, killed. The year of the birth and death is given of many eminent persons who are not mentioned in the body of the work.]

(*Vincent's* Dictionary of Biography *was expressly compiled to give further details than those found in this Index.*)

Abbadies expl. Ethiopia, 1837-45
Abbas, Persia
Abbot, abp. ; Canterbury, 1611
Abbot, Charles ; speaker, 1802
Abbot & Moulin ; Thessalonica, 1876
Abbott, E. ; concordance to Pope, 1875
Abd-el-Kader ; Algiers, 1835
Abderrahman I.—V., caliphs, 755-1023
Abdul-Medjid, Turkey, 1839-61
Abdul-Aziz, Turkey, 1839
Abdul-Rahman (or Abdur-rahman) ; Afghanistan, 1863-81
Abdul-Hamid ; Turkey, 1774, 1876
Abdul-Kerim, Russo-Turkish War, II. 1877
Abel, sir F. A., glyoxiline, 1866, gun cotton, explosives, Imperial Inst.
Abel Oghlan, Dzoungeria, 1864
Abelard, *d.* 1142 ; Abelard, theology
Abercorn, Jas. marquis of, 1811-1885 ; Ireland, ld. lieut. ; 1866 ; (duke) 1874
Abercromby, Jas., speaker, 1835
Abercromby, sir R., 1738 - 1801 ; Trinidad, Alexandria
Aberdeen, earl of, 1784-1860 ; Aberdeen adm., *note* ; Gladstone Adm. 1886
Abernethy, J., surgeon, 1764-1831
Abingdon, earl of ; trials, 1794
Abinger, ld., att.-gen., 1827 ; exchequer
Abney, capt. ; photography, 1882
Abou Saoud ; Egypt, 1872
About, Edm. F. C., Nov. 1828-85 ; France, 1872
Abrantes, duke of ; see *Junot*
Absalom, killed 1023 B.C.
Abubeker ; Ali, 632
Acacius, Acacians, henoticon, 482
Accum, F. ; adulterations, 1822
Achilli *v.* Newman ; trials, 1852-3
Achmet ; see *Ahmed*
Acilius ; statues, temples
Ackermann, R. ; lithography, 1817
Acron ; acromatics, 473 B.C.
Acton, Mrs., Royal Inst., 1838
Actuarius ; purgatives, 1245
Adair, serj. ; Junius, 1769
Adalbert, St. ; Prussia, 997
Adam ; duels, 1779
Adam, R. and bros., architects 1728-92
Adam, W. M. ; mensuration
Adam, W. P. ; Madras, 1880, whip Gladstone adm., 1880
Adams *v.* Coleridge, trials, 1836
Adams, J. C., mathem. ; Neptune,

1845 ; J. (1797) and J. Q. (1825), United States (*presidents*)
Adams *v.* Dundas ; trials, 1831
Adderley, Mr. ; Birmingham, 1856
Adderley, sir C. ; Disraeli administration, 1874
Addington, H., 1757-1844 ; Addington.
Addison, Joseph, 1672-1719, Spectator, 1711 ; Stanhope administration, 1717 ; allegory, Clio, clubs
Adelais ; Adelaide ; England, queens (Henry I., William IV.)
Adeodatus ; pope, 672
Adolphus, Frederic ; Sweden, 1751
Adrian, Rome ; emperor, 117 ; edicts, persecutions ; popes
Aetina, Aetians
Ægeus ; Athens, 1283 B.C.
Ægineta, Paulus ; surgery, 640
Ægisthus ; Mycenæ, 1201 B.C.
Æmilianus ; Rome, 146 B.C.
Æneas ; Italy, Alba, 1182 B.C.
Æschines, Gk. orator, 389-314 B.C.
Æschylus, Greek tragedy, 525-456 B.C. ; drama
Æsop ; fables (about 600 B.C.)
Afranio, bassoon
Africanus ; see *Scipio*
Agamemnon ; Mycenæ, 1201 B.C.
Agathocles, *d.* 289 B.C. ; Carthage, Sicily, Syracuse
Age, proprietor of ; trials, 1844
Agesander ; Laocoön
Agesilaus ; Sparta, 398 B.C.
Agis ; Sparta, 427 B.C.
Agnew, Mr. Vans ; India, 1848
Agnodice ; midwifery
Agricola ; Britain, *d.* 93 ; Lancaster, Caledonia, Roman wall
Agricola, John, *d.* 1566 ; Antinomians
Agrippa, *d.* 12 B.C. ; Pantheon, 27 B.C.
Ahmed I.—III. ; Turkey, 1603, *et seq.*
Ahmed Vefik, Turkey, 1878
Aholiab ; sculpture
Ainsworth, W. H., Nov. 1805-82
Airy, Sir G. B., *b.* 1801 ; Greenwich, 1835 ; pendulum, standard, Royal Society, 1871 ; Albert medal, 1876 ; sun
Aislabie, Mr. ; Sunderland administration, 1718 ; South Sea
Akbar, India ; 1556
Akenside, Mark, poet, 1721-70
Alacocque, M. M. ; sacred heart
Alamayou, Abyssinia, 1868
Alaric, *d.* 410 ; Rome, France
Albemarle, Geo. Monk, duke of, 1608-70 ; administration, 1660
Alberoni, card., 1664-1752 ; Spain, 1715

Albert ; Austria, Bohemia, Germany Hungary
Albert I., assassination, 1308
Albert (prince consort), 1819 - 61 ; England, 1840 ; regency bill, duelling
Albert Edward ; England (royal family), Wales
Albertus, Magnus ; automatons
Alboin the Longobard, killed 573
Albrecht ; Austria, 1866 ; Custozza
Albuquerque (viceroy), *d.* 1515 ; India, 1503
Alcantara, gen. ; Venezuela, 1876
Alcibiades, killed 404 B.C. ; Athens
Alcippe ; Areopagitæ
Alcock, Mr. ; duelling, 1807 ; sir R., Japan
Alcuin (theologian), about 725-804
Aldebert ; impostors, 743
Aldhelme ; Salisbury, 705 ; ballads
Alectus ; Britain, 294
Aleko pasha, Roumelia
Alençon, duc d' ; Agincourt, 1415
Alexander of Paris ; Alexandrine
Alexander the Great, 356-323 B.C. ; Macedon, Egypt, Gordon, Tyre, Memphis
Alexander Severus ; Rome, em., 222
Alexander I., *d.* 1825 ; Russia, 1801 ; Austerlitz, 1805 ; Leipsic, 1813
Alexander II., Russia, 1855, assassinations
Alexander III., Russia, 1881
Alexander ; Scotland (kings) ; Pope Alexander, sir W. ; Nova Scotia, 1722
Alexius, East (emperors), 1081-1203
Alfieri, Victor, Ital. poet, 1749-1803
Alfred the Great, 849-901 ; Ashdown, England, councils, clocks, crown, militia
Alfred, prince ; Godwin, 1053
Alfred, duke of Edinburgh, *b.* 1844 ; aquarium, England (royal family), music, Plymouth.
Aliband ; France, 1836
Alice, princess, 1843-78 ; England ; royal family ; Hesse ; diphtheria
Ali Pacha ; Rosetta ; Turkey, 1820 ; Albania
Alison, Arch., hist., 1792-1867 ; — sir A. (soldier), Ashantees, 1874 ; Egypt, 1882
Allcard *v.* Skinner, trials, 1887
Allen, R., post-office, 1720
Allen and others ; Fenians, 1867
Alleyne, Edwd., *d.* 1617 ; Dulwich
Almagro ; Abancay, 1537
Almansour ; Bagdad, 762

INDEX.

Almeida, L.; Madagascar, 1506
Alphonso; Sicily, Spain, Portugal (kings)
Alsop, Joseph; trials, 1839
Althorp, visc.; Grey administration, 1830; Melbourne, 1835
Alumayû, Abyssinia, 1868-79
Alva, duke of, 1508-82; Antwerp, Holland
Alvanley, lord; duel, 1835
Alvinzi, marshal; Arcola, 1796
Alyattes; Lydia, 761 B.C.
Alypius of Alexandria; dwarfs
Amadeus, Savoy; annunciation
Amadeus, duke of Aosta, b. 1845; king of Spain, 1870-3
Amalric, pantheism
Ambrose, St., d. 397; anthems, Te Deum, liturgies
Ambrosius; Stonehenge
Amenophis; Egypt, 1821 B.C.
Americus Vespucius, 1451-1516; America, note
Amherst, lord; China, 1816; India, 1823
Ammianus Marcellinus, Lat. hist., d. 390
Amontons, W.; 1663-1705, telegraphs
Amos, prophesies about 787 B.C.
Ampère, O. M., 1775-1836; electricity (galvanism and telegraph)
Amulius; Alba, 974 B.C.
Amurath; Turkey, Beyrout
Amyntas; Macedon, 540 B.C.
Anacharsis, 592 B.C.; anchors, bellows
Anacletus; pope, 78
Anacreon, Gr. poet, fl. abt. 557 B.C.
Anastasius; pope; East; emperors
Anaxagoras, 480 B.C.; earthquakes
Anaximander, 547 B.C.; maps
Anaximenes, 548 B.C.; air
Andersen, Hans C., Dan. novelist, 1805-75
Anderson, J.; slavery (in United States), 1853; Wizard of the North, masquerade, 1856
Anderson, Mrs. physic, 1865
Anderssen, chess, 1851-70
Anderwert, M.; Switzerland, 1880
Andrassy; Hungary, 1867
André, maj.; United States, 1780
Andrew; Hungary, kings
Andrews, H., d. 1820; almanacs
Andrews v. Salt; trials, 1873
Andronicus, 240 B.C.; drama
Andronicus; Eastern empire, 1113, 1328
Angela, St.; Ursuline nuns, 1537
Angerstein, J., d. 1823; National Gallery
Anglesey, Henry, marquis of, 1768-1854; Ireland (lord-lieutenant), 1828, 1830
Angus, earl of; Linlithgow
Anjou. Plantagenet, Jarnac, 1569; Naples, 1266
Ankerstrom (kills Gustavus III.), Sweden, 1792
Anna, Santa; Mexico, 1853-76
Anne of Brittany, d. 1514; maids of honour
Anne of Austria, d. 1666; iron mask
Anne, queen, b. 1664; England, 1702-14; semper eadem
Ansell, G.; fire-damp, 1865
Anselm, abp.; Canterbury, 1093
Anson, admiral; Acapulco, 1744; naval battles, 1747
Anson, general; India, 1857
Anthony; monachism, 4th century; —arson, 1871
Antigonus; Ipsus, 301 B.C.; profiles
Antiochus I.—X., 280-65 B.C.; Syria, Jews, 170 or 168 B.C.
Antipater; Cranon, 322 B.C.
Antisthenes; cynics, 396 B.C.
Antonelli, card. 1806-76; Rome, 1848

Antonelli case, Italy, 1877-8
Antoninus Pius, Rome, emperors, 138; Roman wall
Antony, Mark, d. 30; Rome, 43 B.C.; Armenia, Philippi, 42 B.C.; Actium, 31 B.C.
Anviti, col., killed; Parma, 1859
Apelles, painter, 352-308 D.C.
Apollodorus; Trajan's pillar, 114
Apollonius; Syria, 168 B.C.
Appian, hist., fl. about 147
Appius Claudius; Rome, 449 B.C.; aqueducts, decemviri, Virginia
Applegath; printing machines
Apries; Egypt, 571 B.C.
Apsley, ld.; North adminis., 1770
Apuleius, Latin novelist, d. 174
Aquinas, Thos., theol., d. 1274
Arabi Bey; Egypt, 1881-2
Arago, D. F., nat. phil., 1786-1853
Aram, Eugene; trials, 1759
Aratus; Achaia, 245 B.C.
Arbogastes; Aquileia, 394
Arcadius and Honorius; eastern and western empire, 395
Arch, J.; agriculture, 1872
Archdale, J., quaker, 1699
Archelaus; Cappadocia, 20 B.C.; Macedon, 413 B.C.
Archemorus; Nemean games
Archer, F. S.; collodion, 1851
Archidamus; Sparta, 648 B.C.
Archilochus, 708 B.C.; iambic verse
Archimedes, 287-212 B.C.; circle, cranes, mechanics, mensuration, organs, reflectors, screw, spheres
Archytas; math., about 400 B.C.; automaton, pulley
Ardesoif, Mr.; cockfighting, 1788
Ardgillan, lord; Disraeli adm., 1874
Aretin, Gui; musical notes, 1025
Arfastus, chancellor, 1067
Arfwedson, Mr.; lithium, 1817
Argyll, duke of; Dunblane, 1715;— Gladstone adm., 1868, 1880
Ariarathes; Cappadocia (kings)
Ariobarzanes, 322 B.C.; Cappadocia, 93 B.C.
Ariosto, L. Ital. poet, 1474-1533
Aris, gov.; prisons, 1800
Aristarchus, 156 B.C.; sun, globe
Aristæus; conic sections, 330 B.C.
Aristides the Just, d. 468 B.C.; Athens
Aristippus; Cyrenaic sect, 392 B.C.
Aristocrates; Arcadia, 715 B.C.
Aristodemus; biarchy, 1102 B.C.
Aristophanes, d. 380 B.C.; comedy
Aristotle, 384-322 B.C.; Aristotelian philosophy, acoustics, botany, Macedon, mechanics, metaphysics, philosophy
Arius, d. 336; Arians
Arkwright, R., 1732-92; cotton, Manchester, spinning
Arles-Dufour; see Dufour
Arlington, lord; cabal, 1670
Armati; Rome, 1875
Arminius, or Hermann; Teutoburg, 9
Arminius, J., d. 1609; Arminians, Dort
Armitage, sir F.; Manchester, 1876
Armstrong, sir W. G.; electricity, 1840; cannon, 1859
Arne, T., music composer, 1710-78; Rule Britannia
Arnim, H.; Germany, Prussia, 1874-81
Arnold, gen.; United States, 1780
Arnold, Matthew, poet, 1822-88; culture
Arnold, Dr. Thos., hist., 1795-1842
Arnott, Neil, 1788-1874; stove, 1821; bed, 1830; ventilators
Arrian, hist., fl. 148
Arsaces; Arsacidæ, Parthia, 250 B.C.
Arsenius, Armenians, 1261
Artabazus; Pontus, 487 B.C.
Artaxerxes; Persia (kings)

Artemisia; mausoleum, 350 B.C.
Artemon; battering-ram, 441 B.C.
Arthur, king; Britain, 506
Arthur, prince; Connaught, 1874
Artois, count d'; duelling, 1778
Arundel, abp.; Canterbury, 1397-9
Arundel, Henry, earl of; administrations, 1547; Thos., Arundelian marbles
Ascanius; Alba, 1152 B.C.
Ascham, Roger, 1515-1568; archery
Asdrubal; see Hasdrubal
Aselli, G.; lacteals (1622), lymphatics
Ash, Dr.; Birmingham, 1766
Asgill, Mr.; translation, 1703
Ashbourne, ld. chancellor, (Ireland), 1885-1886
Ashburton, lord; Ashb. treaty, 1842
Ashe, gen.; Briar's creek, 1779
Ashford, Mary; appeal, 1818
Ashley, lord; cabal, 1670
Ashley, sir Arthur; cabbages
Ashton, colonel; Wigan, 1643
Aske; pilgrimage of grace, 1536
Aslett, Rob.; exchequer bills, 1803
Aspden, J.; Portland cement
Aspinall; trials, 1876
Assheton, Wm.; clergy charities
Astley, lord; Naseby, 1645
Aston, sir A.; Drogheda, 1649
Astyages; Media, 594 B.C.
Athanasius, d. 373; Athan. creed
Athelstan; England (king), 924; mint, 928
Athenœus, Greek, fl. 228, quotations
Atherton, sir Wm., att. gen., 1861
Athol, duke of; Man, sold by, 1765
Athothes; hieroglyphics, writing
Atlay, bp., Hereford, 1868
Atossa; marriage by sale
Attalus, d. 197 B.C.; seven churches (Pergamus), parchment
Atterbury, bp. F.; banished, 1723
Attila; Hungary, Chalons, 451
Attwood, B.; hospitals
Attwood, T.; chartists, 1838
Atwood, G., d. 1807; Atwood's machine
Atwell, W.; trials, 1857
Auber, D., music composer, 1784-1871
Auchmuty, sir Samuel; Batavia, 1811; Monte Video, 1807
Auckland, ld. bp.; Bath and Wells, 1854
Auckland, lord; Grey administration, 1830; India, 1835
Audiffret, see D'Audiffret
Audubon, J. J., 1780-1851; birds
Auerbach, B., Ger. Nov., 1805-82
Augereau, gen.; Castiglione, 1796
Augustenburg, duke of; Denmark, 1863
Augustin, St. (of Hippo), 354-430
Augustin the monk, abp. Canterbury, 602; Rochester
Augustus (emperor); Rome, 27 B.C.; prætorian guards; calendar
Aulus Gellius, Latin misc., fl. 169
Aumale, duc d'; France, 1871-2; Orleans; assassinations
Aurelian; Rome, emp. 270; Alemanni
Aurelius; Rome, emp. 161
Aurelle de Paladines, Franco-German war; d. 1877
Aurungzebe; India, 1658
Ausonius, Lat. poet, d. 394 (?)
Austin; see Augustin
Austin, capt.; Franklin
Austin, W.; trials, 1855
Austria, John of; Lepanto, 1571
Averroes, med. writer, fl. 1149-1198
Avicenna, med. and phil., 980-1037
Avisa; queens (John)
Ayesha, Mahomet's widow; camel, day of, 656
Ayoob or Ayoub Khan; Afghanistan, Herat, and Candahar

INDEX. 1017

Ayrton, A. A.; Gladstone adm., 1868
—W. harmonica
Azeglio, marchese d'; Italian patriot, 1800-66
Azim; Affghanistan, 1863

B.

Babbage, C., 1792-1871; calculating machine
Babcock, general, United States, 1876
Baber; India, 1525
Babeuf, d. 1791; agrarian law
Babrius; fable
Babyngton (*which see*), 1586
Bach, A.; resonator
Bach, J. Sebastian; passion music; music, 1685-1750
Bachelier, M.; encaustic, 1749
Bacciocchi, princes Piombino
Bachmeier, A.; pasigraphy, 1871
Back, G.; north-w. passage, 1833
Bacon, F., lord, 1561-1626; lawyers, aeronautics
Bacon, sir Nicholas; keeper, ld., 1558; baronet
Bacon, John, sculptor, 1740-99
Bacon, Roger, 1214-1292; astrology, camera lucida, loadstone, magic-lantern, magnet, optics, spectacles
Bacon, T. F.; trials, 1857
Badcock, Mr.; vaccination
Baez, D.; Hayti, 1859-68
Baffin, W. M.; Baffin's Bay, 1616
Bagehot, Walter, essayist, 1826-77
Baggallay, sir R.; solicitor-general, 1873; attorney-general, 1874; justices, lords, 1875
Bagnal, lieut.; duel, 1812
Bagot, bishop; Oxford, 1829
Bagot will case, trials, 1878
Bagration, pr.; Mohilows, 1812
Bagster, Miss M.; trials, 1828; E. longevity, 1877
Bailey, rev. W.; trials, 1843
Baillie, col.; Arcot, 1780
Baillie, general; Alford, 1645
Baillie, Joanna, poet, 1762-1851
Bailly, M., philos., executed, 1793
Bainbrigg, abp.; York, 1508
Bain, A.; education society
Bainbridge, W.; flageolet
Baines, M. T.; Palmerston adm. 1855
Baird, sir David; Cape, 1806; Seringapatam, 1799
Bajazet; Turkey, 1389
Baker, B.; Forth bridge
Baker, colonel; Bull's Bluff, 1861
Baker, H.; Bakerian lecture, 1765
Baker, sir S. W.; Africa, 1864; Egypt, slave trade, 1869-74; col. V., trials, 1875; Russo-Turkish war II., 1878; Egypt, 1882; Soudan, 1883-4
Baker *v*. Loder; trials, 1872
Baker, gen.; Char-asiab
Baker pasha; Turkey, 1879; Egypt, Soudan, 1883-4
Balard, M.; amylene, 1844
Balchan, admiral; Alderney, 1744
Baldwin I.—V.; Jerusalem, 1100-87; East Flanders
Baldwin, prof.; balloons, 1887-8
Bales, P.; caligraphy
Balfe, M. W., mus. comp., 1808-70
Balfour, A. J.; Salisbury adm., 1885, 1886
Balfour, John; Scotland, 1679
Ball, J. T.; chancellor (Ireland), 1874
Ballarat, Melbourne, 1854
Ballard, John; Babyngton's conspiracy, 1586
Ballasteros, gen.; Ximena, 1811
Balliol, Edw.; Scotland, kings. 1329
Balliol, John; Scotland, 1293; Oxford, Dunbar
Balmain, W. H.; luminous paint

Balmerino, lord; rebellion, Scotland, 1745; trials, 1746
Baltimore, lord; America, 1632; trials, 1768
Bancroft, abp.; Canterbury, 1604
Bancroft, G.; Am. hist., b. 1800
Bancroft, Mr. and Mrs., theatres (Haymarket)
Bandmann, M.; trials, 1878
Banks, sir J., 1743-1820; hort. soc., Royal Institution, 1799
Bannerman, H. C.; Gladstone adm., 1880, 1886
Bannister, Mr., actor; retired, 1815
Bar, duc de; Agincourt, 1415
Baradæus; Eutychians, Jacobites
Baranelli, L.; trials, 1855
Barante, A. G. de, Fr. hist., 1787-1866
Barantz, north-west passage, 1594
Barbarossa, Fred. I.; emp. Germany, 1152-90
Barbarossa, d. 1546; Tunis, Algiers
Barbauld, Mrs. A. L., 1743-1825
Barber, Fletcher, Saunders, and Dorey; trials, 1844, and *note*
Barberini; Portland vase
Barbey, M.; France, 1883
Barbou; printers, 1539-1813
Barbour, J.; trials, 1853
Barbour, John, Scot. poet, 1316-95
Barclay, capt.; pedestrianism, 1809
Barclay, Perkins, & Co.; porter
Barclay, Rob., 1648-90; quakers
Barham, lord; admiralty, 1805
Baring, Alex.; Peel administ. 1834; sir F.; London Inst. 1805; Russell adm. 1846
Baring, Mr.; Egypt, 1879
Baring, sir Evelyn; India, 1880; Egypt, 1883
Barker, J. T.; Beaumont trust
Barker, Robert; panorama, 1788
Barkly, sir H.; cape, 1870
Barlaam; Barlaamites, 1337
Barlow; clocks, 1676
Barlow, rev. J.; Royal Institut., 1842
Barlow, sir G.; India (governors), 1805
Barlowe, William; compass, 1608
Barnard, general; India, 1857; judge, United States, 1872
Barnardo, Dr., Barnardo's homes, coffee-palaces
Barnes, T., 1785-1841; Times
Barnett, Geo.; trials, 1816
Barnum, P. T., b. 1810; American showman, elephants, menagerie
Baroux, M.; scrutin
Barrand and Lund; clocks, 1878
Barré, Isaac; Rockingham administration, 1782
Barrett; Cumberland, naval battles, 1811; Fenians, 1868
Barrie, capt.; naval battles, 1811
Barrington, bp.; Durham, 1791
Barrington, Mr.; duel, 1788
Barrington; trials, 1790
Barrios, gen. R.; Guatemala, 1873; America, Central, 1885
Barrot, Odilon, 1791-1873; France, 1848
Barrow, Isaac, theol. and philos., 1630-77
Barry, sir Charles, architect, 1795-1860; parliament, *note*; Reform Club
Barth, Dr.; Africa, 1849
Barthélémy, E.; trials, 1855
Bartholdi, M., sculptor; United States, 1884
Bartlet, W. M.; trials, 1882
Barton, Bernard, poet, 1784-1849
Barton, Dr.; insurance, 1667
Barton, Elizabeth; impostor, 1534
Baschi, Matt.; Capuchins, 1525
Basil, St., d. 380; Basilians
Basil; East. emp. 867; Russia
Basilowitz; Russia, czars, 1462
Bass, M. T., Derby
Bastendorff; trials, 1879

Bastian, Dr., spontaneous generation
Bateman, J. F.; Glasgow, 1859; tunnels, 1869; water, 1867
Bates, M. van Buren; giants. 1871
Bates, W.; United States, 1872
Bath, earl of; Bath admin., 1746
Bathou; Transylvania, 1851, &c.
Bathurst, bp.; Norwich, 1805
Bathurst, earl; Liverpool administration, 1812
Bathyllus; pantomimes
Batman, J.; Victoria. 1835
Batthyany; Hungary, 1848
Battus; Cyrene, 631 B.C.
Baudin, M. Chas.; France, 1851
Baumbos, C. E.; mutinies, 1876
Baumé, areometer, 1768
Baumgarten; æsthetics, 1750
Bavaria, elector of; Ramillies, 1706
Baxter, sir D. 1793-1872; Dundee, 1863
Baxter, miss M. A.; Dundee, 1882
Baxter, G.; printing in colours, 1836
Baxter, Rd., theologian, 1615-91
Baxter *v*. Langley; trials, 1868
Bayard, chevalier, killed, 1524
Bayle, P., d. 1706; dictionary, 1697
Bayley, lieut.; duel, 1818
Baynard, Geoffrey; combat
Bazaine, marshal, 1811-1888; Mexico, 1863-6; Franco-Prussian war, 1870-1; Metz; France, 1873-4; 1883
Bazalgette, J. W., b. 1819; sewers, Thames
Beach, sir M. H., Disraeli adm. 1878; Salisbury adm., 1885, 1886
Beaconsfield; see *Disraeli*
Beadon, bishop; Bath, 1802
Beamish, capt., trials, navy, 1871
Bean aims at the queen; trials, 1842
Beaton, card.; assassinations, 1546
Beattie, Jas.; poet, 1735-1803
Beauclerc, lord Charles, drowned while assisting at a wreck, 1861
Beauchamp, Henry de; Wight
Beauchamp, John de; barons
Beaufort, cardinal, d. 1447
Beauharnais, Eugene, 1781-1824; Italy, 1805; Mockern—Hortense, "Partant pour la Syrie"
Beaulieu, general; Lodi, 1796
Beaumont, sir G., painter, 1753-1827; National Gallery
Beaumont, Mr.; duel, 1821-1826
Beaumont; viscount, 1440
Beau Nash; Bath, ceremonies
Beauregard, P. G., b. 1818; United States, 1861
Beaurepaire, gen.; Verdun, 1794
Beauvoir, sir J. de; trials, 1835
Beers, Dr.; la Crosse
Beck, T.; volunteers, 1881
Beckett, T., *m*. 1170; Becket
Becket (Denison), sir E.; bells, locks trials, 1881
Beckford, W.; Fonthill abbey
Beckwith, Agnes; swimming, 1876
Bedborough, A.; aquarium, 1876
Bede, Venerable, d. 735
Bedford, duke of; duel, 1822; Ireland, lord-lieutenants, 1490-1757; France, 1422; admiralty, 1744; nobility, 1470
Bedingfield, Ann; trials, 1763
Beeby, William; longevity
Beecher, rev. H.; United States, 1874-5
Beeching, J.; lifeboat, 1851
Beethoven, L., mus. comp., 1770-1827; sonata
Begum charge; Chunar, 1781
Behem, Martin; Azores
Behmen; see *Böhme*
Behnes, Wm., sculpt., 1800-64
Behring, d. 1741; Behring's straits
Bela; Hungary, kings
Belasyse, lord L., adm., 1687
Belcher, sir E., 1799-1877; circumnavigation, 1836; Franklin

INDEX.

Belcredl, count Rd., b. 1823; Austria, 1865
Belisarius, d. 565; Africa, east emp.
Belknap, gen.; United States, 1876
Bell, Aud., 1752-1832; Lancasterian schools
Bell, sir C., 1774-1842; nerves
Bell, Henry; steam, 1812
Bell, John Any Bird, the boy; trials, 1831.
Bell, Mr.; cattle, 1873
Bell, A. Melville; visible speech
Bell, A. Graham; telephone, 1877; photophone, graphophone, phonograph
Bell, rev. Patrick; reaping machine, 1826
Bellamont, lord; duel, 1773
Bellamy; trial, 1844
Bellarmine. card., 1542-1621
Bellingham, Perceval adm., 1812
Bellingham, sir Daniel, (mayor of Dublin), 1665
Bellini; Ital. music, 1802-35
Bellot, lieut., d. 1853; Franklin
Belochus; Assyria, 1446 B.C.
Belt v. Lawes; trials, 1881 et seq., 1886
Belus; Assyria, 2245 B.C.
Belzoni, J. B., traveller, d. 1823
Bem, gen. Joseph, d. 1850; Hungary
Benbow, adm.; naval battles, 1702
Benedek, L., 1804-81; Königgrätz
Benedict, Benedictines; popes, 574-1758
Benedict, sir Julius, mus. 1804-85
Bennett, James; Africa, 1872
Bennett, sir John; alderman, 1877; London, 1877
Bennett, sir Wm. Sterndale; mus., 1816-75
Benson and others; trials, 1877
Benson, bp.; Truro, 1877; Canterbury, 1883
Bentham Jer. (1748-1832); savings banks; deontology; panopticon; utilitarianism
Bentinck, lord G., 1802-1848; protectionists.
Bentinck, G. A. F. C.; judge advocate, 1875
Bentinck, ld. W.; Assam, India, 1827; Suttee
Bentley, Rd., scholar, 1662-1742
Beranger, J. P. de, poet, 1780-1857
Berengaria, queen (of Richard I.), d. 1230
Berengarius; fête de Dieu
Berenger, Butt, lord Cochrane, and others; trials, 1814
Beresford, lord; Albuera, 1811
Beresford, lord J.; suicide, 1841
Beresford, Wm.; Derby adm., 1852
Beresford, lord C.; Soudan, 1885
Berg, gen.; Poland, 1863
Bergeret, gen.; France, 1871
Beriot, Ch. A. de; mus., 1802-70
Berkeley; trials, 1811, 1858
Berkeley, hon. C.; duel, 1842
Berkeley, G.; Antigua, Leeward Isles, 1874
Berkeley, lord; admiralty, 1717
Berkeley, lord; America, N., 1644; Brest, 1694; Carolina
Berlioz, L. H., Fr. mus., 1803-69
Bernadotte, 1764-1844; Dennewitz, Sweden (king)
Bernard, Claude, Fr. physiologist, 1813-78
Bernard, St., 1091-1153
Bernard, S.; trial, 1858
Bernard, sir Thomas; British Inst., 1805; Royal Institution, 1799.
Bernini, G. L., Ital. artist, 1598-1680
Berri. duke and duchess of; France, 1820 & 1833, assassinations
Berrington, rev. J.; trials, 1873
Berry, lieut; trials, 1807

Berry, G.; Victoria, 1875
Berryer, P. A., Fr. advt., 1790-1868
Berthelot, P. M., b. 1827; acetylene, olefiant gas, 1862
Berthier, gen.; marshal, 1753-1815
Berthollet, C. L., Fr. chemist, 1748-1822; chlorine
Berthon, rev. E. L.; life-boat, 1882
Bertie, lady G. C.; lord great chamberlain
Berwick, duke of, d. 1734; Landen, Almanza, Newry
Berzelius, Jas., 1779-1848; chemistry, silicium
Besant, Mrs. A.; trials, 1877
Bessel, F.; stars
Bessemer, H.; iron, steel, steam, steam-gun
Bessus; Persia, 331 B.C.
Best, capt.; duel, 1804; Surat, 1611
Beswick, F.; trials, 1869
Bethell, bp.; Gloucester, 1824
Bethell, commander, marriage, 1888
Bethell, sir R., solicitor-gen., 1852, attorney-gen., 1859 (see Westbury)
Bethencourt; Canaries, 1400
Betty, master; theatres, 1804; Roscius
Beulé; France, 1874
Beust, F. F. v., 1809-1886; Austria, 1866
Bevern, prince; Breslau, 1757
Bewick, T., 1753-1828; wood engraving
Bexley, Vansittart, lord; Liverpool administration, 1812
Beza, Theodore, theologian, 1519-1605
Bialobrzeski, abp.; Poland, 1861
Bianconi, C., d. 1875; carriages
Bickersteth, R., bp.; Ripon, 1856
Bickersteth, E. H., bp.; Exeter, 1885
Biddulph, sir R.; Cyprus, 1881
Bidwell and others; trials, 1863
Bidwell, S.; telephotography
Biela, W. von, comet, 1826
Big Sam; giants, 1809
Bingley, lord; Oxford adm. 1711
Binney, rev. Thos., 1798-1874
Birch, J. W.; Straits, 1875
Birch, S., 1813-85; biblical
Bird, L.; Japan
Birde, W.; canon
Birkbeck, Dr. G., 1776-1841; mechanics' institutes
Biscoe, capt.; southern continent, 1832
Bishop; burking, 1831
Bishop, A.; derrick, 1857
Bishop, sir H. 1786-1855; music, ancient concerts; home
Bishop, Irving; thought reading
Bishop, J. F.; Italy, 1862
Bismarck, O. von, b. 1813; Prussia, 1862-76; France, 1870-3; Franco-Prussian War, Germany.
Black, Dr.; duel, 1835
Black, Jos.; chemist, 1728-99; magnesia, air, balloon
Blackburn, abp.; York, 1724
Blackall, Mr.; Queensland, 1868
Blackstone, sir W., 1723-80; law
Blackwood, S. A.; post-office secretary
Blaine, James; Panama, United States, 1884, 1886
Blair, Hugh, 1717-1800; rhetoric, verse;—John, chronologist, d. 1797
Blake, adm. R., 1599-1657; Algiers, Dover straits, Portland isle, Santa Cruz
Blakesley, Robt.; trials, 1841
Blanc, Louis, 1811-82; France, 1848
Blanchard; balloon, 1784-1819
Blanchard, Laman; suicide, 1845
Blanchard, T.; timber bending, 1855
Bland's Silver Bill, U. States, 1878

Blandy, Miss; trials, 1752
Blanqui, France, 1872-79
Bligh, captain; bread fruit tree; Adventure bay, Bounty mutiny
Bligh, captain, v. Mr. Wellesley Pole; trials, 1825
Bligh, Mr.; trials, 1806
Blizard, sir W.; Hunterian soc.
Blomfield, bp.; Chester, 1824; London, 1828
Blondin; crystal palace, 1861
Blood, col., d. 1680; Blood, crown
Blood, Mr.; trials, 1832
Bloomer, Mrs.; dress, 1849
Bloomfield, R., poet, 1766-1823
Blucher, marshal, d. 1819; Janvilliers, Ligny, Waterloo
Blum, R., shot in 1848
Blumenbach, J. F.; physiol., 1752-1840
Blundell, lieut.; duel, 1813
Blunt, Wilfred; Egypt, 1882-3
Boabdil, Abencerrages
Boadicea, d. 61; Britain, Iceni
Boardman, captain; duel, 1811
Boccaccio, 1313-75; Decameron
Boccold, John, anabaptists, 1534
Boddington; trials, 1797
Boden, col; Sanscrit, 1832
Bodley, T.; Bodleian lib., 1602
Boehm, J. E., Tyndale mem.
Boerhaave, H., med. writ., 1668-1738
Boethius, killed, 524
Böttcher (Böttcher); Dresden china, 1700
Bogle v. Lawson; trials, 1841
Böhme, or Behmen, J., mystic, 1612
Bohemia, king of, "Ich Dien;" Crecy, 1346
Boileau, Nic., Fr. poet, 1636-1711
Bois de Chêne, Mdlle.; beards, 1834
Bolan, Mr.; trials, 1839
Bolckow, H. W.; Middlesborough
Boldero, capt.; duel, 1842
Boleslas; Poland (kings), 992
Boleyn, Anne; England (queen Hen. VIII.)
Boleyn, earl of Wiltshire; administrations, 1532
Bolingbroke, lord; Oxford administration, 1711; deism; schism act, 1713
Bolivar, gen., 1783-1830; Columbia
Bolland, Acta Sanctorum, 1643
Bonaparte family; France
Bonaparte, P.; France, 1870;—Napoleon, Jerome; France, 1859-72
Bonar, Mr. and Mrs.; trials, 1813
Bonaventura, 1221-74; conclave
Bonavisa, Anthony; distaff, 1505
Bond; magnetism, 1668
Bond, F. A.; Brit. Museum, 1878
Bond and others; France, 1882
Bond, prof.; photography, 1851
Bonelli; electric loom, 1854
Bonheur, Rosa, Fr. painter, b. 1822
Bonnechose, Emile de, Fr. hist., 1801-74
Bonner, bishop of London; administrations, 1554
Bonnet, C., Fr. naturalist, 1720-93.
Bonnet-Duverdier; France, 1877
Bonnycastle, J., mathematician, d. 1821
Bonpland, A., naturalist, 1773-1858
Bonton and others; France, 1882
Bonwell, rev. J.; trials, 1860
Boole, G.; logic
Boon, colonel; America, 1754
Boosey; copyright, 1854; Dunmow, 1876
Booth, B.; book-keeping, 1789
Booth, Wilkes, assassin; U. States, 1865
Booth, Mr.; theatres, 1817
Booth, W.; salvation army
Bopp, F., Ger. linguist, 1781-1867
Borde, Andrew; Merry-andrew
Borden, Gail; milk, meat

INDEX. 1019

Borelli; mechanics, 1679
Borghese, H.; diamond
Borgia, Cæsar, killed, 1507
Boroimhe, Brian; Ireland, 1014
Borowlaski, ct.; dwarf, 1739-1837
Borrington, lady; trials, 1808
Borromeo, abp. Carlo, 1538-84; Milan, 1576
Borrowes, major; trials, 1888.
Borton, sir A.; Malta, 1878
Boscan, Span. poet, abt. 1496-1544
Boscawen, adm., 1711-60; Lagos
Bosquet, marshal, 1810-61; Inkermann, 1854
Bossuet, J., Fr. theol., 1627-1704
Boswell, sir A.; duel, 1822
Boswell, James, 1740-95, biography
Bosworth, rev. Jos., Ang.-Sax. scholar, 1790-1876
Bothwell, earl of; Scotland, 1567
Bottle conspirators; trials, 1839
Bouch, sir T.; Forth; Tay bridge
Bouchet, Anthony; illuminati
Bourchier; Canterbury, abp. 1454
Boufflers, Fr. marshal; 1644-1711
Bougainville, d. 1811; circumnavigation, New Hebrides
Bouillé, marquis de; Enstatia, 1781
Boulanger; France, 1887-9
Boulby, Mr.; China, 1860
Boulton, Mat., d. 1809; Birmingham
Boulton and others, trials, 1871
Boulton and Watt; coinage, 1788
Bourbaki, gen.; Franco-Pruss. war, 1870-1
Bourbon family; Bourbon, duke of; duels, 1778
Bourgeois, sir F.; Dulwich, 1813
Bourke, sir R.; Victoria, Australia, 1831
Bourmont, marshal; Algiers, 1830
Bourne, Sturges; Canning administration, 1827
Bousfield, W.; executions, 1856
Bovill, sir W., 1814-73; com. pleas, 1866; trials, 1871-72
Bowdler, C. A.; balloons, 1874
Bowen, sir G. F.; Queensland, 1859; Victoria, 1873
Bower, Mr. Elliott; trials, 1852
Bower, G.; gas light, 1884
Bowes, Miss; Strathmore, 1766
Bowley, R.; crystal palace, 1870
Bowman, sir William; Royal Institution
Bowring, sir John, scholar, &c., 1792-1872; Canton, China, Siam
Bowstead, bishop; Lichfield, 1843
Bowyer, bp.; Ely, Chester, 1812
Boxall, sir W.; national gallery
Boyd, captain; duel, 1808
Boyd, Hugh; Junius
Boydell, ald., d. 1804; British Institution
Boyle, earl of Orrery; orrery
Boyle, Rob., 1626-91; phosphorus, Royal Society
Boyle, Henry; Godolphin administration, 1702
Boyton, capt., life-boat, &c., 1875
Brabant, duke of; merchants, 1296
Braddock, gen.; Fort Duquesne
Brabazon, lord, hospital Saturday, 1874; playgrounds
Bradbury, H.; nature-printing, 1855-6
Bradlaugh, C.; Northampton, 1874; trials, 1877, et seq.; parliament, 1880-4; oaths, 1880-9
Bradley, admiral; trials, 1814
Bradley, G. G.; Westminster (dean), 1884
Bradley, Jas., 1693-1762; aberration, astronomy, Greenwich
Bradwardine, abp.; Canterbury, 1349
Brady, capt.; China, 1874
Braganza, John of; Portugal, 1640

Bragg, gen.; United States, 1862-3-76
Braham, John, singer, 1774-1856; theatres
Brahe, Tycho, 1546-1601; astronomy, globe
Braidwood, Jas.; fires, k. 1861
Bramah, J., 1749-1814; hydrostatics, planing-machine, lock (addenda)
Bramwell, sir Frederick J.; Royal Institution
Brand, H. B., speaker, 1872-84; visct. Hampden, 1884
Brande, W. T., chemist, 1788-1866; Royal and London Institutions
Brandreth, the Luddite; Derby trials, 1817
Brandt, count; Zell, 1772
Brandt; cobalt, phosphorus, 1667
Brantome, P., historian, 1527-1614
Brassey, lady, book (cheap); d. 1887
Brassey, Thos.; rail. eng., 1805-70
Brasidas; killed, Amphipolis, 422 B.C.
Braun, K. nephoscope, 1868
Bravo case, Bravo, 1876
Bray, Dr.; Bray's associates
Breadalbane peerage; trials, 1866-7
Breakspeare, Nicholas; pope, 1154
Brederode, H. de; gueux, 1566
Bremer, sir Gordon; China, 1840
Bremer, Fred., novelist, 1802-65
Brendon, St.; Clonfert, 558
Brenn, captain; Hibernia, 1833
Brennus; Rome, 390 B.C.
Brereton, col.; Bristol, 1832
Brereton cases; railways, 1881-4
Bressa, C. A.; Bressa prize
Bresson, count; suicide, 1847
Brett, J. W.; submarine telegraph, 1845
Brett, sir W. B., solic. gen. 1868; master of rolls, 1883
Brewster, sir David, nat. phil., 1781-1868; kaleidoscope, British association; lithoscope
Bridges, Mr.; pecul. people
Bric, Mr.; duel, 1826
Bridgewater, earl; admiralty, 1699
Bridgewater, duke of, 1736-1803; Bridgewater Canal
Bridport, lord; L'Orient, 1795
Brienne, M. de; notables, 1788
Bright, corpulency, 1809
Bright, John, 1811-89; England; Anti-corn-law league, Adullam, agitators, peace congress; Gladstone adm., 1868, 1880
Bright, sir Charles T.; electrician, 1832-88
Bright, T.; shorthand
Brindley, Jas., 1716-72; tunnels, Bridgewater canal, Barton
Brinkleet; trials, 1828
Brinvilliers, madame de, executed, 1676; poisoning
Bristol, mayor of; trials, 1832
Bristol, John, earl of; administ. 1621
Brock, C. F.; fireworks
Brodie, sir B. C., surgeon, 1783-1862; —(son) chemist, b. 1817; graphite, 1862; ozone
Broglie, duc de; France, 1873, 1879
Broke, captain; Chesapeake, 1813
Brome, Adam de; Oriel, 1337
Bromley, sir Thomas; administrations, 1579
Brongniart, A., geol., 1770-1847
Brooke, sir James, 1803-68; Borneo
Brooks, prof.; oysters
Brothers, R., d. 1824
Brough, M. A.; trials, 1854
Brougham, H., 1779-1868; chancellor, charities, impeachment, social science
Broughton v. Knight, trials, 1873
Broughton, lord, 1786-1869; Russell adm., 1846, 1851
Brown, gen.; Prague, 1751
Brown, H., trials, 1858

Brown, sir J.; iron, 1867
Brown, captain John; United States, 1859
Brown, Mrs.; fountain, 1875
Brown, R., d. 1630; Brownists, Independents
Brown, Rob., botanist, 1773-1858; Brownian
Brown, W., 1783-1864; Liverpool, 1857
Browne, American gen.; Chippawa, 1814; Fort Erie
Browne, col. H., China, 1874
Browne, George; Dublin, 1554
Browne, Hannah; trials, 1837
Browning, R., poet, b. 1812
Browning; Mrs. E., 1809-1861
Brownrigg, Eliz.; trials, 1767
Brownrigg, gen.; Candy, 1815
Bruce, baron; Lloyd's, note
Bruce, David; Scotland, king, 1328; Nevill's cross, 1346
Bruce, Edward; Dundalk, 1318
Bruce, H. A.; Gladstone adm. 1868
Bruce, Michael; Lavalette, 1816
Bruce, Robert, d. 1329; Scotland, king, 1306; Bannockburn, 1314
Bruce, com.; Lagos, China, 1851
Bruce, V., traveller, 1730-94; Africa, Bruce, Nile, Palmyra
Brucher, Antonio; coinage, 1553
Brudenell; trials, 1834
Brueys, admiral; Nile, 1798
Brunck, anthology, 1772-6
Brunel, I. K., 1769-1849; blocks, steam, Thames tunnel
Brunel, I. K., jun., 1806-59; steam
Brunetti, prof.; burning dead, 1874
Bruno, d. 1101; Benedictines, Chartreuse, Cologne, tannery
Brunswick, duke of; Valmy, 1792; Quatre Bras, 1815
Brunt, Davidson, Thistlewood, Ings, and Tidd; Cato-street, 1820
Brush, C. F.; electric light, 1878-9
Brutus, Lucius Junius; consuls, Rome, 508
Brutus and Cassius; Philippi, 42 B.C.
Bryan (or Brian) Boroimhe; harp, Clontarf, Ireland, 1014
Bryant, Wm. C., Am. poet, 1784-1878
Bryce, James; Ararat, United States, 1888
Bubb; opera-house, 1821
Buccleuch, duke of; Granton
Buchan, captain; N.-W. passage, 1819-22
Buchan, M.; Buchanites, 1779
Buchanan, J., 1791-1868; pres. U. States, 1856,
Buchanan v. Taylor; trials, 1876
Buckhurst, Thomas, lord; administrations, 1599
Buckhurst peerage; trials, 1876
Buckingham, Stafford, duke of; constable, 1521
Buckingham, G. Villiers, duke of; administrations, 1615, 1621; dress; killed, 1628
Buckingham, duke of; cabal ministry, 1670; Peel administrations, 1841; duel, 1822;—(b. 1823); Disraeli adm., 1868; Madras, 1875
Buckingham, marquis of; Ireland, lord lieutenant, 1787
Buckinghamshire, earl of; Liverpool administration, 1812
Buckland, F.; fisheries, 1863
Buckland, rev. W.; geologist, 1784-1856
Buckle, H. T.; historian, 1822-62
Buckle, capt., Amoaful, 1874
Bufalmaco; caricatures, 1330
Buffet; France, 1873-6
Buffon, G., 1707-88; geology, zoology, 1749
Bugeaud, marshal, 1784-1849; Morocco, 1844

INDEX.

Bulkeley, bishop; Bangor, 1553
Bull, J., "God save the King," 1606
Bull, G., bishop, 1634-1710
Bulwer, see *Lytton, ld.*
Bulwer, sir H. E.; Natal, 1875
Bunbury, E. H.; geography
Bunning, J. B.; coal-exchange, 1849
Bunsen, baron C. J.; Germ. hist. and phil., 1791-1860
Bunsen, R.; voltaic pile, 1842; spectrum, 1860
Bunyan, J., 1628-88; Bedford, allegory, pilgrim's progress
Buonarotti, Michael Angelo, 1474-1564
Burbage, James; plays, drama
Burdett, sir F., 1770-1844; duel, 1807; riots, trial, 1820. See *Coutts*
Burdock, Mary Anne; trials, 1835
Burdon, Mr.; trials, 1841
Burdwan, rajah of; Calcutta, 1878
Bürger, G.; Germ. poet, 1748-94
Burgers, T. F.; Transvaal, 1872
Burgess, bishop; David's, St. 1825; Salisbury
Burgh, Hubert de; Whitehall
Burgoyne, gen.; Saratoga, 1777; sir J. F. 1782-1871; capt. H., Captain, 1870
Burke, Edmund, 1729-97; Rockingham administrations, 1782; Canada, Junius
Burke, sir J. B., b. 1815; armorial bearings, heraldry
Burke, R.; Fenians, 1867-8
Burke and Wills; Australia, 1860-3
Burleigh, lord; administrations, 1558
Burlington, Rd. earl of, 1695-1753
Burmann, P., thesaurus
Burn, H. & others; trials, 1886
Burnaby, col. F. A.; balloons, 1874; Khiva; Soudan, 1885
Burnes, sir A., murdered; India, 1841
Burnet, Dr.; antediluvians
Burnet, bp. Gilbert, 1643-1715
Burnett, Mr., d. 1784; Burnett prizes
Burns, R., Scot. poet, 1759-96
Burnside, gen. A.; U. States, 1862
Burr, colonel; duel, 1804
Burrows, gen. J.; Afghanistan, 1880; Maiwand
Burton, F. W.; national gallery, 1874
Burton, Robt. (*Anat. of Melancholy*), 1576-1640; quotations
Burton, Richd. F.; Midian
Bury, Richard de; libraries, 1341
Bute, earl of, 1713-92; Bute adm.
Butler, bp. S.; Lichfield, 1840
Butler, bp. J., 1692-1752
Butler, captain; Silistria, 1854
Butler, Sam. (*Hudibras*), abt. 1612-80
Butler, gen. B.; New Orleans, 1862
Butt, Mr.; trials, 1871
Butt, I., 1873-79; Ireland, home-rule, 1871-8
Buttevant; viscount, 1385
Button, sir Thomas; N.-W. passage, 1612
Buxton, Mr.; trials, 1829
Buxton, sir T. F., 1786-1845; prisons, 1815
Buxton, E. N., metropolitan school board, 1881
Byng, adm. J., exec. 1757; Gibraltar, Byng, 1757
Byrne, Miss; riot, 1819
Byron, comm.; port Egmont, 1765
Byron, George, lord, poet, 1788-1824; Greece, Missolonghi, swimming; Byron national memorial, 1875
Bysse, Dr.; music (festivals)

C.

Cabot, Sebastian and John; America, 1497
Cabral, Alvarez de; Brazil, 1500
Cabrera, general; Ramon, 1810-77; Spain, 1840
Cade, Jack; Cade's insurrection, 1450
Cadell, Captain; Australia, 1867
Cadmus, 1453 B.C.; alphabet, Bœotia
Cadogan, earl; Salisbury adm., 1886
Cadogan, captain; duels, 1809
Cadwallader; Britain, 678
Cæcilius Isidorus; slavery in Rome, 12 B.C.
Cædmon; Anglo-Saxons, 680
Cæsar, Julius, 100-44 B.C.; Rome, Britain, calendar, Ides, Dover, Pharsalia, Rubicon, Zela
Cæsar, Octavius, 63 B.C.-14 A.D.; Rome, Actium, massacres, triumvirate, Philippi, emperor
Cæsalpinus; blood, circulation, 1569
Cagliostro, d. 1795; diamond necklace
Caillelet, air, gases, 1877; hydrogen
Caird v. Syme; trials, 1887
Cairns, Hugh, earl, 1819-85, att.-gen. 1866, lord chan. 1868-1874
Cairns, W. W.; Queensland, South Australia
Cairoli ministry, Italy, 1878, 1879-81
Caithness, earl of; steam-carriage, 1860
Calaphilus; wandering Jew
Calas, J., judicially murdered, 1761
Calder, sir Robt.; naval batt., 1805
Calderon, P., Span. dramatist, 1601-87
Calderon, Peru, 1881
Calepino; dictionaries, 1500
Calhoun, Mr.; temperance soc., 1818
Caligula; Rome, emperor, 37
Calippus; Calippic period, 330 B.C.
Calixtus, pope; Calixtins, 1656
Callaghan, T.; Falkland Isles, 1876
Callan; trials, 1874, 1886
Callcott, J. W.; music. 1766-1821, glee-club
Callicrates; calligraphy
Callimachus; abacus, architecture, Corinthian, 540 B.C.
Callinicus; Greek fire, wildfire
Callisthenes; Chaldean, Macedon, 328 B.C.
Calonne; notables, 1788
Calthorpe, ld.; Birmingham, 1857
Calverly; pressing to death, 1605
Calvert, F. Crace, d. 1873; carbolic acid
Calvert and Co.; porter, 1760
Calvin, John, 1509-64; Calvinism
Cambacérès; directory, 1799
Cambridge, dukes of; Cumbridge
Cambridge, George, duke of, b. 1819; com.-in-chief, 1856; army, 1872
Cambyses; Egypt, Persia, 525 B.C.
Camden, lord; chancellor, Perceval adm., 1809; exchequer, Ireland (lord-lieut.)
Camden, W., antiquary, 1551-1623
Camelford, lord; duel, 1804
Cameron, H. L.; trials, 1858
Cameron, V. L.; Africa, 1872
Cameron, consul; Abyssinia, 1863
Camillus, Rome; 391 B.C.
Camoens, Port. poet, 1524-79
Campbell, bishop; Bangor, 1859
Campbells; disciples of Christ, 1812
Campbell, sir C.; see *Clyde*
Campbell, John, lord 1781(?)-1861; attorney-general, king's bench, chancellor, Palmerston
Campbell, J. F., sunshine recorder
Campbell, Rev. J.; trials, 1863; Campbellites, 1831

Campbell, major; duel, trials, 1808
Campbell, capt.; marriages, forced, 1690
Campbell, Thos., poet, 1777-1844
Camper, Peter, 1722-89; facial angle
Campion; trials, 1857
Campion, M. Carthagena, 1873; Spain, 1874, Cuba
Canaris; Greece, 1863-4-77
Canaletti, Ven. painter, 1697-1768
Canby, gen.; killed, Modoc, 1873
Canning, George, 1770-1827; Canning, duel, 1809; grammarians, king's speech
Canning, viscount, 1812-62; India, 1855
Canova, A., sculptor, 1757-1822
Canovas del Castillo, A.; Spain, 1874-6
Cantillon; wills (Napoleon's), 1821
Canton, J., d. 1772; phosphorus, phosphorescence, magnetism
Cantor, Theod.; Cantor lectures, 1853
Canute; England, 1017; Alney
Cape Town, Gray, bp. of; Africa, 1866; Church of England
Capel, H.; admiralty, 1679
Capet family; France, 987
Capo d'Istria, count; Greece, 1831
Car; augury
Caracalla; Rome, emp. 211; Alemanni
Caracci, L., painter, 1555-1619; An., 1568-1609
Caraccioli, adm., executed, Naples, 1799
Caractacus; Britain, 50
Caraffa, bishop; Theatines, 1524
Carapanos, M.; Dodona
Carausius; Britain, 281
Cardan, J., 1501-76; algebra
Carden, Mr.; trials, 1854
Cardigan, lord; duel, 1840; trials, 1841 and 1863; Balaklava, 1854
Cardross case; trials, 1861
Cardwell, Edward, visct., b. 1813; Palmerston adm., 1855-59; Gladstone adm. 1868; army, 1872
Carey, bishop; St. Asaph, 1830
Carey, James; Ireland, 1883
Carleton, sir Guy; U. States, 1782
Carlingford, lord; Gladstone adm., 1880
Carlier, fire-annihilator
Carlile, R.; atheist; trials, 1819, 1831
Carlisle, earl of; Ireland, lord-lieutenant, 1859
Carlos, don; Spain, 1833-73
Carlyle, Thos., phil. and hist., 1795-1881; Carlyle
Carmarthen, marquis of; administrations, 1689
Carnarvon, earl of; Salisbury adm., 1885; Disraeli admin., 1874
Carnot, L., French mathematician, 1753-1823
Carnot, M. Sadi; France, 1886
Caroline; queen (George II.), parks
Caroline; queen (George IV.), Brandenburg-house, delicate investigation
Carpenter, W. B., physiologist, 1813-85; deep sea
Carpenter, W. Boyd; bp. Ripon, 1884
Carpenter, gen.; Preston, 1715
Carr, bishop; Worcester, 1831
Carr, Howell; national gallery, 1824
Carrol, balloons, 1878
Carré; congelation, 1860
Carstares, rev. W.; thumbscrew
Carte, D'Oyly; Savoy
Cartier; America, 1534
Cartier, Richard; alchemy, 1476
Carteret; circumnavigator, 1766
Carteret, lord; Walpole adm., 1721

INDEX. 1021

Carthage, St.; Lismore, 636
Cartwright, major; trials, 1820
Carvilius, Spurius; divorces, 231 B.C.
Casella, L.; thermometer, 1861
Cashin, Miss; quackery, 1830
Cashman; Spafields, riots, 1816
Casimir; Poland
Cassagnac, P. de; duels, France, 1877
Cassander; Macedon, 316 B.C.
Cassibelaunus; Briton, 54; chariots
Cassini, 1625-1712; astronomy; Bologna, latitude, Saturn, 1655
Cassius; Philippi, 42 B.C.
Castanos; Spain, 1852
Castel, M.; Dartmouth, 1404
Castelar; Spain, 1869-73.
Castillo, Spain, 1879
Castlereagh, lord; union with Ireland, 1800; Pitt admin., 1804; Liverpool admin., 1812; duel, 1809; suicide, 1822
Castner, H. Y.; Sollum, Aluminium
Catesby, Rob.; gunpowder, 1605
Cateh v. Sheen, trials, 1870
Cathcart, ld.; Copenhagen, 1807
Cathcart, general; Kaffraria; Inkermann, 1854
Catherine; England (queens, Hen. V., VIII., Charles II.)
Catherine; Russia, 1725; Odessa; Sebastopol
Cato (the censor); agriculture; 149 B.C.;—(the tribune), kills himself, 46 B.C.
Catullus, poet, d. abt. 47 B.C.
Catulus; Cimbri, 101 B.C.
Caulaincourt; Chatillon, 1814.
Caus, S. de; steam-engine, 1615
Cautley, sir P., 1802-71; Ganges, 1854
Cavagnari, L.; Afghanistan, 1878-9
Cavaignac, general; France, 1848
Cavalier, camisards
Cavaliere, Emilio di; opera, recitative, 1600
Cave, S., judge-advocate, 1874; Egypt, 1875-6
Cavendish, circumnavigator, 1586; "Whist"
Cavendish, H., 1731-1810; balloons, electricity, chemistry, nitrogen, hydrogen, water
Cavendish, John de; judges, 1382
Cavendish, lord Frederick; Gladstone adm., 1880; murdered, Ireland, 1882
Cavendish, lord John; Portland administration, 1783
Cavendish, W.; Devonshire, 1618
Cavill, Mr.; swimming
Cavour, Camille de, 1809-61; Sardinia, Austria, Italy
Caxton, Wm., about 1412-91; printing
Cayley, sir G.; heat
Caylus, count; encaustic painting, 1765
Cecil, Wm.; administrations, 1572
Cecrops; Athens, 1556 B.C.
Celeste, madame; theatres, 1844
Celestin; popes, 1143
Celsus; midwifery, &c., 37
Cerdic; Britain (Wessex)
Cerinthus; apocalypse
Cernuschi, H.; bi-metallism
Cervantes, M. S., 1547-1616; don Quixote
Cespedes, C. M. de; Cuba, 1868
Cetywayo, (Zulu chief); Transvaal, Zululand, 1872-81; Ulundi
Chabannes, écorcheurs, 1438
Chacornac; planets, 1853
Chad, St.; baths, 667
Chaffers, Alexander, statutory declaration
Challoner, T.; alum, 1608
Chalmers, Dr. T., 1780-1847

Chamberlain, Joseph, Gladstone adm. 1880, 1886; bankrupts; Merchant shipping Act; fisheries, United States, 1887, radical programme
Chamberlain, sir N.; Afghanistan, 1878, Khyber
Chambers, W. O., fish, 1884
Chambers, bishop; Peterborough, 1541
Chambers, encyclopædia, 1728, 1859; Chambers' journal; —R., 1802-71; —W., 1800-83; Edinburgh, 1853
Chambers, sir T.; recorder, 1878
Chambers, sir William; Somersethouse, 1775
Chambord, comte de, 1820-83; France, 1870-6; flag
Chancellor, R.; north-east passage
Changarnier, general, 1793-1877; France, 1851, 1873
Channing, W., 1780-1842
Chantrelle, E. M.; trials, 1878
Chantrey, F., sculpt., 1782-1841; Royal Academy
Chanzy, Fr. gen., 1823-83; Franco-Prussian war, 1870-1; Algiers, 1878
Chaplin, H.; Salisbury adm., 1885
Chapman, Mr.; aranda sermon
Chappe, M.; telegraphs, 1793
Chappell, Thos.; James's, St., Hall, 1859
Chard and Bromhead, lieuts.; Zululand, 1879
Chares; colossus, 268 B.C.
Charlemagne, 742-814; academy, couriers, Avars, Bavaria, Christianity, France, Germany, Navarre
Charles Albert; Sardinia, 1831; Novara, 1849
Charles; England, France, Spain, Savoy, Germany, Sweden, Sicily, &c.
Charles V.; emperor, 1500-58; Spain, Austria, Germany, Spires
Charles V.; Bastile, 1369
Charles VI.; picquet, 1390
Charles XII., 1682-1718; Sweden, Frederickshald
Charles the Bald, Fontenaille
Charles the Bold; Burgundy, 1468, Nancy, Liege
Charles, archduke, 1771-1847; Asperne, Eckmühl, Essling
Charles of Anjou; Naples, 1266
Charles of Lorraine; Lissa, 1757
Charles of Hohenzollern, prince of Roumania, b. 1839; Dannbian principalities; Russo-Turkish war II. 1877
Charles Stuart, prince; pretender, Culloden, 1746
Charlesworth, J. C.; trials, 1861;—Charlesworth, Mr. and Mrs.; convalescent, 1866
Charlotte, queen, England (Geo. III.)
Charlotte, princess of Wales, 1796-1817; Claremont
Charlton v. Hay and others; trials, 1875
Charteris, col.; trials, 1730
Chassé, gen.; Antwerp, 1832
Chateaubriand, viscount, French writer, 1768-1848
Chatham, earl of, 1708-78; Newcastle admin., 1757; Chatham admin., 1766; Walcheren, 1809
Chatterton, T., poet, 1752-70
Chaucer, G., 1328-1400; Canterbury tales
Chaves, marq. of; Portugal, 1826
Chelmsford, ld.; Derby adm., 1858; Zululand, 1879; Ulundi
Cheltenham Chronicle; trials, 1873
Cherubini, music. comp., 1760-1842
Chesham, Sarah; trials, 1851
Cheshire rioters; trials, 1842
Chesney, col.; Assyria, 1835; Euphrates, 1850
Chetwind, capt.; oil on waters

Chetwynd, sir G. r. Durham; trials, 1889
Chevallier, M., 1806-79; Albert medal, 1875, Liverpool, 1875
Chevreul, E., chemist, &c., 1786-1889; candles, glycerine, Albert medal, 1873
Chicheley, archbishop; Canterbury, 1414-1443
Childe, H. L.; dissolving views
Childeric; France (kings)
Childers, H. C., admiralty; Gladstone adms., 1868, 1880, 1886; Greenwich schools, 1870; nat. debt
Chillingworth, W., theol., 1602-44
Ching Noung; China, wine, 1998 B.C.
Chisholm, H. W.; weights, 1877
Chladni, E., 1756-1827; acoustics
Choiseul, E., duc de, 1719-85
Cholmeley, sir R., Highgate
Cholmondeley, gen.; horseguards, 1693
Chopin, F., Hung. mus., 1810-49
Chosroes I.; Persia, 531
Christian; Denmark, Sweden, 1448
Christian IV.; Christiania, 1624
Christian VII.; Denmark, 1775, Oldenburg
Christie, life-raft, &c., 1875
Christie, W. H.; Greenwich (astronomer royal)
Christina; Sweden, 1633; Spain, 1833
Christine, M., twins
Christophe; Hayti, 1811
Christopher; Denmark (kings), 1252, 1320
Christopher, Robt. Adam; Derby adm., 1852
Chrysostom; fathers, 354-407
Chubb, Mr., locks (addenda)
Church, dean, Church of England, 1881
Churchill, C.; satires, 1731-64
Churchill, ld. R.; fourth party, 1880; Salisbury adm. 1885
Cialdini, gen.; Italy, 1860; Castel Fidardo, Gaéta
Cibber, C., 1671-1757; poet-laureate
Cicero, 106-43 B.C.; Athens, Rome, Catiline, Philippics
Cid (Spanish hero), d. 1099
Cimabue, painter, 1240-1300
Cimarosa, musician, 1754-1801
Cimon; Eurymedon, 466 B.C.
Cincinnatus, dictator, 458 B.C.
Cinna, consul, killed, 84 B.C.
Clanny, Dr. Reid; safety lamp, 1817
Clanricarde, marq. of; postmaster, 1846; Russell administration, 1851; Palmerston administration, 1855
Clapperton, Hugh, traveller, 1788-1827
Clare, John, poet, 1793-1864
Clare, earl of; duel, 1820
Clarence, duke of; Anjou, Clarencieux; rebellion, 1478; admiralty, 1827
Clarendon, earl of (Hyde), 1608-74; administrations, 1660, 1685;—earl of, G. F. Villiers, 1800-70;—Ireland, lord-lieut.; Aberdeen, Palmerston
Clare, sir James, phys., 1788-1870
Clarke, Adam, theol., 1760-1832;—Sam., theol., 1675-1729;—Edw. D., traveller, 1768-1822
Clarke, sir Andrew; Straits, 1874
Clarke, sir E.; sol. gen., 1886
Clarke, M. A.; trials, 1814
Clarke, gen.; Cape, 1795
Clarke, J. Algernon; automaton
Clarke, M. C., b. 1809; Shakspeare, concordance, 1847
Clarkson, Thos., 1760-1846; slave-trade, slavery

Claude Lorraine, painter, 1600-82
Claudian, Latin poet, d. about 408; archery
Clandius; Rome, emperor, 41; II., Goths, 269; Naissus
Claudius, App.; decemviri, 451 B.C.
Claughton, bp.; Rochester, Albans, St.
Clausel, marshal; Algiers, 1836
Clausius, R. J., physicist, 1822-28
Claussen, chev.; flax, 1851
Claverhouse; Bothwell, 1679
Clay, F., mus. comp., b. 1840
Clay, Mr.; slavery, U. S., 1820; Liberia; whist
Clayton, Mr.; duel, 1830
Clayton, Dr.; gas, 1739
Clenver, bishop; Bangor, St. Asaph, 1806-1815
Cleisthenes; ostracism, 510 B.C.
Clémenceau, M., Fr. polit.; France, 1882-4
Clemens Romanus; popes, 662;— Alexandrinus, d. abt. 213
Clement; popes, 91; IV.; conclave, 1268;— VII.; pontiff, benefices, Clementines, 1378;—VIII.; index;—XIV. (Ganganelli), 1769; Jesuits
Clement, Jacques; France, 1589;— Joseph; planing machine, 1825;— Julian; midwifery, 1663
Clementi, M., music, d. 1832; sonata
Cleombrotus; Sparta, 380 B.C.
Cleomenes; Sparta, 520 B.C.
Cleon, Athenian demagogue, killed 422 B.C.; Amphipolis
Cleopatra; Egypt, 69-30 B.C.; rose
Cleveland, Grover, b. 1837; president United States, 1884
Clifford, C.; life-boat, 1856
Clifford, J.; trials, 1870
Clifford, lord; Roman Catholics, 1829;—sir Tho., cabal, 1670
Clinton, H. Fynes, 1781-1852; chronology
Clinton, sir H.; Yorktown, 1781
Clinton, Geoffrey de; Kenilworth, 1120
Clive, Robt., lord, 1725-74; Arcot, India, Plassey
Cloncurry, lord, v. Piers; trials, 1807
Close, Mr.; duels, 1836
Clotaire; France (kings), 558
Clovis (Chlodowig, Ludwig, Ludovicus, Louis); France, 481; Normandy, Paris, Clovis, Salique, fleur-de-lis, Alemanni
Cloots, Anacharsis, exec. 1794
Clonet; gas
Clune, &c., trials, 1830
Cluseret, gen.; Lyons, 1870; France, 1871; Fenians, 1872
Clyde, lord, 1792-1863; India, 1857
Clymer; printing-press, 1814
Cobbett, William, 1762-1835; trials, 1809, 1811, 1831
Cobden, R., 1804-65; anti-corn-law league, free trade, French treaty, peace congress
Cobham, ld.; Lollards, 1418
Coburg, prince of; Fleurus, 1794 (see Saxe-Coburg)
Cochrane, lord (afterwards Dundonald), d. 1860; Basque roads, stocks, trials, 1814
Cockburn, sir A., 1802-80; solicitor-general, 1858; attorney-general, king's bench, ch. j., Alabama
Cockerill, J.; Seraing
Cocking, Mr.; balloons, 1837
Codrington, admiral sir E.; Navarino, 1827; — sir W. J., 1804-84; Crimea
Codrus; Athens, 1092 B.C.
Coe; trials, 1876
Coggia; comets, 1874; planets, 1868, 1878
Cohorn, B. van, military engineer, 1641-1704

Coke, sir Edw., 1550-1634; parliaments, 1592
Colbert, J. B., 1619-83; tapestry
Colborne, sir John; Canada, 1838
Colclough, Mr.; duels, 1807
Colcutt, T. E.; imperial institute
Cole and Cox (police); parliament, 1885
Coleman, St.; Cloyne, 6th cent.
Coleman, Mrs.; actress, 1656
Colenso, bp., 1814-83; church of England, 1863; trials, 1866; Natal
Coleridge, Samuel T., poet, &c., 1772-1834; method
Coleridge, sir J., solic.-gen.; att.-gen., 1871; com. pleas, 1873; king's bench, 1880
Coles, capt. Cowper, 1831-70; navy of England, 1855-70; Captain
Colet, J.; Paul's school, 1512
Coligni, admiral, killed, 1572
Collard, dwarf, 1873
Collard, rear-adml.; suicide, 1846
Colley, sir G. P.; Transvaal, Natal, Majuba
Collie, Alex.; London, 1875
Collier, J. P., 1789-1884; Shakspeare, 1849
Collier, Jeremy; eccles.-hist., 1650-1726
Collier, sir R. P.; att.-gen., 1868; baron Monkswell, 1885
Collings, Jesse; restitution bill
Collingwood, lord, 1748-1810; Trafalgar, 1805; naval battles, 1809
Collins, govr.; Hobart Town, 1804
Collinson, sir R., 1811-83; Franklin, 1850
Collucci, V.; trials, 1861
Colman, G., d. 1794;—G., jun., 1762-1836; theatres, 1777
Colonna family flourish, 1288-1555
Colonna, V., poetess, 1490-1547
Colpoys, admiral; mutinies, 1797
Colt, colonel; pistols, 1853
Columba, St., 521-97; isles
Columbanus, d. 614 or 615
Columbiere; armorial bearings, 1639
Columbus, Chr., 1436 or 1442-1506; America, Bahama, Caraccas, Christopher's, Salvador, Domingo
Columbus, Bartholomew; maps, 1489
Columella, medical writer, abt. 46
Colville, sir C.; Cambray, 1815
Colvin, sir A.; India and Egypt, 1883
Colvin, prof. S.; ancient buildings; Slade prof.
Combe, G., 1788-1858; craniology
Combermere, ld.; Bhurtpore, 1826
Comines, Ph. de, Fr. hist., 1445-1509
Commerell, comm.; Ashantees, 1873
Commodus; Rome, emperor, 180
Comneni; eastern emperors, 1057; Pontus, Trebizond, 1204
Comte, A., 1795-1857; calendar, positive philosophy
Comyn, Mr.; trials, 1830
Concha, gen.; Spain, 1868, 1874, Estella
Condé, Louis; Jarnac, 1569
Conflans; Quiberon, 1759
Confucius, 551—477 B.C. Confucianism; China
Congleton, lord; suicide, 1842
Congreve, R.; positive phil.
Congreve, W., dramatist, 1670-1729
Congreve, sir Wm., 1772-1828; fireworks, 1814
Connaught, duke of; Egypt, 1882
Conolly, J., 1795-1866; lunatics, 1839
Conon; Sparta, 394 B.C.; Arginusæ
Conrad; Germany, emperor, 911
Conrad II.; Germany, 1024; Burgundy
Conradin; Naples, Germany, 1268

Constans; Aquileia, 340
Constantine; Rome, emp., 323; Adrianople, aruspices, banner, Britain, Eastern empire, Rome, York, Scotland
Constantine II.; Aquileia, 340
Constantine IV.; monasteries
Constantius; Rome, emps., 305
Contarini (doges at Venice), 1041-1694
Conway, sir Edw.; administrations, 1621;—general, Chatham administration, 1766
Cook, capt. James, 1728-79; Australia, Cook's voyages, Behring's Straits, Botany Bay, Flattery Cape, New Hebrides, New Zealand, Norfolk Island, Otaheite, Owhyhee, Port Jackson, Society isles
Cook, Mrs., murdered; trials, 1841
Cook, J. P., murdered; trials, 1856
Cooke, sir George; Chatham, 1766
Cooke, F. W., R.A., b. 1810
Cooke, Eliz.; trials, 1832
Cooke, Geo. Fred., actor, 1755-1812
Cooke, W. F., electric teleg., 1837
Cooper, Astley, surgeon, 1768-1841
Cooper, J. Fenimore, Am. novelist, 1789-1851
Cooper, Mr.; slave trade, 1787
Cooper, P., philan.; New York, 1883
Cooper; trials, 1805, 1842
Coote, sir Eyre; India, Arcot, 1760; Carnatic, Cuddalore, Porto Novo
Cope, sir John; Prestonpans, 1745
Copernicus, Nic., 1473-1543; astronomy, attraction, solar system
Copleston, bishop; Llandaff, 1827
Copley, J., painter, 1738-1815
Coram, capt. Thos., d. 1751; foundling hospital, 1739
Corday, Charlotte; France, 1793
Corder, William; trials, 1828
Cordova, general de; Granada, 1492
Corelli, A., musician, 1653-1713
Corin; libertines, 1525
Coriolanus; Rome, Volsci, 490 B.C.
Cormac; Cashel, 901
Corneille, P., tragedy, 1606-84
Cornelia, Maximiliana; vestals, 92
Cornelis; Spitzbergen, 1595
Cornelius, P. von; Ger. paint., 1787-1867
Cornell, E.; Cornell univ., 1868
Cornhill, Henry; sheriff, 1189
Cornwall, bp.; Worcester, 1808
Cornwallis, abp.; Canterbury, 1768; Lichfield, 1781
Cornwallis, marquis, 1738-1805; admiralty, India, America, Bangalore, Ireland (lord-lieut.), Seringapatam
Cornwallis, E.; Halifax, N.S.
Corœbus; Olympiads, 776 B.C.
Correggio, A., painter, 1494-1534
Corry; duel, 1800
Corry, H. T. L., 1803-83; admiralty, 1867
Cort, H.; iron, 1781
Corte Real; America, north-west passage, 1500
Cortez, F., 1485-1554; Mexico, 1521
Coryate, Thomas, forks, 1608
Cosmo, I.; Port Ferrajo, 1548
Costa, M., 1810-84; musician.
Coster, L.; printing
Cottenham, lord; chancellor, lord high, 1836
Cottenot, planets, 1878
Cottington, lord; administrations, 1635
Cotton, R.; Cottonian library, 1600
Cotton, M. A.; poisoning, 1873
Cotton, sir Stapleton; Villa Franca, 1812
Cotton, W. J. R.; mayor, lord, 1875
Coulomb, C., 1736-1806; electricity, 1785

INDEX. 1023

Courbet; China, 1884; Tonquin
Courier, P. L.; pamphlets
Courtanvaux; ether, 1759
Courtenay, abp. Canterbury, 1381
Courtenay; Thomites, 1838
Courtenay, sir Wm.; Exeter, 1469
Courtois, M. de; iodine, 1812
Courvoisier; trials, 1840
Cousin, V., Fr. philos., 1792-1867
Coutts, baroness A. Burdett, b. 1814; trials, 1847; Columbia market, 1869; Chichester, 1874; Edinburgh, 1873; flower-girl brigade, 1880; children, 1884; Baltimore
Coventry, sir John; Coventry act, 1670
Coventry; administrations, 1628-1672
Coverdale, Miles, b. 1487; Bible, 1535
Cowan, Mr.; Kookas, 1872
Cowen, J., Newcastle, 1871; democratic federals
Cowles, E.; alumininum
Cowley, Abraham, poet, 1618-67
Cowper, lord; Burford, Halifax, 1714
Cowper, earl; Gladstone adm., 1880
Cowper, E.; printing-machine, 1815 —E. A.; electric telegraph, 1879
Cowper, Wm., poet, 1731-1800
Cox, Walter; trials, 1811
Coxwell, Mr.; balloons, 1862-73
Coyle, Mr. Bernard; duel, 1802
Crabbe, Geo., poet, 1754-1832
Crabtree, W.; Venus
Craggs, Mr.; Sunderland admin., 1718
Crampton, Mr.; United States, 1856
Crane, sir Francis; tapestry, 1619
Cranbrook, lord; Salisbury adm., 1885, 1886
Cranfield, Lionel, lord; administrations, 1621
Cranmer, archbp., 1489-1556; Canterbury, administrations, 1529; homilies, martyrdom
Cranworth, lord; chancellor, 1852
Crassus, Marcus, slain; ovation, 53 B.C.
Craterus; Cranon, 322
Crawford, earl of; Dunecht, trials, 1882
Crawford, divorce case; trials, 1886
Crawford, A. T.; India, 1889
Crawfurd, earl of; Brechin, 1452
Crawley; trials, 1802-1863; steel
Crellin, Miss; trials, 1842
Crespigny, Mr.; duel, 1828
Cresswell, sir C., 1794-1863; probate, 1857
Cresswell v. Walrond; trials, 1877
Creswick, T.; paint., 1811-69
Crewe, bp.; Bambrough, 1778
Crichton, Jas. (the admirable), m. about 1560-1583
Crillon, duc de; Gibraltar, 1782
Crispi, sig.; Italy, 1887
Cristofalli, pianoforte
Cristovitch; Roumelia, 1884
Crockatt v. Dick; trials, 1818
Crockett, Messrs.; leather-cloth
Crœsus; Lydia, 560 B.C.
Croft; impostors, 1553
Croft, sir Richard; suicide, 1818
Crofts, Mr.; dwarfs, 1653
Croke, abp.; Ireland, 1881
Crollius; calomel, 1608
Croly, Geo.; poet, 1780-1860
Crompton, Sam., 1753-1827; cotton; mule, 1779
Cromwell, Oliver, 1599-1658; administrations, 1653; Amboyna, agitators, commonwealth, England, Drogheda, Dundalk, mace, Ireland, Marston Moor, Naseby, Worcester, Manchester, 1875
Cromwell, Richard; administrations, 1658; England

Cromwell, T., lord Essex; administration, 1532; registers
Cronin, Dr.; murder; United States, 1889
Crookes, Wm.; thallium, 1861; spiritualism, radiometer, light, otheoscope, elements
Crosbie, sir Edward; trials, 1798
Cross, E.; Surrey Gardens, 1831
Cross, sir R. A., viscount; Disraeli administration, 1874; Salisbury adm. 1885, 1886
Crossley, F.; Halifax, 1857
Crouch; trials, 1844
Crowse, E.; needles
Crowther, lient.; duel, 1829
Crozier, capt.; N.-W. passage, 1845
Cruden, Alex.; concordance, 1737
Cruikshank, G., 1792-1878; wood-engraving
Ctesias; hist., 398 B.C.
Ctesibius, 140 B.C.; clock, organ, pump
Cubitt, Mr.; treadmill, 1817; J., Blackfriars, 1867
Cullen, Paul, cardinal; 1803-78
Cullen, W., physician, 1712-90
Cumberland, duke of; Closterseven, Culloden, Fontenoy, 1745
Cumberland, R.; comedies, 1732-1811
Cumberland, S.; thought reading
Cumming, lord de Roos r.; trials, 1837
Cumming, Gordon; lion
Cumming, rev. Dr. John, 1810-81
Cummins, Dr.; reformed episcopal church
Cunard, Sam., 1787-1865; steam
Curci, Father; Italy, 1877; Jesuits
Curio; amphitheatres, abt. 50 B.C.
Curran, John Philpot, Irish orator, 1750-1817; duel, 1790
Currell, T. W.; trials, 1887
Cursor, Papirius; dials, 293 B.C.
Curtius, prof. E.; Olympieium, 1875; philology
Curtius, Quintius; earthquakes, 364
Cushing, C., United States, 1878
Custer, gen.; Indians, 1876
Cuthbert, St., d. 686; Canterbury
Cuthbert v. Browne; trials, 1829
Cuvier, G., naturalist, 1769-1832; zoology
Cuyp, A., painter, 1606-67
Cyprian, father, m. 258
Cyriacus; Abrahamites
Cyril, father, d. 386
Cyrus the Great, killed, 529 B.C.; Bactriana, Cyprus, Jerusalem, Media, Persia
Cyrus the younger; Cunaxa, 401 B.C.
Czermak, Dr.; laryngoscope, 1861

D.

Dacier, mad., 1654-1720; Delphin
Dacre, lady Anne; Emmanuel hospital, 1594
Dædalus; labyrinth, axe, 1240 B.C.?
Dagobert; Denis, St., 673
Daguerre, M., 1789-1851; photography
Dahl, professor; dahlias
Dale, Rev. T. P.; public worship, 1877-1881
D'Alembert, Fr. phil., 1717-83; acoustics
Dahlgren, J. A.; engin., 1809-70
Dalhousie, marquis of; India (gov.-gen.), 1848; Gladstone adm., 1886.
Dallinger, W. H.; animalcules, spontaneous generation
Dalmas, A.; trials, 1844
Dalling, H. Bulwer, ld.; 1805-72
Dalmatia; see Soult

Dalrymple, sir Hew; Cintra, 1808
Dalton, John, chemist, 1766-1844; atomic theory, 1808
Damasus, pope, 366; pontiff, crown, pope, tiara
Damian, accordion
Damien, father, ; leprosy
Damiens, Damiens' attempt, 1757
Dampier; circumnavigator, 1689
Dampier, bishop; Ely, 1808
Damremont, marshal; Algiers, Constantia, 1837
Dana, R. H.; United States, 1876
Danaus; Greece, 1485 B.C.?
Danby, earl of; administrations, 1673; physic garden
Dangerfield; meal-tub plot, 1679
Daulcan, chess, concerts
Daniel prophesies, 606 B.C.
Daniel, Sam.; poet-laureate, 1619
Danneker, J., sculptor, 1758-1841
Dannenberg, gen.; Oltenitza, 1854
Dante, Alighieri, Italian poet, 1265-1321
Daulton, G., exec. 1794; clubs, Fren.
Darboy, abp. of Paris; killed, France, 1871
D'Arblay, mad. (Burney), novelist, 1752-1840
Darbon v. Rosser; trials, 1841
D'Arcon, M.; Gibraltar
Dardanus, Ilium, 1480 B.C.
Dargan, W., d. 1867; Ireland, Dublin exhibition, 1853
Darius; Persia, 521 B.C.; Greece
Darling, Grace; Forfarshire, 1838
Darling, sir C.; Jamaica, 1857; Victoria, 1863
Darmes; France, 1840
Darnley, lord; Scotland, 1565
Dartmouth, earl of; Oxford administration, 1711; Rockingham admin., 1766
Darwin, Charles R., naturalist, 1809-82; origin, species, development
Darwin, Erasmus, naturalist, 1731-1802; lunar society
Dashwood, sir Fr.; Bute admin., 1762
D'Aubigné, Merle, ecclesiastical hist., 1794-1872
Daubeny, C.; 1795-1867; atomic theory, 1850
D'Audiffret Pasquier; France, 1875-6
Dauglish, Dr.; bread, 1856
Daun, count, d. 1766, Hochkirchen, Torgau
Davenant, William; drama, opera, 1684
Davenport, Miss; theatres, 1844
Davey, sir H., sol. gen., ; 1826
David; Jews, 1065 B.C.
David, George; impostors, 1556
David I.; Scotland, 1124; Carlisle
David, J., painter, 1748-1825
Davies, C. L.; phonopore
Davila, E. C., Italian historian, 1576-1631
Davis, Jefferson, b. 1808; confederate states; United States, 1861-85
Davis, J.; trials, 1837
Davis; N.-W. passage, 1585; quadrant, China
Davis, N.; Carthage, 1861, 1876
Davitt, M., and Wilson; trials, 1870; Fenian, 1870, 1881; Ireland, 1882; parliament, 1882
Davoust, marshal; Krasnol, Mohilow, Jena, Eckmühl, Ems
Davy, sir Humphry, chemist, &c., 1778-1829; Penzance, Royal Institution, barium, electricity, calcium, magnesium, potassium, sodium, safety lamp, strontium
Davys, bp.; Peterborough, 1839
Dawes, abp.; York, 1714
Dawkins, capt.; navy of England, 1875

INDEX.

Dawkins, W. B. ; caves
Dawson, lieut. ; Africa, 1872
Dawson, J. W. ; Eozoön
Day (Kossuth's notes case), trials, 1860
Day, Mr. ; Fairlop fair
Dazu, H., Bolivia, 1876
Deacle v. B. Baring ; trials, 1831
Deak, F. ; Hungary, 1865-75
Deane, abp. ; Canterbury, 1501
Deane, adml. ; naval battles, 1653
Debain ; harmonium
De Balton ; duels, 1811
De Blignières, M. ; Egypt, 1879
De Brazza ; France, 1882 ; Congo, 1883
De Broglie, France, 1879
De Burgh, Hubert ; Whitehall
De Candolle, A., botanist, 1778-1841
Decazes, duc ; France, 1873-6
Decius Mus sacrifices himself, 295 B.C.
De Courcy, baron ; peers, 1181
Dee, Dr. J., d. 1608 ; astrology
Deerfoot, pedestrianism, 1861
D'Etrees, see D'Estrees.
De Fallières, M. ; France, 1883
De Foe, Daniel, 1663-1731 ; Robinson Crusoe, Juan, plague
De Foix, Gaston ; Ravenna, 1512
De Gasparis, A. ; planets, 1849
De Genlis, mml., 1746-1830
De Giers, chancellor, Russia, 1882
De Grasse, admiral ; Chesapeake, naval battles, Tobago, 1781
De Grey, earl ; Ireland, lord lieutenant, 1427
De Grey, Gladstone adm., 1868
De Groof, V. ; balloons, 1874
De Haven, lieut. ; Franklin, 1850
De Horsey, adm., Peru, 1877
Delabeche, H., 1796-1855 ; geology
De la Clue, admiral ; Lagos, 1759
Delafontaine, M., decipium
Delambre, J., Fr. mathemat., 1749-1822
De la Rive ; Swiss nat. phil., d. 1873
De la Roche, Paul, Fr. paint., 1797-1856
De la Roncière le Noury, adm. ; France, 1875
De la Rue ; trials, 1845
De la Rue, Warren, physicist, 1815-89 ; envelopes ; electric battery ; photography, 1857 ; eclipse, 1860
De la Vigne, C. ; Parisienne
De l'Epee. abbé, 1712-89 ; deaf
De Lesseps, M. ; Suez, 1857
Delille, J. ; Fr. poet, 1738-1813
Delisle ; Venus
De Loundres, Henry ; Dublin, 1205
De Meritens, electric light, 1879
Demetrius ; Athens, Macedon, Impostors, Poland
Democritus, about 400 B.C. ; atoms
De Moivre ; annuities, 1724
De Morgan, A., mathemat., 1806-71 ; almanacs, 1851 ; paradoxies, 1872
Demosthenes, about 382-322 B.C. ; philippica
Denayrouze, M., aërophore, 1875
Denison, archdeacon ; trials, 1856 ; auricular confession, 1873, Church of England, 1873
Denison, bishop ; Salisbury, 1801
Denison, E. B.; bells, 1856
Denison, J. E.; speaker, 1857
Denman, lord, 1779-1854 ; att.-gen. ; king's bench
Denmark, prince George, admiralty, 1702, queens (Anne)
Denner, J., clarionet, about 1690
Dennis, W. ; fire engine
Denny, J.; trials, 1851
Depretis, A.; Italy, 1876, 1884
De Quincey, Thos., essayist, 1785-1859

Derby, countess of; Lathom-house, 1644
Derby, earl of, races, 1779
Derby, earl of, 1799-1869 ; Derby admin., 1852, 1858, 1866
Derby, earl of; Man, Wigan, Derby
Derby, earl of, b. 1826, see Disraeli adm. (Stanley), 1868, 1874 ; Edinburgh, 1874 ; Brussels conference, 1874 ; Turkey, 1876 ; Berlin, 1876 ; Russo-Turkish war, II. 1877 ; Turkey, 1876-7 ; Gladstone adm., 1880
De Roos, lord, v. Cumming ; trials, 1817
De Rossi, catacombs
De Ruyter, adml. ; Sheerness, 1667 ; Chatham, Texel
Dervish pasha, Albania, Dulcigno
Derwentwater, earl of, executions, 1716 ; Greenwich
Des Cartes, René, 1596-1650 ; cartesian, rainbow
Desmoulins, Camille, exec. 1794 ; clubs, 1782
Desnoyers, L. ; charivari
Dessaix, general ; Marengo, 1800
Dessalines ; Hayti, 1803
De Staël, madame, 1766-1817
D'Estaign, count ; Bencoolen, 1760 ; Georgia
D'Esterre, Mr. ; duels, 1815
D'Estrees, adml. ; Texel, 1673
Deucalion ; deluge, 1503 B.C.
De Veres, earls of Oxford ; ld. gt. chamberlain, marquis, duke
Devigne, Hon. ; billiards, 1571
Deville, H. St. C. ; aluminium, 1856 ; platinum, 1859
Devon, W. R., earl of, b. 1807 ; Disraeli, 1868
Devonshire, duke of ; Devonshire administration, 1756 ; Cavendish college
Dewar, prof. J. ; gases ; Royal Institution, 1877 ; elements, 1880-1 ; oxygen ; cold
De Wimpffen, gen. ; Sedan, 1870
De Winter, adm. ; Camperdown, 1797
De Winton, sir F. ; Congo, 1884
De Witt ; chain shot, 1666 ; (pensionary) murdered, 1672 ; Hague
De Worms, baron ; sugar bounties
Dhuleep Singh ; India, 1849 ; Punjab
Diaz, B., discovers Cape of Good Hope, 1487
Diaz, P. ; Mexico, 1867-84
Di Bardi, Donato ; sculpture, 1383
Dibdin, C., 1745-1814 ; ballads
Dibutades ; models
Dicey, W. T. ; steam, 1875
Dick, Mr. ; trials, 1818
Dickens, Chas., novelist, 1812-70
Dickinson, capt. ; trials, 1829
Dickson, col. ; trials, 1859, 1863
Diderot, D., philos., 1713-64
Didius Julianus ; Rome, emp. 193
Dido ; Carthage, 869 B.C.
Didot, M. ; paper-making, stereotype
Diebitsch, gen. ; Balkan, 1829
Diefenbach, L., 1806-83 ; philology
Diesbach ; prussic acid, 1710
Digby, E. ; gunpowder plot, 1605
Digges, L.; optics, 1671
Dilke, C. W.; Athenæum
Dilke, sir C., b. 1843 ; Gladstone adm. 1880 ; corporations
Dilke, lady ; burning dead, 1874
Dillon, Mr. Luke ; trials, 1831
Dillon, Mr., Ireland, 1880-1
Dimsdale and others ; trials, 1878
Diocletian ; Rome, emp. 284 ; Dalmatia
Diodati, J., theologian, 1576-1649
Diodorus Siculus, 50 B.C.-13 A.D. ; Etna
Diogenes, cynic, d. 323 B.C.
Dionysius ; Portugal, anno domini, catapultæ

Dionysius Halicarnassus, Gr. poet, fl. 30 B.C.
Dionysius ; Syracuse, 406 B.C.
Diophantus ; algebra, 370
Dipœnus ; sculpture, marble
Dircks, H. ; ghosts, 1858
Disraeli, I., 1767-1848 :—Benjamin (earl of Beaconsfield, 1876), 1804-81 ; Derby admin., 1852, 1858 ; Disraeli admin., 1868, 1874 ; cottage ; people's tribute
Ditmar, C.; dualin, 1870
Diver, Jenny ; trials, 1740
Dixblancs, M.; trials, 1872
Dixon, capt.; Apollo
Dixon, Hepworth, 1821-79 ; Ebelians, mormonites;—v. Smith (Pall Mall Gazette); trials, 1872
Dixon, J. ; obelisks, (Cleopatra's needle), 1877-8
Dixon, Mr. ; education, 1874, 1876
Dobell, Sydney ; poet, 1824-74
Döbereiner, J. W., nat. phil., 1780-1849 ; diffusion, philos. lamp
Dockwra, Mr. ; penny post, 1683
Dodd, Mr., steamer, 1815
Dodd, Dr. ; trials (executed for forgery), 1777 ; Magdalens, forgery
Dodd, H. P. ; epigrams
Doddridge, Philip, theol., 1702-51
Dodsley, R. ; annual register, 1758
Dodson, sir John ; admiralty court, 1857 ;—J. G.; Gladstone adm., 1880
Dodwell, rev. H. J. ; trials, 1878
Doggett, Thos. ; Doggett prize, 1715
Dolbear, prof. ; telephotography
Dolben, abp. ; York, 1683
Dolce, gen. ; Spain, 1868-9
Dolci, C., painter, 1616-86
Döllinger, Dr. ; papal infallibility, old catholics, 1871
Dollond, John, 1706-61 ; achromatic telescopes, 1753 ; optics
Domenichino, Z., painter, 1581-1641
Domingue, M. ; Hayti, 1874
Dominguez, L. ; Carthagena, Spain, 1873-4
Dominic, St. ; Dominicans, 1215
Domitian ; Rome, emp. 81
Donald of the Isles ; Harlaw, 1411
Donaldson, W. J. ; balloons, 1875
Donatus, grammarian, fl. 355
Donders, phenophthalmoscope, 1870
Donizetti, G. ; music, 1798-1848
Donkin, sir R. ; suicide, 1841
Donne, W. B., examiner (of plays), 1857
Donovan ; duels, 1779
Doré, Gustave, artist, 1832-83
Doria, And., Genoese adml., 1468-1560
Dormer, lord ; Roman Catholics, 1829
Dorregaray, gen. ; Spain, 1874-5
Dorset, duke of ; administrations, 1689 ; Pelham administration, 1744
D'Orvilliers ; Ushant, 1778
Dost Mahomed ; Afghanistan, 1829-42
Douay, gen. A. ; Wissembourg, 1870
Douglas, earl of ; Homildon, 1402
Douglas, James ; British Columbia, 1858
Douglas, Wm.; Otterburn, 1388
Douglass, sir John ; delicate investigation, 1806 ; — sir James, Eddystone
Douiton, strikes, 1876
Douw, Gerard, Dutch paint., 1613-74
Dové, H., b. 1803 ; dichroscope, 1860
Dove, W.; trials, 1856
Dowdeswell, William ; Rockingham administration, 1765
Doyle, sir John ; Portugal, 1828
Doyle, J.; caricatures ; — R., 1826-83 ; Punch
Doyle v. Wright; trials, 1851
Draco, Athens, 621 B.C.; laws, Draco
Drake, Francis, 1545-96 ; Armada, Cadiz, California, Chatham, circum-

INDEX.

navigators, Drake's circumnavigation, Deptford, New Albion
Drayton, M., poet, 1563-1631
Drebbel; optics, 1621; microscope, thermometer
Dred Scott case; slavery, U.S.
Drentelen, Russia, 1878
Dreyse, J. N., 1788-1867; needlegun
Drouet; Varennes, 1791
Druitt, G.; trials, 1867
Drummond, abp.; York, 1761
Drummond, gen.; Chippawa, 1814
Drummond, lieut.; lime-light, about 1826
Drummond, Mr., m.; trials, 1840
Druscovitch, N.; and others (police); trials, 1877
Dryden, John, poet, 1631-1701; poet laureate
Drysdale, Dr.; animalcules
Dubois, cardinal, 1656-1723
Duboscq, M.; electric lamp, 1855
Du Breil de Rays; Port Breton
Dubritius, St.; Caerleon, Llandaff, 612
Duchesne, Père, see *Hebert*
Duchesne; Belgium, 1875
Duckworth, sir J.; Dardanelles, 1807
Duclerc, M.; France, 1882-3
Ducrot, gen., France, 1878; Franco-German war, 1871
Ducrow; theatres, Astley's, 1825
Dudley, earl of Leicester; administrations, 1558
Dudley, lord; administrat., 1551
Dudley, Mrs. M. Y.; Fenians, 1885
Dudley, W., Birmingham, 1876
Duell, William; trials, 1740
Dufaure, J. A. S., France, 1876-9; 1798-1881
Dufay; electricity, 1733
Duff, captain; trials, 1841
Dufferin, ld.; Gladstone adm., 1868, 1880; Canada, 1872; Egypt, 1883; Turkey, 1881-4; India, gov. gen., 1884
Dufferin lady; India, 1887)
Duffy, E. G.; Ireland (Young)
Dufour-Arlès, J. B.; France, 1870-2
Dugdale, W., antiquary, 1605-86
Duggan, Wm.; trials, 1832
Du Guesclin, B.; Montiel, 1369
Duilius defeats Carthaginians, 260 B.C.
Dulong, P. L., 1785-1838; acids
Dumas, A. D., Fr. nov., 1803-70
Dumas, J. B., Fr. chemist, 1800-84; Faraday medal, 1869; Albert medal, 1877
Dumouriez, gen., 1739-1823; Jemmappes, 1792
Dun, John; bailiff
Dunant, H., Geneva convention
Duncan, H.; savings-banks, 1810
Duncan, Dr.; ichnology, 1828
Duncan; Burmah, 1875
Duncan L; Scotland, 1033
Duncan, admiral lord; Camperdown, 1797; Texel
Duncannon, viscount; Melbourne administration, 1834-5
Duncombe, F.; sedan chairs, 1634
Dundas, sir D.; com.-in-chief, 1809
Dundas, sir David; solicitor-general, 1846
Dundas, Henry; Pitt administration, 1804
Dundas, gen.; Kilcullen, 1798
Dundas, lieut.-col.; Prescott, 1838
Dundas, major; trials, 1831
Dundas, sir R.; Baltic, 1855
Dundee, visc.; Killiecrankie, 1689
Dundonald, earl, 1775-1860 (see *Cochrane*)
Dunn, sir David, vice-adm., 1786-1859
Dunn, John, Zululand, 1879
Dunn, Richard; trials, 1847
Duns Scotus, d. 1308; burying alive, Scotists

Dunstan, abp., d. 988; Canterbury, 953; coronation
Dupanloup, F. A. P., bishop of Orleans, 1802-78
Dupetit-Thouars; Otaheite, 1843
Dupont, gen.; Baylen, 1808
Durand, sir H.; India, 1871
Durazzo, Charles of, m. 1386; Naples, kings, 1381
Dürer, A., 1471-1528; engraving
Durham, Joseph, sculptor, 1813-77
Durham, earl of, 1792-1840; Grey admin., 1830; Canada, 1838
Duroc, marshal; Bautzen, 1813
Durnof; balloons, 1870-74
Dutrochet, R. J. H., 1776-1847; endosmosis
Du Val, Claude; robbers, 1670
Duvernois, C.; France, 1874
Dwyer; trials, 1843
Dyce, Wm.; painter, 1806-64
Dyke sir, W. H.; Salisbury adm. 1885
Dymocke family; championship
Dysart peerage, trials, 1681

E.

Eadbald; convents, 630
Eadmer, d. about 1124
Earle, gen.; Soudan, 1885
Eastlake, sir C., 1793-1865; Royal Academy; National Gallery, 1850; —C. national gallery, 1878
Eaton, Daniel; trials, 1796, 1812
Eddy & McGowan; trials, 1870
Eckert; mystic, 1251-1329
Eldy, Mrs.; mind cure
Eden, bp.; Man, 1847
Edgar; England, kings, 958
Edgar, rev. Mr.; temperance, 1829
Edgeley, T.; trials, 1868
Edgeworth, Maria; novels, 1767-1849
Edinburgh, duke of, see *Alfred*, Eddystone
Edison, T. E.; electric pen, &c., microphone, micro-tasimeter, phonograph, telephone
Edmonds; zoology
Edmund; England, 940, 1016
Edmunds, Christians; poisoning, trials, 1872
Edmunds, Mr.; patents
Edward the Confessor; England, kings, 1042; Danegeld
Edward I.; England, kings, 1272; Lewes, Scotland, Wales
Edward III.; England, kings, 1327, Crecy, Sluys, garter
Edward IV.; England, kings, 1461; Barnet, Tewkesbury, Towton
Edward VI.; England, kings, 1547; Christ's hospital
Edward, Black Prince, 1330-76; duke, Cressy, Poitiers
Edwardes, lieut.; India, 1848
Edwards, rev. T., public worship; —Miss A. B., Nov.; Egypt Exploration Fund
Edwy; England, 955
Egan, Mr.; trials, 1843
Egbert; England, kings, 828
Egerton, sir Thomas; chancellor, lord high, 1596
Egerton, Mr.; burnt, Dublin, 1880
Egg, Aug., painter, 1816-63
Eglinton, earl of; Ireland, lord-lieutenant, 1852; tournament
Egmont, lord; administrations, 1763
Egremont, earl of; Grenville administration, 1762
Ehrenberg, C., naturalist, 1795-1876
Eick, H.; trials, 1879
Eirinus, Dr.; asphalt, 1712
Ekenhead, lieut., swimming
Elcho, ld. (aft. earl of Wemyss), b.

1818; Adullam, 1866; cabs, volunteers; liberty and reform, 1884
Elder, John; Glasgow, 1883
Eldon, lord, 1751-1838; chancellor, 1801
Eleanor; queens (Edward I., Hen. II. and III.)
Elgin, Lord; Elgin marbles; d. 1841; —James, lord, 1811-63; Canada, 1846; China, 1857; Japan, Palmerston, India, 1861; govt.-gen., 1861
Elgin, earl of; Gladstone adm. 1886
Elgin, lord, v. Ferguson; trials, 1807
Elijah prophesies about 910 B.C.
Eliott, gen.; Gibraltar, 1781
Eliott, sir Gilbert; North administration, 1770
Elisha prophesies, 896 B.C.
Elizabeth, queen, 1533-1603; England, 1558; goose, poor laws, Richmond, Whitehall
Elizabeth; England, queens (Edward IV. and Henry VII.)
Elizabeth; France, trials, 1794
Elkington; gilding, electrotype
Ellenborough, lord; att.-gen., 1801; king's bench, delicate investigation; lord (son), 1790-1872; Wellington admin., 1828; India, govr.-gen., 1842, 1858, note; Derby adm., 1858
Ellesmere, lord; administrations, 1615; chancellors, ld., 1603
Ellice, E.; Melbourne administration, 1834
Elliot, captain; China, 1840
Elliotson, Dr. J., 1785-1868
Ellis, Agar; trials, 1878
Ellis, sir H., lib. Brit. Mus., 1777-1869
Ellis, A. J.; musical pitch
Ellis, Wellbore; Grenville administration, 1770
Elphinstone, lord; electric light, 1879
Elphinstone, admiral; Cape of Good Hope, 1795; Saldanha
Elsynge, Wm.; Sion college, 1340
Elyot, sir T., "governour"
Elzevir family, printers, 1583-1680
Emerson, R.W.; essayist, poet, 1803-82
Emin Bey; Soudan, 1885
Emmet, Robert; rebellions, conspiracies, trials, 1803; press
Empedocles; suicide
Encke, J. F., 1791-1865; comets, 1818
Enderby, Messrs.; southern continent, 1838
Engels, prof.; lithofracteur, 1869
Enghien, duc d', executed, 1804
Ennius, 239-169 B.C.; stenography
Enraght, rev. R.; public worship, 1880
Eötvos, Joseph; Hung. nov. 1813-71
Epaminondas, 371 B.C.; Leuctra, Mantinea
Epictetus, philosopher, fl. 118
Epicurus, 342-270 B.C.; atoms; philosophy
Epiphanius, St. abstinence, heresy
Erasistratus; anatomy, ab. 300 B.C.
Erasmus, D., 1467-1536; Greek language, Rotterdam
Eratosthenes; degree, 250 B.C.; armillary sphere
Eratostratus (or Herostratus) fires Diana's temple, 356 B.C.
Erechtheus; Athens, 1383 B.C.
Eric; Denmark
Erichthonius; Troy, 1419 B.C., car
Ericsson, capt.; heat, 1853
Erle, sir W.; common pleas, 1859
Ermeland, bp. of; Prussia, 1871
Erskine, sir John; administrations, 1685
Erroll, earl of; constable of Scotland, lord high
Erskine, lord; chancellor, lord Grenville administration, 1806

Erskine, gen.; India, 1795
Esdaile, E.; trials, 1858
Esmonde case; trials, 1868
Espartero, Marshal, Spain, 1841-75; Bilbao, 1836; d. 1879
Esquirol, E.; lunatics, 1810
Essex, earl of; administrations, 1532, 1579; Newbury, 1643
Este, sir Augustus d'; marriage act, royal, 1844
Ethelbert, 560, Canterbury
Etheldreda; Ely, 673
Ethelred, 979; coronation, Danegeld
Ethersey, com.; suicide, 1857
Etty, W. painter, 1787-1849
Euchidas; pedestrianism
Euclid; geometry, 300 B.C.
Eugene, prince, 1663-1736; Belgrade, Turin, Zenta
Eugénie, empress; France, 1853; Marseilles, 1882
Eugenius; popes, Aquileia
Eulenburg, count, Prussia, 1873
Eulenstein, Jew's harp
Euler, L., 1707-83; acoustics
Eumenes; parchment, 190 B.C.
Eumolpus; Eleusinian mysteries
Eupion gas co.; trials, 1876
Euripides, 480-406 B.C.; tragedy
Eurysthenes; biarchy, 1102 B.C.
Eurystheus; Mycenæ, 1289 B.C.
Eusden, L.; poet laureate, d. 1730
Eusebius, of Cæsarea, ab. 275-340
Eustachius; thoracic duct, 1563
Euston divorce case; trials, 1884
Euthalius; accents, 458
Eutyches, fl. 447
Evander; Circensian games
Evans, general de Lacy; British legion, 1835; Spain, 1835; Irun, Sebastian
Evans; trials, 1858
Evans, J.; man, 1872
Evans, M. (G. Eliot), novelist, 1820-80
Evans, W. E.; harmonium, 1841
Evelyn, J., 1620-1706; horticulture, lime-tree, trees
Examiner, the; trials, 1812
Exmouth, lord; Algiers, 1816
Eyre, E. J.; Jamaica, 1864-7
Eyre, John; transportation, 1771
Ezekiel prophesies about 595 B.C.

F.

Faber, F.; oratorians, 1848
Fabius, Quintus; painting, 311 B.C.;
—Maximus; Allobroges, 121 B.C.
Fabii, killed, Cremera, 477 B.C.; Fabii
Fabre, M.; France, 1883
Fahrenheit, G. D., 1686-1736; thermometer, about 1726
Faidherbe, gen.; Franco-Pruss. war, 1871; St. Quentin, 1871
Fairbairn, Mr.; tubular bridge, 1849
Fairfax, T.; Naseby, 1645
Fairland, Miss; trials, 1874
Falck, Dr.; steam-engine, 1779
Falconbridge; London, 1453
Falconer, H.; geologist, d. 1865
Falieri, Marini; Venice, 1335
Falk; Prussia, 1873; Germany, 1878
Falkland, visct.; Newbury, 1643
Falstaff, sir John; taverns
Fancourt, Samuel; circulating libraries, 1740
Faraday, Michael, 1791-1867; Royal Institution, chemistry, electricity, gas, magnetism, magneto-electricity, ice, Albert medal, Faraday
Farewell, lieut., Natal, 1823
Farmer and Wallace, electric light, 1879
Farquhar, Mr., buys Fonthill abbey, 1822

Farr, Dr. W., 1807-83; annuities, 1864; statistics
Farragut, D., 1861-79, admiral, 1866; United States, 1864
Farrar, F. A.; trials, 1868
Farrell v. Gordons; trials, 1873
Farren, Miss, actress, retires, 1797
Farrer; trials, 1859
Fatima; Mahometanism, note
Faulkner, G.; newspapers, 1728
Fauntleroy, H.; forgery, 1824
Faure, Jules, electric battery, 1881
Faust, John; printing, 1442
Faustin I.; Hayti, 1849
Faustulus; Alba, 770 B.C.
Faux, Guy; gunpowder plot, 1605
Favre, Jules; France, 1870-2, d. 1880
Fawcett, col.; duel, 1843
Fawcett, H., 1833-84; Gladstone adm., postmaster, 1880; parcel post
Fazy, J. J.; Switzerland, 1878
Felix, popes, 269 et seq.
Fellows, C.; Lycia, 1840
Felton assassinates Buckingham at Portsmouth, 1628
Fénélon, abp., 1651-1715; Cambray
Fenning, Elizn; executions, 1815
Fenwick, J.; executions, 1697
Feramoz; Afghanistan, 1871
Ferdinand; Austria, Naples, Portugal, Sicily, Spain, Tuscany, Castile, Cordova
Ferdinand of Brunswick, Minden, 1759
Fergus; Scotland, coronation
Ferguson, J.; planets, 1854
Fergusson, sir J.; Bombay, 1880
Fergusson, James, 1808-86; architecture, 1874-76
Fermat; probability
Ferrand; France, 1874
Ferré; France, 1871
Ferrers, earl; trials, 1760
Ferrier, Dr. J., 1811-82; vivisection
Ferry, J.; France, 1879-84
Fessel; gyroscope, 1852
Festing, col.; Ashantees, 1873
Fichte, Germ. philos., J. G., 1762-1814; Im. H., son, 1797-1879
Field, Cyrus; electric telegraph, 1868
Field, J., nocturne
Fielding, H., novelist, 1707-54; magistrates
Fieschi; France, 1836
Figueras; Spain, 1873
Figueroa; Spain, 1868
Fillmore, M.; United States, president, 1850; d. 1874
Finch, D.; admiralty, 1680
Finch, sir John; chancellor, lord; administrations, 1640; Heneage, chancellor, 1673
Finiguerra; engraving, 1460
Finnerty, Peter; trials, 1808, 1811
Finnis, T.; lord mayor, 1856
Finnis, col.; India, 1857, note
Firth, M., Sheffield, 1879
Fish, W.; trials, executions, 1876
Fisher, bp.; administrations, 1509; Salisbury; executed, 1535
Fisher; duels, 1806
Fisk, James; New York, 1871
Fitzgerald, H.; life-boat, 1856
Fitzgerald, lord; attainder, 1798
Fitzgerald, lord, v. Mrs. Clarke; trials, 1814
Fitzgerald, lord; Wellington administration, 1830
Fitz-Osborn; justiciars, 1067
Fitzpatrick; Grenville administration, 1806
Fitzpatrick, Hugh; trials, 1813
Fitz-Roy, R., 1805-65; circumnavigation, 1826; New Zealand, 1843; meteorology, 1857
Fitzwalter, Robert de; Dunmow, 1244

INDEX.

Fox, Henry; Newcastle administration, 1757
Fox, sir Stephen; Chelsea, 1629
Fox, St. G. Lane; electricity (lamplighting by), gas
Foxe, John, martyrologist, 1517-87
Francia, Dr., 1755-1840; Paraguay
Francis, St., 1182-1226; Cordeliers
Francis I., emperor; Germany, 1745; Austria, 1804
Francis I.; France, 1515; duelling, cloth of gold, Marignan, Pavia, Sicily
Francis Joseph; Austria, 1848; assassinations, Hungary, 1848
Francis; trials, 1842
Francis, John, Athenæum (journal)
Francis, sir Philip, 1740-1818; Junius
Francis de Sales, St., 1567-1622, "Devout Life"
Francisco d'Assise; Spain, 1846
Francke, A.; orphan-houses, 1698
Frankfort, lord, v. Alice Lowe; trials, 1842, 1852
Frankland, Edw.; amyl, ethyl, methyl, 1849
Franklin, Benjamin, 1706-90; electricity, 1752; lightning
Franklin, sir John; north-west passage, 1825; Franklin
Franks; suicide, trials, 1825
Fraser v. Bagley; trials, 1844
Freciner, M. de; France, 1885
Frederick; trials, 1874
Frederick, duke of York, 1762-1827; York
Frederick II.; Corte Nuova, 1237
Frederick; Germany, Prussia, Hesse, Nuremberg, Palatinate, Prague, Hochkirchen, Torgau
Frederick III.; Germany, 1888
Frederick-Augustus; Poland, 1697
Frederick-Charles, prince of Prussia, Franco-Pruss. war, 1870-1; Metz, 1870
Frederick-Lewis, prince; Wales, 1729
Frederick William, I.—IV.; Prussia; assassinations
Freeling, S.; Grenada, 1871
Freeman, E. A., conquest, 1870-6
Frelinghuysen, Mr.; United States, 1881
Fremantle, Rev. W. H.; dissenters, 1875
Fremont, J.C., b. 1813; U. States, 1856
Frémy, M.; steel, 1861
French, col.; trials, 1820
Freney; trials, 1749
Frere, sir Bartle, 1815-84; slave trade, Zanzibar, 1872; cape, 1876; Kaffraria, 1878, celibacy
Frère-Orban; Belgium, 1868, 1878
Frewen, abp.; York, 1660
Freycinet, M. de, France, 1879
Frichot, ophicleide
Frith, W. P., painter, b. 1819
Frivell, Wm., post-office, 1631
Frobisher, sir Martin, d. 1594; north-west passage, 1576
Froggatt, E.; trials, 1877-1879
Froissart, historian, 1337-1410
Frost, John, chartist; Newport, 1839
Frost, W. E. R. A., 1810-77
Froude, J. A., historian, b. 1818; South African confederation, 1875
Frumentius; Abyssinia, 329
Fuad Pasha, 1814-69; Damascus, Turkey, 1860-9
Fuller, J.; Royal Institution, 1833
Fuller case; India, 1876
Fulton, R., 1765-1815; steam-engine, 1803
Furley, Mary; trials, 1844
Furneaux, capt.; Adventure Bay, New Holland; returns, 1774
Furness, Mrs. H.; concordance, 1876
Fuseli, H., painter, 1741-1825

G.

Gabelentz, H. C. von der; language, 1874
Gage, gen.; America, 1775
Gaine, W.; parchment paper, 1857
Gainsborough, Thomas, painter, 1727-88
Galba; Rome, emp., 68
Gale, balloons, gunpowder, 1865
Gale, Sarah, and Greenacre; trials, 1857
Galen, 130-200; physic
Galgacus, 84; Granpians
Galileo di Galilei, 1564-1642; acoustics, astronomy, falling bodies, harmonic curve, ice, inquisition, pendulum, planets, sun, telescopes
Gall, J., 1758-1828; craniology
Gallagher, J.; trials, 1883
Galle, Dr.; Neptune, 1846
Gallien; balloons, 1755
Gallienus; Rome, emp. 260
Galton, F.; composite portraits, 1877; heredity
Galvani, Louis, 1737-98; electricity, 1791; voltaic pile
Galway, earl of; Almanza, 1707
Gama, Vasco de, d. 1525
Gambetta, L.1838-82; France,1870-81; opportunists, scrutin
Gambier, lord; Basque Roads, 1809; Copenhagen
Gambier and Rumble, trials, 1869
Gambrill, trials, 1878
Gamgee, A.; Roy. Inst. 1884
Ganigee, J.; glaciarium, 1876
Gamond, Thomé de; tunnels, 1867
Ganganelli; Clement XIV., popes, 1769
Gangeland; apothecary
Gardiner, A.; Natal, 1835
Gardiner, bp.; administrations, 1529
Gardiner, lieut. Alan; missions, 1850
Garfield, gen., U. S. A., United States, 1880
Garibaldi, Joseph, 1807-82; Italy, 1859-76; Solferino, Sicily, Naples, Volturno; Franco-Prussian war, 1870
Garnerin, M.; balloons, 1802
Garnet; gunpowder plot, 1605
Garnet, Dr. Thos.; Royal Institution, 1801
Garrett-Anderson, Mrs.; physic, 1865
Garrick, David, 1716-79; theatres, Drury-lane, jubilees
Garrison, W. L.; slavery in United States, 1831
Garrod, A. H.; Royal Institution, 1875
Garrow, Wm.; att.-gen., 1813
Garth, Dr.; Kit-Cat club, 1703
Gaskell, Mrs. E. C. novelist; 1811-65
Gassendi, 1592-1655; atoms, sun, sound
Gaston de Foix; Ravenna, 1512
Gates, gen.; Saratoga, 1777; Camden, 1780
Gauden, bp.; eikon basilike, 1649
Gauden, M.; sapphire, 1857
Gaunt, John of, b. 1340; Ghent, roses, wars
Gaustus, 335 B.C.; caustic
Gavarni, French caric. 1801-66
Gavestons, beheaded, 1312; rebellions
Gay, John, 1688-1732; fables, operas
Gay-Lussac, J., 1778-1850; balloons
Gayer, J., lion-sermon
Ged, William; stereotype, 1730
Geffcken, Dr.; Prussia, 1888
Geffrard, gen. Fabre; Hayti, 1858
Gelasius L; popes 492; breviary, pall; Candlemas
Gellert, C. F., Germ. fabulist, 1715-69

Gellius, Aulus, Latin miscellany, fl. 117-180
Gelon: Syracuse, 485 B.C. Himera
Genghis khan; see *Jenghis Khan*
Genseric lands in Africa, 429
Geoffroy, M. H.; asbestos
George, David, d. 1536; family of love
George, St.; garter
George L—IV., England; kings, assassinations
George L—V.; Hanover (kings); assassinations
George I.; accession, 1714
George II.; Dettingen, 1743
George, H.; land nationalization, United States, 1886-7
George, king, Bonny
Georgi; dahlia, 1815
Geramb, baron; aliens, 1812
Gerard, J.; physic garden, 1567
Gerbert, d. 1003; arithmetic
Germaine, lord George Sackville; Minden, 1759
Germanus; Sodor, 447
Gerstenzweig, general; Poland, m. 1861
Gervinus, G. G., Germ. hist. 1805-71
Gesler; Switzerland, 1306
Geta; Rome, emp. 211
Gholam Hussein, Afghanistan, 1878-81; India, 1881
Gibbins, Mr., killed; riots, 1831
Gibbon, Edward, historian, 1737-94
Gibbons, Grinling, sculptor, 1648-1721
Gibbons, Orlando; music, 1583-1625
Gibbs, J., architect, 1674-1754
Gibbs, sir V.; attorney-gen., 1807; common pleas, 1814
Gibbs, W. A.; corn, 1868; hay, 1875
Gibbs, W.; Keble college, Christ's hospital, 1877
Gibson, J., sculptor, 1791-1866; Royal academy
Gibson, T.; concordance, 1535
Gibson, T. M., 1807-84; Palmerston administration, 1859
Giesmar, general; Praga, 1831
Giffard, sir Hardinge S.; solicitor-general, 1875; chancellor, ld., Halsbury, 1885
Gifford, lieut. Kildare, 1798
Gifford, R.; attorney-gen., 1819
Gifford; steam-injector
Gifford, Wm., 1757-1826; Quarterly Rev., 1809
Gilbert v. Enoch (*Pall Mall Gaz.*) trials, 1873
Gilbert, archbp.; York, 1757
Gilbert, sir Humphry, 1539-84; Newfoundland
Gilbert, Dr., 1540-1603; electricity, 1600; magnetism
Gilbert, gen.; Ferozeshah, 1845
Gilbert, G.; executions, 1862
Gilbert, W. G.; operas
Gilchrist, earl (of Angus), 1037
Gilchrist, steel
Gildas, historian, 516-570
Gill, D.; star
Gillam, Rd.; trials, 1828
Gillespie, col.; Vellore, 1806
Gillespie, gen.; Kalunga, duel, 1788
Gillott, J.; steel pens
Gillray, J. 1785-1815; caricatures
Ginckel, gen.; Aughrim, 1691
Gintl, Dr.; electric telegraph (duplex) 1853
Gioberti, Italian writer, 1801-52
Gioja, F.; compass, 1302
Giotto, painter, 1276-1336
Giudetti, passion music
Gladstone, rev. Mr.; trials, 1852
Gladstone, J. H.; copper-zinc couple, 1872; physical society, 1874; education society
Gladstone v. Gladstone; trials, 1875
Gladstone, W. E.; b. 1809, Gladstone adm. 1868-86, suspensory act; Eng-

3 u 2

land, 1877-8; Dublin, 1878; parliament, 1881; Kilmainham
Glaisher, J.; meteorology, 1850; balloons, 1862
Glanville, R. de, ch. justice, 1180
Glas, capt., murdered; trials, 1766
Glas, John, 1698-1773; Glasites, 1727
Gleichen, count; England, 1877
Glendower, Owen; Wales, 1400
Glenelg, lord (Charles Grant), d. 1866; Wellington adm., 1828
Glerawley, lord, v. Burn; trials, 1820
Gloucester, duke of; marriage act, 1772
Glover, col.; Ashantees, 1874
Glover, E. A.; trials, 1858
Glover, sir H.; Leeward Isles
Gluck, C.; music, 1714-87
Gobelin, G.; tapestry, Gobelins
Goderich, lord, d. 1859; Goderich
Godfrey, M.; bank of England, 1694
Godfrey of Bouillon; Jerusalem, 1099
Godolphin, earl; Godolphin adm. 1684
Godoy, M., prince of the peace; Spain, 1806; d. 1851
Godwin, sir G.; Pegu, 1852
Godwin, Wm., 1756-1836; politics, novels
Goethe, or Göthe; German miscel. 1749-1832
Goffart, M.; ensilage
Gog and Magog; Guildhall
Gold, F. I., 1881, railways, 1881, trials
Goldoni, Ch., Ital. dramatist, 1707-93
Goldschmidt (Jenny Lind), b. 1821; Nightingale fund
Goldschmidt, H., 1802-66; planets, 1852
Goldsmids; trials, 1873
Goldsmith, Oliver; poet, miscel. 1728-74
Goncourt, naturalism
Gonsalvo de Cordova, gen., d. 1515; Garigliano
Gonzales, F. O., Spain, 1879, Mexico, 1880.
Gooch, lady, trials, 1878
Good, Daniel; trials, 1842
Goodenough, lieut.; massacres, 1875
Goodrich, bp.; administrations, 1551
Goodwin, bp., IL, Carlisle, 1870
Goodyear, C.; caoutchouc
Gordian; Rome, emperors
Gordon, col.; duels, 1783
Gordon, lord G., d. 1793; riots, libel, trials, 1781, 1788
Gordon, gen. Charles George; China, 1863; Egypt, 1874; Abyssinia; Basuto, Congo, Khartoum, Soudan, 1883-4; Gordon memorial
Gordon, sir A. H., 1833-85; Fiji, 1875; N. Zealand, 1880
Gordons, L. and L.; trials, 1804
Görgey, gen.; Hungary, 1849
Gorham v. bishop of Exeter; trials, 1849
Gorst, E. G.; Salisbury adm., 1885
Gortschakoff, gen.; Kalafat, 1854; Silistria, Tchernaya
Gortschakoff, prince A., statesman, 1798-1883; Vienna conference, 1853; Poland, 1861; Russo-Turkish war, II. 1877-8; Russia, 1856-83
Göschen, J. G., b. 1831; Gladstone adm., 1868; Egypt, 1876; Turkey, 1880-1; parliament, 1883; Salisbury adm., 1887
Goss v. Whitake, trials, 1870
Gossett, sir W.; trials, 1842
Gosset, F.; parliament, 1885
Gosset, R. A.; parliament, 1885
Gough, sir Hugh, 1772-1869; China, 1841; India, 1846; Goojerat, Sobraon, Ferozeshah
Goulard; France, 1874

Goulburn, H.; Wellington administration, 1828
Gould, J., 1804-81; birds, works on, 1832-78; humming-birds, 1862
Gould, Jay, New York, 1867
Gould, Miss; trials, 1822
Gould, murderer; trials, 1840
Gourko, gen.; Russo-Turkish war, II. 1878; Schipka
Gourlay, captain; duels, 1824
Gower, earl; Wilmington adm., 1742; North adm., 1770
Gower, F. A., telephone, balloons, 1885
Gower, J., poet; d. 1402
Gracchus, Tiberius, slain, 133;— Caius slain, 121 B.C.
Grady, Mr.; duel, 1827
Graebe and Liebermann, alizarine
Grevius, J. G. and G.; thesaurus
Grafton, duke of; Rockingham adm., 1765; Grafton adm., 1767
Graham, bp.; Chester, 1848
Graham of Claverhouse, 1650-89; Killiecrankie
Graham, A.; planets, 1848
Graham, C. C.; Grenada
Graham, gen.; Barossa, 1811; Sebastian, Bergen-op-Zoom
Graham, Mr.; pendulum, 1715; magnetism, 1722
Graham, H. C., and others; trials; 1886
Graham, Mr.; duels, 1791
Graham, gen. sir Gerald; Egypt, 1882; Soudan, 1884
Graham, sir James, 1792-1861; Grey, Peel
Graham, Thos., 1805-69; mint, diffusion, dialysis, atmolysis
Grammont, duc de, Dettingen, 1743
Granard, Arthur, earl of; Kilmainham, 1675
Granby, marquis of; Chatham adminis., 1766
Grant, Alb.; Leicester square, 1874; trials, 1875-6; painting, 1877
Grant, capt. John; cookery, 1857; cottager's stove
Grant, sir Colquhoun; duel, 1835
Grant, sir F., 1800-78; Royal Academy, 1866-78
Grant, G. B.; calculating machine, 1874
Grant, lieut.; trials, 1816, 1844; Central Africa, 1863
Grant, see Glenelg
Grant, gen. Ulysses, 1828-85; United States, 1863-73; Pittsburg, 1862
Grantham, ld.; Shelburne adm. 1872
Grantley, F. Norton, ld.; attorneygen., 1763
Granville, earl; Russell, Palmerston admin., 1851; Gladstone adm. 1868, 1880, 1886
Gratian; canons, 1151
Gratian, Rome, emp. 367-83
Grattan, Henry, orator, 1750-1820; duelling, 1800, 1820
Grattan, T. Colley, novelist, 1796-1864
Grattoni, Alps (tunnel)
Graves, adm. sir T., Basseterre, 1782
Gray, bp.; Bristol, 1827; see Capetown
Gray, E.; telephone, 1873
Gray, Thomas, poet, 1716-71
Greathead, Mr.; life-boats, 1789
Greatrix, Val.; impostors, 1666
Greaves, lord; suicide, 1830
Grechi, prof.; fire-detector
Greeley, Horace, 1811-72; United States, 1872
Greeley, lieut.; N. E. & W. pass, 1881-4
Green, Charles, 1786-1870; balloons, 1828

Green, rev. S., public worship, 1880
Green, J. R.; hist., 1837-83
Green, J.; seraphine
Greenacre, J.; trials, 1837
Greene, general; Camden, 1781
Greenwood, T.; file, 1860
Gregg, Dr.; reformed episcopa church
Grégoire, M.; national convention 1792
Gregory the Great; chanting Christianity
Gregory I.—XVI.; popes, 590 et seq.
Gregory VII.; Italy, 237
Gregory XI., pope; pallium
Gregory XIII.; calendar, 1582
Gregory Nazianzen, Greek father 326-390?
Grenfell, gen.; Soudan, 1888
Grenville, George; Newcastle ad ministration, 1754; Grenville ad ministration, 1763
Grenville, F.; British Museum, 1846
Grenville, lord; Grenville admin. 1806; delicate investigation
Gresham, sir T., d. 1579; Gresham
Grévy, Jules, France, 1871-8
Grey, bp.; Hereford, 1832
Grey, earl, 1764-1845; Grey, reform
Grey, Henry, earl; Russell adminis tration, 1835
Grey, lady Jane, exec. 1554; England, queens
Grey, lord; Pomfret castle, 1483
Grey, sir George; Russell admin. 1846; Palmerston admin., 1855
Grey, sir G.; Cape, 1856
Grey, Stephen; electricity, 1720
Griesbach, J., critic, 1745-1812
Griffith, sir R., Griffith's valuation
Grimaldi, Joseph, clown; retires 1828
Grimm, Jacob, 1785-1863; Wilhelm 1786-1859; dictionary (German)
Grimm's law
Grindall, abp.; York, 1570; Canterbury, liturgy
Grinfield, general; Demerara, 1803 Tobago
Grinnell, Mr.; Franklin expedition 1850
Grinstead, Capt.; Princess Alice
Grisi, madame, d. 1869
Grissell, C. E., parliament, 1879-80
Grocyn, Wm.; Greek, 1490
Grogan, col., captured; U. States 1841
Gronovius, J., thesaurus, 1657-1702
Gros, baron; China, 1858
Grote, G., historian, 1794-1861
Grotius, II., 1583-1645; philosophy
Grove, sir G.; crystal palace, 1874 music (dict.), 1878
Grove, sir W. R., nat. phil. & judge b. 1811; voltaic battery, 1839; cor relation, 1842; continuity, 1866 antagonism
Groves, W., electric balance, 1879
Growse, Elias; needles
Guelph; Bavaria, Brunswick
Guericke, Otto von, 1602-1686; al electricity, 1647; Magdeburg
Guérin-Méneville, silk (ailanthre 1858
Guernsey, W. H.; trials, 1858
Guesclin, B. du, d. 1380
Guibert, abp.; France, 1876
Guibord, J.; Montreal, 1875
Guicciardini, F., hist., 1482-1540
Guido, Aretino, fl. 1030
Guido, Reni, painter, 1575-1642
Guilford, earl of; trials, 1853
Guillemin, A.; comets
Guillermo; Hayti, 1877
Guinness, sir B., 1798-1868; Patric St., 1863
Guiscard; Naples, 1059; conspir cies, 1710

INDEX.

Guise, dukes of; Guise
Guiteau, C. J., assassin, United States, 1881-2
Guizot, F., 1787-1874; France, 1840-48-70
Gunter, E.; Gunter's chain, 1606
Gurney, G.: Bude light, 1841
Gurney, Messrs.; trials, 1869
Gurney, Russell; recorder, 1856-78
Gurwood, colonel; suicide, 1845
Gutsfeld, Dr.; Africa, 1873
Gustavus Adolphus, killed, Lutzen, 1632; Sweden, Munich
Gustavus Vasa; Sweden, 1521
Gustavus I.—IV.; Sweden
Gutenberg, J., d. 1467; printing
Guter, of Nuremberg; air, 1659
Gutierrez, T., Peru, 1872
Guy Faux; gunpowder plot, 1605
Guy, Thos.; Guy's hospital, 1721
Guyton-Morveau; balloons, 1784-94
Guzman, Dominic de; beads, 1202
Gwynne, Nell; bell-ringing, 1687
Gyges: Lydia, 718 B.C.
Gylippus, 414 B.C.; Syracuse

H.

Habakkuk, prophet, ab. 326 B.C.
Hachette, Jeanne de la; Beauvais, 1472
Hacker, L.; Sunday schools, 1740
Hacker, Matilda, trials, 1879
Hackett, Wm.; impostors, 1591
Hackman, Mr.; trials, 1770
Hackworth, T.; steam, 1825
Haddington, earl of; Ireland (lord-lieut.), 1834
Haden, Seymour; burials, 1875
Hadley; quadrant, 1731
Hadrian; Rome, emperor, 117
Haeckel, prof.; development
Hæcker; magnetism, 1851
Hafiz, Persian poet, fl. 14th century
Haggai prophesies about 630 B.C.
Haggart, David; trials, 1821
Haggarty and Holloway; trials, 1807
Hahnemann, Sam., 1755-1843; homœopathy
Hakluyt, R.; geog., 1553-1616
Hakon; Iceland
Hale, sir Matthew, judge, 1609-76
Hales, Stephen, philosopher, 1677-1761
Halévy, J. E. F., mus. comp. 1799-1862
Halifax, earl of; Halifax administration, 1714; trimmer; see Wood
Hall, A.; astronomy; Mars, 1877
Hall; steam, 1840
Hall, sir B.; health, Palmerston administration, 1855
Hall, John; lead
Hall, sir C., vice-chancellor, 1873
Hall, Marshall, physiol., 1790-1857
Hall, Rev. Robert, 1764-1831
Hall, Sam., d. 1862; lace
Hall v. Semple; trials, 1862
Hallam, Henry, hist., 1778-1859
Haller, A. von; physicl., 1708-77
Halley, Edmund, astronomer; Greenwich, 1719; Venus
Halloran, Dr., transported for forging a frank, 1818 [1886
Halsbury, ld.; Salisbury adm., 1885,
Hamdi Pasha; Turkey, 1878
Hamel, J.; Mont Blanc, 1820
Hamilcar; Carthage, 237 B.C.
Hamilton; duels, 1748, 1804
Hamilton and Douglas cause; trials, 1769
Hamilton, bp.; Salisbury, 1854
Hamilton, duke of; duelling, 1712; trials, 1813
Hamilton, F. W., guards
Hamilton, ld. George; Salisbury adm., 1885, 1886

Hamilton, James, marquis of; administrations, 1640
Hamilton, J.; court of honour
Hamilton, J. B.; vocalion
Hamilton, Mary; trials, 1736
Hamilton, sir W.; Herculaneum
Hamilton, W. R.; Elgin marbles
Hamilton, sir W.; quaternions
Hammond, Mr.; ambassadors, 1791
Hampden, Richard; administrations, 1690
Hampden, John, killed, 1643; ship-money, Chalgrove
Hanlan, E.; boat race, 1882
Hancock, T.; caoutchouc, 1843
Handcock; trials, 1855
Handel, G. F., 1684-1759; Handel, opera, oratorios, Judas, Joshua, Messiah, Rule Britannia
Hannen, sir James; divorce ct., 1872; Parnellites, 1883
Hannibal, Carthaginian, 247-183 B.C.; Rome, Bernard, Saguntum, Spain, Cannæ, Carthage, Zama
Hans Sachs, 1494-1578; minne-singers
Hansom, Joseph; cabs
Hanson, capt.; duels, 1776
Hanway, Jonas, d. 1786; marine society; umbrella
Harcourt, lady; fête de vertu
Harcourt, lord; Oxford administration, 1711
Harcourt, sir W. V., solicitor-general, 1873; Gladstone admin., 1880; London Municipal Bill
Hardicanute; England, 1039
Harding, prof.; planets, 1804
Hardinge, sir Henry (aft. lord), 1846; India
Hardinge, Mr.; journals, 1752
Hardwicke, earl of; Pelham admin., 1744; Derby admin., 1852; Ireland (lord-lieut.), 1801
Hardy, Gathorne, visc. Cranbrook b. 1814; Disraeli administration, 1868 and 1874; Salisbury adm., 1885
Hare, R.; blowpipe, 1802
Hargraves, E.; Australia, 1851
Hargreaves, J.; cotton, 1767
Harley, Robert; Godolphin administration, 1702; Harleian library, see Oxford
Harley, R. W.; Tobago, 1875
Harmodius kills Hipparchus, 514 B.C.
Harney, gen.; United States, 1855
Harold II.; Hastings, 1066
Haroun-al-Raschid, caliph, 765-809
Harpur, W.; Bedford, 1561
Harrington; oceana, 1656; trials, 1878
Harrington, earl of; Pelham administration, 1744
Harriot, T., algebra, 1631
Harris, Mr.; organs, 1682; clocks, apples, fluxions, pendulum
Harris, sir W. S., 1792-1867; lightning conductors, 1820-54
Harrison, B.; United States, 1888-9
Harrison, F.; positive phil.
Harrison, gen.; United States, president, 1841
Harrison, J.; pneumatic loom, 1864;
Harrison, 1714
Harrison, Mr.; congelation, 1857, 1873
Harrowby, earl of; Pitt administration, 1804 et seq.
Harrowby, Dudley F., earl of; Salisbury adm., 1885
Harsnet, archbp.; York, 1628
Hartinger, Mr.; duels, 1820
Hartington, marquis of; Gladstone administration, 1868, 1880, & 1882
Hartland, sir R.; Madras, 1771
Hartmann, Russia, 1880
Harvey, B. Bagenal; trials, 1798
Harvey, Dr. William, 1578-1657;

blood, anatomy, midwifery, gestation
Harwood; porter, 1730
Hasokka, emperor's hymn, 1797
Hasdrubal; Carthage, Spain; Metaurus, 207 B.C.
Hassall, A. H.; food
Hassan and Hussan, drama
Hastings, marquis of; India, gov.-gen. 1813
Hastings, Warren, 1733-1818; India, 1772; Chunar, Hastings
Hatchell, Mr.; duels, 1814
Hatfield fires at George III.; trials, 1800
Hatfield; executions, 1803
Hatherley, ld. chancellor, 1868
Hatton, sir Christopher, d. 1591; chancellor (lord high), master in chancery
Hausmann; Paris, France, 1869
Haüy, R., 1743-1822; crystallography
Haüy, V.; blind school, 1804
Havelock, gen.; India, 1857; Cawnpore
Hawke, adm.; naval battles, 1747
Hawkesbury, lord; administrations, 1807; Amiens
Hawkey, lieut.; duels, trials, 1846
Hawkins, J.; piano
Hawkins, sir John, d. 1595; Guinea, slave trade, 1562; potatoes, tobacco, Chatham
Hawthorne, Nat., Amer. nov. 1804-64
Hay, lord John; British legion, 1835; St. Sebastian's
Haydn, Joseph (first compiler of this book), d. 1856
Haydn, Joseph, mus. comp.; 1732-1809; Creation, Emperor's hymn
Haydon, Benj., painter, 1786-1846
Hayes, Mr.; duels, 1728, 1806; trials, 1802
Hayes, sir H. B.; trials, 1800
Hayes, R. B.; United States, 1876
Hayman, Dr. H.; Rugby; trial 1874
Haynau, gen; Hungary, 1849
Hayter, sir G.; painter, 1792-1871
Hayter, sir Wm., whip
Hayward; trials, 1821
Haywood, W.; Holborn, 1869
H. B.; caricatures
Head, sir Francis; Canada, 1836
Headfort, marquis of; trials, 1805
Hearn, north-west passage, 1769
Heath, archbp.; York, 1555
Heberden, Dr.; Humane Society, 1774
Hebert, J. R. (père Duchesne), executed, 1794
Hector of Troy, slain, 1183 B.C.
Heenan, J.; boxing, 1860
Hegel, G., philosopher, 1770-1831
Hehl; animal magnetism, 1774
Heine, H. German poet, 1799-1856
Helena, St.; cross, 328; Bethlehem
Heliodorus, fl. 398; romances
Heliogabalus; Rome, emp. 218; silk
Helmholtz, H., b. 1821; ophthalmoscope, 1851; acoustics
Héloïse, d. 1164; Abélard
Helps, sir Arthur, hist. and miscel., 1811-75
Helsham, capt; duels, 1829
Hemans, Felicia, poet, 1794-1835
Hencke; planets, 1845
Henderson, sir E., police,—A.; proverbs
Henderson, T.; stars
Heneage, E.; Gladstone adm., 1886
Hengist; octareh, Salisbury
Henley, lord; Grenville admin., 1763
Henley, Jos.; Derby adm., 1852
Henley, orator, d. 1756
Hennessy, J. P.; Bahamas, 1874; Barbados, 1875-6; Mauritius

Hennis, Dr.; duels, 1833
Henrietta; queens (Charles I.)
Henry; kings: England, France, Germany, Spain
Henry I.; Tinchebray, 1106
Henry V.; Agincourt, 1415; Cherbourg
Henry VII.; Bosworth, 1485
Henry VIII.; England, 1509; age, defender, field, monasteries, spurs
Henry II., France; tournaments, 1559
Henry III., France; assassinations
Henry IV.; France, 1589; Nantes, Ravaillac, Yvres, assassination
Henry, Joseph, Am. nat. phil. 1797-1878
Henry, Paul and Prosper; planets, 1872-8
Henry the Lion; Brunswick, 1139
Henshaw, Mr.; duels, 1820
Henty, Mr.; Victoria, 1834
Hepburn, ensign; trials, 1811
Heraclitus, philosopher, fl. 500 B.C.
Heraclius; cross, 615
Herbert, adm.; Bantry Bay, 1689
Herbert, George, ch. poet, 1593-1633
Herbert of Cherbury, lord, 1581-1648; deism
Herbert, Sidney (aft. lord), 1810-61; Peel, Palmerston admins.
Herbert, W., trials, 1880
Hercules Tyrius; purple
Herder, J. G. von, philosopher, 1744-1803
Herkomer, M.; art school, 1883
Hermann (Arminius), Germany, 9
Hero of Alexandria, fl. 284-221 B.C.
Herod; Jews, 42 B.C.
Herodian, hist., fl. 173
Herodotus, b. 484 B.C.; history
Herophilus; anatomy, 302 B.C.
Herostratus fires the temple at Ephesus, 356 B.C.
Herries, J. C.; Peel adm. 1834
Herring, abp.; Canterbury, 1747
Herring, Mrs.; trials, 1773
Herrmann, R.; ilmenium
Herschell, ld.; sol. gen., 1880; chancellor, ld., 1886
Herschel, J. F., 1792-1871; actinometer, photography
Herschel, W., 1738-1822; Saturn, astronomy, telescope, sun, Uranus, nebular hypothesis
Hertford, earl of; administrations, 1547; Pinkey
Hertford, marquis of; his executors v. Suisse, trials, 1842
Hertz, James; cheque bank, 1873
Hervie, H.; doctors' commons, 1560
Hesiod, Greek poet, fl. 850 B.C.
Hess, gen.; Solferino, 1859
Hewett, adm.; Egypt, 1882; Soudan, 1884
Hewett, comm.; Congo, 1875
Heytesbury, lord; Ireland (lord-lieut.), 1844
Heywood, Mrs.; Manchester, 1875
Heywood; pub. worship reg. act, 1883
Hibbert, R.; Hibbert fund
Hicks; life-boat, &c., 1874
Hicks, col.; Soudan, 1883
Hiero, Syracuse, 478-275 B.C.
Hieronymus, see *Jerome*
Hilary; hymns, 431
Hill, lord; commander-in-chief, 1828
Hill, rev. R., Surrey chapel
Hill, Rowland, b. 1795-1879; post-office
Hill, bp. R.; Man
Hillsborough, lord; North administration, 1770
Hilton, James; chronogram
Hind, J. R., b. 1823; planets, 1847; comets
Hindes, lieut.; duel, 1817

Hinds, bp.; Norwich, 1849
Hinrichs, professor; atomic theory, 1855
Hipparchus, fl. 162 B.C.; astronomy, Canary, constellation, degrees, latitude, longitude
Hippias; ostracism, 510 B.C.
Hippocrates, d. 357 B.C.; anatomy, surgery, loadstone
Hirsch, baron; Russia, 1887
Hoadley, B., bp., d. 1761; Bangorian
Hobart, lord; Addington adm., 1801
Hobart, Pasha; admiral, 1823-86
Hobbema, painter, fl. 1681
Hobbes, T., 1588-1679; academies
Hobhouse, sir J. C. (aft. lord Broughton), 1869; Melbourne adm., 1834
Hoche, gen.; Dunkirk, 1793
Hochstade, C. von, Cologne, 1248
Hocker, murderer; trials, 1845
Hödel; Germany, Prussia, 1878
Hodgson, gen.; Belleisle, 1761
Hodgson r. Greene; trials, 1832
Hofer, Andrew; Tyrol, 1809-10
Hoffmann, A., Kladderadatsch
Hofmann, Dr. A. W., b. 1818; chemistry, ammonia, aniline, crith, Faraday
Hogarth, W., painter, 1697-1764
Hogg, James, Sc. poet, 1772-1835
Holbein, Hans, Ger. paint. 1498-1543
Holcombe, lieut.; India, 1875
Holcroft, T., 1745-1809; melodrama, 1793
Holdernesse, earl of; Devonshire administration, 1756
Holgate, abp.; York, 1545
Holinshed, Ralph; d. about 1580
Holkar; India, 1804
Holker, sir J.; solicitor-gen., 1874; att.-gen., 1875
Holland, lord; Melbourne adm., 1835 et seq.; trials, 1797
Holland, sir H., 1788-1873; pres. Roy. Inst., 1865-73
Hollest murderers; trials, 1851
Holloway, T.; Holloway hospitals, 1873
Holmes, adm.; Cape Coast, 1663
Holt, sir John; king's bench, 1689
Holt; trials, 1844
Holtz; electricity, 1865
Holwell, Mr.; suttees, 1743
Holyoake; secularism
Home or Hume, D.; spiritualism; trials, 1868
Home, lieut.; Delhi, 1857
Homer, fl. 962 B.C. (*Clinton*); poetry
Hompesch, baron; duels, 1800
Hone, Wm., 1779-1842; trials, 1817; almanacs
Honey and Francis; riots, 1821
Honorius; West. empire, 395
Hood, admiral; Madeira, 1807; Toulon
Hood, Thomas, comic writer, 1798-1845; Tom, son, 1835-74
Hook, Theodore, novelist, 1788-1841
Hook, W. F. J. D., dean, hist., 1798-1875
Hooke, Rob., 1635-1702; air, boiling, camera, clocks, geology, mechanics, microscope, telegraphs
Hooker, Rich., theol., 1553-1600
Hooker, W., botanist, 1785-1865;—J. D. (son), b. 1816; Kew, 1865;—Gen. R., United States, 1862-3; Fredericksburg
Hopkins, miss Ellice; white cross army
Hopkins, Matthew; witches, 1645
Hopley, T.; trials, 1860
Horace, 65-8 B.C., Latin poet; Athens, satires

INDEX.

Hunt, Henry, reformer; trials, 1820; Clerkenwell, Manchester
Hunt, John and Leigh; trials, 1811-1812; James, d. 1869, anthropology.
Hunt, Wm. Holman, painter, b. 1827; pre-Raphaelite
Hunt, W. T.; trials, 1875
Hunter, John, surgeon, 1728-93:—W., 1718-83
Huntingdon, countess of, 1707-91; Cheshunt, Whitefieldites
Huntingford, bp.; Hereford, 1802
Huntly, earl of; Brechin, 1452
Hunton, Jos., forgery; executions, 1828
Hurd, bishop; Worcester, 1781
Huskisson, Wm., 1770-1830; Wellington admin., 1828; Liverpool, 1830
Huss, John, burnt, 1415; Hussites
Hutchinson, Amy; trials, 1750
Hutchinson, John, d. 1737; Hutchinsonians
Hutchinson, major; Alexandria, 1801
Hutchinson, J. H.; Lavalette's escape, 1815
Hutton, abp.; Canterbury, 1757
Hutton, W., d. 1815; geology
Huxley, T. H., b. 1825; abiogenesis, bathybius, Birmingham, 1874; germ, minimisers, oysters, Roy. Soc. pres. 1883
Huygens, d. 1695; astronomy, optics, pendulum
Hyacinthe (Loyson) father, France, 1869
Hyde, capt.; Chili, 1874
Hyde, sir Edward; chancellor, lord high, 1660
Hyde, Laurence; administrations, 1689 et seq.
Hyder Ali, d. 1782; India, Arcot, Carnatic, Mysore
Hyginus, pope, 139; martyr
Hypatia, philosopher, m. 415 B.C.; hydrometer
Hyperides; Cranon, 322 B.C.
Hyrcanus, John, d. 106 B.C.; Samaritans
Hyslop and Denham; trials, 1877

I.

Ibrahim Pacha, 1789-1848; Antioch, Beyrout, Damascus, Syria, Turkey, Damascus, Wahabees
Iglesias; Mexico, 1876-7; Peru, 1883-4
Ignatief, M.; Russia; resigned, 1882
Ignatius, St., mart., 115; liturgies, 250
Ilbert bill, 1883-4
Ilchester, ld.; Oxford univ.; Slavonia, 1876
Impey, major; duels, 1801
Inachus; Argos, 1856 B.C.
Incledon, C., d. 1826
Inez de Castro; Coimbra, 1355
Ingham, sir J. T.; magistrate, 1876
Ingle, L., trials, 1880
Inglefield, capt.; Franklin, 1852
Inglis, col.; Albuera, 1811
Ingram, Herbert, d. 1860; Illust. London News, 1842—W. J., printing machine, 1877
Inman, W.; steam, 1850
Innocent I.—XII.; popes, 402 et seq.
Innocent III., pope, 1198; transubstantiation
Irenæus, martyr, 202
Irving, E., 1792-1834; Irvingites, trial, 1832; unknown tongues
Irving, H.; theatres (Lyceum), 1874 et seq.
Irving, H. T.; Antigua, 1873; Leeward Isles, 1873

Irving, Washington, 1783-1859
Isaac, major; tunnel (Mersey)
Isabella; salique law, Spain, 1833
Isaiah prophesies about 760 B.C.
Islip, abp.; Canterbury, 1349
Isocrates, Gr. orator, 436-338 B.C.
Iturbide; Mexico, 1821-1865
Ivan; Russia, 1462; czars

J.

Jablochkoff; electricity (electric candles)
Jablonsky; assassin; Russia, 1883
Jack, capt.; Modoc, 1873
Jackson, bp.; Oxford, 1812; Lincoln, 1852; London, 1869-1885; auricular confession, 1873
Jackson, gen.; United States, 1829
Jackson, C. T.; ether, 1846
Jackson, J. B.; printing in colours, 1720
Jackson, Thos., "Stonewall," 1826-63; Manassas, United States, 1862; Chancellorsville, Richmond, 1875
Jackson, T.; executions, 1861
Jacob, Dr.; Christ's hospital, 1854
Jacobi; Baltic, note, electrotype
Jacobs, S.; abstinence
Jacquard loom, 1806
James; England, Scotland, Spain (kings); assassinations
James IV.; Flodden, 1513
James, sir H., 1803-77; photozincography, 1860; ordnance survey
James, sir H.; sol.-general, att.-gen., 1873, 1880
James, W. H., companies, 1876
Jamieson, G.; volunteers (18th meeting), 1877
Jane, England, queens, 1554; Sicily
Janisch, H. R.; Helena, 1873
Jansen, C., 1585-1638; Jansenism
Janssen, M.; eclipse, 1868
Janvier de la Motte; France, 1872
Jardine, sir Wm., naturalist, 1800-74
Jarnac; Jarnac; France, 1874-5
Jason, argonautic exp., 1263 B.C.
Jeans, J. S., steel
Jebb, Joshua, prison reformer, 1793-1863
Jeffcott, sir John W.; duels, 1833
Jefferson, Thos., 1743-1826; United States, president, 1801-8
Jeffery, Robert; Sombrero, 1807
Jeffrey, Francis, critic, 1773-1850
Jeffreys, George (afterwards lord); administrations, 1685; king's bench, chancellor, lord high, bloody assize; d. 1689
Jeffries, Dr. J., colour blindness
Jejeebhoy; Bombay, 1859; Parsees
Jellachich; Hungary, Vienna, 1848
Jenghis Khan; Tartary, 1206; Hungary, India, Moguls, Afghanistan
Jenkin, F., telpherage
Jenkins v. Cook; trials, 1875-6
Jenkins, Henry; longevity, d. 1670
Jenkinson, bp.; David's, St., 1825
Jenks, gaines, 1884
Jenner, E., 1749-1823; vaccination
Jennings, Mr.; tontines, 1798
Jeremiah prophesies about 629 B.C.
Jerningham, Mrs.; blue-stockings, 1760
Jerome, St., Latin father, 345-420; ascension, liturgies
Jerome of Prague; burnt, 1416
Jerrold, Douglas, Nov. Dram., 1803-1857; W. B., 1826-84
Jersey, countess of; delicate investigation, 1806
Jervis, sir John, 1734-1823; Cape St. Vincent;—solicitor-gen., att.-gen., common pleas, d. 1856
Jervois, sir W. F. D.; straits, and South Australia

Jessel, sir Geo. 1824-83; master of rolls, 1873
Jevons, W. Stanley; polit. econ. &c., 1835-82; abecedarium, 1874; method
Joan of Arc, burnt, 1431; Joan.
Joan; queens (Henry IV.), Naples
Joel prophesies about 800 B.C.
Johanni; Abyssinia, 1872
John, St., d. 100; baptism, accusers, evangelists, gospels
John L—XXIII.; popes, 523 et seq.
John of Austria; Lepanto, 1571
John, king; Bohemia, Portugal, Spain, France, Poitiers
John, king; England (1199), charter of forests, magna charta, "B'e"
John of Leyden; anabaptists, 1534
John the Fearless; Burgundy, 1404
Johnson, A.; boats
Johnson, Andrew, 1809-75; United States, 1865-8
Johnson, Sam., 1709-84; dictionary, literary club, 1764
Johnson, capt.; trials, 1846
Johnson, judge; trials, 1805
Johnson, Mr.; swimming
Johnston, capt.; steam, 1825
Johnston, gen.; Ross, N., 1798
Johnston, Albt., k. Pittsburg, 1862; —Jos., U. S., 1863
Johnston, Alex. K., geographer, 1804-71, Africa, 1878
Johnston, Robert; trials, 1818
Johnston, sir John; marriages, forced, 1690
Johnston, W.; orangemen, 1868
Joinville, Jean de, French historian, 1224-1318
Joinville, prince de, b. 1818; Ocean Monarch, 1848
Jomini, baron H., strategist; 1779-1869; Brussels conf., 1874
Jonah prophesies about 862 B.C.
Jones, colonel; Dungan, 1647; Rathmines
Jones, H. Bence, 1813-73; Royal Institution, 1860; fluorescence, spectrum
Jones, Gale; trials, 1811
Jones, sir Horace, 1819-1887; Billingsgate, foreign cattle market, guildhall
Jones, Inigo, architect, 1572-1652
Jones, Jane; trials, 1842
Jones, J. S., Kensington Mus.
Jones, J.; trials, 1870
Jones, J. W.; Brit. Museum, 1866-78
Jones, Mr.; riots, 1819
Jones, Owen, 1809-74, Alhambra, 1842; James's-hall, St.
Jones, T.; book-keeping, 1821
Jones, Mr. Todd; duel, 1807
Jones, sir Wm., 1746-94; Asiatic, chess, Menu, Sanskrit
Jones v. Stannard, trials, 1881
Jones, W. B. T., Davids, St., 1874
Jonson, Ben, 1574-1637; poet-laur.
Joquemin, M.; picquet, 1390
Jordan, J. B., barometer; sunshine
Jordan, Mrs., actress, d. 1816
Jordan, R., gold
Joseph; Germany, Namur, Portugal
Josephine, empress, 1763-1814; France, 1809
Josephus, Jewish hist., 38-100
Jotham; fables, 1209 B.C.
Joubert, gen.; Novi, 1799; Transvaal, 1880
Jourdan, marshal; Cologne, Fleurus, Vittoria, 1813
Jovellar; Spain, 1874-5
Jovian, Rome, emp., 363
Joyce, family murdered, 1882
Juarez, B.; Mexico, 1858-72; d. 1872
Judas Maccabæus rules, 168-160 B.C.
Judith; Abyssinia, 960
Jugurtha, d. 104 B.C.; Numidia, Jugurthine war

INDEX.

Julian; Rome, emp., 360; edicts, Paris
Julianus Salvius; edicts, 132
Julius v. bishop of Oxford, trials, 1879
Julius Cæsar; see *Cæsar, Julius*
Julius, Mr.; duels, 1791
Julius II.; popes, 1503; Rome, Bologna, Laocoön, Cambray
Jullien, M., concerts
Jung Bahadoor; Nepaul, 1857-60
Junot, marshal, 1771-1813; Cintra, Vimiera, 1808
Jussieu, A. L. de; Fr. botanist, 1748-1836
Justin, emp.; Rome, 518 and 565
Justin Martyr, 164; millennium
Justin, St.; Rochester, 604
Justinian; eastern empire, 527
Juvenal, 59-128; satires
Juvigny, flageolet
Juxon, apb.; administrations, 1640; Canterbury, 1660

K.

Kabba Rega; Egypt, 1872
Kalakaua, Sandwich Islands, 1874
Kalkoff, N., journalist; Russia, 1887
Kane, capt.; Samoan isles
Kane, Dr.; Franklin, 1843
Kant, human., 1724-1804; metaphysics
Karaman, Joseph; Syria, 1866-7
Karslake, sir J., 1821-81; att.-gen., 1867-74
Kaspary; humanitarians
Kassas; Abyssinia, 1871
Kastenbein; printing, 1872
Kastner, F.; pyrophone
Kauffman, harmonica
Kaufmann, gen.; Samarcand, 1868; Khiva, 1873; Khokand, 1875; d. 1882
Kaunitz, prince W. A., Aust. statesman, 1711-94
Kaye, bishop; Bristol, 1820; Lincoln
Kean, Charles, 1811-68; theatres
Kean, Edmund, actor, 1787-1833
Keane, lord; Ghiznee, 1839
Kearney, D.; California, 1878
Keats, John; poet, 1796-1821
Keble, rev. John; poet, 1792-1866; Keble
Keenan; trials, 1803
Keet v. Smith; reverend, trials, 1876
Keith, George; earl-marischal of Scotland, Aberdeen, 1593
Keith, George; quakers, 1664
Keith Johnston v. Athenæum; trials, 1875; see *Johnston*
Keller, Dr.; lake dwellings, 1865
Kellerman, gen.; Valmy, 1792
Kellet, capt.; Franklin, 1848
Kellogg; United States, 1874
Kelly; trials, 1869, 1871
Kelly, Miss; theatres, trials, 1816
Kelly, Ned, Victoria, 1880
Kelly, sir Fitzroy, 1796-1880; sol.-general, att.-gen., ch. baron, 1866-80
Kemble, Charles, actor, 1775-1854
Kemble, Fanny, actress, b. 1811
Kemble, John, actor, 1757-1823
Kembles; examiners (of plays)
Kemp, abp.; Canterbury, 1452
Kempe, John; wool, 1331
Kempenfeldt, adm.; Royal George, 1782
Kempis, T. à, 1380-1471; imitation, theology
Kenealy, Dr.; Englishman; trials, 1874
Kennedy, alderman; trials, 1878
Kennedy, Mr.; Franklin, 1851-53
Kennedy, C. R.; trials, 1856 *note*

Kennedy, sir A. E.; Hong Kong, 1872
Kent, Constance, Road murder
Kent, Edw. duke of, 1767-1820
Kent, Odo, earl of; treasurer, 1066
Kent, G.; knives (cleaner), 1844
Kentigern, St.; abstinence, Glasgow, Asaph, 560-83
Kenyon, lord; attorney-general, 1782; king's bench
Kepler, J., 1571-1630; optics, planetary motions, 1609; rainbow, tides, Venus
Keppel, adm.; Belleisle, Ushant, trials, 1799; coalition, naval battles
Keppel, commodore; China, 1857
Keratry, gen.; Franco-Pruss. war, 1870
Kerford, Mr., Victoria, 1875
Kern; davyum
Keshub Sen, deism
Kettel, E.; trials, 1872
Kettlewell, C.; Bartholomew's, St., 1881
Keying; China, 1842-58
Killigrew, Thos.; drama, 1662
Kilmarnock, lord; rebellions, trials, executions, 1746
Kilwarby, abp.; Canterbury, 1272
Kilwarden, lord; king's bench; trials, 1803
Kimberley, earl of, see *Wodehouse*; Gladstone adm., 1868, 1880, 1886
King, Thos.; ventriloquism, 1716
King, Mr. Locke; administrations, 1851
King, Dr.; Cæsarean operation
King, E., bp.; Lincoln, 1885
King, col.; suicide, 1850
King, C.; trials, 1855; gems, 1860
Kinglake, Dr.; trials, 1870
Kinglake, A. W.; hist., b. 1802
Kingsford, A.; hermetic soc.
Kingsley, Rev. C.; novels, &c., 1819-75; socialism; — Henry, nov. 1830-76
Kingston, duchess of; trials, 1776
Kingston, Evelyn, duke of; Walpole, 1721
Kingzett, C. T.; sanitas
Kinnaird, A.; cabmen's rest, 1875
Kirby and Wade, capts. shot, 1702; naval battles, note
Kircher; Æolian harp, 1653; philosopher's stone, trumpet
Kirchhoff, G. R. (1824-1887); spectrum
Kirkman; pianoforte
Kirwan, Richard B.; trials, 1852
Kiss, Karl, Ger. sculptor, 1802-65
Kitchener; Soudan, 1885 *et seq.*
Klapka, general, b. 1820
Kleber, J. B., Fr. gen., 1754-1800; El Arisch
Klein, E.; histology, germ theory
Kleist; electricity, 1745; Leyden
Klopstock, F. T., Germ. poet, 1724-1803
Kluber; cryptography
Kmety, gen. (Ismail Pacha), d. 1865; Hungary, Kars
Knatchbull, sir E.; Peel administrations, 1834-5
Kneller, sir Godfrey, painter, 1648-1723
Knight, Chas., 1791-1873; hist., &c.; diffusion soc., 1827; England
Knight, G.; magnetism, 1756
Knight, Mr.; north-west passage, 1602; South Sea bubble, bribery; free church
Knight v. Wolcot; trials, 1807
Knowles, James; Nineteenth Century
Knowles, J. S., dramat., 1784-1862
Knox, John, 1505-72; Presbyterians, congregation, queen, Scotland
Knutsford, ld. (H. T. Holland); Salisbury adm., 1886

Knutzen, Matthias; atheism, 1674
Koch; germ theory; vivisection
Kock, Charles Paul de, Fr. novelist, 1794-1871
Koffee Kalcalli; Ashantees, 1874
Kohl, F.; execution, 1865
Komaroff, gen.; Russia, 1885
König, F.; printing machine, 1814
König, M.; phonoscope, tonometer, 1862
Körner, Th., Germ. poet, 1791-1813
Kortright, C.; Demerara
Kosciusko; Poland, 1794; Cracow
Kossuth, L., b. 1802; Hungary, 1849-68; United States, 1851
Koster, Laurence; printing, 1438
Kotzebue; north-west passage, 1815; Aug. dramatist; assassinations
Koull Khan; Moguls, India, Persia, 1730
Krapotkine, prince, Russia, 1878; France, 1883
Krell; Kaffraria, 1877
Kruger, P., Transvaal, 1879-81
Krupp, Alfred, 1810-1887; cannon, steel
Kuenen, prof.; Hibbert fund
Kullmann; attempt to kill Bismarck, Prussia, 1874
Kunckel, J., 1630-1703; phosphorus, 1670
Kutusoff, gen. M., 1745-1813; Russia, Borodino, Smolensko, 1812
Kyhl, P.; nature-printing, 1833

L.

Laborde, A. de, "Partant pour la Syrie"
Labouchere, Henry, lord Taunton; Russell administration, 1846; Palmerston administration, 1855
Labourdonnaye; Tournay, 1792
La Bruyère, French essays, 1639-96
Lachaise, Père, 1624-1709; cemetery
Lacon, W. S.; sens
Lacordaire, Père H. D., 1802-61
Lactantius, d. abt. 325; fathers
Ladislas; Bohemia, Hungary
Ladmirault; France, 1873
Laënnec, R., physician, 1781-1826
Lafarge, Madame; trials, 1840
Lafayette, marq.; 1757-1834
Laffitte, d. 1844; wills (Napoleon's)
Lafurge; Tontine
La Fontaine, J., Fr. fabulist, 1621-95
Lagava, &c.; execution, 1856
Lagny, circle, 1719
La Grange, J. L., 1736-1813; acoustics, astronomy, 1780
Laing, Sam., cryst. pal. 1852; India, 1861-2
Laird, Mr.; Birkenhead, Alabama, navy, 1870
Lake, gen.; Bhurtpore, 1805; Delhi, Llucelles
Lake, capt.; Sombrero, 1807
Lalande, J., astron., 1732-1807
Lalanne; abacus
Lally, gen. Thos. de; beheaded, 1766
Lamarck, 1744-1829; species
La Marmora, gen. A., 1804-78; Tchernaya, 1855; Italy, 1862
Lamartine, A. de, 1792-1869, miscel. writer; France, 1848
Lamb, C., 1775-1834; essays
Lamb, Dr., killed, 1623; riots
Lamballe, princesse de; France, 1792
Lamberg, ct.; Austria, 1848
Lambert, Mr., d. 1809; corpulency
Lambert (Latham), J.; trials, 1855
Lambrecht, Mr.; duels, trials, 1830
Lambton, Mr.; duels, 1826
Lamennais, Père, F. R. de, 1782-1854
Laminande, M.; extradition, 1866

Lamm, earl; bellite
Lamoriciere, gen., 1806-65; France, 1851; Rome, 1860
Lamplugh, archbp.; York, 1688
Lanusson, Dr. G. H.; trials, 1882
Lancaster, capt.; Bantam, 1603
Lancaster, duke of; Lancaster
Lancaster, Joseph, 1771-1838; Lancasterian schools, education
Lauder, Richard, 1804-34; Africa
Lane, E. W., orientalist, 1801-76
Landseer, sir E., painter, 1803-73
Lanfranc, archbp. Canterbury, 1070
Lanfrey, Pierre, Fr. hist. 1828-77
Langalibalele; Cape; Natal, 1873
Langara, adm.; naval battles, 1780
Langdale, ld.; master of rolls, 1836
Langdale, sir M.; Naseby, 1645
Lange, sir D.; Suez, 1858
Langham, abp.; Canterbury, 1366
Langiewicz, M.; Poland, 1863-5
Langley, Dr. Baxter; recreative religionists; artisans, trials, 1877
Langley, prof. S. P.; bolometer
Langton, abp.; Canterbury, 1206
Langworthy, E. R.; Owens College, 1874
Lankester, E. Ray; spontaneous generation, 1876-7; spiritualism
Lannes; marshals, Asperne, 1809
Lansdowne, marquis of, 1780-1863; see Petty, Shelburne; Goderich adm. 1827; Russell adm. 1846, 1851; Aberdeen adm. 1852; Palmerston adm. 1855, et seq.; Canada, 1883
Lanyon, sir W. O., Transvaal, 1879
Laomedon; Troy, 1260 B.C.
Laplace, P. de; Fr. mathemat., 1749-1827
Lartigue, M.; railway (balance)
Lasker; Germany, 1884
Lateau, L.; abstinence
Latham, R. G.; philologist 1812-88
Latham, J.; birds
Latimer, bp., burnt, 1555; protestants
Latimer, viscount; administrations, 1672-3
Latorre, col.; Uruguay, 1876
Laud, William, abp., 1573-1645; Canterbury, administrations
Lauderdale, duke of; cabal, 1670
Laura; Petrarch, 1327
Laurent; carbolic acid, 1846
Lautrec, Fr. gen., d. 1528
Lavalette's escape, 1815
Lavater, J., 1741-1801; physiognomy
Lavoisier, A., 1743-94; carbon, hydrogen, nitric acid, phlogiston, water
Law, bishop; Chester, Bath, 1824
Law's bubble, 1720
Lawes, H., mus. comp., 1600-62
Lawless, Mr.; riots, 1828
Lawrence, gen. H., 1800-57; India, 1857
Lawrence, sir J., aft. ld., 1811-79; India, 1863
Lawrence, sir T., painter, 1769-1830
Lawson, sir Wilfrid; permissive bill
Layard, sir A. Henry, b. 1817; Nineveh, Gladstone, 1868; Turkey, 1877
Layer's conspiracy, 1722; Layer
Lazareff, Russia, 1879
Lazzaretti, David; Italy, 1878
Leake, adm., d. 1720; admiralty, Gibraltar, Mediterranean, Minorca
Leatham, W. H.; trials, 1861
Le Clerc; critics, 1696
Lecky, R. J., sunshine recorder
Lecomte, gen.; France, 1871, 1876
Lecoq de Boisbaudran; gallium, 1875
Lechowski, abp. Prussia, 1873-6
Ledru Rollin, A. A., 1808-74; France, 1848, 1874
Lee, Alexander; theatres, 1830
Lee, Ann, shakers
Lee, bp., J. D.; massacres, 1858; Mormonites
Lee Boo, prince; Pelew Islands, 1783

Lee, C. C.; Leeward isles
Lee, John; trials, 1885
Lee, abp.; York, 1544
Lee, W.; stocking-frame, 1589
Lee, gen. Robt., 1808-70; United States, 1862
Leech, John, 1817-64; caricatures; Punch
Leeds, duke of; administrations, 1689
Leeke, H.; Bushire, 1856
Leeuwenhoek, 1632-1723; animalcules, polypus
Lefevre, C. Shaw (ld. Eversley); speaker, 1839-57
Lefevre, G. S.; Gladstone adm., 1880
Lefroy, al. Mapleton, railways, 1881
Leggatt, R.; burning, 1612
Legge, bishop; Oxford, 1827
Legge, H. B., Newcastle adm., 1754
Le Gros, Raymond; Dublin, 1171
Leibnitz, Gottfried, 1646-1716; mathematics, fluxions
Leicester, earl of; administrations, 1558; national associations
Leicester, earl of, v. Morning Herald; trials, 1809
Leighton, Fred.; artist, b. 1830; Royal Academy
Leighton, J. & A.; christmas cards; printing surface, ballot
Leighton, abp. Robt., 1613-84
Leighton, G. C.; printing in colours, 1849
Leitrim, earl of; murd., Ireland, 1878
Le Jay; polyglot, 1628-45
Lelewel; Poland, 1863
Lely, sir P., painter, 1617-80
Le Maire; circumnavigator, 1615
Lemoinne, J.; France, 1873-6
Lemon, Mark, humorist, 1809-70; Punch
Lennox, col.; duels, 1789
Lennox, lord H.; Disraeli adm., 1874-6
Lenoir; gas, 1861
Le Notre; James's-park, St., 1668
Leo; popes, 440; Eastern empire, 457
Leo I.; coronation
Leo IV.; Leonine city
Leo X.; popes, 1513; indulgences
Leo XIII., b. 1810; pope, 1878
Leon, Diego de; Spain, 1841
Leon, Ponce de; America, 1512
Leonarda of Pisa; algebra, 1202
Leonardo da Vinci, painter, 1452-1519
Leonidas; Thermopylæ, 480 B.C.
Leopardi, Italian orat. 1798-1837
Leopold, Germany; Morgarten, 1315; Sempach, 1386; Belgium, 1830; Spain, France, 1870 84
Leopold, prince, 1853-84; England, etc.; Albany, 1881
L'Epée, abbé de. 1712-89, deaf
Lepidus; triumvir, 43 B.C.
Le Pique, M.; duels, 1808
Lepsius, K. R., 1810-84; Egypt
Lerdo de Tejado; Mexico, 1872
Lerothodi, Basuto
Le Sage, French novelist, 1668-1747
Leslie, C. R., painter, 1794-1859
Leslie, H., music
Lesseps, M.; Suez, 1852; Corinth, 1881; Panama
Lessing, G. E., German philosopher, 1729-81
Lestock, admiral; Toulon, 1744
L'Estrange, sir R.; newspapers, 1663
Lethaby, Henry, M.B., chemist, 1816-76
Lettsom, Dr.; Humane soc., 1774
Lever, sir Ashton; museum
Lever, C. J., Irish novelist, 1809-72
Leverson, S. R.; trials, 1868, 1878
Leverrier, U., 1811-77; Neptune, 1846
Levy, Leoni; statistician, 1821-88; wages
Levy, Mr. Lyon; monument, 1810

Lewes, Geo. Hen., philosopher, &c., 1817-78
Lewis, John Fred., R.A., 1805-76
Lewis, Mr.; theatres (Covent-garden), 1773
Lewis, sir G. Cornewall, 1806-63; Palmerston adm., 1855
Lewis v. Higgins, trials, 1876
Lewisham, visc.; Addington adm., 1801
Leybourne, William de; admiral, 1297
Lhoste, M., 1836-7
Liakat, Ali; India, 1871-2
Libanius, Gr. orator, 314-390
Lick, Jas.; observatories
Liddon, lieut.; north-west passage, 1819
Lielner, T.; Erastianism, 1523-84
Liebig, J., 1803-73; acids, agriculture, chemistry, chloroform, chloral
Liebreich, O.; chloral, 1869
Light, F.; Penang, 1786
Ligonier, lord; Bute, 1762
Lilburne, col.; levellers, Wigan, 1651
Lilly, Wm., 1602-81; astrology, 1647
Lily, George, d. 1559; charts
Lily, Wm., grammarian, d. 1523
Lhi; China, 1840
Linacre, Dr., d. 1524; gardening, lectures, physicians
Lincoln, Abm., 1809-65; United States, 1860-5
Lincoln, earl of; administrations, 1759
Lincoln, R. T.; United States, 1889
Lind, Dr.; anemometer, wind
Lind, Jenny (Goldschmidt), b. 1820-87; theatres
Linfield, H. C.; flying
Lindley, John; bot., 1799-1865; horticulture
Lindsay, earl of; Edgehill, 1642
Lindsay, sir C.; Grosvenor gallery
Lindsay, sir John; Madras, 1770
Lingard, J., 1771-1851; historian
Linlithgow, lord; guards, 1660
Linne, Linn, C. von, 1707-78; botany, Linnæan, zoology
Linnell, John; painter, 1792-1882
Linus, poet, fl. 1281 B.C.
Liprandi; Balaklava, Enpatoria, 1855
Lisle, lord; administrations, 1544
Lisle, sir G.; Colchester, 1648
Lisle, visc.; Portsmouth, 1545
Lister, J.; germ theory
Liston, J., actor, retires, 1838
Liszt, F.; music, 1811-86
Little John; Robin Hood
Littleton, Mr.; Melbourne administration, 1834
Littré, M. O. E., 1801-81; dictionaries, positive philosophy
Liverpool, earl of, 1770-1828;—Liverpool adm., 1812
Livingstone, D., 1813-77; Africa, 1856; Edinburgh, 1876
Livius, Titus, Roman hist., d. 18
Lizarraga, gen.; Spain, 1875-6
Llewellyn; Wales, 1194
Lloyd, bishop; Oxford, 1327
Lloyd, Catherine; quackery, 1831
Lloyd, Charles; Junius, 1765
Lloyd, W.; Portland vase, 1845
Lloyd, Clifford; Egypt, 1884
Loch, sir H. B.; Victoria, 1884
Locke, J., 1632-1704; physics, cartesian, coin
Locke, W.; ragged schools, 1844
Lockwood, P. E.; beer
Lockyer, major; duel, 1817
Lockyer, J. N.; eclipse, 1866; Nature, 1869; elements, 1878; meteors, astronomy
Lofting, John; thimble, 1695
Loftus, ld. A., New S. Wales, 1879
Loseman; magnetism, 1851
Logier, J. B.; chiroplast

Lollard, Walter; Lollards, 1315; burned, 1322
Lomakine, gen., Russia, 1879
Lombe, sir Thomas; silk, 1714
Loud, T.; piano, 1802
London dock company; trials, 1851
Londonderry, lord; see *Castlereagh*; suicide, 1822
Londonderry, marquis of; Ireland, ld. lieut., 1886
Long, sir R.; administrations, 1660
Long, Misses Tilney; trials, 1825
Long, St. John; quack, trials, 1830-1
Longden, J. R.; Demerara, 1874
Longfellow, H. W.; Am. poet, 1807-82
Longford v. Purdon; trials, 1877
Longinus, Gr. philos., killed, 273
Longley, abp. York, 1860; Ripon
Longman, W.; Paul's, St., 1873; Publishers' Circular
Longstreet, gen.; Chicamauga, 1863; U. States
Lönnrot, M. E.; Finland
Lonsdale, bishop; Lichfield, 1843
Lonsdale, earl of; duels, 1792; Derby administration, 1852
Lopez; Cuba, 1850; United States
Lopez, gen.; Paraguay; Aquidaban, 1870
Lopez, sir Manasseh; Grampound, trials, 1819
Lorenz, J. F.; cryptography, 1806
L'Orme, Philibert de; Tuileries, 1564
Lorne, marquis of, England, *end.* 1870-1; psalms, 1877; Canada, 1878; United States, 1882
Lorraine, cardinal; assassination, 1588
Lorraine, Chas. of; Lissa, Mohatz, 1687
Lorraine, duke of; Crecy, 1346
Lorraine, Claude, painter, 1600-82
Losinga, H.; Norwich, 1091
Lothian, marquis of; Salisbury adm. 1887
Loudon, C. J., 1783-1843; botany
Lough, John G., sculptor, 1804?-76
Loughborough; att.-gen., coalition, 1783
Louis; France, kings; Spain, 1724
Louis I.—IV.; landgrave, Hesse
Louis XI.; "Christian;" blood, posts, 1470; Provence
Louis XII.; tester, 1513
Louis XIII.; Louis d'or, 1640
Louis XIV.; Dieu-donné, Nantes, 1685
Louis XV.: France, 1757; Damiens
Louis XVIII.; Hartwell, 1807-14; France
Louis, king; Hungary, Buda, 1526
Louis, prince of Condé; Jarnac, 1569
Louis Bonaparte; Holland, 1806
Louis Napoleon; Bonaparte; France, 1848-70; see *Napoleon III.*
Louis Napoleon, France, *end.*; Zululand, 1879
Louis Philippe; France, 1830; assassinations
Louisa Maria, infanta; Spain, 1846
Louise, queen; Belgium, 1832; *d.* 1850
Louth, lord; trials, 1811
Loutherbourg, Mr.; panorama
Lovat, lord; conspiracy, trials, 1747
Lovell; trials, 1812
Lover, Sam., Irish nov., 1797-1868
Lovett, W.; chartists
Lowe, Alice; trials, 1842
Lowe, R.; Gladstone, 1868; London univ.
Lowe, gen. Drury, 1882
Lowell, J. Russell, Amer. sat. poet, *b.* 1819
Löwenthal, J. J.; chess, 1876
Lower, M. A., antiquary, 1813-76; names
Lowther, visc.; Wellington adm., 1828

Loyd; see *Overstone.*
Loyola, Ignatius, 1491-1556; Jesuits, 1534
Lubbock, sir J. W., mathemat., 1803-6; — sir John, *b.* 1834; ancient monuments, bank holidays, bees, proportional representation, biology, pre-historic; early closing
Luby, Thos.; Fenian, trials, 1865
Lucan, earl of; trials, 1856
Lucan, killed, 65; Rome, Cordova
Lucas, Mr.; steel, 1804
Lucian, Gr. satirist, about 120-200
Luciani; Rome, 1875
Lucilius; satire, 116 B.C.
Lucretia, *d.* 47 B.C.; Rome, spinning
Lucretius, Lat. phil. poet, *d.* 52 B.C.; atoms
Luie; trials, 1874
Lully; nitric acid, 1287; (music), 1633-72
Lumby; Athanasian creed, confessions, 1874
Lumley v. Gye; trials, 1854
Lumsden, sir P.; Afghanistan, 1884; Russia, 1885
Lunardi, M.; balloons, 1784
Lushington, S.; admiralty court, 1838
Lusk, A.; mayor, ld. 1873
Lutatius; naval battles, 241 B.C.
Luther, Martin, 1483-1546; Augustins, Lutheranism, Dort, Protestantism, Augsburg, Calvinists, Worms
Luther, R.; planets, 1852
Luvini, G. dietheroscope, 1876
Luxemburg, marshal; Enghien, 1692
Luxmoore, bishop; Bristol, 1807
Lycurgus; Sparta, 881 B.C.
Lyell, sir Charles, 1797-1875; geology, man
Lyell v. Kennedy; trials, 1886
Lyly, W.; euphuism, 1581
Lynall, Thomas; trials, 1877
Lynch, murder; trials, 1817
Lyndhurst, lord, 1772-1863; chancellor; Canning adm. 1827; Wellington adm. 1828; Peel adm., 1834, 1841
Lynedoch, lord; Barrosa, 1811; Bergen-op-Zoom, St. Sebastian
Lyon, capt.; north-west passage, 1821;—general Nathaniel, Springfield, 1861
Lyon, col. F., killed; Shoeburyness, 1864
Lyon, John; Harrow school, 1571
Lyons, lord; Paris, 1887
Lyons v. Thomas; trials, 1869
Lysander; Sparta, 405 B.C.
Lysimachus; Ipsus, 301 B.C.; Corus
Lysippus; Lysistratus, sculpture, busts, 328 B.C.
Lyttelton, lord; chancellor, ld., 1641
Lyttelton, Geo., lord; dreams, 1779
Lytton, E. Bulwer, ld., novelist and poet, 1805-73; guilds
Lytton, R. B., lord, India, 1876

M.

Macadam, J.; macadamising, 1819
Macarthy, sir Charles; Sierra Leone, Ashantees, 1824
Macartney, earl; duel, 1786; China, 1793; India
Macaulay, T. B., ld., 1800-1859; Melbourne adm., 1837
Macbeth; Scotland, 1057
McCabe, abp., Ireland, 1879-80; cardinal, 1882; *d.* 1885
MacCabe; robbers, 1691
McCarthy, Justin, home rule
McHale, abp., 1791-1881
McClellan, gen. George, B. 1826-85; United States, 1861-4

Macclesfield, earl of; chancellor, lord high, 1718
MacCormack; reaping machine, 1831
Macdonald, marshal; Parma, Trebia, 1799
Macdonald, Mr.; Times, printing
Macdonald, capt.; Prussia, 1861
Macdonald, sir J., Canada, 1874
Macdonalds massacred; Glencoe, 1692
Macdonnel, quotations
MacDowell, gen. J.; Manassas, 1861
Macduff, Mr.; duel, 1790
Macfarlane, S.; trials, 1844
Macfarren, sir George, 1813-87; royal academy of music, oratorio, opera
MacGrath; dogs
Macgregor, J.; bank, British, 1849; canoe, 1865
Machiavelli, N., 1469-1527
Machiewicz, abbé; Poland, 1863
Maceo, gen.; Spain, 1882
Mack, gen.; Ulm, 1805
Mackay, gen.; Killiecrankie, 1689
Mackay and Vaughan; trials, 1816
Mackenzie, Henry, novelist, 1745-1831
Mackenzie, bp. C. F.; Africa, 1860
Mackenzie, sir Morell; Germany, 1887-9.
Mackie, A.; printing, 1871
Mackintosh, sir James, 1765-1832
Macklin, C., actor, *d.* 1797
Macklin; Bible, books
Mackonochie, rev. Mr.; Church of England, 1867-76; trials, 1867; ritualists, public worship, holy cross
MacLachlan, Jessie; trials, 1862
Maclagan, bp.; Lichfield, 1878
Maclagan, Dr.; germ theory
Maclean, R.; trials, 1882
Macleod, H. D.; trials, 1858
Macleod, Mr.; United States, 1841
Macleod, Norman, D. D., 1812-72
Macleod, Dr.; glaciarium
Maclise, D., painter, 1811-70
M'Clure, capt.; Franklin, 1850; north-west passage
MacMahon, marshal, *b.* 1808; Magenta, 1859; Franco-Prussian, Sedan, France, 1873-8
McMillan, J.; trials, 1861
MacNamara, capt.; duels, 1803
M'Culloch, J. R., polit. econ., 1789-1864
McCulloch, sir Jas., Victoria, 1875-6
M'Neill, sir J.; Sebastopol, 1855
McCarty, gen.; Enniskillen, 1689
McClintock, capt.; Franklin, 1859
McGill, Mr.; trials, 1842
McKendrick, J. G.; Roy. Inst., 1881-4
McKenzie, Mr.; duel, 1788
McNaghten, sir W., killed, 1841
McNaughten, Mr.; trials, 1761, 1843
McSwiney, Mr., Ireland, 1875
Macready, W.; actor, 1793-1873
Macroath, Mr.; trials, 1841
Macrobius; Lat. writer, *d.* 415
Madan, M.; Peterborough, 1794
Madiai, the; Tuscany, 1852
Madison, James; United States, president, 1809
Mæcenas, *d.* 8; dedications, baths
Mælzel, J.; metronome, 1815
Magee, J.; trials, 1813; Guatemala, 1874
Magee, W. C., bp. Peterborough, 1868
Magellan; killed, 1521; circumnavigation, Philippine
Magi; fire worshippers, Epiphany
Magnin, C.; puppets, 1872
Magnus; king, Norway, Sweden
Maguire, capt.; Franklin, 1848
Magus, Simon; Simonians, heretics
Mahdi; Soudan.

INDEX. 1035

Mahomet, 570-632 ; Hegira, 622 ; Mahometanism, Mecca, Medina, Beder, Turkey, Koran
Mahomet II., d. 1481; eastern empire, Turkey, Adrianople, Constantinople, Albania
Mahony, F. (Prout), d. 1866
Maimonides (Maimoun), Moses, Jewish writer, d. 1208
Maine, sir H. J. S. ; jurist, 1822-88
Maitland, capt. ; France, 1815
Maitland, sir Fred. ; China, 1838
Majendie, bishop ; Chester, 1800
Major ; conchology, 1675
Majorian, coronation
Makart, J. ; painter, 1840-1884 ; Austria
Makomo, Kaffraria, 1873
Malachi prophesies about 397 B.C.
Malcolm ; Scotland, kings, clanships, Alnwick, Dunsinane
Malcolm, Jas. ; trials, 1885.
Malebranche, N. ; philos., 1638-1715
Malherbe ; Fr. poet, 1556-1628
Malibran, madame ; music, 1808-36
Malet, sir E. ; Egypt, 1881; Germany, 1884
Mallet, R. ; earthquakes, seismometer, 1858
Mallory, W. H. ; screw-propeller, 1878
Malmesbury, lord, b. 1807; Derby and Disraeli adms. 1852, 1858, 1874
Malon ; Belgium, 1871 ; 1884
Malpighi, M. ; anatomist, 1628-94
Maltby, bishop ; Durham, 1836
Malthus, T., 1766-1834, polit. econ.
Manasseh, Ben Israel ; Jews, 1657
Manby, capt. ; life-preserver, 1809
Mance, H., heliography
Manchester, bp. of, pub. worship reg. act, 1883
Manchester, earl of ; administrations, 1620
Manchester will ; trials, 1854
Man leville, visct. ; administrations, 1620
Manes, killed, 274 ; Manicheans
Manfred, killed, 1266 ; Naples
Manlius ; Cimbri, 102 B.C., Rome
Mann, Wm., air (compressing), 1829
Manners, lord John, b. 1818; Derby adm., 1852, 1858, 1866; Disraeli administrations, 1868, 1874 ; Reform, 1884 ; Salisbury adm., 1885, 1886, (duke of Rutland, 1888)
Manning, H., b. 1809 ; archbishop, 1865
Mannings ; murderers, trials, 1849
Manny, sir W. ; charter-house, 1371
Mansel, bishop ; Bristol, 1808
Mansell, T. ; executions, 1857
Mansfield, lord ; att.-gen. 1754 ; fictions in law, king's bench
Mansfield, C. B. ; benzole, 1849
Mantegazza, marchese, Italy, 1876
Mantell, G. A., weald
Manteuffel, gen., Franco-Pruss. war, 1870-1
Manuel ; Eastern empire, Trebizond
Manutius, see Aldus
Manzoni, A., Ital. nov., 1784-1873
Mapleson, Mr., national opera house, 1875
Mar, earl of ; Harlaw, 1411; Dumblain, 1715
Mar, earl of ; trials, 1831
Marat, stabbed ; France, 1793
Marbeck, J., concordance, 1550 ; chanting
Marceau, gen., killed, Altenkirchen, 1796
Marcel, S. ; communes, 1356
Marcellus ; Rome, 212 B.C.
March, H. ; executions, 1877
March, Roger, earl of ; rebellions, 1398
March, R. ; rope-making, 1784

Marchmont ; trials, 1858
Marcion ; Marcionites, 140
Marcus Aurelius ; Rome, emp. 161
Marcus Curtius ; Rome, 362 B.C.
Mardonius ; Mycale, Platæa, 497 B.C.
Margaret ; England, queen of Edward I.
Margaret of Anjou, England (queen of Henry VI.), d. 1481; Tewkesbury, Towton, Wakefield
Margaret of Norway ; Calmar, 1393
Margaret (governess of the Netherlands, 1559) ; beards
Margary, Mr., killed ; China, 1875-7
Margraff ; beet-root, 1747
Maria da Gloria ; Portugal, 1826
Maria Louisa, d. 1847 ; France, 1810, first empire; wills (Napoleon's)
Maria Theresa ; Germany, 1711
Marie Antoinette ; France, 1793 ; diamond necklace
Mariño, Hayti, 1880
Marius, d. 86 B.C. ; Ambrones, Cimbri
Mario, G. ; Italian singer, 1808 (?) -83
Marius ; pianoforte
Markham, abp. ; York, 1776
Marks, I. ; execution, 1877
Marlborough, earl of ; administrations, 1628
Marlborough, duchess of, Ireland, 1880
Marlborough, duke of, 1650-1722 ; com.-in-chief, marshals, Blenheim, Donay, Liege, Lisle, Malplaquet, Oudenarde, Ramilies
Marlborough, John, duke of, b. 1822; Derby adm., 1867 ; Disraeli adm., 1868, 1878, gems
Marlowe, Chr. ; dramatist, d. 1593
Marmont, marshal ; Salamanca, 1812
Marmontel, J. F., Fr. novel. 1723-99
Marot, Clement ; Fr. poet, 1495-1544
Maroto, gen., Spain, Vergara, 1839
Marsh, bp. ; Llandaff, 1816
Marsh, Catherine, convalescent institution, 1866
Marsh, professor ; Indians
Marshal, T. R. ; trials, 1859
Marshall, Mr. ; California, 1847
Marshall, capt., naval battles, 1778
Martel, Charles ; France, 714
Martel, France, 1879
Marten, Maria ; trials, 1828
Marth ; planets, 1854
Martial ; epigrams, fl. 100
Martin, John, painter, 1790-1854
Martin, Jon. ; York minster, 1829
Martin, L. H. ; Fr. hist., 1810-1883
Martin ; popes, 640 et seq.
Martin, Rd. ; animals, 1822
Martin, rev. G. ; suicide, 1860
Martin v. Mackonochie, Church of England, 1867-76
Martin, sir Theodore, b. 1816 ; Albert
Martineau, Harriet, hist. novelist, &c., 1802-76
Martyr, Peter, reformer, 1500-62
Marvell, And., d. 1678 ; ballot
Marvin, C. ; trials, 1878
Marx, C., socialists
Mary I., 1516-58 ; England (queen), 1553; Calais
Mary II., 1662-94 ; England (queen), 1689
Mary, queen of Scots, 1542-87; Scotland, Carlisle, Edinburgh, sycamore, Langside, Lochlevencastle, Fotheringay
Maryborough, lord ; postmaster, 1835
Masaniello ; Naples, 1647
Maskelyne, J. N., automaton, 1875
Maskelyne, N., astronomer, 1732-1811; Greenwich, 1765 ; almanacs, Schiehallien, Venus
Mason, Mr. ; U. States, 1861
Mason and Hamlin ; American organ

Mason, Josiah, orphan houses, Birmingham, 1869-75
Massena ; Zurich, 1799 ; Almeida, Busaco
Massey e. Headfort ; trials, 1804
Massey, W. ; India, 1865
Massillon, J. B. ; Fr. preacher, 1663-1742
Masupha, Basuto
Mathew, Theobald, d. 1856; temperance
Mathews, Chas. ; actor, 1776-1835 ; (son) C. J., 1803-78
Mathias ; anabaptists, 1534
Matilda ; England (queen of, William I.) ; Bayeux tapestry, 1066
Matilda ; England (queen of Stephen)
Matilda (empress) ; England, 1135
Matilda ; Denmark, 1772 ; Zell
Matilda, countess ; Canossa, 1077 ; Italy
Matthew, T., abp. ; York, 1606
Matthews, adm. ; Toulon, 1744
Matthews, H. ; Salisbury adm., 1886
Maud ; see Matilda
Maule, Fox (lord Panmure); Russell administration, 1846
Maule, J. B., prosecutor
Maunsell, bookseller ; meal-tub plot, 1679
Maunsell, Capt. C. S. ; trials, 1874
Maupertuis, P. L. de, 1698-1759; latitude
Maurer, J. and G. (German enthusiasts), killed ; Brazil, 1874
Maurice, rev. F. D., 1805-72 ; broad church, working-men's college, 1854
Maury, lieut. M., 1806-73 ; sea
Mausolus, 377 B.C. ; mausoleum, wonders
Maximilian ; emperors, Germany, 1493 ; Mexico, 1864-67
Maximin ; Rome, emp. 235 ; giants, persecutions
May, G. A. C. ; king's (or queen's) bench, 1877
May, S. E. ; parliament, 1886
Mayhew, H. (1812-1887); poor, 1551-2
Mayne, sir Richd., 1796-1868 ; police, 1829
Mayo, earl of, b. 1822 ; Disraeli adm. 1868 ; assassinated, 1872 ; India, Andaman
Mazarin, cardinal ; France, 1643 ; tontines ; printing, 1450
Mazzini, J., Ital. patriot, 1808-72 ; Rome, 1831 ; triumvirate, 1849
Mazzuoli, F. ; engraving, 1524
Mead, Dr. Rich., 1673-1754; inoculation
Mead, Geo., gen., 1816-72 ; United States, 1863
Meagher; Ireland, 1848
Mecklenburg, grand duke, Franco-Pruss. war, 1870-1
Medall, M. ; Alps (tunnel), 1848
Medhurst, Frs. H. ; trials, 1839
Medici ; Medici family
Medicis, Catherine de, d. 1589 ; Bartholomew, St.
Medina-Sidonia, duke of ; armada
Medon ; Athens, 1044 B.C.
Mehemet Ali ; Egypt, Syria
Mehemet Ali ; Russo-Turkish war, II., 1877
Mehemet Ruchdi, Turkey, 1871-2
Meikle, A., threshing machine, 1776
Melanchthon, Philip, 1497-1560 ; adiaphorists, Augsburg confession
Melas, general ; Marengo, 1800
Melbourne, viscount, 1779-1849 ; Melbourne ; trials, 1836
Melikoff, L. Aladja Dagh ; Russo-Turkish war, II., 1877 ; Russia, 1880-1
Mellon, Miss (afterwards duchess of St. Alban's), first appearance, 1795

Melville, lord ; impeachment, 1806
Memnon said to invent alphabet, 1822 B.C.
Menabrea, count L. F. ; Italy, 1867
Menander, d. 291 B.C. ; drama
Mendelssohn, F. Bartholdy, 1809-47
Mendiri ; Spain, 1874-5
Mendizabal ; Spain, 1835
Mendoza, Pedro de; Buenos Ayres, 1530
Menier ; balloons, 1874
Menou, general ; Alexandria, 1800
Menschikoff, prince ; holy places, 1853; Russia, Alma, Russo-Turkish war
Mercadier, M., teleradiophone
Mercator, Ger., 1512-94 ; charts
Mercedes (queen) ; Spain, 1878
Mercier, C. H. ; hospital Saturday, 1874
Mérimée, Prosper, Fr. hist., 1803-70
Merovæus ; Merovingians, France, 448
Mesentzoff, gen. ; assassinated, Russia, 1878
Mesmer, Frederic Ant.; mesmerism, 1766
Metastasio, Pet., It. poet, 1698-1782
Metellus ; Achaia, 147 B.C.
Metius ; telescopes, 1590-1609
Meton ; golden number, 432 B.C.
Metternich, prince, Aust. statesman, 1773-1859
Metz, M. de ; reformatory, 1839
Meux and Co.; porter
Meyer, H. von, archæopteryx, 1861
Meyer, Simon; Saturn, 1608-9-10
Meyerbeer, J. M., Germ. mus., 1794-1864
Meyerstein, E.; printing (in colours), 1876
Mezentius ; Indiction, 312
Miall, E., 1809-81 ; nonconformists
Micah, prophesies about 750 B.C.
Michael Angelo Buonaroti, Ital. artist, 1474-1564
Michael ; eastern empire, assassinations, Servia, 1860-8
Michael, grand duke ; Russo-Turkish war, 1877
Michaelis, J. W., bib. critic, 1717-91
Michaud, abbé ; old catholics, 1872
Michel, Louise ; France, 1883
Michelet, J., Fr. hist., b. 1798
Middlesex, earl of; administrations, 1621
Middleton, Con. ; (Cicero), 1683-1750
Middleton, gen., Canada, 1885
Middleton ; N.W. passage, 1742
Middleton (or Myddelton), sir Hugh, 1565-1631 ; New River
Middleton, John ; giants, 1578
Middleton, rev. T. ; Manchester, 1876
Midhat Pasha, Turkey, 1878-81, Syria
Mieclslas ; Poland, 962
Mieroslawski, L. ; Poland, 1863
Mignet, François, Fr. hist., 1796-1884
Miguel, dom, 1802-66 ; Portugal, 1824
Milan ; Servia
Mildmay, sir J. H. ; trials, 1814
Mildmay, sir Walter; administrations, 1579
Mill, Jas., hist. of Ind., 1773-1836
Mill, John Stuart, 1806-1873, logic
Millais, J. E., painter, b. 1829 ; preRaphaelites
Miller, Hugh ; geology, suicide, 1856
Miller v. Salomons ; trials, 1852
Miller, W.; trials, 1870
Millie, Mr. ; trials, 1839
Milman, H. H., 1791-1868 ; poet and hist.
Milosch ; Servia, 1815
Miltiades ; Marathon, 490 B.C.
Milton, John, 1608-74 ; Paradise Lost, Cripplegate ; press, liberty of
Mina, gen., d. 1836 ; Spain, 1835
Minghetti ministry ; Italy, 1873-6

Minos ; Crete, 1015 B.C.
Minto, earl of; India, gov.-gen., 1807
Miramon, gen.; Mexico, 1859 ; executed, 1867
Mirès, M.; Mexico, 1861
Miraky, L., Russia, 1879
Mister, Josiah; trials, 1841
Mitchell, sir F.; monopolies, victuallers, 1621
Mitchell, D.; aquarium, 1853
Mitchell, adm.; Bantry bay, 1801-2
Mitchell, J.; Ireland, 1848, 1874
Mitchell, S.; Glasgow, 1874
Mitford, sir John; att.-general, 1800; speaker, 1801 ;—W., hist. of Greece, 1744-1827
Mithridates the Great, 131-63 B.C.; Pontus, comets, electuary, massacres, omens
Mitre, gen. B.; Buenos Ayres, 1859-75
Moffat, colonel; wrecks, 1857
Moffat, Dr. C. ; ammoniaphone
Moffat, Rev. R., 1790-1882 ; missionary ; Africa
Mohun, lord; duels, 1712
Moir, capt.; trials, 1830
Moira, earl of; India, gov.-gen., 1813
Moiroso, Basuto
Molé, count, d. 1855
Molesworth, sir William ; Aberdeen adm., 1852
Molière, Fr. comic dram., 1622-73 ; comédie Franç.
Molinos, 1627-96 ; quietists
Molteno, Mr. ; Cape, 1875
Molyneux, Mr.; absentee, 1738
Mompesson, Giles; monopolies, victuallers, 1621
Monasterio, mad. ; France, 1883
Moncasi, J. O., Spain, 1878
Monck, visct. C. S., b. 1819; Canada, 1861
Moncrieff, capt.; cannon, 1868, 1872
Monge, gas
Monk, general ; administrations, 1660 ; guards ; d. 1670
Monk, bishop; Gloucester, 1830
Monmouth, duke of, 1649-85 ; Monmouth, Bothwell, Sedgemoor, iron mask
Monro, James ; police, 1888
Monroe, Mr.; United States, president, 1817-21
Monstrelet, E. de, French historian, d. 1453
Montacute, marquis of ; Man, 1314-43
Montagu, lord ; administrations, 1660-89
Montagu, lady M.W.; inoculation, 1718
Montague, Mrs., d. 1800; May-day
Montaigne, M. de, Fr. essayist, 1533-92
Montalembert, comte de; 1810-70 ; France, 1858
Montanus ; Montanists, polyglot, 1559
Montefiore, sir Moses, 1784-1885 ; Jews, 1837 ; 1883-4
Moutemolin, comte de; Spain, 1860-1
Montero, pres. Peru, 1881
Montesquieu, C. de L., Fr. phil., 1689-1755
Monteverde ; opera, 1607
Montfort, Amauri de ; Albigenses, 1268
Montfort, Simon de; barons' war, commons, Kenilworth, steward, lord high, speaker, Lewes ; killed at Evesham, 1265
Montgolfier, M.; balloons, 1782
Montgomerie, comte de ; tournaments, 1559
Montgomery, Mr. ; suicide, duels," 1803 ; trials, 1873
Montholon, comte de; will (Napoleon's), 1821
Monti, Ital. poet, 1754-1828
Montpensier ; France, Spanish marriage, 1846 ; Spain, 1868-72

Montrose, duke of ; Pitt adm. 1804, Derby adm., 1866
Montrose, marquis of, executed, 1650 ; Corbiesdale, Scotland, Alford, Philiphaugh
Moody and Sankey ; revivals, 1875
Moore, abp.; Canterbury, 1783
Moore ; almanac, 1698-1713
Moore, murdered ; trials, 1853
Moore, capt.; Franklin, 1848
Moore, serjeant; leases, 1535
Moore, Anne ; abstinence, 1808
Moore, Geo. ; mansion house fund, 1871
Moore, sir John, k. at Corunna, 1809
Moore, sir Jonas ; Greenwich
Moore, Thos., poet, 1780-1852
Morales, H. A., Bolivia, 1872
Mordaunt, Charles, viscount ; administrations, 1689
Mordaunt divorce ; trials, 1870, 1874-5
More, sir Thomas, 1480-1535 ; administrations, 1529 ; chancellor, supremacy
More, Hannah, 1745-1833
More, Roger ; rebellion, 1651
Moreau, general, 1763-1813 ; Alessandria, Augsburg, Würtemberg, Dresden
Morelli ; tourniquet, 1674
Moreton, John, earl of; Ireland, 1177
Morgan ; buccaneer, 1668
Morgan, colonel ; Lincoln
Morgan, confederate general ; U. States, 1862
Morgan, Pritchard ; gold, 1887
Moriarty, bp. Ireland, 1877
Morier, sir R. ; Prussia, 1888
Moriones, gen. ; Spain, 1873-5
Morland, Sam., d. 1695 ; capstan, speaking-trumpet
Morland, Geo., animal painter, 1763-1804
Morley, J., b. 1838 ; anti-aggressive ; Pall Mall ; Gladstone adm., 1886
Morley, T.; music ; d. 1604
Morley, ld. ; Gladstone adm., 1886
Morning Chronicle ; trials, 1810, 1830 ; France, 1862
Morning Herald ; trials, 1809
Morning Post ; libel, 1792
Mornington, lord ; India, 1798
Morpeth, viscount (aft. earl of Carlisle) ; Melbourne adm., 1835 ; Ireland, lord-lieut.
Morris, George ; flowers, 1792
Morris, Mr. ; theatres, 1805
Morrison, F. ; Australia, 1882-3
Morse, S. F. B., Am. electrician, 1791-1872
Mortara, E.; Jews, 1858
Mortier, mar. ; Romainville, 1814
Mortimer, E. A.; trials, 1859
Mortimer, earl of March ; Berkeley, 1327
Morton, arch.; Canterbury, 1486
Morton, earl of, regent of Scotland, 1572 ; Tulchan bishops
Morton, sir Albert ; administrations, 1628
Morton, Thomas ; ether, 1846
Morton ; trials, 1852
Moryson, Fynes ; forks
Moscrop, E. H., salmon ova
Moseley, Wolf, &c.; trials, 1819
Moses, 1572-1451 B.C.
Moshesh, cape of G. H., 1879
Mosquera, gen. ; New Granada, 1861
Moss, bishop ; Oxford, 1807
Mosse, Dr. ; lying-in hospital, 1745
Mossol, M., plethysmograph
Most, J., trials, 1881
Mothe-Guyon, madame de la ; quietists, 1697
Motley, J. L., Am. historian, 1814-77
Mouchot, M., sun, 1880
Moule, Rev. H. ; Kimmeridge
Mountaigne, abp. ; York, 1628

Mount-Sandford, lord, killed; trials, 1828
Mouravieff; Kars, 1855
Mourzoufle; Constantinople, eastern empire, 1204
Mozart, W. A.; music, 1756-91
Mudie, C; circulating library, 1842
Muirhead, J. G.; trials, 1825
Mukhtar Pasha, Turkey, 1876; Russo-Turkish war, II. 1877-8
Mulgrave, earl; Liverpool adm., 1812; Ireland, lord-lieut.
Mullens, J.; trials, 1860
Müller, F.; execution, 1864
Müller, F. Max, b. 1823; Vedas, Sanskrit, language, Hibbert fund
Müller, Geo.; b. 1805; orphan houses; scripture knowledge
Mulot, M.; Artesian well, 1841
Mulready, Wm.; painter, 1786-1863
Mummius, L.; Corinth, 146 B.C.; painting
Mundella, A. J.; Gladstone adm., 1886
Mundy, R. M., Honduras, 1874
Munich, marshal; Perekop, 1736
Muñoz, duke; Spain, 1833, 1873
Munro, H.; Buxar, 1764
Munster, earl of; suicide, 1842
Münzer, T.; anabaptists, 1524-5, levellers; Frankenhausen
Murat, Joachim, 1771-1815; Erfurt, Naples
Muratori, L.; hist., 1672-1750
Murchison, sir Roderick I., 1792-1871; geology, Brit. Assoc.
Murdoch, Mr.; gas, 1792
Murillo, Bravo, Spain, 1865, 1868
Murillo, B. S., Sp. painter, 1618-82
Murray, R.; post-office, 1681
Murray, earl of; Scotland, 1567
Murray, lady Aug.; marriage act, 1793
Murray, B.; trials, 1841
Murray, bishop; David's, St., 1800
Murray, James, earl of, Scotland, 1567; assassinations
Murray, John; lighthouse
Murray, sir Geo.; Peel adm., 1834
Murray, sir James; Tarragona, 1813
Murray, Dr. J. H.; dictionaries
Murrell, capt.; wrecks, 1889
Musa; Spain, 712
Musæus, fl. 1413 B.C.
Musgrave, abp.; Hereford. 1837
Musgrave, sir Richard; duel, 1802:—sir A., Jamaica, 1876; Queensland, 1883
Mushat, Mr.; steel, 1800
Muswell Hill, burglary; trials, 1889
Muybridge, E. J.; photography, 1881; zoopraxiscope
Myall, rhubarb
Myddelton, sir Hugh, 1565?-1631; New River
Mylne, R.; architect, 1734-1811; Blackfriars
Myron, sculptor, fl. 480 B.C.
Mytton, general; Wales, 1645

N.

Nabis; Sparta, 206 B.C.
Nabonassar, fl. 747 B.C.; astronomy
Nachimoff, admiral; Sinope, 1853
Nadar; balloon, 1863
Nadir Shah; Persia, 1732; Delhi, Afghanistan, Cabul
Nagel, H., trials, 1872
Nahum prophesies about 713 B.C.
Nana Sahib; Cawnpore, India, 1857
Napier of Merchiston; logarithms; Napier's bones, 1614
Napier, admiral sir C.; Portugal, Sidon, cape St. Vincent, Baltic, 1854
Napier, gen. sir C.; Meeanee, 1843

Napier, lord; China; Edinburgh; United States, 1856
Napier, Mr.; coin, 1844
Napier, sir R., aft. lord (of Magdala), b. 1810; Abyssinia, 1867; Arogee, Magdala, Gibraltar, 1876
Napoleon, Jerome, 1784-1860; son, b. 1822, France, 1851-76; Bonaparte
Napoleon I., 1769-1821, France, abattoirs, Bonaparte, confederation, legion of honour, models, notables, Cairo, Egypt, Elba, Fontainebleau, Malta, Mamelukes, St Helena, Simplon, vaccination; his battles: Acre, Arcola, Asperne, Auerstadt, Austerlitz, Bautzen, Borodino, Castiglione, Charleroi, Dresden, Eckmühl, Essling, Eylau, Friedland, Hanau, Italy, Jena, La Rothière, Leipsic, Ligny, Lodi, Lutzen, Marengo, Montereau, National guard, Pultusk, St. Dizier, Simplon, Tilsit, Troyes, Vienna, Waterloo, Wurtzburg
Napoleon II., king of Rome; France, p. 380
Napoleon III., 1808-73; France, (sovereigns); Boulogne, Strasburg, Cherbourg, Italy, Magenta, Solferino, Sedan, wills, assassinations
Napoleon, imperial prince, b. 1856; Bonaparte; France, 1873-6, Saarbrück
Nares, capt., deep sea, 1872; northwest passage, 1874-8; soundings
Narses; East, empire, 552; Goths, Italy, Rome
Narvaez, gen. Ramon, 1800-1868; Spain, 1846
Nash, Beau, 1674-1761; Bath, ceremonies
Nash, Mr.; theatres, parks, 1818
Nash, Jos., architect, 1812-78
Nasmyth, J.; steam-hammer, 1838; moon
Nasmyth, lieut.; Silistria, 1854
Nasr-ed-Din; Persia, 1848-73
Naville, M. Egypt. expl. fund
Nearchus; sugar, 325 B.C.
Neave and others, trials, 1875
Nebuchadnezzar; Jews, 605 B.C.; Tyre, Babylon
Necho; Egypt, 634 B.C.
Neil, col.; India, 1857; Allahabad, Benares
Neild; legacy to the queen, 1852
Neilson, J., 1792-1865; blowing-machine, 1828
Nelson, Edm.; moon, 1876
Nelson, Horatio, admiral lord, 1758-1805; Nelson
Nero; Rome, emperor, 54
Nesselrode, comte de, Russian statesman, 1780-1862
Newall, R. S.; electric telegraph, 1840
Newcastle, marquis of; Marstonmoor, 1644
Newcastle, duke of; Pelham adm. 1749; Newcastle adm., 1754; Aberdeen adm., 1852
Newcomb, prof. S.; photo-tachometer
Newcomen, T., steam, 1712
Newenham, W. B.; trials, 1844
Newington, H. (Flora Davey), trials, 1871
Newman, rev. J., and Achilli; trials, 1852; Tractarians
Newport, sir John; exchequer, 1834
Newsham, R.; Preston, 1883
Newton, sir Isaac, 1642-1727; air, binomial, coin, diamond, astronomy, royal society, hydrostatics, gravitation, mechanics
Ney, marshal, 1769-1815; Dennewitz, France, Quatre-Bras, Ulm, Ney
Noyle, archbp.; York, 1632

Nez Percés, Indians
Niccoli, Nicholas; libraries, 1436
Nicephori, emperors; east. empire, 802-963
Nicephorus; comets
Nicholas I., Russia, 1825-55
Nicholas V.; popes, 1447-55; St. Peter's, Rome
Nicholas, grand duke, Russo-Turkish war II., 1877
Nicholls, comm. navy, 1884
Nichols, col.; New York, 1664
Nichols, H., Manchester, 1875
Nicholson; trials, 1813
Niebuhr, B. H.; hist., 1776-1831
Niépce; photography, 1814, velocipedes, 1818
Niger, P.; Rome, emp.; killed, 127
Nightingale, F., b. 1820; Scutari, Nightingale
Nikita, Montenegro, 1860
Nilsson, Mr., prehistoric archæology
Ninus; Assyria, 2059 B.C.
Nisbet, sir John; advocates, 1685
Nixon, Alf.; velocipede, 1882
Noad, H. M.; electricity, 1855
Noah, 2347 B.C.; ark, Armenia
Noailles, marshal; Dettingen, 1743
Nobel, Alf.; nitro-glycerine, 1864, dynamite, 1868; blasting gelatine
Nobel, L. & R.; petroleum, 1875
Nobert, F. A.; ruling machine
Nodiling, Dr.; Germany, 1878
Noble, Matt., sculptor, 1820-76
Nordenskjöld, professor, north-east, &c., 1872-3
Norfolk, duke of; administrations, 1540; people; catholic union, 1871
Norman, sir H.; Jamaica, 1883
Norman, sir J.; mayor, 1453
Norman, Robert; magnet, 1576
Norman, justice, murdered, India, 1871
Normanby and Buckingham, duke of; Godolphin adm., 1702
Normanby, marquis of; Ireland (lord-lieut.), 1835; Queensland, 1871; Victoria, 1879
Normandy, Dr.; filterers
North, bishop; Winchester, 1781
North, lord; North adm., 1770
North, sir F.; king's counsel, 1663
North, miss M.; Kew, 1882
Northampton, Henry, earl of; administrations, 1609
Northbrook, ld., India, 1872; earl of, admiralty, 1880, 1885
Northcote, sir Stafford, 1818-87; Derby adm., 1866; Disraeli adm., 1868, 1874; parliament, 1881; Suez, 1883; earl of Iddesleigh, Salisbury adm. 1885, 1886
Northcott and others, trials, 1876
Northmore, gas
Northumberland, Algernon, duke of; Derby administration, 1852; —Algernon George, Disraeli administration, 1878; Royal Institution
Northumberland, Dudley, duke of; administrations, 1551
Northumberland, Hugh, duke of; Ireland (lord-lieut.), 1763
Northumberland, earl of; coaches. Man
Norton, sir Fletcher; att.-gen., 1763
Norton, Jeffrey de; recorder, 1298
Norton v. lord Melbourne; trials, 1836
Nostradamus; almanacs, 1566
Nott, gen.; Ghiznee, 1842
Nottingham, earl of; administrations, 1684
Novalches, marquis de, Spain, 1868, Alcolea, 1868
Nubar Pacha, Cairo, Egypt, 1876-9
Numa Pompilius; Rome, kings 715 B.C.; calendar

1038 INDEX.

Numitor, Alba. 795 B.C.
Nuñez, A.; Paraguay, 1535

O.

Oakley, sir Charles; Madras, 1792
Oakley, R. B., trials, 1876
Oates, T.; Oates' plot, 1678
Obadiah prophesies about 587 B.C.
Obeid-ullah, Kurdistan
O'Brien, king; Limerick, 1200
O'Brien, W.; Ireland, 1886 et seq. trials, 1889
O'Brien, W. S.; Ireland, 1846, 1848
O'Brien, giants, 1785
O'Connell, Mr. Daniel, 1775-1847; duels, 1815; agitators, emancipation, repeal, trials (1831, 1844), Ireland ; Dublin, 1883
O'Connell, Mr. Morgan; duels, 1835
O'Connor, Arthur; press, riots, trials, 1798
O'Connor, Fergus, d. 1855; chartists
O'Connor, Roger; trials, 1817
Ochus; Persia, 359 B.C.
Octavius; Rome, 37 B.C.
Odin; Sweden, 70 B.C.
Odo, earl of Kent; treasurer
Odo, abp.; Canterbury, 941-58
Odoacer; Italy, 476, Heruli
O'Donnell, marshal Leopold, 1808-67; Spain 1841
O'Donnell, Mr.; parliament, 1882
O'Donnell v. Walter; Parnellites, 1888
Œdipus; Bœotia, 1266 B.C.
Œnotrus; Arcadia, Greece, 1710 B.C.
Oersted, H. C., 1777-1851; electricity, 1819
Ofenheim (financier), Austria, 1875
Ogle, George; duel, 1802
Oglethorpe, gen.; Georgia, 1732
O'Grady, Mr.; duels, 1803
Ogyges; deluge, 1764 B.C.
O'Hagan, lord chancellor (Ireland) 1868; Roman catholics; d. 1883
O'Halloran, Dr.; trials, 1818
O'Keefe; trials, 1825
O'Keeffe v. Cullen, trials, 1873
O'Kelly, Mr.; parliament, 1883
Oken, German union, 1822
Okubo, Japan, 1878
Olbers, M.; planet, 1802
Oldcastle, sir J., burnt, 1418; Lollards
O'Leary, pedestrianism, 1877
Oliphant, sir Wm., advocate
Olivarez governs Spain, 1621-43
Oliver; trials, 1858, 1869
Ollendorff, H. G. (linguist); 1803-65
Ollivant, bp.; Llandaff, 1849
Ollivier, E.; France, 1870
O'Loghlen, sir M.; Roman catholics, 1836
Olozaga, Spain, 1871
O'Mahony, Fenians, 1877
Omar, caliph, 634; Alexandria, Ali
Omar Pacha; Citate, Montenegro, Oltenitza, Ingour, Russo-Turkish war, 1855
Ommaney, capt.; Franklin, 1850
O'Moore, Rory; Carlow, 1577
O'Neil, rebellion; massacre, Blackwater, 1598
O'Neil, Miss (lady Becher), appears at Covent Garden, 1814; d. 1872
Onslow, G. and Whalley, G. H.; trials 1872
Onslow, sir R.; Halifax adm., 1714
Opie, John; painter, 1761-1807
Oppian, poet, fl. 171
Orange, William, prince of; Holland, Maestricht, revolution, 1572; England, 1689; assassinations
Orange, prince of; Quatre Bras, 1815
Orbellana; Circassia, 1857
Ord, sir H. St. G., West Australia, 1877

Orellana; Amazonia, 1540
Orestes; Mycenæ, Sparta, 1175 B.C.
Orilia, M. J.; physician, 1787-1853
Orford, earl of; admiralty, 1709
Orloff, count; diamonds, 1772
Ormond, James, duke of; Ireland, lord-lieuts., 1643 et seq.
Ormond, earl of; combat, 1446
Ormond, marquis of; Rathmines, 1640
Orr, Wm.; trials, 1797
Orrery, earl of; orrery
Orrock; trial, 1884
Orsini, Felix, 1819-58; France, 1858
Ortega, gen.; Spain, 1860
Osborn, Sherard; Franklin, 1854
Osborne, sir Thomas; administrations, 1672
Osborne, T., Ireland, young
Oscar; Sweden, 1844
Osgodeby, Adam de; master of the rolls, 1295
Osman Digna; Soudan
Osman Pacha, Plevna, Russo-Turkish war II., 1877
Ospina; New Grenada, 1857
Ossory, lord; tea, 1666
Osymandyas; Egypt, 2100 B.C.; observatories, painting
Othman; Turkey, 1298
Otho; Rome, emp., 69; Germany, 936; Greece, 1832-62
Otto, gas (engine)
Otto, M.; Amiens, 1802
Ottocar; Bohemia, 1197
Oudinot, marshal; Rome, 1849
Oudry, cafeine
Outram, sir James; 1803-63; Mohammerah, India, 1857
Ouvry, F.; antiquaries, 1876
Overbury, sir T., poisoned, 1613
Overdank; assassin, Austria, 1881
Overend, Gurney, & Co.; trials, 1867
Overstone, S., Jones Loyd, lord, financier, 1796-1883; metric system, 1855
Ovid; poet, d. 18
Owden, J. S., mayor, 1877-8
Owen, W. D.; trials, 1858
Owen, Robert; socialists, 1834
Owen, Richard, b. 1804; odontology, palæontology, zoology
Owen, sir P. C.; colonial exhibition 1886
Owens, J., Owens college
Oxenden, sir George; Surat, 1664
Oxford, Edward; trials, 1840
Oxford, earl of; Godolphin adm., 1702; Oxford adm.
Oxford, John, earl of; yeomen, 1486
Oxley; Brisbane, Queensland, 1823

P.

Paciolo; algebra, 1494
Paddon, lieut., takes Cerbère, 1800
Paderborn, bp. of; Prussia, 1874
Page, Flood, crystal palace, 1874
Page, telephone, 1837
Paget, lord; duels, trials, 1807
Paget, lord Wm., v. Cardigan; trials, 1844
Paget, sir A.; trials, 1808
Paget, J.; paradoxes
Paget, sir William; administns., 1547
Pain, O.; Soudan, 1885
Paine, Thomas; trials, 1792
Pakington, sir John, b. 1799; Derby and Disraeli adm.
Palafox, gen.; Saragossa, 1809
Palamedes; alphabet, backgammon, battle, dice, chess, 680 B.C.
Palestrina, 1529-94; music; requiem
Palissa, J.; planets

Palladio, A.; architect, 1518-80
Pallavicino, G., Italy, 1878
Palles, Christ.; exchequer (Ireland), 1874
Palliser, capt., cannon, 1866
Palliser, sir Hugh; Ushant, 1778
Palm, the bookseller; trials, 1806
Palm, cardinal, shot; Rome, 1848
Palmer, J.; mail coaches, 1784
Palmer; duels, 1815; trials, 1856
Palmer, poet, and others murdered; Egypt, 1882; Paul's, St.
Palmer, Roundell; see Selborne
Palmer, S., Times (index)
Palmerston, Henry, visc.; 1784-1865; Palmerston, lady, d. 1869
Panckoucke, C. J.; Moniteur, 1789
Panizzi, sir Antonio; British Museum, 1859
Panmure, lord; Russell adm., 1851
Paoli, Pascal; Corsica, 1753
Papachin, adm.; flag, 1688
Papin; steam-engine, 1681
Papineau; Canada, 1837
Papirius Cursor; sun-dial, 293 B.C.
Pappa, D.; trials, 1870
Paracelsus, 1493-1541; alchemy, physic, theosophists
Pardo, president, Peru, 1879
Pareja, adm.; Chili, 1865
Parini, Guis., Ital. poet, 1729-99
Paris, count of, b. 1838; Orleans
Parke, Mungo, d. 1805; Africa
Parke v. Lewis and others; trials, 1873
Parker, Emily; swimming, 1875
Parker, adm.; Copenhagen, 1801
Parker, Dr.; temple
Parker, abp. Matthew; Canterbury, 1558; liturgy, Nag's Head
Parker (mutineer); trials, 1797
Parker, capt.; Boulogne
Parker, J. H., Rome
Parker, sir Peter; Bellair, 1814
Parker, Thomas, lord; chancellor, lord, 1718
Parkes, sir H., 1828-85; consul; China, 1860-1883
Parma, duke of; Parma
Parma, prince of; Antwerp, 1585
Parmenio; Macedonia, 329 B.C.
Parnell, sir Henry; Melbourne adm. 1835
Parnell, C. S., Biggar, and others; parliament (obstructives), 1877-81; home rule, 1880; trials, 1880-1; Ireland, 1883, et seq.; Kilmainham; Home Rule; Parnellites
Parr, Thomas; 1483-1635? longevity
Parrhasius; painting; fl. 397 B.C.
Parrot, Dr., Ararat
Parry, bp., church of England
Parry, E.; north-west passage, 1818
Parsons, bp.; Peterborough, 1813
Parsons, P.M., brass, manganese, bronze
Parsons family; cock-lane ghost, impostors, 1762
Pascal, B.; 1623-62; air, calculating machine, barometers, probability, hydrostatics
Passaglia, father, 1814-87; Italy, 1862.
Passanante, G., Italy, 1878
Paskiewitch; Silistria, 1854
Pasta, mad., vocalist, 1798-1865
Pasteur, Dr.L.; fermentation, 1861; germ theory; hydrophobia; vaccination
Patch, Mr.; trials, 1806
Pate, lieut.; trials, 1850
Paterculus, Rom. hist., d. 31
Paterson, W.; bank, 1694; Darien
Paton, Miss, at Haymarket, 1822
Paton, Dr., pyroleter
Patrick, St., preaches, 433; Ardagh, Armagh, Dublin, isles, shamrock
Patrocinio, nun; Spain, 1861, 1866

INDEX. 1039

Patten, col. John W., b. 1802; Disraeli adm.
Patteson, J. C., Melanesia, murdered, 1871
Paul, St., martyred, 65
Paul, see *Sarpi*
Paul I.; Russia, 1796
Paul II.; popes, 1464; purple printing, 1819
Paul, sir J., &c.; trials, 1855; fraudulent trustees
Paulinus; bells, 400
Paull, Mr.; duels, 1807
Paululio, Anafesto; doge, 697
Paulus Æmilius; Cannæ, 216 B.C.
Paulus, Marcus; compass, 1260
Paulus; Abrahamites
Pauncefote; United States, 1839
Pausanias; Sparta, 480 B.C.; Platæa, Macedon, 336 B.C.
Pausias of Sicyon, 360-330 B.C.; painting
Pavey, G., trials, 1880
Pavia, gen.; Spain, 1873-4
Paxton, sir Joseph, 1803-65; exhibition of 1851; crystal palace
Payne, L., trials, 1879
Payne, Mr. G.; duels, 1810
Payne, J. H.; home!
Peabody, G., 1795-1869; Peabody
Peace, C., trials, 1878
Peace, the prince of the; Spain, 1806
Pearce, &c.; gold robbery, 1857
Pearson, col., Zululand, 1879
Pease, W., Benwell
Peaucillier; motion
Peckham, abp.; Canterbury, 1279
Pedro; Portugal, Brazil, 1822
Peek v. Gurney; trials, 1871
Peel, A. W.; speaker H. C., 1884
Peel, capt. sir F.; India, 1858
Peel, col.; West Australia, 1828
Peel, sir Robert; cotton manuf., 1750-1830;—(*son*) statesman, 1788-1850; Peel adm. (see *note*), 1834-1841; acts of parliament, conservative, corn bill, duels, 1815; income-tax, tariff; — (*grandson*), b. 1822
Peele, James; book-keeping, 1509
Pelham, H.; Wilmington adm., 1742; Pelham adm., 1744
Pelham, bp.; Bristol, 1807; Norwich, 1857
Pelham, sir W.; engineers, 1622
Pelissier, duc de Malakhoff; 1794-1864; Algiers, Dahra
Pell, Mr.; education, 1876
Pelletier; quinine, 1820
Pellew, sir Ed.; naval battles, 1795
Pelouze, F. J., 1807-1867; formic acid
Peltier, M.; libel, trials, 1803
Peitzen, A. & L., murderers; Belgium, 1882
Pemberton, sir Francis; king's bench, 1681
Pembroke, earl of; Godolphin adm. 1702; lord-lieutenant, Lincoln, protectorates, Salisbury; admiralty
Pengelly, W.; man
Penn, admiral; Jamaica, 1655
Penn, Wm., 1644-1718; Pennsylvania, Quaker
Penny, captain; Franklin, 1850
Penzance, lord (Wilde); arches, 1876; public worship
Pépé, gen. F.; Naples, 1820
Pepin; France, 752; Ferara
Pepper, prof.; Polytechnic, telephone
Pepys, bp.; Worcester, 1841; Pepys
Perceval, Spencer; Perceval
Percy (Hotspur); Otterburn, 1388
Percy, lord; Durham, 1346; Homildon
Percy, John; metallurgist, 1817-89
Perilccas; Macedon, 454 B.C.
Perlita, Mrs. Robinson; theatres, last app., 1779
Péreire, M.; credit mobilier

Pereyra; Uruguay, 1856
Pericles; Athens, 469 B.C.
Périer, C.; France, 1874-6
Perillus; brazen bull, 570 B.C.
Perkin Warbeck; Warbeck, 1492
Perkin, W. H.; aniline, 1857
Perkins; engraving, copper-plate printing, 1819
Perreaus; forgery, trials, 1776
Perring, John; mayor, 1803
Perrotin; planets
Perry, Mr.; trials, 1810
Perry, lieut.; trials, 1854
Persano, adm.; Lissa, Italy, 1866-7
Perseus; Pydna, 168 B.C.
Persigny, J. G., 1808-72; France, 1860
Persius, 34-62; satires
Perugino, Paolo, 1446-1524
Peter the Cruel; Montiel, 1369
Peter the Great; 1672-1725; Russia, Deptford, Petersburg, Narva, Pultowa, wills
Peter the Hermit; crusades, 1094
Peters, C. H. F.; planets, 1862, *et seq.*
Peters, Dr. C.; Zanzibar, 1889
Petion; Port-au-Prince, 1806
Peto, S. M., b. 1809; diorama, 1855
Petrarch, 1304-74; Petrarch, sonnets, humanism
Petre, sir Wm.; administrations, 1547
Petronius; Ethiopia, 22 B.C.
Petronius Arbiter, Lat. satirist, d. 66
Pettigrew, T.; epitaphs, 1857
Petty, lord H.; Grenville adm., 1807
Petty, Wm.; Royal Society, 1660
Pezet, J. A.; Peru, 1863-5
Phædrus writes fables, 8
Phalaris, brazen bull, 599 B.C.
Pharamond; France, 418?
Pharaohs; Egypt, 1899 B.C.
Pharnaces; Pontus, Cappadocia, 744 B.C.
Phayre, col.; India, 1874
Phayre, sir A. P.; Mauritius, 1874
Pheidon, *fl.* 869 B.C.; coinage, silver, scales, weights
Phelps, Mr. S., 1804-78; theatres (Sadler's Wells), 1844, 1878
Phepoe, Mrs.; trials, 1797
Phidias, *fl.* 43 B.C.; statues
Philidor, concerts, chess
Philip; France, Macedon, Spain, Hesse, Orleans, 1640
Philip Neri, St.; oratorios, 1550
Philip the Good; Burgundy, Holland, 1419-67
Philip the Great, killed 336 B.C.; Macedon, Ætolia, Chæronæa, Locri, Thessaly
Philip II.; Spain, 1556
Philippa, England, queen (Edward III.); Durham, 1346
Philipps, T.; Newport, 1839
Phillimore, sir R. J., 1810-85; admiralty
Phillip, gov.; Australia, 1788
Phillips, J.; Brit. Assoc., 1831;—fire-annihilator, 1849
Phillips, John, geologist; Vesuvius, 1869
Phillips *v.* Eyre; trials, 1869-70
Phillips, Wendell; United States, 1884
Philopœmen; Achaia, 194 B.C.
Philpott; bp.; Worcester, 1861
Philpotts, H., bp.; Exeter, 1830
Philpotts *v.* Boyd; reredos, 1875
Phipps, capt.; north-west passage, 1773
Phocas; east. emp., 602
Phocion, killed 317 B.C.
Phoroneus; Argos (1807 B.C.), sacrifice, laws
Photiades, C. J.; Samos
Photius, Gallus; rhetoric, 87 B.C.
Piastus; Poland, 842
Piazzi, M.; planet, 1801

Picard, sir H.; lord mayor, 1357
Pichegru; Manheim; suicide, 1804
Pictet, R., air, gases, 1877, oxygen, hydrogen, distillation; nav. architecture
Picton, gen.; trials, 1806; Quatre-Bras, Waterloo, 1815
Pierce; United States, president, 1853
Pierola, N. de, Peru, 1876-82
Pierre, adm.; Madagascar, 1883
Pierrepoint, Mr.; United States, 1876
Piers, abp.; York, 1589
Pigot, David Richard; exchequer, 1846
Pigot, ld.; India, Pigot diamond, 1802
Pigot, major-gen.; Malta, 1800
Pigott, Mr.; trials, 1871
Pigott, R.; Parnellites, 1889
Pike, Miss; Cork, trials, 1800
Pilkington, bishop; liturgy
Pilpay; Anvar, fables
Pinchbeck, C.; pinchbeck
Pindar, abt., 522-439 B.C., Odes — Peter (Dr. Wolcot), 1738-1819; trials, 1790
Pine, sir B. C.; Natal, 1873
Pinel, M.; lunatics, 1792
Pinzon; America, S., 1500; Peru, 1863
Pisander; naval battles, 394 B.C.
Pisistratus; Athens, 527 B.C.
Pitman, I.; phonography, 1837; stenography
Pitt; diamond, 1720
Pitt, Wm.; see *Chatham, earl of*
Pitt, Wm., 1759-1806; Pitt adm., 1783; India company, E., reform, duels, 1798; income-tax
Pius; popes, 142 *et seq.*
Pius IV.; confession, 1504
Pius VII.; concordat, 1801
Pius IX. 1792-1878; popes; 1846-78; papal aggression, conception
Pizarro; America, 1524
Planché, J. R., 1796-1880; dress
Plato, Gr. phil., 429-347 B.C.; academics, anatomy, antipodes, names, Sicily
Platts, John; executions, 1847
Planté, G., electric battery, 1860
Plautus, Lat., b. 184 B.C.; drama
Playfair, Lyon; Gladstone adm., 1880
Plimpton; rink, 1875
Plimsoll, S.; parliament, seamen, 1873
Pliny the elder, 23-79; pearls, Vesuvius;—the younger, d. 100
Plowden, Mr.; Abyssinia, 1849
Plumer, sir Th.; att.-gen., 1817
Plummer, Eugenia; trials, 1860
Plunket, lord; chancellor, lord (Ireland), 1830
Plunket, D. R.; Salisbury adm., 1886
Plutarch, *fl.* 80; biography
Pocock, admiral; Cuba, 1762
Poerio, C.; Naples, 1850-59-60
Pogson, N.; planets, 1856
Poitevin, M.; balloons, 1852-58
Poitiers, Roger de; Liverpool, 1089
Pole, Wellesley; mint, trials, 1825
Pole, abp.; Canterbury, 1556
Polignac, prince de; France, 1830
Polk, Jas.; United States, president, 1845
Pollen, J. G.; furniture, 1874
Pollio, C.; slavery, 42 B.C.
Pollock, gen. G.; Afghanistan, India, 1842; tower
Pollock, sir Frederick, 1783-1863; attorney-general, exchequer, 1834-1844
Polo, Marco, writes about 1298
Polybius, 207-122 (?) B.C.; signals, telegraphs, Achaia, physic

INDEX.

Polycarp martyred, 166
Polydorus; Laocoön
Pomare; Otaheite, 1799
Pompey, killed 48 B.C.; Rome, Spain, Pharsalia
Pond, J.; Greenwich, 1811
Ponti, G.; academies
Pontius, C.; Caudine forks, 321 B.C.
Pook, E.; trials, 1871
Poole, bp.; Japan, 1883
Poole, A.; auricular confession, 1858
Poole, R. S.; Egypt. expl. fund
Pope, Alex., 1688-1744; Alexandrine verse, satire; Homer, 1714
Pope, gen. J.; Manassas, United States, 1862
Popham, sir Home; Buenos Ayres, Cape, trials, 1807
Popoff, adm.; circular ironclads, 1875
Popp, V., clocks, 1881
Poppæa (wife of Nero); masks
Porsenna; labyrinth, 520 B.C.
Porson, prof., 1759-1808; writing
Porter, sir Charles; Limerick
Porteus, bp.; London, 1787
Portland, duke of, Portland adm., 1783; Ireland (lord-lieutenant), Junius
Portman, sir Wm.; king's bench, 1554
Portsmouth, earl of; trials, 1823
Porus, Hydaspes, 327 B.C.
Posidonius, fl. 86 B.C.; atmosphere, moon, tides, air
Potamon; eclectics, about 1
Potter, abp.; Canterbury, 1737
Potter, Edm.; Manchester, 1883
Pottinger, sir H.; China, 1841
Pouchet, M.; spont. generation, 1859
Pouillet, C. S. M., Fr. nat. phil., 1791-1868
Poussin, N.; painters, 1594-1665
Pouyer-Quertier; France, 1871
Powell, Langharne, and Poyer, colonels; Wales, 1647
Powell; balloons, 1881-3
Power, Mr.; wrecks, 1841
Power, Frank; Soudan, 1884
Powys, bishop; Man, 1854
Poyer, colonel; Wales, 1647
Poynter, E. J., R.A., b. 1836
Prado, M.; Peru, 1824-67
Prado, murderer; France, 1888
Praslin murder, 1847
Praxiteles, fl. 363 B.C.; mirrors
Premislaus; Poland, 1295
Prendergast, gen. H. N.; Burmah, 1885
Prescott, Wm., 1796-1859
Preston, lord; conspiracy, 1691
Pretender, old, 1688-1765; young, 1720-88; Pretender, Falkirk, Prestonpans, Culloden
Pretorius, Natal, 1838; Transvaal, 1880
Pretsch, P.; photo-galvanography, 1854
Prevost, sir George; Plattsburg, 1814
Priam; Ilium, Troy, 1224 B.C.
Price, Mr.; duels, 1816; alchemy; annuities
Price, bp.; B. Free church
Price, adm.; Petropaulovski, 1854
Pride, col.; Pride's purge, 1648
Priessnitz, V.; hydropathy, 1828
Priestley, Joseph, 1733-1804; earthquakes, eudiometer, lunar society, nitrous gas, oxygen, fluorine, colour blindness
Prim, gen. Juan, 1814-70; Castellejos, Guad-el-ras, 1860; Spain, 1866-70; assassinations, 1870
Prince, H. J.; agapemone, 1845
Prior, M., poet, 1664-1721
Priscillian; gnostics, 314
Pritchard, Dr. E. W.; trials, execution, 1865

Probert; trials, 1824
Probus; Rome, emp. 276; massacre
Procles; biarch, 1102 B.C.
Procopius; Nacolea, 366
Procopius, Lat. hist. 500-565; Hussites, 1431
Procter, poets; Bryan W. (Barry Cornwall), 1790-1874; Adelaide, daughter, 1835-64
Propertius, Lat. poet, 26 B.C.
Proudhon, P., socialist, 1809-65; anarchy
Prynne, W., legal antiquary, 1600-69
Psalmanazar, G.; Formosa, 1704
Psammetichus, 650 B.C.; Egypt, labyrinth, languages, sieges
Pseusennes, 971 B.C.; Egypt
Psycho; automaton, 1875
Ptolemy (astronomer), d. 161
Ptolemy; Egypt, Bible, Septuagint, Ipsus, pharos, arithmetic, academies
Ptolemy Epiphanes, 205 B.C.; Egypt, Rosetta
Puckering, sir John; chancellor, lord high, 1592
Pugin, A. W., 1811-52, decorat. art; E. W.; trials, 1874
Pullan, R. P., dilettanti, 1861-70; Priene
Pullen, capt.; Franklin, 1852
Pullinger, G.; banks, joint stock, 1860
Pulteney, Mr.; Halifax adm., 1714
Pulteney, sir James; Ferrol, 1800
Punshon, R.; gunpowder, 1872
Purcell, Henry; music, 1658-95
Purchas, Sam.; 1577-1628
Purdon, col.; Ashantees, 1826
Purefoy; duels, 1788; trials, 1794
Pusey, Dr. E., 1800-82; Puseyism; Oxford univ.
Pyat, F., France, 1880
Pye, Henry J.; poet-laureate, 1790
Pye, J.; engraver, d. 1874
Pym, J.; politician, d. 1643
Pyrrho; sceptics, 334 B.C.
Pyrrhus; Macedon, 287 B.C.; Epirus, 318-272 B.C.; Tarentum, Asculum, 279
Pythagoras, fl. 555 B.C.; acoustics, astronomy, Copernicus, Egypt, the globe, harmonic strings, shoes, solar system, spheres

Q.

Quaritch, B.; books, 1882
Queen v. Lords of Treasury; trials, 1872
Quekett, prof.; histology, 1857
Quentin, col.; duels, 1815; trials, 1814
Quesnay, économistes
Quevedo, Span. writer, 1580-1645
Quinet, Edgar, Fr. philos., 1803-75
Quintilia; Quintilians
Quintin; libertines, 525
Quintus Fabius, 291 B.C.; painting
Quiros; New Hebrides, 1606

R.

Rabelais, F., satirist, 1483-1553
Rachel, mademoiselle, d. 1858:—madame; enamelling; trials, 1868, 1878
Racine, J.; Fr. dramat., 1639-99
Radcliffe, Dr. John; Radcliffe library, 1737
Radetsky, marshal, 1766-1858; Austria, Custozza, Novara, Italy
Radetsky, gen., Russo-Turkish war II., 1878
Radnor, earl of; administrations, 1684
Rae, Dr.; Franklin, 1848

Raffles, sir T. S.; Java
Raglan, lord; Russo-Turkish war, 1857
Ragotski; Transylvania
Raikes, Mr., 1781; Sunday-schools, education, infanticide
Raikes, H. C.; Salisbury adm., 1386
Raleigh, sir Walter, 1552-1618; dress, Pennsylvania, Trinidad, Virginia, England
Ralston, W. C.; California, 1875
Rameses; Egypt, 1618
Ramirez II.; Seniincas, 938 B.C.
Ramsay, David; combat, 1631
Ramsay, sir George; duels, 1790
Ramsden, Jesse, 1735-1800; theodolite, 1787
Rancé; trappist, 1662
Randolph, T.; post-office, 1581
Randolph, bishop; Bangor, London, 1809
Ranger, M.; cotton (a speculator); 1883
Rankin, J., velocipedes, 1878
Ransome, Ransome, filterers, ploughs
Raphael, 1483-1520; cartoons
Raphael, Alex.; Roman catholics, 1834
Rapieff, electric light, 1878
Rarey, J. S.; horse, 1858
Rassam, H.; Abyssinia, 1864; Nineveh; Brit. Mus.
Rathbone, Wm.; Liverpool, 1877
Rattazzi, U., 1808-73; Italy, 1862
Rauch, C.; sculptor, 1777-1857
Rauscher, card.; Austria, d. 1875
Ravaillac kills Henry IV., 1610
Rawdon, lord; Camden, 1781
Rawlinson, col. sir H., b. 1810; Assyria, Babylon, Behistun, 1844
Ray, John, naturalist, 1628-1705
Ray, Peter; volunteers (19th meeting), 1878
Rayhere; Bartholomew's, 1100
Rayleigh, lords, 1879
Raymond, lord; attorney-general, 1725; king's bench
Rayneckers, L.; fuel
Reade, Chas.; Nov. 1814-84
Réaumur, d. 1757; light, steel
Reay, Miss, killed; trials, 1779
Reay, lord; combat, 1631
Reay, lord; Bombay, 1884; London University
Rebeccaites; trials, 1843
Redanies, D.; execution, 1857
Rede, sir R.; Rede lecture
Redesdale, lord; att.-gen., 1800 parliament, 1836
Redpath, L.; trials, 1857
Redwood, T.; analysts, 1874
Reece, R.; bags, 1849; congelation, 1868
Reed, Andrew, 1787-1862; orphan, idiots, incurables
Reed, sir C.; metropolitan school board, 1873-81
Reed, sir E. J., navy, 1862-71
Reeves, Mr. John; levellers, 1792
Regnier, gen.; Kalitsch, Maida, Ximera, 1811
Regulus, 250 B.C.; Carthage
Reich, F., and Richter, T.; Indium, 1863
Reichardt, Wacht
Reichenbach, C., 1788-1869; paraffine, 1831; odyl
Reichenstein; tellurium, 1782
Reichstadt, duke de, 1811-32, France (empire)
Reid, gen.; India, 1857
Reid, R. T.; vivisection
Reinbauer; trials, 1829
Reinkens, Old Catholic bishop Prussia, 1873
Reis, P.; telephone, 1861
Relly, Jas.; universalists, 1760
Rembrandt, Paul; painter, 1608-69

aigias de Fescamp; Lincoln, 1086
nington, type-writers
nissat, C. de; France, 1871-3
ny, St.; Rheims
ard, capt.; balloons, 1884
ata, Maria; witchcraft, 1749
audot, M.; newspapers, 1631
adel, J.; Holyhead, Portland
anie, J. (1761-1831), and sir J.;
reakwater, 1812; Waterloo-bridge,
ondon-bridge
ton, Humphry, landscape gar-
ener, 1752-1818
old Pacha; Turkey, 1853
chlin, J., reformer, d. 1522; Talmud
nu; engraving
ter, J. de; Persia, 1872
ille, Mrs., Slough
ams, Richard; sheriff, 1189
ands, sir Joshua, 1723-92; royal
ademy, 1768
ald, abp.; Canterbury, 1313
nolds, capt.; trials, 1840
nolds, George; duels, 1788
rnolds, O.; explosives
odes, R. G., audiphone
odes, W. B., free hospital, life-boat
alt, gen.; Chippawa, 1814
ard; France, 1876
moli, B., b. about 1803; Italy,
861-7
s, Spring (lord Monteagle); administrations, 1834
h, Richard, lord; chancellor, lord,
847
ard I., England, 1189; Acre,
asalon, Cœur de Lion, Dieu et
non droit, laws, Oleron, naviga-
ion laws
ard III., k. 1485; Bosworth
ard, H.; Eustasia, 1888
ards, Miss; pedestrianism, 1874
ardson, B. W.; hygeiopolis, 1876
ardson, sir John; naturalist,
783-1865; Franklin
ardson, H.; life-boat, 1852
hardson, Sam.; novels, 1689-1761
helieu, card. 1585-1642; France,
624
:helieu, duke of; Closterseven, 1757
:hmond, duke of; Rockingham ad-
inistration, 1782, &c.; Ireland,
uels; Derby and Disraeli admin-
strations; Salisbury adm. 1885
hter, J. Paul, Ger. novel., 1763-1825
lding, Geo., bp.; Southwell
tel, Stephen, 1189; chancellor,
ord, Ireland
er, William; silk hose
geway, C. de, abstinence
ley, bp., burnt, 1555
sdale, Rev. C. J.; public worship
ct, 1876
go put to death; Spain, 1823
l, L.; Hudson's bay; Canada, Ad-
rnda
azi, N., m. 1354; tribune, Rome
g, rev. A., technical education
oni, M.; canal boats
uet, M.; tunnels
uccini, Octavio, b. 1621; opera
on, earl of, 1782-1859; Goderich
lministration, 1827; — marquis
; freemasonry; Gladstone adm.
73, 1886; India, 1880
ikoff, Russia, 1881
c Allah; trials, 1868
ich, Servia, 1880
ebie, D. T.; Salisbury adm.,
86; local government
on, Joseph, critic, 1752-1803
er, Karl, geographer, 1779-1859
er, J. W., electricity, 1812
rs, earl, m. 1483; Pomfret
rs, Mr., Egypt, 1879
ère, R. T.; Tonquin, 1883
lo, David, m. 1566; Scotland,
ance, Naples

Robert, duke of Normandy; Tinche-
bray, 1106; Scotland, 1306
Robert II.; pilgrimages, 1060
Roberts, D., R.A., 1796-1864
Roberts, J. R., Liberia
Roberts, sir F., Afghanistan, 1878-80;
Burmah 1886; Mazra
Robertson, capt.; trials, 1862
Robertson, J. P. B.; Scotland, 1889
Robertson, T. W., dramatist, 1829-71
Robertson, Dr. Wm., hist., 1721-93
Robertson, W., trials, 1878
Robespierre, F. M.; reign of terror,
France, 1793-4
Robin Hood; robbers, archery, 1189
Robinson; see Perdita
Robinson, F.; Goderich, note
Robinson, H. G. R., New Zealand,
1878; Cape, 1880
Robinson, James; ether, 1848
Robinson, R., 1735-90; independents
Robinson, sir Thomas; Newcastle
administration, 1754
Robinson of York, murdered; trials,
1853
Robinson, sir W. C. F.; Straits, 1877
Robiquet and Colin; alizarine, 1831
Robson, W.; trials, 1856
Rochambeau; Yorktown, 1781
Rochebouet, gen.; France, 1877
Rochefort, H.; France 1870-81;
Tunis, 1881
Rochefoucauld, F. De la, phil. 1630-80
Rochester, earl of; administrations,
1679
Rochfort, A. H.; cryptography, 1836
Rock, Dan., 1779-1871; mass
Rockingham, marq. of; Rockingham
administrations, 1765
Roderick; Spain, 709; Wales, 843
Rodney, G.; Eustatia, 781
Rodolph of Hapsburg; Austria, 1278
Rodolph of Nuremberg; wire, 1410;
of Suabia, k. Fladenheim, 1080
Roe, Henry; Dublin, 1878
Roebling, Mr. & Mrs.; New York,
1883
Roebuck, J.; duel, 1835; Sebastopol
Rœmer, light, 1676
Roger; Sicily, Naples, 1130
Rogers and others; trials, 1882
Rogers, John, burnt, 1555
Rogers, Sam., poet, 1763-1855
Rogers, Messrs.; gas lights
Rogers, J. E. T.; wages
Roget, P. M., M.D., philologist, 1799-
1869
Roggewein, circumnavigator; Easter
Island, 1722
Rogier, Charles, d. 1885; Belgium,
1857
Rohan, card.; diamond necklace, 1786
Rollin, Chas., Fr. hist., 1661-1741
Rolt, sir J.; att.-gen., 1866; justice
of appeal, 1867
Romain, M.; balloons, k. 1785
Romilly, sir Samuel; criminal law,
suicide, 1818
Romilly, sir J., aft. ld.; 1802-74;
solicitor-gen., master of the rolls,
1851
Romney, Geo.; painter, 1734-1802
Romulus; Rome, 753 B.C.; calendar,
Alba, aruspices
Romulus Augustulus; western em-
pire, 475
Ronalds, F., 1788-1873; electric tele-
graph, 1823
Ronge, J.; kinder-garten, 1851
Rooke, sir George; Gibraltar, 1704;
snuff, Alderney, Cadiz, Cape la
Hogue, Cape St. Vincent, Vigo
Roper, colonel; duels, 1788
Rosa, Carl; opera, 1889
Rosas; Buenos Ayres, 1852
Roscoe, sir H. E., indigo; technical
education
Roscoe, W., hist., 1753-1831

Rose, German chem., Gustav, 1798-
1873; Heinrich, 1795-1864
Rose, sir Hugh; India, Calpee, 1858
Rosebery, earl of; Gladstone adm.,
1880, 1886
Roseberry, countess of; trials, 1814
Rosencrans, gen.; United S., 1862
Ross, sir J.; Franklin, north-west
passage, 1848
Ross, colonel; duelling, 1817; British
museum, 1876
Ross, gen.; Baltimore, Washington,
1814
Rossa, O'Donovan; Fenians, 1868-83
Rosse, earl of, 1800-67; telescopes,
1828; Royal Society, 1848
Rossel, France, 1871
Rosser, Mr. and Miss Darbon; trials,
1841
Rossi, count, Rome, 1848; assassina-
tions
Rossini, G., mus. comp., 1792-1868
Kostopchin; Moscow, 1812
Rothery, H. C., Tay-bridge
Rothsay; duke, Scotland, 1401
Rothschild, Anselm (the first), d.
1812; Rothschild, Evelina hosp.
Rothschild; Jews, 1849; deaf and
dumb, 1872
Roubiliac; sculptor, 1695-1762
Rouher, E., 1814-84; France, 1863-81
Roupell, W., M.P.; trials, 1862
Rous, F.; psalms
Rousseau, J. J., Fr. phil., 1712-1778
Roustan, M., Tunis, 1881
Routledge v. Lowe; copyright, 1868
Rouvier, M.; France, 1887
Rowan, A. H.; trials, 1794, 1805
Rowe, Nicholas, 1673-1718; poet-
laureate, d. 1715
Rowlandson, Thos., caricaturist, 1756-
1827
Rowley, admiral J.; Bourbon, 1810
Rowsell, C. J.; graphoscope
Roxana; Macedon, 311 B.C.
Roxburgh, duke of, 1812; Boccaccio
Rozier, M.; balloons, 1783
Rubens, P. P.; painter, 1577-1640
Rubery v. Grant; trial, 1875
Ruchdi Pasha; Turkey, 1866-71, et
seq.
Rudbeck, Ol.; thoracic duct
Rudolph; Austria, Germany
Ruhmkorff, induction coil, 1851
Rumford, Benjamin Thompson,
count, 1752-1814; Royal Institu-
tion
Runge, cafeine (eng. caffeine)
Runjeet Singh; Afghanistan, 1818;
diamonds
Rupert, prince, 1619-82; engraving,
Birmingham, Edgehill, Marstou-
moor, Naseby, Newark
Ruric; Russia, 862; Varangians
Rush, Bloomfield, murderer; trials,
1849
Rushworth, E. E.; Jamaica, 1877
Ruskin, John, art critic, b. 1819
Sheffield
Russell, C.; suicide, 1856
Russell, colonel; guards, 1660
Russell, adm. Edw.; La Hogne,
1692
Russell, J. Scott, engineer, 1808-82;
fires, steam-nav., Vienna, wave
Russell, lord John, aft. earl, 1792-
1878; Russell administration, note,
Aberdeen; Germany, 1874; papal
aggression; reform
Russell, Odo, ld. Ampthill; Ger-
many, 1871-84
Russell, sir C., att. gen., 1886
Parnellites, 1888.
Russell, lord W., trials, 1840
Russell, bp. W. A.; China, 1872
Russell, W. H.; Times, 1854, 1857,
1861
Rutherford, J.; lectures

1042 INDEX.

Ruthven, Mr. ; duels, 1836
Rutland, duke of ; Ireland (lord lieutenant), 1784 ; see *Manners*
Ruyter, see *De Ruyter*
Ryder, bp. ; Gloucester, 1815
Ryder, sir Dudley, king's bench, 1754
Rye, Miss ; emigration
Rymer-Jones, A. M., temnograph
Ryvés, Mrs. ; trials, 1866

S.

Sabatta, Levi, 1666
Sabine, gen. sir Edw., 1788-1883 ; Royal Society, 1861 ; magnetism
Sacheverel, Dr. ; high church, 1709
Sackville, lord George ; Minden, 1759
Sadleir, J. ; suicide, 1856 ;—Dr., 1858
Sadler, Mr. ; balloons, 1812
Sadler, Mr. ; Sadler's Wells, 1863
Sadler, sir Ralph ; administrations, 1540
Sadyk ; Turkey, 1878
Safford, Mr. ; planets, 1862
Safvet Pasha ; Turkey, 1877-8
Sagarelli ; Apostolici, 300
Sagasta, Spain, 1871-89
Saget, gen. ; Hayti, 1870
St. Arnaud, marshal ; Russo-Turkish war, Alma, 1854
St. Charo ; concordance, 1247
St. Clair, Bella ; pedestrianism, 1876
St. Cyr, marshal ; Dresden, 1813
St. George, Mr. ; trials, 1798
St. John, John de ; treasurer, 1217
St. John Long ; quack, 1830
St. John, Henry, aft. lord Bolingbroke ; Oxford adm., 1711
St. John, O. ; benevolences, 1615
St. John, William ; chancellor, lord high, 1547
St. Leonards, lord, 1781-1875 ; chancellor, lord high, 1852
St. Mars, M. de ; iron mask
St. Ruth, general ; Aughrim, 1691
St. Vincent, earl ; admiralty, 1801 ; Cape St. Vincent
Sakya Muni, Buddhism
Saladin, sultan, 1136-1193 ; Ascalon, Damascus, Egypt, Syria, Aleppo
Salar Jung, Hyderabad
Sale, lady ; Cabul, India, 1842
Sale, sir Robert ; Moodkee, 1845
Salgar, E., Colombia, 1871
Salisbury, bishop of ; assay
Salisbury, countess of ; garter
Salisbury, Robert, earl of ; administrations, 1603
Salisbury, earl of, 1604 ; coronets, Orleans
Salisbury, Arthur T. G., marquis of ; b. 1830 ; Derby administrations, 1852, 1858 ; Disraeli administration, 1874 ; Turkey, 1877 ; Berlin conference ; conservatives, 1881 ; Salisbury adm., 1885, 1886
Salkeld ; Delhi, 1857
Sallo, Denis de ; critics, reviews, 1655
Sallust, Lat. hist., d. 34 B.C. ; Mauritania, Catiline
Salmasius ; anthology, 1606
Salmeron ; Spain, 1873
Salnave, gen. ; Hayti, 1865-70
Salomons, D. ; Jews, 1835 ; mayor
Salt, Titus ; 1803-76 ; alpaca, 1852, Bradford
Salvator Rosa ; painter, 1615-1673
Salvia'', Dr. ; mosaic, 1861
Salvino degli Armato ; spectacles
Salvius Julianus ; edicts, 132
Sampson, H. : advertisements, 1874
Samuel rules at tel, 1140 B.C.
Samuelson, sir B. ; technical education

Sanballat ; Samaritan, 332 B.C.
Sancho, king ; Portugal, Spain, 970
Sancroft, abp., Canterbury, 1678. ; bishops, England
Sandeman, major ; Beloochistan
Sandeman, R. ; Glasites
Sanderson, Dr. J. B. ; Brown Institute
Sanders, will-forger ; trials, 1844
Sandilli ; Kaffraria, 1877-8
Sandon, lord ; Disraeli admin., 1874, 1878 ; elemen. education, 1876 ; see Harrowby
Sandwich, earl of ; administrations, 1660 ; naval battles, Solebay, Aix-la-Chapelle
Sandys ; administrations, 1742, 1767
Sandys, Edwin, abp. ; York, 1577
Santa Anna ; Mexico, 1853-76
Sapor ; Persia, 240
Sappho writes 611 B.C. ; Sapphic
Sardanapalus ; Assyria, 820 B.C.
Sarmiento, col. D., Argentine confed., 1868
Sarpi, Paul, 1552-1623 ; thermometer, blood
Sassoon, sir A., Bombay, 1879
Sassulitch, V. ; Russia, 1878
Saul, Jews, 1096 B.C. ; Ammonites
Saumarez, sir James ; Algesiras, 1801
Saunders ; trials, 1853
Saunders, com. ; Franklin, 1849
Saunders, sir Charles ; Chatham administration, 1766
Saussure, 1740-1799 ; hygrometer
Saurin v. Star ; trials, 1869
Savage, John ; Babyngton's conspiracy, 1586
Savage, abp. ; York, 1501
Savage, Rich., poet, 1698?-1743
Savage, W. ; printing in colours, 1819-22
Savary, trials, 1825
Savary, capt. ; steam-engine, 1698
Savas Pasha, Turkey, 1880-1
Savonarola, Jerome ; burnt, 1498
Saward, J. ; trials, 1857
Sawtre, sir William ; burning alive, 1401 ; Lollards
Sawyer ; arithmetic, 1878
Saxe, count ; Fontenoy, 1745 ; Laffeldt, 1747
Say, Leon ; France, 1873-7
Say, T. ; colorado beetle
Sayce, A. H. ; Accadians Assyria, 1875 ; Babylonia
Saye and Sele, lord ; administrations, 1660
Sayers, T. ; boxing, 1860
Scanderbeg ; Albania, 1443
Scanlan, Mr. ; trials, 1820
Scarlatti, D. ; spinet
Schamyl ; Circassia, 1859
Scheele, 1742-86 ; nitrogen, oxygen, prussic acid, tartaric acid, photography, glycerine, chlorine
Scheffer, Ary ; painter, 1795-1858
Scheibler M. ; tonometer, 1834
Scheiner, Chr. ; heliometer, 1625
Schenck, gen. ; United States, 1870, 1876
Scheutz ; calculating machine, 1857
Schlaparelli ; planets, 1861 ; comets, 1866
Schiff, Dr. ; vivisection
Schilders, general ; Silistria, 1854
Schiller, F., Ger. poet, 1759-1805
Schimmelpenninck ; Holland, 1805
Schlegel, W., German writer, 1767-1845 ;—F., 1772-1829
Schleyer ; volapük
Schlickmann, gen. ; Transvaal, 1876
Schliemann, Dr. ; Mycenæ, Troy, 1877
Schmidt ; organs, 1682 ; moon, 1874 ; —shot, Spain, 1874
Schœffer, Peter ; printing, 1452
Schönbein, M. ; 1797-1868 ; gun cotton, 1840 ; ozone, 1846

Schomberg, capt. ; nav 1811
Schomberg, duke of ; Boy Londonderry, Carrickf
Schomburgk, sir R. ; Vie 1838
Schopenhauer, A., pessim
Schröter ; pianoforte, 175
Schrötter ; phosph, n
Schonten ; Cape Horn, 16
Schouvaloff, count, Russ
Schubert, F. P. ; Ger. 1828
Schumann, Robert ; Ger. 56
Schwabe, sun
Schwann ; cell theory, 18
Schwartz, C., missionary,
Schwartz, M. ; gunpowde
Schwartzenberg, prince of 1813
Schwatka, lieut., Frankl 1879-81
Schwerin, marshal ; Prag
Scialoia, A. ; Naples. 1877
Scipio Africanus ; honour, Rome, Zama, 202 B.C.
Scindiah, Gwalior
Scobeleff, gen. ; Russo war, 1878 ; Russia, 1882
Scott, sir G. Gilbert ; arch 1878 ; Alban's ; Asaph's ;
Scott, R. H. ; meteorolog
Scott, gen. Winfield, Mexico, 1847 ; Unite 1861-2
Scott ; duelling, 1821, 18
Scott, Walter, 1771-1832 ;
Scott, Dred ; United State
Scott, Miss C. A., Girton
Scribe, E., dramatist, d. r
Scudamore, lord ; apples
Seabury, Samuel ; bishop
Seaforth, earl of ; thistle,
Seal, J. ; trials 1858
Searle ; planets, 1858
Seacon ; Egypt, 737 B.C.
Sebastiani, marshal ; Tal
Sebert ; Westminster Al
Sebright marriage ; tria
Secchi, Padre, A., nat. p
Secker, abp. ; Canterb
Secocœni ; Transvaal, 1
Sedgwick, Adam, d. 187
Sefton v. Hopwood ; tri
Sejanus, d. 31
Selborne, chancellor, ld. 1872-4, appeal ; Glad 1880
Selden, J., 1584-1654 ; laureate
Seleucus Nicator ; Sele omens, Ipsus, 311 B.C.
Selim ; Turkey, Syria, 1
Selkirk, Alexander ; Jua 1705
Sellis, the valet ; suicid
Selmer, M. ; Norway,
Selwyn, sir C. J., justice,
Semiramis ; Assyria, eur B.C.
Semmes, capt., Alabama,
Semple ; trials, 1795, 186
Sen, Baboo, deism, 186
Seneca, put to death, 65 ;
Sennacherib ; Assyria, 7
Sennefelder ; lithography
Sergius ; popes, nativity, fication, Koran
Serrano, 1 arquis de, and Torre, Sj a... 1868-75.
1868
Serrin ; e... l lu p
Bertlurne ; ... l...u, t c
Servetus, Michael, bu Unitarian
Servius T... r B.C.

Sesostris; Egypt, 1618 B.C.
Setalla; burning glasses
Severus; Rome; emp. 193; Britain, Roman walls, Memphis. 202
Sextus Pompeius; Myls, 36 B.C.
Seymour, sir Edw.; speaker, 1678
Seymour, sir M.; China, 1856
Seymour v. Butterworth; trials, 1862
Seymour, Edward, duke of Somerset; administrations, 1547; protectors, admiralty
Seymour, lord; duels, 1835
Seymour, lady; tournament, 1839
Seymour, adm. sir H. (aft. lord Alcester), Egypt, 1882
Sforza, cardinal; Naples, 1877
Shadwell, Thomas; poet-laureate, d. 1692
Shaftesbury, earl of; administrations, 1672; (1801-1885) Chichester; costermongers, Shaftesbury estate
Shakspeare, W., 1564-1616: Shakspeare, drama, mulberry-tree
Shalmaneser; Assyria, 730 B.C.
Shapira, M.; bible, nots
Sharp, A.; circle (squared), 1717
Sharp, archbp.; Scotland, 1679
Sharp, Granville; slavery, 1772
Shaw, rev. Mr.; Madagascar, 1883
Shaw, sir James; mayor, 1805
Shaw, sir John; Greenock
Shaw, capt.; fire brigade
Shaw, W., home-rule, 1879
Sheares, the Messrs.; trials, 1798
Shedden v. Patrick; trials, 1860
Sheepshanks, R.; astronomy, standard, 1855; Sheepshanks' donations, 1857-8
Sheil, R. L.; mint, 1846
Shelburne, earl of; Shelburne administration, 1782; duel, 1780
Sheldon, abp.; Canterbury, 1663
Sheldon, William; tapestry
Shelley, Percy B., poet, 1792-1822
Shepherd v. Bennett; trials, 1870
Sheppard, Jack; execution, 1724
Shepstone, sir T.; Transvaal, 1876-7
Shere Ali, Afghanistan, 1863, 1879; Candahar
Shere Ali, kills ld. Mayo, 1872; Andaman India
Sheridan, gen.; United States, 1883, 1885, 1888
Sheridan, Richard Brinsley, 1751-1816; Grenville administration, comedy, theatres
Sheridan, Dr.; trials, 1811
Sherman, gen.; United States, 1861
Sherwan, Wm.; Norwich, 1869
Shield, Mr.; oil on waters
Shillibeer, G., 1807-66; omnibuses, 1829
Shipley, arts. soc. of, 1754
Shirley, bishop; Man, 1846
Short, bishop; Man, St. Asaph, 1841
Shovel, sir Cloudesley; Scilly, 1707
Shrapnel; bombs
Shrewsbury peerage cases; trials, 1858, 1859
Shrewsbury, duke of; administrations, 1714
Shrewsbury, earl of; Patay, 1429; Castillon, 1453
Shuttleworth, sir U. K.; Gladstone adm., 1886
Sibour, abp.; France, 1857
Sicard, abbé; deaf and dumb, 1742
Siddons, Sarah, actress; retired, 1819
Sidmouth, Henry Addington, viscount, d. 1844; Addington adm., 1800; green bag, speaker
Sidney, sir P., 1554-86; Algernon, 1617-83; Rye house plot
Siemens, sir C. Wm., 1822-83; heat, pyrometer, 1871; Albert medal,
1874; attraction, bathometer, electric telegraph, heat, light, lighthouses, 1878
Siemens, F.; glass, 1885
Siemens, Werner, electricity, electric railway, 1881
Sieyès, abbé; directory, France, 1799
Sigismond; Germany, Bohemia, Hungary, Nicopolis, Poland, Prussia
Silius, Italicus, poet, about 25-99
Sillim, Mr.; trials, 1863
Simeon the Stylite; abstinence
Simmonds; flying, 1875; balloons, 1883
Simmons; trials, 1808
Simmons, sir J. L.; Malta, 1884
Simnel, Lambert; conspiracies, rebellion, 1486; Stoke
Simon Magus; Simonians, 41
Simon, J.; France, 1876-7
Simonides; letters, mnemonics, 477 B.C.
Simplicius, St.; collar of SS., 1407
Simpson, Dr.; chloroform, 1848
Simpson, traveller; suicide, 1840
Sims, G. R.; London, 1883
Sindercomb; conspiracy, 1756
Singh, Runjoor; Aliwal, 1846
Sismondi, C., hist., 1773. 1842
Sisyphus; Corinth, 1326 B.C.
Sixtus; popes, 119
Sixtus V., pope; interdict, 1583
Skene, J. H.; flittites
Skipwith, Mr.; trials, 1872
Skobeleff, gen., Russia, 1880, Senova
Skrzynecki, gen.; Praga, Wawz, 1831
Slade, Dr.; spiritualism, 1876-7
Slade, F., Slade
Slater; forgery case; trials, 1888
Slidell, Mr.; United States, 1861
Sligo, marquis of; trials, 1812
Sloane, sir Hans, 1660-1752; apothecary, Jesuits' bark, British Museum, Chelsea
Sloanes; trials, 1851
Smart, A.; suicide, 1856
Smart, sir G. T., mus., 1776-1867
Smart; chimneys, 1805
Smeaton, Mr.; Eddystone, canal, 1759
Smeaton, sir John; Wigan, 1643
Smethurst, T.; trials, 1859
Smee, trials, 1879
Smirke, R.; 1780-1867; post-office, 1825
Smirke, S.; Bethlehem, British Museum, d. 1877
Smith, Adam, 1723-90; political economy, 1776
Smith, Mr. Beaumont; exchequer, trials, 1841
Smith, Benjamin Leigh; north-west passage, 1871-82
Smith, capt.; duel, trials, 1830
Smith, F. P.; screw propeller, 1836
Smith, Geo.; Assyria, 1866-75; Brit. Museum, 1873; forks; Nineveh; Hittites; d. 1876
Smith, sir J. E.; botanist, 1759-1828; his widow, Pleasance, longevity, 1877
Smith, prof. W. Robertson, free church of Scotland
Smith, J.; bribery, trials, 1854
Smith, Joseph; savings' bank
Smith, Joseph; Mormonites, 1823
Smith, Madeleine; trials, 1857
Smith, Miss v. earl Ferrers; trials, 1846
Smith, Dr. R. Angus; chemist, 1817-84; air, 1858
Smith, Dr. Southwood, 1790-1861; sanitary legislation, 1832
Smith, sir Sidney; Acre, 1799
Smith, rev. Sydney, 1760-1845
Smith, rev. S.; trials, 1858
Smith, Sam. Sidney; trials, 1843

Smith, sir C. Eardley; evangelical alliance, 1845
Smith, sir Harry; India, Aliwal, Kaffraria, 1850
Smith, Mr. Thomas; customs
Smith, Thomas; lord mayor, 1809
Smith, Wm.; geology, d. 1840
Smith, W. H.; admiralty, 1877; Salisbury adm. 1885, 1886
Smith v. earl Brownlow; trials, 1863
Smith, and Markham, captains; duels, trials, 1830
Smithson, J.; Smithsonian Institution, 1846
Smollett, Tobias, novelist, 1721-71
Smyth (will case); trials, 1855
Smyth, W. H., astron., 1788-1865
Snellius; optics, 1624
Snider, Jacob, d. 1866; fire-arms
Snorri, Sturlason; Iceland, killed, 1241
Snow, Dr.; amylene, 1856
Soames; cocoa-nut tree oil, 1829
Soane, sir J., architect, 1753-1837
Sobieski, John; Poland, Cossacks, Hungary, Vienna
Soboleff, gen., Bulgaria, 1883
Sobrero, nitro-glycerine, 1847
Socinus, Lælius (d. 1562), and Faustus (d. 1604); anti-trinitarians, arians, unitarians
Socrates, 468-399 B.C.; Athens, philosophy
Soleil, saccharimeter
Solomon; Jerusalem, 1004 B.C.
Solon; Athens, 594 B.C.; laws, tax
Soloviff, A., Russia, 1879
Solyman; Turkey, Belgrade, Vienna, 1529
Solyman II.; Hungary Buda, Mohatz, 1526
Somers, lord; administrations, 1690; corn
Somers, sir George; Bermudas, 1607
Somerset the black declared free, 1772; slavery in England
Somerset, see Seymour; admiralty, 1859
Somerville, Mary, mathemat., &c. 1780-1872
Sonzogno, R.; murdered, Rome, 1875
Sophia, princess; Hanover, 1659
Sophia Dorothea, d. 1796; England (queens, Geo. I.)
Sophocles, 495-405 B.C.; tragedy, drama
Sorel, Agnes; jewellery, 1434
Soro, Zuan; cipher, 1516
Sostratus; pharos, 280 B.C.
Soto, Ferdinand de; Louisiana, 1541
Soult, marshal, 1769-1851; Albuera, Oporto, Orthes, Pyrenees, Tarbes, Toulouse, Villa Franca, Douro
Southey, Rob., 1774-1843; poet-laureate
Southwell, W.; piano, 1807
Soyer, A. (cook), d. 1858
Spalding, Mr.; diving-bell, 1783
Sparks, George; trials, 1853
Speilman, sir John; paper-making, Dartford, 1590
Speke, capt., 1827-64; Africa, 1863-4; —B.; London, 1868
Spencer, D.; Coventry, 1883
Spencer, earl; Grenville adm., 1806; Roxburghe club; Gladstone adm., 1868, 1880, 1886; Ireland, 1868-73, 1882
Spencer, Mr.; electrotype, 1837
Spener, Phil. J.; theolog. 1635-1705; pietists
Spenser, E., 1553-98; allegory, faery queen, poet-laureate, verse
Spert, sir Thos.; Trinity-house, 1512
Spina, Alexander de; spectacles, 1285
Spinass, J.; trials, 1870
Spinoza, B. de, 1632-77; atheism

1044 INDEX.

Spohr, L., mus. comp., 1783-1859
Spollen, Jas.; trials, 1857
Spottiswoode, Wm. 1825-83; optics, 1871, British association, 1878, Royal institution, 1865, 1873; Royal society, 1878
Sprengel, Dr.; air-pump, *note*
Sprigg, J. G.; Cape, 1878
Spurgeon, C. H., b. 1834; baptists, Surrey gardens, crystal palace, tabernacle
Spurzheim, J. G.; craniology, 1800
Stackpole, capt.; duel, 1814
Stackpoles, trials; 1853
Stael, mad. de, novelist, d. 1817
Stafford, abp.; Canterbury, 1443
Stafford, lord; popish plot, 1680
Stafford, marquis of, d. 1803; Bloomabury
Stahl, G. E.; chemist, 1660-1723; phlogiston
Staines, sir William; lord mayor, 1800
Stair, earl of; Glencoe, 1692; Dettingen, 1743
Staite; electric light, 1848
Stalker, gen.; Bushire, suicide, 1857
Stambouloff; Bulgaria, 1886
Stanberry, John; Eton, 1448
Standen, T.; pedestrianism, 1811
Stanhope, earl; Halifax adm., 1714
Stanhope, Charles, earl, 1753-1816; printing-press; Philip Henry, earl (formerly lord Mahon, historian), 1805-75; antiquaries
Stanhope, col.; trials, 1816
Stanhope, hon. col.; suicide, 1825
Stanhope, lieut.-gen.; Minorca, 1708
Stanhope, Edward; Salisbury adm. 1885-6
Stanislaus; Poland, 1704
Stanley, dean A. P., 1815-81; Sunday, 1877
Stanley, colonel F. A.; Disraeli, 2nd adm., 1878; Salisbury adm., 1885, 1886, (ld. Stanley of Preston); Canada, gov. gen., 1888
Stanley, bishop, Norwich, 1837
Stanley, H. M.; b. 1841; Africa, 1872-82; Congo; Soudan, 1887
Stanley, sir John; Man, 1406
Stanley, sir W.; chamberlain; Bosworth, 1485
Stanley, lord; see *Derby*
Stanley, lord, of Alderley, b. 1802; Aberdeen, Palmerston adm.
Stanley, Edw., lord, b. 1826; Derby, 1866; Disraeli adm. 1868, see *Derby*
Stansfield, James; Gladstone adm. 1886
Stanton, Mr.; velocipede, 1874
Stapleton, J.; trials, 1858
Stapleton, Walter, bp.; Exeter, 1319
Stark; electric telegraph, 1858
Statius, Lat. poet, Æ. 79
Staunton, L. & P., etc.; trials, 1877
Staunton, Mr.; China, 1840
Stead, W. T.; trials, 1885
Stearns; electric telegraph
Steele, sir R., 1671-1729; Tatler, Spectator, clubs, Kit-Cat club
Steele, Mr.; murdered, trials, 1807
Steell, sir J.; Scotland, 1876
Steenchel, Magnus; Sweden, 1314
Stein, Germany, 1819
Steinmetz; chess, 1873, 1883
Stenhouse, J.; dyes, charcoal, 1853
Stephen; popes, England, Hungary, 997; Poland
Stephen, Leslie; biography
Stephens, G.; Runes
Stephens, Miss; theatres, Coventgarden, 1813-1882
Stephens, rev. Mr.; trials, 1839
Stephens, Robert; Bible, 1551
Stephenson, George, 1781-1848; railways, Chatmoss; steam, 1814; Newcastle, 1881

Stephenson, Robert, 1803-59; tubular bridges
Stepniak; Russia, 1884
Sterne, Laurence, humorist, 1713-68
Sternhold, T., d. 1549; Psalms
Stesichorus; choruses, 556 a.c.
Stevens, A.; Wellington (monument), 1853
Stevenson, Messrs.; Granton
Stewart, col.; Trincomalee, 1795
Stewart, gen.; Madras, 1783
Stewart, sir D., Afghanistan, 1880
Stewart, capt.; Franklin, 1850
Stewart, col.; Soudan, 1882
Stewart, gen. H.; Soudan, 1884-5
Stewart, Dugald, phil., 1753-1828
Stewart, Duncan; Cæsarean
Stewarts; trials, 1829
Stifelius; algebra, 1544
Stigand, abp.; Canterbury, 1052
Stillingfleet, B.; blue-stocking
Stirling, W.; Glasgow, 1791
Stirling, capt. "Atalanta"
Stock, Thos.; Sunday-schools
Stockdale; trials, 1826
Stoddart, Dr.; Times, 1812
Stoecklin; Boulogne, 1878
Stokes, E. S.; New York, 1872
Stokes, sir G. G., sunshine recorder; Royal society, 1885
Stone, D. H.; mayor, lord, 1874
Stopford, adm.; Acre, Sidon, 1840
Storace, madame, d. 1814
Storck; anabaptists, 1524; levellers
Storks, sir H.; Ionian Isles, 1859; army, 1868
Stormont, visc.; Portland adm., 1783
Strabo, geog., writes, 14
Strachan, admiral sir Richard; Havre, Walcheren, 1809
Straduarius; viol., 1700-22
Strafford, lord, administrations, 1640; beheaded, 1641
Strafford, earl; admiralty, 1712
Strahan, sir G. C.; Gold Coast, 1874; Windward Isles, 1876; Grenada, 1877; Van Diemen's land, 1881
Strangford, lord; bribery, 1784
Stratford, abp.; Canterbury, 1333
Stratford de Redcliffe, lord, diplomatist, 1788-1880
Strauch, capt.; Congo
Street, Geo. E., 1824-81; architect, law courts
Strelnikoff, gen., assassinated; Russia, 1882
Strickland, Hugh; nat. hist., 1811-53
Stroh, A.; acoustics
Stromeyer; club-foot, 1831
Strongbow; Ireland, 1176
Strousberg, Dr. H. B.; Russia, 1875-6; d. 1884
Struensee, count; Zell, 1772
Strutt, Edw.; Aberdeen adm., 1852
Struve, F., astron., 1793-1864
Strzelecki, count; Australia, 1838; d. 1873
Stuart, Alexander; marquis
Stuart, conf. gen.; United States, 1862
Stuart, gen.; Cuddalore, 1783
Stuart, sir John; Maida, 1806
Stukeley, Dr.; earthquakes
Stum, F.; trials, 1882
Sturmius; magnet
Sturt, capt.; South Australia, 1830
Succoth (St. Patrick) preaches, 433
Suchet, marshal; Valencia, 1812
Sudbury, abp.; Canterbury, 1375
Sudeikin, lieut., murdered; Russia, 1883
Sue, Eug., Fr. novelist, 1804-57
Suetonius, C. T., Lat. hist., 118
Suetonius Paulinus; Menai, 61
Suffolk, Thomas, earl of; administrations, 1540
Suffrein, Thos.; Trincomalee, 1782

e, d. 1405; ludia, Damascus,
.ine
sir T.; Forth bridge; Asia

is; Adamite
lle, Ford, earl of; adminis-
hs, 1699
Dr., abstinence
[opee; India, 1857
; Rome, kings; Sibylline

us Priscus; Rome, kings,
, 588 B.C.
, Abel; circumnavigator,
nlls, 1642; New Zealand,
)lemen's Land
Torquato; It. poet, 1544-95;
ulem Delivered
ahum, d. 1715; poet-laureate
about 170; aquarians, encra-

all, R.; races, 1766
J.; mystic, 1290-1361
ier; pearls, 1633
John; trials, 1845
, H.; trials, 1882
, L.; alphabet
, Mrs.; bells, 1882
, bp. Jeremy, 1613-67
, gen. Zachary; presidents,
ted States, 1849
, Messrs.; oil-gas
, Dr. Brook; acoustics, 1714
, rev. Robert; atheism, trials,
183t
, col. T. E. (after. ld. Ardgillan)
racli adm. 1874
r, rev W.; blind, bells, 1855-6
r, sir W. T.; Andrew's, St.,
3
nayeff; Turkey, 1876; Russia,
2
countess; (empress) France,

i; Austria, 1860; Hungary,
51
phorus; Lent, 130
rd, T. 1757-1834; chain-bridges,
9
William; Switzerland, 1307
el; planets, 1861
ple, earl; Newcastle adm., 1757
ple, sir R.; India, 1869-72;
ngal, 1874
pler, major; trials, 1888
ers, D. (two), 1582-1694
ison, abp.; Canterbury, 1694
nant, Mr.; bleaching, 1798
nent, sir J. E.; 1864-69; Ceylon
niel, John, b. 1820; Punch
nyson, Alfred, lord b. 1809; poet-
ureate
terden, lord; king's bench, 1818
ence, 195-159 B.C.; drama
entius Varro; Cannæ, 216 B.C.
ry v. Brighton aquarium comp.,
rials, 1875
ry, Mr.; boat (tricycle)
rtullian writes 197; cross, Monta-
ists
ucer; Troy, 1502 B.C.
wilk, Egypt, 1879.
xier, F.; drowning
yuham, lord; trials, 1833
ackeray, W. M., novelist, 1811-63
nkombau, Fiji, 1859-74
ales, Miletus; globe, 640 B.C.
Ionic sect, moon, water, world
halestris; queens
hanet, earl of; riots, 1799
hebau; Burmah, 1817-85
hecla; Alexandrine codex
hemistocles; Marathon, Salamis,
480 B.C.
Theobald; civil law, 1138
Theocritus; verse, 265 B.C.
Theodore; Corsica, 1736; Samos,
keys, lathe

Theodore, emperor, 1818-68; Abys-
sinia, 1855-68; Magdala
Theodoric; Spain, Goths, 553
Theodosius; Eastern emp., 379;
Aquileia, Ostrogoths, massacre,
paganism
Theodosius, the younger; academies,
Bologna
Theophilus; Antioch, chronology
Theophrastus, nat. ph., 370-287 B.C.
Theopompus; Ephori, funeral ora-
tions, Sparta, 353 B.C.
Theseus; Athens, 1235 B.C.
Thesiger, sir F.; solicitor-general,
1844; attorney-general, chanc.,
lord high, 1858; trials, 1850; d.
1878
Thesiger, gen.; Kaffraria, 1878
Thespis; drama, 536 B.C.
Thevenot, M.; coffee, 1662
Thierry; Holland, 936
Thiers, A.; 1798-1877; France, 1836,
1871-8; Bordeaux
Thirleby; Westminster, 1541
Thirlwall. bp., Connop, 1797-1865;
St. David's, 1840-74
Thistlewood, A., Cato street consp.
Thom, James, sculptor, 1799-1850
Thomas, Cl.; France, 1871, 1876
Thomas, col.; duel, 1783
Thomas & Gilchrist, steel
Thomas, Mrs., Richmond
Thomé de Gammond, tunnels, 1867
Thompson, E.; life-raft, 1874
Thompson, Eliz.; scientific assoc.
Thompson, sir H.; burning dead,
1873
Thompson, Miss; trials, 1821
Thompson, major; suicide, 1832
Thompson, William; lord mayor,
1828
Thoms, W. J.; folk lore, longevity,
notes and queries, wills
Thomson or Thomas; dynamite, 1875
Thomson, sir C. Wyville, 1830-82;
deep sea, 1868-76
Thomson, Mr. Poulett; Melbourne
administration, 1835; calico
Thomson, R., road steamers, 1868
Thomson, Jas. (the "Seasons"),
1700-48; Richmond, Rule Britannia
Thomson, J. B.; bleaching
Thomson, sir William; electricity,
tides
Thomson, Joseph, Africa, 1880-2
Thornton, Abraham; appeal, 1817
Thornton, sir E.; Turkey, 1884
Thorpe, William de; bribery, 1351
Thorpe, John T.; lord mayor, 1820
Thorwaldsen, Alb., sculp., 1777-1844
Thoth; mythology, 152 B.C.
Thouvenel, E. A., Fr. statesman,
1818-66
Thrasybulus; Athens, 403 B.C.
Thrupp, G.; carriages, 1877
Thucydides, Gr. hist., 470-404 B.C.
Thurlow, lord; chancellor, lord high,
1778; great seal
Thurtell, J.; executions, 1824
Thwaites, sir John, 1815-70; metrop.
board of works
Thyra, Dannawerke
Tiberius, 903 B.C.; Capri, Rome,
emp. 14
Tiberius Gracchus; agrarian law,
132 B.C.
Tibullus, Lat. poet, 50-18 B.C.
Tichborne, trials, 1871-3
Ticknor, G., amer. hist. 1791-1861
Tieck, L., Ger. poet, 1773-1853
Tierney, George; duel, 1798; Gode-
rich
Tighe, Mr.; trials, 1800
Tigranes; Armenia, 93 B.C.; Pontus
Tilden, S. J.; United States, 1876
Tildesley, sir Thomas; Wigan, 1651
Tilghman, B. C.; sand-blast, 1871
Tilloch, Mr.; stereotype

Tillotson, abp.; Canterbury, 1691;
universalists
Tilly; Magdeburg, 1631; Palatinate,
Lech
Times newspaper; Times, trials, 1790
Timoleon; Syracuse, 343 B.C.
Timour; see Tamerlane
Tindal and Coverdale; Bible, 1526
Tippoo Sahib; Arikera, Madras,
Seringapatam, Mysore, 1792
Tirard; France, 1888
Tissandier and others; balloons, 1875;
1883
Tisza; Hungary, 1875-8
Titian, painter, 1477-1576
Titus, Rome, emp. 79; Jerusalem,
Tyre, arches
Todd v. Lyne; trials, 1873
Todhunter, I.; math. 1820-84; pro-
bability
Todleben, gen., 1818-84; Sebastopol;
Plevna, 1877; Russo-Turkish war
II, etc., 1877-8
Tofts, Mary; impostor, 1726
Toler, Mr.; m., trials, 1853
Tolly, Barclay de; Smolensko, 1812
Tolmides; Coronea, 447 B.C.
Tomline, bp.; Lincoln, Winchester,
1820
Tolstoi, count; Russia, 1882; (mini-
ster) Russia, 1883-9
Tom Thumb; dwarfs, 1846
Tompion, Thos.; clocks, 1695
Tone, Theobald W.; trials, 1798
Tonson, Jacob, bookseller, d. 1736
Tonti, Laurence; Tontines
Tooke, J. Horne, 1736-1812; "diver-
sions of Purley," 1786
Tooke, W.; prices
Tooth, rev. A.; public worship, 1876
Topete, adm., Spain, 1868-73
Toro, M. M., Colombia, 1872
Torpey, trials, 1870
Torrence, Mrs.; trials, 1821
Torrens, lieut.; duel, 1806
Torres; Australasia, 1606
Torricelli; d. 1647; air, micro-
scopes
Torrington, Herbert, lord; Walpole
admin., 1727
Toselli, diving, 1871
Totila; Italy, 541
Tourgénéff, T. S., 1818-83; Rus. nov.;
nihilists
Toussaint, 1794; Hayti, St. Do-
mingo
Tower, Mr.; volunteer, 1803, 1860
Townley, G. V.; trials, 1863
Townshend, lord; duel, 1773; Ire-
land
Townshends; Rockingham, Chat-
ham, and Grafton admins., 1765-7
Train, G. F.; street railways, 1860;
Ireland, 1868
Trajan; Rome, emp. 98; Trajan's
pillar, Dacia
Trangott, R.; Poland, 1864
Travers, Samuel; poor knights of
Windsor
Treby, George; Walpole, 1721
Tresylian; king's bench
Trevelyan, sir C.; Madras, 1859-60
Trevelyan, sir G. O.; household suf-
frage Gladstone adm., 1880, 1886;
Ireland, 1882
Trevelyan, W. C.; phonography
Trevethick; steam engine, 1802
Trevor, sir John; speaker, 1694
Tribe, A.; copper-zinc couple, 1872
Troas; Troy, 1374 B.C.
Trochu, gen., France, 1870-1, defence
Trollope, A.; nov., &c., 1815-82
Trollope, Messrs.; tapestry
Tropman, France, 1869
Troubridge, sir T.; wrecks, 1807
"True Sun," prop. of; trials, 1834
Truman, Hanbury, & Co.; porter,
1815

INDEX.

Trumbull, Jonathan
Truro, lord ; chancellor, lord, 1850
Tsêng, marquis, China, 1879-80
Tucker, E. ; vine disease, 1845
Tuckett, capt. Harvey ; duel, 1840
Tufnell, E. C., training schools
Tuite, murderer ; trials, 1813
Tuke, W. ; lunatics, 1792
Tull, William ; posting
Tulloch, col. ; Sebastopol, 1855
Tullus Hostilius ; Alba, saturnalia
Tunstall, bp. ; administrations, 1529 ; arithmetic, privy seal
Turenne, marshal, 1611-75
Turner, Joseph Mallord William, 1775-1851
Turnerelli, T., people's tribute
Turnbull, Dahomey, 1876
Turnbull, W. B. ; trials, 1861
Turner, J. W. ; painter, 1775-1851
Turner, Miss ; trials, 1827
Turner, Richard ; teetotaller, 1831
Turner, rev. Sydney ; 1814-79 ; reformatory schools, 1849
Turner ; trials, 1817
Turpin, or Tilpin, bp. ; writes, 818
Turton, bishop ; Ely, 1845
Tussaud, Mad. ; waxwork
Tasser ; agriculture, 1562
Twyecoss v. Grant ; trials, 1876
Tyce, John ; taffety, 1598
Tycho Brahe, 1546-1601 ; astronomy, platonic year, globe
Tyler, John ; United States president, 1841
Tyler, Wat ; killed, 1381
Tyndale, Wm. ; martyred, 1536
Tyndall, J. ; Roy. Inst., 1853 ; magnetism, Mont Blanc, 1857 ; calorescence, sound, dust, Niagara, United States, 1872, spontaneous generation, germ theory
Tyndarus ; Sparta, 1490 B.C.
Tyrconnel, earl of ; Ireland, 1687
Tyrone ; rebellion, 1599
Tysias, or Stesichorus ; choruses, epithalamium, 536 B.C.

U.

Uchatius, gen. von ; cannon, 1875
Udine ; stucco-work, 1530
Ufrul ; Afghanistan, 1863
Ugolinos, B. ; thesaurus
Uiélas, bp. ; Bible, about 373
Ulloa, Antonio ; platinum, 1741
Ulpian (lawyer) ; slain, 228
Ulysses ; Trojan war
Union Bank ; trials, 1875
Upton, colonel ; Sebastopol, 1830
Urban ; popes, 223
Urban II. ; communion, crusades, 1094
Urban VIII, pope, "Eminence," 1630
Urich, gen. ; Strasburg, 1870
Ursula, St. ; Cologne, Ursulines, 1537
Uriarte, H. ; Paraguay, 1877
Usher, abp. ; articles, 1614
Usher, H. T. ; Labuan, 1875

V.

Valens ; eastern empire, western empire, 364
Valentia, lord ; duel, 1798 ; trials, 1796
Valentia cause ; trials, 1772
Valentine, B. ; antimony, 1410
Valentinian ; western empire, 364
Valerian ; persecutions, 257

Vallaret, Foulques de ; Malta, 1310
Vallière, madame de la ; midwifery, 1663
Valverde, gen. ; Hayti, 1858
Van Artevelde ; Ghent, 1379-83
Vanbrugh, sir J. ; 1670-1726, Clarendon printing office, opera
Van Buren M. (president) ; United States, 1837
Vance & Snee ; trials, 1876
Vancouver ; north-west passage, Vancouver, 1790
Van de Weyer, M. ; Belgium, 1874
Van der Heyden ; fire engines, 1663
Van der Heydt ; Prussia, 1862, 1874
Van der Weyde ; photography, 1876
Vanderbilt, Mr. ; United States, 1885
Vandersmissen, M. ; Belgium, 1886
Vandyck, painter, 1599-1641
Vane, sir Henry ; administrations, 1640
Vanes ; trials, 1876
Van Eyck ; painting, 1366
Van Horn ; buccaneer, 1603
Van Leyden ; engraving on wood, 1497
Van Marum ; electricity, 1785
Van Mildert, bishop ; Llandaff, Durham, 1826
Van Praagh, W. ; deaf and dumb, 1871
Vansittart, Nicholas ; Liverpool adm., 1812
Van Tromp ; Holland, naval battles, Portland Isle, 1653
Varley, C. F., 1828-83 ; electricity, telephone, 1870-7
Varley, John ; water colour painter, 1778-1842
Varley, Cornelius ; nat. phil., 1781-1873
Varole, M. ; optic nerves, 1538
Varro ; writes "de Re Rustica," 37 B.C. ; grammarians, illuminated books
Varus, Alfrenus ; civil law, 66 B.C. ; code, digest
Vasali, or Basil ; Russia, 1270
Vasco da Gama ; Cape, 1497 ; India
Vattel, E. de, publicist, 1714-67
Vauban, S., 1633-1707 ; fortifications, Cherbourg
Vaughan, sir Thos. ; Pomfret, 1483
Vaughan, Mackay, &c. ; trial, 1816
Vauquelin ; chromium, glucinum, 1798
Vaux, Jane, Mrs. ; Vauxhall, 1615
Vega, G. de, 1503-36 ;—Lope de, 1562-1635, poets
Velasquez, painter, 1599-1660 ; Cuba, 1511
Venables, Wm. ; lord mayor, 1825
Venner, T. ; anabaptists, 1661
Venn, J., logic
Vergara, gen. ; New Grenada
Vergennes, M. de ; notables, 1788
Vermandois, count de ; iron mask
Vermuyden, Cornelius ; levels, 1621
Vernet, C. J., 1714-89 ; A. C. H., 1758-1836 ; J. E. Horace, 1789-1863 ; painters
Vernon, adm. ; grog, Portobello, 1739
Vernon, abp. ; York, 1808
Verres ; Sicily, 70 B.C.
Verrocchio, Andrea ; plaster, 1466
Vesalius, 1514-64 ; anatomy, surgery, physic
Vespasian ; Rome, emp. 69 ; amphitheatres, Coliseum, Rhodes
Vespucius, Americus, 1498 ; America
Veuillot ; France, 1883
Victor Amadeus ; Sardinia, 1630
Victor Emmanuel, 1820-78 ; Sardinia, 1849 ; Italy, 1860
Victor, marshal ; Talavera, 1809 ; Barrosa, Witepsk
Victor ; pope, 193
Victoria, queen, b. 1819 ; England, Scotland, Ireland, India

Victory, Espartero, duke of ; Spain, 1840-72
Vidil, baron de ; trials, 1861
Vieta, Francis ; algebra, 1590
Vigilius ; pope, 537
Villars, marshal ; Malplaquet, 1709
Villeneuve, adm. ; Trafalgar, 1805
Villeroy, marshal ; Brussels, 1695, Ramilies, 1706
Villiers, sir George ; administrations, 1615
Villiers, bp. ; Durham, 1860
Vincent de Paul, 1576-1660 ; sisters of charity
Vincent, B., Royal Inst. library catalogue, 1857 ; bible index, 1848
Vincent, C. W., electric light, 1879
Vincent, H. ; chartists
Vincent, Howard ; police, 1884
Vincent, Z. W. ; Cæcilian society
Vinoy, gen. ; France and Franco-Pruss. war, 1870-71 ; d. 1883
Virchow ; development, man
Virgil, Lat. poet, 70-19 B.C.
Virginia ; killed, 449 B.C.
Vitalianus ; pope, 537
Vitellius, Rome, emp. 69
Vitruvius, abt. 27 B.C. ; ink
Vivier ; trials, 1842
Volta, Alex. ; 1745-1826 ; electricity, Volta
Voltaire, F. M. A. de ; 1694-1778
Von Fuchs, Dr., d. 1856 ; water-glass stereochromy
Von der Tann, gen. ; Franco-Prussian war, 1870-1 ; Coulmiers, Orleans
Von Gœben, gen. ; Saarbrück, Franco-Prussian war, 1870-1
Von Groof ; flying, 1874
Von Mohl ; protoplasm
Von Moltke, gen. ; Franco-Prussian war, Sedan, 1870
Von Mühler, Prussia, 1872
Von Stein, Prussia, 1807
Von Swab ; blowpipe
Von Vincke ; Prussia, 1874
Vortigern ; Wales, 447
Voss, poet, 1751-1826
Voysey, C. ; trials, 1870 ; Voysey establishment fund
Vyse, Mrs. A. ; trials, 1862

W.

Waddington ; trials, 1820 ; France 1877-8-9
Wade, Sir T., China, 1875
Wager, C. ; admiralty, 1733
Waghorn, lieut., 1800-50 ; Waghorn
Wagner, R., 1813-83 ; music of the future)
Wainwright, Whitechapel ; trials, 1875
Waithman, Robert ; lord mayor, 1823, obelisk, bank
Wake, abp. ; Canterbury, 1715
Wakefield, Eliz. ; savings banks, 1804
Wakefield, Ed. Gibbon ; marriages, South Australia, trials, 1827
Wakley, T., Lancet, 1823
Waldegrave, earl of ; trials, 1841
Waldegrave, bp. ; Carlisle, 1860
Waldemar ; Denmark, 1157
Walden, abp. ; Canterbury, 1398
Wales, George, prince of, v. Times, trials, 1790 ; regency
Wales, Albert Edward, prince of ; England ; Wales
Walker, A. ; Liverpool, 1877
Walker, Mr. ; Vauxhall, congelation, ice, 1782
Walker, George, Londonderry, Boyne, 1689
Walker, gen. ; filibusters, Nicaragua, 1855, executed, 1860
Wall governor ; trials 1802 Goree

Wall, Mr. Baring; trials, 1833
Wall, Jas.; copying-machine
Wallace, A. R.; development, 1870
Wallace, sir W.; exec. 1305; Falkirk, Cambuskenneth, 1297
Wallace, D. M.; Molokani
Wallaces; trials, 1841
Wallenstein, Albert, general, 1583-1634; Mecklenburg
Waller, G., velocipede
Waller, sir W.; Abingdon, 1644
Wallis, circumnavigator; Otaheite, Wallis, 1766
Wallon; France, 1875
Walpole, Horace, 1717-97; letters
Walpole, sir Robert, 1676-1745; Walpole, adm.; sinking fund
Walpole, Spencer-Horatio, b. 1806; Derby adm., 1852-66
Walsh, abp.; Parnellites, 1889
Walsh, Mrs.; murdered, trials, 1832
Walsh, Nicholas; printing, 1571
Walsingham, lord; att.-gen., 1766; farmers' union, 1874
Walsingham, sir F. administrations, 1587
Walter, E.; commissionaires, 1859
Walter, J., 1739-1812; Times, 1785; printing, 1872
Walthcof; beheading, 1076
Walton, Brian, 1600-61; polyglot
Walton, Izaac, 1593-1683; angling
Walworth; Blackheath, mace, 1381
Warburton, Eliot (lost), Amazon, 1852
Ward, Mr.; forgery, 1726
Ward, E. M., R. A., d. 1879
Ward, N. B.; aquarium, Ward's cases, 1829
Wardle, col.; impeachment, Wardle v. duke of York; trials, 1809
Wardley, James; shakers
Warenne, earl of; Dunbar, 1296
Warham, abp.; Canterbury, 1503; administrations, 1509
Warington, R.; aquarium, 1850
Warner, Mrs., d. 1854; theatre
Warner, Messrs.; bells, 1856
Warren, admiral sir John Borlase; naval battles, 1798
Warren, sir Chas.; Soudan, 1886; Bechuanaland; police
Warren, Sam., novelist, 1807-77
Warrington gang; trials, 1806
Warsop, Geo.; aëro-steam engine, 1869
Warton, Thomas; poet-laureate, 1785
Warwick, earl of; Barnet, St. Albans, Wakefield, 1460
Warwick, John Dudley, earl of; administrations, 1551
Washington, George, 1732-99; United States, York Town, Virginia
Wason, Rigby; trial, 1867
Waterhouse, Mr.; Paul's school, St. Bristol
Waterland, Dr.; Athanasian Creed, 1723
Waters, M.; infanticide, trials, 1870
Waterton, Chas.; naturalist, 1782-1865
Wathen, capt.; trials, 1834
Watson, admiral; India, 1756
Watson, J. C.; planets, 1862
Watson, rev. J. S.; trials, 1871; d. 1884
Watson, bishop; Llandaff, 1782; phlogiston
Watson, Thos., M.D., 1792-1882
Watson, sir Wm.; electricity, 1740; lightning conductor; trials, 1817
Watt and Downie; trials, 1794
Watt, Jas., 1736-1819; lunar society, steam engine
Watteau, Ant., French painter, 1684-1721
Watts, Il., 1815-84; chemistry
Watts, Isaac, 1674-1748; hymns
Watts; theatres, trials, 1850; suicide

Watts, T.; newspapers, 1766
Weare, Mr.; trials, 1824
Weathershed, abp.; Canterbury, 1229
Webb, capt.; swimming, 1875
Webbe, Sam., music, 1740-1817
Weber, Carl von, 1786-1826; music
Webster, C., Richmond murder
Webster, Daniel, d. 1852; United States
Webster, Dr.; trials, 1842
Webster, sir Godfrey; trials, 1797
Webster, Mr.; aluminium
Webster, sir R. E., att.-gen, 1885, 1886; Parnellites, 1888
Webster, T.; painter, 1800-86
Wedgwood, Josiah, 1730-95; earthenware, Wedgwood (porcelain)
Wedgwood, T.; photography, 1802
Weed, Thurlow; United States, d. 1882
Weekes, H., R.A., 1807-77
Weld, Mr.; trappists
Weldon, Mrs.; trials, 1884-8
Weldon, Walter; alkalies, 1877
Wellesley, sir A.; see Wellington
Wellesley, marquis; India, 1798
Wellesley, Mr. Long; duel, 1828
Wellesley, Pole, v. Misses Long; trials, 1825
Wellesley v. Paget; trials, 1809; v. Mornington, trials, 1868
Wellington, duke of, 1769-1852; Wellington; commander-in-chief, duelling, 1824; duels, 1829; trials, 1830
Wells, W.; dew, 1814
Wells, lord Lyon Ireland (lord lieut.), 1438
Weltmann, poisoning, 1859
Wemyss, see Elcho
Wenham; heat
Wensleydale, lord; lords, note
Werdermann, electric light, 1878
Werner, A. G., 1750-1817; geology, 1775
Werner, capt.; Spain, 1873
Weskett, John; commerce, chambers of, 1782
Wesley, J., 1703-91; Wesleyans
West, Benj., 1738-1820; Royal Academy, 1792
Westbury, lord chancellor; Palmerston adm., 1861; 1873-80
Westerton v. Liddell; trials, 1855
Westmacott, sir R., sculpt., 1775-1856; R. 1799-1872
Westmeath, lord; trials, 1796
Westmoreland, earl of; Ireland (lord. lieut.), 1790
Weston, E. P.; pedestrianism, 1874-7
Weston, Richard lord; administrations, 1628
Wetherell, sir Chas.; attorney-gen., 1826; Bristol
Wetherell, rev. Mr.; trials, 1845
Weyland, Thomas de; bribery, 1289
Weymouth; North-West passage, 1602
Weymouth, visct.; Grafton adm., 1768
Whalley will case; trials, 1883-4
Wharncliffe, ld.; Peel adm., 1834
Wharton, Thomas, marquis of; Halifax adm., 1714
Wharton, Miss; marriages, 1690
Whately, abp. R., 1787-1863; logic, political economy, &c.
Wheatstone, sir C., 1802-75; cryptography; stereoscope, electricity, 1834; electric telegraph, and clock, microphone, telephone
Wheeler, sir Hugh; Cawnpore, 1857
Whewell, Rev. W., philosopher, 1794-1866; international law
Whistler v. Ruskin, trials, 1878; impressionists
Whiston, W., theol., d. 1752
Whitaker; almanack, 1874

Whitbread, Samuel; suicide, 1815
White, H. K., poet, 1785-1806
White, Thos., Sion College, 1623; mayor, 1876
White, sir W.; Turkey, 1886
Whitefield, G., 1714-70; Whitefieldites, Wesleyans, 1741
Whitehead, Jas.; ld. mayor, 1823; volunteers, 1883
Whitehead, W. d. 1785; poet laureate
Whitelock, Jno.; Buenos Ayres, 1807
Whitgift, abp.; Canterbury, 1583
Whitney, Eli; cotton, 1793
Whittall; coins, 1884
Whittington; lord mayor, 1405; Leadenhall
Whittlesey, archbp.; Canterbury, 1368
Whitworth, sir Joseph, 1803-87; cannon, plane, Shoeburyness, 1861; Whitworth
Whitworth, earl; Ireland, 1813
Whymper, E., Andes; Matterhorn
Whyte, maj.-gen.; Demerara, 1796
Wickens, sir J.; vice-chancellor, 1871
Wickham, William of, 1324-1405; education, Oxford, Winchester
Wickliffe (Wycliffe), John, 1324-87; Wickliffites, Bible
Wicklow peerage, trials, 1870
Wieland, C.; Germ. miscel., 1733-1813
Wigram, bp.; Rochester, 1860
Wilberforce, bp.; Oxford, 1846
Wilberforce, W., 1759-1833; slave-trade; — S., Winchester, bp.
Wilberforce, bp. E. R., Newcastle-on-Tyne, 1882
Wild, Jonathan; executed, 1725
Wilde, sir James, b. 1816; probate court, 1863; see Penzance
Wilfride, bp.; Chichester, 673
Wilkes, capt.; circumnavigation, 1838; United States, 1861
Wilkes, John; North Briton, obelisk, warrants; duel, 1763; trials, 1764
Wilkie, sir D., painter, 1785-1841
Wilkins, Dr.; Wadham, 1613
Wilkinson, Catherine; baths, 1832
Wilkinson, sir John Gardner, Egyptologist, 1797-1875
Wilkinson, bp. G. H.; Truro, 1883
Wilkinson, Ia.; air (compressing), 1757
William I., England, 1066; Battle-abbey, conquest, Domesday, castles
William II.; England, 1087
William III.; England, 1689, revolution. Boyne, Enghien, Je maintiendrai, New Forest
William IV.; England, kings, 1830; admiral
William I.; emperor; Prussia, 1861; Germany, 1870-88; assassinations
William II.; Germany, 1888.
William; Holland, Scotland
Williams, prof.; Indian inst.
Williams, Ann; trials, 1753
Williams, David, d. 1816; literary fund
Williams, Mr.; Manchester, 1882
Williams, John, dean; adminis., 1621
Williams; see Burking
Williams, Roger; America, 1635
Williams, gen. W. F.; Kars, 1855
Williamson, sir Joseph; administrations, 1629
Willoughby, sir Hugh; north-east passage, 1553
Willoughby de Eresby, lord; chamberlain, lord great, 1626
Willoughby, lieut.; Delhi, 1857
Wills, gen.; Preston, 1715
Wilmot, lieut. E.; Ashantees, 1873
Wilmot, M. A., trials, 1881

Wilmington, earl of; Wilmington adm., 1742
Wilson, capt.; Pelew Islands, 1783
Wilson, sir A.; Delhi, 1857
Wilson, sir James Erasmus, 1809-84; Aberdeen; obelisks (Cleopatra's needle), 1877-8; Egypt expl. fund
Wilson, rev. Carlyle; church army
Wilson, G., colour blindness
Wilson, H. H.; Sanskrit professor, 1832
Wilson, sir C.; Soudan, 1883
Wilson, sir Robert; Lavalette, 1815
Wilson, prof. John, 1785-1854
Wilson, sir John M., Hampstead
Wilson, Mrs. C.; poisoning, trials, 1862
Wilson, capt. W.; United States, 1862, note
Wilson, M.; France, 1887-8.
Wilson, Dr.; sun
Wilton, earl of; trials, 1859.
Wimshurst, James; electricity, 1882
Winchelsea, abp.; Canterbury, 1293
Winchester, gen.; Frenchtown, 1813
Winchester, Henry; mayor, lord, 1834
Winchester, W., marquis of; administrations, 1554
Winchilsea, earl of; duel, 1829
Winchilsea, earl of; Wilmington adm., 1742; Bath adm., 1746
Windebank, sir Francis; administrations, 1635
Windham, general; India, 1857
Windham, W. F.; trials, 1861-2
Windham, Wm.; Grenville adm., 1806
Windischgratz, prince; Vienna, 1848
Winsor, Charlotte; trials, 1865
Winstanley; Eddystone, 1696
Winslow, E. D.; extradition, 1876
Winslow, Dr. F.; trials, 1884
Winter, T.; boxing
Winwood, sir Ralph; administrations, 1612
Winzengerode, gen.; Kalisch, 1813
Wise, prof.; balloons, 1873
Wiseman, cardinal Nicholas, 1802-65; ecclesiastical titles, papal aggression, Rome, Ireland, 1858
Wissman, capt.; Zanzibar, 1889.
Withers, Dr.; libel, 1789
Witherings, Thomas; post-office, 1631
Witherington, W., painter, 1786-1865
Withing, Richard; Glastonbury, 1539
Witikind (Saxon chief), d. after 793
Wittgenstein, gen.; Polotsk, Witepsk, 1812
Witts, De; massacred, 1672
Wodehouse, lord; Ireland (lord-lieut.), 1864
Wodehouse, sir P.; Bombay, 1872
Wodehouse, col.; Soudan, 1889
Woden; Wednesday
Wöhler, F.; 1800-82; aluminium, 1827
Wolcot, Dr., alias Peter Pindar; trials, 1807
Wolf, F. A.; Homer
Wolfe, gen.; Quebec, 1759
Wolff, Dr. J.; Bockhara, 1884; sir H. D., fourth party; Turkey, 1885; Persia.
Wolfius; anemometer, 1709
Wollaston, Wm.; 1766-1828; cryophorus, camera, blow pipe, palladium, rhodium, hypsometer
Wolseley, sir Charles; trials, 1820
Wolseley, sir Garnet (aft. ld.) b. 1833; Hudson's Bay, 1870; Ashantee, 1873; Amoaful, 1874; West Africa, 1873; Cyprus, 1878; Natal; Zululand, 1879; Egypt, 1882; Tel-el-Kebir, 1882; Soudan, 1884
Wolsey, cardinal, 1471-1530; adms., 1514; Hampton, Whitehall, York
Wolverton, ld.; Gladstone adm., 1886.
Wombwell; zoology
Wood, sir Charles (aft. lord Halifax); Russell adm., 1846; Palmerston adm., 1855
Wood, col. sir Evelyn, Zululand, 1879; Egypt, 1882
Wood v. Cox; races, 1888.
Wood, Matthew; mayors of London, 1815
Wood, sir W. P., justice, chancellor, 1868
Wood; Palmyra, 1751-53
Woodford, bp. J. R.; Ely, 1873
Woodfall, Mr.; trials, 1786
Woodmason; ruling machines
Wooler, Mr.; trials, 1817, 1855
Woolley, Mr.; trials, 1863
Worburton; trials, 1885.
Worcester, marquis of; steam, telegraph, 1663
Worcester, Edward, earl of; adms., 1621.
Wordsworth, Wm.; 1770-1850; poet-laureate
Wortley, col. H. Stuart; mansion-house fund, 1871
Wotton, sir Edward; sugar, 1546
Wouvermans, painters, 1620-83
Wray, sir C.; King's Bench, 1573
Wrede, gen.; Hanau, 1813
Wren, sir Christopher, architect, 1632-1723; Chelsea, engraving, Greenwich, monument, St. Paul's, Walbrook
Wren, Matthew; Royal Society
Wrench, Mr.; theatres, 1809
Wright; Mercator's charts, 1556
Wright, sir Rob.; King's Bench, 1687
Wright and Doyle; trials, 1851
Wriothesley, lord; administrations, 1547
Wurmser, gen.; Castiglione, 1796
Wurtz, prof. K. A., 1817-84; chemistry; Faraday medal, 1878
Wyatt, sir Thos.; rebellions, 1554
Wybrow; aquarium, 1876
Wyld, J.; globe, 1851
Wynkyn de Worde; angling, 1496; printing
Wynn, W.; Canning adm., 1827
Wyon, W., medallist, 1795-1851
Wyse, L. A. B.; Panama

X.

Xavier, Francis; 1506-52; Jesuits
Xenophanes, d. 465 B.C.; Eleatic sect, Pantheism
Xenophon; anatomy, couriers, cymbals, retreat of the Greeks, 401 B.C.

Xerxes; Persia, 485 B.C.; Mycale, Salamis
Ximenes, card., 1437-1517; polyglot

Y.

Yakoob, Afghanistan, 1867-79, Kashgar
Yale, Elisha; auctions, 1700
Yarrow, Mr.; spirit motor
Yates, E., nov.; trials, 1884-5
Yeh, commissioner; China, 1857
Yelverton, major; trials, 1860
Yonge, sir Geo.; Shelburne adm., 1783
Yonge, miss C.; names
York, bishop; Ely, 1781
York, cardinal; Scotland, 1807
York, Fred., duke of; 1763-1827 York
York, James, duke of; Solebay, 1672
Yorke, Charles, chancellor, lord high, 1770
Yorke, sir Philip; att.-gen.; king's bench, 1733
Yorke, Mr. Redhead; trial, 1795
Youl, J. A., salmon ova
Young; impostors, 169a
Young, Brigham, 1801-77; Mormonites
Young, major; Prescott, 1838
Young, Charles; theatre, 1807
Young, Edw., poet, 1684-1765
Young, Thos., 1773-1829; Royal Institution, colour, spectrum
Youngman, W.; executions, 1860

Z.

Zabala; Spain, 1874
Zacharias; pope, 741
Zaleucus; sumptuary laws, 450 B.C.
Zamoyski, count; Poland, 1862
Zankoff; Bulgaria
Zasulitch, V.; Russia, 1878
Zazel; Aquarium
Zechariah prophesies about 520 B.C.
Zeno (stoic), fl. 299 B.C.; eastern empire, 474
Zenobia; Palmyra, 263
Zenon; Armenia, 18
Zephaniah prophesies abt. 630 B.C.
Zephyrinus; pope, 202
Zetland, earl of; Salisbury adm., 1886; Ireland, ld. lieut., 1889.
Zeuxis, fl. 455-400 B.C.; painting
Zimmerman; physiognomy, 1776
Zinzendorf, 1700-60; Moravians
Ziska; Bohemia, 1417
Zoh; eastern empire, 1034
Zola, E., naturalism
Zollicoffer, gen.; U. States, 1861
Zorilla, R.; Spain, 1872-3
Zoroaster (supposed author of "Zendavesta"); about 555 B.C., fire-worshippers
Zosimus; alchemy, 410
Zukkertort, J. S., chess
Zumalacarregul (Carlist); killed near Bilbao, 1835
Zumpte, M.; pianoforte, 1766
Zurbano, gen.; Spain, 1844

ADDENDA.

5. ABYSSINIA.—The Negus is stated to have been defeated in his attack on the dervishes, 10 March; and to have been attacked and killed by them, 12 March, 1889.
7. ACHEEN.—The natives attacking the Dutch garrison, defeated; 160 killed, reported 15 May; another engagement in which the Dutch lose 19 killed; reported 2 Aug. 1889.
9. ADELAIDE.—Population 1886, 128,377.
21. AGRICULTURE.—The Act for establishing the Board of Agriculture, with a minister, received the Royal Assent, 12 Aug. 1889.
23. ALABAMA.—Population 1880, 1,262,505.
24. ALASKA.—Population 1880, 33,426.
24. ALBANIA.—The Albanian society established at Bucharest for the political, moral, and intellectual development of the Albanians has been reorganized, and the sultan has been asked to accept the protectorate, May, 1889.
26. ALDERSHOT.—The queen reviews 11,945 of all ranks . . . . . . 31 May, 1889
A sham fight and review, in which about 25,530 troops, regulars and volunteers, were engaged, took place here in the presence of the emperor William II., the princess of Wales, the duke of Cambridge, and others of the royal family . . . . 7 Aug. ,,
27. ALEXANDRA PARK.— Re-opened for the season; exhibition of nearly 1,000 monkeys, balloons and parachutes, &c., professor Baldwin, Mr. Young, and others 1 June, 1889
Comic opera by Mr. C. Wibrow, 17 June, et seq. ,,
French national fête, gen. Boulanger present 13 July, ,,
Professor Baldwin, after 98 ascents and descents, retires with intention of returning to America, about . . . 17 July, ,,
The London Financial Association apply for the appointment of a provisional liquidator pending the winding-up of the Alexandra Palace and park company. Mr. C. L. Nichols appointed . . . . . 27 July, ,,
50. ARIZONA.—Population 1880, 40,440.
50. ARKANSAS.—Population 1880, 802,525.
84. BANK discount raised to 3 per cent. 8 Aug., to 4 per cent. 29 Aug. 1889.
105. BELFAST.—Prince Albert Victor of Wales opens the new Alexandra docks 20 May, and lays the foundation of Albert bridge, 22 May, 1889.
105. BELGIUM.—State trials of 27 socialists at Mons, nearly all acquitted, 25 May; the minister of justice was censured for the prosecution, May, 1889.
121. BLIND.—According to the census of 1881, the number of blind in the United Kingdom was about 32,101. England and Wales 22,832, Scotland 3,158, Ireland 6,111. The royal commission to enquire into their condition was appointed 28 July, 1885, and on the 20th of Jan. 1886, additional members were appointed, and its inquiries were extended to the deaf, dumb, and imbeciles in the United Kingdom, Paris, Germany, Switzerland, and Italy. The commission, after 116 sittings, and many visitations and examinations of witnesses, issued their first report July, 1889. The number of the deaf under instruction in the United Kingdom was in 1851 1,300, in 1888 3,138. The commission met with great uncertainty in regard to idiots and imbeciles.
129. BOTANY.—Royal botanic society's jubilee fête; floral parade and feast of roses, 15 July, 1889.
133. BRAZIL.—The emperor fired at by Adriano Valte, a republican, Portuguese; not injured, 15 July, 1889.
137. BRISBANE, Queensland. — Population in 1887 about 73,000.
150. BURMAH.—A great fire at Mandalay, 450 houses burnt . . . . . 11 May, 1889
Mr. Dyson, assistant commissioner, and others, killed in an unsuccessful attack upon the Dacoits reported . . . . 2 June, ,,
Savage tribes beyond the frontier of Burmah Proper; incited by rebel Burmese chiefs; reduced to submission by the police and military . . . . . Jan.-June, ,,
Frequent engagements with bands of Dacoits June-July, ,,
Mr. MacDonnell appointed chief commissioner in the absence of sir. C. Crosthwaite, announced . . . . . 3 Aug. ,,
155. CALAIS.—The president Carnot opened the new harbour, docks, &c., 3 June, 1889.
155. CALCUTTA.—Trade paralyzed by strike of about 30,000 native bullock-carters for a few days, 30 June, et seq., 1889.
163. CANDIA (Crete). — The population in 1889 estimated at 210,000. Anarchy through party strife of Christians and Mahometans, May-June; Turkish troops sent to Crete, 13 June; provisional government formed to restore order . . . . 3 June, 1889
Mahmoud Djellalledin, pasha, Turkish commissioner well received; agitation calmed by his inquiries, June 14, et seq. An insurgent assembly demands a constituent assembly, judicial reforms, and dismissal of the governor, the people neutral about 1 July; the sultan sends 20,000 T., 6 July; Mahmoud Djellalledin, pasha, informs a deputation that their demands must be referred to the sultan, 8 July; he is suddenly recalled, 8 July, ,,
State of affairs becomes worse; increase of revolutionary bands, reported . 18 July, ,,
Asserted influence of Greek agitators, 22 July; insurrection increasing; call for annexation to Greece, or British protection about 25 July; Djavad pasha arrives to take command of the troops, two ships of war coming, reported . . . . . 1 Aug. ,,
Riza pasha appointed temporary governor, with extra powers for repressing disorder 4 Aug. ,,
Fighting going on, villages burnt, reported 5 Aug. ,,
Note from the Greek government to the powers, urging intervention in Crete, 6 Aug.; they decline, leaving the settlement to the Sultan, 9-12 Aug.; about 17,000 Turkish troops in Crete, reported . . . 7 Aug. ,,
A Turkish note denies the charges in the Greek note . . . . 12 Aug. ,,
Riza Pasha the governor recalled; replaced by Shakir Pasha, who arrives with plenary powers, 13 Aug.; proclaims martial law 14 Aug. ,,
Partial submission of the insurgents; amnesty promised . . . . . 17 Aug. ,,
166. CANTERBURY.—Reed and others versus the bishop of Lincoln, before sir J. Parker Deane, 23 July, 1889.
168. CAPE OF GOOD HOPE.—Sir H. Brougham Loch appointed governor and high commissioner for South Africa about 22 June, 1889
169. CARBO-DYNAMITE. — A powerful explosive of the nitro-glycerine class, invented by Messrs.

ADDENDA

Reid and Borland, was tried in 1888, and in July, 1889, was said to be practically perfect.
171. CARLYLE SOCIETY, founded in 1879, consists of students and admirers of Carlyle's works, desirous of extending his influence; they meet monthly to read papers, &c. They have a branch at Montreal.
185. CHESS.—International Chess Tournament, New York, closed; equal prizes awarded to Herr Weiss (Vienna) and M. Tischigorin (Russia) . . . . . 27 May, 1889
192. CHINA.—Hsu Ta Jen appointed minister for London, Paris, Brussels, and Rome, announced . . . . . 4 June, 1889
Luchow, in the province of Szechuen, destroyed by fire, about 1,200 persons perish, 27 June, „
The Yellow river bursts its banks at Shantung, and inundates the country, and countless lives are lost, reported . . 26 July, „
194. CHRIST'S HOSPITAL.—The appeal of the governors against the Charity Commissioners' scheme, was submitted to the judicial committee of the privy council 18 June, 1889
210. COAL.—Explosion of fire-damp in Verpilleux mine, near St. Etienne, about 184 deaths 3 July, 1889
210. COAL DUES.—An act for the abolition of these dues received the royal assent 9 July, 1889. Provision was made for the continuance of these dues another year to enable the corporation to pay debts due for the Holborn Viaduct and various city improvements.
212. COIN.—Mr. Göschen introduces a bill for the withdrawal of light gold coin issued before June, 1837, and the substitution of coin of full weight provisionally, at the expense of the mint, July; passed . Aug. 1889
224. CONGO.—The State appeals to Belgium for an annual subsidy of 1,500,000 francs for ten years, about . . . 12 Aug. 1889
225. CONSERVATIVES.—The National Union of Conservative Associations was held at Salisbury . . . . 25 July, 1889
226. CONSTANTINOPLE.—Great fire, about 200 houses destroyed . . 18 July, 1889
233. CORNWALL.—Receipts from the duchy in 1888 107,572l.; paid to the prince of Wales as duke, 61,971l.
236. COTTON.—In Lancashire and Cheshire the mills put on half time, to limit the production and check speculations to raise the price of cotton, &c. . . about 15 July, 1889
249. CYPRUS.—Long drought in 1887-8; bad harvest, great distress, relieved by government, trade and revenue decline, expenditure increased, increase of crime, government report . . . . . July, 1889
258. DELAGOA BAY.—The Portuguese government in 14 Dec. 1883, granted a concession to a Portuguese company for the construction of a railway from the bay to the Transvaal territory. The prospectus of the East African Railway Company (capital 500,000l.) was issued 7 March, 1887. As the construction went on, more money and time were required. As the railway was not completed in the specified time, the works were confiscated by the Portuguese government 25 June, who cancelled the concession (see *Portugal*) . . . . 26 June, 1889
263. DERVISH.—Probably a corruption of der-pish or der-bish, one in advance. The dervishes of the present time, fanatical enthusiasts, unrecognized by orthodoxy, originated in Persia, whence they spread over the Mahommedan world. Those now attacking Egypt are said to be subject to a disciple of the late Mahdi of Obeid or Khartoum. The dervishes have great influence over the ignorant masses. See *Soudan*.
266. DICTATORS, line 3, erase "Flavius."
270. DOCKS.—New Barry docks, 7 miles west of Cardiff, Bristol channel (which with break-water, &c., cost 850,000l.), opened 18 July, 1889.
286. EARTHQUAKES.—Shocks in N. France and S. England . . . 30 May, 1889

Shock at Djarkend, government of Semiretchinsk; half the town destroyed reported 12 July, 1889
Severe shocks at Kumamoto, Japan, great loss of life and property . reported 30 July, „
291. EDINBURGH.—Naval and military exhibition opened . . . . 18 June, 1889
Freedom of the city presented to Mr. C. S. Parnell (18,000 municipal electors protest against it) . . . . 20 July, „
294. EDUCATION.—Bill for enforcing the new education code withdrawn . . July, 1889
299. EGYPT.—Proposed conversion of the 5 per cent. Egyptian preference debt fails because opposed by France, unless a time be fixed for the evacuation of Egypt by the British 24, 25 June; much irritation at Cairo 27 June, *et seq.* 1889
The Egyptian government appeals to the French without effect . . July, „
333. EXETER Bishops: 1830. H. Philpotts *not* Philpotta.
344. FIRE BRIGADE.—The London County Council orders the appointment of 138 additional firemen and 4 new stations with the usual appliances . . early Aug. 1889
348. FIRES.—Messrs. W. H. & F. Croker, builders, and Messrs. Bonsey, corn merchants, extensive buildings near great dover-street, borough . . . . 7 July, 1889
378. FRANCE.—New army bill reducing the term of service from five years with exemptions to three years, nominally without exemptions, passed by the chamber . . July 9, 1889
M. Quesnay de Beaurepaire hands in the indictment against gen. Boulanger 7 July, „
Sale (at Paris) of the pictures, tapestries, china, &c., of M. Secrétan (ruined by speculations in copper); enormous prices realised, 1-4 July; 17 of M. Secrétan's pictures were sold by Messrs. Christie in London for 27,824l. 10s. . . . 13 July, „
Anniversary of the fall of the Bastille celebrated in France, the United States, &c. 14 July, „
Bill prohibiting a man to be candidate for more than one place in the chamber passed by the senate . . . . 15 July, „
Cantonal elections: republicans, 752; conservatives, 497; gen. Boulanger, 12; 28 July, „
The chamber votes 2,400,000l. for the increase of the navy (3 ironclads, &c.); the session closed . . . . 15 July, „
Indictment against gen. Boulanger, charging him when director of infantry in 1882, with courting popularity by corruption, &c., and when minister of war in 1886 with malversation of public money, and plotting against the state, with count Dillon, H. Rochfort and other confederates; they are cited to appear before the High Court of Justice on 6 Aug.; non-appearance to be followed by loss of civil rights and sequestration of property . . . 17, 28 July, „
Gen. Boulanger appeals to the people in reply to the indictment . . . 6 Aug. „
The trial of Gen. Boulanger, Count Dillon, and H. Rochefort begins . . 8 Aug. „
Sentenced to deportation to a fortress, and payment of costs of the trial . 14 Aug. „
396. GAMES.—At the Bedford club, charterhouse-street, E.C., said to be a common gaming house. Mr. John Bertenshaw and 65 persons arrested by the police . . 25 July, 1889
409. GERMANY.—33 Silesian miners engaged in the strikes; sentenced to various terms of penal servitude, (Enkel, the ringleader, to 7 years for riotous conduct). . 24 July, 1889
Prince Bismarck's bill to compel the working class, with the assistance of the state and their employés, to provide for sickness (passed 1883), for accidents (passed 1884), for old age and infirmity, passed . 24 May, „
The emperor with a fleet arrives at Spithead 1 Aug., and proceeds to the queen at Osborne 2 Aug.; created a British admiral; present at the grand naval review 5 Aug. and at a

ADDENDA. 1051

sham fight at Aldershot, 7 Aug.; queen Victoria made colonel of a German regiment to be called "The Queen of England's Own," about 3 Aug.; the emperor leaves England . . . . 8 Aug. 1889
The emperor of Austria and his heir at Berlin, 12–15 Aug. ,,
415. GLOUCESTER.—An act was passed in 1884 to provide for the disunion of the sees of Gloucester and Bristol.
425. GREECE.—Marriage of the princess Alexandra and the archduke Paul of Russia, 16 June, 1889.
426. GREENLAND.—Dr. Nansen described his journey across Greenland at a meeting of the royal geographical society, 24 June, 1889.
440. HAYTI.—The blockade of Haytian ports, of November last declared to be non-effective, and the ports to be open; *London Gazette*, 12 July, 1889
Unsuccessful attacks of gen. Hyppolite on Port-au-Prince 11, 12, and about 25 July, ,,
453. HOSPITAL SUNDAY, 1889, 23 June; amount received up to 29 July, 41,107*l.* Hospital Saturday, 1880, 13 July; amount received up to 7 Aug. 5,080*l.*
459. HYDROPHOBIA. — Reported number of patients by M. Pasteur since 1885, 6,950, up to . . . . 28 June, 1889
Meeting of eminent men at the mansion house, London, to establish a fund to support the Pasteur institute . . . . 1 July, ,,
See *Mansion House Funds*.
474. INDIA.—Proposal for a new 4 per cent. loan (20,000,000 rupees) issued . 1 July, 1889
Subscription list closed . . . 30 July, ,,
489. IRELAND. — Resisted evictions on the Vandeleur, Lansdowne, Smith - Barry, Ponsonby, and other estates . May–July, 1889
Mr. A. J. Balfour explains his bills for the improvement of Ireland (drainage of the Bann, Barrow, and Shannon, by grants of 383,000*l.*, and the construction of light railways was also proposed . . . . 31 May, ,,
Appeal of Mr. Conybeare (who had been sentenced to three months' imprisonment 3 May) disallowed . . . . 5 July, ,,
Mr. William O'Brien arrested for speech at Clonakilty . . . . 30 June, ,,
Mr. W. O'Brien and Mr. Parnell announce the formation of a New Tenants Defence League, which see . . . . 10, 11 July, ,,
Dr. Tanner sentenced to one month's imprisonment for an assault, and to three months for contempt of court . . . 29 July, ,,
The light railways bill read second time 19 July, ,,
The mission of Mr. Dillon and other delegates to Australia to obtain for home rule, reported unsuccessful; meetings at Sydney, Melbourne, and Brisbane, protest against them July, ,,
The Bann drainage bill, and the light railways bill proceed, the Shannon and Barrow bills dropped about 6 Aug.; the Suck drainage bill and the light railways bill passed Aug. ,,
499. ITALY.—Death of Benedetto Cairoli, aged 63, patriot and statesman, associated with Victor Emmanuel, Cavour, and Garibaldi, in the unification of Italy, deeply lamented, 8 Aug. 1889
514. KANSAS.—Uniontown destroyed by the bursting of a dam caused by heavy rains, several lives lost, reported 17 June, 1889.
517. KIEF (Kiov or Kiow), chief town of a province of the same name in European Russia, made a principality 1137, annexed to Poland 1386, and after several changes was ceded to Russia 1686. The cathedral of St. Sophia was founded in 1037, the Greek academy 1588, and the university in 1834.
526. LAND.—The lord chancellor's land transfer bill dropped 5 July, 1889.
544. LIVERPOOL.—Strike of sailors and firemen end of May, they set up picketing, which is suppressed by the police 5 July, strike virtually ended 12 July, 1889.
Loyal and patriotic union established in Dublin to oppose the national league, 1 May, 1885; Mr. Houston, the secretary, acknowledged before the special commission, the purchase of the copyright of "Parnellism unmasked by Richard Pigott," the basis of "Parnellism and Crime" (in 1885), 12 July, 1889.
558. LUNATICS in charge in England and Wales 84,340 . . . . . . 1 Jan. 1889
Lunacy acts amendment bill read 3rd time in the commons . . . . 30 July, ,,
563. MADRAS.—Lord Connemara reports improvement in the condition of Ganjam; employed on works, 15,425; deaths from cholera in a week 602; reported . . . 9 July, 1889
Prospects improving; rain general; on works 8,751; deaths from cholera 343 . 13 Aug. ,,
572. MANSION-HOUSE, LONDON.—Pasteur institute fund established (see *Hydrophobia*), 1 July, 1889; received from the prince of Wales 105*l.*, the duke of Westminster 200*l.*, the duke of Northumberland 100*l.*, and many others.
623. NAVY OF ENGLAND.—Grand jubilee naval review by the queen at Spithead; 135 vessels, 20,200 men and about 500 guns (accidentally omitted at page 623) . . . 23 July, 1887
The fleet assembled for the autumn manœuvres, inspected by the emperor William II. (and his brother prince Henry), the prince of Wales, and members of both houses of parliament. The display consisted of 20 battle ships (9 first class, 9 second class and 2 third class), 38 first class torpedo boats and other vessels, in all 106 vessels (the queen inspected the fleet later in the day) . 5 Aug. 1889
The naval manœuvres begin; sham declaration of war, 15 Aug.; "H.M.S. *Sultan* is afloat," announced . . . . . 20 Aug. ,,
629. NEW RIVER.—An entire freehold adventurer's share of the company was sold by auction for 122,800*l.* to the Prudential Assurance Company . . 17 July, 1889
The annual income of the company from land and water was stated to be 511,356*l.* in . 1888
634. NEW ZEALAND.—The debate on the Representation Bill to increase the number of country members of parliament at Wellington lasted 76 hours, adjourned 27 July; amicable arrangement between town and country parties . . . . 29 July, 1889
635. NICARAGUA.—Death of sig. Carazo; Dr. Sacasa elected president; reported 2 Aug. 1889
663. PANAMA —Canal bill passed by the French senate . . . . . 11 July, 1889
672. PARNELLITE COMMISSION.—101st sitting Michael Davitt examined . 4 July, 1889
106th sitting: Mr. Houston, secretary of the "Loyal and Patriotic Union" (established in 1885), states that in 1885 he purchased the copyright of "Parnellism Unmasked" (by Richard Pigott). The court refuses to accede to the application of sir C. Russell to inspect the books of the "Loyal and Patriotic Union" . . . . 12 July, ,,
107th sitting: Mr. Parnell and his friends with their counsel withdraw from the case 15 July, ,,
112th sitting: examination of the Land League account books and documents; adjournment to 24 Oct. . . . . 25 July, ,,
680. PENNSYLVANIA. — Latest statistics state the result of the Johnstown disaster to be about 6,000 deaths . . . 26 July, 1889
683. PERSIA.—The shah at Hatfield 7, 8 July; other seats 9 July, *et sq.*; at Birmingham 11 July; Sheffield 12 July; Liverpool and Chester 13 July; Manchester 15 July; Glasgow 18 July (inspected the Forth bridge); at Edinburgh 23 July; Newcastle 24 July; Bradford 24, 25 July; Leeds 26 July; Brighton 27, 28 July; Osborne 29 July; Paris 30 July; dines with the president 1 Aug.; goes to Baden 10 Aug.; at Munich 19 Aug.; at Vienna . . 23 Aug. 1889
713. PORTRAIT GALLERY.—North extremity of the National Gallery chosen for the site of the new building . . . July, 1889
Bill passed . . . . . 26 July, ,,
715. PORTUGAL.—The wine trade much disturbed by the government proposing to grant bounties to wine-growers, and support a monopolizing company . June, July, 1889

ADDENDA.

726. PRISONS.—The committee appointed to inquire respecting prison rules, reported in favour of their continuance in regard to dress and hair-cutting, for sanitary, disciplinary and general reasons . June, 1889
741. QUEENSLAND.—1888-9 revenue 3,636,000l.; expenditure 3,51,000l.
751. RAILWAYS.—Bill for their regulation in regard to public safety, relating to the block system, brakes, points, signals, coupling, &c., introduced by sir M. Hicks-Beach July; passed . . . . Aug. 1889
Great swing railway bridge, span 140 ft., over the Dee declared open by Mrs. Gladstone 3 Aug. ,,
[It gives a direct route to the Manchester, Sheffield and Lincolnshire Railway into Wales, and also to the Great Northern and Midland systems.]
775. ROYAL GRANTS, to members of the royal family.—The queen on July 2 applied to parliament for a grant to prince Albert Victor of Wales for his maintenance, and for one to the princess Louise of Wales on her proposed marriage with the earl of Fife, a select committee was appointed consisting of 23 members, (including Mr. Göschen, Mr. W. H. Smith, Lord Hartington, Mr. J. Chamberlain, Mr. Gladstone, Mr. John Morley, Mr. Labouchere, Mr. Burt, Dr. Cameron, Mr. Parnell, and Mr. Sexton) 8 July, the committee first met 10 July, 1889.
After several meetings at which there was much discussion on various propositions, a report was submitted to the house of commons, who eventually resolved, after several amendments had been rejected, that 36,000l., out of the consolidated fund should be paid annually (through trustees) to the prince of Wales for the support and maintenance of his family, the same to continue till six months after the queen's decease, 29 July 1889. An act of parliament to this effect was passed shortly after.
797. SAVOY.—The magnificent Savoy Hotel on the Thames Embankment opened by a company 6 Aug. 1889, the directors include the earl of Lathom, Mr. R. D'Oyly Carte, and sir Arthur Sullivan.
802. SCOTLAND.—Local Government Act and the Universities Act passed Aug. 1889.
823. SNOWDON, mountain peak N. Wales with the valley, hotel, buildings, quarries, &c., sold by auction to sir Edward Watkin, for 5,750l. 10 July, 1889.
831. SOUDAN.—The Dervishes, suffering from thirst are repelled from the river . July, 1889
Reinforcements sent from Malta to strengthen the garrison at Assouan . . . July, ,,
Dervish deserters come in; prisoners sent to Cairo; their loss estimated to be since 1 July 2,500 killed and wounded about . 14 July, ,,
Dervishes reinforced by about 1,500 . ,,
Gen. sir F. W. Grenfell arrives at Col. Wodehouse's camp at Bellana; the enemy hold a strong position at Khor their fighting force estimated at 2,500 . . . . 15 July, ,,
The R. Irish Rifles arrive at Assouan 16 July, ,,
Gen. Grenfell summons Wad El N'jumi to surrender, all lives to be spared; the messenger beaten . . . . . 17 July, ,,
Reconnoissance parties of the enemy cut off Wad-el-N'jumi calls on the Egyptians to surrender, and threatens them with the fate of gen. Gordon, reported . . . 19 July, ,,
A large number of additional troops sent from Cairo . . . . 20 July, ,,
British field force at Assouan commanded by major gen. hon. R. H. de Montmorency 23 July, ,,
Party of 300 Dervishes repulsed with loss; reported . . . . 21 July, ,,
Frequent skirmishes; many killed and prisoners 25-31 July, ,,
Dervishes defeated with loss of 70 men by lieut. D'Aguilar at Anabi . . 31 July, ,,

Battle of Toski; after seven hours' hard fighting about 3,000 Dervishes are defeated by gen. sir Francis Grenfell. Wad-el-N'jumi with his principal emirs, and about half his army are killed, the other half are either wounded or fugitives; the repeated desperate charges of the Dervishes are chiefly repulsed by the 20th Hussars and the Egyptian cavalry who pursue them till they are utterly routed and their arms and standards captured. (The commanders under gen. Grenfell were col. Kitchener mounted troops; col. Wodehouse, infantry; Rundle artillery, Irwin and Beech, English and Egyptian cavalry; Settle, sen. staff officer; the British loss 17 killed (1 English 16 Egyptians); wounded, 131; above 1,000 Dervishes prisoners and wounded; parts of the Shropshire and Lancashire regiments and the Royal Irish Rifles were engaged 3 Aug; gen. Grenfell arrives at Cairo . . . . 17 Aug. 1889
The Egyptian troops occupy Matuka; the British ordered to return to Cairo . 7 Aug. ,,
832. SOUTH AUSTRALIA.—Revenue 1883-9, 2,202,510l. expenditure 2,273,203l.
843. SPANISH EXHIBITION.—In July, 1889, it cluded representations of the Alhambra, Mad market-place, panorama of a journey throu Spain, a Spanish band and strolling players, &c
860. STRIKE of part of the dock labourers of the po of London about 16 Aug.; about 25,000 out, 2 Aug. 1889.
871. SWITZERLAND.—Loan for 25,000,000 francs, to supply new arms for the Federal troops, subscribed for by Berne alone, reported 23 July, 1889.
872. SYDNEY.—Rev. Canon William Saumarez Smith, D.D., announced as the new Bishop and Metropolitan of Australia, 9 Aug. 1889.
880. TENANTS' DEFENCE LEAGUE.—At a meeting in the house of commons, Mr. Parnell and the Irish parliamentary party declare that a new league is necessary to protect by legal means the tenant farmers of Ireland against the "Landlords' conspiracy," (this is to supersede the national league and the plan of campaign) 14 July, 1889.
A committee met and agreed upon a constitution and rules; the tenants are invited to contribute to a fund, with a promise of help from the league branches are to be established, and officers elected 22 July, 1889.
894. TITHES.—Much agitation against tithes in Wales, 1889. A tithes rent recovery bill, introduced into the commons; withdrawn 16 Aug. 1889.
918. TRIALS.—Mrs. Florence Elizabeth Maybrick charged with poisoning her husband, James Maybrick, at Aigburth, by arsenic, tried at Liverpool by Mr. Justice Stephen; convicted 21 July-7 Aug.; sentence of death commuted to penal servitude for life 22 Aug. 1889.
929. TURKEY.—On account of the disturbances in Crete and the complications in the Balkans, the calling out of 80,000 men of the reserves has been ordered; active movements in the dockyards about 1 Aug. 1889.
949. UNITED STATES.—The British sealer, Black Diamond, seized by the U. S. revenue cutter Rush (captain Shepard), in Behring sea, (for an alleged violation of the law forbidding the killing of fur-bearing animals in Alaska waters). The Triumph was overhauled and discharged about . . 31 July, 1889
Declared legal by secretary Blaine 1 Aug.; the Black Diamond escapes, and sails to Victoria, British Columbia, about . . . 4 Aug. ,,
Reception at Liverpool of 50 representatives of American industries (on a tour of trade observation in Europe) . . . 1 Aug. ,,
The national monument at New Plymouth, Massachusetts, commemorating the landing of the "Pilgrim Fathers," which see, dedicated . . . . . . 1 Aug. ,,
The Sioux, and the Chippewa Indians, sell a large part of their reservations, which are to be opened for settlement, Aug. 1889.

THE END.

BRADBURY, AGNEW, & CO., PRINTERS, WHITEFRIARS.

www.ingramcontent.com/pod-product-compliance
Lightning Source LLC
Chambersburg PA
CBHW031905220426
43663CB00006B/779